ISBN 978-0-282-54968-8
PIBN 10856234

For support please visit www.forgottenbooks.com

1 MONTH OF
FREE
READING

at

www.ForgottenBooks.com

By purchasing this book you are eligible for one month membership to ForgottenBooks.com, giving you unlimited access to our entire collection of over 1,000,000 titles via our web site and mobile apps.

To claim your free month visit:
www.forgottenbooks.com/free856234

English
Français
Deutsche
Italiano
Español
Português

www.forgottenbooks.com

Mythology Photography **Fiction**
Fishing Christianity **Art** Cooking
Essays Buddhism Freemasonry
Medicine **Biology** Music **Ancient**
Egypt Evolution Carpentry Physics
Dance Geology **Mathematics** Fitness
Shakespeare **Folklore** Yoga Marketing
Confidence Immortality Biographies
Poetry **Psychology** Witchcraft
Electronics Chemistry History **Law**
Accounting **Philosophy** Anthropology
Alchemy Drama Quantum Mechanics
Atheism Sexual Health **Ancient History**
Entrepreneurship Languages Sport
Paleontology Needlework Islam
Metaphysics Investment Archaeology
Parenting Statistics Criminology
Motivational

SCYTHIANS AND GREEKS

A SURVEY OF ANCIENT HISTORY AND ARCHAEOLOG
ON THE NORTH COAST OF THE EUXINE
FROM THE DANUBE TO THE CAUCASUS

by

ELLIS H. MINNS, M.A.

Late Craven Student and Fellow of Pembroke College, Cambridge
Member of the Imperial Russian Archaeological Society
Member of the Imperial Historical and Antiquarian Society of Odessa

Cambridge:
at the University Press
1913

Cambridge:
PRINTED BY JOHN CLAY, M.A.
AT THE UNIVERSITY PRESS

OPTIMO PATRI

OPERIS FAVTORI PRAECIPVO

PIGNVS PIETATIS

PREFACE

THIS book offers a summary of what is known as to the archaeology, ethnology and history of the region between the Carpathians and the Caucasus. The region is of varied importance for different branches of knowledge touching the ancient world, yet about it the scholars of Western Europe have had a certain difficulty in obtaining recent information, because each found it unprofitable to master Russian for the sake of pursuing his subject into an outlying corner. The language difficulty, therefore, first suggested this work, and my original intention was merely to supply a key to what has been written by Russian scholars, since they have been insisting upon the right of their language to scientific use. But such a fragmentary account of things would have been most unsatisfactory, and, though the time has not really come for a complete synthesis, enough advance has been made since the last attempt to review the subject, to justify a provisional summary.

Though the geographical limits to which I have confined myself have confessedly been dictated by considerations of language—i.e. I have, in principle, kept to the area within the Russian Empire which has naturally attracted the attention of scholars writing in Russian—yet the frontier of Russia towards the Carpathians and the Danube answers nearly to a real historico-geographical boundary, the western limit of the true steppe. The Caucasus, again, is a world in itself, having little in common with the steppe, nor has the time yet come to bring any sort of system into its archaeology ; so I have reason enough for leaving it alone. On the other hand, the unity of the Asiatic and European steppe has led me on occasion right across to Siberia, Turkestan and China without any feeling that I was trespassing beyond my borders.

My limits in time are, I hope, equally intelligible : an attempt to begin at the beginning has resulted in Chapter VII, which, I trust, will not be useless: since it was printed off, more material has accumulated than I was able to cope with in the Addenda. The Great Migrations form a good lower limit, as they made a radical change in the population of the steppe and interrupted the continuous life of the Greek cities on the Euxine coast. In the case of Chersonese alone there was no such break and I have therefore followed its history to the end.

Just these same limits were contemplated by K. Neumann in his *Die Hellenen im Skythenlande* (Berlin, 1855), but he only lived to publish the first volume and that is nearly sixty years ago. In the first three parts of Kondakov and Tolstoi's *Russian Antiquities in the Monuments of Art* (St P. 1889–) reissued by Reinach as *Antiquités de la Russie Méridionale* (Paris 1892, henceforward cited as *KTR.*) is provided a more recent summary. This, intended as an introduction to a more or less popular account of Christian art in Russia, leaves something to be desired in arrangement and in bibliographical indications of the sources for the facts presented, but I have no idea of superseding it, as its limits in time and space are much wider than mine, and, though I have been allowed to reproduce a great many of its illustrations, it remains the most accessible book in which to find many more.

When the above work was compiled, the policy of publishing in Russian had just become dominant (from about 1889, v. p. xxv) and it was difficult for Europe to know of discoveries in Russia from then until 1904, when Pharmacovskij began contributing year by year to the *Archäologischer Anzeiger* his very full and well illustrated reports. It is just from the period before 1904 that the main bulk of my unfamiliar matter is taken, as the greater part of the illustrations (e.g. those borrowed from the Archaeological Commission) had been selected by then and the earlier part of the book drafted.

Other obligations and work having nothing in common with this have made the writing, and also the printing, of the book a very slow business, further delayed by the continual flow of fresh material, the incorporation of which, especially at the later stages, has presented some difficulty : there have also resulted certain unavoidable inconsistencies. Important facts which I have learnt since the earlier sheets were printed off are briefly indicated in the Addenda, to which I would ask the reader's attention, but these supplements, necessarily, have been kept down rather jealously.

A great cause of delay has been the miscellaneous content of the work : its unity being merely geographical, the composition of the different chapters has meant incursions into different branches of knowledge, in each of which the specialist will find me wanting. He also may say that what interests him has not received sufficient space, but there is no denying that the book is big enough already. The notes give him chapter and verse for every fact mentioned and indications as to where further information may be found on any particular point : I believe that even Russians may find these convenient. For readers requiring less detail, I have endeavoured to make such a representative selection of material as to supply a general account of each subject treated and thus to make the book intelligible without the necessity of

looking up any references. Accordingly I have shewn enough coins to give an idea of the whole series and have even taken up space with an Appendix of Inscriptions, though Latyshev's *Inscriptiones Orae Septentrionalis Ponti Euxini* is fairly accessible.

With regard to illustrations, I have deliberately sacrificed quality to quantity : I could not afford to reproduce photographically the hundreds of objects of which I have made rough and ready tracings for Chapters VIII—XII ; the source of each being given, those who want finer detail will know where to find it. Illustrations of objects from a tomb will be found where the tomb is described.

Critics may point out books and articles that I have overlooked, and such indications will always be welcome. Omissions are inevitable in view of the wide survey necessary. I fear I have not extracted all I might have done from Serbian, Bulgarian, Polish, Rumanian and Hungarian authorities, but these lie somewhat on one side ; even in Russian I have found it impossible to hope for completeness, while in the archaeological literature of Western Europe I must have missed endless articles which would have enriched my work ; but had I waited to read them all, the book would never have been published.

I am very anxious to direct the attention of the reader to the table for transliterating Russian on p. xxi, in order that he may have all possible help in grasping the many unfamiliar names he will meet with in the text, and also to the Preliminary Bibliography and List of Abbreviations (pp. xxiv —xxxv) which explain such references in the notes as may not be clear at first sight.

A book like this is not written without incurring many obligations which can only be repaid by sincere thanks and a readiness to render service for service if opportunity arise.

Most of all I am indebted to the Imperial Archaeological Commission at St Petersburg : during my stay there, I was given a place of my own in its library and was presented with a complete set of its more recent publications, and these have been sent me regularly year by year ever since ; full leave was granted me to reproduce any of its illustrations and over 130 blocks were sent to England for my use. Its individual Members have done all that could be done for me, especially the President, Count A. A. Bobrinskoj, who gave me his magnificent volumes on *Smêla* and his *History of Chersonese*; the Vice-President, Academician V. V. Latyshev, who by a long series of letters and articles has kept me informed of epigraphic progress ; the Senior Member, Professor N. I. Veselovskij, Mr A. A. Spitsyn and Mr B. V. Pharmacovskij who by sending me his articles has kept me up to date in his own special studies.

M.   *b*

At the Imperial Hermitage, I have pleasant recollections of the courtesy of the late Dr G. von Kieseritzky; Mr E. M. Pridik and Mr O. F. Retowski have rendered me valuable help and so has Mr J. I. Smirnov, whose most generous offer to read my proofs unfortunately came too late. Count I. I. Tolstoi and Academician N. P. Kondakov graciously agreed to my reproducing illustrations from *KTR.*, and from the latter I have received kindnesses more than I can recount. I should also like to mention the names of Professor M. I. Rostovtsev and especially of the late Baron Victor R. Rosen, without whose kindness my stay in Petersburg would have been far less profitable.

In the Historical Museum at Moscow, Mr A. V. Orêshnikov made me very much at home, and ever since by most valuable letters, articles and casts of coins has been my chief help in numismatics; Mr V. A. Gorodtsov has supplied me with unpublished material for Chapters VII and VIII. Professor Vs. Th. Miller, Director of the Lazarev Institute, has earned my gratitude both personally and by his books.

At Kazan, the late Professor I. N. Smirnov first made me acquainted with Volga-Kama antiquities.

From Kiev, Mr N. Th. Bêlashevskij of the Town Museum and especially Mr V. V. Chvojka have sent me books, letters and photographs of which I have made full use, and Professor J. A. Kulakovskij has been constant in help and encouragement.

At Odessa, the Imperial Historical and Antiquarian Society did me the honour to elect me a member: its Director, Dr E. R. von Stern, now Professor at Halle, put its coin collection at my disposal and its Secretary, Professor A. A. Pavlovskij, has supplied me with its *Transactions.* These two scholars have besides rendered me important private services.

At Nicolaev, Mr A. Vogell entertained me and shewed me his beautiful collection, now, alas, dispersed. At Kherson, Mr V. I. Goszkewicz has kept me abreast of the progress of archaeology in his district.

At Chersonese, the late Director of the Excavations, Mr K. K. Kosciuszko-Wałużynicz, shewed me round the site and sent me photographs and reports from time to time: I am also under very definite obligations to his successor, Dr R. Ch. Löper, and his draughtsman Mr M. I. Skubetov. From General A. L. Bertier-de-La-Garde at Jalta, I have received books, articles, letters and other help on many points archaeological and numismatic: my constant references to his work are a measure of what I owe him. Dr K. E. Duhmberg, Director at Kerch, assisted me while I was there, and his successor, Mr V. V. Škorpil, has answered questions and sent me valuable articles, while Dr I. A. Terlecki gave me my first real introduction to Bosporan coins.

Outside Russia, I have found similar assistance : from Mr A. M. Tallgren at Helsingfors, from Professor A. von Lecoq and the authorities of the Antiquarium at Berlin, from Professor P. Bieńkowski at Cracow, Dr Vasić at Belgrad, and Professor M. Rosenberg at Karlsruhe. In Paris, my special gratitude is due to Professor Paul Boyer, Director of the School of Living Oriental Languages, my first guide in Russian studies, also to Mr E. Babelon at the Cabinet des Médailles, and to Mr S. Reinach, who helped me at the St Germain Museum, joined in allowing me to copy figures from *KTR.* and encouraged me in other ways.

In the British Museum, Mr O. M. Dalton of the Medieval Department, who has traversed much of the same ground in his *Treasure of the Oxus*, has been to me a constant moral support and has besides helped me in many ways ; in the Coin Department, I have always been sure of assistance from the late Mr Warwick Wroth, from Mr G. F. Hill and from Mr H. Mattingly ; I have been also specially beholden to Sir Cecil Smith and Mr F. H. Marshall, both formerly of the Greek and Roman Department. To Professor W. M. Flinders Petrie I am indebted for one of my most valuable illustrations. At Oxford, I have received help and encouragement from Sir A. J. Evans, Sir M. A. Stein and Professor J. L. Myres.

In Cambridge, my thanks are first due to the Managers of the Craven Fund, who enabled me to make my original archaeological visit to Russia, and to my College, which allowed my work upon this book to qualify me for holding my Fellowship. I cannot say how much I owe to my masters, the late Mr R. A. Neil who encouraged me at the beginning—I had hoped to talk over many a point with him—and Professor Ridgeway, who has ever been urging me forward. My thanks are also due to the Masters of St Catharine's and Emmanuel Colleges, to Sir Charles Waldstein, Professor J. B. Bury, Professor H. A. Giles, Professor A. A. Bevan, Professor E. J. Rapson, Miss Jane E. Harrison, Mr A. B. Cook, Mr S. A. Cook, Professor C. H. Hawes, now of Dartmouth College, U.S.A., and other scholars to whom I have had occasion to turn for information.

Much of the photographic work was done by the late Mr H. A. Chapman of the Fitzwilliam Museum, the staff of which has aided me in the matter of coins. The trouble that I have given to the staff of the University Library has amounted to something that deserves special recognition from me.

My very deepest gratitude is due to Mr A. J. B. Wace, who has read the proofs right through, successive batches coming to him at the most widely different places, and to Mr F. W. Green, who has made assurance more sure for the second half of the book by eliminating errors which had crept in after Mr Wace's reading.

If I have omitted to acknowledge either here or in the text any

obligations incurred within these thirteen years, may the lapse of time be some excuse for me.

The Syndics of the University Press I can but thank for undertaking a book by nature unremunerative and ask their pardon for having expanded it beyond reasonable convenience and delayed it almost beyond endurance: from the staff, especially from Mr Norman Mason, whom I have troubled with an endless series of petty details, I have received invaluable help given with unfailing patience, while the press-readers have saved me from many slips.

The work is dedicated to my Father, who has enabled me to devote myself to it, has very largely supplemented the liberal allowance for illustrations made by the Syndics, and has contributed to the expenses incidental to making the scale of the book less inadequate to its subject.

E. H. M.

24 *April*, 1913.

CONTENTS

ILLUSTRATIONS

MAPS AND PLANS

COIN PLATES

ILLUSTRATIONS IN THE TEXT

In view of my special obligations to the Imp. Archaeological Commission which gave me full leave to copy everything and actually entrusted me with 130 blocks I have marked these (AC.): the British Museum and the Society of Antiquaries allowed me to have electrotypes of those marked (BM.) and (SA.) respectively. The numerous figures marked (K.) are copied by the gracious permission of Messrs Kondakov, Tolstoi and Reinach from their *Antiquités de la Russie Méridionale*. Other such obligations to modern works I have acknowledged in their place.

All illustrations of objects from one find are grouped where that find is described, although any particular object may be treated of in some other part of the book and to this reference is, as far as possible, given.

TRANSLITERATIONS.

Greek.

Greek names and words appear in the traditional Latin transliteration much as is recommended to contributors to *JHS.*, i.e. names that the Romans themselves did not fully Latinize, e.g. *Delos,* and certain words which are more familiar in the Greek form, e.g. *Nike, Boule,* are treated inconsistently. Greek words in the index mostly appear where they would if transliterated into Latin, but if actually next each other are put in the Greek order.

Russians transcribe Greek by tradition as if it were modern Greek (no *h*; ι, η, υ = i etc.): a reform party represents the Erasmic view but has not attained to a consistent system: it is hampered by having no *h* for which Γ i.e. *g* is used.

Latin is pronounced after the German fashion and transliterated accordingly.

Russian.

The use of diacritical marks has been avoided for typographical reasons, and they only appear in Polish, Bohemian or Serbo-Croatian names of which they are an integral part. This has involved the frequent use of two letters in English for one in Russian which is apt to make the unfamiliar words very long and hard to grasp. To avoid this has seemed more important than to attempt to give the pronunciation exactly and I have aimed at using as few letters as are consistent with a fair rendering. The vowels are of course to be pronounced as in Italian except *e* and *y* (see below); the English mode of expressing consonants fits Russian better than does the German or French, but I have had to depart from it by using *j* for consonantal *y* as *y* is wanted for a special vowel: I have not ventured to use *c* for *ts* (nor of course *ch* for *kh*, except in a few Greek words) as is done in scientific transliteration of Slavonic. To keep the words short I have represented Russian e and ѣ by *e* and *ê* instead of *je* and *jê*, the *j* being nearly always present before an *e* sound in Russian: so when я or ю (ordinarily *ja* or *ju*) follow an i I have omitted the *j*. The *j* looks unfamiliar and I have sometimes yielded to temptation and substituted *i* in diphthongs *aj, oj,* e.g. Tolstoi.

When names of Russians are really French, German or Polish, I have restored to them their own spelling: when Greek or Latin enter into the composition of Russian words or names I have as far as possible written them as I write Greek or Latin (e.g. Pharmacovskij but Funduklej) so as to bring out their derivation, the terminations being transcribed normally. This has led me into many inconsistencies (e.g. two values of *ch*), but anything which makes Russian names less unfamiliar and so easier to distinguish is valuable, Westerners being inclined to confuse them. It has also enabled me to make a difference between *Cherson* the Byzantine form of Chersonese and *Kherson* the modern Russian town at the mouth of the Dnêpr.

The accent is not written in Russian, so I have not made a practice of indicating it, but I have occasionally (especially in the index) put it as a guide to pronunciation: unaccented vowels are much less clear in quality, e.g. *o* is indistinguishable from *a*; when, as often, *ê* has the tonic accent I have not put an extra mark; *ê* (=*jo*) only arises under the accent.

Latin letters.	Russian letters.	Pronunciation.
a	а	*a* as in *father.*
ai, aj	ай	*ai* in *aisle.*
b	б	*b* as in *boy.*
c		Not used alone except to represent κ or *c* in Greek or Latin.
ch	ч (х)	*ch* as *church* (but when representing χ it is to be pronounced *kh*).
d	д	*d* as in *debt*, or rather Fr. *dette.*
e	e	At the beginning of all but a few modern loan-words as *ye* in *yet* or *ya* in *Yale*: after a consonant the *j* (*y*) is less distinct but always present except after *sh, ch, zh* and *ts.*
e	э	*e* as in *equator*: confined to obvious modern loan-words.
ë	ё	Accented e in certain cases assumes the sound of *jo, o*, and so I have sometimes written.
ⸯ	ѣ	A special letter now identical in sound with e but never turning to ë.
ej	ей	*ey* in *grey.*
f	ф	Only in foreign words; if the origin is Greek 1 use *ph.*
g	г	Hard as in *get.*
gh	г	г sounded as a spirant, at the end of words (e.g. *Bugh*) as *ch* in *Loch.*
h		Not in Russian. Latin &c. *h* is represented by г or sometimes х. Greek ʻ is sometimes rendered by г, more often left out.
	и, i	*i* as in *machine*. (Sometimes = й in diphthongs, e.g. *Ainalov, Tolstoi.*)
i (ia, ie, ië, iu)	ь (ья, ье, ьё, ью)	ь + я is almost identical with i + a and I have made no distinction, so with other vowels except ьи = *ji.*
ij	ий	*ee* in *free* but after *k* as *y* in *whisky.*
j	й (ай, ей, ой)	*y* at the end of diphthongs as in *ay, grey, boy.*
j (ji)	ь (ьи)	*y* before *i* after a consonant, as in *Goodyear.*
ja, ju	(я, ю)	*y* before *a, u*, as in *yarn, yule.*
(e, ë, ê)	(е, ё, ѣ)	I do not write the *j* in these cases but it is to be pronounced.
k	к	*k* except in Greek or Latin words, in which where possible I write *c.*
kh	х	German *ch* in *ach*: but in Greek words I use *ch* for χ.
l	л	*l* "hard" between *l* and *w* as in *people*, "soft" between *l* and *y* as in Fr. *ville.*
m	м	*m.*
n	н	*n.*
o	о	*o* accented open as *oa* in *broad*: unaccented as *ă* in *balloon.*
p	п	*p.*
ph	ф	I have written *ph* in words of Greek origin.
q		Not in Russian.
r	р	*r*, strongly trilled: when soft between *r* and *y* but not like *ry.*
s	с	*s* as in *size, case*, never as in *cheese* (I have left it in words like *Muséj, numismática*, written with *z* in Russian).
sh	ш	*sh* in *shut.*
shch	щ	*shch* in *Ashchurch.*

Latin letters.	Russian letters.	Pronunciation.
th	ѳ	*f*; I have written *th*, as ѳ only occurs in words borrowed from the Greek, but the pronunciation in Russian is *f*.
ts		*ts* as in *its*: ц often represents a Latin *c* through German influence.
	у	*u* in *rule*.
	в	*v*, at the end of words pronounced as *f*, hence the common spelling *-off*.
		Our *w* does not occur in Russian but Germans use the letter to render в.
	кс	ξ, and also ψ, have been dropped from the Russian alphabet.
	ы	A peculiar vowel between *i* and *u* not unlike its value in *rhythm*.
y	..	Representing Greek υ as in *Sympheropol*.
z		English *z*. But Germans transliterating Russian use it for ц = *ts*.
zh	ж	French *j*, English *z* in *azure*.
(ʻ)	ъ	Keeps preceding consonant "hard": I have only used it in the middle of words.
(ʼ)		Makes preceding consonant "soft": when a vowel follows I write *i*.

Consonants before *a, o, u, y,* (ʻ) are mostly pronounced hard, i.e. more or less as in English : before *i, e, j* and (ʼ) soft, that is with a *j* sound, but this must not be overdone.

Russians writing their own names in Latin letters are generally quite inconsistent, mostly using a French or German system, often a mixture of the two or alternately one and the other : the only thing is to disregard their individual usage and reduce all names to one system.

Chinese, etc.

The forms in which Chinese names appear have been revised by Professor Giles, to whom my best thanks are due, in accordance with the Wade system. The transliteration does not attempt to restore lost final consonants but neither does it render some of the Pekinese innovations (e.g. Hsiung-nu, Tʻu-chiü for Hiung-nu, Tʻu-küe): also *zh* is put for Wade's (French) *j*. A convenient table of transliterations from Chinese, including that used by Russians, is in *TRAS.* Oriental Sect. xviii. i. p. 074.

Other Oriental names have been rendered rather haphazard, mostly as found in the books from which I took them.

Russian Weights.	*Russian Measures.*
1 dólja = ·675 gr. troy = ·044 grm.	1 vershók = 1·75 inch = 4·445 cm.
96 dóljas = 1 zolotník = 64·8 gr. troy = 4·265 grm.	16 vershóks = 1 arshín = 28 inches = 71·12 cm.
3 zolotníks = r lot = { 194·4 gr. troy / ·45 oz. avdp. } = 12·78 grm.	3 arshíns = 1 sazhén = 7 feet = 2·134 m.
	500 sazhéns = 1 verst = 1166 yds, 2 ft = 1·067 km.
32 lots = 1 funt = ·9 lb. avdp. = 409 grm.	(3 versts = 2 miles : 15 versts = 16 km., cf. Scale on
40 funts = 1 pud = 36·11 lb. avdp. = 16·36 kgr.	Map IX.)
(3 puds = 1 cwt.)	

I have avoided using these, but many of the books to which I refer do so, others use our feet and inches or of late years the Metric system.

PRELIMINARY BIBLIOGRAPHY OF RUSSIAN PUBLICATIONS.

In view of the mutual independence of various parts of the book sectional bibliographies have been appended to each of Chapters II—IV, XIII—XIX, although this has meant a certain amount of repetition: the notes throughout give much bibliographical information but they contain a certain number of abbreviations, some of these it has been thought better to expand in § C below even though they be fairly familiar to archaeological readers, but it is only a list of abbreviations, not a bibliography of periodical literature, and does not contain titles cited in a form about which there can be no mistake.

Titles of works in Russian appear in the notes in English *Translations* (not always, I fear, quite consistent), the Russian character has been avoided as generally unintelligible, and even transliterations are difficult for those unfamiliar with the language to grasp. The title of every Russian serial (A) and independent work (B) to which reference has been made, is here given both in the original Russian language and character and in a Latin transliteration. Articles published in serials of which the Russian title is given, can be readily identified by their English titles, and it has not been thought necessary to give the Russian. As the place of publication of every work or else that of the serial in which it is published has been given in every case, a reader may be expected to infer that a work published in Russia is written in Russian in spite of its being cited by an English title, and if he wishes to know the exact form of the Russian title he will find it in A or B. Certain Russian works, mostly official publications, have recognised French titles and are cited by these mostly in an abbreviated form, v. § C. The titles of the magazines *Propylaea* (Пропилеи) and *Hermes* (Гермесъ, not to be confused with the German *Hermes*, Berlin, 1866—) have been distinguished by the warning (Russian). Latyshev's Ποντικά is a collection of articles in Russian, his *Scythica et Caucasica* has a Russian translation and notes and so has his *Christian Inscriptions from S. Russia*, which by an oversight I have cited as "Inscr. Chr." The titles of works in French, German, etc. are of course left unaltered; to those in Slavonic languages which use Latin letters a translation has been added. The citation of Russian authorities will enable anyone who can command the help of an interpreter to look up any particular point with as little difficulty as possible.

By far the greater part of work on the antiquities of S. Russia appears in the publications of some institution or society, nearly always a serial, and these may conveniently form one class (A) and the independent books another (B). I have not made any effort to include books older than 1860 and quite superseded, nor have I aimed at any completeness in this practical guide to a wide literature. I have inserted one or two books which have appeared since the printing of the section for which they would have been useful. A helpful book of reference is

Прозоровъ, П. (Prozorov, P.). Систематическій Указатель Книгъ и Статей по Греческой Филологіи напечатанныхъ въ Россіи съ XVII столѣтія по 1892 годъ на русскомъ и иностранныхъ языкахъ, съ прибавленіемъ за 1893, 1894 и 1895 годы. Спб. 1898. (*Sistematícheskij Ukazátel' Kníg i Statéj po Grécheskoj Philológii napechátannykh v Rossíi s* XVII *stolětia po* 1892 *god na rússkom i inostránnykh jazykákh, s pribavlěniem za* 1893, 1894 *i* 1895 *gódy* = *Systematic Index of Books and Articles on Greek Philology printed in Russia from the* XVIIth *century to* 1892 *in Russian and other languages, with a Supplement for* 1893, 1894 *and* 1895. St P. 1898.)

See also *IosPE*. II. pp. 339—344, and the half-yearly Supplement to *BCA*. (v. inf. p. xxvi).

A. *Official Publications and Serials issued in Russia.*

The IMPERIAL ACADEMY OF SCIENCES (Императорская Академія Наукъ, Imperátorskaja Académia Naúk), St P., publishes the Записки (*Zapíski*, *Mémoires*) of the Historico-Philological Class, also a *Bulletin* from which were collected articles in *Mélanges Gréco-Romains*, 1855— (also *Mélanges Asiatiques*), a Сборникъ (*Sbórnik*, *Miscellany*) and Извѣстія (*Izvêstia*, *Bulletin*) Отдѣленія русскаго языка и словесности (Otdêlénia rússkago jazyká i slovésnosti, of the Department of Russian Language and Literature), 1900— , and the Византійскій Временникъ (*Vizantíjskij Vremenník*, Βυζαντινὰ Χρονικά), 1894— . Also Prozorov's book above mentioned, but I have not often had occasion to cite its publications.

The IMPERIAL ARCHAEOLOGICAL COMMISSION (Императорская Археологическая Коммиссія, Imperátorskaja Archeologícheskaja Commíssia[1]) is the central organ of Russian archaeology. The movement which led to its establishment produced two works which may be classed with its publications :

Antiquités du Bosphore Cimmérien [**ABC.**] *conservées au Musée Impérial de l'Ermitage*, large folio, St P. 1854, published in Russian and French facing each other. This rare book was reissued in large 8ᵛᵒ by S. Reinach in his "Bibliothèque des Monuments Figurés," Paris, 1892, with new introduction and descriptions to the plates, which are reduced almost to half size. Except where fine detail or colour are important I have used this convenient edition instead of the cumbrous original.

Извлеченіе изъ всеподданнѣйшаго отчета объ археологическихъ розысканіяхъ въ 1853 г. (*Izvlechénie iz vsepóddannêjshago Otchéta ob Archeologícheskikh Rozyskániakh v* 1853 *godú* = *Extract from a most humble Report on the Archaeological Explorations in* 1853), by Uvarov and Leontiev, 4ᵗᵒ, St P. 1855.

The Commission is constituted as a part of the Ministry of the Imperial Court, as is also the Hermitage Museum. Its most important publication is :—

Compte Rendu [**CR.**] (Отчетъ, *Otchêt*) *de la Commission Impériale Archéologique*.

From 1859 to 1881 the text (4to) of this contained a Report (in French) of the excavations conducted in each year, and a Supplement by L. Stephani in German (1859 is in French) dealing with various objects either yielded by recent excavations or preserved in the Hermitage ; there were occasional woodcuts (unnumbered) and very few plates except in the text for 1872, which has as a second supplement V. Stasov's French account of a catacomb illustrated with 18 plates ; each part is accompanied by an atlas of six magnificent plates. Each part has a superficial index, and in Reinach's *ABC.* there is a short summary of the contents of this series and a meagre index to the whole.

The Reports for 1882—1888 were all issued at once (sm. folio) with an atlas of the same type, a description of its six plates and an index ; this volume appeared in a French and a Russian edition.

CR. from 1889 to 1898, henceforward in Russian (sm. folio without an atlas but with many cuts in the text), contained the Reports year by year, an appendix with fuller reports of particular excavations but no index : indices to the years 1882—1898 form a separate volume. From 1899 the fuller reports have been transferred to *BCA.* and each volume has been supplied with an index. *CR.* comes out four or five years after date.

---

[1] To be distinguished from the Imp. Archaeographic (Археографическая) Comm., which publishes documents dealing with Russian history, e.g. versions of Ps. Nestor's *Chronicle*, and in its *Chronicle* (*Lêtopis*) articles upon such subjects.

The Imp. Archaeological Commission has also issued:—

Antiquités de la Scythie d'Hérodote [**ASH.**], two Parts, 1866, 1873, 4to, text (in French) and large atlas, forming the first two numbers of

Матеріалы по Археологіи Россіи [**Mat.**] (*Materiály po Archeológii Rossíi, Materials for the Archaeology of Russia*), Nos. III.— (*ASH.* being reckoned as Nos. I. and II.), 1888— (sm. folio), contain monographs with excellent plates, dealing with the following particular finds or classes of antiquities:—

South Russia: Nos. I., II. (= *ASH.*); VI., XIX. Kulakovskij, Catacombs at Kerch, v. p. 308 n. 4; VII., XII. Malmberg and Orêshnikov, Bertier-de-La-Garde, Chersonese Finds, v. pp. 363 n. 1, 553, 509 n. 1; VIII. Strzygowski and Pokrovskij, Shield (?) from Kerch, v. p. 320 n. 3; IX., XVII., XXIII. Latyshev, Inscriptions; XIII. Malmberg and Lappo-Danilevskij, Karagodeuashkh, v. p. 216; XXIV. Zhebelëv, Panticapaean Niobids, v. p. 370; XXXI. Pridik, Melgunov's Find, v. p. 172 n. 1; XXXII. Zhebelëv and Malmberg, Three Archaic Bronzes, v. p. 374 n. 4.

South-West Russia: XI. Antonovich, Excavations in the country of the Drevljane (all dates, Sc. to Slav).

North-West Russia: IV. Avenarius, Drogichin Cemetery (Govt. Grodno); XIV. Spítsyn and Romanov, Ljutsin Cemetery (Govt. Vitebsk); XXVIII. Sizóv, Gnêzdovo near Smolensk (Liv (?) and Slav graves X.—XI. cent. A.D.).

Novgorod Frescoes: XXI. Examination of Suslov's scheme for restoring Frescoes in S. Sophia; XXX. Pokryshkin, Report on restoration of S. Saviour's, Nereditsa.

North Russia: XVIII. Brandenbourg, Barrows S. of L. Ladoga (Finnish, VIII.—XI. A.D.); XX. Spitsyn and Ivanovskij, Barrows of St P. Govt.; XXIX. Glazov, Barrows at Gdov (Slav or Finnish, XI.—XV. A.D.).

East Russia: X. Cemeteries at Ljada and Tomnikovo (Tambov Govt.); XXV. Spitsyn, Antt. of the Kama and Oka (Finnish, X.—XI. A.D.); XXVI. Spitsyn, Antt. of the Chud' folk on the Kama (Finnish, I.—XIV. A.D. v. p. 257 n. 3); XXII. Chwohlson, Pokrovskij and Smirnov, Syrian Dish from Perm (VI.—VII. A.D.).

Siberia: III., V., XV., XXVII. Radloff, Antiquities of Siberia, v. p. 241 n. 1.

Transcaspia: XVI. Zhukovskij, Ruins of Ancient Merv.

Herat: XXXIII. N. I. Veselovskij, Cauldron dated A.H. 559.

Извѣстія Имп. Арх. Комм. [**BCA.**] (*Izvêstia Imp. Arch. Comm.* = *Bulletin—Mitteilungen—de la Commission Imp. Archéologique*), large 8vo, 1901— (45 Pts in Aug. 1912, indices in Nos. XX. and XL.), contains fuller reports of particular excavations, various articles not important enough for *Mat.*, reports of decisions of the Commission with regard to proposed changes in churches and other ancient buildings (forming a special series called Voprósy restavrátsii, Questions of Restoration). Two numbers a year are furnished with a Прибавленіе (*Pribavlénie* = *Supplement*), in which are collected reprints of newspaper articles touching Archaeology and a list of Archaeological publications for the half-year.

Besides these the Commission has issued

Альбомъ рисунковъ помѣщенныхъ въ Отчетахъ за 1882—1898 годы (*Albóm risúnkov pomêshchënnykh v Otchëtakh za 1882—1898 gódy* = *Album of Illustrations that appeared in CR. 1882—1898*), St P. 1906.

Also Kondakov's *Russian Hoards*, Smirnov's *Argenterie Orientale*, Kulakovskij's *Past of Taurida*, Latyshev's Ποντικά, Rostovtsev's *Decorative Painting* and von Stern's *Watercolour Vases*, v. § B.

The IMPERIAL RUSSIAN ARCHAEOLOGICAL SOCIETY (Императорское Русское Археологическое Общество) of St P., founded in 1846, has issued several different series of publications (v. Polênov, D. V., Библіографическое Обозрѣніе Трудовъ И. Р. А. О., *Bibliographical Survey of the Works of the I.R.A.S.*, St P. 1871, and N. I. Veselovskij, *History of the I.R.A.S.* 1846—1896, St P. 1900, pp. 97—142). Those touching the subject of this book are:—

Mémoires de la Société d'Archéologie et de Numismatique de St P., Vols. I.—VI. 1847—1852, French or German articles, sometimes identical with those appearing in

Записки Санктпетербургскаго Археологическо-Нумизматическаго Общества, after Vol. III. Имп. Археологическаго Общ. (*Zapíski = Transactions—Sanctpeterbúrgskago Archeologíchesko-Numismatícheskago Óbshchestva*, afterwards *Imp. Archeologícheskago O.*), I.— XIV. 1847—1858.

Извѣстія И.А.О. (*Izvéstia I.A.O. = Bulletin*), I.—X. 1857—1884, but little concerned with Prehistoric or Classical Antiquities, then took their place.

Записки (*Zapíski* [З.И.Р.А.О. = **TRAS.**], new series), revived by a resolution made in 1882 and coming out in three parallel sets, Oriental (1886—), General (Vols. I.—VI. 1886—1895), Russian and Slavonic (Vols. III. and IV. 1882, 1887, Nos. I. and II. being in the old series). This last was united with the General, so that its Vols VII.—IX. 1896—1901 are each in two parts, i. Russo-Slavonic, ii. Classical and West European, but restored and the old numeration resumed with Vols. V.— 1903— , and the Classical, etc. started afresh with Vols. I.— 1904— . A Numismatic section began to publish *Zapíski* in 1906.

The Society also published Koehne's *Chersonese*, Sabatier's *Souvenirs de Kertsch*, Latyshev's *IosPE, Inscr. Christ.*, and *Sc. et Cauc.* v. § B.

It has a small Museum, *Catalogue* by A. A. Spitsyn, 1908.

The IMPERIAL MOSCOW ARCHAEOLOGICAL SOCIETY (Императорское Московское Археологическое Общество = Imp. Moskóvskoe Arch. Ob.) has not produced very much with which we are concerned in Древности (*Drévnosti = Antiquities*), as its Труды (*Trudý* or *Transactions*, lit. *Labours*) are called, Moscow, 1865— .

Археологическія Извѣстія и Замѣтки (*Archeologícheskia Izvéstia i Zamétki = Arch. Bulletin and Notes*), 1893— .

Матеріалы по Археологіи Восточныхъ Губерній (*Materials for the Archaeology of the Eastern Governments*), 1893— .

Матеріалы по Археологіи Кавказа (*Mat. for the Arch. of the Caucasus*), 1894— .

Памятники Христіанскаго Херсонеса (*Pámjatniki Christiánskago Chersonésa = Monuments of Christian Chersonese*), Pts I., II., III. (1905—1911), however, promise to form a most important series, v. Ainalov, Lavrov, Shestakov in § B.

It has been chiefly instrumental in organizing the Archaeological Congresses (Съѣздъ, S'ézd), of which the *Trudý* (*Trans.*) in 4to are most valuable. They were held I. Moscow, 1869; II. St P. 1872; III. Kiev, 1875; IV. Kazan, 1878; V. Tiflis, 1881; VI. Odessa, 1884; VII. Jaroslav, 1887; VIII. Moscow, 1890; IX. Vilna, 1893; X. Riga, 1896; XI. Kiev, 1899; XII. Kharkov, 1902; XIII. Ekaterinoslav, 1905; XIV. Chernigov, 1908; XV. Novgorod, 1911. Preliminary reports of papers are published in the *Izvéstia* or *Bulletin* of the Congress.

The MOSCOW NUMISMATIC SOCIETY (Московское Нумизматическое Общество, Moskóvskoe Numismatícheskoe Óbshchestvo) publishes Труды (*Trudý, Transactions*), 1897— , and a Нумизматическій Сборникъ (*Numismatícheskij Sbórnik = Numismatic Miscellany*), 1908— .

Moscow UNIVERSITY published Miller's *Ossetian Studies* and Orêshnikov's *Catalogue of its Coins*, v. § B.

The IMPERIAL ALEXANDER III. HISTORICAL MUSEUM OF RUSSIA, Moscow (Имп. Россійскій Историческій Музей Имени Императора Александра III.) issues *Reports* (Отчетъ, Otchët), 1899— .

The IMPERIAL HISTORICAL AND ANTIQUARIAN SOCIETY OF ODESSA (Имп. Одесское Общество Исторіи и Древностей = Imp. Odésskoe Óbshchestvo Istórii i Drévnostej) published Vol. I. of its Заниски [З.О.О. = **Trans. Od. Soc.**] (*Zapíski = Transactions*) in 1844; Vols. I.—XV. are 4ᵗᵒ; Vols. XVI.—XXX. (1912) in 8ᵛᵒ have separate paginations for: i. *Investigations*, ii. *Materials*, iii. *Miscellanea*, iv. *Obituaries*, v. *Minutes* (Протоколы) *of Meetings*.

    It has also issued in sm. folio, text in German and Russian :—
Das Museum der Kaiserlich Odessaer Gesellschaft für Geschichte und Alterthumskunde :—
   i. (1897), ii. (1898), *Terracotten* [**Od. Mus. Terra-cottas**], by A. A. Derevitskij, A. A. Pavlovskij and E. R. von Stern; iii. (1906), *Theodosia und seine Keramik* [**Theodosia**], by E. R. von Stern.

Краткій Указатель Музея Имп. Од. Общ. Ист. и Др. [**Od. Mus. Guide**] (*Krátkij Ukazátel' Muséa Imp. Od. Obshch. = A Short Guide to the Museum of the Imp. Od. Soc.*), ed. 2, 1909, by von Stern, mentions some important objects not yet published.

The MUNICIPALITY OF KHERSON is issuing V. I. Goszkewicz's Херсонскій Городской Музей (*Khersónskij Gorodskój Muséj = Kherson Town Museum*), i. (Coins) 1910; ii. (Chronicle 1909–11) 1912.

The TAURIC RECORD COMMISSION (Таврическая Ученая Архивная Коммиссія, Tavrícheskaja Uchënaja Archívnaja Commíssia) publishes its Извѣстія (*Izvêstia = Bulletin*) since 1887, 46 numbers, 8ᵛᵒ.

The MINISTRY OF PUBLIC INSTRUCTION in St P. publishes its Журналъ [Ж.М.Н.П. = **Journ. Min. Pub. Instr.**] monthly since 1834; it contains some articles concerning S. Russia in the body of the magazine and many in a special Classical Section with separate pagination.

KIEV UNIVERSITY (the University of S. Vladimir) publishes Извѣстія (*Izvêstia = Bulletin*), 1861— , in which Antonovich's *Description* of its coins appeared.

The RUSSIAN ARCHAEOLOGICAL INSTITUTE IN CONSTANTINOPLE (Русскій Археологическій Институтъ въ Константинополѣ) publishes Извѣстія (*Izvêstia*) but they are not concerned with our region.

Private Magazines in Russian.

Пропилеи (*Propylaea*), ed. P. Leontiev, v. vols. 8ᵛᵒ, Moscow, 1851—1856.

Филологическое Обозрѣніе (*Philologícheskoe Obozrênie = Philological Review*), Moscow, 1891— , now defunct.

Гермесъ, Научно-популярный Вѣстникъ Античнаго Міра (*Germes*, i.e. *Hermes, a Popular Scientific Messenger of the Ancient World*), St P. 1907— , ed. A. I. Malein and S. O. Cybulski.

Археологическая Лѣтопись Южной Россіи (*Archeologícheskaja Létopis' Júzhnoj Rossíi, Arch. Chronicle of S. Russia*), published by N. Th. Bêlashevskij as a supplement to *Kíevskaja Stariná*, 1899—1901, and then independently, Kiev, 1903—1905.

B.   *Full Titles of Books published in Russia, etc.*

AINÁLOV, D. V. (Айналовъ, Д. В.).   Памятники Христіанскаго Херсонеса, I. Развалины Храмовъ (*Pámjatniki Christiánskago Chersonésa, I. Razváliny Khrámov = Monuments of Christian Chersonese, I. Ruins of Churches*).   Moscow, 1905.

ANTONOVICH, V. B. (Антоновичъ, В. Б.).   Описаніе Монетъ и Медалей хранящихся въ нумизматическомъ музеѣ Университета св. Владиміра (*Opisánie Monét i Medálej khranjáshchikhsja v numismatícheskom Muséé Universitéta sv. Vladímira = Descr. of coins and medals preserved in the Numism. Museum of the Univ. of S. Vladimir*).   Kiev, 1896.

ARKAS, Z. (Аркасъ, З.).   Описаніе Ираклійскаго Полуострова и Древностей его (*Opisánie Iraklíjskago Poluóstrova i Drévnostej egó = Descr. of the Heraclean Peninsula and its Antiquities*).   Trans. *Od. Soc.* Vol. II. and Nicolaev, 1879.

ASHIK, A. (Ашикъ, А.).   Воспорское Царство (*Vospórskoe Tsárstvo = The Bosporan Kingdom*).   4to.   Odessa, 1848—1849.

—— Керченскія Древности.   О Пантикапейской Катакомбѣ украшенной фресками (*Kérchenskia Drévnosti. O Pantikapéjskoj Catacómbé ukráshennoj fréscami = Antt. of Kerch. A Panticapaean Catacomb adorned with frescoes*).   Folio.   Odessa, 1845.

BERTIER-DE-LA-GARDE, A. I. (Бертье-Делагардъ, А. Л.).   Поправки Общаго Каталога Монетъ П. О. Бурачкова (*Poprávki Óbshchago Catáloga Monét P. O. Burachkóva = Corrections of P. O. B.'s General Coin Cat.*).   4to.   Moscow, 1907.

BOBRINSKOJ, Ct A. A. (Бобринской, Графъ А. А.).   Смѣла (*Sméla* [**Sm.**], v. p. 175 n. 1), III. vols.   Folio.   St P. 1887—1901.

—— Херсонесъ Таврическій (*Chersonesus Taurica*).   8vo.   St P. 1905.

—— Сборникъ Археологическихъ Статей поднесенный Гр. А. А. Б. въ день 25 лѣтія Предсѣдательства его въ Имп. Арх. Комм. 1886—1911 (*Sbórnik Archeologícheskikh Statéj podnesénnyj Gr. A. A. B. v den' 25 létia predsédátel'stva egó v Imp. Arch. Comm. = Miscellany* [**Misc.**] *of Archaeological Articles presented to Ct A. A. B. on the 25th anniversary of his Presidency of the Imp. Arch. Commission, 1886—1911*) [résumé, *Arch. Anz.* 1912, pp. 147—153].   8vo.   St P. 1911.

BONNELL, E.   *Beiträge zur Alterthumskunde Russlands.*   8vo, II. vols.   St P. 1882, 1897.

BRAUN, FR. (Браунъ, Ѳ. А.).   Разысканія въ области Гото-славянскихъ отношеній (*Razyskánia v óblasti Goto-Slavjánskikh Otnoshénij = Investigations in the province of Gotho-Slavonic Relations*), Pt I. *Sbórnik,* Russian section of the Ac. of Sc. St P. Vol. LXIV. 12, 1899.

BROCKHAUS-JEFRON (Брокгаузъ-Ефронъ).   Энциклопедическій Словарь (*Entsiclopedícheskij Slovár' = Encyclopaedia*).   8vo.   St P. c. 1900 and Supplements.

BRUUN, F.   Черноморье (*Chernomórje = The Black Sea Region*).   2 Pts.   From Записки Имп. Новороссійскаго Университета (*Zapiski Imp. Novorossíjskago Universiteta*), Vols. XXVIII., XXX.   Odessa, 1879, 1880.

BURACHKOV, P. O. [**B.** or **Bur.**] (Бурачковъ, П. О.).   Общій Каталогъ Монетъ принадлежащихъ Эллинскимъ Колоніямъ...въ предѣлахъ нынѣшней южной Россіи (*Obshchij Catálog Monét prinadlezháshchikh Ellínskim Colóniam...v predélakh nýnéshnej Júzhnoj Rossíi = General Catalogue of Coins belonging to the Greek Colonies...within the bounds of what is now S. Russia*).   4to, Pt I. (all issued).   Odessa, 1884.

FUNDUKLEJ, I. (Фундуклей, I.).   Обозрѣніе Могилъ, Валовъ и Городищъ Кіевской Губерніи (*Obozrénie Mogíl, Valóv i Gorodíshch Kíevskoj Gubérnii = Survey of Barrows, Banks and Camps in Kiev Govt*).   Kiev, 1848.

GIEL, CHR. [**G.**].   *Kleine Beiträge* [**Kl. B.**] *zur Antiken Numismatik Südrusslands.*   4to. Moscow, 1886.

GOERTZ, K. K. (Гёрцъ, К. .К.).   Археологическая Топографія Таманскаго Полуострова (*Archeologícheskaja Topográphia Tamánskago Poluóstrova = Arch. Topogr. of the Taman Peninsula*). Ed. I. *Drevnosti*, II. (1870). Ed. II. 8vo, Acad. of Sc. St. P. 1898.

—— Историческій Обзоръ Археологическихъ Изслѣдованій и Открытій на Таманскомъ Полуостровѣ...до 1859 г. (*Istorícheskij Obzór Arch. Izslědovanij i Otkrýtij na Tamánskom Poluóstrové...do 1859 g. = Hist. Conspectus of Arch. Invest. and Discoveries on Taman Pen. up to 1859*). Ed. I. *Drevnosti*, IV. (1876). Ed. II. 8vo, Acad. of Sc. St P. 1898.

GOLUBÍNSKIJ, E. E. (Голубинскій, Е. Е.).   Исторія Русской Церкви (*Istória Rússkoj Tsérkvi = Hist. Russ. Ch.*). Ed. II. Moscow, 1901—1904.

GORODTSÓV, V. A. (Городцовъ, В. А.).   Первобытная Археологія (*Pervobýtnaja Archéologia = Primitive Arch.*). Moscow, 1908.

—— Бытовая Археологія (*Bytovája Arch. = Cultural Arch.*). М. 1910.
    These books came too late for me to make use of them in Chapters IV.—IX.

GOSZKEWICZ, V. I. (Гошкевичъ, В. И.).   Клады и Древности (*Klády i Drévnosti = Treasure-trove and Antiquities*). Kherson, 1903.

GRIGORIEV, V. V. (Григорьевъ, В. В.).   Россія и Азія (*Rossía i Ásia*). St P. 1876.

JAGIĆ, I. (Ягичъ, И. В.).   Четыре Критико-Палеографическія Статьи (*Chetýre Critico-Paleo-graphícheskia Statjí = Four Critico-palaeogr. Articles*) in No. XXXIII. of the *Sbornik* of the Acad. of Sc. St P. 1884.

KARAMZÍN, N. (Карамзинъ, Н.).   Исторія Государства Россійскаго (*Istória Gosudárstva Rossíjskago = Hist. of the Russian State*). St P. 1816—1826.

KHANÉNKO, B. I. and V. I. (Ханенко, Б. И. и В. И.).   Собраніе Ханенко (*Sobránie Khanenko = Collection Khanenko*). Folio. Kiev, 1899— .

KLEMENTZ, D. (Клеменцъ, Д.).   Древности Минусинскаго Музея (*Drévnosti Minusínskago Muséja = Antt. of Minusinsk Museum*). Tomsk, 1886.

KOEHNE, B. de.   Изслѣдованія .объ Исторіи и Древностяхъ Города Херсонеса Таврическаго (*Izslědovania ob Istórii i Drévnostjakh Góroda Chersonésa Tavrícheskago = Investigations into the History and Antiquities of the city of Chersonesus Taurica*). Published by the St P. Archaeologico-Numismatic Soc. St P. 1848. The German text had appeared in its *Mémoires*, v. inf. p. 551.

—— *Description du Musée de feu le Prince Kotschoubey* [**MK.**]. 2 vols. 4to. St P. 1857.

KONDAKÓV, N. P. (Кондаковъ, Н. П.), with Ct I. I. TOLSTÓJ (Гр. I. I. Толстой), Русскія Древности вя Памятникахъ Искусства (*Rússkia Drévnosti v Pámjatnikakh Iskússtva = Russian Antt. in Monuments of Art*). VI. Pts, 4to. St P. 1888—1899.
    S. Reinach issued Pts I.—III. as *Antiquités de la Russie Méridionale* [**KTR.**]. 4to. Paris, 1891.

KONDAKÓV, N. P.   Русскіе Клады, Изслѣдованіе Древностей Великокняжескаго Періода (*Rússkie Klády, Izslědovanie Drévnostej Velikoknjázheskago Períoda = Russian Hoards, an Investigation into the Antiquities of the Grand Ducal Period*). Folio. Pt I. (Pt II. has not appeared). Issued by the Arch. Comm. St P. 1896.

KULAKÓVSKIJ, J. A. (Кулаковскій, Ю. А.).   Карта Европейской Сарматіп по Птолемею (*Kárta Evropéjskoj Sarmátii po Ptoleméju*). Folio. Kiev, 1899.

KULAKOVSKIJ, J. A.   Прошлое Тавриды (*Próshloe Tavrídy* = *The Past of Taurida*).   Issued by the Arch. Comm.   8ᵛᵒ.   Kiev, 1906.

LAMÁNSKIJ, V. I. (Ламанскій, В. И.).   Сборникъ Статей посвященныхъ его поклонниками В. И. Л. (*Sbórnik Statéj posvjashchënnykh egô poklónnikami V. I. L.* = *Miscellany of Articles dedicated by his admirers to V. I. L.*).   2 vols.   St P.   1908.

LAPPO-DANILÉVSKIJ, A. S. (Лаппо-Данилевскій, А. С.).   Скиѳскія Древности (*Skýthskia Drévnosti* = *Sc. Antt.*).   *TRAS.*   Slav. Sect. Vol. IV.   1887.

LÁTYSHEV, V. V. (Латышевъ, В. В.).   Изслѣдованія объ Исторіи и Государственномъ Строѣ города Ольвіи (*Izslêdovania ob Istórii i Gosudárstvennom Strôê góroda Ol'vii* = *Investigations into the History and Constitution of the city of Olbia*).   Reprinted from *Journ. Min. Publ. Instr.*   St P. Jan.—Apr. 1887.

——— *Inscriptiones Antiquae Orae Septentrionalis Ponti Euxini* [IosPE.].   4ᵗᵒ.   Vol. I. 1885, Vol. II. 1890, Vol. IV. 1901.   Vol. III., which is to contain inscriptions on amphorae, graffiti and such like, is being prepared by E. M. Pridik.   Vol. V., containing inscriptions found during this century and published in *BCA.*, is said to be contemplated.

——— Сборникъ Греческихъ Надписей Христіанскихъ Временъ изъ Южной Россіи [Inscr. Christ.] (*Sbórnik Grécheskikh Nádpisej Christiánskikh Vremën iz Júzhnoj Rossíi* = *Collection of Greek Inscriptions of Christian Times from S. Russia*).   8ᵛᵒ.   1896.   More recent inscriptions are in *IosPE.* IV. or *BCA.*   Both *IosPE.* and *Inscr. Christ.* are published by the Imp. Russ. Arch. Soc. St. P.

——— *Scythica et Caucasica* [Sc. et Cauc.] *e veteribus Scriptoribus Graecis et Latinis collegit et cum versione Rossica edidit B. Latyschev.*   Vol. I. Greek, Vol. II. Latin.   Issued in parts, 1890—1906, as a Supplement to *TRAS.* or as Vols. XI. ii. and Vol. II. of the Classical Series.   No index.

——— Ποντικά (Russian.   A selection of his scientific and critical articles on the History, Archaeology, Geography and Epigraphy of Scythia, the Caucasus and the Greek Colonies on the shores of the Black Sea).   8ᵛᵒ.   Issued by the Imp. Arch. Comm.   St P. 1909.

LÁVROV, P. A. (Лавровъ, П. А.).   Житія Херсонскихъ Святыхъ въ Греко-Славянской Письменности (*Zhitiá Chersónskikh Svjatýkh v Greco-Slavjánskoj Pís'mennosti* = *Lives of the Chersonian SS. in Graeco-Slavonic Literature*).   No. II. of *Monuments of Chr. Chersonese.*   Moscow, 1911.

MANSVÉTOV, I. D. (Мансветовъ, И. Д.).   Историческое Описаніе древняго Херсонеса и открытыхъ въ немъ памятниковъ (*Istorícheskoe Opisánie drévnjago Chersonésa i otkrýtykh v nëm pámjatnikov* = *Hist. Descr. of Anc. Chersonese and the monuments discovered in it*).   Moscow, 1872.

MILLER, VS. TH. (Миллеръ, Вс. Ѳ.).   Осетинскіе Этюды (*Osetínskie Etjúdy* = *Ossetian Studies*).   3 Pts, 8ᵛᵒ.   Published by the Univ. of Moscow, 1881—1887.

NESTOR (so-called).   Лѣтопись по Лаврентіевскому Списку (*Létopis' po Lavrèntievskomy Spísky* = *Chronicle according to the Laurentian Version*).   Ed. III. issued by the Archaeographic Comm.   St P. 1897.   French Translation by L. Leger, Paris, 1884.

NIEDERLE, DR L.   Lidstvo v dobĕ předhistorické (*Man in Prehistoric Time*).   Prag, 1893.   Translated into Russian as Человѣчество въ доисторическія времена (*Chelovêchestvo v doistorícheskia vremená*) [Preh. Man] by Th. K. Volkov and ed. by D. N. Anuchin, St P. 1898.

NIEDERLE, DR L. Staroveké Zprávy o zemĕpisu východní Evropy se zřetelem na zemĕ Slovanské (*Descriptio Europae Regionum quae ad orientem spectant veterum Scriptorum locis illustrata*), Čech, from " Rozpravy české Akademie Císaře Františka Josefa pro vĕdy, slovesnost a umĕní" (*Trans. Čech Acad. of Emp. Francis Joseph for Sc., Lit. and Art*), VII. i. I. Prag, 1899.

—— Slovanské Starožitnosti (*Slavonic Antiquities*) [Slav. Ant.]. Prag, 1902— .

ORÊSHNIKOV, A. V. (Орѣшниковъ, А. В.). *Zur Münzkunde des Cimmerischen Bosporus.* 8ᵛᵒ. Moscow, 1883.

—— Каталогъ Собранія Древностей Гр. А. С. Уварова; Вып. VII. Монеты Воспорскаго Царства и Древнегреческихъ Городовъ находившихся въ предѣлахъ нынѣшней Россіи (*Catálog Sobránia Drévnostej Gr. A. S. Uvárova, Vyp. VII. Monéty Vospórskago Tsárstva i Drevnegrécheskikh Gorodóv nakhodívshikhsja v predélakh nynêshnej Rossíi = Cat. of the Coll. of Antt. of Ct A. S. Uvarov, Pt VII. Coins of the Bosporan Kingdom and of the ancient Greek cities within the limits of modern Russia*) [Cat. Uvarov]. 4ᵗᵒ. Moscow, 1887.

—— Описаніе Древне-греческихъ Монетъ принадлежащихъ Имп. Московскому Университету (*Opisánie Drevne-grécheskikh Monét prinadlezháshchikh Imp. Moskóvskomy Universitétu = Descr. of ancient Greek coins belonging to the Imp. Moscow Univ.*). Published by the Cabinet of Fine Arts, Moscow Univ., 8ᵛᵒ, 1891.

—— Матеріалы по Древней Нумизматикѣ Черноморскаго Побережья (*Materiály po drévnej Numismátikê Chernomórskago Poberézhia = Mat. touching the ancient Numismatics of the Black Sea Coast*). [Mat. for Num.] 8ᵛᵒ. Moscow, 1892.

PODSHIVÁLOV, A. M. (Подшиваловъ, А. М.). *Beschreibung der unedirten und wenigbekannten Münzen von Sarmatia Europaea, Cher. Taur. und Bosp. Cimm. aus der Sammlung A. M. P.* Moscow, 1882.

—— Нумизматическій Кабинетъ Московскаго Публичнаго и Румянцевскаго Музеевъ, I. (*Numism. Cabinet of Moscow Public and Rumjantsev Museums, I. Sarm., Cher. T., Bosporus*). Moscow, 1884.

POMJALÓVSKIJ, I. V. (Помяловскій, И. В.). Сборникъ Греческихъ и Латинскихъ Надписей Кавказа (*Sbórnik Grécheskikh i Latínskikh Nádpisej Kavkáza = Coll. of Gr. and Lat. Inscrr. of the Caucasus*). Made for the vth (Tiflis) Arch. Congress, St P. 1881.

ROSTÓVTSEV, M. I. (Ростовцевъ, М. И.). Исторія Государственнаго Откупа въ Римской Имперіи (*Istória Gosudárstvennogo Ótkupa v Rímskoj Impérii = History of State Contracts in the Roman Empire*). St P. 1899. Also in German, Leipzig, 1902.

—— Античная Декоративная Живопись на Югѣ Россіи (*Antíchnaja Decoratívnaja Zhívopis' na Júgê Rossíi = Ancient Decorative Painting in S. Russia*). Folio, many coloured plates. Issued by the Arch. Comm. too late for my use. St P. 1913.

SABATIER, P. *Souvenirs de Kertsch et chronologie du royaume du Bosphore.* Issued by the Arch. Num. Soc. St P. 1849. A Russian translation appeared in 1851.

ŠAFAŘÍK, P. Slovanské Starožitnosti (*Slavonic Antiquities*). Prag, 1862-3.

SAMOKVÁSOV, D. J. (Самоквасовъ, Д. Я.). Исторія Русскаго Права (*Istória Rússkago Práva = Hist. of Russian Law*). Pt II. Warsaw, 1884.

SHESTAKÓV, S. P. (Шестаковъ, С. П.). Очерки по Исторіи Херсонеса въ VI—X вѣкахъ по P. Хр. (*Ócherki po Istórii Chersonésa v VI—X vékákh po R. Chr. = Sketches of the Hist. of Chersonese in the VIth—Xth centuries A.D.*). No. III. of *Monuments of Chr. Chersonese.* Moscow, 1908.

SIBIRSKIJ, PR. A. A.   *Catalogue des Médailles du Bosphore Cimmérien précédé d'études sur l'histoire et les antiquités de ce pays.* Vol. I. all produced. 4to. St P. 1859. A Russian translation was produced next year but only three or four copies of either exist. Fragments are published in *Trans. Od. Soc.* and *TRAS.* first series.

ŠKORPIL, V. V. and MARTI, J. J.   Керамическія Падниси хранящіяся въ Мелекъ-Чесменскомъ Курганѣ въ гор. Керчи (*Keramícheskia Nádpisi khranjáshchiasja v Melek-Chesménskom Kurgánê v gor. Kérchi = Ceramic Inscrr. in the Melek-Chesme Barrow, Kerch*). 4to. Odessa, 1910.

SMIRNÓV, J. I. (Смирновъ, Я. И.).   Восточное Серебро. Атласъ Древнѣйшей Серебряной и Золотой Посуды Восточнаго Происхожденія найденной преимущественно въ предѣлахъ Россійской Имперіи (*Vostóchnoe Serebró. Átlas Drevnéjshej Serébrjanoj i Zolotój Posúdy Vostóchnago Proiskhozhdénia najdénnoj preimúshchestvenno v predélakh Rossíjskoj Impérii = Argenterie Orientale. Recueil d'ancienne vaisselle orientale en argent et or trouvée principalement en Russie*). Short introduction in Russian, table of localities in French. Folio, 130 plates. Issued by the Arch. Comm. St P. 1909.

SPÁSSKIJ, G. A. (Спасскій, Г. А.).   Археолого-Нумизматическій Сборникъ (*Arch.-Num. Sbórnik = Arch.-Num. Miscellany*). 4to. Moscow, 1850.

STERN, E. R. VON.   Акварельныя Вазы (*Aquarél'nya Vázy = Watercolour Vases*). Folio. To be issued by the Arch. Comm. St P. 1913. See too Odessa Soc. in § A.

SUMARÓKOV, P. (Сумароковъ, П.).   Досуги Крымскаго Судьи (*Dosúgi Krýmskago Sudjí = Leisure of a Crimean Judge*). 4to. St P. 1803-5.

TOLSTÓI, Ct I. I. (Толстой, Гр. И. И.).   v. Kondakov.

UVÁROV, Ct A. S. (Уваровъ, Гр. А. С.; also transliterated Uwarow and Ouvaroff).   Археологія Россіи: Каменный Вѣкъ (*Arch. Rossíi: Kámennyj Vék = Arch. of Russia: Stone Age*). II. vols. Moscow, 1882.

VINOGRÁDOV, V. K. (Виноградовъ, В. К.).   Ѳеодосія (*Theodosia*). 8vo. Theodosia, 1884.

ZABÈLIN, I. E. (Забѣлинъ, И. Е.).   Исторія Русской Жизни (*Istória Rússkoj Zhízni = History of Russian Life*). II. vols. Moscow, 1876.

C. *Abbreviations.*

Ordinary abbreviations of classical authors and their works, and titles which have not been cut down very short, have been left unexplained.

AA.SS. *Acta Sanctorum* (Bollandi). Antwerp, 1643— .

ABC. *Antiquités du Bosphore Cimmérien.* v. § A, p. xxv.

Anon. *Anonymi Periplus Ponti Euxini*, in *GGM.* or *Sc. et Cauc.* v. p. 25.

Ant. Gem. A. Furtwängler, *Die Antiken Gemmen.* Berlin, 1900.

Ant. Sib. W. Radloff, "Antiquities of Siberia" in *Mat.*, Nos. III., v., XV., XXVII.

Arch. Anz. *Archäologischer Anzeiger*, Suppl. to *Jahrb. d. k. deutschen Archäologischen Instituts.* Berlin, 1886— .

Arch. Chron. of S. Russia. v. § A, p. xxviii.

Arch. Congress. Russian Archaeological Congresses held in connexion with the Imp. Moscow Arch. Soc., q.v. in § A, p. xxvii.

ASH. *Antiquités de la Scythie d'Hérodote.* v. § A, p. xxvi.

Ath. Mitt. *Mitteilungen des k. deutschen Arch. Instituts.* Athens, 1876—

Aus Sib. W. Radloff, *Aus Sibirien.* Leipzig, 1884.

A.V. E. Gerhard, *Auslesene Gr. Vasenbilder.* Berlin, 1840.

M.

B., Bur. (coins).　Burachkov. v. § B, p. xxix.
BCA.　*Bulletin de la Commission Impériale Archéologique.* v. § A, p. xxvi.
BCH.　*Bulletin de Correspondance Hellénique.* Athens, 1877— .
B.de-La-G. }
BG. (coins).}　Bertier-de-La-Garde.
Beschr.　*Beschreibung*, e.g. Podshivalov, § B, p. xxxii, and *Berlin Coin Cat.*
B.M.　British Museum : *BMC.* = *Cat. of Greek Coins* : *BM. Jewellery*, v. p. 386 n. 6.
Bobrinskoj Misc.　v. § B, p. xxix, s.v. Bobrinskoj.
BSA.　*Annual of the British School at Athens.* London, 1896.
Bulletin of Kiev University.　v. § A, p. xxviii, s.v. Kiev.
Bull. of XII. Arch. Congress.　v. § A, p. xxvii, s.v. Imp. Moscow Arch. Soc.
Bull. of Russian Inst. in C-ple. }
Bull. Taur. Rec. C. }　v. § A, p. xxviii.
Bull. Imp. Ac. Sc. St P.　v. § A, p. xxv.
Cat. Moscow Univ. Coins. }
Cat. Uvarov. }　v. § B, p. xxxii, s.v. Orêshnikov.
Cher.　Chersonese.
CIAtt.　*Corpus Inscriptionum Atticarum* (= *IG.* I, II).
CIG.　*Corpus Inscriptionum Graecarum* (Boeckh).
CIL.　*Corpus Inscriptionum Latinarum.*
Cl. Rev.　*Classical Review.* London, 1887— .
Coll. Khanenko.　v. § B, p. xxx, s.v. Khanenko.
CR.　*Compte Rendu de la Comm. Imp. Arch.* v. § A, p. xxv.
DA.　K. Müllenhoff, *Deutsche Altertumskunde.* Berlin, 1870—1900.
Dar. et Saglio.　Daremberg et Saglio, *Dictionnaire des Antiquités.* Paris, 1877— .
D.N.V.　Eckhel, *Doctrina Numorum Veterum.* Vienna, 1792–98.
Drevnosti.　v. § A, p. xxvii, s.v. Imp. Mosc. Arch. Soc.
ʼΕφ. ʼΑρχ.　ʼΕφημερὶς ʼΑρχαιολογική. Athens, 1837— .
Eph. Epigr.　*Ephemeris Epigraphica.* Rome, 1872— .
FHG.　C. Müller, *Fragmenta Historicorum Graecorum.* Paris, 1841–70.
Furt.　A. Furtwängler, *Vettersfelde.* Berlin, 1883.
FW. (coins).　Fitzwilliam Museum, Cambridge.
G. (coins).　Giel.
GGM.　C. Müller, *Geographi Graeci Minores.* Paris, 1855–61.
H.　Hudson.
H. (coins).　Hermitage.
Her.　Herodotus.
HN.　B. V. Head, *Historia Numorum.* Oxford, [1]1887, [2]1911.
IG.　*Inscriptiones Graecae.*
Inscr. Chr.　*Christian Inscriptions of S. Russia.*　}v. § B, p. xxxi,
IosPE.　*Inscriptiones Antiquae Orae Septentrionalis Ponti Euxini.*} s.v. Latyshev.
J. (coins).　Jurgiewicz, v. p. 449.
JHS.　*Journal of Hellenic Studies.* London, 1881— .
Journ. Min. Publ. Instr.　v. § A, p. xxviii.
JRAS.　*Journal of the Royal Asiatic Society.* London, 1834— .
J⟨R⟩AS. Bengal.　*Journal of the Asiatic Society of Bengal.* Calcutta, 1832— .
Khan.　Khanenko. v. § B, p. xxx.
Kl. B.　Ch. Giel, *Kleine Beiträge.* v. § B, p. xxx.
KTR.　N. P. Kondakov, I. I. Tolstoi, S. Reinach, *Antiquités de la Russie Méridionale.*
　　　　Paris, 1891.

KW.	G. von Kieseritzky, C. Watzinger, *Griechische Grabreliefs aus Südrussland.* Berlin, 1909.
Lat.	V. V. Latyshev.
L.-D.	Lappo-Danilevskij. v. § B, p. xxxi.
M. (coins).	Minns.
M.	Moscow.
Mat.	*Materials touching the Archaeology of Russia published by the Imp. Arch. Com.* St P. 1888—. v. § A, p. xxvi.
Mat. Arch. Cauc.	*Materials touching the Archaeology of the Caucasus published by the Imp. Mosc. Arch. Soc.* v. § A, p. xxvii.
Mat. for Num.	Orêshnikov, *Materials for the Numismatics of the Black Sea Coast.* Moscow, 1892. v. § B, p. xxxii.
MK.	B. de Koehne, *Musée Kotschoubey.* v. § B, p. xxx.
Mon. Ined.	*Monumenti Inediti dell' Instituto Archeologico.* Paris, Rome, 1857— .
Mon. Piot.	*Monuments Piot.* Paris, 1894— .
Mosc. Coin Cat.	v. § B, p. xxxii, s.v. Orêshnikov.
Mus. Borb.	*Real Museo Borbonico.* Naples, 1824.
NH.	Pliny, *Naturalis Historia.*
Num. Misc.	*Numismatic Miscellany.* v. § A, p. xxvii.
O. (coins).	Odessa.
Od. Mus. Guide. *Od. Mus. Terra-cottas.*	v. § A, p. xxviii.
Or. (coins).	Orêshnikov.
Os. Studies.	Vs. Th. Miller, *Ossetian Studies.* v. § B, p. xxxi.
P. (coins).	Pick. v. p. 449.
Per. P.E.	*Periplus Ponti Euxini,* after Latyshev, *Sc. et Cauc.* pp. 271—288, cf. inf. p. 25.
Ποντικά.	v. § B, p. xxxi, s.v. Latyshev.
Preh. Man.	L. Niederle, *Prehistoric Man.* v. § B, p. xxxi.
Propylaea.	v. § A, p. xxviii.
P.-W.	Pauly-Wissowa, *Encyclopädie.* Stuttgart, 1894— .
Rep. Hist. Mus. Mosc.	*Report of the Historical Museum at Moscow.* v. § A, p. xxviii.
R.G.	Mommsen, *Roemische Geschichte.*
Rh. Mus.	*Rheinisches Museum für Philologie.* Bonn, 1827–41; Frankfurt-a.-M., 1842— .
Röm. Mitt.	*Mitteilungen d. deutschen Archäologischen Instituts.* Rome, 1886— .
Samml.	J. Böehlau, *Sammlung Vogell.* v. p. 339 n. 6. Cassel, 1908.
SB.	*Sitzungsberichte.*
Sc. et Cauc.	V. V. Latyshev, *Scythica et Caucasica.* v. § B, p. xxxi. St P. 1890—1906.
Sc. Antt.	A. S. Lappo-Danilevskij, *Scythian Antiquities* in *TRAS.* v. § B, p. xxxi.
Sib. Ant.	v. *Ant. Sib.*
Slav. Ant.	L. Niederle, *Slavonic Antiquities.* v. § B, p. xxxii.
Sm.	Ct A. A. Bobrinskoj, *Smêla.* v. § B, p. xxix, and p. 175 n. 1. St P. 1887—1902.
St. Byz.	Stephanus Byzantius.
St P.	St Petersburg.
Syll.	Sylloge, e.g. Dittenberger.
Trans. Mosc. Num. Soc.	*Transactions of the Moscow Numismatic Society.* v. § A, p. xxvii.
Trans. Od. Soc.	*Transactions of the Odessa Historical and Archaeological Society.* v. § A, p. xxviii.
Trans. (Imp.) Russ. Arch. Soc. *TRAS.*	*Transactions of the Imp. Russian Archaeological Society.* St P. v. § A, p. xxvii.
U. (coins).	Uvarov Coll. v. § B, p. xxxii, s.v. Orêshnikov.
ZMDG.	*Zeitschrift der deutschen morgenländischen Gesellschaft.* Leipzig, 1845— .

MUSEUMS

Objects (apart from coins for which see p. 661) from S. Russia are well represented in the following Museums —:

The *Hermitage at St P.* receives the best things from the excavations of the Archaeological Commission and largely from chance finds. Far the greater part of objects mentioned below are, unless it is otherwise indicated, in the Hermitage. Objects from South Russia are also represented in the *Alexander III Museum.*

The *Historical Museum at Moscow* has much Palaeolithic and Neolithic material and some Scythic, from the Greek Colonies the Burachkov Collection and many new acquisitions. Attached to the University is the *Alexander III Museum of Fine Art.*

The *Town Museum at Kiev* has received the results of Chvojka's excavations and has incorporated with it the Khanenko Collection and that of Count Bobrinskoj as published in their works, in fact nearly everything from the Kiev district except the Ryżhanovka find which went to the Academy of Science, Cracow.

The *Museum of the Odessa Society* is the best place for studying Petreny, Tyras, Theodosia, Berezan and perhaps Olbia as it has most of the material from those sites except Pharmacovskij's finds at Olbia: it has also a good deal from Bosporus. Things published in *Trans. Od. Soc.* are mostly in this Museum.

The *Town Museum at Kherson* is concentrating the finds from the lower Dnêpr.

Chersonese has two museums, one in the Monastery containing the finds made before the Archaeological Commission began digging, the other those made by it as far as they are not sent to the Hermitage.

Theodosia has a small Museum supported by the Odessa Society.

At *Kerch* there is the Museum of the Archaeological Commission and its collection of Inscriptions in the Royal Barrow; the Odessa Society has inscriptions in the Melek Chesme Barrow. But the best things go to the Hermitage.

At *Kazan* the Town Museum has objects illustrating the Volga-Kama culture.

At *Minusinsk* is the best collection of Siberian bronzes, etc.

The provincial Universities and the St P. and Moscow Archaeological Societies have small museums.

Private Collections of importance are Ct Uvarov's at Porêchje (everything), Ct Stroganov's at St P. (Permian Plates), Teploukhov's (Permian Culture) near Perm, Suruchan's (Greek) at Kishinëv, Terlecki's (Bosporus), Novikov's (Eltegen) at Kerch, Mavrogordato's, Konelski's (Olbia) at Odessa. Vogell's at Nicolaev (Olbia) was mostly dispersed at Cassel in 1908 (v. p. 339 n. 6), the things chiefly went to German museums. The first museum in S. Russia was established at Nicolaev by the Scottish Admiral Greig.

On the whole things from our area have not found their way outside Russia to any great extent, they are best represented at Berlin, there is little at the Louvre but much from the Caucasus at St Germain.

The British Museum has MacPherson's and Westmacott's finds made during the Crimean War and a few purchases: the Ashmolean, Oxford, the things published by E. A. Gardner (*JHS.* 1884, Pl. XLVI, XLVII) and others since given by Mr Wardrop: the Fitzwilliam, Cambridge, three inscriptions (v. App. 67, 68, 69) and one or two stelae brought back by Dr E. D. Clarke.

ADDENDA AND CORRIGENDA

p. 5 l. 27, nn. 6, 7, otters and watersnakes, v. p. 105 n. 5.

p. 7 l. 32, gold from Urals and Altai, v. p 441.

p. 8 sqq. esp. p. 34 and Chapters II.—VI. *passim*, v. How and Wells, *A Commentary on Herodotus*, Oxford, 1912, I. pp. 302—344, 424—434.

p. 41 n. 1. A. M. Tallgren, *Zt d. Finn. Altertumsges.* XXVI, thinks this stopped axe older than those from Hallstatt and all such, even in Britain and the Urals, Mediterranean in origin.

p. 44 sqq. That Greeks had met people with Mongolian blood is shewn by the caricatures on Fig. o. The cyrbasiae shew these figures to be Scythians, probably Sacae from the Persian forces quartered in Egypt. No. 1 has the sloping eyes, No. 2 the high check-bones, No. 3 the round face of the Mongol, but their beards shew them no longer as Hippocrates describes them (v. p. 46) but intermixed with other blood yet not more than the Hiung-nu on p. 96 f. 27. Nos. 4 and 5 shew the almost Iranian type of the Kul-Oba Vase p. 201 f. 94. For a brilliant account of Nomad life in general v. J. Peisker, *Camb. Mod. Hist.* 1.

Fig. o. Caricatures of Scythians from Memphis, Vth century B.C. W. M. Flinders Petrie, *Memphis*, 1. (1909), p. 17, Pl. XL. 42, 44 (3 and 4); 11. (1909), p. 17, Pl. XXIX. 78, 79, 80 (1, 2, 5), cf. *Meydum and Memphis*, III. (1910), p. 46, Pl. XLII. 136—138. My very best thanks are due to Professor Flinders Petrie who sent me these photographs before his Vol. II. was published.

(Cambridge, 1911) pp. 323—359 and more fully *Vierteljahrschr. f. Social- u. Wirtschaftsgesch.* III. (1904), " Die älteren Beziehungen der Slawen zu Turkotataren und Germanen und ihre sozialgeschichtliche Bedeutung," pp. 187—360; 465—533: most of his conclusions as to Sc. (pp. 187—240) are much the same as mine, i.e. that the true Sc. were Turkotartars imposed upon a more or less Aryan population represented by the Georgi, etc. and themselves strongly mixed with Aryans not only thereby but during the men's domination in Media, which he fully accepts, when they adopted Iranian speech from Median wives. These women as not nomads could not ride but had to be carted and also had different bathing customs from the men. A careful examination of the forms underlying the straight hair in the Greek portraits (l.c. pp. 216—224) shews them not Aryan but just like e.g. Kara-kirgiz. Hippocrates may have seen purer Turkotartars but the Greeks even in Upper Asia mostly came in contact only with a border of half-castes. Vegetarian Sc. in Ephorus ap. Strab. VII. iii. 9 are Aryans raided by Sc., cf. Tadzhiks.

p. 50 n. 4.   Other carts, v. inf. p. 370 n. 3 and Addenda thereto.
p. 61 l. 43.   Rostovtsev (v. Add. to p. 218) regards the "woman" on all these plaques as a goddess.
p. 66 n. 7.   *For* stone *read* bezel, v. p. 427 f. 318 *top*.
p. 67 l. 16.   Bow-cases.   *After* "p. 284" *add* and Addenda to p. 287.
p. 70 n. 12.   *For* D. A. Anuchin *read* D. N. Anuchin.
p. 71 n. 2.   *Add* for this and two more sheaths v. p. 567 n. 3.
p. 74 l. 13.   *For* Bezchastnaja *read* Bezschastnaja.
p. 78 n. 7.   *Add* Ul, *Arch. Anz.* 1910, pp. 199—201 ff. 3, 4.
p. 80 n. 5 col. 2.   *For* Zamazaevskoe *read* Zamaraevskoe, dist. of Shadrinsk.
p. 85.   Mr A. B. Cook pointed out to me this sentence from the *Etym. Mag.* s.v. πόποι· οἱ γὰρ Σκύθαι, ἀγάλματα τινὰ ἔχοντες ὑπόγαια τῶν θεῶν, πόπους αὐτὰ καλοῦσι, but there is probably a confusion with the Dryopians who had gods called πόποι, *Class. Rev.* 1904, XVIII. pp. 83, 84, perhaps helped by the word Papaeus. For Argimpasa v. Add. to p. 218.
p. 100 l. 29.   v. Addenda to p. 44.
  „   ll. 31, 37, 48.   *For* Le Coq *read* Lecoq.
p. 123 l. 20.   For these Getan(?) kings, v. p. 487.
p. 130 n. 1.   *Add* V. A. Gorodtsov, *Primitive Archaeology*, Moscow, 1908: *Cultural Archaeology*, 1910.
p. 131 n. 4.   *For* G. A. Skadovskij *read* G. L. Skadovskij.
p. 134 n. 1 col. 2.   *After* civilization of Servia *add* and *Glas Srpske Kraljevske Akademije* (*Voice of the Serbian Royal Acad.*) LXXXVI., " Gradac," where he finds this culture surviving to La-Tène times.
        At end add, cf. Wace and Thompson, *Prehistoric Thessaly*, pp. 231—234, and 256—259; Gorodtsov, *Cultural Arch.* pp. 133—151; E. Meyer, *Gesch. d. Altert.*[2] I. 2, pp. 734, 741, 742.
p. 142 l. 16; p. 143 n. 5.   Veselovskij found on the Ul a model waggon and long-necked female statuettes of alabaster like Aegean types, *BCA.* XXXV. Pl. I., II., IV., *Arch. Anz.* 1910, p. 195.
p. 144.   Majkop.   Pharmacovskij (Hist. Congr. London, 1913) shewed the bulls, etc. to belong to a portable canopy and the cups to exhibit the earliest (B.C. 1400—1000) East-Anatolian or Urartu style preceding ordinary Hittite.   A. M. Tallgren, *Zt d. Finn. Alt. Ges.* XXV. 1, " Die Kupfer- u. Bronzezeit in Nord- u. Ostrussland," arrives at this date independently.
p. 148 n. 1.   *For* VIII. 2 *read* VIII. 1.
p. 155 last line.   Anuchin, Veselovskij and Pharmacovskij (*Bobrinskoj Misc.* p. 63 n. 2) agree that Zabêlin was wrong in thinking Chertomlyk barrow to have been plundered.
p. 165 l. 21.   Pharmacovskij (l.c.) shews that this pottery points to about the middle of the IInd cent. B.C., e.g. a cantharos like p. 349 f. 254.
p. 168 n. 1.   *Add* cf. silver vessels from Chmyrëva, p. 383, *Arch. Anz.* 1910, pp. 215—226 ff., 12—25 and Vs. Sakhanev *BCA.* XLV. pp. 111—131, who refers their ornament to the IInd cent. B.C.; he thinks the horses killed as usual, cf. Lemeshóva Mogila, *Arch. Anz.* 1912, pp. 376, 377.
p. 173 n. 2.   Martonosha crater.   *For* IV *read* VI.   Cup from Vorónezh v. Add. to p. 200.
p. 175 n. 1.   Ct Bobrinskoj's excavations.   *After* XX. p. 1 *add* XXXV. pp. 48—85; XL. pp. 43—61; *Arch. Anz.* 1912, pp. 378, 379.
p. 192 l. 3.   *For* Pomashki *read* Romashki.
p. 200 f. 93.   The Kul Oba vase has a close analogue in one of silver gilt found near Vorónezh in 1912.
  „   n. 1.   *For* v. p. 39 f. 3 *bis read* v. Addenda to p. 44 f. o for physical type of Scythians.
p. 210 n. 3.   *For* Dionysius *read* Dionysus.

pp. 218, 219. Karagodeuashkh. Rostovtsev, *BCA*. XLIX. "The Idea of Kingly Power in Scythia and on the Bosporus" (= "Iranism and Ionism," Hist. Congr. London, 1913), sees on the rhyton, f. 121, two horsemen face to face each above a prostrate foe but one holding a sceptre, the other adoring him, i.e. to judge by Sassanian investiture scenes, a mounted form of Mithras conferring divine right on a king: on f. 120 R. sees at the top the king's Τύχη or *hvareno*, then Mithras with a quadriga and below Aphrodite-Argimpasa-Anahita-Astarte (cf. pp. 85, 617—619 and Pl. VIII. 12, 14) receiving in communion the sacred rhyton and round-bottomed vase, cf. analogous scenes of communion and unveiling, pp. 158, 203 ff. 45, 98. On the Bosporus reiranized by the IInd and IIIrd centuries A.D. this conception of kingship is symbolized by sceptres and crowns, v. p. 434 and f. 325, and on coins like Pl. VIII. 10.

p. 232 l. 36. *For* Parthlan *read* Parthian.

p. 232 n. 4. Kuban Barrows. *Add CR.* 1906, pp. 91—95; *Arch. Anz.* 1909, p. 148 (cf. inf. p. 382); 1910, p. 197 (Ul); 1911, pp. 193, 194, ff. 1, 2 (Kasinskoe, Govt Stavropol).

p. 235. Fig. 144, the Uvarov cup, ff. 140, 141 and the Ust-Labinskaja bottle are all figured in Smirnov, *Arg. Orient.* X. 25 (cf. 26), 27, XI. 29, 30 (cf. XII. 31—34), IX. 280 (cf. 281).

p. 254 n. 1. *For JRAS. Bengal read JAS. Bengal.*

p. 257 n. 2. *For* Vol. XXVI. Helsingfors, 1910 *read* Vol. XXV. 1, Helsingfors, 1911.

„ n. 5. H. Appelgren-Kivalo, *Zt d. Finn. Altertumsges.* XXVI. "Die Grundzüge des Skythischpermischen Ornamentstyles," derives the eagle from a Ganymede subject by a jug from Nagy-sz.-Miklós and traces the further degeneration of the deer into a row of men.

p. 266 l. 15. *Add* Beak-heads are quite Greek, e.g. a girdle-mount from Olbia, *Arch. Anz.* 1911, p. 223, f. 30; so is a mirror like the Romny one, ib. p. 224, f. 31. Indeed nearly all Sc. motives are finding their source as we learn more of Ionian art with its Minoan survivals.

p. 270 f. 186. This sheath is from Elizavetovskaja, v. p. 567.

p. 271 sqq. Siberian plaques, v. G. Hirth, *Formenschatz*, 1909, No. 85 (cf. 40); 1910, No. 1.

p. 273 n. 3. *For* f. 333 *read* p. 507, f. 339.

p. 287 l. 35. Pharmacovskij, "The Gold Mountings of the Bow-cases from the Iljintsy and Chertomlyk Barrows," *Bobrinskoj Misc.* pp. 45—118, sets the whole matter on a fresh footing. The Iljintsy grave had the usual wooden chamber, which collapsed when being plundered: the chief object besides the sheath was a set of horse's gear like p. 185 f. 78 but ruder in workmanship. He says that the Iljintsy cover was made by preparing first the wooden foundation and carving the design upon it, then beating into the carving a plate of base gold with a pure gold face and finally touching up with a graver, whereas that from Chertomlyk was produced by laying a slightly inferior gold plate over the Iljintsy sheath and beating it into its lines: this is shewn by the traces of the Iljintsy engraving on the wrong side of the Chertomlyk cover and by the design not always having come out on the latter particularly where it is rather weak in the former. The finishing of the Iljintsy cover was the less elaborate (much of it pointillé) and pathetic, but the more intelligent. The plate from the butt end of the bow-case was found at Iljintsy (that from Chertomlyk is figured *ASH*. II. p. 118): each is rounded below and has a midrib flanked by affronted griffins rampant and acanthus-flowers above; so the thickness of the bow-case, greatest 4 cm. from the bottom, was 6·5 cm. (2·6 in.) as against a breadth of 21—25 cm. (8·25—9·8 in.) and a length of 43 cm. (17 in.). The midrib answers to the division separating the bow (put in string upwards) from the arrows (said to be in bundles point upwards): at Iljintsy there were 142 bronze and 12 bone arrows.

The subject of the reliefs is the whole life of Achilles, not merely his time at Scyros, and so does not go back to one great composition e.g. of Polygnotus, but consists in Hellenistic wise of scenes divided by adjacent figures being set back to back: reckoning from left to right we have, above, 1, 2, Phoenix teaching Achilles to shoot; 3—8 Achilles (6) seizing arms from Odysseus (5), 3 being the Scyran queen with Neoptolemus, 7 a nurse and 8 Deidamia: the next scene is cut in two, 9 is Lycomedes (his right arm is clear upon the Iljintsy sheath) parting with Achilles (10) while the four women to the left below ought to be looking at them; they are the queen between two daughters and a nurse marked off as a group indoors by dotted curtains; in the following scene we have Agamemnon and Achilles now reconciled by Odysseus and Diomede; Achilles is putting on a greave before going out to avenge Patroclus; the last figure is Thetis bearing away her son's ashes.

The animals, especially the lank griffins, are in the Hellenistic manner while the ornament shews exactly the same elements as the base of a column at Didyma near Miletus (Pontremoli-Haussoullier, *Didymes*, p. 145): Lesbian cyma, acanthus, twist and palmette all

in a late stage not before the middle of the IInd century B.C. which agrees with the pottery (v. Add. to p. 165). So Pharmacovskij refers the gold work to Miletus in that century and the tombs themselves and with them most of the big Scythic tombs to a slightly later time.

pp. 293—435. Additions to almost every page of Chapters XI. and XII. might be made from Pharmacovskij, *Arch. Anz.* 1911, pp. 192—234; 1912, pp. 323—379.

p. 295 l. 18. *For* p. 566, f. 345 *read* p. 565.

p. 298 l. 31. A head of Egyptian work from Kerch, B. A. Turaev, "Objets égyptiens et égyptisants trouvés dans la Russie Méridionale," *Revue Archéologique*, 1911, II. pp. 20—35.

p. 304 l. 7; p. 310 l. 30. Deified dead and chthonian divinities, v. p. 606 n. 10.

p. 320 l. 25. *After Mat.* VI. *add* and *Röm. Quartalschr.* VIII. pp. 47—87; 309—327, Pl. II., III.

p. 338 n. 4. Egyptian Porcelain. Cf. Addenda to p. 298 l. 31.

  „   n. 5. Ionian Pottery. Cf. inf. p. 564 n. 3.

  „   n. 6. *Add* Naucratis, *BCA.* XL. pp. 142—158; XLV. p. 108, f. 5.

p. 339 nn. 7, 8. Ionian Pottery, *Arch. Anz.* 1911, pp. 223, 224, ff. 29, 32; 1912, pp. 354—371, ff. 41, 44, 46—51, 61. Early pottery inland; v. inf. p. 441 n. 1.

  „   n. 9. *Add* cf. *Arch. Anz.* 1912, p. 360, f. 51.

  „   n. 14. *Add* Milesian sherds from Chersonese itself, *Arch. Anz.* 1912, p. 349.

p. 340 n. 6. *Substitute* Mr J. D. Beazley refers it to Oltus.

p. 347 n. 5. Panathenaic Amphorae, Kerch, Tanais, v. p. 626; Chersonese, Add. to p. 516.

p. 348 l. 20. Von Stern's *Watercolour Vases* (v. p. xxxiii) will deal fully with the whole class.

p. 349 n. 1. *Add BCA.* XL. p. 430, bl. f. cotyle from Cherkassk.

  „   n. *For* Reliefkeramite *read* Reliefkeramik.

p. 362 n. 4. Polychrome glass, cf. *Arch. Anz.* 1911, p. 199, f. 6.

p. 367 n. 14. Bes, cf. *BCA.* XLV. pp. 71—75, Pl. II.—IV. and Add. to p. 298 l. 31.

p. 370 n. 3. *Add* For toys see von Stern "From the Children's Life on the N. coast of the Euxine," *Bobrinskoj Misc.* pp. 13—30 = *Arch. Anz.* 1912, pp. 147—148, feeding-bottles, dolls, dolls' sets of furniture, etc., animals, waggons, an eicositetrahedron with the alphabet, some things Milesian ware.

p. 379 l. 3. *Add* a tortoise-shaped bronze lyre-body from Kerch deserves notice, *Arch. Anz.* 1911, p. 203, ff. 11, 12.

p. 383 n. 9. Chmyrëva vessels, v. Addenda to p. 168 n. 1.

p. 386 l. 11. For a large hoard of Byzantine and Sassanian plate (VI.—VII. cent.) from Malaja Pereshchépina near Poltava v. I. A. Zarětskij, *Trans.* (Труды) *of the Poltava Record Comm.* IX. 1912, N. E. Makarenko, *BCA.* XLVI. and a future publication of the Imp. Archaeol. Comm.

p. 390 n. 7. These crowns support Rostovtsev's theory of Bosporan kingship, v. Add. to p. 218.

p. 395 n. 5. *Add* early earrings, Olbia, *Arch. Anz.* 1911, p. 222, f. 27; 1912, p. 355, ff. 42, 43; Bosporus, ib. pp. 333, 346, ff. 16—18, 31.

p. 412 n. 12. Scarabs from Berezan, cf. B. A. Turaev, *BCA.* XL. pp. 118—120 and Add. to p. 298.

p. 415 *below cuts. Add* Burial at Olbia came in about 550 B.C. before which burnt bones were put into amphorae in special pits among the houses, v. *Arch. Anz.* 1912, p. 351: an excellent early grave ensemble, ib. p. 354, f. 41 sqq.

p. 458 n. 1. *Add* A similar house just to the S. of this is described in *Arch. Anz.* 1912, p. 363 sqq.

p. 468 n. 4 ⎫ *IosPE.* I. 97¹ as supplemented in IV. p. 271, *Trans. Od. Soc.* XIV. p. 22, *BCA.*
p. 476 l. 26 ⎪ XLV. p. 1 = *Arch. Anz.* 1912, p. 366, dedicates τοὺς νηοὺς (i.e. three cellae) σὺν
p. 478 l. 20 ⎬ τῇ στοᾷ on behalf of Alexander Severus, the Roman Senate and the prosperity of
p. 479 bottom ⎭ Olbia θεοῖς ἐπηκόοις Sarapis, Isis, Asclepius, Hygiea, Poseidon (and Amphitrite).

p. 471 l. 10. *For* φρατίραι *read* φρατρίαι.

p. 479 l. 15. *Add* and *BCA.* XLV. p. 7, No. 2, Αὐρ. Χρύσ[ιππος τοῦ δεῖνος?]/Μητρὶ θεῶν [ἀνεθήκεν?].

p. 486 l. 16. Bertier-de-La-Garde casts doubts upon this Pallas type in silver.

p. 497 l. 7 ⎫ The foundation of Chersonese is put back to the VIth century B.C. by Ionian
p. 515 l. 21 ⎭ sherds and archaic terra-cottas found on its "New" site, *Arch. Anz.* 1912, p. 349.

p. 516 l. 9. *After* 380) *add* and a Panathenaic vase, *Arch. Anz.* 1912, p. 349.

p. 524 l. 28. *After* Dia... *add* and Thrasymedes, *BCA.* XLV. p. 40, No. 2, c. 100 A.D.

p. 541 l. 23 ⎫ *BCA.* XLV. p. 40, No. 2 shews that there were only three νομοφύλακες and that
p. 542 l. 27 ⎭ ὁ ἐπὶ τᾶς διοικήσεος regularly acted with them and must be restored in *BCA.* III. p. 21, No. 1; XIV. p. 104, No. 9.

p. 544 n. 11. *After* IV. 84 *add BCA.* XLV. p. 65, No. 12, a dedication to the Chersonesan Maiden.

p. 598. n. 7 l. 8. *For* βίνο *read* βίον.

p. 620 n. 4. *Add* cf. reprint of this *defixio* by R. Wünsch, *Rhein. Mus.* LV. pp. 232—236.

CHAPTER I.

PHYSICAL GEOGRAPHY AND NATURAL PRODUCTIONS.

THE scope of the present work includes the History of the Greek Settlements on the north coast of the Euxine from the mouth of the Danube to that of the Kuban, and the Ethnology of the country at the back of that coastline from the slopes of the Carpathians to the lower course of the Volga and the foothills of the Caucasus.

This tract extending through twenty degrees of longitude is quite different from any other tract in Europe, wherein the only region at all similar is that of the Hungarian Puszta, which is in a sense its westerly continuation and has always been deeply influenced by the neighbourhood of the greater plain. But this greater plain is itself but a continuation, almost a dependency, of the still wider plains of Northern Asia, and this continuity is the governing condition of its historical development. It is only within the last hundred years or so that Southern Russia has been definitely added to Europe. Before that time Asiatic tribes have been more at home in it than European. In Europe and Asia it is one continuous belt of steppe or prairie. The most striking feature of this broad stretch of country is the absence of mountains; they only come in as forming its border on the west and on the south-east, where the coast range of the Crimea is a continuation of the Caucasus, just as the plain of its northern region is really one with the mainland plain beyond the Isthmus[1].

But though the whole region may be broadly regarded as a plain, this must not be taken to mean that it is one dead level. Right across from the Carpathians to the coast of the Sea of Azov near the Berda there runs a belt of granite, which crops out wherever it is crossed by one of the great rivers. To the north of the granite belt is a limestone formation. Where these rocks occur the plain attains a considerable elevation, to the west in Podolia it becomes diversified with hills, and again further east about the Donets, where are the chief coal-mines of Russia, there is hilly country that ends in steep cliffs about Taganrog. Even where the rise of the plain is gradual, it attains a height of

---

[1] Much the best survey of the Physical Geography of Scythia is to be found in K. Neumann's *Hellenen im Skythenlande*, pp. 14 to 99. He is inclined to exaggerate the former extent of the woodlands. Cf. also Elisée Reclus, *Nouvelle Géographie Universelle*, Vol. v., and L. Bürchner, *Die Besiedelung der Küsten des Pontos Euxeinos*, Pt I. Introduction, pp. 5–22.

300 feet above the sea, as in Ekaterinoslav. In general it slopes gently towards the south-west: so that the cliffs which are a few feet high near the Danube are not less than a hundred and fifty at the mouth of the Dnêpr. To the east of the Dnêpr the coast plain is very low. Between the Crimea and the mainland the boundaries of land and water are so ill defined that a change of wind will make the sea encroach, but the steppe reaches the level of the western plain about the forty-seventh parallel, and further north it attains four hundred feet south of the Great Meadow[1].

In spite therefore of the general flatness the actual heights reached by some parts of the plain are far too great to allow any talk of serious changes in the course of the rivers during the last two thousand years. These have not been able to do more than deepen their beds and very slowly edge westwards. The outlines of their course have been fixed by the geological formation which has made the remarkable correspondence of the sudden bends from ESE. to WSW. round which Dnêpr, Donets and Don have to find their way to the sea. The plain and the rivers are the features of the country that specially struck the Greeks, they had nothing of the sort in their own land[2].

It is the great rivers that shew up the heights to which the plain rises. Each has a steep or "hilly" bank to the west and a flat or "meadow" bank to the east, and flows winding along a broad valley, which at the lower end has been cut down to below the level of the sea forming the *liman*[3] so characteristic of Russian rivers. If the river has to cross the granite belt it has there failed to make its course easy for itself and is broken by rapids, most important in the case of the Dnêpr. The lesser streams have made proportionate valleys and into these leads a whole system of ravines, which carry off the melting snow but are dry during most of the year. All these depressions make no difference to the view of the steppe, as they are not noticeable until the traveller comes to the edge of one of them, but they present considerable obstacles to anyone not acquainted with the precise places where they can be crossed conveniently. They provided much too complete a system of drainage and the now diminished rainfall is carried off at once from the surface of the steppe, compare the expression of Hippocrates, ἐξοχετεύουσι. For the inhabitants of the steppe they are of the utmost importance. In them the flocks can find shelter in the winter, and in them the first beginnings of agriculture can be made. There is little doubt that the agricultural tribes of which we read in Herodotus confined their attempts to these valleys, and it was not till the other day that the open steppe was cut up by the plough. Till then it had been merely pasture, but some of it pasture unsurpassed in the world, at any rate during its season.

[1] The marshy widening of the valley about Nicopol.
[2] Her. IV. 82, Θωυμάσια δὲ ἡ χώρη αὕτη οὐκ ἔχει χωρὶς ἢ ὅτι ποταμούς τε πολλῷ μεγίστους καὶ ἀριθμὸν πλείστους. τὸ δὲ ἀποθωύμασαι ἄξιον καὶ πάρεξ τῶν ποταμῶν καὶ τοῦ μεγάθεος τοῦ πεδίου κ.τ.λ. So

Hippocrates, *De aere*, etc. 25, Ἡ δὲ Σκυθέων ἐρημίη καλευμένη πεδιάς ἐστι καὶ λειμακώδης καὶ ψιλή, καὶ ἔνυδρος μετρίως· ποταμοί γὰρ εἰσὶ μεγάλοι, οἳ ἐξοχετεύουσι τὸ ὕδωρ ἐκ τῶν πεδίων.
[3] An estuary or lagoon cut off from the sea by a strip of sand with or without openings.

From the time of the snow's melting to the middle of summer the
growth of the grass in the richer regions seems by all accounts to have
been marvellous: but even so the sun would scorch it up and animals
had to come near the streams until the autumn rains: and again they
had to find shelter in the valleys for the depth of the winter, so that
the nomad life was not quite as free as is represented, for these wintering
places are quite definitely the property of particular tribes. Throughout
great areas of the steppe, especially towards the south and east, the
rich pasture gives way to barren lands offering but wormwood and silk
grass, or tussock grass that does not even cover the surface of the sand.
Worse still in the government of Astrakhan, at the eastern boundary of
our area, there is but unrelieved salt sand : here the only land of any
value is that along the lower Volga. This is why the trade route of
which Herodotus gives particulars goes so far to the north. Yet com-
mentators gaily assign such a district as the only local habitation of more
or less important tribes. A great characteristic of the whole region is
lack of trees, but in the river valleys, besides the meadows which kept
the cattle alive in the winter, there were some woods at any rate. Especially
was this the case on the lower Dnêpr where much land, since invaded
by sand-dunes, was formerly wooded. In the north also the forest belt
seems to have come further south down to the edge of the glacial
deposit, along the line shaded on the general map, and to have sent
outliers into the open plain. The retreat of the woods is due partly to
man and partly to the drying up of Eurasia[1] to which it has itself
contributed. This drying up of the interior has also had a strange effect
even upon the coastline.

The shores of such a country as we have described do not naturally
offer facilities for commerce. To begin with the gentle slope of the
plains continues in some parts under the sea : hence the shore between
the mouths of the Dnêpr and the Don, if we leave out of account
the southern part of the Crimea, as ever a strong contrast to the rest
of the region, is not to be approached by ships. This initial difficulty
is increased by the deposits of the great rivers, deposits which are
heaped up with the more ease in that there is no tide to carry them
away. As soon as the stream meets the dead mass of motionless sea,
still more some current of the sea or of another river, it drops its load
of silt along gentle curves mathematically determined by the meeting
places of the opposing currents. So the Sea of Azov acts as a kind
of settling tank for collecting the silt of the Don. The coarsest falls
to the bottom at once to add to the growth of the delta, the finer has
to pass successively the dead points produced by the opposing currents
of the various streams that fall in from each side : hence the spits
running out between the river mouths and especially the strange Arabat
spit that encloses the Putrid Sea[2] and makes an alternative entrance to
the Crimea.

[1] Cf. Prince Kropotkin in *Geographical Journal*,   [2] Σαπρὰ λίμνη, Strabo, VII. iv. 1.
London, Aug. 1904.

Hence too the fact that during certain winds vessels have to lie ten miles from the shore off Taganrog[1], and the complaints of the silting up of the Maeotis expressed by Polybius[2] who regarded the completion of the process as not very distant, and the recent Imperial commission on the subject[3].

After all this the current that flows out of the Maeotis has left only 4·25 metres on the bar at Kerch.

The same process goes on at the mouth of the Dnêpr. There is the bar and delta below Kherson, another bar (6 metres) at Ochakov running across from Kinburn spit (Ἄλσος Ἑκάτης), and a third, the Tendra, Δρόμος Ἀχιλλέως, along the line where it meets a coast current from east to west.

The Dnêstr only just keeps open. Here the bar has long been dry land, save for two small openings of which that used by ships has a depth of only five feet.

The small rivers such as the Kujalnik and Tiligul are entirely closed. Yet this process is quite modern. In 1823 the Tiligul was open, now the highroad runs along its bar. Within the bar in every case is an estuary (liman) which used once to be open. This inconvenient phenomenon of shut river mouths is due partly to the unequal flow of rivers which have to carry snow water; more however to their inability to keep a sufficient current in a channel that they had excavated in ages of more abundant rainfall. It is one more evidence of the drying up of the country.

The Greek colonies of Tyras and Olbia were founded on the steep side of a liman where the current came near the coast, the position of Tanais was somewhat similar. All the other ports depended on the entirely exceptional formation of the Crimea: Chersonese had the use of the many harbours about Sevastopol, some of which are steep to. Theodosia had a small harbour and fine roads, and the towns on the Bosporus though troubled with shoals were not yet strangled by accumulating silt. Beyond the Bosporus Bata (Novorossijsk) and Pagrae (Gelendzhik) had clean harbours, but the former suffers from a unique disadvantage, the Bora, a wind which blowing from the mountains covers ships with such a coating of ice that they have been known to sink under the weight[4].

Of modern towns Odessa is comparatively free from silt, but its harbour is entirely artificial. In fact the headland that sheltered the roads is being washed away. But both Nicolaev and Kherson suffer from the shoals and bars encouraged by the drying up of their respective rivers.

This drying process has tended to make the climate of Scythia more extreme in character. Of course most of the ancients regarded only its cold, and regarded it as cold all the year round[5]: just as it requires an effort

---

[1] Clarke's *Travels*, I. p. 428.
[2] IV. 40. So too Aristotle, *Meteorologica*, I. xiv. 39.
[3] The Don delta gains 6·70 metres yearly. The gulf below is 1 ft 6 in. less deep than 200 years ago. The sea should last another 56,500 years,

E. Reclus, op. cit. p. 789.
[4] N. A. Korostelev, The Bora at Novorossijsk. *Mém. de l'Acad. Imp. des Sciences de St Pétersbourg*, *Classe Physico-Mathématique*, VIIIᵉ sér., T. XV. No. 2, St P. 1904.
[5] Her. IV. 28. Hippocrates, *De aere*, c. 26.

for most of us to think of Russia and Siberia as very hot in the summer. Strabo[1] even refuses to believe in the heat, arguing that those who found it hot did not know real heat[2]. A curious fact is that the Greeks undoubtedly looked on Scythia as damp and foggy, whereas it suffers from oft-recurring drought. Probably there was more wood and so there was more moisture, and probably also the Greeks connected the north with cold and wet and thought that further to the north there must be more cold and wet. Also there certainly were marshy foggy tracts at the mouths of the big rivers, the points where they had most commerce with Scythia, and the readiness with which people believe the worst of foreign climates accounts for the permanence of this idea.

One or two little points served to confirm this impression. A Greek felt a kind of horror of a country in which the myrtle and bay did not grow[3], and the attempts to make them grow at Panticapaeum were probably not very skilled, for the vine did not do well, and that succeeds there quite easily nowadays[4].

So too the fact of the sea freezing struck them as evidence of an intolerable climate. Actually this tends to come about chiefly in places where the fresh water contributed by the rivers has made the sea hardly more than brackish. But this again was just in regions where the Greeks were most likely to see it. Also the uncertainty it introduced into commerce at certain times of the year would bring it home to the Greeks of Hellas, and every Greek had heard of the brazen pot split by the frost and dedicated by Stratius in the temple of Aesculapius at Panticapaeum and the epigram thereon[5].

The Fauna of the steppe region is not specially striking. It is on the whole poor. The ancients were interested in the accounts of the Tarandus, a beast with a square face and a power of changing colour, apparently the reindeer with its summer and winter coat[6]: that no longer comes so far south. So too the otter and beaver have retreated with the forests though place-names shew the former extent of the latter[7].

The wild white horses about the source of the Hypanis may either have been the western extension of the grey pony of Upper Asia or they may have merely run wild[8].

Strabo (VII. iv. 8) mentions that in the marshes there were hunted deer and wild boar, and on the plains wild asses and goats. He also mentions the Colus, a kind of buffalo or bison.

On domesticated animals the climate was supposed to have such an effect that asses (in spite of Strabo's wild asses) and mules succumbed[9], and horned cattle lost their horns[10].

---

[1] VII. iii. 18.
[2] Aristotle, *Problem.* XXV. 6, recognises the hot summer.
[3] Theophr. *Hist. Plant.* IV. v. 3. Pliny, *NH.* XVI. 137.
[4] Until Byzantine times the Greeks never seem to have gained occupation of the mountains of the Crimea and their warm southern valleys with Mediterranean vegetation. Besides these were quite an exception on the north coast of the Euxine.

[5] Strabo, II. i. 16.
[6] Arist. *de Mirabilibus*, c. 30. Theophr. Frag. 172; Her. IV. 109.
[7] Her. l.c.; Strabo, III. iv. 15; Th. P. Köppen, On the Distribution of the Beaver in Russia, *Journ. Min. Publ. Inst.* St P., June, 1902.
[8] Her. IV. 52.
[9] Aristotle, *de Animalibus*, VIII. 25.
[10] Arist. op. cit. VIII. 28. This circumstance was explained by the statement that the cold prevented

Very characteristic of the steppe are the various rodents, *susliks* and *baibaks*, relations of the jerboa, but regarded by the ancients as exaggerated mice : hence the story that skins of mice were used for clothing[1]. Such creatures with their curious watchful attitude, along with Indian ants and Babylonish garments, may have their part in the origin of griffin legends.

We may also mention adders and snakes[2], bees[3] and ephemera[4].

More important than the land animals were the fish that abounded in the rivers and formed the main object of export[5].

The most important species were the Pelamys, a kind of tunny, and the ἀντάκαιοι or sturgeons. Of the former Strabo (VII. vi. 2) has an idea that they were born in the Maeotis and made their way round and began to be worth catching when they got as far as Trapezus, and were of full size at Sinope. The difficulty is that I am assured by Mr Zernóv, Director of the Marine Biological Laboratory at Sevastopol, to whom I offer my best thanks, that no sort of tunny does this; that a kind of herring does so; but that the *scumbria*, which answers to the general description of the pelamys, and a mackarel now called *palamida*, do not go into the Sea of Azov at all. The palamida is quite rare in the Black Sea though common in the Mediterranean. Moreover the tendency is for the Mediterranean fauna gradually to conquer the Black Sea, so it is not likely that this particular species was commoner in ancient times. Yet Strabo from his birthplace ought to have known all about it.

The ἀντάκαιοι or sturgeons are first mentioned by Herodotus (IV. 53) at the mouth of the Dnêpr. This fishery does not seem very abundant now. The other great locality was in the Maeotis, both along the eastern shore at the mouths of the rivers Rhombites[6] (this is now represented by fisheries at the same points and at Achuev which is just at the mouth of the Anticites) and at the Cimmerian Bosporus, where the Greeks were much struck by the fishing carried on through the ice and believed that fish as big as dolphins were dug out of the solid[7]. As a matter of fact though ice is collected on the shore every year the strait does not freeze over very often : this happens more regularly in the upper part of the Maeotis at the mouth of the Don.

There are three kinds of sturgeon. *Accipenser Stellatus* (*sevrjúga*) with a sharp nose forms the bulk of the catch in the Sea of Azov. *A. Huso* (*Bêlúga*) has whiter flesh and used to be common at Kerch and at the delta of the Dnêpr. This seems to be the one that Strabo means when he talks of its being as big as a dolphin. Finally we have *A. Sturio* (*osjotr*), our sturgeon, which is more characteristic of the Volga. It has a blunt nose, and so differs from the fish represented on the Greek coins (Pl. v. 18, 20).

The ancients thought that the fish went into the Pontus to escape the larger fish that preyed upon them outside and to spawn, as the

their growth. Yet we have Greek representations of the saiga with its splendid horns, and the tarandus or reindeer was known with its horned hind.

[1] Justin II. 2, pellibus murinis utuntur, cf. Hipp. *de aere*, c. 26.

[2] Arist. *de Mirabilibus*, c. 141 ; Her. IV. 105.

[3] Her. v. 10. Arist. *de Animalibus*, v. xxii. 8.

[4] Ib. v. xix. 14.

[5] Cf. especially M. Koehler, ΤΑΡΙΧΟΣ in *Mém. de l'Acad. des Sciences de St Pétersbourg*, VIᵐᵉ sér. T. I. p. 347, St P. 1832.

[6] Strabo, XI. ii. 4.

[7] Strabo, VII. iii. 18.

fresher water was more favourable to the young. That is true of the coastline, but the middle of the sea is full of bacteria which produce sulphuretted hydrogen, so that the fishes from the Mediterranean can only make their way round gradually and have not yet elbowed out of existence the archaic but excellent species proper to the Aralo-Caspian-Euxine basin.

As to the Flora of the northern coast of the Euxine, leaving aside the Crimean mountains, we have already spoken of the scarcity of wood, a scarcity which seems to have increased in modern times. What trees do grow are confined to the river valleys and include deciduous species only, as indeed is noticed by Theophrastus[1] who speaks of figs and pomegranates growing if earthed up, also excellent pears and apples, and among wild trees of oaks, limes and ashes; but no firs or pines. There is however a special *Pinus Taurica*. In the open country the ancients noticed the luxuriance of the grass or when they wished to find fault the stretches of wormwood[2], to which however they ascribed the good quality of the meat[3]. They speak also of eatable roots and bulbs[4] and of various drugs, also of hemp used both as a fibre and as a narcotic[5].

A special lack in Scythia was that of good stone. About Odessa and Kerch there is a soft local limestone easy to work but only durable if protected from the weather by a coat of plaster: in the Crimea, especially at Inkerman, there occurs a stone of higher quality: but in general stone is not to be found, and this has been one reason for the absence throughout the whole region of important architectural monuments.

Of other natural productions we need mention but amber[6], which is occasionally found near Kiev, but does not seem ever to have been systematically worked; salt[7], given as occurring at the mouth of the Dnêpr, and indeed spread over a whole section of the steppe (the carting of salt into the interior was a great industry until the railways came, and followed immemorial tracks, the Greeks must have profited by it in their time), and gold which does not occur in Scythia itself, but has been abundant to the west in Transylvania whence the Romans obtained much gold, and to the north-east in the Urals where the mines of the ancient inhabitants (*Chúdskia kópi*) have been worked by the Russians, and further towards the middle of Asia, in the Altai, where also the modern miner has come across traces of former exploitation. In ancient times there were no doubt placer workings that yielded gold more readily than it can be attained now. These regions also contained ancient copper mines: and the turquoise of the east country was not without influence on the development of decorative art in the whole region.

So we may conclude a very hasty survey of the natural conditions which the Greeks met on the north coast of the Euxine and which governed the evolution and history of the native tribes they found there.

[1] *Hist. Plant.* IV. v. 3.
[2] Ovid, *Epist. ex Ponto*, III. 1. 23.
[3] Pliny, *NH.* XXVII. 45. Theophrastus, *Hist Plant.* IX. Xvii. 4.
[4] Ib. VII. Xiii. 8, IX. Xiii. 2.
[5] Her. IV. 74.
[6] Th. P. Köppen, On the Finding of Amber in Russia, *Journ. Min. Publ. Inst.* St P., Aug. 1893.
[7] Her. IV. 53. Dio Chrys. XXXVI.

CHAPTER II.

SEAS AND COASTLINE.

BEFORE we even approach the coast of Scythia and discuss the knowledge of it possessed by the ancients, something must be said of their ideas concerning the Euxine Sea and its subordinate the Palus Maeotis[1].

Herodotus[2], for instance, takes the former to be 11,100 stades in greatest length, measured from the mouth of the Thracian Bosporus to that of the Phasis, and in greatest breadth 3300 stades reckoned from Themiscyra at the mouth of the Thermodon to Sindica. Moreover he thought that the neck between the Halys and Cilicia was only five days' journey "for a well girt man[3]." That means that he imagined the Euxine as stretching too far to the south at the eastern end: naturally, for this part, protected by the Caucasus, has a much warmer climate than the western[4]. As a matter of fact the broadest part is from the mouth of the Dnêpr to Heraclea in Bithynia, but Herodotus was evidently ignorant of the great bay along the south side of his square Scythia, whereas we may put the Rugged Chersonese and Sindica opposite to it some way up the eastern coast of the same. In the figure he gives for the greatest breadth Herodotus is not very far out, it being (but in the western half) 325 geographical miles or 3250 stades; but between the points he mentions it is only 235 geographical miles or 2350 stades.

His error with regard to the length is more serious. The extreme E. and W. points are Batum and the bay south of Mesembria, but he neglects the westerly bight of Thrace and makes a straight line from the Thracian Bosporus to the Phasis 11,100 stades, about double the real distance. We may take it that in reckoning 70,000 fathoms for a ship's journey in a day and 60,000 for a night he was taking the utmost possible, wherein he made no allowance for contrary winds and other obstacles. The cross measurement is more correct, as a ship could often take a straight passage north to south. She would not go for long out of sight of land, for a little to the west at the narrowest part of the sea the highlands of the Crimea (Criu Metopon) and Cape Carambis may be seen at the same time.

This exaggerated idea of the size of the Pontus present to the mind of Herodotus must have reacted on his view of Scythia and induced him

[1] E. Bunbury, *History of Ancient Geography*, I. pp. 175-636, II. 261-282.
[2] IV. 85, 86.
[3] I. 72.
[4] H. Berger, *Gesch. d. wissenschaftlichen Erdkunde der Griechen*, Leipzig, 1903, p. 103.

to lay it out on too large a scale, another reason for our not extending it very far into the interior. In later times after the publication of Peripli and the advance of geography the ancients had a very good practical knowledge of the shape of the Euxine, comparing it justly to the asymmetrical Scythian bow[1].

They naturally exaggerated its size, but their methods of calculation always produced this effect: yet they paid much attention to the subject. Pliny[2] gives five different reckonings of the circumference of the Pontus, they vary between 2000 and 2425 m.p. (= 16,000 to 19,400 stades), the real amount is about 1914 geographical miles (= 2392 m.p. or 19,136 stades). He also quotes Polybius for the distance of 500 m.p. across from one Bosporus to the other, which is approximately correct.

One curious error persisted. Eratosthenes and Strabo[3] both regarded Dioscurias (Sukhum Kale) as the extreme point of the whole sea, lying in a corner (μυχός) 600 stades east of the mouth of the Phasis, which some old poet, Herodotus and Ptolemy make the extreme point. This should really be at Batum, which is still further south. The error seems to rest on a commercial superiority of Dioscurias which lasted during Hellenistic and early Roman times. It was the last point of the navigation of the right side of the Pontus: the mountainous coast between it and the Cimmerian Bosporus being dangerous and unprofitable.

For all their familiarity with it the Greeks never forgot that the Euxine's first name was Axenos and most of them regarded a journey across it with some trepidation. To this day it is not a favourite sea with sailors, who dislike its fogs, its sudden storms and the scarcity of good harbours along the greater part of its coast. These causes tended to isolate the Greeks of its northern shore; in spite of the close commercial connection with the homeland no one voyaged to Olbia or Panticapaeum except on business, and Herodotus and the exile Dio Chrysostom are the only extant ancient authors of whom we can say that they visited the north side of the Euxine.

Maeotis.

Wrong as was Herodotus with regard to the Euxine, his ideas of the Palus Maeotis were even more erroneous[4]. He thought of it as not much smaller than the Pontus, whereas its real area is about one twelfth. He knew that it was nearly twenty days' journey to the Tanais, elsewhere he gives 4000 stades from the Bosporus, and this he seems to have imagined as its width rather than the longest line that could be drawn in a narrow triangle. Already Scylax was a little less wild and thought of it as half the size of the Euxine[5]. The distance across to the Tanais was usually put at 2200 stades[6], not so very much more than the actual distance of 1700: but most authors continue to give its circumference as 9000 stades[7], a very strange exaggeration. Right on into mediaeval times

[1] Hecataeus, Eratosthenes and Ptolemy, ap. Amm. Marcell. XXII. viii. 10. Dion. Perieg. l. 157, and Eustathius ad loc., Pliny, *NH.* IV. 76.
[2] *NH.* IV. 77.   [3] XI. ii. 16.
[4] IV. 86.   [5] § 68.

[6] Strabo, VII. iv. 5, Agathemerus, 18.
[7] Pliny, *NH.* IV. 78; Strabo, l.c.; Agathemerus, 10; Schol. in Dion. Perieg. *GGM.* II. p. 457; Peripl. Anon., 118 (92), etc.

the mouths of the Tanais were supposed to be exactly on the same meridian as the Bosporus, though Hippocrates speaks of the lake as stretching towards the summer rising of the sun. The ancients consistently regarded it as a lake or marsh and as the greatest lake they knew : hence perhaps their exaggerated idea of its size. Some even went so far as to regard the Cimmerian Bosporus as the true mouth of the Tanais[1]. On the other hand, some authors could not disabuse themselves of the notion that the Maeotis was connected with the Northern Ocean or at any rate with the Caspian[2].

Caspian.

With regard to the Caspian Herodotus and Ptolemy agree in making it an inland sea, though the former shews a tendency to make it balance the "Red" sea or Indian ocean[3]. But Strabo[4], Mela[5], Pliny[6], and Plutarch[7], all going back to Eratosthenes and perhaps to the Ionian geographers[8], make it connected with the northern ocean. Considering how little they knew about it, it is remarkable that both Herodotus and Strabo had a very fair idea of its size. The latter's information came from Patrocles, who was sent exploring by Seleucus. The idea of a passage from the northern ocean was due to the Greek belief in the symmetry of the world[9], and the existence of an arm of the sea running not so much north as east. Of this Patrocles seems to have been aware, but no one ever got near the Volga mouth, which indeed with its seventy channels is singularly unlike a sea strait. Herodotus seems to have thought of the Caspian as having its greatest length from north to south, but later authors put it from east to west[10].

Survey of Coastline.

The ancients never had a settled idea of the shape of the Scythian coast. The inaccuracy of the outline given by Ptolemy is a measure of the difficulty they found in getting their bearings. The requirements of their navigation demanded no more than a rough knowledge of the distances separating the cities, harbours and chief headlands as measured across the openings of unimportant or unnavigable inlets. Such knowledge they possessed in a very fair degree. The accuracy of the figures given by Ps.-Arrian and the anonymous compiler of the *Periplus Ponti Euxini* is remarkable when we consider the chances of corruption arising from the Greek methods of writing numbers. Of the inside of the country the Greeks knew hardly anything. They knew the appearance of the steppe and that great rivers made their way through it to disembogue in broad

[1] e.g. Ps.-Arrian, *Per. P. E.*, 29 (19 H.).
[2] Plutarch, *Alexander*, XLIV. For the silting up of the Maeotis, v. supra, p. 4.
[3] Her. I. 202, 203; IV. 40. Arist. *Meteorologica*, II. i. 10.
[4] XI. vi. 1 ; vii. 1.
[5] I. 9.
[6] *NH.* VI. 36.
[7] l. c.
[8] Berger, op. cit., p. 57.
[9] v. J. L. Myres, *Geogr. Journal*, VIII. (1896) p. 605, On the maps used by Herodotus.
[10] For the Araxes question and the rivers running into the Caspian v. infra, p. 30.

shallow estuaries, but of the real direction of these streams' flow they had no notion. They imagined a symmetrical scheme of rivers coming down at right angles to the coast. The supposed flatness of the steppe would of course offer no obstacle to channels running from one stream to another, a hypothesis representing trade routes connecting the lower course of one river with the upper part of another. Such portages have always been in S. Russia. The granite ridge that runs from Podolia to Taganrog causes the well-known rapids of the Dnêpr and bends that stream into such an elbow that its upper waters are more conveniently approached either from one of the lesser rivers that fall into the Maeotis, or from the Ingul or Ingulets. Hence the confusion between Hypanis and Borysthenes, the difficulties with the Panticapes and Gerrhus. But it is better to discuss the position of rivers with that of the tribes so intimately bound up with them in the description given by Herodotus. Till the time of Ptolemy we have no details of the *Hinterland* save the schematic picture of the river system and the names of innumerable tribes, whether assigned to localities or indeterminate. Herodotus just mentions the point Exampaeus and the city of the Geloni, but these would be fixed by the river and tribe scheme, if any determination of their place could be reached. Before adventuring ourselves in the boundless interior let us see how much the ancients knew of the coast between the mouths of the Danube and the steep slopes of the Caucasus where they overhang the sea[1].

Different accounts of the Danube mouths[2] are given by different authors[3], and none of them agree with the present state of things, but a comparison between the actual lie of the country and the various descriptions of its ancient condition renders it possible to account for the apparent contradictions of our authors and to trace the history of geologic change since the time of Herodotus.

The delta begins between Isakcha and Tulcha, where the Kilia and St George arms separate, and forms a triangle with two sides of 46 miles and a base of 33 miles long, to which is added a four-sided piece enclosed by lake Rasim, the Dunavets, the sea, and the St George arm. All this space is marsh, subject to floods except for five sandbanks upon which

---

[1] For the sake of convenience in handling, I have reproduced the central part only of Latyshev's combination of Ptolemy's maps of European and Asiatic Sarmatia, Dacia and the Caucasus. With the outlying parts from the Baltic shore to the NW. round by W. and S. to Transcaucasia on the SE. we are not concerned. To the N. are very few names which represent living information, but mostly they are the Herodotean tribes which obviously could not be accommodated in the comparatively well-known central regions. I here give some interesting points to the N. and E. as placed by Lat.; Ptol. does not locate tribes exactly. Borusci long. 63°, lat. 58°; Rhipaei Montes 63°, 57° 30'; Alexandri Arae 63°, 57°; Nasci 63°, 57°; Fontes Tanaidis 64°, 58°; Modocae 67°, 60° 30'; Zacatae 67°, 59° 30'; Caesaris Arae 68°, 56° 30'; Asaei 68° 50', 59° 40'; Perierbidi 68° 30', 58° 50'; Fontes Rha Occidentales et Finis Montium Hyperboreorum 70°, 61°; Svardeni 71°

30', 59° 30'; Chaenides 74°, 59°; Epistrophe Rha 74°, 56°; Confluentes Rha 79°, 58° 30'; Zinchi 74°, 48° 30'; Montes Hippici 74°, 54°—81°, 52°; Finis M. Coracis 75°, 48°; Caucasus M. 75°, 47°—85°, 48°; Alexandri Columnae 77°, 51° 30'; Fontes Vardanis 78°, 48° 30'; Portae Sarmaticae 78°, 47° 30'; Alterae P. Sarm. 81°, 48° 30'; Sacani 82°, 51°; Ceraunii M. 82°, 49° 30'—84° 52'; Epistrophe Rha 85°, 54°; Ostium Rha 87° 30', 48° 40'; Fontes Rha Orientales 90°, 61°.

[2] Braun, *Investigations*, pp. 182 sqq.

[3] Herodotus IV. 47, Ps.-Arrian *Peripl.* 35 (24 H.), Ephorus ap. Strab. VII. iii. 15, Dionysius Perieg. l. 301, and Anon. 93 (67) give five mouths; Pliny, *NH.* IV. 79, Ptolemy III. X. 2, who has a completely wrong idea of the Delta's shape, six; Strabo VII. iii. 15, Pomponius Mela II. 8, seven. Nowadays we have but three; Kilia Mouth, Sulina Mouth, and St George's Mouth.

poor villages are built. This tract cannot correspond to the ancient delta, which included the island Peuce whereon the Triballi with their wives and children took refuge from Alexander when he drove them from their country[1]. For the banks of this island were steep and the current, confined by the high banks, swift. Alexander only prevailed by crossing the main stream and discomfiting the Getae on the left bank.

Peuce then was an island with high banks: and therefore outside the present delta. Still most of our authorities say that it was between two arms of the river and the sea. Some[2] put it between the St George mouth (Ostium Peuces, Ἱερὸν στόμα) and the next to the N. (Naracu stoma, Ναράκιον στόμα), on what is now called St George's Island: and Dionysius has much the same idea (l. 301). But Strabo (VII. iii. 15) says merely that it lies near the mouths and that there are other islands above and below it, i.e. it is not directly on the sea, but even 120 stades = 15 miles up stream. We have no data for exactly determining the amount the delta has grown in the last 2000 years, except that according to the Peutinger Table Noviodunum (Isakcha) is 65 Roman miles = 520 stades from the Sacred mouth along the course of the river; Ptolemy makes it about 477 stades or 60 miles in a direct line. This brings us to just about a line of sandbanks reaching from Vilkov by Ivancha to Teretsa, and representing an old coastline which we may take as the coastline at the beginning of our era. This line gives about the right amount, 47 versts (31 miles = 279 stades), which we get as the distance between the old mouths from N. to S. in Arrian (280 stades) and Strabo (300 stades). If now we measure our 15 miles up stream from our ancient Sacred mouth we come upon rising ground which takes up the rest of the Dobrudzha up to Tulcha.

Braun supposes that formerly an actual branch of the Danube cut off this triangle from the main land and fell into the sea somewhere opposite the channel Portitsa, within twelve miles or so of Istropolis (? Karanasup), having sent off an arm into a marsh, now represented by lake Babadagh, and having formed lake Rasim. Bruun[3] anticipates Braun and says there exist traces of such a channel. This state of things is represented by Pliny's confused account[4]. When this branch got silted up confusion arose in the mind of Ptolemy, who found the southernmost mouth given variously as the Peuce mouth and the Sacred mouth, and he identified them and so was brought to seek the island Peuce in the modern delta and to throw out all the measurements and distort the shape of the whole delta to try and reconcile different accounts both founded on fact but referring to different times.

Without detailed investigation of the actual lie of the land between the main course of the Danube and Babadagh it is impossible to say whether Dr Braun has really disentangled the labyrinth of the Danube mouths. If it is at all possible, such a solution would best fit the case.

---

[1] Arrian *Anab.* I. 2—4.

[2] Scymnus, l. 787, Anon. 94 (68), Pliny and Ptolemy. Under the name of Ptolemy we may quote data due to Marinus of Tyre whose work formed the basis of Ptolemy's. For our purposes no distinction can be made between them.

[3] *Chernomorje*, I. pp. 48—59.

[4] l. c. Primum ostium Peuces, mox ipsa Peuce insula in qua proximus alveus [nomen deest] appellatus xix m. p. magna palude sorbetur: ex eodem alveo et supra Histropolin lacus gignitur lxiii m. p. ambitu, Halmyrin vocant.

II] Mouths of Danube 13

It is just conceivable that within historic time Peuce never was a real island or Portitsa a real mouth of the Danube, but that the first was defensible across a short isthmus and along the course of a minor stream flowing into Babadagh lake, and so gained the name of island, to be a refuge for the Triballi and later (when it almost certainly was no longer separate) for the division of the Bastarnae hence called Peucini. So there may have been a false mouth to the south of the delta as there was to the N. or ships may once have gone in by Portitsa and across lake Rasim to ascend the stream now represented by the Dunavets. We can see by the varying accounts of authors that the real mouths of the river closed and shifted, as has happened with all the Black Sea rivers, but that old names and old descriptions lived on in Geography books and led compilers astray. Only Strabo who prided himself on direct up-to-date information and avoided padding copied from other books, gives an intelligible account of the district as it was in his time. The question of the number of mouths is never settled, to-day one may count anything from three to twelve and no doubt it was the same in ancient times. We may take it then that while it is hopeless to identify the lesser mouths (we have ten different names preserved in various authors) Peuces ostium was originally what is now Portitsa, Ostium Sacrum (later also called Peuce) corresponded to St George's mouth, Naracu stoma was half-way between that and Calon stoma, the Sulina mouth (lately canalised and made really navigable); that Pseudostoma, Boreon stoma, Spireon stoma corresponded to branches of the Kilia mouth, and Psilon stoma was a still more northerly channel running out through the marshes (Thiagola) at Zhebriany.

The stretch from the Ister to the Tyras is not important. Strabo tells us of two lakes, one open and one shut, corresponding to Sasyk and probably Alibey, two limans now communicating with the sea by narrow channels.

Between them came the place τὰ Ἀντιφίλου of Peripl. Anon. and next his Cremnisci, which Pliny also gives with Aepolium and Montes Macrocremni, which seems a very grand name for the low cliffs of this coast. Near the corner of the Dnêstr Liman we have Hermonactis vicus (Strabo and Ptol.) and Turris Neoptolemi (Strabo and Anon.). Of this latter there seem some traces left in the foundations of a tower. It is ascribed to Neoptolemus the Admiral of Mithridates, and appears to have been a lighthouse[1].

A difficulty is in the distance given by our authorities for the space between Danube mouth and Dnêstr mouth. Strabo and Anon. make it 900 stades. Really it comes to about 600. Ps.-Arrian obviously left the coast at Portus Isiacorum (Odessa) and cut straight across to the Danube mouth, making it 1200 stades, probably by adding on half the distance for possible curves of the coast. He says that there were no settlements in that space ἔρημα καὶ ἀνώνυμα, whereby he did an injustice to Tyras, which was still coining in Arrian's time[2]. Anon. filled in the gap with names gleaned we

[1] Becker, *Trans. Odessa Soc.* III. p. 151, On the coast of the Euxine between the Ister and the Borysthenes with reference to ancient settlements.

[2] An argument for its not being the real Arrian, v. p. 24, n. 3.

know not whence, and made the total distance agree with Ps.-Arrian. But why Strabo should be 300 stades out it is hard to say, unless he applied a measurement stretching to the southern and most used Danube mouth to the northern nearest one. Pliny gives 130 m.p., that is 1040 stades, from Tyras to Pseudostoma. The ancients all seem to have overestimated this unattractive piece of coast. Ptolemy on the other hand makes too little of this very distance. From Thiagola (Zhebriany) to the Dnêstr mouth he gives what represents 390 stades, while further to the E., e.g. between Dnêstr and Dnêpr, he is substantially correct. Dr Braun has well shewn that just here comes the break in his bearings, due to his having Byzantium two degrees too far to the N., in the same latitude as Marseilles. Harpis, the other point he gives, is still orientated from the S., and represents Eskypolos, the town at the end of the Roman wall that guarded the lower Danube.

Strabo says that 140 stades up the river Tyras are the towns of Niconia on the right and Ophiussa on the left. Pliny says that the town Tyras was formerly called Ophiussa. We need have no doubt that it is the present Akkerman, mediaeval Moncastro or Bêlgorod. What we know of its history and coinage will be found further on (ch. XIV.). Niconia would be Otarik, where some antiquities have been found. Strabo adds another datum, 120 stades, for the distance between Tyras town and the mouth of the river, more close than the figure he has first given and agreeing with Anon., who says that τὰ Νεοπτολέμου was 120 stades from Tyras river, surely a mistake for Tyras town[1].

The position of the island Leuce, now Phidonisi, is accurately defined by Strabo, who says it lies 500 stades from the mouth of the Tyras, and Demetrius (ap. Anon. 91 (65)), who gives 400 stades as its distance from the mainland at the Danube mouth. This is fairly correct. Other authors confuse it with the Δρόμος Ἀχιλλέως, or the nameless island near the mouth of the Borysthenes, now called Berezan. First mentioned by Arctinus, Leuce is spoken of by Stesichorus in his *Palinode*, by Pindar (*Nem.* IV. 49), Euripides (*Androm.* 1259), Lycophron (*Alexandra* 186), and gradually the romantic legend grew that we find in its fullest form in Philostratus Junior[2].

To the E. of the Tyras the next place mentioned is Physce in Ptolemy, probably at the mouth of the Baraboi, and Ps.-Arrian's Portus Isiacorum, interesting as being the forerunner of modern Odessa, and 50 stades (Anon. 87 (61)) further on Istrianorum Portus, probably by the mouth of the Kujalnik or Hadzhi Bey limans, once estuaries navigable from the sea.

The cliffs gradually rise along this coast, and the name Scopuli (Anon. 87 (61)) may be justified. The next point is Ordessus (Ptol.) or Odessus (Ps.-Arr. and Anon.), probably at the mouth of the Axiaces or Asiaces (Mela), now the Tiligul, cut right off by a bar, but once open. Here, near Koblevka, Uvarov found traces of ancient habitation[3].

---

[1] Vide E. von Stern, On the latest excavations at Akkerman, *Trans. Od. Soc.* XXIII. p. 58.
[2] Heroicus XIX. 16 (pp. 327—331). Latyshev, *Scyth. et Cauc.* I. p. 637. V. account of Leuce in Ukert and *Trans. Od. Soc.* I. p. 549, II. p. 413,

and a discussion of the whole question and of the worship there paid to Achilles by the Olbiopolites, in Latyshev, *Olbia*, pp. 55—61 and inf. chap. XV.
[3] Cf. A. S. Ouvarov, *Recherches sur les Antiquités de la Russie Méridionale*, Pl. XXVI. and XXVII.

Opposite the liman Berezan is the island of the same name referred to by Strabo and Ps.-Arrian. This island was early settled by the Greeks, as upon it have been found vases of Milesian type and archaic asses of Olbia[1]. It is constantly confused with Leuce. From here it is just 60 stades (Anon.) on to the mouth of the great liman in which the Bugh and Dnêpr join. Altogether the distances along this coast are very much what Ps.-Arrian and Anon. make them.

The common estuary of the Bugh and Dnêpr is one of the finest in Europe, its very size prevented casual observers understanding how the land lies. Dio Chrysostom (*Or.* xxxvi.) gives us the best description. Herodotus and Dio alone grasped the fact that the city which its citizens called Olbia, and strangers Borysthenes, lay upon the Hypanis, the Bugh, not upon the Borysthenes river, the Dnêpr. The confusion was natural, but the site of Olbia could never have been determined from the texts. The mounds, coins and inscriptions dug up at Sto Mohil (the hundred Barrows), a mile to the south of the village of Iljinskoe or Parutino, have settled the matter. Alector mentioned by Dio must be Ochakov opposite the long spit of Kinburn, well known in the Crimean war. Between them is a bar with a very narrow channel under the guns of the fort. When you have passed the fort the great liman is spread before you and even at Olbia the opposite side of the Bugh is so far distant that the impression produced is that of a lake rather than a river. Hence the variations of distance given by the authorities, Scymnus and Anon. making it 240 stades up from the mouth of the river, Strabo (who says Borysthenes) and Dio 200 stades. Pliny with his 15 m.p. must have measured from the point where a ship leaves the Dnêpr channel and begins to ascend the Bugh. On the Borysthenes itself there seems to have been no important settlement. On its left bank and on the islands of the river still survived into last century remains of the woods which gained the district the name of Hylaea, of which Herodotus, and after him Mela and Pliny, speak. It hardly required many trees to attract attention in the bare steppe land. We need not suppose that Valerius Flaccus meant anything when he wrote (*Arg.* vi. 76):

> Densior haud usquam nec celsior extulit ulla
> Silva trabes: fessaeque prius rediere sagittae
> Arboris ad summum quam pervenere cacumen.

He had read in his Mela:

> Silvae deinde sunt quas maximas hae terrae ferunt[2].

The position of the Hylaea is a favourite subject for discussion, but the difficulty only arises if we put the Panticapes[3] (which flows into the Hylaea) to the west of the Borysthenes and identify it with the Ingulets, so as to give room for the Georgi between it and the Dnêpr. But if

[1] V. chapters XI. XII. and XV.
[2] For the former extension of trees where now there are none, see Burachkov (who spoke from personal knowledge); On the position of Carcinitis, *Trans. Od. Soc.* IX. p. 3; K. Neumann, op. cit. pp. 31 and 74 sqq., who has collected various testimony to shew that trees did really exist along the river valleys, but is inclined to make too much of it, and W. W. Dokoutchaiev, Les Steppes russes autrefois et aujourd'hui, *Congrès International d'Archéologie préhistorique et d'Anthropologie, II*. Session à Moscou, Vol. I. 1892.
[3] Her. IV. 54. Vide infra, p. 29.

we suppose that it was the Konka across the Dnêpr valley it would flow precisely into the wooded region to the south of the estuary[1].

Ptolemy puts Olbia on the Borysthenes. In face of such a mistake it seems risky to assign positions to the other cities he mentions. But near Great Znamenka and Little Znamenka overlooking the well-watered flats of the so-called "great meadow" we find the remains of fortified settlements with Greek pottery[2], which may mark his Amadoca and Azagarion.

At the mouth of the Dnêpr liman we have Kinburn spit, which is probably the site of Ptolemy's Ἄλσος Ἑκάτης[3], which Anon. puts on the next spit, the west end of the Tendra or Δρόμος Ἀχιλλέως, whereupon there seems to have been a sanctuary of the hero mentioned by Strabo. A stone with a dedication to Achilles was dredged up off Kinburn[4], and others with his name were found on the Tendra[5]. The formation of Kinburn spit and the Tendra is unstable and channels in them open and shut so that what has been an island becomes joined to the mainland and again becomes an island according to the caprice of the currents. The Island of Achilles mentioned by Pliny hereabouts may well be of such formation. Some authors, e.g. Ps.-Arrian, have hence confused the Δρόμος with Leuce. But in the main the descriptions are accurate, telling of the sword-like stretch of sand curving at each end and serving as the race-course of the fleet-footed hero. Dzharylgach, the other end, seems to be what we must understand by Tamyrace. Between it and the place where the Tendra joins the mainland Ps.-Arrian gives ἐκρόα λίμνης, probably a temporary gap in the continuity of the beach. Behind Tamyrace spit was some sort of shelter for the few ships that came that way. Between Tamyrace and the opposite coast of the Crimea is the gulf called the gulf of Tamyrace or Carcinitis running up to Taphrae on the Isthmus of Perekop. How little the ancients visited these parts is shewn by the vagueness of the measurements given. Tendra is about 80 m. long or 750 stades, but Strabo calls it 1000, Ps.-Arrian 980, Anon. 1200, Agrippa 80 m. p. = 640 stades. The 60 stades given as the distance from the shore is not far out.

So with the gulf called Carcinites or Tamyrace the 300 stades is not far out for the distance across the mouth, but the ancients had the most exaggerated idea of its extent to the eastward. Strabo puts this at 1000 stades and says some multiplied this amount by three.

On the other hand, Pliny and Strabo both give the breadth of the Isthmus of Perekop, Taphrae, at 40 stades (5 miles) which is very near. Strabo adds that others reckoned it at 360 stades, which is about the distance from the gulf of Perekop on the w. to Genichesk on the sea of Azov[6]. Again they give a very good description of the Putrid Sea (Sivash), but make it very much too big. This is one of the most unmistakeable

---

[1] Cf. Niederle, *Starověké Zprávy o zeměpisu východní Evropy* (Ancient Information as to the Geography of Eastern Europe), p. 35 sq.

[2] *CR.* 1899, p. 28, and Braun, op. cit. p. 211 sqq., 371–3, also Ouvarov, op. cit. Pl. D.

[3] Later called ἄλσος alone and afterwards the Island of S. Aetherius, upon which the Russians refitted their dug-outs [Const. Porph. *de adm. Imp.*

[4] c. IX., cf. Latyshev, 'Island of S. Aeth.' in *Journ. Min. Pub. Instr.* St P., May 1899, p. 73].

[5] *IosPE.* IV. 63. V. ch. XV.

[6] *IosPE.* I. 179–183.

[7] This is probably the site of Asander's wall, v. ch. XIX., no doubt on the site of a former ditch that gave its name to the place.

features of the whole coast line and naturally impressed those who came
near[1]. At this point Pliny[2] gets hopelessly confused. He mixes up the
Putrid Sea, the liman of the Utljúk or Molóchnaja and the Hypanis
(Bugh) with one of the limans about the Peninsula of Taman at the
opposite corner of the Sea of Azov and the Hypanis (Kuban), and one can
make no sense out of his jumble of names. *Lacus Buces...Coretus Maeotis
lacus sinus...amnes Buces, Gerrhus...* hardly tally with *regio Scythia Sindica
nominatur.* One cannot help thinking that as now, so formerly, the same
geographical names were repeated along this coast. Every other salt lake
is called Sasyk, the cutting through a spit of sand is called Bugas, there
are two Kujalnik rivers, an Ingul and an Inguléts (a diminutive though it
is the bigger river), a Don and Donéts, two sandspits called Dzharylgach,
two places called Ak Mechet, two Sivash lakes, two rivers Salgir, and two
Karasu, so in old days there were two rivers Hypanis, Bugh and Kuban,
perhaps two Gerrhus, more than one Panticapes and several Eiones, Insulae
Achillis and so forth. Just as the Russians have adopted Tartar words as
names, so the Greeks took native words meaning river or salt lake or
channel. Hence the confusion produced by the attempts of Ptolemy or
Pliny to distinguish these names without local knowledge.

In the Gulf of Carcinites Pliny[3] mentions the islands Cephalonnesus,
Spodusa and Macra, and Ptolemy gives position to the first of these. Mela,
Pliny and Ptolemy also mention a town, Carcine, which is merely the Carcinitis of Herodotus (IV. 99) and Hecataeus (fr. 153). Herodotus says that the
Hypacyris here falls into the sea and Mela (II. 4) copies him inaccurately,
*sinus Carcinites, in eo urbs Carcine, quam duo flumina Gerrhos et Ypacares
uno ostio effluentia adtingunt.* Pliny is still further removed and speaks of
the Pacyris (sic)[4]. The only stream that runs into the gulf is the Kalanchák,
now quite unimportant, but from its mouth hollows and what were once
water-courses may be traced far inland almost to the Dnêpr about the land
called Gerrhus. This may have been a way of getting quickly up to that
district, but it must have been early abandoned owing to the failure in
water of which we can trace the effect all over the steppe region.

The position of Carcinitis town has been a great bone of contention
because it has been assumed that it must have been situated on the gulf
Carcinites, whereas the town Cercinitis is plainly put in the western Crimea
by Ps.-Arrian and Anon. (who adds a name Coronitis). Across the gulf 300
stades from Tamyrace we find mentioned Calos Limen, 700 stades further
on Cercinitis, and 600 stades beyond Chersonese. Reckoning back exactly
from the well-known site of the latter we get Cercinitis at the mouth
of the closed estuary Donguslav, the position approved by Bruun and
Burachkov. Another 700 stades brings us too far round the corner to give
the required 300 more to Tamyrace. If we take all the distances to
be as usual somewhat exaggerated we may put Cercinitis just to the west
of the modern Eupatoria on a spot where there are traces of a Greek
town (v. Chapter XVI.)[5]. Coins occur marked ΚΕΡΚΙ and ΚΑΡΚ, similar in

---

[1] Strabo VII. iv. 1.
[2] *NH.* IV. 84.
[3] *NH.* IV. 93.

[4] *NH.* IV. 84.
[5] Excavations of N. Ph. Romanchenko, *TRAS.*
VIII. pp. 219—236.

M.

type to the coins of Chersonese (Pl. IV. 1, 2, 3, cf. IV. 17), and even an inscription[1] has been found ; and we can put Calos Limen at Ak Mechet or at
the next little bay along the coast.   So Cercinitis is another example of the
curiously inaccurate naming of places along this coast by which the town
Borysthenes (Olbia) was not upon the Borysthenes and Istrus not actually
upon the Ister.   The gulf Carcinites was the gulf just beyond Carcinitis, up
which the men of that town traded by way of the Hypacyris until the latter
dried up, and so it was thought of as standing at the mouth of that river.
Later Ptolemy calls Carcinites itself a river.   If this was the view of
Herodotus we can see why he had no idea how much the Crimea is
divided from the mainland, and a river being provided we need not trouble
about Donguslav lake.

At Chersonese we again reach a definite point.   A discussion of the
topography of the district lying immediately about it will best go with the
sketch of its history and remains that will be given in Chapter XVII.

Strabo (VII. iv. 2) gives 4400 stades as the distance we have come
from the Tyras.   But with moderate allowance for the curves of the coast
the distance can hardly come to more than 3000 stades.   Strabo must have
reckoned in the circumference of the Carcinites gulf and made his ship
go right up to Olbia and other places of call on the way.   Anonymus (83
(57)—87 (61)) adds up to 3810 but gives 4110 (89 (63)), having missed
300 stades somewhere about Tamyrace.   He says that Artemidorus gives
4220, but that is going round Carcinites gulf.

Beyond Chersonese Strabo (l.c.) rightly mentions the three deep bays
and the headland now C. Chersonese.   C. Fiolente is much more picturesque,
but not so important geographically as C. Chersonese, and is not likely
to be meant by Strabo.   Portus Symbolon is clearly Balaklava, and by
it was Palacion or Placia, built by the natives as a menace to the whole

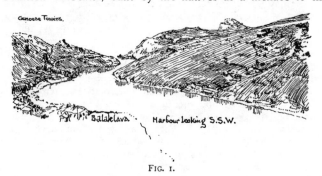

FIG. I.

Minor Peninsula.   The fancy that this narrow inlet is the harbour of the
Laestrygones has nothing for it but the names of Dubois de Montpéreux,
after Pallas the first scientific explorer of these parts, and K. E. von Baer[2]
who was rather a scientist than a historian.

---

[1] *BCA.* x. 20.   [2] *Ueber die homerische Localitäten in der Odyssee,* Brunswick, 1878, v. inf. Ch. XIII.

The southernmost cape of the Crimea was called by the ancients Criu Metopon and was very well known. It was supposed to be just opposite to Carambis on the coast of Asia Minor and they could both be seen from a ship in mid sea. The high land behind the capes can really be seen. This comparatively narrow part was reckoned to divide the Euxine into two basins, but it is hard to settle what particular headland was the actual Ram's Head. Pliny[1] gives it as 165 m.p., i.e. 1320 stades from Chersonese town, which would bring it to Theodosia; and 125 m.p. = 1000 stades on to Theodosia, which would bring it back to C. Sarych. Anon. (81 (53)) makes it 300 stades from Symbolon Portus. That would be about Aju Dagh. But he also makes it 220 stades from Lampas (Lambat), which would bring it again to near Aj Todor, not in itself a very prominent cape, chiefly interesting for a Roman station of which M. I. Rostovtsev has given an account[2]. But above it Aj Petri rises high and can be seen further than Aju Dagh, and the latter is considerably to the north, so that perhaps it is best to call Aj Todor Criu Metopon. The most southerly point is actually Kikeneis or Sarych, still further to the west.

The position given by Ptolemy also leans in favour of Aj Todor. Ptolemy's Charax—Pliny[3] mentions Characeni—may well have been the settlement on Aj Todor. In the interior Strabo mentions Mount Trapezus, Chatyr Dagh (VII. iv. 3), and it is at least as much like a table as a tent.

Chatyr Dagh . Trapezus Mons. from N.W.

FIG. 2.

The modern place-name Partenit near Aju Dagh suggests that here may have been a sanctuary of the virgin goddess to whom all the Tauric mountains were holy. Lampat, the next village, has also preserved its Greek name mentioned by Ps.-Arrian (30 (19 H.)) and Anon., and Alushta is the Ἀλοῦστον of Procopius[4]. Beyond Lampas 600 stades further east we have what Ps.-Arrian calls λιμὴν Σκυθοταύρων ἔρημος, 200 stades short of Theodosia. Anon. (78 (52)) calls it also Ἀθηναίων. These 200 stades bring us to Otüz, the most probable site, for 600 stades from Lampas makes the site too close to Theodosia. The name of Sugdaea, Sudak, so important in mediaeval times, does not occur before Procopius (l. c.).

Theodosia is again a certain site, and has recovered its old name (v. Ch. XVIII.).

From near Theodosia an earthwork goes across to the beginning of the Arabat Spit on the Maeotis. This seems to represent the boundary of

[1] *NH.* IV. 86.
[2] *Journ. Min. Pub. Instr.* St P., May 1900, v. inf. Ch. XVII.
[3] *NH.* IV. 85.
[4] *De Aed.* III. 7.

the kingdom of Leucon as against the Scyths and Tauri of the peninsula rather than the Wall of Asander[1].

At 280 stades from Theodosia Ps.-Arrian (30 (19 H.)) and Anon. (77 (51)) give Cazeca, clearly Kachik the eastern headland of the bay of Theodosia, about 30 miles from that city following the coast round; 180 stades further east, according to Anon., was Cimmericum, evidently Opuk, where Dubrux[2] discovered traces of a fortified town with a harbour. This is rendered quite certain by the existence opposite here of two skerries mentioned by Anon. (76 (50)). From the head of Lake Uzunlar, once an arm of the sea, goes another embankment to Hadzhibey on the Sea of Azov. At a distance of 60 stades Anon. gives Cytae, also mentioned by Pliny[3] and called Cytaea by Scylax (68). The 60 stades would bring it to Kaz Aül. Acra[4] or Acrae (Pliny) would come at Takil Burun, 30 stades from Cytae on the headland marking the entrance of the Cimmerian Bosporus. The site of Hermisium[5] is uncertain. After another 65 stades we reach Nymphaeum, undoubtedly Eltegen, where there are evident remains of a city and harbour (v. Chapter xviii.). Tyritace[6] seems to have been at the head of Churubash Lake, once an arm of the sea. Dia of Pliny is uncertain, but must have been between Tyritace and Panticapaeum. This latter was more than the 85 stades from Nymphaeum by Tyritace, given by Anon., but there seems no reason to question these identifications. As to Panticapaeum, there can be no doubt that its Acropolis was the hill now called Mount Mithridates (v. Chapter xix.).

The identification of the several small settlements about the Cimmerian Bosporus, and on the Peninsula of Taman, is rendered difficult by the uncertainty as to changes in the one case in the position of sandbanks and spits which would necessarily modify the distances reckoned from one place to another, in the other to still more considerable changes in the water-courses which intersect the peninsula, deriving from the Hypanis or Kuban, and subject not only to ordinary silting up, but to the more unusual action of the mud volcanoes that abound in the district.

Next to Panticapaeum, on the west side of the strait, we have Myrmecium, mentioned by most of the authorities as being 25 (Anon.) or 20[7] stades away. This would fairly bring us to the place called the Old Quarantine, just the other side of the bay. Somewhere near must have been the town which early issued coins marked ΑΠΟΛ and ΑΠ (Pl. ix. 10), and which seems to have been absorbed in Panticapaeum, unless Apollonia was indeed the Greek name for that city. Forty stades further on (Strabo) we have Parthenium, while Anon. makes it 60 from Myrmecium to Porthmium. Probably these both represent the site of Jenikale lighthouse at the narrowest point of the channel, whose breadth is regularly given as 20 stades, which is about right. It is really about 90 stades from Panticapaeum.

Ps.-Arrian and Anon. reckon the strait to be the mouth of the Tanaïs, and this is not unreasonable according to the view that makes the Maeotis a mere marsh and no sea.

[1] Strabo VII. iv. 6, cf. supra, p. 16, n. 6.
[2] *Trans. Od. Soc.* IV. p. 69 and Pl. I.
[3] *NH.* IV. 86.
[4] Anon. and Strabo XI. ii. 8.

[5] Pliny, *NH.* IV. 87, Mela II. 3.
[6] Steph. Byz. s.v.; Ptol. Τυρικτάκη ; Anon. 76 (50) Τυριστάκη.
[7] Strabo VII. iv. 5.

On the west of the Maeotis, between the Bosporus and the Don, except for Herodotus and his Cremni (IV. 20, 110, perhaps near Genichesk), Ptolemy is the only authority, and the names he gives are mere names not to be identified, for he has a wrong idea of the lie of the land, and in any case there seems to have been no important settlement on this coast. Only at the headland Zjuk, about 40 miles to the west of the entrance to the straits, we have remains of a Greek village[1], which may have been Heracleum or Zenonis Chersonesus. So too no purpose can be served by endeavouring to identify the rivers of this coast.

The mouth of the Don is a more interesting point. Of Tanais town and its inscriptions we will treat later (Ch. XIX.). Its site in the second and third centuries A.D. was clearly near Nedvigovka on the Dead Donets, but it is quite probable that the original Tanais town destroyed by Polemo was on the site of Azov, or in the delta at Elizavetovskaja Stanitsa[2]. We cannot identify the island Alopecia, mentioned by Strabo (XI. ii. 3), Pliny[3] and Ptolemy. It has probably been joined to the delta, which is growing very fast. In any case it is hard to see how it can have been 100 stades below the town.

The east coast is more important because of its fisheries, which supplied much of the τάριχος exported from the Pontus[4]. The first, 800 stades from the Tanais, was at the Great Rhombites, probably the Jeja. At Jeisk, at its mouth, is still a great fishery. After another 800 stades came the Little Rhombites by Jasenskaja Kosa, where there once flowed into the sea the Chelbasi and Beisug rivers which now reach it only during the spring floods; 600 stades more past the northern delta of the Kuban brings us to Tyrambe, possibly Temrjuk or Temrjuk Settlement, between which an important branch of that river (the Anticites or Hypanis) reaches the Maeotis. At a distance of 120 stades was Cimmerice or Cimmeris village, probably the NW. point of the island Fontan. This was the point from which vessels reckoned their course across the Maeotis. 20 stades beyond was Achillis vicus, at the narrowest point of the strait, opposite Parthenium. These figures all seem put too low by Strabo (XI. ii. 4—6). Perhaps the current that flows down the Sea of Azov helped the vessels along and led the navigators to underestimate the distance. The natural course would be for ships to go right straight across to Tanais and come down the east coast to take in their cargoes of fish. Ptolemy mentions these same points as Strabo, but his authority is not to be preferred.

The topography of the Taman Peninsula is, as we have said, particularly difficult. The interweaving of land and water made it hard for Strabo (XI. ii. 6—10) to describe, and the changes since his time, both in his text and in the land surface, make it still harder to apply his description[5]. In general the very greatest caution should be used in explaining difficulties of ancient topography by geological changes, but here three powerful

[1] A. A. Dirin, *Trans. Od. Soc.* XIX. ii. p. 121.
[2] Strabo XI. ii. 3.   [3] *NH.* IV. 87.
[4] Strabo XI. ii. 4.
[5] The best account is in Goertz, *Archaeological Topography of the Taman Peninsula*, Moscow,

1870, and *History of Archaeological Investigations in the Taman Peninsula*, M. 1876, both repr. St P. 1898; but cf. I. E. Zabélin, *Trans. Third Arch. Congr.* (Kiev) 1874, II., Explanation of Strabo's Topography of Bosp. Cim.

agencies have been at work. Something has been done by the mud-volcanoes found on both sides of the strait, but most active to the east of it. Their activity is not mentioned by the ancients, they may have been quiescent during classical times : since then there have been thrown up the cone of Kuku Oba, which is the most striking object of the Bosporus, and some of the cones just south of Sennája, the site of Phanagoria. One of these it was that cast up, in 1818, a Greek inscription[1], referring to the construction of a temple of Artemis Agrotera[2].

Another agency in changing the face of the land is the action of the Kuban. Whereas the northern branch, the Protoka, has formed an ordinary delta in what was once a bay of the Maeotis, the southern branch flowed into what must have been a group of islands and found its way to the sea through channels and sounds which itself it has done much towards silting up.

Lastly the sea itself has encroached on the side towards the Bosporus. Here the shifting currents have alternately washed the shore away and deposited new sandbanks, there is even reason to suppose that the level of the land is sinking. Columns, the remains of a temple, are seen in the sea along the northerly spit opposite Jenikale, and again off the site of the ancient Phanagoria.

Along the coast from Tuzla to C. Panagia barrows are seen in section upon the cliff. The latter cape takes its name from a church now swallowed up by the waves. At Taman itself the cliff, with remains of an ancient town, is being washed away. The statues from the monument of Comosarye[3] were found in the sea, because the headland of SS. Boris and Glêb on which it was built had been encroached upon.

In the district, then, there are three main bodies of water, the Gulf of Taman, Akdengis (or Akhtaniz) Liman, and Kizil Tash Liman. Branches of the Kuban flow into the two limans, but the Gulf of Taman is at present cut off from it. But there can be little doubt that a depression running east from the cove Shimardan by Lake Janovskij to the Akdengis liman represents an old channel[4].

The only certain points in the whole peninsula are Phanagoria[5], the great masses of débris and rows of barrows about Sennája leave no doubt where we must seek the capital of the Asiatic half of the Bosporus kingdom, and Gorgippia, long supposed to be Anapa and recently proved to be so by inscriptions[6].

If we take the Gulf of Taman to be Strabo's Lake of Corocondame, the village of that name must have stood at the base of the southern sandspit that partly cuts the gulf off from the Bosporus[7]. But Strabo says (XI. ii. 14) that Corocondame is the point from which begins the eastward sail to Portus Sindicus, and marks the beginning of the Bosporus strait, corresponding to Acra.

If then we suppose that C. Tuzla extended a little further west and

[1] App. 29=*IosPE*. II. 344.
[2] Goertz, *Topography*, p. 45.
[3] App. 30=*IosPE*. II. 346.
[4] v. Map in *ABC.=KTR.* p. 108, f. 141, after Dubois de Montpéreux.

[5] Suvórov's Fort Phanagoria by Taman was named according to the view current in his time, cf. Clarke's *Travels*, II. pp. 81—83.
[6] *IosPE*. IV. 434. *BCA.* XXIII. 32.
[7] Anon. 64 (23).

from it ran out a spit like the southern spit for a little over a mile (XI. ii. 9),
we get about 80 stades across to Acra instead of 70 (§ 8), 130 stades
bring us to Patraeus and the monument of Satyrus (Ruban's Farm and
perhaps Kuku Oba) ; 90 stades from there would be Achillis vicus, on the
northern spit, where columns are seen in the sea, just opposite Jenikale[1].
Cimmeris would be 20 stades further, at the base of the northern spit,
just at the point where the navigation of the Maeotis begins. Only the
distance to Tyrambe is much more than 120 stades, but this seems wrong
in any case.

The actual site of Corocondame seems to have been washed away.
It has been usually placed at Taman, inasmuch as that was the site of a
very ancient Greek settlement, and some have seen in Tmutarokan, the
mediaeval Russian name of Taman, an echo of the ancient Corocondame,
but Taman does not lie on the Bosporus itself. It is impossible to say
that from it one sails eastward to Sindicus Portus, and it is much more
than 10 stades from any possible entrance to the gulf.

"Above Corocondame," says Strabo (XI. ii. 9), "is a fair-sized lake" (or
liman), "which is called after it, Corocondamitis. It debouches into the sea
10 stades from the village. Into this lake flows a channel of the Anticites river,
and makes an island surrounded by the lake, the Maeotis and the river...."

§ 10. "When one has sailed into Lake Corocondamitis one has Phanagoria, an important city, and Cepi, and Hermonassa, and the Apaturum, the
temple of Aphrodite. Of which Phanagoria and Cepi are built on the said
island on the left as one sails in, the rest of the cities are on the right
beyond the Hypanis" (= Anticites), "in the land of the Sindi. In the land
of the Sindi is also Gorgippia, the royal city of the Sindi, and Aborace."

§ 14. "From Corocondame you sail straight off to the east 180 stades to
Portus Sindicus" (probably at the entrance to Lake Kizil Tash (170 stades)).
"It is 400 stades further to what is called Bata, a harbour and village" (now
Novorossijsk (500 stades)).

From this it is clear that Phanagoria being at the bottom of the Gulf
of Taman, the channel of the Kuban came just south of it, and somewhere
on the same island was Cepi, usually put at Artjukhov's farm. But there
is no way of identifying Hermonassa, Apaturon, or Pliny's Stratoclia, nor
of giving names to the large number of sites of ancient settlements.
The district was very thickly populated in antiquity and is covered with
villages, forts, earthworks and barrows, from which latter some of the
most beautiful objects have been recovered.

Anon. (62 (21) sqq.) gives us more details of this part[2]. He gives
the distance from Hieros Limen (another name for Bata or Patus) to what
he calls Sindica or Sindicus Portus as 290 stades (it is rather more than
300 to Anapa), and says it is 540 on to Panticapaeum, which is about
right. Next he speaks of Corocondame and its liman, which he says is
also called Opissas : and the circumference he gives at 630 stades ; this
is about right if we reckon in the shores of Lake Akdengis. It is hard
not to wonder whether Opissas was not the name of this liman—"the

---

[1] On the Euxine coast such spots were connected with the name of Achilles.

[2] Cf. Bruun, *Chernomorje*, II. 242—270.

backwater." He adds that Hermonassa is 440 stades from the entrance of the lake and 515 by it to the entrance of the Maeotis. It seems as if he measured by Lakes Corocondame and Akdengis and some passage of the Kuban into Lake Kizil Tash, so that Hermonassa would be one of the sites on the north shore of that liman.

Of the Greek settlements in this peninsula Phanagoria (Ch. XIX.) was a colony of Teios, Cepi of Miletus, and Stephanus Byzantius calls Hermonassa a settlement of Ionians, repeating what Dionysius (l. 553) says of all these places, ἔνθα τε ναετάουσιν Ἰωνίδος ἔκγονοι αἴης.

The coast east of Anapa hardly comes into our province. The ridge of the Caucasus leaves such a small distance between itself and the sea that there is no space for rivers or harbours or anything but a narrow tract of steep ground inhabited by tribes which have always been well known for savagery. The piratical row-boats that Strabo (XI. ii. 12) calls camarae were still in use in the last century, according to Taitbout de Marigny[1], and the coast always had a bad reputation until the Russians were forced almost to clear it of inhabitants. About 300 stades from Gorgippia (Anapa), the last city of the Bosporan kingdom, Strabo gives Bata, called by Scylax Patūs, and later by Ps.-Arrian and Anon. Hieron, now Novorossijsk[2]; 180 stades further they give Pagrae, Gelendzhik. This whole coast is described in detail by Ps.-Arrian (26—28 (18 H.)), but it was never occupied by the Romans, who left the country between the Bosporus and Dioscurias untouched. Probably there was something of the nature of a sphere of influence. Arrian's jurisdiction as legate of Cappadocia only extended as far as Dioscurias. He could not have interfered with the Bosporus, which was in relation with Lower Moesia. The periplus that bears his name has been unskilfully tacked on to the account of his real expedition: a reference to the death of King Cotys does not come in at all well. The addition seems to date from Byzantine times, and to have used sources open to Anon., who did not, however, copy Ps.-Arrian[3].

Strabo (XI. ii. 12—16) gives all detail necessary for this coast. According to Artemidorus first came the Cercetae for 850 stades after Bata. Then the Achaei for 500 stades, the Heniochi for 1000 stades, as far as Pityūs, now Pitsunda, and 360 stades further on was Dioscurias, Sukhum Kale. But the writers on the wars of Mithridates gave the order Achaei, Zygi, Heniochi, Cercetae, Moschi, Colchi, with Phthirophagi and Soanes further inland.

There seems to have been some shifting of population, for Arrian and Anon. give also Macrones, Zydritae, Lazi, Apsilae, Abasgi and Sannigae, and speak of an old Achaea and an old Lazice west of the later positions of those tribes. Some of these peoples certainly still remain. Cercetae may very well be the Circassians (Cherkes). The Lazi are the Lesghians; the Soanes the inhabitants of Svanetia; the Abasgi, the Abkhazes. Strabo says that at Dioscurias were kept seventy interpreters, each for a different tribe of the interior with which business was done, and others raised the

---

[1] For the pirates of this coast see de Peyssonel, *Traité sur le commerce de la Mer Noire*, Vol. II. p. 10. Paris, 1787.

[2] For its harbour, v. supra, p. 4.
[3] v. C. G. Brandis, in *Rheinisches Museum*, LI. p. 109. C. Patsch in *Klio*, Vol. IV. (1904), disagrees.

number to three hundred. It would scarcely be impossible to come up to the former number nowadays by taking all the dialects of the Caucasus, and in Kerch, for instance, twenty different tongues are in quite common employ at the present time.

For the racial affinities of the tribes East of the Sea of Azov, v. p. 127.

LOCI CLASSICI.

Hecataeus, *Phanagoria, Apaturum,* ap. Steph. Byz. s.vv.

Herodotus, IV. passim.

Ps.-Scylax, *Periplus Maris Interni,* 68—81 (second half of IVth c. BC. *GGM.* I. pp. xxxiii—li, 57—61).

Aristotle, *De Animalibus* V. xix. 14.

Polybius, IV. 38—42.

Ps.-Scymnus, *Periegesis,* ll. 767—957 (c. 90 BC. *GGM.* I. pp. lxxiv—lxxx, 227—234).

Strabo, *Geogr.* VII. iii. 1—19, iv. 1—7 (pp. 295—312 C.), XI. i. 5—7, ii. 1—16, 19 (490—507 C.).

Dio Chrysostomus, XXXVI.

Dionysius Periegetes, ll. 142—168, 541—553, 652—732, and Eustathius in ll.

Ps.-Arrian, *Periplus P. Euxini* 1—16 (1—11 H.), 25—37 (19—25 H.) (v. p. 24 n. 3; *GGM.* I. pp. 370—401).

Ptolemy, *Geogr.* III. v. vi. x., V. viii., VIII. x., xviii.

Stephanus Byzantius, sub nominibus urbium, etc.

Anonymi *Periplus Ponti Euxini,* 47 (6)—118 (92). (Vth c. AD. *GGM.* I. pp. cxv—cxxii, 402—423, also *FHG.* V. pp. 174—187.)

Pomponius Mela, I. 110—115, II. 1—15.

Pliny, *NH.* IV. §§ 75—93, VI. 15—22.

Solinus, XIII. 1—3, XIV. 1, 2, XV. 1—29, XIX. 1—19.

Ammianus Marcellinus, XXII. viii. 10—26.

Avienus, *Descr. Orbis,* ll. 214—254, 720—733, 852—891.

Priscian, *Periegesis,* ll. 138—158, 557—566, 644—721.

Jordanes, *Getica,* v. (30—46).

Anonymus Ravennas, I. 17, II. 12, 20, IV. 1—5, V. 10, 11.

CHAPTER III.

GEOGRAPHY OF SCYTHIA ACCORDING TO HERODOTUS.

In the preceding survey of the coasts of Scythia we have had many tangible points by which to test the accounts of the ancients and have been able to fix the position of most important names occurring in the authorities. But it is far otherwise with regard to the interior. A whole series of ingenious investigators has endeavoured for instance to draw a map of Scythia according to Herodotus, and the different results to which they have come prove that in this it is hopeless to seek more than the establishment of a few main facts. Well has Pliny said "*Neque in alia parte maior auctorum inconstantia, credo propter innumeras uagasque gentes*[1]," and he proceeds to give whole lists of names derived from all kinds of authors from Hecataeus to Agrippa. Herodotus is the main authority, and no lover of Herodotus can deny that he might have used more system and consistency in his account without interfering with the charm of the narrative. The mistake made by most writers is in striving to wrest the different geographical sections of Book IV., composed at various times from various sources and introduced in various connections, into a seeming consistency with each other and with the modern map—generally to the unfair treatment of the modern map. It is useless to attempt to give any résumé of the views which have prevailed from time to time as to the geography of Scythia. As any particular problem is treated the views of different writers may be quoted, but a systematic setting forth of all the theories that have been advanced would take up a great deal of space without much helping matters. Some idea of the variety of the solutions may be gained from the Bibliography to this chapter; it does not claim to be complete, for no useful purpose would be served by seeking out all the obscure or aberrant authors who have dealt with the subject.

In Chapters VII. and VIII. I shall enumerate the various civilisations that have left traces or rather tombs on the soil of S. Russia, but so far no one has succeeded in establishing any close link between the series of names or groups of names furnished by history and the remains which archaeology has unearthed in the steppe region. As will be pointed out there are correspondences between the culture revealed by tombs of the so-called Scythic type and the culture ascribed by Herodotus to the Scyths; but this culture certainly belonged also to other tribes, particularly the Sarmatians. No one has applied so much common sense to the examination of Herodotus as Mr Macan, and I am deeply indebted to his masterly excursus on the geography of Scythia.

[1] *NH.* VI. 50.

Most writers take the passage cc. 99—101 as their main guide in setting out their map. But this passage rests on the radical error that the line of the coast from the Don mouth to Perekop is about at right angles to that from Perekop to the Danube mouth. This latter line is one side of a square including all Scythia, and the former is another; each side being reckoned at 20 days journey = 4000 st., about the actual length of the s. side, but a square with two of its sides almost in the same straight line makes an awkward foundation for any further construction. Indeed this square Scythia is merely a chess-board for the game of Darius and the Scythians, on which they can make their moves untroubled by any of the real features of the country, notably the rivers (Map IV.).

A much more satisfactory account is furnished by cc. 16—20, starting characteristically from Olbia and giving an intelligible survey of the inhabitants, the western half going from s. to N., Callippidae, Alazones, Aroteres, the eastern half from w. to E., Georgi who may well be the same as Aroteres, Nomades and Royal Scyths; above them from w. to E. the same row of non-Scythian tribes that we get in 99 sq., Agathyrsi, Neuri, Androphagi, Melanchlaeni, with the Sauromatae beyond the Tanais and the Budini, etc. further to the NE. No geometrical boundaries are mentioned, only a rather doubtful desert (Map V. p. 34).

The real boundary of Scythia was no desert but the edge of the forest[1]. As far as the open steppe, whether cultivated or no, extended, so far were the nomads masters, so far went the boundaries of Scythia. The same line which bounded the dominions of the Khazars, the Pechenêgs, the Cumans, and the constant incursions of the Tartars, formed the real limit of Scythia. Time may have pushed northwards the forest zone as he has destroyed the Hylaea on the lower Dnêpr, but a line running ENE. from Podolia to the Kama must be just about the upper limit of the steppe. If there was a desert, it was one made by the incursions of the steppe men, like the desert belt to the s. of Muscovy in the xvth century, kept clear of settled habitations by the menace of the Golden Horde.

The excursus on the rivers does very little to clear up our ideas of Scythia[2]. Of the eight main rivers, five, the Ister, Tyras, Hypanis, Borysthenes and Tanais, can be identified with certainty as the Danube, Dnêstr, Bugh, Dnêpr and Don, but one can by no means say the same of the Panticapes, the Hypacyris and the Gerrhus nor of the numerous tributaries of the Danube.

The whole question of the Danube has been complicated by the attempt to take square Scythia (IV. 99—101) as the base for the descriptions of tribes and rivers given in chapters 17 to 20 and 47 to 57.

Since the time of Niebuhr it has been generally received that because the tributaries Porata, Tiarantus etc. flowed into the Ister out of Scythia, therefore the Ister formed the boundary of Scythia: which is no doubt true if interpreted in the sense that the nomad Scyths lorded it over the Rumanian steppes as well as over the Russian: but it does not follow that the boundary of this Scythia ran more or less north and south, and so Herodotus conceived

---

[1] Shewn by the shading on Map I.   [2] Her. IV. 47—57.

of the Danube as taking a great bend to the south : for he says consistently that it flows from w. to E., and the boundary running N. and S. belongs only to square Scythia which is erected from the coast and is not concerned with anything more than the mouth of the Danube, there rightly regarded as making a bend to the SE. and so entering Scythia[1]. Once the idea of a great southern bend had been formulated it was confirmed by elaborate theories of symmetry[2] and accepted even by Macan and Niederle who know so well the impossibility of reconciling all the geographical data.

Given that the Ister of Herodotus flowed more or less west to east the identification of the tributaries[3] is a mere matter of detail. The Pyretus-Porata is evidently the Prut; the survival of this name justifies us in calling the Ordessus Ardzhish : it is impossible to say which of the many left bank tributaries correspond to the Tiarantus, Naparis and Ararus. The Maris among the Agathyrsi is certainly the Maros which reaches the Danube by way of the Theiss. This settles the Agathyrsi in Transylvania, and not so far north as they are put in square Scythia.

The Tyras is quite clearly the Dnêstr[4] but equally clear is it that Herodotus did not know anything about its upper course. As soon as it reaches the woods of Podolia it is lost sight of and a lake is invented for its source. The Greek feeling was that a great river must rise either from a high mountain or from a great lake. Herodotus knew that there were no mountains to the N. of Scythia, accordingly he has provided most of the rivers with suitable lakes. True to his wrong bearings he makes the Dnêstr come down from the N. instead of the NW.

The Hypanis or Bugh[5] is set E. of the Borysthenes by Strabo, Pliny, Vitruvius (VIII. ii. 6), and Ptolemy. This mistake is owing to the confusion of the town Borysthenes or Olbia on the Hypanis with the river Borysthenes. Also if the mouth of the common liman be regarded as the mouth of the Borysthenes it actually is to the w. of the Hypanis. Further trouble is caused in Pliny by the existence of the other Hypanis, also called Anticites, now the Kuban. As to Exampaeus and the bitter spring supposed to spoil the river water for four days journey seawards it must have been some stream impregnated with salt from the steppe. Both the Sinjukha and the Mertvyavody (or dead waters) have this quality and either would suit fairly well: but if Exampaeus is about the point where the Tyras and Hypanis are nearest each other it must be far inland in Podolia.

In his description of the Borysthenes (Dnêpr)[6] the chief difficulty is that Herodotus omits to mention the well-known cataracts which would have come in so well in comparing it to the Nile. Constantine Porphyrogenitus first mentions them[7]. It seems as if the old routes had left the main river before

---

[1] Her. IV. 99 ὁ Ἴστρος ἐκδιδοῖ ἐς αὐτὴν (sc. Σκυθικήν) πρὸς εὖρον ἄνεμον τὸ στόμα τετραμμένος.
[2] J. L. Myres, op. cit. p. 614.
[3] In the geographical introduction to his article on the European expedition of Darius (*Cl. Rev.* XI. July 1897, p. 277), Prof. Bury makes Oarus=Ararus=Buzeo and so keeps Darius in the west of Scythia, v. inf. p. 117.
[4] Δάναστρις, Const. Porph. *De Adm. Imp.* 42.

(For the bearings of these river names see inf. p. 38.)
[5] Βογοῦ, Const. Porph. l.c.
[6] Δάναπρις, Anon. 84 (58).
[7] *De Adm. Imp.* c. 9 gives a lively account of the difficulties offered by them, more than they would seem to present nowadays: in ancient times perhaps they were quite impassable.

arriving at them, going perhaps up the Ingulets, and as if the water route which followed the Dnêpr was due to the Variags, who would be the first to draw attention to the Rapids.

The land Gerrhus must have been at the bend of the stream about Nicopol. In this district were the tombs of the Scythian kings and here the finest barrows have been opened. The Gerrhus river was fourteen days up stream from the Hylaea, the extent of the country of the Nomads (c. 19) on the E. side of the Borysthenes, while on the west for 10 or 11 days stretched the country of the Georgi and above them was a desert. Moreover the Borysthenes was supposed to flow from the N. as far as the land of Gerrhus, to which was forty days sail[1]. Its source like the Nile's was unknown.

The description of the Borysthenes is true to this day. The Hylaea indeed has almost disappeared, but the rich pastures are still there; the fisheries and the salt trade survived till the other day. It is curious that there has never been a great port at the mouth of the Dnêpr. Olbia and Nicolaev are both on the Bugh, and Kherson was one of Potemkin's mistakes both in name and in site. The channel is too shoaly for a satisfactory harbour, whereas of late years Nicolaev has begun to rival Odessa.

The Panticapes is a puzzle. The natural meaning of the words of Herodotus suggests a river flowing s. and running into the Dnêpr towards its lowest reaches on the E. side, but such a river does not exist. Some see in it the Konka a kind of alternative channel of the Dnêpr which it accompanies for the last 150 miles of its course, others maintain that it is the Ingulets, which would answer very well except that it is on the right bank of the Dnêpr. The question is bound up with the position of the Scythae Georgi. If the Ingulets is the Panticapes, the natural meaning of c. 18 is that they lived to the w. of it, but in that case they would hardly touch the Borysthenes and would not have been called Borysthenitae by the Olbian Greeks. Also Herodotus says distinctly that they lived between the Panticapes and the Borysthenes. But between the Konka and the Dnêpr there is scarcely any space at all, certainly not three days journey. However this small space, the valley of the Dnêpr, would be singularly suited for agriculture, and the statement does not preclude their occupying an expanse of steppe to the west. Anyone ascending the Borysthenes might well think on seeing its confluence that the Konka was an independent stream. On the whole we may suppose that the informants of Herodotus knew but the mouth of the Konka, and its course was purely hypothetical; if ground be sought for its mother-lake, it might be the marshes of the Great Meadow.

The sixth river, the Hypacyris, also does not occur on the modern map. Either there once was a considerable river represented by the Kalanchák and the dried watercourses which formerly fed it, over one of these there used to be a large stone bridge : or Herodotus regarded the gulf of Perekop as the estuary of a river and deduced the river therefrom. So too with the Gerrhus the seventh river. It separated from the Borysthenes in the land called Gerrhus and flowed into the Hypacyris, according to c. 56 dividing the Scythian Nomads from the Royal Scyths. This gives no space for the fourteen

---

[1] So apparently c. 53. It would be easier to reconcile the Greek with actuality could we read 14 for 40, $\overline{\iota\delta}$ for $\overline{\mathrm{M}}$: not a great change, giving just the distance up to Gerrhus.

days journey which they are supposed to stretch from w. to E. (c. 19). These fourteen days may perhaps be reckoned up the stream of the Dnêpr and Konka, but Herodotus would regard this as S. to N. So that either the Gerrhus does not really flow into the gulf of Perekop and join the Hypacyris at all, but flows into the sea of Azov as the Molochnaja, Berda or Kal'mius all of which come close to tributaries of the Dnêpr that join it above Nicopol (e.g. the Samára), or else there is no real distinction between Nomads and Royal Scyths, which may well be the same tribe under different names. Perhaps the easiest solution is that the Panticapes is the Konka more or less where Herodotus puts it. This agrees with the natural position of the Hylaea. The Gerrhus as the Molochnaja flowed into the sea of Azov as Pliny and Ptolemy (but not Mela) believed and formed a short cut from the sea to the upper Dnêpr and the land Gerrhus. Another such short cut was furnished by the Hypacyris now the Kalanchak. Such short cuts reached by portage were actually used by the Cossacks in their raids against the Turks and must have been still more convenient when there was a greater extent of forest and consequently more water in the rivers.

No one but Bruun[1] has doubted that the Tanais was always the Don or at any rate the Donets, and the Hyrgis would be the other branch now regarded as the true Don. Or this may well be represented by the Oarus which is almost certainly the Volga[2] in the upper part of its course: I mean that merchants following the trade route towards the NE. might well understand that the river they crossed above Tsaritsyn flowed into the Azov sea instead of making its sudden bend S.E. to the Caspian. The Tsaritsyn portage must have always been a place where trade was transferred from one river to the other. As to the Lycus and the Syrgis, which may or may not be the same as the Hyrgis, no one has given names to them so as to carry conviction; the former may perhaps be the Ural. In later times there was such confusion[3] that the Caspian was represented to Alexander as being the same as the Maeotis[4].

The question of the other rivers running into the Caspian is very difficult. On the west we have the Kur and the Aras now joining at their mouths, these are clearly the Cyrus and the Araxes properly speaking.

In the mind of Herodotus there seems some confusion because the Armenian Araxes answers in direction (IV. 40), but neither in importance nor in position, to another Araxes upon which he puts (I. 201) the Massagetae; especially does it come short in the matter of its delta in which there should be islands the size of Lesbos (I. 202). This greater Araxes seems to be the Oxus or a running-into-one of the Oxus and Jaxartes[5]. The latest

[1] *Chernomorje* II. i. 104 and Appendix to *Anti-quités de la Scythie d'Hérodote*.

[2] Cf. Ptolemy, V. viii. 12, 13. 'Pâs, Raw in the language of the Finnish Mordva.

[3] De Plano Carpini (ap. Rockhill, Rubruck, p. 8, c. ix.) thinks the Volga finds its way into the Black Sea, and even in the 16th century Mathias a Michov, a Pole who knew most of Russia well and has no mercy on those who believed in the Rhipaean Mountains, repeats several times that the Volga falls into the Euxine. (Mathiae a Michov de Sarmatia, Lib. I. c. vii. p. 493 in *Nouus Orbis* of Simon Grynaeus, Basileae, 1537.)

[4] Strabo, XI. vii. 4.

[5] Stein will have but one Araxes, thought of by H. as running out of Armenia past the south coast of the Caspian into which it sends an arm, to marshes far to the E. The Scyths forced over the river would be Sacae invading Persia (cf. J. L. Myres op. cit.). Westberg (*Klio, Beitr. z. alten Gesch.* Bd IV. H. 2, pp. 182—192, Zur Topographie des Herodots) makes the Araxes of I. 202 the Volga and puts the Massagetae upon that, v. inf. pp. 111, 113 n. 3.

investigations seem to shew that two thousand years ago the Caspian ran up a valley (the Uzboi) in the direction of the Aral sea and communicated with it by means of a lake or depression Sary Kamysh into which an arm of the Oxus flowed. Between this arm and the main stream going into the Aral sea there would be room for large islands[1]. Further it is a question whether the Araxes mentioned (IV. 11) as having been crossed by the Scyths may not be the lower Volga, as it seems hard to think of them as ever having been south of the Oxus and displaced northwards by tribes coming from the east. If the Jaxartes were meant it would be just conceivable. They would find no satisfactory abiding place between the Jaxartes and the Don. We can never tell whether Herodotus be using Europe in the ordinary sense of the NW. quadrant of the old world or in his own special sense of the whole northern half.

Seeing there are such difficulties in identifying the rivers, which must have remained substantially the same, we cannot hope to fix the place of the various Scythian tribes (cc. 17—20) with any accuracy: we can determine their relative positions but we have no idea of the relative extent of the lands they occupied and only one or two definite statements. We cannot even say whether the Georgi and Aroteres may not be the same people traversed and described by different travellers, and so too with the Nomad and Royal Scyths. On the modern map we may put the Callippidae quite close to Olbia: the Alazones have no boundaries that we can fix[2], we may place them in the central part of the Government of Kherson, while the northern part of the same and some of Ekaterinoslav and perhaps some of Kiev were occupied by the Aroteres. These three tribes lay on one route from Olbia towards the north. To the west we only know of the Greek Tyritae about the mouth of the Dnêstr: whether the same native tribes occupied the *Hinterland* and Rumania we cannot tell. Travellers towards the ENE. from Olbia passed the Scythae Georgi occupying the valley of the lower Dnêpr included in a belt three days journey wide and extending ten or eleven days upstream to about the borders of Ekaterinoslav. Hence they would seem to have been continuous with the Aroteres and very likely identical. That is to say the two names between them represent a congeries of tribes in the same more or less agricultural stage.

The centre of Ekaterinoslav, by the great bend of the river, is the land Gerrhus which marches with the country of the Georgi and the Nomad Scyths. These with the Royal Scyths from which they cannot be clearly distinguished held the mainland part of Taurida, the western part of the land of the Don Cossacks, and probably also Kharkov and Vorónezh.

The flat northern part of the Tauric peninsula, which Herodotus thought continuous with the mainland, also belonged to them as far as the slaves' ditch, wherever that may have been. These eastern tribes lay on the route which led into Central Asia, and information about their

[1] Cf. P. Kropotkin, *Geogr. Journal* XII. (1898), p. 306, The old beds of the Amu Daria; and W. W. Tarn in *JHS*. XXI. (1901) p. 10, Patrocles and the Oxo-Caspian trade route.

[2] We cannot reconcile the statement that they lived where the Tyras and Hypanis come close together, which would be somewhere in Podolia, with the position of Exampaeus on their northern boundary, as this must have been further down stream (c. 52).

position was hardly as definite as that about the central region north of
Olbia.   Indeed their position was perhaps indefinable; where the grass
grew for their cattle, there was the land of the Nomad Scyths; as the
most numerous and powerful tribe they did not need to respect their
neighbours' boundaries.

BIBLIOGRAPHICAL SKETCH.

Our ideas of the Geography of Scythia have gradually grown clearer. Thus
we have slowly eliminated the views which brought the boundaries of Scythia well
up into central Russia far beyond the limits of the Steppe, we have given up the
attempt to bring Herodotus into agreement with the present condition of things by
allowing great changes in the courses of the rivers and a former eastern extension
of the Maeotis—our countrymen Rennell and Rawlinson were most ready for such
explanations: we have forgotten such extravagancies as Lindner's view that the
Scyths proper were to the west of the Dnêpr, or Kolster's that Herodotus did

FIG. 3.

not clearly distinguish between the Don and the Danube[1], or even more pardonable
eccentricities such as Bruun's, that the Tanais was not the Don, but the Molochnaja.

[1] Both writers I judge by Neumann's statement of their views (op. cit. pp. 96 n. 2 and 204).

Most writers now agree as to the general orientation of the Scythia of Herodotus, but mention must be made of Krechetov's ingenious view, which figures the Scythian Square as washed by the sea along the halves of two adjacent sides only : the remaining halves of those sides running inland along the lower Ister and the coast of the Maeotis, which he reckons a mere marsh and no sea[1] (fig. 3).

The square thus obtained with its corner at Cercinitis, placed by Krechetov at Donguslav lake in the Crimea, would be inclined slightly so as to have the E. sides facing ESE., so the sea along the south coast of the Crimea would be the eastern sea of c. 100. But when translated into the terms of the correct modern map, it works out to have much the same real meaning as the more usual interpretations which count the Maeotis as a sea for the nonce. And after all, what is important to us is not the shadowy idea of Scythia that floated in the mind of Herodotus, incapable of being consistently represented on our map, but the real state of affairs of which Herodotus and Hippocrates give so interesting but so tantalizing accounts.

Who wishes to follow the various attempts at drawing a map of Scythia *ad mentem Herodoti*, or at disposing the ancient names about the modern map, may consult the following books as I have done. I omit the eighteenth century attempts as being controlled by too slight a regard for the geography of the regions concerned.

BIBLIOGRAPHY.

Rennell, James. *The Geographical System of Herodotus examined.* London, 1800. pp. 47—163. Map III.

Niebuhr, B. G. *On the Geography of Herodotus and on the History of the Scythians, Getae and Sarmatians.* Oxford, 1830. =*Kl. Schr.* Bonn, 1828. I. p. 132.

Bobrik, Hermann. *Geographie des Herodot.* Königsberg, 1838. pp. 84—123. Map VI.

Dubois de Montpéreux, F. *Voyage autour du Caucase.* Vol. I. Pl. 9. Paris, 1839 ; Neuchâtel, 1843.

Lindner, F. L. *Skythien und die Skythen des Herodot und seine Ausleger.* Stuttgart, 1841.

—— Skythien und die Skythen des Her.; Nachtrag (VIII. Supplement-Bd d. *Neuen Jahrb. d. Phil.*, 1842).

—— Explication Nouvelle des données géographiques d'Hérodote concernant la Scythie (*Annales des Voyages*, 1845. I.).

Nadezhdin, N. I. The Scythia of Herodotus explained by comparison with the localities. In *Trans. Od. Soc.* Vol. I. (1845), pp. 3—114.

Ukert, F. A. Skythien. Being Vol. III. Pt II. of his *Geographie der Griechen und Römer.* Weimar, 1846.

Kolster, W. H. Das Land der Skythen bei Herodot und Hippocrates (*Jahrbuch für Philologie und Pädagogik.* Bd XII. 568, XIII. 1—77 (1846-7); also *Jahrb. f. Phil. u. Päd.*, LXXVII. 331).

Dumshin, G. Of the Rivers of Scythia according to Herodotus. In *Publications of the Students of the Richelieu Lycée.* Odessa, 1852.

Blakesley, J. W. *Herodotus with a Commentary.* London, 1854.

Wheeler, J. T. *The Geography of Herodotus.* London, 1854. pp. 137—170, 178—194.

Neumann, K. *Die Hellenen im Skythenlande.* Berlin, 1855.

Abicht, K. *Herodotos.* Leipzig, 1869.

Bruun, F. An Essay to reconcile conflicting opinions as to the Scythia of Herodotus and the lands marching with it. 1st in Russian in *ASH.* Pt II. St P. 1872. Next in French edition of the same. St P. 1873. Reprinted in *Chernomorje.* Vol. II. pp. 1—120 and Map I. Odessa, 1880.

Burachkov, P. I. On the Position of the ancient City of Carcinitis and its Coinage. In *Trans. Od. Soc.* IX., 1875. pp. 1 sqq.

Zabêlin, I. E. *History of Russian Life.* Moscow, 1876. Vol. I. p. 227 sqq.

Rawlinson, G. *History of Herodotus*, translated with notes. London, 1880. Vol. III. pp. 1—114, 178—209.

---

[1] This is a fresh interpretation of τῶν δύο μερέων μεσόγαιαν φέρον καὶ τὸ παρὰ τὴν θάλασσαν, Her. κατηκόντων ἐς θάλασσαν, πάντῃ ἴσον τό τε ἐς τὴν IV. 101.

M.

Kiepert, H. *Manual of Ancient Geography*, Eng. ed. London, 1881.

Bonnell, Ernst. *Beiträge zur Alterthumskunde Russlands.* Bd I. St Petersburg, 1882.

Bunbury, E. H. *History of Ancient Geography.* Ed. 2. London, 1883. Vol. I. pp. 172—217. Map IV.

Voevodskij, L. F. Map of Scythia prepared for the VI. Russian Archaeological Congress (Odessa), 1884.

Dzieduszycki, W. Information of the Ancients as to the Geography of Polish lands. (Polish) in *Rosprawy i Sprawozdania z posiedzeń Wydziału hist.-filozof. Akad. Kraków.* T. XIX. 1887, p. 141 sqq.

Lappo-Danilevskij, A. Scythian Antiquities. *Trans. Russ. Arch. Soc.* Slavonic Section. Vol. IV. (1887), p. 352 sqq.

Tomaschek, W. Kritik d. ält. Nachr. über Skythischen Norden. *Sitzungsber. Akad. Wien, Phil. Hist. Cl.* 116, 117. 1888.

Krechetov, P. N. Letters on the Scythia of Herodotus; in *Trans. Od. Soc.* Vol. XV. (1889), pp. 457—495.

—— Boundaries and Outlines of the Scythia of Herodotus; in *Drevnosti=Transactions of Moscow Archaeological Soc.* Vol. XIII. (1889), p. 179.

Latyshev, V. V. *IosPE.* Vol. II. St P. 1890. Map II.

Macan, R. W. *Herodotus, Bks IV.—VI.* London, 1895.

Krashenínnikov, M. *Disposition of Ancient Scythia according to Modern Localities.* Slutsk, 1895.

Stein, H. *Herodotos erklärt.* Buch IV. 4te Aufl. Berlin, 1896.

J. L. Myres. An Attempt to reconstruct the Maps used by Herodotus. *Geographical Journal.* London. VIII. (1896), p. 605.

Míshchenko, Th. G. Ethnography of Russia according to Herodotus. *Journ. Min. Publ. Instr.* St P. 1896, May.

—— Information of Herodotus touching lands outside Scythia. *Ib.* 1896, December.

NIederle, L. *Descriptio Europae Regionum quae ad orientem spectant veterum scriptorum locis illustrata.* Prag, 1899.

—— *Slavonic Antiquities.* Vol. I. Pt II. p. 215 sqq. Prag, 1904 (both in Čech).

Braun, Fr. *Investigations in the province of Gotho-Slavonic relations.* I. St P. 1899, pp. 69—99.

Westberg, Fr. Zur Topographie des Herodots. *Klio, Beitr. z. alten Gesch.* IV. (1904), pp. 182—192.

Shuckburgh, E. S. *Heroaotus IV., Melpomene.* Cambridge, 1906.

CHAPTER IV.

THE SCYTHIANS, THEIR CUSTOMS AND RACIAL AFFINITIES.

PERHAPS no question touching the ethnography of the ancient world has been more disputed than that of the affinities of the Scythians[1]. It would seem at first sight that with the mass of details supplied by Herodotus and Hippocrates and the evidence derived from archaeological investigation of their country we ought to be able to arrive at a definite conclusion, but so far no perfectly satisfactory reconciliation of the various views has been reached. Perhaps the first doubt that arises is whether such a reconciliation is to be sought for; whether the mistake common to almost all writers on the subject may not be that they have rashly attempted to find one answer to the riddle, have said that the Scythians were Mongols or Slavs or Iranians, whereas the truth seems to be that the word Scythian had no ethnological meaning even in the mouth of Herodotus. With him, as I take it, it had a political meaning, whereas with the other authors who make use of the term it is merely geographical.

For most Greeks a Scythian, Σκύθης, was any northern barbarian from the east of Europe, just as Γαλάτης was any such from the west.

Herodotus wishing to give a more exact account of the peoples to the N. of the Black Sea tried to draw a line between Scyths and non-Scyths, but he found it hard to make his line consistent. For instance in IV. 81, when he tries to give us some idea of the numbers of the Scythians, he has in his mind two conceptions of the meaning of the term, for he says that he heard that they were exceeding many and also that they were few in number, that is to say the real Scyths (ὀλίγους ὡς Σκύθας εἶναι). At other times he makes careful distinctions between the peoples he calls Scythians and those to whom he denies the name, even when they have Scythian customs and Scythian dress; yet some of these tribes are called Scythian by other authors. We may take it that Herodotus used the word in a narrow sense to include only the Royal Scyths, possibly together with the Nomads, for it seems hard to establish any clear distinction between them; and in a wide sense to denote all those tribes, whatever their affinities or state of civilisation, that were under the political domination of the Royal Scyths. Each of these uses is more definite than the ordinary Greek use against which there is an under-current of protest in the repeated asseverations of Herodotus that such and such a tribe is not Scythian: perhaps he is contradicting Hecataeus. After the time of Herodotus the vague use returns. Thucydides[2]

[1] For a short history of the Scythian question, and the chief solutions that have been proposed, see the Appendix at the end of this chapter.
[2] II. 96, 97.

for instance must mean all the people of Scythia together when he says that, uncivilised though the Scythians were, no single nation of Europe or Asia could stand against them in war, if but they were all of one mind.

In late writers such as Trogus Pompeius[1] and Diodorus Siculus (I. 55, II. 43) we have what purports to be very early history of the Scythians, who according to Trogus always claimed to be the most ancient of races. These authors speak of conquests pushed by the Scythians to the borders of Egypt and of an empire of Asia lasting fifteen hundred years and ending with the rise of Ninus. Fr. Hommel (v. inf. p. 99 n. 10) thinks that this is an echo of the Hittite rule, but it would be rash to conjecture what may be the foundation for these stories, which come in a suspicious company of Amazons and Hyperboreans. They look like the reflex of the Egyptian stories in Herodotus (II. 103 and 110) who speaks of Sesostris having conquered the Scythians and Thracians. These are mere exaggerations of the real campaigns of Rameses pushed to the limits of the world and slenderly supported by mysterious rock carvings and such facts as the resemblance between the Colchians and the Egyptians. Trogus Pompeius idealizing the Scythians has made their exploits balance and surpass those of the nation whose claim to greater antiquity he dismisses.

The greater part of the information as to manners and customs given by Herodotus and the physical details in Hippocrates evidently refer to the Royal Scyths. On the other hand some statements seem quite inconsistent with their manner of life, and we are in our rights in supposing that such details apply to the settled tribes in Western Scythia about whom information would be easily available at Olbia. Less information is given about them because they did not offer so much novelty to interest the Greeks and also they do not play a prominent part in the story of the expedition of Darius, wherein *ex hypothesi* nomads and nomads only could be the protagonists.

Are we then to take the Scythians settled and nomad to be one race in two states of culture, or have we to do with the subjection of a peaceful agricultural people established in an open country and the domination of an intrusive horde of alien nomads?

If the wider sense of Scythian in Herodotus is taken to be political, the sharp line drawn by Herodotus between the agricultural Scythians and the Neuri, Agathyrsi and Getae need not have any ethnological significance, that is that even if we suppose the Neuri to be Slavonic and the latter two Thracian, there is no reason against taking these "Scythians" to belong to either of these races. The general view is that both agricultural and nomad Scythians were Iranian[2]. There can be no doubt that up to the coming of the Goths and later the Huns, the Euxine steppes were chiefly inhabited by an Iranian population, and even in the steppes population does not change as easily as it used to be thought. It took the long continued storms of the great migrations from the coming of the Huns to that of the Tartars to sweep away this Iranian population and pen its survivors into the high valleys of Ossetia.

---

[1] ap. Justin, I. i., II. i. sqq.   [2] For other possibilities v. pp. 97—100.

Professor Vsevolod Miller[1] has given the clearest demonstration of the process by which this retrenchment of the Pontic Iranians came about. He shews that the place-names about the Ossetes in countries now peopled by Tartar-speaking tribes prove that they formerly extended over a greater area. Next he shews their identity with the Jasy of Russian chronicles, the Ossi of the Georgians.

Klaproth first proved in 1822 that the Ossetes are the same as the Caucasian Alans, and this is supported by the testimony of chroniclers Russian, Georgian, Greek and Arab[2]. From Ammianus Marcellinus (XXXI. ii. 16—25) we know that at the time of the Huns' invasion these Alans pastured their herds over the plains to the N. of the Caucasus and made raids upon the coast of the Maeotis and the peninsula of Taman. The Huns passed through their land, plundering them, but afterwards made alliance with them against Ermanrich the king of the Goths. Ammianus means by Alans all the nomadic tribes about the Tanais and gives a description of their habits borrowed from the account of the Scythians in Herodotus. For the first three centuries of our era we find these Alans mentioned[3] as neighbours of the Sarmatians on this side or the other of the Don, living the same life and counting as one of their tribes. That is that Ossetes, Jasy, Alans, Sarmatians, are all of one stock, once nomad now confined to the valleys of the central chain of the Caucasus. The Ossetes are tall, well made, and inclined to be fair, corresponding to the description of the Alans in Ammianus (XXXI. ii. 21), and their Iranian language answers to the accounts of the Sarmatians whom Pliny calls "*Medorum ut ferunt soboles*[4]."

In a large number of inscriptions from the Greek cities along the Euxine shore we meet with several hundred barbarian names, and these give more or less trustworthy material for investigation. The first to examine them scientifically was K. Müllenhoff[5]. He compared the names with the Old Persian and arrived at satisfactory results, but Vs. Miller has been more successful through taking Ossetian as the basis of comparison[6]. On comparing the number of names which offer easy derivations from the Ossetian we may get some clue to the distribution of Iranian population along the coast. At Tyras we have no certain Iranian name among the five barbarian names we know: in Olbia out of about a hundred names half can be explained (App. Nos. 11–13 give samples): in Tanais out of 160 names a hundred are intelligible (cf. App. 56): in Panticapaeum out of 110 only 15 give ready meanings and these are mostly also found at Tanais, so from near Taman only two names out of thirteen, from Gorgippia only seven or eight out of forty (v. App. 69) are demonstratively Iranian, and these mostly occur at Tanais. Furthermore we must make a distinction between

---

[1] *Ossetian Studies* III., Moscow, 1887.

[2] Cf. Josafa Barbaro, *Viaggio alla Tana* ap. Ramusio, *Navigationi*, Venice, 1559, vol. II. p. 92, = f. M. iiij, "Alani li quali nella lor lingua si chiamano As."

[3] Pliny, *NH.* IV. 80, Dionysius Periegetes 305, 306, Fl. Josephus, *Bell. Jud.* VII. vii. 4, Ptolemy etc.

[4] *NH.* VI. 19.

[5] "Ueber die Herkunft und Sprache der ponti-schen Scythen und Sarmaten," *Monatsbericht der k. Preuss. Akad. d. W.* 1866 p. 549 sqq., reprinted in *DA.* III. p. 101 sqq., 1892. Cf. Sir H. Howorth, *Journal of Anthrop. Inst.* VI. 1877, p. 41 sqq.

[6] First in an article in *Journ. Min. Publ. Instr.* St P. Oct. 1886, p. 232, entitled "Epigraphic Traces of Iranian Population on the North Coast of the Euxine," and again in the third volume of his *Ossetian Studies.*

names shewing Old Persian forms and those which resemble Ossetian. The former are mostly names very familiar to the Greek world and in common use in the Hellenised provinces of the Persian Empire, especially Asia Minor: they are many of them royal names and testify to the political and general influence of the Persian Empire rather than to an Iranian population. Such would be Ariarathes, Ariaramnes, Arsaces, Achaemenes, Orontes, Pharnaces, Mithradates, Ariobarzanes, Machares and many more. The true native Iranian names are almost confined to Olbia and Tanais, others in the Bosporan kingdom may well have found their way in through Tanais. New Inscriptions (e.g. in *IosPE.* Vol. IV) supply more barbarian names but do not materially alter the results attained by Vs. Miller except that we find in them several more names certainly Thracian both at Olbia and on the Bosporus. The unintelligible names at Gorgippia seem to recall Caucasian languages rather than Indo-European.

All these names are late in date, mostly of the II. and III. centuries A.D., the time when the Sarmatians spread from Hungary to the Caspian. At that time no doubt there was a broad band of Iranians right across, but it looks as if along the coast there long remained representatives of some other population, Getae in the west about the Ister and Tyras, and perhaps in the Olbia district, Tauri in the Crimean mountains, and tribes of the Caucasus stock to the south-east of the sea of Azov. From the western aboriginal tribes the Greeks may have heard the names of the rivers Borysthenes, Hypanis, Tyras, and Ister, names for which no satisfactory explanation has been suggested, and once sanctioned by classical usage these names continued to be used by the Greeks as long as they were in continuous occupation of this coast. But this tradition was broken by the destruction of the colonies Tyras and Olbia, and when the Greeks again had dealings with this coast they learnt other native names which only appear in authors who preferred actuality to classical correctness—Δάναπρις in Periplus anonymi (86 (60)), Βογοῦ and Δάναστρις in Constantine Porphyrogenitus (*de adm. Imp.* 42). Now these names seem to contain the Ossetian Don a river, at least they have never been satisfactorily explained from the Slavonic; and the occurrence of *Dan* in river names just coincides with the extension of the Iranians in South Russia. The mouth of the Tanais being already in Iranian hands the Greeks at once adopted its Iranian name. The Iranian names for the western streams may be just as old, but they were not current on the seaboard and only found their way into Greek speech when the Greeks had, as it were, to rediscover the region after considerable changes of population. Maybe by then they learnt them not from the Iranians, but from Slavs who had borrowed them. The name of the Bugh has its counterpart in the Northern Bugh, also a Slavonic river, but it may be the same as *Bogh* = God, which is regarded as a loan-word from the Iranian *Baga.* I have never seen any other explanation of the curious fact that the present names for these rivers being apparently Iranian are first recorded just about the time that the Iranian population was succumbing to Slavonic and other invaders. In later times we get a fresh set of river names of Turkish origin.

Only in the east part of the Crimea the Iranians seem to have touched the

Black Sea coast, for Ἀρδαβδα = Ἑπτάθεος (Anon. 77 (51)), "Tauric" or Alan for Theodosia, seems clearly to contain Ossetian *avd* = seven, and *ard* may be according to Müllenhoff *eredhwa* high, Lat. *arduus*. Vs. Miller says seven-sided, but that does not seem a near translation. So Σουγδαῖα, Sudak is no doubt Os. *suydäg* holy, cf. Sogdiana.

Whereas the Iranian character of the Sarmatian language and even a numerically preponderant Iranian element in the population has been generally accepted, the case of the Scyths is by no means as clear. What reliance can be put on the statement of Herodotus (IV. 117) that the Sarmatians speak the same language as the Scyths, but speak it incorrectly? While Herodotus is not altogether to be trusted in his statements about language, still he occasionally notices points bearing upon it, for instance when he mentions the seven languages required along the trade route to the NE. up to the Arimaspians. And the fact of the resemblance and the difference between the Scythian and Sarmatian dialects is the only explanation for the invention of the aetiological myth about the Sarmatians being descended from young Scyths and Amazons (IV. 110–7). The other main difference between the two peoples, the free position of women among the Sarmatians, is also accounted for by the myth. Curiously enough the Ossetes still have legends of warlike women, and such stories are abroad throughout the Caucasus : among the Circassians is a literal reproduction of this tale in Herodotus.

When we come to examine the Scythian names and words in the Greek texts it is disappointing to find how few are readily to be explained from Iranian. Some words are quite clear, e.g. Ἐνάρεες = Ἀνδρόγυνοι (Hippocrates, *De aere*, 29, speaks of the ἀνανδρείη of his ἀνάριες) from *a* privative and Sk. Zd. *nar, nara* man. So Ἐξαμπαῖος = Ἱραὶ ὁδοί from Zd. *asha, ashavan* pure, *pathi* path. *Arimaspi* may be connected with Zd. *airima* loneliness, oneness, and *spu* may be from the root ϻραϻ, Lat. *specio*. Müllenhoff objects to these and wants e.g. to translate Arimaspi "having obedient horses," saying that the others would be *Arimaspui*, but it seems more likely that a Greek would make a mistake in dropping a termination and yet get the meaning right, than that he should invent an entirely wrong meaning which should still yield a form so near to what he reported. In οἰόρπατα = ἀνδρόκτονοι there seems to be possibly a misunderstanding. The first part is clearly Zd. Sk. *vîra* man : the second half is rather *paiti* lord than from *pât* to fell, causative of *pat* to fall. Some of the Sarmatians were regularly called Γυναικοκρατούμενοι. The fact that Herodotus has in these cases furnished a translation is decisive. Also one or two of the proper names are evidently Iranian, e.g. Ariapithes, Spargapithes. So most of the names in the "Scythian" legend of their own origin (IV. 5, 7) have quite an Iranian look. Targitaos (?Tirgataos, cf. Τιργαταώ, queen of the Maeotae)[1] may well be *Tighra tava* sharp and strong : and the names of the three brothers in -ξαις recall Avestic χ*shaya* lord ; so Colaxais would equal Archistratus[2].

Whereas no satisfactory Iranian explanation of the names of deities

---

[1] Poliaenus, VIII. 55.   [2] Vs. Miller, op. cit. p. 126 and Müllenhoff op. cit., v. inf. p. 43.

has been put forward, on the other hand Schiefner absolutely annihilated K. Neumann's attempts to derive any Scythian words from Mongolian[1].

Making all allowances for the inaccuracy with which Herodotus represented Scythian sounds, the corruption of the forms in our MSS. and the fact that we have to place beside these forms languages considerably removed either in time or collaterally from what Scythian may have been, we must allow that the comparative success attained with Sarmatian forms suggests that there were foreign elements in Scythian which exercised much influence on the stock of names in use or in tradition. Founding any argument on personal names is singularly unsatisfactory. All history tells us that easily as nations change their language, they change their names still more easily. There are hardly a dozen English personal names in use or a dozen Russian, we must not therefore infer that Russians or English are descended from Greeks and Romans and Jews. So Persian names were common all over the East far beyond the extension of the Persian nationality, and it is hard to say whether the Persian names that we find in Herodotus as borne by Scythians are due to an original community of origin, or a borrowing at a time when the Scyths had warlike dealings with Persia either in Europe or Asia, or whether they are not merely given to personages in the same way as figures are given names on Greek vases. The Darius vase would be a peculiarly apt example, for on it Greek and Persian names are given indifferently to the barbarians hunting griffins and other monsters, just to lend them more individual interest. Such must almost certainly be the case with Spargapithes the Agathyrse[2].

Knowledge of the nationality of the Cimmerians whom the Scyths dispossessed would throw some light on the affinities if not of the Scyths themselves at least of the steppe population they found at their coming. The resemblance of the name Cimmerius with Cimber already made Poseidonius[3] imagine that there was some connection between them and the barbarians from the far north-west[4], and modern writers have further compared the name of the Cymry and supposed that these were one and the same people, Kelts[5]. There is no impossibility in a migration from Central Europe to the steppes of the Black Sea in times before history, just as in historic times Central Europe has sent out conquerors to every corner of the continent, and Kelts actually did reach the neighbourhood of Olbia in the time of Protogenes, not to speak of their raids upon Delphi and Asia Minor. Further the bronze civilisation of the Koban necropolis certainly offers such analogies with that of Hallstadt that it is hard to believe that they are not connected. If only there were any finds of Hallstadt types between Hungary and the Caucasus offering evidence that the people who owned the Koban bronzes had settled in the steppes, the Cimmerians might have been thought of, but people who settled long enough to leave the earthworks of which

[1] "Sprachliche Bedenken gegen das Mongo-lenthum der Skythen," *Mélanges Asiatiques*, t. II. p. 531, St Petersburg, 1856, but see inf. pp. 85, 100.
[2] Her. IV. 78.
[3] ap. Str. VII. ii. 2.
[4] Cf. Aristophanes, *Lysistrata* l. 45 Κιμβερικά, but this is an easy corruption palaeographically.
[5] Ridgeway, *Early Age* I. p. 387 sqq.

Herodotus makes mention (IV. 12) must have left weapons by which their course could be traced. And save for a single stopped axe-head from Kerch figured by its owner Canon Greenwell[1] no Koban or Hallstadt implements seem to have been found in South Russia. The flat-ended hair-pins found by Count Bobrinskoj at Gulaj Gorod[2], and the spirals found by him at Teklino[3], seem to be rather eastern outliers from Central Europe than links between it and the Caucasus.

H. Schmidt[4] has the same difficulty to face in maintaining that the makers of the late bronze things from Hungary were Thracians and that these Thracians were the Koban people in the Caucasus (v. inf. p. 259) and that the Cimmerians of the plains between were Thracians as well. It is true that the Cimmerian raids were made in common with the Thracians, but we have to account for the Iranians north of the Euxine.

Müllenhoff[5] supposes that there never were any Cimmerians at all north of the Euxine, that they are only known in Asia Minor, that their name was traditionally assigned to the earthworks and settlements about the Bosporus, just as now earthworks in eastern Europe are assigned to Trajan far beyond the limits of the Roman Empire, and that they were really invaders from Thrace or the parts beyond, men of darkness who joined with Treres and other Thracian tribes in invading Asia Minor. It is hard to think that Herodotus simply invented all the story of the Cimmerians coming from the N. side of the Pontus, though even so it is at first sight difficult to see precisely how things happened; how if the Cimmerians fled SE. there should have been their kings' tomb on the Tyras; and how they should have formed their connection with the Treres. But that invaders from the east should have cut them into two is not inconceivable. Part went into Thrace, produced a turmoil there and finally, with Thracian tribes they had disturbed, entered Asia Minor by the NW.; part were pressed towards the Caucasus and passed it, not as Herodotus says along the coast of the Black Sea, for no army has ever passed that way (Mithridates in his famous flight was accompanied only by a small guard), but by the central pass of Darial, through which, as the Georgian annals shew, the northern peoples have often forced their way. Though the idea of the Cimmerians being cut in two seems hard to accept, the analogy offered by the fate of the Alans shews that it is not without the bounds of possibility. On the coming of the Huns part of these was forced westward, joined the Germans against whom they were thrown and ended as the inseparable companions of the Vandals in North Africa. Part of them was, as we have seen, pressed up against the Caucasus and remains there to this day: and about them are the Tartar tribes that penned them in. So likewise the Magyars were driven by the Pechenêgs partly w. across the Dnêpr, partly through the Caucasus, where they were called Sevordik'[6]. So the Scyths drove

---

[1] *Archaeologia*, Vol. LVIII. Pt I. p. 12.
[2] Govt of Kiev, *Sm.* I. No. XLI. p. 102 and 115 and pl. IX. 7, 8.
[3] *Sm.* III. CCCLXVII. pp. 19 and 23 and pl. II. 4 and 9.

[4] *Zt. f. Ethnologie*, XXXVI. (1904), p. 630.
[5] *DÄ.* III., p. 19 sqq.
[6] J. Marquart, *Osteuropäische und Ostasiatische Streifzüge*, p. 36.

the Cimmerians through the Caucasus and followed them. Then both peoples came within the sweep of Assyrian policy[1].

Here we get another view of them. We find the Cimmerians, Gimirrai, first N. of Urartu (Ararat). Hence they are driven out by Aš-gu-za-ai (Asarhaddon) or Iš-ku-za-ai (Sun Oracle). These names are גמר and אשכנז of Genesis x., where the latter form is miswritten for אשכנו. The first syllable is added as usual in Semitic languages to help out such a combination as šk at the beginning of a word, so that the identity with the Greek Κιμμέριος and Σκύθης is almost complete. So too the leader of the Ašguzai Bartatua is Protothyes father of Madyes in Herodotus (I. 103) and Tugdammi the Cimmerian is Λύγδαμις in Strabo (I. iii. 21) for Δύγδαμις. Lygdamis was a familiar name and the copyist was misled. The Cimmerians driven S. from Urartu attacked Man a kingdom under Assyrian suzerainty. The Assyrians supported their vassals and found allies in the Scythians who were already enemies of the Cimmerians. This hostility turned the Cimmerians westward against Gugu, Gyges of Lydia (Herodotus says Ardys I. 15), and one horde was destroyed by Madys (Strabo) in Cilicia, whereas Lydia was under their dominion till the time of Sadyattes, and Sinope and Antandrus were long occupied by Cimmerians. Meanwhile the Scythians as allies of the Assyrians tried to raise the siege of Nineveh which was being prosecuted by the Medes; hence a conflict between Scythians and Medes and apparently an overrunning of Media by the Scythians[2]. Scyths also made their appearance further to the sw., apparently being sent by Assyria against Egypt, but bought off by Psammetichus. Thus they are referred to by the Hebrew Prophets[3] and engaged in the sack of Ascalon where some contracted a disease ascribed by Herodotus (I. 105) to the hostility of Aphrodite. A colony of them is said to have settled at Beth-shean hence called Scythopolis[4]. Evidence of intercourse between Assyria and the Scyths may be seen in the gold dagger sheaths from the Oxus (p. 255, f. 173), from Melgunov's Barrow (p. 171, ff. 65—67) and from Kelermes, and also the unique axe from the latter (p. 222; cf. p. 263).

It has been supposed that the Scythians that overran western Asia were Sacae from the E. of the Caspian, and that such incursions were always possible we learn from subsequent history, but the Assyrian evidence goes to shew that Scythians had penetrated through the Caucasus. A curious point is that the son of Tugdammi, Sandakhšathra[5], has a name clearly Iranian, and it is hard to suppose that the Cimmerians had yet come under Median influence. Does it mean that the Cimmerians had Iranian affinities? It looks as if the "Royal" Scyths, whoever they may have been, were invaders from the far North-east who found in the steppes a population of Iranian stock whom they called men of darkness, i.e. Westerners (cp. p. 100), partly nomad and partly settled, drove some of this population out, and established a dominion over the remainder.

[1] Winckler, H., *Altorientalische Forschungen*, I. p. 484 sqq., "Kimmerier, Ašguzäer, Skythen."
[2] v. N. Schmidt, s.v. Scythian in *Encyclop. Biblica*, Vol. IV., Lond. 1903.
[3] Cf. Jer. iv. 3—vi. 20. Cf. Driver, *Introd. to Lit. of O.T.*, p. 237, who suggests that a description originally meant for the Scythians was worked over to make it do for the Chaldaeans. Ez. xxxviii. and xxxix. to 16 is even less exact.
[4] Josephus, *Ant. Jud.* XII. viii. 5.
[5] Sa-an-dak-šat-ru, Justi, *Iranisches Namenbuch*, p. 283.

By the time of Herodotus they may have become almost blended with their nomad underlings; such blending takes place far more easily with nomads than with agricultural populations: they may have even adopted their language, retaining the names of persons and gods which are so difficult of interpretation in the light of Iranian vocabularies. The conception of displacements of whole populations is being superseded by the recognition of the fact that in most countries the mass of the people has remained much the same as far back as we can trace its characteristics. The general type of skull and build in any given locality does not easily alter. From time to time conquests change the national name, the language talked by all, the ethnological character of the upper classes or even of all the warrior caste: to outside observers it seems as if a new race had been substituted for a former one, but in a few generations the aborigines again come to the top and in time the physical type of the invaders becomes almost extinct. Only a long succession of conquests of a country peculiarly open to attack can really sweep away a whole population, where that has been at all thick and where the disparity of development is not too great. We are so used to the cases of the North American Indians, the Tasmanians, and other instances of utterly barbarous tribes really disappearing before the invader, that we do not realize that such conditions rarely obtained in the old world. To the north of the Euxine it took the successive hordes of the Huns, Avars, Khazars, Pechenêgs, Polovtses and Tartars, to say nothing of less important tribes, to sweep the Iranian folk clean off the plains over which they had wandered; and they only succumbed to this fate because they were living in perfectly open country upon a highway of nations.

Four legends as to the origin of the Scythians.

In the first, which is told by the Scythians of themselves[1], they say that they are the newest of races and spring from Targitaus son of Zeus and a daughter of the Borysthenes. Targitaus had three sons, Lipoxais, Harpoxais and Colaxais, of whom the youngest obtained the kingdom by the ordeal of approaching four sacred gold objects that fell burning from heaven. These sacred gold objects were a plough and a yoke and an axe and a cup. From these three sons three tribes, Catiari, Traspies and Paralatae, are descended, and the whole nation is called Scoloti; Scythae being the Greek name: and the gold objects are kept sacred until this day. The next story (c. 8 sqq.) is told by the Pontic Greeks. In it Heracles plays the part of Zeus; Echidna, half woman, half serpent, bears three sons to him. The ordeal is the stringing of the bow left by the hero and the knotting of the belt with its cup attached. The two elder sons, Gelonus and Agathyrsus, fail and become fathers of peoples outside Scythia, the third Scythes remaining in the land.

These two stories are substantially the same. Only the second has been even more Hellenised than the first. The Scythians are represented as autochthonous even though Targitaus only dates back a thousand years before Darius. Three sons in each case submit to an ordeal in

---

[1] Her. IV. 5 sqq.

which, as usual in folk tales, the youngest is successful. From the sons
tribes are descended; in the one case well-known neighbouring nations
whose names the Greeks knew, in the other obscure septs among the
Scythians, to whom as a whole is given the native name Scoloti. None of
these names meet us elsewhere except a bare mention in Pliny[1] taken
from Herodotus. The scene of both stories is laid in West Scythia:
in both there comes a mention of a golden cup—now no representation
of a Scythian with a cup at his belt has been found—and more remarkable
still a golden plough is one of the holy objects. The man who keeps
them is given land for his very own, as much as he can ride round in
a day. This legend in two forms can only apply to the agricultural
West-Scythians. Hitherto writers who wished to be more than usually
exact have called the Royal Scyths Scoloti, but this legend would suggest
that just these did not call themselves Scoloti, which was really the
native name for the royal clan among some tribe of the western Scythians
about Olbia[2]. Mishchenko[3] examining these legends thinks they apply
to the reigning clan of the Royal Scyths, but that perhaps their real scene
is central Asia. He takes Pliny as a serious witness to the survival of
these clans. I cannot follow him in this, though I have come to much
the same conclusions in most things.

Another account in Herodotus (IV. 11), to which he himself chiefly
inclines, definitely names the nomad Scyths and brings them out of Asia
(that is to say Asia in the ordinary sense, not according to the Herodotean definition of it), across the Araxes (apparently the Volga), into the
land of the Cimmerians; and then follows the story of how the latter
fled into Asia across the Caucasus and the Scythians pursued them.
This account represents the Massagetae as responsible for the first impulse,
but Aristeas says that it was the Arimaspians that fell upon the Issedones
and that these fell upon the Scyths and drove them against the
Cimmerians. At any rate it is clearly stated that the Scyths came from
the East. Diodorus Siculus has made a contamination of these accounts
and while letting the Scythians come from Western Asia has brought
in the Echidna of the Greek legend (II. 43 sqq.). His story with its
explanation of the history of Sarmatians and Amazons reads plausibly,
being eked out with details which apply to the rise of every tribe that
ever rose to power in Asia; compare the accounts of how Chingiz
Khan became great and spread abroad the dominion of the Mongols;
but his anachronisms enable his reader to estimate his account at its
real worth. Of course the Asiatic origin of the nomad Scyths is no bar
to their Iranian affinity, but it makes a non-Aryan derivation conceivable.

Physical characteristics.

The supporters of the Mongol theory of the Scyths rely chiefly on the
evidence of Hippocrates in his treatise on Airs, Waters and Places[4]. The
evidence of the first of Greek physicians ought to be conclusive, but

---

[1] Cotieri, *NH.* VI. 50.
[2] For Iranian tales in which the youngest of
three brothers succeeds cf. Spiegel, *Érân. Altertumsk.* I. 544, who compares Echidna and Dahâk.

[3] *Journ. Min. Pub. Instr.* St P., 1886, Jan.
[4] cc. 24—30. There is a translation by F. Adams
in *Transactions of the Sydenham Society*, Vol. I.
pp. 187–8, 207—218.

unfortunately, in spite of much medical detail, it does not give us a clear idea of Scythian characteristics.   The fact is that he was trying to prove a theory, emphasizing the effect of the environment upon a race, and it is a question whether he does not rather twist his facts to meet his theory.   And inasmuch as his notion of the environment is faulty—he takes Scythia to have a climate almost uniformly cold throughout the year—the facts that suit his theory are rather open to doubt.

Hippocrates begins by describing the Sauromatae whom he calls a Scythian tribe living about the Maeotis and differing from the other tribes. He goes on to tell of their women's taking part in war—the usual story. He draws a very clear line between them and the rest of the Scyths of whom he says that they are as different from all other men as are the Egyptians. But this difference which he ascribes to their monotonous mode of life, the men riding on horseback and the women on waggons, and to the continuous cold and fog of their country, he hardly defines in a convincing way.   It amounts to a tendency to fatness, slackness and excess of humours, and a singular mutual resemblance due to all living under the same conditions. This slackness they counteract by a custom of branding themselves on various parts of the body[1].   Further he says that the cold makes their colouring πυρρός, which seems to mean a reddish brown, the colour that fair people get from being much in the open.   It cannot be any kind of yellow[2].   The colour of the Tartars was not far from reddish.   Kublai Khan had a white and red complexion, yet Chingiz Khan was surprised at his being so brown, as most of his family had blue eyes and reddish hair[3].   So too Batu is described by Rubruck as *perfusus gutta rosea* which du Cange takes = *rubidus in facie*; so Hakluyt and Bergeron, but Rockhill is probably right in translating "his face was all covered with red spots[4]."   The Chinese describe one of the five tribes of Hiung-nu as fair.   Lastly Hippocrates observes in both men and women a sexual indifference that amounts in some of the men to actual impotence ; these are the Anaries of whom Herodotus also speaks, ascribing their disease to the wrath of the goddess at Ascalon whose temple they had plundered at the time of their invasion of Asia[5].   But Hippocrates will have none of this, and says this is a disease just like any other disease[6] and due to excessive

---

[1] Cf. J. G. Frazer, *Golden Bough*[2], III., p. 217. The Indians of St Juan Capistrano in California used to be branded in certain parts of their bodies ...because they believed that the custom added greater strength to their nerves and gave a better pulse for the management of the bow.
[2] H. Kiepert, *Manual of Ancient Geography*, Eng. ed., London, 1881, p. 196, translates "dusky yellow." He takes the Royal Scyths to be Turkic in spite of the philologists.
[3] Rashid-ed-Din ap. Yule[3], *Marco Polo*, I., p. 358 n. 1, cf. inf. p. 100.
[4] Rubruck, p. 124.
[5] Her. I. 105.
[6] Cf. Reineggs (Jacob), *Allgemeine historisch-topographische Beschreibung des Caucasus*, Bd I., p. 270.
"Der Mann (der Nogajen) hat ein fleischiges aufgetriebenes aber breites Gesicht, mit sehr hervorstehenden Backenknochen, kleine tiefliegende Augen und keine fünfzig bis achtzig Barthaare. Wenn nun nach Krankheiten eine unheilbare Entkräftung folgt oder das Alter zunimmt, so wird die Haut des ganzen Körpers ausserordentlich runzlich und die wenigen Barthaare fallen aus und der Mann bekommt ein ganz weibliches Ansehen.   Er wird zum Beischlaf untüchtig und seine Empfindungen und Handlungen haben allen Männlichen entsagt.   In diesem Zustande muss er der Männer Gesellschaft fliehen: er bleibt unter der Weihen, kleidet sich wie ein Weib, und man könnte tausend gegen eins wetten dass dieser Mann würklich ein altes Weib und zwar ein recht hässliches altes Weib sei."
Neumann, p. 164, quotes curiously enough from an English translation which I have not seen, and translates back into German.
The disease described by Pallas (*Voyages en plusieurs provinces*, Paris, II. 8°, II., p. 135 sqq.) does not appear cognate with this, though some

riding. But all this, he says definitely, applies only to the most noble and rich among them. With the common folk it is entirely otherwise. This whole description seems to suggest the condition of an Asiatic race in the last stage of degeneration, when the descendants of a small band of conquerors have reached a state of effete sloth and are ready to make way for a more vigorous stock.

The chief question that is raised by this description is as to the amount of trust that can be put in the statement that the ruling caste of Scyths is quite unlike any other kind of man. In the representations on works of art (v. p. 57 n.) the nomads do not appear so very unlike any other northern people, their resemblance to modern Russian peasants has often been pointed out; though this resemblance is superficial, due rather to certain similarities of costume and to the way in which an abundant growth of hair disguises the individuality of a type, than to a deep-seated likeness. The similarities of costume are due to the fact that the Russians have borrowed many details of their dress from nomad tribes through the intervention of the Cossacks, whose mode of life had much in common with that of their hereditary foes. The words for clothes in Russian are mostly of Tartar origin[1]. Still the bearded warriors on the vase from Kul Oba could not possibly be described as εὐνουχοειδέστατοι ἀνθρώπων. If these are in any sense Scythian they must belong to a later time when the N. Asiatic blood had become completely mixed in. The Tartars of Kazan and the Uzbegs of Turkestan, races in which Altaic blood has been much diluted with Finnish or Iranian, are fully bearded. The Chinese drawings of Kara Kitans (p. 96, f. 27) shew them with full beards. The representations of nomads from Kul Oba seem to belong to about the middle of the fourth century B.C. and by then the peculiar type described by Hippocrates might well have become almost obliterated by intermarriage with earlier inhabitants. Ammianus Marcellinus (XXXI. 11) uses a similar expression of the Huns "*spadonibus similes*," and he is not likely to be copying Hippocrates in the same way that he applies to the Alans the description Herodotus gives of the Scythians. It seems as if the Huns, almost undoubted Altaic, produced the same impression on Ammianus as the Scyths on Hippocrates[2].

The osteological characteristics of the skeletons found in Scythic graves throw very little light on the questions at issue. Had the skulls discovered been uniformly short or long, such uniformity would have been a weighty argument for assigning them to Tartars or Europeans respectively. But the rather scanty observations made hitherto tend to shew that there was considerable variety among individuals who used objects of defined Scythic type. The best known case is that of the five skulls found in Chertomlyk and discussed by K. E. von Baer in *ASH*. Of these two were short and two were long and one was intermediate, and the data were not sufficiently exact to shew that either lords or servants were one or the other. And even had there been such data they would not have cleared up the question, as it would

---

symptoms are alike. My friend Dr L. Bousfield suggests that it was very bad orchitis and that Hippocrates may have been right in putting it down to constant riding.

[1] V. V. Stasov in his review of Maskell's Russian Art, *Works*, Vol. II. iii., p. 823.

[2] For the types of variously proportioned mixtures of Iranian and Turko-Tartar blood v. Ch. de Ujfalvy, *Les Aryens au Nord et au Sud de l'Hindou Kouch*, Paris, 1896. An Uzbeg with a beard is illustrated in Keane's *Ethnology*, p. 312.

be possible to argue the greater purity of blood of either rulers or servants; *a priori* the latter might be supposed to be imported slaves, but Herodotus distinctly says that they were native Scyths, and he tells of the marriage of Scythian kings with various foreign women. So too some of the skulls illustrated by Count Bobrinskoj in *Smêla* slightly suggest Mongolian forms, others are purely European[1]. To this same conclusion came Professor Anatole Bogdanov[2], who says that in Scythic tombs the skulls are mostly long though occasionally Mongoloid and notes a general tendency towards brachycephaly during the Scythic period. For strangely enough although Slavs and Finns are now short-headed they seem to have become so only during the last few centuries[3]. In Hungary e.g. at Keszthely the cemeteries which are referred to the Sarmatians are full of bow-legged skeletons, a characteristic which may be accounted for either by their horsemanship or by a mixture of Altaic blood[4].

The process of gradual amalgamation of Central-Asian rulers with an alien subject population under very similar circumstances may be observed in the case of the coins of the Kushanas. Not that a change of racial type can be followed unless Miaus represents the purer blood, but the Indian name Vāsudeva, along with the Kushana Vasushka, succeeds to Kujula and Hima Kadphises, Kanishka and Huvishka, without a break to mark a change of dynasty. Their successors the Ephthalite Huns answer decidedly to the type described by Hippocrates but in their case the evolution was cut short by the Turks[5].

Manner of Life.

If we consider the customs which Herodotus ascribes to the Scythians it becomes evident that they form no coherent whole. Although it is hard to say what various usages may coexist in any given nation, what survivals from an earlier state may continue into a high civilisation, the parts of the picture drawn by Herodotus do not fit together. We see that he has mixed together information drawn from different sources and applying to different tribes. When it comes to endeavouring to determine according to these various customs the affinities of their users we are on very uncertain ground. Analogues for every detail can be found among various nations and as readily among Aryans as among non-Aryans. Most of the usages mentioned are inseparable from a nomadic life and throw no light on the affinities of the people among whom they obtain. The characteristic dress of the Scyths which struck the Greeks so much, is almost the only possible one for a nation of riders living in a cold climate, so too the use of various preparations of mare's milk, butter, kumys and cheese, the felt tents, bows and

[1] *Sm.* II., pl. XXVII.—XXX. Dr W. H. Duckworth, of Jesus College, kindly examined these for me.

[2] *Congrès International d'Archéologie Préhistorique et d'Anthropologie*, IIme *Session à Moscou*, T. I., Moscow, 1892, p. 5. "Quelle est la race la plus ancienne de la Russie Centrale?"

[3] Niederle, *Slavonic Antiquities*, I. pp. 89 sqq.

[4] G. Nagy, *The Nationality of the Scyths*, p. 31. Cf. L. Fligier, *Archiv f. Anthropologie*, XVII. (1888), p. 302. For the Macrocephali with their artificially elongated skulls v. D. Anuchin, *Sur les crânes anciens artificiellement déformés de la Russie*, Moscow Congress, p. 263; *BCA.* XX. p. 85, f. 41;

for a shortened skull *Ib.* XXV. p. 126 f. 18, both from Chersonese.

[5] *B. M. Coin Cat.*, *Greek and Scythic Kings of Bactria and India*, by P. Gardner, XXIV. 7, XXV. 1—9, XXIX. 10. E. J. Rapson, *Grundr. d. Indo-Arischen Phil. u. Altertumsk.*, Bd II. Heft 3 B, Pl. II. 1, 8—12, IV. 18. I am very grateful to Professor Rapson for indicating this series to me, but cf. O. Franke, "Zur Kenntnis d. Türkvölker u. Sk. Zentral-Asiens," p. 79 in *Abhandl. d. k. pr. Akad.* Berlin 1904. The Ephthalites' coins have *tamgi* very like those that occur in the Crimea, v. inf. ch. XI. § 4.

arrows, curious methods of cooking owing to the absence of proper fuel, and so on, were conditioned by their general mode of life and could be nearly paralleled among any nomad tribe.   As a matter of fact the medieval travellers found all these things in use among the Mongols, and some of the coincidences with facts recorded by Marco Polo, de Plano Carpini, de Rubruck and others are striking.   These agreements are not restricted to such necessary similarities; the accounts of cemeteries and funeral customs, of the religion of the Mongols, of their personal appearance, of the polyandry of the Tibetans, of their way of disposing of the aged, suggest that though it may be going too far to declare positively that the Scyths were Mongolian, we must admit that the Mongols before their conversion whether to Islam or Buddhism were their closest possible analogues.   And their fate in western Asia and eastern Europe has been analogous.   Already the hordes that Batu led against the West had very few pure Mongols save among the chief leaders, and this strain soon merged in the mixed multitude that it ruled, so that the later khans of the Golden Horde were just like any other west Asiatic monarchs, a mixture of the Turk and the Circassian[1].

This seems the place to give a summary of what our authorities tell us as to the life of the Scythians, especially the Nomads.   The main bulk of information is contained in Herodotus (IV. 59—75), and the reader is prayed to have him at hand: some details are filled in from other passages and other authors (especially Hippocrates, *De Aere, etc.*).   In order to give as complete a picture of nomad life as is possible within narrow limits I have anticipated the archaeological results set forth in the later chapter which describes the tombs found in the Scythic area.   Professor Lappo-Danilevskij[2] has arranged the accessible material under convenient headings.   In preparing the following summary I have everywhere been indebted to him, though much has been discovered since his book was written.   Count Bobrinskoj (*Smêla* passim) also gives a convenient view of what is known of various classes of objects.

In spite of the well-known existence of tribes of agricultural Scythians, Scythian always suggested to the Greek the idea of nomadic life.   The governing condition of the nomads' existence was the necessity of finding natural pasture for their cattle, hence their moving from place to place, and this necessitated everything from the form of their dwellings to the cut of their clothes, from their tactics in warfare to their method of cookery.

Their chief occupation was looking after their many horses, and of this we have a splendid illustration on the famous Chertomlyk vase (v. pp. 159—162, ff. 46—49), on which we see pourtrayed in greatest detail the process of catching

---

[1] In the confusion of nomenclature used for the races of northern Asia it seems impossible to arrive at a satisfactory terminology. By Mongolian in the broader sense is meant belonging to the eastern branch of the Uralo-Altaic peoples as opposed to the Finno-Ugrian branch. This eastern branch can be further divided into a western section to which belonged the Hiung-nu or Huns and the Turks, and an eastern section of whom the best known representatives are the Mongol tribe and the Manchus. But in dealing with western Asia and Europe the two sections are indistinguishable, as any movement of the eastern section produced its chief effect upon the West through the instru-

mentality of the western section. Hence from our point of view Hunnish or Turkish comes to the same thing as Mongolian, though a confusing of them may seem to Turcologues unpardonable. But the nature of the material does not allow of greater accuracy seeing that we have an actual case of 100,000 Huns who took the name of the Sien-pi—eastern Mongols—when defeated by them. For the gradual shading of Mongols into Turks (v. p. 91 sqq.), Turks into Ugrians and Ugrians into Finns, and the various crossings of all these races with the "Caucasic" stock, see A. H. Keane, *Ethnology*, p. 295 sqq., also Franke, loc. cit.

[2] *Scythian Antiquities*, pp. 383 sqq.

the wild horse of the steppes or breaking him in. Others have been reminded by it of the story in Aristotle[1] of the Scythian king's practice of horse-breeding. On the vase we have two breeds represented; the tame horse which is being hobbled and the wild ones with hog manes. Professor Anuchin[2] thinks the former is like the Kalmuck breed and the latter the half-wild horses of the royal stud. Professor Ridgeway[3] compares with the former the shaggy horses of the ancient Sigynnae and those of the modern Kirgiz, descendants of the "Mongolian" pony. The indocility of this race made the practice of gelding necessary, otherwise it was unknown in the ancient world[4]. Horses were also used for food. Scythians were supposed to like them very high. Next in importance to their horses came the cattle used for drawing their great waggons. Both Hippocrates and Herodotus say that they were hornless. The latter ascribes this to the cold (IV. 29). They had sheep as well, for mutton bones are found in cauldrons in the tombs, as for example at Kul Oba. They made no use of pigs either in sacrifice or in any other way. So the early Turks regarded swine as tabu[5].

Besides looking after their cattle the Scyths of course engaged in hunting, and we have gold plaques[6] with representations of a Scyth throwing a dart at a hare, reminding us of the story of how the Scyths when drawn up in battle array over against Darius set off after a hare[7]. As hunters they had a taste for representations of animals, especially in combat, and these are very characteristic of objects made for their use. Representations such as those on the Xenophantus vase (ch. XI. § 7) are purely fantastic: more realistic is a hunting scene that appears on the wonderful fragments of ivory with Greek drawing found at Kul Oba (p. 204^D: *ABC.* LXXIX. 10).

Hunting supplied some of their food, more was produced by their cattle especially by their horses. Most characteristic were the products of mare's milk especially kumys ὀξύγαλα, the cheese called ἱππάκη, butter and butter-milk[8], also horse-flesh and other meat. Their methods of cooking were conditioned by the scarcity of fuel. Very characteristic are the round-footed cauldrons in which have been found horse (e.g. Chertomlyk, p. 162, f. 50) and mutton bones (e.g. Kul Oba). They also used some vegetable food such as onions, garlic, and beans[9] as well as grain, and the people about the Maeotis dug up a sweet bulb[10] just as the Siberian tribes do with the Martagon lily[11]. Besides kumys they drank wine readily enough, and Greek amphorae penetrated far into the country: such jars were part of the provision put in a dead man's tomb: few of the amphorae found far from the coast bear stamps (ch. XI. § 7): it would seem as if the commoner sorts did for the barbarians. Their habit of drinking it neat especially excited the contempt of the Greeks.

[1] *Hist. Anim.* IX. 47.
[2] *On the question of wild white horses* (*Her.* IV. 52), St P. 1896.
[3] *Thoroughbred Horse*, p. 130.
[4] Strabo, VII. iv. 8; use of mares, Pliny, *NH.* VIII. 165.
[5] Her. IV. 63. Vambéry, *Die primitive Kultur der Turko-Tataren*, p. 38, 199, but cf. inf. p. 182.
[6] p. 197, f. 90, *KTR.* f. 162, p. 154, *ABC.* XX. 1, silver *ASH.* XIII. 10.

[7] Her. IV. c. 134.
[8] Cf. Hippocrates, *De Morbis*, IV. c. v. § 20, and Strabo VII. iv. 6, hence the Homeric epithets Ἱππημόλγοι and γλακτοφάγοι, *Il.* XIII. l. 5, 6. Cf. Rubruquis c. 6, ap. Hakluyt p. 97, Rockhill p. 62.
[9] Her. IV. 17.
[10] Theophrastus, *Hist. Plantarum* VII. xiii. 8 and IX. xiii. 2.
[11] For the eating of bulbs among the Turks v. A. Vambéry, op. cit., p. 220.

M.

Waggons.

As everybody knows, the home of the Scyth was on his cart. Already Hesiod[1] speaks of the waggon-dwellers. Hippocrates[2] gives the fullest description, saying that the smaller ones had four wheels, the larger six, that they were covered with felt and arranged like houses divided into two or three compartments and drawn by two or three yoke of hornless oxen. In these the women lived, whereas the men accompanied them on horseback. Aeschylus sums up their whole life in three lines[3]:

> Σκύθας δ' ἀφίξῃ νομάδας, οἳ πλεκτὰς στέγας
> πεδάρσιοι ναίουσ' ἐπ' εὐκύκλοις ὄχοις
> ἐκηβόλοις τόξοισιν ἐξηρτυμένοι.

"And thou shalt come to the Scyths, nomads who dwell in wattled huts high in the air upon their fair-wheeled wains, equipped with far-shooting bows."

We have remains of waggons in various Scythic tombs but they seem perhaps rather open funeral cars than the wheeled dwelling (p. 75). It is an open car also that we see on the coin of Scilurus struck at Olbia.

Coin of Scilurus Mus. Kotschp.28.

FIG. 4.

Some light may be thrown by the toy carts found in Greek graves at Kerch treated of by Professor P. Bieńkowski of Cracow[4]. Some are clearly

FIG. 5. *BCA.* IX. Pl. V[d]. Kerch. Toy model cart.

mere country carts, not unlike those still in use in the Crimea, a body of wicker or skin with wooden framing set upon a pair of axles. Others

---

[1] ap. Str. VII. iii. 9 Γλακτοφάγων ἐς γαῖαν, ἀπήναις οἰκί' ἐχόντων. Cf. Hor. *Carm.* III. XXiv. 10 "Scythae, Quorum plaustra vagas rite trahunt domos."
[2] *De Aere* c. 25.
[3] *Prom. Vinc.* l. 735.

[4] *Wiener Studien*, XXIV., p. 394, and *BCA.* IX., pp. 63—72 and pl. IV.—VIII. I have much pleasure in thanking him for allowing me to copy his pictures in the former paper and for sending me an off-print of the latter. Of course the wooden axles have been supplied.

are more like our idea of waggon dwellings, being not merely tilt carts as No. 2 in Fig. 6, but remarkable structures such as No. 1 *b*, with a kind of tower in which were windows before and behind set upon a body which itself had windows in the sides between the wheels and also behind. The pyramidal tower may be a tent whether fixed or moveable like those of modern nomads. Or this may have been an arrangement for defence; for the method of making a lager of waggons has always been a resource of

FIG. 6.

the nomads. The waggons always had a hole in front for the dissel-boom, and in one case were furnished with a pair of oxen also on wheels. .They seem rather late in date, but the types are probably old[1]. If we may judge by the analogy of other Asiatic nomads it is at least a question whether the Scyths were always on wheels, like the gipsies in England. We have no artistic representation of any vehicle quite suitable for such a life. It seems more likely that they carried their tents all standing upon their carts and set them down upon the ground when they came to a halt. The Sarmatian tent represented on the walls of the catacomb of Anthesterius[2] is set upon the ground, and this is the arrangement described by Rubruquis[3]. "Their houses wherein they sleepe they ground upon a round foundation of wickers artificially wrought and compacted together: the roofe whereof consisteth (in like sorte) of wickers meeting above into one little roundell, out of which roundell ascendeth vpward a necke like vnto a Chimney, which they couer with white felte....The sayd houses they make so large that they conteine thirtie foote in breadth. For measuring once the breadthe betweene the wheele ruts of one of their cartes, I found it to be twenty feete ouer: and when the house was upon the carte it stretched over the wheeles at each side fiue feete at the least: I told 22 oxen in one teame drawing an house upon a cart....And a fellow stood in the doore of the house, vpon the forestall of the carte driuing forth the oxen....When they take down their dwelling houses, they turne the doores alwayes to the South." Evidently everything was on a much larger scale than with the Scyths, but probably the principle was the same. There were also small permanently covered carts. In later times the clumsy

---

[1] Compare Mr Hill's cart, which is Greek or Oriental, coming from Alexandria, *JHS.* XVII., p. 88. Miss Lorimer's country carts are mostly two-wheeled, not like those figured here, v. *JHS.* XXIII., p. 132.
[2] ch. XI. § 4, *CR.* 1878, pl. I. I.
[3] op. cit. c. 2, Hakluyt p. 95, Rockhill p. 54 sqq.

standing tent lifted down bodily from the cart has given place to the folding Jurta of the Kirgiz. The transition is shewn in the annexed picture[1]. It gives a view of a body of Kundure Tartars who in Pallas's time were just adopting the Kirgiz dwelling such as is shewn on the extreme left, whereas they had used small white tents which were put bodily on to bullock carts and could be taken off again and set down on the ground. They also had Arbas or two-wheeled waggons with wooden sides and a rounded top, and similar ones are described among the medieval Tartars.

The picture gives as good an idea as may be of what must have been the general appearance of a body of Scyths.

Towns.

Of the towns mentioned by Greek authors as being in Scythia we know neither where they were nor what. The agricultural Scythians may well have had settlements worthy of the name, and even nomads have always had some kind of capital (e.g. Karakorum) and places for trading. In any case they mostly seem to have been either on the coast as Cremni[2], or in the western half of Scythia[3].

[1] P. S. Pallas, *Travels in the Southern Provinces of the Russian Empire in the years* 1793-4, Eng. Trans. London, 1802, vol. I. pl. 6, p. 172. Cf. E. D. Clarke, *Travels*, London, 1817, vol. I., p. 394. The covered carts are well described by Josafa Barbaro in his *Viaggio alla Tana*, ff. 93 sqq., in Ramusio, *Navigationi et Viaggi*, vol. II., Venice, 1559. Marco Polo, I. lii., Yule² i. p. 252, 254, n. 2.

[2] Westberg, l.c., puts Cremni at Eskykrym, the old capital of the Crimea, to which it has given its name. It seems better to take the name as Greek and the place as a trading station. Besides Herodotus certainly thought of it as on the coast of the Maeotis, for the shipload of Amazons landed there in the Sauromatae legend (IV. 110). Even so it is hard to imagine how they should have found their way through the Bosporus: still St Ursula sailing from Britain to Rome was wrecked at Cologne.

[3] About Smêla are many *gorodishcha*, entrenchments serving as refuge camps, and some have yielded Sc. objects, e.g. *Sm.* II. pp. 52—61. V. A. Gorodtsov's excavation of one at Bêlsk is not yet published, but v. inf. pp. 119, 147.

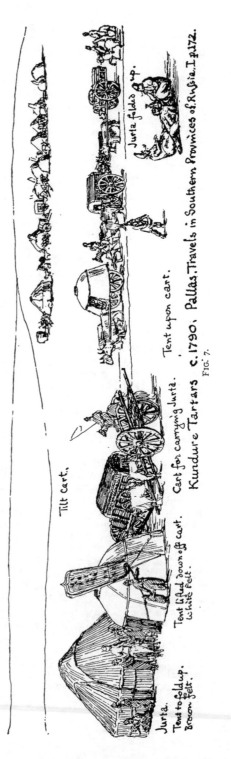

Jurta folded up.

Tent upon cart.

Cart for carrying Jurta.

Tilt cart.

Tent lifted down off cart. white felt.

Jurta.

Tent to fold up. Brown felt.

Kundure Tartars c. 1790. Pallas. Travels in Southern Provinces of Russia. I. pl. 72.

FIG. 7.

The ancients tell us nothing of the dress of the Scythians except that they wore belts and trousers and pointed caps. We must therefore rely on representations which may be more or less certainly regarded as intended for Scythians. These fall into two classes, those presumably executed north of the Euxine—they are mostly in repoussé gold or silver and give us genre scenes—and those, very nearly all vase-paintings, due to Greeks in less close contact with the Scythians. The latter class is thoroughly untrustworthy, as might be expected, and chiefly depicts battle scenes.

Among the various barbarians which appear on Greek vases of only two can it be said on the artist's own authority that he was thinking of northern nomads. On the well-known François vase[1] we have three archers (p. 54, fig. 8), one labelled Euthymachos, one Toxamis and one Kimerios. Toxamis, whose name according to one authority "klingt echt skythisch," perhaps on the analogy of Lucian's very suspicious Toxaris, wears a patterned tunic, a quiver and a high pointed headdress. He is shooting with a bow whereon seems to be shewn the lacing which is essential in a composite bow though in its more developed forms it is usually concealed. Kimerios, about whose name there can be no doubt, is similarly equipped but has a bow-case instead of a quiver. But Euthymachos, who may well be a Greek archer, is dressed just the same, and in later vases archers, even though probably Greek, wear barbarian costume[2].

In the case of another painting of barbarians attempts have been made to identify them as Cimmerians. Dr A. S. Murray sees them in a horde of cavalry who are slashing down Greeks on a sarcophagus from Clazomenae[3].

But these people are using great swords such as were not developed in S. Russia until after the Christian era. It is true that they have bow-cases, but these again seem not quite like the gorytus, the combination of bow-case and quiver which is peculiar to the Scythic area. It is hard to judge by mere silhouettes, but the swords and the caps seem much more like those of Central Europe; may not we call these folk Treres, the Thracian allies of the Cimmerians?

There is another vase (p. 55, fig. 9) which might conceivably represent Cimmerians rather than Scythians as they have hitherto been called by F. Dümmler who published it and others like it which form his class of "Pontic" vases[4]. It is certainly tempting to see in these wearers of peaked hoods some East European Nomads. But all these vases are found in Italy and it would be rash to decide where they were made[5].

Another case of referring to our region unidentified barbarians is seen

[1] *Mon. Ined.* IV. 54, *Wiener Vorlegeblätter* VI. 1888, pl. I.—V.

[2] e.g. Hartwig, *Die Griechischen Meisterschalen*, pl. XIV., Gerhard, *Auserlesene Vasenbilder* III. 264.

[3] *Terra-cotta Sarcophagi in Brit. Mus.* pl. I.

[4] *Röm. Mitth.* II. p. 171, pl. IX. I am indebted to Mrs H. F. Stewart, of Newnham College, for calling my attention to this and to the Agathyrsi

vase. She has even been good enough to allow me to reproduce her drawing. Miss Jane Harrison has also helped me very much in this question of vase-paintings. To both I wish to offer my best thanks.

[5] Prof. Furtwängler, *Ant. Gemmen*, III. p. 88, would assign them to a local Italian make, and Mr H. B. Walters, *Hist. of Anc. Pottery* I. p. 359, will not decide between Kyme and Italy.

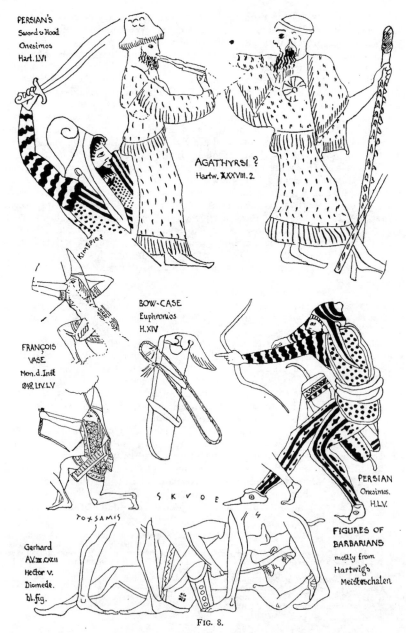

PERSIAN'S
Sword & Hood
Onesimos
Hart. LVI

AGATHYRSI ?
Hartw. XXXVIII. 2

KIMEPIOΣ

FRANÇOIS
VASE
Mon. d. Inst
1848. LIV. LV

BOW-CASE
Euphronios
H. XIV

PERSIAN
Onesimos.
H. LV.

ΣΚΥΘΕ

ΤΟΧΣΑΜΙΣ

Gerhard
A.V. III. CXII
Hector v.
Diomede.
bl. fig.

FIGURES OF
BARBARIANS
mostly from
Hartwig's
Meisterschalen

FIG. 8.

FIG. 9. " Pontic " Vase with Cimmerians (?).

in the case of a cylix (Fig. 8, top) figured by Hartwig[1]. He guesses that
these strange people are Agathyrsi, but he does not adduce any evidence :
in his discussion he treats Herodotus in the most cavalier fashion and
entirely ignores his distinctions between the various neighbours of the
Scythians. He thinks the knowledge of detail points to the master having been
a Scythian. That there was such an one we know[2] from a signature. One
of the supposed Agathyrsi is wearing on his chest just such a rayed
plate as was found at Nymphaeum (v. p. 213, f. 114).

We have a tangible reason for referring to a Scyth the fallen figure
labelled ϟΚΥΟΕϟ that occurs in a black-figured vase (Fig. 8, below) with the
combat of Hector and Diomede[3]. His hood with a high point behind and
perhaps his bow-case, seem accurately remembered, but inasmuch as he
wears a sleeveless tunic adorned with crosses and no trousers but greaves,
he does not agree with more exact pictures. This freedom of treatment
shews that we are not to expect accuracy in cases defined by no inscription, and therefore we cannot deny that a barbarian is meant for a
Scythian just because his clothes do not exactly tally. On the other hand
figures are much too often described as Scythians. I know of no figure
upon a red-figured vase which I could be sure was meant for a Scythian.
Phrygians, Persians, Greek archers equipped in Asiatic guise, most frequent
of all, Amazons have a common dress which is not so far removed
from that of the Scythians but that a Greek might apply it to the latter.
These people all have a headdress with more or less of a point, but there
are nearly always lappets which could be tied about the chin (Fig. 8, top).
Their clothes seem made of a thin material, the trousers (or perhaps stockings)
usually fitting quite close to the legs and the jersey having sleeves often of
the same striking pattern. The close-fitting tunic over these is usually
plain and sleeveless, sometimes patterned and sleeved (Fig. 8, below).
Another form of tunic is rather flowing and then is generally sleeved
or its place is taken by a cloak with sleeves that wave empty behind—
perhaps this is the *candys*. The wearers mostly have axes as well as
bows. Their bow-cases have no place for arrows (v. p. 67, f. 17) and their

[1] op. cit. pl. XXXVIII., XXXIX. 1, p. 421.   [2] *Jahrb. d. k. deutschen arch. Inst.* 1887, p. 144.
[3] Gerhard, *A.V.* III. 192.

swords are not at all like any Scythic type. Only when they are labelled or when they are hunting griffins or engaging in any other distinctive occupation can we say who they may be.   There is no doubting the Persians on Hartwig's plates LV., LVI., nor the young Athenians on his plate XIV., so on the well-known vase with a δοκιμασία of horsemen the central figure is surely not an outer barbarian[1]. Likewise the Amazons are often clear enough[2], in other cases, e.g. Hartwig's II. 2 and XIII., they are only to be distinguished by the inscriptions[3]. The list of Scythians in Walters (p. 179) contains the examples which I have discussed and others which all appear to me Persian as far as I have been able to see them; so too with Reinach. It is much safer to call such figures oriental archers[4]. An Arimasp such as we find on the calathos from the Great Bliznitsa (ch. XII.) is no doubt an Arimasp, but his dress is purely fantastic. The crowning example of the decorative use of barbarian costume is on the Xenophantus vase, and here we know that all are Persian. Yet Clytios would pass for an Amazon (ch. XI. § 7).

So likewise with engraved stones. There is one[5] which represents a barbarian with a long cloak and a tunic leaning on a spear, and there is that signed by Athenades with a man sitting on a folding stool and trying the point of an arrow[6]. Both come from Kerch, yet neither is specifically Scythian but rather Persian: the latter is even closely paralleled by a coin of Datames satrap of Tarsus[7].   Terra-cottas found in the Crimea give us very generalised figures wearing it would seem the native hood and trousers

FIG. 10.   Terra-cotta Barbarian or Greek in local costume, Kerch. *KTR.* p. 204, f. 188 ; *CR.* 1876, VI. 8.

and the Greek chiton : much what we should expect from Dio Chrysostom's account of the Olbiopolites[8].   But again this is very like Phrygian dress and may be merely another example of influence from Asia Minor, always strong on the northern Euxine.   The last classical representation of conventional Scythic dress is on an ivory diptych of the 6th century A.D.[9]

[1] *Jahrb.* 1889, pl. 4.
[2] v. Reinach, *Répertoire de Vases*, sub v.
[3] So too Walters, op. cit. II. p. 176, f. 137.
[4] e.g. Walters, pl. XXXVII. 2 ; Ashmolean 310, pl. 13 ; Louvre, Pottier, II. F. 126. K. Wernicke, "Die Polizeiwache auf der Burg von Athen" (*Hermes*, XXVI. 1891, f. 51—75) points out that the policemen in the fifth century were ever-present

models of Scythic dress.
[5] ch. XI. § 13 : *KTR.* p. 207, f. 190 = *ABC.* XVII. 9.
[6] *KTR.* p. 188, f. 178 = *CR.* 1861, pl. VI. 11.
[7] *KTR.* f. 179.
[8] *Or.* XXXVI. p. 50, v. ch. XV.
[9] *Mon. Piot*, VII., p. 79, pl. X.: Dar. et Saglio s.v. Diptychon.

Even in the other class of monuments apparently made by Pontic Greeks although they bear every appearance of accuracy we cannot be sure of every detail. Also we must remember that none of the folk represented need necessarily be Scyths in the narrower sense of the word, they are most of them in all probability Sarmatians. They are almost always shewn with beards. They wore close-fitting coats with narrow sleeves, cut rather short behind, but in front coming down much lower to a point. The flaps folded over so that the coat was in some sort double breasted without coming up to the chin. It was apparently trimmed and probably lined with fur.

It was adorned with, as it were, orphreys or bands of either embroidery or gold plates following the seams at the inset of the sleeves, down the middle of the back and at the sides. At the sides were little slits to allow free movement as in some modern coats. The round dots on the Kul Oba coats seem rather ornaments than actual buttons in both cases. The belts kept them to. The coat was apparently the only upper garment, for the man facing on the Chertomlyk vase has for some reason freed his right shoulder of his coat and this leaves it bare. The under side of the coat is of different texture from the upper. The belt is apparently of leather and a strap run through a slit in it carries the bow-case. Trousers are either full enough to hang in folds and adorned just with a stripe down the seam, or tighter and covered with stripes round or lengthwise (Kul Oba). They were tucked into soft boots which were tied round the ankle and sometimes the instep as well. The fuller variety were so tucked in as to come down and partly conceal the boot[1].

Such clothes had no need for fibulae, but we find pins with ornamental heads in Scythic graves.

Headdress.

We find these men with long hair and considerable beards. They either went bare headed or wore hoods more or less like the Russian *bashlyk*. It is difficult to tell which forms belong to the nomads and which to the Persians. The Asiatic nomads had very high pointed headgear, according to Herodotus and the Bisutun bas relief of Sakunka the Saka (p. 59, f. 12). But in other cases the apex of the hood is allowed to hang down, and that this is intended is shewn by the pattern on a band round the end of the chief's hood found at Karagodeuashkh. It contains griffins whose heads are towards the longer side of the band[2]. A somewhat similar band from Kul Oba goes the other way up and is adorned with figures and foliage[3]. A very remarkable object, which seems to be a

---

[1] These details can be best seen on the Kul Oba Vase (pp. 200, 201, ff. 93, 94), the Chertomlyk Vase (pp. 159—162, ff. 46—49), and the Kul Oba Necklet (p. 202, f. 97). Other representations are added from Kul Oba plaques bearing a man shooting a hare (p. 197), two men shooting in opposite directions (p. 197), man and woman with mirror (p. 158, f. 43), man with gorytus (p. 197), two men drinking out of one rhyton (p. 203). Also two men one with a severed head and one with a sword from

Kurdzhips (p. 223, f. 126, *CR.* 1895, p. 62, f. 140), the seated man from Axjutintsy (p. 182 f. 75 *bis*) and two wrestlers from Chmyrev barrow (p. 169, f. 62, *CR.* 1898, p. 27, f. 24); l.c. f. 26 is an obscure figure which seems to have on a sleeved coat without putting its arms into the sleeves; this seems a Persian fashion. Cf. Persepolitan sculptures, the "Alexander" sarcophagus, etc. Pins, p. 191, f. 83.

[2] p. 219, f. 122 = *Mat.* XIII. viii. 1, 2.

[3] p. 202, f. 96 = *ABC.* II. 1.

headgear, is a golden truncated cone about 10 in. high made of four
hoops separating three bands of pierced orna-
ment, two of griffins and one between of
palmettes set with garnets.   This alone shews
that its date is comparatively late.   It was
found by Prof. N. I. Veselovskij at Beslenêevskaja Stanitsa on the Kuban.   Another
strange head ornament, which may be put down
to native influence, though found in a grave
near Panticapaeum, is the heavy gold pilos[1]
ornamented with volutes.   But these stiff metallic headgears must have been rare.   More
commonly the stuff head covering is adorned
with gold plaques, as we see on the Kul Oba
vase and find in actual fact.   For instance,
a man's skull covered with gold plates of two
patterns *in situ*, which must have been sewn on
to a stuff cap.   It was found at Sinjavka on
the Rossava (Kiev Government)[2].

FIG. 11.   Gold Tiara with Garnets.
Beslenêevskaja Stanitsa. *CR.* 1895,
p. 28, f. 43. ½.

Asiatic Nomads.

Almost as instructive as the accurate
Greek representations of European Scythians
are those of Asiatic nomads : perhaps the best
of these is on a large gold plate from the
Oxus Treasure[3]. Although the man who made
it could draw, the style of execution is curiously
lacking in character ; we cannot call it Persian or Scythic, though other plates
of the treasure shewing more or less similar figures, women's as well as men's,
do appear quite barbarous : also the distinctions of texture which would make
the dress more intelligible are not rendered.   The costume is almost identical
with that we have been examining, save for a difference of cut in the
lower border of the coat and the arrangement of the bashlyk which has
bands covering the mouth[4].   The man carries a bundle of rods in his
right hand.   These last details recall the regulations of the Avesta for
preventing the breath from defiling the sacred flame and the *barsom*
carried by the Mage.   Therefore the presumption is that we have before
us a Persian : but he is wearing a nomad's clothes, and his dagger makes
clear for us the arrangement of the typical Scythic daggers with their
side projections.

[1] ch. XI. § 12; *KTR.* p. 49, f. 56=*CR.* 1876,
pl. II. I.
[2] p. 192, f. 84; *Sm.* III. p. 139, f. 71, and pl.
XVIII. 2.

[3] p. 255, f. 174, Dalton, No. 48.
[4] Cf. the "Alexander" sarcophagus and the
Pompeii Mosaic of Issus (Mus. Borb. VIII. pl.
XXXVI. sqq.).

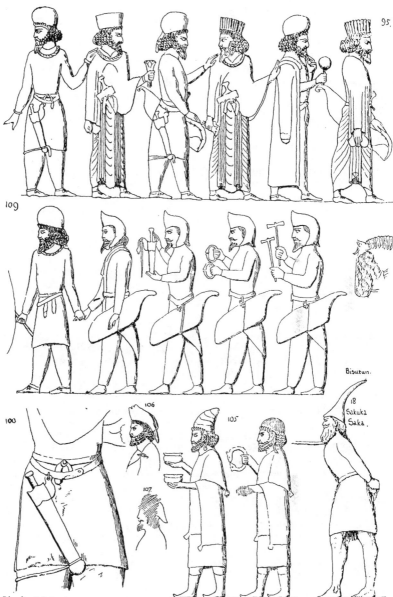

Flandin et Coste. Palace N°2. Persepolis.

FIG. 12.   Persian bas reliefs shewing Nomad Costume.

Bisutun and Persepolis.

On the bas relief of Bisutun we have a Saka labelled as such in
the inscription of Darius: unfortunately being a prisoner he is without
his weapons and his national dress.   The only thing distinctive about
him is the very tall cyrbasia upon his head.   He is fully bearded[1].

The bas reliefs of Persepolis representing court ceremonies shew rows
of figures[2] wearing flowing robes with full sleeves and skirts, high headdresses, daggers with curious broad guards stuck into their belts, and laced
shoes, alternating with men wearing the nomad costume, close-fitting coat
and trousers, round-topped bashlyk without lappets, the Scythic dagger with
its complicated attachment to the belt and shoes tied with a thong round
the ankle.   Both have the same way of wearing their hair, the same
torques, and the same bow-cases decidedly unlike the Scythic gorytus.
They are taking the same part in guarding the king, introducing persons
to whom audience was to be granted.   The difference of costume must
go back to an original difference of race, but what relation they bear to
each other we cannot say.   It has been suggested that we have Medes
and Persians, or that one sort are nomads hired to be a palace guard like
the Turks at the court of the Caliphs.

At Persepolis, besides the men in nomad costume that appear to be
palace guards, we have on the same platform which supported the Great
Hall of Xerxes representations of strange peoples bringing tribute.   Those
for instance on No. 105 have pointed caps, and are carrying cups such as
are used for kumys: also they have rings or bracelets quite similar to
Scythic types (cf. p. 257, f. 178, No. 140 of the Oxus Treasure) and lead
a cart with them.   On No. 109 we have bowmen with metal objects, hammers
and rings and daggers of the Scythic form.   They are clothed in a kind
of coat cut away in front and long behind, which irresistibly recalls Radloff's
description of the curious garment in the big tomb on the Katanda (v. inf.,
p. 248).   It just answers to his comparison of a dress-coat.

On the staircase of the Palace No. 3, or dwelling palace of Darius
or Artaxerxes, we have similar people, but this time they are leading
a sheep[3].   When the great king is represented on a throne supported by
various peoples, such figures occur again[4], so on the king's tomb to the
S.E. of the platform called No. 10[5].

The peoples on these monuments are unfortunately only to be distinguished by their attributes, by the animals that accompany them, and
by what we already know of Asiatic dress.   The inscriptions do not help
us to put names to them, but in some of these tribes we can surely see
the Sacae, whom Herodotus puts among the subjects of the great king,
and other northern tribes who were tributary or represented as such by
the Persian court.   Herodotus (VII. 60—66), in his review of the army
of Xerxes, gives most of the tribes of Iran and its northern borders
much the same clothes, that he says the Persians borrowed of the Medes;

[1] p. 59, f. 12=Flandin et Coste, *Voyage en Perse*, I. pl. 18.
[2] Ib.=II. pl. 95, 96, 97, 100.
[3] op. cit. III. pl. 119.
[4] op. cit. III. pl. 155.
[5] op. cit. III. pl. 164.

the differences seem mainly in the headdresses, tiaras among Medes, Persians and Hyrcanians, Cissii with mitrae, Bactrians and Arii much like the Medes, so too Parthians, Chorasmians, Sogdi, Gandarii and Dadicae, while Sacae had tall-pointed caps.

Another picture of Persians and nomads is on a cylinder and represents a Persian king stabbing a nomad whom he holds by the top of his hood. The attitude is exactly the familiar one of the king slaying a lion or other beast. The barbarian is trying to hit the king with a battle axe. He is bearded, wears a short sleeved coat, trousers and a gorytus just like the men on the Kul Oba vase. Behind each protagonist is an archer shooting. The bows are the typical Asiatic, sigma-shaped, asymmetrical bow suitable for use on horseback. Above all the symbol of the deity lends its countenance to the king's victory.

FIG. 13. Persian Cylinder. Combat between Persians and Sacae. Rawlinson, *Five Great Monarchies*, IV. p. 321.

With all their differences these costumes are essentially the same, the costume which climate and custom force on the nomad, and it is probable that the Persians borrowed it from their nomad neighbours or kept it from the time that they were nomads themselves.

A later form of the same costume and especially of the headdress as worn by the Parthians, descendants of conquering nomads, is shewn on the annexed coin.

FIG. 14. Coin of Tiridates II. of Parthia B.C. 248—210, shewing pointed bashlyk encircled by diadem and with lappets below. R. Arsaces as Apollo on the Omphalos with hood, trousers and asymmetrical bow. Dalton, *Treasure of the Oxus*, p. 48, f. 32 b.

Women's Dress.

Of the women's dress we have only a vague idea. In Kul Oba and Chertomlyk were found identical plaques with the figure of a woman seated holding a handled mirror and a nomad standing before her and drinking out of a horn[1]. Over her dress she wears a cloak with hanging sleeves and her head is covered with a kerchief.

The dancers figured on a plaque from Kul Oba[2] are Greek and go back to Scopas (compare the dancers on the tiara from Ryzhanovka[3]) though their kerchiefs rather recall the Scythic fashion.

The best view of women's dress is that furnished by the three-cornered gold plaque from the headdress of the queen at Karagodeuashkh[4]. On this we see the queen herself sitting as it were in state with a woman attendant on

[1] p. 158, f. 45 = *ABC.* XX. 11. Front view, indistinct. Ib. = *ASH.* XXX. 20.
[2] p. 197, f. 90 = *ABC.* XX. 5.
[3] *Sm.* II. pl. XVI. 3.
[4] p. 218, f. 120 = *Mat.* XIII. iii. 1.

each side behind her and a man on each side in front.   Unluckily the plaque
has suffered much from the falling in of the tomb's roof, but we can still make
out that the lady wore a tall conical headdress such as that to which this
very plaque belonged.   From it a kind of Veil fell down behind ; the whole
effect being like that of the medieval headdress in which fairies are often
represented.   Her dress can hardly be seen as she is almost shrouded in
a great mantle adorned with dots, which may well represent gold plaques.
Some such headdress belonged to the woman in Kul Oba, and about the
woman's head at Chertomlyk could be traced a line of gold plaques (pp. 161
and 158, f. 45 = *ASH*. xxx. 16) forming a triangle with a rounded top and lines
going down thence to the hands, the vestiges of a kind of mitre with long
lappets[1].   She was covered with a purple veil of which traces were found.

Gold Plaques and Jewelry.

Both men and women among the Scythians adorned their clothes with
the gold plaques so often referred to.   Poorer people wore bronze instead
(e.g. the grooms at Chertomlyk), but gold is the characteristic material.   The
Hermitage is said to possess over 10,000 specimens.   The plaques were
sewn on to the clothes chiefly along borders and seams, more rarely as it
were scattered over the field.   They were of every shape and size, and bore
figures of men, animals, and conventional patterns, such as palmettes, rosettes,
and the pyramids of grains, called wolf's teeth.   Enough specimens to shew
their extraordinary variety are illustrated below (e.g. pp. 158, 178, 184, 192,
197, 208, etc., cf. p. 157).   Of a special character are the strips which seem
to have chiefly adorned headgear.   They seem rather of barbarian work, being
less adaptable than the plaques, and therefore made on the spot[2].   The plaques
are mostly found on the floors of tombs, not *in situ* but fallen from clothes
that have rotted away hanging on pegs in the walls.

Solid gold also the nomads, both men and women, wore in every
conceivable ornament.   Herodotus mentions this of the Massagetae (i. 215),
and Strabo of the Aorsi (xi. v. 8).   Besides the high headgear of which we
have already spoken, the women wore frontlets of gold mostly of Greek
workmanship, and these were used also to support temple ornaments which
took the place of earrings.   This fashion is best illustrated by the finds at
Kul Oba[3].   So at Ryzhanovka[4] and Darievka[5].

Earrings were also largely worn.   Men it seems only wore one[6], women
had sometimes several pairs buried with them, at Kul Oba for instance;
where the finest pair may be either true earrings or temple ornaments[7],
Ryzhanovka[8], Karagodeuashkh[9], Chertomlyk, Zvenigorodka[10].

This magnificence is still more marked in the torques and necklaces.
The latter, as indeed most of the women's adornments, are chiefly of Greek

---

[1] Cf. *ASH*. ii. p. 107, *KTR*. p. 263.

[2] e.g. p. 157, f. 44.   Alexandropol, *KTR*. p. 252,
f. 231 = *ASH*. xv. 3.   Chertomlyk, *KTR*. pp. 309,
310, ff. 269--271 = *CR*. 1864, v. 3--5.   Darievka,
Sm. ii. pl. X. XI.   Axjutintsy, inf. p. 182.

[3] p. 195, f. 88 = *ABC*. ii. 3, xix. 1, 4, 5, including the well-known Athena heads.

[4] *Sm*. ii. xvi. 3, xvii. 1, xviii. 14.

[5] *Sm*. ii. X. 3.

[6] p. 237, f. 147 = *Vettersfelde*, I. 5, e.g. Chertomlyk, *KTR*. p. 264.

[7] p. 195, f. 88 = *ABC*. xix. 5.

[8] p. 178 = *Sm*. ii. xvi. 4 and 5.

[9] p. 217, f. 119 = *Mat*. xiii. pl. iii. 6 and 7,
iv. 10.

[10] *KTR*. p. 290.

work, or imitations of it, and present some of the most wonderful examples of goldsmith's skill that exist. The simplest are such plain circlets as that from Axjutintsy[1], just a thick gold wire, or with nothing more than simple grooves or other mouldings, as at Karagodeuashkh[2]: or a wire adorned at the end with rude animals' heads, such as one found in Stavropol government[3], at Akhtanizovka on the Taman Peninsula where the wire went round the neck several times and made a kind of collar opening by hinges[4], and at Volkovtsy[5]. At Chertomlyk were gold, silver-gilt and bronze torques, the latter for grooms and servants, the former with lions at the ends or all along the hoop for the king and queen[6]. At Alexandropol a servant had a bronze hoop[7]. Better work, purely Greek, we find on the Salgir in the Crimea[8], and at Karagodeuashkh[9]; here the ends represent a lion fighting a boar. The best known specimens are those from Kul Oba[10]. Of these, the first, belonging to the king, ended in the excellent representations of nomad horsemen, to which we have already referred. The second belonged to the queen, and ends in lionesses. Of the third only the ends remain, adorned with a lion's head and bands of enamelled palmettes. So the warrior at Vettersfelde had a gold neck-ring (III. 3). The composition of these rings ending in lions' heads seems to be a Greek execution of the Iranian design exemplified in the collar and bracelets found at Susa by J. de Morgan[11]. In feeling near akin to the Iranian, are two neck-hoops from Salamatino (Sarátov)[12], in style they are almost identical with the Oxus Treasure.

Besides the solid gold hoops we have wonderful gold plaits and chains and necklaces, as at Karagodeuashkh[13] and Ryzhanovka[14], but they do not equal those found in purely Greek graves as the Great Bliznitsa on the Taman Peninsula and at Theodosia[15].

Even more varied than the neck rings are the bracelets. At Kul Oba the king had in the sphinx bracelets on his wrists a pair of the most beautiful personal ornaments existing[16]. But even here under the Greek execution lies an Iranian base; they recall the armilla published by Mr Dalton[17]. More purely Greek are his queen's armlets with griffins and deer, and that with Peleus and Thetis from above his right elbow[18].

Very pleasing are those from Karagodeuashkh[19] ending in sea horses. A pair found near the station Golubínskaja in the country of the Cossacks of the Don, just where it approaches the Volga, is interesting as offering a close analogy both in design and colouring of enamel to armlets from the Oxus Treasure. Simplest of all are mere wire circlets, such as those from Ryzhanovka, in bronze[20] and in silver[21]. Unusual in type are the ribbon-like

[1] *Sm.* II. xxii. 1.
[2] *Mat.* XIII. v. 1 and viii. 3.
[3] *CR.* 1897, p. 72, f. 167.
[4] p. 215, f. 118=*CR.* 1900, p. 107, f. 210.
[5] p. 184, f. 77=*Sm.* III. p. 83, f. 23.
[6] p.158,f.45=*ASH.* XXXVII. 2,7; cf. pp. 157, 161.
[7] *KTR.* p. 246.
[8] *CR.* 1891, p. 78, f. 58.
[9] p. 217, f. 119=*Mat.* XIII. pl. II. 7—9.
[10] p. 202, f. 97, p. 197, f. 90=*ABC.* VIII. 1, 2, 3.
[11] p. 271, f. 187. Cf. *La Délégation en Perse du Ministère de l'Instruction Publique* 1897 à 1902, Paris, 1902, pp. 95 and 97, *Mémoires*, T. VIII. (1905),

Pl. IV. v., and E. Pottier, *Gazette des Beaux Arts*, 1902, p. 32.
[12] *CR.* 1902, p. 139, ff. 246, 247.
[13] p. 217, f. 119=*Mat.* XIII. iv. 4, 3 and 1.
[14] p. 179, f. 74, ib. p. 37, f. 7=*Sm.* II. xvi. 9.
[15] ch.XI.§ 12,XII.=*CR.*1869, I. 13; *ABC.* XII[a]. 3,4.
[16] p. 199, f. 92=*ABC.* XIII. 1.
[17] *Archaeologia*, vol. LVIII. (Oxus Treasure, No. 116).
[18] p. 199, f. 92=*ABC.* XIII. 2 and 3.
[19] p. 217, f. 119=*Mat.* XIII. iii. 8 and 9.
[20] *Sm.* II. xvii. 5 and 6.
[21] ih. xviii. 8 and 12.

armlets found *in situ* at Volkovtsy and Axjutintsy [1]. The Vettersfelde warrior had his arm ring [2].

As well as his Greek armlets the Kul Oba king had almost plain native ones in pale gold or electrum [3], one large pair worn upon his upper arm and four as a defence below the elbow.

Finger rings were also much worn. For instance at Chertomlyk the queen wore ten rings in all, one on each finger; the king seems to have

FIG. 15. *CR.* 1890, p. 118, f. 71. Golubinskaja Stanitsa. Golden bracelet with enamel inlay.

had two, and the servants mostly one each [4]. They occur of all materials, gold, silver, glass, iron, copper, even stone. Good specimens were found at Karagodeuashkh [5] and Ryzhanovka [6]. Three of these are specially interesting as having bezels set with Greek coins whose aesthetic beauty was appreciated in this way (Pl. v. 16).

Besides these regular species of adornments, the nomads had a taste for amulets or charms as we call them. Besides various pendants there have occurred animals' teeth, a natural gold nugget, a flint implement at Vettersfelde (I. 3), an Assyrian engraved cylinder [7], even a rough stone (Ryzhanovka).

Those who could not afford the precious metals used beads, either home-made of clay or stone, or of glass imported from the Mediterranean area; even cowrie shells found their way so far north [8]. The best coloured plate shewing the variety of beads found in S. Russia is given by Count Bobrinskoj [9]. As materials, he enumerates paste, rock crystal, shells, stones, carnelians, gold, silver, amber, birds' and beasts' claws and teeth [10], and there seems to be also Egyptian porcelain. The glass beads comprise most of

[1] v. p. 184, f. 77, No. 425 = *Sm.* III. p. 85, f. 24; *Rep. Hist. Mus. Moscow*, 1906. I. 17.
[2] Furtwängler, I. 4.
[3] v. p. 197, f. 90 = *ABC.* XXVI. 3.
[4] Lappo-Danilevskij, *Sc. Antiquities*, p. 420.
[5] *Mat.* XIII. iii. 10 and 11.

[6] *Sm.* II. xviii. 5, 9, 10, 11, 13.
[7] p. 193, f. 85 = *Sm.* I. p. 77.
[8] *Sm.* II. v. 1.
[9] *Sm.* III. pl. xiii.
[10] p. 208, f. 106 below = *CR.* 1877, ii. 13, No. iv. of VII Brothers.

the ordinary types. Further south corals have been found. The annexed cuts offer as good a representation as can be given without colour.

Рис. 44. ¹/₄.   Рис. 45. ¹/₁.   Рис. 46. ¹/₁. Рис. 47.¹/₁. Рис.48.¹/₁. Рис.49.¹/₁. Рис. 50.¹/₁.   Рис. 51.¹/₁.

p29. Glass and Agate Beads from near Besleneevskaja Stanitsa. (Kuban') CR.1895

Рис. 52.¹/₁. Рис.53. ¹/₁. Рис.54.¹/₁. Рис.55.¹/₁. Рис. 56.¹/₁.   Рис. 57.¹/₁.   Рис.58.¹/₁.   Рис.59.¹/₁. Рис. 60.¹/₁. Рис.61.¹/₁.

FIG. 16.

Mirrors.

To admire themselves in all this finery the Scythian women had metal mirrors.   These were of three types, that of the ordinary Greek mirror with handle in the same plane; that with merely a loop behind; and that in which the loop has been exaggerated to make a kind of handle at right angles to the plane of the back of the mirror[1].

In almost every rich tomb in which a woman was buried, there has been found a mirror.   The first type is far the most frequent and corresponds to the common Greek type (there are none like the round handleless Greek mirrors in boxes), and many are of actual Greek work or direct imitations of it: we even get, as in Kul Oba, Scythian patching of Greek objects.   It is a mirror of this type that is held by the woman on the plaque already mentioned (p. 158, f. 45).   Three very simple examples are figured by Count Bobrinskoj[2], one has a bone, and one a bronze[3] handle nailed on to the bronze disk.   Equally clumsy in a different material is that from Kul Oba, on which a gold handle of native work has been added to the Greek disk of bronze[4].

Greek mirrors of this type early found their way into Scythia, for some specimens (ch. xi. § 10) belong to the archaic period.   Those of which the execution is purely Scythic, shew a reminiscence of Greek models, not merely in the general shape, but in the division of the handles into panels that were filled with characteristically Scythic beast forms[5].   More often there has been worked out an arrangement thoroughly in the spirit of Minusinsk art, the end of the handle being adorned by an animal in the

---

[1] Cf. Bobrinskoj, *Sméla*, III. p. 67, and K. Schumacher, Barbarische und Griechische Spiegel, *Zeitschrift für Ethnologie*, XXIII. (1891), p. 81 sqq.; J. Hampel, Skythische Denkmäler aus Ungarn in *Ethnologische Mittheilungen aus Ungarn*, Bd IV. (1895), Heft 1; P. Reinecke, Die skythischen Alterthümer im mittleren Europa, *Zeitschrift für Ethnologie*, XXVIII. (1896), p. 1, and Ueber einige Beziehungen der Alterthümer China's zu denen des skythisch-sibirischen Völkerkreises, *Zt. f. Ethn.* XXIX. (1897), p. 141.

[2] *Sm.* II. xiv. 5, and I. X. 2.
[3] *Sm.* III. p. 95, f. 44.
[4] p. 201, f. 95 = *ABC.* XXXI. 7.
[5] Cf. *Arch. Anz.* 1904, p. 22, f. 1; Khanenko, op. cit. XLVI. 351 b, and those from Hungary, Pokafalva, and Transylvania, Olach Zsakoda, Hampel, l.c. ff. 25—29.

round (bear or wolf, v. p. 178, f. 73) or two beak-heads facing (p. 191, f. 83, No. 351, cf. daggers, p. 249, ff. 169—171, v. p. 266). Thoroughly Scythic are the mirrors with a loop at the back (v. p. 190, f. 82, No. 237). These are mostly smaller and may have developed from the phalerae, from which it is hard to distinguish them. In Siberia and in China, to which this type penetrated, the loop is sometimes in the shape of an animal, and this form was exaggerated in the west, so that the animal is disproportionately raised [1] or the loop develops into a handle at right angles to the plane of the mirror [2].

Bows, Bow-cases and Arrows.

The most characteristic weapon of the nomads was the bow. Owing to its material we cannot depend on actual remains for exact knowledge of it. Two bows have been found in S. Russia [3], one at Michen near Elisavetgrad, the other near Nymphaeum, but they were not in such perfect preservation as to give us an exact idea of the shape. But we have many representations and descriptions by ancient authors. The Scythic bow is compared by Agathon [4] to the letter sigma, probably the four stroke one, not the C, which is suggested by Ammianus Marcellinus (XXII. viii. 37) who likens it to the waning moon. The shape of the Black Sea is continually compared to that of a Scythic bow, the Crimea representing the handle with unequal curves on each side bending round to the string represented by Asia Minor [5]. This agrees fairly well with the bows on the Kul Oba vase (p. 200, f. 93), especially that which the archer is stringing, and with those on the coins of Olbia and Cercinitis (Pl. III. 4, IX. 1), and of Leucon of Panticapaeum (Pl. VI. 16). Compare the bow held by Arsaces, who on the Parthian coins takes the place of the Seleucid Apollo on the Omphalos [6]. The asymmetry is best seen in a bow wielded by an Amazon, and quite possibly copied from a Scythian bow [7]. It is harder to judge of its shape when it is represented at the moment of aim being taken, as on the handle of the sword from Chertomlyk (p. 163, f. 51), and on the plaque with two nomads shooting in opposite directions [8]. More often we see it represented in the gorytus or combined bow-case and quiver as on the Kul Oba vase, and the coins of Olbia [9].

This complicated curve of the bow made it more convenient to use on horseback (the Scyths are called ἱπποτοξόται, yet we have no view of one; on pp. 278, 279, ff. 201, 203 we have Siberians), and allowed it to be carried comfortably in the gorytus. The modern Tartar bow seems the very counterpart of the Scythic, and the bows pictured by Chinese artists in the hands of the Hiung-nu are also similar. These latter had bow-case and quiver separate, and the Manchu bow-cases in the British Museum are quite unlike the Scythic ones in all details of their construction [10].

[1] v. p. 193, f. 85 top = *Sm.* III. xii. 3.
[2] Cf. p. 193, f. 85 bottom, *Sm.* III. p. 113, f. 62 = Khanenko, op. cit. LVII. o.
[3] Lappo-Danilevskij, *Sc. Antiqq.*, p. 434.
[4] ap. Athenaeum, p. 454 d.
[5] Strabo, II. v. 22.
[6] p. 61, f. 14. *BM. Cat. Parthia*, Artabanus I., pl. v. 4—7; Mithradates II., pl. VI. 1, etc.
[7] Gerhard, *Auserlesene Vasenbilder*, II. ccxxii.

Cf. snake drawing bow on ring stone, ch. XII. = *CR.* 1861, VI. 8, and the Persian's bow on p. 54, f. 8.
[8] p. 197, f. 90. *KTR.* p. 135, f. 150 = *ABC.* xx. 6.
[9] Cf. a little model of a bow and bow-case, p. 244, f. 152 = F. R. Martin, *L'âge du bronze au Musée de Minoussinsk*, XXX. 15, where the asymmetry is well shewn.
[10] p. 96, f. 27. Certainly the Scythic bow was not a simple or "self" bow, but composite. For

These combined quivers and bow-cases (γωρυτός) were peculiar to the Scythic culture, except in so far as they were borrowed by neighbouring nations. They were worn on the left side. The wooden model from a tomb at Kerch supplements the numerous representations on vases (Kul Oba, p. 201, f. 94) and gold plates (Kul Oba, p. 197, f. 90, Axjutintsy, small

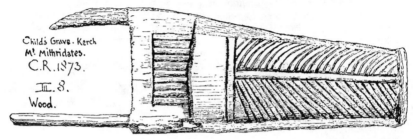

Child's Grave. Kerch
M! Mithridates.
C.R.1873.
Ⅲ.8.
Wood.

FIG. 17.

barrow, p. 182, f. 75 *bis*), on the coins of Olbia (Pl. III. 4), a Greek grave-stone from Chersonese (ch. XVII.), and frescoes from Kerch (ch. XI. § 4), also on a cylinder representing the Great King fighting Sacae (p. 61, f. 13), whereupon the latter only have them. The Persians, as shewn on the bas reliefs (p. 59, f. 12), seem to have had simple bow-cases, and of such we have a model in bronze from Minusinsk (p. 244, f. 152). All these enable us to recognise as gorytus-covers three richly repoussé gold plates (from Chertomlyk p. 164, f. 53, Karagodeuashkh p. 221, f. 125, in very bad preservation, and from Iljintsy[1], district of Lipovets, government of Kiev, a replica of that from Chertomlyk), upon which the adaptation of Greek ornament to Scythic form is specially remarkable (v. p. 284). Less rich was the specimen from Volkovtsy (v. p. 183) of leather with five small gold plates instead of one complete cover. Such plates are the dots in the pictures named above. The quivers were likewise made of leather and adorned with gold plates, but we have none completely covered: at Axjutintsy, large barrow, the deer took up most of the surface (p. 181, f. 75). The three-cornered gold plates found in the VII. Brothers (pp. 209, 211, 213, ff. 108, 111, 114), and one of similar shape

this type see H. Balfour, *Journal of Anthrop. Inst.* XIX. (1890), p. 220 ff., XXVI. (1896), p. 210 ff. The Chinese character Kung (inf. l.c.)=bow suggests the four-stroke sigma. An unsymmetrical Manchu bullet-bow from Mukden in the Pitt-Rivers Museum at Oxford exactly resembles the pictures of the Scythic bows.

As an indication of the range of such a bow we have an inscription from Olbia, published and discussed by von Stern (App. 6=*Trans. Od. Soc.* XXIII. p. 12=*IosPE.* IV. 460), making a prize shot to be 282 fathoms, about 660 yards, according to von Luschan (ibid.) too far for a self-bow but not unprecedented with a Turkish bow. Mr C. J. Longman gives 360 yards as the utmost for an English bow, and for a Turkish mentions 482 yards attained by Mahmud Effendi in London in 1795, and 972 yards shot by Sultan Selim in 1798 in the

presence of the British Ambassador to the Porte. Selim could shoot farther than any of his subjects (*Badminton Archery*, pp. 103 and 427). Major Heathcote, a practical archer, suggests to me that for use in war where only point blank shots could be effective, our self-bow would not be as inferior as appears from the above figures: also it did not require such careful protection from damp. Cf. also F. von Luschan, "Über den antiken Bogen," in *Festschrift für Otto Benndorf*, 1898, pp. 189—197 ; and Zusammengesetzte und verstärkte Bogen in *Verhdl. d. Berlin. Anthrop. Ges.* XXXI., 1899, p. 221, as noticed in *Centralblatt für Anthropologie, Ethnologie und Urgeschichte*, v. (1900), p. 84.

The Persian bows were long (μεγάλα), Her. VII. 61, probably self-bows, the Sc. having their local (ἐπιχώρια) bows, c. 64.

[1] *Arch. Anz.* 1903, p. 83; *BCA.* III. App. p. 51.

from Karagodeuashkh (p. 219, f. 123), are usually explained as the ends of quivers. Their number need not surprise us, seeing that a common man-at-arms among the Mongols was required to have three quivers[1]. In each quiver were very many arrows. At Volkovtsy there were about 300, and similar numbers in those found in other tombs. Each Scyth could well spare an arrow-head for the king's monumental cauldron[2]. The arrows were made usually of reed, sometimes of wood, and were about 30 in. long (e.g. at Chertomlyk). The bow was about the same length. The gorytus is 49½ cm. and about a quarter of the bow sticks out beyond in the illustrations, so the whole would come to 60 or 70 cm., say 2 ft. 6 in. The fragments of the Nymphaeum bow made up about that amount. The breadth would be about 30 cm., say a foot[3].

The arrow-heads are of stone, bone[4], iron, and especially of bronze. A few are the shape of small spear-heads with two cutting edges, but the typical shape is of triangular section. Count Bobrinskoj discusses the various types and illustrates a very varied series[5]. The triangular ones seem the latest, being furthest from the stone forms. Some have a small socket, others also a kind of barb or thorn on one side. Many a head has a hole for a sinew to bind it to the shaft. Doubtful traces of feathers have been found by Count Bobrinskoj[6]. In general arrow-heads are far commoner in Scythic graves than in those of any other people. Of the 200 found in Kul Oba[7] most were gilt, and the bronze is perhaps the hardest known[8].

Spear-heads were found in most of the well-known tombs, copper in the Round Barrow at Geremes, in Tsymbalka bronze, most often iron, e.g. the Stone Tomb at Krasnokutsk, Chertomlyk and Tomakovka. So, too, many in Count Bobrinskoj's district about Smêla. The shape is that of a leaf with a socket running up into a kind of midrib[9]. In the frescoes of the tomb of Anthesterius (ch. XI. § 4) the spears are painted of enormous length, 15 or 20 feet apparently, but at Chertomlyk was found one about 7 feet which is much more reasonable. They also used shorter darts, which are mentioned by the ancients, and are represented in the hand of the hare hunter[10] and on the Kul Oba vase. Apparently the weapons grew longer with time, for Tacitus[11] speaks of the great Sarmatian spears (*conti*).

Swords, Daggers and Sheaths.

At close quarters the Scythians used swords or daggers, less charac-teristic than the bows, but in themselves interesting for their form. Hardly any of them are worthy to be called swords. The longest specimen of the type comes from outside the ordinary region for Scythic finds. It is 113 cm. long, and its haft is 18 cm. It was found at

---

[1] De Plano Carpini ap. Rockhill, p. 261, n. 3.
[2] Her. IV. 81.
[3] Lappo-Danilevskij, *Sc. Antt.*, p. 434.
[4] p. 158, f. 45; p. 190, f. 82 = *Sm.* II. xiv. I.
[5] p. 190, f. 82 and *Sm.* III. p. 9 sqq. and pl. XVI. Cf E. Lenz, *BCA.* XIV. p. 63 sqq.
[6] *BCA.* XIV. p. 31.   [7] *ABC.* XXVII. II.

[8] ib. 20 gives an arrow nock. The shaft was of ash.
[9] v. p. 190, f. 82 and *Sm.* II. xxv. 6 and 7; III. ii. 8; *Collection Khanenko*, vol. II., pt 3, XXXviii. 164, 165.
[10] p. 197 = *ABC.* XX. 9.
[11] *Hist.* I. 79.

Aldoboly, in the county of Háromszék, Hungary[1]. To judge by their sheaths those from Kul Oba, Chertomlyk and the Don had blades about

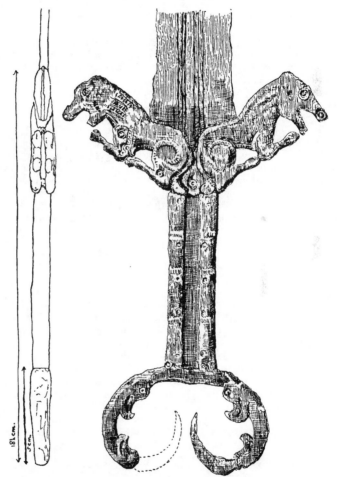

J. Hampel. Skythische Denkm. aus Ungarn. p. 19. f. 22. Iron Sword from Aldoboly (ce Háromszék) Total Length 113½ cm.

FIG. 18.

54 cm. long, and most specimens of daggers are shorter than this. Almost every Scythic grave has yielded one or more such daggers. The pommels

[1] J. Hampel, *Ethnologische Mittheilungen aus Ungarn*, Bd IV. (1895), Heft 1; Skythische Denk-   mäler aus Ungarn, f. 22 a, b, c.

are usually plain knobs, sometimes they have a pair of beak-heads or beasts curled round towards each other; these curls degenerating in the later and longer specimens into a likeness of the *antennae* of Hallstadt swords; but the make of the weapon is quite different[1]. The guard is narrow and heart-shaped, rarely projecting enough to be any protection. The hilts are often overlaid with gold as at Vettersfelde[2], Chertomlyk (both the king's great sword and three others, p. 163, ff. 51, 52), Kul Oba[3] and Karagodeuashkh where the blade was rusted right away[4]. In western Scythia about Kiev these swords have occurred very often, e.g. at Darievka[5], Axjutintsy[6], several at Volkovtsy and Prussy near Cherkassk[7], and one in the district of Dubno in Volhynia[8].

As we go west swords of this type grow steadily longer. The Siberian dagger is the short sword of Chertomlyk and the long sword of Aldoboly, which would almost merit the description in Tacitus of the swords of the Sarmatae[9]. This seems to correspond to an evolutionary progress, the Minusinsk daggers are certainly early compared with the Hungarian swords[10]: in between come one from Ekaterinenburg (54 cm.), from Izmailovo (Samara, 63 cm.) and another from near Samara (83 cm.)[11]. Such swords also made their way to the north to Ananjino and the basin of the Kama[12]. The above examples all have iron blades and hilts of iron, gold or bronze: a whole bronze dagger was found by chance at Kamenka, district of Chigirin[13]. The all bronze dagger is rare in Europe though common in Siberia[14].

This type of sword had a special sheath to suit it, marked in the older examples by special adaptation to receive the heart-shaped guard, in others by a special tip or chape made separately and often lost (it was this separate tip (μύκης) that caused the death of Cambyses, by coming off as he jumped on his horse and allowing his dagger to run into his thigh[15]) and a projection on one side by which it was hung to the belt[16] in the manner shewn by the Oxus plaque (p. 255, f. 174), and the Persepolitan reliefs (p. 59, Nos. 95, 100). The sheaths have of course perished, but they were often covered with gold plates which enable us to judge of their shape. An early plate of this type forms part of the Oxus Treasure (p. 255, f. 174). It is in very bad preservation, having been snipped up into small pieces, some of which as well as its tip are lost. It is decorated with hunting scenes in which the king appears under the familiar winged disk, all in a rather mechanical style, bearing the same relation to Assyrian bas reliefs that the Chertomlyk bow-case bears to Greek marbles. The costume of the figures is rather

[1] p. 189, f. 81=*Sm.* I. vii. 2 and 5; but cf. E. Lenz, *BCA.* XIV. p. 62.
[2] Furtwängler, III. 5.
[3] *ABC.* XXVII. 10. Cf. ibid. 9 from the otherwise Greek tomb of Mirza Kekuvatskij.
[4] *Mat.* XIII. v. 4.
[5] *Sm.* II. xv. 7.
[6] *Sm.* II. xxii. 4.
[7] *Coll. Khanenko*, Vol. II. Part 2, pl. II., III.; Part 3, pl. XXXVIII. 166.
[8] ib. 167.
[9] *praelongos, Hist.* I. 79.
[10] e.g. others from Pilín, Bereg and Neograd. Hampel, op. cit. ff. 16—18.

[11] Béla Pósta in Gr. Eugen Zichy, *Dritte Asiatische Forschungsreise*, Bd III., Budapest, 1905, p. 102, f. 57.
[12] v. p. 258, f. 179. D. A. Anuchin, On certain forms of the oldest Russian swords, *Trans. VI. Russian Arch. Congress*, Odessa, 1886, Vol. I., p. 235 sqq.; very late one 3 ft long from Koshibeevo, Tambov Government, A. A. Spitsyn, Antt. of Kama and Oka, *Mat.* XXV. pp. 11, 59, pl. XII. 3.
[13] p. 189, f. 81, *Sm.* III. xi. 5.
[14] p. 243, f. 150=*Mat.* III. vii. 10; p. 249, f. 169.
[15] Her. III. 64.
[16] The bow-case being worn on the left side, the sword was on the right, not a common practice.

Scytho-Persian than Assyrian, and the patterns which mark the structure of the sheath are distinctly queer, suggesting a barbarization of Greek models. Doubts have been cast on its authenticity, but it shews a combination of motives upon which a forger would hardly hit, and which may be explained by our supposing its maker to have been a craftsman trained in the Assyrian traditions and working for a nomad.

This view is supported by the analogies presented by the Melgunov dagger and sheath (pp. 171, 172, ff. 65—67) which, being of the same Scythic shape, is regarded as being a product of Assyrian work of the early vith century B.C. The blade was 43 cm. long. The illustrations make a long description unnecessary. At the tip were two lions rampant facing each other, along the sheath eight monsters with fishes for wings shooting towards the hilt. The fifth from the tip is lost on both sides, but his tail appears on that not shewn. At the hilt end is the familiar composition of two figures and the tree of life. The projection for hanging has a typical Scythic deer, otherwise the workmanship seems purely Assyrian.

In 1903 a very close parallel to this hitherto unparalleled decoration was found by Mr D. Schulz at Kelermes near Majkop. The description of the sheath sounds identical, but the motive of two beardless winged genii adoring a tree at the upper end is repeated upon the guard, while the grip is adorned with a geometrical design. The work is finer than in Melgunov's example[1].

Another sheath, important for its forming a link between these and the later Siberian style, was found in 1901 near the Don[2].

Of Greek work we have such plates from Vettersfelde (p. 237, f. 146), Kul Oba (p. 203, f. 98) and Chertomlyk (p. 164, f. 53). For the same kind of dagger quite a different sheath, without the side projection, is one from Romny (government of Poltava, p. 186, f. 79, No. 461).

Another type of smaller dagger and sheath, apparently of Greek work, occurs at Tomakovka[3] and Vettersfelde[4].

As to the custom of setting up a sword and worshipping it[5], the attendant circumstances seem rather to suggest its belonging to some Thracian tribe in western Scythia within reach of trees. The ascription of the same custom to the Alans by Ammianus Marcellinus (XXXI. c. ii. 23) is of a piece with his wholesale borrowing of details from Herodotus to adorn his account of Sarmatia. That Attila regarded the finding of a sword as a good omen of his warlike might does not prove that the Huns actually worshipped a sword as the incarnation of the god of war[6]. However, Geza Nagy[7] cites something of the sort among the Bolgars, the Voguls, the Tunguz and the ancestors of the Magyars. Elsewhere (VII. 64) Herodotus says of the Sacae, whom he identifies with the Scyths, that they had daggers ἐγχειρίδια, though in IV. c. 70 he speaks of their putting an *acinaces* into the bowl from which they are to drink for the ceremony of blood brotherhood. But even acinaces need not mean a very long sword, it is usually applied to the Persian sword, which is represented as short

[1] v. p. 222 and B. V. Pharmacovskij in *Arch. Anz.* 1904, p. 100. This find is not yet illustrated.
[2] v. p. 270, f. 186, Kieseritsky, *Arch. Anz.* 1902, p. 45 f.
[3] p. 158, f. 45 = *ASH.* XXVI. 16.
[4] Furt. III. 2.
[5] Her. IV. 62.
[6] Jordanes, *Get.* c. XXXV., quoting Priscus, fr. 8, Müller, *FHG.* IV. p. 91.
[7] op. cit. p. 49 sqq.

on the reliefs of Persepolis.   Had he meant an ordinary sword he would
have said ξίφος.   The archaeological evidence therefore exactly bears out
the natural inference that the Scyths used short swords, hardly more than
daggers, and similar to those of the Persians.

Besides swords or daggers we find knives in Scythic tombs, seemingly
knives for general use rather than weapons.   The best example of the type
is that from Kul Oba[1], which has an ornamented gold handle and a steel
blade.   The whole is not unlike a modern table-knife.   Usually, as in the
country about Kiev, they have plain bone handles[2].   Two similar ones were
found at Chertomlyk.   Near Zhurovka was found an iron knife, quite
recalling the Minusinsk "cash" knife[3].

Axes.

Herodotus further speaks of the Scyths as having axes, sagaris; they
formed part of the equipment of the Sacae of the Persian host (VII. 64)
and were used with the sword in the ceremony of blood brotherhood.   The
Greeks mostly thought of these as double axes, and it is such that we find
in the hands of Amazons and of barbarians, vaguely meant for Scythians,
on fantastic works of art.   On the coins of Olbia (Pl. III. 4) we find weapons
with one cutting edge, and on the other side of the handle a curious projection
whose nature it is somewhat hard to make out.   On coins of Cercinitis and on
the plate from Axjutintsy (p. 182, f. 75 *bis*) a seated figure holds such an axe.
Moreover, actual finds do not help us much to determine the real shape of
Scythian axes.   It may be noted that most of these finds and the coins likewise come from western Scythia, and it is in the western legend that special
mention is made of axes[4].

Earliest in type are axe heads from west Russia about Smêla, all
unfortunately chance finds.   They include a very simple one with the
beginnings of flanges[5], and three socketed specimens, distinguished from
the ordinary European types by a double loop[6].   Such an one was also
found at Olgenfeld[7] (Don Cossacks).   Much the same types extend across
to Siberia (p. 243, f. 151).   A single-looped axe occurred at Pavlovka in
Bessarabia[8].   Very modern looking iron axe-heads found by Mazaraki at
Popovka (Romny, government Poltava) seem to belong to late Sarmatian
times[9].   More characteristic is a bronze model axe-head from Jarmolintsy;
it is not known from what particular barrow.   The wrong end is in the
form of an animal's head.   Another such model[10] has the haft preserved.
These objects seem to have been symbolic and call to mind the model
picks from Siberia[11].   The real axes most like those on the coins are an
iron specimen from near Romny[12], and one in bad preservation from the
banks of the Salgir[13].   It is certainly remarkable that the axe is so rare in
characteristically Scythic graves, seeing that the Greeks evidently associated

[1] v. p. 197=*ABC.* XXX. 10.
[2] v. p. 190, f. 82, *Sm.* II. xv. 4 and 6.   Cf. I.
iv. 11.   Lappo-Danilevskij, *Sc. Antt.*, p. 425.
[3] *BCA.* XIV. p. 21, f. 52.   Cf. infra, p. 246.
[4] Her. IV. 5.   [5] *Sm.* I. vi. 1.
[6] ib. Nos. 3, 17, 18 = p. 190, f. 82.
[7] *CR.* 1891, p. 80, f. 59.   [8] Ib., p. 85, f. 64.
[9] *Sm.* II. xxv. I, 8, 14.
[10] *Sm.* II. xxiv. 20; III. xi. 1, both on p. 179,

f. 73.   A model axe to serve as check-piece of a
bit, ib. = *Sm.* II. iv. 12, and p. 214, f. 115 top.
[11] p. 242, f. 150; Radloff, *Sib. Ant.* I., pl. XVI.
and XVII.
[12] Khanenko, op. cit. II. Pt 3, pl. XXXVIII. 170.
[13] *CR.* 1891, p. 78, f. 56.   V. A. Gorodtsov
gives a survey of all types of axes found in Russia
in *Rep. Hist. Mus. Moscow*, 1906, pp. 94—135.

the Scyths with axes. At last in 1903 a really fine axe, overlaid with gold work in the Assyrian style, has been found at Kelermes[1].

Besides axes the Scyths may well have used maces, for instance that figured by Count Bobrinskoj[2], but as this was a chance find it cannot be certainly referred to the Scythic period[3]. The use of lassos by the Sauromatae is mentioned by Pausanias (I. 21. 5). Also sling stones have been found, but to whom they belonged is not clear[4].

To keep his weapons sharp the Scyth always carried with him a perforated whetstone, and no object is so characteristic of the Scythic graves. So de Plano Carpini (c. 17 § 6) says of the Tartars that they always carry a file in their quivers to sharpen their arrow-heads. Often the hone is set in gold, plain as at Karagodeuashkh[5] and Vettersfelde[6], more usually adorned with palmettes and other Greek patterns, as at Kul Oba[7], Chertomlyk, Salgir[8], and Zubov's barrows[9]. At Kostromskaja[10] and Grushevka (p. 177, f. 72) were found large slabs of stone which had served as whetstones.

Shields and Armour.

On the Kul Oba vase (pp. 200, 201, ff. 93, 94) we find long-shaped shields, oblongs with rounded corners. Hence Furtwängler has supposed that the Kul Oba deer and the Vettersfelde fish adorned shields of this shape. But at Kostromskaja, a deer very similar in outline to the Kul Oba deer was found attached to a thin round iron shield, 33 cm. across[11], and it is quite probable that this gives the size and form of the Kul Oba and Vettersfelde shields. Iron scales were found round the gold panther at Kelermes. In any case the shields were quite small and suitable for use on horseback. The oblong gold plate with a deer from Axjutintsy[12] may have been a shield ornament or may have decorated a quiver, inasmuch as there was a heap of arrows below it. The round gold saucer from Kul Oba[13] was certainly a drinking cup, not a shield boss. Stephani calls it a breast-plate. The oval shields with a lozenge boss borne by combatants on catacomb paintings and shewn on gravestones can hardly be called Scythic. (Ch. XI. §§ 3, 4.) Aelian[14] says that the Scythians covered their shields with Tarandus (reindeer) skin.

The only certain breast-plate which appears to have been made for a Scythian is that from Vettersfelde[15]. Another possible breast-piece is the silver relief of a golden-horned hind with her fawn and an eagle below found in the second of the Seven Brothers[16]. This seems to have belonged to a coat of scale armour from the same tumulus and it is clear that scale armour was characteristic of the nomads. Pausanias gives an interesting description of the Sarmatian armour, which seems to have struck him by its ingenuity (I. 21. 6). He and Ammianus Marcellinus (XVII. xii. 1) say

[1] Cf. p. 222 and *Arch. Anz.* 1904, II. p. 100.
[2] *Sm.* III. Xii. 1.
[3] Cf. a statuette at Odessa. Lappo-Danilevskij, op. cit. p. 432.
[4] L.-D. loc. cit.
[5] *Mat.* XIII. vii. 7.
[6] p. 237, f. 145 = Furt. II. 2.
[7] p. 197, f. 90 = *ABC.* XXX. 7.
[8] *CR.* 1891, p. 78, f. 57.
[9] *BCA.* 1902, I. p. 103, f. 31.

[10] p. 225, f. 128 = *CR.* 1897, p. 12, f. 44.
[11] Ibid. and p. 226, f. 129 = *CR.* 1897, p. 13, f. 46.
[12] p. 181, f. 75 = *Sm.* II. xxi. 3 and p. 163.
[13] p. 204, f. 99 = *ABC.* XXV., *KTR.* p. 85, f. 114.
[14] *De Animal.* II. 16. Thoraces, Pliny, *NH.* VIII. 124.
[15] p. 237, f. 145 = Furt. II. 1.
[16] v. p. 207, f. 105 = *KTR.* p. 195, f. 183 = *CR.* 1876, IV. 1.

that it was of horn or horses' hoofs. Of this material we have no specimens, but iron[1], bronze and bone are common enough. The scales were sewn on to a leathern or stuff backing, being arranged like feathers or "like the scales of a dragon. And if any one may not have seen a dragon he must have seen a green fircone." Apparently the backing was always present, the arrangement of the holes does not permit the scales being held in place by a system of thongs plaited and intertwined as in Japanese and Tibetan scale armour. But in the specimens at Oxford the scales are held so well by interlaced thongs that the backing might have been left out.

Examples in iron and bronze have been found in almost all the tombs of Scythic type, Kul Oba[2], Alexandropol[3], Seven Brothers[4], Krasnokutsk and Tsymbalka[5], Bezchastnaja[6]. From Popovka come scales of bone polished on one side. There are other such in the Historical Museum at Moscow. Bronze (Kul Oba) and iron (Alexandropol) scales were sometimes gilt.

Further defensive armour consisted in greaves which are always of purely Greek form and work; such were found at Chertomlyk. Unique are a cuirass and a pair of brassarts of vth century Greek workmanship found near Nicopol in 1902 : at Kul Oba were sollerets for the king's feet[7].

A helmet of pure Greek work from Galushchino (Kiev) is figured by Khanenko[8], and another Greek helmet was found at Volkovtsy.

The native helmet seems to have been covered with scales. Lenz (l.c. p. 61) figures what may be part of one, and they are well shewn on the frescoes of the catacombs at Kerch, whereon the people wear scale helmets and coats of scale armour. The latter were so long and awkward that the wearers had to sit their horses sideways. The Greeks wear shorter mail covered with some kind of surcoat[9]. The pictures are an instructive commentary on the remarks of Tacitus (l.c.) on the clumsy arms and mail of the Sarmatians, which rendered them helpless against the handy weapons of the Roman legionaries. The resemblance of this kind of mail to that worn by the Tartars and to that ascribed by the Chinese to the Hiung-nu need be insisted upon.

Horse trappings.

The horse trappings of the Scythians are perhaps the most characteristic of their belongings. In some cases the horse must have been most richly caparisoned, in a style that recalls the magnificence of Oriental equipment from the time of the Assyrians to the present day; especially the fashions of the Sassanian kings as pourtrayed on dishes and bas reliefs[10].

When Scythian horsemen are represented by the Greeks they seem equipped quite simply. Those on the Kul Oba torque[11] and the Hare

[1] Cf. Tacitus, *Hist.* I. 79.
[2] *ABC.* XXVII. 3—6.
[3] p. 158, f. 45 = *ASH.* XI. 13.
[4] *KTR.* pp. 273, 276, 277.
[5] ib. pp. 268, 270.
[6] ib. p. 278. Illustrations shewing the construction may be found in *ABC.*, l.c., *JHS.* 1884, XLVI. (from Kerch, now in the Ashmolean); inf. p. 231, f. 134 (Zubov's Farm); *CR.* 1897, p. 13, f. 45; Khanenko, op. cit. II., Part 2, pl. VII, Part 3, pl.

XXXIX.; *Sm.* III. viii. 15—21, cf. II. p. 173 ; v. inf. p. 188, f. 80. The subject is discussed by E. Lenz, publishing scales from Zhurovka, *BCA.* XIV. p. 54.
[7] *Archaeol. Chron. of S. Russia*, No. 1, 1903, p. 36, pl. v.; *ABC.* XXVIII. 9.
[8] op. cit. II. 2, pl. IX. 218.
[9] v. ch. XI. § 4 = *CR.* 1872, text pl. IX.; and = *KTR.* p. 211, f. 193.
[10] Cf. *KTR.* pp. 414, 416, ff. 372, 373.
[11] p. 202, f. 97 = *ABC.* VIII. 1.

hunter[1] seem even to be riding bareback; the very spirited sketch of a Scythian being dragged by the reins shews a saddle with some kind of saddle cloth cut into vandykes[2], but is very vague about the girths and so is no evidence as to stirrups.   On the Chertomlyk vase (p. 161, f. 48) we have a man hobbling a hog-maned pony with a simple saddle, with a girth and martingale but no crupper, and as it seems no stirrups, though a thong hanging from the girth looks rather like a stirrup leather.   So on the Kerch frescoes there seem to be no stirrups.   The bridles look much like modern ones, except that the cheek pieces are usually longer than nowadays and generally have three loops in them, probably for two pairs of reins and something answering to a curb.   The actual bit is made in two pieces like a modern snaffle.   They were sometimes made more effective with ports (ἐχῖνοι)[3].   The types of bits and cheek pieces (*Psalia*)[4] are the same right across to the upper Jenisei.   Horses slain to accompany their owner into the next world are mostly provided duly with all necessary harness, though in some cases the front row of a number of horses is so equipped, but not the back row, or there is a regular gradation from harness elaborately adorned with gold, to silver, bronze and iron bits.   There is said to be a Scythian saddle in the Hermitage, but its provenance does not seem clear[5].

When driven in carts, horses seem to have had much the same bridle, but no saddle.   There must have been some kind of collar, but our only view of a Scythian cart, that on the coin of Scilurus[6], shews neither this nor shafts.

Of the carts, especially the funeral cars, we have considerable remains, in the Alexandropol barrow a space seven feet long was covered with fragments of the car, at Krasnokutsk and Chertomlyk the pieces were piled in a heap about four feet long by three feet broad and two feet high.   Here were found fragments of tires, naves of wheels, nails and bolts, rivets and various strips of metal.   At Krasnokutsk there seem to have been eight wheels, but perhaps here were two cars, or else one so great as to compare with those described by Hippocrates or even Rubruquis, as used for carrying the dwelling houses.   In most cases the car had been broken up on the site of the tomb, at Karagodeuashkh so effectually that hardly anything was left[7].   Harness and cars were decorated with all imaginable metal plates of gold or bronze.   Especially important were the frontlets and cheek ornaments on the horses' heads.   The finest specimens of all are perhaps those found in Chmyreva barrow[8].

[1] p. 197, f. 90 = *ABC*. XX. 9.
[2] p. 204 D, f. 103 = *ABC*. LXXIX. 9.
[3] v. p. 214, f. 115 = *CR.* 1876, p. 133, VII. Brothers, No. VI.; Voronezhskaja, *CR.* 1903, p. 71, f. 152.
[4] Stephani calls them ψάλια, and this term is usual in Russian archaeological literature.   But E. Pernice (LVI. Winckelmann's Programm, Berlin, 1896, *Griechisches Pferdegeschirr*, p. 34, note 30) shews reason to believe that the cheek pieces (Seitenknebel) were called λύκοι, whereas ψάλιον was a vague word for a bit as a whole.   From the cheek pieces I would distinguish the cheek ornaments something in the shape of a lop-sided leaf, which with the long frontlets and round phalerae served merely for adornment (cf. the specimens from Volkovtsy, p. 185, f. 78, and others).   The elaboration of the bit and bridle was occasioned by the indocility of the northern horse.   Hence it is that much the same devices were needed over the whole of his area—whereas the thoroughbred was docile and obeyed a mere halter. (Cf. W. Ridgeway, *The Origin of the Thoroughbred Horse*, passim.) So too the Scythians alone among the ancients rode geldings: a practice which is described as originally Turkish. (Vámbéry, op. cit. p. 195.)
[5] v. Lappo-Danilevskij, op. cit. p. 456.
[6] p. 50, f. 4 = *KTR.* p. 175, f. 170.
[7] *Mat.* XIII. p. 50.
[8] p. 166, ff. 54, 55 = *KTR*. pp. 269—272, ff. 241—243, from Tsymbalka; *Sm.* III. p. 83 sqq., ff. 32,

Harness was also adorned by *phalerae*[1] chiefly at points where strap met strap. These may be plain or be decorated, sometimes with the most exquisite Greek work, as in those from Chmyreva. The plain phalerae are hardly to be distinguished from the looped mirrors, and may well have given rise to the type. Many of the plates of bronze and gold found in various graves seem to have decorated straps rather than garments; and the whole class of so-called Siberian gold plaques seems to have adorned horse trappings. The nomads have always loved to decorate these as well as themselves. As Herodotus says of the Massagetae (I. 215), they adorn their bits and bridles with gold phalerae.

Most interesting for their purely Scythic style are the cheek pieces. Something of the sort was necessary if only to prevent the bit being dragged sideways out of the horse's mouth: specimens which occur without trace of cheek pieces[2] may have had them of bone, or possibly some more effective arrangement of straps. They can be well seen in place in the specimens from Bobritsa near Kanëv[3], and others from the district of Verkhne-dnêprovsk[4]. At Bobritsa there were three bits, and the bridle of one was adorned with four big round silver plaques which came on the horse's neck, two smaller ones from above his mouth, two long-shaped ones for cheek ornaments and a frontlet 24 cm. long and more or less triangular, adorned with a gold crescent[5]. At Axjutintsy[6] the cheek pieces were still

FIG. 19. *BCA.* IV. p. 33, f. 7. Bronze bit from Constantinovo (Kiev Government).

attached to the bit itself, so at Constantinovo[7] and Zubov's Farm[8]. Separate cheek pieces of interesting style were found in most of the Seven Brothers[9], and at Nymphaeum in what seemed otherwise a Greek grave[10]. The silver trappings from Krasnokutsk are specially remarkable[11].

33, 35, 41, or better Khanenko, II. 2, pl. XXI.— XXIII. 401—403 = p. 185, f. 78 from Volkovtsy; *Sm.* III. p. 99, f. 56 = Khanenko, II. Pt 3, pl. LVI. from Berestnjagi; from Chmyreva, p. 169, ff. 60, 61, *CR.* 1898, pp. 27, 28, ff. 27, 30, 31, 37; a frontlet of the same type, but native style, from Alexandropol, p. 158, f. 45 = *ASH.* XIII. 6.

[1] Chmyreva, p. 168, ff. 58, 59. Bagaevskaja, *CR.* 1904, p. 125, ff. 217, 218. Janchekrak, *Rep. Hist. Mus. Moscow*, 1907, p. 13, pl. I.
[2] e.g. *Sm.* I. v. 10 and 12.
[3] *Sm.* III. xix. 4, and p. 128.

[4] p. 191, f. 83 = Khanenko, op. cit. Vol. II. Pt 3, pl. XLI. 334.
[5] *Sm.* III. pp. 127, 128, ff. 64—67.
[6] *Sm.* II. xxiii. 9 and 17.
[7] *BCA.* IV. 1902, p. 30, f. 1 and p. 33, f. 7.
[8] p. 231, f. 135, *BCA.* I. 1901, p. 98, f. 16.
[9] p. 214, f. 115, *KTR.* p. 50, ff. 57—62, p. 517, f. 476, p. 532, f. 478 = *CR.* 1876, pp. 124—126, 132—137, and 1877, p. 14.
[10] v. p. 215, f. 116, *KTR.* p. 52, ff. 63—65 = *CR.* 1877, pp. 230—2.
[11] pp. 167, 168, ff. 56, 57.

In the western district we find cheek pieces made of bone and various other patterned bone ornaments. These give us specimens of the Scythic beast style executed in a fresh material[1]. The most common pattern which has parallels in bronze[2] has a horse's head at one end and a hoof at the other. Others have drawings of horses, deer, or beaky birds, the flat shape necessitated by the weaker material giving a good space for a repeated pattern. There are also bone plaques in the same style. The varieties of metal cheek pieces are more numerous as the material allowed more license. Besides the horse-head and hoof pattern we get model axes[3], pick-axes, various monstrous creatures, and merely ornamental shapes[4].

For pictures of cheek pieces in use see the Issus Mosaic at Pompeii[5], giving a view of the general arrangement of the bridle, and the plaque of the Hare hunter from Kul Oba (v. p. 197, f. 90).

In the central tomb and in Chamber III. of Chertomlyk were found what appear to have been whip handles, and in Kul Oba there was one decorated with a gold band twisted round it spirally[6]. Herodotus speaks of the Scyths' whips in the legend of the slaves' trench (IV. 3). They were like the *nagajkas* the Cossacks have adopted from the Tartars.

"*Standards.*"

With the horse trappings seem to go various ornaments whose exact use is not clear. They all agree in having sockets for mounting them upon staves, and it has been suggested that they are all ornaments for elaborate funeral cars. Others have seen in some of them standards, in some maces or staves of office.

For instance, at Alexandropol there were found bronze sockets like those of spear heads crowned two of them with a kind of three-pronged fork with birds on the top of each

FIG. 20. *CR.* 1898, p. 80, f. 143. Bronze Standard from Bélozérka.

prong and bells in the birds' mouths[7], two pair with an oblong plate of pierced work with a griffin and a row of oves[8], also with pendant bells; others with simple birds[9], five with a kind of tree of life and little silver roundels hanging from each branch[10]; others had a winged female figure very rude in style[11]. Such are winged monsters from Krasnokutsk[12], birds, griffins

---

[1] pp. 188, 189, ff. 80, 81. *Sm.* I. xi., III. p. 76, vii., viii.; Khanenko, op. cit. Vol. II. P't 3, XLVIII.—LI., LXI. Bone knops from the Kuban (Kelermes); *CR.* 1904, p. 91, ff. 145—150, p. 94, ff. 155—160.

[2] *KTR.* p. 50, f. 57, from the Seven Brothers.

[3] p. 178, f. 73 = *Sm.* II. iv. 12, XXiv. 20.

[4] *Sm.* III. x. 11—14; Khan. II. 3, XLII.

[5] *Mus. Borb.* VIII. pl. XLII.

[6] Lappo-Danilevskij, op. cit. p. 459.

[7] p. 154, f. 41 = *ASH.* II. 1—3; *KTR.* p. 241, f. 218.

[8] *KTR.* p. 243, f. 220 = *ASH.* III. 1—4, IV. 1—4.

[9] *ASH.* II. 6—8.

[10] *KTR.* p. 243, f. 221 = *ASH.* V. 2.

[11] p. 154, f. 40 = *KTR.* p. 241, f. 217.

[12] *ASH.* XXIV. 1, 2, XXVI. 1—4.

from Slonovskaja Bliznitsa[1]. At Chertomlyk were four standards with lions[2], four with very much degraded deer[3], and some with birds like those from Alexandropol[4]. Pierced figures of a deer in a like style even more characteristically Scythic were found at Bêlozérka near Chmyreva barrow[5]. Arrian[6] speaks of the dragon standards of the Scythians, but these he describes as being of stuff, and they need bear no relation to the bronze griffins. Still these socketed figures may have crowned the standard staves, as we read of the T'u-küe, that a young wolf was upon the top of their standard, because they traced their descent from a wolf. Conceivably deer or griffins held the same place in the estimation of various Scythian tribes as the wolf among the early Turks. Certainly the re-occurrence of representations of these beasts, almost always in much the same attitude, seems due to something more definite than mere decorative fitness. The explanation that in the combats of griffins and deer it is a case of Panticapaeum versus Chersonese cannot of course commend itself in spite of the occurrence of these animals on the coins of the two cities (e.g. Pl. v. 13).

On the other hand these ornaments were found by the heap of fragments of the Alexandropol chariot, and with them were other pieces that could only have been nailed on to something, possibly the sides of the chariot. Most of them have something jingling about them, and this is a further point of resemblance to the other class of so-called maces of office. (In Russian *Bunchukí* or *Bulávy*, from the word for a Cossack Hetman's mace.) The general disposition of these is a socket merging into a kind of hollow bulb pierced by three-cornered openings and containing a metal ball which rattles: above all is the figure of an animal.

These Bunchuki occur chiefly in West Russia, but some come from the Kuban, from Majkop and Kelermes[7]. The best account of them is given by Count Bobrinskoj[8]. They have been found in Bessarabia, Rumania and Hungary as well as in Russia[9].

Hampel, following J. Smirnov, thinks that from their occurring in pairs or in sets of four these objects cannot be signs of rank, but that they probably adorned the tent upon the waggon. A pair found near Zhurovka shewed no signs of staves but were apparently riveted together in the middle like scissors[10]. Reinecke in a second paper[11] suggests a likeness to a kind of rattle figured in Kin-shih-so (Vol. II.), but there seems a want of intermediate links, and as no one knows what the Chinese object was for, it does not help matters much. The characteristic animal top is also lacking. In the Scythic examples this is always some sort of deer or bird of prey.

Here may be mentioned two bone or ivory knobs of Ionic work, both representing lions' heads[12]. The style is orientalising, the amber eyes being typical, and the date about the viith century B.C.

[1] *ASH.* XXIV. 3—5; XXVI. 1, 2.
[2] ib. XXVIII. 3 and 4.
[3] *ASH.* XXVIII. 1 and 2.   [4] ih. II. 6—8.
[5] p. 77, f. 20 = *CR.* 1898, p. 80, ff. 143, 144.
[6] *Tactica*, 35. 3. They seem really to have been Dacian (v. Pauly-Wissowa s.v. *Draco*) and appear on M. Antonine's Column, Petersen, p. 71, pl. LXIV., LXV.
[7] *Sm.* III. p. 66, f. 20. *CR.* 1900, p. 37, ff. 96, 97 : 1904, pp. 88, 89, ff. 139, 140.
[8] *Sm.* III. p. 63. Cf. pl. IX. and XVII. 5, also Khanenko, op. cit. II. 2, pl. XI. 224, and 3, pl. XLIII.

347. v. inf. p. 186, f. 79, also p. 183, f. 76.
[9] Cf. J. Hampel, Skythische Denkmäler aus Ungarn in *Ethnol. Mittheil. aus Ung.*, Bd IV. 1895, ff. 1, 2, 3, 5, 6, 7, 8, and P. Reinecke, Die Skythischen Alterthümer im Mittleren Europa in *Zt. f. Ethn.* XXVIII. (1896).
[10] *BCA.* XIV. p. 34, f. 78.
[11] Ueber Einige Beziehungen u. s. w., *Zt. f. Ethn.* XXIX. 1897.
[12] *Sm.* I. and II. frontispieces, for latter v. inf. p. 193, f. 85. Bobrinskoj calls them staff-heads.

Cauldrons.

Of other gear beside what we have named the Scythians possessed but various kettles or cauldrons or pots. Of these the bronze or copper cauldrons are the most characteristic in form, being with the special daggers and horse trappings the particular marks of Scythic culture. They are found from Krasnojarsk to Budapest, and the type is constant though the workmanship is sometimes native, sometimes quite Greek. Their distinguishing feature is that the body of the cauldron is roughly speaking hemispherical and is supported upon a truncated cone which forms a foot or stand. The handles project upwards from the upper rim. The whole stands from 1 to 3 feet high, and is 2 ft. 6 in. across. Evidently the people who devised this base had not thought either of suspending the cauldron from a tripod or making it stand on three legs of its own. Therefore it is hard to believe

FIG. 21. *CR.* 1897, p. 82, f. 200. Raskópana Mogila near Mikhailovo-Apostolovo. Kherson Government. Bronze cauldron. ⅛.

FIG. 22. *CR.* 1899, p. 50, f. 96. Khatazhukaevskij Aul. Bronze cauldron. ¼.

in Reinecke's idea that this form is derived from that of the Chinese sacrificial

three-footed cauldrons figured in Po-ku-t'u-lu, Kin-shih-so, and the like[1].
True, the handles are set on in much the same way, but the difference in the
supports seems decisive. These cauldrons are regularly put in tombs and
contain mutton or horse bones, shewing that once there was in them food
for the use of the dead. An interesting specimen is that from Chertomlyk[2],
which has six goats round its rim instead of handles; in the same tomb
was found a kind of open work saucepan, which may have been used for
fishing meat out of the water in which it had been boiled, or for grilling
it over the fire[3]: another curious example coming from Mikhailovo-Apostolovo in Kherson government and district[4] has pure Greek palmettes
decorating its surface[5].

This type is also common in Siberia, and it is there only that the same
form occurs in earthenware[6]. Herodotus speaks of the Scythian cauldrons
(IV. 61) and compares them to the Lesbian ones. But this does not help us
much. And again (IV. 81) he speaks of the monumental one at Exampaeus
as containing 600 amphorae, and being six fingers thick, but such dimensions
would make it perfectly useless.

Herodotus goes on to say that when they had no cauldron the Scyths
boiled the animal in his own skin, making a kind of haggis, as is done by
sundry savage nations. He seems scarcely right when he speaks of the
bones burning excellently and taking the place of wood. Nowadays the
steppe dwellers use *kirpich*, bricks of dried cow dung, and that answers the
purpose, but is ill spared from the enrichment of the fields. But Gmelin

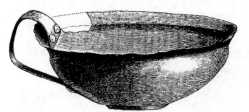

FIG. 23.   *CR.* 1891, p. 85, f. 63.   Cup from Pavlovka.   ½.

describes ceremonies of burning a victim's bones and of cooking in skins
by means of heated stones as practised by the Buriats in his day[7].

[1] *Zt. f. Ethnol.* XXIX. (1897), Ueber einige
Beziehungen u.s.w.
[2] p. 162, f. 50=*KTR.* p. 262, f. 238.
[3] *KTR.* p. 259, f. 236=*ASH.* XXVII. 1.
[4] p. 79, f. 21 = *CR.* 1897, p. 82, f. 200.
[5] Further examples : Kul Oba, *ABC.* XLIV. 11,
13; Axjutintsy, *Sm.* II. p. 163, f. 19; Volkovtsy,
Sm. III. p. 84, f. 30; Hungary, Ó Szöny, J. Hampel,
Ethn. Mittheil. aus Ungarn, Bd IV. f. 11 (other
cauldrons called Scythic by Hampel do not seem
to deserve the name); Alexandria (Kherson govt),
CR. 1890, p. 115, f. 64; to the east of the sea of
Azov, Jaroslavskaja Stanitsa, *CR.* 1896, p. 56, f.
277; Khatazhukaevskij Aul, *CR.* 1899, p. 50, f. 96;
Vozdvizhenskaja, *CR.* 1899, p. 46, ff. 77, 78;
Zubov's Farm, *BCA.* I., p. 96, f. 10; inf. p. 230,
f. 133; further north near Vorónezh, at Mazurka,
CR. 1899, p. 101, f. 197; even as far as Perm at

Zamazaevskoe, *CR.* 1889, p. 93, f. 45 ; see also *Sm.*
III. p. 72. Béla Pósta ap. Zichy, *Dritte Asiatische
Forschungsreise,* Bd IV. p. 514 sqq. f. 287 sqq. figures
many and works out a theory of their development,
which appears to apply mostly to the later specimens. Vol. III., p. 69 he says that they occur up
to the Xth century A.D. and still survive among the
Kirgiz about Turuchansk.
[6] inf. p. 246, f. 159, Klements, *Antiquities of
the Minusinsk Museum,* Tomsk, 1886, pl. XIX. 14
and 19. There also we find an improved form
with a spout, op. cit. pl. XIII. 1. Cf. Zichy, op. cit.
IV. p. 398, f. 230.
[7] *Reise in Sibirien,* III. pp. 22—25, 74—76,
ap. K. Neumann, p. 264 sqq. De Plano Carpini
says that the Mongols never break an animal's
bones but burn them (§ iii. Bergeron, Hague, 1735,
p. 30, Rockhill, p. 81, n.).

Most of the drinking vessels found in Scythic graves whether they be of metal or of fine pottery are of Greek workmanship and Greek shape. However, the Kul Oba vase (p. 200, f. 93) seems of native shape, at least it has no counterpart in pure Greek design, save in the companion vases found with it, in one from Katerles[1] and one from Ryzhanovka[2]. It is from such a cup that a nomad is drinking[3]. From Volkovtsy (p. 186, f. 79, No. 451) came two such cups of native work and from Galushchino a similar one but shallower (ib. No. 450); the form is common in clay in the Kiev district (p. 82, f. 25). The Scyths also seem to have liked shallow bowls or cylices, and saucers with a boss in the centre. These were all of pure Greek design[4].

At Pavlovka in Bessarabia was found a shallow cup or saucer of bronze, with a handle riveted on to one side[5]. This and another more or less like it are the only cups that could be carried at the belt according to the legend in Herodotus[6].

Very common in Scythic tombs are the so-called rhyta or drinking horns. They are mostly not the true Greek rhyta, which had a hole in the pointed end from which a stream was let flow into the mouth, as may be seen represented on Greek vases, but horns from the broad ends of which the liquor was drunk. On gold plaques we see pictures of Scythians drinking from such horns, e.g. the man standing before the lady with a mirror[7], and the group of two Scythians apparently drinking blood brotherhood[8]. Actual specimens were found, two at Kul Oba[9], three at Seven Brothers[10] and at Karagodeuashkh[11]. Others have been found in a less perfect condition or of a less characteristic form, e.g. one from Kerch shaped as a calf's head with scenes in relief on the neck of the vase[12]. It is remarkable for its extraordinary resemblance to a small bronze vessel figured in Po-ku-t'u-lu. This has been noticed by P. Reinecke[13], but the objects are not really comparable, as the exceedingly small size of the Chinese specimen makes it quite a different sort of thing. Moreover that from Kerch does not seem to have occurred in a Scythic grave (v. ch. xi.-§ 11).

Unique in its way is the famous Chertomlyk vase (pp. 159—161, ff. 46—48 and pp. 288, 9) evidently meant for kumys, as it has a sieve in its neck and at each of the three spouts, shaped two of them as lions' heads and one as a winged horse. Besides these we have various ladles, colanders, pails, bowls, and other vessels of Greek make. But the most famous Scythian drinking vessels were not made of gold or silver, but of the skulls of their enemies. Something of this sort has been found in Siberia in the government of Tomsk, a human skull adapted to form part of a cup[14].

---

[1] inf. p. 198, f. 91 and *ABC.* xxxiv. and xxxv.
[2] *Sm.* II. xvi. 7.
[3] p. 97, f. 90, middle = *ABC.* xxxii. 1.
[4] Kul Oba, p. 204, f. 99 = *ABC.* xxv.; Seven Brothers, p. 209, f. 107 = *CR.* 1876, p. 157, and IV. 9 and 10; Zubov's Farm, p. 231, f. 136 = *BCA.* I. p. 99, f. 18; Karagodeuashkh, *Mat.* XIII. p. 153 and VI. 4.
[5] *CR.* 1891, p. 85, f. 63.
[6] IV. 10. Cf. Congrès International d'Archéologie Préhistorique et d'Anthropologie, xime Session à Moscou, M. 1892, Vol. I. p. 108; N. Brandenbourg, *Sur la coupe des ceintures des anciens Scythes.* A saucer with a loop from near Mariupol.

[7] p. 158, f. 45 = *ABC.* xx. 11.
[8] Kul Oba, p. 203, f. 98 = *ABC.* xxxii. 10.
[9] p. 197, f. 90; *ABC.* xxxvi. 4 and 5.
[10] pp. 211, 213, ff. 110, 114 and *CR.* 1876, IV. 8, 1877, I. 5, 6, 7; *KTR.* p. 318, f. 286.
[11] p. 219, f. 121, *Mat.* XIII. p. 140 sqq., ff. 16—23.
[12] *ABC.* xxxvi. 1 and 2 = *KTR.* p. 87, f. 116.
[13] Einige Beziehungen u. s. w. p. 161 in *Zt. f. Ethn.* xxix. (1897).
[14] Her. IV. 65, v. inf. p. 83, f. 26 = *CR.* 1898, p. 83, f. 154.

Scythic pottery has not received much attention. It is always hand-made and mostly very rough both in fabric and material. Only in the west, where it really belongs to the native inhabitants, not to the Scythic elements, we find considerable variety of form, and even decoration applied by incising a pattern and filling up the lines with white. The most interesting products

FIG. 24. *BCA.* IV. p. 33, f. 4.
Constantinovo. Scythic cup.

FIG. 25. *BCA.* IV. p. 31, f. 3. Constantinovo. Scythic pottery.

are cups with high handles[1] which have analogies to the south-west[2], and others of the same shape as the Kul Oba vase. They also used dishes made of stone[3]. But the best pottery they imported from the Greeks. Besides the amphorae which were brought merely for the sake of their contents, we have more artistic products occurring far inland (ch. XI. § 7): that they were highly valued we can judge from their having been mended after ancient breakages. Large vases are comparatively rare, but smaller specimens are not uncommon. They are some help in dating the tombs in which they occur, but not much, as it is hard to say how long they had been in use before being buried. They are mostly of the last period of red-figured ware. Some are evidently manufactured in the Pontic colonies, and not sent from Greece[4]. There is, for instance, a kind of small ugly cantharos with inferior glaze that is peculiar to the Euxine coast and its sphere of trade influence (figured in ch. XI. § 7). Except in beads, glass does not occur until quite late, probably Roman, times. Vessels were also made of wood; to this day the Kalmucks value old wooden saucers, something like mediaeval mazers, extravagantly highly, especially if they are well coloured. Herodotus mentions that milk was kept in wooden vessels[5].

[1] *BCA.* IV. 1902, p. 33, ff. 4—6; *Sm.* I. xiii.—xv., II. vi. and vii., III. p. 37, f. 6; Khanenko, op. cit. II. 3, liii., liv., lxii., lxiii. Bobrinskoj, *BCA.* IV. p. 32 and *Sm.* II. p. xvii., says that this pottery belongs to the earlier Scythic period when iron was still rare: same form at Ladozhskaja on the Kuban, *CR.* 1902, p. 75, f. 160.
[2] Niederle, *Slav. Ant.* I. p. 498.
[3] *Sm.* II. p. 136, f. 21, and III. p. 141, f. 78.

[4] *Trans. Od. Soc.,* Vol. XXII. 1900; E. R. von Stern, *On the importance of Ceramic finds in the South of Russia,* p. 10; *Sm.* II. viii. (Axjutintsy), and xix. (Ryzhanovka), and III. xx. (Bobritsa); cf. II. p. 126.
[5] IV. 2. The particular ferment which made kumys would be better communicated by wooden or leather vessels than by clean metal or earthen-ware.

Of the ways of the Scyths in war Herodotus tells us in chapters 64 to 66. A Scyth who has slain an enemy drinks his blood, and cuts off his head, which acts as a voucher in the allotment of booty[1]; then he takes the scalp, scrapes it with the rib of an ox and wears it at his bridle, or even, when he has taken many scalps, and is hence accounted a great warrior, makes a cloak of them. Others use the skins of their enemies' hands to cover their quivers, or stretch whole skins upon wooden frames and carry them about. Furthermore, they take the skulls of their very greatest enemies or of their own people with whom they have been at feud and whom they have vanquished before the king, saw them off above the eyebrows, clean them out and mount them in ox leather, or if they are rich enough, in gold, and use them as cups. Furthermore, once a year, the headman of each pasture land (may we not say *ulus*?) mixes a bowl of wine and there drink of it all who have slain a man. But those who have not are kept away and disgraced accordingly. And those who have slain very many men drink from two cups at a time[2].

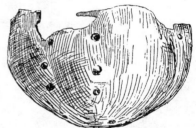

C.R. 1898. p.83 f. 154.b Government of Tomsk.
Part of skull cup with holes for leather lining.

FIG. 26.

More important information as to how Herodotus imagined the Scyths waging war we can gather from the accounts of the contest with Darius, and can supplement by the general testimony of antiquity and Oriental history as to the tactics of the nomads. There is no need to enlarge upon the policy of retirement before the regular troops of the invader, of harassing his rear, cutting his communications and enticing pursuit by pretended flights. In defence, the strength of the nomads lies in the fact that there is nothing for the invader to destroy and no source from which he can get supplies, and he is helpless in the face of the superior mobility of his opponent: for the offensive[3] the nomads are powerful because their whole population can take part in battle, no one is left on the land, as with settled peoples, for there is nothing to defend in detail, also the host carries its own provision with it, and is very mobile. Still the nomads have rarely been successful against settled states in a sound condition. Their inroads have been irresistible only when internal division or decay laid the civilised countries open to them. They are at a great disadvantage when it is a question of walled towns, forests or mountains, and only by becoming settled have they been able to keep moderately permanent dominion over agricultural countries: though they have often exacted blackmail or tribute from powerful states on the borders of their natural sphere of influence, the Euro-Asiatic plain[4]. Thucydides (v. sup. p. 35) exaggerates their power.

---

[1] Cf. Kurdzhips, inf. p. 223, f. 126, also p. 173, n. 6.
[2] σύνδυο κύλικας ἔχοντες πίνουσιν ὁμοῦ. Looking at p. 203, f. 98 inclines one to translate "drink in twos, sharing their cups together."

[3] Arrian, *Tact.* 16, 6 ascribes to the Scythians attacks in wedge-shaped (ἐμβολοειδέσι) columns.
[4] H. C. Mackinder, The Geographical Pivot of History, *Geogr. Journal*, XXIII. (1904) p. 421.

Their raids brought the Scyths slaves, employed in herding the cattle and making kumys, but among nomads master is not far above man, and so thought the mistress when the master was away. Upon the kings only native Scyths attended[1].

In Chapters 73 to 75 Herodotus seems to describe three different customs as one: a ceremonial purification from the taint of a corpse; this may not have been separate from the second, the usual vapour bath enjoyed much as it still is in Russia, in spite of the ridicule of St Andrew[2]. Thirdly, a custom of intoxicating themselves with the vapour of hemp. He adds that the women whitened their skins with a paste of pounded cypress, cedar and frankincense wood; something very like the Russians' lye.

Position of Women.

Herodotus goes on to say that the Scyths were very much averse from adopting foreign customs: and quotes the lamentable ends of Anacharsis and Scyles. But one might take this rather as evidence of the attraction the higher Greek civilisation exercised over some of them. Incidentally we learn that the Scythian kings were polygamous, that a son succeeded to his father's wives, and that some had married Greek women.

We have already noticed that the chief difference between the Scyths and the Sarmatians was in the position of the women. Among the former they were apparently entirely subject to the men and were kept in the waggons to such an extent that, as Hippocrates says, their health suffered from want of exercise. Whereas among the Sarmatians they took part in war, rode about freely and held a position which earned for some tribes the epithet of women-ruled, and gave rise to the legend of the Amazons. This is in some degree the natural position of women among nomads, they have to take charge of the Jurtas when the men are absent rounding up strayed cattle, and are quite capable of looking after everything at home, entertaining a stranger and even beating off an attack by robbers[3]. It does not argue primitive community of women or Tibetan polyandry, such as the Greeks attributed to the Scyths and Herodotus to the Massagetae (v. p. 111). The queens who are so prominent in Greek stories about nomads, Tomyris, Zarinaea[4], Tirgatao, can hardly be quoted as historical proofs of woman rule, though they might be paralleled in Tartar history. We must regard the confined condition of women among the Scyths as exceptional, due to the position of all women being assimilated to that of those captured from conquered tribes, this being possible because the exceptional wealth of the leading men among the Scyths enabled them as members of a dominant aristocracy to afford the luxury of exempting their women from work, and so to establish a kind of *purdah* system even in the face of nomad conditions, which are naturally unfavourable to seclusion.

[1] Her. IV. 1—3, 72.

[2] *Laurentian Chronicle* (so-called Nestor) ed. 3, St P., 1897, p. 7. "I saw wooden baths, and they heat them exceeding hot, and gather together and are naked and pour lye (*kvas usnianyi*) over themselves and beat themselves... And this they do every day, not tortured by any man, but they torture themselves."

[3] E. Huntington, The Mountains of Turkestan, in *Geographical Journal*, Vol. XXV. 2, Feb. 1905, p. 154 sqq.; de Plano Carpini ap. Bergeron (Hague), § IV. p. 39, Rockhill, p. 75, n. 3. The maids and women ride and race upon horseback as skilfully as the men....They drive the carts and load them...and they are most active and strong. All wear trousers, and some of them shoot with the bow like men.

[4] Ctesias, fr. 25 ap. Diod. Sic. II. xxxiv. v. Müller, pp. 42, 44.

Religion.

All that we know of the Scythian's religion is contained in three chapters of Herodotus (IV. 59, 60, 62). The following deities were common to all, Tabiti—Hestia who was the principal object of their veneration, next to her Papaeus—Zeus with Apia—Ge, husband and wife, after them Goetosyrus—Apollo, Argimpasa—Aphrodite Urania, and Ares. Thamimasadas—Poseidon was peculiar to the Royal Scyths. They raised no statues, altars or temples to their gods, save to Ares alone. They sacrificed all sorts of animals after the same manner, but horses were the most usual victims. The beast took his stand with his fore feet tied together and the sacrificer pulling the end of the rope from behind brought him down. Then he called upon the name of the god to whom the sacrifice was offered, slipped a noose over the victim's head, twisted it up with a stick and so garrotted him : then he turned to flaying and cooking. Sacrifices were made to Ares after another ritual described below.

The catalogue of gods hardly tells us more than that the Scyths were no monotheists. The forms of the names are very uncertain, being variously read in different MSS. of Herodotus and in Origen, who quotes them from Celsus[1]. Also as Origen says, we cannot tell what meaning we are to attach to the Greek translations; e.g. Apollo or Poseidon. For instance, the latter may have been either the horse-god or the sea-god.

However, Zeuss and his followers find that a list including Hestia, Zeus and Earth, Apollo and the Heavenly Aphrodite, and further Poseidon, has an Aryan, even a distinctly Iranian look. So when Theophylactus (VII. 8) says of the Turks " they excessively reverence and honour fire, also the air and the water : they sing hymns to the earth, but they adore and call god (i.e. the heaven, *tängri*) only him who created the heaven and the earth : their priests are those who seem to them to have the foretelling of the future—" Zeuss[2] has to explain that these Turks were really only Tadzhiks—Iranians under Turkish rule. But this can hardly be said of the Tartars of whom de Plano Carpini says "Les Tartares adorent donc le soleil, la lumière et le feu comme ainsi l'eau et la terre, leur offrant les prémices de leur manger et boire[3]."

G. Nagy, besides pointing out the general analogy between Scythic and Uralo-Altaic religious conceptions, even makes an attempt to explain the actual god-names and succeeds better than those who have sought Iranian derivations : he suggests, for instance, as analogies for Tabiti = Hestia, the Vogul *taüt*, *toat*, fire : for Papaeus = Zeus, *baba* = father in most Uralo-Altaic languages, but of course in most other tongues there is something similar ; for Thamimasadas or Thagimasadas (Origen) = Poseidon, the Turkish *tengiz*, Magyar *tenger* = sea, and Turkish *ata*, Magyar *atya* = father ; the word for sea also occurring in Temarinda (= *mater maris*[4] with Turkish *ana*, Ostjak *anka*, mother) and Tamyrace (sup. p. 16). The phonetic change is similar to that in *cannabis*, probably a loan word from the Scythic, and Magyar *kender* hemp. Less convincing than these but more plausible than the Iranian comparisons are Apia = Ge, cf. Mongolian *Abija*, fruitful, and Artimpasa = Aphrodite Urania,

---

[1] c. *Celsum*, V. 41, 46, VI. 39, Γογγόσυρος, 'Αργίμπασα, Θαγιμασάδα, for MSS. Οἰτόσυρος, 'Αρίππασα, Θαμιμασάδας, Hesych. Γοιτόσυρος, 'Αρτιμήασα.

[2] op. cit. p. 285 sqq. (v. inf. p. 98, n. 8).
[3] Bergeron (Hague), § III. p. 31.
[4] Pliny, *NH.* VI. 20, native name for Maeotis.

cf. Cuman *erdeng* = maiden, and Mordva *paz* = god. (G)oetosyrus = Apollo is so uncertain in form that it is useless to propose etymologies for it. Certain it is that the Scythic pantheon offers nothing like the complete series of analogies which may be established between the other Aryan pantheons.

The method of sacrifice by hobbling the victim, throwing him down and throttling him may be compared with the Buriat ritual with its precautions against the blood falling upon the earth[1]. The favourite sacrifice was a horse, so also it was a horse that the Massagetae offered to the sun[2]. For similar ritual at sacrifices of reindeer, horses and cattle among the Voguls, Ostjaks, Votjaks and Altai Turks, compare Nagy[3].

Herodotus goes on to say that Ares was worshipped in the form of an *acinaces* set up on a platform of bundles of brushwood, three furlongs square, heaped up one in each district. Besides horses and sheep they sacrificed to him one man out of every hundred prisoners, pouring his blood upon the sword on the top of the mound, and below cutting off the victim's right arm and throwing it into the air.

This worship of Ares seems to stand apart from the other cults. The most probable derivation for it is Thrace: it was most likely commonest among the western Scythians who had close relations with Thrace, e.g. Ariapithes[4] had to wife a daughter of the Thracian Teres, father of Sitalces. In the treeless steppes of Eastern Scythia it would have been impossible to make mounds of brushwood of anything like the size described by Herodotus (IV. 62), whence were the 150 loads of brushwood to come every year when the people had not even the wood for cooking-fires? Each mention of Ares and his worship has the appearance of a later insertion added by Herodotus from some fresh source. He does not give the Scythian word for Ares. Heracles also, for whom likewise no Scythian name is given, is not so well attested as the other gods. He may well have been put in because of the "Greek" legend which made him the ancestor of the race. Nagy, however (p. 45), finds a similar figure in Finno-Ugrian mythology, e.g. in the Magyar Menrot or Nimrod.

Witchcraft.

Herodotus (IV. 67—69) gives a fuller account of the witchcraft of the Scyths than of their religion, and the account seems to apply to the Royal Scyths. He says that their wizards prophesied with bundles of rods which they took apart, divined upon separately, and bound up again. It is remarkable that the man represented on the plaque from the Oxus Treasure (p. 255, f. 174) carries a bundle of rods: and hence Cunningham[5] calls him a mage, for he says the mages had sacred bundles of rods (*barsom*). This would suggest that the wizards came from the Iranian population, that the invaders left this department in the hands of the people of the country, as so often happened. The Enarees also claimed power of divination by plaiting strips of bast. But something similar was practised by Nestorian priests among the Mongols[6].

Characteristic of the low state of culture is the belief that if the king fall sick it must be by the fault of some man of the tribe who has sworn

[1] Neumann, op. cit. p. 262.   [4] Her. IV. 76 sqq.
[2] Her. I. 216.   [5] *JRAS. Bengal,* Vol. L.
[3] op. cit. p. 47.   [6] Yule[3], I. pp. 241, 242, n. 2, Rubruck, p. 195.

by the king's hearth, and forsworn himself, bringing down on the king the vengeance of the offended deity. A man whom the wizards definitely accused of this according to the results of their divinations could only hope to escape if other and yet other wizards declared their colleagues' accusation false. We can hardly doubt that the decision was generally upheld, and the accused beheaded, and his property distributed among his destroyers. The horror of the punishment meted out to wizards whom their colleagues did not support, makes us think that it could not have been inflicted often. Bound hand and foot and gagged they were set in a pyre of brushwood upon a cart, and oxen dragged them until themselves set free by their traces burning. It looks like a kind of scapegoat ceremony by which the guilt of dishonest wizardry was purified by fire and scattered over the face of the earth.

With their witchcraft goes their rite for taking oaths, and swearing blood brotherhood. They pour wine into great earthenware cups and mix with it blood drawn from the parties to the oath ; then they dip therein a sword, arrows, an axe and a dart, and after praying long over it the contracting parties drink it off together with the chief of their followers[1].

Parallels for the divination ceremonies and the mode of discovering the man responsible for any disease of the king's, also for the oath ceremony, may be found in almost any race from Kamchatka to the Cape of Good Hope, and such parallels prove nothing but that the human mind works on similar lines in different countries. We may, however, mention divination by sticks among the early Turks[2]. So the ceremonies of blood brotherhood may be also paralleled among the Parthians[3], also apparently an Uralo-Altaic tribe, the Magyars and the Cumans or Polovtses, whose prince made such a covenant with Philip, son of Nariot de Toucy, and Andronicus the Greek Emperor[4]. But it is in their burials that the Scyths and the Hunnish nations most resemble each other.

Funeral Customs.

The account of Scythic funerals given by Herodotus (iv. 71—73) agrees so well with the archaeological data, as summarised below in the survey of the principal Scythic tombs of South Russia (ch. viii. p. 149 sqq.), that the two sources of information may be used to supplement one another.

As to the burials of the kings, Herodotus says that they take place in the land of the Gerrhi (v. p. 29). Here when their king dies they dig a great square pit. When this is ready they take up the corpse, stuff it full of chopped cypress, frankincense, parsley-seed and anise, and put it on a waggon. Their own ears they crop, shear their hair, cut round their arms, slit their foreheads and noses, and run arrows through their left hands. Thus they bring their king to the next tribe on the way to the Gerrhi and make them mutilate themselves in the same way and follow with them, and so with the next tribe until at last they come to the Gerrhi. There in the place prepared they lay the body upon a mattress, and drive in spears on each side of it in line, and rafters across and make a roof of mats (or wicker work). They strangle and lay in the

---

[1] For a remarkably exact parallel among the Hiung-nu, see infra, p. 93.

[2] Nagy, op. cit. p. 51.

[3] Tacitus, *Annals*, xii. 47.

[4] Nagy, op. cit. pp. 53, 54 ; Rockhill, Rubruck, p. xxxiii, quoting from Joinville, *Histoire de S. Louys*.

vacant room within the tomb one of the dead man's concubines, and his cupbearer, his cook, his groom, and his messenger and horses, and cups of gold (they use none of silver or copper), and firstlings of all his other possessions. When they have done this they make a great mound, vying with each other to make it as great as possible. After the lapse of a year they take fifty of the king's best attendants (and these are Scyths born, whomsoever he commands to serve him: no bought slaves serve the king), and fifty of the finest horses, slay them, and stuff them with chaff. Next they fix the felloes of wheels on posts, with the concave side uppermost in pairs, run a stake through each horse lengthwise, and set him on each pair of felloes, so that one supports the shoulders of the horse, the other the hind-quarters, and the legs hang down freely. Bits are put in the horses' mouths and the reins taken forward, and fastened to a peg. One of the fifty strangled youths is then put astride of each horse, a stake being run up his spine and fixed in a socket in that which runs horizontally through the horse. So these horses are set in a circle about the tomb.

Thus are the kings buried. Ordinary Scyths are carried about on a waggon for forty days by their nearest kin and brought to their friends in turn. These feast the bringers and set his share before the dead man (who presumably has been embalmed), and so at last they bury him.

It is by the general correspondence of funeral customs that we are enabled to say that certain of the barrows opened in South Russia belonged most probably to the people whom Herodotus and Hippocrates describe. Much has been made of small differences of detail and of the decidedly later date of the works of Greek art found in the tombs of which we have good accounts, but that substantially the very people, of whose funeral ceremonies Herodotus gives so full an account, raised the mounds of Kul Oba, Chertomlyk and Karagodeuashkh, is not open to reasonable doubt.

When Herodotus uses the present and speaks as if each of the details he describes were repeated at every king's funeral there is no need to believe anything but that he has generalised from the current account of the last great royal burial. If we have not yet found remains of a circle of fifty impaled young men upon impaled horses standing on ghastly guard about a Prince's tomb, it does not mean that the tombs opened so far belong to a different nation, but that we have not come on that in which was laid Octamasades, or whoever it may have been, whose funeral was narrated to Herodotus. Even did we find it we might well discover that rumour had exaggerated the number of sacrifices.

Burial Customs of Mongols and Turks.

Yet even such wholesale slaughter can be paralleled from Marco Polo[1].

"All the great Kaans and all the descendants of Chingis their first lord are carried to the mountain that is called Altay to be interred. Wheresoever the Sovereign may die he is carried to his burial in that mountain with his predecessors no matter an the place of his death were an hundred days' journey distant, thither must he be carried to his burial. Let me tell you a strange thing too. When they are carrying the body

[1] I. li. Yule[3], I. p. 246.

of any Emperor to be buried with the others, the convoy that goes with the body doth put to the sword all whom they fall in with on the road saying 'Go and wait upon your Lord in the other world.'...They do the same too with the horses: for when the emperor dies they kill all his best horses in order that he may have the use of them in the other world as they believe. And I tell you as a certain truth that when Mangou Kaan died more than 20,000 persons who chanced to meet the body were slain in the manner I have told." Mangu died in the heart of China. So Rashid-ud-din (ap. Yule, l.c.) says forty beautiful girls were slain for Chingiz.

William de Rubruck[1] says of the Comanians or Polovtses, "They build a great toomb ouer their dead and erect the image of the dead party thereupon with his face towards the East, holding a drinking cup in his hand before his nauel. They erect also vpon the monuments of rich men Pyramides, that is to say, litle sharpe houses or pinacles....I saw one newly buried on whose behalfe they hanged up 16 horse hides; vnto each quarter of the world 4, betweene certain high posts; and they set besides his grave Cosmos for him to drink and flesh to eat; and yet they said that he was baptized."

So Ibn Batuta[2], who travelled in China in the middle of the fourteenth century, thus describes the funeral of a Khan slain in battle. "The Khan who had been killed, with about a hundred of his relations was then brought and a large sepulcre was dug for him under the earth, in which a most beautiful couch was spread, and the Khan was with his weapons laid upon it. With him they placed all the gold and silver vessels he had in his house, together with four female slaves and six of his favourite Mamluks with a few vessels of drink. They were then all closed up, and the earth heaped upon them to the height of a large hill. Then they brought four horses which they pierced through at the hill until all motion ceased; they then forced a piece of wood into the hinder part of the animal until it came out at his neck and this they fixed in the earth leaving the horse thus impaled upon the hill. The relatives of the Khan they buried in the same manner putting all their vessels of gold and silver in the grave with them. At the doors of the sepulcres of ten of these they impaled three horses in the manner thus mentioned. At the graves of each of the rest only one horse was impaled." This was all at El Khansā—Shen-si.

And de Plano Carpini[3], of the Mongols, says in Bergeron's words:

"Quand le capitaine est mort on l'enterre secretement en la campagne auec sa loge. Il est assis au milieu d'icelle auec vne table deuant luy et un bassin plein de chair et vne tasse de lait de jument. On enterre aussi auec lui vne jument auec son poulain & vn cheual sellé & bridé et mangent vn autre cheual dont ils remplissent la peau de paille puis l'esleuent en haut sur quatre bastons....Ils enterrent de mesme auec luy son or & son argent. Ils rompent le chariot qui le portait et sa maison est abattue et personne n'ose proferer son nom iusqu'à la troisième generation.

[1] Cap. 10, p. 100 in Hakluyt's translation, 2nd ed., London, 1598, Rockhill, p. 81, v. inf. p. 239, f. 149.
[2] Trans. S. Lee, London, 1829, p. 220, quoted by Blakesley and Macan on Her. IV. 72.
[3] Paris, 1634, c. iii. The reader will lose nothing by the French translation, though I have learnt since this was in type that it was made from Hakluyt's English. Cf. Rockhill, p. 81.

" Ils ont vne autre façon d'enterrer les Grands. C'est qu'ils vont secrette-
ment en la campagne et la ostent toutes les herbes iusqu'aux racines puis
font vne grande fosse: à costé ils en font vne autre comme vne caue sous
terre: puis le seruiteur qui aura esté le plus chéry du mort est mis sous
le corps....Pour le mort ils le mettent dans cette fosse qui est à costé auec
toutes les autres choses que nous auons dites cy dessus, puy remplissent ceste
autre fosse qui est deuant celle la et mettent de l'herbe par dessus.

" Et en leur pays ils ont deux lieux de sepulture, l'un auquel ils enterrent
les Empereurs, Princes, Capitaines et autres de leur noblesse seulement
& en quelque lieu qu'ils viennent à mourir on les apporte la tant qu'il est
possible et on enterre auec eux force or et argent. L'autre lieu est pour l'en-
terrement de ceux qui sont morts en Hongrie. Personne n'ose s'approcher
de ces cemetieres là. Si non ceux qui en ont la charge et qui sont establis
pour les garder. Et si quelqu'autre en approche il est aussitost pris battu
foüetté et fort mal traitté."

Nearly every detail of these passages can be paralleled from Herodotus
or the excavations. Only the Mongols could do things on a more magnificent
scale than the Scyths, who could not rival the horrors of Mangu Khan's funeral.
The mutilation of those who met the funeral car of a Scythian king is mild
compared to the wholesale slaughter we find in Asia fifteen hundred years later[1].

Such customs we can trace 800 years earlier among the T'u-küe or
Turks as reported by the Chinese[2].

In the second of the inscriptions of the Orkhon, the earliest monu-
ments of Turkish speech, erected by Jolygh Tigin in memory of Bilgä or
Pitkia, the Khan of the Turks, brother of Kül Tigin, the Khan says " My
Father the Khan died in the year of the dog in the 10th month the 36th day.
In the year of the pig in the fifth month the 37th day I made the funeral.
Lisün (or Li-hiong) tai sängün (a Chinese ambassador) came to me at
the head of 500 men. They brought an infinity of perfumes, gold and
silver. They brought musk for the funeral and placed it and sandalwood.
All these peoples cut their hair and cropped their ears (and cheeks?): they
brought their own good horses, their black sables and blue squirrels without
number and put them down[3]."

This inscription is dated A.D. 732, Aug. 1st. It recalls Herodotus also
in a passage in which the Khan warns the Turks against the charm of
the Chinese and their insinuation, and blames the Turkish nobles who had
abandoned their Turkish titles and bore the Chinese titles of dignitaries
of China. That is, that the Turks had their Anacharsis and Scyles attracted
by the civilisation of the South. And the warning of the Khan was too
late, for ten years afterwards the Turkish empire was conquered by the
Uigurs, their western neighbours and former subjects[4].

Nagy[5] supplies further parallels from among Uralo-Altaic tribes. For

[1] For the stuffing and impalement of horses
among men of the Altai, cf. Witsen, *Noord en Oost
Tartarye*, and W. Radloff, *Aus Sibirien*, II. p. 26
and pl. 1 ; v. inf. p. 251, bottom.

[2] Cf. Vilh. Thomsen, Inscriptions d'Orkhon dé-
chiffrées, No. v. of *Mémoires de la Société Finno-
Ougrienne*, Helsingfors, 1896 ; Stanislas-Julien,

Documents Historiques sur les Tou-kiue extraits
du Pien-i-tien, *Journal Asiatique*, VI.e série, T. III.
et IV., Paris, 1864.

[3] Thomsen, op. cit., p. 130.

[4] Cf. E. Blochet, Les inscriptions Turques de
l'Orkhon, *Revue Archéologique*, 1898, p. 357, 382.

[5] op. cit. pp. 54—57.

self-mutilation he instances the Huns at the death of Attila[1], and says that it is still practised among the Turks of Central Asia, who also set up spears in the grave, a custom of which traces survive in Hungary. The horse-burial as practised among Indo-Europeans he ascribes entirely to nomads' influence, and quotes examples among the Avars, Magyars, Old Bolgars and Cumans in Europe. The funeral of a Cuman as described by Joinville, A.D. 1241, very closely recalls the Scythic custom, as with the dead man were buried eight pages and twenty-six horses; upon them were put planed boards and a great mound quickly heaped up by the assembly. The horses are still stuffed and set over the grave among the Jakuts, Voguls, Ostjaks, and Chuvashes: while among the Kirgiz a horse is devoted to the dead at the funeral and sacrificed on the first anniversary. The interval of forty days before the funeral recalls the identical interval which comes between the death and the wake among the Chuvashes, and the fact that the Voguls believe that the soul does not go to its home in the other world until forty days have elapsed.

Nomads of Eastern Asia.

Since it is a question of the Scyths coming out of Asia it is worth while to see what the Chinese have to say as to their north-western neighbours. The accounts they give resemble wonderfully the accounts of the Scyths given by the Greeks, but inasmuch as integral parts of China, not mere outlying colonies, were always exposed to serious inroads of the nomads, the latter's doings were observed and chronicled with far more attention, so that we can watch the process by which the name of one empire succeeds the name of another, while the characters of all are precisely similar. If it be allowed to say so " Plus ça change, plus c'est la même chose." The most convenient account of the series is that given by Professor E. H. Parker in *A Thousand Years of the Tartars*, 1895. The same writer has given literal translations of the original texts in the *China Review*[2].

In the earliest times we have mention of raids which plagued the Chinese as far back as their traditions went. They say, for instance, that in the time of Yao and Shun, and later under the dynasties T'ang and Yü, B.C. 2356—2208, there were nomads to the north with the same customs as the later Hiung-nu—Hien-yün and Hün-küh (or Hun-yŏk) to the west, and Shan Zhung to the east. The Emperor Mu of the Chou dynasty, 1001—946 B.C., received as tribute or present from the Si Zhung or western nomads, a sword of K'un-wu or steel, which is said to have cut jade like mud[3]. The Hiung-nu, who are perfectly historic, were supposed to trace their descent from Great Yü the founder of the Hia dynasty, B.C. 2205—1766. At this time one Duke Liu took to the nomads' life and drove them back with their own tactics.

They made fresh encroachments, but were once more driven out by Süan, 827—781. Just before the ascent of the Ts'in dynasty c. 255 B.C.

---

[1] Jordanes, *Get.* XLIX.
[2] Vols. XXI. sqq. The latest account is O. Franke, Zur Kenntnis der Türkvölker und Skythen Zentral-asiens in *Abhandl. d. k. pr. Akad. d. W.* Berlin, 1904.
[3] F. Hirth, *China and the Roman Orient*, p. 250, according to Lieh Tsê, ap. Yüan-chien-lei-han.

the nomads were decoyed into an ambush and defeated. Several times the Chinese have treated them just as the Medes treated the Scyths.

During the troubles arising on the fall of the short-lived dynasty of Ts'in, T'ouman, the head or Zenghi (Shan-yü) of the Hiung-nu, raised their power very high and was succeeded by his son Mao-tun[1], who extended their empire to Kalgan and the borders of Corea.

East of the Hiung-nu were the Tung-hu (Tunguz) or eastern nomads, who have produced the ruling tribes of the Wu-huan or Sien-pi, the Kitans or Cathayans and the Manchus. These were reduced to subjection, and Mao-tun also extended his dominions over the tribes represented by the Kao-ch'ê or High Carts, later called Uigurs and the Kirgiz. He also conquered the Yüe-chih between K'i-lien and Tun-huang (Western Kan-su) and the Wu-sun by Lop-nor and drove them westward. So he could boast that he was lord of all that use the bow from the horse. By the next Zenghi Kayuk (or Ki-yük), now allied with the Wu-sun, the Yüe-chih were driven part into Tibet, part yet further, out of the Tarim basin to the west of Sogdiana, whence they extended southwards to the Oxus. From Oxiana they moved on and established a lasting kingdom just north of the Hindu Kush. From the chief of their five tribes they took the name of Kushanas. In their advance to the south they drove before them the Sai (Sek, i.e. Saka). Between them they crushed the Graeco-Bactrian state and finally advanced their dominion to India, wherefore they were known to the west as the Indo-Scyths[2]. In all this the settled Iranians were not displaced. The movement is singularly like that to which Herodotus ascribes the coming of the Scyths into Europe, only the line of least resistance led south and not north from the Oxus. Kayuk made a cup of the skull of the Yüe-chih king, and it became an heirloom in his dynasty. He died in B.C. 160.

The Chinese sent an ambassador Chang K'ien to the west, 136—126 B.C., to try and make an alliance with the Yüe-chih against the Hiung-nu and the Tibetans. They did not succeed but they established intercourse with the west, and at this time various Greek products first found their way to China[3]. About 110 B.C. the Hiung-nu were defeated, and in B.C. 90 the eastern nomads, who had recovered their independence, invaded the Hiung-nu territory and desecrated the tombs of former Zenghis: that being the worst injury that could be done, as in the case of the Scyths[4]. Forty years later it looked as if the Hiung-nu dominion was just about to fall, as there was a quarrel between Chih-chih and Hu-han-ya, two heirs to the throne, but Hu-han-ya established his position by a treaty with China in 49 B.C. The Emperor Yüan-Ti's ambassadors were Ch'ang and Mêng. They went up a hill east of the Onon and killed a white

---

[1] Written variously Mê-t'ê, Mo-t'ê, Bagator, Meghder and Moduk! Franke, op. c. p. 10, n. 3. Not knowing Chinese I cannot answer for correct or even consistent transliteration. Thanks to Professor Giles I have been saved many mistakes, but he is not responsible for such as may be left.

[2] *Journal Asiatique*, VIII.ᵉ série, T. II., 1883, p. 317; E. Specht, "Études sur l'Asie Centrale d'après les historiens chinois." His sources are Ma Tuan-

lin's Encyclopaedia and that called Pien-i-tien. See Skrine and Ross, *The Heart of Asia*, p. 14 sqq.; E. J. Rapson op. cit. (v. p. 47), p. 7; v. inf. pp. 100, 110, 121.

[3] Cf. H. A. Giles, *China and the Chinese*, New York, 1902, p. 130; and F. Hirth, *Ueber fremde Einflüsse in der chinesischen Kunst*, München and Leipsig, 1896, p. 2 sqq.

[4] Her. IV. 127.

horse[1]. The Zenghi took a king-lu knife, some gold and a rice spoon, made with them a mixture of wine and blood, and drank of it with the envoys, himself using the skull of the Yüe-chih king who was killed by Kayuk Zenghi. Soon after this the Hiung-nu divided into a northern and a southern state; in 87 A.D. the Sien-pi of the eastern nomads attacked the northern horde and took the Zenghi, and skinned him to make a trophy. About 196 A.D. the last remnants of Hiung-nu power were swept away and the people are said to have been driven west, to reappear as the Huns we know in eastern Europe two generations later (inf. p. 122). In the east they were ousted by the Sien-pi; it is said that when these conquered the northern Hiung-nu 100,000 of the latter submitted and called themselves Sien-pi, though these being eastern nomads differed from them more than any of the western tribes[2].

The eastern tribes were more democratic than the westerners, also dirtier, and they disposed of their dead on platforms instead of burying them. They held their power till about 400 A.D. when they gave way in exactly the same manner to the Zhu-zhu or Zhuan-zhuan, a mixed multitude of western nomads, known to Europe as Avars, but not the false Avars who once ruled Hungary: they held under them an obscure tribe called T'u-küe or Turks, who did metal work for them. They were a clan of Hiung-nu called A-she-na: and took the title Turk from a mountain near. T'u-mên, their Khagan or Khan, having defeated a neighbouring tribe, asked the daughter of the Khan of the Zhuan-zhuan in marriage. He replied, "You are common slaves whom we employ to work us metal, how dare you ask to wed a princess?" But T'u-mên married a Chinese princess and rose against the Zhuan-zhuan power and destroyed it in A.D. 546. Se-kin his successor is described as having a very broad dark red face, and eyes like green glass or lapis lazuli. He defeated the Yi-ta and extended Turkish sway from the Liao Sea to within measurable distance of the Caspian. These Yi-ta, more fully Yen-tai-i-li-to, were formerly called Hua; in the west they are known as the Ephthalite Huns; a very mixed race, they probably had something in common with the true Huns. They had supplanted the Yüe-chih, and destroyed the kingdom of the Kushanas. We hear of their polyandry, a primitive Malthusianism which seems to have been endemic in their country, as it is ascribed to the Massagetae, to the Yüe-chih and T'u-huo-lo or Tochari, and to the Yi-ta[3].

So to the Turks succeeded the Uigurs, whose ancestors are called Kao-ch'ê, High Carts, Ἀμαξόβιοι: after them came Kitans from the east. They in turn gave way to the Mongols, and the Manchus have been the last of the nomad tribes to establish an empire.

The process is always the same, the great bulk of the conquered horde amalgamates quite readily with the victors, the ruling class and their dependants, if not caught and skinned by their enemies, retire towards China

---

[1] Cf. Her. IV. 70.

[2] Cf. the description of nomad life and the history of the Huns given by Gibbon at the beginning of Chap. XXVI. of the *Decline and Fall.* His authority for the identification of the Hiung-nu is de Guignes, and it is upheld by modern writers, in spite of the attacks made upon it by certain later critics. The modern Peking pronunciation Hsiung-nu has no bearing on the question.

[3] Franke, op. c. p. 45, n. 2, thinks the Ephthalites were true Huns, much mixed. In Sanskrit they were called Huṇa.

or to the West, where they often retrieve their fortunes. Hence the invasions of Huns and Avars and Turks: it was only the Mongols that themselves extended their empire so far. To the north also this influence reached so that most of the Jenisei tribes and most of the Finno-Ugrians have been so much Tartarised that it is hard to reconstitute their original mutual relations. We have only to take the series back one more term and the movement which brought the Scyths into Europe and all the effects of their coming fall perfectly into line.

The foregoing sketch of Central Asia from the Chinese standpoint recalls many details in Herodotus, and the complete picture as drawn by the Chinese agrees precisely with his. Take for instance the accounts of the T'u-küe (c. 550 A.D.). They begin by saying that these are descended from the Hiung-nu and have exactly the same mode of life: that is that details which do not happen to be given as to one tribe may be inferred from their applying to the other. The various Tung-hu or eastern nomads differ considerably. The T'u-küe were then a tribe of the Hiung-nu and traced their descent from a she-wolf, hence they had a she-wolf on their standards. (We can imagine them to have been like the animals on sockets found at Alexandropol.) Their habits are thus described. They wear their hair long, and throw on their clothes to the left: they live in felt tents and move about according to the abundance of water and grass. They make little of old men and only consider such as are in the prime of life. They have little honesty or proper shame; no rites or justice, like the Hiung-nu. Perhaps this is only one point of view; another passage says that they are just in their dealings, suggesting the Greek view of nomads, δικαιότατοι ἀνθρώπων (v. p. 109).

Their arms are bow, arrows, sounding arrows (used for signals), cuirass, lance, dagger and sword. On their standards is a golden she-wolf. Their belts have ornaments engraved and in relief. This reminds us of the universal Scythic gold plates. So Zemarchus at the Turkish court remarked on the profusion of gold[1]. They use notches in wood for counting: elsewhere it says they have an alphabet like other Hu or barbarians.

When a man dies he is put dead in his tent. His sons, nephews and relations kill each a sheep or horse and stretch them before the tent as an offering. They cut their faces with a knife[2]. On a favourable day they burn his horse and all his gear[3]. They collect the ashes and bury the dead at particular periods. If a man die in spring or summer they wait for the leaves to fall, if in autumn or winter they wait for leaves and flowers to come out. Then they dig a ditch and bury him. On the day of the funeral they cut their cheeks, and so forth as on the first day. On the tomb they put a tablet and as many stones as the dead man has killed enemies. They sacrifice a horse and a sheep and hang their heads over the tablet. That day the men and women meet at the tomb clothed in their best and feast. These feasts seem to be the occasions when the young men see girls to fall in love with them and ask their hands of their fathers. This whole account seems rather to describe a funeral in two parts or funeral

---

[1] Menander, f. 20; *FHG.* IV. p. 227.
[2] Cf. Menander, f. 43; *FHG.* IV. p. 247.
[3] Radloff says this must be a mistake, as he has found no traces of cremation. Some tombs both in Siberia and in Russia have the wooden erection partly burnt, cf. A. Heikel, Antiquités de la Sibérie occidentale in *Mém. Soc. Finno-Ougrienne* VI. (1894), and Radloff, *Aus Sibirien*, II. chap. vii.

and after-funeral than really to imply that the dead were kept according to the time of the year. It corresponds generally with what is found in Scythic tombs and with the account in Herodotus. Hieh-li, the last Khan, was buried under a mound, and an attendant willingly sacrificed himself to serve him in the next world[1]. When a man dies his son, younger brother or nephew takes his wives and their sisters to wife. This was the case with the Scyths, e.g. Scyles married Opoea, wife of his father Ariapithes[2].

Although the T'u-küe change places, yet they have special land for each family. Agriculture is not unknown to them. The Khan lives at Tu-kin Shan. They revere demons and spirits and believe in magicians. Their food of milk and cheese and kumys is just what Herodotus describes.

A curious point of likeness already referred to is the attraction civilisation exercised upon them, so that individuals were continually trying to imitate Chinese ways, they married Chinese wives, and some could even talk Chinese, and occasionally it required the good sense of Chinese deserters to prevent the nomads giving up their ways and so rendering themselves open to attack. On the other hand, when the Chinese tried to make them adopt small details, Sha-poh-lioh the Khan, 581—587, replied, "We have had our habits for a long time and cannot change them[3]." Just the same opposition is characteristic of the Scyths, some of whom were always hankering after Greek ways, in spite of the disapproval of their fellows. So Marco Polo[4] speaks of the degeneracy of the Tartars, who by his time had adopted the customs of the idolaters in Cathay and of the Saracens in the Levant.

Géza Nagy[5] remarks on another point of resemblance between the Scyths and the Turks, their very concrete metaphors. Just as the Scyths replied to the Persians' defiance by sending the Great King a bird, a mouse, a frog and five arrows, which is rightly interpreted by Gobryas to mean that they will fall by the arrows, unless like birds they can fly into the air, or like mice burrow underground, or like frogs jump into the waters[6], so the Turks threatened the Avars that, flee as they might, they would find them upon the face of the ground, for they were not birds to fly up into the air nor fishes to hide themselves in the sea.

In just the same way, in A.D. 1303, Toktai sends to Nogai as a declaration of war a hoe, an arrow and a handful of earth; which being interpreted is, "I dig you out, I shoot you, better choose the battlefield[7]."

So the familiar story of Scilurus and his counsel to his sons, illustrated by a bundle of faggots, is told by Hayton the Armenian of Chingiz Khan[8].

Pictures of Hiung-nu.

Not only the verbal accounts agree but also the pictures. In the Pien-i-tien and I-yü-kuo-chih we have pictures of Hiung-nu. They have more

[1] *China Review*, XXV. p. 242.
[2] Her. IV. 79. Cf. de Plano Carpini of the Mongols, c. 6, ap. Hakluyt, Rockhill, p. 78, Yule[3], I. p. 253.
[3] *China Review*, XXV. p. 11.
[4] Yule[3], Vol. I. c. liv. p. 263.

[5] op. cit. p. 58.
[6] Her. IV. 130—132.
[7] Yule, *Marco Polo*[3], Vol. II. p. 498, quoting Hammer von Purgstall.
[8] *Haithoni Armeni de Tartaris Liber* in *Novus Orbis* of Grynaeus, Basel, 1537, c. xvii.

FIG. 27.

beard than we might expect. Their tunics lined with fur are not unlike the Scythic tunics on the Kul Oba vase, their soft boots tied about the ankle with a string are very similar, and the bow and bow-case are very much like the western representations. Scyths are always bare-headed or wear a hood, but the Hiung-nu have conical fur-lined caps. The Kara Kitan in the latter book, sitting between the hoofs of his horse who is lying down, reminds us of some of the Siberian gold plates. The bow-case is well shewn on the Pa-li-fêng, a kind of Tartar. The horns on the head of the women of the T'u-huo-lo and their neighbours, adorned as they were with gold and silver, resemble the headdress of the Queen at Karagodeuashkh. But these resemblances do not go deep and many of the coincidences in customs may be merely due to like circumstances, still the likenesses are so great and the barriers between South Russia and Central Asia so often traversed, that it is harder to believe that entirely separate races developed such a similarity of culture than that a horde driven west by some disturbance early in the last millennium B.C. finally found its way to the Euxine steppes. And the character of the objects they had buried with them on their way from the Altai to the Carpathians sets the matter almost beyond doubt.

So far we have used no more evidence than was before K. Neumann, the champion of the Mongolian theory, the strength of whose case rests upon coincidences of custom, very close indeed but not sufficient to prove that the Scythians had any real connection with upper Asia, for his philological comparisons have been rejected by serious students of Mongolian, or was before Müllenhoff, chief defender of the dominant Iranian theory, who supported it on philological grounds, stronger indeed than Neumann's, but affording too narrow a basis for the weight it has to bear. Neither of these writers has given due weight to the analogies between the remains found in the tombs of Scythia and those that occur in southern Siberia, in the basin of the Jenisei, far beyond the limits of Aryan population. Until the affinities of that civilisation and of the tribes that were influenced by it have been cleared up, the final word cannot be said on the position of the Scythians[1].

SCYTHIAN PROBLEM.

BIBLIOGRAPHICAL SUMMARY.

So many different views as to the affinities of the Scythians have been propounded that their enumeration seemed too much of a burden for the text of Chapter IV. At the same time their succession has a certain historical interest and space had to be found for a short account of the more important theories. The older writers are more fully dealt with by Dr L. Niederle[2], but one or two useful books have escaped even his marvellously wide reading.

The traditional view regarded the Sarmatians, and the Scythians naturally went

---

[1] However Neumann, op. cit. p. 236, quotes Gmelin's account of the graves on the Abakan.

[2] *Slovanské Starožitnosti* (Slavonic Antiquities), Prag, 1902—, Vol. I., Appendix p. 512.

with them, as the ancestors of the Slavs. For one thing the Byzantine writers applied to the latter these classical names which had already served for the Goths: for another there was no more obvious ancestry for the Slavs to be discerned among nations mentioned by ancient writers, and the Scythians and Sarmatians, though great nations, did not seem to have left any other descendants. This theory naturally appealed to the tendency of chroniclers to push the ancestry of their own nation as far back as possible, and accordingly it is accepted by most of the Slavonic historiographers. Since the appearance of later hypotheses it has been almost dropped in Germany, Cuno, with his fanciful Slavonic etymologies, being a solitary exception in later times[1]. In Russia, however, national feeling has kept it still alive. It gained support from the undoubted superficial resemblance of the Russian *muzhík* and the figures on the Kul Oba and Chertomlyk vases. The chief exponent of it has been Zabêlin[2].

During the eighteenth century there appeared· one or two dissentients, but the first to gain general approval with a new theory was B. G. Niebuhr[3]. He made a careful examination of Herodotean geography and referred the Scyths to a stock akin to the Tartars and Mongols. His main arguments were based upon similarity of customs. Grote[4] gives a good statement of this view. Boeckh, in the introduction to *Inscriptiones Sarmatiae, etc.*[5], regards the Scyths as Mongolian and the Sarmatae as Slavs with Mongolian mixture, but admits the Iranian element. Niebuhr's line of proof was carried further by K. Neumann[6], who also adduced etymologies from the Mongolian which were promptly demolished by the great Turcologue Schiefner[7].

Meanwhile Kaspar Zeuss[8] had advanced the view that all the steppe peoples as far as the Argippaei were Iranian. His main argument was the similarity of Scythian and Iranian religion, but he also proposed Iranian etymologies for a certain number of Scythian words. This view gained general favour when supported by K. Müllenhoff, who supplied a large number of Iranian etymologies[9]. Duncker[10] states Müllenhoff's view without reservation as fact. W. Tomaschek[11] accepted this theory and developed the geography of the subject. Much the same general position was taken by A. von Gutschmid[12], and Th. G. Braun[13] follows Tomaschek closely. So, too, Dr Niederle (op. cit.) seems to have not a doubt of the broad truth of Müllenhoff's view on this matter, though generally inclined to disagree with him[14]. L. Wilser[15] takes the Iranian character of the Scythian language as proven and tries to prove in his turn that it has also special affinities with German. In fact he regards Germans, Scyths, Parthians, Persians and Medes as a series without very considerable gaps between the neighbouring terms,

[1] J. G. Cuno, *Forschungen im Gebiete der alten Völkerkunde.* I. Theil, *Die Skythen,* Berlin, 1871, described by Gutschmid in his review of it as the worst book he had met for fifteen years (*Kl. Schr.* III., p. 446—452). He had never met *Scythia Biformis das Urreich der Asen* by Wajtes Prusisk, Breslau, n. d.

[2] I. E. Zabêlin, *History of Russian Life,* I. 243 sqq.; also D. J. Samokvásov, *History of Russian Law,* Pt II. 1—69, Warsaw, 1884.

[3] *Kl. Schriften,* 1828, I. p. 352 sqq., in English, *A Dissertation on the Geography of Herodotus and Researches into the History of the Scythians, Getae and Sarmatians,* Oxford, 1830.

[4] *History of Greece,* ed. 3, 1851, Vol. III. p. 216 —243.

[5] *CIG.* Vol. II., Pt XI. p. 81.

[6] *Die Hellenen im Skythenlande,* Berlin, 1855.

[7] "Sprachliche Bedenken gegen das Mongolenthum der Skythen," *Mélanges Asiatiques,* T. II. p. 531, St Petersburg, 1856.

[8] *Die Deutschen und die Nachbarstämme,* München, 1837.

[9] "Ueber die Herkunft und Sprache der Pontischen Scythen und Sarmaten." *Monatsber. d. k. Preuss. Akad. d. W.* 1866, p. 549, reprinted in *Deutsche Altertumskunde,* Berlin, 1870—1900, III.

p. 101 sqq.

[10] *History of Antiquity,* Eng. Trans. 1879, Vol. III. pp. 228—246.

[11] "Kritik der ältesten Nachrichten über den Skythischen Norden. I. Ueber das Arimaspische Gedicht des Aristeas," *Sitzungsber. d. kk. Akad. zu Wien,* 1888, CXVI. pp. 715—780. II. "Die Nachrichten Herodot's über den Skythischen Karawanenenweg nach Innerasien." *Ib.* CXVII., pp. 1—70.

[12] "Die Skythen," in *Kl. Schriften* III., p. 421, Leipzig, 1892, from this the article in the ninth edition of *Encyclopaedia Britannica* is shortened.

[13] *Investigations in the province of Gotho-Slavonic Relations,* St Petersburg, 1899.

[14] See also Sir H. Howorth, *Journ. of Anthrop. Inst.* VI. (1877), pp. 41 sqq.; H. d'Arbois de Jubainville, *Les premiers habitants de l'Europe,* Paris, 1889, II. pp. 223—264; F. W. Thomas, "Sakastana," *JRAS.* 1906, p. 204 regards "Scythic" as an E. Iranian dialect, but he mostly means Indo-Scythic.

[15] Cf. *Internationales Centralblatt für Anthropologie u. s. w.* VII. (1902), Heft 6, p. 353, review of L. Wilser; "Skythen und Perser," in *Asien—Organ der Deutschen Asiatischen Gesellschaft,* 1902.

whereas he entirely denies the close connection between the speakers of Sanskrit and the speakers of Zend. Unfortunately, not having seen his paper, I cannot give his arguments for this novel position. Something similar is J. Fressl's view[1], and E. Bonnell seems to waver between assigning Germans, Lithuanians, Slavs, and Kelts as descendants of the Scythians, whom yet he calls Iranian[2]. Likewise Fr. Spiegel[3] thinks the bulk of Scythians Indo-European, but will not decide between Iranians and Slavs; still he admits a possibility of Uralo-Altaic Royal Scyths. So, too, Professor Lappo-Danilevskij, in his convenient collection of material concerning Scyths, gives rather an uncertain sound as to their ethnological affinities[4].

Meanwhile Niebuhr's theory lived on in spite of the Iranian hypothesis of the philologists[5], especially in Hungary, where A. Csengery referred the Scyths to the Uralo-Altaic folk[6], perhaps to the Sumer-Akkadians, and Count Géza Kuun[7] to the Turco-Tartars on the ground of the god-names, and A. Vámbéry on the ground of customs[8]. This view finds its most complete expression in a monograph by Géza Nagy[9].

A Magyar has a hereditary right to speak on any question concerning Finno-Ugrians, but he is apt to have his racial prejudices, which act as a corrective to those of the German or the Slav. Accordingly Mr Nagy maintains that the Scyths were Uralo-Altaic, and thinks that an Uralo-Altaic language has always been dominant in the Steppes, save for the comparatively short interval during which the Aryan branch of the Indo-Europeans was making its way from its European home towards Iran and the Panjáb. This view he supports by destructive criticism of the etymologies proposed by Müllenhoff and other advocates of the pure Iranian view, criticism that in truth shews up their mutual disagreement and the arbitrary character of their comparisons. But he in turn advances Uralo-Altaic etymologies equally arbitrary, and in them has recourse to Sumer-Akkadian, a language whose existence is hardly so strongly established as to allow it to lend support to further fabrics of theory[10].

There follow further arguments drawn from physical type, manner of life, custom and religion, much the same as those advanced above, with the general result that although the author does not deny the existence among the steppe-dwellers of a strong Iranian influence and of a certain Iranian element supplied by the leavings of the great Aryan migration, he takes their main mass to have been Uralo-Altaic in speech, and even distinguishes among them different layers, Finno-Ugrian and Turco-Tartar, and different stages of social development, matriarchal and patriarchal.

[1] *Die Skytho-Saken die Urväter der Germanen*, München, 1886.

[2] *Beiträge zur Alterthumskunde Russlands*, St Petersburg, I. 1882, II. 1897 : a book of useful material used uncritically. Rawlinson *Herodotus*, III. p. 158 makes Sc. a special branch of Indo-European.

[3] *Éranische Alterthumskunde*, II. p. 333 sqq.

[4] *Trans. Imp. Russ. Soc.*, Slavonic Section, Vol. IV. (1887), p. 352 sqq.

[5] e.g. E. Bunbury, *Hist. of Ancient Geography*, I. 215 ; H. Stein, *Herodotus*, Vol. II. p. 13 ; Fligier, *Archiv f. Anthropologie* XVII. p. 302.

[6] *A Szkithák Nemzetisége* (The Scyths' Nationality), Budapest, 1859.

[7] *Codex Cumanicus*, Budapest, 1880.

[8] *A Magyarok Eredete* (The Origin of the Magyars) (Chap. i.), Budapest, 1882 : for these references to Magyar books I am indebted to G. Nagy. Cf. also Vámbéry's *Die primitive Kultur der Turko-Tataren*, Leipsig, 1879.

[9] *Archaeologiai Értesitö* for 1895, reprinted as No. 3 of *Néprajzi Füzetek*, Budapest, 1895. "A Szkithák Nemzetisége" (The Scyths' Nationality). Without the aid of Mr S. Schiller-Szinessy, of Cambridge, I could not have learnt to read this valuable essay.

[10] With regard to affinities with the early population of SW. Asia various writers have already pointed out resemblances between the Hittite and the Scythian dress. Some have brought in the Etruscans too, hoping to solve the three chief problems of the ancient world under one. But there is no physical impossibility about North Asiatics in Asia Minor, as is shewn by the incursions spoken of by the Hebrew prophets and supposed to have changed Beth-shean to Scythopolis. Fr. Hommel ("Hethiter und Skythen und das erste Auftreten der Iranier in der Geschichte," in *Sitzungsber. d. k. Böhm. Ges. d. Wiss. Phil.-Hist. Classe*, Prag, 1898, VI.) proposes Iranian derivations for the Hittite names on Egyptian and Assyrian monuments, and on this basis goes on to identify Hittites and Scythians, taking the Iranian character of the latter for granted, arguing from the late Greek inscriptions with barbarian names. In support of this surprising hypothesis he quotes the mythical accounts of combats between Sesostris and the Scythians, Herodotus, II. 103, 110 ; Justin, I. 1 and II. 3 ; Diodorus, I. 55, II. 43, 46, and says that these Scythians were really Hittites (v. p. 36). Karolides, *Die sogenannten Assyrochaldäer und Hittiten*, Athen, 1898, suggests something of the same sort, to judge by Jensen's review in *Berl. Phil. Wochenschr.* 1899, p. 1034.

Even in etymology he makes out a very good case for the Uralo-Altaic origin of some of the Scythic god-names (v. supra, p. 85). Other words with a likely Uralo-Altaic origin are the Greek τυρός, cf. Magy. *turó*, "curd," and Κιμμέριοι, the men of the darkness, cf. Magy. *komor*, "dark," Zyrjan *kimör*. On the other hand some of the etymologies proposed by the Iranian party are reasonable and G. Nagy's substitutes very far-fetched. As he applies all the stories of origins to the Altaic tribes and makes even the Cimmerians and agricultural Scythians Altaic, he has to find suitable meanings for Colaxais and his brothers, which leads him very far afield. So too with Oiorpata, Arimaspi, Enarees, Exampaeus, all of which are either obviously or very probably Iranian.

The upshot of all this is to prove from the other side that no one etymological key will open all the locks that bar the way to a full understanding of the Scythian problem. This Jurgewicz[1] saw, but endeavoured to explain too much from Mongolian, even those names in the Greek inscriptions that most easily yield Iranian meanings. These have been most satisfactorily interpreted from the Ossetian by Professor Vs. Th. Miller[2]. But his successful use of Iranian has not blinded him to the presence of other elements and he takes an eclectic view, allowing a strong influence and possibly rule exercised upon the Iranians by Uralo-Altaic folk. Professor Th. I. Mishchenko, the Russian translator of Herodotus, sets forth a similar theory in various articles[3], and with these authors' general views I am in very close agreement. However they have mostly regarded the Sarmatians as an Iranian tribe that has swept away the supposed domination of the Uralo-Altaic horde: but I find it hard to draw any real line of demarcation. Many of the archaeological finds on which I have largely relied for evidence of Uralo-Altaic influence undoubtedly belong to the Sarmatian period. Each people probably consisted of an Iranian-speaking mixed multitude, dominated by a clan of "Turks" whose language died out but supplied many loan-words, particularly special terms touching the official religion and the necessities of Nomad life. The Iranians who took to that life had no such words of their own and had to borrow them of the real steppe folk, together with their customs, dress and art.

New possibilities are opened by the surprising discovery made by Dr E. Sieg and Dr W. Siegling[4] that among the MSS. brought by Dr A. von Le Coq[5] from near Turfan in Eastern Turkestan are fragments of an Indo-European language which as a "*centum*" language, and, so far as deciphered, in vocabulary, is rather European than Asiatic, but which in its case-formation seems to follow Altaic models. The decipherers call it "Tocharian, the language of the Indo-Scyths," i.e. of the Yüe-chih, on the ground of the colophon of an Uigur MS. noting a translation made from Indian through "Toχrï̈[6]." In view of the numerous languages represented in the Le Coq, Grünwedel and Stein MSS. from E. Turkestan, there is not evidence enough for putting a name to the new language (the more that the Uigur for Yüe-chih is Kitsi, v. p. 111, n. 2), but its existence and perhaps also the pictures of a blonde race formerly in these parts make us ready to believe that migrations from Europe, subsequent to those of the Indo-Iranians, penetrated the heart of Asia. Any of the peoples of whom we know neither the physical characteristics nor the languages, but only the names upon the map of Scythia in the widest sense, may have been Indo-Europeans of this or some other new branch. One thinks at once of the Wu-sun with red hair and blue eyes set deep in the face, who made the same impression on the Chinese as do Europeans, and of the fair Budini among whom were the Geloni talking something like Greek. We may hope any day for specimens of Saka speech as Dr Le Coq tells me, but I still hold the above view of the Scyths in Europe.

[1] *Trans. Odessa Soc.* VIII., 1872, pp. 4—38.
[2] *Journ. Min. Publ. Instr.*, St P., Oct. 1886, p. 232, "Epigraphic traces of Iranian population on the North Coast of the Euxine"; and again in his *Ossetian Studies*, Vol. III., Moscow, 1887.
[3] *Bulletin of Kiev University*, 1882, No. 11; 1883, No. 9, "On the question of the Ethnography and Geography of Herodotean Scythia"; *Journ. Min. Publ. Inst.*, St P., Classical Section, 1888,
January, pp. 39—47, "Legends of the Royal Scyths in Herodotus"; 1896, May, pp. 69—89, "Ethnography of Russia according to Herodotus," November, pp. 103—124, "The Information of Herodotus as to the lands in Russia outside Scythia."
[4] *SB. d. k. pr. Akad. d. W.* Berlin, 1908, p. 915.
[5] *Zt. f. Ethnologie*, 1907, p. 509.
[6] F. K. W. Müller in *SB. d. k. pr. Akad. d. W.* Berlin, 1907, p. 958.

CHAPTER V.

TRIBES ADJOINING SCYTHIA ACCORDING TO HERODOTUS AND ARISTEAS.

On the South, Tauri and Getae.

BEFORE treating in detail of the archaeological evidence as to the population of the Euxine steppes, it seems suitable to consider the statements of
Herodotus and other ancient authors as to the different peoples that surrounded those whom he called Scythian. In spite of the confusion in the
account of the rivers, they are our best guide in locating the various tribes
both within and without the ill-defined outlines of Scythia proper. (Maps
I., IV., V.)

On the mountainous south coast of the Crimea lived the Tauri, some have
called them Kelts, comparing the name of the Taurisci : but some theorists
find Kelts everywhere. We have no data whatsoever for giving relations to
the Tauri. They probably represent the earliest inhabitants of S. Russia,
perhaps akin to the aborigines of the Caucasus ; possibly they would be
Iranians if Ἀρδάβδα was their name for Theodosia, which lay on their
borders[1]. Then we could understand their later mixing with the Scythians,
when in the latter the Iranian element had again come to the top. Otherwise we must take the Scytho-Tauri to be like the Celto-Scythae and the
Celtiberians, products of the Greek belief that a race of which not much
was known was best named by combining the names of its neighbours.

The Tauri were chiefly famous for their maiden goddess[2], to whom
they sacrificed shipwrecked sailors. They seem always to have been pirates
and wreckers. In the second century B.C. they were the dependent allies
of Scilurus, and though their name survives on the maps their nationality
seems to have merged in the surrounding tribes.

Along the lower Danube the western Scythians marched with the Getae[3],
a tribe of whom Herodotus and Strabo have much to say. Our authorities
generally agree in making them a branch of the Thracians, though it is
doubtful how far Thracian is more than a geographical expression. There
seem to have been two races there with different customs and different
beliefs as to a future life[4]. The Getae would be akin to those whom
Professor Ridgeway regards as invaders from Central Europe, with light
complexions, and a religion shewing decided resemblances to Druidism.
But they do not come into our subject except in connection with the
history of Olbia, which they destroyed about 50 B.C. The Kelts on the
lower Danube and also the Bastarnae belong to a later distribution of races.

---

[1] Anon. Peripl., § 77 (51), it is more probably
Alan.

[2] Her. IV. 103, v. inf. Chapter XVII.

[3] For Getae v. Müllenhoff, *DA.* III. pp. 125—163;
W. Tomaschek, " Die Alten Thraker," I. p. 92 sqq.,
in *Sitzungsber. d. kk. Akad. zu Wien,* CXXVIII.,
1893, and P. Kretschmer, *Einleitung in die
Geschichte der griechischen Sprache,* Göttingen,
1896, p. 212 ; Niederle, *Slav. Ant.* I. p. 318, II.
p. 62, v. inf. p. 122, for their invasions of Scythia.

[4] W. Ridgeway, *Early Age,* I. p. 351 sqq.

On the West, Agathyrsi and Sigynnae.

The Agathyrsi[1], the westerly neighbours of the Scythians, are said by
Herodotus (IV. 104) to resemble the Thracians in most of their customs,
and are taken by all writers to be closely connected with them in race, as
later the Getae and the Dacians, whose names we afterwards find in the
same region, the modern Transylvania, out of which flows the Maros (Μάρις)[2]
to join the Danube. It is just conceivable that they were Iranian, at least
the name Spargapithes has such a look[3]. The effeminacy of the nation
does not agree with the general character of the Thracians, but the weight
of opinion assigns them to that stock[4]. F. Hartwig[5] seeks to identify the
Agathyrsi with people in curious fringed gowns on a cylix from Orvieto.

The Sigynnae whom Herodotus (v. 9) mentions quite in another connection
as living beyond the Danube and stretching westward to the land of the
Enetae, would be more likely to be Iranian, for he says that they called themselves colonists of the Medes and that they wore Median dress. He says
he cannot tell how Median colonists should come there, but that anything
may happen, given sufficient time. This expression certainly suggests that
Herodotus had no idea that from the Carpathians to the confines of Media
there stretched a whole row of nations, more or less akin to the Medes, for,
as I take it, the Iranian character was disguised by the Scythic element
which gave the tone to the whole. Strabo (XI. x. 8) puts the Sigynni (*sic*)
on the Caspian, and Niederle[6] seems inclined to think him right, supposing
a confusion to have arisen through the use of the word Sigynna in Ligurian
in the sense of pedlar: but Herodotus, by mentioning this fact, makes it
unlikely that he should have been led astray by it; a national name may
well gain such a meaning[7]. A point about the Sigynnae which is mentioned
by both Herodotus and Strabo is their use of small shaggy ponies for driving.
The Median dress may mean no more than that they wore trousers. It
seems as if trousers were introduced to Europeans by immigrants from the
steppes to the east. The form of the word "*braccae*" suggests that they
were adopted first by the Germans and then by some of the Kelts[8].

Northern Border.

The Neuri[9] marched with the Agathyrsi. Their position would be
about the head waters of the Dnêstr and Bugh and the central basin of the
Dnêpr. The Neuri are perhaps the most interesting of the Scythians'
neighbours, for we can hardly fail to see in them the forefathers of the
modern Slavs. This is just the district that satisfies the conditions for the
place from which the Slavonic race spread in various directions. The one
distinguishing trait that Herodotus gives us, that each man became a wolf

---

[1] In treating the neighbours of the Scyths I have
mostly followed Tomaschek, "*Kritik*" II. v. supra,
p. 98, n. 11.
[2] Her. IV. 48.
[3] Her. IV. 78, cf. the Scythian S. IV. 76, and
Spargapises, king of the Massagetae, I. 211 : but it
may have been supplied to give individual circumstance to the story of Scyles. Their community of
wives also recalls the Massagetae.

[4] Niederle, *Slav. Ant.* I. p. 263.
[5] *Die Griechischen Meisterschalen*, p. 421, Pl.
XXXVIII., XXXIX., v. supra, pp. 54, 55.
[6] op. cit., I. p. 238.
[7] e.g. Lithuanian *Szatas*, i.e. Scot = pedlar.
[8] v. d'Arbois de Jubainville, op. cit. II. p. 264 ;
Sophus Müller, *Urgeschichte Europas*, Strassburg,
1905, p. 161 sqq.
[9] Her. IV. 105.

for a few days every year (IV. 105), recalls the werewolf story that has always been current among the Slavs; even now the word for werewolf is one of the very few Slavonic loan-words in Modern Greek. Everything points to this identification. Braun (op. cit. p. 79 sqq.) puts the case very well. Valerius Flaccus (*Argon.* VI. 122) speaks of "*raptor amorum Neurus*," which calls to mind the account of the Drevlians and other Slavonic tribes of this region who carried off their wives at water[1], but we do not know if he had any foundation for the expression. When Herodotus says that the Neuri had Scythian customs, it might well describe the frontiersmen on whom the Scythic culture had evident influence (v. p. 175). The geographical names of the district are purely Slavonic, whereas immediately further east the occurrence of Finnish words for rivers shews that we are no longer in territory originally Slavonic[2]. Tomaschek suggests that the invasion of snakes which drove the Neuri eastward to the Budini, said by Herodotus to have happened one generation before the campaign of Darius, an invasion usually taken to mean an attack from a hostile tribe[3], was really a movement of the East Germans, and Braun[4] goes so far as to say that it was a movement of the Bastarnae, forced down between them and the Carpathians by the expansion of the Kelts at their time of greatest power for aggression. He sees in the occupation of the Desná the first movement of Slavonic conquest. For here we have a river bearing a Slavonic name, the Right-hand river, clearly approached by the Slavs from the south and flowing through a country of which the other river-names are Finnish. That the Slavs came to know the Kelts through the Germans is clear from loan-words, especially Russian *volokh*, O. Slav. *vlakh*, from Gothic *walhoz, our "Welsh," the German name for Kelts and later for Romance speakers[5].

Eastward of the Neuri in the general description of Scythia[6] and in the other passages where they are referred to, come the Androphagi. But in the account of the Neuri, c. 105, it is said that the latter, when invaded by snakes, migrated to the Budini, that is past Androphagi and Melanchlaeni. Either then the Budini changed their abode, perhaps in consequence of this invasion, or there were two tribes of Budini, eastward and westward. This might help to account for the genesis of the story about the march of Darius across Scythia. If the tale went that Darius marched to the land of the Budini, it would be readily thought to speak of the eastern Budini, well known because of the town Gelonus and its connection with Greek trade. We must then allow a probability of a second tribe of Budini near the Neuri[7].

[1] Ps.-Nestor, Laurentian MS., ed.[3], p. 12, умыкиваху у воды дѣвица.

[2] N. P. Barsov, *Outlines of Russian Historical Geography,* Warsaw, 1885, p. 75.

[3] Niederle, *Slav. Ant.* I. p. 295, vehemently protests against this interpretation, and takes the account literally.

[4] op. cit. p. 247.

[5] The identification of Neuri and Slavs seems first to have been well established by P. J. Šafařík (Slovanské Starožitnosti), *Slavonic Antiquities,* Prag, 1862—63, I. p. 224 sqq. He regards their land as the very kernel or heart of the region originally settled by the Wends. He takes the Budini (ibid. p. 215) to be Slavs also, and their name to mean Waterfolk, from *vodá*. Gelonus reminds him of the typical spread-out Slav settlement. His tradition is carried on by Niederle, *Slav. Ant.* I. p. 266.

[6] Her. IV. c. 102, 106.

[7] This expedient of supposing doubled tribes is excused by many instances of tribes with similar names, especially in Eastern Europe, under conditions which make it easy for part of a nation to split off, e.g. Royal Scyths and colonist Scyths in Herodotus, three or four tribes called Huns, so too with Alans, Turks, Bolgars, Tartars, Kalmucks, Nogai, all of which have had subdivisions living at one time far apart from each other. This list might be almost indefinitely extended.

The Androphagi were probably Finns, and the most barbarous of them, as no trade route passed through their land. Theirs would be central Muscovy and southwards towards Chernigov. Hence, too, the most exaggerated stories would be told of them. But we need not believe that they were cannibals any more than the Samoyeds, Finns also, whose name means the same. Tomaschek ingeniously suggests that the Amadoci of Pseudo-Hellanicus[1] and of Ptolemy are the same as the Androphagi, *āmâdaka*, cf. Skr. *āmâd*, eater of raw meat. He would propose to identify them with the Mordva of the present day, which is very possible, for there is no doubt that all the Finnish tribes now found on the middle Volga and on the Kama once lived far to the west or south. But when Tomaschek (II. p. 10) sees in Mordva another Iranian nickname meaning cannibal, he hardly carries conviction. The necessary sound changes are as unlikely as that a nation would take such a nickname to itself. Still Mordva is a loan-word from the Iranian (= *Mensch*), and many other words shew that these Finnish tribes, now so far separated from any Iranian nationality, once had close dealings with some such. That the Mordva once marched with speakers of the Baltic group far to the west of their present place is shewn by loans from an early stage of Slavonic and from Lithuanian.

If the Androphagi are Finns, Mordva, the Melanchlaeni are Finns also, Merja and Cheremis. The former were early absorbed by the advance of the Slavs, and the latter have been so strongly subjected to Turkish influence that all earlier traces have been wiped out. But archaeological evidence proves that some such tribe occupied the region corresponding to that assigned by Herodotus to the Melanchlaeni about Riazan and Tambov[2]. It may be a coincidence that the Cheremis wore black till a hundred years ago. Dark felt is the natural product of the coarse dark-woolled sheep of the country. So we need not see any connection with the Σανδαράται of the Protogenes inscription (Ossete *sau* black, *daras* garment) who were almost certainly a Sarmatian tribe. For the kind of name compare the Caucasian Melanchlaeni, who have tended to the confusion of later writers, and in modern times the Kara Kalpaks, White Russians, and such like.

Next to the Melanchlaeni and now above the Sarmatians, well to the east of Scythia, lived the Budini, fifteen days' journey from the corner of the Maeotis. The Oarus seems to have flowed through their country, coming from that of the Thyssagetae. If then we measure fifteen days' journey up the Don to the portage by Tsaritsyn and then up the Volga, we come to the lower part of the governments of Saratov and Samára, and not far to the north begins the forest region. The territory of the Budini probably included the lower courses of the Bêlaja, Vjátka and Káma. The inhabitants are most likely represented by the Permiaks, driven north and east by the spread of the Slavs and the irruptions of the Tartars.

Near the junction of the Kama and Volga there has always been an important trading post, Kazan since the coming of the Mongols, in early mediaeval times Bolgary. Gelonus seems to have been the first of the

---

[1] Steph. Byz. ad voc.

[2] Count Uvarov, *Les Mériens*, St P., 1875; however A. A. Spitsyn, *BCA*. xv. 164, urges that the particular barrows that Uvarov assigns to the Merja belong rather to early Russians, but he does not deny a still earlier Finnish population.

series. We have the name of another town among the Budini, Καρίσκος[1].
Tomaschek compares Permian *karysok*, little fortress. The wide commercial
relations of this district are shewn by the wonderful silver plates found in the
government of Perm, splendid specimens of Graeco-Roman, Syrian, Byzantine,
Sassanian and even Indian work being dug up in these remote forests, as
well as coins of Indo-Scythian kings[2], evidence of connection with Central
Asia. All these precious wares must have been paid for with furs. There
may well have been a sufficiently lively trade to tempt the Greeks to establish
a factory in the interior of the country, even as far from the coast as the
land of the Budini[3]. Herodotus probably exaggerated the number of the
Greek population, as he has most clearly exaggerated the extent of the
town of Gelonus. Three miles and a half square is an impossible size,
three miles and a half about would be plenty for warehouses and temples
and gardens and space for folding the local sheep of which Aristotle speaks.
The establishment must have been like one of the forts in Canada, inhabited
by a mixed population of traders and trappers, or the *Ostrogi* in Siberia,
round which towns like Tomsk and Tobolsk have grown[4]. The description
of the Budini themselves tallies with that of the Permiaks, grey-eyed and
reddish-haired : φθειροτραγέουσι—compare what Ibn Fadhlān says of the
Bashkirs, "*Pediculos comedunt.*" The otters and beavers of Herodotus
have become rarer with assiduous hunting, but they were common when the
Russians first came, and found a home by the many rivers of the country[5].
His lake may be the marshes on the course of these, for instance about
the lower Kama.

It is barely conceivable that the Neuri should have come so far for
refuge as to the middle Volga, hence the probability of there having been
other Budini near the Dnêpr. These Darius may perhaps have reached ;
Ptolemy's Bodini seem the mere survival of an empty name.

Niederle[6], while admitting that the Androphagi and Melanchlaeni are
Finns, is inclined to think the Budini Slavonic. He regards them as
stretching from the Dnêpr to the Don behind the Androphagi, although
Herodotus says distinctly that beyond these is a real desert and no men at
all. Budini looks cèrtainly very like a Slavonic tribe-name with the common
suffix -*in*-, and there are plenty of Slavonic names from the root *bud*-. But
they certainly stretched further east than Niederle allows, for they lived
fifteen days up the Don above the Sauromatae. By bringing them west
he puts Gelonus on the site of Kiev.

---

[1] Aristotle, ap. Aelian *de Nat. Anim.* XVI. 33.
[2] e.g. Kadphises I., *CR.* 1896, p. 132 ; *KTR.* p.
411–436 ; *Arch. Anz.* 1908, p. 150 sqq.
[3] J. Abercromby, *The Pre- and Proto-historic
Finns*, Vol. I. p. 124, describes the trade routes
followed by the mediaeval Arabs, both directly up
the Volga to Bolgary, and, when the Khazars
hindered, across the Kirgiz steppe from the Amu-
Daria, and so to the west of the Urals : he suggests
that the Persian plate found the same way, and in
yet earlier times the foreign imports found at
Ananjino, v. inf. p. 257. If the Geloni spoke
something like "Tocharian," a Greek hearing the
numerals might think them bastard Greek.
[4] For a view of such a wooden-walled town in

Europe in mediaeval times, v. *Nuremberg Chronicle*
(1493), fol. CCLIII., "Sabatz in Hungaria." The
gorodishche or camp at Bêlsk (v. p. 147) excavated
by Gorodtsov is 20 miles round, much larger than
Gelonus.
[5] Her. speaks of a marsh in which are taken
ἐνύδριες καὶ κάστορες καὶ ἄλλα θηρία τετραγωνο-
πρόσωπα. The last I wrongly identified with the
Tarandus or reindeer, v. sup. p. 5 and nn. 6, 7, but
the marsh and Theophrastus l.c. rule this out.
The ἐνύδριες usually translated otters are watersnakes, v. Pliny, *NH.* XXX. § 21, XXXII. § 82, and
the square faced beasts are the otters ; a gloss
to this effect has been misapplied.
[6] op. cit. I. p. 275.

The late Professor I. N. Smirnov[1] of Kazan, the chief authority on the Volga Finns, directly denies that the ancestors of the Cheremis and Mordva were the Melanchlaeni and Androphagi.   But he does not advance any very valid objections, and admits a contact with Iranians which argues a seat further to the south.   He denies any contact with Greeks such as we must suppose in the case of the Budini.   Incidentally he describes many customs among the Finns that recall Scythian usages : among the Cheremis the sacrifice of a horse forty days after death and the stretching of its skin over the tomb : the soul does not really leave the body for forty days and even later comes back to it by a hole left for the purpose.   On this fortieth day is the wake, at which the dead man assists, and is taken back to the grave on a cart with bells : among the Mordva again, after forty days there is a wake and a horse sacrifice and a washing of the funeral car.   In both cases many things are put in the grave, or the dead will come and fetch away both things and people.   This is all in favour of the existence of an Uralo-Altaic element among the Scyths, although there was a clear line of distinction drawn between them and these Finns : for the Finns lived in the forest and the mixed multitude of Scythians in the steppe.

South of the eastern Budini were the Sauromatae, stretching east and north from a point three days' journey to the east of the Tanais (which Herodotus takes to run southwards), and the same distance north of the corner of the Maeotis.   Hippocrates says they are a special tribe of Scythian, and Herodotus, deriving them from a marriage of Amazons and Scyths, shews that they spoke a language akin to that spoken by the Scyths but gave their womenfolk more freedom[2].

North-Easterly Trade Route.

·Herodotus derived his account of these nations, Agathyrsi, Neuri, Androphagi, Melanchlaeni, Budini and Sauromatae, from two sources and gives particulars of them in two places.   In the one (cc. 100—109, Map IV. p. 27) he is keeping in view the story of Darius and his expedition, but these tribes, although set out according to the scheme of the square, are not wrested far from their places as given by the less detailed account which goes with the less schematic description of the lie of the land (cc. 16—26, Map V. p. 34).   This he supplements with much information, partly due to Aristeas, as to tribes living in a north-easterly direction far into Central Asia (Map I.).   Due north of the European tribes Herodotus imagines a continuous desert, occasionally diversified with the lakes necessary for the southward-flowing rivers : this desert is a real desert as opposed to the patches of thinly peopled land separating hostile tribes.   Probably this real desert was actually uninhabited, as the forests of the far north were only peopled comparatively lately, when these very tribes were driven up by new comers from Asia, or the Lapps and Samoyeds crossed from the far NE.

---

[1] "Les Populations Finnoises du Bassin de la Volga et de la Kama, 1ère Partie, Les Tchérémisses, Les Mordves," Paris, 1898, tr. by P. Boyer in *Publications de l'École des Langues Orientales Vivantes,* IVᵉ Série, T. VIII.   I should like to express my gratitude to the author of this book for his kindness to me at Kazan, and especially to the translator, to whom I am indebted for my knowledge of Russian and for many favours, including the loan of this very book. Abercromby, op. cit., mostly follows Smirnov.

[2] Her. IV. 21, 110—117, also infra, p. 119, for their migration west of the Tanais.

The land of the next tribe, Thyssagetae, is beyond a desert seven days' journey across, lying to the N. or rather E. of the Budini[1]. From their country run the four rivers Lycus, Oarus, Tanais and Syrgis into the Maeotis. This last detail is not to be reconciled with geography (cf. p. 30). We can only think that it was a country with several rivers running SW., down which people got to the Maeotis across the Tsaritsyn portage. This would give us the western slope of the Ural from Ufá to Orenburg. Herodotus says nothing of the Urals. Their incline is so gentle that they do not strike a traveller as mountains. Here is a river, Chussovaja, which may have the same root as Thyssagetae. The termination of this latter form is Scythian or Sarmatian, cf. Tyragetae, Massagetae. In Ossetian, *-gä-* is an adjectival affix and *-tä* the plural termination. Tomaschek identifies the Thyssagetae with the Voguls.

The trade route described by Herodotus passed far to the north and crossed the Urals, avoiding the barren Caspian steppe. Herodotus knew that hereabouts was no channel leading to the Northern Ocean, and in this he was in advance of the more scientific geographers down to Marinus of Tyre.

To the south lived tribes of more or less Iranian affinities, Sauromatae, later Aorsi and Alans, marching with the Finnish and Ugrian tribes above them and with the Caucasians to the south. They carried on a profitable trade between the mines of the Ural and Iran, and also between the Mediterranean world and the Far East. In the Chinese annals the Yen-ts'ai or Aorsi, afterwards called A-lan-na, held the country from the Aral sea to the borders of Ta-Ts'in (Roman empire), and their traders even reached China.

With the next tribe, the Iyrcae (IV. 22), we get beyond the stage for the wanderings of Darius. They are interesting for their name, which can hardly be other than the Sarmatian form of Jugra[2], the word whence we have Hungarian. The ancestors of the Magyars were a tribe between the Voguls and the Ostjaks, swept from their place by the Turkish invasions and now a racial erratic block in the middle of the Slavs. Here we have the first notice of them[3]. Their peculiar method of hunting, represented on a gold plaque in the Hermitage[4], required a country full of trees but not a thick forest: such would be the basins of the Tobol, the Ishim, and the Irtysh, just to the E. of the southern Ural and the land of the Thyssagetae[5].

As neighbours of the Iyrcae, Herodotus speaks of a tribe of Scyths that had separated from the Royal Scyths of the Euxine Steppes. Considering the ease with which a nomadic nation divides and sends off one part to a surprising distance (e.g. the Kalmucks, the majority of whom in the reign of Catherine II. of Russia left the lower Volga for the frontiers of China[6]), it is impossible to say that a part of the Royal Scyths could not have migrated

---

[1] Her. IV. 22, 123; Tomaschek, II. p. 32.

[2] Such a transposition of mute and liquid is regular in Ossete, cf. Tirgatao = Tighratava, and Vs. Miller, *Os. Studies*, III. p. 83.

[3] Cf. also Dr Bernhard Munkacsy, "Die älteste historische Erwähnung der Ugrier," in *Ethnol. Mitth. aus Ungarn*, Bd IV., Heft 4—6, p. 152, and Bd v., Heft 1—3, p. 7.

[4] p. 278, f. 201 = *KTR.* p. 395, f. 358.

[5] The conjecture Τύρκαι is an anachronism.

The name Turk had not yet come into existence, though it would be no proved anachronism to say that races kindred to the Turks had passed this way. "Turcae" in the MSS. of Mela, I. 116, and Pliny, *NH.* VI. 19, may well be due to intelligent copyists.

[6] De Quincey's account is mostly fancy, but vividly presents the possible circumstances of the great migration. Corrections are made in vol. VII. of Masson's Edinburgh edition.

north-eastwards.   That there is a connection between inhabitants of these mutually remote regions is rendered probable by the similarity of many objects found here on the upper waters of the Jenisei and in the Scythian graves.   Perhaps an easier way of supposing the conditions is to imagine that here again travellers found a subject population ruled over by a tribe with customs and language similar to those of the original royal caste of the Scyths.   It is hard to imagine Iranians so far to the north beyond the utmost bounds of the Aryan world.   If the Scyths were Ugrian rather than Turko-Tartar, this would be just the place from which they should come.   The Scythian traders finding these Scyths far in upper Asia recalls how the mediaeval Magyar missionaries found again their kin the Voguls and Ostjaks.

Argippaei.

As far as these Scyths, says Herodotus, all the land is flat and deep-soiled ; henceforward it is stony and rugged.   That is, we are coming to the outliers of the Altai mountains.   On the upper Irtysh the steppe ceases about Bukhtarminsk.   The trade route from the Ural came down from almost a north-westerly direction, and continuing the line we should be brought to Dzungaria and the country about Kuldzha well described as lying beneath lofty mountains, the Altai on one side and the T'ien Shan on the other.   Here we meet with the Argippaei (c. 23), (the exact form of the name is uncertain: Argimpaei, Arimphaei, Orgiempaei, etc.).   To the E. of them again, or rather to the SE. following the same general line, come the Issedones[1].   The position of the Issedones can be approximately fixed from Ptolemy's account which has been well interpreted by Tomaschek[2] as placing them in the Tarim basin.   That is that the northern route followed by the informants of Herodotus, and a more direct way by which went Maës Titianus, the Syrian merchant, bring us to the same region.

In the Argippaei we have undoubtedly pure Mongols.   Herodotus says of them that they are bald from their birth both men and women, have flat noses and large γένεια, translated by Tomaschek cheek-bones, and speak a language of their own, but wear the dress of the Scythians.   The baldness may well be a misunderstanding of the custom of shaving the head, or an exaggeration of the scantiness of hair which distinguishes the Mongolian race : the other details point clearly to Mongols and are borne out by what is told us of their food and manner of life[3].

They live off a tree called *Ponticum* about the size of a fig tree, bearing a fruit like a bean but with a stone.   When this is ripe they rub it through a cloth and a thick black juice runs off from it.   This juice is called *Aschy*.   This they use as it is or mix it with milk, and of the pulp of the fruit they make cakes and eat them.   For they have not much cattle as their pastures are not excellent.   This ponticum seems to

---

[1] Tomaschek, II. p. 54.
[2] I. p. 734, see infra, pp. 110 and 114 n. 3.
[3] Γένεια might be taken to mean chins, cf. in the letter of Yvo of Narbonne to Giraldus, Abp

of Bordeaux, Matthew Paris, 1243, "menta prominentia et acuta" of the Tartars (Keane, *Ethnology*, p. 350, Note 2); Hakluyt, p. 21, "long and sharpe chinnes."   Mongol as defined sup. p. 48 n. 1.

be an Iranian word meaning the way-tree, "travellers' joy" as it were :
but "aschy" is Turkish and seems closest to *áčí*, sour[1]. It appears to be the
Bird Cherry, *Prunus Padus*, which is treated in exactly this way by the
Bashkirs.   But many other steppe berries are similarly used by various
tribes.

The tree covered with felt in the winter is a picturesque account of the
felt tent supported by a light and portable framework now universal among
the nomads of Asia.   It has entirely superseded the waggons in which the
Scyths lived, being more roomy, more adaptable and in every way superior,
except that it has to be taken up and down, and affords no shelter during
the actual journey (v. supra p. 32 and f. 7).

The most remarkable point about the Argippaei is the respect in which
they were held by their neighbours. Says Herodotus, "No man at all wrongs
these men. For they are said to be sacred. Nor have they any weapon of
war. And they both act as adjusters of differences among their neighbours,
and if any man take refuge from pursuit with them he can be touched
by no one."   Tomaschek supposes that these were the frontier officials
of a well-organised Turkish kingdom, set to prevent the interruption of
commerce by the quarrels of the various tribes upon its borders.

In general, however, the Greeks had a tendency to idealize the life
of nomads.   One might almost say they found in them the noble savage.
Hence Homer speaks of the Mare-milkers as the most just of men[2], and
Strabo (XI. viii. 7), speaking in particular of the Massagetae, but in general
of all who live in Scythic wise, says, "Such have a manner of life common
to them all, which I have often spoken of, and their burials are much the
same, and their customs and all their life together, independent but rude,
wild and warlike, however as to contracts they are straightforward and
honest."   So the Chinese speak alternately of the treachery and honesty
of their nomad neighbours.

Herodotus (IV. 24) says that all is perfectly clear and definite as far
as the bald people, that Scyths and Greeks from the Pontic trading towns
can tell about them; further that these Scyths use seven interpreters to
make their way through seven tongues.   It is not quite clear how the
number seven is made up.   The tribes that may come in are Scyths,
Sarmatae, Budini, Geloni, Thyssagetae, Iyrcae, other Scyths, Argippaei
and perhaps Issedones.   In such a tale there is a great temptation to bring
in as many tongues as possible, and the informants may well have reckoned
in the Scyths themselves, or made Sarmatian into a separate language, or
likewise Eastern Scythian, or counted in the Geloni, whatever their jargon
may have been : in any case seven is a fair total, though five would probably
have done.

Beyond the Argippaei (c. 25) to the north as it seems are indeed
great and high mountains, the main ranges of the Altai : the goat-footed
men need not be snow-shoe men, as Tomaschek suggests, but any active
mountaineers, and the folk who sleep six months in the year always mark
the bounds of knowledge or rather inference towards the north.

---

[1] Or *akší*, Vámbéry, op. cit. p. 98.   [2] *Il.* XIII. 6.

Issedones.

To the East, or rather SE. of the Argippaei, are the Issedones (c. 26)[1], apparently Tibetan tribes in the Tarim and Bulunggir basin.

The customs of these people as related by Aristeas exactly recall those ascribed by mediaeval and modern travellers to the Tibetans. As Zenobius sums it up (v. 25) the Issedones eat their parents except their heads: their heads they cover with gold. Compare Rubruck translated by Hakluyt (p. 116):

"Next vnto them" (i.e. the men of Tangut) "are the people of Tebet men which were wont to eat the carkases of their deceased parents: that for pities sake they might make no other sepulchre for them but their owne bowels. Howbeit of late they have left off this custome, because that thereby they became abominable and odious vnto all other nations. Notwithstanding vnto this day they make fine cups of the skuls of their parents, to the ende that when they drink out of them they may amidst all their iollities and delights call their dead parents to remembrance. This was told mee by one that saw it. The sayd people of Tebet haue great plentie of golde in their land." In the British Museum may be seen skull cups richly mounted such as are used in Tibet in the Lamaist ceremonies.

Further ἰσοκράτεες δὲ ὁμοίως αἱ γυναῖκες τοῖσιν ἀνδράσιν. Not so much as it seems from their taking part in war and chase like the Sarmatian women, as from the importance naturally gained by the one woman of a polyandrous household. The Chinese even speak of states in this region in which the women held all the political authority.

If the testimony of Ptolemy according to all interpreters could not be adduced for putting the Issedones on the Tarim the positions of all the tribes along the trade route would lose a very important confirmation. The chief difficulty is that the Chinese describe wholesale changes of population as occurring between the times of Aristeas and of Ptolemy: the encroachments of the Hiung-nu (v. pp. 92 and 121) had in the second century B.C. driven the Yüe-chih from the Bulunggir basin into that of the Tarim. The Yüe-chih are said to have customs similar to those of the Hiung-nu, but polyandry is ascribed to them and they appear rather to have been nomad Tibetans, perhaps with Hunnish chiefs, at least they use the Turkish title *jabgu*. To the west of Lop-nor they found a town-dwelling population called T'u-huo-lo (Tochari)[2]. Later we meet with both peoples in Trans-Oxiana and Bactria (hence the name Tokharistan) and they apparently leave the Tarim basin to the Hiung-nu[3]. Had not the Yüe-chih been driven out of the country long before Ptolemy's time their identification with his Issedones would be

---

[1] Ἰσσηδοί ap. Tz., v. p. 112, n. 4; Alcman ap. St. Byz. Ἐσσηδόνες.

[2] Of them the Wei- and Sui-shu say, "Brothers have one wife in common: she wears on her cap so many horns...as there are brothers; when one brother enters her chamber he puts his shoes before the door as a token. The children belong to the eldest brother." This likewise sounds Tibetan and we can never clearly distinguish between the Yüe-chih and the T'u-huo-lo, but it is written of them in Bactria when they had long ago coalesced

[3] They cannot have been cleared out completely. We know that some, the Little Yüe-chih, remained behind among the Tibetan K'iang. The inaccessible oases of the Tarim basin have harboured the relics of many races. From his last journey Dr M. A. Stein brought back MSS. in twelve languages (*Times*, Mar. 8, 1909), but the Tibetan element seems the oldest at least along the South, having been present in Khotan before the historic invasion (Stein, *Ancient Khotan*, I. p. 147).

obvious: perhaps the name had clung to two settlements Issedon Scythica (Ak-su?) and Issedon Serica (Lou-lan near Lop-nor?), reason enough for him to put the well known tribe on to his map. This is not on a par with his haphazard insertion of antiquated names towards the edges of Sarmatia: he had, as I shew below, a very good knowledge of the Tarim basin[1].

So Ptolemy's Issedones represent the Yüe-chih in their second position on the Tarim, but Aristeas knew them on the Bulunggir and probably included the Tochari under them. So his Issedones might extend to the Pamir, where they would be opposite to the Massagetae just over the pass into the Jaxartes basin[2].

Massagetae.

Like tales are told of the Massagetae N. of the Oxus, of their way of eating their parents, not even having left them to die a natural death, and of their marriage customs[3]. They are described as living opposite the Issedones[4], that is, just across the mountains to the west of them, and are often coupled or even confounded with them. In IV. 13 Herodotus says, when speaking of the movement that drove the Scyths out of Asia, that according to Aristeas the Arimaspi attacked their neighbours the Issedones, and these drove out the Scyths: whereas in c. 11 he says that the Scyths were pressed by the Massagetae. The Massagetae are evidently a mixed collection of tribes without an ethnic unity, the variety of their customs and states of culture shews this, and Herodotus does not seem to suggest that they are all one people. They are generally reckoned to be Iranian. But it is probable that at any rate part of them were practically identical with the Issedones: that just as the Yüe-chih were driven by pressure from the Huns over the mountains into Bactria, so before them another Tibetan tribe had trodden the same path under the same pressure and gained the country of the two rivers: perhaps this was the very movement of which Herodotus and Aristeas speak. Other Massagetae may well have been Iranian, or as some thought[4], much the same as the Scythians; whereas the inhabitants of the islands of the Araxes (Oxus or Jaxartes, v. sup. p. 30) were aboriginals connected perhaps with the tribes of the Caucasus. The picture drawn of the nomad Massagetae seems very like that of Scythians in a rather ruder stage of development. The tale of Tomyris may bring to mind either the Tibetan gynaecocracy or that of the Sarmatians. Certainly it appears more closely linked with the latter. The name Massagetae seems to mean belonging to the great (horde), and probably just as all the tribes north of

[1] p. 114, n. 3. In the same way the name Tochari survived in Ptolemy's Thaguri, Thagurus Mons and the town Thagura (v. l. Θόγαρα, cf. Justin's Thogari and Tib. Thogar), and still later attached to the ruined towns ascribed by Hüan Tsang to the vanished T'u-huo-lo.

[2] Even phonetically the identification, hinted at by Tomaschek, is not impossible. Iranians and Greeks might make Issedi out of Ngüt-shi, the oldest form of Yüe-chih, cf. Canton. yüt, Jap. getsu, Franke, op. cit. p. 23; Uigur, Kitsi, Mong. Gači, F. K. W. Müller, "Uigurica," p. 15, n. 1, in *Abh. d. k. pr. Ak. d. W.*, Berlin, 1908.

[3] Compare Her. I. 215, 216, γυναῖκα μὲν γαμέει ἕκαστος, ταύτῃσι δὲ ἐπίκοινα χρέωνται. ὁ γὰρ Σκύθας φασὶ Ἕλληνες ποιέειν, οὐ Σκύθαι εἰσὶν οἱ ποιέοντες ἀλλὰ Μασσαγέται· τῆς γὰρ ἐπιθυμήσῃ γυναικὸς Μασσαγέτης ἀνήρ, τὸν φαρετρεῶνα ἀποκρεμάσας πρὸ τῆς ἁμάξης μίσγεται ἀδεῶς, p. 110, n. 2, and Marco Polo, Yule[3], Vol. II. Bk II. c. xlvii. p. 54. G. Nagy, op. cit. p. 7 sqq., takes the Massagetae to be essentially the same as the Scyths, but the latter having attained to the idea of exclusive property in women who had been seized in war, had passed out of the stage of community of women.

[4] Her. I. 201.

the Pontus were for the Greeks more or less Scythians, all the tribes that were under the "great horde" were regarded by the Persians, from whom the Greeks mostly got their ideas of the peoples on the northern border of Iran, as all more or less Massagetae; again it may have been the Scyths' name for them.

Sacae.

For we must confess that no word like Massagetae occurs in the Old Persian inscriptions in which as we should expect from Herodotus (VII. 64) we find *Saka*. In the epitaph of Darius at Naksh-i-Rustam (a) we have *Saka Tigrakhauda*, *Saka Humavarka*, and *Saka [t]yai[y ta]radaraya (transmarini)*[1]. Oppert explains Tigrakhauda as "cunning with arrows." It is usually taken to mean "with pointed caps," and Humavarka has been compared with Σκύθαι Ἀμύργιοι; the transmarine Sacae may be beyond either the Aral or the Caspian or even, as F. W. Thomas[2] suggests, Lake Hamun, as well as the Euxine, so that we are not much helped.

On the rock of Bisutun[3] Darius says himself (v. 22) "I went against the land of the Saka...Tigris...to the sea: I crossed it on a bridge, I slew the enemy, I seized...by name Sakŭnka...I seized also other rulers"; but the lacunae make it impossible to know to what expedition this refers. Saka are also mentioned as having revolted. At Persepolis (I. 18) Saka are named as bringing tribute. But which of these may be among the varied nations sculptured we cannot say. Those whose clothes have any resemblance to Scythic dress have been reproduced (p. 59, f. 12). Most interesting is the figure at Bisutun inscribed *Iyam Sakŭnka hya Saka*; "this is Sakunka the Saka." But of his national costume only the cyrbasia is left him.

Arimaspians and Hyperboreans.

As far as the Issedones reached there was a quite practicable trade route, and as it seems nearly allied Iranian tongues served as a medium of intercommunication beside the native idioms. As far as the Issedones it is quite possible that Aristeas of Proconnesus penetrated. From them he heard of other men living yet further east, but what he tells of these shews that we are coming to the lands where travellers' tales flourish with most luxuriance. In the quotation from the *Arimaspea* preserved by Tzetzes, the Issedones say, "Above us[4] to the north dwell men whose borders march with ours, many are they and mighty warriors indeed, rich in horses, wealthy in sheep, wealthy in cattle, shaggy of hair, sturdiest of all men; and each has but one eye in his fair forehead—the Arimaspi." Whatever the word

[1] Spiegel, *Érânische Altertumskunde*, Leipzig, 1871, I. p. 223 and *Die altpersischen Keilinschriften*, Leipzig, 1881, p. 54 and Glossary, s.vv. He takes Sk'udra = Σκολοτοί.
[2] *JRAS.* 1906, p. 181. He thinks that from early times the Sacae reached down into Sistan.
[3] Spiegel, op. cit. p. 41. The third column at Bisutun is only called Scythic on the general principle "*Omne ignotum pro Scythico.*"
[4] So Tomaschek, I. p. 758, combines the lines

and translates, putting all into nominatives which do not seem to me to scan. Latyshev (*Sc. et Cauc.* I. p. 322 = Tzetz. *Chil.* VII. 686) gives them thus:
Ἰσσηδοὶ χαίτησιν ἀγαλλόμενοι ταναῇσι....
καί σφεας ἀνθρώπους εἶναι καθύπερθεν ὁμούρους
πρὸς Βορέω, πολλούς τε καὶ ἐσθλοὺς κάρτα μαχητάς,
ἀφνείους ἵπποισι, πολύρρηνας, πολυβούτας....
Ὀφθαλμὸν δ' ἐν ἔκαστος ἔχει χαρίεντι μετώπῳ.
χαίτῃσιν λάσιοι πάντων στιβαρώτατοι ἀνδρῶν.

means, whether or no it be a folk-etymology, we cannot go behind the statement of Herodotus that the Scythians took it to mean one-eyed. The Chinese still say of the Khalkas, these people have but one eye, one hand[1], thus describing their awkwardness, and some such metaphor probably lies at the bottom of this tale. Beyond the Tarim basin to the north, we come precisely to the cradle of the Mongolian race. In this region the Chinese annalists of the Chou (B.C. 1155—255) and Han dynasties put the Hien-yün or Hiung-nu stretching from Shan-si across the Sha-mo far to the north of the T'ien Shan range. These are they whom we know in Europe as the Huns. Shorn of the poetic epithets, the description of Aristeas applies to them. They often joined into a well-organised state as often destroyed by the dissensions of the tribes. When united they controlled the commerce between China and the west and regulated it. The Bald-heads of Herodotus (IV. 23) would be their outpost to the west. True, Aristeas calls the Arimaspi χαί-τῃσιν λάσιοι but the warriors may well have been unkempt, while the custom officials would be shaved and smooth. Also in that western part in the gate of Dzungaria there would not be the abundance of flocks and herds that marked them on their native plains. Whether the Issedones received of them gold from the eastern Altai, or whether it did not rather come from the south from the mountains above India, and whether the griffins are not the ants or baibaks, that according to the story threw the gold out of their burrows, is more than can be said. Certainly the representations of Arimaspians and griffins in art belong to Western Asia. The griffins come from eastern stuffs (= *cherub*), and their name is Semitic; the Arimaspians are dressed in barbarian costume, as conceived by the Greeks, on the model of the barbarians most familiar to them, Phrygians and Persians. Still the subject was felt to belong to Scythia, and was used to adorn goods destined for the Scythian market.

Beyond the griffins, says Aristeas[2], live the Hyperboreans, reaching down to the other sea. Herodotus doubts this, for he says he heard nothing about them from the Scyths[3]. The Hyperboreans are always the people beyond knowledge towards the north. They must always figure as the last term of any series that stretches in that direction. Still, as Tomaschek suggests,

[1] Cf. the Hou-yen-kuo, lit. Back-eye-people.

[2] Her. IV. 13, 32; Damastes ap. St. Byz. s.v.

[3] By ignoring Ptolemy (v. p. 114, n. 3) F. W. Thomas (op. cit. p. 197) puts the Issedones in Farghana and the Arimaspi (=Ariaspi) in Sistan, which hardly suits Her. and his κατύπερθε. F. Westberg, *Klio* (Bd IV., 1904, pp. 182—192, "Zur Topographie des Herodots"), by giving up the same *point d'appui* and restricting the area under consideration, has to use excessive ingenuity in fitting in the various tribes. He puts the Budini about Saratov on the steep or right bank of the Volga, and identifies them with the Burdas of Ibn Rusta; further he believes that Darius reached the Volga in this region. The desert above them is the high ground of the Zhigulóv Hills, and the Thyssagetae are on the Samara bend of the Volga and about the lower Kama with the Iyrcae on the Bêlaja and in the southern Urals. The Bashkirs are the Argippaei, although they would appear to have reached their present position only in some later migration of Turko-Tartaric peoples. The names due to Aristeas he regards as mere alternatives of other tribal names known to Herodotus, so he identifies the Massagetae, whom he puts N. of the Jaxartes, with the Arimaspi, and opposite them the Issedones, whose women were so independent, with the Sarmatians. The Araxes of Herodotus I. 201 is for him the Jaxartes, but in c. 202, the Volga with its delta among the islands of which the fish-eaters live, and the Rhoxolani, whom we meet in later times, are *Araxalani, called after the river. Such a scheme seems to me to wrest the data given by Aristeas and Herodotus from their natural meaning, whereas something like Tomaschek's view is far less arbitrary. Most original is d'Arbois de Jubainville (op. cit. I. p. 241 note); he supposes that the Arimaspi migrated from upper Asia to the Alps or Rhipaean mountains above Friuli. His object is to identify the Kelts with the Hyperboreans.

some faint account of the civilised empire of China may have penetrated to Aristeas or his Issedon informants.

Aristeas also mentions the Rhipaean mountains, but again Herodotus does not believe in these. He is right in rejecting them to the north of the Euxine, but in upper Asia the difficulty is rather that among so many ranges we cannot tell which was intended by the name.

Always it has been at the apogee of the dominion of some Turko_ Tartaric tribe that it has been possible for westerners to traverse central Asia. The voyage of Aristeas (c. 650 B.C.) comes at the time of the early nomad power which troubled the Chinese under the Chou dynasty. Those of Zemarchus and the Nestorian Alopen coincide with the greatest extent of the early empire of the western Turks which likewise gave Hüan Tsang his opportunity to journey westwards[1]. De Plano Carpini, Rubruck and Marco Polo were enabled to travel by the organization of the great Mongol Empire[2], and since its fall, till the other day, no European had followed in all their footsteps, just as for seven hundred years no Greek followed Aristeas[3].

[1] Chavannes, E., "Documents sur les Tou-kiue (Turcs) occidentaux recueillis et commentés," in *Results of the Orkhon Expedition*, St P., 1903.

[2] v. Heyd, *Hist. du Commerce du Levant au Moyen Âge*, Paris-Leipzig, 1886, Vol. II. p. 215 sqq.

[3] PTOLEMY'S SERICA. As it is physically possible for Aristeas to have penetrated as far as the Tarim, the question whether Ptolemy's Issedones can guide us in locating his, is a question of how much real knowledge of Central Asia Ptolemy shews, and requires a brief examination of his map of Serica &c. in the light of recent travel (Ptol. *Geogr.* I. xi. xii., VI. xiii.—xvi., cf. Maps I. and VI.; see Yule, *Cathay and the Way Thither*, pp. xxxix. and cxlvii.; Richthofen, *China*, I. p. 477—500 and Map 8; Bunbury, *Hist. Anc. Geogr.*, II. p. 529 sqq.; Tomaschek, op. cit. I. p. 736; Marquart, "Erān-šahr" (*Abh. d. k. Ges. d. Wiss. zu Göttingen*, Bd III. No. 3, Berlin, 1901), p. 154, and lastly for one or two new points M. A. Stein, *Ancient Khotan*, I. p. 54). Richthofen seems most nearly right, Tomaschek gets everything too far to the E., Marquart hopes too much for a mechanical formula for reducing Pt.'s degrees to modern measurements. This is a fundamental mistake. In these regions all his knowledge is derived through Marinus of Tyre from Maës Titianus (60—80 A.D.) a Syrian merchant, who himself appears to have reached the "Stone Tower" and to have sent agents on to Sera Metropolis seven months' journey: this distance Marinus naively reckons at 36,200 stades, which Pt. is about right in halving, but this he does on general grounds, not on definite information. Hence we cannot take figures beyond the "Stone Tower" seriously. The more important is it that his map gives the general shape of the Tarim basin very fairly. The Imaus is clearly the Pamir, the only cross range in Central Asia, though of course it does not stretch indefinitely northwards. On it is set ὁρμητήριον τῶν ἐς τὴν Σήραν ἐμπορευομένων, and Irkeshtam the Russian Custom-station commanding the passes both towards Farghana and towards the Alai plateau (Stein, p. 55) suits very well; the "Stone Tower" 5° W. must be on the Alai road. The Αὐζάκια ὄρη are the T'ien Shan and the Ἀσμιραῖα to the S.E. of them the Kurruk

Tagh: the Κάσια ὄρη are not about Kashgar but the W. K'un-lun from which comes jade (Turk. kash); Thagurus Mons to the E. is Altyn Tagh or perhaps Nan Shan. Between the two mountain lines flows the Oechardes or Tarim with its important source (Ak-su?) in the T'ien Shan, its sudden turn S. towards Lop-nor (ἡ ὡς ἐπὶ τὰ Κάσια ὄρη ἐκτροπή, v. S. Hedin's Map in *Through Asia* II.), and its tributary from the K'un-lun, the Charchan Darya; the eastern part of it with its source in long. 174°, lat. 47° 30', would perhaps be the Bulunggir which Stein says once joined the Tarim in Lop-nor (*Geogr. Journ.* XXX. 1907, p. 503: Dr Hedin tells me he doubts this). Outside the Tarim basin the physical features are not so clear, but we may recognise the Ἄννιβα ὄρη as the Altai, Emodus and Ottorocorrhas* as the Himalaya and North Tibetan ranges, the Bautius being the Upper Brahmaputra, but information as to this Southern side came from India, and Pt. not realising Tibet has made this river one with the Huang-ho crossed by the agents of Maës towards their journey's end. The limit between Scythia extra Imaum and Serica represents if anything the extent of Chinese power in the 1st cent. A.D.: Αὐζακία πόλις may be Kashgar and Issedon Scythica, Ak-su; Issedon Serica, Lou-lan by Lop-nor (Tomaschek brings it within the old western extension of the Chinese wall, Stein, l.c.); the Issedones between, the memory of the Yüe-chih: it is tempting to see in Χαύρανα, Khotan and in Ἀχάσα χώρα the Khašas, confusion being produced by the combination of Indian and Seric information: the Thaguri though far to the E. may represent the Tochari (v. supr. p. 111, n. 1): Aspacarae would be an Iranian term for nomads probably Tibetan; Bautae, the Indian for Tibetans, cf. Bhotan, Sera Metropolis is more likely Ch'ang-'an the capital of the Elder Han near Si-'an-fu, than Lo-yang in Ho-nan Pt.'s Sinae Metropolis (long. 180°). The Annibi, Garinaei (? Mountaineers) and Rhabbanae would be Huns and perhaps Sien-pi; the Σίζυγες, Kao-ch'ê. It is noticeable that fancy names like Abii and Anthropophagi are confined to the N. border of the map, so Issedon is not of that class.

* Please correct Otto(ro)corrhas, etc. on Map VI.

MAP VI.

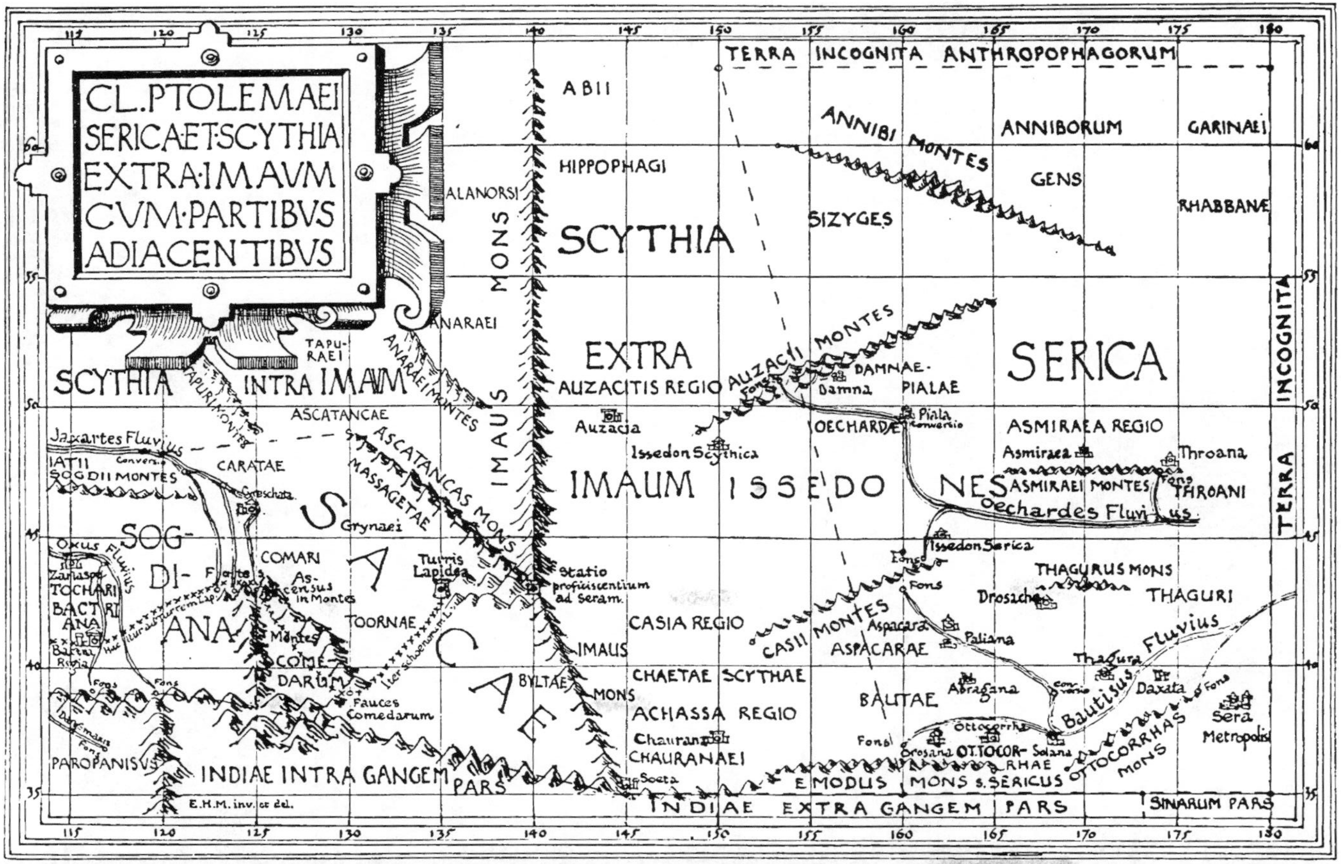

CL. PTOLEMAEI
SERICAE·TSCYTHIA
EXTRA·IMAVM
CVM·PARTIBVS
ADIACENTIBVS

CHAPTER VI.

HISTORY OF SCYTHIA, LATER MIGRATIONS.

In the preceding pages has been given a sketch of the position, and as far as possible ethnology, of the inhabitants of the great steppes and their neighbours, according to Herodotus and his informants, especially Aristeas, who enables us to extend our knowledge as far as the borders of China. Aristeas gives us the first recorded example of one of those movements which have altered the names on the map of Asia from that day to the day of Tamerlane. The fate of the Greek settlements on the north coast of the Euxine is so intimately bound up with these changes of population that a brief survey of them is indispensable.

The Chinese chronicles of the Chou dynasty speak of the restlessness of the Hiung-nu interfering with communications with the west in the VIII. century B.C. : and Aristeas says that the incursions of the same people whom he calls Arimaspi drove the Issedones to fall upon the Scyths and make them enter Europe. We have supposed this in conjunction with Herodotus (IV. 11) to mean that Issedones forced themselves into the country to the west of the Tarim basin and joined with the Massagetae or impelled them against the Scyths. These latter, crossing the Volga and Don, pressed the inhabitants of the land, probably Iranians, towards the west, where they joined Thracian tribes, Treres, and invaded Asia Minor, and towards the SE. where they passed the Caucasus and attacked vassals of the Assyrians. These called them Gimirrai, in Greek Cimmerians. The eastern horde was followed by Scyths, Ašguzai, who appeared as allies of the Assyrians, effected a diversion of the siege of Nineveh and made a raid over a great part of western Asia. It seems impossible to get a more detailed view of the movements of these various northern invaders from the accounts in Herodotus (I. 103–6), the Assyrian monuments, and the Hebrew Prophets (v. pp. 41, 42).

In SW. Asia the Scyths, broken by the Median Vespers still commemorated in Strabo's Sacaea (XI. viii. 4, 5), disappeared without leaving any traces, the Cimmerians finally vanished after having held their ground for many years at various points such as Sinope and Antandrus, but to the north of the Euxine the Scyths established themselves as the ruling caste of nomads in the eastern part of the plain, exacting tribute from various tribes in the western half. Above the steppe belt, the row of forest tribes, Slavonic Neuri, Finnish Androphagi, Melanchlaeni and Budini, Ugrian Thyssagetae and Iyrcae, take no part in the changes which swept the open steppe. In the time of Herodotus and Hippocrates the Scyths seem on the down grade, on their eastern frontier appear the Sarmatae, nomads from the Caspian steppes, pressing the Maeotae and allied, probably Caucasian, tribes towards the mountains, and threatening their neighbours across the Tanais.

Though we have so full an account of the customs of the Pontic Scyths we know few events in their history; still from Herodotus we can construct a kind of genealogy of their reigning house. We cannot tell whether this was in any way related to Madyes and his father Protothyes (Bartatua), whose exploits were in Asia. But we have the succession Spargapithes, Lycus, Gnurus, Saulius (with his brother Anacharsis), Idanthyrsus, who was probably father to Ariapithes. This latter had three wives, the Istrian woman by whom he had Scyles his immediate successor, the Scythian Opoea, who bore him Oricus, and the daughter of the Thracian Teres, mother to Octomasades, who eventually slew Scyles and reigned in his stead. We have no means of placing Ariantas, who made the cauldron out of arrow-heads, or Scopasis and Taxacis, who were kings under Idanthyrsus at the time of Darius [1].

Invasion of Darius.

Except for one incident we know nothing of the reigns of these kings, save the stories of Anacharsis and Scyles, shewing the attraction exercised by Greek life on the more advanced Scyths and the tragic result. But to that incident, the famous invasion of Scythia by Darius about 512 B.C. [2], we are indebted for the introduction of the Scythian episode into the history of Herodotus.

After what has been said of the geography of Scythia there is no need to insist on the impossibility of the story as related to us. Its whole basis is inconceivable and the tale is adorned with improbabilities of every kind. We may take it as true that Darius crossed the Danube and disappeared for a time into the steppes. It may well be that he was severely harassed by his mobile enemy; but it cannot be believed that he went further than the Dnêstr, the crossing of which would have involved a bridge and dangerous operations in face of an active foe. Strabo [3] indeed says (VII. iii. 14) that the desert of the Getae was the scene of the expedition, but this may be only the outcome of his own reasoning, not independent historical evidence. However, he must be substantially right: Darius can hardly have done more than make a demonstration against the northern barbarians, with a view to securing his frontier on the Danube. It may well be that the ruling race gathered the western tribes to oppose him, so he may have come in contact with the western Budini (if as is suggested above there were two

[1] Her. IV. 76—81.

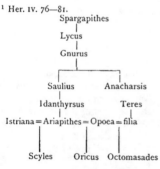

. That Scyles took his father's wife Opoea (c. 78) is in accordance with the almost universal custom of polygamous countries. Still we may remark that this custom shocked de Plano Carpini, Rubruck (c. 6) and Hayton (op. cit. c. xlviii.) among the Tartars, and is noticed by the Chinese.

[2] v. Macan, *Herodotus*, Books IV.—VI. Vol. II. App. 3.

[3] Ctesias, Frag. 29, §§ 16, 17 (Müller) says Darius advanced 15 days' march, and returned on finding the Scyth's bow stronger than the Persian, cf. the tale of the Khazar and Russian swords in Ps.-Nestor.

divisions of these), and this may have brought into the narrative a confusion which Herodotus turned to account to enforce several of his favourite notions, the condign punishment of the Great King's overweening pride, the servility of the Ionians, and the solitary merit of Miltiades. In this latter Mr Macan, as Thirlwall before him, sees the chief motive of the whole tale. He thinks it an echo of the defence made when he was on his trial for tyranny in 493 B.C.

Darius can never have meant to reduce all European Scythia. The device of keeping his communications open sixty days and no more, if it meant anything, would mean that Darius intended to return by the Caucasus, if he found the path open. But with his experience of nomads on his north Asiatic frontiers, to say nothing of the fate of Cyrus (the common story may well be unhistorical), he would never have trusted himself unsupported in an unknown country, even supposing that he was absolutely ignorant as to the extent and character of the countries he must traverse. He reduced Thrace, received the submission of Macedonia, and made a demonstration, perhaps not entirely successful, against the northern neighbours of his new territories; that is sufficient justification for his European expedition, and we need not regard this as part of a scheme to gain profit from the gold of the griffins, and round off his empire by making the Euxine a Persian lake.

A most original view is that advanced by Professor Bury[1]. According to him the real objective was the gold of Transylvania, afterwards worked so profitably by the Romans. Had Darius meant to go east he would never have left his fleet at the Danube, but it could support him no further in a north-westerly direction. His idea then would seem to have been to build a line of forts along the Oarus = Ararus = Buzeo to keep his communications open, but upon realising the difficulty of permanently defending such a line, he abandoned his plan and returned. Confusion of the Ararus and the Oarus would then be the foundation of the story bringing Darius all across Scythia : also a more definite object for his expedition would be furnished, and an explanation of his attempted fort-building. One only wonders if the Great King in Susa had heard of the gold mines in the land of the Agathyrsi.

Duncker[2] rationalises the story and suggests that the sixty days was merely an arbitrary limit given out by the Ionians to prevent daily discussion of the question whether Darius should not be abandoned. He does not think Darius went far. It is surprising what a good defence of the traditional account is made by Rawlinson (ad loc.) who strongly urges the independence of commissariat shewn by an Asiatic army, and its power of crossing rivers without difficulty. But in this case it is too much to believe.

Herodotus (VI. 40, 84) tells us that in revenge the Scyths made a raid which reached the Thracian Chersonese and drove out Miltiades, and even proposed to Cleomenes a joint invasion of Asia.

Decline of Scyths. Advance of Sarmatae.

After the time of Octomasades, who may be reckoned a contemporary of Herodotus, we can trace the Royal Scyths no farther with any certainty. The name Scyth seems to move westward giving place to those of eastern

---

[1] *Classical Review*, XI. (1897), July, p. 277, "The European Expedition of Darius."   [2] *History of Antiquity*, Eng. ed., 1879, Vol. VI. p. 272 sqq.

tribes, but then it spreads again over all the steppe countries, and embraces all the nomad peoples. These changes of connotation make it hazardous to make any statement as to the fate of the true owners of the name, save that they moved west and were absorbed between the Getae and Sarmatians.

When exactly these latter crossed the Don is not quite clear. As Niederle[1] says, it was probably a gradual process. In § 68 of the Periplus ascribed to Scylax, dated by K. Müller[2] about 338 B.C., a tribe of Syrmatae is given in Europe close to the Tanais, but in § 70 Sauromatae are in Asia, just over the river. Stephanus Byzantius cites this rare form Syrmatae from Eudoxus of Cnidus, and gives it as the same as Sauromatae, Sarmatae. Braun[3] wishes to make these Syrmatae Finns, and to distinguish them from the Iranian-speaking Sauromatae. But it seems more probable to suppose the mention of "Syrmatae" west of the river to be put in by a later hand than that of the compiler of the periplus. In the second half of the fourth century the Sarmatae are still east of the Don or just crossing, for the next century and a half we have very scanty knowledge of what was happening in the steppes. Probably an era of mutual strife had broken out which made impossible, not merely journeys into upper Asia such as Aristeas had accomplished, but even regular communication with the *hinterland* of the Euxine. The Scyths had shewn readiness to trade and an appreciation of Hellenic culture, in spite of the statement of Herodotus (IV. 76) that they were hostile to foreign influences, for no nation ever thinks another sufficiently ready to adopt its customs. But now they were fighting a losing conflict with the ruder Sarmatae[4], and the latter were not to be such good neighbours to the Pontic Greeks.

The first definite mention of Sarmatae in Europe is in Polybius (xxv. ii. (xxvi. vi.) 12). Gatalus ὁ Σαρμάτης is one of the rulers in Europe who joined a great league of states in Asia Minor and on the coast of the Euxine, B.C. 179. This is the first occurrence of the form Σαρμάτης in place of the earlier Σαυρομάτης which continues to be used as a proper name[5].

The centre of gravity of the Scyths' power, and it may well be the representatives of the Royal Scyths, shifted westward for a while under the pressure from the east. They even extended their borders in this direction, and crossed the Danube, so that the Dobrudzha gained the name of Little Scythia[6], which was also applied to all West Scythia as far as the Borysthenes. Demetrius of Callatis early in the second century B.C. speaks of Scythians near Tomi[7]. They may have appeared here when their king Atheas[8], after successful struggles with the Triballi and with Istrus, concentrated his power on this side, only to be defeated by Philip of Macedon, 339 B.C. (v. p. 123). We find Scythians also mentioned in the decree in honour of Protogenes at Olbia[9], in such a fashion as to shew that their power was no longer what it was. There it is a case of their seeking protection from other invaders. The names of tribes mentioned with them,

---

[1] *Slav. Ant.* I. p. 322.
[2] *GGM.* I. p. xxxviii sq., 15 sq.
[3] op. cit. p. 87. He gives a good sketch of these changes of population.
[4] Diod. Sic. II. xliii. 7.
[5] Sarmata is the Latin save in poetry.
[6] Strabo, VII. iv. 5.

[7] Quoted in *DA.* III. p. 36.
[8] Justin IX. 2, Frontinus, *Strateg.* II. 4, cf. Polyaenus, V. 44; Ateas, Str. VII. iii. 18. They may have crossed earlier, Scythic tombs occur in Bulgaria, v. inf. p. 150, n. 1.
[9] App. 7 = *IosPE.* I. 16.

Saii, Thisamatae and Saudaratae, recall the forms of Sarmatian names. From this time forward the word Scythian becomes a purely geographical designation for any northern nation, Sarmatae, Goths, Huns, Russians all have applied to them the name sanctioned by classical usage.

For instance, it is hard to define the Scythians ruled over by Scilurus and his son Palacus. Strabo (VII. iv. 3) and the Diophantus inscription[1] call them Scythians, and they are in close alliance with the Sarmatians and with the Tauri; they may perhaps be the people loosely termed Tauroscythae or Scythotauri; they were scarcely a homogeneous tribe, but more likely a casual aggregation of the dwellers along the coast between the Dobrudzha and the Crimean mountains. Scilurus struck coins in Olbia, and the other barbarian kings, whose names we find on coins struck in that city, were probably lords of the same power, but whether before or after Scilurus we cannot say, the style is all we have to go by, and this is so barbarous that it can be no sure guide as to date. A reasonable view is that of A. V. Orêshnikov[2], according to which there were kings of the Scythians about the Danube-mouth Canites[3], Cau-, Sarias and Aelis[4], who had not full control over Olbia. Later, about 110 B.C., Scilurus, who must have organised a considerable power sufficient to give much trouble to Chersonese and Mithridates, and appears to have had something of a capital at Kermenchik by Sympheropol[5], became suzerain of Olbia, and put his name upon its coins. Pharzoeus and Inismeus (Ininsimeus) also struck coins with the name Olbia, but style and lettering appear considerably later, and these kings seem to belong to the time when the city arose from the Getic devastation, and existed under the tutelage of the natives who had missed its commercial services. After a period of hostility towards the natives, as described by Dio Chrysostom, who calls them vaguely Scythians, this tutelage was exchanged for Roman protection. Latyshev is inclined to put Pharzoeus and Inismeus before Scilurus. If the coins are genuine which are figured by P. Vacquier[6], Scilurus and his dynasty ruled at Cercinitis also, as is in itself very probable.

This disappearance of the true Herodotean Scyths does not denote any great destruction of population, merely that the ruling caste lost its vitality and merged in the mass of the people, and another tribe having defeated it assumed its place and spread its power over much the same group of tribes as had owned the sway of the Scyths. The difference cannot have been great. Objects found in tombs which must be referred to the Sarmatian period are often preeminently Scytho-Siberian. The leaders of the Sarmatae were again probably Uralo-Altaic, though it is just possible that they represent an Iranian reaction. We are unable to make any distinction between

---

[1] App. 18 = *IosPE.* I. 185.

[2] *Trans. Russ. Arch. Soc.*, New Series, Vol. IV. pp. 14—24.

[3] Cf. βασιλεῖ Σκυθῶν ΓΚΑΝΙΤΑ on Varna Inscr. *CIG.* 2056; Latyshev, *Olbia*, pp. 129—135, v. inf. ch. XV.

[4] v. ch. XV. end, Coin Pl. III. 20—25. Orêshnikov, *Materials touching the ancient Numismatics of the Black Sea Coast*, Moscow, 1892, p. 29.

[5] Neapolis? cf. *IosPE.* I. 241—244, IV. 191, 192. The two inscriptions with kings' names are unfortunately very imperfect. *IosPE.* I. 241,

ΒΑΣΙΛΕΥΣ ΣΚΙΛΟΥΡΟΣ ΒΑΣ . . . . . Ε . . . . Δ . Σ |
. . . . ΛΕΑΥ . . . . . / ΒΑΣΙΛΙΣ . Α . . . Ν . . Ρ . . . .

looks as if Scilurus were dedicating a statue of his queen, evidently we have only just missed the name of the king his father. IV. 191,

Βασ]ιλεὺς Χωδ[αρζος?
'Ομ]ψαλάκου

is not sufficiently certain to warrant our adding these names to history.

[6] *Numismatique des Scythes et des Sarmates, Kerkinitis et Tannais* (sic), Paris, 1881.

the various tribes of Sarmatae, two or three names occur frequently and probably denote conglomerations of tribes upon which the name of a successful tribe has been imposed; the names of the lesser tribes, of which Pliny and Ptolemy have preserved many, can never mean anything to us.

Scythia according to Strabo.

The superficial accounts of these countries that we find from the time of Herodotus to that of Strabo offer compromises between the state of things learnt from the former and the actual state of things in the author's own day. Strabo found this so changed that he dismissed all the information given by Herodotus as pure invention, and has given us a fresh description of the population to the north of the Euxine. But his information only embraces the belt of open steppe, and he knows nothing of the northern peoples beyond. He says (VII. iii. 17):

"Of all the country lying above the said interval between the Ister and the Borysthenes the first part is the desert of the Getae, next come the Tyregetae, after them the Iazyges-Sarmatae, and those called Royal and Urgi, the greater part nomads, but some engaged in agriculture. They say these also live along the Ister, often on one side and on the other. In the back country are the Bastarnae marching with the Tyregetae and with the Germans, and indeed themselves having something of German race about them; they are divided into several tribes, some are called Atmoni and Sidones, and those that hold the island Peuce in the Ister, Peucini. But the Rhoxolani are furthest to the north and hold the plains between the Tanais and the Borysthenes....But we do not know if any one lives above the Rhoxolani."

He goes on to give the stock description of nomad arms and mode of life, adding that the Rhoxolani winter in the marshes by the Maeotis and spend the summer on the plains. Still further E. beyond the Tanais, between it, the Caspian and the Caucasus, Strabo places the Aorsi and Siraci[1], the Sirachi of an inscription at Tanais (193 A.D.) in which Sauromates II. claims to have conquered them[2]. These people are also rich in horses and mostly nomadic though not quite without agriculture. They were just then specially prosperous owing to the overland trade with India. The Aorsi seem to be mentioned as Yen-ts'ai by the Chinese historians and to have later been known as A-lan-na[3]. Whereby we may identify them with the Alans or Alanorsi in Ptolemy. Pliny[4] is the first writer in the west to speak of Alans, and the Rhoxolani themselves are interpreted as Blond Alans. The personal names of Aorsi and Siraci preserved by Strabo bear an Iranian stamp. Strabo does not mention the name of the Iazamatae, the first tribe of the Sarmatae, which we meet as their extreme western out-post towards the Tanais; the name occurs in various forms, Hecataeus calls them Ixibatae; Ephorus who distinctly refers them to the Sarmatae, Iazabatae[5]; Polyaenus

---

[1] XI. ii. 1; *BCA.* x. no. 69, Siraces Str. XI. ii. 8, Siraceni, Ptol. v. viii. 17; v. Introd. to *IosPE.* II. p. xiv.

[2] App. 52 = *IosPE.* II. 423.

[3] Tomaschek II. 37 and Hirth, op. cit. inf. p. 122, n. 6.

[4] *NH.* IV. 80, Braun, p. 95.

[5] Both ap. Steph. Byz. s. vv.

(VIII. 55) makes them Ixomatae and by mistake Maeotian, he speaks of a time when they were living to the E. of the Maeotis. But Müllenhoff is probably right in regarding Iazyges as a later form of the same word[1].

So the chain of Sarmatian tribes according to Strabo is Iazyges, Royal Sarmatians, Urgi of which we know nothing more, and chief of all Rhoxolani[2] with the Aorsi and Siraci beyond the Tanais. These nations gradually pass westwards. Ovid still knows the Iazyges in W. Sarmatia[3], but in Tacitus[4] they appear as allies of the Suevic king Vannius, that is they are already on the middle Danube in A.D. 50. Ptolemy has them in two places, along by the coast of the Maeotis and Iazyges Metanastae, between the Theiss and the Danube, the result of combining information of different dates[5].

In Western Sarmatia the Iazyges are succeeded by the Rhoxolani. Tacitus[6] tells how they made an unsuccessful raid into Moesia, A.D. 70, and clearly shews the inferiority of their long swords or spears and heavy coats of mail to the handy equipment of the legionaries[7]. Later they fought Hadrian on the Danube and their land extended to the borders of Dacia.

East of the Rhoxolani came the Alans who crossed the Tanais and finally found themselves neighbours of the Goths and Vandals, with whom the name of their western division becomes so closely linked.

Westward Movement of the Huns.

All these movements from the East, like that which brought in the Scyths, seem to have had their origin in Mongolia. Towards the end of the Chou dynasty (c. 1155—255 B.C.) the Hiung-nu were pressing both upon China and south-westwards upon the Yüe-chih (Issedones? v. p. 110) and Wu-sun. The Ts'in dynasty (255—209) resisted the Nomads and secured China against them by building the Great Wall. Hence the Hiung-nu turned westwards and c. 176 B.C. drove the Wu-sun into the mountains about Ili and the Great Yüe-chih into the Tarim basin. Here the latter seem to have amalgamated with the earlier population, the T'u-huo-lo (Tochari). After their defeat by Kayuk c. 160 B.C. we find the Yüe-chih probably including the T'u-huo-lo 2—3000 *li* w. of Ta-Yüan (Farghana), N. of the Kuei (Oxus); w. of them is 'An-si(k) (Arsaces, i.e. Parthia), N. the nomadic K'ang-kü and again N. of these the Yen-ts'ai (Aorsi). To the s. of the Kuei, 2000 *li* sw. of Ta-Yüan, is Ta-Hia, and se. of this again Yen-tu (Panjáb)[8], so Ta-Hia must be Bactria (v. inf. p. 129, n. 4). The appearance of the Yüe-chih in Trans-Oxiana displaced the Sai (Sek = Sacae) southwards, but may also have exercised pressure northwards, as in the following century we find the Aorsi on the borders of Europe. Next we hear in the Han Annals that the Yüe-chih have moved south of the Kuei and conquered

[1] *DA.* III. 39, cf. Ukert, *Skythien*, p. 546.
[2] Cf. Appian, *Mithr.* 69, Σαυρομάτων οἵ τε Βασίλειοι καὶ Ἰάζυγες καὶ Κόραλλοι, and Diophantus inscr. (App. 18) 'Ρευξιναλῶν.
[3] *Tr.* II. 191, ubi codd. Zaziges : Owen pessime Sidones.
[4] *Ann.* XII. 29, 30.
[5] For the later history of these Sarmatae on the Theiss v. Niederle, *Slav. Ant.* II. 127.

[6] *Hist.* I. 79.
[7] For pictures of Sarmatians on the walls of the vaults of Anthesterius and others near Kerch, *CR.* 1872; *KTR.* p. 203 sqq., v. inf. ch. XI. § 4.
[8] Chang K'ien, c. 126 B.C., ap. Shih-ki c. 123. The first character of Yen-tu (= India) is commonly read *Shên*, body, hence the identification Sindhu, but here we are specially directed to pronounce it *Yen* or *Yüan* (H. A. Giles).

Ta-Hia. This would be soon after the unsuccessful attack of Artabanus on the Tochari (c. 124 B.C., Justin XLI. 2), as it seems to be the movement Strabo (XI. viii. 2) records, whereby the Asil, Pasiani (in these names lie hid Yüe-chih and Wu-sun), Tochari and Sacarauli (v.l. Saracauli) from over the Jaxartes drove the Greeks out of Bactria[1]. Of the five Yüe-chih tribes the Kushanas eventually came to the front and their power also gravitated towards India, replacing the Greek dominion in Afghanistan. Hence in western usage they shared the name of Indo-Scyth with the Saka states on each side. Meanwhile we catch glimpses of the westward movement of the Hiung-nu[2] due to pressure from the Sien-pi, their eastern neighbours, who finally absorbed part, penned part in the Altai to reappear as the Turks, and drove the main body to the far west. About 200 B.C. the Phauni are coupled with the Seres as the limits of Graeco-Bactrian ambition, that is the Huns were in their original position[3]. Amometus[4] puts them to the N. of the Indians by the Tochari: Ptolemy or rather Marinus of Tyre places them as Chuni on the borders of Europe, and gives the Ural river its Turkish name $\Delta\alpha\ddot{i}\xi$[5], now Jajyk. So from the other side the Hou-han-shu tells of the Huns spreading westward, c. 100 A.D., and subduing the A-lan-na, c. 250 A.D., and the Wei-shu of their taking the land of the Yen-ts'ai[6].

Finally, in 375 A.D., the storm of the Huns' invasion fell upon the Alans and afterwards on the Goths, and all the peoples of Eastern Europe were involved in confusion. It is beyond my purpose to follow their fate.

Invasions of Scythia from the West.   Getae.

But not only from the east did peoples enter the steppe land. The force of the backwash of the Iranians and advance of Huns was not sufficient entirely to prevent the western peoples from moving down towards their end of the great plain.

The Getae may almost count as original inhabitants. Certainly we have very early traces of their presence to the N. of the Danube. Whenever their nation was strong and united they seem to have extended their sway to the Dnêstr, in times of decadence their borders would fall back to the Danube, and as we have seen, sometimes the Scythians crossed even this. To the Getae belonged very likely the Tyragetae, not from the similarity of name which seems to be but Sarmatian for men of the Tyras, but

---

[1] Tr. Pomp. Prol. XLI. "Saraucae et Asiani" attack Diodotus of Bactria; XLII. "reges Thogarorum Asiani interitusque Saraucarum."

[2] All the Chinese forms, v. sup. p. 91, including Hua the older name for the Yi-ta or Ephthalites, the Yüe-chih's successors, called in Sanskrit Hūṇa but generally regarded as no true Huns, go back to an original *Hun*. In western authors we have Chuni, Phuni, Χοῦνοι, Φοῦνοι and Οὖννοι; the interchange of *ph, kh,* and *h* is found in Turkish dialects and Tomaschek (I. p. 759) may be right in identifying all these forms.

[3] Strabo XI. xi. I, on authority of Apollodorus. Codd. Φαυνῶν, Müller Φρυνῶν. H. Brunnhofer, *Iran und Turan,* p. 204, sees in Dribhika, Cumuri and Dhuni, beggar folk of the Veda, nomad tribes

Derbiccae and Θοῦννοι, the form preferred (he says) by Eust. ad v. 730 of Dion. Perieg., but this is but to strengthen his view of the late invasion of the Panjàb by the Âryas, Eust. really rejects the Θ.

[4] ap. Pliny, *NH.* VI. 55; Detlefsen reads "Thuni et Focari," adding "al. Chuni, Phuni vel Phruri, et Tochari"; similar var. ll. in Dion. Perieg. v. 752; so much for arguments founded on the supposed etymology of tribal names.

[5] Γέηχ in Constant. Porph. *de adm. imp.* 37.

[6] See F. Hirth, "Ueber Wolga-Hunnen und Hiung-nu," in *Sitzungsber. d. phil.-hist. Classe der k. bayer. Akad. d. Wiss.* 1899, Bd II., Heft II., pp. 245—278, Munich, 1900, and review of same by Prof. K. Inostrantsev in *TRAS.* Oriental Section, Vol. XIII. p. 068, St Pb., 1900.

from there being no other stock to whom the Tyragetae can be referred. They seem clearly distinguished from any variety of Scythian[1].

In the time of Philip of Macedon we read that Atheas had spread the power of the Scythians to the south of the Danube, but this power was, it seems, destroyed by the defeat inflicted by Philip[2], B.C. 339. For in 336 Alexander[3], having driven the Triballi to take refuge in the island of Peuce, crossed the Ister, defeated the Getae on the north bank to the number of 10,000 foot and 4000 horse, and took their town. It seems hardly possible that in three years' space the Scythians should have thus disappeared and left in their place another nation with a town and large forces, and that this nation should continue the war with Macedon. The question arises, was not Atheas a Getan, called a Scythian just because he lived N. of the Danube? Alexander's attack was merely a demonstration, and later the Getae gave much trouble to the rulers of Macedon. While Alexander was conquering the east his lieutenant in Thrace, Zopyrion, made an expedition against the Scythians[4] and was annihilated. This again suggests that the authorities did not clearly distinguish Scythians and Getans in this region. About 291 B.C. Lysimachus undertook an expedition against Dromichaetes, king of the Getae, was defeated and taken prisoner with his whole force in the space between the Ister and the Tyras in which, according to Strabo, Darius had suffered defeat (VII. iii. 8 and 14). Tacchella[5] refers to successors of Dromichaetes coins bearing the names of Acrosandrus, Canites, Adraspus and Sarias, also perhaps Scostoces. We hear little of the Getae for the next two hundred years, for the Galatian invasions weakened all the Thracian and neighbouring tribes. Then about the time of Sulla[6] there arose a vigorous king among the Getae, as Latyshev thinks, or according to others among the Daci. The fact is that these were two closely connected peoples, and the Romans were apt to apply the name Daci to both because they approached the pair of them from the west, whereas the Greeks called both Getae, having come in closest contact with these[7]. It is with this king Byrebista[8] that Strabo (VII. iii. 11) begins his account of the Getae. He found his people oppressed and weakened by continuous wars but united them and trained them till he had subdued the greater part of their neighbours. He harried the Roman provinces and Thrace, destroyed the Keltic Boii and Taurisci, and took Olbia and the other Greek towns along the coast as far as Apollonia[9]. At least the time given by Dio for this destruction, 150 years before the delivery of his speech, between 67 B.C. and 50 B.C., agrees with the time of Byrebista's power which ended with his death about 44 B.C. Caesar intended an expedition against him, but when Augustus sent one, the king

---

[1] For a good account of the Getae see Müllenhoff, *DA.* III. pp. 125—163; also Kretschmer, *Einl. in d. Geschichte d. Gr. Spr.*, p. 213, and Tomaschek, *Thraker*, I. p. 93; Latyshev, *Olbia*, p. 72, note 12, and p. 149 sqq.

[2] Justin, IX. ii.

[3] Arrian, *Anab.* I. iii. 1, 2; Str., VII. iii. 3—8.

[4] Justin, II. iii. 4; XII. i. 4; ii. 16; cp. XXXVII. iii. 2. Getae in Q. Curtius, X. i. 43. Thucydides, II. 96, already classes both together as ὁμόσκευοι, πάντες ἱπποτοξόται.

[5] *Revue Numismat.* 1900, p. 397; 1903, p. 30, but Canites is king of the Scythians in *CIG.* 2056, v. sup.

p. 119, n. 3.

[6] Jordanes, *Get.* c. XI.

[7] Cf. Dio Cassius, *RH.* LXVII. 6.

[8] This form Βυρεβίστα indecl. is used in a contemporary inscr. from Dionysopolis, N. of Varna, Latyshev, *Journ. Min. Publ. Inst.* 1896; Ditt.[2] I. 342. Strabo has Βοιρεβίστας, VII. iii. 11; Trogus Pomp. *Prol.* XXXII. 10 Burobustes, or something like it; Jordanes, *Get.* XI., Burvista.

[9] Dio Chrysostom, *Or.* XXXVI. p. 49. He seems to have had a peaceful suzerainty over Dionysopolis, Ditt.[2] I. 342.

had been murdered and the country was divided into four or five warring states, so that the power of the Getae sank as quickly as it had risen.

To the Getae belong the Carpi, Carpiani (Ptol. III. v. 10), Harpii (*ib.* III. x. 7) between the Tyras and Ister, with the town Harpis on the coast. Niederle[1] puts them further inland and connects their name with Carpathian, and suggests that they were Slavs, the same as the enigmatical Khorvate or Croats. They are not mentioned by Strabo, whereas they were known to Marinus of Tyre. They could hardly have come in after the annexation of Bessarabia to the Roman Empire under Nero (v. chap. XIV.), so that their appearance coincides in time with the migration of the Iazyges into the basin of the Theiss, and there may well have been causal connection between the two events[2]. Geographus Ravennas (I. 12) speaks of *Sarmatum Patria* which may be either the Theiss valley or Sarmatia E. of the Carpathians, and adds, *gens Carporum quae fuit ex praedicta in bello egressa est.* That the Carpi were Dacians is shewn not so much by the form Καρπόδακαι[3] as by the characteristic place-names in *-daua* given by Ptolemy in their country. The forms with *H* came through the mouths of Germans, Bastarnae[4].

Bastarnae and Sciri.

These Bastarnae[5] are the next invaders from the w. who came to join the mixed population of this part of Scythia. They were the easternmost outpost of the Germanic world, the first Germans to come in contact with the Greeks. These latter at first regarded them as a variety of Kelt and the earlier authors speak of them as Γαλάται, but the clear statements of Strabo and others[6] who had learnt the difference between Kelt and German have given Müllenhoff and Braun good grounds for confidently affirming their German blood. They are also interesting as having stood between the Keltic and Slavonic worlds in the place afterwards occupied by the Goths.

Whether or no they were the serpents who drove the Neuri from their country (p. 103), the first position in which we can clearly trace them is on the E. slopes of the Carpathians, which they must have reached before the first great sound-shift, for from them must have come the form Harfaða in which the word Carpathians occurs in Norse epics[7]. At the beginning of the second century B.C. they moved down to the Danube and were employed by Philip of Macedon against the Thracians. Being defeated the greater part returned home, but a part settled in the island Peuce, near the mouth of the Danube (p. 12), and never rejoined their fellow tribesmen, though consciousness of their affinity continued for centuries, and geographers, mistakenly identifying Peucini and Bastarnae, placed the former in the interior in the places occupied by the latter. Strabo is the first to say where the main body of the Bastarnae lived after leaving the Carpathians. He locates them in the interior bordering on the Tyragetae and the Germans,

---

[1] *Slav. Ant.* I. p. 424 sqq., II. 107, 122.
[2] Braun, p. 174 sq.
[3] Zosimus, IV. xxxiv. 6.
[4] Carpidae, given by Ephorus ap. Scymnum 841 in *Peripl. Anonymi* § 75 (49), is probably a mistaken correction of Callippidae, for E. follows Herodotus, and the change might be made by Anon. or one of his authorities who knew the late Carpi.

[5] Braun, p. 99 sqq.   Cf. Niederle, op. cit. I. p. 289 sqq. ; Müllenhoff, *DA.* II. 104 sq.
[6] Str. VII. iii. 17 ; Pliny IV. 100; Tac. *Germ.* 46.
[7] Niederle takes the snakes literally, and will not allow the Bastarnae on the Carpathians before 250 B.C. Trogus Pomp. XXVIII. mentions them about 240. N. will not grant any defined date to the sound-shifting.

that is in Galicia and upper Bessarabia.   In this position, though they
retained their German speech, manner of life and houses, living a settled
life and going afoot as opposed to the Sarmatians who spent their time in
waggons or on horseback, still by mixed marriages they took on something
of the dirty ways of the Sarmatians[1].   In spite of the words mixed marriages,
we must beware of thinking of the Bastarnae as bastard Germans, as Braun
has shewn that this use of the root *bast* is only mediaeval.   Also they are
not to be identified with the Galatae of the Protogenes inscription[2].   If
Γαλάται there meant Germans, we should not have Γαλάται καὶ Σκίροι, as
these latter would be included in the greater denomination[3].

These Sciri offer no great difficulty, although they are not mentioned
again until the time of Pliny[4], who puts them on the Vistula to the s. of the
Goths, between them and the Bastarnae: we may suppose that they, with
their companion Kelts, were partakers in the movement which brought the
Bastarnae into Thrace, but instead of continuing as far as that more distant
objective they turned aside to plunder Olbia.   Being foiled in their attempt
the Sciri probably returned to the Vistula with the chief mass of the
Bastarnae, whereas the Kelts who came from Northern Hungary remained
on the Danube together with the Peucini.   It seemed as if the Sciri remained
among the most remote Germanic tribes, until these at last moved south
in the wake of their more advanced countrymen.   But some Sciri are found
among the tribes subject to the Huns about 381 A.D., and again in 409, when
they were caught in a flight and destroyed or sold as slaves[5].   The Huns
could scarcely have reached the Sciri on the Vistula ; perhaps some of them
had settled further south.   Ptolemy does not mention any Sciri[6].

Kelts and Goths.

Finally, beside the Germanic Bastarnae and Sciri there were Kelts on
the lower Danube.   Ptolemy puts them above the Peucini, between them and
the Harpii, calling them Britolagae, v.l. Βριτογάλλοι.   Their towns were
Noviodunum and Aliobrix, names whose Keltic character is evident.   Various
views have been taken as to how Kelts came there, and whence and when,
and with these questions is bound up that of the date of the Protogenes
inscription[2].   The eastern movements of the Kelts had brought them to
three positions from which a detachment might have moved down to the
lower Danube.   From the Eastern Alps, occupied about 400 B.C., they
spread further, and in 281 attacked Thrace along the western border, and
in 279 made their great descent upon Delphi.   On their way back the
remnants occupied SE. Thrace, and founded a kingdom under Comontorius
with a capital Τύλη or Τύλις, near Mount Haemus.   This kingdom continued
till 213 B.C. when a rising of the Thracians utterly destroyed them[7].   These
are the Kelts who are supposed by W. A. S. Schmidt[8], and after him Latyshev[9],

---

[1] Connubiis mixtis nonnihil in Sarmatarum
habitum foedantur, Tac. *Germ.* 46.
[2] App. 7 = *IosPE.* I. 16, cf. ch. XV.
[3] A. Spitsyn refers to the Bastarnae the stray
objects of La Tène style found in Russia, *BCA.*
XII. p. 78, but it is as likely that they are due to Kelts.
[4] *NH.* IV. 97.
[5] Zosimus, IV. xxxiv. 6 : Sozomen, IX. 5.

[6] Braun, p. 117 sqq. ; Niederle, op. cit. I. p.
302 sqq.
[7] Polybius IV. xlv. 10 ; xlvi. 1.
[8] "Das olbische Psephisma zu Ehren des Protogenes," *Rheinisches Museum für Philologie* IV.,
Bonn, 1835-6, p. 357 sqq., 571 sqq.
[9] *Olbia*, p. 66 sqq.

to have extended their devastations as far as Olbia.   Boeckh thought that the assailants were Scordisci from Pannonia.   In each of these cases the incursion must have been pushed very far from the base of the people making it, and they must have returned to their own place again.   Moreover it is hard to see how they should have come into combination with the Germanic Sciri.   Whereas if we suppose that there was a general southward movement of Keltic tribes settled in northern Hungary, and Germanic tribes from over the mountains in Galicia, Britolagae, Bastarnae and Sciri, this combination could be well understood and the assailants would be found again in the Britolagae on the Danube.   That would put the Protogenes inscription in the second century B.C., not in the third, and this agrees best with the general character of the lettering which still does not preclude its belonging to the third century according to Latyshev's view[1].

To Keltic influence we may attribute the presence in S. Russia of fibulae derived from the La Tène type[2], but Spitsyn (l.c.) puts them down to the Bastarnae.   Keltic too, if we may trust the engraving, is a coin from the Crimea figured by Waxel[3].

Yet one more nation entered Sarmatia from the west, the nation which brought about the fall if not the absolute annihilation of the Greek colonies on the mainland.   The Goths appear in the steppes early in the third century A.D., and by 238 already receive a stipend from the empire[4].   This aroused the envy of the Carpi, who claimed to be as good as they, and on being treated by the Romans with contempt they crossed the Danube and destroyed Istropolis, A.D. 241.   Under Philip the Arabian the stipend to the Goths was unpaid and they in their turn invaded the empire and laid siege to Marcianopolis.   After defeating the Gepidae who had tried to follow them into the rich plain, but were forced to return to their seat in Galicia, the Goths under Cniva again invaded the empire in 249, took Philippopolis in 250, and the following year defeated and killed the emperor Decius.   In the war which followed the Goths, whom the historians with characteristic pedantry call Scythians, used boats to harry the coasts not merely of the Euxine from Pityus to Byzantium, as the Russians were to do after them, but also those of the Aegean, sacking even such towns as Ephesus and Athens, as well as "Trojam Iliumque vix a bello illo Agamemnoniaco quantulum se reparantes"[5]! But a great combined invasion, rather a migration by land and sea with women and children, was destroyed by Claudius, who well earned the title Gothicus. Aurelian ceded Dacia to the Goths and peace was made in 270, a peace which lasted with slight interruptions till the eve of the Hunnish invasion. But before crossing the Danube the Goths had worked their will upon Olbia and Tyras.   Coining comes to an end with the first half of the reign of Alexander Severus, and the latest inscription (App. 14) is of the time of Philip the Arabian : Olbia was not quite deserted, for later coins, even Byzantine ones, have been found on the site, but it ceased to be a Hellenic

---

[1] v. Braun, p. 126 sqq.; Niederle, I. p. 303 sqq.
[2] B. Salin, *Die Altgermanische Thier-Ornamentik*, p. 5 sqq. R. Hausmann, "Einige Bemerkungen über neuere Fibelforschung und über die Fibeln im Odessäer Museum," *Trans. Od. Soc.*

XXI. p. 255 ; *Sm.* III. i. 1—7.
[3] *Suite du Recueil d'Antiquités*, f. 57.
[4] Cf. Hodgkin, *Italy and her Invaders*[2], Vol. I. p. 46.
[5] Jord. *Get.* XX., cf. Zosimus, I. XXXV. sqq.

city[1]. The Goths probably obtained from it, as from Panticapaeum, some of the ships they used in their distant sea expeditions[2]. But from the time of the coming of the Goths the history of the Pontic Greek states is at an end, save only for Chersonese on its well-defended peninsula. For her these new tribes mostly meant new markets for her commerce.

Crimea and Caucasus.

At the other end of the region whose history we are considering, about the west end of the Caucasus, we find another group of tribes whose position it is again very hard to determine. Here the causes are just the opposite to those which produce difficulty in the great plain. The mountainous country has cut up the inhabitants into tribes so small that the number of names furnished by the ancient authors conveys no idea to our minds. Pliny, for instance (*NH.* IV. 85), speaks of thirty tribes in the Crimea, and hardly any of his names occur in any other author, they seem to be the designations of the inhabitants of particular valleys and villages. This region appears to have preserved some relics of the Scyths, possibly joined with the Tauri. Scythotauri may mean but the Scyths living in or near the Tauric Chersonese, or it may be just the Tauric natives, loosely called Scythians. It is hard to see how the Scyths could have really amalgamated with the mountain people. However, Scilurus as ruler of the western steppes in the time of Mithridates made his power felt against Chersonese, and had occupied Balaklava, so that he had penetrated to some extent into the Tauric territory. The Scythae Satarchae in the Crimean steppe may be either relics of Scyths or a Sarmatian tribe.

Our written authorities draw no clear line of distinction between Sarmatae and Maeotae on the one hand, and on the other between the Sindi, who were almost certainly Maeotae, and their SE. neighbours. But the barbarian names found in the inscriptions at Phanagoria and Gorgippia shew a much smaller proportion of Iranian derivatives than those of Tanais, and these few are either widely distributed Persian names or names of particularly common occurrence at Tanais that seem to have spread about the Bosporan kingdom. This would seem to point to the indigenes of the Euxine coast being of a different stock from the Sarmatian natives surrounding Tanais, and so presumably Caucasian. This is Müllenhoff's view. On the other hand, Professor Lappo-Danilevskij[3] points out the substantial identity of customs and civilisation of the people who heaped up barrows along the Kuban and along the Dnêpr and, assigning his Karagodeuashkh barrow to the Sindi, refers these to the same stock as the Sarmatians. Possibly a ruling tribe, nearly related to the Scyths, played the same part to the east of the Maeotis that their cousins played to the west, and dominated many tribes of various origin, some Iranian and some Caucasian. This would account for the similar customs used at the burial of kings in two regions so widely separated[4].

[1] Latyshev, *Olbia*, p. 210.
[2] Zosimus, I. XXXI. For remains of the Crimean Goths v. MacPherson's *Kertch*, pl. v., and *BCA.* XIX. p. 1—80, N. Répnikov's excavations near Gurzuf.

[3] *Mat.* XIII. St P. 1894, pp. 96—111, v. inf. p. 206 sqq.
[4] Strabo, XI. ii. 16, says of the people above Dioscurias that the greater part are Sarmatae

East of the Sea of Azov the tribes along the coast where the Caucasus comes close to the Black Sea were certainly the ancestors of the people that inhabited the district till the other day. The best account of these, and of the Maeotae too, is in the first chapter of Latyshev's introduction to the Inscriptions of the Bosporus[1]. But he only takes notice of the tribes mentioned in his inscriptions.

As we have seen, the Sarmatae really included the Iazamatae, whom some authorities give as Maeotae: Iranian too were the Aorsi and Siraci, of whom Strabo says that they came down from the north (XI. v. 8). They seem to have encroached upon the Maeotae, who appear once to have reached as far as the Tanais along the Palus that bore their name.

Earlier (XI. ii. 11) Strabo gives a list of tribes among the Maeotae, Sindi, Dandarii, Toreatae, Agri, Arrhechi, Tarpetes, Obidiaceni, Sittaceni, Dosci, and the people called Aspurgiani. Of these the Sindi are much the most interesting. They first fell under Greek influence, their territory, the Taman peninsula and a little to the E. of it by the southern mouth of the Kuban, being full of Greek towns, hence they alone have left us coins (Pl. IX. 25—27) and they are first mentioned in the inscriptions of the Bosporan kings apart from the other "Maitae[2]," that is they became so Hellenized that they hardly counted as Maitae (*IosPE*. II. 6—8, 10, 11, 15, 36, 344—347, IV. 418)[3]. After the Sindi the Maeotae are taken together, e.g. Σινδῶν καὶ Μαιτῶν πάντων[4]. Next are mentioned Toreatae[5], Dandarii[6], Tarpetes[7], Doschi[8], Sirachi[9]. Strabo omits to mention the Thateis[10], and the name is found in the text of no author, but Boeckh restored it for Θρακῶν Diodorus XX. 22 and in Ptolemy for MSS. Θερμαιῶται, Θετμῶνται put Θατ(εῖς) Μαιῶται. The inscriptions give also the name Pses[s]i[11]. Of these tribes the Toretae seem to have lived on the coast just E. of the Sindi, the Dandarii N. of them near the upper branch of the Kuban, the others cannot be well located except the Aspurgiani between Gorgippia and Phanagoria, and these appear to have been not a tribe but rather a political party or a military colony founded by Aspurgus[12].

Along the coast next to the Toretae (at Bata) came the Cercetae, says Artemidorus, then the Achaei, Zygi and Heniochi; but the authors who treated of the wars of Mithridates put the Cercetae to the east of these latter, between them and the Moschi. Last of the coast series come the Colchi[13]. The Cercetae may well be the Circassians. There may have been a change of population here in spite of the natural difficulties, or Artemidorus may have confused the Cercetae and Toretae, whom Anon. Periplus (63 (22)) makes the same. Further up in the mountains Strabo (XI. ii. 1, 19; v. 7, 8) tells of Macropogónes, Phthiro-

---

and all Caucasian. So even in his time some Sarmatian tribes had taken to the mountains like their last representatives the Ossétes. Tirgatao, queen of the Maeotae, had an Iranian name, v. supra p. 39.

[1] *IosPE*. Vol. II. p. ix, as usual amplifying the work of Boeckh, *CIG*. II. p. 100.

[2] Her. IV. 123, Μαιῆται.

[3] Cf. App. 27, 29, 29[a], 30, 31, 35, 42.

[4] App. 29[a]=*IosPE*. II. 11.

[5] App. 27=*IosPE*. II. 6; App. 29=*IosPE*. II. 344; App. 42=*IosPE*. II. 36, *ib.* IV. 419.

[6] App. 27, 29.

[7] Τάρπειτες. App. 42.

[8] Last in *IosPE*. II. 347, ll. 4, 5, [κ]αὶ βασιλεύον-τος Σινδῶν, Μαιτῶν,/[Θ]ατέων, Δόσχων.

[9] Not Maeotae, v. sup. p. 121.

[10] App. 30=*IosPE*. II. 346; App. 31=*IosPE*. II. 8; App. 35, *IosPE*. II. 15; *ib.* 347.

[11] App. 27 and 42; cf. St. Byz. s.v.

[12] Latyshev, *IosPE*. II. introd. p. xxxix, and Rostovtsev in *BCA*. x. p. 15. Ptolemy's Asturicani are very likely the same, v. ch. XIX.

[13] Strabo, XI. ii. 14.

phagi, Melanchlaeni, Soanes above Dioscurias, in what is now Svanetia, and barbarous Troglodytes (in the Caucasus there are great cave cities of unknown date[1]), Chamae-coetae, Polyphagi, Isadici, and to the north of the chain Nabiani and Panxani; other authors add many names in their lists, but they cannot be identified. The Melanchlaeni and Phthirophagi occurring here have been identified with the Melanchlaeni and Budini[2] in the interior beyond Scythia, and have accordingly added to the confusion. The descendants of these tribes have not moved or have only been moved of late years by the Russian administration, which found the Circassians too little amenable to its rule. The survival of the names Cherkess, Svan, Abkhaz (the Abasgi)[3] shews that there has been no great change of population, although most of the modern tribal names are not to be identified with those mentioned by the ancients.

This completes a general view of the peoples of the north coast of the Euxine and their chief movements down to the period of great migrations.

---

[1] e.g. Uplostsikhe, Dubois de Montpéreux, Vol. IV. pl. I. sqq., and Haxthausen, *Transcaucasia*, London, 1854, p. 424.

[2] Her. IV. 109, sup. p. 105.

[3] Anon. 51 (10).

[4] TA-HIA, v. p. 121. Marquart (*Ērānšahr*, p. 199 sqq. Exc. III. Toxāristān) tries to shew that Ta-hia is an attempt of the Chinese to write Tukhāra, the form T'u-huo-lo (in Hüan Tsang, A.D. 629—645, and Wei- and Sui-shu) belonging to a later date when they were rather more successful in expressing foreign sounds. The old equation Ta-hia = Dahae (A. Rémusat and others) had been disproved by Gutschmid (*Gesch. Irans*, p. 62, n. 2), for the Dahae were far to the NW. near the Caspian (Str. XI. vii. 1 et al.) whereas the data (supra, p. 121) make it clear that geographically Ta-Hia = Bactria. Marquart explains his own identification by supposing that the Tochari left the Tarim basin in a migration earlier than that of the Yüe-chih, and that these caught them up and conquered them in Bactria; but we have no Chinese account of such a separate movement of the Tochari, nor does Strabo or Justin support it (v. p. 122). I have supposed (mainly following Franke, op. cit. p. 30) that the Yüe-chih when driven w. by the Huns conquered the Tochari in the Tarim basin, and the two tribes, whatever the former differences between them, became politically one, then together they were forced through Farghana (rather than Dzungaria, v. Shih-ki l.c.) to Trans-Oxiana and later moved S. to Bactria. The Chinese went on using the name Yüe-chih for the combination, among the Westerners (and Southerners, Skt Tukhāra) the word Tochari was the more familiar (cf. Getae and Daci, p. 123), so that it clung to their new country and so got into later Chinese. As to the name Ta-Hia, we have T'u-huo-lo already as the Chinese transcription of Tukhāra and *Ta* = great was, as I understand from Professor Giles, too familiar an ideogram often to be used as a mere phonogram (Ta-shih = Tadzhik used for Arabs being understood as Polyphagi), so that Hia is all we have to deal with, and by its tone there is no reason to suppose any lost final consonant. It would therefore do for the first syllable of Yavana (Gr. 'Ιάϝονες, Pers. Yauna, cf. Ar. *Ach.* 104) the name by which the Bactrian Greeks were known in India. The Ta would distinguish these Hia from the Hia nearer home, cf. Ta-Ts'in = the Roman empire and Ta-Yüan = Farghana. This latter might seem more like Yavana, but F. Hirth, *Ueber fremde Einflüsse in der chinesischen Kunst*, München, 1896, p. 24, gives good reasons against this interpretation.

130

CHAPTER VII.

PRE-SCYTHIC REMAINS IN SOUTH RUSSIA.

I OUGHT perhaps to ask forgiveness for mentioning remains that have no direct connection with Greeks or even with Scythians, but these paragraphs make accessible to English readers what it is difficult for them to read for themselves, and give a certain completeness to this hasty survey of Russian archaeology. Also the interest of the Tripolje culture soon to be described is so general that exception can hardly be taken to some account of it being given.

No satisfactory attempt can yet be made to sum up the prehistoric antiquities of Russia. The time has not come. As compared with Western Europe the series still has many gaps that will be filled up in due course: we cannot yet tell whether the absence of certain stages be due to their never having existed in Eastern Europe, or to the fact that it is only within the last thirty years that this vast area has been seriously investigated. Even now for the Stone Age we are chiefly dependent on chance finds, and very little has been done towards examining the remains of these early periods *in situ*[1].

Palaeolithic Remains.

The first finds of palaeolithic weapons were made in 1873 near Gontsy (district of Lubny, government of Poltava). They were followed by others in the same part of the country. The remains were associated with the bones of mammoths[2]. Next Count Uvarov[3] found others near Murom (government of Vladimir) by the village of Karacharovo and along the course of the Oká. Further, a station has been discovered on the Don, near Kostenki (government of Vorónezh), and another not far off at Borshev[4]. Bone implements of the same periods have occurred in caves near Kalisz in Poland.

---

[1] See *Archaeological Chronicle of S. Russia*, no. I. 1903, p. 6, N. Th. Bélashevskij, "Current Problems of S. Russian Archaeology"; also Dr Niederle, *Lidstvo v době předhistorické*, Prag, 1893 ("Man in Prehistoric Time"), or better its Russian translation by Th. K. Volkov, ed. by Prof. D. N. Anuchin, Moscow, 1898, pp. 53 sqq. (quoted as Niederle, *Preh. Man*) and *CR. du Congrès Intern. d'Archéol. préh. et d'Anthrop. XIᵐᵉ Session à Moscou*, Vols. I., II. (1892–3). Professor Anuchin's résumé made for Brockhaus & Ephron's *Encyclopaedia* has been

published in German in the *Internationales Centralblatt für Anthropologie u.s.w.* 1903, pp. 65 sqq., 129 sqq. For Western Russia and its connection with Western Europe see Niederle, *Slavonic Antiquities*, Part I. Prag, 1904, pp. 435 sqq.

[2] Count A. S. Uvarov, *Archaeology of Russia, Stone Age*, Moscow, 1881, Vol. I. p. 104. For similar finds made by Kan'shin at Umrikhino near Kursk v. *BCA.* XXI. suppl. p. 10.

[3] op. cit. Vol. I. p. 112.

[4] *CR.* 1905, p. 84.

But by far the most trustworthy information as to the Early Stone Age in Russia is due to the careful investigation by Mr V. V. Chvojka of a station on the very site of Kiev, known as the Cyril Street Settlement[1].

At a depth of 19 metres from the top of a steep slope forming the S. side of the Dnêpr valley, underneath layers of black mould, *löss*, clay, streaky sand and sand with boulders and above a tertiary stiff blue clay, were found very many mammoth tusks, bones of mammoths, and in a less quantity of other animals contemporary with them, mostly broken and shewing traces of fire, places where fires had been made, that is patches of mixed earth and charcoal often several yards each way and two or three feet thick, and finally mammoth tusks with traces of definite handiwork, even a rude attempt at a drawing[2], together with flint implements of the earliest type.

The conditions under which the finds were made are best satisfied by the supposition that here was a settlement of man living in the interglacial age a little to the south of the great glacier that covered all N. Russia: the original limits of steppe and forest seem to answer to the line reached by the said glacier. Man settled in the valley of the Dnêpr and hunted the mammoth who furnished the chief means of his subsistence, The great amount of the remains shews that he must have lived on this spot for many years. It was probably sheltered from the cold winds and convenient for hunting purposes. Occasional floods marked by layers of sand drove him from his place, but he returned again and again. In the streaky sand above the main layer of remains we find a few patches of charcoal with bones of lesser animals, no longer the mammoth; no doubt a change of climate or of physical conditions made this spot uninhabitable and drove away the earlier fauna, so that man could no longer occupy the site permanently. Th. K. Volkov[3] has endeavoured to prove that these remains belong to the period called by French archaeologists La Madeleine, the latest palaeolithic period, but Chvojka, in an article in the same journal, makes out a good case for an earlier date. Flint implements of a similar type to those found in Cyril Street have been picked up in various parts of Russia, but this is the only palaeolithic settlement that has been excavated, at any rate in the south of Russia[4].

Finds of the very latest palaeolithic period, possibly indicating a transition to the neolithic, have been more frequent and extend much further north as the retreating ice-sheet allowed man to occupy more country. Such have been made on the banks of Lake Ládoga by Prof. Inostrántsev and about the Oká by Count Uvarov. Cave dwellings with chipped flints have been investigated along the Dnêpr near Kiev by Prof. V. B. Antonóvich and by K. S. Merezhkovskij in various parts of the Crimea[5].

[1] *Transactions of the XIth Russian Archaeological Congress at Kiev*, Vol. I. Moscow, 1902, "The Stone Age on the middle course of the Dnêpr."

[2] *Trans. Od. Soc.* Vol. XXIII. p. 203, and *Arch. Chron. S. Russia*, I. pl. 1—4.

[3] Vol. XLVI. *Transactions of the Shevchenko Scientific Society*, Lemberg, in Little Russian, trans. into Russian in *Arch. Chron. of S. Russia*, no. I.

[4] *Transactions of VIIIth Russian Archaeological Congress*, Moscow, Vol. III. p. 88 sqq. Mr G. A. Skadovskij's finds of palaeolithic implements in Kherson govt quoted by Bobrinskoj, *Sm.* III. p. iii.

[5] Niederle, *Preh. Man*, pp. 53—57. The scarcity of Palaeolithic finds in Russia is exemplified by the fact that V. A. Gorodtsov enumerating all the types of axes in the Moscow Hist. Mus. (*Report for* 1906, p. 97) gives none of this period.

Early neolithic stations are also found in all parts of Russia from the so-called Winter Shore (Zimnij Béreg) on the White Sea and the borders of Lake Onéga to Kazan on the Volga, and to Júrjeva Gorá near Smêla, with many other points in the basin of the Dnêpr about Kiev. The pottery is very rude and shews no special points of contact with other cultures[1].

In the far west of Russia, between the Carpathians and Kiev, we find in the neolithic period distinct traces of connection with the coasts of the Baltic, pottery with string patterns (*Schnurkeramik*), northern types of axe and amber, but such finds are few and poor. This gives way in transitional times to banded ware, which seems to have come in from the south and has analogies in central Europe[2].

Close by the palaeolithic station at Cyril Street, Kiev, Chvojka investigated the most important neolithic site in S. Russia. Whereas palaeolithic man preferred the lower slopes of the valley, neolithic man chose the plateaus above. Here were found the remains of a village which must have existed long. The more primitive dwellings were as it were caves cut in from the edge of the slope; the great majority was formed by digging out a shallow pit oblong or round from three to five and a half yards across and about a foot or eighteen inches deep[3]. In the middle of this they dug a hole from 2 ft. 6 in. to 5 ft. deep, 6 ft. 6 in. to 8 ft. across, with a way down into it made with steps, and at the other end a niche in the face of the inner pit with a hearth and a hole for smoke to escape. Round the outer shallow pit were walls of wattle and daub, and over all a roof. The inhabitants threw all the remains of their food into the central pit, shell-fish, bones of deer of various kinds, wild boar and beaver, and to some extent horses and cows. But they were also acquainted with agriculture, for we find several examples of hand-mills and lumps, which Chvojka supposes to be cakes. Also they seem to have kept tortoises as pets. Spindle whorls shew that spinning, and probably weaving in some simple form, were known. Most weapons and tools are made of stone or horn of deer or elk. The latter are well made, but the flint implements are very slightly ground. There is a remarkable absence of arrow-heads. Most characteristic is the pottery, in which is to be traced progress from very ill-baked, formless, cracked vessels, made of the first earth that came to hand, such as are found in the cave dwellings, to fairly graceful pots of considerable size, adorned with dots and lines and made of a careful mixture of clayey sand and pounded shells. Some few pieces approach to the finer kinds found on the "areas" next described.

On this same site between two of the huts was found an early mould for casting copper or bronze axes, and near it was a horn axe of exactly the same type, but inasmuch as no metal was found in the houses themselves we may be allowed to class them as neolithic[4].

[1] Niederle, *Preh. Man*, p. 78; *Slav. Ant.* I. 445; Bobrinskoj, *Sm.* I. pl. 1, 2; III. p. 49 sqq.; Spitsyn, "Stone Age Station at Bologoe," *TRAS.* Russo-Slav. Section, V. Pt I (1903) p. 239; at Balakhny on the Oka, Spitsyn and Kamenskij, ib. p. 94, VII. Pt I (1905) pp. 1—72; Abercromby, *Finns*, pp. 58 sqq.

[2] Niederle, *Slav. Ant.* I. p. 452.
[3] Inf. p. 137, f. 31 = Chvojka, *Stone Age*, p. 24, f. 11.
[4] Spitsyn gives a Map of the stations of the earliest copper age in Central and North Russia, *TRAS.* Russo-Slav. Section, VII. Pt I, p. 73.

The next class of remains distinguished by the "areas" hereafter to be described with their remarkable pottery and figurines is of very special interest because of the wide range of its affinities, considering its rather special character.

Area at Veremje. A.
Chwjk . p. 94. f. 30.

Area near
Shcherbanevka
A.

Plan of
Area-group
near
Shcherbanevka
A.
1901.
p. 6. f. 6.

View of Area-group at Zhukovtsy. B. p. 34. f. 15.

FIG. 28.

Tripolje Culture.   Areas.

The actual "areas" are about Kiev but the culture occurs in Russia in the governments of Chernigov, Kiev, Poltava and Kherson, in Podolia and in Bessarabia.   Pottery of the same type has been found long since in Galicia at Wygnanka and Złote Bilcze, in Bukovina, in Moravia, in Transylvania

and in northern Moldavia near Cucutenï. Something similar occurs in Serbia
and at Butmir in Herzegovina. A southern extension has been traced through
Thrace to Thessaly and across the Dardanelles to Hissarlik and Yortan on
the Caicus[1]. The first finds were made about the village of Tripolje on the
Dnêpr forty miles below Kiev, whence this is called the Tripolje culture. The
remains consist of so-called "areas" (*ploshchádka*). These are arranged in
groups of a circular form, sometimes the circle is double or triple for part of its
circumference, in any case the areas are closer together on s. and SE. than on the
N. and W.; in the middle of the circles are usually two or three areas of larger
size than the rest. The group is always on high ground dipping down to water
on the south side. Each "area" is a space from 5 to 10 yards long or even,
if it be in the centre, more than 20 yards long by 6 or 8 or even 12 broad.
The distinguishing mark is found in one or more layers of clay lumps spread
over its surface and mixed therewith a surprising number of pots of various
sizes and shapes. Also there appear pedestals like inverted cones or pyramids,
sometimes shewing traces of having been coloured red or white several times,
axes of deer's horn and of flint, sling stones, corn-grinders, shells, bones of
animals among others of horses and tortoise shells, and little figures in clay
that distantly recall those from Hissarlik.

The construction of an area seems to have been as follows. The space
to be occupied was marked and dug out to the depth required from two feet to
about four, then walls were built of wattle and covered with clay which was
fired when dry. Sometimes we seem to have a lean-to with only one wall and
a roof; others had walls on two, three or four sides. In some cases the walls
were whitewashed or coloured red or bear layers of alternate colour, and there

[1] Niederle, *Preh. Man*, pp. 154—167; *Slav.
Ant.* I. pp. 455—466; Chvojka, *Stone Age*, and
TRAS. Russian Section, Vol. V. pt 2, p. 1, St P.
1904; also *Archaeol. Chron. S. Russia*, 1904, pp.
116, 221; Khanenko, *Antiquités de la Région du
Dnièpre*, Part I. Kiev, 1899; Th. Volkov, "With
regard to our neolithic finds with pottery of pre-
Mycenaean type," *Arch. Chron. S. Russia*, 1900,
131; I. A. Linnichenko, "On the latest excavations
of Mr Chvojka," *Trans. Od. Soc.* XXIII. Minutes,
p. 75; "On a pot from Tripolje with signs upon it,"
ib. text, p. 199; E. von Stern, "Excavations in N.
Bessarabia in connection with the question of Neolithic settlements with pottery of a pre-Mycenaean
type," *Bulletin of XIIth Russian Archaeolog. Congress* (Kharkov, 1902), p. 87; A. A. Skrylenko,
"On Clay statuettes from Tripolje," ib. p. 223;
A. Spitsyn, "Report of V. N. Domanitskij's Excavations of Clay Areas near Kolodistoe, Govt of
Kiev," *BCA.* XII. p. 87; *CR.* 1906, pp. 106—108,
ff. 141—151, M. K. Jakimovich, Staraja Buda near
Zvenigorodka. Von Stern has published and illustrated with excellent plates the results of his
excavations at Petrény (district of Bĕltsy in Bessarabia) and has given his general views at length
in his article "Die prämykenische Kultur in
Süd-Russland" (Russian and German) in Vol. I.
of *Transactions of the XIIth (Kharkov) Congress
of Russian Archaeologists*, Moscow, 1906. His
finds are in the Society's Museum at Odessa,
Chvojka's in the town Museum at Kiev. The
central European finds are discussed by H. Schmidt
in *Zt. f. Ethnologie*, XXXV. (1903), pp. 438—469,
"Tordos"; XXXVI. (1904), 608—656, "Troja,
Mykeňe, Ungarn"; XXXVII. (1905), 91—113,
"Keramik der makedonischen Tumuli"; the Tran-
sylvanian (Priesterhügel) by J. Teutsch, *Mitth. d.
Anthrop. Ges. in Wien*, 1900, pp. 193—202; the
Rumanian by ·M. Hoernes, *Urgeschichte d. bild.
Kunst*, p. 210; the Serbian by M. Vasić, *Starinar*, I.
ii. (1907) "Žuto Brdo," and *BSA.* XIV. pp. 319—342
"The South-Eastern Elements in the Prehistoric
Civilization of Servia." The whole question is well
set forth by R. M. Burrows, *The Discoveries in
Crete* (London, 1907), pp. 184—202, and his résumé
gives all that the English reader requires but wants
illustrations; see too D. G. Hogarth, *Ionia and the
East* (Oxford, 1909), p. 113; and Peet, Wace and
Thompson in *Classical Rev.* 1908, pp. 232—238 for
further literature. For Thrace (Tell Racheff near
Jamboli, see Fr. Jérôme, "L'Époque Néolithique
dans la Vallée du Tonsus" in *Revue Archéologique*
3, XXXIX. (1901), pp. 328—349, and *CR. du Congrès
International d'Archéologie*, 1905, Athens, p. 207),
also Seure-Degrand, *BCH.* 1906, pp. 359 sqq.
Tsountas and Stais have found neolithic stations
near Volo, Αἱ προιστορικαὶ ἀκροπόλεις Διμηνίου καὶ
Σέσκλου, Athens, 1908, esp. pl. XI; and Wace and
Droop at Zerélia in Thessaly, *Annals of Archaeology and Anthropology* (Liverpool), 1908, p. 116
sqq.; *BSA.* XIV. p. 197 sqq.; for imported ware at
Matera, S. Italy, see T. E. Peet, *The Stone and
Bronze Ages in Italy*, (Oxford, 1909), p. 108, f. 36.

is every trace of the structure existing a considerable period and being restored and beautified from time to time. Remains are also found of a kind of cornice to the walls. Sometimes there had been a floor of hardened clay. The layers of clay lumps seem to be the remains of the walls and perhaps the roof, and

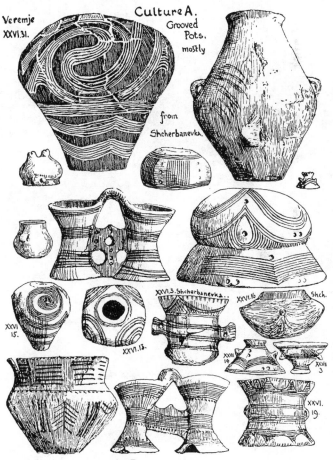

FIG. 29. v. p. 137.

where there are many layers it is probable that the structure has been destroyed and reedified. Occasionally there seem to have been interior walls. Amid the clay lumps, standing or lying or upside down on the original floor, are the remarkable vessels which give chief interest to the discovery, as in them and the figures some have seen an analogy to the early Aegean culture. As many as eighty have been found together. Chvojka divides the areas into two classes

Culture A.

V.V Chvojka. Stone Age on the Middle Dnepr.

Tripolje.
Copper. XXI.10.

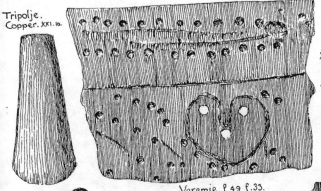

XXVIII
8.
Deep
Yellow
u
Brown.

Veremje. P.49 f.33.

XXI .11

XXVIII.1.
White u Brown
Black outlines.
Veremje.

Shcherbanevka.
Dark red
Clay.
XXII.2.

XXVIII 2

XXVIII.11.
White u Brown
Outlines dark
Brown or
Black.

XXVIII.10,
Cream and
Dark brown.

Painted Potter. Culture A.

that he calls *A* and *B*, without wishing to prejudge the question which of them comes first in point of time.

A (ff. 28—30) is distinguished by pottery of very various shapes, e.g. a double jar-stand (?) like an opera-glass or twin bottomless dice-boxes, pyri-

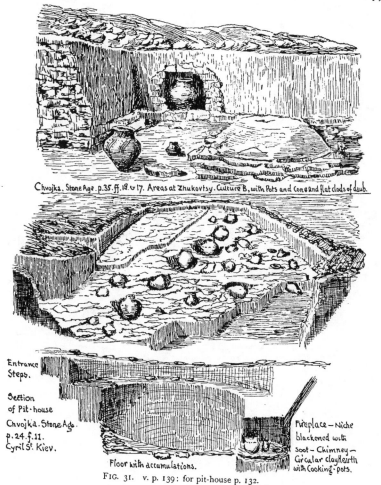

Chvojka, Stone Age. p.35. ff.18. & 17. Areas at Zhukovtsy. Culture B, with Pots and Cones and flat clods of daub.

Entrance Steps.

Section of Pit-house Chvojka. Stone Age. p.24.f.11. Cyril St. Kiev.

Floor with accumulations.

Fireplace — Niche blackened with Soot — Chimney — Circular clay Hearth with Cooking-pots.

FIG. 31.   v. p. 139: for pit-house p. 132.

form pots with small openings above, conical pots on little rims to support them, rude faces made by a pinch of the fingers and three dots on a round or heart-shaped projection of clay, stone axes bored through and even one or two copper ones, most of all by the adornment of the pots either with graceful and

M.

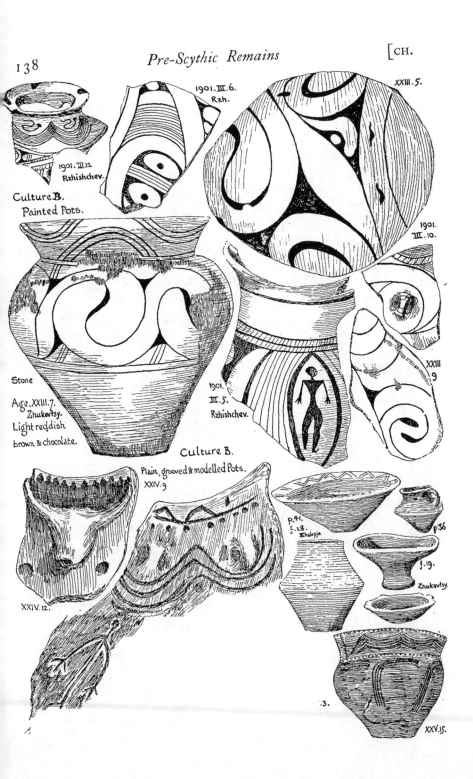

1901.III.6.
Rzh.

XXIII.5.

1901.III.12.
Rzhishchev.

Culture B.
Painted Pots.

1901.
III.10.

XXIII
9

Stone
Age.XXIII.7.
Zhukovtsy.
Light reddish
brown & chocolate.

1901.
III.5.
Rzhishchev.

Culture B.

Plain, grooved & modelled Pots.
XXIV.9

p.41.
f.28.
Khalepja.

p.36

f.19.

Zhukovtsy.

XXIV.12.

.3.

XXV.15.

free spirals or wavy patterns made by four or five parallel grooves giving a ribbon-like effect, or with equally easy spirals painted on a yellow or reddish ground with reddish or brownish paint and polished to a smooth and pleasant surface. Also the idols are more like crosses than human beings.

In *B* (ff. 31—34) on the other hand the shapes of the pots are more angular, the ornament especially when incised is less free and chiefly confined to the upper half of the pot, the rim of which is sometimes adorned with heads of animals and birds in relief. There are no axes with holes bored in them and no metal whatsoever, by so much *B* seems inferior, but the statues of women are very

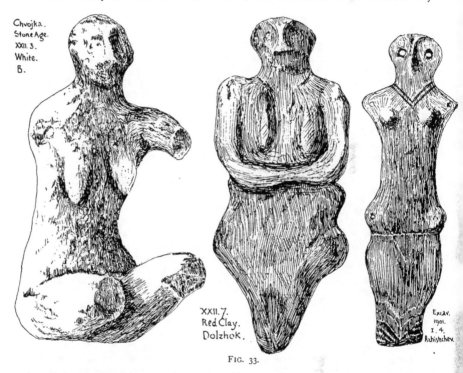

Chvojka.
Stone Age.
XXII. 3.
White.
B.

XXII. 7.
Red Clay.
Dolzhok.

Excav.
1901.
I. 4.
Rzhishchev.

FIG. 33.

much better than the cruciform idols of *A*. Also *B* has curious pedestals of clay which have been painted several times, or stands of clay supporting a stone basin. In *B* also have been found remains of half-cooked corn hidden below the general level of the platform. Moreover in *B* have been found marks, some occurring singly upon vessels and perhaps denoting ownership as the *Tamgi* of the Caucasian tribes, in one case[1] set in a row and presenting a remarkable resemblance to an inscription. It would seem as if *A* were superior to *B* and later than it, but the difference in the statuettes is most remarkable.

[1] Figured in the *Trans. Od. Soc.* Vol. XXIII. p. 202.

Chvojka thinks that the cultures *A* and *B* belonged to the same people but that *A* has mostly imported from the south the elements that distinguish it.   Perhaps the occurrence of metal in *A* proves it to be the more modern.

As to the object of the areas, they cannot be dwellings, because about them are none of the traces of habitation, no remains of food or pottery thrown away, hardly any implements or signs of a perpetual hearth.   Though no urns of ashes or interments were found in the earlier diggings Chvojka came to the conclusion that they must be tombs or chapels of the dead.   It is a remarkable conception that on the highest suitable hill near the village there should have been the circle of little chapels dedicated to the departed of each family.   Except in one case we have not happened upon the village.   The culture of the pit houses on M. Sventoslavskij's ground near the site on Cyril Street, Kiev, of which we first spoke, seems to occupy a half-way position between the period of the earlier pit houses and that of the areas, having similar pottery and also arrow-heads which are not found in the earlier houses.   The pottery rather resembles *A* than *B*.   Later excavations about Rzhishchev and Kanëv[1] have shewn that the same people lived in the more advanced pit dwellings and built the areas. Better preserved specimens of these unspoilt by the plough have yielded urns full of human ashes and thereby placed their purpose beyond a doubt : bodies some scorched and some untouched by fire shew that cremation was not the exclusive custom, but it is not clear whether it was going out or coming in[2].

Superior especially in range of colour to anything from Tripolje is a pot from Podolia of which Chvojka has recently sent me a photograph.   This pot which he classes with *B* stands 2 ft. 6 in. high and its surface is covered with light brown slip.   On the upper slope are two bands of ornament in dark red, the lower curvilinear, the upper having drawings of a he-goat, a nanny goat, a deer and a dog. It was full of scorched wheat grains.   Other vases from Podolia have on a ground painted black, light brown, yellow or grey, spirals and curves in three colours, white, light or dark red, orange or brown according to the ground[3].

FIG. 34. Pot from Podolia from a drawing by Chvojka.

Von Stern's finds at Petreny likewise surpass Tripolje ware in range of colour.   There is little incised work and the figurines are few and very rude, one of them is striped : most of the attempts at modelling in the round come from one single area.   The shapes too of the vases are not so varied as further north.   The painting however is very abundant and of a high order.   In a few cases on the natural red or yellow surface of the clay the patterns have been painted directly in black or violet brown.   More often the natural clay is covered by a slip, polished if it be red or brown, dull if it be white or yellowish : on this the painting is applied in black or violet brown (often with a greenish tinge to judge by the plates), rarely yellow or red.   In a few cases

[1] *TRAS.* Russo-Slav. Section, Vol. v. Pt 2, St P. 1904.

[2] Chvojka, *Arch. Chron. S. Russia*, 1904, p. 223.

[3] Private letter from Mr Chvojka, Jan. 8, 1907.

I take this opportunity of thanking him most deeply for sending me reprints of his articles, unpublished photographs and very kind letters to enable me to keep abreast of his researches.

both black and red are used together. The designs are mostly of much the same character as those here illustrated, especially those of culture *B* (p. 138, f. 32). They are founded on the spiral executed with wonderful skill, simpler curves also come in, arcs of circles and fairly straight lines. The attempts at the human figure scarcely come up to those illustrated above, and the animals including oxen, dogs and goats are not equal to those on the Podolian pot. There are the same knobs and tiny handles. The potter's wheel is strange to the whole culture.

Chvojka, the first discoverer, thought that this was an autochthonous civilisation developed by the Indo-Europeans before they differentiated, perhaps more particularly by that section of the race which was to become the Slavs. Those who studied the Western regions, where somewhat similar spirals occur, did not at first dare to think that northerners could have been so artistic without external influence, and ascribed the highly developed decoration to the influence of the Aegean exercised through traders and the importation of wares. Independently M. Much, H. Schmidt and von Stern advanced the view that the movement was the other way, that the northern finds are earlier in date than the similar objects in the Aegean region—in fact von Stern even entitles the Russian version of his paper " Pre-historic Greek Culture in the S. of Russia," and thinks that the artistic people who made the Petreny pots moved south and conquered even as far as Crete. .

The difficulty here is that we can trace back continuous development on such sites as Cnossus to a neolithic stratum far inferior in artistic power to the pots at Petreny : that is, that the supposed northern immigrants must have gone back in their art on reaching new countries, and afterwards raised it again to the height of Kamares ware or ware from Phylakopi which according to von Stern recall Tripolje and Petreny. This is of course possible ; the wars of conquest may have caused a setback in art. But the fact is that we do not know enough yet to talk of movements or affinities of races. Still, having regard to the artistic gifts of the Mediterranean as opposed to the Northern race, it may be that the basis of the Tripolje population was a geographically northern outlier of the former subjected to the strong influence of its neighbours, the varying strength of this influence accounting for the differences presented by similar cultures to the westward. The inconsistency of funeral customs argues the same mixture. Cremation would seem to have come in from the north, but not yet to have put an end to the vivid consciousness of the dead man's continued presence and needs which goes with primitive interment. Hence the numerous offerings. Under their less favourable conditions pottery painting was the one art which the Tripolje folk brought to a high standard, that and the modelling of some *B* figurines[1]. Before they could advance further they seem to have come absolutely to an end. There is nothing in S. Russia which can claim to be in any sense a successor to the Tripolje-Petreny culture. They may have moved south or they may have been overwhelmed by newcomers. They were agriculturists long before the date of the agricultural Scythians, but the next people to dwell in their land were thorough

[1] For a fuller statement of the various views of Wosinsky, Schmidt, and Hoernes, see Burrows, op. cit. pp. 189—196. He regards the art as due to an outlier of the Mediterranean race.

Nomads. At Khalepje one area had been spoilt by its materials having been used to pile a barrow for a man of the nomad race buried doubled up according to custom with only one pot by him, but with his bones coloured with the characteristic red[1].

Niederle[2] reviewing the whole subject with very wide knowledge of the Central European finds comes to no very certain conclusions. He is disinclined to hold to the view at first current in Russia that the Tripolje culture evolved entirely on the spot. He takes it to be a special development of the South European band pottery (*Bandkeramik*) already approaching the Tripolje forms at Butmir and other sites across to Transylvania. This development may have been called forth by intercourse with the Aegean area and Asia Minor going by way of Rumania and Bessarabia, but the gap in our knowledge of these countries makes it so far impossible to trace its progress. A distant resemblance to forms from the Mediterranean region is undoubted, but investigators of Aegean styles seem to see it less clearly than those who have dealt with N. Europe[3]. The statuettes also recall Southern forms. The *B* culture moreover shews analogies with the Northern style before mentioned, especially in the wide open flower-pot shaped vases[4]. A consideration of these relationships inclines Niederle to put the whole culture at about 2000 B.C., which would give time for the period of coloured skeletons to follow. But it seems premature to attempt to assign dates, only we must allow a long period for the red skeletons.

Coloured Skeletons.

Right across South Russia from Podolia and Kiev to the slopes of the Crimean mountains and the Caucasus, the most primitive type of grave commonly met with is distinguished by the fact that the skeletons are coloured bright red, mostly with ochre or some other earth containing iron. The colour is found in a thick layer most abundant upon the upper part of the body and head, and even occurs in lumps lying to one side. The body usually lies with the legs doubled up in a position "making our last bed like our first[5]." The interment is in the untouched earth, not in the mass of the barrow. The size of the barrows raised over them shews that these men were great chieftains in their day, though they took so little with them into the tomb[6]. Often later peoples have used their barrows, putting their own dead into a shallower grave in the heap[7]. Also we find various interments of this type in one great mound, which suggests that within the limits of this period men had had time to forget the first owner of the barrow. Often, but not always, above the body there are the remains of a kind of wooden shelter, more rarely a stone cist. Few objects are found in the tomb, at most one or two round-bottomed pots[8], more rarely chips of flint, still more rarely copper or bronze arrow-heads. This gives their

---

[1] Chvojka, *Stone Age*, p. 41.
[2] *Slav. Ant.* I. p. 460.
[3] Cf. however some of the vases from Cnossus illustrated by Mackenzie, *JHS*. 1903, 157 sqq. esp. p. 189, ff. 2 and 3.
[4] Cf. p. 138, f. 32 (right hand bottom corner) and the northern pots figured by Niederle, *Slav. Ant.* I. p. 444, g and r.

[5] Sir T. Browne, *Hydriotaphia*, chap. III.; shewn in side tomb, p. 177, f. 72, but no colour was found there.
[6] e.g. Bezschastnaja Mogila 15 m. high and 230 round. *KTR.* p. 278, *CR.* 1883. p. xliv.
[7] e.g. Geremes Barrow, *KTR.* p. 253.
[8] A good example, Mastjugino (Voronezh) *CR.* 1905, p. 97, f. 123.

date as belonging to the latest stone age, and the first beginnings of metal. But much more metal is found with the colouring of the skeleton in the south at the foot of the mountains.

There seems no doubt that the colouring matter was very thickly smeared on the body at burial, and that after the decay of the flesh it impregnated the bones when they had become porous with age. The colour is almost always red, sometimes whitey yellow. The circumstances of the finds preclude the idea that the flesh was taken off the bones and the latter stained on purpose, or that the colouring matter is the remains of paint on the coffin or dye in clothes or cere cloth. Probably these people painted themselves with ochre during life, and when they died they wished to enter the other world in full war paint, and even had a supply for future use put with them. Professor Kulakovskij[1] compares the painting red of the face of Jupiter Capitolinus and of the hero of a Roman triumph, suggesting that this is an instance of Roman conservatism going back to the most primitive times; the practice was common in Neolithic Italy[2].

In the Kuban district richer tombs with the characteristic colouring accompanied by pottery and axes and spear heads of copper were found by N. I. Veselovskij at Kostromskaja[3], Kelermes[4], Kazanskaja, Tiflisskaja and Armavir[5]. Many have intruded Scythic interments as that at Vozdvizhen-skaja (inf. p. 229, f. 131). Of unexampled richness was a tomb at Majkop[6], so much so that one might doubt whether it have any connection with that of the typical coloured skeletons. Here we have associated with the colouring, in this case by means of red lead, gold vessels and other objects testifying to remarkable artistic progress. The style in some cases, e.g. the plates with lions and bulls[7], recalls the Scythic, in others rather the products of the Caucasus. Still the wooden covering and the characteristic doubled up position offer some resemblance to the simpler coloured burials. Archaic objects are a vessel made of stone, but mounted in gold and with a gold stopper, and implements of stone and copper, as well as bronze; also the pottery is not unlike that found in other graves. Quite unlike anything else, and so far unexplained, is a set of silver tubes about 40 in. long, four with golden end-pieces: upon these were threaded, through a hole in their backs, solid golden bulls (p. 144, f. 35). There were also fourteen silver vessels, of which two had engraved ornament, recalling faintly the compositions of Western Asia. One is shewn here (p. 144, f. 36), the other[8] has a more conventional frieze and no landscape.

It is probable that we have here relics of a people which formerly stretched all over S. Russia, and buried its dead after daubing them with red colour. We have seen that many tribes were pressed towards the Caucasus when enemies entered their land, and this may have been the case with this people. Here they would be in contact with the Caucasian tribes, and

[1] J. A. Kulakovskij, "On the question of coloured skeletons," *Trans. of the XIth Russian Archaeological Congress* (Kiev), Vol. I.; Count A. A. Bobrinskoj, *Sm.* II. pp. 24—33, and III. p. iii. and for a very full list, A. A. Spitsyn, *TRAS.* XII. (1899), pp. 53—133.

[2] Pliny, *NH.* XXXIII. 111, 112; T. E. Peet, op. cit. pp. 120, 168, but there the bones were stripped of flesh before the colour was applied.

[3] *CR.* 1897, pp. 15—17, ff. 53—62.

[4] *CR.* 1904, p. 96, ff. 163, 164, one axe double looped, the other of Koban type.

[5] *CR.* 1900, p. 45, f. 105 ; 1901, pp. 66—86 ; 1902, pp. 66—75, 86—89, ff. 193, 198 ; 1903, pp. 61—71 ; 1905, p. 69; the ff. noted shew the three-legged clay incense-burners (?) peculiar to these tombs.

[6] *CR.* 1897, pp. 2—11.

[7] ib. p. 3, ff. 1—3.

[8] ib. p. 8, ff. 27—29.

FIG. 35.   Golden Bull.   Majkop.   *CR.* 1897, p. 5, f. 14 a.   ¼.

FIG. 36.   Silver Cup from Majkop.   *CR.* 1897, p. 7, f. 26.   ⅓.

through them with Western Asia, also sooner or later they would have to do with the "Scythic" culture, whether the Scyths were their immediate displacers, or whether other movements of population intervened. Hence an intelligible mixture of original customs, Scythic dress shewn by the many gold plates in the form of lions, and Caucasian metal work shewn in the gold and silver bulls and the engraved vessels.

We must beware of trying to give this race any historic name. Professor D. J. Samokvásov wishes to call it Cimmerian and date it up to the vith century B.C., but this is going further than is safe[1]. Mr V. I. Goszkewicz of the Kherson museum unhesitatingly applies the name Cimmerian to graves of this class, which he enumerates fully as far as they occur in the government of Kherson. He says[2] that in particular cases the position of the bones makes it appear that the colour was applied after the flesh had been removed, and suggests that there existed some arrangement like the "Towers of Silence." But there are too many suppositions concerned for this to be an argument in favour of the Iranian affinities of the Cimmerians. I take it these are the people Professor J. L. Myres calls "the Kurgan people," and declares to have been blonde longheads. He gives a map shewing such burials right across from the upper waters of the Obj to the Elbe, and as far south as Thessaly and Anatolia. As kurgan is just the Russian for barrow, the name Kurgan people would suit any one between these early folk and the nomads of the xiiith century[3].

In the neighbourhood of Kiev, according to Professor V. B. Antonovich[4], these people were dolichocephalic[5]. He mentions two other types of very early burials that occur at any rate in his district, small barrows with the bodies lying straight and often wrapped in elm bark, no objects therewith; and graves without barrows but with stone cists, bodies burnt accompanied by rude pottery. Both these types are comparatively rare and do not seem to offer any data for putting them before or after the widely spread people with coloured skeletons. The early date of the latter is shewn by the invariably bad preservation of the bones.

Megalithic Monuments.

The Dolmens[6] of Russia have not yet been duly investigated, but it seems probable that they are to be referred to a very remote date. They offer close analogies to those in Western Europe, but any direct connection is hard to suppose, because there is a gap in their distribution. That similar forms may arise independently is shewn by the occurrence of dolmens

[1] *History of Russian Law*, Warsaw, 1888, p. 134 sqq., cf. Bobrinskoj, *Sm.* II. p. Xiii.
[2] *Treasure Trove and Antiquities*, Bk I. Kherson, 1902, p. 137.
[3] *Geographical Journal*, XXVIII. (1906) p. 551, "The Alpine Races in Europe." The geological changes described in this ingenious paper come before anything with which this book can deal.

[4] Niederle, *Slav. Ant.* I. p. 449.
[5] Talko-Hrincewicz, J., *Przyczynek do poznania świata Kurhanowego Ukrainy* (A contribution to the knowledge of the barrow-world of the Ukraine), Cracow, 1899, says that the percentage of long heads in these graves is 71, in Scythic, 43, in early Slavonic, 96. v. *Arch. Chron. S. Russia*, 1900, p. 116.
[6] *KTR.* pp. 446–8; *CR.* 1896, p. 163; 1898, p. 33.

in India, the Sudan, Algeria and Syria.   It is with these last that O. Montelius' would connect those in the Crimea and the Caucasus.   At Tsarskaja
in the latter the further detail is found of a hole in one of the side slabs
agreeing with a disposition remarked in Western Europe and also in India.
To those who see Kelts in the Cimmerians the dolmens are a welcome
confirmation, but in both ends of Europe these monuments probably precede
any population to which we can put a name.   In a barrow at Verbovka
(Kiev government) was found a circle of twenty-nine stones about four feet
high, with engravings something like those of Gavr'inis, but no objects[2].

Diagram of Dolmen. Tsarskaja. CR. 1898. p.36. f. 53.

Fig. 37.   Total length 3·11 metres = 10 ft. 2½ in.
Dolmens with similar holes near Tuapse, *BCA.* XXXIII. pp. 83—86, ff. 14—16.

Earthworks.

Sheer want of stone might prevent the erection of dolmens on the
steppes, but no country could better suit earthworks.   Besides the innumerable funeral barrows which generally reveal their date on excavation, are
many works meant either for look-out stations or for defence.   These are
of all dates, from the earliest times to the works thrown up by Charles XII
of Sweden or the Russian expeditions against the Crimea under Münnich
or Suvórov.   But merely defensive considerations will not explain the
singular forms of some of these great works; their extent suggests that they
were the work rather of settled people than of nomads, moreover, they occur
in the wooded country beyond the steppe.
      The first account of them was that by A. Podberezskij[3].   They occur
about Kharkov, Poltava[4], and in the south of the government of Chernigov,
but are specially common in that of Kiev[5] and so westwards into Podolia.
Some seem to have been occupied in Scythian times from the pottery picked

[1] "Orienten och Europa" in *Antiqvarisk Tidskrift för Sverige*, XIII. I.
[2] *BCA.* XX. p. 12.
[3] *Trans. Od. Soc.* Vol. VII. 1868, p. 256, mostly reproduced by Count Bobrinskoj, *Sm.* II. p. iv.
[4] In *BCA.* XXII. pp. 55—88, N. E. Makarenko gives plans and descriptions of eight such forts
mostly near Romny.   In *BCA.* v. pp. 1—95, A. Spitsyn gives short particulars of them in many governments.
[5] l. Funduklej's *Survey of Barrows, Banks and Camps in the Government of Kiev*, Kiev, 1848, is not quite superseded.

up upon them, but of those that seem built for defence the lie of the land makes it probable that they were designed by people who had very feeble missile weapons. Matrónenskij Gorodishche, the greatest of them, goes down into a ravine in such a way that part of the bank would be entirely commanded by good bowmen[1].

At Bêlsk (Poltava) is a camp of another type, the largest in Russia; it has been specially well excavated by Mr V. A. Gorodtsov[2]. It is six-sided, like a truncated octagon, one long side running N. and S. by the river Vorskla, which defended it from the E. whence attack was most to be feared. This side, which is seven miles long, is broken by a fort, a stronger fort is at the salient angle away from the river, the greatest breadth (four miles) being measured between them; there is a smaller fort to the N.E. The whole circumference is some 20 miles. The site had been inhabited in the Tripolje period and yielded the typical pottery and statuettes. With these came early Scythic things, pots with white incrustation (v. p. 82), bone and bronze psalia and a whole hoard of arrowheads, besides Ionian vases and beads of "Egyptian paste": from this we can distinguish a later Scythic period with black figured and later Greek vases and glass beads; to this the earthworks belong, for the older remains are used up as material in the banks; the whole comes under the special form of Scythic culture described on pp. 175 sqq. About were barrows of all sizes, most of them plundered. Some had the queerest resemblance to spiders or crabs, consisting of a small circle with one or more openings, on either side of which stretch out claw-shaped banks, sometimes two or three, one within the other. Such are found elsewhere and called *Majdans*, and were long unexplained. One of the first to be carefully excavated, that at Tsvêtno (Kiev government), was quite of a spider shape (see plan, p. 148, f. 38). Within the enclosure was found a typical grave of a Scythian woman, and near by other Scythic remains of the IV.—II. centuries B.C., but in connection was a barrow with a red skeleton. The combination offered no clue to date or purpose.

But Mr Gorodtsov[3], after examining a considerable number of such earthworks, came to the conclusion that they were merely barrows which had been plundered for their contents, the peculiar form assumed by the earth that had to be moved being due to the conditions of working with *volokushi*, wheeless carts or sledges used by the Russians in the XVIIth century.

A. A. Spitsyn has cleared up the whole mystery. In the XVIth and XVIIth centuries saltpetre was regularly extracted from the grave mounds: the earth was boiled on the spot and the liquor again boiled. The banks are merely spoil-heaps trending away from the barrow, so as not to get in the way of the operators. Spitsyn shews how a certain amount of system producing fair symmetry was rendered necessary, and describes exactly how the process was carried on. He supports his case by many extracts from contemporary authors and documents referring to it as quite a common

[1] Plan in *Sm.* II. p. 52.
[2] He is to publish an account of it in the *Transactions of the XIVth* (1908) *Russian Archaeological Congress* (Chernigov), but he has been good enough to give me private information, for which my best thanks are due.

[3] *Drevnosti*, = *Trans. Mosc. Arch. Soc.* XX. 2, pp. 29—39. L. V. Padalka, *Archaeological Chronicle of S. Russia*, 1904, pp. 128 sqq., dissents strongly, but by his article I have been made acquainted with Gorodtsov's view.

thing, and coins of the time are found in the banks, e.g. near Bêlsk. The centre of the mound was naturally the richest, and the flanks were left

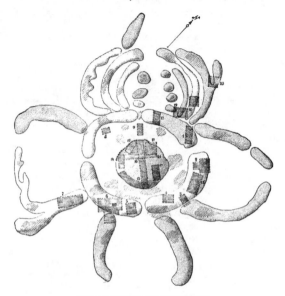

Bobrinskoj's Trenches.   Plunderers' Pits.   Site of Grave.
Scale 128 ft. to the inch.
FIG. 38. *CR*. 1896, p. 213, f. 606. Majdan at Tsvêtno.

as not worth boiling. Hence the ring form. Most likely the application of the process to the Siberian barrows first shewed their richness in gold, of which the Siberian collection at the Hermitage is almost the sole relic[1].

[1] A. A. Spitsyn, *TRAS*. Russo-Slavonic Section, VIII. 2, pp. 1—28. He gives plans of about fifty majdans and a very good bibliography of the question, which can now be taken as settled.

CHAPTER VIII.

SCYTHIC TOMBS.

IF Herodotus is the main source of our information as to the population of the north shore of the Euxine during the flourishing time of its Greek Colonies we are hardly less indebted to the finds made in the barrows of the country, finds which on the whole bear out what Herodotus has said and supplement it with many details throwing much light upon the elements which went to make up the mixed culture of the inhabitants. From about the viith century B.C. to a little after our era is the period to which may be referred a series of tombs that seem to belong to peoples all closely connected with each other in funeral customs and general mode of life. To give any ethnic name to this class of grave is begging the question of their origin, yet it is impossible to habitually refer to them as "graves of nomadic tribes in contact with central Asian and Greek civilisations." They are generally called "Scythian" or "Scytho-Sarmatian," or those shewing Greek influence are called "Scythian," those with Roman manufactures or coins "Sarmatian." This latter distinction is certainly unsatisfactory, for the name of Sarmatian had spread over the European steppes certainly before Roman influence had been brought to bear on these countries. In fact as will be seen the greater part of the tombs usually called "Scythian" appears to belong to a time when the Scyths of Herodotus had disappeared. On the other hand the general agreement between the archaeological evidence and the information furnished by Herodotus argues the substantial identity of the cultures described in these different sources. This all points to there being but little real difference between Scyth and Sarmate. The latter were apparently nearer the Iranians of Iran both in language and dress, but in both there seems to have been an Altaic element.

I propose then to call the class of tombs, which I shall now describe, "Scythic," not wishing to assert thereby that they belonged exclusively to Scyths, but suggesting that they are the most typical tombs of the inhabitants of Scythia, when that was the general name for the Euxine steppes; still there can be little doubt that the true royal Scyths of Herodotus were among the tribes that buried in this fashion, although no tomb has been found which could be referred to the particular generation observed by him.

Unfortunately in spite of the enlightened efforts made by the Russian government to protect these remains, and in turn to explore them with the best archaeological skill, we cannot point to any first-class normal Scythic tomb which fate has reserved for quite satisfactory exploration. The great majority was plundered long ago, as it seems in most cases, shortly after the very funeral, in other cases the discovery has been made by peasants searching for treasure, or amateurs who have neglected to keep a minute account of all details as to the position in which everything was found; finally it has happened that an excavation already almost brought to a successful conclusion has been ruined by the insufficiency of the guard set over it. Hence our picture of a Scythic interment must be pieced together from the best preserved

parts of many tombs.   It is impossible to take one tomb, even Kul Oba or Karagodeuashkh, describe it fully, and make it a norm, treating all others as varieties.   Besides, enough remains to shew that each great tomb had its own peculiar features which have their interest in filling in the general outlines of Scythic life.

In the following enumeration of the most important tombs the older finds, particulars of which are more accessible, will be treated as briefly as possible; further particulars can be found in books so easily obtainable as S. Reinach's reprints of the *Antiquités du Bosphore Cimmérien* (*ABC.*) and of Kondakov and Tolstoj's *Antiquités de la Russie Méridionale* (*KTR.*). Descriptions derived from the *Antiquités de la Scythie d'Herodote* (*ASH.*), from the *Compte Rendu de la Commission Archéologique* (*CR.*), especially since it has been published in Russian, from the *Bulletin de la Commission Archéologique* (*BCA.*) and from other Russian publications will be given more fully.

The distribution of these Scythic barrows reaches from Podolia and the Kiev government southwards to the Euxine and eastwards to the valley of the Kuban on the northern slopes of the Caucasus.   The finest of them are about the bend of the Dnêpr, near Alexandropol, near where we should put the land of Gerrhus; a special character marks those in the governments of Kiev and Poltava; a few occur about the Greek towns of the Bosporus on each side of the strait, and the Kuban series is hardly second to the Dnêpr group.   Isolated is the remarkable find of Vettersfelde in Lower Lusatia. Also a burial of somewhat similar type has been found in Thrace, Dukhova Mogila near Philippopolis[1].   Further, as has been said, objects of a type resembling the barbarian element in Scythic tombs can be traced right across to Krasnojarsk beyond the Altai.   To the west also, in Hungary, objects of Scythic type have been found[2].

The question of dating and classifying these tombs is very difficult.   Our only criteria are the objects of Greek art found in them.   Yet these only give us the earliest date possible.   And even as to this there is some doubt, for various judges make more or less allowance, for barbarous influence, for the difference between the best art and that of articles made for export, and for the time necessary for new fashions in art to penetrate to such remote regions.

Moreover, unfortunately none of the tombs with the most archaic Greek objects have been opened by skilled archaeologists.   For instance, the tomb at Martonosha (p. 173) may well have belonged to a contemporary of Herodotus. The amphora handle seems to be vith century work, and the other objects are not definitely late in date; but we shall never know, for our account of the excavation is derived from peasants nearly twenty years after the event, and we know yet less of the circumstances under which were discovered the archaic "Cybele"[3] or the mirror handle with almost the earliest nude female of archaic (rather than primitive) Greek art[4].

In the account which follows the barrows are arranged rather geographically than chronologically, though in the first group their dates would seem to

---

[1] *BCH.* xxv. (1901), p. 168, G. Seure.
[2] Dr P. Reinecke, "Die skythischen Alterthümer im mittleren Europa," *Zt. für Ethnologie,* XXVIII. 1896, pp. 1—42, and J. Hampel, "Skythische Denkmäler aus Ungarn," *Ethnologische*

Mittheilungen aus Ungarn, IV. 1895, pp. 1—26.
[3] *CR.* 1896, p. 82, f. 337.
[4] *CR.* 1897, p. 78, f. 186.   All these three bronzes are illustrated in Chap. XI. § 10, ff. 278—281.

be in the order I have given. Each barrow described has its own features of interest, and from them all some idea of the Scythic type can be formed. Fewer descriptions would have left out interesting points, more would have wearied the reader without attaining completeness ; many important excavations have for this cause been necessarily omitted, for them the reader must be referred to the *CR.*, *BCA.*, and other special publications.

Poor Class. Twins.

Professor A. Lappo-Danilevskij[1], in his review of the various types of Scythic graves, divides them into four classes. His first class seems not clearly to be distinguished from the class of coloured skeletons of which we have already treated, except that the colouring is not predominant. The bad preservation of the bones, the poverty of the objects found with them, the large number of burials in one mound, rank tombs like the Pointed Tomb on the Tomakovka, the Round Kurgan (= barrow) at Geremes (variously written Guérémesov, Hérémesse, Germesov), the Long Tomb near Alexandropol, all on the right bank of the Dnêpr near the great bend, with the Bezschástnaja (unlucky) Tomb on the opposite bank, which distinctly contained coloured bones[2]. It is remarkable that all these are near the land Gerrhus, it seems as if the Scyths had adopted the sacred burial district of earlier inhabitants. Lappo-Danilevskij takes these great barrows with as many as fourteen separate interments to have been burying places of comparatively obscure families which heaped up great mounds when enough dead had been accumulated : but more probably the distinction between these and the following graves is one not merely of social position, but of time and race. We may put them down as of the last pre-Scythic phase, for the skeletons are not coloured, and are not all doubled up, and there are a few objects of copper or bronze ; but there are no chambers hollowed out, no horse graves, and none of those mines by which the rich booty of the true Scythic type of graves was carried off by men who well knew what they were doing. In this class there was nothing to tempt them.

An isolated example recalling this type is the barrow called Perepjatikha, in the district of Vasilkóv (Kiev government), opened in 1845. It is far to the west of the central Scythic group, but cannot be classed with the generality of Scythic barrows in Kiev government. It contained fourteen skeletons under a wooden roof upon which stones had been piled ; by four of them were lumps of paint, necklets, metal disks, one bronze arrow, two iron axes, an earthen vessel with a stone stand, and 24 gold plaques of griffins once sewn on to a whitey-yellow stuff. This is not a normal Scythic tomb, and the paint suggests an early date ; perhaps the Scythic objects belong to an intruded interment[3].

A fairly simple example of a Scythic grave (Lappo-Danilevskij's second class)[4] is the Stone Tomb (*Kámennaja Mogíla*) near Krasnokutsk, between

[1] Scythian Antiquities, *TRAS.* Russo-Slav. Section, Vol. IV. (1887), pp. 352—543 ; p. 467 sqq.
[2] v. *ASH.* passim.
[3] A. Kohn and C. Mehlis, *Materialien zur Vorgeschichte des Menschen im Östlichen Europa*, Vol. I. pp. 367—375, Pl. III.—XI. Illustration also in *KTR.* p. 289, f. 254, shewing a very steep barrow surrounded at some distance by a bank and a group of lesser mounds. Cf. too Lappo-Danilevskij, op. cit. p. 487 sqq., who classes it rather with the other west-Scythic barrows.
[4] op. cit. p. 470; *KTR.* p. 268 ; *ASH.* plan E.

Nicopol and Ekaterinoslav. The tomb derives its name from the fact that all the skirts of the heap and the central portion above the actual grave consist of stone. The main grave contained a human skeleton and those of two horses, three spears, scales from armour, fragments of amphorae, and of an alabastron and a jug, but all was in confusion. In a separate grave was the skeleton of another horse with a bridle adorned with bronze plates and with an iron bit. This would appear to be the grave of an ordinary cavalier whose position did not allow him the elaborate funerals of greater men. Yet the barrow is a considerable size, 19 feet high and 200 in diameter.

The third class consists of so-called twins (*Bliznitsy*)[1]. Best known are the Geremes, Tomakovka and Slonovskij twins, all in the same district. In these we have two mounds close to each other, one flat-topped with steep sides fortified with stone, containing one human grave, horse graves and various gear including Greek wares, the other round-topped with many poor graves. Moreover, only in the chief mound are there traces of thieves' mines; about the chief of the Geremes and Slonovskij twins is a ditch and bank: in these chief twins also there seem to have been one grave chamber and a side chamber for the horse grave. But as all have been plundered in ancient times we cannot be sure of their disposition or

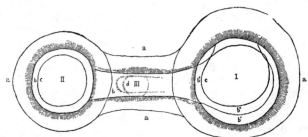

FIG. 39. · *CR*. 1891, p. 161, f. 195. Double barrow at Pavlovka. I. Barrow with core *c* of rammed earth. Circumference 160 paces. Diameter about 36 m. Height 3·5 m. II. Barrow with core *c* of stones. Circumference 100 paces. Diameter 20 m. Height 2 m. III. Joining bank with small tumulus *d*, 30 paces long, 15 m. broad, 1·4 m. high. *aaa*. Extreme circumference. *b, b'* pits dug. The original interments were of red skeletons, others of later nomads, but none, it seems, Scythic.

contents. They offer close analogies to the next class, but are on a smaller scale; it is suggested that in them small tribal chieftains were buried, and that the ordinary folk of the tribe rest in the lesser twin alongside.

Big Barrows.

The fourth and chief class is that of the so-called Big Barrows (*Tólstya Mogíly*)[2]. Chief of these are that near Alexandropol, often called the Meadow Barrow (*Lugovája Mogíla*), and the Chertomlýk or Nicópol Barrow. Others are that at Krasnokutsk, the Tsymbalka, the Orphan's Grave (*Sirotína Mogíla*), Chmyreva barrow, Ogüz near Serogozy in the

[1] Lappo-Danilevskij, p. 471; *ASH*. plans E, D.
[2] Strictly speaking *Kurgán* (Turkish = OE. burh) is used in Great Russian for a barrow and

Mogíla for a grave, but in the language of Lit. Russia where all the Sc. tombs are, *Mohíla* = barrow.

Melitopol district (Tauric govt), and Martonosha in that of Elisavetgrad (Kherson govt). In height they vary from 30 to 70 feet, and they may be from 400 to 1200 feet round at the base. On the top there is always a flat space some 50 feet or more across. Hence the sides are rather steep, especially on the north. The heap during its progress was rammed down hard and further fortified by a basement of stones; about the mound would be a ditch and bank with gaps for entrance. The grave chamber is from 9 ft. 6 in. to 15 ft. long by 7 or 7 ft. 6 in. broad and sunk into the earth itself to the level of a layer of clay that runs under the black soil at a depth of from 9 ft. 6 in. to 42 ft. (at Chertomlyk barrow). The sides of the grave chamber were sometimes smoothed and plastered with clay, in other cases traces may be seen of the narrow wooden spade with which they were dug out; such a spade was found near Smêla[1]. Beside the main chamber there are side chambers ("catacombs"), varying in number. In the Krasnokutsk barrow one only beside a horse grave, in Tsymbalka two, five each at Alexandropol and Chertomlyk. These chambers are generally on the north side of the main chamber. Beside these chambers for the burial of the king's servants and the storing of his gear were horse graves, always to the w. of the central grave, and in the Chertomlyk barrow two graves near them for the grooms. These chambers are roofed with unsquared tree trunks.

The king was brought to his tomb on a funeral car, of which the remains have been found, well bearing out the description of Herodotus. The car was left for the dead man to use, being broken up and buried in the heap or led down into the grave chamber. So too the horses, whose lives were even more prodigally wasted at these funerals than those of human beings. In the Ulskij barrow on the Kuban were found over four hundred horses (v. p. 227). At Krasnokutsk and Alexandropol the remains of a second car were found. On this probably the dead man's favourite wife rode to her fate.

None of the Big Barrows have been left unplundered, so we cannot know the exact disposition of the most precious objects about the principal bodies, but in chamber No. v of Chertomlyk king's and queen's things seem put apart from each other in niches. Amphorae and other vessels, mostly of Greek workmanship, were put on the floor and clothes hung on pegs in the wall. The body was usually laid on some kind of mattress which at Chertomlyk was covered with a pall adorned with gold plates. In the Alexandropol barrow there were only two servants buried with their master, in Chertomlyk five with their feet towards him ready to stand up and face him at his call. In the Krasnokutsk and Alexandropol tombs were also found heaps of human and horses' bones. When the way into the tomb had been filled up, upon the flat space where the barrow was soon to be raised was held the funeral feast, well marked at Chertomlyk and elsewhere by fragments of amphorae, horses' bones, and things lost by the revellers. After that the barrow was heaped up; but, as it seems, before all knowledge of plan and contents was lost, daring robbers sank mines into it from the north side, the side on which the heap was steepest, towards which there were always extra chambers, and braved not only the vengeance of the dead man and that of his successors (the Mongols had guards to watch their burial places), but

[1] *Sm.* III. p. 53, f. 12.

the chance of a fall of those tunnels, that the secrecy of their operations made it impossible to support properly.   Since then, Genoese on the coast and Cossacks on the plains, and in modern times the neighbouring peasants, have made a regular practice of seeking the dead men's gold.   It is no wonder that the archaeologist often finds himself forestalled.   His only comfort is that the bronzes are almost as interesting as the gold work, and that the thieves left everything but the precious metal.   If only they had not thrown everything about in seeking for that[1], we should be better pleased.

Alexandropol Barrow.

Of the barrows about the Dnêpr, those most remarkable for the variety of their contents are that near Alexandropol and that at Chertomlyk, twelve miles N.W. of Nicopol.

The full report of the excavation of the former is given in *ASH*. with plan and sections and many plates, and a well illustrated summary in *KTR*.

FIG. 40. Alexandropol. Bronze standard? *KTR*. p. 241, f. 217 =*ASH*. I. 8.

FIG. 41. Alexandropol. Bronze standard? *KTR*. p. 241, f. 218=*ASH*. II. I.

(pp. 238—251), but the exploration was so desultory and the sepulchre itself and all the objects belonging to it had been so thoroughly ransacked by thieves who, after an unsuccessful attempt, finally reached the central chamber, that it is hard to get a clear idea of the whole, and the main interest belongs

---

[1] For a description of Italian (in this case Venetian) enterprise in robbing a barrow near the mouth of the Don in 1436, see "Viaggio di Josafa Barbaro alla Tana," in Ramusio, *Navigationi et Viaggi*, Vol. II. Venice, 1559, ff. 91 sqq.

to the accessories, the remains of two chariots, the horse tombs, and the bronze "standards" (ff. 40, 41), while little is left of the riches of the actual occupant but gold plates, many very similar to those of Kul Oba (f. 42, others on p. 158, f. 45, also a horse frontlet, an armour scale and a bone arrowhead). Clearly the plunderers had not time to seek trifles. For dating

Fig. 42. Gold plate from Alexandropol. *KTR.* p. 249, f. 228 = *ASH.* XII. 6.

Scythic things, certain round and oblong silver plates that formed part of the harness are very important, as their style seems late Hellenistic[1]. Other things in the tomb look at first sight almost archaic, but they are only degradations of the Ionian strain.

Chertomlyk.

At Chertomlyk the thieves were less fortunate, one of them was found crushed by a fall of earth at the mouth of his mine, but here again the central interment had been much disturbed. The objects worth carrying away seem to have been mostly heaped up in various corners of v (see plan), and by mere chance the king's things were still apart from the queen's.

---

[1] Unfortunately the figures of them in *ASH.* pl. XIV do not reproduce well; cf. *KTR.* p. 251, f. 230; *TRAS.* VII. pl. XIII, XV, XVI. Stephani, *CR.* 1865, p. 167 makes these and phalerae from the Great Bliznitsa (l.c. v, VI, cf. inf. ch. XII.) IVth century; F. H. Marshall, *JHS.* XXIX. (1909) p. 157 publishing some from Elis in the British Museum concurs, but their sets are better in style. For other Sc. phalerae v. Spitsyn *BCA.* XXIX. pp. 18—53.

In looking at the annexed plan it must be remembered that only the central part of the tumulus is given; for a complete plan the reader is referred to *ASH*. plate F.   Round the whole must be supplied the stone plinth, and it must be borne in mind that the plan is engraved so that the north comes to the right instead of being at the top.

West

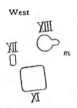

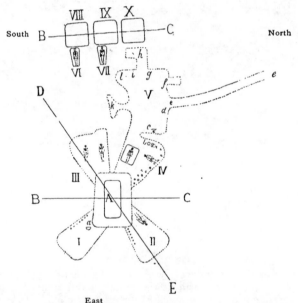

Fɪɢ. 43.   Plan of centre of Chertomlyk barrow.   *KTR*. p. 257, f. 235=*ASH*. Plan F.

The barrow was 60 feet high and 1100 feet round, surrounded by a stone plinth, and a kind of stone alley led up to it across the steppe.

A is the central shaft descending 35 ft. 6 in. below the original surface of the ground, 15 ft. × 7 ft. at the top and widening downwards.   At the bottom opened out four lateral chambers, ɪ, ɪɪ, ɪɪɪ, ɪᴠ, one from each corner.

The N.W. chamber IV communicated with a large irregular chamber V into which debouched a narrow passage *ee*, the mine of ancient plunderers. To the west of all this were three square pits in a line from S. to N., VIII, IX, X, and to the E. of VIII and IX two graves, VI and VII. Later graves, XI, XII, XIII, were sunk in the heap for persons who had nothing to do with its original possessors.

In A everything had been thrown into disorder by the plunderers. There were only found traces of a coffin or bier painted red and bright blue. In I to the S.E. were a small cauldron, at *a* the remains of a skeleton converted into lime, by it remains of a quiver with arrows and five iron knives with bone handles, not unlike p. 190, f. 82 *below*; against the wall in a corner 150 more arrows with remains of their shafts, 28 inches long, and what once was a carpet; about the floor many gold plates and strips which had adorned clothes hung from iron hooks in wall and ceiling.

In No. II to the N.E. were six amphorae along the wall, in the middle a bronze mirror with an iron handle, by the door a skeleton with a bronze torque and a gold earring and finger ring, on his left an ivory handled knife and a leather quiver with 67 bronze arrow-heads, near his head ivory and gold remains of a whip handle, also a silver spoon and the fragments of an ivory box, besides innumerable plates and strips of thin gold for sewing on to clothes. The enumeration of the plates found in one side chamber of a single tomb will shew the variety of these plates and the prodigal use made of them. Figures of many of them are in *KTR.*, still more in *ASH.* In II were found 25 plates with flowers, 64 with a fantastic animal, 7 with a lion tearing a stag, one with a calf lying down, 10 with a barbarian combating a griffin, 31 with a griffin alone, 12 with a rosette, 130 with a bearded man's head, 24 with a gorgon's head and 5 pendants, 27 with a plain gorgon's head, 6 with the heads of Athena and a lion back to back (p. 158, f. 45, XXX. 6), 33 of Heracles strangling a lion (ib. xxx. 10), one of a lion combating a sphinx, 24 triangles made up of grains (cf. p. 197, f. 90, *ABC.* XXII. 7). Besides these a great number of hollow pendants, tubes, beads, buttons, and other golden ornaments to be sewn on to clothes. These plates are very characteristic of Scythian dress, and occur in great numbers in all barrows; less wide-spread was the use of strips of gold repoussé or ajouré with plant patterns or combats of animals and monsters, sometimes as much as 14 inches long. All these thin gold objects have little holes near the edges for sewing on to textiles.

FIG. 44. Gold band. Chertomlyk. *KTR.* p. 310, f. 271 = *CR.* 1864, v. 5. ¼.

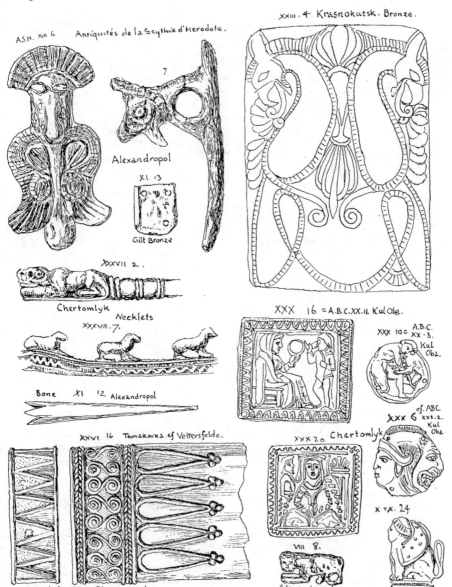

XXIII. 4. Krasnokutsk. Bronze.

A.S.H. XIII 6   Antiquités de la Scythie d'Herodote.

7

Alexandropol

XI 13

Gilt Bronze

XXXVII 2.

Chertomlyk
                Necklets
XXXVII. 7.

Bone   XI 12 Alexandropol

XXX 16 = A.B.C. XX. 11. Kul Oba.

XXX 10c A.B.C.
         XX. 3.
         Kul
         Oba.

cf. ABC.
XXX 6 XXI. 2.
       Kul
       Oba

XXVI 16 Tomakovka. cf. Veltersfelde.

XXX 20 Chertomlyk

x rx. 24

VIII 8.

Alexandropol

Dotted Surface – Blue enamel.

Objects from Scythic tombs on the Middle Dnêpr. (Gerrhus)

FIG. 45.   Gold: Horse's Frontlet (cf. Greek version of same type, p. 169, f. 61): Necklets (p. 63, 161):
Plates (pp. 61, 155, 157, 161, 266): Dagger (p. 71, cf. 236).   Bronze: Plate (p. 167, 282): Armour
Scale (p. 74).   Bone Arrow-head (p. 68).

FIG. 46. (v. pp. 161, 288), Chertomlyk Vase, silver, parcel gilt. Front view.
KTR. p. 297, f. 257 = *CR.* 1864, pl. 1. 70 cm. (26⅜ in.) high.

FIG. 47. Chertomlyk Vase. Side view. *KTR.* p. 296, f. 256=*CR.* 1864, pl. II.

In III, the S.W. chamber, lay a skeleton wearing a golden torque with twelve lions upon it, shewing signs of long wear (*ASH.* XXXVII. 7 on p. 158). About the head could be traced the form of a hood outlined by 25 gold plates with griffins and fastened at a couple of smaller ones, a flower and a gorgoncion. He wore the usual bracelets and rings, and a belt with brass plates, and greaves (which are not so general); by his head were two vessels, a bronze cup, and a silver ewer with a string to hang it up by, and lower down the quiver with arrows, and a whip. By him lay another skeleton with much the same equipment. In the N.W. chamber (IV) were found remains of a bier painted dark and light blue, green and yellow. Upon it lay a woman's skeleton in rich attire. On each side of her head were heavy earrings, and upon it were 29 plates in the shape of flowers, twenty rosettes and seven buttons. The head and upper part of the body were covered by a purple veil with 57 square gold plates representing a seated woman with a mirror, and a Scyth standing before her (v. p. 158 = *ASH.* XXX. 16). The line of these plates made a kind

FIG. 48. Frieze of Chertomlyk vase. *CR.* 1864, pl. III. ¼.

of triangle reaching a foot above her head and descending to her breast, out-lining a hood or pointed headdress with lappets falling down on each side of the face; such lappets seem shewn on a plaque of inferior execution figured on the same page (*ASH.* XXX. 20). Something of the same sort was worn by the queen at Kul Oba, and by that at Karagodeuashkh where the triangular gold plate which adorned it has a scene representing a queen wearing just such a one (p. 218, f. 120). The Chertomlyk lady also wore bracelets and a ring on each finger; by her hand was a bronze mirror with an ivory handle, with traces of some blue material. By the woman's skeleton was a man's with iron and bronze bracelets and an ivory-handled knife (the knives are always on the left hand side), a little further were the usual arrow-heads. Along the wall were ranged thirteen amphorae. In the west part of this chamber (*b*) was made the most precious find of the tomb, the famous Chertomlyk or Nicopol vase (ff. 46—49, cf. p. 288 sqq.). By it was a great silver dish with an elaborate pattern engraved within, and two handles formed by a kind of palmette of acanthus leaves with the figure of a woman wearing a

FIGURES FROM THE CHERTOMLYK VASE. C.R. 1864. Pl. III.

FIG. 49, cf. p. 57.

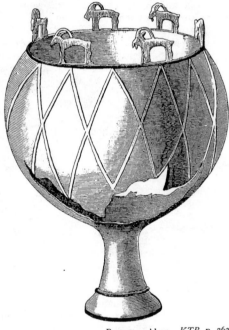

FIG. 50. Chertomlyk. Bronze cauldron. *KTR.* p. 262, f. 238=*ASH.* Text, p. 112.

calathos in the middle[1].   This chamber (IV) opened into another (V) to
the west of it; V had suffered so much from the falling-in of the roof and

FIG. 51. Chertomlyk. Golden hilt of king's sword.
    KTR. p. 304, f. 264=*CR.* 1864, v. 2, better
    Pridik, *Melgunov*, pl. v. 1, cf. p. 270. ⅓.

FIG. 52. *Mat.* XIII. p. 54, f. 30=*ASH.*
    XL. 12. Lesser sword from Cher-
    tomlyk found at *k* on plan. ⅓.

still more from the operations of the tomb-thieves, that it is impossible to
say what may have been its original plan.   It can hardly be entirely due
to the thieves.   The thieves' mine (*ee*) opened into it and all round were

[1] *KTR.* pp. 263-4, ff. 239-40=*ASH.* XXIX. 5, 7.

21—2

Chertomlyk.
Gold Plates for
Bowcase and
Dagger. From
Electrotypes
at South
Kensington
Museum.

FIG. 53, cf. p. 284. A little over ⅓.

niches (*f, h, l, k*) apparently due to them.   If on their entrance they found
the way into IV blocked up, they probably tried the walls in various directions
and finally broke into IV and obtained access to the central tomb.

They seem to have begun to pile their booty in heaps in the corners
of V ready to take it away, when the roof, disturbed by their operations,
fell in and caught one of them, whose skeleton was found at *e* by the entrance
of his mine; at *c* was a six-wicked lamp he may have been using : the
plunderers at Alexandropol had only potsherds with rags in them.   At *d*
was a cauldron of the Scythic type 3 ft. high with goats as handles on the
edge; the outside blackened with fire; within the head, ribs and leg-bones
of a horse (f. 50).   Near it was another, smaller, containing a foal's bones.
At *f* was a niche in the wall with a heap of gold ornaments, at *h* another
with a woman's things, as far as may be judged, at *g* and *i* were remains
of boards, at *l* another heap of gold, at *k* the objects taken from the tomb
of the king himself.   Three swords had been stuck into the wall, where
their blades remained while the handles had rusted off and fallen down (f. 52).
Below were the great gold plate that adorned the king's gorytus, a strip of
gold that went along the side of it, and the plate of gold which covered his
sword sheath (f. 53); two more swords with gold hafts (f. 51), a hone with
a gold mounting, and many other gold plates and a heap of arrow-heads.
About the floor were fragments of Greek pottery.

Of the horse graves, in VIII were three horses saddled and bridled, one
with gold ornaments, the others with silver; in IX were four horses, two
saddled and bridled with gold, two only bridled and with silver.   In X
were three horses saddled and bridled with gold, one without a saddle and
bridled in silver.   The grooms in VI and VII had each his torque, one of
silver gilt and one of gold, and each his quiver with arrows.

In the heap itself, early in the excavations, was found an immense
number of objects pertaining to harness.   At the top of the barrow was
a mass of such ornaments rusted together, silver had almost perished, bronze
was in bad condition, of gold there was little but 29 pair of horse's cheek
ornaments.   In bronze there were animals upon sockets (the so-called
standards), horse frontlets, buckles, buttons, bells, tubes, strips, crescent-
shaped pendants, and about 250 iron bits, also a curious open-work saucepan, as it would appear for fishing meat out of one of the big cauldrons[1].
This description of the finds in the Chertomlyk barrow, though far from
detailed, gives some idea of the barbarous prodigality with which the steppe
folk buried their kings.

· *Krasnokutsk and Tsymbalka.*

In the same neighbourhood as Chertomlyk is the Krasnokutsk barrow[2].
In its mound Zabêlin found the fragments of a funeral car broken up and piled
in two heaps, and the usual remains of harness and trappings: in a special
tomb were four horses with frontlets (ff. 56, 57 and p. 158, f. 45; *ASH.* XXIII.

[1] *KTR.* p. 259, f. 236.
[2] Cf. *ASH.* plan C; *KTR.* p. 254 (not the same as the " Stone Tomb" there).

FIGS. 54, 55. Horse's frontlets, gold. Tsymbalka. *KTR.* p. 269, f. 241, p. 272, f. 243.

4). These ornaments are interesting because of their remarkable resemblance to the northern beast-style usually associated with the early middle ages. Other two tombs had been completely stripped by plunderers who only left enough to let us judge that the contents were of the usual Scythic type.

FIG. 56, cf. p. 267. Krasnokutsk. Horse's cheek ornament. Silver. *KTR.* p. 256, f. 234=*ASH.* XXIII. 5.

On the S. side of the river, in the district of Melitopol, government of Taurida, is the barrow Tsymbalka[1] near Bêlozérka. As usual the main tomb had been violated by a mine from the north, but in the side tomb were six horses, four with bronze trappings and silver frontlets, two with very interesting gold frontlets, one of fine late IVth century Greek work with a *Schlangenweib*, the other barbaric with griffins (ff. 54, 55, cf. p. 269).

[1] *CR.* 1867, p. xxi ; 1868, p. xix ; *KTR.* p. 268.

FIG. 57. Krasnokutsk. Silver bridle ornament. *KTR*. p. 255, f. 233=*ASH*. XXIII. 7.

Chmyreva Mogila.

Chmyreva Mogila, two miles from Tsymbalka, was investigated in 1898 by Dr Th. G. Braun[1]. Here again the main tomb had been rifled, this time by

FIG. 58. *CR*. 1898, p. 28, f. 28. Chmyreva Mogila. Gold plate from harness, cf. p. 269.

FIG. 59. *CR*. 1898, p. 29, f. 32. Chmyreva Mogila. Gold plate from harness. ¼.

means of a shaft sunk from the top of the mound, and a later burial for which the barrow had been used was also cleared, but the horse interment was the best met with. An inclined plane led to an oblong pit 7·10 m. × 3 m. × 2·15 m. Ten horses had been led into the pit which was then shut up with boards and

[1] *CR*. 1898, p. 26; *BCA*. XIX. p. 96.

heaped over. They had evidently struggled towards the outlet, and their skeletons lay one upon another. Their trappings were adorned with the usual metallic plates, but some were of the finest Greek workmanship of about

FIG. 60. *CR.* 1898, p. 28, f. 30. Chmyreva Mogila. Gold cheek ornament for a horse. ¼.

FIG. 61. *CR.* 1898, p. 27, f. 27. Gold frontlet, side and front. Chmyreva Mogila. ¼.

FIG. 62. *CR.* 1898, p. 27, f. 24. Gold plate. Chmyreva Mogila. ¼.

300 B.C.[1] (ff. 58—60): there were also specimens of native attempts to imitate them. Very strange is a frontlet of a type which has occurred in several of the Gerrhus tombs[2], but this is the only one of skilful execution (f. 61). In the main tomb was picked up an interesting plate with two Scythians wrestling (f. 62).

Ogüz, Dêev and Janchekrak.

In the same district further to the south near Lower Serogozy, Ogüz, a very large barrow, has been investigated by Professor Veselovskij[3]. A plan and section of the stone corbelled vault are given overleaf. The interior is 21 ft. square, surrounded and upheld by a solid mass of stone work 50 feet square. The stones of the corbelled vault itself were bound by iron clamps of a ⌐ shape. Unfortunately the tomb had been rifled three times. The first time the plunderers knew what they were doing, for they approached along the gallery from the s. instead of as usual from the N. The last plunderers came down from above and took off the top stone of the vault. Hence it all filled with earth. The plunderers could do their work much more effectually in the stone vault than in unlined earthen pits and left very little behind them, just a few gold plates, some from the same dies as at Chertomlyk, Kul Oba and Theodosia (e.g. *ASH.* xxx. 6 on p. 158 and *ABC.* xxii. 28), and other ornaments, also some horses' bones coloured green with copper, but no bronze objects with them.

At the sides of the great stone mass were small niches; in the eastern one nothing was found, in the northern one was a woman's skeleton with a mirror and one or two poor ornaments. In the niche to the west lay two

---

[1] *CR.* 1898, figs. 28—34. [2] v. p. 158 = *ASH.* XIII. 6 and 7. [3] *CR.* 1894, p. 77.

skeletons with no objects but a bronze earring.

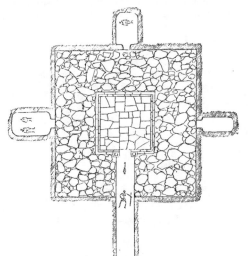

At the entrance of the main vault lay a man's skeleton with a long spear, an iron knife and bronze and bone arrow-heads. He seems to have been as it were a sentry outside the tomb moved to one side by the thieves. This would shew that they had penetrated very soon after the heaping of the tomb. Veselovskij points out that such a work as the stone vault must have been built in the king's lifetime though the heap may have been raised after his death. In 1902 further excavations by N. W. Roth led to considerable discoveries in this same barrow, but the objects found are of the same types, save for some new forms of arrow-heads[1].

Figs. 63, 64. *CR.* 1894, p. 78, ff. 110, 111. Plan and section of vault in Ogüz barrow.

Near by was Dêev barrow[2], 500 ft. round but only 14 ft. high. The main tomb was empty, but a woman's (?) still untouched contained mostly poor copies of Hellenistic work, e.g. two diadems, one with a rich leaf pattern, the other with Neo-Attic maenads, also a frontlet with pendants and Sphinx earrings, all to be closely paralleled at Ryzhanovka (p. 179). There was a very fine gold and enamel necklace with alternate ducks and flowers and an armlet like that from Kul Oba on p. 197 (*ABC.* XXVI. 3).

[1] *Arch. Anz.* 1904, p. 106 ; *CR.* 1902, p. 63 sqq. ;   [2] *BCA.* XIX. p. 168, pl. XIII. XV.
1903, p. 166, f. 323; *BCA.* XIX. p. 157.

From Janchekrak in the N.E. of the district of Melitopol come phalerae of late Roman date, one with the type of winged figure which was adopted for the Christian angel : they were found with a hone and were probably from a late Scythic grave[1].

Melgunov's Barrow.

Of the barrows which have been excavated without proper account having been kept of the disposition of their contents we can regret none more than that called Litój Kurgan, opened in 1763 at Kucherovy Bueraki, about 20 miles from Elisavetgrad, by order of General A. P. Melgunóv, who sent the spoil up to Petersburg for Catherine II to view. Preserved with the Siberian antiquities in the Museum of the Academy of Science the objects have with them found their way to the Hermitage.

FIG. 65. Melgunov's barrow. Golden sheath and fragment of sword hilt. Pridik, pl. III. ⅔.

They included a very interesting dagger and sheath of Scythic forms, but Assyrian style; here is a view of one side of the sheath and a fragment of the

---

[1] *Rep. Imp. Russ. Hist. Museum, Moscow, for* 1907, p. 13, pl. I. ; *Arch. Anz.* 1908, p. 190, ff. 21, 22.

much damaged dagger hilt (ff. 65—67[1], cf. p. 71) with a restoration (f. 68), parcel gilt feet and fittings of a couch, and one of 17 golden birds displayed (f. 69). There were also a golden diadem or necklet in the form of a triple chain

FIGS. 66, 67. Details of Melgunov sheath. Natural size. From S. Kensington electrotype.
Dalton, *Oxus Treasure*, p. 56, f. 38, p. 38, f. 26.

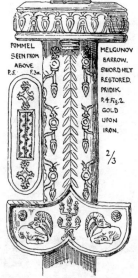 

FIG. 68.

FIG. 69. Couch fittings, ⅔ ; Bird, ⅓.

[1] In *Mat.* XXXI. with Pharmacovskij's "Kelermes," E. M. Pridik will publish a complete account of the find with excellent plates. He has had the extreme kindness to send me a preliminary copy of his part (St P. 1906), from which the annexed illustrations are taken. Cf. also *Trans. Od. Soc.* VI. p. 601 ; *TRAS.* XII. Pt I. (1901), p. 270 sqq., A. A. Spitsyn. The sheath had previously only been published by Maskell, *Russian Art*, p. 112, from the S. Kensington electrotype, which lacks the side projection, a

separate piece, by its style a Scythic addition ; for the use of Mr Dalton's blocks I gladly thank him and the authorities of the British Museum.

In order to try and obtain more light, V. N. Jastrebov undertook further explorations in 1894, but does not seem to have lit upon the right barrow.

A copper belt with a pattern very like that on the sword hilt was found at Zakim (Prov. of Kars) *CR.* 1904, p. 131, f. 239. For the couch foot v. Perrot and Chipiez, *Chaldaea &c.*, II. p. 315, f. 193.

with rosettes set with onyx ; parts of silver disks with a pattern of roundels (they seem to have to do with the suspension of the dagger), 40 bronze arrow-heads of types more or less like Nos. 4, 29, 35, 36, on p. 190, f. 82, a golden strip with figures of an ape, two ostriches (?) and a goose in rather a naturalistic style, 23 gilt iron nails and a short gilt bronze bar ending in rude lions' heads[1], apparently like a hussar button. The style of all these things seems to go back to early in the vith century B.C., perhaps the chain and the repoussé strip are later, but this must have been a very early Scythic tomb.

Martonosha.

In 1870 at Martonosha in the district of Elisavetgrad on the borders of the governments of Kherson and Kiev some peasants excavated a barrow and found a man's skeleton, by his thigh a hone, about him spears and arrows, and in the heap various pots crushed by the earth, four whole amphorae buried standing up, an enormous cauldron full of cow's bones, and a bronze amphora with an archaic Greek running or flying Medusa in the pose of the Nike of Archermus. These particulars were collected in 1889 by Mr Jástrebov, who made a further exploration of the tumulus and found another grave plundered in antiquity. He gives the height of the barrow as 28 feet and the circumference of a high bank round it as more than 800 feet. It is clear that the interment was a Scythic one of the ordinary type though not very rich. The interesting point is the amphora handle which is Greek work of the vith cent. B.C., perhaps the most archaic piece found in the steppes[2].

Eastern Governments.

The governments to the east of Ekaterinoslav have been very imperfectly investigated. Still chance finds in those of Khárkov and Vorónezh and the land of the Don Cossacks[3], also beyond upon the Volga in the governments of Samara, Sarátov[4] and Astrakhan[5], and further in Ekaterinenburg and Orenburg[6], shew that there is no serious gap in the continuity of Scythic occupation stretching to within a measurable distance of the West Siberian area (v. p. 252). This region supplies interesting terms in the series of swords[7] and cauldrons[8].

[1] Cf. Kelermes, *Arch. Anz.* 1905, p. 58.
[2] Ch. XI. § 10, f. 278, *Gazette Archéologique*, 1888, A. Podshivalov, p.79, pl. 13; *Trans. IVth Russ. Arch. Congress*, Odessa, 1886, Vol. I. pl. I. p. lxxi; *CR.* 1889, p. 30, f. 12; *Mat.* XXXII. p. 37, pl. IV.
[3] Fedulovo near Bagaevskaja (Cherkassk). *CR.* 1904, pp. 124—126, ff. 217—223, fine Hellenistic phalerae, cf. *BCA.* pp. 23, 24, 39—41, ff. 42—49. Taganrog, ib. pp. 27, 41, 42, ff. 51—57. Starobélsk (Kharkov), ib. pp. 27, 28, 43—45, ff. 58—69.
[4] Spitsyn in *TRAS.* Vol. VIII. pp. 140 sqq., 154 sqq., 162 sqq. ff. 33—41. A complete interment

of late Scythic type at Salamatino near Kamyshin, Saratov. *CR.* 1902, p. 138 ff. 246—252.
[5] Kishe, district of Chornyj Jar, *CR.* 1904, p. 133, ff. 245, 246.
[6] Krasnogorsk, *CR.* 1903, p. 126, ff. 256, 257. A special point was the absence of the dead man's skull, suggesting Her. IV. 64 and p. 83 supra.
[7] Graf Eugen Zichy, *Dritte Asiatische Forschungs-Reise*, Bd III. Budapest, 1905; *Archaeologische Studien auf Russischen Boden*, by Béla Pósta, p. 102; *CR.* 1902, p. 142, f. 259.
[8] Zichy, op. cit. Bd IV. p. 514.

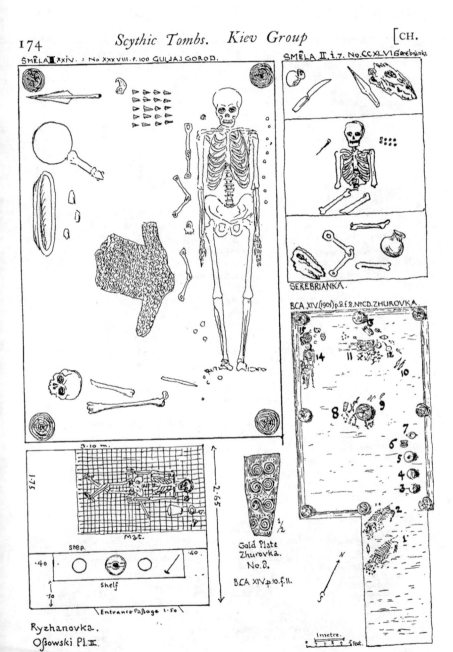

SMÊLA XXIV. : No XXXVIII. P. 100 GULJAJ GOROD.

SMÊLA II. i. 7. No. CCXLVI Serebrjanka

SEREBRIANKA.

BCA. XIV. (1905) p. 8. f. 8. No CD. ZHUROVKA.

Gold Plate
Zhurovka.
No. ð.

BCA XIV p. 10. f. 11.

Ryzhanovka.
Ossowski Pl. II.

Much the same culture which we find in the tombs on the lower Dnêpr is brought to light higher up the river in the governments of Kiev and Poltava. This country is no longer pure steppe, here we have the beginnings of the forest and the people are not so exclusively nomadic as further south. There is no longer such waste of horses at a funeral, no longer indeed such richness in gold and metal work, whereas the bone objects so characteristic of Finnish remains in N. Russia occur here also. Moreover, this is the country of earthworks (*gorodíshche*), and in these earthworks are found things of Scythian type, and great barrows are often near them. This all points to there having long existed here a nation having much in common with the steppe folk, but with some progress towards agriculture, a condition like that ascribed by Herodotus to the agricultural Scythians, whom however he seems to put further south.

This country has been investigated by Count A. A. Bobrinskoj, whose volumes on excavations round about Smêla, his estate on the Tjasmin in the s, of Kiev government, have supplied me with particulars of the Scythic tombs of the district[1]. Here also the greater part of the barrows has been plundered at some time or other. A typical simple grave unplundered is No. CCXLVI.[2], near the River Serebrjanka. Under a mound 2·4 m. high and 97 m. round was a rectangular pit 4·1 m. long by 3·35 m. broad and 25 cm. deep. The pit had been floored, lined and covered with wood; at each end were as it were shelves. Upon one lay a horse's skull, on the other an earthen pot. In the upper part of the tomb was a rusted bit, some bones and a broken pot, further down a horse's lower jaw, fragments of an iron spear, a bone-handled knife, and an iron nail. Below all lay the skeleton and by it a bronze needle and sixty tiny yellow beads. The wooden floor was strewn with white sand and the hole filled in with black earth.

Such was a typical poor grave not far to the west of Smêla. The same type is rather more developed in another good example in this part of the country[3] near Guljaj Gorod. Sufficient description is an explanation of the plan. The mound was 7 ft. high: in the midst was a pit 9 ft. 6 in. × 7 ft. and 7 ft. deep with the remains of a wooden erection supported on four posts and floored with wood. Along the E. wall lay a skeleton N. and S.; W. of it were bits and other remains of harness in bronze, iron and bone, and in the middle an iron coat of mail. In the N. part of the pit lay a small bronze brooch in the form of a boar and the remains of a leathern quiver with over 150 bronze arrow-heads. Along the W. wall going S. were, a long iron spear-head, a bronze mirror with a handle, and a long oblong stone dish and by it pieces of red and yellow colour. At the south end were the remains of another skeleton and an extra skull.

Essentially similar but more elaborate are the tombs near Zhurovka S. of Shpola. The example No. CD at Krivorukovo, two miles from Zhurovka,

[1] Count A. A. Bobrinskoj, *Barrows and chance Archaeological finds about the Village of Smêla*, I. St P. 1887, II. 1894, III. 1902 (cited as *Sm.* I gladly take this opportunity of thanking Count Bobrinskoj for his liberality in sending me his beautifully illustrated volumes). Continued in *BCA.* IV. p. 24, XIV. p. 1, XVII. p. 77, XX. p. 1: cf. *Archiv f.*

Anthrop. XIX. (1891), p. 110. B. Khanenko, *Antiquities of the Region of the Dnêpr Basin, Period before the great Migration,* Vol. II. Pt II. and Pt III. Kiev, 1900. Bobrinskoj's finds are at Smêla, Khanenko's in the town Museum, Kiev.

[2] *Sm.* II. p. 2, pl. I. 7 on f. 70.

[3] *Sm.* I. p. 100, No. XXXVIII. pl. XXiv. 22 on f. 70.

was chosen because of the special interest of a Greek cylix with a vth century inscription Δελφινίο ξυνὴ 'Ιητρō.   It was probably a little valued offering got rid of by an Olbian shrine of Apollo, just as is done at the present day ; it is not likely to have been lost.   We may allow some time for its coming into the possession of its Scythic owner and finding its way into a grave, so that the interment may be put in the ivth century B.C.   The annexed plan (f. 70) gives the general disposition, and the objects found are mostly figured by Count Bobrinskoj[1].   The barrow was 4·20 m. high and 164 m. round. Just above the natural surface of the ground were found the remains of a flat wooden roof reaching out far beyond the grave pit.   The latter went down 2·22 metres.   It was taken up by a wooden erection with nine posts supporting the roof.   The sides of the pit were defined by ditches in which were fixed the lower boards of a wooden lining.   The floor was of oak[2]. At the SE. corner entered the approach in which were two horse skeletons with bits (1, 2) and other trappings.   To the right of the entrance stood two big amphorae (3, 4) and a native vessel (5), beyond a gold plaque with a crouching deer (cf. p. 214, f. 115 = *CR*. 1876, p. 136) (6), and the cylix above mentioned (7).   On the central post had hung two sets of horse trappings, including a gold plate (8) with interesting spirals and dots[3].   By the post was a piece of meat (9) of which the bone had survived, and from near it there pointed a pair of spears (10) northwards towards the principal skeleton (11), which lay surrounded with the trappings of man and beast, including a mirror (12) and a quiver with 463 arrows (13).   A second skeleton of a young man lay along the SW. wall (14).   Close to his head was a shirt of iron mail (15), and by him bits and ornaments.   The objects found in this tomb recall in style those from the VII Brothers (inf. p. 206), as well as those across the Dnêpr in Poltava (v. p. 180 sqq.).

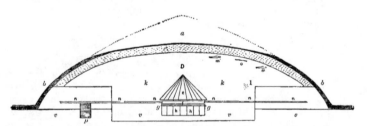

FIG. 71. *CR*. 1891, p. 169, f. 200. Scythic barrow near Kalnik, government of Kiev. Original height, 6 m. Circumference 193 paces.   *a.* Top of barrow levelled for ploughing.   *b.* Humus. *c.* Decayed turf.   *D.* Black earth (Chernozëm) making the main mass of the heap.   *e.* Wooden tabernacle partly burnt.   *f.* Wooden flooring under *e.*   *g.* Mass of yellow green clay with burial. *h.* Pit full of black earth and decayed oaken piles.   *k, k.* Orange and black spots.   *l.* Pocket of charcoal.   *m, m'.* Human skeletons.   *n, n.* Wooden floor extending over almost the whole area of barrow.   *o.* Patch of red clay.   *p.* Section of ditch.   *v.* Subsoil of yellow clay.

[1] *BCA*. XIV. pp. 8—13, ff. 8—26. The cylix is treated by Ct. I. I. Tolstoj, ib. p. 44, v. inf. Ch. XV.
[2] On *BCA*. XIV. p. 14, ff. 28, 29, 30, we have section, plan, and conjectural elevation of such an erection, but in this case the roof is slightly sloping.
[3] Spirals are not common in Scythic ornament. *BCA*. XIV. p. 20, f. 51; XVII. p. 98, f. 37. *CR*. 1904, p. 89, ff. 142, 143.

The next two figures explain themselves. Kalnik was excavated by Professor Antonovich. The section gives a good idea of the elaborate wooden floors and tabernacles sometimes found in the midst of a Scythic barrow. The objects found were not of special interest.

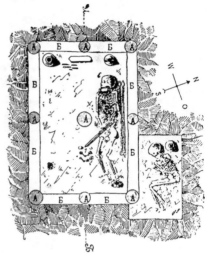

FIG. 72. *BCA.* IV. p. 42, f. 16. Grushevka, district of Chigirin, excavated by Ct. Bobrinskoj No. CCCLXXXIII.

A, wooden posts ; *B*, ditches.

In the older tomb, that to the SE., lay a crouching skeleton, behind his head a single pot and below a beef bone, but there was no red colouring.

In the later Scythic tomb the skeleton, which shewed signs of fire, lay extended. Above, between two pots, a grindstone and some bronze clamps: by the head, mutton and horse bones and an earring like No. 455 on p. 191, f. 83: round the neck an electrum hoop and beads of gold, silver and crystal. The spears had iron heads and spikes. The iron sword was 64 cm. long, by it was a pierced hone. At the knees, two iron psalia and bronze ornaments ; at the feet, a clay pot and bronze clasp.

Darievka.

To the SW. of Smêla towards Zvenigorodka at a place called Darievka[1], near Shpola, Madame J. Th. Abaza excavated a large barrow and found a typical Scythic grave, with the usual gold plates to the number of 270, with griffins (f. 73), deer, lions, triangles with grains, palmettes, strips (ib.) etc.: the types are very similar to those found further south though the workmanship is not quite so fine : there was also found in bronze, a large mirror, 41 arrowheads (fewer than is usual in the south) ; in iron, a long spear-head, a javelin-head and knives in bone hafts ; 38 bone arrow-heads, some glass beads and two black-glazed Greek vases. The excavation does not seem to have been conducted very scientifically, and it is not apparent whether there was a woman buried as well as a man, moreover there is a strange absence of all horse gear. At Vasilkov near by were found a dagger of the Scytho-Siberian type with heart-shaped guard and a wonderful lion's head in stained ivory apparently of Greek workmanship (p. 193, f. 95, cf. p. 266) : also bone spoons and knobs with good specimens of the Scythic beast style.

Ryzhanovka.

Still richer were the results attained by the Polish archaeologist Godfryd Ossowski in 1884 and 1887, at Ryzhanovka, to the w. of Zvenigorodka[2] (f. 70,

[1] *Sm.* II. p. 128 sq.
[2] "Zbiór wiadomości do antropologii krajowej" (Collection of information touching the anthropology of the country) of the Cracow Academy, Vol. XII.; and "Wielki Kurhan Ryżanowski według badań dokonanych w latach 1884 i 1887" in Polish, French Abstract, Cracow, 1888 (The Great Ryzhanovka Kurgan according to investigations made in 1884 and 1887). *Sm.* II. p. 137 sqq., pl. XVI.—XIX.

M. 23

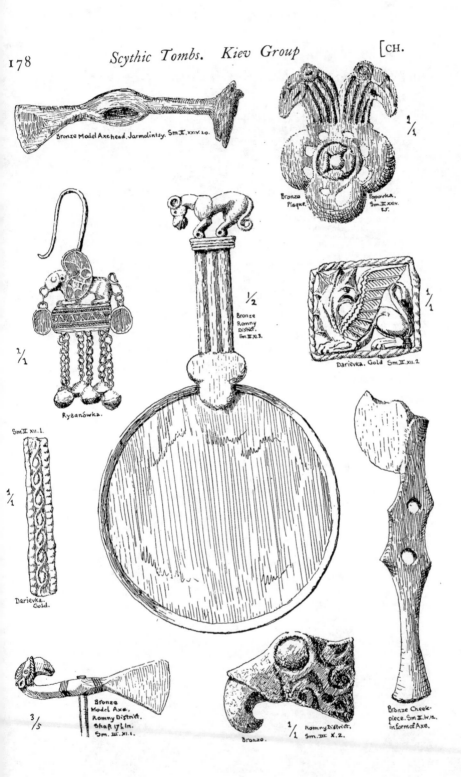

Bronze Model Axehead, Jarmolintsy. Sm.II.XXIV.10.

Bronze Plaque. Popovka. Sm.II.XXIV.15.

2/1

Ryżanówka.

Bronze Romny District. Sm.II.XI.3.

1/2

Darievka. Gold Sm.II.XII.2.

1/1

Sm.II.XII.1.

1/1

Darievka. Gold.

Bronze Model Axe. Romny District. Shaft 17½ in. Sm.III.XII.1.

3/5

Bronze.

1/1 Romny District. Sm.III.X.2.

Bronze Cheek-piece. Sm.II.iv.12. in form of Axe.

below). His accounts have been summarised by Count Bobrinskoj, without the plan and section. I have adopted the dimensions given on Ossowski's plan. The great kurgán (barrow) was explored in 1884 by a trench cut through the middle of it, but only horses' bones and amphora sherds were found. But in 1887 the side of the trench fell in, exposing the top of a complete amphora, a bronze vessel, a mirror, and some gold plates. The peasant who found all this then caught sight of a human skull, was frightened, gave up digging and handed over his finds to the lord of the manor, Mr Grincewicz. The latter gave them to Mr Ossowski for the Cracow Academy. Then happily a horse fell into the hole and died there, preventing any further attempts on the part of unauthorised plunderers. Ossowski proceeded to investigate the tomb systematically, and it proved one of the most perfect Scythic tombs known.

A passage led down to a depth of 3·1 m. and then continued horizontally for 6 m., being 1·50 m. broad and rather more than a metre high. It led into a rectangular chamber 3·10 m. long and 2·65 m. broad, high enough to stand up in. The chamber was divided into two unequal parts by a step 40 cm. high. In the northern part into which the passage led lay a narrow board 2 m. long with a hole to hold the bottom of the amphora discovered by the peasant. Along it were ranged the bronze vessel, the mirror and a bronze pin. In the w. corner of the southern division was the skeleton of a young woman of weak build in a half-sitting position, one leg bent under the other. She lay upon some kind of woollen stuff under which was a layer of moss. She wore upon her head a golden tiara, with a thrice repeated scene of maenads, well-known Neo-Attic types[1] going back to Scopas, a golden frontlet with pendants[2], a long ribbon of gold with rude griffins and palmettes, three gold plates, a pair of gold earrings or temple ornaments shaped like griffins (f. 73) hung from the diadem, four little gold beads, and a big bead of carnelian.

Round her neck she had an elaborate gold necklace, upon her belt 21 gold rosettes, on her arms two bracelets, one silver and one gold; she

FIG. 74. Mat. XIII. p. 37, f. 7 = *Sm.* II. xvi. 9. Part of gold necklace. Ryzhanovka.

wore eight rings, two seal rings, two set with gold staters of Panticapaeum (rather like Pl. v. 16), one set with an unworked piece of limestone, and three

---

[1] Rather like Nos. 25 and 27 or 32 in F. Hauser, *Die Neo-Attischen Reliefs.*   [2] Cf. *ABC.* pl. VI. 2.

quite plain.   The seals are a winged quadruped and a dagger, and Hercules'
club and bow, both of them suggest coins of Panticapaeum.   Across between
the shoulders were three rows of the triangles of grains (called wolf's teeth,
as on p. 197, f. 90), points downwards.   Upon the rest of her clothing space was
found for three big flat rosettes, 44 big convex ones, 21 rayed ones, 47 small
convex ones, two small flat ones, 230 large knots, three small ones, 20 silver
tubes and two bronze rings.

By the skeleton were found in bronze a pail and plate, in silver an
object that fell to pieces, a saucer and a fluted cup with three gilt rings and
a frieze of dogs round it, a clay saucer, bottle and spinning whorl, a black-
glazed cantharos (mended) and two bone bodkins.   We have already mentioned the amphora, mirror, cup and pin found on a shelf by the entrance
of the chamber.

I have enumerated all these things because there is no rich tomb
whereof the disposition had remained untouched and was noted down with
such exactness.   It is not quite normal because it is the tomb of a woman
only, but it gives a good idea of how the innumerable gold plates beloved
by the Scythians were applied.

To judge by Count Bobrinskoj's plates the greater part of the Ryzhanovka objects are imitations of Greek work made by native workmen or
by inferior artizans in Panticapaeum; there is little distinctively Scythic
about them, but it is noticeable in other tombs that the Scythic work is
best represented on horse trappings and weapons, both of which are naturally
absent in a woman's grave.   In this and in detail, the earrings, the strips with
leafwork and with griffins, and the frontlets with Maenads and with pendants,
it agrees with the Dêev barrow (p. 170).   The parcel gilt silver cup recalls
by its shape and decoration the series of similar vessels from Kul Oba[1].   The
form seems native, though Greeks may have imitated it to order.   The earrings have an archaic, almost oriental, touch about them; the two coins are
put between 350 and 320 B.C. (v. Ch. XIX.); the bronze pail, though it has
been rudely supplied with an iron handle, is a beautiful piece of Greek work,
perhaps of the IIIrd century.   The figures on the tiara, already degraded by
repetition, and the cantharos (cf. Ch. XI. § 7, f. 254) might be later, so that the
whole interment may be put in the IInd century.

Government of Poltava.   Axjutintsy.

On the left side of the Dnêpr near Romny (Poltava government) at
Axjutintsy, S. A. Mazaraki dug up an interesting barrow about 1885.   In
this district the course of the Sula cuts off from the steppe a district rich
in wood and water, and it seems as if any nomads that did cross the river
tended to settle down to some degree, being protected by the river from other
nomads, and henceforward finding no necessity to change their pastures at
various seasons; hence the barrows thickly grouped along the river escaped
speedy plunder and so their investigation promises well[2].

The spoils of the chief barrow (No. 2) at Axjutintsy (10 m. high, 156 m.

---

[1] pp. 198, 200, ff. 91, 93, cf. p. 287, *ABC.* XXXIV. XXXV.   [2] Zavitnevich ap. Bobrinskoj, *Sm.* II. p. 101.

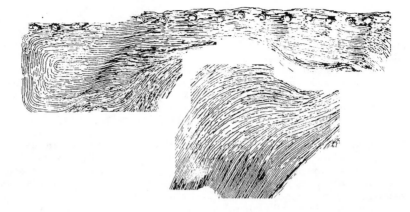

,XXI. Axjutintsy. Gold Quiver Cover.

FIG. 75.

about)[1], found in a central pit 8·5 m. × 4·2 m. and 1 m. deep, offer a great contrast to those at Ryzhanovka, inasmuch as the tomb being that of a warrior, almost all the objects are arms or trappings, and all are most purely Scythic. There was a wooden erection over the burial place, under it lay the skeleton much decayed with its head to the south. By its left shoulder were two leathern quivers with 400 bronze arrow-heads, by its head on the right five iron spear-heads and a javelin, in the SE. corner of the grave three iron bits with bronze ψάλια (others were of bone, v. p. 189, f. 81), 18 bronze plates from horse trappings and some ornaments with fantastic beast heads. In the NW. corner was a bronze Scythic cauldron weighing 40 lbs., a perished bronze dish, a terra cotta cylix, an amphora with 15 gold faces in it, a small oblong gold plate with a deer on it, five stones for throwing and the remains of textile ; in the NE. corner was a small urn. The skeleton wore bronze armour and a plain gold open neck hoop, 1 lb. in weight; by the pelvis were an iron sword of Scytho-Siberian type and a large gold oblong plate with a crouching deer (f. 75), the cover of a quiver or bow case, for under it lay a heap of bronze arrow-heads. There was another grave in the barrow lower down, the skeleton much decayed and by it only animals' bones, and 40 bronze arrow-heads. The only purely Greek object seems to be the cylix, which may be referred to

FIG. 75, *bis.* Axjutintsy, Gold Plate from Belt. *Rep. Hist. M. s. Moscow*, 1906, I. ⅓. ⅓.

the Vth cent. B.C. The same date may be given to the great plate with the deer, which recalls the Kul Oba deer (put by Furtwängler in the middle of that century[2]) and Minusinsk designs (p. 251, f. 172).

A barrow[3] opened in 1905 had been robbed, but not till the wooden chamber had rotted, so only the servants' division suffered. The other held two skeletons and much the same set of grave goods as the chief barrow of Volkovtsy (v. inf.). Most noticeable were nine gold plates from a belt (f. 75 *bis*), a diadem strip, bronze greaves and the bones of swine as well as sheep (v. p. 49). A Greek cylix had Vth century letters scratched upon it, but as the pattern on the strip goes back to IVth century work, this smaller barrow cannot be older than the IIIrd century.

Volkovtsy.

In 1897 and 1898 Mazaraki excavated at Volkovtsy, the next village to Axjutintsy, a rich tomb which Count Bobrinskoj has illustrated and described[4]. The barrow was 13 m. high and some 150 m. round ; about it was a bank. In the midst was an oaken chamber 5 m. × 3·5 m.

The plan (f. 76) gives a singularly complete view of the contents of a Scythic tomb in this part of the country. The skeleton lay with its head to the S. About its neck was a gold torque (p. 184, f. 77, No. 424), by its collar-bone a gold tube (No. 418), about its right arm a gold ribbon (No. 425), by its left forearm a quiver adorned with gold plates (Nos. 406, 410, 413, 417) and containing three hundred arrows. By its left

[1] *Sm.* II. p. 163.
[2] p. 203, f. 98 = *ABC.* XXVI. 1, cf. p. 266.
[3] For description, plan, section and illustrations of chief objects v. *Report of Imp. Russ. Hist. Mus.*

Moscow for 1906, pp. 14—17, ff. 1, 2, Pl. I. II.
[4] *Sm.* III. p. 82 sqq. ff. 22—42. See also B. Khanenko, op. cit., Vol. II. Pt II. p. 6.

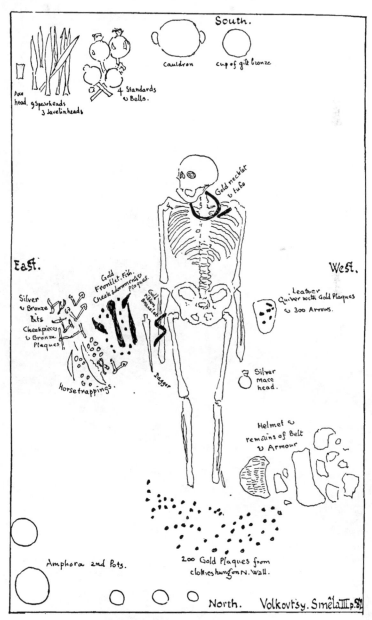

FIG. 76. Plan of tomb at Volkovtsy. N.B. The "Mace Head" is the cup f. 79, No. 451.

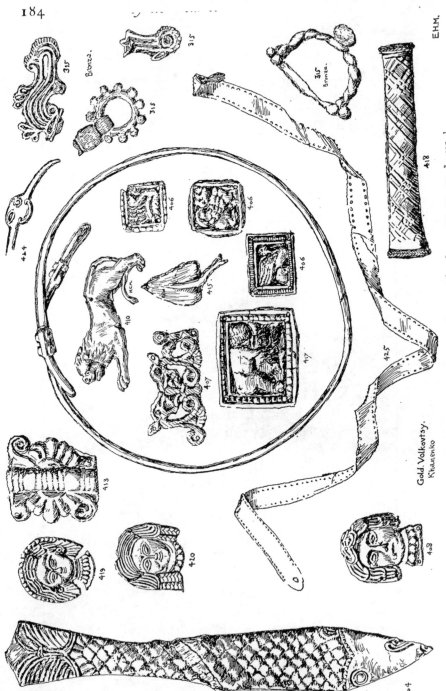

FIG. 77. Objects from Volkovtsy (pp. 182, 187), 413, 418, 425, ⅞; 404, 406, 408, 410, 419, 420, 424, ¾; 315, ½.

Gold. Volkovtsy.
Khanenko.

E.H.M.

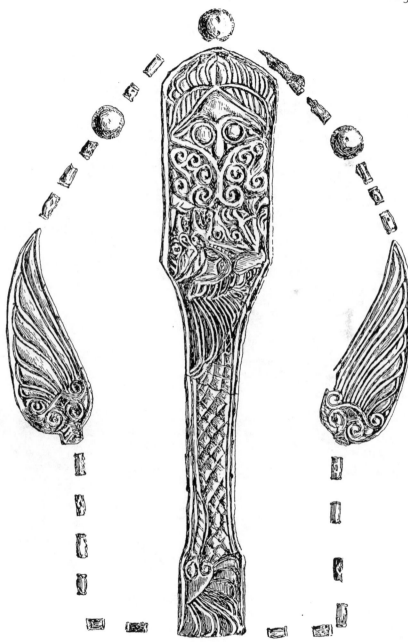

Gold. Volkovtsy. 403. Khanenko

FIG. 78. Horse's frontlet, cheek and bridle ornaments (v. p. 187, 283). ¼.

M.

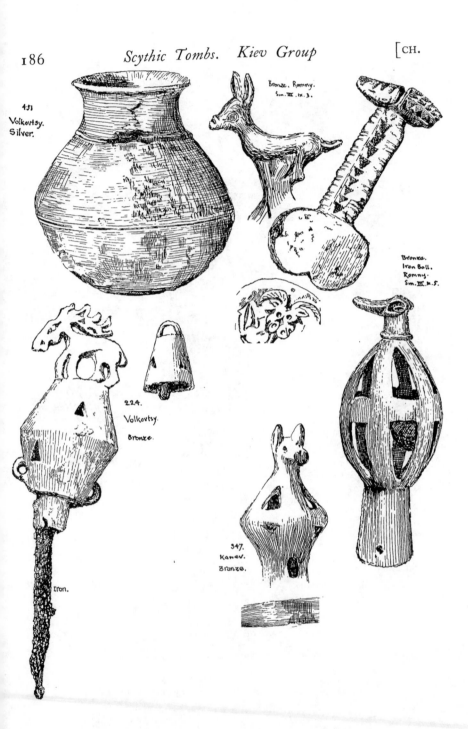

451
Volkovtsy.
Silver.

Bronze. Romny.
Sm. III. ix. 3.

Bronze.
Iron Ball.
Romny.
Sm. III. x. 5.

224.
Volkovtsy.
Bronze.

Iron.

347.
Kanev.
Bronze.

hand was a silver cup (f. 79, No. 451). The NE. corner of the tomb was given up to the remains of armour, bronze and bone, and a great bronze helmet. In the NW. corner stood an amphora, a black-glazed vessel and three other pots between, at the dead man's feet hung his clothes whose gold plates strewed the ground (f. 77, Nos. 408, 415, 419, 420). To his right were a dagger and a collection of horse trappings (No. 315), including six bits with bronze psalia, horses' cheek ornaments and frontlets of gold (f. 78), a large gold fish (f. 77, No. 404) and other fragments. In the SW. corner were nine iron spear-heads, three javelin-heads, and an iron battle-axe, and by them along the s. wall four maces or standards[1] (f. 79, No. 224), and further a big Scythic cauldron and a saucer of gilt bronze. The manner in which the Greek motives have been degraded is well exemplified by the horse's frontlet with a gorgoneion at the top end and two griffins which I did not distinguish until I came to draw them. Compare the pair of horse frontlets from Tsymbalka (p. 166, ff. 54, 55).

Popóvka. Later Tombs.

About Popóvka, also on the Sula, Mazaraki likewise carried on excavations in a large group of barrows[2]. These belong to a later period as is shewn by the abundance of iron used for arrow-heads as well as for swords and spears, which themselves differ somewhat in type from those found in more ancient graves. An interesting find was one of bone scale armour made of pieces of various sizes, sewn on much as were the common bronze scales. That the Sarmatians used such armour we know from Pausanias (I. 21. 5) who says that a Sarmatian hauberk of scales made of horses' hoofs was preserved as a curiosity in the Temple of Aesculapius at Athens. In one barrow there was also found a mirror with a loop in the middle of the back such as is common in tombs of the time of the great migrations. The figures of stone-bucks and birds of prey recall Siberian objects and the finds in NE. Russia. There seem no Greek objects but amphorae, and no objects of Roman manufacture. Still these graves may be probably assigned to the first two centuries A.D. just before the great apparent changes of population in these parts. Further Scythic finds from the Kiev and Poltava governments are published in the catalogue of B. I. Khanenko's collection now in the town Museum at Kiev. The interest of these is that they lead on to the mediaeval and northern beast style, which owes much, may be even its origin, to influence exerted through the Scythians.

The Scythic graves are succeeded in this region[3] and to the north of it by graves containing very similar objects, but occurring in cemeteries without barrows over the interments. The imported objects become Roman and even include coins (e.g. of Faustina and Gordian), dating these burials as of the IInd and IIIrd centuries. Cremation is practised and skeletons are sometimes found in the early huddled position. The native pottery improves, but on the whole not much of value was buried with the dead; there is

---

[1] Supply on p. 78 references to Greek analogues to both bird and beast *bunchuki* like those on f. 79, *Olympia*, IV. XXiii. 410—417, *Delphes*, v. xv. 4.

[2] *Sm.* II. p. 168 sqq.

[3] We cannot yet speak of a La Tène period in Russia; for scattered objects in that style, v. p. 259.

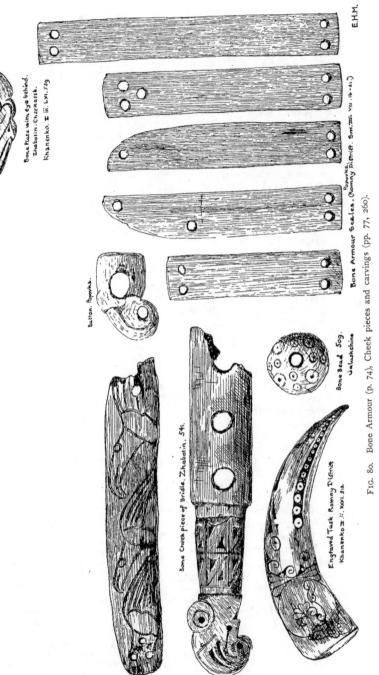

Bone Plate with eye behind.
Zhabotin. Chernassk.
Khanenko. II iii. LXI. 589

Bone Armour Scales. Popovka.
(Romny District. Sm. III. viii. 16-21.)

E.H.M.

Button. Popovka.

Bone Bead Sog.
Ialukchine

Bone Cheek piece of Bridle. Zhabotin. 541.

Engraved Tusk Romny District
Khanenko II K. xxxi. 512

FIG. 80. Bone Armour (p. 74), Cheek pieces and carvings (pp. 77, 260).

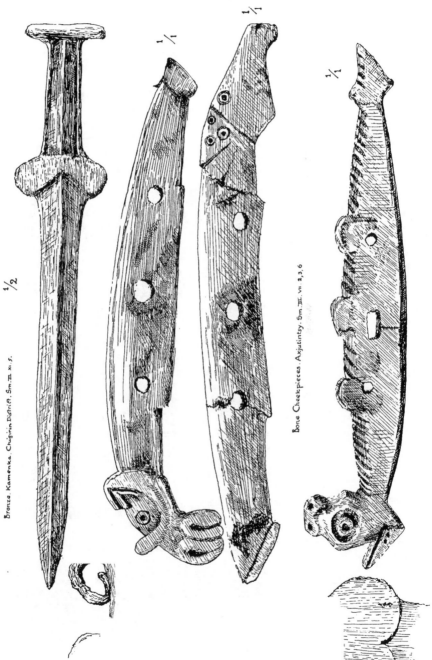

Bronze. Kamenka. Chigirin District. Sm. III. xi. 5.

½

Bone Cheekpieces. Axjutintzy. Sm. III. vii. 2, 3, 6

¹⁄₁

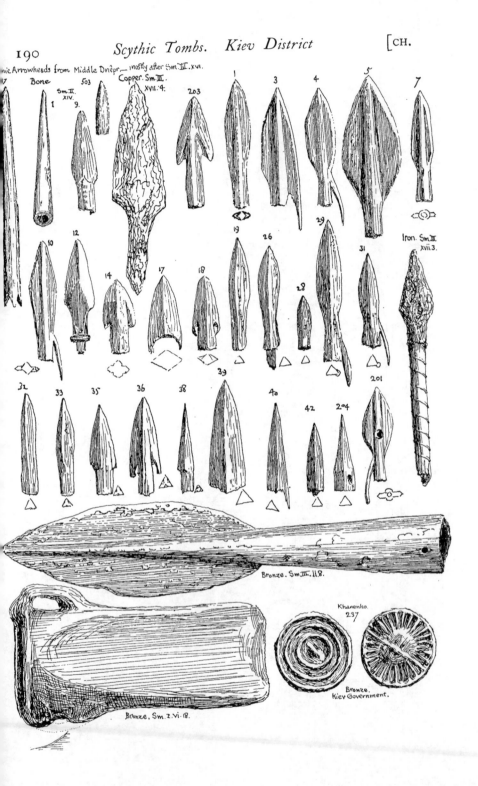

Scythic Arrowheads from Middle Dnêpr.— mostly after Sm. III. xvi.

Bone   Copper. Sm. III.
            XVII. 4.

Sm. II.
XIV.

Iron. Sm. III.
xvii. 3.

Bronze. Sm. III. ii 8.

Khanenko.
237

Bronze.
Kiev Government.

Bronze, Sm. I. vi. 18.

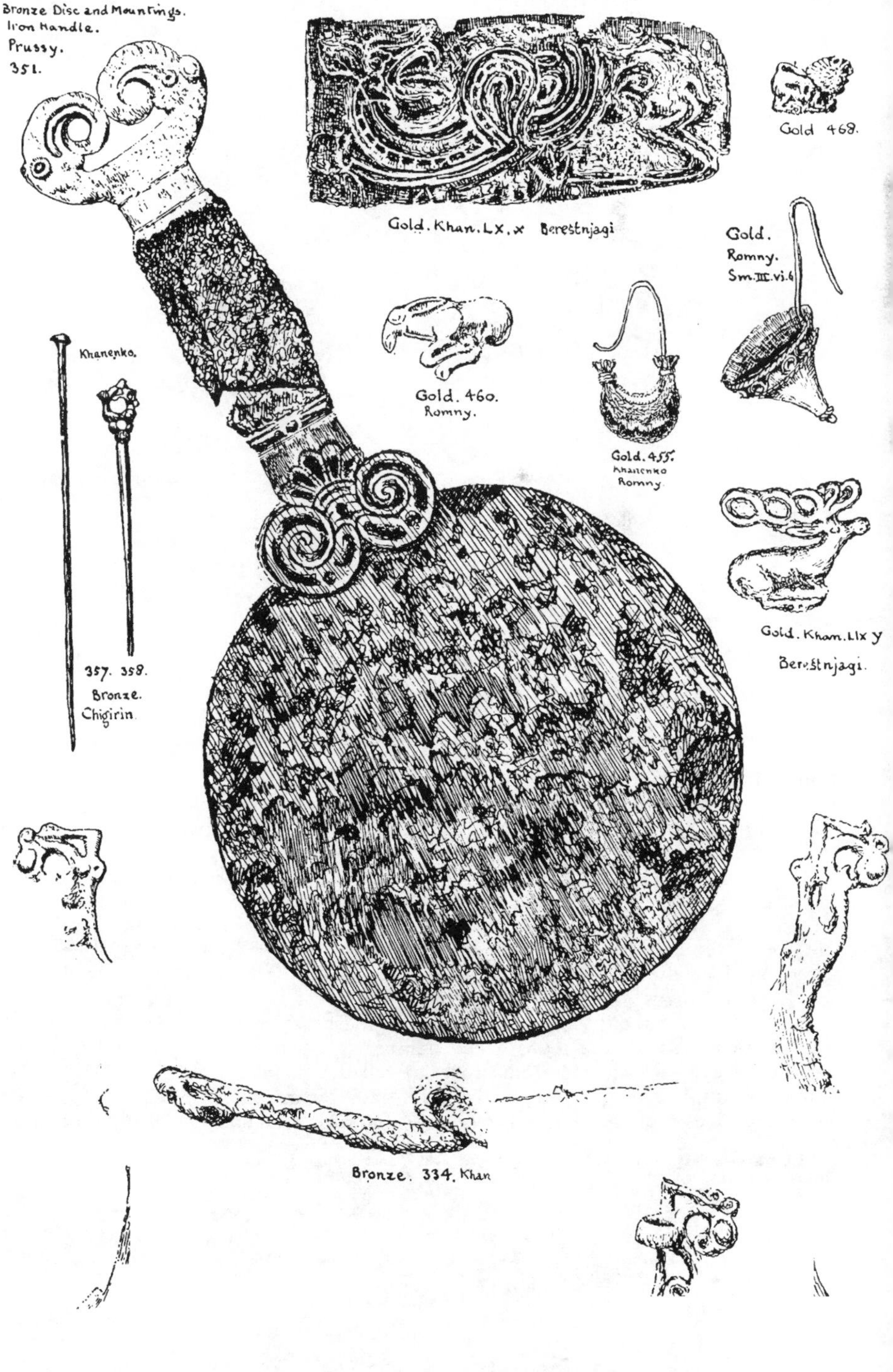

Bronze Disc and Mountings.
Iron Handle.
Prussy.
351.

Gold. Khan. LX. x Berestnjagi

Gold 468.

Gold.
Romny.
Sm. III. vi. 6

Khanenko.

Gold. 460.
Romny.

Gold. 455.
Khanenko
Romny

357. 358.
Bronze.
Chigirin.

Gold. Khan. LIX y
Berestnjagi.

Bronze. 334. Khan.

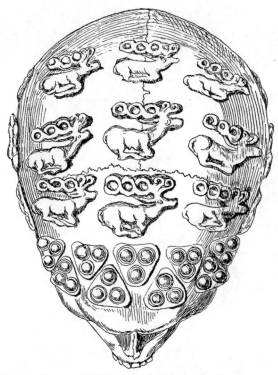

FIG. 84. Sinjavka No. 100. Gold plates on Skull (v. p. 58). *Sm.* III, p. 139, f. 71. ⅔.

a remarkable absence of weapons, and of horses, the bones found being
exclusively those of food animals.   Thus the cemeteries of Zarubintsy,
Cherniakhovo, and Pomashki[1], excavated by Mr V. V. Chvojka, form a
bridge connecting the Scythic type of these regions with the Slavonic type
of later times.   There is much to be said for the view well put forward
by Chvojka that the basis of the population was the same always, that
we have in fact the Slavonic Neuri for a time under strong Scythian
influence, even lordship possibly, at other times under Roman or Gothic
attraction, but always reverting to their own ways.   Certainly the inland
NW. Scythic graves which occur north of the forest line are by no means
so typical as those about the Dnêpr bend, and these are less characteristically
nomadic than those on the Kuban; the number of horses sacrificed increases
steadily as we go east.   It seems rash to call the makers of the Neolithic
"areas" Slavs, they might be yet undifferentiated from other kindred stocks,
but there does not seem good evidence for any fundamental change of

[1] Cf. "Cemeteries of the mid Dnêpr," by V. V.   Slav. Section, pp. 172—190.
Chvojka. *TRAS.* XII., Pt I., St P., 1901, Russo-

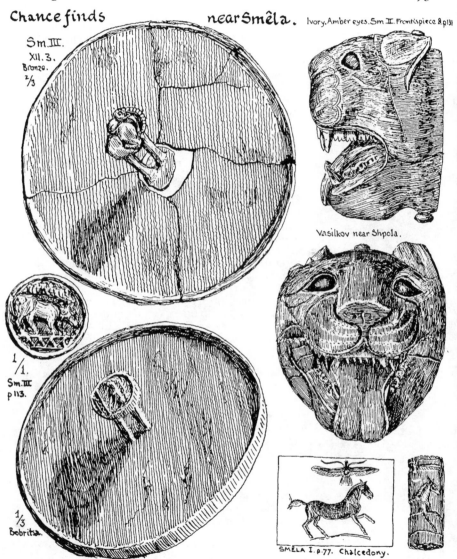

Chance finds near Smêla. Ivory. Amber eyes. Sm II. Frontispiece & p.131

Sm.III.
XII.3.
Bronze.
2/3

Vasilkov near Shpola.

1/1.
Sm.III
p.113.

1/3
Bobritsa.

SMELA I. p.77. Chalcedony.

FIG. 85. Looped Mirrors (p. 66), Lion's Head (pp. 78, 266), Cylinder, Kholódnyj Jar No. XIX (p. 271).

population. The agricultural folk remained on the land though they had to submit to aristocracies of warlike foreigners coming upon them alternately from the steppes to the SE. and from the forests and seas to the NW.

M.

Royal and Golden Barrows.

Tombs of the Scythic type are also found where we should least expect them, in the immediate environs of Panticapaeum. But for the great finds of Kul Oba we should not ascribe the vaults of the Golden Barrow (Altyn Oba) or the Royal Barrow (Tsarskij Kurgan) to natives but they all belong to the same class and probably once hid similar contents, though the first alone preserved them to our day. The masonry of all is clearly Greek, though the plan rather suggests the Mycenaean period. Are we to see in it a survival of the old method of burial among the Milesian descendants of the ancient race? Are we to ascribe this way of building

Entrance to Royal Barrow.
from a Photograph.

FIG. 86.

tombs to the influence of Asia Minor, if this be not saying the same thing in other words, or should we not rather regard these as the translation into stone of the wooden roof and earthen pit with a gallery leading down to it which formed the typical Scythian grave? The Tsarskij Kurgan may be said to be the only impressive architectural monument left by Greek builders on the north coast of the Euxine, with the possible exception of the town walls of Chersonese. The great barrow is three miles to the NE. of Kerch, a little inland of the Quarantine, the site of Myrmecium. It has a circumference of 250 m. (820 ft.) and a height of 17 m. (55 ft.). A curious feature in the heap is the layer of seaweed which occurs also in barrows near Taman[1]. Into one side of it leads a gallery 116 ft. long, 11 ft. broad and 23 ft. high, the walls being for

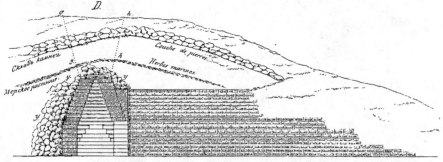

FIG. 87. Kerch. Section of Royal barrow. *ABC*. Pl. A^b, D.

six courses (10 ft.) perpendicular, and then for twelve corbelled out one above another until they meet at the top, all being of great stones hewn in the rustic manner. At the end of the gallery is a doorway 13 ft. high and 7 ft. broad, leading into a chamber 21 ft. square and 30 ft. high, roofed by a circular Egyptian vault ingeniously adapted to the square plan. But the whole has been plundered and has lain open from time immemorial.

[1] E. D. Clarke, *Travels*[1], II. p. 73.

Altyn Oba, or the Golden Barrow to the w. of Kerch along the line of Mount Mithridates, resembles the Tsarskij Kurgan, except that the gallery is much shorter and the vault is round on plan. It contained two subsidiary chambers and had a stone revetment. It also was plundered long ago and the masonry is in no way so well preserved as that of the former tomb[1].

Kul Oba.

Kul Oba. Temple Ornament & Earring in Gold and Enamel. ABC. Pl. XIX.

Breast Roundlet. Kerch.

FIG. 88. ⅔.

This is also true of the famous Kul Oba from which much stone has been taken to build an adjacent village, so that the balance of its Egyptian vault was disturbed, and the ransacking that its riches brought upon it has reduced it to utter ruin. For the circumstances of the opening of the tomb in 1830 the reader is referred to the account of Dubrux[2], but we here reproduce the plan and section on a larger scale.

[1] *ABC.* plan A[n], B, 1.   [2] *ABC.* pp. 4—16 of Reinach's reprint.

Koul-Oba. Plan and Section from North to South. A.B.C. Plan A
Sommet du Tumulus.

a—e (not shewn here) refer to details of the exterior of the mound on *ABC.* Plan A, A, B.

f. Are four amphorae, one with the stamp of Thasos.

g. A Scythic cauldron containing mutton bones[1].

h. Two silver gilt basins (lost) containing three little round bottomed silver vessels[2], two rhyta[3] and a cup marked ΕΡΜΕΩ[4].

i. Sunk space in which were the bones of a horse, a helmet and greaves.

k. Skeleton of groom, (?) about him many gold plates.

l. Woman's skeleton.

m. Electrum vase with reliefs of Scythians[5].

n, n. Great coffin of cypress or juniper wood.

o. King's skeleton.

p. Board dividing off the compartment 5 in which were the king's arms.

q. Bronze hydria. Bronze amphora. Lesser Scythic cauldron[6].

r. Bronze dish about 9 inches across.

s. Two iron spear-heads, 1 ft. 3 in. long.

tt. (Not shewn here). Pegs in S. wall from which hung clothes, from which fell gold plates[7].

u. Wooden ceiling.

V. Keystone of vault.

x. Places where the walls had given.

y. Hole above the door by which Dubrux entered.

z. Beams which held the stones of the door and vestibule.

aa. Under-tomb in which the deer was found[8].

bb. Dry stone wall closing entrance.

cc. Rough stone exterior.

1. Walls of tomb.
2. Vestibule.
3. Door.
4. Seven courses of vault closed by *V.*
5. Compartment in which lay the king's arms.

Scale of Feet

Plan et Coupe du Nord au Sud.
План и разрезъ отъ Сѣвера къ Югу.

FIG. 89.

[1] *ABC.* XLIV. 11.   [2] *ABC.* XXXIV. 1, 2; 3, 4 [fig. 91], XXXV. 5, 6.   [3] *ABC.* XXXV. 4 [on fig. 90], 5.
[4] *ABC.* XXXVII. 4.   [5] *ABC.* XXXIII. [figs. 93, 94].   [6] *ABC.* XLIV. 7, 12, 13.
[7] *ABC.* XX. XXI. XXII. [fig. 90].   [8] *ABC.* XXVII. 1 [fig. 98].

Gold Objects
from Kul Oba.

Gold Plate. Kul Oba. ABC. XX. 5.

Gold Plate. Kul Oba. ABC. XX. 9.

ABC.   XXI. 10

Kul Oba. Queen

ABC. VIII. 2. Ends of Gold Necklet

ABC. VIII. 3.

Kul Oba. Gold Plate.
ABC. XXXII. 10.

ABC.
XX. 10

Gold, blue & green Enamel. End of Copper
Necklet from below the floor. Kul Oba.

Kul Oba. Gold.
Hollow Figure with
Cup & Quiver.

ABC. XX. 2.

ABC. XXX 7 & 10. Kul: Oba
Whetstone
Mounted.

Knife.

ABC. XXVI. 3. Kul Oba.
King's Gold Armlet.

Gold.

Gold

ABC. XXII. 7.

Slaty
Schist.

Gold Plate. Wolf's
'Tooth' pattern com-
mon to all Scythic tombs.
ABC. XXVI. 4.

Rusty
Iron.

Kul Oba.
Silver.

ABC.Pl. XXXIV.

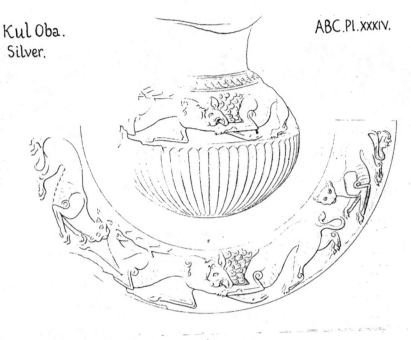

Silver, parcel
gilt.

FIG. 91. ¾

FIG. 92.   Bracelets from Kul Oba. *ABC*. XIII. 1, 3, King.   2, Queen.   ⅔.

Kul Oba, the mound of ashes, is about 4 miles w. of Kerch beyond Altyn Oba and with it was incorporated in ancient defences of the peninsula. It is long shaped, contains traces of several minor interments and at the east end had twin peaks. In one the chamber almost vanished long ago, in the other was a vault in construction similar to that of Altyn Oba, except that its plan was square, and it preserved its square section up to the summit. The vault was 15 ft. × 14 ft. and 17 ft. high, the gallery only 7 ft. long. The section (p. 196, f. 89) shews the construction and the plan gives the distribution of the objects as they were found, and

FIG. 93. Electrum vase from Kul Oba[1]. *ABC.* XXXIII. I. ⅓.

should be compared with that of Chertomlyk (p. 156) and Karagodeuashkh. The system of construction, sumptuous though it was, did not allow of the

---

[1] These figures find new analogues in terra cottas of Scythians from Egypt c. 300 B.C.   W. Flinders Petrie, *Memphis*, I. (1909), Pl. XL. and p. 17, v. supra p. 39 f. 3 *bis*.

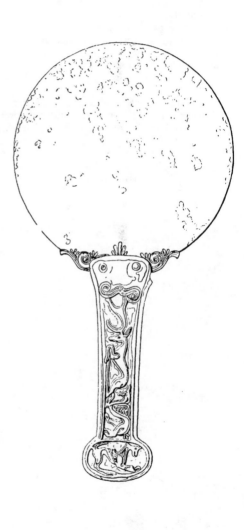

FIG. 94. *CR*. 1864, p. 142. Kul Oba Vase.
Two groups. ½.

FIG. 95. Kul Oba. Bronze mirror with gold
handle = *ABC*. XXXI. 7. ½.

many side chambers or of space for horse graves and groom graves in the true Scythic style.

Upon the woman's head was a diadem of electrum with a pattern of palmettes and hippocamps[1], and with enamelled rosettes. About her neck was a gold necklace finely braided, and a neck ring with lion ends[2]. Near the waist were two medallions of Athena with pendants and three smaller such decorated with flowers[3]. These are all earrings or temple ornaments hung from the ends of a diadem; why they occurred in this position does not appear. By her side were two bracelets with a pattern of griffins seizing deer many times repeated[4]; between her knees the vase with Scythians[5]. She was laid upon the floor and covered with five inches of black mould. Between her and the groom lay six knives with long handles of ivory, and a seventh with its haft plated with gold[6]. This is the only object near her of distinctly Scythic type. She had also a Greek mirror with a handle of Scythic work[7]. About her were fragments of turned wood and painted planks, probably part of her coffin[8].

The king and his belongings lay in a great box 9 ft. 4 in. square and 10½ in. high. The side towards the woman was open. The king wore on his head a pointed felt cap adorned with two strips of embossed gold (*ABC.* II. 2 and f. 96). His neck ring ended in mounted Scythians (f. 97). On his right upper arm was a bracelet an inch broad with alternate scenes of Peleus and Thetis and Eos and Memnon, and blue forget-me-nots between[9]. On each fore-arm were two electrum armlets[10], and on his wrists bracelets with sphinxes at the ends[11]. To the left of the king a narrow board cut off a compartment for his arms between him and the open side of the great box.

Fig. 96. *ABC.* II. 1. Kul Oba. Gold band round king's hood. ½.

There was his sword of Scythic style with a blade nearly 2 ft. 6 in. long

Fig. 97. Kul Oba. Gold and enamel necklet=*ABC.* VIII. 1. ⅔.

and 3½ in. broad[12]; his whip with gold thread plaited into the lash; a gold plate from the sword sheath[13]; a greave, the other being on the king's

[1] *ABC.* II. 3.
[2] *ABC.* VIII. 2 on fig. 90.
[3] *ABC.* XIX. 1 and 4 on fig. 88.
[4] *ABC.* XIII. 2 on fig. 92.
[5] *ABC.* XXXIII. figs. 93, 94.
[6] *ABC.* XXX. 9, 10 on fig. 90.
[7] *ABC.* XXXI. 7 fig. 95.
[8] *ABC.* LXXXIII. LXXXIV. 1, v. inf. Ch. XI. § 4.
[9] *ABC.* XIII. 3 on fig. 92.
[10] *ABC.* XXVI. 3 on fig. 90, perhaps Dubrux means one on each: ten smaller ones (ib. 4) may have come down to the wrists.
[11] *ABC.* XIII. 1 on fig. 92.
[12] Haft *ABC.* XXVII. 10.
[13] *ABC.* XXVI. 2, fig. 98.

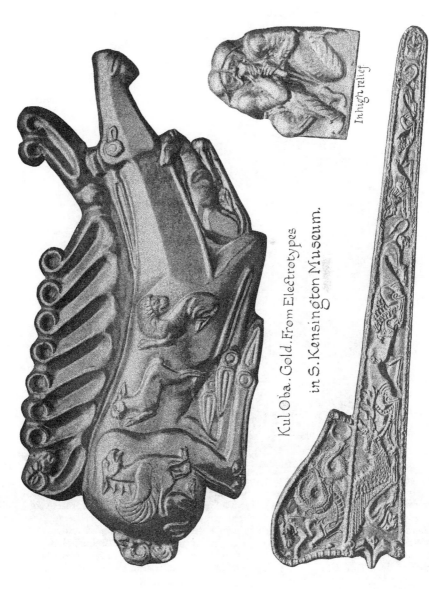

In high relief

Kul Oba. Gold. From Electrotypes in S. Kensington Museum.

FIG. 98. Deer (¾), inscribed ΓΑΙ and Sheath (¾), inscribed ΠΟΡΝΑΧΟ. *ABC.* XXVI. 1, 2 : Group ⅓, ib. XXXII. 10.

right, a hone pierced and mounted in gold[1], and a round drinking cup with
a boss in the middle (f. 99).   Under the king's head were four gold statuettes
of a Scythian with a bow càse[2], and one of two Scythians drinking out of
the same horn[3].   In the engravings it is hard to .distinguish these from the
ordinary stamped gold plates, but they are in the round.   As usual the whole
floor was strewn with these stamped plates[4], shewing all the types we have
already met; sometimes it seems from the same dies as those found at
Chertomlyk, Ogüz and VII Brothers[5].   Also many bronze arrow-heads were

FIG. 99.   Phiale Mesomphalos.   Gold.   Kul Oba=*ABC.* XXV.   ½⅔.

found, too hard for a file to bite on them.   In sifting the earth in the vault
there were found the remains of the ivory veneer from an inner coffin with
fragments of perhaps the most beautiful Greek drawings extant, representing
the judgment of Paris (ff. 100, 101), the rape of the daughters of Leucippus
(f. 102), preparations for the race between Pelops and Oenomaus[6], and other
pieces in a more sketchy style with a Scythian dragged by the reins[7], shewing
that these bits at any rate were made for the Scythian market, if not in Panticapaeum itself (inf. Ch. XI. § 5); also pieces with quasi-architectural decoration,

[1] *ABC.* XXX. 7 on fig. 90.
[2] *ABC.* XXXII. I, reference· omitted on fig. 90.
Back view, Sabatier, *Souvenirs de Kertsch*, v. 4.
[3] *ABC.* XXXII. 10, fig. 98, cf. p. 83, n. 2.
[4] *ABC.* XX. XXI. XXII. some on fig. 90.

[5] p. 158, f. 45,·*ASH.* XXX. 6, 10, 16; p. 208,
f. 106, No. 3.
[6] *ABC.* LXXIX. 13, 14 on f. 103.
[7] *ABC.* LXXIX. 9 on f. 103.

Fig. 100. Kul Oba. Drawings upon ivory. Judgment of Paris. *ABC.* LXXIX. 1. ½.

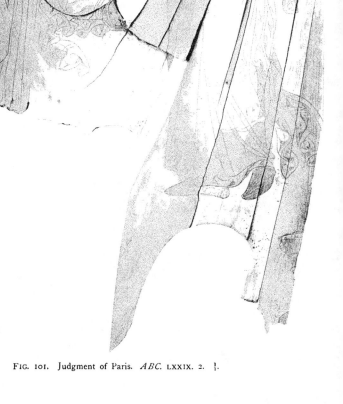

FIG. 101. Judgment of Paris. *ABC.* LXXIX. 2. ⅓.

Ivory from Kul Oba. ABC. LXXIX. 17.
All one piece.

FIG. 102. Rape of Leucippides. ⅓.

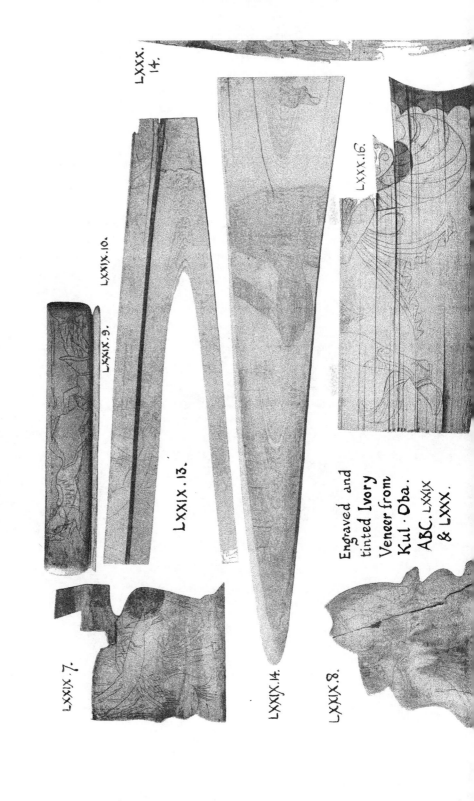

LXXX.
14.

LXXIX.10.

LXXIX. 9.

LXXX.16.

LXXIX. 13.

LXXIX. 7.

LXXIX.14.

LXXIX.8.

Engraved and
tinted Ivory
Veneer from
Kul · Oba.
ABC. LXXIX
& LXXX.

including a kind of Ionic capital (f. 104). Before the careful examination and registration of the contents of the vault had been completed, this latter began to fall about the head of Dubrux to whom we owe the account. Unhappily during the third night the guards set over the chamber left their post, and Greeks and peasants of the neighbourhood risked entering into the danger and began to collect the remaining gold plates. This led them to dig up the floor, and under it they found another tomb in the

Ivory Veneer from Kul·Oba: half real size. Disks of green Glass. *ABC.*Lxxx.19.

FIG. 104.

earth itself and not lined in any way. The skeleton was almost decayed away. In this tomb there was much gold and electrum. The story goes that out of 120 lbs. of gold found the government only rescued 15 lbs., and that there was not a woman about Kerch but had ornaments of the spoil. Of the treasury in the undertomb there were recovered only the well-known deer[1], and two gold lions' heads[2] which formed the ends of a great neck ring of gilt copper. Next day the whole tomb was a wreck. In what relation the undertomb may have stood to the upper one no man can say. The dead man has been supposed to be an ancestor of the king that lay above, or conceivably it was a *cache* and the skeleton was a guard for it. The deer seems to have been the ornament of a shield; a very similar one has been found at Kostromskája near the Kuban with traces of a round shield about it (v. pp. 225, 226, ff. 128, 129).

The cauldrons, the queen's mirror handle, the sword hilt and some of the gold plates alone shew purely Scythic workmanship, but many of the things made by Greeks were clearly intended for the Scythian market, e.g. the deer, the sword-sheath (if indeed these be not of native work, v. p. 265 sqq.), the adornments of the king's pointed cap, the hone, the cups and some of the neck-rings, for the forms of the objects are Scythic, even though the style be Greek. Therefore we need hardly hesitate to believe that the man buried in Kul Oba was just as much a native chief as that in

---

[1] *ABC.* XXVI. 1 on fig. 98.   [2] *ABC.* VIII. 3 on fig. 90, coloured figure, Sabatier, op. cit. pl. IV.

Chertomlyk barrow.   But he must have come within the attraction of Greek civilisation, just as Scyles did, or just as a Sultan of Johore or a Dhuleep Singh puts on the external trappings of another civilisation and buys its products.   The house of Spartocus, the rulers of the Bosporus, though of barbarian origin, were if anything Thracian, and certainly far more truly Hellenized than the king of Kul Oba, with whom the veneer is very thin, as testify the slaughtered slave and wife and the very mutton bones in the cauldron.

Kuban Group. Seven Brothers.

To the east of the Bosporus the same culture prevailed and along the course of the Kuban many tombs have been opened.   These tombs seem to have been less thoroughly ransacked in former times, so that they have now offered many interesting objects.   The first group to be explored in this district was that called the Seven Brothers lying on the steep side of the Kuban 10 m. SSE. of Temrjuk.   These barrows were excavated by Baron B. G. von Tiesenhausen in 1875 and 1876[1].   Of them No. 1 was almost a blank.   No. 11[2] contained a stone chamber with one corner set apart for the man, in the remainder 13 horses.   The bits, psalia and trappings of three horses offer most remarkable forms, e.g. the fore part of a horse at one end and a hoof at the other[3], others are in the shape of axes or of beak-heads (f. 109), some of the bits themselves have cruel ἐχῖνοι upon them with spikes to make them more effective[4].   The man's skeleton was wearing a hauberk with scales, some of gilt iron, some of bronze[5], and by him was a spare cuirass of iron, once adorned with a splendid pectoral in silver, a horned hind suckling a fawn with an eagle displayed beneath (f. 105). About his neck he wore a torque of gold and two necklaces[6]; upon his clothes innumerable various gold plates exemplifying the Scythic love of animal forms (f. 106).   Some of these go back to the beginning of the vth cent. B.C., for there is the turn-up nose and the long eye of the archaic period (ib. No. 1).   Some, e.g. No. 3, are identical with those at Kul Oba, but most are earlier in style, compare the winged boar on f. 106 with that on f. 90. By his side were the remains of a very long and heavy sword and of a lance, a rhyton ending in a lion's head[7], a φιάλη μεσόμφαλος (f. 107), other cups, spoons, colanders, vases[8] and a silver gilt cylix with Bellerophon and the Chimaera[9]; also a gold plate in the shape of a triangle with rounded apex decorated in the middle with a winged panther devouring a goat, with nail-holes all about the edge (f. 108).   Plates of a similar form were found in the other graves of the group, five in No. iv, and it seems most likely that they adorned the ends of quivers, since no other trace of quivers has been found though arrow-heads occur, and we have other cases of a superfluity of some object being placed with the dead.

The third barrow had been plundered, but there were left gold plates; the style is decidedly later than in No. 11, a sword hilt[10], some amber beads,

[1] *CR.* 1875—77.
[2] Plan, *CR.* 1876, p. 117 on fig. 114.
[3] ib. p. 124 = *KTR.* p. 50, f. 57.
[4] *CR.* 1876, p. 123—126, cf. those from No. iv. on f. 115.   [5] ib. II. 15—18.
[6] ib. iv. 6, 7 and III. 26 on f. 106.
[7] ib. iv. 8.   [8] ib. iv. 11, 12.
[9] *CR.* 1881, I. 3, this exquisite vth cent. engraving came to light on subsequent cleaning.
[10] *CR.* 1877, p. 9 and I. 1, 2 on f. 105.

FIG. 105. Silver, parcel gilt, pectoral. Seven Brothers, No. 11.=*CR*. 1876, IV. 1. ⅜.

CR. 1876. III　Seven Brothers. Nos. 1–21 No II. Nos. 23–33 No. VI.

Kul Oba.

1877. III
Nymphaeum.

Engraved Glass.

No. VII

Gold & Rock-crystal.

1877. I. 1. No III Silver ♡ Gold.

No III

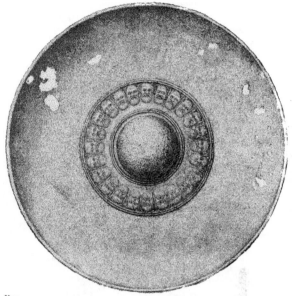

FIG. 107. *CR.* 1876, IV. 9. Seven Brothers, No. II. Silver phiale. ½.

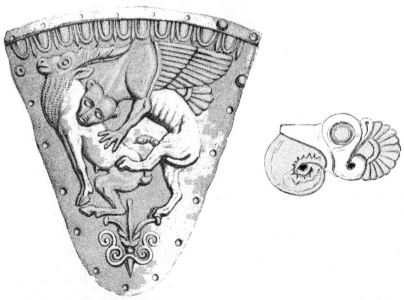

FIG. 108. *CR.* 1877, II. 3. Seven Brothers, Nos. II
and IV. Golden quiver tip. ⅓.

FIG. 109. *CR.* 1876, p. 126. Bridle
ornament. Seven Brothers No. II.

M.

27

parts of a broken silver vessel, and to the east of the chief tomb was the tomb of five horses with bridles adorned with bronze.

The fourth barrow had a horse tomb yielding further varieties of bits and bronze plaques with fantastic animals contorted in the typical Scytho-Siberian taste (f. 115). The central vault had been pillaged partly, but not completely ; by the head of the skeleton were found two gold rhyta, ending, one in a sheep's head, the other in the forepart of a dog[1], and a great silver one with winged ibex of Perso-Greek style[2]: five (ff. 108 same as one in No. II, 111, 112, 114) triangular plates, a silver cylix engraved with Nike gilt[3], three amulets mounted in gold and a gold bracelet[4]. In a compartment boarded off lay a leather jerkin with a crescent-shaped gorget and a gorgoneion on the breast (f. 114), and bronze scales sewn all over it, a candelabrum[5], a bronze cauldron containing a sponge, some fur, a cloth and a stuff with a branching pattern upon it[6], a bronze dish and a ladle handle in the form of Hermes Criophoros[7]. This tomb and the second are the oldest of the group and may well belong to the vth century. The fifth barrow had untouched only the horse tomb with the usual bridles[8].

The sixth tumulus had not been opened. The chamber was divided into four compartments by thin stone walls (f. 114). In No. 1 lay the dead man, in Nos. 2 and 3 his various gear, in No. 4 his seven horses. Over his coffin was stretched a woollen stuff roughly painted (not embroidered) after the fashion of black-figured vases[9]. It had been in long use, for it was patched and mended (f. 113). There was very little upon the dead man, scale armour, remains of furs, perhaps boots and cap, some good beads, a pair of gold "twists" (v. Ch. XI. § 12), the usual gold plates and, most interesting, a crystal intaglio of a sow[10]. In the small compartment (No. 2) was a bronze mirror, some gold buttons, the sherds of two amphorae, a silver gilt cylix with a genre scene[3] and a red figured vase with ephebi; No. 3 held a chest with engraved ivory panels, some vases of bronze and pottery and pieces of a basket ; in No. 4 the horses wore bits adorned with bronze cheek-pieces and phalerae. The seventh tumulus had but a horse-tomb, in it was picked up an early earring[11]. In none were there any remains of women's burial.

The main interest in the Seven Brothers is in their undoubtedly early date (v. inf. p. 265) and in the beast style, which is applied to the adornment of the horse trappings. At Eltegen (Nymphaeum) about the same year Professor Kondakov found similar pieces in two tombs, which must be classed with the Seven Brothers owing to the surprising identity of both gold and bronze objects yielded by them. It looks, however, as if in this case we had rather Greeks with Scythic horse gear, than Scythians with Greek tastes (ff. 106, 114—116)[12]. The pattern on the coffin sunk for inlay (f. 115,

[1] *CR.* 1877, I. 6, 7 ; *KTR.* p. 318, f. 286.
[2] *CR.* 1877, I. 5 ; one end fig. 111, the other on fig. 114: cf. Furtwängler in *Arch. Anz.* 1892, p. 115.
[3] *CR.* 1881, I. 12 ; cf. p. 206 n. 9: similar cylices, I. 4 from No. VI. and I. 5 (Dionysius and Maenads) from a group near are of unsurpassed IVth cent. work.
[4] *CR.* 1877, II. 13 (tusk on f. 106), 14, 15 ; ib. II. 10.

[5] ib. II. 7, 8.
[6] *CR.* 1878–9, pl. V. I.
[7] *CR.* 1877, I. 9.
[8] *CR.* 1876, pp. 136–7.
[9] Or rather transitional red-figured of the class treated of by Six, *Gaz. Arch.* 1888, p. 193 ; H. B. Walters, *Hist. Anc. Pottery,* I. p. 393 ; Rhomaios, *Ath. Mitt.* 1906, p. 186 ; *JHS.* XXIX. (1909), p. 333.
[10] *CR.* 1876, III. 28—33 on f. 106.   [11] ib. III. 42.
[12] *CR.* 1876, pp. 220–40 ; *KTR.* p. 52.

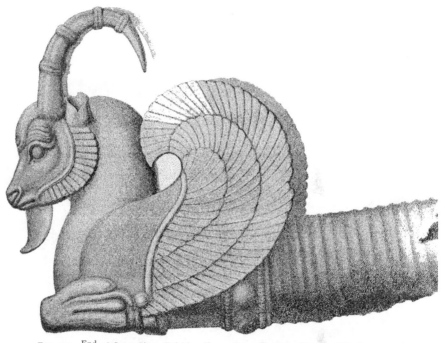

FIG. 110. End of Great Silver Drinking Horn. Seven Brothers, No. IV. *CR*. 1877, I. 5. ⅓.

FIG. 111. Gold Plate. Seven Brothers, No. IV.
CR. 1877, I. 8. ½.

FIG. 112. Gold Plate from Seven Brothers,
No. IV. *CR*. 1877, II. 5. ½.

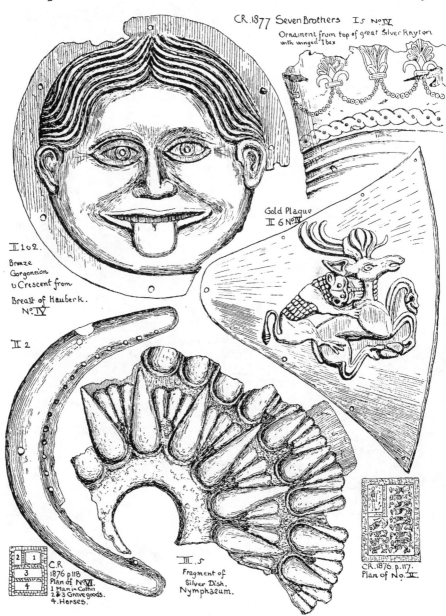

CR.1877 Seven Brothers Is Nº IV

Ornament from top of great Silver Rnyton
with winged Ibex

Gold Plaque
II 6 Nº IV

II 102.
Bronze
Gorgoneion
v Crescent from
Breast of Hauberk.
Nº IV

II 2

III .5
Fragment of
Silver Dish.
Nymphæum.

C.R
1876 p 118
Plan of Nº VI.
1 Man in Coffin
2 & 3 Grave goods.
4. Horses.

2	1
3	
4	

CR.1876. p. 117.
Plan of No. II.

Fig. 114. ⅔.

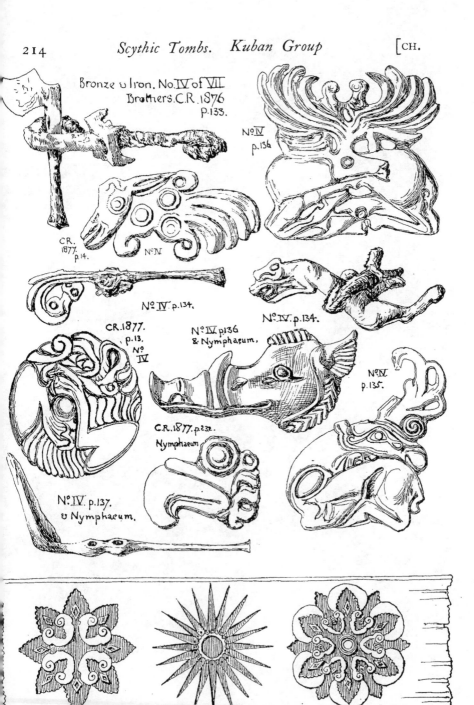

Bronze v Iron. No. IV of VII
Brothers. C.R. 1876
p.133.

N° IV
p.136

C.R.
1877.
p.14.

N° IV

N° IV. p.134.

N° IV. p.134.

C.R.1877.
p.13.
N°
IV

N° IV p.136
& Nymphaeum.

N° IV
p.135.

C.R.1877. p.32.
Nymphaeum

N° IV. p.137.
v Nymphaeum.

cf. Ch. XI. § 5), and the gold plates[1] are Greek. The rayed silver dish (f. 114)[2], the engraved ring and the plate with a winged being on f. 106 (Nos. 8 and 30 *below*), shew Iranian affinities.

A most remarkable mixture of Scythic and Greek grave-goods was that found by a peasant in 1900 at Akhtanizovka[3], NE. of Phanagoria. A brooch (f. 117) and still more a big intaglio shew that we have to do with the first centuries A.D. Quite Greek are a conical helmet with a gold wreath and cheek-pieces, phalerae and glass vessels. But the necklets, one of five turns, one of three, and one of nine (f. 118), are quite Siberian in character, and the hone is perhaps the latest example of a Scythic hone. So in place and in contents this tomb came between the Bosporus and the Kuban.

At Siverskaja[4], Kuban district, Cossacks found a similar mixture, glass vessels mounted above and below in gold and garnets—from the upper rim carnelians and gold beads hung by chains—a roundel in technique like Fig. 117, one with a curled-up griffin, a large phalera with rude figures and coins of the last Paerisades.

FIG. 116. *CR.* 1877, p. 231. Cheekpiece. Nymphaeum.

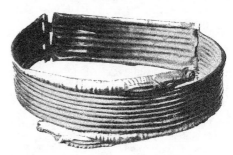

FIGS. 117, 118. Akhtanizovka. Brooch with stone ($\frac{1}{1}$), and Gold Necklet ($\frac{1}{3}$). *CR.* 1900, p. 107, ff. 210, 211.

---

[1] Even the lion with serpent-headed tail, f. 106, cf. Spartan bronze fibula, *BSA.* XIII. p. 114, f. 4.
[2] Cf. that found at Susa by de Morgan, *Mém. de la Délégation en Perse du Min. de l'Instr. Pub.*, T. VIII. (Paris, 1905), Pl. III.

[3] *CR.* 1900, pp. 104—108, ff. 190—219, cf. Spitsyn, *BCA.* XXIX. pp. 19—23, 30—36, ff. 1—35.
[4] ib. pp. 24—26, 37, 38, ff. 36—41; *KTR.* 448—451, f. 394, the phalera.

Karagodeuashkh.

Of late years excavations have been carried on with much success on the E. side of the Bosporus higher up the Kuban than the Seven Brothers. The most important find is perhaps that made in the barrow Karago-deuashkh, and it has been particularly well treated from the general point of view by Professor A. S. Lappo-Danilevskij, and from the point of view of art criticism by Professor W. Malmberg[1]. This is perhaps the most important contribution to the question of Scythian ethnology for the last fifteen years, and I am much indebted to it. .

Karagodeuashkh barrow is near the post and railway station Krýmskaja about 20 miles NE. of Novorossijsk, just at the point where the Adagum, a tributary of the Kuban, flows into the plain. The valley of the Adagum is the pass by which the railway to Novorossijsk crosses the ridge of the Caucasus, here not much more than 1500 feet high. The barrow was about 33 ft. high and 672 ft. round. In 1888 a hole appeared in one side of it disclosing stonework. E. D. Felitsyn, a local archaeologist, informed the Archaeological Commission and proceeded to excavate the barrow[2]. There appeared a row of four chambers leading one into the others, built of squared stones, of varying heights. The first was 11 ft. 6 in. by 9 ft. 9 in. and 6 ft. 6 in. high, the next 14 ft. long by 11 ft. broad. Both these chambers were plastered: the next room was 21 ft. long and 7 ft. broad, plastered and frescoed. The last chamber was about 10 ft. 6 in. square and 8 ft. high; between the chambers were doorways with stone lintels.

In the first room by the door were the remains of a funeral car, in the middle of the chamber were two or three horse skeletons, one with a bit in its mouth; the bones shewed signs of fire. In the right-hand half of the chamber were a heap of ashes and some bones of a domestic animal, and in the corner a big amphora, 46 cm. high; by it a silver vessel, a copper spoon and some pottery, also 150 various beads and three engraved pastes set in silver[3]. Along the left-hand wall lay the skeleton of a young woman in full array. By her head was a thin gold plate (f. 120) roughly cut into a triangle so as to mutilate the subjects on it, Tyche or Nike, a *biga*, and a queen surrounded by attendants and wearing just such a headdress. About it 16 ajouré plates in the shape of a dove (III. 5 on fig. 119) and 50 round Medusa heads, by her temples beautiful Greek earrings (ib. III. 6, 7), on her neck a golden hoop and a necklace (ib. IV. 1, 2). Upon her wrists were spiral bracelets ending in hippocamps (ib. III. 8), and on her right hand a ring with a woman playing the lyre engraved upon the bezel[4]. Beside her lay a golden chain ending in a lion's head, a second plaited gold necklace (ib. IV. 3), and the silver roundel with Aphrodite's head (ib. III. 12). About her were the remains of a coffin. The second chamber was absolutely empty.

[1] No. XIII. of *Materials for the Archaeology of Russia, published by the Imp. Archaeological Commission*, St P. 1894.

[2] *CR.* 1882—1888, pp. ccxvi—ccxx.
[3] *Mat.* XIII. iv. 6, 8, 9.
[4] ib. iii. 10.

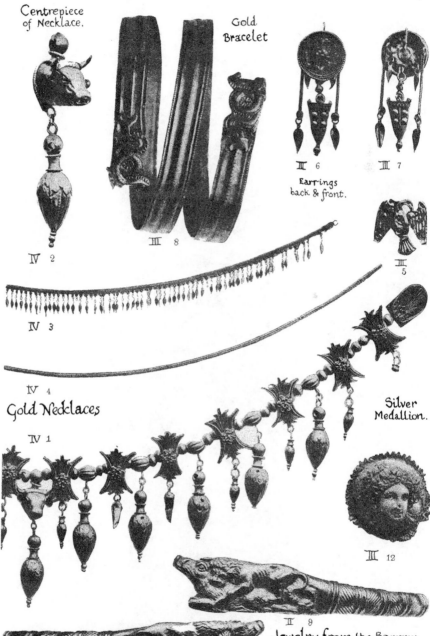

Centrepiece of Necklace.

Gold Bracelet

IV 2

III 8

Earrings back & front.

III 6   III 7

III 5

IV 3

IV 4

Gold Necklaces

IV 1

Silver Medallion.

III 12

II 9

Jewelry from the Barrow Karagodeuashkh. Mat. XIII.

Ends of Gold Torque II 8

FIG. 120.   Karagodeuashkh.   Gold plate from headdress.   *Mat.* XIII. iii. 1. $\frac{18}{20}$.

In the third long and narrow chamber were frescoes that crumbled away upon discovery. A pasturing deer was distinguishable. In the further corner were the bones of a horse with iron and bronze trappings.

FIG. 121. *Mat.* XIII. p. 150, f. 23. Karagodeuashkh. Silver Rhyton, restored. ⅓.

In the fourth or square chamber, also frescoed, were the fragments of several big amphorae and one whole one; along the right wall various broken vessels, a great copper jug, a smaller one, two copper cauldrons,

FIG. 122. *Mat.* XIII. p. 29, f. 1. Gold strip round hood. Karagodeuashkh.

FIG. 123. Karagodeuashkh. Gold plate from quiver. *Mat.* XIII. Pl. viii. 9, pp. 56, 134. ⅓.

28—2

FIG. 124.   *Mat.* XIII. p. 125, f. 2.   Karagodeuashkh.   Part of bow-case. $\frac{9}{10}$.

and a clay lamp. Near it a great copper dish with two crossed rhyta upon it, and by them a silver cylix and scyphus[1], and further on a great bronze plate (possibly a shield; it fell to pieces in being brought out) with two more crossed rhyta upon it (f. 121), a silver colander and a silver ladle[2]. Along the left wall lay a man's skeleton, by his head gold rosettes and faces and a strip from his hood (f. 122), about his neck a gold hoop with ends in the form of lions devouring boars (Fig. 119, II. 8, 9). At his side an iron sword with a gold haft of the Scythic type and a cylindrical hone in a plain gold mount[3]. On the right of his head lay a bow-case adorned with a plate of silver covered with gold and ornamented with figures in relief of the same disposition as the Chertomlyk plate (ff. 124, 125). In the quiver part 50 copper (?) arrow-heads. On the left side was another quiver, adorned with little gold plates, and containing 100 arrow-heads (f. 123). Above the head by the wall lay twelve iron spear-heads. About were the remains of a coffin, but it cannot be said whether the arms lay within it or without.

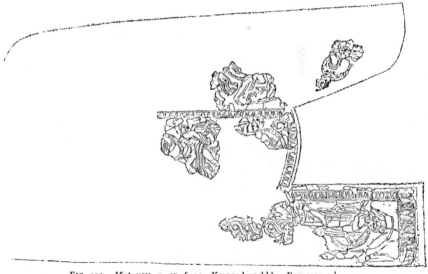

FIG. 125.   *Mat.* XIII. p. 57, f. 34.   Karagodeuashkh.   Bow-case. $\frac{1}{3}$.

The stone roof of all the chambers had fallen in and filled them up with earth and stones, severely damaging many objects. Also the objects found were not registered as carefully as might be, so that the details of their original disposition are no longer to be restored. For instance there is an interesting fragment of a phiale mesomphalos with concentric patterns round the perished boss[4].

On comparing this with the other rich Scythic tombs we may notice the absence of armour scales and of a gold plated dagger-sheath.

[1] *Mat.* XIII. v. 2 and p. 151, f. 24.   [2] ib. vi. 2, 3.   [3] ib. vii. 7.   [4] ib. vi. 4.

Kelermes.

A little further to the east about Majkop are many barrows just where various tributaries of the Kuban enter the plain[1]. The oldest in date, near the Kelermes, was excavated by D. Schulz in 1903 : no details or illustrations are to hand, and the novel character of the objects makes it hard to picture them to oneself even by the careful description[2].

The horse grave in this case had been plundered, but the man's body was untouched. He wore a bronze helmet, surrounded by a broad gold band as a diadem with rosettes, flowers and falcons soldered on to it ; in the middle was a stone apparently amber ; above and below ajouré rosettes and falcons. There was a second diadem with repoussé flowers. At the skeleton's right hand lay a short dagger of the usual Scythic type with a gold haft and a gold sheath with a row of monsters and genii, and on the usual side-projection a crouching stag, the whole much like Melgunov's sheath (pp. 71, 172), but of a more purely Assyrian style. The haft had similar decoration. There was also found an iron axe, which is unique, enriched on haft and head with elaborate decoration of genii and beasts, wrought in gold ; into this the Scythic elements seem to have entered more than into that of the sheath. About a yard to the left was a panther of cast gold surrounded by iron scales, corresponding exactly to the shield ornaments of Kul Oba and Kostromskaja. The eyes and nostrils were filled with glass pastes which had themselves stones let into them ; the ears had pastes of different colours, separated by gold *cloisons*, a very important instance of this interesting technique. Near the feet were arrow-heads of bronze. There were also gold buttons, bronze bridles and big iron lance-heads. The chief pieces are referred to Mesopotamian art of the VIIth or VIth century, fresh evidence of direct contact between Scyth and Assyrian.

In 1904 Mr Schulz opened another barrow in which lay a man and a woman[3]. With the former were found a gorytus cover in gold, adorned with crouching stags in squares, and two rows of panthers, a silver rhyton with centaurs and Artemis, the Lady of the Beasts. The woman had a most remarkable belt with gold adornments set with amber, a diadem with a griffin head in front, recalling very closely the griffin from the Oxus treasure (v. p. 256)—from the diadem's hoop hung by chains rams' heads and flowers enamelled blue—and a silver gilt mirror bearing various groups of animals, monsters and centaurs, together with a similar Artemis. In neither tomb had there been a wooden tabernacle. The two silver pieces belong to Ionian art when it was chiefly occupied with beasts and still had much in common with non-Hellenic art in Asia, and the diadem belongs to the Perso-Greek style. The belt and gorytus are more like the Scythic work, and the former strangely anticipates some details of the so-called Gothic jewelry, although it must be several centuries older.

---

[1] The usual modern settlement in this district is the Cossack post or Stanítsa, mostly named either after some Russian town, e.g. Jaroslávskaja or Kostromskája, or from the river upon which it lies, as Kelermesskaja or Kurdzhipskaja (sc. Stanitsa). In the names derived from rivers I have dropped the Russian adjectival ending -skaja.

[2] *Arch. Anz.* 1904, p. 100 sqq. Pharmacovskij is to treat of these finds in *Mat.* XXXI.

[3] *Arch. Anz.* 1905, p. 57 sqq. figs. 1—4.

In two other barrows opened by Veselovskij[1] standards and bone work recall W. Scythia. Phalerae with cold inlay and with spirals are also interesting[2], but wooden tabernacles had made plunder easy and only horses were left, 24 in one, 16 in the other, arranged in ⌐_ shape. Other barrows held coloured skeletons. At Voronezhskaja the 30 horses were set as a horse-shoe and had trappings recalling the VII Brothers[3].

Kurdzhips.

On the Kurdzhips, a tributary of the Bêlaja, another affluent of the Kuban, in the Majkop district, again just where the river reaches the plain, are many barrows. One was opened without authorization in 1895, but most of the objects found were secured for the Archaeological Commission[4]. They comprised the usual selection of gold plates, mostly of rather rude

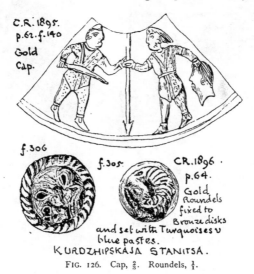

KURDZHIPSKAJA STANITSA.

FIG. 126. Cap, $\frac{2}{3}$. Roundels, $\frac{1}{1}$.

work, but worthy of note are a gold nugget pierced for suspension as an amulet, some round carnelians slung round with gold wire, and especially a kind of cap with a rosette pierced with a hole above, and on each side a group of two men in Scythian dress, each holding one spear set up between them; in the free hand of one is a sword, of the other a human head cut off (f. 126). It might almost illustrate what Herodotus (IV. 64) says of Scyths bringing scalps to their king to claim their share of the booty. This find moved the commission to send Mr V. M. Sysoev to investigate the barrows thoroughly[5]. This one proved to be 9 ft. 6 in.

[1] _CR._ 1904, pp. 85—95.
[2] ih. pp. 88, 89, ff. 138, 142.
[3] _CR._ 1903, pp. 73, 75, ff. 139—153.

[4] _CR._ 1895, pp. 62, 63, figs. 140—153.
[5] _CR._ 1896, pp. 60 and 149.

high and about 84 ft. from E. to W. and 70 ft. from N. to S.   A curious
feature was that the heap was half and half of stone and earth.   Nothing
in the way of a definite burial was found, but many objects occurred in a
thin layer going under the greater part of the area of the tumulus.   The
bronze and iron objects were in too bad a state to preserve, and the
clay vessels were all broken.   The Greek objects, e.g. a little glass amphora
of variegated streaks, and bronze reliefs under the handles of a deep
bronze dish, would make the date of the deposit about the last century B.C.
No objects suggested Roman times.   The most beautiful thing was an
elaborate buckle in three parts, adorned with knots and enamelled rosettes
(f. 127).   There were more gold plates, and imitations of them in the shape
of Medusa heads of gilt plaster.   But the most interesting detail was the

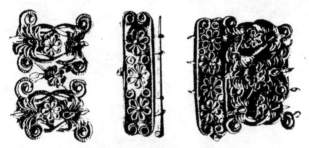

FIG. 127.   Buckle from Kurdzhips.   *CR.* 1896, p. 62, f. 295.   ⅓.

occurrence of two round repoussé gold plates, fixed to large bronze roundlets.
On one was a lion curled up, on the other a tiger or lioness (f. 126).   In
the former were two turquoises set and holes for them in the latter.   The
workmanship, and especially the manner of treating turquoise, recalls the
plates from Siberia, whose affinities with the Scythic are undoubted but
difficult to define.   This was the first appearance of such work so far SW.
but it has again been found at Zubov's Barrow, and elsewhere in the district[1].

Kostromskája.

In the same country, at Kostromskaja, Veselovskij excavated a very
interesting barrow[2], see plan and section (f. 128).   In the centre of the barrow
was erected a kind of tabernacle as follows.   Four thickish posts were driven
into the ground.   Four great beams were laid about them so as to form
a square of 3·20 m. = 10 ft. 6 in.; within these, along each side, were put
six vertical posts of less thickness; and outside, opposite to the spaces
between these last, five such sloping up so as to meet high above the
middle.   In the square thus formed were found the dead man's belongings
about 7 ft. from the original surface.   In the S. part was an iron scale
hauberk with copper scales on the shoulders and along the lower margin.

[1] v. p. 230, f. 132 and p. 232 n. 6.   [2] *CR.* 1897, p. 11.

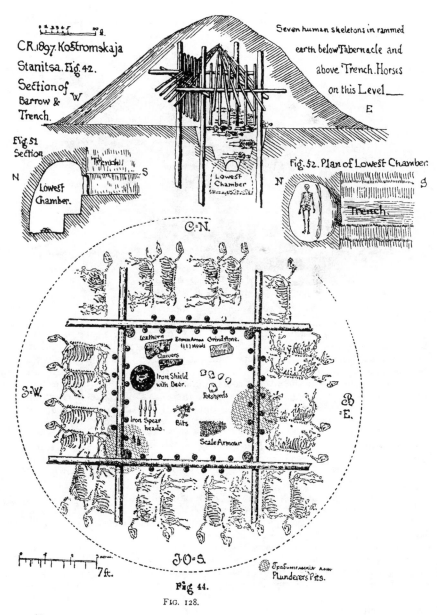

CR.1897. Kostromskaja
Stanitsa. Fig. 42.
Section of
Barrow &
Trench.
W

Seven human skeletons in rammed
earth below Tabernacle and
above Trench. Horses
on this Level ——
E

Fig. 51
Section
N   S

Lowest
Chamber.

Trench

Lowest
Chamber

Fig. 52. Plan of Lowest Chamber.
N   S
Trench.

C. N.

Leathern   Bronze Arrow   Grindstone.
Quivers   Heads.

Iron Shield
with Deer.
Potsherds
S. W.
Iron Spear
heads.   Bits
Scale Armour
&
E.

7 ft.

J. O. S.

Грабительские ямы
Plunderers' Pits.

Fig 44.
FIG. 128.

To the w. lay four iron spear-heads; N. of these a thin round iron shield, adorned in the centre with a cast deer, like the Kul Oba deer (f. 129). In

FIG. 129.   Golden deer from Kostromskaja.   *CR.* 1897, p. 13, f. 46.   ⅜.

the NW. corner two leather quivers, one worked with beads, and by them bronze arrow-heads. In the NE. corner lay a big sharpening stone broken into two pieces, all about pottery purposely broken, and in one place several copper and iron bits. Outside the square were 22 horse skeletons arranged in pairs, with the legs of one under the body of the next, except that at the two outside angles to the north there was only one horse each. Some of the horses had bits in their mouths. The tabernacle seems to have been daubed over with clay and the whole structure set on fire and then the earth heaped upon it. The square space had been dug out to 7 ft. below the surface and then filled in with earth rolled hard. In this earth were found 13 skeletons, but nothing with them. The pit ended in two steps on each side going longways N. and S., so that the bottom of all was a ditch a couple of feet wide. On each step lay a skeleton. At the N. end of the ditch stood two small slabs of stone that closed the way into a small chamber going down with two steps again, this time E. and W. In the chamber there was just room for a skeleton lying at full length. Nothing was found with it.

No doubt this burial is very unlike most of the Scythic type, but the deer is a distinct link and the ideas expressed by this ritual are very similar to those expressed by that we have found in Scythic graves. The principle of breaking objects or burning them so as to despatch them to the other world is more logically carried out than usual. The slaughter of men and horses is greater than any we have met, though we shall

meet a worse horse sacrifice in the next tomb dealt with. The bareness of all the human remains and the ingenious arrangement of the dead man's grave-chamber almost suggest that an attempt was made to secure a quiet resting place by withdrawing the body from the valuables which experience had found to tempt the sacrilegious.

Ulskij Barrow.

A barrow excavated by Professor Veselovskij in the same district of Majkop, where the Ul runs into the Laba, yielded a yet more astonishing

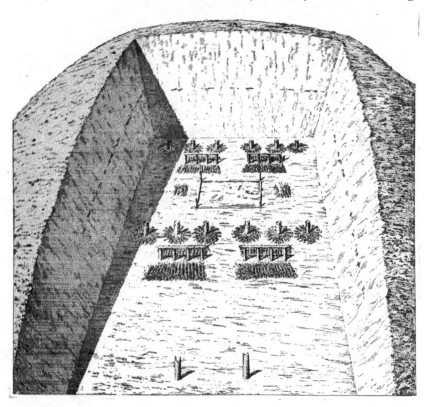

FIG. 130. Diagram of Ulskij barrow. *CR.* 1898, p. 30.

example of sacrificing horses[1]. The barrow was 15 m. high and had a long south slope, but its shape had been disfigured by a battery erected upon it

[1] *CR.* 1898, p. 29.

during the Russian conquest. A trench 25 m. by 60 m. was cut through it (v. f. 130). This shewed that the barrow had been partly heaped up and then more than fifty horses laid upon its surface, and these had been covered with another mass of earth. The barrow had been plundered, but in the plunderers' hole were found a gold plaque of Scythic style with griffins and deer[1], fragments of copper cauldrons, Greek vases and scale armour very similar to that found at Kostromskája. But the plunderers had not destroyed the general disposition of the grave; first two thick stakes had been driven in 5·35 m. (17 ft. 6 in.) apart, making as it were an entrance gate, 15 m. (49 ft.) beyond were two rows of posts in one line, each row joined by bars across, leaving the 5·35 m. avenue in the middle. On each side of each of these fences lay 18 horses with their tails to the bars (72 in all); 4·25 m. (15 ft.) further on were three posts on each side of the central avenue, and about each post, radiating with their heads away from the posts, again 18 horses (108 in all); 4·25 m. beyond was an oblong, set crosswise (7·45 m. × 5·70 m. = 24 ft. 6 in. × 18 ft. 6 in.). As at Kostromskaja there were perpendicular posts at the corners and four horizontal beams, and along the sides holes (4 and 6 respectively) for smaller rods. Evidently here was such a tabernacle as in the former case. But this had been plundered. At each side of the oblong were the skeletons of two bulls and some horse bones lying in confusion. Beyond in the same order were the fences with horses and the posts with them radiating therefrom. The horses near the oblong had bits in their mouths.

Thus we arrive at something over four hundred horses sacrificed at this one burial. The plundering of the grave prevents us knowing how many human beings shared the same fate. The distances given above appear to have been set out on a standard of 1·07 m., a little over 43 in. This was divided into three parts of about 1 ft. 2½ in. The measurements are all nearly divisible by these amounts. Another barrow close by had also been plundered, there too were horses' skeletons arranged in rows 2·15 m. apart shewing the same unit. In this tomb were found fragments of a black figured vase giving a presumption of an early date, making it the more regrettable that the grave had been ransacked[2].

Vozdvízhenskaja.

Among various other interesting barrows in this district should be mentioned that at Vozdvizhenskaja dug up by Veselovskij in 1899[3]. Here the original interment was that of a single skeleton doubled up and stained dark red; he was buried without any objects. Above him lay four skeletons also stained and doubled up, one of them apart, the others on a space paved with cobbles. By these were an earthen pot and a spear, palstaff, axe, chisel and pin, all of copper. In the upper part of the barrow was another stained skeleton and not far from it a complete Scythic interment.

---

[1] *CR.* 1898, p. 301, f. 42.
[2] *CR.* 1898, p. 32, ff. 47 a and b; another black-figured vase in a plundered tomb at Voronezhskaja,

CR. 1903, p. 73, f. 138.
[3] *CR.* 1899, p. 44, ff. 67—72 and pl. 2.

Under a wooden tabernacle once supported by four posts at the corners,
covered by a pall with stamped gold plates, lay a man's skeleton.   By his
head was the usual iron and copper scale hauberk and iron arrow-heads,
on his breast a golden brooch with a large carnelian and other adornments;

FIG. 131.   Diagram of Vozdvizhenskaja barrow.   *CR.* 1899, p. 44, Pl. 2.

under his heels two plaques with a six-headed snake attacking a wild goat,
on his right two iron swords, a hone, a mirror, an alabastron, at his belt
a dagger of the type suggesting the Siberian.   By his knees were found
tinsel threads, perhaps a fringe.   On his left one or two vessels of silver
and clay and glass, further down two pair of iron bits with wheel- and S-
shaped psalia adorned with gold and an iron brooch with a gold plate in

the form of a curled up animal with settings for turquoises.   Along one side
stood three copper vessels, a big cauldron upside down so that the handles
had got bent in, another such, smaller and right way up, and a large copper
basin.   The glass shews their burial not to be very early.   The whole barrow
is interesting as an example of the same tumulus being used several times.

Zubov's Barrows.

The last find of this type in this district that need be described is that
made in 1899 by the peasants of Zubov's farm[1] 14 m. E. of Tenginskaja
between the Kuban and the Zelenchuk.   Two barrows were excavated.
A large proportion of the booty was secured for the Hermitage.   In Barrow
No. 1 by the skeleton there lay seven roundels of gold with a large circle
of many coloured glass in the centre in a border set with small coloured
stones and pastes and adorned with gold wire soldered in patterns on the
surface, rather like that from Akhtanizovka (p. 215, f. 117) but better.   These
were ornaments of a strap or belt as is shewn by a flat loop at the back.
They were of Greek work and would seem to belong to the time about the

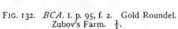

FIG. 132.   *BCA.* I. p. 95, f. 2.   Gold Roundel.   FIG. 133.   *BCA.* I. p. 96, f. 10.   Zubov's Farm.
        Zubov's Farm.   ¼.   Bronze cauldron.   ⅙.

Christian era when such many coloured jewels had become fashionable.
Five other roundels were of pure Siberian type with monsters and characteristic incrustations: they too adorned a strap (f. 132).   There were also
the end pieces of the strap and buttons belonging.   On the arms were
two open gold bracelets, on the breast a hemispherical cup of glass, by the

[1] *BCA.* I. pp. 94—103, ff. 1—31 and pl. II.

feet a Scythic cauldron (f. 133), by the head a copper jug (to look at it might be English XVIIth century work), along the side an iron sword with a gold hilt, on the left a scale hauberk (f. 134), silver plaques, iron bits with curious psalia overlaid with gold (f. 135), a large stone hone, an earthen jug and iron

FIG. 134. *BCA.* I. p. 97, f. 15. Zubov's Farm.
Bronze armour. ⅓.

FIG. 135. *BCA.* I. p. 98, f. 16. Zubov's Farm.
Iron bit with gold mounts. ⅓.

FIG. 136.

FIG. 137. *BCA.* I. p. 99, f. 18. Phiale from Zubov's Farm. ⅘.

arrow-heads. The most interesting object was a silver φιάλη μεσόμφαλος about 8 in. across (ff. 136, 137). Upon the boss is a coiled serpent, about it "*stabornament*," round the hollow thirteen deer heads facing in relief, about the edge the inscription

ΑΠΟΛΛΩΝΟ΢ΗΓΕΜΟΝΟ΢ΕΙΜΙΤΟΜΦΑ΢Ι

’Απόλλωνος ‘Ηγέμονος εἰμὶ τὸμ Φάσι. "Apollo the Leader's am I who is at Phasis[1]." The work of the bowl is very similar to that found in the second of the Seven Brothers (p. 209, f. 107), and referred by Stephani to the early vth century. The inscription belongs to the end of the century or the beginning of the ivth. What was the temple of Apollo the Leader at Phasis we know not, but how a bowl belonging to it came into this tomb is no mystery, when we think that this Kuban district is the hinterland of that very coast whose piratical inhabitants are described by Strabo (xi. ii. 12).

In the second barrow the tomb was covered with wood: the earrings, pendants, bracelets, beads, mirror and especially three small jugs, two adorned with a little animal crawling up the side by way of a handle, and containing rouge and white paint, make it appear that it was a woman's though she had a miniature copper-headed spear. Besides there were glass and earthen vessels and gold plates for sewing on to dresses.

It is a pity that the excavation was not made by an expert. For Kieseritzky[2] wishes to use the phiale to date the roundels as of the vith century B.C. and supposes that an early barrow and one of Roman date have had their contents mixed, but the phiale is a chance survival and nothing else in the find is contemporaneous with it. The cases of the archaic lamp, tripod and stand from Ust-Labinskaja[3] and perhaps of the black-figured vases (p. 228 n. 2) seem similar.

In this Kuban district a more or less Scythic culture seems to have continued later than in the west of what is now South Russia. This is what we might expect if the Alans are indeed much the same as the Sarmatians of whom we hear in earlier times and the Ossetes of our own day. The tombs of the first three centuries A.D.[4] often introduced into the barrows of red skeletons (p. 143) are characterised by the substitution of Hellenistic or Roman industrial products[5] for the more artistic Greek work; at the same time communication with Central Asia was kept up and we find specimens of the Siberian style, with its beasts and turquoise or garnet incrustations[6] also a Parthian coin c. 43 A.D.[7], so that the mixture of things at Zubov's barrows need not awake suspicion.

[1] The inscription can hardly be meant for an iambic trimeter as the writer in *BCA*. suggests, the trochee in the second foot, the dactyl in the third, and the spondee at the end make it intolerable.
[2] *Arch. Anz.* 1901, p. 55.
[3] *CR*. 1902, p. 79, ff. 166—168; *Arch. Anz.* 1903, p. 82, ff. 1, 2.
[4] N. I. Veselovskij, "Barrows of the Kuban district in the time of Roman dominion in the Northern Caucasus," *Bulletin of the XIIth Archaeological Congress*, Kharkov, 1902; and the accounts of his excavations at Kazanskaja, Tiflisskaja, Ust-Labinskaja, Armavir and Nekrasovskaja in

CR. 1901, pp. 66—86; 1902, pp. 65—91; 1903, pp. 61—70; 1905, pp. 73—75: *Arch. Anz.* l. c.; 1906, p. 109; 1907, p. 126.
[5] e.g. silver cups, *CR*. 1902, pp. 70, 78, ff. 143, 165; white bronze basin with copper *emblema*, *CR*. 1905, p. 74, f. 95; *Arch. Anz.* 1906, p. 111, f. 1; vessel in form of ram such as is common at Olbia, *CR*. 1902, p. 67, f. 136, of a duck (?), p. 72, f. 152; *Arch. Anz.* 1902, p. 83, f. 3.
[6] e.g. roundels, *CR*. 1902, pp. 67, 77, 78, 82, ff. 139, 140, 161, 164, 177; figures of rams, p. 87, f. 196; 1903, p. 62, f. 96; v. inf. pp. 277, 279, f. 205.
[7] *BCA*. xxxii. App. p. 99, Stavropol.

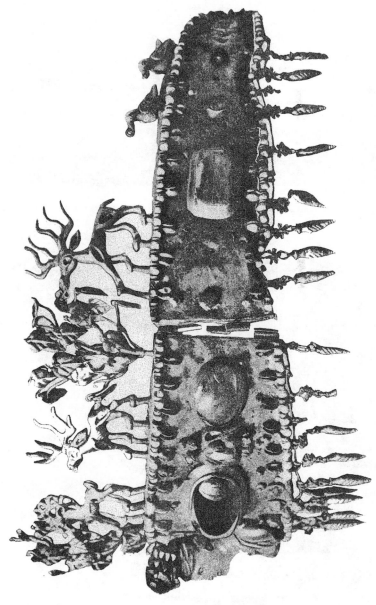

FIG. 138. Diadem in gold set with a bust of a Roman empress in chalcedony and large amethysts and garnets. Novocherkassk. *KTR.* p. 489, f. 441.

FIG. 139. Collar in gold encrusted with coral and topaz from Novocherkassk. *KTR.* p. 491, f. 443. $\frac{6}{7}$.

FIG. 140. Side view of circular box from Novocherkassk. *KTR.* p. 492, f. 445. $\frac{1}{1}$.

FIGS. 141, 142. Gold bottle from Novocherkassk, side and top. *KTR.* p. 493, ff. 447, 448. $\frac{7}{9}$.

FIG. 143. Gold strip encrusted with light and dark blue and green. Treasure of Novocherkassk. *KTR.* p. 494, f. 450.

These objects were not merely imported as is shewn by the well-known Novocherkassk treasure. The main bulk of this find is in the Siberian style, but in the front of the principal piece, a crown (f. 138), is the bust of a Roman empress in chalcedony of the iind or iiird century A.D. and attached to its lower rim are pendants after the fashion of those found in Panticapaean work of about that time. Also the work cannot very well be much later because in the following centuries the so-called Gothic jewelry was dominant in these regions (v. pp. 280—282).

This treasure was found in 1864 near Novocherkassk on the lower Don and included the crown mentioned above, a collar (or diadem, f. 139) even more Siberian in style, a spiral bracelet ending in animals, two little boxes (f. 140) and a scent bottle (ff. 141, 142, of the same shape as that found in a tomb of a Bosporan queen at Glinishche near Kerch[1]) adorned with beasts, another in the shape of a feline with a body of agate, a statuette of Eros (iind cent. A.D.), some little gold plates recalling typical Scythic fashions, a slip of gold attached to a chain and encrusted with bright blue, turquoise and pink, recalling Central Asia in colouring and the "Gothic" style in make (f. 143), some gold vases, one with a handle formed of an animal (f. 144) and an object like a spectacle-case attached to a chain and adorned with animals' heads[2]. The circumstances of this find render it

FIG. 144. Golden cup from Novocherkassk. *KTR.* p. 495, f. 452. ⅓.

doubtful whether these objects were buried with a dead man or were a *cache.*

Similar in shape and style to the cup here figured and found in the same neighbourhood is a cup in the Uvarov Collection inscribed

ΞΗΒΑΝΟΚΟΥΤΑΡΟΥΛΑϹΕΠΟΙΕΙ ⚡ΜΗ

in dotted letters: Xebanocus is the name of the owner rather than that of

[1] *ABC.* XXIV. 25, v. inf. Ch. .XII. end, f. 326; cf. a plainer example in *CR.* 1902, p. 83, f. 184, from Ust-Labinskaja.

[2] *KTR.* pp. 488—496, ff. 441—454 gives all these except the Eros and the vases. Maskell, *Russian Art*, p. 83 sqq.

the maker's father: MH is more probably 48 than a misspelling of μϵ and so ⸓ would seem to stand for χρυσοῦ. It is all very obscure, but we learn from it that a thing of this style was made for a Sarmate or Alan (cf. some seventy Sarmatian names in -ακος in *IosPE*.) by a man who wrote Greek.

Vettersfelde.

There is one find which belongs to the class of Scythic antiquities but was made in a region so far distant from the localities where Scythic remains are usually to be looked for, that it naturally comes in at the end of this survey although in date it may be almost the earliest of the rich Scythic equipments[1]. In October 1882 there were ploughed up near Vettersfelde in Lower Lusatia and acquired for the Antiquarium in Berlin the fragments of a great jar and the complete equipment of a Scythian chief. It included the centre ornament of his shield, a fish 41 cm. × 15 cm. made of pale gold repoussé and covered with animals in relief (f. 146), a gold breastplate 17 cm. square formed of four roundels each with a boss in the middle and animals in relief all round it, set about a fifth smaller roundel or boss (f. 145. 1), a gold plate to cover the sheath of a dagger of the typical Scythic shape with a projection on one side (f. 147), the handle of the said dagger as usual covered with a gold plate and shewing the characteristic Scytho-Siberian heartshaped guard, a golden pendant, earring (f. 148), arm-ring, neck-ring, chain, knife sheath with remains of the iron blade, gold ring, small stone wedge set in gold, a hone bored through and set in gold (f. 145. 2), and some fragments. Professor Furtwängler has treated these things in a masterly fashion and they are all duly illustrated by him. All of them have their analogues in the South Russian finds except the breastplate, but such an object is quite in keeping with the tastes of people who covered themselves with gold plates of various sizes. The earring is declared by Hadaczek to be of an Ionian type and earlier than any found in South Russia and the knife sheath is identical with the one from Tomakovka figured on p. 158.

The fish is the most remarkable of these things. It corresponds in style (v. p. 264) and destination to the Kul Oba deer, and Furtwängler's decision that they are both shield ornaments has been satisfactorily borne out by the finding of the Kostromskaja deer still in place upon remains of the shield, only this was round instead of long shaped as had been supposed on the evidence of the Kul Oba vase[2].

The inventory of the find is typically that of the personal effects in the Scythic tombs of kings except that the horse trappings are absent, and of course the women's things. The whole may be dated rather earlier than the older objects from Kul Oba and put in the first decades of the vth century.

---

[1] *XLIII*ᵗᵉˢ *Winckelmannsfestprogramm*, A. Furtwängler, Der Goldfund von Vettersfelde, Berlin, 1883. I wish I could still express to Professor Furtwängler my gratitude for his kind permission to reproduce his pictures. Fig. 147 I owe to Mr Dalton and the authorities of the British Museum.

[2] supra pp. 203, 226 ; *CR.* 1897, p. 12. V. Gardthausen's view that the fish was a Tessera Hospitalis is an extraordinary instance of the errors of even famous scholars, *Rhein. Mus.* XXXIX. p. 317

How these things including the brittle whetstone found their way so far from home without loss is unexplained.   Save for some little damage by

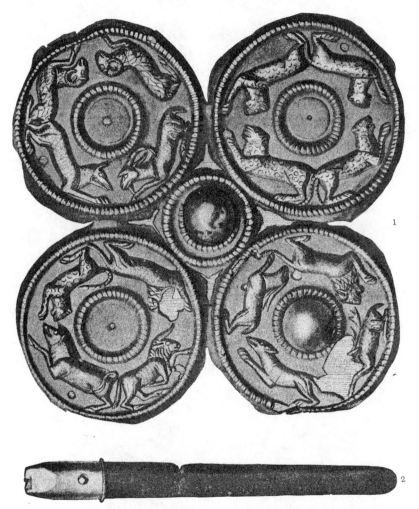

FIG. 145.   1. Gold breastplate (?) from Vettersfelde.   2. Hone set in gold.   Furtwängler, pl. II.   ⅕.

fire and rust they are as good as new.   Furtwängler guesses that their coming may have to do with the Scythians' northward retreat before Darius.

FIG. 146. Gold fish from Vettersfelde. Furtwängler, pl. I.
Rather less than half size.

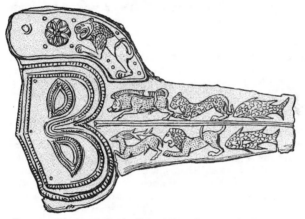

Vettersfelde, I.5.
Gold Earring.

FIG. 147. Gold dagger sheath. Vettersfelde. Pl. III. 1. After Dalton,
Oxus Treasure, p. 33, f. 22. ½.   FIG. 148. $\frac{9}{11}$.

Kámennya Báby.

With the tombs of the Scythic type many investigators have
been inclined to connect the mysterious stone figures known
as *Kámennya Báby*—stone women—rude figures hewn out of
blocks of stone and almost always representing women, rarely
nude, more often wearing a short skirt and jacket and a kind
of pointed hat with a veil or hood hanging from it and the hair
hanging down in a thick plait behind. The dress is sometimes
shewn in some detail and an elaborate necklace is a common
feature[1]. The face is round and rather Mongolian in aspect,
but the execution is too rude to let this be any criterion.
The men's dress sometimes distantly recalls that of a Roman
soldier. Nearly all the figures agree in holding a cup rather
like a dicebox before them. This does not seem to be for the
receipt of the offerings of the living because often it is not
made concave on the top. A very rare form belonging apparently to the same class is a statue in a lying posture as it
were swathed in a winding sheet[2]. These figures, which have
been objects of a superstitious reverence till recent times, used
to be common about the Steppes, frequently occurring upon
Scythic barrows, for instance such famous ones as those at
Alexandropol and Chertomlyk, Zubov's, Melgunov's and others.
Further their limit of distribution is just that of the Scytho-
Siberian culture from Galicia across South Russia to the basins
of the Obj and the Jenisei, in the Crimea and on the Kuban.

FIG. 149. *CR.*
1895, p. 76, f.
199. Murza
Bek, Crimea.
Kamennaja
Baba. 6 ft.
8 in. high.

[1] M. Guthrie, *A Tour through the Taurida*,
London, 1802, pl. II. p. 406; P. S. Pallas, *Southern
Provinces*, I. p. 444.
    [2] Zubov's Barrow, *CR.* 1900, p. 39, f. 100, cf.
N. I. Veselovskij, "A New Type of Kámennya

Báby" in *Bulletin of XIIth Russian Arch. Congr.*
(Kharkov), 1902, p. 222, and "So-called Kámennya
Báby" in *Messenger (Věstnik) of Archaeology ana
History*, Pt XVII. St P. 1905.

Professor Lappo-Danilevskij[1] shews that they cluster most thickly just about the bend of the Dnêpr, just in the land Gerrhus. This would all suggest that there was a real connection between the Scythic tomb and the statue upon its summit.

It is not important that Herodotus does not mention the setting up of such figures; the golden statue erected to Zarinaea their queen by the Sacae[2] might be a glorified "*baba*" but is not enough to prove others having really been set up by Sacae. However Rubruck says distinctly (v. supra p. 89) that the Polovtsy or Cumans set up figures holding cups before them[3], and cases occur of "*báby*" being found upon barrows of the mediaeval nomads, e.g. at Torskaja Sloboda, district of Kupjansk, government of Kharkov (Veselovskij, l.c.). Further in the Orkhon inscriptions very similar figures are designated as *balbals*, memorial statues.

It seems then clear that *kámennya báby* were set up by a mediaeval Turkic tribe, presumably the Cumans as Rubruck says so, and this is the opinion of Tiesenhausen and Veselovskij the best authorities on the relations of Russia with the Orient. Anyone setting up such a statue would naturally choose a commanding position such as is afforded by a high barrow. The coincidence in area of their distribution with that of Scythic remains is due to the fact that, as has been already remarked, the range of the Cumans was limited by the same physical conditions as that of the Scyths when they were the dominant nomad power. We cannot however assert that the Scyths set up no such figures, since *a priori* they might be expected to agree in this as in other customs with the later nomads, but there is no specimen to which we can point as probably being Scythic.

---

[1] *Scythian Antt.* p. 475 sqq. where he quotes the literature of the subject, esp. Piskarev's list in *TRAS.* (old series), Vol. III. pp. 205—220 (I have not seen this), and Burachkov's sensible account in *Trans. Od. Soc.* IX. pp. 65—70.

[2] Ctesias, fr. 25 (Müller, p. 43) ap. Diod. Sic. II.

xxxiv. 5.

[3] Spitsyn, *TRAS.* X. (Russo-Slav. section, 1898), p. 342, figures a male baba from Vêrnyj (Semi-rêchensk) bearing a cup of well-known mediaeval (XIIIth cent.) Mongol type.

CHAPTER IX.

SIBERIA AND SURROUNDING COUNTRIES.

In the foregoing pages mention has been made of the resemblances between the culture I have called Scythic and that of early inhabitants of Siberia. These resemblances are so great that it is impossible to treat the archaeology of South Russia without touching that of Siberia. This may be called a case of explaining *ignotum per ignotius*, but in a sense the ethnology of Siberia is less open to question than that of the Euxine steppes, inasmuch as the north of Asia is not exposed to invasions from so many quarters as Eastern Europe and is inhabited by peoples who, whatever their mutual differences, have more ethnological affinity than those we find side by side at the junction of the two continents.

The best account of the chief forms of tombs in Siberia and of the civilisations to which they correspond is given by Dr W. Radloff[1].

Radloff describes various types of graves in Siberia, of which the most important division is into graves marked by barrows and graves marked with stones mostly set in rectangles. In the basins of the Irtysh, Tobol and Obj and again in the Kirgiz steppe and in south-west Siberia we mostly have mounds larger or smaller. In the river valleys of the Altai, on the banks of the Jeniséi and in the Abakan steppe are found the stone graves, as well as over the Chinese border in Mongolia. In the Altai and on the Bukhtarma we find cairns of stone.

These graves may be referred to four epochs:

(i)   All the stone graves in the vale of the Jenisei and the Altai and many of the mounds of the Kirgiz steppe belong to the Copper or Bronze age.

(ii)   Most of the barrows and big cairns belong to the earlier Iron age.

(iii)   The smaller barrows called Kirgiz graves are of the later Iron age.

(iv)   These shade into barrows which contain even XVIIth century coins and modern Russian objects.

In graves of the first period are found many weapons and tools of cast copper and bronze, they have nearly all been plundered so that it is very rare to come upon gold. Similar tools are found in old gold and copper workings in the Altai mountains, and there is no doubt that these people worked the metals themselves and had attained very considerable

---

[1] *Aus Sibirien*, Leipzig, 1884, Vol. II. chap. VII. pp. 68—143; trans. into Russian and re-published by Count A. Bobrinskoj in *TRAS*. VII. (1895) p. 147 sqq. Dr Radloff is now publishing for the Archaeological Commission a fully illus-trated work on the Antiquities of Siberia. *Materials for the Archaeology of Russia*, Nos. III. v. xv., form Vol. I., and Vol. II. begins with XXVII. See also D. Klements, *Antiquities of the Minusinsk Museum, Objects of the Metal Ages*, Tomsk, 1886: a cata-logue with very good introduction and with illustra-tions. These latter are rather superseded by those in Martin, F. R., *L'âge du Bronze au Musée de Minoussinsk*, Stockholm, 1892.

Siberia

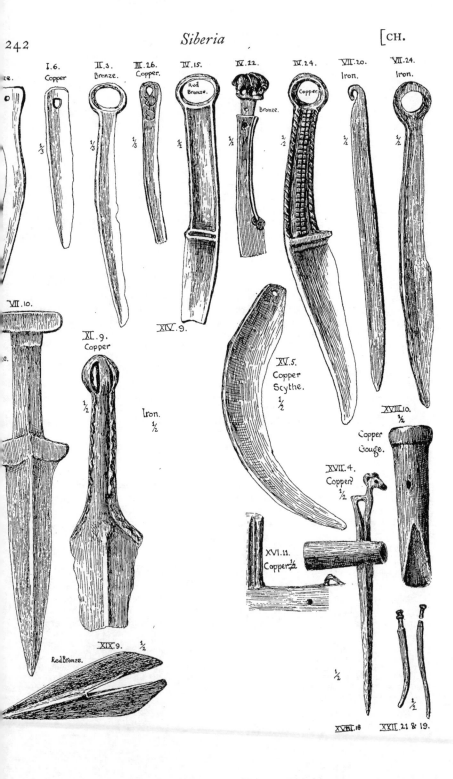

I.6.
Copper

II.3.
Bronze.

III.26.
Copper.

IV.15.
Red Bronze.

IV.22.
Bronze.

IV.24.
Copper

VII.20.
Iron.

VII.24.
Iron.

VII.10.

XI.9.
Copper

XIV.9.

Iron.

XV.5.
Copper
Scythe.

XVIII.10.

Copper
Gouge.

XVII.4.
Copper?

XVI.11.
Copper

XIX.9.

Red Bronze.

XVII.16.

XXII.21 & 19.

II.4.
Red
Bronze.
½.

III.5. Red Bronze. ½.

Radloff,
Siberian Antiquities,

Vol. II = Mat. 27.

Axe heads from Upper

Jenisêj.

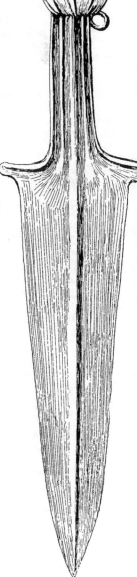

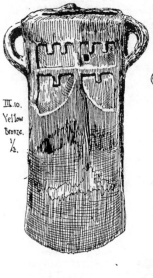

III.10.
Yellow
Bronze.
½.

VI.3.

VI.9. ½.
Yellow Bronze.

IV.7.
Yellow
Bronze.
⅛.

Bronze Knife & Dagger from

skill. The old workings consist of simple shafts not more than fifty feet deep and indifferently propped up. Working even to such a depth was dangerous and skeletons of miners have been found with pickaxes and sacks to hold the ore. Miners seem to have been in high regard, for Radloff figures a copper statuette of one[1] and also wherever these people lived we find elegant models of pickaxes, too delicate for actual use and apparently serving as ornaments or insignia[2]. Their tools are found in the gold washings as well as in the shafts (called Chud mines). Smelting furnaces have also been found in the Altai, and everywhere about the Abakan, Jenisei and upper Obj we have fragments of copper such as are trimmed off castings. Their bronze, when they made bronze, is of very great hardness, and their castings hardly ever have flaws in them, although they cast cauldrons up to 75 lb. in weight. Well finished and rough tools are found together in the same grave. The chief objects found comprise knives and daggers but few arrowheads or spear-heads. Axe-heads especially the double-looped type (f. 151, cf. p. 261) are common, and pickaxes both serviceable and ornamental. They

Bronze Objects from about Minusinsk: from F.R.Martin.

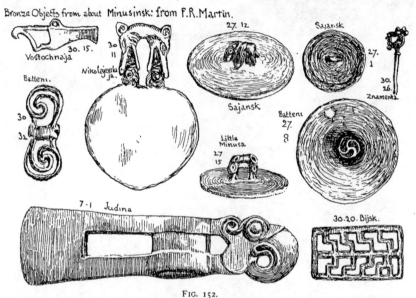

30. 15. Vostochnaja
Battem.
30
32
Nikolajevskaja.
7·1 Judina
27. 12
Sajansk
Little Minusa
27 15
Sajansk
Battem
27
8
Sajansk
27. 1
30. 26. Znamenka
30.20. Bijsk.

FIG. 152.

also made scythes and sickles and copper cauldrons. For their own adorn-ment they had earrings of gold and copper, carnelian and metal beads, beast-headed pins, belt pieces, and disks with loops behind serving either for mirrors or for ornaments. The pottery is very rude and falls far below[3] the skill shewn in metal work. They were acquainted with weaving, but

[1] *Aus Sib.* II. pl. IV. 1 and [2] on fig. 172, p. 251.   [2] *Sib. Ant.* I. xvi. 11, xvii. 4 on fig. 150.
[3] v. Klements, op. cit. pl. XIX.

FIG. 153. *Mat.* III.=*Sib. Ant.* Vol. I. p. 12, ii. 18. Yellow bronze knife. ¼.

FIG. 154. *Mat.* III.=*Sib. Ant.* Vol. I. p. 10, ii. 10. Copper. ½.

FIG. 155. *Mat.* III.=*Sib. Ant.* Vol. II. p. 18, iii. 9.
Golden bronze plated with tin. ¼.

FIG. 156. *CR.* 1900, p. 123, f. 275.
Bronze axe-head. Angara. ½.

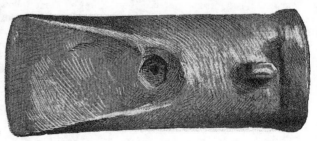

FIG. 157. *Mat.* XXVII.=*Siberian
Antiquities*, Vol. II. p. 2, i. 3ᵃ.
Stone mould for axe. ⅔.

FIG. 158. *Mat.* XXVII.=*Sib. Ant.* Vol. II. p. 33. Bronze axe-head. ¼.

their stuffs were also coarse. They do not appear to have kept cattle, but they do appear to have engaged in agriculture for they have left many copper sickles about the fields, and these fields often have traces of irrigation works. The bone arrow-heads found with their objects and their love of beasts in their ornament suggest that they were hunters as well. They do not seem to have been nomads in any sense. So they had few horse-trappings, and the rock carvings ascribed to them shew the men all on foot.

But it is their metal work which makes them interesting. They appear to have originated many types that were afterwards spread far and wide. Their knives (v. the series on f. 150), in their simplest form mere slips of copper, as it were long narrow triangles with a hole towards the base, were improved into excellent instruments with a well formed ring at one end, sometimes in the form of an animal, a firm handle separated from the blade by a well marked fillet and projection, and a blade bent forward so that the edge made an obtuse angle with the haft. Such a knife recalls irresistibly the Chinese knife which afterwards shortened down into the round cash[1]; and so P. Reinecke[2] thinks it an imitation of the Chinese, but just as possibly it came into China by some early raid from the north (v. p. 91).

Then the bronze cauldron upon a conical base round which the fire was built, a type characteristically Scythic, was made by these people; they alone made the same shape in pottery so they were probably the originators of it. They also seem to have invented the disc with a loop in the middle of the back, which grew, as it appears, into the mirror used over all northern Asia and in Scythia and the Caucasus. This mirror Reinecke (loc. cit.) also calls a Chinese invention, but it was only introduced into China about 140 B.C. along with other western products. Together with this new form of mirror the Chinese began to use a new name for mirrors with an ideogram suggesting metal[3].

f. 19.　　f. 14

Klements. Minusinsk Museum Pl XIX. Clay Pots.

FIG. 159.

The Chinese even followed their models in decorating these mirrors, the loop being formed of the body of an animal just as with the mirrors and knife handles of the Jenisei people (v. f. 152).

Furthermore these early inhabitants of the Jenisei developed a dagger with a curious heart-shaped guard and a well defined knob at the end of the haft, which type is found in Scythic tombs and on the monuments of

---

[1] Cf. the specimen in the British Museum, on f. 151; Ridgeway, *Metallic Currency*, p. 157, f. 21.

[2] *Zt. f. Ethnol.*, XXIX. 1897, pp. 140 sqq., "Ueber einige Beziehungen der Alterthümer Chinas zu denen des Skytho-Sibirischen Völkerkreises." But cf. same shape arisen independently in Iseo lake-dwelling, T. E. Peet, *Stone and Bronze Ages in Italy*, v. 3, and a knife from Nordenford, Bavaria, in the Maximilian Museum, Augsburg, kindly brought

to my notice by Mr Reginald A. Smith of the British Museum.

[3] Prof. H. A. Giles, *China and the Chinese*, New York, 1902, p. 132; cf. *Po-ku-t'u-lu*, in which such mirrors are figured; Hirth, *Fremde Einflüsse*, ff. 2—16. I am much indebted to Professor Giles for the information about mirrors and for help in consulting Chinese archaeological works.

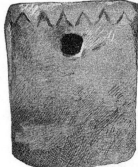

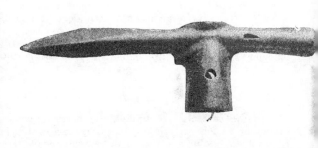

FIG. 160. *Mat.* XXVII.=*Sib. Ant.* Vol. II. p. 4, i. 6². Copper Axe-head. ⅟₁.

FIG. 161. *CR.* 1900, p. 123, f. 276. Bronze pick from Angara, Siberia. ⅟₂

FIG. 162. *Mat.* XV.=*Sib. Ant.* Vol. II. p. 82, xv. 3. Copper Siberian scythe. ½.

FIG. 163. *Mat.* XV. *Sib. Ant.*, Vol. I. p. 131. Bronze bit from Siberia. ½.

FIG. 164.
Mat. V.=*Sib. Ant.*
Vol. I. p. 31, v. 8.
Copper knife. ⅟₁.

FIG. 165.
Mat. III.=*Sib. Ant.*
Vol. I. p. 22, iii. 23.
Reddish bronze knife.

Persepolis[1]. But the interest of these objects is not merely in the types of their weapons but in the style of their ornament. Besides zigzags and simple patterns of straight lines they developed a beast style remarkable for its simplicity and naturalism. They pourtray chiefly bears (ff. 150, 152), deer (f. 165), and argali or ibex (ff. 166—168, 172) and have no tendency to the fantastic combinations of incongruities found in western Asiatic and also in Scythic work.

Early Iron Age. Katanda.

In the next class of graves, the barrows, we find a different culture belonging to the early iron age. The barrows as usual occur in groups. In such a group on the river Katanda not far from where it falls into the Katunja a tributary of the Obj, Radloff[2] came upon many tombs with interments of men, women and horses, and one in particular yielded very important remains.

The barrow was heaped up of stones and 7 ft. high by 100 ft. in diameter. Attempts had been made to plunder it and in the heap were found in disorder bones of at least six horses, human bones likewise, six iron bits, various iron and bone arrow-heads, an iron spade, an iron and a copper knife, an iron sabre, a mass of blue glass beads and two heart-shaped carnelians from earrings. In the midst of the heap was found the grave pit, 14 ft. long, filled up with big stones and earth; 2 ft. 6 in. below the original surface of the ground the excavators were stopped by coming to earth permanently frozen: water meanwhile trickled into the excavation from all sides and continuance of the work became very difficult: the earth had to be melted with fires and the water and mud baled out. Two fathoms deep they came upon bones of men and horses and also found an iron bit with large rings. Further down were the remains of an oblong erection of larch wood, of which the roof had been destroyed by former plunderers. Across this building went two thick beams and upon one of them was a big bundle of leather enclosed in a rind of ice six inches thick. The bundle turned out to be a kind of coat of silken stuff, much like a dress coat in shape, lined with sable and edged with leather and little gold plates. The first plunderer had not penetrated beyond this level, at which a layer of birch bark covered the whole tomb. In this was another garment of ermine dyed green and red and adorned with gold buttons and plates; this was likewise rolled up into a bundle and encased in ice. It had a high collar and very narrow sleeves. In it was an ermine gorget, a band of silk on which were fastened horses and monsters of wood, a carved wooden saucer and fantastic deer, bears, etc. Under the birch layer was reached the bottom of the pit whereupon were two low tables hewn out of wood and upon each table an unadorned skeleton. Some fragments of clothing and gold plates were picked up in the bottom of the grave. The skeletons were absolutely decayed. Although the state of the skeletons

---

[1] v. pp. 59, f. 12, 61, 189, f. 81 and f. 150=*Sib. Ant.* I. vii. 10, xiv. 9; a variety with an open hollow knob (ib. xi. 9) has a close parallel in China, f. 151, and also suggests the *Bunchuki* on p. 186, f. 79.
[2] *Aus Sib.* II. p. 104 sqq.

FIGS. 166, 167. *Mat.* xv.=*Sib. Ant.* Vol. I.
App. p. 126. Bronze Argalis. ½.

FIG. 168. *Mat.* v.=*Sib. Ant.* Vol. I. p. 60,
x. 11. Bronze knob inset into haft. ⅓.

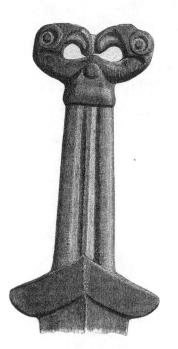

FIG. 171. *CR.* 1899,
p. 136, f. 271. Siberia.
Iron dagger. ½.

FIG. 169. *Mat.* xv.=*Sib. Ant.* Vol. I.
p. 68, xii. 1. Reddish bronze. ⅓.

FIG. 170. *Mat.* xv.=*Sib. Ant.* Vol. I. p. 69,
xii. 4. Iron handle. Copper or bronze
blade. ⅓.

M.

shewed that the grave was of early date, the frozen condition of the ground had preserved the furs and textiles in a manner unparalleled in warmer countries. The same cause also prevented the complete plundering of the grave, although the thief found that which was in the upper layer and threw some of it aside.

Another field of barrows was explored on the river Berel, near the Bukhtarma, an affluent of the Irtysh. In the heap of stones composing one barrow, about 20 feet high and 100 feet across, was found the skeleton of a horse with an iron bit and two iron stirrups. In the natural earth was a great pit 20 × 24 ft., and the ground was frozen: when it was cleared there appeared a layer of wood at the s. end and of birch bark at the N. end, under this latter sixteen horse skeletons in four rows with their heads to the east. The two easternmost rows had iron bits, and were covered with wooden and birch bark ornaments mostly overlaid with gold. In the middle of the wooden platform at the s. end was a tree trunk hollowed out, adorned at each corner with four birds cast in copper. Under this was a grave-pit with a horse's and a man's skeleton. By the latter were traces of copper and gold. To all appearance this part of the grave had been plundered in antiquity. Other graves about were found to be arranged like those on the Katanda, horse skeletons above and men's below, and objects of silver and iron, with well-made pottery. The iron knives and daggers were made after the exact fashion of the bronze ones, only the iron hafts were covered, each with a thin gold plate. In one case were found scales of iron armour for sewing on to a leathern jerkin.

The earthen barrows about Barnaul agreed mostly with these, except that they were smaller and the horses were not always buried with the men. They contained similar layers of birch bark and wood. Most of these graves had been plundered.

The graves of the later iron age are much smaller than those already described. They are called Kirgiz graves and may well belong to that people. They shade off into quite modern interments containing e.g. Russian xviith century coins.

The people of the early iron age are evidently quite different from those of the bronze age. Their burials are different and their manner of life likewise. Evidently the horse played a great part in their existence. Also they have many more weapons found with them. That is to say that they were a nation of warlike nomads. Still their civilisation had much in common with that of their predecessors. They adopted from these the characteristic dagger, the characteristic knife, the cauldron, the mirror; they seem even to have continued their agriculture to some extent, and they also engraved representations of themselves upon cliffs; this time we find the figures predominantly on horseback in place of going afoot. The new comers seem to have brought a knowledge of silver and of iron, and also a distinct taste for the monstrous. With them begins the liking for winged quadrupeds, for horns ending in birds, for inconsequent beak-heads, for conventionalised creatures quite unlike the naturalistic style of their predecessors. Yet the similarity in technique, the imitation of bronze forms in iron (ff. 169—171)—we find even such strange cases as bronze daggers with iron handles—the similar love

Aus Sibirien. Vol. II. Objects from the Altai.

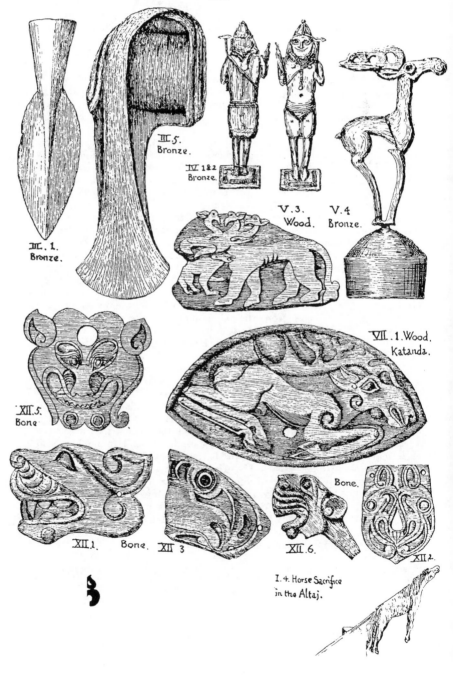

III.1.
Bronze.

III.5.
Bronze.

IV 1&2
Bronze.

V.3.
Wood.

V.4
Bronze.

VII.1. Wood.
Katanda.

XII.5.
Bone.

XII.1.　　Bone. XII 3

XII.6.　　Bone.

XII 2.

I. 4. Horse Sacrifice
in the Altai.

of gold plates as adornments, make it clear that the old tradition lived on. It seems as if this new warlike immigrant people conquered the old miners and metal workers, and used their inherited skill in the carrying out of its own taste and thereby formed a mongrel style which is indistinguishable from the Scythic.

Everything points to this immigrant population having been of what may be called Hunnic stock. Their mode of life, their burial customs, their type as seen in statues and rock carvings, correspond with what we know from Chinese sources of the Hiung-nu, the T'u-küe, the Tartars, and all other tribes of that stock (see p. 88 sqq.).

The burial customs do not correspond, inasmuch as the Chinese speak of them as burning their dead, whereas no cases of complete cremation have been found. Still near Tobolsk A. Heikel found in a tomb which had much in common with these middle Siberian barrows, that the wooden erection set over the body had been set on fire before the heap was raised[1].

It looks as if they had already learned something from their southern neighbours before they enslaved their northern ones. This would account for much that is in common between Scytho-Siberian art on the one hand and Iranian on the other, and likewise Chinese. This latter resemblance has already been dealt with by P. Reinecke[2], in the article already quoted, and by S. Reinach in the *Revue Archéologique*[3]. The former takes for granted that the northern barbarians were only passive, receptive. This may be true in a sense. But inasmuch as they received from all directions it is possible that they transmitted something to the Chinese, whether it was derived from the west or from the Altai miners to the north.

As to the affinities of these latter it is hard to give any opinion. It would be natural to refer them to the Uralo-Altaic tribes and argue that there is much in common between their civilisation and that of the tribes of that race all across from Finland, central Russia and Perm to the Altai, and that to this day most of those regions are peopled by that race where it has not been encroached upon by intrusive Turks. But Radloff is rather inclined to see in them the ancestors of what he calls the Jenisei tribes, who speak a language quite distinct from Uralo-Altaic and Turkish, and who have been mostly assimilated by one or other of the great tribes about them, yet still in some cases have preserved a hereditary skill in metal-working, for instance the Kuznetsy or Smith Tartars, who talk a Turkish tongue but belong to the older race. The Uralo-Altaic peoples never reached so high a state of civilisation. Moreover we know that the T'u-küe in the vith century A.D. had long since held a metal-working race under subjection. This employment of alien craftsmen is characteristic of the nomads. For the T'u-küe there worked Chinese, for Chingiz Khan's successors Chinese, Persian, even German miners and armourers and a French jeweller[4]; for Timur were set up the most perfect productions of purely Persian architecture.

[1] Axel Heikel, "Antiquités de la Sibérie Occidentale" in *Mémoires de la Société Finno-Ougrienne*, No. vi. Helsingfors, 1894.
[2] *Zt. f. Ethnolog.* XXIX. 1897, p. 140 sq.
[3] XXXVIII (1901), p. 27 sqq. *La Représentation du Galop dans l'art ancien et moderne.*
[4] Rockhill, *Rubruck*, pp. 137, 177.

Besides the few objects which have been recovered from tombs excavated by a competent archaeologist, there is a whole class of antiquities
nearly all of gold, some set with stones, whose provenance is vaguely
given as Siberia. Spitsyn refers them more particularly to the basins of
the Ishim, the Irtysh and the upper Obj. They came to the Hermitage
from the collection of the Academy of Sciences of St Petersburg, and they
represent the first attempt at an Archaeological Museum, surviving from the
Kunstkammer of Peter the Great. They were saved because the attention
of his government was at last called to the great spoils collected by the
bugrovshchiki, or mound-diggers, who went out in large parties and systematically robbed the ancient graves, which must have been astonishingly rich
in gold. Nowadays no one has hit on such a rich grave still unrifled so
as to describe its disposition. Radloff, in an appendix to his "Siberian
Antiquities," gives extracts from the works of early European travellers in
Siberia who tell of the work of spoliation[1].

The collection includes collars, frontlets, figures of birds, animals and
men, buckles and plates of various shapes, some with loops behind for
straps. The commonest forms are oblong and a kind of ᙍ shape which
is made to suit the favourite subject of an attack by a carnivore on a
pasturing animal very well. Plates of bronze, but exactly similar in shape
and design, have been found still nailed symmetrically on to coffins, but
they seem too solid for mere funeral furniture and had probably served
some purpose in the life of their owner, most likely they had some part
in the adornment of his horse or were nailed on to coffers in which he
kept his goods. Some idea of date was furnished by their being found
with coins of the Han dynasty which circulated from B.C. 118 to A.D. 581[2].
Witsen, to whom some specimens now lost found their way, figures them
in company with coins of the Roman emperors, e.g. Gordian, and there
is no reason against their belonging together: only his plates give a
most miscellaneous lot of things, and we cannot be sure which was
found with which. In accordance with these data M. Hoernes[3] thinks that
the Siberian Iron Age came in with the Christian Era, but the South Russian
analogies point to a much earlier time.

These Siberian gold objects have never been satisfactorily published;
Dr Kieseritzky, the late curator, who referred them to the Massagetae,
promised an illustrated Catalogue of all the Scythian and Siberian Antiquities: meanwhile the best pictures of them, some of which I have reproduced below (pp. 272—280), where I treat their style in detail, are in *KTR*.[4]

---

[1] Witsen, *Noord en Oost Tartarye*, 3rd ed.
Amsterdam, 1785; Messerschmidt, *MSS. of Acad.
Sc. St Pet.*; P. J. von Strahlenberg, *Description of
Siberia and Great Tartary*, London, 1736, p. 364;
J. Bell of Antermony, *Travels from St Petersburgh
to various parts of Asia*, Edinburgh, 1806, p. 154;
Archaeologia, II. p. 272, pl. XIV.—XVIII., "Some
account of some Tartarian Antiquities in a letter
from P. Demidoff, dated Sept. 17, 1764," pl. XIV.
gives a prince buried with wife and horse quite
in Scythic style, pl. XV. the eagle figured on p. 273.
Pallas also treats of them and figures the commoner
types, *Voyages dans plusieurs Provinces de l'Empire*

de Russie, Paris, l'an II. 8vo, Vol. V. p. 13, pl. 40;
Vol. VI. p. 287, pl. 98. A. A. Spitsyn, *TRAS.*
Russo-Slav. Section VIII. i. (1906), p. 227, reprints
Witsen and Messerschmidt's accounts, and also
inventories of such objects sent to the Tsar in 1716
and still to be recognised.

[2] Excavations of J. D. Talko-Hryncewicz on
R. Dzhida in the Transbaikal District, as summarised by A. A. Spitsyn, *TRAS.* XII. (1901) p. 277.

[3] *Natur- und Urgeschichte des Menschen*, Wien,
1909, II p. 304.

[4] pp. 379—400, ff. 332—365; cf. also Ch. de
Linas, *Origines de l'Orfevrerie Cloisonnée.*

Oxus Treasure.

From the southern borders of Siberia, where the steppe marches with Iran, comes a collection of objects in the British Museum. It claims to be one hoard discovered in 1877 near the middle Oxus either at Kabadian or between it and Khulm[1]. It includes a few pieces in style similar to the Siberian Plates, some objects whose artistic affinities are not yet cleared up, several examples of Persian jewelry, and some Greek work including coins. It is most unfortunate that this find was not made within reach of any trustworthy authority. We cannot even be sure that all the objects really belong to the same *cache*. They found their adventurous way down to India into the hands of ingenious native dealers, who added to their number by forgeries, and by duplicating real antiques in more precious materials. One thing is clear, that of the vast number of objects and coins purporting to be part of the treasure no specimen which belongs to a known art and can be dated approximately is later than about 200 B.C.: there are no Parthian coins and none of Eucratides, though they are common in those parts; the latest coin belongs to Euthydemus, whereas some of the things go back at least to the vth century B.C. The barbaric pieces recall the undoubted Iranian ones closely, and it is almost inconceivable that if they were imitations of Sassanian work and belonged to the ivth century A.D., chance and the caprice of dealers should have associated just these and no others with this definable find.

Mr Dalton's identification of the purely Persian style of the griffins and other objects that he published in his preliminary article was afterwards triumphantly vindicated by Mr J. de Morgan's excavations at Susa. There, in a tomb proved by coins to belong to the early ivth century B.C., were found armlets and other jewels precisely similar to some from the Oxus, save that their preservation is incomparably better. They are adorned with inlays of light and dark blue and red[2].

For a catalogue of the treasure the reader is referred to Mr Dalton's work. Its chief glory, the pair of griffin armlets (No. 116), of exactly the same style as the collar from Siberia (p. 272, ff. 188, 189) and the best example of the kind of model which inspired later Siberian plates, has no Scythic character and so no place here[3]. The sheath (No. 22) has already been discussed (p. 70, v. inf. pp. 263, 270). It is 10·9 in. = 27·6 cm. long.

The gold plaque (No. 48) with a figure of a man probably a Persian in a costume resembling the Scythian is very valuable as illustrating the latter, but its purpose is not quite evident and in spite of its clearness it lacks artistic style. The ring (No. 111), on the other hand, has very definite Siberian analogies in the manner in which the animal is bent round, and in the hollows left for precious inlays.

---

[1] O. M. Dalton, *The Treasure of the Oxus*, London, 1905 (cf. also *Archaeologia*, LVIII. (1902), p. 237, "On some points in the History of Inlaid Jewellery"), gives a full account of it with an illuminating discussion and excellent plates, quite superseding General Cunningham's in *JRAS. Bengal*, L. (1881) p. 151, LII. (1883) pp. 64, 258, from which are taken *KTR.*'s drawings and some of mine prepared before the publication of Mr Dalton's book. He and the Trustees of the British Museum have kindly allowed me to make use of the blocks of Nos. 23 and 111.

[2] inf. p. 271, f. 187, J. de Morgan, *Délégation en Perse du Ministère de l'Instruction Publique*, 1897—1902, p. 93 sqq. and *Mémoires* T. VIII. pp. 29—58, pl. IV. v.; E. Pottier, *Gazette des Beaux Arts*, 1902, p. 17, "Les Fouilles de Suse."

[3] v. coloured plate XVI. in *Archaeologia*, LVIII.

FIG. 173. Gold plate from sword sheath. *Oxus Treasure*. Dalton, no. 22. ½.

FIG. 175. Gold ring. *Oxus Treasure*, no. 111. ⅓.

FIG. 174. Gold plaque from *Oxus Treasure*.
Dalton, no. 48. ⅓. v. p. 58.

FIG. 176. Gold griffin (from Tiara?), front and side views. *Oxus Treasure*, no. 23. ¼.

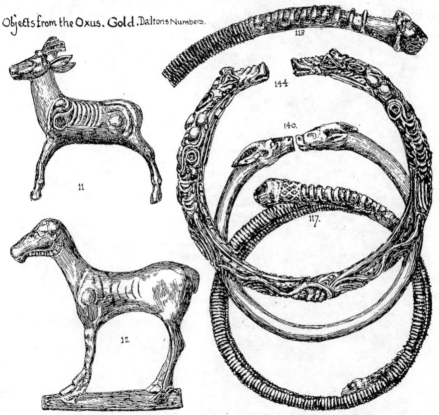

FIG. 177. Nos. 11, 12, 140, ⅓; No. 117, ⅔; Nos. 118, 144, slightly enlarged.

The same may be said of the griffin ornament (No. 23), though it is nearer to its Iranian originals. The armlet (No. 144) is again more barbaric. The beasts upon it are broken-down griffins with intertwined tails. Other armlets (Nos. 117 and 118) are, on the other hand, purely Persian. No. 140 has less definite style. It is singularly like those brought as tribute on Persepolitan sculptures (p. 59, f. 12). The two figures of deer (Nos. 11 and 12) are very like such figures from Siberia (inf. p. 272, f. 190). They are given to shew the muscle lines in an early stage before they had become exaggerated. Whatever doubt may be cast on the genuineness[1] of some of the Oxus treasure these pieces appear to me certain.

Anánjino, and Perm.

Besides the Altai region and western Siberia, finds of objects of the Scytho-Siberian type are made in the Urals and in the forest region to the west of them. Evidently there was intercourse but no regular domination, such as is suggested by the finds in Little Russia. The best example of a mixed Finno-Scythic culture (it may be premature to name it so, but all likelihood points to such a name being near the mark) is the cemetery of Anánjino, on the river Tojma near Elábuga, on the lower Kama[2]. Anánjino belongs to the transition from bronze to iron: there are bronze axes and pick-axes, spear and arrow-heads, and iron daggers of Siberian type (f. 179) and some beast style ornaments recalling Siberian forms, for instance a twisted up beast (f. 180) whose analogues come from the Crimea (f. 181) and from Siberia (p. 274, f. 194). On the other hand some things recall the remains found further to the north about Perm and everything is rudely made. The costume on an incised tomb-stone is not unlike the Scythic (f. 178).

Further north and west the Siberian dagger penetrated among purely Finnish people such as dwelt in the upper basin of the Kama[3]. This is the country in which are found the wonderful pieces of Graeco-Roman, Byzantine and Sassanian silver plate kept chiefly in the Hermitage and the Stroganov palace at St Petersburg[4]. In this country are found bronze and copper "idols" which have some connection with things Scythic; they seem rather poor relations than imitations, but the outspread eagle with a human face upon its breast, the emblem of the God of heaven, certainly recalls a favourite Scythic motive, and the many-headed deer is, as it were, an exaggeration of the type best exemplified by that from Axjutintsy[5].

[1] M. Dieulafoy, *Journal des Savants* 1906, p. 302, condemns it, but cf. M. Rosenberg, *Monatshefte d. Kunstwissenschaftlichen Literatur*, 1906, p. 229.

[2] Baron J. de Baye, "La Nécropole d'Ananino," *Mém. de la Société Nationale des Antiquaires de France*, Série VI. T. VI. 1897, pp. 1—26, and *KTR*. p. 434 sqq.; also J. Aspelin, *Antiquités du Nord Finno-Ougrien*, p. 105 sqq., Helsingfors, 1877. A. M. Tallgren promises a full account of "Die Bronzezeit im ostlichen u. nördlichen Russland" in *Finska Fornminnesföreningens Tidskrift* Vol. XXVI. Helsingfors, 1910.

[3] Cf. "Antiquities of Chud folk on the Kama from the Collection of the Teploúkhovs," published

by A. A. Spitsyn in *Mat.* XXVI. St P. 1902. Pl. XXVII. 8, a characteristic Scythic iron dagger; pl. XXXV. copper axe-heads. A. Likhachov in *Trans. of VIth Russian Archaeological Congress* (Odessa, 1886), I. p. 135.

[4] *KTR.* pp. 408 sqq.; *Arch. Anz.* 1908, pp. 150—162, ff. 1—6. Mr J. I. Smirnóv of the Hermitage has made a complete publication of them in his *Argenterie Orientale*, St P. 1909.

[5] J. Abercromby, *Finns*, Vol. I. p. 118 sqq., p. 240; A. A. Spitsyn, *TRAS.* Russo-Slav. Section, Vol. VIII. (1906), pp. 29—145, ff. 1—496, has given a full repertory of such Shaman objects.

Ananjino
KTR p.435
f.389

FIG. 178.

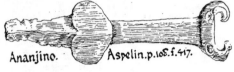

Ananjino.   Aspelin.p.108.f.417.

FIG. 179.

FIG. 180.   Bronze beast from Ananjino.
KTR. p. 435, f. 390.

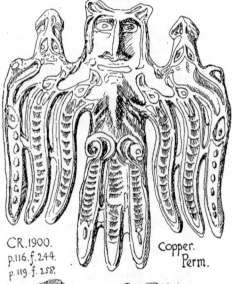

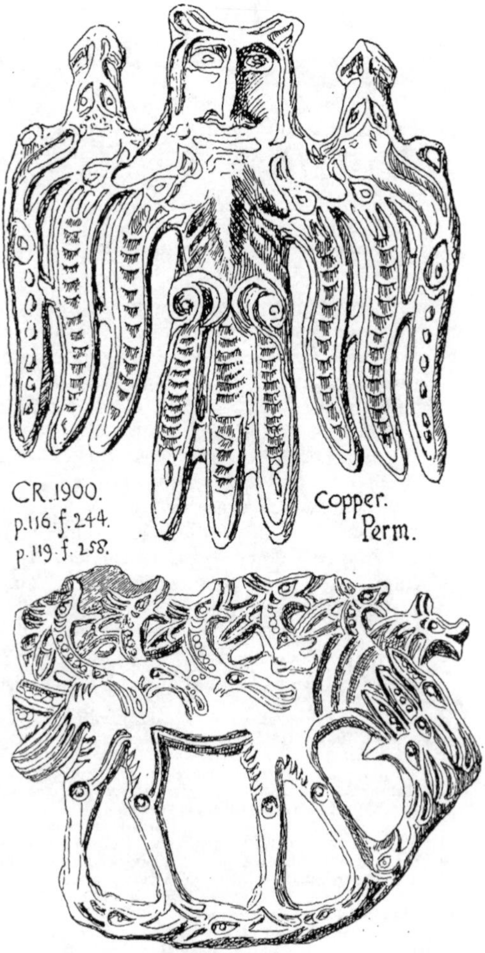

CR.1900.
p.116.f.244.
p.119.f.258.

Copper.
Perm.

C.R.
1895
P.18.f.32

Bronze
from near
Sympheropol.

FIG 181. ½

FIG. 182. ¾ and ⅔

La Tène.

On its western border the Scytho-Siberian style met with the Hallstatt and later with the La Tène styles. There seems to have been no inter-action, but Scythic objects spread into Hungary[1], perhaps in consequence of such movements as that of the Iazyges Metanastae (v. p. 121). The La Tène objects found in Russia (hitherto very few) were brought by western invaders, whether German Bastarnae or real Kelts (v. pp. 125, 127). Their incursions were, as we have seen, less important than those from the east. So far we can speak of the La Tène culture as having been established in Poland and even in Galicia, but as merely sporadic in Podolia and on the lower Dnêpr, where the Protogenes inscription is the only witness to the westerners' raids[2]. It must have been in S. Russia that the Scythic beast-style, applied to types developed from La Tène, produced the style of the Migration period. Here too perhaps had arisen the fibula with its foot bent back that gave rise to the cross-bow shape. Salin supposes that different modifications of this form, e.g. the radiated and square-headed types, mark different streams of culture diverging from the Crimea as a centre, but he thinks that the Germans' beast-style was their own and not indebted to the Scythic[3].

Caucasus.

Resemblances have been seen between the metal work of the Caucasus[4] and that of the Scytho-Siberian style, but they do not amount to much: they might be expected when we consider that Assyrian influence reached the Caucasus on one side and dominated Iran on the other, and also that some tribes of the northern plains undoubtedly passed through the mountains (v. supra p. 42). Most curious is a perfectly Minusinsk knife from Kortsa, a little west of Koban[5]. At a comparatively late period the Caucasians seem to have borrowed the characteristic looped mirrors[6], and along the northern foot-hills finds of Scythic type are constant. Moreover Gothic jewels have

---

[1] J. Hampel, "Skythische Denkmäler aus Un-garn" in *Ethnologische Mittheilungen aus Ungarn*, Bd IV. (1895); P. Reinecke, "Die skythischen Alterthümer im mittleren Europa," *Zt. f. Eth-nologie* XXVIII. (1896), v. supr. pp. 65, 68, 78.

[2] A. A. Spitsyn in *BCA*. XII. p. 78, "Monuments of La Tène Civilisation in Russia," speaks of La Tène finds in Poland and also at Gromovka and Great Ternava in Podolia, Zalêsje near Kiev, and Vodjanoe near Nicopol.

[3] Bernhard Salin, *Die Altgermanische Thier-ornamentik*, üb. v. J. Mestorf, Stockholm u. Berlin, 1904, p. 12 sqq.; R. Hausman, "Ueber neuere Fibelforschung," *Trans. Od. Soc.* XXL p. 255, quoting O. Almgren: cf. fibulae inf. Ch. XI. f. 284, XVII. f. 333; *Sm.* III. pl. i. and Baron J. de Baye, *Industrial Arts of the Anglo-Saxons*, p. 38 and pl. III.—VII.

[4] For the earlier Archaeology of the Caucasus see *Materials touching the Archaeology of the Caucasus*, published by the Moscow Archaeological Society, Part I with several short articles, and esp. Part VIII, Moscow, 1900, which contains a very full summary and many excellent plates, edited by Countess P. S. Uvarov; E. Chantre, *Recherches Anthropologiques dans le Caucase*, Paris, 1885-7; J. de Morgan, *Mission Scientifique au Caucase*, Paris, 1889; J. Mourier, *L'Art au Caucase*, Odessa, 1883; R. Virchow, *Das Gräberfeld des Kobans*, Berlin, 1884; "Ueber die Culturgeschichtliche Stel-lung des Kaukasus," *Abhandl. d. kön. pr. Akad. der Wiss. zu Berlin*, 1895, I.; G. Radde, *Museum Caucasicum*, Bd V, bearbeitet von Gräfin P. S. Uwarow, in Russian and German, Tiflis, 1902; see also *KTR*. p. 437 sqq. There is a good repre-sentative collection of objects from Koban and elsewhere in the Museum at St Germain-en-Laye, near Paris.

[5] Countess P. S. Uvarov, *Mat. Arch. Cauc.* VIII. p. 180 and pl. LXXVI.

[6] op. cit. pl. LIV., Dergavs.

occurred in a great find at Rutkha[1] on the Urukh well in the mountains, and typical fibulae and bird's head ornaments have been found in several localities. Sometimes types characteristic of the mountains are found sporadically in the plains, for instance the singularly elegant axes of the Koban[2] recall one or two specimens from Perm, that backwater to which all kinds of flotsam drifted[3]. But it seems as if the Caucasus threw no light on the early population of the northern steppes. The objects of the Koban cemetery have their analogues in central Europe, whatever the connection may have been[4]; later sites shew products of Roman craftsmanship, but on the whole archaeology is even more at fault in the mountains than in the plains.

[1] op. cit. pl. CI. CII.
[2] op. cit. pl. III.—VIII.; *KTR.* p. 462, f. 407.
[3] Aspelin, p. 60, f. 237 ; J. Abercromby, *Finns,*
Vol. I. p. 240, regards these as evidence of the early existence of the Permian trade route.
[4] H. Schmidt, *Zt. f. Ethn.* XXXVI. (1904), p. 620.

FIG. 182 *bis.* Ivory Ibex and Boar from Ephesus, v. p. 263. Constantinople Museum.

D. G. Hogarth, *Excavations at Ephesus,* London, 1908. Ch. IX. "The Ivory Statuettes," by Sir Cecil Smith. Ibex, p. 163, No. 23, pl. XXI. 5, XXIII. 2. Boar, p. 164, No. 26, pl. XXVI. 3; cf. p. 177, f. 33, bronze ibex and boar from the Troad. My best thanks are due to the Trustees of the British Museum and to Sir Cecil Smith for leave to reproduce these objects, and to Mr Dalton who called them to my notice. The pictures came too late to go into their right place in the text.

The resemblance of these animals to the Scythic is exceedingly close. In the Ibex the attitude of the feet and the way they are conventionalised is just that of the Scythic deer. The manner in which its head is turned round is a Mycenaean survival; Sir Cecil Smith compares the ibex on the Enkomi casket in the British Museum, but in the Scythic area it can be paralleled by a plaque from the Kuban (p. 279, f. 205), and a cheek-piece and a plaque from Zhabotin (p. 188, f. 80, Nos. 540, 539). On this last a mare with her foal bears upon her shoulder a star applied in the same way as the circles upon the ibex. Both star and circles may go back to a swirl of hair such as is just visible upon the shoulders of the lions flanking the tip of the Melgunov sheath (p. 171, f. 65, cf. a rosette in the same position, Layard, *Monuments of Nineveh,* I. 31). More probably it is due to the practice of adorning the plain surfaces of figures with various decorative motives, a practice common to the Ionian (Sir C. Smith, p. 156) and Scythic styles, and pushed to its furthest in the Kul Oba deer and Vettersfelde fish and in the Siberian plates (e.g. p. 273, f. 197). The boar is also very like Scythic work especially about the feet: it has some resemblance to a gold boar from Alexandropol (*KTR.* p. 244, f. 223=*ASH.* VI. 3). Gold work like some of that from Ephesus, particularly the repoussé plates (Hogarth op. cit. Pl. VIII. IX.), more especially a roundel with a griffin (VIII. 3) in which Hogarth sees a Central European look, may have served as a model for similar work in Scythia.

CHAPTER X.

SCYTHIC ART AND GREEK ART IN THE SERVICE OF SCYTHIANS.

SCYTHIC art has a character of its own. When we have made all allowance for foreign influence there remains something unlike anything else, the basis of the whole development, that to which imported elements had to conform or else quickly degenerate beyond recognition. This native element is at its purest in the art of the basin of the upper Jenisei and its centre may be reckoned Minusinsk. Until the true date and affinities of Minusinsk art have been made clear the Scythic problem cannot be said to be solved.

Unhappily we are not yet in a position to frame even plausible theories on the subject. In the last chapter I have given the few data available : but they do not take us far. The objects there figured give a fairly representative collection of the different classes of Minusinsk work : sufficient to judge of its character, sufficient to let the reader see for himself affinities with the products of other lands. Mr Seebohm's *Siberia in Asia* is, I believe, the only English book in which any of them have been figured. The few specimens he brought home are in the British Museum. Otherwise these things are inaccessible to British archaeologists.

Almost all the types are peculiar. The knife seems to be a local development, at least we seem able to trace it through many stages : but this type was not spread over the Scythic area, and in China only, as has been said, seems to have its counterpart. The dagger does not seem to have attained its development at once. Its less perfect form also appears in China ; but its fully developed type spread westwards as far as Hungary. The mirrors also spread to China and to S. Russia : likewise the cauldrons. The arrow-heads appear nearly all to be of the four faceted[1] as against the later triangular shape. The axe heads seem a final improvement of the socketed celt, having a peculiar second loop (p. 243, f. 151). This also spread over the Scythic area (p. 190) ; later would be that with one loop in the middle of the broad side (p. 243, p. 245, f. 158). Finally we have the beautifully shaped head with a transverse hole for the haft (III. 5 on p. 251). All these types suggest that bronze casting was developed longer and further than in most countries : that an out-of-the-way district was left undisturbed to let its bronze craft evolve independently. Something similar seems true of Hungary.

But the ornament has the chief claim to interest and is the greatest puzzle. It is not quite clear which way it is going ; whether animal forms are being degraded into easy curves or curves have suddenly been seen to have animal possibilities. To me this latter seems the case. The

---

[1] More or less similar to Nos. 203 to 18 on p. 190, f. 82, but without side spurs.

loops of a mirror (p. 244, f. 152) or the ring of a knife handle (ff. 150, 165)
suggested, perhaps at first owing to the chances of casting, the shape of an
animal with its head down, or of two heads neck to neck ; the loop of an
axe-head (f. 151) joined to another small ring looked like a beak and eye
and was improved to bring out the resemblance. So the ends of pommel
and guard struck the imagination as being ready to make beak-heads, and
beak-heads became the regular decoration of the dagger (ff. 169—171).
The wrong end of an axe became a beak-head or an argali schematically
rendered (ff. 152, 150). Animals so derived from loops and knobs and
handles remained simple and geometrical in their lines. The eyes remain
ring-like ; the beaks are always curved right round, the bodies lumpy and
the limbs thick. Sometimes pure line was sufficient, zigzags in the knife
handles (ff. 153, 155), even spirals as on the ornament and mirror from
Batteni (f. 152). The ornament from Bijsk (ib.) shews a favourite pattern
for incrusted jewelry. When this eye for chance resemblances was turned
on to representations of animals it saw them also in antlers or tails in
which it was ready to fancy a likeness to other creatures' heads; but this
development seems subsequent to the introduction of iron and the conquest
of the metal workers by nomads who exploited their skill. It is the distinguishing mark of the Scythic style.

There does not seem to me to be anything in the earlier Minusinsk
art which need have come in from outside, except perhaps the socketed
celt[1]. It was the nomads who brought beasts and monsters from sw. Asia,
and perhaps from the coasts of the Euxine. M. Salomon Reinach has
seen resemblances between Siberian art and certain points of Mycenaean.
If there be such they are in the later Minusinsk, which is identical with
Scythic. But this had received Mediterranean elements into itself; archaic
Greek art as practised in Ionia had penetrated to it at an early period,
and before that there may have been other influences from the Aegean
region. These affected Scythic art from the first and would account for
any resemblances. So that there may be truth in M. Reinach's fascinating
theory that the representation of a flying gallop in which the animal sticks
his legs out in all directions at once, spread from Mycenaean art to some
lost Central Asian art and hence through Siberia as far as China, to
return to the West and English sporting prints with the *Chinoiseries* of
the xviiith century[2].

Influence of Western Asia and Ionia.

Whatever the ultimate origin of the Minusinsk style, whatever influences it may have felt in spite of its remoteness, upon the coming of the
iron people it became the foundation of their taste and was spread by
them over all the steppes. Thereby it emerged from its isolation and

[1] Sophus Müller, *Urgeschichte Europas*, p. 161, brings the style up from S. Russia.
[2] S. Reinach, "La Représentation du Galop dans l'art ancien et moderne," *Revue Archéologique*, XXXVI. (1900), pp. 216 and 440 ; XXXVII. p. 244 ; XXXVIII. (1901), pp. 27 (Scythic style) and 224; XXXIX. p. 1, and *BCH*. 1897, pp. 5—15, "Un Monument oublié de l'art Mycénéen."

became exposed to the influences of the arts of south-western Asia.   But it is beyond us to disentangle these influences, because we are not yet able to clear up the mutual relations of these arts, Assyrian, perhaps N. Syrian and finally Iranian on the one hand, on the other Mycenaean (in survivals) and early Greek.   If, for instance, we take the Ephesus[1] and the Nimrud[2] ivories referred to the viiith and ixth centuries, Sir Cecil Smith[3] is inclined to make both groups Greek: Mr Hogarth[4] finds the former Greek under Assyrian influence exerted through the N. Syrians, the latter N. Syrian.   Seeing that very similar ivories come from Sparta[5], perhaps rather too much has been made of the Orientalism in the Ionian finds, though the very material suggests the East: that Greeks should have had a hand in the Nimrud ivories seems thereby less probable.   The difference touches the Scythic question nearly, inasmuch as one or two of the Ephesus beasts (v. p. 260) are in a style almost identical with the Scythic.   With the Ephesus Lions[6] may be classed the lion-head from Vasilkov (p. 193, f. 85).   But it is precisely in the beasts that Assyrian influence appears most plausible at Ephesus ; yet the features which recall the Scythic do not seem to extend to the basreliefs of N. Syria[7] and Assyria, though the small figures in the round are not so very unlike[8].   It seems therefore justifiable to distinguish two quasi-independent strains that met in Scythic art, the Assyrian to which the Iranian succeeded and the Ionian which never quite gave way to the Attic.

The earliest objects from Scythia that we can date, the Melgunov and Kelermes sheaths, referred to the viith and vith centuries B.C., are under overwhelming Assyrian influence, yet their general forms are Scythic and the crouching deer upon the side projection is Ionian : in the sheath from the Don (p. 270, f. 186) the two strains are blended.   In the Oxus sheath the Scythic element is weaker.   Pieces of Iranian work are few in European Scythia, the hilt of the Chertomlyk sword is the best example[9]; further east we can name the better specimens from the Oxus and one piece of Siberian treasure (p. 272, ff. 188, 189), but its imitation is universal in the Asiatic steppes and is carried by tribal movements into Europe.   In the viith and vith centuries B.C. Greek and Oriental art were still closely allied, and even later certain classes of objects seem to stand between the two, especially engraved cylinders and gems such as those from S. Russia illustrated in Ch. xi. § 13, f. 298, and others like them from western Asia[10], and certain silver work (v. p. 265).

In the Greek influence we must distinguish two periods, that of the Ionian archaic art and that of the fully developed Attic art afterwards practised throughout the Greek world.   There is something almost barbaric about the Ionian art that makes us barbarians think of our own mediaeval

[1] Hogarth, *Excavations at Ephesus*, pp. 155—185, pl. XXL—XXVII.
[2] Cecil Smith, ih. p. 182, pl. XXVIII. XXIX. ; Perrot and Chipiez, *Chaldaea*, &c. I. pp. 212, 301, 363, ff. 80, 129, 130; II. pp. 119—122, ff. 56—59; Dalton, *Archaeologia*, LVIII. pp. 246, 247.
[3] l.c. p. 184.
[4] *Ionia and the East*, Oxford, 1909, p. 59.
[5] *BSA*. XII. pp. 320—328, XIII. pp. 70—107.

[6] *Exc. at Eph*. XXI. I, 3, XXIII. 3, XXV. 12.
[7] e.g. the deer at Sindzherli, K. Humann u. O. Puchstein, *Reisen in Kl. Asien*, XLIV. 1, XLV. 3.
[8] e.g. many with the Nimrud Ivories in the British Museum, cf. Perrot and Chipiez, op. cit. II. p. 315, f. 193.
[9] Yet cf. for the hilt Perrot and Chipiez, op. cit. I. p. 334, two calves' heads addorsed from Nineveh.
[10] Furtwängler, *Antike Gemmen*, III. p. 116 sqq.

work, a decorative quaintness which does not demand for its appreciation so high a level of aesthetic development as that required by the perfect art of the vth century.   Hence its easy adoption by neighbouring Asiatic nations and the employment of Greek craftsmen by the Achaemenians. Hence too its spreading among the Scythians.   Prepared by the Minusinsk culture and perhaps by some contact with survivals of Mycenaean art, the Scythians made the Ionian archaic style as employed for the representation of beasts their own, and continued to practise it with much spirit, but too little restraint, incorporating into it Minusinsk feeling.   The elements that they thus joined were not hopelessly incongruous, but combined to make a whole, with a distinct character of its own and no small decorative merit. Moreover, even when the Pontic Greeks had left it behind, the Scyths having made it their own kept to it fairly consistently : when their models were not beyond them they were capable of assimilating them.   So this descendant of Ionian archaic art lived on until after the Christian era and spread from Siberia to Hungary.

The story of Aristeas and the account of the trade route running north-east from the Euxine shews us that there was every reason why products of Ionian art of the viith and vith centuries B.C. should quickly penetrate into the interior of northern Asia, and their style become the property of all the nomad tribes.   Hence we can readily admit the possibility that objects of this date found as far north as Minusinsk should recall details of ivory carvings found at Ephesus, and that the Scythic crouching deer itself should be originally Greek.   Accordingly in the older period it is very hard, strange as it may appear, to distinguish between Greek and Scythic.

Herodotus (IV. 79) bears witness to a Scyth's use of Greek style by mentioning the griffins and sphinxes in the palace of Scyles in Olbia ; we may picture them as like the griffins from Olympia[1].

Archaic Greek Objects in Scythia.

Specimens of this archaic Greek art which penetrated to the Scythians and called forth their imitation are not infrequent.   They have with them only the Assyrian work at Kelermes and Melgunov's Barrow, in cases such as Vettersfelde and the Seven Brothers they make up the greater part of the find, though there are already some later things.   Mostly the older pieces are few compared to the products of the later art.   Their interest for the moment being the effect they exercised upon the native style we may leave aside such as produced no imitations ; such are the Greek pots, technically as well as artistically inimitable (Ch. XI. § 7), and some of their bronzes (Ch. XI. § 10, ff. 278—281).   Furtwängler long ago pointed out that the Vettersfelde objects (v. p. 237) were of pure Greek work, and shewed that the details, especially the Triton on the fish, the friezes of animals rather quietly attacking and flying, the convention by which quadrupeds seen from the side have only two legs, the use made of the graver to put in surface details, the eyes on the sheath so suggestive of *Augenschalen*, and

---

[1] *Olympia* IV. pl. XLIX., cf. Hogarth, *Excav. at Ephesus*, pl. XVI. 4 ; *Delphes*, v. pl. X.

the whole spirit of the three chief pieces, belong to Ionian work of the late archaic period. The earring is put down by Hadaczek to an earlier period and is purely Ionian : the dagger sheath just like the one from Tomakovka (p. 158 below) is perhaps later, but likewise entirely Greek. But the chief pieces, as shewn by the shape of the sheath and perhaps by the use of small animals to decorate the big fish, mark the interference of the Scythian customer. The Kul Oba deer (p. 203) has only this last point to make it Scythic, its general character is just like the Ephesus ibex down to the details of the feet, which might strike one as barbarous. The Kostromskaja deer (p. 226) represents a decided conventionalising of the same type, and in spite of the grace of line and skill of execution must be native work. The Seven Brothers also yielded much archaic Greek work. Almost all the gold plates on p. 208 are of this class ; such an array of animals would delight a Scythian, and the Asiatic element in Ionian allowed monstrous forms which were not less welcome. On two of the triangular plates, that with the eagle and hare (a well-known design, e.g. the coins of Agrigentum) and that with a lion and ibex, there is only just a touch of archaism (p. 211, f. 112 and p. 209, f. 108) ; whereas upon a third (p. 213, II. 6) we can see an archaic model through barbarous execution, and upon another (p. 211, f. 111) though the execution is skilful the incongruous monster suggests barbarism. The breastplate with a gorgoneion (p. 213, II. 1) offers a type which is very popular on the small plates of gold : the Scythians could attain to such a grotesque. The great silver rhyton (p. 211, f. 110) with a winged ibex from the same tomb, like the lesser golden dog[1] rhyton and those from Kul Oba (p. 197), is a fine specimen of Graeco-Asiatic art, having decided Ionian affinities both in its main lines and in its decoration : compare that from Erzingan in Armenia figured by Dalton[2]. The figure of a sow engraved in rock crystal (p. 208, No. 33) is typically Ionian, as Furtwängler points out[3]. Altogether the Seven Brothers give us Greek things just as they best suited Scythic taste without going out of their way to meet it. The gold saucer (p. 204, f. 99) from Kul Oba appears to me Greek work almost as early, but calculated for a Scythian purchaser, witness the bearded heads. The general scheme of rays or petals recalls the dish from the tomb at Nymphaeum which agrees in so much with the VII Brothers (p. 213, III. 5), or a dish found with the Erzingan rhyton[4]. The manner in which the rays are filled is ingenious : archaic Greek art shared with the barbarians a natural abhorrence of void : but the various elements are rather incongruous, and the leopard-heads upside down shew a disregard of the fitness of things which would hardly have pleased a Greek. Kul Oba had one or two early gold plates for sewing on to clothes, but these are hardly archaic : just these patterns occur also at Alexandropol

---

[1] *KTR.* p. 318 f. 286=*CR.* 1877, I. 7.

[2] *Oxus Treasure*, No. 178. He calls it Perso-Greek. Much the same technique is exemplified by the great vessel of uncertain provenance with two handles, each a winged ibex or antelope, one of which is in the Berlin Antiquarium (Furtwängler, *Arch. Anz.* 1892, p. 115), the other in the Louvre (W. Froehner, *La Collection Tyszkiewicz*, Munich, 1892, pl. III.). This is referred by Furtwängler to

the vth century, but a slightly inferior ibex (No. 10 in the *Oxus Treasure*) of the same style has a palmette on its lower attachment which Dalton puts in the IVth century. All these have the muscle-markings brought out in gold (v. p. 268).

[3] *Vettersfelde*, p. 23 (v. inf. p. 270).

[4] Dalton, *Oxus Treasure*, No. 180 ; cf. *Les Arts*, I. (1902), p. 18 ; cf. No. 18 of the treasure itself.

and the Seven Brothers; probably the dies were in use a long time.   In
general the Medusa-head plates were best imitated : others produced the
poor result we see at Volkovtsy (p. 184).   The Ryzhanovka earrings (p. 178)
shaped like dumpy griffins with curled-up wings are called by Hadaczek[1]
masterpieces of Graeco-Scythic work of the IIIrd century B.C. : they look
to me earlier, and certainly go back to archaic originals.   Sphinxes from
Alexandropol (p. 158, xxx. 24) and from Dêev Barrow near Sêragozy[2]
have similar wings.   In the case of one or two types we have not found
actual Greek originals in the Scythian district, though they are familiar
enough elsewhere : such is the winged goddess from Alexandropol (p. 154,
f. 40) and the animal on the mirror from Romny (p. 178, f. 73).   The ivory
lion heads from near Smêla[3] are, at any rate that shewn on p. 193, good
examples of the orientalising Greek style.   The mounting of the mirror from
Prussy also looks quite Ionian, being identical with a mirror-mount from
Olbia, though the beak-heads are very Scythic and perhaps not original[4].

Scythic Beast-style.

When the Scythians set to work for themselves one way of attaining
decorative effect was the reducing of organic curves to abstract ones as
we see on such mirrors as that from Romny or on the Kostromskaja deer.
Another was to imitate the practice of the makers of the Vettersfelde fish
and the Kul Oba deer and cover the beasts with secondary ornament or turn
extremities into heads of other creatures.   This we see on the Axjutintsy deer
(p. 181) on which the curve of the belly has afforded space for a bird's eye
and beak, and the antlers end in griffins' heads.   The extreme case is seen
in the gold plate of another reindeer from Verkhne-udinsk (p. 275, f. 197) which
is all over small animals fitted in to cover every space.   And the addition
of incongruous extremities, especially claws (which give such a good excuse
for stone settings), has rendered it impossible for us to define the species
of some of the Siberian beasts.   However for sheer incongruity nothing
can surpass the gryllus from the Seven Brothers (p. 211).

In the adorning of men's things, especially in horse trappings, this older
naturalised style remained supreme.   It seems as if the Greeks recognised
its suitability, for in what was apparently a purely Greek grave at Nymphaeum
there were many psalia quite similar to those from the Scythic Seven Brothers
(v. p. 214).   So too the hilts of the characteristic Scythic swords and knives
are almost all worked in this style, and again are sometimes the only objects
of the kind in the tomb[5], or else they are Assyrian, as in Melgunov's Barrow
and Kelermes, or Iranian as at Chertomlyk, never as it seems Greek.

Besides the absolutely bizarre and apparently meaningless combinations
which seem merely due to the desire for decorative detail or the impulse
to complete the chance resemblance which an antler or tail of one animal
may bear to the head of another, we also find the well-defined monsters
which go back to the symbolic creations of western Asia, sphinxes, griffins

[1] *Der Ohrschmuck der Griechen und Etrusker*,
Wien, 1903, p. 41, f. 16 ; *Sm*. II. p. 143, xvi. 4.
[2] *BCA*. XIX. p. 170, pl. xiii., v. p. 170.
[3] Frontispieces of *Sm*. I. and II.

[4] p. 191, No. 351, cf. *CR*. 1905, p. 34, f. 32.
[5] e.g. Mirza Kekuvatskij, near Kerch, *ABC*.
Reinach, p. 21, pl. XXVII. 9.

and such like. The Greeks were prepared to supply these, already themselves sharing them with the East, and they became the stock decoration
of objects destined for the Scythian market, and were in high honour among
the colonists themselves who put the griffin on the coins of Panticapaeum.

Besides going to the extreme of making an animal more decorative
by adding to him the attributes of another, the Scyths were inclined to
insist on surface details and use them to make a pleasing pattern. There
is this element in one of the little silver gilt vessels from Kul Oba[1], and
on the dagger sheath from the same grave inscribed ΠΟΡΝΑΧΟ[2]; in spite of
the Greek model, still archaic though already too far advanced in style for
satisfactory imitation, the native taste comes out in the way that the line which
indicates musculature on Ninevite sculptures is represented by a volute or

FIGS. 183, 184. Gold plates. Ak-Mechet. *KTR.* pp. 284, 285, ff. 249, 250.

S curve. We see the same thing on a gem from the Crimea[3]. This tendency
when carried further leads to designs like the plates from Karagodeuashkh
(p. 219, f. 123) or Berestnjagi[4]; without looking into them one is not sure that
animals are really intended, so far have they degenerated into mere decorative arrangements of curves. The deer from Ak-Mechet is tending this
way, but on the other plate vegetable forms are taking the likeness of a
snail. A more interesting example of this conventionalising of animal forms
is shewn by certain horse trappings from Krasnokutsk[5]. Here the design
most clearly foreshadows the northern European beast-style. Very similar
are designs from Siberia[6].

[1] *ABC.* XXXIV. 1 on p. 198.
[2] *ABC.* XXVI. 2 on p. 203.
[3] Ch. XI. § 13, f. 298, Furtwängler, *Ant.
Gemmen*, XI. 26.
[4] *Sm.* III. xviii. 11, xix. 2 = Khanenko, II. 3, LX.

x. on p. 191; so Volkovtsy, p. 185, f. 78.
[5] pp. 167, 168, ff. 56, 57 and *ASH.* XXIII. 4 on
p. 158.
[6] Radloff, *Aus Sibirien*, II. p. 128, v. on p. 251,
XII. 1—6.

On statuettes in the Oxus treasure we have the muscle markings emphasized decoratively though without entire disregard of natural modelling (p. 256, Nos. 11 and 12). But when the beast came to be felt as merely part of the pattern, there was no reason why this line should not be brought out in colour as well as in form, and on the ibex (No. 10, v. p. 265, n. 2) gilt is used, and finally it became the custom among the Asiatic nomads to adorn the flanks of creatures with blue stone or coral inlaid, and the round or pearshaped forms suggested by the prominence of the muscle were combined into one motive of a dot between two triangles, which has suggested to some writers an eye, to others a beak-head doubled for symmetry[1]. All these modifications and departures from naturalism were due to horror of empty space, which also led to the creatures being twisted about in every way so as exactly to fill the space available.

The species represented in Scythic art are many[2]. The lions and other felidae preying upon deer are after Asiatic or Greek models. Their species are hard to define, because the artists did not care to be accurate as to spots and manes and tasselled tails, such details they delighted to add even to lionesses. Chief of the true Scythic beasts is the reindeer who is constantly occurring, mostly in a crouching position with his legs bent under his body— he figures upon quiver covers, breastplates, shields, standards, gold plates for sewing on to clothes, mirrors, bridle cheek-pieces and other trappings, and upon the one Scythic gem, and in Siberia upon a wood-carved saucer (v. p. 251) and another wooden fragment. So too a bird of prey is a favourite subject, sometimes with wings deployed to form a gold plaque for sewing on to clothes, more often a mere head and beak, upon standards, horses' cheek-pieces, no more than beak and eye at Nymphaeum (p. 215, f. 116), ending the horns of the deer or the tail of a monster, the hilt of a sword or the handle of a mirror, second but to the deer. He even occurs double-headed (double-headed eagles seem natural in Russia) on a bronze plaque[3].

FIG. 185.

Besides these the ibex is common, especially on Siberian things, and mostly in the round, as an adornment to edges, as it were upon the sky line, e.g. on the Chertomlyk cauldron (p. 162, f. 50) and the Novocherkassk crown (p. 233, f. 138) side by side with the deer. Characteristic are the bell-like objects with an ibex perched upon them (p. 249, ff. 166, 167); such a one serves also as a mirror handle (p. 193). The horse is rare except on his own cheek-pieces, which so often end with a hoof at one end and an admirably conventionalised horse's head at the other (p. 189). The hare is not uncommon (p. 186). In the Siberian plaques the fauna is yet more varied, for we get many different beasts of prey, serpents, eagles, oxen and the yak, as well as horses, dogs and boars, and even human figures.

There is in the productions of this adopted style a unity in the design and execution, an adaptation of the ornament to the form of the object to be

---

[1] Cf. Dalton in *Archaeologia*, LVIII. p. 237; *Oxus Treasure*, p. 30 sq.
[2] Cf. Ch. de Linas, *Origines de l'orfèvrerie*

cloisonnée, Vol. II. p. 158, on the Fauna of the countries where Scythic and Siberian art prevailed.
[3] p. 178, cf. *BSA*. XIII. p. 85, f. 21, Spartan ivory.

décorated, which makes quite rude things satisfactory. It shews that the style had become the natural expression of the people who had developed the characteristic forms of the objects themselves. It is far otherwise with the occasional attempts to apply the fully developed Greek style to these same objects. The things begin to lose their original shape, and at the same time violence is done to the Greek design which is being borrowed from elsewhere and applied to a new field; hence the shortcomings we shall have to notice in some of the more ambitious pieces of Greek work from S. Russia. When an actual Greek form suited their purposes the Scythians used it readily enough, as in the case of various pieces of armour and some decorations for horses (e.g. at Tsymbalka and Chmyreva barrows, pp. 166—169, ff. 54, 58—61). This was always the case with women's belongings which served for pure decoration, so that their forms were not conditioned by necessities of use. Hence we find plenty of later Greek work at the women's sides, e.g. at Kul Oba and Ryzhanovka. But at the latter we see the miserable attempts of the natives to imitate the higher style, *corruptio optimi pessima*. Other examples of the same failure are the second frontlet from Tsymbalka (f. 55), and that from Volkovtsy (p. 185), and the plate from Berestnjagi (p. 191, Khan. LXX. x.) in which one can just trace the elegant IVth century griffins.

Especially in representations of the human form did the Scythians fail. They did not do so badly with masks because these derive from the gorgoneion which they received in the archaic phase (v. p. 208), but the Ionian decorative art was not specially fond of the human figure, and the attempts to imitate later models are grotesque without being spirited. Such are plates from Geremes[1] and Kurdzhips[2]. The badness of the figures on the Karagodeuashkh headdress (p. 218) may be due to the treatment the plate has received. Most of the thin gold figures in the Oxus treasure, though they are not exactly Scythic, are equally bad[3], but one is fairly good (p. 255, f. 174).

As with the early Turks so with the Scyths, gold is the favourite material. We know of hardly anything but their gold work. A certain number of similar objects in bronze, a few silver cups and horns, their iron sword blades, some bits of carved wood from Siberia, and the interesting carved bone work from the Kiev and Kuban districts, make up all that is left in any other material[4]. We can well believe that their tents were spread with carpets of their own make, and their garments may have had other decoration more suitable than the innumerable gold plates: but of this we have no remains[5]. In the western district, where pottery had been successfully practised before the Scythic period, some of their earthenware was pleasing in shape, with a dark ground and incised patterns filled in with white (p. 82, ff. 24, 25), but native work could not compete with Greek pottery; for a nomad with close communication with the Ural and the Altai gold was the special medium for artistic work, accessible, portable and instantly effective.

---

[1] *KTR.* p. 253, f. 232 = *ASH.* XXII. 9, and p. 33.
[2] p. 223 = *CR.* 1895, p. 62, f. 140.
[3] Dalton, Nos. 49 to 100.

[4] pp. 188, 189, ff. 80, 81, and p. 223.
[5] *Sm.* I. p. 73, No. XXVI. A woollen garment embroidered in red, blue and yellow.

Scythic Style in Northern Asia.

In the borders of European Russia the place of discovery makes very little difference as to style. There may be a rather greater proportion of pure Greek things about the Bosporus, but as pure a Greek style occurs round Kiev or on the Dnêpr bend, and some objects even at Kul Oba are absolutely Scythic. As against the Asiatic steppes there is a difference: there the Iranian influence is much stronger, and objects made in Iran, so rare in the West, can be quoted from the Oxus treasure and the Siberian finds: whereas actual Greek work has not been found beyond the Oxus, though we have seen that Ionian art made its influence felt far to the North East.

Still the first art, to which we can point and say that we have actual examples which found their way into the possession of the Scyths and therefore could attract them, was the Assyrian. This contact must have taken place in Asia, and the Melgunov and Kelermes finds must have travelled westwards, the Oxus sheath, which may be Iranian, eastwards. The mixture of Assyrian and Scythic motives is much more intimate upon the sheath from the Don. As regards form it does not seem to have possessed the characteristic projection by the hilt, but agrees with the other early specimens in its shortness and broadness. Upon it are three beasts; a boar, whose muscles and ear are rendered in a way which will soon let them degenerate into merely decorative curls—his mane has not the gap seen upon the Vettersfelde hog—is pursued by a lion. The lion's mane is represented as though it were a separate cape put on; his tail looks like a string of vertebrae ending in a beak-head (on Melgunov's sheath we have cape-like manes and scorpion tails, pp. 171, 172, ff. 65, 67); his muscles have the S curve and similar mannerisms. The last beast is a lion, just like the other, save that his hindquarters are twisted round so as to bring the feet against the top margin—a most Siberian attitude—and M. Reinach would say most Mycenaean[1]. In this sheath, which cannot be later than the vith century B.C. because of its closeness to Assyrian models,

Gold Scabbard from the Don. Archäologischer Anzeiger 1902. p. 45

FIG. 186.   My thanks are due to Dr A. Conze for leave to copy this.

we see the Scythic style already sufficiently independent to introduce considerable modifications into the model provided by a higher art, modifications dictated by a spirit we can trace for another eight centuries.

The Iranian art was a more permanent neighbour than the Assyrian, just so much higher than the Scythic as to encourage imitation. In Europe its direct contributions are limited to the Chertomlyk hilt[2] and a seal cylinder

---

[1] Cf. inf. p. 276, f. 198=*KTR*. p. 391, f. 351; Reinach, *Rev. Arch.* XXXVIII. p. 39.

[2] p. 163, f. 51, but see the photographic reproduction in Pridik, *Melgunov*, pl. v. 1, and compare the round silver plaque from the *Oxus Treasure*, No. 24.

(p. 193, f. 85) found at Kholodnyj Jar near Smêla[1]; but to the eastwards Iran is supreme. We can see what part it played by merely looking at the pictures of the Oxus treasure. Here, discovered on the borders between Iran and the steppes, we have an ensemble of objects which includes, on the one hand, the most considerable, till de Morgan's find at Susa, almost the only collection of ancient Persian goldwork known : on the other, barbarous imitations of the Persian style strongly coloured by the Scythic character, shading off into the regular Scytho-Siberian work : the Greek things are as it were intrusive, isolated : other objects are unfamiliar in style, and cannot be referred to any known school, though there is no reason to doubt their genuineness. A comparison of these objects from Susa with Nos. 117 and 118 of the Oxus treasure shews their identity in general composition and even in style, allowing for the rough treatment suffered by the latter. Everything in the Oxus treasure has lost its stones. It almost looks as if the things had been prepared for melting down. The mutilated necklet from Kul Oba (p. 197) with enamel in place of stone inlay shews the same scheme as treated by a Greek ; the original model was Assyrian[2].

Bracelet. Susa. Gold, Lapis Lazuli, Turquoise, Mother of Pearl. Achaemenian IV cent. B.C. De Morgan. p. 95.

End of Torque. Susa. p. 97.

FIG. 187 from J. de Morgan's preliminary publication (Paris, 1902), better in *Ministère de l'Instruction publique, Délégation en Perse, Mémoires*, T. VIII. (1905), p. 44, ff. 70, 71, pl. IV.; p. 48, f. 76, pl. V.

Siberian Goldwork.

Of purely Persian style, identical with that of the great Oxus griffin-bracelet which Dalton puts in the vth century B.C., is one piece from Siberia acquired in the same way as the generality of Siberian plates (v. supra, p. 253). It is hardly needed to prove that Persian originals penetrated far northwards, we could deduce that from the imitations, but its presence makes quite certain. It is a necklet[3] in the shape of an overlapping ring, 19 cm. across, made up of two hollow gold tubes, each of which ends in a winged lion. The picture shews the hollows prepared to receive precious stones, turquoise or lazulite; they mark the lines of the face, the ridges of the horns, the shaggy mane, to which is applied a scale ornament which is so effective in any cloisonné technique, the shorter feathers of the wings, the curves of the ribs and, specially typical, the muscles of the hindquarters. Here already the intelligible lines of such a figure as the Oxus deer have given rise to a roundel representing the projection of the hip bone, flanked by hollow triangles that only distantly recall muscle lines (v. above, p. 268). Perhaps the true origin of this pattern is in the purely inconsequent decoration

[1] Perhaps it is rash to call this or Nos. 8 and 30 *below* on p. 208 specifically Iranian.
[2] Layard, *Mon. of Nineveh*, XXIV. LI. 11; cf.

Perrot and Chipiez, *Sardinia, etc.*, II. p. 243, f. 370, N. Syrian bracelet.
[3] ff. 188, 189, cf. *Oxus Treasure*, p. 28, f. 18.

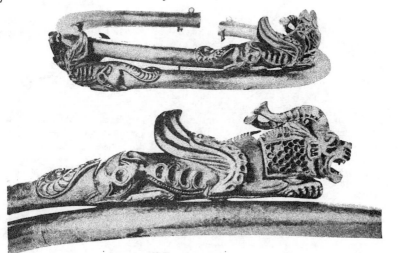

FIGS. 188 (½), 189 (¼). Golden necklet from Siberia. Hermitage. Pridik, *Meigunov*, v. 2 *a*, *c*.

FIG. 190. Gold figure of a reindeer from Siberia. Hermitage. *KTR.* p. 381, f. 335.

FIG. 191. Ends of a torque in gold from Siberia. Hermitage. *KTR.* p. 383, f. 339.

of the Zhabotin horse or the Ephesus ibex : but the deer here figured (f. 190) has markings which might well develope into such as adorn the lion.

Another torque is not far removed from the Persian style of the first, but in spite of their spirit the lions that form its ends are distinctly inferior to it, especially in fineness of execution (f. 191).

A similar falling off is noticeable in a great figure of an eagle[1] with a kind of reptile head devouring an ibex. Especially coarse are the *cloisons* on the neck, breast and upper wings. They were once filled with red stones. The tail feathers seem to have been supplemented by real feathers slipped in. The ibex has the ; ornament. His hindquarters are slewed round in a way that can be better seen on other examples (e.g. p. 276, f. 198).

FIG. 192. Gold Plate from Siberia, probably a crest. Hermitage.
From an Electrotype in S. Kensington Museum.

Of unusual form is a buckle (p. 274, f. 193), of which the pierced work distinctly recalls the late Roman pierced work figured by Riegl[2], and a buckle from Chersonese[3]. This, with the Novocherkassk treasure and the coins of Gordian and the Younger Han, confirm the belief that this style lasted well on into the time of the Roman empire.

[1] First figured in *Archaeologia*, II. pl. XV., also Dalton, ib. LVIII. p. 255, f. 19. I have to thank him and the Society of Antiquaries for an electrotype of his block. *KTR.* p. 379, ff. 332, 333 ; De Linas, *Origines*, II. p. 196.

[2] *Die Spätrömische Kunstindustrie nach den Funden in Oesterreich-Ungarn*, pl. XII.

[3] Ch. XVII. f. 333 = *CR.* 1894, p. 74, f. 107.

Another curious form is a strap ornament formed of a lioness, bent right round until she has almost lost the shape of a beast. Yet exactly the same pattern in bronze and with less complete conventionalising comes from Sympheropol, and another example of still ruder workmanship from Ananjino (p. 258, ff. 180, 181), shewing how even the less important Scythic types spread just beyond the borders of the steppes.

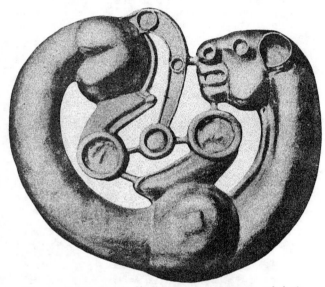

FIG. 193. Gold buckle from Siberia. Hermitage. *KTR.* p. 385, f. 342. ⅔.

FIG. 194. Gold beast from Siberia. Hermitage. *KTR.* p. 398, f. 362.

It has been remarked (p. 253) that the typical plates of this style are either in a kind of oblong frame or of a ∞ shape. As a specimen of the former we have a combat between a boar (bear?) and a great serpent (f. 195). The boar has claws, but all animals in this style have claws, they give such a good excuse for inlaying. In this case there are comparatively few stones. The next (f. 196) is more typical; upon it a griffin and another monster, as it seems a carnivore with horns ending in beak-heads, attack a tiger whose stripes give excellent excuse for inlays.

Of the ∞ shape a simple instance is a figure of a deer with antlers ending in beak-heads, a tail ending in the same and with the fore part of its body covered by a whole bird, and its hinder parts decorated with an entirely inconsequent head. Some sort of small carnivore is attacking it in front. Attention has already been called to the analogies offered by this to the Kul Oba and Axjutintsy deer. This particular example is interesting because its provenance is known; it was brought from Verkhne-udinsk A specimen much like it found its way to China and is figured in *Kin-shih-so* as a coin with the type of a hind suckling her fawn[1].

[1] p. 251, f. 172, cf. S. Reinach, "Représentation du galop," *Rev. Archéol.* 1900—1901, P. Reinecke, "Ueber einige Beziehungen, u.s.w.," *Zt. f. Ethnol.* XXIX. (1897) p. 161; Odobesco, *Petrossa*, p. 512.

FIG. 195. Gold plate from Siberia. Hermitage. *KTR.* p. 386, f. 344.

FIG. 196. Gold plate from Siberia. Hermitage. *KTR.* p. 387, f. 345.

FIG. 197. Gold plate from Verkhne-udinsk. Hermitage. *KTR.* p. 389, f. 348.

35—2

In the combat of griffin and horse we have a good instance of the favourite mannerism, by which creatures' hindquarters are decorated with a pattern of a circle between two triangles, and of another by which an animal is represented as having twisted its hindquarters right round in the

FIG. 198. Gold plate from Siberia. Hermitage. *KTR.* p. 391, f. 351.

FIG. 199. Gold plate with coloured inlay from Siberia. Hermitage. *KTR.* p. 393, f. 354.

agony of combat. The ibex in the grasp of the eagle above exhibits both features. The griffin's wings are becoming rudimentary. Next we have an eagle and another creature attacking a yak whose presence shews that these plates must have originated in the higher parts of Asia.

Very decorative is another version of the combat between boar and serpent. The fellow to this was brought to Holland by Witsen, but is now lost[1].

FIG. 200. Gold plate with coloured inlay from Siberia. Hermitage. *KTR*. p. 394, f. 357.

Interesting for its subject is the following plaque (f. 201)—a boar hunt— a perfect illustration to Herodotus (IV. 22, v. p. 107) and his account of the Iyrcae. We have the man ambushed in the tree with his horse waiting quietly below him and the dog in the corner, and then later we see him pursuing his quarry at full gallop.

In the last (f. 202) we have a representation of the people for whom these were made and of their horses. They are not much like representations of Scyths. They had real saddles with hanging straps that might serve for stirrups. The bow-case is still much the same; the figure that may well be a woman wears a tall cap, like the Karagodeuashkh queen (p. 218, f. 120) or the Chinese pictures of T'u-huo-lo (v. p. 110, n. 2).

There is a small statuette (ff. 203, 204) of a mounted horseman of this race, but the only clear point about his dress is the heart-shaped panel on his back, shewn also on the boar hunt.

The style of these Siberian plates with coloured stones does not penetrate far into Europe. On the Kuban it occurs most generally on circular plates or bosses with an animal twisted round upon itself[2]. On a larger scale we

[1] Figured in his *Noord en Oost Tartarye*, Amsterdam, 3rd ed. 1785, pp. 748 sqq., and copied by Radloff, *Siberian Antiquities*, Vol. I. App. p. 130.
[2] Kurdzhips, v. p. 223, f. 126; Zubov's Barrows, p. 230, f. 132; Kazanskaja, *CR*. 1901, p. 71, f. 137; Ladozhskaja, *CR*. 1902, p. 77, f. 161, and Ust-Labinskaja, ib. p. 78, f. 164, p. 82, f. 177; v. p. 232, nn. 4, 6.

see it on a plate of which the exact provenance is not given. It shews us a most typical Siberian griffin with rather ill-developed wings. To judge from the photograph the gold lacks ·the extravagant solidity of the Siberian work. The griffin is no longer upon his native gold mountains (f. 205)·

FIG. 201. Gold plate inlaid with blue and pink: eyes in black. *KTR.* p. 396, f. 359.

FIG. 202. Gold plate from Siberia. Hermitage. *KTR.* p. 397, f. 360.

FIGS. 203, 204. *Mat.* XV.=*Sib. Ant.* vol. I. p. 123, Appendix. Gold.
Siberian Horseman. *KTR.* p. 383, f. 338.

FIG. 205. Gold late from the Kuban district. *KTR.*   8(f   o

Finally we have the Novocherkassk treasure (v. p. 233). In this the great crown shews a strange mixture of elements. The animals along the upper edge and the birds between the great stones on the hoop are typically Siberian, even recalling early Minusinsk productions; the idea of the whole is perhaps Asiatic, the beading along each edge and the pendants below are debased Greek, and in the middle of the front is a Graeco-Roman bust of an empress, shewing that the whole must be of about the IIIrd century A.D. On the collar, shallow box (p. 234, ff. 139, 140) and bracelet[1] we have the Siberian style, but it has not the expression of ill-regulated vigour that even the rudest of the former plates presented. The animals are rectilinear, and the settings for stones are nearly all of the simple pear shape. In spite of the complications there is no more the same play of fancy. The bottle (f. 141) is interesting because it also offers some indication of date, for a bottle of just the same shape and of similar technique, though not covered with animals, was found in the tomb of the queen with the gold mask. In it was also found a dish[2] inscribed with the name of Rhescuporis, and it is ascribed to the Rhescuporis who reigned from A.D. 212—229. This would agree with the date assigned to the Novocherkassk treasure, but it does not go for much as there were so many kings called Rhescuporis (v. Chapter XIX.). Among the Novocherkassk objects some (e.g. p. 235, f. 143) presented the usual technique of the well-known jewelry inlaid with garnets that has been called Gothic, before which the Siberian style gave place. This is the final stage of its development under predominant Iranian influence.

The remarkable art of which the examples have been discussed in the preceding pages evidently flourished in the Asiatic steppes. One specimen (p. 251), generally similar to the plate from Verkhne-udinsk, found its way to China and is figured in the Chinese archaeological work *Kin-shih-so*. There is some resemblance in character between Siberian and Chinese art; it may be due to some community of race, or perhaps one may have influenced the other; the connection may go back even to Minusinsk days. Or again, the resemblance may be due to both having borrowed from Iranian or some other central Asian art: in each case we seem to have an intrusion of monsters ultimately derived from Mesopotamia, the great breeding ground of monsters. And so they finally penetrated to the borders of China, just as the Aramaic scripts twice traversed the same stretch in the cases of the Turkish and Uigur alphabets. The early Chinese bronzes and jade earrings, figured in such books as *Po-ku-t'u-lu* and *Kin-shih-so*, are very much conventionalised; we have the face *T'ao-t'ieh*, or else the patterns are for the most part merely geometrical. The Dragon, Tiger, and Phoenix only come in under the Han Dynasty and decidedly recall Persian types, e.g. the Simurg[3], but the way in which their bodies are twisted about is rather in the Siberian spirit[4].

The westward movement of the central Asian tribes, described above, brought the users of this style into Europe, but here there were neither the gold nor the precious stones, nor perhaps the skill to make the things. For we

---

[1] *KTR.* p. 492, f. 444.
[2] Bottle and Dish, *ABC.* XXIV. 25, XXX. 11, see Ch. XII. ff. 325, 326.
[3] Hirth, F., *Ueber fremde Einflüsse in der*

Chinesischen Kunst, p. 10.
[4] e.g. Jade roundels figured 20 pp. from the end of Huang Hsiao-fêng's *K'ao-ku-t'u.*

must suppose that the nomads employed some other race, either their original helots from Minusinsk or, very possibly, Tadzhiks, men of Iranian blood from the borders of Iran and Turan, if one may still speak of Turan. Through all their history the nomads have been ready to borrow or rather seize their neighbours' tastes. In Europe the objects are decidedly decadent both in material, size and style. For the evolution and decay of the art we have to allow many centuries. The description of the panther from Kelermes (p. 222) sounds as if it was either an early specimen or a direct model, and that is referred to the vɪth century B.C. The Novocherkassk treasure belongs to the ɪɪɪrd century A.D. The names of the peoples in the steppes change many times during these eight centuries: it is clear that we cannot connect the style with any single historical name. Kieseritzky thought that the objects belonged to the Massagetae, of whom Herodotus says that they wear gold upon their belts and headdresses (ɪ. 215): others have mentioned the gold ornaments of the Aorsi[1], and the gold ornaments of the Turks as seen by Zemarchus[2]. The latter are of course too late in date, but both the former attributions may be right. A nomad has no other use for gold but to make of it personal adornments. The Scyths of Herodotus presumably used the Scythic style which shews traces of Ionian archaic art; in time they or the earlier Sarmatians imported much made in the fully developed or Hellenistic styles: but towards the end of the ɪɪnd century B.C. the intercourse of coast and hinterland became less friendly, and the new tribes which arrived—Iazyges or Alans—brought with them their own things and had less to do with the Greeks. These Alans came into close touch with the Teutonic tribes pressing down from the north-west: and the latter acquired from them a taste for gold and jewels, which they could not have developed in their own country, and some new elements of a beast-style. Hence a decided resemblance between the art of the Great Migration period and the Scytho-Siberian. Riegl (op. cit.) maintained that this art of the western barbarians was really an art of the Roman provinces developed according to a new "colouristic" principle. By this he meant that taste had shifted away from an appreciation of the delicate gradations of light and shade, the subtle modelling and the absolute disregard of the background which mark Classical art with its essentially plastic basis, towards strong contrasts either of light and shade (obtained by deep undercutting in plastic work) or of opposed colours, and towards a care for the shape of the background as well as for the subject or pattern, so that when the evolution is complete one cannot say which is background and which pattern. Modern decoration has shewn a very similar tendency. This is true of Roman art and to a much greater degree, especially as regards colour, of barbarian art of the period, so that the change of taste in the Graeco-Roman world prepared it to receive the foreign elements that came in from the east and north. But Riegl wanted to make out that the character of the barbarian things was the result of the Roman change of taste. Hence he had to make the Siberian style, in which if anywhere the "colouristic" principle is predominant, late enough to be an effect of a process which began about the Christian era. How he would have done it we cannot

[1] Strabo, XI. v. 8.   [2] Menander, Fr. 20 in Müller, *FHG.* IV. p. 228.

tell, for the volume in which he was to have treated of the barbarian arts has never appeared : and now it never can.

This much seems clear: that the Siberian art as exemplified in the Novocherkassk treasure would naturally lead on to the "Gothic" style, the ornamental style of the barbarians that overran the Roman empire. Specimens of this work are distributed from Stockholm to Spain and from Ireland to the Caucasus, but there seems good reason to suppose that it arose in southern Russia, where alone could be a meeting point for the various influences of which it shews traces. The chief characteristics of the style are great love for beast-forms especially those of birds of prey, whose representations, reduced to a hooky beak and an eye, persist when all the other lines have become purely geometrical, and a way of incrusting the surface of an object with flat plates of stones or pastes, especially garnets or their equivalents, separated by *cloisons* of gold. The beast-style seems to derive from the Scytho-Siberian, the bright stones from the east, probably from Persia: but the mixing of these streams was not effected without Greek help, probably that of the goldsmiths of Panticapaeum who under oriental influence had long moved in the direction of a prodigal use of various coloured stones, especially almandines. That the origin of the style is to be sought in the east is shewn by the regular degradation of form, material and technique as we go westward, until in Anglo-Saxon graves we have stiff rectilinear designs, mere beak-heads, red glass and gilt bronze instead of conventional but spirited animals and garnets or emeralds upon gold.

The beast patterns already foreshadowed by the horse trappings from Krasnokutsk held their own longest as "Island varieties" in Ireland and Scandinavia, where they came to be thought autochthonous and characteristically Keltic or Northern. The way in which the handle of a bell from Llangwynodl Church, Carnarvonshire[1], is treated might be Scythic. It has a head at each attachment just like the mirror from Sajansk and the ornament from Nicolaevskaja on p. 244, whereas the ornament on the same page from Bijsk has a pattern of right angles which is a very favourite one on the Teutonic *cloisonné* work[2].

Scythic Copies of developed Greek Style.

Thus the Ionian style or an adaptation of it survived in Scythia for many centuries after giving place in its own country and among its own people to the style of the great Attic masters. The Greeks in S. Russia followed the fashions of Hellas, so the productions of the finest period and later of the Hellenistic found their way to the Scythians who evidently admired and valued them. But here was something too high for them to make their own,

[1] J. Romilly Allen, *Celtic Art in Pagan and Christian Times*, London, 1904, p. 210.

[2] Ch. de Linas, *Origines de l'orfèvrerie cloisonnée*, Paris, 1877, 8; A. Odobesco, *Le Trésor de Petrossa*, Paris, 1889–1900; N. P. Kondakov, *Geschichte und Denkmäler des Byzantinischen Emails; Sammlung A. W. Swenigorodski*, Frankfurt a/M. 1892 (also in Russian and French); J. Hampel, *Der Goldfund von Nagy Szent Miklos*, Budapest, 1885; O. M. Dalton, "On some points in the History of Inlaid Jewellery," *Archaeologia*, LVIII. (1902), p. 237 (bibliography, p. 239, n. b.); *Treasure of the Oxus*, London, 1905, p. 24. Finds in S. Russia; E. R. von Stern, "On the question of the origin of the 'Gothic' Style of Jewelry," *Trans. Od. Soc.* XX. p. 1; D. MacPherson, *Kertch*, pl. v.; A. A. Spitsyn, *BCA.* XVII. p. 115; N. I. Répnikov, *BCA.* XIX. p. 1: Caucasus, supra, p. 260.

and when they tried imitation the result was, as we have observed, hopelessly barbarous and made no approach to style, even the Kul Oba sheath[1] shews something of this.

Fairly good specimens of the more advanced style in barbarous versions are the quiver-cover from Prussy[2], the Karagodeuashkh head-piece (p. 218), and many of the small gold plaques, e.g. the griffins from Darievka[3], others from Ogüz[4], also perhaps the gold band with dancers, a native interpretation of two of the Neo-Attic types[5], and the necklace from Ryzhanovka (p. 179, f. 74), and the plaques from Dört Oba near Sympheropol[6].

The two horse frontlets from Tsymbalka (p. 166, ff. 54, 55), one of Greek work, the other an imitation of a very similar design, let us gauge the difference precisely. The Volkovtsy frontlet is another such curious perversion of the gorgoneion and two griffins (p. 185, f. 78). But mostly the Scythic interpretations of Greek motives are beyond words barbarous. Sometimes perhaps they were produced, like the indications from coins so common on Bosporan gold wreaths, by laying a slip of gold upon a relief, and so taking an impression. Such very thin leaves are peculiarly liable to crumpling in the earth, and when they are crumpled photographs do them even less than justice, so that they may not have looked as bad as the pictures of them do now. Also such flimsy work may well have been done just for funeral purposes, yet, all allowance made, the later Scythian craftsman made astonishingly bad copies of Greek originals of the free style. Nothing could be worse than some of the gold strips from Chertomlyk[7], Kul Oba[8], or Ryzhanovka[9], and some of the plates for sewing on to clothes, more especially the masks[10]. So too nearly all other things from Volkovtsy (v. p. 183 sqq.) shew a singular miscopying of Greek originals. The wearers just wanted the sparkle of the gold and did not much care about the design. This rudeness makes it particularly difficult to detect forgeries of Graeco-Scythic work. The forger and the ancient barbarian copyist were so much in the same position towards their models that the results are much the same. All such work is infinitely inferior to the barbarous but spirited productions of the old native art, marked by a distinct and constant style, or its adaptation of archaic Greek work.

Greek Work for Scythian Market.

In sharp contrast with the Scythic attempts to copy Greek work come the objects which, be they never so Scythic in shape and purpose, were evidently executed by Greeks on purpose for the Scythian market. Though some of them are disappointing on closer examination, yet they bear witness to the facile skill of Greek craftsmen and the energy of the Greek trader who studied the necessities of his barbarian customer and secured for him what would be a delight to his eyes, and at the same time useful and fitted

[1] p. 203 = ABC. XXVI. 2.
[2] Khanenko, op. cit. II. 2, viii. 217.
[3] Sm. II. xii. 2, on p. 178.
[4] CR. 1894, p. 80, ff. 114—124, v. p. 170.
[5] Sm. II. xvi. 3, Hauser, Nos. 26, 29, from Dêev Barrow, BCA. XIX. pl. xiii.

[6] CR. 1892, p. 9, ff. 4 and 5.
[7] p. 157, f. 44 and KTR. p. 309, ff. 269, 270.
[8] ABC. II. 2.
[9] Sm. II. xviii. 14.
[10] e.g. Sm. II. pl. XI. and XXII.; ABC. XXII. etc.

for the necessities of his life.   Some of the finer things may well have been
presented by the Dynasts of the Bosporus or the governments of other Greek
states to important chieftains among the natives, such presents as the tiara
of Saitapharnes professed to be; some were probably executed on the spot
by craftsmen who had tried their fortune in the service of native chiefs; but
the greater part probably found their way through Bosporan middlemen from
the workshops of Asia Minor or Panticapaeum to the treasures of Scythian
chieftains.   The details of such pieces as the Chertomlyk and Kul Oba vases
and the Kul Oba necklet, as well as of several minor representations of Scyths,
shew that some Greek artists must have been familiar with people and
country, and the presence of Greek workmen in the interior of Scythia is
evidenced by the existence of such tombs as Ogüz (p. 170, ff. 63, 64) with
carefully fitted stones and characteristic Greek clamps.   But that objects were
exported from Greece itself on purpose for the Scythian market, is shewn
by the occurrence far in the interior of the productions of Attic ceramics,
and the disproportionate frequency upon them of griffins and such like
subjects supposed to be specially suitable.

Chertomlyk Bow-case and Sheath.

The most famous object made by Greek workmen to a Scythic pattern
is the gold plaque from Chertomlyk that once covered the king's Gorytus
(v. p. 164, f. 53 for the style, ff. 206, 207, for the compositions).   Stephani[1],
who first wrote about it, took it to be Attic workmanship and interpreted
the scene by the obscure Attic legend of Alope.   This opinion was usually
accepted[2], until Furtwängler, in treating of the Vettersfelde find (op. cit. p. 47),
pointed out that its true affinities are rather with Ionian work than with Attic,
previous critics having been led astray by the evident reminiscence of the
Parthenon frieze seen on the left of the lower tier of figures.   Furtwängler,
and after him F. Hauser[3], were unnecessarily hard upon the composition, the
first accusing the maker of having merely filled up a given space with perfectly
meaningless and unconnected figures from his sketch book ; the latter making
out that he did not even draw the figures himself, but that both they and the
ornamental members were produced from ready made dies.   A. N. Schwartz[4]
quotes Furtwängler and Hauser, and agrees with the latter, and at the same
time points to the peculiar squat proportions of the figures, the prudish
arrangement of the drapery[5], and the luxuriance of the ornament, all of which
can be matched in later Ionian art, while the reminiscences of Attic compositions remodelled according to Ionian taste remind him of the treatment of
Attic themes on the coinage of Cyzicus[6].

[1] *CR.* 1864, p. 144 sqq.
[2] e.g. Beulé, *Fouilles et Découvertes*, Paris, 1873, Vol. II. p. 378, makes all *ABC.* Attic, so Sir C. T. Newton, *Essays*, p. 373 sqq.; cf. O. Rayet, *Études*, p. 230 = *Gaz. des Beaux Arts*, Jan. 1882.
[3] *Die neo-attischen Reliefs*, p. 126.
[4] *Drevnosti* (i.e. *Trans. of the Moscow Archaeo-logical Society*), Moscow, 1894, Vol. xv. Pt 1, pp. 17—34, "On the History of ancient Greek reliefs on gold objects found in S. Russia."
[5] Cf. B. Graef, " Die Schamhaftigkeit der Skythen," in *Hermes*, XXXVI. (1901), pp. 86—94. Graef is very hard on the composition and even on the patterns, which he makes out to be very late.
[6] He quotes Canon Greenwell, "Coinage of Cyzicus," *Numismatic Chronicle*, 1887, p. 1.

More recently Prof. C. Robert[1] has, to some extent, restored the reputation of the artist by proposing a new interpretation of the subject. He suggests that it is the discovery of Achilles among the daughters of Lycomedes in Scyros, only that the scene has been snipped in half so that the figures of seated women ought to come on the right side of the girl rushing to the right. So we have Achilles, with his hair done like a woman's, seizing a dagger and restrained by Diomede, while an elderly nurse holds back Deidamia. This latter, her secret discovered, is rushing towards her mother who sits between her other daughters attended by another maid-servant. Further to the right we have Lycomedes in a chair and by him two other men of Scyros examining arms brought by Ulysses, who has disguised himself as a crutched pedlar. More arms are justifiably used to fill in vacant spaces. The corners of the design are taken up with a scene of teaching a boy to shoot, and with the nurse bearing away Neoptolemus. All this goes back, according to Robert, to a picture of Achilles in Scyros painted by Polygnotus[2],

FIG. 206.   *Mat.* XIII. p. 57, f. 35 = *CR.* 1864, pl. IV.   Chertomlyk bow-case.

and such episodes would be just in the manner of that artist. Hence coincidences with the Gjölbashi Heroum well known to reflect his school. But the craftsman who made the relief was singularly awkward in his manner of adapting the design to the space he had to fill. He did not use ready made dies, traces of their edges would have shewn on the plate, and the ornamental strips narrow towards the left side, so that no arrangement like a bookbinder's roll could be used. But he has cut the composition in half at

[1] *Archäol. Anzeiger*, 1889, p. 151.   [2] Pausanias, I. xxii. 6.

᷾a critical point, so that the women
are looking at nothing at all ; and
he was quite at a loss to fill in the
right hand acute angle.   The best
he could do was to repeat the reclining young Scyran from below
and put in a perfectly inconsequent
elderly man sitting on a camp-stool
with a staff against his right shoulder, but no right arm whatsoever.
So again the left end of the animal
frieze is very clumsily managed; and
yet through all the imperfections of
the copy the grace of the single
figures of the original shines clear.

Robert's interpretation is fully
accepted by W. Malmberg[1], who
shews also that enough of the Karagodeuashkh cover (pp. 220, 221,
ff. 124, 125) is left to make us sure
that it was identical in style and
similar in disposition to the perfect
Chertomlyk specimen. He suggests
that it is derived from the Iliu Persis
of the same master, but there is not
enough left to judge by and certainly Robert's restoration of that
picture does not endorse his view.

Malmberg takes the two as a
text for a detailed study in the
affinities of this whole class of objects and accordingly deals with the
Chertomlyk sheath which is of much
the same character.   He begins
by pointing out that the subject
of the latter is not, as has been
supposed, a combat of Greeks and
Scyths, but of Greeks and Persians,
and refers it likewise to the school
of Polygnotus, to the Marathon
painted in the Στοὰ ποικίλη at
Athens by his pupils Micon and
Panaenus.   Here again the craftsman has not arranged his material
with much skill.   For instance the

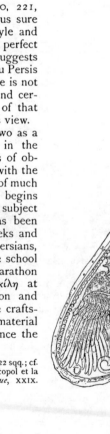
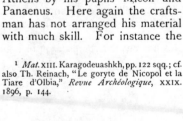
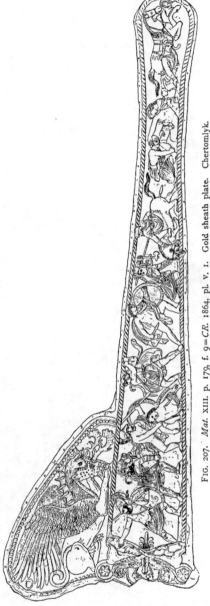

Fig. 207.   *Mat.* XIII. p. 179, f. 9=*C.R.* 1864, pl. v. 1.   Gold sheath plate.   Chertomlyk.

[1] *Mat.* XIII. Karagodeuashkh, pp. 122 sqq.; cf.
also Th. Reinach, "Le goryte de Nicopol et la
Tiare d'Olbia," *Revue Archéologique*, XXIX.
1896, p. 144.

two first figures on the left are known elsewhere, one at Gjölbashi, the
other in the guise of an Amazon on a vase which he figures; but the
Greek is calling forward his men, and his attitude has no meaning if there
be no men on that side, whereas he pays no attention to the Persian who
is about to cut him down, for he does not belong here but to a scene of
single combat with an antagonist in a corresponding position[1]. So too the
Persian horseman farther along has no lower part to his body, his shoulders
are immediately above the saddle. His horse can be paralleled from Gjölbashi. The horse at the end fills the space rather well but the helmet
does not come in satisfactorily. The two griffins at the hilt are not very
happy, and in the original, which must have been something like the group
on the Chertomlyk vase, the griffin upon the characteristic projection could
not have been occupied merely with the head of a deer[2].

In a review of Malmberg's essay[3] S. A. Zhebelëv enters a protest
against his tendency to assign everything to Polygnotus and warns us not
to attribute everything to Ionia and nothing to Athens. He does not
however offer any definite valid reasons against putting these pieces down
as Asiatic.

The whole question receives fresh light from the discovery made by
General Brandenbourg of an almost exact replica of the Chertomlyk cover
in a Scythic grave near Iljintsy (government of Kiev). Kieseritzky[4] says
that the only differences are that the quality of the gold is much inferior
and that there is different application of dotted work. He maintains that
the two objects were made upon the same die, instead of being repoussé
freely. This argues that the Scythian trade was important enough for it
to be worth a Greek's while to make not merely isolated specimens of
objects for specifically Scythian use, but to prepare for producing several
replicas of one pattern. It emphasizes the distinction between the first-rate
works of art destined for the Scythians, works which may be taken to be
presents from Greek rulers, and the mere trade productions exported for
barbarians whose critical faculty was not too highly developed. It does not
touch the question whether the designer of the die had heaped together
absolutely unmeaning figures or spoilt a ready-made composition in adapting
it to fill a strange space. Kieseritzky rejects Robert's interpretation and
regards the design as *disjecta membra* of various cycles of representations.

Kul Oba Vase.

Of quite another character is the work on the well-known electrum
vase from Kul Oba (p. 200, f. 93). The form of the vessel is apparently
Scythic. It can be paralleled by three others from the same tomb, two
others from near Kerch[5], one from Ryzhanovka[6], and two from Volkovtsy[7].
It may well be developed from such round bottomed pots as are figured

[1] op. cit. p. 188, f. 30 and p. 185, f. 28 = Baumeister, p. 2000, f. 2151.
[2] Yet cf. *CR.* 1898, p. 69, f. 117, carnivore and
ram's head on a copper plate from Jenisei.
[3] *TRAS.* Vol. IX. (1897) p. xlvii.; B. V. Pharmacovskij, "Vase-painting just before the Persian

Wars," ib. X. (1899), p. 114, supports Malmberg.
[4] *Arch. Anz.* 1903, p. 83; *BCA.* III. app. p. 51.
[5] p. 198, f. 91, *ABC.* XXXIV. and XXXV.
[6] *Sm.* II. xvi. 7.
[7] Khanenko, II. 2, XXX. 451 and 452 on p. 186.

by Bobrinskoj[1]. An intermediate stage is furnished by a wide-mouthed silver vessel from Galushchino (p. 186, No. 450), resembling the rest of the silver ones in material, but decorated much in the same way as the clay pots. One scheme of ornament is common to almost the whole class, a simple fluting and a guilloche which may go back to Assyrian models : the more elaborate examples have a frieze with beasts, and this one specimen genre scenes from nomad life. There can be no question but that these were executed by a Greek in the ivth century, when the tendency to realism had succeeded to the period of ideal art. The artist must have enjoyed pourtraying a subject so full of local colour, and he has taken pleasure in representing every detail. Characteristic of the stage of art is the accuracy with which the expressions of pain, care and effort are rendered on the faces. Of the other vases of the type, one with a beast frieze is of Scythic work as has been seen, the other Kerch examples seem rather Greek, those from Little Russia apparently of native execution. The technique is always the same, repoussé and parcel gilt.

Chertomlyk Vase.

Not less than the artist of the Kul Oba vase, that of the Chertomlyk (often called Nicopol, pp. 159—161, ff. 46—49[2]) vase must have studied the Scythians at first hand. But in this case there has been no native influence upon either form or design. Only the purpose is Scythic, for there can be little doubt that the vase was meant for kumys. It stands about 2 ft. 4 in. (·70 cm.) high with a greatest breadth of about half as much and is in the form of an amphora with a base instead of a point below. In the neck is a fine strainer and there are strainers in the three outlets. Of these the principal in the midst of the main front of the vase is in the form of a horse's head, itself treated realistically but surrounded by a kind of frill taken from the rayed comb (*Strahlenkamm*) of griffins, flanked by great wings. The side outlets are rather conventional lion-heads. Each outlet was furnished with a plug attached by a chain. This arrangement suggests that the vase was meant for some liquid with scum or dregs, most probably kumys : strainers are common in rich Scythic graves. Below the neck, which is left plain, the shoulders of the vase are decorated by two bands of reliefs. The upper one, slightly repoussé and heightened with gilding, offers on each side a scene of two griffins attacking a stag. The band below this goes continuously round the vase and bears the well-known scene of breaking in a filly, or whatever it may be (v. p. 48); the technique is curious. The figures have been separately cast solid, gilded and soldered on to the ground. Lassos and reins were in silver wire now broken away but remaining in the grasp of some figures. It is not necessary to insist on

---

[1] p. 82, f. 25=*BCA.* IV. p. 31, f. 3; *Sm.* II. vii. 17—20.
[2] The pictures of this vase (e.g. *KTR.* pp. 296—298, ff. 256—258) all go back to the same outline drawings in *CR.* 1864, pl. I.—III. and *ASH.* It would be well if photographs could be reproduced, but for this we must await the Hermitage catalogue. This applies to most of the Scythic antiquities found about that period. Maskell's figure (*Russian Art*, London, 1884, p. 44) is independent but unsatisfactory, better in Rayet, op. cit. p. 225.

the ethnographic importance of this scene, nor on its artistic perfection. Its exactness is shewn by the care with which two different breeds of horses are distinguished. These cast figures are in equally high relief on all sides, but the repoussé work is higher at the front and shades off so that behind forms are only indicated by engraving and gilding. Below the band of Scythians the whole surface of the vase is covered with arabesques made up of palmettes, flowers, tendrils and leaves of acanthus with storks and other birds about the branches. Some have found this a reminiscence of the luxuriant vegetation of the steppe!

The whole work is perhaps the finest extant example of toreutic at the moment of its most consummate mastery, when it was ministering to the suddenly blown luxury of the newly founded Hellenistic kingdoms. An artist of such skill could hardly have been under the necessity of seeking his fortune in the perilous chances of nomad life. Shall we not rather see in it a gift ordered of some Asiatic master by a ruler of the Bosporus or of Olbia, who gave him opportunities for studying the natives, whom he wished to delight with a suitable present? This is no mere botching for commercial purposes such as we have already discussed. This is a master-piece produced when the very highest art was no longer flourishing, but such decorative work as this was at its very best. Prof. Furtwängler in an *obiter dictum*[1] assigns the vase to the end of the vth century, but he gives no grounds and it is hard to think that either figures or ornament can be anything like so early. It corresponds with the naturalistic treatment of barbarians characteristic of the Pergamene school, as in the statues set up by Attalus at Athens, e.g. the motive of the Scyth with one shoulder bared which recalls the Persian at Aix[2].

Other ornaments made for Scythians.

We may say something similar of the Kul Oba king's necklet (p. 202, f. 97) that ends in Scythic horsemen. The artist had probably seen Scyths and worked in their country: also in his design he has probably but improved upon a native model. The ordinary ending is a lion's head as with the broken specimen[3]. This cannot fail to recall the disposition of the inlaid Persian necklets and bracelets above illustrated (p. 271), and the resemblance is increased by the occurrence of colour, blue enamel in the palmettes, in the Kul Oba example, though enamel is not unknown in Greek work outside South Russia. The queen's necklet with a whole lion and the simple bead ornament also suggests native models[4]: and similar treatment occurs on the necklet from Karagodeuashkh[5] with its particularly spirited treatment of a lion and boar. Very like the Kul Oba lion-head necklet is that from the Salgir[6]. Identical design and execution are seen on the whetstone mountings, for instance one from that same tomb[7], from Kul Oba[8] and others, all no doubt made for Scythian use (v. p. 73).

[1] *Arch. Anz.* 1892, p. 115.
[2] Dr C. Waldstein and Mr A. J. B. Wace confirm me in this view. Mr A. B. Cook compares the patterns on Apulian vases, e.g. Furtwängler u. Reichhold, *Gr. Vasenmalerei*, Ser. II. f. 52, pl. 88—90; so too Riegl, *Stilfragen*, p. 235. For fresh light on Chertomlyk, esp. the gorytus, v. Addenda.
[3] *ABC.* VIII. 3 on p. 197; cf. p. 205, n. 2.
[4] *ABC.* VIII. 2 on p. 197.
[5] II. 5, 8, 9 on p. 217.
[6] *CR.* 1891, p. 78, f. 58.
[7] l.c. f. 57.
[8] *ABC.* XXX. 7 on p. 197.

Another ornament which could not very well have been made for any other than barbarian use is the curious three-storied tiara from Besleneêevskaja (p. 58, f. 11); its work is rather mechanical and the use of almandines suggests a late date: but only a Greek could have made it.

A Greek design, which may yet go back to underlying Scythic ideas, is that of the silver pectoral, or whatever it may be, from No. 11 of the VII Brothers (p. 207, f. 105). Above we have the hind with the golden horns, which must have come into Greek mythology from the North—for among deer only the reindeer female has horns—suckling her fawn, below an eagle displayed with gilt wings and tail. This latter is conventionalized in the archaic spirit which recalls the Scythic manner, and the horns are treated much in the same way; but we cannot be sure that it was definitely made for Scythians; the like is true of the rhyta from the same barrows (p. 211, f. 110, p. 210, n. 1, 2), from Kul Oba (p. 197, f. 90, p. 196 *h*) and from Tanais[1], all archaic in feeling.

The three rhyta from Karagodeuashkh are in the free style. They are not in very good preservation but appear to have been of excellent work. One of them bears figures of barbarian horsemen which would indicate special preparation for its destined owners[2]. Malmberg makes a great point of the particular species of deer represented on one of them, a deer with palmate antlers (πρόξ) confined, he says, to Asia Minor and unknown to the European Greeks. Hence the artist must have come from Asia. This argument would apply to the Chertomlyk sheath and gorytus.

A curious example of Greek work made on a purely Scythic model is the unique cauldron found by Prof. D. I. Evarnitskij in a barrow called Raskopana Mogila (the dug-out tomb) near Mikhailovo-Apostolovo in the district of Kherson (p. 79, f. 21). It is more regular in shape than any other and has three bands of ornament produced by applying thick wire to the surface of the vessel. The upper band has conventionalized bucrania and roundels, the lower is a simple zigzag, between them runs a row of palmettes. The superior workmanship of the whole proves a Greek artificer. The palmettes and especially the bucrania suggest a comparatively late date. As it weighs more than forty pounds this can hardly have been an article for export. It may have been made in the country under the direction of a Greek adventurer.

As has been already remarked the Greek style influenced horses' gear least of all, but one horse's frontlet of Greek work from Tsymbalka has already been mentioned in connexion with a very similar design of Scythic execution from the same tomb, and it is accompanied by a cheek-piece also apparently Greek[3]. These are quite elegant, but are far surpassed by the set found in Chmyreva barrow in the same district by the bend of the Dnêpr[4]. Here we have a curious forehead ornament (purely Scythic examples of the same type were at Alexandropol, Krasnokutsk, Chertomlyk and Ogüz[5]) that has a distinctly eastern look, and one or two pieces are barbarous imitations of Greek originals: but we have round and oval plates embossed

[1] *Arch. Anz.* 1910, p. 204, f. 5, *BCA.* XXXV. p. 86 sqq.
[2] p. 219, f. 121; *Mat.* XIII., Lappo-Danilevskij, p. 76, and Malmberg, p. 140.
[3] p. 166, ff. 54, 55 and *KTR.* p. 270, f. 242.
[4] v. p. 168; *CR.* 1898, p. 27 sqq. ff. 27—34.
[5] p. 158, f. 45=*ASH.* XIII. 6, 7; ib. VII. 5; XXIII. 2, 3; XXVIII. 5, 6; *BCA.* XIX. p. 159, Nos. 9, 10.

and then finished with the burin, large ones representing the head of Hercules in his lion's skin, smaller ones with Medusa and cheek plates both of the common wing shape (as at Tsymbalka and Volkovtsy) and of a special singularly elegant pattern.   All are executed in the manner of the best early Hellenistic style.   Interesting is the treatment of the gorgoneion.   As has been seen, the Scyths had long been accustomed to the archaic round-faced type with the tongue out, and here we have the same type translated into the less naive forms of later art without approaching the refined beauty of the Rondanini type[1].   Finally one cannot but think that the great mass of gold embossed plates was consciously intended for the Scythian market : such a large proportion of them bear Scythian scenes (pp. 158, 197) or the monsters connected with Scythia in the popular mind, that it is fair to say that most of them were always destined thither.   By these plates alone we could trace Greek art from the late archaic stage, to which belong some of the Medusa-heads[2] and others[3] recalling early vth century coin types down to the Hellenistic times.   Those found in Scythic graves are of precisely the same style as most of the others and all were probably prepared by the same set of merchants trading with Scythia[4].

Strips of gold[5], popular as they were with the natives who largely imitated them (p. 157, f. 44), were also worn as head bands by the Greeks themselves and occur in purely Greek graves both in Kerch and near Olbia (p. 392, ff. 288, 289).   They did not require to be made specially.

A more difficult question is raised by some pieces that have nothing barbaric about them except that they were found in Scythic graves and shew a certain prodigality of gold that hardly agrees with our idea of Greek taste.   But this taste for heavy ornaments, were it in its origin barbarous or no, was certainly shared by inhabitants of the Greek coast cities.

The weight of the Kul Oba temple-ornaments with the medallions of Athena does not far surpass those with Nereids carrying the arms of Achilles found in the Taman Bliznitsa, the tomb of a priestess of Demeter : and this lady's calathos and other head-gear were heavier than anything in Kul Oba (pp. 425, 426, ff. 315, 316).   Other large ornaments have been found in un-Greek graves at Theodosia (p. 401, f. 294) and in the tomb under the town wall at Chersonese (pp. 397, 422).   The Kul Oba Sphinx bracelet in spite of its massiveness seems too elegant to have been made for a barbarian king : much more the Peleus and Thetis bracelet with its reminiscence of archaic art, and perhaps the queen's bracelet of griffins in spite of its subject.   The same is true of the more delicate jewelry from Karagodeuashkh and Ryzhanovka. Here a curious example of Greek art work, produced with no thought of Scythians' taste, yet appreciated by them, is afforded by the Panticapaean staters set in rings[6].   In general the Greek things found in Scythic tombs are just those which were in use among the Greek coast population and so were on the spot to be offered in barter to the natives and to attract their taste.   Of such the next chapter treats.

[1] Yet this was not unknown, v. *CR.* 1892, p. 20, f. 9, Chersonese.
[2] e.g. *ABC.* XXI. 17; *CR.* 1877, III. 9, 10 on p. 208.
[3] *ABC.* XX. 1, 2, 3, on pp. 158, 197, 208.
[4] The British Museum has plates from Kul Oba (?), Marshall, *Cat. of Jewellery* (v. p. 386, n. 6), XL. 2104-7, and Ogüz (?), LXIX., LXX. 3073—3080, 3085.
[5] e.g. *ABC.* II. 3.
[6] p. 180, cf. Pl. V. 16; *Sm.* II. xviii. 5, 11.

FIG. 208. Hygiea (?). Olbia. ¼. *BCA*. XIII. Pl. II. v. p. 297. Nose restored.

CHAPTER XI.

ART IN THE GREEK COLONIES.

§ 1. *General Characteristics.*

SCYTHIC art has a special interest because it is one of the most important sources of information as to the origin of the nomads of South Russia, and its productions are all that is left us of a great nation : accordingly its remains have been examined in some detail.   The specimens of Greek art found in Scythia or in the coast settlements are, on the contrary, but a small part of the total mass of Greek art-work known, this small part being selected from the greater whole by the taste and commercial connexions of the three or four chief colonies.   Still, this comparatively small part has yielded what is absolutely an enormous number of works of art, and it will be impossible to treat these as fully as the Scythic objects.   It might be thought safe entirely to ignore the finds made in such obscure towns as being unlikely to tell us anything which would not be more satisfactorily attained by investigations at the great centres of Greek art and civilization, but it just happens that certain crafts of the ancient world have left better specimens in this region than in any other.   Whereas we shall find hardly any architecture or sculpture worth serious attention, decorative painting in its latest form is represented ; almost the only Greek carpentry, inlaying and drawing on wood and almost the only textiles preserved have been saved for us in South Russian graves ; the later styles of ceramics can be well studied, and some special developments observed, and terra-cottas without attaining to a high level shew how the Bosporan artists followed at a distance the movements of taste and fashion in the main centres of life.   In bronze work also we have artistic specimens of mirrors and mirror cases, horse-trappings and various vessels with relief work dating from the early vth century onwards.   But it is in the precious metals that the South Russian discoveries are richest.   In silver, besides the peerless Chertomlyk vase, we have vessels of all kinds of shapes and very varied decoration dating from the late archaic to Roman times.   In gold work not even Etruscan tombs have furnished such perfect specimens.   In their own way the necklets from Kul Oba, from Theodosia and the Great Bliznitsa, the earrings from Theodosia and Chersonese, one or two of the gold wreaths, the calathi from the Bliznitsa, the Nereid temple-ornaments from the same tomb, and those with Athena Parthenos and the Sphinx bracelets from Kul Oba, have never been surpassed as triumphs of the goldsmith's art.

It is possible to guess at some of the causes that determined the character of the finds, at least that of those made about the Cimmerian Bosporus. Here we had Greeks living under strong barbarian influence, their archons were of barbarian extraction, and ruled as kings over neighbouring barbarous

tribes. The Milesians themselves were largely crossed with Asiatic blood : the barbarians both of Asia and of Scythia had very strong beliefs in the necessity of providing the dead with a permanent dwelling and with all that they could want in the next world. Hence the Ionian colonists in Scythia were especially likely to raise solid memorials to their dead and fill the well-built sepulchral chambers with precious things, more likely than the home Greeks, whose notions of the next world were more exposed to scepticism. The Bosporans, too, were rich with the riches of a commercial class and had a taste for ornaments of gold upon their apparel. Moreover, their land produced little fine stone (hence the wooden sarcophagi), but easily worked coarse stone (hence the vaults that often kept all these things in good preservation). Further, we must not forget that the most precious things of all come from frankly barbarian graves. The combination of circumstances is best paralleled by the state of Etruria, where the wealthy lucumones had a taste for Greek art, and fitted up their everlasting abodes with beautiful things of Greek, or imitation Greek, style. But the time of Etruscan wealth, though in all it lasted longer, came to an end sooner than Bosporan and Scythian prosperity, and the one region yields products of stiff archaic art, the other, mostly objects which shew the most delicate and fanciful, if rather overblown, art of the times succeeding Alexander. In this the resemblance is rather to Grecian Egypt, from which many parallels will be quoted.

§ 2. Architecture.

It is difficult completely to account for the lack of monumental art. No doubt it existed to some extent, but nothing like what there must have been in most Asiatic Greek towns. Had there been many great buildings adorned with sculpture they could not have perished entirely, troublous though the history of Panticapaeum and Olbia may have been. So the general results have in this respect been disappointing throughout the whole coast, but the new systematic excavations at Olbia give us hope. The Hellenistic house and Prytaneum (?) (pp. 455—457) do present considerable interest, and there is a good Hellenistic anta capital[1]: also one or two fragments, e.g. a marble cyma[2], date from quite early times. The city walls too are reported to be of impressive solidity, but city walls are rather engineering than architecture. So too the great tombs, whether ancient as the Royal Barrow[3] and others near Kerch, or of the Roman period like those at Olbia (inf. pp. 417—420, ff. 308, 309), are also rather engineering works, though some of them have architectural embellishments, e.g. the first tomb in the Great Bliznitsa near Taman had an elegant cornice, but painted only (v. p. 423, ff. 312, 313).

Chersonese stands on a different footing. As a Dorian city it has singularly little in common with the other Scythian colonies. Also the greater part of its site having rock just under the surface, buildings were more likely

---

[1] *BCA.* XXXIII. p. 127, ff. 47, 48 = *Arch. Anz.* 1909, p. 174, f. 36.
[2] *CR.* 1905, pp. 14, 15, ff. 13, 14 = *Arch. Anz.* 1906, p. 122, f. 7.
[3] Supra p. 194, ff. 86, 87. On Mycenaean sur-
vivals in their disposition and the real place they take in the history of architecture, v. R. Durm in *Jahreshefte der k. Arch. Instituts zu Wien,* X. (1907), p. 230. He seems to put them too early, VI.—V. B.C., but Kul Oba cannot be so old.

to be cleared away and their materials worked up into new ones. The first attempt at a city wall is well preserved because it was treated as a mere retaining wall to support a road across a piece of swampy ground, and accordingly earthed up in Roman times. Now that it is uncovered it produces quite an imposing effect. Of strictly architectural work we have but fragments, a few bits of cornice (one in painted terra-cotta)[1] and architrave, an Ionic capital and some late poor pillars built into Uvarov's basilica[2]. The Byzantine remains are another matter, and because of their definite interest will be treated briefly in their place (inf. p. 508). The cave churches at Inkerman and other sites in the Crimea are beyond my scope[3].

From Panticapaeum we have a few pieces in the Hermitage, and some bits lying about Mount Mithridates or stored in Melek Chesme barrow[4]. Ashik figures a few more, now lost[5]. The temple of Artemis Agrotera[6] has left no trace ; the building in which the inscription was found at Akhtanizovka cannot have been a temple[7]. So too with the other temples of whose existence we know. At Anapa a coffer with a Medusa-head from the ceiling of a large building has been dug up[8]. Baths have been excavated at Panticapaeum (v. inf. p. 566, f. 345) and Chersonese (v. inf. p. 506).

§ 3. *Sculpture.*

As with architecture so with sculpture. Not a single good life-size statue has ever been found in South Russia. No large bronzes are known at all, and the few marble statues are of very little value, so I have felt it my duty to enumerate fragments that would scarcely claim attention elsewhere. On the other hand, we have any quantity of funeral bas-reliefs varying in quality from bad to a badness such that there might be some doubt whether they represent the human form at all[9]. Yet it is but just to say that comparatively few gravestones have survived from before the 1st century B.C., and hardly any of these bear figures.

We have evidence in a signature of Praxiteles[10] that at any rate the Olbiopolites tried to secure good work, but of the work itself we have not a fragment. We know from Pliny that an Eros by the same hand existed as near as Parium on the Propontis[11]. We have in an inscription from Chersonese the name of another well-known artist, Polycrates, who may well be the Athenian famous for representing athletes[12]. We can better spare the various statues of whose former existence we know by the whole series of inscriptions from Panticapaeum and Phanagoria, though portraits of the

---

[1] *BCA.* xx. p. 47, f. 23.

[2] Dubois de Montpéreux, Sér. III. Pl. xxxii. *bis.*

[3] ib. IV. vi.: *Trans. Od. Soc.* XIV. pp. 166—279, A. L. Bertier-de-La-Garde, "Remains of ancient Erections in the neighbourhood of Sevastopol and the Cave-towns of the Crimea."

[4] *ABC.* Frontispiece ; *IosPE.* IV. 202.

[5] *Bosporan Kingdom,* III. p. 56, ff. cix.—cxvii.

[6] App. 29 = *IosPE.* II. 344.
  Ashik, op. cit. I. f. x. Goertz, *Taman,* p. 156.

[8] *CR.* 1903, p. 78, f. 162.

[9] G. von Kieseritzky und Carl Watzinger (*K W.*) *Griechische Grabreliefs aus Südrussland,* Berlin, 1909, v. inf. p. 299.

[10] *IosPE.* I. 145.

[11] *NH.* XXXVI. 22 (4); Latyshev, *TRAS.* IV. p. 146; Loewy, *Inschr. Gr. Bildhauer,* p. 383, No. 76 a.

[12] *IosPE.* IV. 82, Pliny *NH.* XXXIV. 91 (19). Cephisodotus who made the statue of Ariston, App. 19 = *IosPE.* I. 199, is thought by Loewy, op. cit. p. 237, No. 337, to have been an Athenian but only of the Roman period.

Spartocid kings would have been interesting, especially as the heads are gone from the bas-relief above the Athenian decree in honour of the sons of Leucon[1].

Of the figure subjects actually preserved, the oldest is a little bit of back hair from Olbia, Milesian work like the Croesus columns at Ephesus[2]; second seems to rank a piece of a sepulchral relief from Kerch with a youth's head and shoulders, Attic work of the early vth century[3]. Next come more fragments from Olbia, a bit of hair and brow in the style of the Parthenon[4], a mutilated head of the end of the century[5], and a larger piece now in the Historical Museum at Moscow[6], part of a ivth century grave-relief in Pentelic marble with a mistress like the seated figure of Demetria and Pamphile[7] and a maid behind her chair, but the heads are gone and the stone split, after which the back was used for *IosPE.* i. 64, a dedication to Apollo Prostates, with a figure of extraordinary barbarity; so that of the good work hardly anything is left. Something similar happened to the stone of *IosPE.* iv. 36, also from Olbia, and bearing reliefs of young men.

To the ivth century belonged the monument of Comosarye[8], with its statue of Astara, which is figured by Ashik[9], but has since been lost. We still have from Chersonese a girl's torso at Odessa[10], of which Zhebelëv says that after the manner in which the zone and diploidion are arranged and the folds treated, it would seem to go back to a good ivth century original: he suggests as its nearest analogue a statue at Corfu[11], which recalls the middle period of Praxiteles. O. Waldhauer publishes a torso of a draped woman from Theodosia, which he dates between 470 and 460 B.C. (he means 370—360)[12]. In the same collection we have a female head from Olbia in very poor preservation, but also of ivth century date[13]; and to the same period seems to go back a sleeping Eros with a torch, similar but inferior to one at Vienna[14]. A bearded male head from Olbia in the Historical Museum at Moscow, in type not unlike Asclepius, is referred by O. Waldhauer[15] to Scopas himself, but it looks later in his picture, and is in any case very fragmentary. To the end of the ivth century belongs the most interesting statue from South Russia, the replica of the Phidiac Athena Parthenos in Pentelic marble dug up at Olbia in 1903. Pharmacovskij[16] judges it Attic work, though rather careless and mechanical, placing it between the Somzée and Patras replicas[17]. Another piece in Pentelic marble is a Hellenistic head from Kerch[18].

From Olbia, from the Hellenistic house at ix on the plan (p. 450, f. 331), come the most attractive of sculptures from these parts, the three heads, of

[1] *BCH.* v. Pl. v. p. 194, v. inf. App. 28.
[2] *CR.* 1906, p. 32, f. 24.
[3] *ABC.* Frontispiece, 15, Reinach, p. 40; *KW.* 441, pl. XXXI.
[4] *BCA.* XXXIII. p. 125, f. 45.
[5] ib. p. 126, ff. 41—44 = *Arch. Anz.* 1908, p. 183, f. 17.
[6] *KW.* 156, pl. XI.
[7] Conze, *Attische Grabreliefs,* 109, pl. XL.
[8] App. 30 = *IosPE.* II. 346.
[9] *Bosporan Kingdom,* I. f. ix.
[10] S. A. Zhebelëv, "Monuments of Classical Sculpture preserved in the Museum of the Odessa Society," *Trans. Od. Soc.* XXII. p. 66, f. 1: for Furtwängler's account of the same collection, v.

Philologische Wochenschrift, 1888, p. 1516.
[11] Arndt-Amelung, *Photogr. Einzelaufn. Ant. Sculpt.* II. 603.
[12] *Trans. Od. Soc.* XXVI. p. 203, f. 1.
[13] Zhebelëv, op. cit. p. 70, f. 4.
[14] ib. p. 69, f. 3, cf. Sacken u. Kenner, *Die antiken Sculpt. d. kk. Münz- u. Antiken-Cabinets in Wien,* 1866, Pl. v.
[15] *BCA.* XXIII. pp. 76—102, Pl. I.
[16] *BCA.* XIV. pp. 69—93, Pl. I.—III.
[17] O. Waldhauer in *BCA.* XVII. p. 99 wishes to refer it to the school of Philiscus c. 250 B.C., but Pharmacovskij, ib. p. 109, successfully defends his own view.
[18] *Arch. Anz.* 1910, p. 210, f. 8.

about half life-size, dug up by Pharmacovskij in 1902[1]. He has no difficulty in shewing the first to be that of Asclepius, and finally comes to the conclusion that it is Alexandrian work of the middle of the IIIrd century, recalling as it does the style of Bryaxis, e.g. his Serapis, but shewing some influence of Lysippus. The expression is mild and compassionate, without the exaggerated passion of Pergamum or Rhodes. The wonderfully beautiful

FIG. 209. *CR.* 1899, p. 23, f. 33. Kerch.   FIG. 210. *Mat.* VII. p. 21. Marble Head of Archaistic
Bearded Hermes.   Hermes. ¾. Chersonese.

female head (p. 292, f. 208) has less defined characteristics, but agrees with the first. The only reason for its being named Hygiea is that it was found with the Asclepius. The third head is that of a child, but shews only the beginning of that accurate study of infant forms which reached its perfection in Boethus: one hesitates to give it a name, but it may be an Eros.

To the IInd century belongs a pair of Herms from Kerch, one headless, representing Heracles, another with the Bearded Hermes (f. 209). Another such Hermes (f. 210) in marble, of a more archaistic character, was found at

[1] *BCA.* XIII. pp. 191—215, ff. 151, 153, 155, 156, Pl. I.—III.

Chersonese in 1890, and is very closely related to the original from which the artificer whose moulds were found there that same year had taken his cast[1]. It distinctly recalls the Hermes of Alcamenes from Pergamum[2].

To the class of the late Hellenistic genre. subjects belongs a statuette from Akkerman, now at Odessa. It represents a hunter in a chlamys[3]. The execution is rough, belonging to the last century B.C. To a model originating in the same sort of taste goes back a statue dedicated by the Olbian strategi to Apollo Prostates in the IInd century A.D.—a boy with a wine-skin, from which the water of a fountain is to gush[4].

Of the Odessa collection perhaps the most pleasing specimen is a bas-relief from Kerch, with Artemis, Apollo Daphnephoros, Hermes and Peitho or Aphrodite[5]. Reinach sees in it Attico-Ionian sculpture of about 470 B.C. But the figure of Peitho in its transparent dress seems to betray the taste of a later time, and the relief would more likely belong to the archaistic class; its poor preservation makes it hard to be quite sure. It recalls the lost Corinth puteal[6], which was almost certainly Neo-Attic. So Hauser says, and Kondakov would seem to agree.

Of whole statues perhaps the best are those of a man and a woman of the Ist century A.D. discovered at Glinishche, near Kerch[7]. They are rather over life-size and of regular Roman work. The woman generally resembles the well-known woman from Herculaneum; the type also occurs in terra-cotta. At Odessa is a female head from Theodosia bearing some relation to this group, but earlier in execution[8]. From Kerch comes an elaborate sarcophagus on which recline the mutilated figures of a man and a woman[9]; the position is that so common on Etruscan sarcophagi; on the sides are interesting reliefs with scenes from the life of Achilles. There is also a statue of Cybele in poor preservation[10]. Both these are also illustrated by Ashik, who gives some other fragments, but his drawings are so bad as to be almost worthless[11]. A good Roman portrait head at Odessa comes from Olbia. It belongs to the IIIrd century A.D., and Zhebelëv[12] sees in it Paulina, and von Stern, in a note to Zhebelëv's article, Julia Maesa.

Animals have not fared better than men. There is a very stiff lifeless lion from Kerch in the Hermitage (f. 211), rather a better one from Chersonese[13], and a pair of rather worse ones from Olbia, chiefly interesting for the mysterious marks scratched upon them[14]. A griffin's body at Odessa might have once adorned the palace of Scyles[15]. In the little museum at Theodosia is an elegant bas-relief of a griffin, but it came from Kerch; a marble table-leg in the form of a lion from Chersonese is good as mere decoration[16]. The British Museum has some specimens from Kerch, sent home by Colonel Westmacott in 1856; they include figures of a lion and lioness, a relief of Tritons and some typical grave stelae[17].

[1] v. p. 367, f. 267, *Mat.* VII. p. 20·
[2] *Sitzber. Berlin. Akad.* 1904, p. 69: *Ath. Mitt.* 1904, W. Altmann, p. 179, Pl. XVIII.—XXI.
[3] Zhebelëv, op. cit. p. 68, f. 2.
[4] *CR.* 1905, p. 15, f. 16=*Arch. Anz.* 1906, p. 119, ff. 5, 6. Inscr. App. 11=*BCA.* XVIII. p. 103, No. 5.
[5] Kondakov, *Trans. Od. Soc.* X. p. 16 and Pl. I. 3; S. Reinach, *Monuments Piot,* II. p. 57, Pl. VII. v. Stern, *Od. Mus. Guide,* p. 102, makes it IVth cent.
[6] *JHS.* VI. (1885), p. 48, Pl. LVI. LVII.

[7] *ABC.* Frontispiece 7, 8, Reinach, p. 39.
[8] O. Waldhauer, *Trans. Od. Soc.* XXVI. p. 191: Reinach, *Rép. de la Statuaire,* II. p. 613. 4, 666. 8.
[9] *ABC.* Frontispiece 9, Reinach, p. 38. [10] ib. 12.
[11] *Bosp. Kingdom* III. ff. cxviii. xcix. c.—cviii.
[12] op. cit. p. 71, f. 5.
[13] *CR.* 1905, p. 46, f. 43.
[14] v. p. 317, f. 227: *CR.* 1872, Text, Pl. XVII. 19.
[15] *Museum Guide,* p. 17, No. 9, cf. Her. IV. 79.
[16] *CR.* 1890, p. 31, f. 16.
[17] MacPherson, *Kertch,* pp. 48—51.

These stelae have been comprehensively studied by Watzinger[1]. His first class[2] consists of those without figures.   Besides the plain stelae or those with a simple horizontal moulding along the top, referred to any century between VI B.C. and I A.D.,—these may have the further adornment of two rosettes or weapons,—we have in the IVth century B.C. a simplification of a cornice with eaves, and at all periods a pedimental top.   A more interesting termination is the palmette in its varieties.   Here belongs the oldest piece of carving from Kerch, not later than the VIth century B.C., an arrangement

FIG. 211.   *CR.* 1894, p. 5, f. 1.   Marble Lion from Kerch.

of palmettes and volutes, recalling early Ionian pottery or even Cypro-Phoenician work[3].   More ordinary forms were at first probably painted : the favourite variety is a palmette rising from a pair of ∞ volutes commonly not lying horizontally as in most Attic work, but set vertically back to back, an East-Greek form[4].   Between the volutes there gradually grow up acanthus leaves and flowers until the palmettes are disintegrated into sprays of volutes[5]. About the middle of the IVth century Attic fashions come in again ; e.g. an anthemion from Chersonese in Pentelic marble (f. 212), and imitations from Kerch.   All these types are copied unintelligently in the Ist century A.D. and caricatured in the next[6].

The figured stelae Watzinger[7] first classifies by their architecture : they offer curious examples of degradation.   The actual relief is usually in a

[1] *KW.* (v. p. 295, n. 9) is mostly his work though he has used Kieseritzky's materials. He describes over 800 reliefs and illustrates some 350, but often older cuts, e.g. some in *CR.*, Latyshev's in *IosPE.* IV. and *BCA.* x. and MacPherson's in *Kertch* are clearer.

[2] *KW.* 1—155, Pl. I.—X.

[3] *KW.* 87, Pl. IV., cf. O. Montelius, *Die älteren Kulturperioden,* I. Nos. 319, 323, 371, 381.
[4] *KW.* Pl. V.
[5] *KW.* Pl. VI. VII.
[6] *KW.* Pl. IX.
[7] *KW.* pp. 22—28.

rectangular panel frequently flanked by pilasters; above is a kind of entablature, often with three rosettes on the frieze.   Above this, again, the composition is in a few cases, in the 1st and IInd centuries A.D., finished off with an anthemion; more usually by a pediment with acroteria, occasionally giving the top a gabled outline.   Far more commonly above the pediment is another horizontal moulding.   The acroteria are sometimes left flat as it were for painted palmettes (Figs. 214, 216), later they degenerate into shapeless lumps: more often an attempt at a palmette is carved upon them, usually without the base volutes (Fig. 215).   Between the acroteria and in the pediment we generally have rosettes.   The most elaborate composition (II century B.C.)[1] has to flank the relief Ionic columns supporting an architrave

FIG. 212. Anthemion from Chersonese.   *KW*. 128, pl. VIII. (cf. ib. 129 from Olbia).

with circles incised upon it.; above this is an Ionic portico, with rails and large shields between the five columns, a bust of Demeter in the pediment and large rosettes above.   Instead of the rectangular field we very often find a niche with an arched top, and the treatment of this arch in conjunction with the pilasters and architrave shews how early the Eastern Greeks began to try and reconcile the two principles, for these rude imitations follow more accomplished Hellenistic models; but we have all the combinations which elsewhere play a greater part, the arch rising from the pilasters themselves as on Fig. 213, or from an inner order or else from brackets; in the spandrels we have long-stemmed volutes or rosettes.   Above the arch come the same upper members as above the rectangular fields.

The reliefs themselves—sometimes there are two on one stone—offer the ordinary types.   The feminine figures, which occur singly or in all possible combinations, are all represented on Fig. 213, the lady sitting or standing

[1] *KW*. 407, Pl. XXVIII.

in an attitude of dejection and the basket-bearing maid often on a smaller scale. The man appears as taking leave of the woman, at other times he is standing alone, and then is usually armed. In Fig. 214 he is resting his elbow on a pillar against which his shield leans while his gorytus hangs behind him. At other times we see him riding out to war with his groom

Fig. 213. *Ios PE.* IV. 391 = *CR.* 1890, p. 29, f. 15; *KW.* 201, Pl. XIV. Stele of Chreste. ¹⁄₁₁. Kerch.

Μελλόγαμόν με κόρην ἀπενόσφισε βάσκανος Ἀ(ι)δης
Χρήστην καὶ γ[νω]τῶν δὶς δύο καὶ γενέτου,
μητρὸς ἐμῆς φθιμένης ὃς νηπίαχόν με κομίσσας
εἰς φλόγα καὶ σποδίην ἐλπίδας ἐξέχεεν.
(l. 2 = four brothers and a father.)

Fig. 214. *CR.* 1876, p. 214 = *Ios PE.* II. 62, *KW.* 454, Pl. XXXIII. Stele of Mastus. ¹⁄₁₅. Kerch.

Ἡ σύνοδος ἡ περὶ ἡρέαν Παντάγαθον καὶ συναγωγὸν Μίκαν καὶ φιλάγαθον Εὐρήμωνα καὶ παραφιλάγαθον Ἧλιν καὶ πραγματᾶν Φαρνάκην Μαστοῦν Μαστοῖ μνήμης χάριν.

(ἡρέαν = ἱερέα.)

following on foot or on horseback (Fig. 215). Both these stelae have been set up by the society to whom the deceased belonged (v. Ch. XIX.). The galloping type like Fig. 218 is rare; usually the horse is walking. When

there are two reliefs they may represent two different aspects of the dead
man's life, e.g. on the stele of Gazurius (p. 507, f. 339), above the relief of
arms typifying his warlike side, is a group shewing him with his wife, a boy

FIG. 215. Kerch. Stele of Daphnus in coarse local stone. $\frac{1}{10}$. *KTR.* p. 217, f. 197: *CR.* 1872 (Text), XVII. 3:
KW. 627, Pl. XLII. = *IosPE.* II. 65. Δάφνε Ψυχαρίωνος | ἐπὶ τῆς αὐλῆς | χαῖρε. | οἱ συνοδεῖται.

and a child. In the case of Fig. 216 the name of Dionysius and his relief
have been added after that of Diophantus. The armed horseman is often
combined on one stele with the so-called "Funeral Feast" (*Totenmahl*),

ΔΙΟΦΑΝΤΕ ΥΙΕ
ΚΟΣΟΥ ΧΑΙΡΕ

ΔΙΟΝΥΣΙΕ ΥΙΕ
ΔΙΟΦΑΝΤΟΥ
ΧΑΙΡΕ

FIG. 217. *Mat.* XIX. p. 49: *Selections from the most
humble Report on Archaeological Investigations made in
1853* (St P. 1855), p. 168: *KW.* 734, Pl. LIV.: Latyshev,
Inscr. Christ. p. 23, No. 12. Tombstone from Chersonese
used again in Christian times. ⅓.

φος
ζοη
κυριε βοηθη
τον υκον τουτον αμην

i.e. Φῶς. Ζωή. Κύριε, βοήθει τὸν οἶκον τοῦτον. Ἀμήν.

FIG. 216. *CR.* 1890, p. 26, f. 14: *IosPE.*
IV. 300: *KW.* 624, f. 15. Stele of
Diophantus. ₁/₁₁. Kerch.

a very common subject[1]; we have a man reclining on a couch, a woman
sitting at the end of it, a servant offering him a cup, a three-legged table
before him, and other minor figures. The scene is universal throughout the
Greek world. Besides Panticapaeum, where it also occurs painted on the
walls of "catacombs" (pp. 312—321, ff. 223, 224, 229, 231), we meet it at Tyras

---

[1] *KW.* 687—737, Pl. L.—LIV., cf. Kulakovskij, *Mat.* XIX. "Two Kerch Catacombs," p. 44 sqq.

(IIIrd century B.C.)[1], Olbia[2], and Chersonese (Fig. 217); this last in Christian times was let into the walls of a basilica, hence the crosses and inscriptions. Originally the type exhibited the dead man as a hero, as in the well-known Sparta reliefs[3]; but the specimens on the Bosporus have become purely conventional; if they represent anything it is rather the dead man in his family circle. Soracus, for instance (p. 321, f. 231), holds a lyre instead of the usual cup or the bunch of grapes that often takes its place. The idea of the deified dead man still survives on the tombstone with elaborate architecture, quite an *aedicula*, described above[4]; on it the man is being crowned by Nike, and his wife appears as a goddess (Aphrodite?).

Unusual subjects are those on the stele of Glycarion and Polysthenes[5]—two men in red in a blue and red boat upon a blue sea—and the memorial of a poet with a lyre and book-chest[6].

FIG. 218.   Tanais.   Votive Relief.   ⅓.   *KTR*. p. 14, f. 12 : *ABC*. Vol. I. p. 278, v. inf. p. 369.

Rather like a grave relief is Tryphon's dedication from Tanais (Fig. 218). The type recalls the coins of Cotys II (Pl. VIII. 4), terra-cottas from Kerch[7], and a clasp in the form of a horseman from Sympheropol[8]. From this latter site come reliefs of Tauri (?), one a trousered rider, early IVth century, the other with two fields, in one a horseman, in the other a spearman in a doublet with a small targe[9].

The ordinary stelae with reliefs date from the IInd century B.C. to the IInd century A.D. Two, clearly among the latest in style[10], bear the actual date 426 of the Bithynian, Pontic or Bosporan era (A.B.) = 130 A.D. Hardly one of them has any artistic merit; the great majority come from Panticapaeum,

[1] *KW*. 687, Pl. L.
[2] Kulakovskij, p. 50, ff. 13, 14; Uvarov, *Recherches*, Pl. XIII. takes the dead man for Asclepius, cf. Furtwängler, *Ath. Mitt*. 1883, p. 368.
[3] Tod and Wace, *Catalogue of Sparta Museum*, pp. 102-113, cf. J. E. Harrison, *Prolegomena to the Study of Greek Religion*, pp. 350—360.
[4] p. 300 = *KW*. 407, Pl. XXVIII.

[5] *IosPE*. IV. 238; *KW*. 550, Pl. XXXVII.
[6] *ABC*. I. p. 279, Reinach, p. 96, not in *KW*.
[7] *ABC*. LXIV. 2, v. p. 369, n. 3.
[8] *CR*. 1889, p. 26, f. 11.
[9] *KW*. 557, Pl. XXXVIII. 442, Pl. XXXII.
[10] *KW*. 272, Pl. XVIII.; 614, Pl. XLII. = *BCA*. x. p. 81, No. 94; *IosPE*. II. 301.

a few from Olbia and Chersonese. I cannot detect any local distinction of style. The very last stage of degradation would seem to be reached in the stones set up by Roman soldiers at Chersonese, e.g. to Aurelius Victor and the son of Aurelius Viator[1], if it were not for rude plates in the shape of head and shoulders[2] something like Muhammadan tombstones but flat. There are a few attempts at sepulchral effigies[3], but they are very poor. The stelae from Kerch not only crowd the Hermitage and the Kerch, Moscow and Odessa Museums, but are preserved, many of them, in the Royal and Melek Chesme Barrows; some twenty-five are in the British Museum.

MacPherson[4] tells us how two statues, one of an orator, the other of a woman, both double life size and of marble and so presumably imported work, were lost in the Volga on the way to Petersburg, and we may regret their loss, as that of Astara mentioned above, but they were probably of late date.

§ 4. *Painting.*

Of painting we have more remains than of sculpture. It is to this rather than to its carpentry that the coffin of the Kul Oba queen[5], the most elaborate early example, owes its interest. The top plank (Pl. LXXXIII. 1*a*) is much the most important for colour and composition; the ground colour is not clear, but beginning from the left we have a mass of green for the chariot, whitey-green horses with red straps, a man's figure with reddish-brown flesh in a red chiton, pursuing a girl in a green dress; a second girl (on 1*b*) has a yellow dress, then comes a man in a blue and white chiton with a red border running after a yellow and brown swan; the next figure, green and brown, is rather being attacked by a swan; there follow a figure in green and brown, and one in a red chiton with a blue border; finally, on the last division (1*c*) a grey female figure, pursued by a brown-fleshed man in a white and blue chiton, and beyond him another chariot, brown, with whitish horses. The hunting scene on the plank below (LXXXIV. 1*b* and 1*e*) has a primrose ground, the chariot is neutral tint, the driver green, the two horses grey; in front a red-fleshed man runs after a bird with a neck outlined in red and wings of white and green. The lowest plank (1*c*, 1*f*) has a red ground; upon it are yellow griffins with white wings, yellow lions and other yellow beasts. Below is a plain yellow band. The end fragment (1*d*, 1*g*) is brown, with a kind of red panel; upon it are a griffin and a lion, both yellow. I have given this colouring at length as the original *ABC.* is very rare and Reinach's reprint accessible, so his plates are worth supplementing; for this is a richer and more subtle range of colour than we find elsewhere in IVth century work[6].

[1] *IosPE.* IV. 120, 122.
[2] *KW.* LV. LVI.
[3] *KW.* LIV. LV.
[4] *Kertch*, p. 85.
[5] *ABC.* Reinach, pp. 10, 127, Pl. LXXXIII. LXXXIV. We have four planks of it left shewn in their mutual relation in LXXXIV. 1. Three of them 1*a*, 1*b* and 1*c* came one above the other along one side: 1*d* was part of the framing of an end: 1*a* is reproduced on a larger scale at the top of Pl. LXXXIII., and on a still larger scale, so that it had

to be taken in three pieces, on the same plate 1*a*, 1*b*, 1*c*; it represents the rape of the daughters of Leucippus. The other two long planks (with a hunting scene, 1*b* and 1*c* of Pl. LXXXIV.) are repeated on a fairly large scale on Pl. LXXXIV. as 1*e* and 1*f*. The end piece 1*d* of Pl. LXXXIV. is enlarged alongside as 1*g*; cf. Dubois de Montpéreux, IV. xxv. xxvi.

[6] For a discussion of the drawings on ivory, pp. 204, A—D, ff. 100—103, and the polychrome decorations of other sarcophagi, v. p. 330 sqq.

Simpler in every respect and therefore presumably earlier in date is the stele
of Apphe, wife to Athenaeus (Fig. 219),
found in January 1887 on the way from
Kerch to the Quarantine. The lines are
lightly incised on the stone, and the spaces
were filled in with colour, since vanished.
According to Gross's drawing, here reproduced, we have a life-sized picture of a
woman looking down at an infant that she
holds in her arms. Her cloak which
covers her head is brown with a red
border: the child wears a red cap and a
white-sleeved shirt. In front of her stands
a Herm with a wreath painted on it, but
Kieseritzky saw therein a woman with a
pine-cone and a box. Above is the inscription traced in red upon a brown
band: the whole was surmounted by a
wreath of bay leaves in white, now mostly
broken away. The work cannot be later
than the first half of the ivth century:
even as interpreted by Gross it is a
charming drawing: nothing else like it
has survived on Scythian soil.

The architectural patterns on the stele
of Apaturis, wife of Thynus[1], are painted,
a cymation in green and blue upon red,
and a bay wreath blue and green with a
red stalk and dark berries; both go round
to the sides of the stele. The inscription
is in red. The stele of Xeno and Xeno-
peithes[2] has at the top a red cymation (?),
under it the inscription, incised but filled in
with red, and below this a red fillet tied in
a knot with its ends hanging right down.
Both stelae are of the ivth century.

We have no good wall painting from
houses: the Hellenistic house[3] at Olbia,
which had an interesting design in the
pebble-mosaic of its peristyle[4], and the
baths at Panticapaeum[5] only yielded architectural patterns and marbled plaster.

FIG. 219. Painted Stele of Apphe. Kerch. *CR.*
1882–8, p. 20; *KW.* 284, f. 6; *IosPE.* II. 217.
Height 1 m. 98 cm.

---

[1] *IosPE.* IV. 363; *Mat.* XVII. Coloured Plate.
[2] *BCA.* XVIII. p. 130, No. 47; *KW.* 34, Pl. II.
[3] v. p. 457, *BCA.* XIII. p. 62, f. 34.
[4] ib. pp. 40—43, ff. 22—25.
[5] *CR.* 1898, p. 14.

But it was on the walls and roofs of grave chambers that the greater part of ancient paintings—hence loosely called frescoes—in South Russia have survived. The earliest seem to be in the Taman Peninsula. In the second chamber of the Great Bliznitsa there were elegantly painted cornices (v. p. 423, ff. 312, 313), and in the middle of the roof a woman's head on a dark blue ground. About her neck was a string of gold beads, and behind fell a light and dark red veil. Her hair, eyes and brows were dark brown, and about her head and in her right hand were leaves and flowers, red, yellow and white. This is one of the very few examples of late ivth-century painting. The head is probably that of Persephone[1].

In the same district, about a mile and a half to the west, Tiesenhausen found in Vasjurin hill the next term in the series of S. Russian wall paintings. In the outer corridor (for the tomb was in two parts) a pattern representing blocks of masonry went almost to the top of the wall, and was crowned with a very realistic cornice shewing a row of oves and dentels, with lions' heads for gargoyles, and above them the line was broken alternately by swallows and ornaments representing meagre conventionalized antefixes. Within the chamber the masonry courses only went up to a dado, above which there was a broad brown band below the cornice. Other colours used were red, grey, black, blue and green[2].

To this early class the traces of fresco at Karagodeuashkh (v. sup. p. 216) seem to have belonged.

"Catacombs" at Kerch.

The sepulchral chambers of Kerch itself offer curious specimens of the later stage of wall painting as practised far from the centres of Hellenistic art, but yet in accordance with its traditions. Something of the same kind was universal in the Graeco-Roman world and is most familiar to us from the wall paintings of Pompeii. Other well-known examples have been found in Rome, the discovery of some of them being of importance in the history of the Renaissance. The fashion has long been supposed to originate in Alexandria, and the earliest examples of the fully developed architectural style are two graves lately found there[3], in which the architectural motives being logically worked out produce a much more satisfactory decoration than the rather mechanical architectural style and later baroque extravagances of the Pompeian examples. It is, however, just as likely that the real birthplace of the style was one of the magnificent cities of Asia Minor. There is no doubt that in each case the tomb reflected as faithfully as convenient the local style of house decoration and even arrangement. We must, however, never forget that these paintings were hurriedly executed by artificial light under unfavourable conditions and that it is hardly fair to judge them as if they were the highest of which their makers were capable.

---

[1] Coloured Frontispiece, *CR.* 1865, Text.
[2] *CR.* 1868, p. xiii.: 1869 Text, pp. 174-5, with illustrations: reopened in 1907, *BCA.* xxxv. p. 47.
[3] H. Thiersch: *Zwei Antike Grabanlagen bei Alexandria*, Berlin, 1904: but cf. Wiegand-Schrader, *Priene*, p. 308 and M. Bulard, "Peintures Murales et Mosaïques de Délos," *Mon. Piot*, XIV. 1908.

The closest parallel to the Kerch tombs is a great sepulchral cave at Palmyra[1], where the mixture of Greek and Oriental races offered some analogies to Bosporan conditions, but the whole being on a much larger scale than anything in Kerch gave much greater scope for the artist who distinctly foreshadows some of the typical effects of the Byzantine style. Another very close parallel is offered by the decoration of a tomb in the northern necropolis of Cyrene; here the flat pattern on the walls resembled very much the carpet-like pattern of the later Kerch examples[2].

At Kerch the sepulchral chambers, generally called "catacombs[3]," occur on the north side of the ridge running west from Mount Mithridates where a bed of calcareous rock overlies one of stiff clay. A perpendicular shaft was sunk through the rock and the chamber dug out in the clay. From the shaft a passage usually leads into a main room from the sides of which open out recesses with couches on which the dead were placed. In the walls there were generally one or two niches to hold lamps or vases. In most cases there was no attempt at decoration and the contents of the catacombs are not often very interesting, since all date from after the Christian era. Moreover nearly always they have been plundered, because it was so easy to violate a whole series of them by breaking through the partition walls. How they stand to one another may be well seen by the section given as MacPherson's frontispiece. In one or two examples of sepulchral vaults the walls which are adorned with paintings are of real masonry; the usual practice was to cover the natural clay with plaster to afford a satisfactory ground, only in a few late cases very simple decorations or crosses and inscriptions were traced directly upon the clay.

The decoration of the chambers may be classified into three styles according as the walls are treated mostly to represent masonry or marble lining or embroidered hangings respectively[4]. The styles succeeded apparently in this order, though Rostovtsev in his last article asserts that the textile style came between the masonry and the marble lining and overlapped both. In all there persists a low band of plain colour or uniform marbling running along the base of the wall and representing a plinth.

[1] *Bulletin of the Russian Archaeological Institute in Constantinople*, Vol. VIII. Pt 3, Sophia, 1903, B. V. Pharmacovskij, "Painting in Palmyra," an account of the Megaret-Abu-Skheyl. J. Strzygowski, *Orient oder Rom*, p. 11 sqq., Leipzig, 1901, has less satisfactory illustrations. Both refer to Østrup, *Historisk-topografiske-Bidrag til Kendskabet til den syriske Ørken*, Kjøbenhavn, Lunos, 1895; I copy the title just as they give it.

[2] Smith, R. M. and Porcher, E. A., *History of the recent Excavations in Cyrene made during the Expedition to the Cyrenaica in 1860–61*. Pl. XXI. p. 31.

[3] This term was given them by the early explorers and has clung to them ever since, although they are not really like the Roman Catacombs: there is sometimes a fortuitous resemblance, owing to grave-robbers having broken through from chamber to chamber, so making a kind of passage instead of sinking a fresh shaft.

[4] A. Ashik, *Antiquities of Kerch; a Panti-*

capaean Catacomb adorned with Frescoes, Odessa, 1845, was the first to publish a Kerch catacomb; Stephani, as occasion offered, described or illustrated in *CR*. those found from year to year, but V. V. Stasov was the first to go into the subject in *CR*. 1872, pp. 235—328, his XVIII plates are in the Text not the Atlas of *CR*.; J. A. Kulakovskij after publishing "A Christian Catacomb of 491 A.D. at Kerch," in *Mat*. VI. (1891), made a fresh survey of the question in *Mat*. XIX. (1896), "Two Kerch Catacombs with Frescoes; also a Christian Catacomb opened in 1895," upon this my account has been mainly based. M. I. Rostovtsev reviewed Kulakovskij in *TRAS*. IX. (1896), Pt II. p. 291, and added much of his own; he has made a new classification and given fresh details in *Journ. Min. Pub. Instr.*, St P. 1906, May, pp. 211—231, "Decorative Painting at Kerch," and it is this article that I have in mind when I refer to him. He is preparing a comprehensive work on the subject.

Among the very earliest vaults are the two with a masonry lining. Of one we did know only by MacPherson's very untrustworthy sketch[1], but Rostovtsev describes a drawing preserved in the Hermitage. The stones below the dado were jointed in black with red rustication, one course was sham marble, another had birds on sprays, above were horsemen with red and blue cloaks : the figures outside the door, shewn by MacPherson as lion-headed, were probably Hermes and Calypso, typical of parting. The other frescoed masonry tomb was opened by Kareisha in 1832. The description is very vague and it is hard to trust the published pictures[2]; the date seems to be the 1st century A.D.; the chief subject was the contest of Pygmies and Cranes.

FIG. 220.   *CR.* 1868, p. 114.   View of the Catacomb of Alcimus.   Kerch.

In an ordinary plastered tomb of the first class, which corresponds in some degree to Mau's first style at Pompeii, we have above the dark plinth an imitation of four or five unequal courses of big blocks of stone treated a little decoratively. This reaches almost to the height of the lowest spring of the irregular roof and is finished off by a broad band representing a cornice and

---

[1] *Kertch*, p. 76.   [2] Dubois de Montpéreux, Sér. IV. Pl. xviii. 2.

leaves but little space above itself where the roof is low, but considerable *lunettes* or spandrels where the roof rises. This space above the cornice is at the free disposal of the artist. To this class belongs the tomb of Alcimus, son of Hegesippus, found in 1867[1]. The free wall space opposite the entrance was adorned with the rape of Core. Four brown horses draw a red chariot with blue wheels: the driver above may be either Eros, who should have wings, or Hermes, who usually leads the horses. On the car stands Pluto in a short red chiton and flying chlamys holding the blue-draped figure of Persephone whom he has seized from among four women. Of these one with a blue veil falling back is probably Demeter, the others, Persephone's usual companions. The cornice is adorned with swags of foliage and birds. In the

FIG. 221.   *CR.* 1868, p. 116.   Ceiling of Catacomb of Alcimus.   Kerch.

middle of the roof was a woman's head surrounded by green leaves and red, white and blue flowers (f. 221), recalling the head in the Great Bliznitsa (p. 307). Another catacomb (Zaitsev's) with the rape of Core was opened in 1895. Its frescoes have stood well and one can still see a head in the middle of the ceiling labelled Δ]Η ΜΗΤΗΡ, and a side scene of Hermes and Calypso[2].

Of much the same date as the catacomb of Alcimus is the vault opened in 1891[3]; above a plinth treated as a perfunctory imitation of marble are four courses of large stones, the joints marked with blue lines and the outline followed in brown. The top course has the thickest stones and each of them is treated as a panel filled with a garland hanging from two hooks. The garlands are alternately simple brown fillets and swags of fruit with flowers, the remainder of the oblong being filled with fluttering ribbons, the whole having a very graceful effect. Above the broad brown cornice band, we have peacocks and other birds on the long walls, on the entrance wall Hermes and Fortune and a deer under a tree. The principal wall opposite the entrance is divided into two by a niche, above which is the familiar motive of two peacocks drinking from a standing cup. On the right of this, but not well preserved, are the frequent scenes of a horseman and his companions and a sacrifice with a man and woman (Rostovtsev calls them Serapis and Isis) wearing calathi. On the left we have the familiar "funeral feast" with the unusual addition of a cradle with children, and beyond a picture of a tent. The whole is flanked by decorative trees and beasts. Something similar must

[1] f. 220, *CR.* 1868, pp. 114 and 116.
[2] *Trans. Od. Soc.* XIX. *Minutes*, p. 56.
[3] Fig. 222; Kulakovskij, *Mat.* XIX. pp. 34—43, Pl. VIII.—XI.

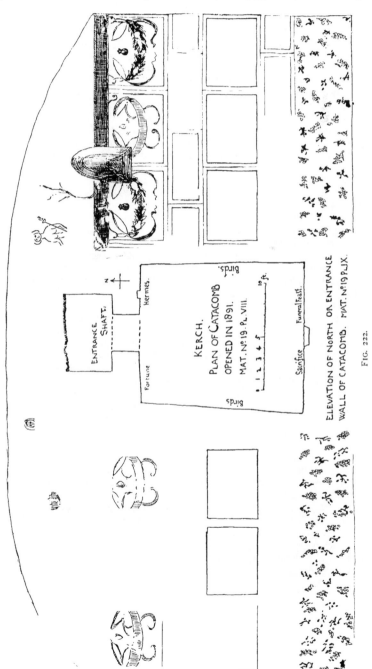

ENTRANCE SHAFT.

Hermes.

Fortune.

KERCH.
PLAN OF CATACOMB
OPENED IN 1891.
MAT. Nº 19. PL. VIII.

Birds.

Birds.

0 1 2 3 4 5   10 ft.

Sacrifice   Funeral Feast.

ELEVATION OF NORTH OR ENTRANCE
WALL OF CATACOMB.   MAT. Nº 19 PL. IX.

FIG. 222.

have been a catacomb opened in 1852, of which the only account is in an article by P. Becker on "Kerch and Taman in July 1852[1]." He mentions two horsemen and birds above, and birds painted on the stones of the wall-pattern. Here seems to belong one opened in 1908; the walls were covered with broad stripes, yellow, dark red and yellow again with a narrow white band between and a white cornice: all round were painted alabastra, round vessels, garlands, olive crowns, Hercules clubs, and embroidered cloths represented as hanging from nails[2].

But much the most interesting of this class, though perhaps the latest, is that of Anthesterius, the son of Hegesippus, discovered in 1877[3]. Whether this Hegesippus was the same as the father of Alcimus cannot be decided, but there is sufficient resemblance in style between the tombs to make it not unlikely. Rostovtsev makes this vault earlier than that of Alcimus. Above the plinth we have four courses of stones separated by black lines and outlined in brown, the whole suggesting rustication. The stones of the top course, which are far the largest, are treated as panels, two of them bear figures with leaves in their hair and caducei in their hands, one (Fig. 223, No. 3) wears brown, the other (No. 4) green and red. Above the black and brown cornice is the chief scene (No. 1): Anthesterius in a blue and white shirt (conceivably steel mail) and brown trousers on a black horse with white patches is shewn receiving a blue cup from a boy in a brown shirt and red hose. Behind this latter is a woman shrouded in red sitting upon a high wooden chair with a blue cushion at her back: on each side stands a girl, one with a long blue dress and white shirt over, the other with these colours reversed. Next we have the tent, brown with reddish people within and apparently a blue floor: against it leans an inordinately long spear, brown with a blue head. Beyond stands a conventional tree with a gorytus hanging on it, and round the corner on a side wall are a brown and a green horse flanking a similar tree (No. 2). With the exception of the green horse the objects seem coloured according to nature. Here we evidently have a contamination of the funeral feast and the scene of the horseman's departure, so the slave and the three-legged table with vessels on it have been supplied on one of the top stones beneath the cornice band. On the right-hand side of a niche we have a man clothed like Anthesterius, but with a blue (steel) cap and a long spear riding a light-brown horse and leading a black one. Behind follows another lightish-brown horse.

In the shaft of the catacomb found in 1891 was found a coin of Mithridates VIII; this goes towards dating this class any time in the second half of the first century A.D.

A transitional stage in which we miss the imitation of a wall built with solid stone blocks, but still have the high cornice, is exemplified by a fine specimen discovered in 1841 and published by Ashik[4]. Unfortunately the drawings then made were anything but exact, and it is hard to see what we may take as authentic in them. Attempts to reopen the chamber have hitherto

---

[1] *Propylaea, A Russian Classical Magazine,* III. p. 362.
[2] *Arch. Anz.* 1909, p. 149, where for some reason it is put down to the early IVth century B.C.

[3] f. 223, coloured in *CR.* 1878–9, Pl. I. f. 1 and Frontispiece.
[4] op. cit., his most important drawings have been reproduced in *KTR.*, pp. 211, 212, ff. 193, 194 and in Stasov XVIII. 35.

FIG. 223, v. pp. 51, 68, 312.

failed. In this case the wall surface below the cornice was divided up by Ionic pillars, between which were various scenes, while there were more scenes above the cornice.   Accordingly more space was taken up with figure-work than in any catacomb known.   There were also purely decorative panels with sprigs, peacocks, masks, and architectural adornments.   The scenes represented included a specially full version of the funeral feast and a cavalry engagement wherein some combatants wear short scale-coats, sometimes partly hidden by a surcoat, others coats of mail so long that they have to ride side-saddle.   The surface of these latter is not indicated with typical scale pattern, but with oblongs just like masonry, perhaps they were quilted and

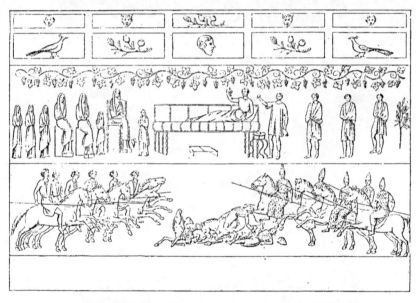

FIG. 224. Wall Painting from catacomb at Kerch (1841) after Ashik.   *KTR.* p. 211, f. 193.

not covered with scales at all.   Which are Bosporans and which barbarians is not clear.   Other scenes shew the funeral, the dead man carried high in a covered litter, also various scenes from daily life and even gladiatorial combats.   All with a Roman touch which may be genuine or may be due to the training of the copyist.

Typical specimens of the second class were those discovered in 1872 and 1875.   They are characterized by the disappearance of the plain wall of apparently solid blocks: in its place we find an imitation of as it were high wainscoting made with panels of many-coloured marbles rendered architectural with pilasters.   A similar change of taste is observed at Pompeii.   The favourite pattern for the wainscot panels seems to be a rayed circle within a larger circle inscribed in a lozenge in its turn inscribed in the oblong of the

panel[1]. The wainscoting is not as high as the former wall pattern and leaves more space for free decoration above.

Judging from the description a good early example of this style was a tomb excavated in 1902 on the way to Katerles[2]. It is interesting for the painting of Medusa's head on the inner side of the door slab, and for a very pretty and natural design of a vine with grapes that adorned the long front of one sarcophagus. These give an idea much higher than usual of the skill of Bosporan painters. It is a pity that the decoration of the other original sarcophagus and of the vault itself has only left very small traces.

Another sarcophagus[3] had interesting painting on its inside: upon one end was depicted a garland, upon the other a table with vessels and two comic dancers; each side was divided by Composite pilasters into three panels, bearing (1) a man with a horse and arms hanging behind him, (2) a painter at work in his studio, (3) the funeral feast, (4) a lady seated and two servants,

FIG. 225. *CR.* 1872, Pl. III. (Text). Section of Stasov's Catacomb.

(5) two horsemen opposed to each other, (6) musicians; the lower face of the cover was adorned with roses. Thus the interior of this coffin presented all that a catacomb could do; it is referred to the 1st century A.D.

The richest specimen of a catacomb and the best illustrated was found in 1872 and published with very full treatment by V. V. Stasov. This author is too much inclined to see Oriental influence in every detail: the fact is that there is nothing but what can be paralleled from Hellenic sources, save the actual portraits of barbarians and the barbarous costume of the Bosporans themselves.

The greater part of the surface of the tomb above the panelling is taken up with trees, birds and beasts, among which the peacock, boar, dog, deer,

---

[1] Stasov, Pl. XII. : a photograph of something like this pattern on an actual wall, *CR.* 1901, p. 58, f. 118.

[2] *BCA.* IX. p. 151, Pl. IX.—XI., coloured.
[3] *CR.* 1900, pp. 27, 28 ; *Arch. Anz.* 1901, p. 57.

lion and leopard can be distinguished, also two winged Genii or Erotes, one of whom has an orthodox Greek chlamys, but the other is arrayed in a brown coat and knickerbockers[1]. The background of walls and ceiling (op. cit. Pl. XIII.) is semé of an ornament in the shape of a light and dark pink heart associated with pairs of green leaves (apparently a conventionalized rose), and has besides long yellow things like centipedes with ribbons at each end and sometimes leaves sticking out of them : these appear to be garlands of a kind or rather bags stuffed with flowers worn as garlands. These two motives occur in all the late Kerch catacombs and can be paralleled from Sicily and from textiles made in Egypt under Greek influence. For this habit of strewing a background is certainly derived from textiles, and the whole scheme of decoration was influenced by the custom of hanging tapestries on the walls of rich rooms[2].

To us the chief interest of Stasov's catacomb consists in the pictures of combats between what we may take to be Bosporans and natives. In these the difficulty again arises that the Bosporans had so far adopted barbarian arms that it is hard to say which side is which. First we have people with long coats of steel mail and buff jerkins under them, with loose brown trousers and conical caps on their heads[3]. When on horseback these ride astride, have long spears and saddles with a kind of tail sweeping back on each side, and resemble Anthesterius. Their footmen (f. 227) bear round shields and two spears apiece, but not all have the coats of mail. In front of them goes a standard-bearer with a standard which recalls both the labarum and the standard on Parthian coins[4]. The principal personage, probably the owner of the vault, always has a red chlamys flying behind him. These people have round faces and no beards. Against them fight folk on horseback who do not wear the clumsy mail but coats and trousers. They use short nomad bows, but so did the Bosporans to judge by Anthesterius and the grave reliefs. Finally, we find the principal figure in all his glory fighting a bearded fellow in coat, knickerbockers and stockings, with a short sword and a lozenge-shaped shield; he would seem to be a rude mountaineer. That there was not much difference in

FIG. 226. *Mat.* XIII. p. 30, f. 3. Coin with Standard and *Candys*[4].

armament between Bosporans and Sarmatians or whoever their enemies may have been is evident; probably they found that the best way to combat nomads was to adopt their ways, and so they suffered the same outer assimilation that has made the Terek Cossacks so like their hereditary enemies among the mountaineers[5].

In one place the surface layer of plaster with its painting had cracked off and disclosed signs scratched on the wall just like those on the Olbia lions[6] and (occasionally upside-down) on certain gravestones[7], all idle scribbles, but thus proved to be ancient. Similar separate signs or modifications of these, occurring one or two at a time on coins, slabs, buckles and strap-ends,

[1] op. cit. Pl. v. VII. VIII. XL, v. f. 227.
[2] Rostovtsev, *TRAS.* IX. ii. pp. 296, 297, e.g. the embroidered sheet from Akhmîm in the British Museum, 2nd Egyptian room, No. 29771.
[3] Pl. VIII.=*KTR.* p. 210, f. 192.
[4] *ZMDG.* XXI. 1867, p. 460, Pl. I. 2; Levy,

"Beiträge zur Aramäischen Münzkunde Erans."
[5] Baddeley, J. F., *The Russian Conquest of the Caucasus*, London, 1908, p. 11.
[6] f. 227, cf. p. 298, *Trans. Od. Soc.* III. p. 247, Pl. vi.; IX. p. 191, Pl. xiv.; XV. pp. 504, 505.
[7] *IosPE.* II. 219, 232.

must have had some real meaning analogous to that of the *tamga* or brand of possession among Caucasian tribes[1].   One particular device ⋔, that to the left

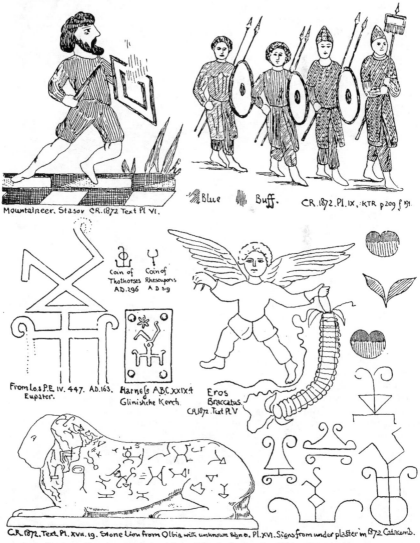

Mountaineer. Stasov CR.1872 Text Pl VI.

🌾 Blue 〽 Buff.   CR. 1872. Pl. IX, KTR p209 ſ 191.

Coin of
Thothorses
A.D.296

Coin of
Rhescuporis
A D sig

From Los P.E. IV. 447. AD.163.
Eupator.

Harneſs ABC xxIx4
Glinishche Kerch.

Eros
Braccatus
CR1872.Text Pl.V

CR. 1872. Text Pl. XVII. 19. Stone Lion from Olbia with unknown sign Ø. Pl. XVI. Signs from under plaster in 1872 Catacomb.

FIG. 227.   Paintings from Stasov's Catacomb.   Various *Tamgi*.

on Fig. 227, almost seems to have been the Bosporan "broad arrow," as it heads

[1] *Trans. Od. Soc.* XV. p. 50 sqq.: cf. the marks on Kushana and Crim-Tartar coins.

an official inscription and appears crowned by Nike upon bas-reliefs[1]; other patterns sometimes used in conjunction with it look like the marks of individuals, kings or citizens.

Very similar to Stasov's is a catacomb entered in 1875 (f. 229)[2]; it has much the same sham wainscoting and the same rose background; the scenes include Apollo in green with a lyre riding upon a blue-grey griffin facing Artemis (?) also in green and sitting on a bull, the conventional funeral feast and the horseman's stirrup cup.

FIG. 228. *CR.* 1891, p. 53, f. 29.
Kerch. Part of bronze buckle
with *Tamgi*, ⚏ and another. ⅓.

FIG. 229. *CR.* 1876, p. 218. Catacomb found in 1875.

A vault (Feldstein's) opened in 1906 shewed both the first and second styles: the first chamber was poor and only had the masonry pattern, the second had sham marble incrustation, the top of the wall offering squares with garlands and flowers or circles and rhombs, and the roof, coffers with birds and rosettes; the third chamber was much spoilt, but its plinth bore columns with purple curtains between them.   Rostovtsev classes with this a vault that Lutsenko found in 1860 but did not record very clearly[3].   It was the burial place of the Ulpii who were well known in the Bosporan kingdom, being ἐπὶ τῆς νήσου and ἐπὶ βασιλείας (v. Ch. XIX.) about A.D. 107.

[1] V. V. Škorpil, *BCA.* XXXVII. pp. 23—35, collects examples of this mark (which I denote by ⚏): it is hard to tell mere varieties from true species; so many, like mediaeval merchants' marks, have the same top. Official inscrr. with different marks, each except ⚏ personal to a king: *IosPE.* II. 423 (App. 52), Sauromates II (those on 428 seem private); 431, Rhescuporis; 433, 434 (App. 59), Ininthimaeus (cf. mirror, *CR.* 1904, p. 75, f. 115); IV. 447 ⚏, Eupator v. f. 227. Reliefs on which Nikai flank the mark, *Inscr. Chr.* No. 99, Pl. XI., ⚏ with another mark both defaced, and Škorpil, f. 1, ⚏, alone; less careful carvings on stone slabs: ib.

ff. 2, 3 shew ⚏ and another mark, the same two as f. 228; gravestones: *IosPE.* II. 84 ⚏ (cf. *KW.* 626, f. 16), 219 (⚏ ?), 232 (⚏ ?), IV. 237, 283, 359, *BCA.* x. p. 36, No. 28 (⚏ ?); buckles etc.: f. 228, ib. XXV. XXIX. 4 ⚏ (f. 227), XXXII. 19 (⚏ ?), 20 ⚏; the four strap-ends have the same tip, it may be a mark: cf. *TRAS.* Slav. Sect. IV. (1887) p. 519, Orient. Sect. I. (1886) p. 304: *KW.* l.c. calls these marks "Gothic."

[2] Stephani in *CR.* 1875, pp. xxiv—xxvi, 1876, pp. 218—222; *KTR.* p. 37, ff. 37—39.

[3] *CR.* 1860, p. vi.

In the 1902 catacomb were coins of Cotys II (123—131 A.D.), and in that of 1875 coins of Rhoemetalces and Eupator (131—153—170 A.D.), so as far as our evidence goes this class of tomb went right through the IInd century A.D.

The third class is represented by the tomb found in 1873 and that of Soracus. In these the architecture is reduced to a mere plinth and all the wall space given up to fancy patterns. In the former (Fig. 230)[1] the style of these patterns differs little from that of those in the second class. We have the same roses and peacocks and garlands as in Stasov's; new are figures of four women dancing and three people under a tree. There is the usual combat, but less well drawn than in Stasov's. The enemy is represented as

FIG. 230. *CR.* 1874, p. 115. Combat from Catacomb found in 1873. Kerch.

almost identical with the victor. On the roof is a Hermes head with blue wings set as a medallion within a flower-sack garland brought round to form a circle: near by is a brown dog with a green collar. There is a kind of cornice pattern, but that is the only concession to architectural feeling.

The tomb of Soracus son of Soracus (f. 231) published by Kulakovskij[2] comes last in the series: a painted *tabella ansata* (op.cit. Pl. VII.) bore an inscription in lines alternately red and black, a curious specimen of Bosporan Greek; both writing and language point to the IIIrd century A.D. and can tell us a good deal as to the pronunciation of that time and place; e.g. αἰ = ἦ and ἱερϣιον appears to be for ἡρῷον, so that Soracus regarded himself as joining the ranks of heroes and his sepulchral chamber as a shrine. Yet that did not prevent a

▶ ἀ[γ]αθ[ῆ] τΥΧΗ ◀
cωρακὸc Β' ΔικϢν πράκτωρ,
οἰκοΔομήcαc τὸ ἱερϢιον
τοῦτο ἐκΧ θεμελίϢν καινὸν
καὶ μΗΔένΑΝ ἔξο ΒΑλϢΝ ἕτερον
5 οcτέον τινὸc. ἐΝθΆΔε κΑτοικϢΝ-
τά με μΗΔεὶc μοι πΑρΥΒρίcει μΗ-
Δέ μοΐ τιc cκΥλεῖ τὰ 'ὸcτέΑ· ὡc ἅΝ
Δέ μέ τιc πΑρΥΒρίcει, Αἰ cκΥλεῖ τὰ ὸcτέ-
Α, Αἰ ἔξω ΒΑλεῖ, μΉτε ἐΓ ΓΗ̂c κΑρπὸΝ
10 λάΒοιτο, μΉτε ἐΧ θΑλάcHc, μΉτε
θΑνϢΝ εἰc ᾅΔοΥ ΧωρΉcοιτο[3]. ◀

[1] *CR.* 1874, pp. 112—118; *KTR.* pp. 34—36, ff. 32—36.
[2] *Mat.* XIX. pp. 16—33, Pl. I.—VII.: references to these, but the details can be seen on Fig. 231.
[3] Spelling unchanged, but accents etc. supplied: l. 9, so Kulakovskij; Latyshev, *IosPE.* IV. 342, βάλει.

justifiable fear that the shrine might be plundered and his heroic bones cast out, and the inscription contains the usual comprehensive curses to guard against this. He seems to have amassed some wealth as an exactor of legal fines.

As regards the decoration, except for the brown plinth which goes right round there is no architecture left (Pl. II.). The whole wall is covered irregularly with the heart-shaped rose, whose leaves are not quite so much conventionalized as usual : we also have the brown garlands sometimes pecked at by a pair of birds; a fresh pattern is one of crossed palms (Pl. IV.). On the left of the entrance stood Hermes (Pl. III.) on a pedestal with money-bag and caduceus painted on a kind of buttress or pier supporting the roof. To this corresponds on the right an actual square pier which bears on one side the inscription and below it two Erotes (Pl. VI. *b*)[1], on another a dancing Satyr with flutes (Pl. V.). At the back of the Hermes buttress, looking towards the couch on which no doubt was placed the body of Soracus, we have the inevitable funeral feast with some apparent attempt at portraiture of the principal figure (Pl. VI. *h*).

This is the latest catacomb with frescoes, but that method of burial went on for another two hundred years. To this interval belong such as have rude drawings or patterns executed directly upon the clay[2]. In unadorned catacombs have been found coins of a whole series of sovereigns from Sauromates I (92—124 A.D.) to Valentinian III (424—455) and later still a silver shield with a splendid figure of Justinian on horseback[3].

Sometimes in Christian tombs crosses and extracts from the Psalms and hymns covered the walls. Such a case was published by Kulakovskij in his first monograph (*Mat.* VI.) and was important for the definite date 788 A.B. = 491 A.D. The names of the dead pair Sauagas and Phaeisparta are clearly of the same Iranian or Ossetian type that we have said to be characteristic of the earlier Bosporan citizens[4]. This and the continued use of the Bosporan era proves that there had not been such a break-up as had been hitherto supposed. The greater part of the walls is covered with Psalm XC., but the writing is so inaccurate that it is of no importance for the Greek text ; the presence of ɥ is so much against that form being Egyptian.

In another Christian catacomb, discovered near by in 1895, we have the same Psalm XC. (but written much more correctly), the Trisagion and various crosses but no names; the writing again points to the Vth century A.D.[5]

At Chersonese, with the exception of three Christian vaults[6], only one chamber with frescoes has been discovered, and that in such bad condition that it is hard to judge of date, style or subject. It was only possible to distinguish the figure of a woman, half nude, turned away from the spectator, and a group that suggests the winged figures bearing away a dead man, so common upon white lecythi[7]. At Olbia practically no remains of painting have survived[8].

---

[1] The figures and inscription recall tomb paintings near Tripoli, *Arch. Anz.* 1904, p. 118.

[2] Cf. *CR.* 1873, p. XI; 1890, pp. 28, 29; 1894, p. 89, f. 148; 1907, p. 76, f. 63.

[3] J. Strzygowski and N. V. Pokrovskij in *Mat.* VIII.

[4] Sauagas seems actually to occur in *IosPE.* II. 49[1] (inf. App. 66), 389, Phaispharta, in a Christian

amulet, *Trans. Od. Soc.* XXI. *Minutes*, p. 8.

[5] Kulakovskij in an appendix to *Mat.* XIX. p. 61. Mr N. McLean kindly informs me that the text offers no points of interest.

[6] *BCA.* XVI. p. 98, No. 1494, XXV. pp. 166—169, Nos. 2086, 2114.

[7] *CR.* 1894, pp. 71, 72, ff. 103, 104.

[8] Two rude figures *BCA.* XIII. p. 26, f. 16.

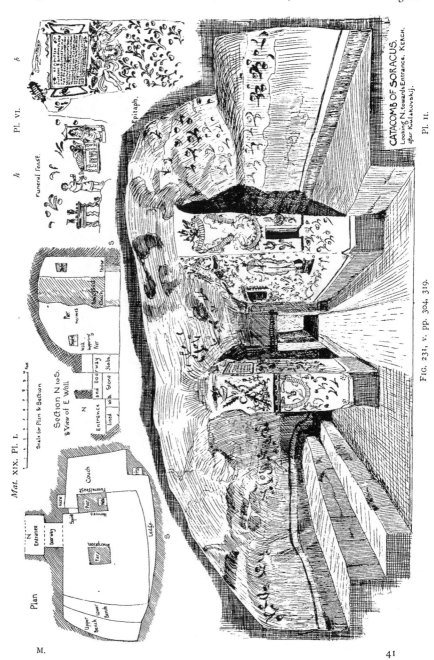

CATACOMB OF SORACUS.
Looking N. towards Entrance. KERCH.
after Kulakovskij.

Pl. II.

FIG. 231, v. pp. 304, 319.

§ 5.   *Woodwork.   Coffins.*

The solidity with which the tombs were built about the Bosporus has preserved for us a large number of coffins which rank as among the best specimens of Greek woodwork extant[1].   They are mostly constructed in a manner suited to the material, with framing and panelling : the enrichments are like those used in stone architecture, which had itself borrowed some from wooden construction, but are applied with due regard to the material.   Only rarely do we find an instance of a wooden coffin clearly imitating a stone sarcophagus in its turn designed after the pattern of a small temple.   The Niobid coffin (pp. 332—334, ff. 241—244) is evidently put together on the pattern of such a stone sarcophagus as the well-known one from Sidon[2] called Les Pleureuses, and both reproduce the columns round a temple or mausoleum,

Fig. 232.   *CR.* 1900, p. 103, f. 183.   Wooden Coffin from Olbia in Odessa Museum.

the statues between them (e.g. the Nereid monument) and the railings put from column to column.   Simple wooden treatment we have in that from Olbia, a little more elaborate in that from Jüz Oba.   In this already we have the application of colour which is such an interesting feature.   Panels and frames were painted with figure subjects, enriched with elaborate marquetry, and even had applied to them wooden, plaster or terra-cotta figures and adornments coloured and gilt, until the more splendid coffins when fresh must have presented a magnificent combination of colour and form.

The plain chest from Olbia (f. 232), probably made to hold clothes, is very like an old English hutch, except that the front has such broad framing that the single panel bordered with beading that runs along the middle of the side is not half the breadth of the enclosing frame, being in fact not an inserted

---

[1] C. Watzinger, "Griechische Holzsarkophage aus der Zeit Alexander's des Grossen," Heft 6 *der Wissenschaftlichen Veröffentlichungen der Deutschen Orient-Gesellschaft,* Leipzig, 1905, has treated the whole subject thoroughly in connexion with the coffins found in 1902–4 at Abu Sir in Lower Egypt. He enumerates over 60 coffins, of which nearly 50 come from S. Russia.   I have only noticed those of which there are published drawings or considerable remains.   W. gives many illustrations and a most interesting analysis of technical and decorative development ; his work has rendered this section almost unnecessary, cf. *Catalogue Générale des Antiquités Égyptiennes du Musée du Caire.* C. C. Edgar, "Graeco-Egyptian Coffins," Cairo, 1905, pp. 1—10, Nos. 33101—33123, Pl. I.—V.

[2] O. Hamdy Bey et Th. Reinach. *Une Nécropole Royale à Sidon,* Paris, 1892, Pl. IV.—XI. p. 238 sqq.

panel but one with the frame. The lid had two slopes and there were bronze handles on it[1] : the end view was very like Fig. 233.

Simple also, but very effective, is a coffin (f. 233)[2] found in a splendid stone chamber under one of the Jüz Oba barrows to the south of Kerch. The sarcophagus took the form of an immense chest crowned by a roof of two slopes with a cornice along the sides and pediments at the ends. In each side and end of the chest was a panel of bright red set in the framework of dark brown and surrounded by a carved and gilded cymation : all the other mouldings were equally carved and gilded, and the whole produces an effect perhaps all the better for the loss of decorations stuck onto the panels. There was an inner coffin with simpler mouldings. Within this was found among other things the curious ring bearing on its bezel a serpent drawing a bow[3] and vase fragments of the end of the vth century[4].

FIG. 233. *CR.* 1860, VI. 2 and p. iv. Coffin from Jüz Oba. Brown ; mouldings and pegs, white ; panel, red.

Of similar general construction, with a long narrow panel down each side, was a coffin discovered by Ashik in the barrow of Mirza Kekuvatskij near Kerch in a chamber with an "Egyptian" vault. The framing of the panel was of cypress and the panel set in an egg-and-dart border of red and gold. On the ground of the red panel were gilt wooden figures of griffins attacking various animals. These have mostly come off the one panel that has been preserved, and we have Α Β Γ Δ Ε Ι Θ incised on the places from which they came, as a guide to the workman in fixing them on. Stephani suggests that the normal Ionic alphabet had not yet come into use, hence the absence of H. This would argue for an early date, but the style can hardly be much before the middle of the ivth century[5].

A more elaborate and better preserved example of somewhat the same design was found by Tiesenhausen in 1868 in the stone chamber of a barrow, about a mile and a half from Taman on the way to Tuzla[6]. The coffin was built with three long panels in the sides one above the other, each surrounded with beading, but only the centre one, the narrowest, was decorated with wooden groups of griffins and panthers attacking deer. As usual the ground was red and the animals coloured and gilt. The framing was further adorned with inlaid arabesques and the corner posts with rosettes representing pegs. The cover was of two slopes with cornice and at each end a pediment ; one of the latter is preserved ; it has a winged figure and arabesques in marquetry, and is surmounted by acroteria on the gable and at each angle.

---

[1] Watzinger, p. 38, No. 15, ff. 67, 68, shews its relation to No. 1 coffin from Abu Sir, which appears actually to have been used as a chest ; cf. Edgar, op. cit. Pl. I. III.

[2] Watzinger, p. 35, No. 10, f. 63.

[3] *CR.* 1861, VI. 8 on p. 427, f. 318.

[4] ib. Pl. III.—v.

[5] *ABC.* LXXXIV. 2 shews the panel and griffins, 3, a part of the cornice ; cf. also p. 21 of Reinach's reprint. Watzinger, p. 38, No. 14. For I perhaps we should read Ⅰ.

[6] f. 234, *CR.* 1868, p. x, and 1869, pp. 177 and 178 : *KTR.* pp. 40, 41, ff. 44, 45. Watzinger, p. 37, No. 13, ff. 65, 66.

In 1882 the same explorer found the best specimen of this-type near Anapa towards Vitjazevo and Blahovêshchenskaja[1]. The lid is lost and nothing is known of it. The framing and panels, of which there are two one above the other, have been left uncoloured, but the architrave, the corner-posts and the broad horizontal band between the panels have as it were

FIG. 234. *CR.* 1869, p. 177. Taman. Wooden Coffin, v. p. 323.

subsidiary panels with a dark red ground sunk into them (Fig. 235). On the corner-posts these are filled with beautiful arabesques of acanthus leaves, tendrils and palmettes of carved and gilt wood. Under the cornice the red band forms a kind of frieze and bore small figures of barbarians in combat (Fig. 236).

[1] *CR.* 1882—1888, pp. xxi—xxvi, Pl. VI. 5, p. 71 sqq. Watzinger, p. 36, No. 12, f. 64.

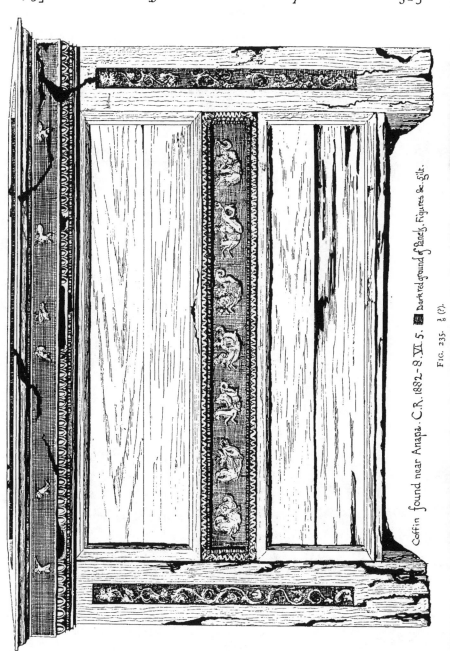

Coffin found near Anapa. C.R. 1882-9. VI. 5. ▦ Dark red ground of Panels. Figures &c. gilt.

Fig. 235. ⅛ (?)

Upper Frieze of Combatants from Coffin, Anapa. Wood, blocked out & painted. CR. 1882-1888 Pl. V.

FIG. 236. Figures, ¼: acanthus pattern, slightly reduced.

CR. Text.
1882 1883, p.72.
Coffin from
Anapa.
Gilt Wood on
r d round.

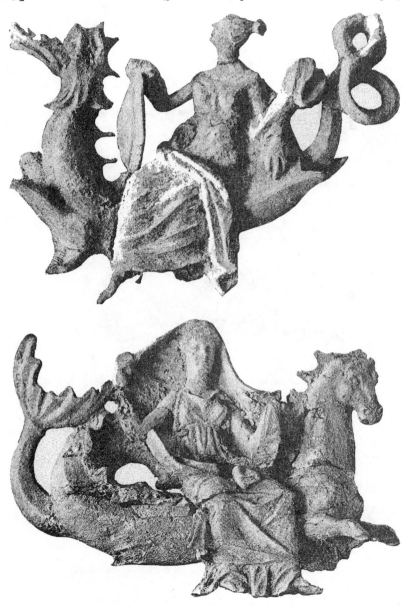

FIGS. 237, 238. *CR.* 1882-8, pp. 50 and 61. Wooden Nereids from Coffin found near Anapa. ¼.

The broad band half way up each side has a row of Nereids bearing the arms of Achilles and riding upon sea monsters[1]. These were adjusted by letters of the alphabet. This band is enclosed by the usual cymatia and beadings, made separately[2]. Among the lady's belongings found within was a coin of Lysimachus, dating the find as of the IIIrd century B.C. which just agrees with the style of the Nereids ultimately derived from Scopas.

FIG. 239   *CR.* 1882–8, pp. 74, 75, A, B, C.   Mouldings from Anapa Coffin.   ⅓.

Of more complicated design, though scarcely more rich in execution, is a great coffin found by Ashik in the Serpent Barrow (Zmêínyj Kurgan) near Kerch in 1839[3] (Fig. 240): Stephani took the design to represent a house with a flat roof enclosed by a kind of railing and with many windows in the side walls. Accordingly the chief horizontal moulding, made up of a large bead moulding, then egg-and-dart, another bead and another smaller egg-and-dart, all enriched with red and gold, does not run along the extreme top, but some eight inches down ; a smaller top moulding has alternate squares of red and brown and a cymation with reversed palmettes in red and white on a black ground. Between is a kind of chessboard three rows deep chequered red and green, all forming as it were an attic. The main order, so to speak, has panels filled with varied blind trellis patterns between grooved styles almost like triglyphs. Below is another row of egg-and-dart and a base moulding. At the ends the trellis gives place to three panels of brown ground colour, bearing gilt figures : Hera with a sceptre balanced by Apollo with a bay branch and between them a panel of acanthus arabesques with palmettes. Watzinger[4] is probably

---

[1] ff. 237, 238, *CR.* 1882—1888, Pl. III.—v. 15, 17, 18, and Text pp. 48 sqq.
[2] f. 239, l.c. pp. 74, 75, A, B, C, D.
[3] f. 240. *ABC.* Pl. LXXXI. 6, 7 and p. 22 of

Reinach.   Coloured in Sabatier, *Souvenirs de Kertch*, Pl. VIII.
[4] op. cit. p. 40, No. 18.

right in thinking this to be an ordinary box-coffin which has lost its end-posts (the feet shewn are not original), has a kind of triglyph frieze instead of its main long panel and an extra board framed above it.   The main body of the sarcophagus is of cypress-wood, the carved parts are of yew.

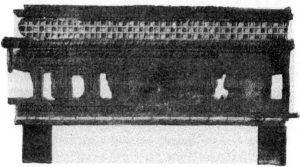

FIG. 240.   *Mat.* XXIV. p. 20, f. 26.   Wooden Coffin.   Serpent Barrow, Kerch. $\frac{1}{20}$.

Of perfectly plain construction was the outer coffin of the Kul Oba king, it was just a great box about nine feet square and eleven inches high (v. p. 202), with one side left open; the elaborate inner coffin belongs to the next class.   The queen's coffin[1], which Dubrux calls a catafalque, had turned pillars at the angles, but otherwise seems to have been quite simply made. Its paintings have been noticed already (sup. p. 305).

Of unusual type was the ornament of a sarcophagus found in 1876 between Churubash and Eltegen (Nymphaeum)[2].   Instead of the architectural patterns derived from stone, the framing was ornamented with inlaid rosettes and stars at intervals in quite an original style.   So in mediaeval times orna-ment applied to wood occasionally escaped from the tyranny of stone forms and suddenly shewed a certain independence and designs adapted to the material.   Watzinger regards the marquetry as preceding the application of figures in relief and this as the earliest coffin extant.   He illustrates a very elegant example of inlay from Kerch[3] with a simple olive-wreath pattern.

The coffins with more ambitious architecture being built up of a very large number of small pieces whose forms were not dictated by the simpler necessities of construction have on the whole suffered more than the artistically framed boxes.   The application of strictly stone forms to the decoration of the coffins had to struggle against the important place that construction gave to the corner-posts, and this prominence was never quite got over.   The simplest way to use stone forms was just to plaster them on to the frames and leave the wooden panels between.   We have such an arrangement in the coffin found on Cape Pavlovskij as mentally reconstructed by Watzinger[4].   Here the ends were left much as on the box coffins, they had a panel with particularly rich marquetry work.   The long sides had at each

[1] Watzinger, p. 44, No. 24.
[2] v. p. 214, f. 115, *CR.* 1876, pp. xvii—xix, 1877, p. 221; Watzinger, p. 39, No. 17.
[3] p. 39, No. 16, ff. 69, 70.
[4] p. 45, No. 26, ff. 81—85.   *CR.* 1859, p. 29 Text: inside it a coin like Pl. v. 14.

M.   42

end and in the middle an elegant Ionic column with inlaid palmettes on the neck and glass centres to the curls of the capitals. These columns must have stood on some sort of base and had above them some sort of entablature to which belonged sundry pieces of moulding enriched with marquetry. In the wide intercolumniations were panels similar to those in the end walls. The roof has left very little but seems to have had acroteria and a sima-like ornament along the eaves.

Watzinger (p. 56, No. 41) has shewn with some ingenuity that the beautiful ivory veneers from Kul Oba would suit such a coffin very fairly well. The wood seems all to have perished and the ivories were not noticed until late in the process of collecting the finds. The unfortunate history of the exploration (v. p. 205) prevented the possibility of seeking any more fragments[1]. The discoverers thought that they had found parts of a box or of a musical instrument, but the size of the capitals with their glass eyes[2] shews that we have to do with a large composition, for corresponding pilasters must be more than a metre high. We may suppose that there were two pilasters at each corner. The subject of the Judgement of Paris (pp. 204 A, B, ff. 100, 101) would take the main panel on one side, and the corresponding panel would have the meeting of Paris and Helen[3]. Or if there were a pilaster in the middle as on the Pavlovskij sarcophagus, the two incidents of the Paris story would be one on each side of it. The pieces with Herms[4] would do for the end- or back-panels. The narrow strips with the rape of the daughters of Leucippus and the preparations for the race of Pelops and Oenomaus (pp. 204 C, D, ff. 102, 103, LXXIX. 13, 14) may have run along the frame above a broader panel. The short thick pieces with a Scythian dragged by his horse and a hare pursued by a dog rather like a Russian borzoi would fit in across the breadth of the corner-posts (ib. LXXIX. 9, 10).

To the posts and frames rather than to panels would belong such decoratively treated pieces as the sitting women (ib. LXXIX. 7, 8), Hermes or a Boread (LXXX. 16), the lion[5] and such mere decoration as the candelabrum (ibid. 14) with patterns like the egg-and-dart and the quatrefoil border[6].

The main pieces here regarded as panels are engraved with the point upon ivory hardly more than a millimetre thick. They are delicately tinted, the colouring, which is chiefly noticeable at the outlines, being in very subtle greys and browns. It must have been brighter once but was probably always restrained, as the drawing is before the time of a varied palette.

The drawing is very like that of red-figured vases of the finest style save for one or two mannerisms (e.g. the treatment of the hands) which suggest the ivth century[7]. Still more like these ivories because of a similarity in technique are the engraved silver cylices from the VII Brothers[8], but if we

---

[1] Thanks to the great kindness of Mr E. M. Pridik I have reproduced on pp. 204 A—D, ff. 100—103, photographs of the most interesting of the fragments. They do better justice to the originals than even Piccard's beautiful drawings in *ABC*. to which all other pictures of them go back. References to pieces which I have not reproduced have been enclosed in square brackets.

[2] p. 205, f. 104, *ABC*. LXXX. [1, 5, 18,] 19.

[3] [*ABC*. LXXIX. 11, 12.]
[4] [*ABC*. LXXX. 11, 12, 15.]
[5] [*ABC*. LXXX. 17.]   [6] [ibid. 8, 13.]
[7] This was pointed out to me by Professor Waldstein, who referred me for an example of early archaistic treatment, such as we get in the Hermes, to a relief at Epidaurus (Defresse et Lechat, p. 87).

[8] v. pp. 206, 210, 382, *CR*. 1881, I. 1—4.

are to judge of these too, photographs are a necessity, for the drawings fall far short, as Stephani complains.

There is considerable difference of style between the fragments, but perhaps it is not more than is to be explained by the more ambitious rôle that the panels would play in the original composition. The presence of the Scythian looks as if the work was done either at Kerch or definitely for the Scythian market, but he is so spirited that we cannot regard him, though different, as inferior to the more finished panels. Watzinger (p. 91) thinks the work Milesian because of the Asiatic look of the capitals, the fame of Milesian furniture and the resemblance to a sarcophagus found at Gordium : but in the ivth century Miletus had lost its commercial predominance and it is at least as likely that we have Attic work. In any case these fragments are unsurpassed as specimens of Greek drawing.

The coffin of the Priestess of the Great Bliznitsa by Steblêevka has left but fragments including the capitals of two pilasters once curiously adorned with inlaid work, one with a palmette, the other with a group of two griffins and a deer[1] and also an Ionic fluted column, another shaft not fluted, thirteen greenish glass roundels from the eyes of Ionic capitals and a large number of pieces of ivory or bone for inlaying. Also various pieces of moulding, egg-and-dart, etc. with traces of red colour. These would make up into something not unlike the Pavlovskij coffin.

Also from the same Bliznitsa come the fragments of a man's coffin which was utterly destroyed by the falling in of the vault above it[2]. They include a very large number of pieces of ivory for inlaying, having the forms of human figures, male and female, parts of Fauns, Erotes, birds, horses, deer and three figures of Sirens playing the drum, the cymbals and the flute, also a butterfly, leaves, grape bunches and palmettes, and purely architectural pieces with traces of colour, egg-and-dart mouldings, cymatia and Ionic capitals duly garnished with glass eyes to the volutes (v. p. 424, f. 314). In spite of the large number of fragments no attempt can be made to restore the general design. Very similar fragments were discovered by MacPherson[3].

The next step towards a temple form is when there are large pilasters or piers at the corners and along the sides small pilasters, usually five, supporting a fully-developed entablature and resting on an imposing plinth. A good example of such a type is figured by Watzinger[4]. It was found by Kareisha in 1842 and a drawing has been preserved, but the original has perished entirely. The pilasters were Corinthian with Attic bases. Along the eaves were triangles representing antefixes and on the gables strange acroteria[5]. Under the projecting upper member of the plinth were turned balusters supporting the corners. Of the same type is a coffin from Kerch in the Antiquarium at Berlin[6]. The capitals, this time Ionic (?), were moulded in stucco which has fallen away, the lid is lost.

---

[1] p. 424, f. 314, *CR.* 1865, Pl. vi. 4, 5 and p. 9. Watzinger, p. 47, No. 28, ff. 87, 88.

[2] *CR.* 1866, Pl. I. and II. 1—26 and pp. 5—68 of the Text. Watzinger, p. 56, No. 40.

[3] *Kertch*, Pl. I. p. 55.

[4] op. cit. p. 46, No. 27, f. 86.

[5] Compare the solid flat corner acroteria of a marble sarcophagus found at Kerch, *CR.* 1905, p. 58, f. 66. Probably these were painted, cf. those of grave reliefs, supra, p. 301, f. 214.

[6] Watzinger, p. 48, No. 29, ff. 89—91.

In these the corner-posts are still flat as natural construction demands, but the straining after stone effects led to the substitution of a round pillar at the corners. The simplest example had just a base moulding and a friezeless architrave and seven Ionic pillars along each side. In each of the panels between them hung a wreath of stucco, and two on each end-panel (compare the wreaths in the catacomb on p. 311, f. 222). The lid had two slopes[1]. To this class belongs a sarcophagus found near the Kerch Almshouse of Zolotarev in 1883. It was in rather bad condition but was remarkable for the great variety of applied figures that it once bore. At the angles there seem to have been turned pilasters on a flat carved base, the usual cornice and slender colonnettes along the sides. Along the frieze seem to have been

FIG. 241.   *Mat.* XXIV. p. 19, f. 24 = *CR.* 1875, Frontispiece.   Niobid Coffin.   Kerch. $\frac{1}{18}$.

wooden figures of Centaurs, dolphins, hippocamps, pegasi, wolves attacking bulls, dogs, a horse, a lynx and a barbarian spearing a lion, and above at the corners wooden dolphins. In the panels were plaster appliques coloured white, blue and brown, including winged Naiads, Medusa-masks, bucrania and dolphins[2]. The Hermitage exhibits a model coffin set up to shew off the plaster appliques; the coffin and arrangement are not to be regarded, but the photograph gives a good idea of the variety of the appliques found together[3]. Somewhat similar was one found by Kulakovskij in 1890 at Glinishche near Kerch, but its preservation was not very good[4]. The same kind of thing comes from near Cape Zjuk to the north of Kerch[5].

The most elaborate wooden sarcophagus that we possess has been already referred to as that of the Niobids. It was found in 1874 on Mount Mithridates. Were it not that it lacks its cover it would be a regular little temple of the Ionic order. Along the side (f. 241) are six intercolumniations with five complete columns and two half ones against the angle piers. At the ends

[1] Watzinger, p. 49, No. 30, f. 92, from a drawing in the Archaeological Commission. The coffin, found in 1864, has perished.
[2] *CR.* 1882-8, p. xl: this seems to be Watzinger's p. 49, No. 32, ff. 94—107, which shew very rude work, but subjects agreeing with the above description.
[3] inf. pp. 371—373, ff. 269—277. Another with great variety is Watzinger's p. 51, No. 33, ff. 108—111.
[4] *CR.* 1882-8, p. 74, Note 1 and 1890, p. 25.
[5] *Trans. Od. Soc.* XIX. Pl. IV. *Materials*, p. 127.

(f. 242) we have two half columns and a single whole one; these end columns stand in front of pilasters with imposts from which arches are turned across. Above the columns run a narrow frieze and a cornice with dentels. From column to column, about a third of the way up, go rods holding trellis work in place below them, answering to the railings put in this position in actual temples. The statues usual on the stylobate are represented by figures of coloured plaster

FIG. 242. *Mat.* XXIV. p. 19, f. 25 = *CR.* 1875, p. 5. End view of the same coffin. $\frac{1}{12}$.

stuck on to the surface of the panel immediately above the trellis. They belong to the series of the Niobids, and the Pedagogue (f. 243) was found actually in place. Most were rather broken, but their places could be traced on the panels. Within were found glass vessels and a gold wreath with an indication of a coin of Vespasian. On the whole the sarcophagus is a fine piece of work, although perhaps its design goes beyond what is legitimate in wood[1].

Joinery and Ivory-work.

It just happens that by far the greater part of Greek woodwork left to us consists of coffins. But the few fragments left of other pieces of furniture make us regret their rarity. In 1842 Kareisha discovered a three-legged table

[1] *CR.* 1875, p. 5 sqq. Watzinger, p. 54, No. 35. The identification of the indication made by Mr Markov has degraded the sarcophagus from being the first example of the combination of arch under architrave: Stephani had put it down to a Diadochus and dated it in the IIIrd century, B.C.

in a tomb by the Kerch Public Garden.   On being touched it fell to pieces, but one leg was saved, and the whole can easily be restored from this and from the pictures.   For this is just the type of table commonly represented in the funeral feast scene[1].   The same technique as was applied to coffins was used in making boxes for daily use.   To such a box belonged a piece of ivory inlay representing Eros and Aphrodite.   The drawing is wonderfully free, especially considering the material (v. p. 424, f. 314).

FIG. 243.   *Mat.* XXIV. pp. 12, 16, ff. 14, 20.   Plaster Niobid and Pedagogue from the same coffin.   ½.

Some interesting ivories come from Olbia, archaic engravings of Eros and the " Persian " Artemis[2], a statuette of a seated woman about 2 in. high[3],

[1] *ABC.* LXXXI. 1—5, p. 126; *Jahrb. d. k. deutschen Arch. Inst.* 1902, pp. 125—140, C. Ransom, " Reste Gr. Holzmöbel in Berlin," p. 127, f. 2.

[2] Vogell, *Sammlung* (v. inf. p. 339 n. 6), Nos. 1145, 1146, ff. 54, 55.

[3] *BCA.* XXXIII. p. 106, f. 4 = *CR.* 1907, p. 57, f. 47

and a box the bits of which bear Erotes playing the double flute and juggling
with balls[1].   Unexpected are the remains of another box made up of fourteen
narrow panels apparently representing a Sassanian king and his court watching
nautch girls and child acrobats dancing and tumbling to the music of winged
boys.   Pharmacovskij cites Alexandrian analogues for the work, but they are
not convincing and it is as likely to have come from somewhere further east,
almost outside the classical tradition[2].   From Chersonese come some late bone
fragments carved with animals, a barbarian soldier and a statuette[3].

We may also mention some sets of men for playing games, one with heads
of nine gods, Augustus, L. Caesar, and a lady of their house, two wreaths
and the Eleusinium, numbered on the reverse I—XV in Greek and Latin, all
found at Kerch in a box complete, another at Odessa, most of a set of eighteen,
also from Kerch[4], and one from Chersonese consisting of fifteen black and fifteen
white draughtsmen in glass[5].

Very neat joinery is shewn in a toilet box found at Kerch with little compartments containing a round bronze mirror, a comb and spaces for putting
jewelry[6].   Still higher skill went to making the comb with the words in open
work ΑΔΕΛΦΗ ΔϢΡΟΝ[7].

So much for the remains of Greek woodwork found in South Russia to
which Blümner[8] rightly points as to perhaps the most important source for
our knowledge of Greek carpentry.

It is curious to notice how much the Greek interpretation of stone forms
in wood forestalled the ways of the Renaissance artists.   For instance, the
table-leg might well have been the work of a XVIth-century Italian, and the
same may be said of details such as those of the Niobid sarcophagus.   Only
the Italians could not remain so long at the stage of satisfying simplicity and
degenerated much sooner into rococo.   In the wall paintings resemblances are
not always mere coincidences, for discoveries of ancient frescoes in Rome had
an important effect in guiding Italian decoration: but the case of woodwork
shews that without them the development would have been very similar.

§ 6.   *Textiles.*

The special conditions that have preserved wooden objects for us in
Bosporan graves have also allowed the survival of a few specimens of
textiles: for the older time before our era little has been found elsewhere,
later on Grecian Egypt has furnished us with some examples.   Stephani has
reproduced and discussed the best pieces[9].   He prefaces his description with
an account of the representation of textiles in art, especially vase-paintings.

The oldest piece (p. 212, f. 113, l.c. Pl. IV.) covered the sarcophagus in
No. VI of the VII Brothers, which dates from the IVth century.   The stuff

[1] *CR.* 1904, p. 39, f. 57.
[2] *Arch. Anz.* 1907, pp. 149—151, ff. 15—28;
CR. 1906, pp. 39—44, ff. 35—48; *BCA.* XXXIII.
p. 134 sqq., cf. *Bull. Soc. Arch. d'Alexandrie,*
V. Pl. I. II. p. 3.
[3] *CR.* 1895, p. 93, f. 239; 1901, p. 39, ff. 77, 78; 1902,
p. 39, f. 64; 1903, p. 35, ff. 45—47; 1904, p. 62, ff. 94, 95.

[4] M. I. Rostovtsev, *BCA.* X. pp. 109—124, Pl.
III. IV., cf. *Rev. Archéol.* 1905, V. pp. 110—124: *Arch.
Anz.* 1910, p. 238, f. 41.
[5] *BCA.* IV. p. 109.   [6] *CR.* 1899, p. 129, f. 251.
[7] *ABC.* Reinach, p. 136.
[8] *Technologie,* II. p. 329.
[9] *CR.* 1878-9, Pl. III.—VI., Text, pp. 111—114.

must be much older as it has been darned in places.   It is made of several
strips sewn together and then covered with the design by means of some stain.
There was a broad border of large palmettes, and six or more strips across
filled with complicated figure-subjects separated by narrow patterned bands.
The names NIKH, EPI[Σ, AΘHNAIH, IOKAΣTH, I]OΛEΩΣ, MOϒOΣ,
I]ΓΓOMEΔΩN, EVΛIMEΗN, AKTAIH and ΦAIΔ[P]H shew both that many
various tales were represented and that the dialect of the maker was Ionic.
The stuff was yellow, but the ground of the design is black, and red is used
also.   The whole suggests some Ionian form of red-figured vase whereon
the traditions of black-figured technique had survived more than they did
at Athens (v. p. 210, n. 9).

From the same tomb comes a piece (Fig. 244, v. 2) with a pleasing
pattern of ducks on a purple ground and a border of stags' heads ; something
of the same black-figured spirit survives in the manner in which the ducks are
rendered.   They are yellow with streaks of black and green, and green was
used for the stags' eyes : the trimming was of fur.

The finest piece left, from the Pavlovskij Fort Barrow, has a dark purple
ground embroidered mostly with a pattern of spirals and palmettes, but also
bearing the figure of an Amazon and edged with a green border of the
texture of rep.   The tendrils and stalks are pinkish-yellow, leaves are green,
the Amazon has a green chiton with a red and yellow border.   The drawing
of it all is very free, considering that the design was to be carried out in satin
stitch (Fig. 244, III. 1, 2).

On the same plate, III. in *CR.*, we have specimens of golden leaves sewn
on to a bark foundation covered with stuff to make a crown, a cheaper form
than the all-gold crowns illustrated on pp. 388, 389, ff. 285, 286.   In one case
the gold was itself covered with fine woollen crêpe : one bore an indication
of a coin marked B̊ÅE common also on the gold crowns.   Thus I would
date them about the middle of the 1st century A.D., assigning them to
Mithridates VIII, but they are more usually put down to Mithridates Eupator
(v. coin-plate VII. 14—18 and Ch. XIX.).

Other interesting pieces not reproduced on Fig. 244 may be mentioned ;
v. 3 is silk found with the three-legged table (v. p. 333) ; v. 4 is embroidery
in gold on slate colour, making an ivy pattern.   Other pieces on this and the
following plate are mostly stripes and mat-like patterns : VI. 2 is a conical
cap with a tassel at one end and stripes round the other : VI. 3 (Fig. 244)
has its stripes enriched with simple arabesques which look thoroughly in
the *Empire* style.   In several of these pieces remarkable skill is shewn in
making the red shade into the green by delicate gradations.   The texture
is mostly similar to what we call rep[1].

Byzantine textiles, some inwoven with figures of men and animals
interesting when compared with Coptic work, have been found at
Chersonese[2].

---

[1] VI. 5 and 6 shews an ancient shoe adorned
with gold sequins and not more than 6½ in. long.
Other shoes have been found at Pavlovskij barrow,
CR. 1859, p. 30, No. 15, and in the Great Bliznitsa
in the tomb of the Priestess of Demeter, *CR.* 1865,
p. 11, No. 16.   Wooden soles of Roman date are
figured, *CR.* 1878–9, p. 143.   All are very like our
shoes ; cf. Watzinger, op. cit. p. 14, ff. 25, 26.
[2] *CR.* 1891, p. 5, f. 2 ; 1904, p. 51, ff. 63, 64 :
BCA. XVI. p. 38, ff. 1, 2.

V. 2.

III. 1.

C.R. 1878-79.

Wool.
Embroidered.

Purple, Red
or Brown.

Green.

Yellow.

III 2. Pavlovskij
Barrow,
Kerch.

III 2.

§ 7. *Ceramics.*

For the history of the Ceramics of the Greeks the finds in South Russia have no such superlative importance as for the study of their carpentry, textiles or goldwork. Yet they have yielded much material towards filling up outlines traced by investigators working in other regions, and they have no small historical interest as determining the relations between the coasts of Scythia and other parts of the Greek world at various periods[1].

In view of the endless number of specimens any attempt at an enumeration even of the most important is hopeless, and for finds made in Stephani's lifetime the reader is referred to *CR.* from 1859 to 1881 and to his Catalogue of Vases in the Hermitage.

Early Vases.

One Geometric vase is said to have come from Berezan[2]; with, as far as I know, this single exception the earliest kind of Greek vase that occurs in South Russia is that referred by Boehlau to Miletus. From the environs of Kerch such vases are very rare, first published was that from Temir Gorá[3]. A Corinthian aryballus was found at Kerch in 1902, and with it one of "Egyptian porcelain" with a kind of cartouche upon it, not, it seems, Egyptian work but after the Saite type as Mr F. W. Green tells me[4]; another Corinthian and a Milesian (?) aryballus were found there the next year[5].

But these early finds are few on the Bosporus: the rather desultory excavations carried out in that region in spite of their long continuance do not seem to have happened upon the oldest cemeteries. Perhaps there was no considerable Greek population before the vith century, or it is just conceivable that the older diggers who were looking for productions of the "finest" periods took no notice of earlier and less elegant objects.

Be that as it may, the careful diggings of the last few years have produced plenty of early fragments from the Olbia district. They were first reported in any quantity from the island Berezan, from which were derived the collections of Father Levitskij[6], soon to be published in *Materials*, and of Mr Voitinas[7]. Excavations were there carried on in 1900 and 1901 by G. L. Skadovskij and since 1902 by von Stern. The summaries of results published yearly mention Theran, Milesian and Samian[8], Naucratis, "Egyptian porcelain," Clazomenian, Proto-Corinthian and Corinthian, Cyprian, Early Boeotian, Attic black-figured and a few severe red-figured vases: there is

---

[1] Professor E. R. von Stern summed up the whole results to 1899 in a paper read before the xith Russian Archaeological Congress at Kiev, *Trans. Od. Soc.* XXII. pp. 1—21, "On the significance of Ceramic Finds in South Russia for elucidating the Cultural History of the Black Sea Colonization," and this with additions to bring it up to date has been the basis of the following section: but he has since remodelled it with much the same additions as mine and presented it to the International Congress of Historical Sciences at Berlin (1908), *Klio*, IX. (1909), pp. 139—152, "Die Griechische Kolonisation am Nordgestade des Schwarzen Meeres im Lichte archäologischer Forschung." Since Stephani's death nearly all advance in our

knowledge of S. Russian Ceramics has been due to von Stern and his pupil B. V. Pharmacovskij.

[2] *Arch. Anz.* 1910, p. 227, f. 27.

[3] *CR.* 1870-1, Pl. IV; Prinz, *Klio*, Beiheft VII., "Funde aus Naukratis," p. 134.

[4] *CR.* 1902, pp. 53, 58, ff. 89, 120.

[5] *CR.* 1903, p. 47, ff. 71, 72; cf. *Arch. Anz.* 1908, p. 170.

[6] *CR.* 1901, p. 133: two late Milesian sherds, N. Radlov, *BCA.* XXXVII. p. 81, coloured Pl. III. IV.

[7] *CR.* 1903, pp. 152, 153, ff. 303, 304.

[8] So J. Boehlau, *Aus Jonischen und Italischen Necropolen*, Leipzig, 1898, p. 52 sqq., renames Rhodian and Fikellura.

also a new ware most nearly allied to Naucratis and so probably Milesian, it consists of bowls, yellow or yellowish-grey outside, red, black, dark-brown or chocolate within : round the outside run three red or dark rings. Attic wares are confined to the top layers ; among these were two signatures of Tlesus[1].

Olbia itself yields a not less abundant harvest of much the same sorts[2] : the best specimens seem at first to have fallen into the hands of the predatory diggers, as von Stern laments[3], but now Pharmacovskij has found very numerous fragments and some whole vases. He has grouped them temporarily and published some of the best pieces, recording the occurrence of Samian[4], Naucratis, Corinthian, Chalcidian and the unknown Ionian fabric with creamy ground and red decoration[5] : such already existed in Mr Vogell's collection at Nicolaev[6]. More recently specimens of Milesian, Clazomenae and Daphnae wares have turned up, and lastly vases in the shape of a man with a hedgehog in "Egyptian porcelain" probably made at Naucratis or Miletus[7].

Fragments of Milesian pots even penetrated into the interior as far as the government of Ekaterinoslav and the districts of Chigirin and Zvenigo-rodka in Kiev[8]. A very early black-figured vase of curious shape like the weight on a steel-yard was found in a barrow near Ulskaja (Kuban) in 1898. It would appear to be of some Asiatic make, but is not quite like the Milesian[9].

Black- and Red-figured Vases.

Ordinary black-figured vases come from all the sites in South Russia, Kerch[10], Theodosia[11], Berezan and Olbia[12], even Eupatoria (Cercinitis)[13] and Chersonese[14]. These Attic vases shew that the Athenian potters had conquered this market in the latter part of the vith century. Von Stern correlates this with the foreign policy of the Pisistratids. With the expulsion of the tyrants this pre-eminence was apparently lost, for the severe red-figured vases of about the time of the Persian wars are very scarce. From

[1] References for finds at Berezan, v. inf. p. 451, n. 1, also for the pots, von Stern, *Trans. Od. Soc.* XXIII. p. 28 ; *Klio*, IX. pp. 142—144.
[2] For the first example, v. G. Loeschke, *Arch. Anz.* 1891, p. 18, f. b.
[3] *Trans. Od. Soc.* XXII. *Minutes*, p. 119: the collection of which he speaks was acquired by the Hermitage and published in *CR.* 1901, pp. 129—131, ff. 219—227: it includes most of the kinds mentioned above, but it is not certain that they all really came from S. Russia.
[4] *BCA.* XIII. pp. 217—220, ff. 157—160.
[5] ib. p. 148, f. 94 ; cf. von Stern, l.c. p. 120.
[6] This was mostly dispersed in May, 1908, but a fully illustrated record of it exists in J. Boehlau, *Sammlung A. Vogell*, Cassel, 1908 ; the early pots are Nos. 16—47, Pl. I. II. Some now at Munich, *Jahrb. d. k. d. Arch. Inst.* 1910, p. 58, ff. 10, 11. I gladly came this opportunity of thanking Mr Vogell for his kindness to me at Nicolaev and for sending me his catalogue.
[7] *BCA.* XXXIII. pp. 118—120, ff. 23—27, cf. *CR.* 1902, p. 53, f. 89 ; *Arch. Anz.* 1909, pp. 171, 175,

ff. 33, 34, 39; 1910, pp. 234, f. 33, 238, 239.
[8] Von Stern, *Trans. Od. Soc.* XXIII. *Minutes*, p. 13; *Klio*, IX. p. 141; Bobrinskoj, *BCA.* XX. p. 7, f. 9.
[9] *CR.* 1898, p. 32, f. 47.
[10] *ABC.* XLVIII. 6, 7 ; LXIIIa. 1 ; MacPherson, Pl. IX. ; *CR.* 1898, p. 17, f. 16 ; 1899, p. 27, ff. 38—40 ; 1902, pp. 53, 54, ff. 90—93; 1903, p. 162, f. 132 ; 1905, p. 64, f. 80.
[11] Von Stern, *Das Museum der kais. Odessaer Ges. d. Gesch. u. Altertumsk.* III. "Theodosia und seine Keramik," Odessa, 1906, Pl. II. 1—9.
[12] *CR.* 1873, p. xxii; 1897, p. 79, ff. 187, 188; 1902, p. 7, f. 3: *Trans. Od. Soc.* XXII. *Minutes*, p. 119: *BCA.* XIII. p. 149, f. 95, pp. 155—159, ff. 103—108, p. 184, f. 136, p. 187, f. 143 ; XXXIII. p. 121, ff. 28—30; *Arch. Anz.* 1909, p. 173, f. 40. Vogell, *Samml.* Nos. 59—107, Pl. I. II.
[13] *BCA.* XXV. p. 185, f. 26.
[14] A fragment, *Mat.* VII. p. 24: the Milesian sherds from Inkerman in the British Museum, A. 1675, Prinz, l.c. and letter from Mr H. B. Walters, were probably in native hands.

43—2

Leuce we have part of a cantharos made by Nicosthenes and painted by Epictetus with a symposium[1]; from Olbia a pelice with a flute-player and Nike[2], an amphora *a colonnette* with Dionysus and Maenads[3], and one or two bits[4]; from Kerch a shallow cup with Menelaus and Helen that von Stern[5] puts down to Amasis II[6], an amphora *a colonnette* like that from Olbia[7], and the fragments figured on *CR.* 1873, III., of which Fig. 245 is an example.   A beautiful alabastron, made by Hilinus and painted by Psiax, with a warrior on one side and an Amazon on the other, though in the Odessa Museum was not certainly found in South Russia[8].

Among all the fragments of red-figured pottery found by General Bertier-de-La-Garde during the harbour works at Theodosia, not one belonged

M! Mithridates. Kerch.

C.R. 1873 II 6

FIG. 245. ⅓.

FIG. 246.   Side view of Fig. 247. ½.

to the severe style.   It seems likely that upon the interruption of the trade with Greece the colonies in Scythia were no longer in a position to indulge in such luxuries as the finest painted pottery.   We have no hint as to their fate during this disturbed period which included the expedition of Darius, an event which must have excited anxiety among the men of Olbia.   Athens did not regain the market at once, her attention was diverted to the West,

[1] Pharmacovskij, *Trans. Od. Soc.* XVI. p. 39, Pl. II. 3.

[2] Von Stern, ib. XXII. p. 93, Pl. III. 2.

[3] Vogell, *Samml.* No. 109, Pl. II. 5.

[4] *BCA.* XXXIII. p. 122, ff. 32, 33.

[5] l.c. p. 73, Pl. III. 1.

[6] J. D. Beazley, *JHS.* XXX. (1910), p. 38 would call him Kleophrades.

[7] *CR.* 1903, p. 159, f. 318.

[8] Von Stern, *Trans. Od. Soc.* XVII. p. 37, Pl. II.

to Italy and Sicily, and vases of the transitional style are also rare[1]. But with the introduction of the free style, South Russia becomes one of the richest sources. The ware destined for it was singularly like that exported to Cyrene. From this time forth we can study the changes in fashion of Greek pottery by innumerable examples drawn from Olbia[2], and still

FIG. 247. Lecane from Kerch. $\frac{3}{10}$. I have much pleasure in thanking Miss J. E. Harrison for the loan of the block made from a drawing by Mrs H. F. Stewart after *Trans. Od. Soc.* XVIII. Pl. I.

more from Kerch and its environs[3]. From Theodosia we get fragments[4]; from Chersonese two or three late vases[5] and some fragments[6], of importance in their way as the first proof that the site of the "New" Chersonese dated from at least the ivth century B.C.

Among the various classes of free-style vases found at Kerch the lecanae are quite a speciality. Half of those extant come from the Bosporus, and

[1] Olbia, *BCA.* XXXIII. pp. 122, 123, ff. 34, 35; cf. von Stern, *Theodosia*, Pl. II. Nos. 10, 11.

[2] e.g. *CR.* 1902, p. 7, ff. 2, 4; 1906, pp. 47, 48, ff. 55—57; *BCA.* XIII. p. 189, f. 145; XXXIII. pp. 123, 124, ff. 36, 37; Vogell, *Samml.* Nos. 110—183, Pl. III.; *Arch. Anz.* 1908, p. 187, f. 20.

[3] e.g. a fragment by Andron, Pharmacovskij, *Trans. Od. Soc.* XVI. p. 14, Pl. II. 1; a pelice, Heracles crowned by Nike, von Stern, ib. XIX. p. 94, Pl. I.; *CR.* 1903, p. 47, f. 73, p. 157, f. 314,

&c. Pharmacovskij classifies all vases of these styles known down to 1901 in a wonderful appendix to his "Vase Painting and its relation to Monumental Art in the period directly after the Graeco-Persian Wars," *TRAS.* XII. (1901, 2): all found in Russia are indexed s.v. Россія.

[4] Von Stern, *Theodosia*, Pl. III.—V.

[5] *CR.* 1903, p. 32, f. 33, p. 39, f. 55.

[6] *CR.* 1904, p. 68, f. 104; *BCA.* IV. p. 78, ff. 28, 29; *Mat.* VII. iv. 2, 3, 4.

they are almost always marked by singular elegance[1].   Their use for washing
face, hands and feet in perfumed water just suited the luxurious tastes or
the Bosporan ladies.

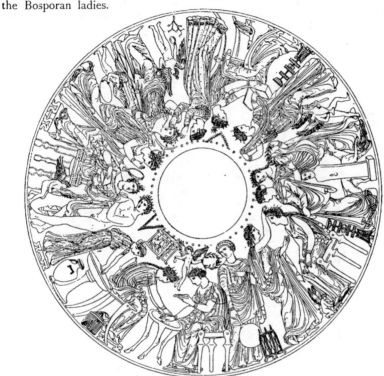

FIG. 248.   Jüz Oba Lecane.   *KTR.* p. 77, f. 106.   ⅓.

In Panticapaeum as in South Italy the simple contrast of black and red
at last ceased to satisfy customers, and vase-painters took to heightening
the effect of their wares by adding white details and gilt accessories.   This
is almost universal upon a second type of lecane with high body and vertical
handles[2].   Lastly came the use of relief that was finally to oust the styles
which relied on mere painting.   A famous example of this relief-work, with
the further addition of bright colour, is the vase that reproduces, as is
supposed, not only the subject of the west pediment of the Parthenon, the
contest of Athena and Poseidon, but also its composition[3].

[1] e.g. those published by Pharmacovskij, *Trans.
Od. Soc.* XVI. p. 29, Pl. II. 2, and von Stern, ib.
XVIII. pp. 19—63, Pl. I. (Figs. 246, 247), also *CR.*
1860, I. (=*KTR.* pp. 76—78, ff. 105—107, v. Fig.
248) p. 5 sqq., 1861, I. II. &c. : plain ones from Olbia,
CR. 1900, p. 9, f. 18 ; *BCA.* XIII. p. 137, f. 79: list
in Pharmacovskij's "Vase Painting" App. p. 73.

[2] Pharmacovskij, op. cit. App. p. 75, but Boehlau
Samml. Vogell, No. 181, Pl. III. 4, calls them
amphorae.   The best was found at Kerch in 1906,
Arch. Anz. 1907, pp. 131—136, ff. 3—7 ; another
ABC. LII. Reinach, p. 104.

[3] *CR.* 1872, Pl. I. 1=*KTR.* p. 78, f. 108 and
many books since.

The same kind of work adorns the equally well-known vase[1] signed round the neck just where it rises, below the palmettes which decorate it,

ΞΕΝΟΦΑΝΤΟΣΕΠΟΙΗΣΕΝΑΟΗΝ

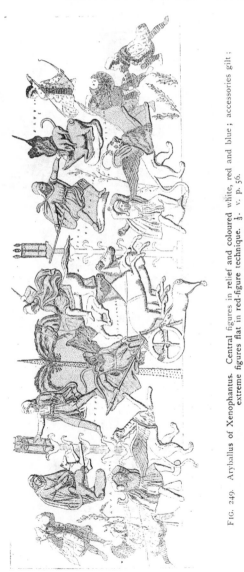

FIG. 249. Aryballus of Xenophantus. Central figures in relief and coloured white, red and blue; accessories gilt; extreme figures flat in red-figure technique. ⅓. v. p. 56.

The last word of the signature has been usually completed ᾽Αθηναῖος not ᾽Αθήνησι, and it is supposed that Xenophantus was an Athenian artist working at Panticapaeum, but it is quite conceivable that he worked at Athens and exported his wares. Round the shoulders comes a narrow frieze in gilt relief—a biga with attendant figures thrice repeated, a gigantomachy and a centauromachy in between. The main subject (f. 249) belongs to the world of pure phantasy: the dress and the names of the figures are more or less Persian, the date-palm and silphium in the background are Libyan—even in Libya tripods do not grow on silphium stems—only the griffins suggest Scythia, and one of these is of quite a strange type[2].

The less elaborate colour effects of white lecythi did not find much favour outside Attica, but we have one or two examples from Kerch[3], and one apparently from Olbia[4].

[1] *ABC.* XLV. XLVI., Reinach, p. 98 = *CR.* 1866, IV.   Rayet et Collignon, *Céramique Grecque*, pp. 264, 265, ff. 100, 101, &c.
[2] For another aryballus in much the same style, v. *ABC.* XLVIII. 1, 2, 3: and one just slender enough to be called a lecythus, *Arch. Anz.* 1908, pp. 173, 174, ff. 10 *a, b.*
[3] ib. p. 170; *CR.* 1902, p. 55, f. 97.
[4] Vogell, *Samml.* No. 145, Pl. III. 13.

Vases in the Shape of Statues, Animals and Heads.

Something of the same taste which rejoiced in the many-coloured vases decorated with reliefs also approved of vases actually made in the form of

FIG 250. Phanagoria. Tinted Vase. *KTR.* p. 81, f. 110. ¾.

human figures and beasts or monsters, and these, also beautifully coloured, are rather a speciality of South Russia, although they do occur elsewhere. Particularly beautiful specimens are a Sphinx and an Aphrodite Anadyomene,

both found in a tomb near Phanagoria[1]. The former (f. 250) has preserved
its colours specially well : the handle and mouth of the vessel are the ordinary
black ; the Sphinx herself wears a red diadem with gilt flowers, gilt also are
her hair and necklaces with touches on wings and tail : these last are white
with blue streaks : blue also are her eyes : her body is a warm white, shading
up from her breast to the delicate flush of her face : the base is red and blue,

FIG. 251.   Phanagoria.   Tinted Vase = *CR*. 1870-71, I. 3.   From a photograph kindly
sent me by Mr J. I. Smirnov.   ¾.

and between the feet it is adorned with white palmettes on a red ground.
It is a pity that this vase is not published in colours before it fades, as it
must do in spite of the great care taken to shield it.   The Aphrodite
(Fig. 251) is in much the same style but not so well preserved.   She is

[1] *CR*. 1870-1, I. 1, 2 and 3, 4 = *KTR*. pp. 81, 82,
ff. 110, 111 ; Rayet et Collignon, pp. 273, 271, ff.
104, 103 ; G. Treu, *XXXV^{tes} Winckelmannsfestprogramm*, "Griechische Thongefässe in Statuetten-
und Büsten-form," Berlin, 1875, Pl. I. 5 ; cf. W.
Froehner, *Collection Tyszkiewicz*, Pl. XLI.   I am
indebted to the late Mr Kieseritzky for shewing me
these figures.   For the types of this class of vase,
v. *Die Antiken Terrakotten*, herausg. v. R. Kekulé
von Stradonitz ; Bd III. 1, 2, "Die Typen der figür-
lichen Terrakotten," bearb. v. F. Winter, Berlin
1903, 1, p. 228. 6 ; 2, p. 158. 2, p. 203. 3, 4.

coming out between two valves of a shell, white without and red within. The type is common in terra-cottas[1]. The same idea of a figure made into a vase is less well carried out in the Dancer Vase[2] from the Pavlovskij Barrow a little to the south of Kerch. Another such vase represents a Siren, but the mixture of woman, bird and fish is clumsily managed[3].

A whole series of vases somewhat similar in conception and in colouring was found in 1852, likewise by Phanagoria, but they differ in that they have the form of upright human figures. One presents a winged dancer with castanets standing by an altar: each of the next two, a girl without wings: the last, a young man, perhaps Dionysus. The back in each case has the black or brown of an ordinary vase, and the neck projects above the figure's head. The colouring may have faded from these, the flesh tints have not the delicacy of the former vases[4]. Still less delicate in colour is a group of a goddess riding upon a goat[5], and a charming vase from Kerch at Odessa[6] relies entirely upon modelling for its effect.

In quite a different style are vases made in the form of a Silenus reclining on a wineskin[7] or leaning against it[8]. Another vase from Olbia takes the shape of a female bust[9] and brings us to a whole class of vases in the form of heads[10] from the Quarantine road at Kerch[11], from Chersonese[12], and from Olbia heads of a Maenad, Silenus, Pan, a negro, a child and women[13]. Another form of head-cup furnished with handles comes from Kerch[14]. Cups shaped like a horse's head occur at Kerch[15] and Olbia[16], also a boar's head at Olbia[17]. Whole animals are specially common there—the earliest is a black-figured askos in the shape of a bird[18]—a bull[19], many rams[20], a dog[21], a lion[22] and a cock[23], made in fine red clay. Mr Vogell[24] had replicas of pretty well all these types and more, a crouching negro, swine, hedgehog, ape, etc. They mostly belong to about the IInd century B.C. Similar examples from Kerch are an eagle[25], a wolf[26], a nondescript animal with an old man's head[27], and an elephant[28]. Some also come in Scythic graves (v. supra p. 232, n. 5).

Rhyta in the form of human or animal heads have in them something of the same idea, and besides the well-known silver examples clay specimens occur at Kerch[29].

[1] *CR.* 1870–71, pp. 5, 161, 170, 177, 181, 197.
[2] *KTR.* p. 192, f. 182 = *CR.* 1859, III. 1: for the costume see E. Pottier and S. Reinach, *La Nécropole de Myrina*, Pl. XXVIII. 3, XXXI. and p. 393.
[3] *CR.* 1870–71, Pl. I. 6.
[4] *ABC.* LXX. 1—8; cf. Kekulé-Winter III. 2, p. 156. 7.
[5] *ABC.* LXXI. 4, 4a; cf. Treu, op. cit. II. 5. Kekulé-Winter III. 2, p. 197. 1.
[6] *Odessa Museum, Terra-cottas* (v. p. 363 n. 1), I. xii. 4.
[7] ib. II. Xii. 2.
[8] *BCA.* XXXIII. p. 132, f. 56.
[9] *CR.* 1900, p. 8, f. 16.
[10] The earliest example of this idea is from Berezan, a helmeted head of "Rhodian" ware, *Arch. Anz.* 1908, p. 180, f. 14.
[11] *CR.* 1900, p. 27, f. 64; 1905, p. 66, f. 86 = *Arch. Anz.* 1907, p. 141, ff. 11, 12, a fine head of Heracles.
[12] *CR.* 1891, p. 149, f. 183.

[13] *Arch. Anz.* 1908, p. 186, f. 19; 1910, p. 235, f. 36; *CR.* 1897, p. 80, f. 195; 1904, p. 40, ff. 60, 61; *Od. Mus.* II. Xii. 1, 3. For glass heads v. p. 362, n. 3.
[14] ib. Xiii. 2.　　　　[15] ib. X. 1.
[16] op. cit. I. Xvii. 4.
[17] *CR.* 1902, p. 27, f. 45.
[18] *Arch. Anz.* 1909, p. 175, f. 40; Tritons, ib. 1910, p. 214, f. 14.
[19] *Od. Mus.* I. Xvii. 2.
[20] op. cit. II. xvi. 3, 4; *Arch. Anz.* 1891, p. 19, f. 4; *CR.* 1902, p. 11, f. 14.　　[21] ibid. f. 13.
[22] *Drevnosti*, XV. ii. p. 11, f. 10, v. p. 420.
[23] *BCA.* VIII. p. 54, f. 55.
[24] *Samml.* early, Nos. 45, 46, Pl. I. 2, 6; later, Nos. 523—541, Pl. VIII. 1—18.
[25] *Od. Mus.* II. xvi. 2.
[26] *ABC.* LXXI. 5, 5a.
[27] *CR.* 1906, p. 86, f. 95; *Arch. Anz.* 1907, p. 130, ff. 1, 2.
[28] *Arch. Anz.* 1910, p. 214, f. 13.
[29] *Od. Mus.* II. Xiii. 1, 3.

Late Painted and Distempered Vases.

But the plastic feeling did not suddenly destroy the taste for painting. The red-figured technique survived longest in little aryballi with women's heads or palmettes hastily touched in (e.g. f. 252)[1], or else in various vases which seem to have been imported from South Italy. In one grave at Kerch[2] we have one of the ordinary plates with fishes and a squid for decoration and a lecane of the same style, and from Chersonese a fish plate[3]. Pieces of Italian ware have been sold as from Olbia, but their provenance is not certain; there were, however, many specimens in the Vogell collection, an Apulian " Pracht-amphora," pelicae, craters, jugs and fish plates[4].

To the latter part of the ivth century belong the Panathenaic vases that have been found at Kerch[5]: their technique is black-figured, but their style readily betrays their date: rather an earlier one was found at Nymphaeum and is in the possession of Mr A. V. Novikov. Another, from Olbia (?), was

FIG. 252. Late Vase from Olbia. *CR.* 1901, p. 10, f. 12ᵃ. ½.

in the Vogell collection[6]. It is interesting to think that Greeks from these distant towns won prizes at the Panathenaea. Something similar is a prize vase with pictures of a horseman and of a quadriga in the old black-figured technique; it was found by Pharmacovskij at Olbia[7], and there are other such in the Odessa Museum. There is nothing so far to shew at what contest they were awarded. The subsidiary decoration seems to be in the Hellenistic manner.

When moulded ware took the place of painted in most parts of the Greek world, the Pontic Greeks seem to have wished to continue the custom of depositing painted vases with their dead. Accordingly, since the supply of Attic vases had ceased, they endeavoured to provide a substitute, and produced a kind of vase which has never been found south of the Euxine. Such vases are of a badly prepared clay and have thick sides so that they weigh three times as much as good Greek vases, and their surface could never be brought to the smoothness of the old ware. This clay was sometimes coloured black,

[1] Cf. MacPherson, Pl. viii. *CR.* 1862, ii. 1—40.
[2] *CR.* 1902, p. 54, ff. 94, 95.
[3] *CR.* 1903, p. 32, f. 34.
[4] *Samml.* Nos. 546—574, Pl. iv. v.

[5] *CR.* 1876, i. pp. 5—108; 1881, p. 127 sqq.
[6] *Samml.* No. 108, f. 6 and Pl. iv. 5.
[7] *CR.* 1901, pp. 10, 11, f. 13.

sometimes left its natural dirty yellow.   To this ground they applied their
painting in something of the nature of tempera, but they did not know how to
fix the colours, which accordingly brush off very easily, and it is rare to find a
well-preserved specimen.   The best according to von Stern is at Berlin; the
examples at Odessa, one of which comes from Olbia (hitherto these have been
found at Kerch only), have but single figures left, yet the Hermitage is not
without fair pieces, reproduced by Stephani[1].   Upon another (f. 253) we
have a combat of a Greek with an Amazon.   The Greek has reddish brown
flesh with high lights, a red chiton, blue scarf, whites to his eyes and black
pupils, a bluey white shield, a brown helmet and spear and a red plume: the

FIG. 253.   Distemper Vase.   Kerch.   *CR.* 1878-9, Pl. I. 5.   ⅓.

Amazon is painted with a blue helmet, yellow flesh, brown chiton, red scarf and
a bluey white shield with a gorgoneion in the centre.   Another good vase of the
kind is represented on the Frontispiece of *CR.* 1863[2].   It is not the drawing
or colouring that is so bad in this curious class of vase as the technical side,
the knowledge how to prepare clay, make a pot and apply colours so that they
shall stand properly.   There can be no doubt that they were made on the
north coast of the Euxine, probably at Kerch, in spite of one being found at
Olbia, and this shews that the Panticapaeans had a fair share of skill in
drawing, and raises the question whether we must really put down most of the
artistic objects found in South Russia as foreign importations.

We have seen (p. 339) that even Milesian vases found their way up into
the interior of the country.   The Attic vases are naturally of far more frequent
occurrence (p. 82, n. 4).   Early examples are a black-figured cylix from
Gorobinets[3] and a white lecythus with black patterns from near Shpola[4]: later
a red-figured aryballus and crater from Bobritsa[5], a fine crater with Europa
and the Bull from Galushchino[6], another crater from near Kanëv in Kiev

[1] *CR.* 1874, Pl. II. 5, 6, black clay, a garland;
7 and 8, natural coloured clay, two Sirens and a
tripod, v. Text, p. 42 sqq.
[2] *KTR.* p. 72, f. 95.
[3] *BCA.* xx. p. 7, f. 7.

[4] *Smêla*, II. viii. 1, p. 117.
[5] *Sm.* III. xx. 5, 6.
[6] Khanenko, *Antiquités de la Région du
Dniepre*, II. 2. xxxvi. No. 809.

University Museum, a careless cylix with a dedication from Zhurovka (pp. 176 and 361), and a number of pieces of mere black-glazed pottery ; the care with which they are mended shews how much they were valued. All these places are in the Government of Kiev, but there are plenty of Greek pots from Poltava, Ekaterinoslav and the Kuban[1].

Plastic Decoration.

While the belated distemper-vases were being put in graves by those who regarded old customs, plastic decoration became more and more usual for vases used by the living. After becoming hasty in order to be cheap, and gaudy in order to be attractive, vase painting gave up the struggle and yielded to various wares which could receive rich ornament from a mould without the labour involved in hand-painting. A last survival of painting was a practice of putting a wreath round a vessel's neck or a kind of necklace in white paint, giving almost an effect of relief. This was often done in local work, which is betrayed by the poor quality of its glaze. There is a large amphora of such work in the Museum at Chersonese. Better work, probably imported, recalls the style associated with Gnathia in Apulia[2]. The main cause of the change of fashion was that the wealthy classes in the Hellenistic states had now

Fig. 254. *CR.* 1901, p. 12, f. 17. Cantharos, Olbia. ⅓. Such are found in Scythic tombs (v. p. 82), e.g. Chertomlyk.

within their reach great masses of gold and silver, some of which they applied to the making of plate, and Toreutic became a far more important art than it had been. The common people who could not afford these precious materials could at least copy the metal forms in clay, an imitation which at its best produced some undeniably elegant pots, but when coarsened to suit common clay and poor workmanship led to a loss of that adaptation of form to material which makes quite rude work satisfactory.

Vessels which shew this imitation of metal work specially clearly are similar to those which, when found in Italy, are called Cales ware[3]. They are characterized by the use of medallions (*emblemata*) as ornaments whether

---

[1] pp. 165, 182, 228 n. 2 ; von Stern, *Trans. Od. Soc.* XXIII. *Minutes*, p. 11, "The action of Ancient Civilization on the region outside the range of the Colonies on the Euxine Coast," cf. *Klio*, IX. p. 141.

[2] Rayet et Collignon, p. 328 ; *ABC.* XLVII. 4, 5 ; Vogell, No. 572, Pl. v. 4 ; R. Pagenstecher, *Arch. Anz.* 1909, p. 1.

[3] Pharmacovskij, *BCA.* II. p. 73, "A fragment

of a cup from Olbia adorned with a relief." A perfect example from Olbia, *BCA.* XIII. p. 164, f. 114 ; Rayet et Collignon, p. 348. H. Dragendorff in *Bonner Jahrbücher*, XCVI. XCVII. (1895), "Terra Sigillata," pp. 23—26 f. ; *Arch. Anz.* 1910, p. 213, ff. 11, 12, p. 235, f. 35 ; R. Pagenstecher, *Jahrb. d. k. d. Arch. Inst.* Erg. heft VIII. (1909), "Die calenische Reliefkeramite," pp. 12, 120, Pl. IV.

let into the bottoms of cups or into the sides of larger vessels.   Exactly similar medallions are used in the silver plate that has survived.   In plate their use began in Hellenistic and went on into Roman times, so that the Bosco Reale and Hildesheim treasures offer perfect parallels.   Such a medallion in silver has actually been found at Olbia[1], and at Chersonese was found a whole series of moulds apparently made from such metallic originals[2].   That these Olbian clay pots were not imported from Cales is shewn by the fact that they are closer to the metallic originals and finer in their workmanship than the Italian examples.   The fashion probably spread from Asia Minor.   A curious trace of the making of pottery at Chersonese is a kind of triangle with a pyramid on each point, itself made of clay, and used to keep apart the different shallow vessels in a pile while they were being baked in the kiln[3].

FIG. 255. *CR.* 1896, p. 208, f. 594.   FIG. 256. *CR.* 1901, p. 13, f. 20.
Pelice. Olbia. ¼.   Cylix. Olbia. ½.

The influence of metal work is further shewn in a growing tendency to flute vessels, to make the handles very thin, often to imitate in clay the methods of riveting a metal handle to its body, and in general to apply a style of ornament more suited to repoussé work.   At the same time the varnish gets less and less beautiful; instead of the hard black smooth varnish of former times, it is brownish or greyish with metallic lights and unevenly put on.   This kind of stuff is well represented and fully illustrated in Pharmacovskij's account of his excavations in Olbia in 1901[4].

The question of Hellenistic pottery and the transition from the characteristic black varnish and painted style of classical Greek times to the red varnish and plastic style of typical Roman ware has received much illustration from excavations near the west end of the Athenian acropolis[5].   Evidently the

[1] Pharmacovskij, *BCA.* II. p. 75, f. 2.
[2] v. p. 365. f. 265. W. K. Malmberg, *Mat.* VII. "Antiquities from Chersonese," Pl. I. 1, 2, 3, II. 4, 5, 6, thinks that some were taken from mirror boxes, but Pharmacovskij's view seems more probable. For examples of such medallions from Egypt, rather later in date, v. *LVIII*ᵗᵉˢ *Winckelmannsfestprogramm*, E. Pernice, "Hellenistische Silbergefässe im Antiquarium," Berlin, 1898, Pl. II. IV.; and C. Waldstein *JHS.* III. (1882), p. 96, Pl. XXII.
[3] *BCA.* I. p. 44, f. 41.
[4] *BCA.* VIII. pp. 33—40, ff. 16—38; Vogell, *Samml.* Nos. 296—388, Pl. VI. Some at Munich, *Jahrb. d. k. d. Arch. Inst.* 1910, pp. 58, 59, f. 12.
[5] *Ath. Mitt.* XXVI. (1901), pp. 50—102, C. Watzinger, "Vasenfunde aus Athen."

new-fashioned vases were made even in Athens, and they correspond fairly closely to the various types from South Russia[1], but the change of fashion seems to have come in from Asia Minor, which had led the way in the metallic originals.

Watzinger points out very clearly how a set of silver vessels such as the cantharos, cylix, jug and standing saucer found in a tomb on the Quarantine Road at Kerch[2], or those in Artjukhov's Barrow[3], can be paralleled in clay. Both these tombs contained a coin of Lysimachus, in the latter case one coined in Byzantium shortly after his death in B.C. 281, shewing that the burials belong to about the middle of the century. So Watzinger gets dates for the potsherds, comparing *ABC*. XXXVIII. 5 with the Calenian style, XXXVIII. 1 with the inscribed canthari, *CR*. 1880, p. 19 with the cups upon which raised decoration is just beginning, and *ABC*. XXXVII. 5 or XXXVIII. 3 with those wares upon which the plastic principle has triumphed. To this transitional period, or some half century later, belong vases with a light surface and decoration in red or brown rather carefully put on. In this style are jugs with sketches of objects, e.g. one from Kerch with a jug like itself, an amphora, a basket, a lyre, a harp and pan-pipes[4]. The most extraordinary example of a metal shape in clay is a kind of stand from Olbia. It is like a candlestick with a disproportionately large sconce, from the underside of which hang loose rings: the whole is supported by high claw feet. A fragment of a similar one was found at Chersonese. It is wonderful that pottery should have been strong enough to hold together in such a shape[5].

Megarian Bowls.

One class of ware with rather rich ornament in relief is that most commonly represented by the small hemispherical or shallow cups called Megarian bowls[6]. The Russian dealers call them *Jermolki*, skull-caps, which has the advantage of not begging the question of their origin. A cup of similar shape in silver occurred in Karagodeuashkh Barrow, but it may be of barbaric make and it lacks decoration[7]. These cups are dark grey, brown or almost black, and have a dull surface. They were formed in moulds, themselves covered with patterns by means of stamps in relief, and the makers shewed much ingenuity in adapting the same moulds to the production of various-shaped vessels by adding bases, necks and handles to the fundamental

[1] Watzinger's pelice, op. cit. Pl. III., is like Olbian pelicae, f. 255; *CR*. 1900, p. 6, f. 5; 1901, p. 14, f. 23; Vogell, Nos. 302—306, Pl. VII. 16—19: others, from Kerch, *Annali dell' Instituto*, 1840, Pl. C. 4 (Ashik's report of excavations) and from Artjukhov's Barrow (v. p. 430), *CR*. 1880, p. 14 and extra plate, 4, 5. His cantharos (op. cit. p. 74, f. 18 n. 1) is like cylices from Olbia, f. 256, inscribed ΦΙΛΙΑΣ; *Arch. Anz.* 1891, p. 19, f. 2, ΑΘΗΝΑC, *CR*. 1896, p. 80, f. 333, ΔΙΟΝΥΣΟΥ, f. 334, ΥΓΙΕΙΑΣ; Vogell, Nos. 334—340, f. 14, Pl. VI. 13, 1, 3, 9, 7, 11, 15 and the canthari Nos. 313, 314, Pl. VI. 31, with similar inscriptions and also ΔΩΡΟΝ and ΑΦΡΟΔΙΤΗΣ; cf. *Trans. Od. Soc.* XXIII. p. 23: Watzinger's saucer, p. 80, No. 29, is like *Arch. Anz.* 1910, p. 211, ff. 9, 10.

[2] v. p. 384, *ABC*. Reinach, p. 20, XXXVII. 5, XXXVIII. 1, 3, 4, 5; *Annali dell' Instituto*, 1840, p. 13.

[3] *CR*. 1880, pp. 17, 22, Pl. II. 19, 20, 21, IV. 8, 9; v. p. 431, f. 321.

[4] *CR*. 1906, p. 90, f. 108 = *Arch. Anz.* 1907, p. 138, ff. 8, 9; cf. one with wreaths and pots, Vogell, No. 389, Pl. V. 17, cf. p. 353 n. 6.

[5] *BCA*. XX. p. 26, f. 9.

[6] Dragendorff, op. cit. p. 28 sqq.: *Bonner Jahrbücher*, CI. (1897), p. 142: R. Zahn, *Jahrb. d. kais. deutschen Archäol. Inst.* 1908, pp. 45—77, "Hellenistische Reliefgefässe aus Südrussland," describes and illustrates some 35 examples from the Vogell Coll., cf. Vogell, *Samml.* Nos. 245—295, mostly figured on p. 28 and Pl. VII. 1—12 : others illustrated in *ABC*. XLVII. 1, 2, 7, 8, XLVIII. 8—10; *CR*. 1876, p. 185; 1899, p. 124, f. 235.

[7] *Mat.* XIII. p. 43, f. 8, cf. the gold Graeco-Bactrian (?) bowl from Transcaucasia, Smirnov, *Argenterie Orientale*, VII. 20 = *KTR*. p. 449, f. 393.

bowl¹. The conditions of extracting the moulded vessel determined the
shapes that this process could produce.   In any case, the manufacture seems
to have been carried on somewhere in Central Greece, Dragendorff says
Chalcis, whereas von Stern points out that the attribution to Megara,
which is now universally discredited, rested for a while on much the same
evidence as that which now points to Chalcis: nothing short of the discovery
of an actual potter's workshop with broken moulds and pots of this make can
really settle the question.   In any case, the same firm sent identical bowls to
Vulci and Panticapaeum.   But undoubtedly there were imitators on the spot.
Zahn makes out that only his Nos. 1 and 2 were made in Greece, but no
doubt the moulds for others came from abroad, as his Nos. 4 and 5 are of
native clay but identical with examples from Montefiascone and Megara.

FIG. 257. *CR.* 1901, p. 15, f. 26, identical with Vogell,   FIG. 258. *CR.* 1900, p. 12, f. 24. "Megarian
No. 288, Zahn, 6. "Megarian bowl." Olbia. ⅔.   bowl." Olbia. ⅔.

Demetrius² and Menemachus³ are well-known names in this trade, but they may
have worked in Greece; Menemachus ware occurs in Italy⁴.   But the stamps
for pots with the strange word KIP BEI must have been made on the Euxine,
for only in this region do we find genitives in -ει from nominatives in -εις
according to some native declension⁵, and in one of the Pontic colonies there
must have been a potter with the barbarous name Κίρβεις.   These bowls and

¹ Pelicae thus made Zahn, Nos. 28, 29; *CR.*
1903, p. 157, f. 315; a jug, Zahn, No. 32; handled
cups, Nos. 30, 31; a deep vase on a foot with
several bands of ornament, von Stern, *BCA.* III.
pp. 93—113, Pl. XIV. XV.
² e.g. *BCA.* I. p. 31, f. 24, Chersonese.
³ Malmberg, *Mat.* VII. p. 27.
⁴ Dragendorff, XCVI. p. 27.
⁵ e.g. Γάστεις gen. Γάστει in *IosPE.* II. 267,

403 and many others: v. *BCA.* IV. p. 141, B. B.
Latyshev, "On the question of ancient pottery with
the inscription KIP BEI": Zahn, p. 49, points out
that the letters come round the head of a bust like
that of Tyche (Demeter?) on Olbian coins (Pl. III.
3 and its degradation III. 27), but his pictures,
on pp. 55, 56, 60, 61, 67 or *Arch. Anz.* 1910, p. 234,
f. 34, do not establish an identity of type: for the
grammatical form he compares Doric genitives in -α.

their like are placed in the IIIrd and early IInd century B.C. Von Stern (l.c.) suggests that they are the Vasa Samia, a name that has long been familiar and used to be applied to the bright red Arretine ware. He argues that there was an important class of what we should term Hellenistic ware called after Samos, and that the affinities of the compositions reproduced on "Megarian" ware are rather with Asia than Europe, so that Samos would suit as the place of its manufacture.

Closely connected in technique is this same Arretine ware. The chief difference is caused by the discovery that more intense baking produced a harder substance and a uniform bright red colour much more attractive than the dull surface of the "Megarian" ware. This discovery was probably made in some Greek country[1]; but Arretium became a great centre of the industry, and imitations were made in France, Germany, and even Britain. That products of the Italian factories were exported as far as South Russia is proved by the stamps of Roman makers, both in Latin and Greek letters (e.g. CCELLVM and ΓΑΙΟΤ[2]), from Olbia, and I have myself a broken lamp from Chersonese with Latin letters upon it[3].

This ware is the first witness of the intercourse with Italy and Rome, which ended in the Roman protectorate over Olbia[4] and Chersonese and suzerainty over the Bosporus.

Alexandrian Vases, Painted and Glazed.

Vases were imported not only from Greece and Italy, but also from Alexandria, whose artistic influence we have already seen in the frescoes of tombs. One class said to have come from there is that of vases on which the body has been covered all over with white to receive painting in red, pink, yellow and black[5]. Ornament consisted e.g. in a bay garland of alternate red and black leaves about the neck, on the shoulders another of various coloured leaves upon a black ground, and on the body a panther and a round medallion which has lost its decoration. These vases seem mostly amphorae, sometimes put upon most curious stands[6].

The same white ground and bright-coloured decoration distinguishes a unique amphora found at Olbia in 1901[7]. But in this case there is the addition of plastic decoration which marks the vase as belonging to the IInd century. Body and base were of the ordinary late varnish, only marked by fluting and by as it were a whorl of sepals above the base. Shoulders and handles were covered with white, and the latter adorned with masks with gilt diadems and brown hair, and the former with elaborate patterns of acanthus and vine in relief, coloured pink and blue and gold. Upon the neck were figure subjects.

---

[1] The intermediate steps were well represented in the Vogell Coll. Nos. 438—518, ff. 30, 31 and on p. 48, Pl. VII. 20—33, cf. Dragendorff, XCVI. p. 96, ff. 2—12.

[2] *Trans. Od. Soc.* XXII. *Minutes*, p. 88, *BCA.* XVI. p. 57.

[3] Cf. Zahn, op. cit. p. 73, a late cup with OYIΛΙΣ = Vilis; *CR.* 1896, p. 185, f. 565 a lamp with MAP-KOY and one with two gladiators, *CR.* 1892, p. 25, f. 20; from Kerch a saucer with POY ΦOY, *Trans. Od. Soc.* XXIII. p. 29, and C. CORV. S. on a lamp,

ABC. Inscr. LXVI. Reinach, p. 135.

[4] Very good specimens from Olbia, *CR.* 1906, p. 35, ff. 27—29.

[5] *CR.* 1900, pp. 11, 12, f. 22; Vogell, Nos. 395, 396, Pl. v. 8, 12.

[6] Cf. *Amer. Journ. of Archaeology*, I. (1885), p. 18, A. C. Merriam, "Inscribed Sepulchral vases from Alexandria," Pl. I. No. 1: ib. 1909, R. Pagenstecher, p. 387.

[7] ff. 259—261, *BCA.* VIII. p. 31 and Pl. III. The vase is to be published in colours in *Materials.*

From Alexandria too comes, at a still later date, a class of vases to which much attention has been drawn of late[1].   It is distinguished from all other ancient pottery by being covered with a metallic glaze somewhat similar in composition to modern lead glaze[2].   The best Russian specimen, published

FIGS. 259, 260. *BCA*. VIII. Pl. III.   Olbia. Dark glaze below, white ground, gilt and coloured above, v. p. 353. ⅕.

by Schwartz[3], was found at Olbia in 1891.   It is of red clay covered with green glaze, and is more or less the shape of an inverted bell or a brass mortar[4], furnished with a handle made up of two snakes intertwined.   Round

---

[1] *Drevnosti*, i.e. *Trans. of Moscow Archaeolog. Soc.*, Vol. XV., Pt II. 1894, p. 14, Pl. II. IV. A. N. Schwartz "With regard to a vase with representations in relief found at Parutino (Olbia)"; *Trans. Od. Soc.* Vol. XXII. p. 22, Pl. I. II. E. von Stern, "Ancient glazed Pottery in South Russia"; Pharmacovskij, *BCA*. VIII. p. 50; Dragendorff, CI. p. 144, ff. 5—13; further literature ap. Zahn, op. cit. p. 76 n. 33.

[2] Cf. Rayet et Collignon, op. cit. p. 372, f. 139, Berenice vase.

[3] See also von Stern, loc. cit., Pl. I. 1 and 1 *a*.

[4] Cf. a silver original from Bosco Reale, *Monuments Piot*, V. Pl. VII. VIII.

the base go three tori and a pattern of oves and lotuses very hastily
indicated.   Above this is the figure subject, also roughly but cleverly
modelled—a caricature of the judgement of Paris, in which Hermes and
Paris are in the usual attitude, but treated in the comic style, and the three
goddesses are represented by sketches of three low-class Alexandrians who
are not distinguished by any particular attributes.   Hera is giving Athena
a slap in the face, and preparing the insulting gesture ἀνάσυρμα ; Athena has
started back from her and is making the usual sign to ward off the effect of
bad language.   Aphrodite is also giving way before Hera's fury, and holds
what seems to be a flower before her face.   The whole is a good instance
of the boldness with which the Greeks caricatured their gods.   In the same
tomb was found another example of the same technique, now in the possession

FIG. 261.   *BCA.* VIII. Pl. III.   Upper part of the same vase.   ⅓.

of Mr Pierpont Morgan (Fig. 262)[1], whom I heartily thank for allowing me
to take the photograph.   In form it is an oenochoe, about 7 inches high, with
the usual trefoil lip ; round the neck is the same adaptation of oves as on
the last vase ; at the setting on of the handle is a mask, with horns rather large
for a Silenus and rather small for a Zeus Ammon.   On the body of the
jug are three skeletons wearing conical hats ; the middle one has also a
necklace ; they seem to be dancing some obscene dance ; between them are
ravens ; the whole is covered with a brownish green glaze.   The skeletons
recall the Bosco Reale cups, to which reference has been made.   The imitation
of metal originals is unusually clear in this ewer.   Everything joins to put

[1] It has been lent to S. Kensington since Dec.
1905 and I there recognised that it must be by the
same hand.   The investigations of Professor von
Stern (*Trans. Od. Soc.* XXVII. pp. 87—100 "A
Tomb-find made at Olbia in 1891") have shewn
that it is from the same tomb, for an account of
which v. inf. p. 420.

the date of the tomb at about 100 A.D.   Mr Vogell sent me a fragment which
must have come from a replica of this oenochoe.   Its glaze is cream coloured.

Another example of the same ware comes from Kerch, and is in
I. K. Suruchan's Museum at Kishinëv.   Its glaze is brown, but the heads
of the figures are inserted in some white material.   The subject is the flight
of Iphigenia, twice repeated with slight variations[1].   It is argued from this
that the Alexandrian maker consciously designed this and all from the same

FIG. 262. Jug with Metallic Glaze. Olbia. ⅔. v. pp. 355, 420.

mould for the Pontic market, hence that the trade between these distant
points was really worth special consideration.   This may have been so, but
it is quite possible that the maker of the vase had no such idea, and that its
being found upon the Euxine is due to chance or to the choice of the
exporter.

In the Odessa Museum is another piece with figures; it comes from

[1] von Stern, *Trans. Od. Soc.* XXII. Pl. I. 2.

Olbia[1]. On it, repeated more than once, we have the battle of Cranes and Pygmies. The groups were formed in plaster in a mould and applied to the vessel after baking, but before it was covered with its yellow glaze. The vase is too much broken to judge of its exact form. A replica of it in the Vogell collection[2] shews it to have been like a teacup with two handles. A porringer from Olbia, also at Odessa, has a kind of cornice and a row of oves, from which droop four swags, two encircling the handles and two enclosing with their arcs pairs of Erotes. All this was made in a mould, save that the Erotes were added in plaster. The work is very rough indeed, but the design good[3].

Other pots made after the same fashion (f. 263)[4] have no figured adornment but simple patterns mostly made with dabs of slip of different colour applied before the glazing: they all have a curiously modern appearance and do not at all suggest ancient work, but their genuineness is universally acknowledged. Their technique seems to go back to some of the glazing processes of ancient Egypt, and such vases from Egypt are in S. Kensington Museum.

Fig. 263. *CR.* 1901, p. 16, f. 32. Olbia. Decoration *en barbotine*, Metallic Glaze. $\frac{3}{4}$.

It leads on by such specimens as have been found in Chersonese and Theodosia[5] to the Byzantine glazed vessels and ceramic ornament, and so to all the faiences of the nearer East and the Mediaeval West. A similar glaze applied to a different material is exemplified by the fragments of a vase of the so-called Egyptian porcelain, so far unique in South Russia, found by Pharmacovskij in the vault of Heuresibius at Olbia; it too comes from Alexandria[6].

[1] von Stern, loc. cit. II. 1.
[2] No. 520, Zahn, loc. cit. No. 37.
[3] von Stern, loc. cit. p. 50, f. 1; for a similar design in silver, cf. *ABC.* XXXVII. 1.
[4] von Stern, op. cit., Pl. II. 2 (Kerch), 3 and p. 53, f. 2: Pharmacovskij, Olbia, *BCA.* VIII. pp. 50, 51, ff. 50, 51; *CR.* 1905, p. 13, f. 12; Vogell, No. 521, Pl. VII. 14.
[5] *CR.* 1895, pp. 3, 4, 92, ff. 2—4, 237, 238; 1896, p. 166, f. 532; p. 199, ff. 578, 579; 1899, p. 110, ff. 220,

221; 1901, p. 49, f. 98; 1902, p. 38, ff. 59, 61; 1903, pp. 33, 34, ff. 37—39; 1906, p. 79, f. 78; cf. N. P. Kondakov, *Russian Hoards*, St P. 1896, pp. 36—42, ff. 9—17, 23; W. de Bock, "Poteries vernissées du Caucase et de la Crimée," *Mémoires de la Société nationale des Antiquaires de France*, LVI. Paris, 1897, pp. 193—254; Tolstoi and Kondakov, *Russian Antiquities*, Vol. v. St P. 1897, p. 28; von Stern, *Theodosia*, p. 52 sqq. and Pl. VI—VIII.
[6] *BCA.* III. p. 12, f. 4.

Clay Lamps.

Besides the vases of innumerable shapes clay was used to make lamps in great variety.   Illustrations of such are scattered through the pages of reports of the excavations at Olbia, Chersonese and on the Bosporus, but very little has been done towards examining the types prevalent at different times[1]. Lamps with the old black glaze are comparatively infrequent.   The oldest is that with a vith century *graffito* from Berezan (v. p. 361) ; commonest are those in ware similar to the Arretine vases and their imitations.   They are made also in a kind of dull black ware.   Besides the familiar type like a double-bottomed saucer with a handle on one side and the projection for the wick on the other, we have them ingeniously arranged for three or four wicks.   In general their forms are just alike over the whole of the ancient world, and the decoration impressed upon the round saucer part is the last stage in the vulgarization of familiar types.

A lamp that does call for notice is one from Olbia in the form of a negroid Silenus sitting doubled up and leaning against an amphora.   The whole is cleverly adapted for a lamp, the neck of the amphora doing well for pouring in the oil and the wick coming out at its shoulder[2].   Pharmacovskij compares a figure of an old woman from Scyros ; she is hugging an amphora, and so forms a small vase[3] ; and likewise a little vase from Olbia with Silenus on a wineskin[4].   The style points to the IInd century B.C. and recalls the later Pergamene school with its love of barbarian types.   Another unusual lamp from Olbia is in the form of a sandalled foot[5].   But generally there is just a rosette with a hole in the middle, or a poor reproduction of the most commonplace ancient motives[6].

With lamps go lampstands.   The most curious of these is one from Olbia in the British Museum[7].   It has the shape of a four-pillared shrine upon a high base : in the front is a niche in which stands the figure of an actor in a woman's part.   The stand supports a moveable bowl and the lamp was for warming food in this, not for giving light.

Amphorae.

Rather apart from other ceramic remains come the large amphorae in which wine was kept and exported[8].   A small proportion of these bear stamps,

[1] A fine series from Delos, W. Deonna, *BCH.* XXXII. (1908), pp. 133—176 : cf. Wiegand-Schrader, *Priene*, p. 449 sqq.

[2] *BCA.* VIII. p. 47, Pl. IV. ; *CR.* 1901, p. 14, f. 25.

[3] R. Weisshäupl, Παραστάσεις γραίας μεθυούσης, Ἐφημερὶς Ἀρχαιολογική, 1891, p. 145, Pl. X.

[4] *Odessa Museum, Terra-cottas* (v. p. 363, n. 1), II. xii. 2.

[5] *CR.* 1901, p. 14, f. 24, cf. *CR.* 1894, p. 100, f. 174 ; for one in the form of a boar's head, v. *CR.* 1896, p. 81, f. 335.

[6] Nevertheless they have been very fully illustrated : cf. MacPherson, *Kertch* Pl. VII. : *CR.* 1891, p. 143, f. 161 ; 1892, pp. 23–5, ff. 16—21 ; 1895, p. 106, f. 256 ; pp. 108–9, ff. 261—266 ; p. 111, f. 271 ; p. 115, f. 288 ; 1896, p 182, f. 561 ; p. 185,

f. 565 ; 1897, p. 114, f. 226 ; p. 117, ff. 229—231 ; p. 119, f. 234, on a stand ; p. 128, ff. 248–9 ; 1899, p. 7, f. 8 ; 1900, p. 6, ff. 6—9 ; 1901, p. 135, f. 238 ; 1903, pp. 27, 42, ff. 23, 57 ; *BCA.* IV. p. 85, f. 34 ; p. 102, f. 51 ; *KTR.* pp. 103, 104, ff. 138, 139. These are mostly from Chersonese, some from Kerch, as also *Od. Mus.* I. X. 5, II. XVIII. 12 ; from Olbia come those figured ib. I. XVII. 1, II. XVII. 1, *CR.* 1896, pp. 204, 206, 208, ff. 586—589, 596 ; 1904, p. 33, ff. 41—46, in *BCA.* VIII. p. 41, ff. 39, 40 ; p. 47, f. 47 ; p. 55, f. 59 ; p. 57, ff. 61, 62 ; Vogell, Nos. 575—642 with 21 illustrations and *Arch. Anz.* 1910, p. 236, f. 37.

[7] *JHS.* XXIX. (1909) p. 164, f. 17.

[8] P. Becker, *Mélanges Gréco-Romains*, St P. (1855) I. pp. 416—521, "Ueber die in Südlichen

symbols, monograms and inscriptions with proper names in full. The interpretation of these stamps has not been successfully attained. Mr E. M. Pridik, in the forthcoming Volume III. of *IosPE.*, is making a complete collection of them and of other inscriptions upon pottery, and we may expect that he will be able to offer some satisfactory explanation. Meanwhile it is not very hopeful to go into the subject at great length.

At first sight it might be supposed that the stamps have to do with the wine contained in the vessels, that they take the place of our labels, and that the name of a magistrate appearing upon the vessel was a guarantee of the authenticity of the commodity or of the vessel's containing full measure, and at the same time among those who knew would serve as a date mark. The amphorae without marks would either have contained *vin ordinaire* or had their distinguishing signs applied on the clay with which the opening was stopped, or written on some part of their surface. But the fact that similar stamps with the same names both of magistrate and of private persons occur upon tiles makes it apparent that it was a matter for the potter and the authorities who supervised him; and at the same time deprives us of any intelligible explanation. Is it conceivable that the same potter making amphorae and tiles, and putting the stamps on the amphorae for certain wine producers, stamps accordingly associated with his factory, should have transferred them also to tiles[1]?

Whatever may have been their use, the stamps do allow us to learn something of the wine trade among the Pontic colonies. Quite clear are those of Rhodes and Thasos, which occur in large quantities on all the Greek sites. Clear too are those of Cnidos and Paros, which are very much less frequent[2]. Plain amphorae may be referred to these cities by similarity of make or material. The difficulty arises in assigning those which bear two names or even three, the third the patronymic of one of the other people; in agreement or apposition to one of the names is the word ἀστυνόμου or ἀστυνομοῦντος, very rarely ἀγορανόμου, with or without ἐπί, and this comes either at the beginning or between the names, in such a way that it is hard to distinguish who is astynomus and who potter. One class of these with the inscription in a peculiar narrow depression may be referred to Chersonese because of its being found in greater proportion in the neighbourhood of that city and because of the occurrence of Doric forms in the names. It is usually

Russland gefundenen Henkelinschriften auf Griechischen Thongefässen." *Trans. Od. Soc.* V. p. 18 sqq. = (Fleckeisen's) *Jahrbuch für klassischen Philologie,* Suppl. Bd IV. (Leipzig, 1862), pp. 451 sqq., 'Ueber eine Sammlung unedierter Henkelinschriften aus Südlichen Russland." *Trans. Od. Soc.* VII. p. 3 sqq. = *J. f. kl. Phil.* Sup. Bd V. (1869) p. 445; "Ueber eine zweite Sammlung u.s.w." *J. f. kl. Phil.* Sup. Bd X. (1878), p. 1; "Ueber eine dritte Sammlung u.s.w."; *Trans. Od. Soc.* XI. p. 12, "Inscriptions on handles of Greek amphorae in the collection of I. K. Suruchan." L. Stephani, *Mél. Gréco-Romains,* St P. (1866), II. pp. 7—26 and 206—216, and *CR.* passim. D. MacPherson, *Kertch,* Pl. X. XI. W. N. Jurgiewicz, *Trans. Od. Soc.* XI. p. 51 sqq.: "Collections of I. I. Kuris and Odessa Soc."; ib. XV. p. 47, "Handles

from near Chersonese"; ih. XVIII. p. 86, "Amphorae and Tiles from Theodosia." E. von Stern, *Trans. Od. Soc.* XXII. *Minutes,* p. 84; XXIII. p. 30. V. V. Škorpil, *BCA.* III. p. 122; XI. p. 19 "Ceramic Inscriptions" mostly from the north slope of Mount Mithridates at Kerch; with J. J. Marti, *Ceramic Inscrr. preserved in the Melek Chesme Barrow, Kerch,* Odessa, 1910. See also Latyshev, *Olbia,* p. 299.

[1] For tile stamps v. Ch. Giel, *Kleine Beiträge zur Antiken Numismatik Südrusslands,* p. 41.

[2] For the special points of the Rhodian, Thasian and Cnidian amphorae (the latter are common at Athens though rare on the Euxine) v. A. Dumont, *Inscriptions Céramiques de Grèce,* Paris, 1872, pp. 13—15; Rayet et Collignon, p. 360, ff. 133, 134: for the wine trade from other cities, v. inf. p. 441.

without any emblem[1]. On this class names appear which also mark some coins of Chersonese. A kiln for baking amphorae was found there by Tower *B* on p. 505, f. 338.

By far the greater part present no special peculiarities of dialect or have sporadic Ionic forms, but are further distinguished by an emblem of a bird of prey attacking a dolphin or fish. Emblems may often be the devices of particular magistrates or potters, and particular ones go with certain names; but those which accompany various names and are common throughout a whole class of stamps evidently have to do with the city. Such are the balaustium of Rhodes and this eagle and dolphin. Unfortunately this very mark is common to the coins of several cities round the Euxine coast: it seems to have belonged to Sinope first and to have been adopted thence by Istrus and Olbia, and the question arises, to which it is to be referred in this case. P. Becker wished to call amphorae with this mark Olbian and it is certain that some of them must have come from Olbia: Jurgiewicz the other chief authority of the last generation put them down to Sinope: Kosciuszko-Walużynicz follows him when treating of certain amphorae with "astynomus" found at Chersonese[2].

Though we have tiles with the stamps of the Archons of Panticapaeum[3] and it is tempting to connect with some Spartocid Satyrus a handle found at Chersonese[4], whereon one stamp had ΕΠΙΣΑΤΥΡΟ, the other, a good example of the canting stamp, ΣΑΤΥΡΟΣ and a Satyr's head like Pan's on the coins of Panticapaeum, yet there are no amphorae which we can certainly refer to that city. This makes it look as if it were a matter of wine-making rather than pottery. The districts devoted to vine culture in ancient times did not quite correspond to those now noted for it; some change of conditions has occurred. Strabo (II. i. 16) mentions the difficulty of cultivating the vine at Panticapaeum certainly as if it were not grown in sufficient quantities to make wine, though now there are considerable vineyards in the neighbourhood. On the other hand, we know from the Agasicles[5] inscription and from actual remains that the territory of Chersonese was covered with vineyards, whereas now they grow only in one or two favourable spots, and it seems possible that wine was an important factor in the prosperity of the colony, as it had too small and too dry a territory to grow corn with success. Whether the Greeks ever made use of the southern slopes of the Crimea where are now the best vineyards is not quite clear; it rather seems as if they never got firm possession till quite late times. Bessarabia produces good wine, and may have supplied the Olbian trade: the vine district may have extended further to the N.E. than it does now. In any case the wine of the country did not satisfy the inhabitants, and they did a large trade with Rhodes and Thasos. A curious use of amphorae, not uncommon in very early Greece, is that for roofing over grave-cists[6].

With the amphorae and tiles go the great store-jars found in all Greek towns; from Olbia some have been extracted whole, or at any rate completely pieced together[7].

---

[1] *BCA.* II. p. 18.
[2] Ibid.: *CR.* 1896, p. 169. *BCA.* XVI. p. 57, cf. XXV. p. 93, tile from Sinope.
[3] MacPherson, pp. 72, 75, Pl. VII. XI.
[4] *Mat.* VII. p. 26.
[5] App. 17=*IosPE.* I. 195.
[6] Olbia, *CR.* 1905, p. 34, f. 31.
[7] *CR.* 1902, p. 21, ff. 30, 31.

Graffiti.

In Pridik's third volume of *IosPE.* we shall find besides the stamps all the "*graffiti*" scratched on pottery: this kind of material is well dealt with by Professor von Stern in treating a collection of such scratches in the museums of Odessa and Chersonese. They result from the excavations on Leuce made in the forties, from the works in connection with the harbour at Theodosia, from the present diggings in Chersonese, and from various sources, so that they give a satisfactory sample of what is to be found[1].

Von Stern divides those which can be more or less deciphered into inscriptions dedicatory, inscriptions of owners, and marks of dealers[2]. The first class offers most interest, including dedications to Achilles at Leuce[2], e.g. ΓΛΑΥΚΟΣΜΕΑΝΕΘΗΚΕΝΑΧΙΛΛΗΙΛΕΥΚΗΜΕΔΕΟΝΤΙΓΑΙΕΣΓΟΣΙΔΗΟ explained as "Glaucus has dedicated me to Achilles Lord of Leuce: O boy into the Temenos of Poseidon." It is conceivable that the writer, who combines exalted style with some carelessness (e.g. Λεύκη for Λεύκης after μεδέοντι, cf. App. 26 = *IosPE*. ii. 343, iv. 418), put in an extra E, meaning by the final words merely "the son of Posideus[3]": ΓΛΑΥΚΟΣΕΣΓΛΙΝΑΙΔΕΟ = "Glaucus take care how you sail in" is on the reverse. Other sherds had [γ]έρα Ἀχιλλέως and ΑΙΤΟΙCΥΝΝΑΥΤ = κ]αὶ τοῖς (σ)υνναύτ[αις: I had rather supply ὁ δεῖνα ἀνέθηκε κ]αὶ τοὶ συνναῦτ[αι. Vases with dedications somehow fell into the possession of the natives. We have a cylix of the careless redfigured style with Δελφινίο(υ) ξυνῆ Ἰητρô(υ) from Zhurovka (v. p. 176), and the silver vase from Zubov's farm (v. p. 232) once belonging to Apollo in Phasis. From Theodosia we have fragments with ΑΓ, ΑΘΗ, ΑΡΙ, ΗΡ, ΑΡΤ, ΑΣ, ΣΩ, ΗΔ, which may be taken as dedications and would then give us the names of gods worshipped in Theodosia, and ΗΡΑ, CΩΤΗ, ΔΙ, ΔΑΜΑ, ΔΙΑΙ, ΑΘΑ, ΑΡΙ, ΑΡΤ, in Chersonese, but since there are proper names of men as well as gods beginning with these letters we have no right to assume this. These may all belong to the class of owners' inscriptions, which is represented by less doubtful examples, but does not give any very interesting results. Then we have the marks of the dealers in pottery, denoting the price and what numbers they had of any particular sort. Two abecedaria from Theodosia are not of much account, one is ΑΒΓΔΕΗΙΟΙΚΛΜΝ only, and the other ΑΓΒΕΔΙΗΘΥΚΛΜΝΞΟΓΡΣΤΥ+ΦΨΗ. Very early *graffiti* interesting for an alphabet agreeing with that of Miletus in the vith century B.C. come from Berezan, ΣΜΙΚΗΣ ΕΙΜΙ[4], ΜΗΔΕΙΣΜΕΚΛΕΨΕΙ[5] and on a lamp ΩΣΛΥ+ΝΟΝΕΙΜΙΚΑΙΦΑΙΝΩΘ[ΕΟΙΣΙ]ΝΚΑΝΘΡΩΓΟΙΣΙΝ[6]. Another verse ΗΔΥΠΟΤΟΣΚΥΛΙΞΕΙΜΙΦΙΛΗΓΙΝΟΝΤΙΤΟΝΟΙΝΟΝ is pleasing with a Homeric word as befits Olbia[4]. Lastly there are the suitable mottoes painted on by the maker such as ΦΙΛΙΑΣ etc. (v. p. 351 n. 1). Interesting palaeographically are the boldly dashed-in letters on two cups from Chersonese (ii—iii cent. A.D.), ειλεοςμοιοθεος and πεινεε[γ]φραινου[7].

---

[1] *Trans. Od. Soc.* xx. p. 163: from Olbia and Berezan, ib. XXIII. p. 18 sqq.

[2] Dedications found elsewhere are given in the account of the cults of each deity in the different towns.

[3] I find this suggestion has been anticipated by l. T., *Journal of the Ministry of Public Instruction*,

St P., Dec. 1902, Classical Section, p. 291.

[4] *Trans. Od. Soc.* XXIII. p. 26.

[5] *Arch. Anz.* 1907, p. 145, *CR.* 1906, p. 55.

[6] *Trans. Od. Soc.* XXIX. *Minutes*, p. 88; *Arch. Anz.* 1910, p. 227, f. 26.

[7] p. 507, f. 339, *CR.* 1896, p. 186, ff. 566, 567.

§ 8.   *Glass.*

Glass in a measure took the place of the finest pottery in later times.   It did not come in till about the IInd century B.C., except in the form of beads (p. 65, f. 16) and of small glass vessels of many colours usually shaped like amphorae or alabastra, with the rods for extracting the unguents they held.

But in the early centuries of our era it was exported in enormous quantities from Egypt and Syria, and a great deal has been preserved in the Euxine colonies.   There are some magnificent specimens of both plain and coloured glass in the Hermitage, mostly from Kerch, and a representative series from Olbia in the Odessa Museum.   But the best collection was Mr Vogell's[1], which included some wonderful examples of the millefiori technique and an amphora two feet high made in two pieces and mounted in bronze engraved and gilt[2].

FIG. 264.   Glass from Olbia.   ⅜. *CR.* 1900, p. 9, f. 19.

Coloured glass was worked into the most varied shapes, from the simple tube in which unguents were sold to pieces in the form of heads[3] or decorated with frills and laces, like those on Venetian glass, or even elaborate vine-leaf patterns such as that signed by Ennion.   The same maker's wares have been found in Italy[4].   Though the capacities of the material were at length understood, many of the shapes are reproductions of forms already made in clay, stone (e.g. f. 264) or metal, such as the common cup or porringer which answers to the silver example from Artjukhov's barrow[5].

Glass from the Euxine coast has no special features ; probably it was all imported[6].   From the colonies it found its way to the natives, and we have had many instances of its occurring in their graves (supra, pp. 82, 224, 229—232), even the early kinds, as at Kurdzhips[7]. The most interesting case is that of Siverskaja (v. p. 215) where an ordinary glass jar and a porringer of the silver type described above have been treated as if they were made of rare stone and elaborately mounted in gold and garnets, just as Chinese porcelain has been treated in Europe.   A grave at Mtskhet in the Caucasus furnished the piece of highest technical mastery though of late Roman date—a silver cantharos with a pierced frieze and decorative patterns had blown into it a lining of dark purple glass[8].

[1] Richly illustrated in his *Sammlung*, Nos. 742 —1083, Pl. X.—XIII.

[2] Polychrome glass is figured in colours in *ABC.* (orig. ed.) LXXVII., cf. LXXVIII. 5, 6, also the interesting medallions from Zubov's barrows in *BCA.* I. Pl. II. and a fish-shaped bottle from Chersonese, ib. XVI. p. 95, Pl. VI. Beads, MacPherson, Pl. VII. VIII. : *Smēla*, III. Xiii. Ordinary photographs of coloured glass, even with full descriptions annexed, such as we have in Vogell, loc. cit., esp. Nos. 997, f. 51 and 1003, Frontispiece, in *CR.* 1900, p. 12, f. 26, or *KTR.* p. 93, f. 127, are not of much use.

[3] e.g. from Chersonese, Janus, *CR.* 1897, p. 126, ff. 242, 243: woman's head, *CR.* 1902, p. 44, f. 77.

[4] *ABC.* LXXVIII. 1—4 ; *KTR.* p. 94.

[5] *CR.* 1880, p. 9=*KTR.* p. 90, f. 119, a plainer form of IV. 8 on p. 431, f. 321.

[6] Other pieces ; Kerch, MacPherson, Pl. IV. VI. : *CR.* 1874, I. 9, 10 ; 1896, p. 158, f. 528 ; 1900, p. 28, ff. 65—67 ; 1903, p. 49, ff. 80, 82 ; 1905, p. 63, f. 74 ; *Arch. Anz.* 1907, p. 139, f. 10 : Chersonese, *CR.* 1891, p. 138, ff. 142, 143, p. 140, f. 151, p. 154, f. 191 ; 1895, pp. 111, 112, ff. 269—273 ; 1899, p. 9, ff. 12, 13 : Olbia, *CR.* 1901, p. 18, ff. 36—38 : 1902, p. 12, ff. 16, 17 ; *Arch. Anz.* 1908, p. 187, f. 20 ; 1910, p. 238, f. 38 : but the best pieces seem never to have been figured.

[7] *CR.* 1896, p. 152, f. 505.

[8] *CR.* 1872, II. I=*KTR.* p. 225, f. 201.

§ 9. *Terra-cottas.*

In spite of the spirited defences made by the Russian archaeologists it must be admitted that the terra-cottas[1] of the Northern Euxine, if not worthy of the wholesale condemnation meted out to them by Pottier[2], and repeated by Mr Huish[3], do not come up to the level attained at Athens, Myrina or Tanagra. The few exceptions are either actual imports or copies or even imitations made by taking casts of imported figures. That quite good figures were produced in these northern parts, that not all the tolerable specimens were imported, we know from the discovery of a coroplast's workshop with moulds at Kerch close by the cemetery[4] and at Chersonese. But the ease with which given types could be reproduced is shewn by the success of modern forgers. This being so, it is natural to find that by far the greater part of South Russian terra-cottas though of native manufacture can be paralleled in other Greek districts, particularly at Myrina, the necropolis of which corresponds in date to that in which the best class of Kerch statuettes occurs.

In view of this agreement there is no need to consider the debated question of the reason why the Greeks put terra-cottas in their graves. The various views are well summed up by Derevitskij in his article, and again in his introduction to the Odessa Terra-cottas. This latter publication, with its text in German as well as Russian, makes a very representative collection accessible to Western archaeologists who wish illustrations on a larger scale than those in Kekulé-Winter. In view of the existence of these works and the generally second-rate character of Euxine terra-cottas, I have treated this section rather shortly.

As with other departments of Greek art, the early development of the art of moulding clay is not to be studied in the Euxine colonies. We cannot point to many undoubtedly early specimens. We have in plenty types which by their disposition and rudeness go back to the first attempts at modelling, but these we must regard as survivals preserved under the influence of hieratic tradition. Speaking broadly, we find but few instances of the severe style, and can merely witness a steady decline from the making of quite satisfactory imitations of the best products of Attica or Asia Minor to the rudest lumps in which any plastic intention can be traced.

The different towns have distinctly their several characteristics in terra-cottas. The highest average belongs to Theodosia, because nearly all its specimens belong to one fairly early find, hence a superiority in material, a firm yellowish carefully washed clay, design, characteristic of the best period,

---

[1] *ABC.* Pl. LXIV. to LXXVI. *CR.* passim. *KTR.* p. 94 sqq. N. P. Kondakov, *Trans. Od. Soc.* XI. p. 75—179: "Greek Terra-cotta Statuettes." A. A. Derevitskij, *Trans. Od. Soc.* XVIII. p. 203—250: "Some Greek Statuettes from the Collections of the Odessa Archaeological Society and of Al. Iv. Nelidov." (Mostly a series of actors.) A. A. Derevitskij, A. A. Pavlovskij, E. von Stern, *Das Museum d. kais. Odessaer Gesellschaft für Geschichte und Altertumskunde,* I. 1897, II. 1898, "Terracotten."

W. K. Malmberg, *Mat.* VII. "Antiquities found in Chersonese in 1888 and 1889." S. A. Zhebelëv, *Mat.* XXIV. "The Kerch Niobids." A. Vogell, *Sammlung,* Nos. 643--738, figs. 39—42, Pl. IX. Kekulé-Winter (v. p. 345 n. 1), III. 1, pp. xl—xliv, gives a most excellent review of the S. Russian terra-cotta types.

[2] *Les statuettes de terre cuite dans l'antiquité,* p. 147, quoted by Derevitskij, p. 212.

[3] *Greek Terra-cotta Statuettes,* p. 184.

[4] *CR.* 1878, p. xxxi; *KTR.* p. 98.

and execution, careful and artistic.   One head[1] has even a decidedly archaic feel, and another[2] is as severe. as possible.   So too the interesting acroterium[3].   The other pieces belong to the ivth and iiird centuries, the best time of the art.

The Olbian figures are of a reddish, rather crumbly clay, with a smooth surface.   A grotesque old woman from Berezan[4] and a mask and fragments from Olbia[5] are earlier than anything from Theodosia; a head of a youth[6] is still almost archaic.   Some of the figures found here are clearly brought from Athens[7], not being made of the local clay, and there is sometimes a certain doubt whether the importation was made in ancient or modern times.   We have just a few specimens of the best period[8]; perhaps the most interesting terra-cotta from Olbia is a Hellenistic model altar with groups on each face[9], Poseidon and Amphitrite, Nike before a trophy, and Dionysus, a Maenad and a Satyr.   Somehow it seems as if there were less taste here for clay figures; perhaps their place was taken by vases shaped like figures or animals (v. p. 346). At any rate Pharmacovskij, while speaking (l.c.) of numerous Hellenistic terracottas, has published very few, though his excavations have yielded so rich a series of vessels of just those centuries when figures were most abundant. The Vogell collection[10] offered examples of terra-cottas of every period, but many of them were from Kerch, some perhaps from abroad.   Figures of the Roman period, including unmistakable Roman soldiers[11], are fairly common.

At Chersonese at the east end of the site (*Z* on Plan vii) was made a remarkable find throwing much light on the way the ancient potter worked: in one room was his kiln perfectly preserved, in another his stock of clay moulds, many broken but about forty more or less whole: from these casts have been made to let us judge better of his work[12].   These moulds he seems to have made not by independent modelling but by taking impressions from metal, stone or clay.   The general style points to the second half of the iiird century B.C., when medallions in high relief were much in fashion for adorning the bottoms of silver vessels and were imitated. in clay (v. pp. 350 and 385); several of these moulds, made from *emblemata* in silver vessels, were intended for producing such imitations.

The best of these (i. 1 on f. 265) represents Omphale teaching Heracles to spin: it must have been taken from an earlier original than anything else in the collection.   Other roundels with Nike and Eros, Heracles and Telephus, Satyrs' heads and a pair with young Satyrs[13]—these last perhaps not immediately from metallic originals—are not equal to the first either in style or preservation.   The Athena head (f. 265, 1. 4) resembles closely Konelsky's *emblema* (p. 385); another piece seems to be an impression from a cheek-piece of a helmet[14].

[1] Kekulé-Winter, III. 1. 236. 8 *c*. : *Odessa Museum*, I. X. 6.
[2] ib. I. ix. 1.
[3] ib. I. vi, vii.
[4] *Arch. Anz.* 1909, p. 161, ff. 23, 24.
[5] *CR.* 1902, p. 22, f. 33; *BCA.* XXXIII. p. 117, ff. 17—21.
[6] *CR.* 1902, p. 18, f. 26.
[7] *Od. Mus.* II. i.

[8] e.g. *Arch. Anz.* 1909, p. 173, f. 37.
[9] ib. p. 170, ff. 31, 32 : *BCA.* XXXIII. pp. 128, 129, ff. 49—52.
[10] *Samml.* Nos. 643—738, Pl. IX.
[11] *Od. Mus.* II. xiv.
[12] *CR.* 1882—1888, p. ccxvi. Malmberg, *Mat.* VII. pp. 3—26: cf. Pharmacovskij, *BCA.* II. p. 73.
[13] *Mat.* VII. 1. 3, 2, II. 3—6.
[14] ib. p. 11.

I.1. I.4.

III.2.

III.3. Casts from the
Terra-cotta Moulds
found at Chersonese.
Malmberg,
Mat.VII

IV.
5a. IV.
5b.

FIG. 265. ⅔, but IV. 5 is ⅓.

Another roundel with a male and female head (Fig. 266) is interesting because it shews metallic details specially clearly and because there comes from Olbia a very similar piece of silver work, which again has a still closer analogy with a more recently discovered pottery fragment from Chersonese[1].   Other moulds have been taken from marble sculpture, especially a fragment of a Bacchic procession[2] and a head of an archaic type of Hermes (Fig. 267) of which Kondakov and Malmberg believe that we possess the battered original in Fig. 210 on p. 297 ; they point especially to similar curls in the left moustache and beard and to the fact that, allowance being made for the double shrinking of the clay, the sizes of the two pieces tally exactly.   Most of the moulds reproduce terra-cotta originals, not only the pretty but senti-

FIG. 266. *Mat.* VII. p. 12. *Emblema* from mould found at Chersonese. ⅓.

mental heads on Fig. 265—III. 3 rather recalls the familiar Niobe—but various rough heads and figures[3], and purely decorative pieces, attachments of handles and lips, borders and the like[4].   In view of such a method of working we can hardly credit this potter with a distinct style.

Other pieces of terra-cotta from Chersonese mostly have a bold free character, rough but not barbarous, just what we should expect in a town which, without any claims to artistic life, still kept itself much freer from barbarous admixture than any other on the north coast of the Euxine[5].

[1] *BCA.* II. p. 75, f. 2 ; p. 19, f. 19.
[2] *Mat.* VII. II. I.
[3] ib. III. I, 4, 5, pp. 17, 18.
[4] ib. pp. 22, 23.

[5] *CR.* 1896, p. 175, ff. 546—550; 1898, p. 111, f. 10; 1899, p. 8, ff. 10, 11, p. 9, f. 14; 1900, p. 18 sqq., ff. 34—38, 42; 1905, p. 54, ff. 58, 60: *Arch. Anz.* 1906, p. 115, ff. 2, 3.

By far the greater part of the terra-cottas from South Russia are found in the environs of Kerch.   Here they occur in the greatest numbers and in the greatest variety, but it is hard to characterize their style except when it becomes barbarous and produces some types unknown in purely Greek lands.

We have of course the usual Aphrodite Anadyomene[1] with or without a Herm, a dolphin or an Eros, she often wears a disk-shaped head-dress peculiar to Kerch[2]; Eros alone or with Psyche[3]; Dionysus and his crew[4] or their masks[5];

FIG. 267. · *Mat.* VII. p. 21.   Head of Hermes from mould found at Chersonese.   ⅔.

Demeter and Core[6]; Muses[7]; actors[8]; theatrical masks[9]; gorgoneia[10]; Nereids and Tritons[11]; Heracles[12]; Pan[13]; Bes[14]; of everyday types, mother and child[15];

[1] e.g. *ABC.* LXV.   *CR.* 1870–71, II. 6, III. 1, 4—6; 1880, V. 6—8, VI. 10—12.   *Od. Mus.* I. iv.
[2] *ABC.* LXV. I, LXVI. I; *CR.* 1873, I. 5.
[3] *CR.* 1864, VI. 2—4; 1874, I. 1—5; 1878–9, II. 6, 7; 1881, IV. 1, 2, 6.   *KTR.* p. 99, f. 134=*ABC.* LXIV. 9.
[4] ibid. 5; *CR.* 1875, II. 27; 1877, VI. 1.
[5] *ABC.* LXVI. 3, LXXIV.   *CR.* 1878–9, II. 1—5, pp. 23, 24=*KTR.* pp. 96, 97, ff. 131, 132.
[6] *CR.* 1870–71, II. 1—4.

[7] *CR.* 1873, I. 4; 1880, VI. 7; 1881, IV. 7.
[8] Derevitskij, *Trans. Od. Soc.* XVIII. Pl. II.: with dancers, *CR.* 1906, p. 87, ff. 96—102.
[9] *ABC.* LXXV. 3; *CR.* 1881, IV. 2, 3; 1882–8, VI. 1.
[10] *ABC.* LXXV. 1, 2, 4—7.
[11] *Od. Mus.* I. Xii. 4, xvi. 5.
[12] *ABC.* LXIV. 8; LXX *a*. 5.
[13] *Od. Mus.* I. Xii. 5.
[14] *Od. Mus.* I. Xiii. 2.
[15] *CR.* 1859, IV. 3. .

cloaked ladies in sentimental poses walking or talking[1]; veiled dancers[2]; young men too walking or talking or out with their dogs[3]; girls at their games (e.g. ἐφεδρισμός or κατάγουσα)[4]; scenes of children with animals and birds[5]; in fact all the stock subjects familiar from the books on Greek terra-cottas (Kekulé-Winter, passim) and common to the whole Greek world, executed in styles varying from good to bad. But again we do have other compositions of more historical interest, though it is not among them that we get the best artistic execution.

Some of these recall us to Asia Minor and its religions, and may there-fore be likewise spread over the Greek world, but there is reason to think that either there was an original community of ideas between the Bosporus and Asia or the latter exerted its influence there sooner than anywhere else.

Perhaps the general Nature goddess does not belong much more to Asia Minor than to any other region, but her worship was much celebrated there under various names. This seems to be the deity represented by a kind of triangle of clay which serves as a background to a figure of which one can but distinguish the face, the breasts and the knees; the arms are nearly always broken off, but in one specimen they hold out a fruit and a dish in just the attitude in which a goddess sits on the later Bosporan coins (e.g. Sauromates II, v. inf. Pl. VIII. No. 12). A similar ruder figure bears before itself a smaller nude female figure, and was explained as Moloch by a former writer. It seems to represent the Mother and Daughter that are one[6].

The same mother goddess, more definitely Asiatic, is represented[7] with her hands upon her breasts. The execution is distinctly better, and in one case the brilliant colouring has been to some extent preserved. An Asiatic analogue is furnished by a terra-cotta bust that has found its way from Smyrna to Odessa, and is exactly the same in conception[8]. Something similar is a very barbaric bust covered with a green glaze such as we have already met on some pottery and referred to Egypt, but this is unlike any definite school[9].

Incontestably Asiatic is the group of a man with a conical cap, a sleeved coat and tight hose kneeling on the back of a bull in the act of slaying it[10]. This must be one of the earliest renderings of the Mithras group so common in late Roman times, for its style is good and with it were found other well-modelled figures[11]. It seems as if the first conquests of the Mithraic cult, which for a time seemed a serious rival to Christianity, were on the Bosporus[12].

Another Asiatic type represented in terra-cotta statuette and also in an anthropomorphic vase is that of the dancer in a similar costume[13]. Reinach calls him Men Atys, Stephani had no good reason to make him a Scythian.

[1] *ABC.* LXVIII. 1—3 = *KTR.* p. 102, f. 137; *CR.* 1859, IV. 4; 1868, I. 16, 17; 1874, III. 3; 1876, VI. 3; 1880, V. 9, VI. 8, 9; *ABC.* LXIX. 2: seated, *CR.* 1860, IV. 5.

[2] *CR.* 1870–71, III. 2; 1876, VI. 2, 4.

[3] *ABC.* LXX a. 3; *CR.* 1870, IV. 2; 1882–8, VIII. 4; *ABC.* LXIV. 6, 7; *CR.* 1868, III. 8, 9.

[4] *Od. Mus.* II. vii. 2; *CR.* 1872, IV. 2; 1880, VI. 2.

[5] *ABC.* LXXIII. *CR.* 1859, IV. 6; 1863, I. 4—6; 1868, III.; 1873, II. 2; 1876, VI. 9; 1878–9, V. 2—4. *Arch. Anz.* 1909, p. 153, f. 13.

[6] *ABC.* LXXII. 5: *Od. Mus,* I. xiii. 1, 3; *CR.* 1876, VI. 10 bearing Herm instead.

[7] *ABC.* LXIX. 4, LXX a. 4.

[8] *Od. Mus.* II. iii. 1. Cf. H. B. Walters, *Brit. Mus. Cat. of Terra-cottas,* Pl. XXII.

[9] *Od. Mus.* II. xv. 2.

[10] *CR.* 1880, VI. 6. *Od. Mus.* II. v. 1. The same more impressionistically rendered II. v. 3.

[11] ib. II. ii. 2: iv. 2—5.

[12] A good example, a Nike slaying a bull, from which this type was taken, on a gold ring, *ABC.* XVIII. 4, 7; cf. *JHS.* VII. (1886), Cecil Smith, p. 275 and F. Cumont, *Mystères de Mithra* (Bruxelles, 1899), I. p. 179, II. p. 191, f. 17, similar Mithra group from Kerch in the Hermitage.

[13] *ABC.* LXX a. 7, *CR.* 1859, III. 1, Pottier et Reinach, *Nécropole de Myrina,* p. 393, Pl. XXVIII. 3: cf. XXX. 1. Kekulé-Winter, III. 2, p. 158. 2, 8.

Other subjects are harder to define. As has been remarked in dealing with representations of barbarians in other materials, it is very difficult to distinguish between studies from the life of real South Russian natives, vague barbarians with a general outlandish style of costume chosen according to the Greek conventional idea of barbarians, and finally faithful representations depicting the local Greeks who had partly adopted barbarian clothing. They had clearly taken to trousers and hoods (*bashlyki*), and the population being mixed the facial type does not go for much: the more that it is not readily distinguishable in small figures hastily executed. The figure standing at ease leaning on his oval shield, clothed in a hood, a chiton and trousers[1], has a shield just like that on the gravestone of Gazurius at Chersonese, who certainly counted himself a Greek to judge by his epitaph and office (inf. p. 507, f. 339, p. 541, πρωταρχοντεύων). A man with similar headgear and shield is represented nude, a convention a Greek would never apply to a barbarian warrior[2].

The same question arises with regard to a type of galloping horseman (cf. p. 304, f. 218) which occurs in stone, bronze and terra-cotta, and also on coins. The fact that a man with a Greek name put it on his dedication seems against its being barbarian. The terra-cotta versions are not clear enough to help[3]. When the horse stands on four separate legs the whole becomes rather a toy than a work of art[4]. The barbarian can, however, be recognised without any doubt when he is caricatured. Such caricatures we have in the figures of slaves looking after children[5]. One, for instance, wears a moustache.

These caricatures were carried to very great lengths among the Bosporans, even further than among other Greeks. From some of the tombs have been taken the most extraordinary figures, notably that of the second lady in the Great Bliznitsa near Taman, explored in 1869[6]; the lady was apparently a close relation of the priestess of Demeter, whose grave was found in the same barrow in 1864, and was herself initiated; she possessed also the most beautiful jewelry, but with all this was found a whole collection of terra-cottas representing comic actors in all the obscene extravagance of their costume, athletes and slaves and women likewise, all with every indecent detail. Stephani explains that everything ἄτοπον καὶ γελοῖον served to avert the evil eye, and that the object of these grotesques was to keep off evil influences: others think that this was just her taste, and she wished to have with her in the grave what she had found amusing in life, and that other caricatures were due to the same feeling in other people, though in no one was it so exaggerated[7].

In many tombs, especially in the later period, we find figures with movable limbs. Some are made like articulated dolls, that is, like an ordinary statuette with some of the limbs working on pieces of wire[8].

A more typical class is made so that the trunk, in the shape of a kind of hollow cone, ends about the hips, and the legs and phallus are hung separately

---

[1] p. 56, f. 10. Several replicas exist, e.g. *ABC.* LXIV. 3. *Od. Mus.* I. xv. 1, 3.

[2] *Od. Mus.* I. xv. 5.

[3] *ABC.* LXIV. 2; *CR.* 1870-71, II. 7, 8; 1873, II. 4. *Od. Mus.* II. Xi. 1, 3: but *Od. Mus.* II. X. 2, 3 have the horse moving slowly.

[4] *Od. Mus.* II. Xi. 2.

[5] *KTR.* pp. 100, 101, 206, ff. 135, 136, 189 = *CR.*

1870-71, v. 9, 1859, IV. 7, 1869, II. 2, cf. *CR.* 1877, v. 11; 1880, VI. 4.

[6] *CR.* 1869, II. III., v. inf. p. 428.

[7] *Od. Mus.* I. xiv. 4, 5, 6; Kekulé-Winter, III. 1, p. 172, 1—6; *CR.* 1865, VI. 6, 7; 1868, I. 15; 1874, I. 8; 1882-8, VI. 1, 2.

[8] *ABC.* LXXIV. 8 is quite rudely made but *CR.* 1868, I. 18 is more artistic, cf. 1877, VI. 8, 12, 15, 16.

M.

on to wires and could be moved about by strings through a hole in the back.
These almost certainly served as marionettes[1].   Mostly they are very rudely
modelled, but there is an excellent caricature of a conjuror from Kerch, and
from Olbia come models of Roman soldiers made on the same principle[2].
Some of the coarsely made ones have as it were rays coming from their heads,
and hence they have been called idols, but there is no reason to suppose that
they represent anything but some strange head-dress (f. 268).   The model
waggons were also toys (v. pp. 50, 51, ff. 5, 6[3]).

It has been said that we have no clear idea what was the object of putting
terra-cottas into graves, and we do not know of any definite arrangement
according to which they were disposed.   They were evidently thrown into a
heap in no sort of order: sometimes broken on purpose and with the fragments

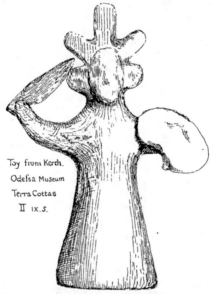

Toy from Kerch.
Odessa Museum
Terra Cottas
II IX. 5.

FIG. 268.   ½.

at opposite ends of the grave: but in South Russia the object of a large class
both of terra-cottas and of plaster figures is quite clear.   They served to
decorate coffins, and mention has been made of the traces left by them on the
panels.   The most usual series for this purpose was that of the Niobids, and in
various Russian Museums several separate sets from Kerch are preserved in a
more or less incomplete condition (ff. 269, 270, also pp. 332—334, ff. 241—243[4]).
Similar figures have been found at Gnathia in Apulia, and published for
comparison by Mr Zhebelëv in his exhaustive treatment of the subject.   The

---

[1] *CR.* 1873, II. 6—10; 1880, V. 5; *Od. Mus.* I.
xiv. 1, 2, 3.

[2] ib. II. xiv. 1, 2, 3.

[3] Veselovskij found better model waggons at

Ulskaja, *Arch. Anz.* 1910, p. 196, f. 1; *BCA.*
XXXV. p. 3, associated with a red skeleton, copper
pins and "pre-Mycenaean" figurines, ib. Pl. I, II.

[4] Cf. *CR.* 1861, III. IV.; 1868, II. 1—9; 1874, I.

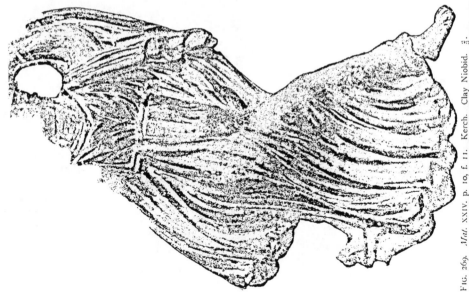

FIG. 269. *Mat.* XXIV. p. 19, f. 11. Kerch. Clay Niobid. ⅜.

FIG. 270. *Mat.* XXIV. p. 7. f. 6. Kerch. Clay Niobid. ⅜.

FIGS. 271—275. *CR.* 1891, p. 45, ff. 21—25. Plaster Coffin Ornaments. Kerch. ⅔.

FIG. 276.   Plaster Ornament.   Kerch.   *CR*. 1891, p. 56, f. 35.   ¾.

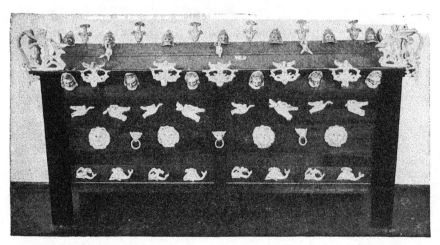

FIG. 277.   *CR*. 1901, p. 59, f. 119.   Model of Coffin from Kerch with plaster ornaments.

different series vary considerably in their style, and these variations on a familiar type throw light on the methods which workmen practising a minor art applied in copying examples of fine statuary.   Besides the Niobids there were used for the same purpose various masks, especially those of Medusa and models of theatrical masks; also flat figures of lions and griffins and conventional ornaments such as palmettes; these have often survived when all trace of the wooden coffin had long vanished or did vanish at the touch of fresh air (ff. 271—276; f. 277 shews what the whole looked like): but these modellings, whether in plaster or clay, though sometimes spirited and skilful, are too hasty to be of very great interest or beauty[1].

With these flat-backed figures may be mentioned flat lead castings from Olbia, the commonest are bucrania; double axes and a biga also occur, and the British Museum has the figure of a Scythian[2].

The only other objects of clay that remain to be mentioned are the little pyramids with holes in them which are picked up on the beach near Greek sites, and apparently served as weights for nets and for the threads of the warp in weaving.   Sometimes they have stamps with emblems like those on coins or on amphorae[3].

§ 10.   *Bronzes.*

On the whole, South Russia is not distinguished for Greek bronze work. No bronze statues have ever been found there, and but few statuettes: the reason seems to be that few bronze things have so close a personal relation to any individual that his relatives should wish to lay them with him in the grave, and it is from graves that the antiquities found in South Russia are taken. Remains of towns have yielded comparatively little, for bronze is too valuable a material to find its way to the rubbish heap, and has always been melted down to suit new needs.   There is no reason to suppose that there was any lack of beautiful bronzes in Olbia or Panticapaeum, only when those towns ceased to flourish the bronzes were carefully taken away.   At Chersonese, which was less rich in classical times, bronzes may well have been comparatively rare, and the conditions of the soil make it unlikely that any finds of bronzes will be made on that site.

The early Greek bronzes found in South Russia have all been found in Scythic graves, and have thus been mentioned already, but as products of pure Greek art, whose presence in barbarian hands was accidental, not designed by their makers, they must be treated here.   We have, in fact, a specimen of the three most familiar types of Greek vith-century art[4].   There is, for instance, the six-winged Gorgon in the posture of the Nike of Archermus, whether running or flying it is impossible to tell: we have seen that the Medusa head was very popular among the Scythians, but the whole monster is of rare occurrence : the two chief examples are a gem from Jüz Oba[5] and the handle

---

[1] *CR.* 1902, p. 51, f. 80. Watzinger, *Griechische Holzsarkophage*, passim, esp. pp. 60—62 and 89.

[2] Vogell, *Samml.* p. 94, f. 63: *CR.* 1874, I. 11—24 and p. 32: Brit. Mus. MS. Cat. 1907. 5. 20: cf. lead at Sparta, *BSA.* XII. p. 322, f. 3 ; XIV. p. 24, f. 9.

[3] MacPherson, p. 103: Malmberg, *Mat.* VII. p. 30: *BCA.* I. p. 35, ff. 30—36.

[4] The three bronzes here illustrated have been newly republished with excellent photogravures in *Mat.* XXXII. The Gorgon is treated by W. Malmberg, the Koré mirror by the same and S. A. Zhebelëv, the other mirror by the latter alone.

[5] v. p. 427, f. 318, cf. *CR.* 1860, IV. 6. Furtwängler, *Die Antiken Gemmen*, VIII. 52.

of a crater from Martonosha (f. 278)[1].   The whole must have been a fine piece
of work : the rim, neck and upper part of the body, adorned with spirals and
Stabornament, are in the Odessa Museum, the handle in the Hermitage.   The
latter is very massive; where it rested on the vase's shoulder the junction is
masked by the four-winged Gorgon in a characteristic vith-century chiton.
She is running along a kind of abacus as of an Ionic capital, which in its turn

FIG. 278.   *CR.* 1889, p. 30, f. 12.   Martonosha.   Handle of Bronze Crater.   ¼.

is connected with the vase by serpents.   The angle between the lower part
of the handle and the vase, on a level with the Gorgon figure, is filled up by
another wing on each side so that the monster should appear winged from
every point of view.   The whole style points to Ionian work of the vith century.
It is very sad that this handsome piece should have been so broken at the time
of its discovery, and that further the fragments should be separated by all the
length of Russia.

Another familiar archaic type is that represented by a statuette found in
secret diggings about two miles from the Government town, Kherson, in
1896 (Fig. 229)[2].   The fragment is 25 cm. high, and formed the handle of a
mirror.   We have a figure standing in the accustomed attitude of the Acropolis

[1] v. p. 173, n. 2 (where read *Trans.***VI***th Russ. Arch.
Congress*, Odessa,): Reinach, *Rép. Stat.* II. p. 442.
II.   For its nearest analogue, v. *Catalogue of an
Exhibition of Greek Art, Burlington Fine Arts
Club*, London, 1904, p. 32, No. 65, Pl. XXXVI.: this
is now it seems at Munich, *Jahrb. d. k. d. Arch. Inst.*
1910, p. 50, f. 3: the handle of another, de Ridder,

Collection de Clercq, Tome III. "Les Bronzes," p.
267; cf. H. B. Walters, *B.M. Cat. Bronzes*, p. 85,
No. 583, and one in the Louvre *Gazette Archéologique*, 1887, Pl. 33.
[2] *Mat.* XXXII. pp. 1—24, Pl. 1: Goszkiewicz,
Treasure Trove, p. 44, Pl. VIII.: Derevitskij, *Trans.
Od. Soc.* XIX. *Minutes*, p. 105 sqq., ff. 1, 2, 3.

Korai and agreeing with them in all details.   Her left hand as usual holds a
fold of her skirt, her right hand bears a human-headed bird.   The manner of
attachment to the circumference of the mirror is elaborate.   The artist did not
see his way to breaking with his model and lifting her arms to hold the arc
above her head, but managed the transition by interposing a whole system of
animals.   Two jackals (?) with their forefeet on each side of the lady's head
and their hind feet on her shoulders support with their heads and the lady's a
strip of metal which is the ground for the familiar group of two lions tearing
an ox as he lies on his back.   These in turn support a strip of bronze adapted

FIGS. 279, 280.   *CR.* 1896, p. 82, ff. 337[a, b].   Kherson.   Bronze Mirror Handle.   ½.

to the arc of the mirror and curling round in volutes to touch the lions' backs.
In this strip are holes for rivets; the palmette which supported the disk from
the back has become detached.   The figure clearly stood on some sort of base
now lost.   There is also a small antelope which was probably fixed to the
circumference of the disk as in other examples.

The general type of mirror is fairly common[1].   The treatment of the
figure, the *coiffure*, the beast group and the human-headed bird all point,
according to Messrs Malmberg and Zhebelëv, to Ionian art of the latter part

[1] e.g. Reinach, *Rép. Stat.* II. Aphrodite, p. 327
—330: some of these have animals on the rim but
mostly Erotes supporting the disk, cf. also H. B.
Walters, *B.M. Bronzes*, Pl. III. 238, IV. 243, 241;
Arch. Anz. 1904, p. 23, f. 2; *Burlington Catalogue*,
1904, XLV. A. 8, and one in the Hermitage, *Mat.*
XXXII. Pl. II.

of the vith century, being much earlier than a very similar piece occurring in Etruria, which has been ascribed to native artists[1] and dated by de Ridder as late as the middle of the vth century[2]. Our figure was at first called Cybele, then Aphrodite, but it is better not to give it a name.

Much more simple in general disposition is a similar mirror found the following year at Annovka (Fig. 281)[3]. Here we have a nude female figure holding the disk with her hands raised on each side above her head, which

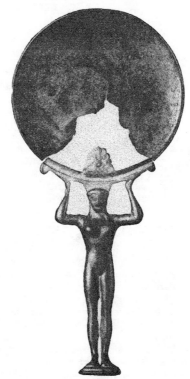

FIG. 281. *CR.* 1897, p. 78, f. 186ᵃ. Bronze Mirror. Annovka near Odessa. ⅔.

itself bears the palmette that supported it behind. Unlike the Egyptian figure-handles this stands on a base, and so derives from a separate statuette. In spite of her sex, in type she resembles the so-called archaic Apollo. The proportions of the body and the whole treatment recall that type, made female because the object it adorned was designed for women's use. Zhebelëv shews that while nude female statuettes of a hieratic type are general, such very early artistic presentations are exclusively Peloponnesian. For the figure,

[1] H. B. Walters, *B.M. Bronzes*, No. 493.
[2] *BCH.* XXII. (1898), Pl. III. p. 204.
[3] *Mat.* XXXII. Pl. III. pp. 25—35.

the closest analogy he quotes and illustrates (likewise a mirror handle) is at Munich; for the general scheme, a mirror at Aegina[1].

An attempt at the same motive is found in a mirror from near Romny in the Government of Poltava. In this case we have a relief instead of a complete figure, and the arms seem clumsily put behind the head instead of being stretched outwards and upwards:—also the legs are much too long in proportion. The handle ends below in a medallion on which is a Sphinx. The mirror disk is perfect. This does not seem so old as the former mirrors, but it is hard to judge of its style because its surface is in an unsatisfactory state. It hardly seems quite barbarous work, yet it is a very poor reproduction of its prototypes[2]. For other more or less Greek mirrors, v. p. 266.

A similar case of a traditional plastic type (Apollo) being used as a mere handle is the Hermes who served to hold a saucepan from the VII Brothers[3]. The transition to the disk is made by two rams on each side of the god's head, so he may be considered a kind of Criophoros.

Another early bronze is a candelabrum from Ust Labinskaja, found in a grave with plaques of the Siberian style such as it appears on the Kuban (e.g. Zubov's barrows, p. 230, f. 132). At the top of the shaft which was lost was a human-headed bird, with long archaic locks of hair, its waves indicated by nicks: above rose the convolvulus-shaped sconce for the lamp. The base was bell-shaped, with fluting and oves, and stood upon three bustard feet. The whole cannot be later than the vith century[4].

These specimens of archaic bronzes have all occurred in native tombs. Those worthy of notice from Greek tombs are of much later, even Hellenistic, date. Most artistic are the examples of repoussé work, especially the mirror boxes. One of these boxes bears Bacchus and Ariadne, accompanied by Eros and a panther: the inside is decorated with engraving, but is in poor preservation[5]. From each of the two women's graves in the Great Bliznitsa came a mirror box with a group of Aphrodite and Eros[6]. Perhaps the most decorative is one from Artjukhov's barrow with a magnificent figure of Scylla[7]. A later mirror with the familiar group of the three Graces was found on the slope of Mount Mithridates[8]. From Olbia we have one with Demeter's head[9].

In the first grave of the Great Bliznitsa were four sets of phalerae for horses, making up twenty roundels and four pointed ovals, all adorned with the battles of Amazons and Greeks[10]. This kind of work was heightened with gilding.

In the same technique were made the adornments of a couch discovered at Phanagoria. The chief piece[11], in the shape of ∫, masked the end of the

[1] de Ridder, 'Εφημ. 'Αρχ., 1895, Pl. 7.
[2] Khanenko, II. 3, Pl. XLVI. 351 *b*: compare a mirror figured in *Arch. Anz.* 1904, p. 22, f. 1, which has a sphinx above on a square plaque, then a human figure for the length of the handle, and a spread eagle below in the medallion. The work is much more archaic.
[3] *CR.* 1877, I. 9. Reinach, *Rép. Stat.* II. p. 88. 8, cf. 2, 5; p. 89. 1, 2, 8.
[4] *Arch. Anz.* 1903, p. 82, ff. 1, 2: *CR.* 1902, p. 79, ff. 166—168.
[5] *ABC.* XLIII. and *CR.* 1881, II. 1.
[6] *CR.* 1865, v. 1; 1869, I. 29; cf. *Coll. Tyszkiewicz*, Pl. v. from Corinth.

[7] *CR.* 1880, III. 13.
[8] *CR.* 1894, p. 45, f. 68; another mirror from Kerch with Eros tying Aphrodite's sandals, *CR.* 1901, p. 60, f. 124.
[9] *CR.* 1902, p. 13, f. 20.
[10] *CR.* 1865, v. 2—6, cf. those from Elis in the British Museum, *JHS.* XXIX. (1909), p. 157, and supra p. 155, n. 1.
[11] *CR.* 1880, IV. 10; C. Ransom, "Reste gr. Holzmöbel in Berlin" in *Jahrb. d. k. arch. Inst.*, 1902, p. 134, f. 11; cf. a close analogy in the British Museum, *JHS.* XXIX. (1909), p. 162: also Wiegand-Schrader, *Priene*, p. 380, f. 481.

pillow-rest, and bore Aphrodite in the middle and little busts at each end; the other fragments were plain but sufficiently preserved to allow the wooden parts to be restored and the whole to stand in the Hermitage.

It is the repoussé work also which gives artistic interest to a helmet from the Quarantine road[1], which bore a triangle upon the brow with a head of Athena, a gorgoneion of the later beautiful type on each side and a well-designed figure of Scylla with a torch and an oar filling the shape of the cheek pieces. The work is graceful, apparently of early Hellenistic time. Another fine helmet, a perfect specimen of its kind but quite plain, came from the Mirza Kekuvatskij barrow[2], together with a plain pair of greaves[3] and a Scythic sword, the one barbarian object[4]. A similar helmet of pure Greek work was found up country at Galushchino near Kiev[5]. Very like is another helmet from Nymphaeum[6]. Of quite an original type is one found in the man's tomb in the Great Bliznitsa and shaped as a Phrygian cap, making permanent the soft felt *bashlyks* of the country[7].

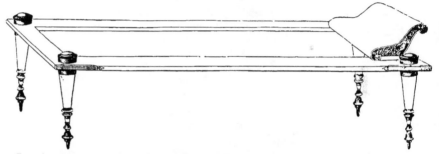

FIG. 282. Phanagoria. Couch. Restored woodwork: ancient bronze mountings. *CR.* 1880, p. 88.

Besides the greaves mentioned above the Hermitage has a more ornamental pair adorned above with a gorgoneion[8], not unlike a leg in the British Museum bronze room. The gorgoneion is of an archaic type, but as such appears rather to be a survival than a very early example. Mention has already been made of an elegant Greek cuirass and brassart of vth-century work found near Nicopol[9]. The scale armour and arrow-heads, most of which were certainly of Greek work, are treated on pp. 68, 74, for they have no artistic interest and were as it were naturalized among the Scythians.

A certain number of bronze vessels has been found in various graves; comparatively few are extracted whole, but the rim above and the handles, on which the decoration is concentrated, have generally been preserved. The commonest type is that of a hydria, which was a convenient vessel

[1] *ABC.* XXVIII. 1, 2, 3. Baumeister, p. 2036, f. 2214.
[2] *ABC.* XXVIII. 4, Reinach, p. 21.
[3] ib. XXVIII. 8.
[4] ib. XXVII. 9.
[5] Khanenko, II. 2, Pl. IX. 218.
[6] *KTR.* p. 48, f. 54=*CR.* 1877, p. 234.
[7] *KTR.* p. 48, f. 55=*CR.* 1866, Frontispiece;

other interesting helmets, *BCA.* XXIX. pp. 30, 31, ff. 1—3.
[8] *ABC.* XXVIII. 7.
[9] v. p. 74, S. Pavlutskij, "Objects of ancient armour from the district of Ekaterinoslav," in *Archaeological Chronicle of S. Russia,* I. (1903), p. 37, and Pl. V.

for receiving the ashes of the dead. For instance, in the passage under the wall of Chersonese by the gate[1] *E* stood six urns, Nos. 1—3 of clay entire, Nos. 4—6 of bronze broken : No. 4 as a prize from the Attic festival Anacia bore on its rim AΘΛΟΝΕΞΑΝΑΚΙΣΥΝ in dotted letters very like those of the Timotheus papyrus ; it held the best jewelry, No. 1 the next best.

Sometimes these urns were secured most carefully against any sort of damage, for instance there is in the Kerch room at the Hermitage a kind of stone box arranged to receive such a hydria and protect it from injury, and it is

FIG. 283. Stone box containing a clay urn. *CR.* 1891, p. 35, f. 16, from Hadzhi Mushkai near Kerch.

still untouched (cf. f. 283). Fragments of a very artistic hydria, with decorated foot and side handles and a Siren at the base of the middle handle, were found in the Babý barrow near Mikhaílovo-Apóstolovo[2]. A perfect specimen is well illustrated in MacPherson (Pl. III.) ; this was gilt as many others were, for instance the hydria in Kul Oba ; by it stood a great rarity, a bronze amphora of almost the same form as the earthen ones and also gilt[3].

Another form that often occurs in bronze is the ewer, oenochoe : a good specimen with a well-worked handle ending in an archaistic bearded head was found at the Khatazhukáevskij Aúl on one of the tributaries of the Kuban[4]. Among other objects found with it was a polished stone axe, which points to a

[1] v. pp. 397 sqq., 422, 499, Plan VII. inset, *BCA*. I. pp. 1—9, *CR.* 1899, p. 4, ff. 3, 5 : cf. *New Palaeo-graphical Soc.*, Pl. 22, especially the Ω.
[2] *CR.* 1897, p. 135, ff. 264—266.
[3] *ABC.* XLIV. 7, 12.
[4] *CR.* 1899, p. 49, ff. 92, 93.

strange mingling of different cultures.   In the same year was found at Chersonese a ewer of rather unusual form, having a very high handle embellished
with a dog above and a woman's face below[1].   jugs like an oenochoe but
with lids survived till the iiird century A.D., occurring in the queen's tomb at
Glinishche near Kerch; in the same tomb was a handsome dish or shallow
bowl with handle formed of snakes curling out of a winged head[2].   A similar
shallow bowl 47 cm. ($18\frac{1}{2}$ in.) across was found at Majkop; it also had snakes
about the handles and below them repoussé plaques representing Pylades and
Thoas (?)[3].   A basin of pale bronze 50 cm. across with a pretentious Hellenistic
emblema in copper representing a warrior, his mourning wife and a goddess
of death, comes from a plundered tomb at Nekrásovskaja Stanitsa on the
Kuban[4].   In one of the V I I Brothers an oenochoe was found with a Satyr above
the handle and a crouching figure below.   Another from the same group had a
handle ending in an elegant Siren[5].   Of a similar type is a vessel from the
Kuban district with Eros and a torch at the base of the handle[6].   From the
V I I Brothers also comes one of the few good statuettes found in South
Russia, a young Apollo crowning a tall columnar stand like a candelabrum[7].
   Quite isolated are some statuettes from the land of the Don Cossacks, a
pair of wrestlers, a Satyr and a young Dionysus[8].   The latter is rendered rather
curious by having a Byzantine inscription round his middle and Christian
monograms engraved upon his chest.   Very few of the common statuettes that
fill museums in the West have been found even in the town excavations.   We
may mention Zeus with a thunderbolt[9] and a bust of a woman from Chersonese[10], statuettes of Athena and of Osiris from Eupatoria[11], and a Hermes from
Balaklava[12], but nothing of any merit.
   It is curious that perhaps the most graceful small bronzes found in all the
extent of the North Euxine coast came long ago from Tanais (Nedvigovka),
which has yielded no other works of art, the more so that the remains of
the town then investigated date from the iind century A.D.   They include a
pretty lamp, an imperfect candelabrum, and a kind of standing vase[13].
Another fragment from the same site is the fluted handle of some vessel: at
the end is a ram's head, and on the plate by which it was riveted to the body
of the vessel are two figures affronted of Greek potters moulding pots: the
style seems as early as the ivth century B.C.[14]   A good lamp was found in
Artjukhov's barrow[15], another on a stand at Kerch[16].   Worthy of mention as an
evidence of trade with Italy is a saucepan found near Kagarlyk (Kiev Govt)
with a Latin inscription N GRANIPLOCAS[17].
   Of Roman date is an interesting vessel from Tyras cemetery in the form

[1] *CR.* 1899, p. 8, f. 9.
[2] *ABC.* xliv. 8, 2, cf. *BCA.* xvii. p. 69 ; xxxvii.
p. 34, *temp.* Rhescuporis IV (?).
[3] *CR.* 1896, p. 150, f. 500.
[4] *Arch. Anz.* 1906, p. 111, f. 1 ; *CR.* 1905, p. 74,
f. 95 : Pagenstecher, *Calen. Reliefkeramik*, p. 161.
[5] *CR.* 1877, iii. 1—4.
[6] *Arch. Anz.* 1903, p. 84, f. 4.
[7] *CR.* 1877, iii. 17, 18.
[8] *CR.* 1867, I. 1—4 ; Reinach, *Rép. Stat.* ii. p.
125. 4.
[9] *CR.* 1891, p. 12, f. 9.

[10] *CR.* 1896, p. 169, f. 537.
[11] *CR.* 1897, p. 74, f. 171 ; *BCA.* xxv. p. 179, f. 14.
[12] *CR.* 1891, p. 131, f. 138.
[13] *KTR.* pp. 91, 92, ff. 120, 123, 122 = *Report of
Archaeological explorations made in* 1853, Nos. 40,
42, 39.
[14] *Archaeological Bulletin and Notes published
by the Moscow Archaeological Soc.* vii. 1900, p.
360, note by the Countess Uvarov.
[15] *KTR.* p. 55, f. 69 = *CR.* 1880, p. 19.
[16] *CR.* 1904, p. 75, f. 116.
[17] *CR.* 1891, p. 91, f. 70.

of the head and bust of a negro girl; the handle above is a half circle with loops in the shape of chenisci.   The whole shews Alexandrian influence[1].

The poorer classes used bronze for their adornment: very common are simple bracelets from Kerch, just bronze wire twisted round the wrist and then round itself, and of no artistic interest[2].   There is little more of this in the bronze rings with engraved bezels[3].   None in mere instruments such as strigils, ear-picks and what not.   Buckles give some field for fancy in the various pierced patterns with which they were decorated; one from Chersonese is a good example of the change of taste of which Riegl makes so much[4]; the *tamga* is sometimes ingeniously worked into the design (v. supra, p. 318, f. 228).

§ 11.   *Silver.*

Silver oxidizes with time so that comparatively little has been preserved in good condition.   Small pieces have nearly always perished, with the exception of coins which the pressure of the die makes more resistant.   Special circumstances have rendered possible the great finds of ancient plate made in Western Europe, and nothing comparable has been discovered in South Russia.   As in the case of bronzes, the earliest specimens come from barbarian or semi-barbarian graves.   From Majkop come pieces which are apparently pre-Greek: the curious cup (p. 144, f. 36) and its fellows, and a "Cypro-Phoenician" vase with lotus pattern round the top and birds on the base[5]. Most of the older gold and silver plate in Kul Oba and the VII Brothers, rhyta, cups, phialae, torques, pectoral, plates for various weapons and clothes, having an Oriental or Scythic touch about it, as well as the later work from Chertomlyk, has been discussed in Chapter x. (pp. 262—269, 283—291). Perhaps the oldest Greek silver is the φιάλη μεσόμφαλος found in Zubov's barrow (p. 231, ff. 136, 137) and the similar one from No. II of the VII Brothers (p. 209, f. 107).   These may be referred to the earlier part of the vth century, although the inscription on the former may be later.   A vessel of the same type but of later style occurred at Dêev barrow, but this is simply fluted[6].

Early cylices with the most beautiful engravings inside were found in the VII Brothers[7]: one from No. IV has Nike gilt; that from No. II, Bellerophon, an early representation, for both cups belong to the vth century: a *scène de famille* on that from No. VI, put by Stephani early in the next century, is ranked by him as a drawing with the Kul Oba ivories, but he explains that the illustration in *CR.* does it scant justice: it is one of the cases that cry aloud to be reproduced by photography, excellent as may be the drawings in *CR.*; we see the objects in the earlier issues through the style of Piccard, the later drawings make us regret him.   Another ivth century cylix from a barrow near

---

[1] Von Stern, *Jahreshefte d. österr. Archäol. Inst.* VII. p. 197; again with corrections *Trans. Od. Soc.* XXVI. p. 183: an analogous piece of Mr Pierpont Morgan's, lent to S. Kensington, comes, as Mr B. Rackham kindly tells me, from Alexandria.

[2] Cf. *Sm.* II. xvii. 5, 6, from Ryzhanovka.

[3] *ABC.* XVIII. 12, 13, both of Roman date.

[4] p. 507, f. 339; cf. Riegl, *Die spätrömische*

Kunst-Industrie, Pl. XII.

[5] *Arch. Anz.* 1909, p. 151, f. 11: Smirnov, *Argenterie Orientale,* Pl. I. Nos. 1—11; Pl. CXXX. Nos. 326—331; Pl. CXIX. No. 303.

[6] *CR.* 1897, p. 33, f. 103, v. sup. p. 170.

[7] p. 206, n. 9, p. 210, n. 3 where please read "Dionysus": *CR.* 1881, I. 1—5.

by bears Dionysus and Maenads. The whole series is very interesting as furnishing examples in Greek engraving of the best time, and with the Kul Oba ivories shews how the methods familiar to us on vases were also used in other branches of art. Rather later is the Kul Oba cylix with the Ionic dedication EPMEΩ: the cover (or bottom plate) is engraved with palmettes[1].

The classification of later Greek plate is difficult, because not only did the old simple shapes live on or from time to time return into favour,—even in a rich tomb like the Great Bliznitsa[2] we find nothing more elaborate---but actual pieces can be shewn to have survived for hundreds of years, as indeed Pliny and Juvenal tell us[3].

FIG. 284. Silver Canthari, Colander and Hairpin, bronze Fibula. Olbia. v. p. 420.

For instance, the cylix was always a popular shape, and the plain specimens from Olbia[4] and Ryzhanovka[5] are on much the same lines as the older pieces. That from Karagodeuashkh is distinguished by its high base: from the same tomb come late examples of rhyta, a φιάλη μεσόμφαλος and an elegant ladle and strainer[6], with cheniscus handles[7]. Chmyreva Mogila has furnished a whole set of plate, three such φιάλαι, two with palmettes, one with a Bacchic frieze round the boss, a tall cylix with a Nereid inside, a fluted two-handled bowl with a frieze of birds and fishes, a globular fluted cup[8], two bottles, a ladle, a saucer and a barbaric jug with gold lid and handles[9].

We see reversion to type, Roman copies of good Attic models, in the two canthari and the strainer (f. 284) found at Olbia with the glazed jug (p. 356, f. 262) and now belonging to Mr Pierpont Morgan. The cup to the left

[1] *ABC.* XXXVII. 4.
[2] *CR.* 1869, pp. 8, 11 = *KTR.* p. 90, ff. 118, 119.
[3] *NH.* XXXIII. 157 (55): *Sat.* VIII. 104 and Mayor in loc.
[4] *BCA.* VIII. pl. IV. 2.
[5] *Smêla,* II. xvii. 4.
[6] *Mat.* XIII. pp. 140-152, ff. 16, 18--24, vi. 2—4,

v. sup. p. 219, f. 121, p. 290: cf. *ABC.* XXX. 1, 2; XXXI. 4, 5. 10 from Kerch.
[7] v. *CR.* 1863, p. 49.
[8] Like p. 198, f. 91, but without the friezes.
[9] A new excavation published in *Arch. Anz.* 1910, pp. 215—226, ff. 15—25 since my Ch. X. was printed off.

shews the more graceful shape and more enrichment about the top.   The handles have come off and lie beside the cups.   The other objects are a bronze fibula and a big silver hairpin[1].

Of more richly wrought Greek plate, besides such triumphs as the Chertomlyk and Kul Oba vases which have already been discussed, the finest pieces are two great dishes.   One found at Chertomlyk had elaborate handles supported by a female bust rising from a great palmette flanked by acanthus spirals, while the inner surface is entirely covered with a rich arabesque of acanthus.   Underneath are bobbin-shaped feet[2].

More simple and more elegant is a dish found at Glinishche near Kerch in the tomb of the queen with the golden mask (p. 434, f. 325).   Its only adornments are in the centre a medallion with a monogram surrounded by a bay wreath and round the rim the same wreath with the same monogram. This latter seems made up of the letters ΑΝΤΟΒ standing for ΑΝΤΙΟΧΟΣ or ΑΝΤΙΓΟΝΟΣ ΒΑΣΙΛΕΤΣ.   The latter is the more probable.   The Bosporus was out of the way of Syria and more likely to have had friendly relations with Macedon.   The Bosporan kings put the B first in their monograms upon coins.   The decoration is executed in niello and engraving.   The historical interest of the dish is much enhanced by a *pointillé* inscription on the back, which, in addition to some unintelligible marks probably denoting the weight, has the words ΒᴬϹΙΛΕ(ꞶϹ ΡΗϹΚΟΥΠΟΡΕΙ, apparently a very late Rhescuporis, for the formation of the genitive is incorrect or incomplete as it is on the coins of the last king of the name[3].   The queen's jewelry (v. p. 434, ff. 326, 327) with its barbarous use of garnets suggests the Novocherkassk treasure or the so-called Gothic jewels, and all points to the end of the iiird century A.D., that is to say that the great dish was in use for four or five hundred years before it found its final resting place.   Other pieces of old plate that the same queen possessed are a fiagon with a Medusa-head of late Hellenistic style below its handle and a covered vase with Erotes, garlands and masks of rather tasteless Roman work[4].   A rare object is a silver sceptre from the same grave[5].

From Kerch too comes a good set of plate found in a woman's tomb on the way to the Quarantine[6].   She had a gold wreath, earrings (No. 12 on p. 396, f. 290), necklaces, finger-rings, the two best with busts of Athena in gold with the faces cut in garnet[7], a ladle, a spoon and a strigil, a hairpin and toilet instruments, and a stater of Lysimachus important as giving a *terminus post quem*, but his coins went on being struck after his death and remained in circulation not much less than a century.

Two pieces of the plate seem early Hellenistic, one, an elegant cylix with a gilt and engraved drawing of Helios and his four horses on a loose plate fitting in the bottom of it, is according to Watzinger the model for a class of Cales ware[8]: the other, a cantharos with a necklace below its rim, is just like the clay

---

[1] von Stern, *Trans. Od. Soc.* xxvii. p. 88, "A Tomb-find made at Olbia in 1891."

[2] *ASH.* xxix. 5—7 ; *KTR.* pp. 263, 264, ff. 239, 240.

[3] Cf. *TRAS.* vii. p. 228; perhaps this is a native genitive of the type ΓΑΣΤΕΙ ΚΙΡΒΕΙ (v. p. 352, n. 5) with more right to exist than the usual 'Ρησκου-πόριδος : at that period -ις and -ιις sounded the same.

[4] *ABC.* xxxvii. 1, 2, cf. p. 357, the glazed porringer ap. von Stern, *Trans. Od. Soc.* xxii. p. 50.

[5] *ABC.* ii. 5.

[6] Ashik, *Bosporan Kingdom*, Pt iii. p. 70, n. 2, ff. xliv—xlix ; *ABC. Introd.*, p. lxiii., Reinach, p. 20, xxxvii. 5, xxxviii. 1, 3, 4, 5 ; *Annali dell' Instituto*, 1840, p. 13.   Watzinger, *Ath. Mitt.* xxvi. (1901) p. 92, v. supra p. 351.

[7] *ABC.* xv. 15 ; Ashik, ib. and f. 184, very like p. 365 supra, f. 265, 1. 4.

[8] Pagenstecher, *Calen. Reliefkeramik* (v. p. 349, n. 3), p. 130.

cylix from Olbia (p. 350, f. 256) except that its base is adorned with a Lesbian cyma like the necklace gilt. Simple too is a saucer upon a square base and fluted stem; it has a cover but no handles. But two of the pieces are quite baroque, one a jug with a twisted handle ending in a mask, an oak wreath round the neck and a vine pattern on the shoulder; the other, even more overloaded, has the vine pattern, fantastic handles in the shape of Satyrs, a spout made like a comic mask, and altogether suggests bad Renaissance work. Though found in the same grave these pieces must represent two different periods of silver ware.

Between them come two porringers and a flask from Artjukhov's barrow[1], in which the engraving technique has not entirely given way to the relief work: indeed some pieces from there are quite plain, the saucer on a stand just like that mentioned above, and a porringer with thumb-piece handles whose form is so common in glass.

An Olbian find, containing a gold necklace with no special features, a ring and a silver-gilt *emblema*, offers certain analogies to the Quarantine-road tomb. The *emblema*, 12 cm. ($4\frac{1}{2}$ in.) across, a splendid bust of Athena set in a frame of egg-and-dart so deep as to resemble *Stabornament*, corresponds to the plate with Helios above-mentioned; the dish into which it fitted has vanished. The ring has a similar Athena-head in gold repoussé, and exactly recalls the two biggest rings from the Kerch tomb. Von Stern[2] puts these things in the first half of the IInd century B.C.

To a late period belongs a rhyton in the shape of a calf's head which has upon its cylindrical cup extraordinarily bad figure subjects, whereas the animal's head is rendered excellently well, so that it is difficult to understand how the whole could have been made at one time[3]. Really the figures almost equal the culminating horrors of Dorohoe[4].

Fragments of interesting work, remains of *emblemata* and other embellishments of Hellenistic silver vessels, have been mentioned in connection with the clay wares that copied them (p. 364), indeed, as there pointed out, the best of the moulds found at Chersonese have really more to do with silver work than with ceramics. Actual fragments of silver are two heart-shaped pieces with women's heads and a round one with two heads kissing, all from Chersonese[5], and two reliefs of Tritons from Jaroslavskaja on the Kuban[6].

The latest productions of antique silver work come from two curiously similar finds made in catacombs at Kerch in 1904: each included a silver dish inscribed DNCONSTANTIAVGVSTI ♥ VOTIS ♥ XX♥ (i.e. his Vicennalia A.D. 343), a gold wreath with an indication from a coin of Sauromates II (A.D. 174—210)—also in one case others of Gordian and Valentinian—a dagger hilt set with red glass and many other specimens of garnet jewelry

[1] v. p. 431, f. 321, *CR.* 1880, II. 19; IV. 8, 9.
[2] *Aus der Sammlung Konelsky. Ein Athena-Medaillon aus Olbia*, Odessa, 1907, with a most beautiful coloured plate by M. Pharmacovskij, the best delineator of antiques in Russia: cf. the Athena from Mahadiyya, *Arch. Anz.* 1910, p. 263, f. 3.
[3] *ABC.* XXXVI. 1, 2; *KTR.* p. 87, f. 116; a similar rhyton from Sophia but not quite as atrocious is figured in *CR.* 1880, Text, pp. 56, 73. It is in the form of a deer's head and bears a Bacchic

scene. A still closer analogue is seen in another deer's head from Tarentum now in Trieste shewing the same inferiority of figure-work, L. de Laigue, *Rev. Archéologique*, Sér. 3ᵉ, XXXIX. (1901), p. 153, Pl. XVI.—XVIII.: such western analogues dispose of Reinecke's Chinese comparison, v. supra, p. 81.
[4] *ABC.* XXXIX.--XLII.
[5] *BCA.* II. p. 17, ff. 16, 17, p. 19, f. 1, v. p. 350.
[6] *CR.* 1896, p. 57, f. 280.

M.

49

and a silver-gilt shield boss: one tomb had two interesting silver spoons[1], the other two good ewers and a gilt bronze statuette of a priestess[2].

There should be mentioned also, although it occurred in the district of Baku far from the Hellenic colonies, a fine dish representing Amphitrite riding on a hippocamp attended by Tritons and Erotes; its style suggests the beginning of the decline[3]. Similar dishes of late classical[4] and Byzantine work also form part of the strange collection of silver plate that has found its way from all directions to the depths of the Perm forests, although they are mostly Oriental (v. p. 257, n. 4): the Klimova find includes a round dish with a goatherd sitting in landscape recalling Theocritus and the "Hellenistic relief[5]."

§ 12.   *Goldwork and Jewelry.*

It is to the magnificent examples of goldwork found in them that the excavations in South Russia owe their world-wide fame. The Hermitage possesses by far the richest collection of such work. It is therefore impossible to mention at all a large proportion of the specimens exhibited there or described in the various publications, and even such very indifferent completeness as has been reached in other departments is in this unattainable.

Moreover, owing to the absence of any treatise dealing generally with Greek goldwork and jewelry, it is harder to determine exactly what relation the style of objects found in South Russia bears to that current in the rest of the Greek world[6]. Eugène Fontenay's book[7], attractive from its style and many illustrations and important because of its author's technical knowledge gained by actual practice, covers too wide a field and in the ancient part loses by the author's want of familiarity with archaeology. If Dr Hadaczek will make such monographs upon other jewel-forms as he has upon earrings[8] we may hope that he will finally write an all-embracing history of jewelry in the ancient world. Much material for comparison is furnished by the Nelidov Collection, which includes a small number of objects from South Russia but was mostly formed in Constantinople and Rome[9]. Two works by Froehner have the same kind of interest[10], but none of these books give any view of the development of Greek jewelry or the geographical distribution of various types.

The classification of styles in goldwork is rendered particularly difficult by the transportability of the objects. Identical forms occur in South Russia, on the coasts of Asia Minor, in Cyprus, in Syria, in Egypt, in Athens, in South Italy and in Etruria, and there is very little means of judging where we

---

[1] *Arch. Anz.* 1905, p. 60, f. 5; *CR.* 1904, pp. 71—74, ff. 106—113, *BCA.* xxv. p. 32 sqq.

[2] *CR.* 1904, pp. 78—83, ff. 123—133.

[3] *CR.* 1896, p. 114, f. 410.

[4] e.g. Nilometer, *CR.* 1867, II. 1—3; Meleager, ib. 4, 5 = *KTR.* p. 412, f. 371; Satyr and Maenad, *CR.* 1878-9, VII. 1.

[5] *Arch. Anz.* 1908, p. 156, f. 3: the back, p. 157, f. 4 has VI—VII century Byzantine punches.

[6] This want has at last been admirably met by Mr F. H. Marshall's *Catalogue of the Jewellery, Greek, Roman and Etruscan, in the Department of Antiquities, British Museum,* 1911; but though he very kindly let me see an advance copy, I could but put in a few references to it, as this section was

already in type; there is not much from S. Russia: M. Rosenberg's *Gesch. d. Goldschmiedekunst auf Technischer Grundlage,* Frankfurt a/M., 1910, also came too late for me.

[7] *Les Bijoux Anciens et Modernes,* Paris, 1887.

[8] Karl Hadaczek, " Der Ohrschmuck der Griechen und Etrusker," Wien, 1903 in *Abhandlungen des Archäologisch-Epigraphischen Seminars der Universität Wien,* Heft XIV.

[9] *Klassische Antike Goldschmiede-arbeiten im Besitze Sr. Excellenz A. I. von Nelidow beschrieben und erläutert von L. Pollak,* Leipzig, 1903.

[10] *Collection du Château Goluchów. L'orfèvrerie décrite par W. Froehner,* Paris, 1897; and *La Collection Tyszkiewicz,* München, 1892.

are to seek the centres of distribution.   The provenance of a given object is no evidence as to its origin unless in one place we find many specimens of some type which occurs nowhere else: the material gives no such clue as can be derived from marble or clay: there are no inscriptions such as we find on statues and pots and gems: finally we seem to know least about the jewels of those very districts in which we may suppose that the best were made.   For, speaking broadly, it is from the edges of the Greek world, where the Greek met the barbarian, that the jewels come—from Cyprus, from Etruria and from South Russia; few from Asia Minor, fewer still from historic Greece.   Of Mycenaean jewels there is here no question.

In spite of their richness in this department the South Russian colonies only yield good work of a comparatively late period: as with other arts (save pottery) we must go elsewhere for early specimens, our first examples already belong to the time of highest mastery.   No early gold has been found at Berezan, from Olbia we have one find of the vith century B.C. (v. p. 400) and one or two rings from the next.   From Greek graves on the Bosporus there does not seem to be any goldwork of the archaic period: there ought to be some, for the coins of Panticapaeum begin fairly early and the pieces found in native graves like Vettersfelde, Melgunov's barrow, Kul Oba, Kelermes and the VII Brothers must have come in through the Greek ports (v. Chap. x).

We have already discussed the reason for the richness of the finds in South Russia.   The Scythians carried out to its farthest logical conclusion the principle of surrounding the dead with all they loved and needed during life, even more than the Etruscans, whose graves are the other great source of Greek jewelry: and from contact with the natives there seems to have been a strengthening of this feeling in the Greeks among whom it already existed. The example of Kul Oba was, as it were, felt at the Great Bliznitsa.

In attempting therefore to characterize the jewels of South Russia in general we must beware of regarding them too much as one whole and indivisible.   Some were probably made in Athens, many in Asia Minor, others shew Egyptian influence, most were very likely made upon the spot. Also they nearly all belong to a time when the early severity was out of fashion.   Nevertheless, taking them all round, especially the jewels found about the Bosporus and those in the possession of natives, we are justified in seeing in them a prevalent taste for colour and florid workmanship as against the general Greek feeling for form and restraint.   It cannot be mere chance that in this region, with its close and friendly connexion with the Orient, we get the best specimens of Greek enamel (used merely as a filling in patterns of soldered wire which occur equally well without it), the first examples of true cloisonné and the first cameo, as well as an early welcome given to the Oriental love for many-coloured precious stones as opposed to plain gold be it never so cunningly worked.

This taste went on flourishing, and all later jewels depend upon colouristic effects, so that to the jewellers of Panticapaeum has been put down the not quite unwilling elaboration of the "Migration" style with its reminiscences of Persian, Scythic and Greek and the production of the Treasures of Petrossa and Nagy Szent Miklós and the models imitated by the Goths and other Teutonic conquerors of Europe (v. supra p. 282 n. 2).

Crowns.

Crowns or wreaths, usually found in place upon the brows of the dead, both men and women, form the most continuous series of gold objects yielded by South Russia. They are surpassed in number by the earrings, but they form a series in that so many of them bear their own approximate date in the shape of an "indication" or impress of a coin which often formed the centrepiece. There must be nearly fifty known, for many have been discovered since Stephani gave a list of nineteen in the Hermitage[1]. The earlier crowns are sometimes of quite artistic workmanship, studies of olive, bay and oak treated both conventionally and naturalistically. Good specimens of conventional treatment are the crowns worn by both man and woman in the second tomb in Artjukhov's barrow[2]. Here we have intertwined oak and bay with what appear to be acorn-cups forming the centre. More naturalistic is a crown of the same date—IIIrd century (both graves had coins of

Fig. 285. *CR.* 1878, p. 115. Kerch. Gold wreath with indication of BAE Coin, cf. inf. Pl. VII. 17. ⅓.

Lysimachus)—with bay leaves. In front the stems were joined in a reef-knot adorned with enamel[3]. The leaf-stalks were inserted into the hollow stems and soldered. In a rather similar but even more naturalistic example[4] they were twisted round the stems. Most beautiful, only surpassed by a wonderful example from South Italy in the Louvre[5], is a gold crown consisting of two olive sprays tied together at the back: the rendering of sprays, leaves and berries is well-nigh perfect[6]. Equally beautiful, and to be referred to about the same date, is a kind of aigrette made of barley ears[7]. Perhaps it was such crowns as these that were granted as rewards to those who had deserved well of the state, Diophantus at Chersonese[8], Protogenes and later Theocles and many others at Olbia[9] with Cocceius at Tyras[10].

[1] *CR.* 1875, p. 19 sqq.
[2] *CR.* 1880, II. 1 and III. 1: cf. *BM. Jewellery*, XXVII. 1633, XXVIII. 1628.
[3] *ABC.* IV. 3 on f. 286, cf. Nelidov, I. 1: *BM. Jewellery*, XXVII. 1607—1609.
[4] *ABC.* V. 3.
[5] Cf. Daremberg et Saglio, s.v. *corona* f. 1976; also Tyszkiewicz, I. 4.

[6] *ABC.* IV. 2 on f. 286; Fontenay, p. 389, cf. ib. p. 387.
[7] *ABC.* V. 1 on f. 286; Fontenay, p. 390.
[8] App. 18=*IosPE.* I. 185, cf. ib. IV. 68; and the carved crowns of Agasicles App. 17=ib. I. 195.
[9] App. 7, 10=ib. I. 16, 22.
[10] App. 3=ib. I. 2.

Gold
Aigrette
and Wreaths.
Kerch. ABC.

V. 1.

IV. 3.

IV. 2.

Most of the series belongs to Roman times and is the merest funeral furniture. The crown then consists of a strip of gold leaf, wider in the centre than at the sides, mounted on a foundation of bark or leather, with parsley leaves pointing towards the centre, which is decorated with an indication or a gem or sometimes a repoussé plaque. Often the only remains of the crown lie in scattered parsley leaves once sewn on to a stuff ground. For instance, in one case the band was of some dark red material and over the whole there was a kind of veil of the finest crêpe[1]. In the centre was an indication of a coin with the monogram B̊ΑΕ and a Herm. This indication is particularly common on crowns (Fig. 285)[2], and is sometimes imitated in freehand drawing[3]. Another king whose coins make indications was Sauromates II[4]. Sometimes coins of distant cities, e.g. Heraclea Pontica[5], very often of Roman emperors[6], served the same purpose. Other wreaths of late date have a square plaque with a gem at each corner[7], or a gorgoneion[8], a head of Helios[9], an engraved gem[10], or a plain one[11]. Some crowns have not even the parsley leaves but only the προμετωπίδιον or centre-piece.

Mask and Cap.

With the funeral crowns may be mentioned the repoussé funeral mask[12] of the queen whose tomb was found at Glinishche near Kerch (v. inf. p. 433). It is evidently a portrait executed with the least possible departure from the original, probably from a plaster model. Its use seems to have been to let the dead face appear at the funeral ceremony in a case where that would have been otherwise impossible. The same device has been resorted to independently among many nations, and the parallels of Mycenae and others do not shed any light on the question why this almost unique mask was made in this case. We have seen that the queen also wore a funeral wreath[7]. Another golden mask more elaborate but not so well made has been found at Olbia, but its date does not seem defined in the slightest[13].

Another piece quite unlike anything else is the gold cap found near Cape Ak-burun in 1875 (Fig. 287). It is in the shape of half an egg lined with leather and felt and made of pierced work; above a narrow acanthus-leaf, stem and tendril border, the design, which is thrice repeated, consists of a pair of broad nautilus spirals curling outwards from an acanthus bract: from between them grows the flower which is usually associated with the

[1] *CR.* 1878–79, III. 4—7, Mount Mithridates.

[2] One from Olbia, *BM. Jewellery*, LXIX. 3072.

[3] *CR.* 1902, p. 51, f. 86.

[4] *CR.* 1904, pp. 71, 79, ff. 106, 123.　[5] ib. p. 79.

[6] Agrippina and Nero, *BM. Jewellery*, LXX. 3081; Vespasian in the Niobid coffin, v. p. 333; M. Aurelius, *ABC.*III. 1; Commodus, *ABC.*IV. 1; Philip, *CR.* 1875, p. 24=*KTR.* p. 43, f. 48; Gallienus, *CR.* 1875, II. 2; the same with Valerian as on Pl. VIII. 22, ib. II. 7; Salonina, *BM. Jewellery*, 3082, 3083; Maximian, *CR.* 1875, II. 5; Galerius, *Trans. Od. Soc.* XX. i. 1; Gordian and Valentinian in one grave with Sauromates II, shewing how little evidence of date they furnish, *CR.* 1904, p. 72, ff. 108, 107.

[7] e.g. *ABC.* III. 3=*KTR.* p. 46, f. 52 found with indications of Rhescuporis, A.D. 211—228, v.

p. 434, n. 1, or that found in the tomb of the queen with the mask, ib. f. 325=*ABC.* III. 4.

[8] *CR.* 1875, p. 24=*KTR.* p. 47, f. 53.

[9] *CR.* 1875, p. 21=*KTR.* p. 44, f. 50.

[10] Artemis with her bow, *CR.* 1875, p. 16=*KTR.* p. 45, f. 51.

[11] *CR.* 1875, p. 23=*KTR.* p. 43, f. 47.

[12] *ABC.* I., *KTR.* p. 70, f. 94. See Benndorf, "Antike Gesichtshelme und Sepulcralmasken," *Denkschr. d. Phil.-hist. Cl. d. k. Akad. d. W. zu Wien*, XXVIII. (1878), p. 7, No. 7, and Pl. II.

[13] Published by Count Uvarov, *Recherches sur les Antiquités de la Russie Méridionale*, Paris, 1851, Pl. XIV., and Benndorf, op. cit. p. 9, No. 8, and Pl. XV. 1; cf. Nelidov, VII. 40, Sidon. Some Siberian tribes masked the faces of their dead.

acanthus flanked by curved stems. All the elements are Greek, but the whole is most unusual. But that its owner was a Greek we may judge from his having a Panathenaic amphora buried with him, and a coin of Alexander gives us some idea of the date.

FIG. 287. Gold Cap from Ak-burun. *KTR.* p. 49, f. 56 = *CR.* 1876, II. 1. ¾.

Calathi and Frontlets.

More normal and very magnificent are the golden calathi found in both the tombs of the Great Bliznitsa. The better of them[1], in the first tomb, was covered with thirteen plates of gold nailed on to a light foundation. Along the top was nailed a strip with oves, along the bottom one with a maeander and blue enamelled rosettes. The main space, slightly curved outwards, was decorated with Arimaspians and griffins each made in repoussé, cut out and nailed on separately. The whole is effective but rather mechanical. The technique did not encourage any real unity in the pairs of combatants; for instance, in the centre group, in which there are two griffins to one Arimaspian, each of the griffins is symmetrically looking away

[1] *CR.* 1865, I. 1—3, v. p. 425, f. 315.

from their opponent whose stroke will obviously go near neither of them,
His clothing is just that of the conventional barbarian—short cloak, chiton
and trousers; he is no Scythian.

The decoration of the other lady's calathos[1] is if anything still less
original.   The wooden or leather foundation was covered with stuff on which
was nailed a row of Bacchic figures, Maenads, griffins and such like.   These
figures are merely stumpy versions of the usual Neo-Attic types.

The calathos, though mostly associated with deities, was evidently
commonly worn by real women.   These actual specimens are perhaps unique,
but we see models of it on such figures as the dancing statuette from the
Great Bliznitsa[2] and of the nearly allied stephane on the elegant pendants
or earrings in the shape of women's heads[3].   Both forms have survived in
the Russian *kokoshnik* which is derived from Byzance.

FIGS. 288, 289.   Gold diadems.   Olbia.   *CR.* 1897, pp. 79, 80, ff. 191, 192.   ½.

The calathos was certainly kept for high days and holidays.   For less
important occasions was reserved the στλεγγίς or ἄμπυξ.   Both the ladies
in the Great Bliznitsa had such imitating the texture of the hair either with
close archaic-looking curls, these latter were prolonged downwards over the
temple[4], or with more artistic wavy lines[5].   Quite common were strips of thin
gold which must have been mounted on something and served as frontlets.
Usually their only decoration is some ornament stamped in the gold, for
instance two from Olbia, one with pairs of affronted Sphinxes (f. 288), the
other (f. 289) rising gracefully to a point in the middle, with a pattern of
berried ivy and palmettes[6].   In the Nelidov Collection are several of this type
from the Crimea.   One of early ivth-century work has a representation of
the Lampadedromia, Nike and a youth on horseback, and is ascribed to an
Attic master; others have a composition of Aphrodite between two Erotes[7].

[1] *CR.* 1869, I. 1—9=*KTR.* p. 54, f. 67.
[2] *CR.* 1865, III. 27 on p. 427, f. 318.
[3] *ABC.* VII. 10, 11, 11 *a* on p. 396, f. 290; Fontenay, p. 111; MacPherson, *Kertch*, Pl. I. and on the Sphinx, *ABC.* XII[a]. 2 on p. 401, f. 294.
[4] *CR.* 1869, p. 17, Pl. I. 11=p. 428, f. 319.
[5] *CR.* 1865, I. 4, 5, p. 36 with a Nike at each

end; cf. 1859, III. 2, Pavlovskij Barrow; 1882-8, I. I. p. 31, Anapa, with lion-masks at the ends and pendants all along in front.
[6] Cf. *BM. Jewellery*, XXVIII. 1610, and several from Cyme, p. 172, Nos. 1612—1614*, ff. 52—54.
[7] Nelidov, v. 12, 15—19.

Sometimes the simple repoussé strip is embellished with rosettes in enamel, as on the elaborate arabesque of the Kul Oba queen[1], or a figure and rosettes riveted on[2]. Such a strip may also be set off with a knot of filigree[3] or stones and even tassels in the middle; the pattern (e.g. Demeter looking for Core, and the rape of Core—or a commonplace arrangement of Maenads, tripods and dolphins or of mere arabesques) is often made by being engraved upon a cylinder. In one case we can see where the cylinder had a flaw in it[4].

A last type of frontlet is one with little pendants dangling whether from the lower edge[5] or from little stalks like davits adorned with rosettes[6].

The diadem from Artjukhov's barrow (p. 432, f. 322), the most elaborate of all with its big carnelians and tassels, belongs to the later style (v. p. 404).

Temple-Medallions.

To the end of calathi or heavy frontlets were hung medallions covering the temples—these did not take the place of earrings but were worn in addition to them; the lady of the first tomb of the Great Bliznitsa was wearing both. Their great size and weight must have made these temple plaques inconvenient, and they are comparatively rare. Far the finest are the famous specimens from Kul Oba so often reproduced for their importance in determining the details of the head of Athena Parthenos as made by Phidias[7]. Dubrux says they were found on the queen's breast, but they must be the same as those of the Bliznitsa which were found on the pillow. The two heads are identical save that on one Athena is seen in three-quarter face to the right, on the other she is looking to the left. She wears a decorated stephane and above it a helmet surmounted by three crests, the centre one Scylla, the side ones pegasi; it is flanked by ear-pieces bearing griffins, and these are not drawn symmetrically. Above the rim of the stephane is a row of griffins' heads[8]. Her hair falls on each side in corkscrew curls. Her earrings are of the type with a disk and inverted pyramid such as was found at Karagodeuashkh[9]. She wears a necklace with pendants. She is attended by her owl and snake.

The close similarity to the head of the Varvakion statuette and other known reproductions of the great Parthenos make the identity of the type beyond cavil: the only question is who is responsible for the precise interpretation of the type. Kieseritzky saw in it the work of Attic masters, of representatives of the school which had actually worked at the chryselephantine original. But the proportions of the face are not those of Attic work, being much rounder and plumper. This might perhaps be explained as an accommodation to the shape of the medallion; and the same explanation

[1] *ABC.* II. 3.
[2] Olbia, *CR.* 1903, p. 151, f. 301.
[3] *ABC.* VI. 3, 4, cf. *BM. Jewellery,* XXVII. 1607—1609.
[4] Fontenay, p. 507.
[5] *ABC.* VI. 1.
[6] ib. VI. 2, Ryzhanovka, *Sm.* II. xvii. 1, both types, Dêev Barrow, v. p. 170, *BCA.* XIX. xiii. 4, xv. 10.

[7] p. 195, f. 88 = *ABC.* XIX. 1, the heads alone reproduced in the text of Reinach, p. 63 from Kieseritzky, *Ath. Mitth.* VIII. (1883), Pl. XV and pp. 291—315, see Reinach for other reproductions.
[8] Cf. one figured on p. 427, f. 318 = *CR.* 1869, I. 28, from the third lady's tomb of the Great Bliznitsa.
[9] v. p. 217, f. 119, III. 6, 7; Hadaczek, p. 28.

might be applied to the proportions of faces upon the Cyzicene staters whose small area gave less freedom than the broad flat silver coins of other states. In fact most full faces on coins are rather round except the curious topsy-turvy types of Istrus, where a long narrow face was equally necessitated by the design[1]. The fashionable account is that we have an imitation of Attic types in Ionian proportions, that it is in Asia Minor that we are to seek for the centre of export of gold-work into South Russia[2]. So much more attention has been given to the study of style in sculpture than to that of mere decorative jewelry, that it is to the specimens with reliefs that we must look for light on the question of the origin of all.

In this case the frame is worthy of the picture. About the medallion is a border with a wavy pattern of leaves and spirals of twisted wire soldered on, enriched with blue and green enamel. Along the lower edge of the border are enamelled rosettes and leaves disguising loops from which hangs a whole network of fine chains, with other rosettes at the knots serving as points of attachment for pear-shaped vases in the meshes. Each vase has its neck and a little knop at its pointed lower end, and is covered with patterns of gold threads and grains soldered on.

In the first tomb of the Great Bliznitsa (p. 426, f. 316) were found similar temple ornaments, slightly smaller but of coarser workmanship. The medallions have Thetis or Nereids riding on sea-horses and bearing arms to Achilles. The composition is again a craftsman's version of great sculpture, perhaps going back to an original by Scopas: but there is no Scopaic character about the execution. The palmette border again has blue enamel. The arrangement of the network below is very like the Kul Oba work but a little inferior.

Unworthy to be mentioned with these are the rough roundels with rough pendants found at Darievka near Shpola, but they must have served the same purpose[3]. They seem to be rude Greek work rather than a native imitation, but it is hard to say. They each consist simply of a large rosette surrounded by a guilloche border to which are hung vase pendants.

Earrings.

No jewels offer so many varieties as earrings, and they have been well classed by Hadaczek[4]. Examples of most classes occur in the Graeco-Scythian area. The oldest piece of pure Greek goldwork, put by him about 600 B.C., is an earring from Vettersfelde[5], for Vettersfelde must be considered as an outlier of Scythia. Another archaic type well represented is a kind of double twist such as would just go round two fingers. Each end is adorned with spirals and patterns of gold wire soldered on and finished off with a pyramid of grains. These occur in bronze and silver, but the greater part are in gold. The Hermitage has seven pairs, and Stephani was never sure whether they were earrings, or served to keep thick plaits of hair or possibly

---

[1] *Brit. Mus. Coins, Thrace, etc.*, p. 25, No. 8.
[2] A. N. Schwartz in *Drevnosti (Trans. of Moscow Arch. Soc.)*, XV. i. p. 17.
[3] *Sm.* II. X. 3.
[4] Cf. Marshall, *BM. Jewellery*, pp. xxxii—xxxvi.
[5] p. 239, f. 148; Hadaczek, p. 20, f. 36.

folds of drapery in place[1]: but Hadaczek proves by coins that they hung from the ear. MacPherson's plate shews green enamel adorning his specimens[2].

Another early type that Hadaczek derives from Ionia, was the "woolsack" or "leech," a kind of crescent not flat but thick and hollow; from one end rose a wire which went through the ear and caught on the other end. This seems to have existed in the East from time immemorial[3] and to survive still; in the Middle Ages it developed into the Russian *kolt* with its enamel decorations[4]. In Greek hands it was chiefly adorned with patterns of grains soldered on to it[5], or wire spirals and plaits[6]. More ingenious was the device of a goldsmith who saw in it the likeness of a bird and put a head on to the hook end[7]. Allied in technique is the cone-earring from Romny[8].

A great many ancient earrings have the hook fixed to a disk. This is usually adorned with a rosette[9] and a border. Commonly it has something hung to it in turn. One of the simplest motives is a kind of inverted pyramid. Such an earring is worn by Athena on the Kul Oba plaque. An actual pair comes from Karagodeuashkh[10], and another without the disk from the same grave[11]. Such a one Aphrodite wears as engraved on the inlaid box (p. 424, f. 314). Hadaczek (p. 28) quotes similar specimens from Cyprus, which has very often produced duplicates of South Russian jewelry. In the first Karagodeuashkh specimen little chains hang down on each side of the pyramid[12].

Very common indeed is the type in which the pendant below the disk takes the shape of a vase with little S handles of wire and grain decoration soldered on to the body[13]. One in the Athens Museum is just like one from Kerch (f. 290. 19)[14]. Modifications arise by which the vase is flattened into a mere setting for a stone (f. 290. 20) or the handles are absent (ib. 17). More ambitious forms of the disk and pendant type have the half-moon hanging from the disk[15] and from it again a network of chains and vases and rosettes such as hangs from the temple ornaments but very much smaller. This development gave room for decorative figures though on the most extraordinarily small scale. The Kul Oba queen had two pair of this type: one has a comparatively simple rosette above and grains upon the crescent

---

[1] *CR.* 1876, III. 32, supra, p. 208, f. 106; *ABC.* XXXII. 14; MacPherson, *Kertch*, Pl. 1 = *BM. Jewellery*, XXX. 1649, cf. p. 176; E. A. Gardner, *JHS.* v. (1884), p. 69, Pl. XLVII. 5, "Objects from Kerch in the Ashmolean": cf. Nelidov, X. 210 from Gizeh; Hadaczek, p. 15.

[2] Such from Cyprus, *JHS* XI. p. 55, Pl. v. 3; Myres-Ohnefalsch-Richter, *Cat. Cyprus Museum*, Nos. 4108 sqq. Ohnefalsch-Richter, *Kypros, the Bible and Homer*, Pl. LXVII. 8, and here statues have shewn them used as earrings twisted into the ears but the coils seem closer: ib. XLVIII. 2, LV. 7. They are always found near the head of the dead, e.g. at Praesus, *BSA.* XII. p. 68.

[3] *Cat. Cyprus Museum*, Nos. 4008 sqq.; *Kypros, etc.*, Pl. CLXXXII. 5; Munro, *JHS.* XII. (1891), p. 313, Pl. XV. I am indebted to Professor J. L. Myres for the Cyprian comparisons.

[4] Many examples in N. P. Kondakov's *Russian Hoards*, I. (St P. 1896), and his *Zvenigorodskij Enamels*, v. supra, p. 282, n. 2.

[5] Hadaczek, p. 22, f. 40 from VII Brothers = *CR.* 1876, III. 42 supra, p. 208, f. 106; Hadaczek, f. 41, Eltegen = *CR.* 1877, III. 33; Grushevka, v. p. 177, *CR.* 1901, p. 105, f. 187; Romny, Khanenko, No. 455, on p. 191, f. 83; Chmyreva, with a duck at each point and nineteen suspended by chains, *Arch. Anz.* 1910, p. 215, f. 15; cf. Nelidov, X. 191, 192.

[6] Olbia, *CR.* 1903, p. 148, f. 288.

[7] Hadaczek, p. 22, f. 42 = *JHS.* v. (1884), XLVI. 6.

[8] p. 191, f. 83 = *Sm.* III. vi. 6.

[9] Vogell, *Samml.*, No. 1231, p. 91, f. 60e.

[10] p. 217, f. 119, III. 6, 7, cf. *CR.* 1876, v. 7.

[11] *Mat.* XIII. iv. 10.

[12] Cf. *BM. Jewellery*, p. 180, ff. 58, 59, Pl. XXX. 1666-7, Cyprus; 1662-5, 1670-3, Cyme. Nelidov, X. 200—202.

[13] Hadaczek, p. 34, f. 56; *CR.* 1878, p. 35. 3, 4.

[14] Cf. Fontenay, p. 114; Nelidov, XI. 215 sqq.; Gołuchòw, VIII. 46; Tyszkiewicz, XI. 9 = *BM. Jewellery*, LI. 2331.

[15] ib. XXX. 1653, Eretria.

FIG. 290. *ABC.* VII. Gold Earrings from the Bosporus: from various tombs on the Quarantine
Road, 1, 7, 9, 12, 13; Hadzhi Mushkai, 6, 8, 11, 15, 16, 23; Podgornyj Post, 2, 10, 20; Kherkheulidzev's
works, 17, 24; near Kerch, 4, 5, 18, 19; Phanagoria, 3, 21, 22; Olbia, 14: 11 has blue enamel,
17 a carnelian, 19 and 23 garnets, 20 an emerald, 24 a turquoise. $\frac{11}{20}$. v. pp. 395—398, 408, 409.

with palmettes at its ends, from which spring winged Nike-figures[1]. The other[2] has richer decoration throughout and hidden in the leaves of the upper rosette are figures of Thetis and the Nereids with the arms of Achilles. It seems to have lost similar side figures, there remain but the stalks to bear them. The lesser rosettes are alternately dull gold and blue enamel; the egg-and-dart mouldings and some details of the pendants, dark and light blue.

Even more wonderful examples of the same kind of work were found at Theodosia. With a similar general design the tiny space above the crescent gives room for a chariot and four horses driven by a winged Nike and containing another figure and flanked by Erotes[3]; with the earrings was a necklace (Fig. 294. 3, 4) to match. Almost identical earrings, still unpublished, were found under Chersonese wall in urn 4 ; at the side of the quadriga a Muse with a lyre sat in a high spray of foliage[4]. Earrings of this same type also occurred in the two women's graves of the Great Bliznitsa[5]. In the first they were found *in situ* worn along with temple-plaques shewing an extraordinary accumulation of jewelry upon one head: in the other tomb only one earring has survived.

In these cases the figures are merely a decorative detail not an independent element in the design, but often the pendant which hangs from the disk takes the form of a human or animal figure. Commonest of these are winged human figures, especially Nike[6] or Eros. The Erotes are innumerable in all kinds of attitudes, dancing (f. 290. 18), playing the lyre (f. 294. 13), with a mask[7], with a butterfly[8], riding on a bird[9], as cupbearers (f. 290. 9, 13), with a caduceus (ib. 12), or a shepherd's crook[10], gesticulating or just quiet[11]. Less common figures are Sirens (f. 290, 14, 15, 16), Pegasus (ib. 2), Maenads[12] and Artemis-Selene[13].

Another favourite form shews a bird instead of the human figure suspended from the disk. The figure of the bird is generally enamelled white or blue, we have for instance a swan from Taman[14] and from Kerch (f. 291), and a dove from Artjukhov's barrow[15].

Besides the comparatively light earring-figures hanging from a disk we have whole figures or heads attached to a single hook. Among these it is somewhat difficult to distinguish between a pendant that formed the centre-piece of a necklace and an earring. When they occur in pairs it is clear that they are earrings, e.g. the Ryzhanovka earrings (p. 178, f. 73) which Hadaczek[16] calls Graeco-Scythic of the IIIrd century B.C. : but they would seem to be earlier. Their closest analogues are the Sphinxes from

[1] *ABC.* XIX. 4 on p. 195, f. 88, Hadaczek, p. 36.

[2] *ABC.* XIX. 5 = *KTR.* p. 234, f. 208 ; Fontenay, p. 112.

[3] p. 401, f. 294. 5 = Fontenay, p. 112.

[4] *BCA.* I. p. 7 ; inf. inset of Plan VII. and p. 422 : for all such cf. *BM. Jewellery*, XXX. 1655, Crete ; Berlin Antiquarium, No. 65, Cyme.

[5] *CR.* 1865, II. 3 ; 1869, I. 12.

[6] *Arch. Anz.* 1909, p. 150, f. 10 Tanais ; Hadaczek, p. 38, f. 66 (= *CR.* 1859, III. 3), cf. p. 39, f. 68 ; Daremberg-Saglio, s. v. *inaures*, f. 4013 ; Nelidov, IX. 103 ; Tyszkiewicz, I. 2 ; *BM. Jewellery*, XXXII. 1845—1850.

[7] f. 290. 6, cf. *Abhdl. d. Phil.-hist. Cl. d. k. sächs. Gt d. W.* XIV. (1894), Th. Schreiber, "Die alexan-

drinische Toreutik," p. 306, f. 36.

[8] *CR.* 1878—79, Text p. 35. 2.

[9] *CR.* 1889, p. 8, f. 1.

[10] p. 427, f. 318 = *CR.* 1868, I. [8], 9.

[11] ibid. [6], 7 ; 1876, III. 41 ; cf. Nelidov, VIII. 56 sqq. ; *BM. Jewellery*, p. XXXV., Pl. XXXII. 1858—1915.

[12] f. 318 = *CR.* 1860, IV. 4, Hadaczek, p. 40, f. 73.

[13] f. 318 = *CR.* 1868, I. 2, 3 = Hadaczek, p. 40, f. 74, Reinach, *Rép. Stat.* II. p. 319. 7.

[14] *CR.* 1870, VI. 12 = Hadaczek, p. 45, f. 84.

[15] p. 431, f. 321 = *CR.* 1880, III. 4, cf. Nelidov, X. 179 ; *BM. Jewellery*, XXXI. 1677—1682, Vulci.

[16] p. 41, f. 76 : *Sm.* II. xvi. 4, 5.

Dêev barrow[1] and lions from the Vogell collection[2]. Something similar but purely Greek is a Sphinx found at Theodosia (f. 294. 2) which seems to be a necklace pendant, another similar pendant comes from Olbia (f. 292) representing a boy. In all these cases the figure is sitting on some kind of base. A free standing figure is an Eros with a mask and a butterfly[3] larger than most earrings and alone, but found upon the dead woman's pillow.

With these go the many women's heads in stephanae[4] which certainly served as earrings : yet they cannot but recall the equally common bulls' heads[5] which still remain hanging to their necklaces.

Perhaps the simplest type of all is the earring that is literally a ring[6]. Such we find perfectly plain and also decorated, whether by a twist or plait[7] or by one end of the ring being enlarged into the head of an animal : a lion[8],

Kerch.
Gold i̇
blue
enamel.

FIG. 291. *CR.* 1871, VI. 13, 13a. ¼.

FIG. 292. *CR.* 1897, p. 79, f. 190.
Gold Earring or Pendant. Olbia. ¼.

FIG. 293. *CR.* 1896, p. 80, f. 331.
Olbia. Gold Earring. ¼.

a bull[9] or a lynx (f. 290. 3). Also we get this thickening formed into a human figure, Eros[10] or Priapus (f. 290. 22).

From these rings we get various charms suspended ; a favourite one is the club of Hercules or a bunch of grapes, but these rather coarse additions mostly belong to the later style when stones had come into fashion (v. p. 409)[11].

Rather like some earrings are pin-heads decorated with heads or busts of animals. Such are the half-griffin from Theodosia[12] or the negro heads from Phanagoria (f. 294. 14) and Kerch[13]. To a later period belong some found at Chersonese crowned with a bird, a hand and a vase[14].

[1] *BCA.* XIX. xiii. 18, cf. p. 170.
[2] *Samml.* No. 1229, p. 92, f. 61 *b*.
[3] *CR.* 1897, p. 118, f. 233, Chersonese, grave 893, found with a coin like IV. 22.
[4] f. 290. 10, 11, 11*a* : MacPherson, Pl. I : Fontenay, p. 111 : cf. *BM. Jewellery*, XXXII. 1855.
[5] f. 294. 9 ; *CR.* 1863, I. 7, 8 ; 1873, III. 15 ; Karagodeuashkh, p. 217, f. 119, IV. 1, 2 : Olbia, *BM. Jewellery*, LXVIII. 2971.
[6] Cf. ib. pp. xxxiv, 184, f. 60, Pl. XXXI. XXXII. 1684—1824 : Hadaczek, p. 46.
[7] f. 290. 4 ; Vogell, *Samml.* p. 90, f. 59.
[8] Kerch, f. 290. 1 ; *CR.* 1877, V. 14 ; Olbia, f. 293 (horned) ; *BM. Jewellery*, LIII. 2444, with onyx vase ; Vogell, *Samml.* p. 91, f. 60 ; Chersonese,

CR. 1900, p. 17, f. 31 ; *BCA.* I. p. 7, urn I in the wall ; cf. Ohnefalsch-Richter, *Kypros, etc.*, Pl. CLXXXII. 8, CCXVII. 13—17, p. 492 sqq.
[9] f. 290. 5 ; *CR.* 1865, III. 38 : from Olbia, *CR.* 1899, p. 124, ff. 236, 237, cf. Nelidov, IX. 139.
[10] f. 290. 7, 8 ; *CR.* 1876, III. 40 ; 1880, IV. 5, 6.
[11] Other pendants from Olbia, a bird, *CR.* 1903, p. 148, f. 289 ; a stone wedge, ib. p. 150, f. 297 ; a negro's head, ib. p. 151, f. 300 ; fica, *BM. Jewellery*, LXVIII. 2964 ; fica from Kerch, *CR.* 1866, II. 34, III. 11 ; cf. Nelidov, XX. 531.
[12] f. 294. 12, cf. Nelidov, VI. 33.
[13] *Report of Arch. Investigations for* 1853, No. 74=*KTR.* p. 66, f. 86.
[14] *CR.* 1892, p. 21, ff. 12—14.

Necklets.

As wonderful as the work of the temple-ornaments and earrings is that of the necklets, and the variety of patterns is very great. The chief classes are the torque, the necklace of beads, the necklace of plates, the chain necklace, the necklace with simple pendants, and that with a whole network of chains and pendants hanging from the main string. The first hardly occurs in Greek graves, those from native graves have been dealt with above (p. 289). There is one in the Artjukhov barrow, an imitation of the form we meet in Kul Oba, but hollow and inferior (p. 431, f. 321 *below*). Of the necklace of beads a good example is one from Kerch[1]. The beads are alternately plain and covered with little spirals, while others imitate the shape of a gourd: the work is like that of f. 294. 3. Similar in principle is the necklace from the third lady's tomb in Great Bliznitsa[2] with a wonderful variety of beads, some of which are artistically worked amulets, in the shape of flies, rams' heads, negroes' heads, frogs, bunches of grapes, bearded heads and others. Of simple chains the simplest is such a one as was found at Bulganak, just a chain with a lion's head at each end[3]. More artistic are round plait chains like those from Melgunov's barrow—the earliest, perhaps a diadem (p. 172)—Karagodeuashkh (p. 217, f. 119, IV. 4), Theodosia (f. 294. 1) or Chersonese wall, urn 4. In urn 1 the necklace was made up of two flat plaits ending in lion-heads hooking on to a centre-piece, a filigree reef-knot containing an Eros holding a lyre[4]: the design foreshadows the Artjukhov crown (p. 432, f. 322).

Of simple pendants the best usually hang from a string of beads such as one from Theodosia (f. 294. 3) with vase-like drops, or one from Kerch with various charms, lions, combs, birds, shells or amulets against the evil eye: such also hang from plain chains[5]. When we have beautiful plaited ribbons, e.g. the Kul Oba queen's and its twin from Kerch[6], and those from Karagodeuashkh (p. 217, f. 119, IV. 3) and Chersonese wall, urn 4[4], we generally find the place of the vase-shaped drop taken by a tiny pendant whose outline is the same but whose section is like a three-rayed star, thus giving six surfaces to catch the light at various angles and being more effective than the much more elaborate hollow vase.

Necklets in which the chain is more important than the pendants we find in the second best of the third lady in the Great Bliznitsa[7] which has a row of beads of three chief types and two sizes, the larger alternately plain and adorned with rosettes about the string hole, the smaller plain towards the end and adorned with spirals in the middle beads—from every larger bead hangs a rosette and from it alternately a plain and a decorated vase.

The ingenious arrangement of the best necklace at Karagodeuashkh (p. 217, f. 119, IV. 1, 2) forms a transition to the necklace of plates. The greater part of the beads are small and plain: from certain larger ribbed ones hang large vase pendants, to the front of intermediate ones are fixed X-shaped,

---

[1] *ABC.* XII. 4 = *KTR.* p. 320, f. 289.
[2] v. p. 427, f. 318, *CR.* 1869, I. 15.
[3] *ABC.* XI. 7, Olbia, *CR.* 1903, p. 150, f. 296.
[4] Unpublished, cf. *BCA.* I. pp. 6—9.
[5] *ABC.* XII. 3; XI. 1.

[6] *ABC.* IX. 1: the two varieties were called ὅρμος ἀμφορέων and λογχωτός, v. *BM. Jewellery*, p. xxxvi., cf. Pl. XXXIV. 1943—1948, two from Cyme.
[7] v. p. 427, f. 318 = *CR.* 1869, I. 14.

(or "double-axe") plates each with a rosette in the middle and a palmette above and below, from the lower edge of these plates hang lesser vases.

This device of masking the actual string with plates is carried further in the well designed but rudely executed necklace from Ryzhanovka which is made up alternately of round rosette-plates and X-shaped pieces fitting into them (p. 179, f. 74). A like arrangement occurs in the necklace from Kerch in the Ashmolean, Oxford; this has acorns hanging from the rosettes[1]. As usual Dêev barrow supplies an analogue to Ryzhanovka, its necklace is as it were double: instead of the rosettes it has fourteen twin half-beads and the plates between them an inch high are cut out on each side to fit into them, so 8⊦8⊦. These plates are of two varieties, in each at the top is a large rosette and at the lower angles two such, but in six the middle space has a whorl of large leaves supporting a rosette, in seven a duck with niello eyes is as it were swimming on it. From each pair of beads and from each plate hangs a vase-pendant: two strings half an inch apart ran through beads and plates alike[2]. The same double effect is seen in a necklace from Kerch: the plates are of much the same shape with forget-me-nots at each end and a woman's mask in the middle but two separate rows of beads fitted into them, each bead of dull gold representing a knot tied in a textile[3]. The ducks and rosettes reappear at Chmyreva Mogila but on rectangular plates[4].

A necklace from Olbia, apparently Ionian work of the vith century B.C. and so perhaps the oldest piece of goldwork found in a Greek grave in South Russia, has no beads or chain, but consists of eleven plates, two terminal triangles decorated with palmettes, five squares with rosettes in wire soldered on, and four tall narrow plates with stamped Sphinxes: to each of these hang two barleycorn pendants and to each square three[5]. With this were found two pendants in the shape of lion-heads.

Finally instead of a row of vase pendants, varied though they may be in shape, we may have continued along the whole length of the chain a rich network of chains and vases like that below the more elaborate temple-plaques and earrings. A simple example is the second-best necklace from the first tomb of the Great Bliznitsa. Here we have the plaited ribbon and two rows of the vase-like pendants (cf. Karagodeuashkh), the points of attachment being covered with the usual forget-me-nots. More elaborate is the same lady's best necklace with three rows of real Vases, each vase being covered with ornament of wire soldered on[6]. The most perfect specimen of this style was found at Theodosia with the wonderful earrings (f. 294. 4, 4 a): in this case the upper row of smallest vases gives place to a row of tiny images of the Ephesian Artemis each hanging from a demi-horse put between the enamelled forget-me-nots that mask the attachments of the network chains.

Quite unique as a necklet is that found in the third lady's tomb of the Great Bliznitsa serving her for best (p. 429, f. 320). Its affinities are perhaps rather with the torque than with the necklace. It is in shape a

---

[1] *JHS.* v. (1884), Pl. XLVII. 4, so *ABC.* Reinach, p. 137; *BM. Jewellery*, XXXV. 1951, 1952.
[2] p. 170, *BCA.* XIX. p. 171, Pl. XIII. 14—17; *CR.* 1897, p. 31, f. 94: duck from Kerch, Sabatier, IV. 7.
[3] *ABC.* XII. 1, 2.

[4] *Arch. Anz.* 1910, p. 216.
[5] *CR.* 1903, pp. 149, 150, f. 295, cf. Hadaczek, p. 58, f. 106—108: *BM. Jewellery*, IX. 888, Ephesus; XI. Camiros.
[6] *CR.* 1865, II. 5, 4 = Fontenay, p. 173: cf. *BM. Jewellery*, XXXV. 1947, Melos.

FIG. 294. *ABC.* XII a. Gold Objects from Theodosia, 6 electrum, 7 silver spiral, gold ends,
8 chalcedony, 14, 15 from Phanagoria. $\frac{3}{3}$. v. pp. 397—402, 409, 410, 414.

crescent formed by two twists of gold that make the inner and outer circumferences. In the space between them framed by a kind of egg-and-dart we have figures of rams and goats ajouré with poppy plants and rosettes in the background. At each end a dog is pursuing some rodent. The ends of the crescent die into a flat collar, linked by a plait pattern to the lion-heads which hold the fastening rings. These lion-heads are also exceptional, for in general a string of beads, or a necklet whose section is round, has lion-heads, whereas the flat necklaces or ribbon chains end in U-shaped pieces each decorated with a palmette. In spite of its strange form there is no doubt that this was a necklet, it recalls most closely the metal neck ornaments (*tsata*) put on to icons.

Armlets. Various Goldwork.

Armlets do not shew so much variety as necklets. The general form is either a smaller torque, a twist encircling the wrist once with animals' heads at each end, or else a spiral of two or three turns with either a flat section and palmettes as finials or a general representation of a snake.

To the first type belongs the magnificent bracelet from Kul Oba worn by the king (p. 199, f. 92. 1). The bold twist wormed with small strands ends in palmette collars which form the transition to the foreparts of Sphinxes whose paws hold a knot between them. Their style is so restrained that they must surely go back to originals of the vth century, although the actual work may belong to the ivth. Somewhat similar are the bracelets from the Great Bliznitsa ending in lionesses (p. 426, f. 317) and silver ones with gold lions' and rams' heads from Kerch and Chersonese wall, urn 4, respectively[1].

Among the flat-sectioned spiral bracelets a similar mixture of material is found in a pair from Theodosia (f. 294. 7); each has three turns and ends in flattened lion-heads. Examples of the same type with antelopes' heads we have from Kerch[2] and with a whole lion from the Great Bliznitsa[3]. At Karagodeuashkh similar armlets end in sea horses with curled tails (p. 217, f. 119, III. 7, 8). Whole serpents appear at Artjukhov's barrow, tombs I and II[4].

Rather special are the armlet of the queen from Kul Oba, a broad thin plate of gold with two bands of repeated groups—griffins attacking deer, finishing off at each end with four lion-heads in low relief, and a second worn by the king, also a flat band but narrower with a little moulded edge and archaic groups of Eos and Memnon alternating with Peleus and Thetis; the whole studded with blue forget-me-nots (p. 199, f. 92. 2, 3).

Among other pieces of Greek goldwork may be mentioned the sheath from Tomakovka and its replica from Vettersfelde (p. 148, f. 45, cf. p. 236). The belt clasp from Kurdzhips seems so far unique (p. 224, f. 127). It is made up of two strips of gold adorned with enamelled rosettes and circles, hooking on to each other, and two side-pieces with an elaborate decoration of intertwined spirals, palmettes and rosettes; one side-piece was firmly united to one strip, the other hooked on to the free strip.

---

[1] *ABC.* Text, Reinach, p. 138 = *KTR.* p. 65, f. 85. Unpublished, *BCA.* I. p. 9, perhaps with more than one turn.

[2] *ABC.* XIV. 1 = *KTR.* p. 317, f. 285.
[3] *CR.* 1869, I. 16.
[4] *CR.* 1880, I. 9, II. 14: 1873, III. 7, Kerch.

Mention must also be made of the gold repoussé and engraved work, the phalerae[1] for adorning horses, mostly of Hellenistic date, found in native graves such as Chmyreva barrow (pp. 168, 169, ff. 58—61), Akhtanizovka and Siverskaja (p. 215), Fedulovo, Taganrog and Starobêlsk (p. 173, n. 3), and latest, Janchekrak (p. 171), and of the smaller plates of greater range in time used for sewing on to clothes[2], and of the innumerable buttons, studs and other small pieces of gold found in some of the richer Greek graves as well. This is particularly the case in the Great Bliznitsa and is one of several points of resemblance which link it on to the Scythic graves in spite of the pure Greek character of everything found in it except one plate from the pyre of the second lady with a combat between a griffin and a lioness represented quite in the Scythic manner. How this piece found itself in such company it is impossible to say[3].

Transition from Goldwork to Stone Jewelry.

The goldwork considered hitherto has been goldwork that relied for its effect upon the gold: contrasts of colour were only introduced by the use of enamel which though more general than in other Greek districts was applied in the same primitive way, being run into the spaces it was desired to colour and allowed to keep its natural surface instead of being ground flat. The colours used were also primitive, limited to a light and dark blue and green. This use of gold by itself is characteristic of the Greeks in the best age. Stones only appear in rings (v. p. 410) and occasionally separately as beads. The difficulty of guessing the chief export centre among old Greek lands which supplied the Euxine market with goldwork has been already mentioned. No doubt there is great resemblance between some of the little Attic jewelry known to us and some of the simpler specimens from South Russia. But Athens had no special reputation for ordinary goldwork nor any natural advantages such as she had in silver. The great chryselephantine statues stood quite apart. There is on the other hand a remarkable identity between the elaborate goldwork from South Russia and that found at Cyme in Aeolis[4]. The excessive complication of detail, the insertion of figures on a scale which did not allow of their being satisfactorily executed, the luxuriant curls of the vegetable ornament, the actual material (electrum) of one or two of the older pieces (e.g. f. 294. 6), such details as the Ephesian Artemis on the Theodosian necklace, all suggest Asia Minor. The undoubted supremacy of Athens in its own speciality—pottery—does not preclude the retention by Ionia of its natural importance in other departments. In works which can be judged by the canons applying to sculpture the subjects which are of Attic origin have been reinterpreted in the Ionian manner (v. pp. 284 and 394), and we may well believe that the greater part of the goldwork found north of the Euxine was either imported from Asia Minor or made on the spot by artists under the predominant influence of Asia. But this must not be taken to be

---

[1] *BCA.* XXIX. pp. 18—53.
[2] *BM. Jewellery*, p. xxxvii, Pl. XL. 2104—2107 Kul Oba (?); LXVIII. 2886, LXIX. LXX. 3072—3085, Ogüz(?) and Olbia.

[3] v. p. 427, f. 318, *CR.* 1865, III. 1—32.
[4] v. pp. 392, n. 6; 395, n. 12; 397, n. 4; 399, n. 6; 406, n. 3: *B.M. Jewellery*, p. xxxviii, the great find contained an Alexander coin.

without exceptions.   Athens had special relations with the Bosporus and there
is no need to put everything down to Ionia.   As time went on provincialisms
tended to disappear in the Greek world, and just as the κοινή dialect spread
everywhere so a common acceptance of artistic and industrial fashions spread
the patterns which arose in one town throughout the rest.   Hence we find in
the British Museum and the Louvre jewelry from Etruria and South Italy
identical with that from South Russia preserved in the Hermitage.

But as the Greeks came into closer contact with the Eastern barbarians
after the conquests of Alexander they suffered to some extent the influence of
the people they were ruling.   From them they learned to rate much higher
the beauty of precious stones.   At the same time, perhaps from the same
cause, they were learning to appreciate colour as well as form, at least
their love of colour took a new direction, gratified itself in new ways.   They
came to prefer sharp contrasts to delicate gradations; as Riegl puts it the
colouristic principle with its instant appeal to the senses replaced the tectonic
with its appeal to the understanding[1]: it is curious that in ceramics they
abandoned painting and took to plastic decoration just at this very period.

The question arises as to what part of the barbarian world had most part
in this revolution.   No doubt the accumulations of the Persian realm in Iran
and nearer Asia supplied material for it: for instance, the garnet, the most
characteristic jewel of the new movement, is usually referred to Syria: but
it is a question whether the impulse was not equally due to Egypt whose
artistic influence has been so ably championed by Professor Schreiber[2].

In South Russia the new fashion may be said to make its appearance
in the splendid contents of Artjukhov's barrow (v. p. 430).   In that barrow
we have for the first time a general use of precious stones, both set and
pierced for use as beads, the first cameo, the first example of Greek cloisonné
enamel.   Such a use of precious stones was common in Egypt from time
immemorial: the cloisonné process closely resembles effects produced in
Egypt from an early period, the decoration of one of the earrings though in
general design quite Greek has among its ornaments the feather and cow-horn
crown of Isis-Hathor[3].   Also there were beads of Egyptian manufacture with
Egyptian emblems such as the god Bes.   At this moment too the reef-knot
came into fashion and occurs on very many objects of the second and third
centuries B.C.   This very pattern occurs in Egypt and on Greek soil seems
accompanied by a fashion for tassels very characteristic of the Artjukhov finds[4].

At first the introduction of the new element of precious stones did
not make much difference in the jewelry into which it entered.   The goldwork of the Artjukhov crown and earring is nearly as fine as that of the
pure gold technique of the Bliznitsa.   But as time went on, less attention
was paid to the gold, and it became coarse and clumsy, and the forms of
objects were also changed to receive the stones better.   On the whole,
however, the same forms went on.

[1] *Die Spätrömische Kunst-industrie*, p. 172 sqq.
[2] In many works e.g. *Alexandrinische Toreutik*: see however the protest against the exaggeration of this point of view, in A. J. B. Wace's "Apollo on the Omphalos," *BSA.* IX. (1902–3).
[3] v. p. 431, f. 321 = *CR.* 1880, III. 4, 5. Schreiber,

op. cit. p. 290 and Pl. II. f. 8 B′, *BM. Jewellery*, LI. 2328 (Calymnos), 2329—2331.
[4] Cf. a necklet (?) from Ithaca, Fontenay, p. 430: a reef-knot with a figure in it from Syria, *BM. Jewellery*, XXXIV. 2001, cf. XXVII. 1607—1609: for the whole change of taste, ib. p. xlii sqq.

We have only one crown of the new style; those described above belong to the late period, but except the one or two which have a square centrepiece with stones at the corners[1], they shew its distinguishing features only by their progressive decadence. This Artjukhov crown (p. 432, f. 322) consists of a hoop formed of three parts joined by hinges, two fluted side-pieces adorned with a wave ornament and finishing in collars with enamel, and a centrepiece in the shape of a reef-knot made of large garnets joined by gold bands. The middle of the knot is taken up by a group of an eagle lifting an Eros: the eagle's outspread wings are enamelled. From the lower margin of the crown hang six characteristic tassels each consisting of a round or heart-shaped garnet, from which depends a round bead set in gold, the immediate head of the tassel which is made up of six garnets hung on gold chains and wire stalks. It has been doubted whether this can be a diadem because the tassels would get so much in the way of the wearer's eyes, but it would not be worse than some of the pearl fringes on old Russian headdresses.

For neckgear in this Tomb I, we have, beside a simple neck-ring (p. 431, f. 321, I. 2), a chain[2], a row of small amulets[3], and three necklaces, one of carnelians and gold beads, one of garnets held in gold rosettes (ib. I. 5)[4] and one of which the main part is gold chain, but each end has a garnet heart and the centre an emerald between two garnets flanked by lion-busts with bodies of banded stone (ib. I. 6). The same lady had an armlet of chalcedony balls quite in the barbaric manner[5]. She also had a pin (f. 321, I. 17) with a head in the form of a disk decorated with a rosette in real cloisonné enamel offering a smooth surface: from the disk hangs down even such a tassel as hangs from the crown. Her left hand bore a ring with the bezel embellished by a rosette like that on the disk of the pin (ib. I. 13) and her right a ring with garnets[6]. This same taste runs through all the graves of the barrow: each lady had such a pin, the lady in the second grave had the earrings with the Egyptian motive (f. 321, III. 5), the well-known ring with a bezel in the form of a shoe-sole bearing the inscription ECTIAIOC MAMMIAI carried out in black enamel and gold cloisons (ib., III. 7, 8) and the cameo of Eros and the butterfly[7]. The Artjukhov barrow is dated at about halfway through the IIIrd century by the coins of Lysimachus and Paerisades found in it. This gives just the date for the change of style, for in it not everything has yet conformed to the new fashion. For instance, the ordinary Kul Oba type of neck-ring with lions' heads at the ends is here but hollow and poor, suggesting that though the form still existed it was no longer held in its old esteem (f. 321 *below*). Quite in the old manner are the snake bracelets[8], the Erotes earrings[9] and the necklaces of the lady in the second tomb[10]. The work and general type of the earring with the Isis headdress (f. 321, II. 4, 5) is just that of the former period but for the introduction of that one detail.

An ornament common to all the Artjukhov ladies, and occurring in other contemporary graves, seems to have come in rather late although it does not shew any distinct trace of the new style. It is a round plaque usually with a border of enamel and bearing some subject such as Aphrodite and Eros.

---

[1] p. 434, f. 325, *ABC*. III. 3—5.
[2] *CR*. 1880, I. 3.
[3] ib. I. 7.
[4] Cf. *BM. Jewellery*, XXXVIII. 1961.
[5] *CR*. 1880, I. 8.
[6] ib. I. 14.
[7] ib. III. 9 on f. 321; Furtwängler, *Ant. Gem.* III. p. 152, f. 106.
[8] *CR*. 1880, I. 9.
[9] ib. I. 11, 12.
[10] ib. II. 9, 10, 11.

It appears to have been worn at the intersection of the cross-bands[1] over the breast, just where the terra-cottas often indicate a large ornament[2]. Two examples come from Egypt, and this would seem to be one more indication of a connexion between that country and the new fashions.   Still we have in two plaques from Kerch (p. 195, f. 88)[3] roundels executed in the old manner with wonderful filigree and quite suitable for the same purpose as the Aphrodite reliefs.   One rather similar roundel from a man's grave in Artjukhov's barrow (f. 321, II. 3[4]) is an unmistakable example of the new style, having pastes as well as patterns in gold soldered on.

It has been noticed that a love of reef-knots is characteristic of the things found in Artjukhov's barrow.   This same love is exemplified by other jewels which, whether adorned with stones or not, appear to belong to about the same time.   The knot became a favourite motive for the middle of diadems[5] and necklaces[6].   In some of these the tassels also occur, and these continue in favour in a simplified form until the barbarous ages when we cannot tell if the dangling chains and stones derive from Greek originals or from the general Finnish love of all kinds of jingles.

Necklaces with coloured stones.

The Artjukhov necklace (f. 321, I. 6) is the first of an interesting series. The distinguishing feature is that the middle or front of the necklace consists of several large oval or lozenge-shaped stones of different colours set in gold box-settings and joined by hinges[7]: the two ends are the ordinary plaited chains.   This fashion went on for three hundred years, for a later phase of it is seen in three necklaces which may be dated in the 1st century A.D. The first was found at Olbia in 1891 in the tomb with the glazed pottery (v. p. 420)[8].   It is the most developed of the series and shews the love of bright-coloured stones and pastes pushed very far.   A necklace precisely similar I saw recently in the possession of Messrs Spink in Piccadilly, London.

The chains on each side end in lynxes with crystal bodies and golden heads.   Between them are five blue pastes, three oval and two square, set in broad bands of gold with lesser pastes and granular patterns.   From the middle oval paste hangs a butterfly[9] of gold with a paste body, an emerald head, and wings each set with three blue and green pastes.   On each side from the square pastes of the main row hang first a round emerald and then a pear-shaped drop of pink paste, each duly set in gold.   From the lynx-heads to the square pastes, and from these to the butterfly's wings, hang light chains of gold.   In the same grave was found a pair of earrings consisting each of a garnet body set in gold, from which hangs a crystal amphora and several light gold chains (v. p. 408).   The distinguishing

---

[1] Cf. *BM. Jewellery*, XXXVIII. 1984.
[2] *CR.* 1880, I. 16; II. 13: Karagodeuashkh, the first and best, p. 217, f. 119, III. 12 : Chersonese, associated with a polychrome necklace, f. 295 Γ; Kurdzhips, *CR.* 1895, p. 62, f. 141; cf. Schreiber, op. cit. p. 311, f. 51; *BM. Jewellery*, LXVIII. 2883, Egypt.
[3] Cf. ib. XXXVIII. 2059, Cyme; *ABC.* XIX. 2, 3.
[4] Cf. *BM. Jewellery*, LX. 2945.

[6] e.g. ib. XXVII. 1607-9; *ABC.* VI. 3, 4.
[6] *ABC.* IX. 2, 3, this latter had two knots and is better illustrated in Fontenay, p. 174, where one knot is shewn with the Medusa face that fills it, and the tassels that hang from it; *ABC.* X. 1, 2, cf. Nelidov, XIII. 329; Gołuchòw, VII. 36.
[7] Cf. *BM. Jewellery*, LVIII. 2747; LXI. 2749.
[8] Orêshnikov, *Drevnosti*, XV. ii. (1894) Pl. I.
[9] Cf. *BM. Jewellery*, LXI. 2746, Rome.

Garnet
Paste
Amethyst
or Sapphire

Garnet
Paste
Amethyst

Emerald
|
Garnet

Emerald
|
Paste

Topaz Garnet Topaz

Garnet
Garnet Emerald Garnet
Garnet

FIG. 295. *CR.* 1896, p. 76, f. 323. Chersonese, Tomb No. 630. a, Gold ring with engraved Amethyst. b, Gold ring with Garnet. B, Gold plates. Γ, Gold roundel with Aphrodite and Eros. Δ, Gold Necklace with coloured stones. ⅓.

feature of this chain is the elaboration of the settings of each great paste.

In the next butterfly necklace, found at Chersonese in 1896 (f. 295), the stones are smaller, all oval and put in simple settings.   The variety is even greater.   With this necklace were found two roundels with Aphrodite to wear upon the breast and a wristband[1] made of gold tubes soldered to each other side by side and so building up hexagons and strips which could be threaded together.   In 1898 a very similar necklace was found in a leaden urn at Chersonese[2].   It consisted of seven garnets and two green pastes, with two pendants with green pastes and a light blue paste in the head of the butterfly which had a garnet on its wing.   There had been other pendants, now lost, and more stones in the butterfly, but the whole shewed signs of having been long used and roughly mended.   With it was found other jewelry of much the same character as accompanied the fellow necklaces and also a coin of Domitian and one of Chersonese[3], so that the objects may be referred to the 1st century A.D. confirming the conclusions independently arrived at on the evidence of the other similar finds.   Another necklace in the same taste was found at Hadzhi Mushkai near Kerch[4].   This has chain all the way round save for a medallion with an engraved garnet and a fastening disguised by the figure of a ram with its wool curiously rendered by small circles of gold wire soldered on.   From the chain hang emeralds, aquamarines and turquoises in box-settings.   The ram has been compared to a little lion found at Kurdzhips[5] and recalls another ram on a bracelet from Armavir on the Laba a tributary of the Kuban : but this last is frankly barbarous[6].

Jewelled Earrings.

Whereas these many-coloured necklaces are the most extreme examples of the new taste in jewelry, the earrings are the commonest.   Inasmuch as almost every grave yields a pair it is useless to multiply references.   The interesting point is to observe how the necessity for accommodating the stones led to modifications in design and the weeding out of types unsuited to the new decoration.

In the earrings and other minor pieces we meet almost exclusively with garnets.   There remained a desire for some contrasting colour, but it could not often be gratified.   The disk and amphora earring lent itself well to garnets : one would make the centre of the disk, another perhaps adorn the vase flattened to receive it[7]; more often, however, it was of gold merely and rather degraded[8].   In a more ambitious type the disk tends to become a triangle (cf. f. 290. 20), from the base of which hangs a row of chains with an amphora of onyx or crystal in the middle[9].   The skill to make good figures became rare, and the Erotes had to give way.   But the ring-shaped

[1] *CR.* 1896, p. 180, f. 556.
[2] *CR.* 1898, p. 121, No. 1009 between *F* and *E*[1] on p. 505, f. 338.
[3] Laureated head right.   XEP in wreath. Burachkov, XVI. 91.
[4] *ABC.* X. 3 = *KTR.* p. 316, f. 282.   v. inf. p. 434, n. 1 : cf. Nelidov, XIV. 396, from Ismid.

[5] *CR.* 1896, p. 62, f. 296.
[6] *CR.* 1902, p. 87, f. 196 ; cf. p. 232, n. 6.
[7] *ABC.* XXIV. 19.
[8] e.g. *CR.* 1892, p. 109, f. 67 ; 1894, p. 63, f. 89, both from Chersonese.
[9] Olbia, same tomb, *Drevnosti*, XV. ii. Pl. 1 ; Kerch, *CR.* 1903, p. 45, f. 62.

type with a lion's head continues, a setting for the stone being put below the lion's mouth as at Chersonese, a double lion's head (p. 507, f. 339), but in general the thick end of the ring is turned merely into a setting for a round or pear-shaped stone[1].

FIGS. 296, 297. *CR.* 1891, pp. 37, 54, ff. 17, 31. Kerch. Earrings in Gold and Garnet. }.

To this shape a pendant is often hung, the old amphora (ff. 290. 19; 296) or a bunch of grapes (f. 290. 24, cf. f. 294. 11), a club of Hercules[2], and most characteristically a bunch of chains whether forming a tassel (f. 290. 17) or all in a line (ib. 20; f. 297)[3]: by a survival Eros is even left hanging in the midst (f. 290. 18).

Garnet Style.

This garnet style becomes more and more barbaric. It is applied to harness[4] and to buckles[5]. Some buckles are interesting for the *tamga* they bear such as has been already mentioned on bronze examples[6]. Other buckles lead on to absolutely barbaric types[7]. The harness mentioned, which also had the same *tamga*, was found in the famous tomb at Glinishche (v. p. 433) in which, alongside of the Hellenistic plate already described, was found an armlet which retains some traces of Greek technique, but is directly related to the little bottle found in the same grave (p. 434, ff. 326, 327), and so all such bottles are classed as Greek by Smirnov[8] though—with the exception of one from Olbia with a rude lion stopper[9]—found in most barbarian company, e.g. in the Novocherkassk treasure (p. 234, ff. 141, 142[10]) and the late Ust Labinskaja barrows[11]. This is in fact the end of Greek jewelry unless, as von Stern thinks, it was the Greeks of Kerch that began to make the jewelry of the barbarians[12].

[1] *KTR.* p. 66, f. 86a; *CR.* 1894, p. 64, f. 93; Hadaczek, p. 52, f. 96.
[2] f. 290. 21, 23; Vogell, *Samml.* p. 91, f. 60; *BM. Jewellery*, LII. 2412, 2420*, Olbia; cf. 2417; armlets, *ABC.* XXIV. 3, 4: *CR.* 1892, p. 119, f. 74.
[3] Also *CR.* 1892, p. 111, f. 169.
[4] p. 435, f. 328; *ABC.* XXIX. 1—5.
[5] *ABC.* XXXII. 16 = *KTR.* p. 315, f. 280. It is an ox head.
[6] *ABC.* XXXII. 19, 20, cf. supra p. 318, n. 1.
[7] ibid. 13, 15: *Trans. Od. Soc.* XX. i. 11, 13.
[8] *Argenterie Orientale*, p. 5, Pl. XII. 32.

[9] *CR.* 1868, I. 10 = Smirnov, XII. 31.
[10] Smirnov, XI. 29, gives better photographs of this, also of the box, XI. 30, the cup, X. 25, and the Uvarov cup, XI. 27, v. supra pp. 234, 235, ff. 140, 144.
[11] *CR.* 1902, p. 83, f. 184 = Smirnov, CX. 280; others from Siberia, XII. and CX. 33; Mozara, Kamyshin (*CR.* 1898, p. 78, f. 137), XII. 34; Starotitorovka, Kuban, CXIII. 242; Novopetrovka, Kherson (*CR.* 1903, p. 154, f. 305), CXIII. 279; unknown place, Coll. Botkin, St P., CX. 281.
[12] *Trans. Od. Soc.* XX. p. 1.

M.

Finger-rings.

One more jewel must be mentioned, the finger-ring. In this the occurrence of stones is, of course, no criterion of date. There are rings of the ordinary shape with a bezel set with a stone whether plain or engraved. Others have a gold bezel likewise engraved[1]. Sometimes these engravings afford by their rubbed condition interesting evidence of the continued use of the ring, and warn us afresh that a stone too may have been worn a very long time before being buried with some possessor[2]. Besides ordinary rings there should be noted the rings with a stirrup-like outline[3]. They are usually early, before the ring and the stone had adapted themselves to each other. Interesting are those which have instead of a flat bezel[4] an animal or insect formed in the round. Then there are double rings like that of the masked queen (p. 434, f. 325) and one with four lions upon it[5]. Many of the later ones have dotted inscriptions especially XAPA[6]. A special form is that of the serpent-ring sometimes forming a pendant to a serpent-bracelet[7]. Some rings such as that with Aphrodite and a trophy and that with a large head of Athena[8] both found with silver vessels on the way to Kerch Quarantine are too big to wear and were probably votive.

§ 13.   Gems.

The gems found on the north coast of the Euxine are not on the whole of very great importance[9]: but the two specimens of work by Dexamenus are sufficient to redeem the whole class from insignificance.

Of special local interest are the oriental gems. In many of them strong Greek influence is traceable, and Furtwängler in his discussion attributes almost all of them to Greek artists[10]. Perhaps the earliest of them is a cylinder from Kerch[11] upon which a priest is worshipping a sacred dragon that rises from the symbolic "sea" Apsu; behind are the symbols of Marduk: the elements of the name inscribed are " Marduk" or " Šamaš" and "iddin" or "šum...": Menant[12] assigns this to the Neo-Chaldaean Empire. Other specimens are Achaemenian. Perhaps the most interesting is explained by Menant[13] as a forerunner of the scene represented at Bisutun : Darius is slaying Gaumata the Mage and behind him four figures with ropes round their necks represent four rebels subdued ; behind them is a palm tree with fruit. Another notable example comes from Anapa out of the Nereid coffin[14] and bears

[1] e.g. *BCA.* I. pp. 6, 9, Chersonese wall, urn 1, Athena, cf. Lysimachus coins on Pl. VI. 19—21 ; urn 4, Aphrodite on silver ring, cf. p. 217, f. 119.

[2] e.g. *ABC.* XVIII. 3.

[3] e.g. p. 208, f. 106 ; *ABC.* XVI. 1, 2, 4, 7—12, 14, 15, v. f. 298 ; p. 427, f. 318, p. 431, f. 321 ; Vogell, *Samml.* No. 1242, p. 92, f. 62, gold bezel with double palmette.

[4] *ABC.* XVI. 11. *CR.* 1865, III. 23, 24, v. f. 318 ; Fontenay, p. 28.

[5] *ABC.* XVIII. 6.   [6] ibid. 20—25.

[7] Kerch, *ABC.* XVIII. 10, 11 ; Bliznitsa, *CR.* 1869, I. 19 on f. 318, Artjukhov's barrow, *CR.* 1880, II. 14, 16: Theodosia, in electrum, f. 294. 6.

[8] *ABC.* XV. 9, 15 ; also Konelsky's, v. pp. 384, 385.

[9] The largest publication, T. de Kibaltchitch, *Gemmes de la Russie Méridionale,* 1910.

[10] v. p. 56 ; cf. Stephani's list in *CR.* 1881, pp. 81 –88, also 1882–88, pp. 62—66 sqq. ; Furtwängler, *Die Antiken Gemmen,* III. p. 116 sqq.

[11] *CR.* 1881, v. 6, 7 on f. 298.

[12] *Glyptique Orientale,* Vol. II. p. 71, Pl. X. 4 and Furtwängler, loc. cit. For the interpretation I am much indebted to Canon C. H. W. Johns, Litt.D., Master of S. Catharine's College.

[13] op. cit. Vol. II. ix. 1 and p. 168, f. 147=*CR.* 1881, v. 9 on f. 298.

[14] *CR.* 1882–8, v. 3, on f. 298, v. p. 324.

a king with crenelated crown[1] adoring Anaitis who walks upon a lion and is surrounded with rays.   The worship of Anaitis was first allowed by Artaxerxes Mnemon[2].   In the same tomb was a very curious gem, not a cylinder, but a four-sided prism[3].   One face bears a Persian distinguished as such by the shape

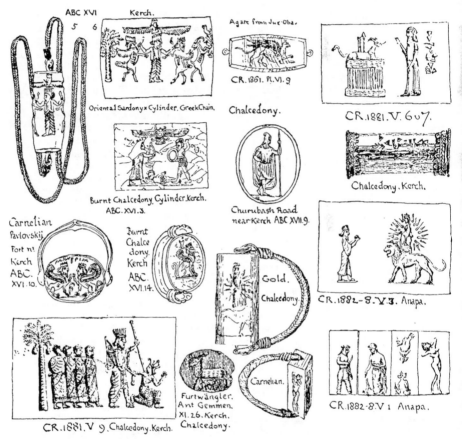

FIG. 298.   Oriental and Perso-Greek Gems found about the Bosporus.   ½. v. pp. 263, 267.

of his hood, flat on top with its tip hanging backwards[4]; the next has a man with a dog jumping up at him, closely recalling the composition of an Attic grave relief, upon the next is represented a cock fight much as it occurs upon the cylices of the lesser Attic masters, and the last shews a nude woman dancing.   The style of the latter cannot be much before the end of the fourth

[1] Cf. Dalton, *The Treasure of the Oxus*, p. 75.
[2] Menant, op. cit. Vol. II. p. 175.
[3] *CR*. 1882–8, v. 1, on f. 298.
[4] Cf. Dalton, op. cit. p. 48 sqq.

century. The whole prism has been at some time shortened so that the feet
of the figures and the tail of one cock have been cut off.

Of other cylinders one from Kerch[1] seems purely Persian, shewing a king
struggling with two crowned human-headed winged bulls under the over-
shadowing of the Deity; beyond is an ibex and a palm tree. Of purely
Greek workmanship but clearly made for a Persian is a cylinder bearing
a Persian King, his shoulders somewhat damaged by the fire through which
the stone has passed, fighting for the body of a slain Greek against another
Greek over whom his victory is assured by the protection of the Deity[2].
Stephani gives several plain cylinders in his list. The Greek settings in
which these gems are found consist of little gold mouldings round each
end of the cylinder and a half hoop ring of twisted gold. The poor cylinder
from Kholódnyj Jar (p. 193, f. 85) is interesting mainly for its provenance.

Beside the cylinders we have scaraboids with oriental compositions.
Very typical is a longshaped octagon bearing the traditional combat of a king
and a lion found in the third lady's tomb of the Great Bliznitsa[3]. Very
typical too is an oval of engraved glass from Nymphaeum out of the tomb
which offers such analogies with the VII Brothers. Upon one side of this
is a cow, upon the other the emblem of the Deity[4]. To this class also belong
two specimens—one with a winged and crowned Sphinx, another with two
such affronted with an uninterpreted inscription in what is said to be Lycian[5].
Hence they may both be referred to Asia Minor. With them may be
mentioned the chalcedony with a winged monster now at Oxford[6] and one
with a winged human-headed ox[7]. The occurrence of these Persian gems
does not really seem an evidence of any love of Persian forms due to a
community of origin between the natives of these parts and the Iranians, but
is merely due to Iran's having exerted upon Asia Minor and its dependency
the Bosporus a general influence, which is most clearly shewn in the distribution of pure Persian proper names. Figures of barbarians occur upon
gems of undoubted Greek workmanship made apparently for Greeks, but as has
been remarked they are merely generalized barbarians of the Phrygian type[8]
or definitely Persian as the Athenades gold bezelled ring which is nearly
connected with the coins of the Persian Satrap Datames[9]. A head with
a Phrygian cap has the artist's name ΓΕΡΛΛ Perga[mos][10]. It is said to be
too early to have anything to do with the city Pergamum.

The work of a broken scarabeoid[11] bearing a cow seen from behind is so
rude, shewing clearly the use of a coarse drill, that it is hard to say whether it
is very early or very late. The meaningless combination of Egyptian elements
seen on a broken carnelian—above, the winged disk, on each side, a hawk
wearing the double crown, in the midst, a lotus bud instead of a scarab, and
below a boat, all within a twisted border—betrays an Asiatic workman[12].

[1] *ABC.* XVI. 5, 6, on f. 298.
[2] ibid. 2, 3 : Perrot-Chipiez, *Persia*, p. 457, f. 226.
[3] p. 427, f. 318=*CR.* 1869, I. 18, cf. Menant,
Vol. II. p. 165, f. 143.
[4] *CR.* 1877, III. 8 on p. 208, f. 106.
[5] *ABC.* XVI. 14, 10, on f. 298.
[6] *JHS.* v. (1884), XLVII. 8.
[7] *Arch. Anz.* 1908, p. 170, f. 9. *CR.* 1907, p. 79,
f. 68.
[8] e.g. *ABC.* XVII. 9 on f. 298, cf. p. 56.

Furtwängler, *Ant. Gem.* XIII. 5.
[9] *ABC.* Reinach, p. 137 : *CR.* 1861, VI. 11 :
KTR. p. 66, f. 88, p. 88, ff. 178, 179 : Furtwängler,
Jahrb. d. deutschen Archäol. Inst. 1888, p. 198 and
Pl. VIII. 3 : *Ant. Gem.* X. 27.
[10] *ABC.* XVI. 4 and Reinach, p. 58. Furtwängler,
Jahrb. 1888, p. 198, Pl. VIII. 5 ; *Ant. Gem.* XIII. 2.
[11] *ABC.* XVI. 15.
[12] ibid. 13, my authority is Mr F. W. Green :
more Egyptian is *CR.* 1872, III. 16.

Greek Gems.

The oldest undoubted example of absolutely Greek work is a large chalcedony[1] found in the same grave, in Jüz Oba, as the beautiful lecane (p. 342, f. 248); it bears Medusa in the archaic pose of the Nike of Archermus and the Medusa from Martonosha, she has snakes in her hands and four wings. The dry careful manner is typical of the archaic style, yet it is already shewing signs of coming freedom and has been assigned to the beginning of the vth century. Most of the things in the same grave seem to be of the end of the century and a pair of Maenad earrings still later (f. 318); so the gem must have been worn for a hundred years before burial.

Another gem shewing archaic feeling is a crystal with a sow from No. IV of the VII Brothers[2], noticeable is a nick in its mane seen also on the Vettersfelde boars, this Furtwängler[3] says is a characteristic of Ionian art.

FIG. 299, Jüz Oba, Chalcedony; FIG. 300, Taman, Agate.   Gems by Dexamenus of Chios. $\frac{2}{1}$.

Of the severe style we know no better master than Dexamenus of Chios: there are four known specimens of his signed work and two of them are from South Russia: a heron flying[4], and a heron standing with a cicada before him[5]. This latter has been damaged in the funeral fire, but the former is the best study of a bird in Greek art; in some ways it rather recalls Japanese work.

Of the other Dexamenus gems one at Cambridge shews a lady Mica and her servant, just such a group as served as a model to put on a gravestone, the other has the portrait of an unknown Greek[6], one of the first portraits known. Sir A. J. Evans (loc. cit.) calls it Cimon without obtaining Furtwängler's agreement. The four gems are placed by Furtwängler (p. 137) in the following chronological order, Mica, the standing heron, the portrait head and the flying heron: he assigns 430 to 420 B.C. as the time when Dexamenus flourished[7]. This gives a definite point of the utmost use in determining the development of gem-engraving, and the two herons are

---

[1] *CR.* 1860, IV. 6 on p. 427, f. 318. Furtwängler, *Ant. Gem.* VIII. 52.

[2] *CR.* 1876, III. 33 on p. 208, f. 106.

[3] *Vettersfelde,* p. 24, v. pp. 237, 239, ff. 145, 147.

[4] f. 299; *CR.* 1861, VI. 10 = *KTR.* p. 66, f. 87: *Ant. Gem.* XIV. 4: a smaller replica that may perhaps be by the same hand, ib. XIV. 2.

[5] f. 300; *CR.* 1865, III. 40: *Ant. Gem.* III. p. 137, f. 94. I am much obliged to Sir A. J. Evans for leave to reproduce his enlarged photographs, *Revue Archéologique,* XXXII. 1898, p. 337, Pl. VIII.

[6] *CR.* 1868, I. 12: *Ant. Gem.* XIV. 1, larger LI. 8.

[7] See also his "Gemmen mit Künstlerinschriften," *Jahrb. d. k. d. Arch. Inst.* 1888, pp. 199—204.

among the most important ancient gems in existence because of the undoubted genuineness of their inscriptions, seeing that they have never been bought or sold. Another standing heron or stork on chalcedony from Theodosia does not come up to that by Dexamenus (p. 401, f. 294. 8).

A very interesting early ring already mentioned as from Jüz Oba bears engraved upon the gold bezel the curious device of a snake twined round a bow so as to draw an arrow[1]. Another gold bezel with Nike before a trophy adorns the only good ring from Kerch in the British Museum[2].

Rather later in style come the Asiatic gems spoken of above, that shewing a Phrygian supposed to be Paris, and those with the names Athenades and Perga[mos]. The latter was found in the same grave as a Lysimachus stater and a large burnt chalcedony bearing Apollo Citharoedus (or perhaps a Muse)[3]. Other specimens of Hellenistic work are a Venus *accroupie* mounted on a beautiful chain[4] and the two votive rings before noticed (p. 410), Aphrodite crowning a trophy and the ambitious Athena head in garnet which recalls the ring and *emblema* in the Konelsky collection, and to a less degree two Athena heads from Chersonese, the mould for terra-cottas (p. 365, f. 265, I. 4) and another garnet[5]. To this period belong two archaistic gems; one with Artemis[6], the other a blue chalcedony with a remarkable attempt to reproduce the ancient Apollo type[7] ascribed to Canachus; but all the archaic points are ridiculously exaggerated; on the arm is a bird in place of the usual stag.

A cameo from Artjukhov's barrow—the earliest known—Eros with a butterfly[8], is dated by coins of Lysimachus and Paerisades and the style of the silver vessels (v. p. 351) to about the middle of the IIIrd century. A fine piece of work from Chersonese is a Medusa head of the beautiful suffering type[9] cut in onyx. The same site has produced a pair of ordinary cameo portrait busts[10]. In this connexion we may mention a brooch with a magnificent portrait of L. Verus in rock crystal though it was found at Batum: the head was sunk from behind and then gilt and so from in front appears as it were in relief[11].

A very large number of poor gems with commonplace heads, animals or even whole figures, have been found about Kerch, but of recent years few that seemed worth figuring in *CR.*; the best in *ABC.* have been noticed.

To stones of Roman date there is no end, but it is curious to find one with a Roman warrior offering a wreath to Hecate, at Nóvgorod Sêversk north of Chernigov in Central Russia (Fig. 301).

Cutting coin-dies is an art nearly allied to gem-engraving: what measure of success it attained north of the Euxine, Plates I.—IX. shew: the gold staters of Panticapaeum are good, some of the rare early types of Chersonese, especially the full-faced ones, and one or two issues of Olbia and Phanagoria are passable, but on the whole the interest that can be claimed for these coins is historical and not artistic.

FIG. 301. *BCA.* III. p. 114. Carnelian. Novgorod Sêversk. ⅔.

[1] *CR.* 1861, VI. 8 on p. 427, f. 318.
[2] F. H. Marshall, *Catalogue of Finger-rings, Greek, Etruscan and Roman, in the B. M.*, 1907, No. 51, Pl. II., inscribed [Π]αρμένων βασιλεῖ.
[3] *ABC.* XV. 10.   [4] ib. XVII. 19.
[5] *CR.* 1906, p. 81, f. 81.
[6] *ABC.* XVII. 8.

[7] *CR.* 1882–8, II. 13, 14 and p. 41. Furtwängler, *Ant. Gem.* Vol. III. Text p. 161, ff. 114, 115.
[8] v. p. 431, f. 321; *CR.* 1880, III. 9 and p. 78: Furtwängler, op. cit. Vol. III. p. 152, f. 106.
[9] *CR.* 1892, p. 102, f. 59.
[10] *CR.* 1901, p. 46, ff. 87, 88; 1906, p. 81, f. 84.
[11] *Arch. Anz.* 1908, p. 163, f. 7.

CHAPTER XII.

REPRESENTATIVE GREEK TOMBS.

ALMOST all the objects of Greek art from South Russia occur in tombs, so it seems worth while for that alone to give some account of them and their disposition: on the whole we cannot say that we gain therefrom any knowledge of the special peculiarities among the Greeks of the Scythian coast. About Kerch graves are noticeably rich in their contents, which may point to a specially lively sense of the duty of providing all necessary for the departed in the next world: also the number of conspicuous barrows seems greater: but speaking broadly such a necropolis as that excavated by Pharmacovskij outside Olbia[1], or by Duhmberg near Kerch[2], is similar e.g. to the well-known necropolis of Myrina[3].

Berezan.

Everywhere, though cremation was practised, burial was the more usual rite. The only exception is the very early cemetery on the island Berezan[4]. Here were found large hollows with smaller ones about them. These latter proved to be grave-pits about 1·40 m. (4 ft. 6 in.) deep and divided by stone walls: in them were urns with ashes, fragments of vases and Olbian *asses* or fish-coins. The larger proved to be crematoria: one such pit 3·55 m. (11 ft.) deep having its chimney still preserved. In it were found successive layers of cinders and sherds of Ionian and black-figured Attic vases dating the finds as from the VIIth to the early Vth centuries B.C. (v. supra, p. 338). In some cases the sherds belong to vases of which other fragments were found by the cinerary urns. Each body was burnt at the crematorium, and upon the fire were cast pots, weights, fish-hooks, even a charred semi-circular cake has been preserved; afterwards all was gathered up and laid in a small pit together with arrow-heads, bits of rouge, coins, lamps and terra-cotta figures, one of which is usually a pot-bellied grotesque[5]: in large low barrows were several funeral pits together, each containing a number of urns with ashes and similar offerings. Yet even at Berezan burials are not unexampled. One was covered by a deposit datable c. 600 B.C., but it was without any offering save the skeleton of a bird[6]: in general the burials are rather poor and belong to the last period of the island's being inhabited, as with them the vases are of

---

[1] *BCA.* VIII. p. 1 sqq., cf. *JHS.* XVI. (1896), pp. 345, 346; and *CR.* 1904, p. 34 sqq. where ff. 48, 49, plan and section of a late barrow, shew very well how the different types of grave are intermixed.

[2] *CR.* 1899, p. 27; *BCA.* I. p. 80.

[3] E. Pottier et S. Reinach, *La Nécropole de Myrina*, Paris, 1888.

[4] v. inf. p. 452, n. 1, and esp. *CR.* 1904, pp. 41 —49; *Arch. Anz.* 1905, p. 61.

[5] *Arch. Anz.* 1909, p. 161, f. 24.

[6] *Trans. Od. Soc.* XXIX. *Minutes*, p. 82: *Arch. Anz.* 1910, p. 225.

Attic rather than Ionian make : they are set at the feet of the dead and in his
hand is put an Olbian fish-coin.   Burials are found in small flat barrows and
in the large barrow to the east of the island.   The transition to burning is
exemplified by partly cremated bodies[1], as when only a single vertebra was
charred[2].   An interesting point about Berezan is that the interments were often
made not in the necropolis but close to or in the houses, in pits similar in form
to the rubbish pits but distinguished from them by the absence of kitchen
refuse, the completeness of the pots they contain and the presence of terra-
cotta statuettes and other offerings[1].

Olbia.

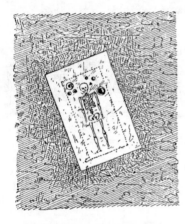

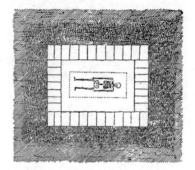

FIGS. 302, 303. Olbia. Simple Pit-grave.
        BCA. VIII. p. 9, f. 8.

FIGS. 304, 305. Olbia. Pit-grave with plank
        ceiling. *BCA.* VIII. p. 19, f. 11.

At Olbia Pharmacovskij (l.c.) describes three main types of grave ; the
simplest is that of graves súnk perpendicularly into the earth, the coffin lying
at the bottom and having the earth heaped directly upon it (ff. 302, 303): by
a development of this to avoid direct contact with the earth, the pit is lined
with stones and planks laid across to make a kind of chamber (ff. 304, 305):
the place of such planks has been taken by five amphorae likewise laid

[1] *Trans. Od. Soc.* XXIX. *Minutes,* p. 45.   [2] ib. XXVIII. *Minutes,* p. 141.

across[1], or more usually above the lining slabs was a double row of carefully fitted slabs forming a two-pitched roof[2]: such tombs vary in length from 2·70 metres (8 ft. 10 in.) to 5·22 metres (17 ft. 3 in.).

A different constructional principle is applied by undercutting one of the long sides of the grave-pit and making a recess for the coffin: this was then walled up and the shaft or pit filled in with earth (ff. 306, 307).

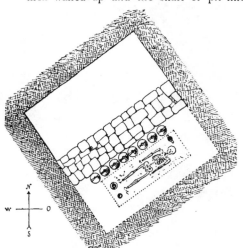

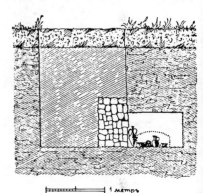

1 metre.

FIGS. 306, 307. Olbia. Undercut grave.
BCA. VIII. p. 11, f. 9.

Under special geological conditions at Kerch this form developed into the roomy funeral chamber or catacomb approached by a shaft piercing the particular limestone layer which conveniently held up the roof (v. p. 308). At Olbia, where there was no special advantage in going so deep, the undercut grave did not in its development get beyond a simple δρόμος leading down by earthen steps to the entrance of a bare grave chamber which never approached the size and decoration possible at Kerch: the body was put within, the entrance blocked with a rough wall, the dromos filled up with rammed earth and a monument placed alongside[3].

When a more splendid resting place was desired at Olbia a stone vault was built: a late Roman example (c. 200 A.D.) is that of Heuresibius and Arete[4], which is identical in plan with the common earthen chamber, save for the addition of a vestibule. Here, as may be seen by the plan and section annexed (ff. 308, 309), the approach with steps cut out of the earth led down to an elaborate erection entirely below the original surface of the ground. A corridor, with its outer door tightly closed by a stone, led through a door flanked by architectural pilasters into the main chamber. Both corridor and inner chamber were covered with true barrel-vaults and adorned with simply

[1] *CR.* 1905, p. 34, f. 31; *Arch. Anz.* 1909, p. 170, f. 30.
[2] *CR.* 1904, pp. 34—39, ff. 48—55; *Arch. Anz.* 1905, p. 64, ff. 11—13; 1909, p. 167, ff. 28, 29.
[3] *JHS.* XVI. p. 346; *BCA.* VIII. p. 12, f. 10.
[4] At XI on the Plan of Olbia, p. 450, f. 330; v. *BCA.* III. (1902), pp. 1—20.

M.

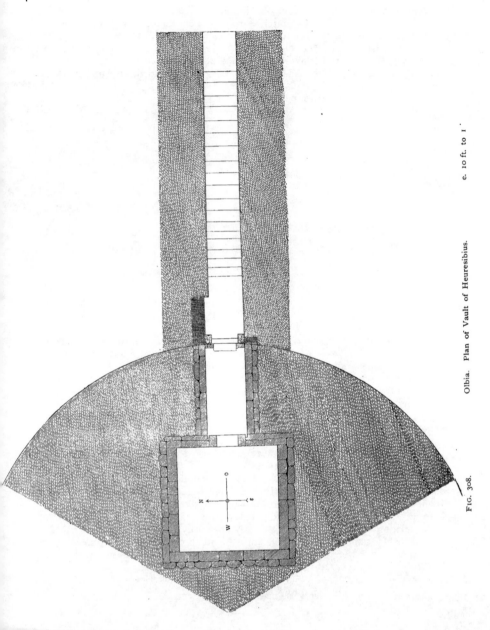

FIG. 308.   Olbia.   Plan of Vault of Heuresibius.   e. 10 ft. to 1´

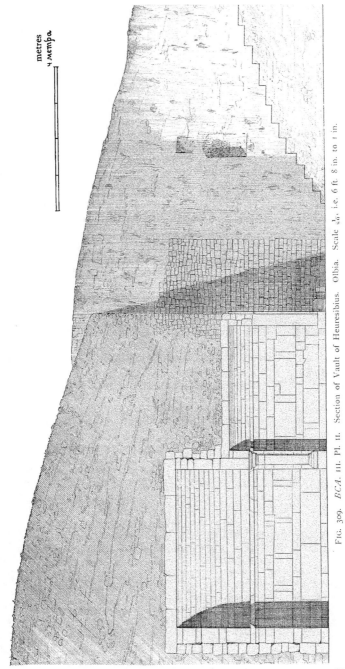

metres
4 метра

FIG. 309. *BCA.* III. Pl. II. Section of Vault of Heuresibius. Olbia. Scale ¹⁄₅₀, i.e. 6 ft. 8 in. to 1 in.

moulded cornices.   The tomb had been opened both by ancient and modern
robbers: the last only found fragments of a bench and a marble table inscribed:

ΕΥΡΗΣΙΒΙΟΣΚΑΛΛΙΣΘΕΝΟΥΣΚΑΙΑΡΕΤΗΠΑΠΙΟΥ

ΤΟΜΝΗΜΑΖΩΝΤΕΣΕΑΥΤΟΙΣ   ΙΖ̄

ΚΑΤΕΣΚΕΥΑΣΑΝ ΕΝΗΜΕΡΑΙΣ

Von Stern, who first published the inscription[1], took the ἐν ἡμέραις ιζ'
to be the addition of modern forgers, and in spite of Latyshev's defence of
them[2] they seem to be the work of the Brothers Hochmann through whose
hands the stones had passed.   Pharmacovskij when he carried out his scientific
exploration only found one or two bits of a glazed vase (v. supra, p. 357) and
of millefiori glass, also a coin of the end of the IInd century A.D.[3]   The approach
was filled in with earth as could be seen from the unbroken edges of the
earthen steps, and the whole structure covered by a barrow enclosed by such
a solid stone plinth that some took it for the foundation of a defensive tower[4].

In the case of another barrow[5] much the same in type just enough of the
plinth was preserved to make its restoration possible.   It consisted of a rough
foundation in the form of two steps, a course of long plain stones laid on their
sides, another course of broad rusticated stones laid alternately as headers and
stretchers and a simple cornice, making a total height of 1·88 m. (6 ft. 2 in.): the
stones came from the ruins of the town-wall.   The diameter of the circle was
37 m. (120 ft.) and the original height of the heap some 15 m. or 50 ft.   The
chamber consisted of an outer and inner room of the same breadth roofed with a
barrel-vault.   It was absolutely empty, but the resemblance to the masonry of the
former barrow argues that it belongs to the same time ; in spite of its imminent
fall Olbia must have been flourishing to allow of its citizens having such expensive monuments.   The two barrows can be distinctly seen on my view of Olbia
from the river (p. 450), but since that was taken they have necessarily been
almost destroyed.   In the necropolis of Olbia burials are almost universal and
cremation occurs only in isolated instances.   Except in the very simplest
interments the body was put into a shell which was enclosed in a monumental
wooden coffin : but Olbia has not yielded any fine· coffins in good preservation[6].

One grave discovered at Olbia in 1891 deserves mention because of its
exceptional character and the interesting fate of its contents[7]; unluckily it was
ransacked by peasants, so we cannot be sure of its exact arrangement.   In a
chamber lined with stone lay two skeletons with gold leaves upon eyes, mouths
and ears (cf. p. 507, f. 339).   Of the man we know no more : the woman, laid on
a wooden couch with bronze feet, wore also a funeral wreath, a necklace with
many-coloured stones and pastes and a butterfly pendant (cf. p. 406), another
of transparent beads, gold and garnet earrings, a silver roundel with Aphrodite
and Erotes, and two gold rings with engraved garnets: on her dress were
sewn repoussé gold plates: in her mouth was a silver coin rather like
Pl. III. No. 6 with a countermark dated Ist century A.D.   There were also
found a plain bronze mirror, a bone spoon, a clay lamp, a small black vase,

---

[1] *Trans. Od. Soc.* XXIII. *Minutes*, p. 5.
[2] *IosPE.* IV. 461 ; more strongly *BCA.* III. p. 53.
[3] Burachkov, VII. 168 or IX. 226, cf. inf. Pl. III. 15.
[4] e.g. Uvarov, *Recherches*, Pl. VIII. A.
[5] IX on the plan, p. 450; cf. *Arch. Anz.* 1904, pp. 102, 103, ff. 1, 2 ; *BCA.* XIII. pp. 7—39, ff. 4—18,

Pl. V.—IX.; XXXIII. pp. 107, 108.
[6] A simple one on p. 322, f. 232.
[7] Mostly figured by A. V. Orêshnikov, *Drevnosti*, XV. ii. pp. 1—13, "Remarks on antiquities found at Parutino in 1891," or von Stern, *Trans. Od. Soc.* XXVII. p. 88, "A Tomb-find made at Olbia in 1891."

a pot shaped like a seated lion (v. p. 346) and a glazed mug with the Judgement of Paris (v. p. 354). In 1905 I saw certain objects professing to come from Olbia, which had been lent to S. Kensington Museum by Mr Pierpont Morgan and obtained by him from Messrs Spink. I was at once struck by their resemblance to the above and had photographs sent to Professor von Stern who proved that they came from this same grave. They include two silver canthari, a bronze hairpin with a silver head (v. p. 383, f. 284) and a glazed oenochoe with dancing skeletons (p. 356, f. 262). The couch, mouthplates and butterfly necklace recall Chersonesan customs so nearly that we may believe that here we have the tomb of a Chersonesite living in Olbia.

Chersonese.

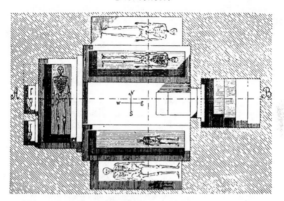

FIGS. 310, 311. *CR.* 1897, p. 125, ff. 240, 238. Plan and Section of tomb No. 982 at Chersonese.

At Chersonese K. K. Kosciuszko-Waluźynicz has given full descriptions of over two thousand graves; they include simple pit-graves, undercut graves and sepulchral chambers, of which the most usual type is square with a pillar in the middle and loculi in the walls[1]. Figs. 310, 311 which explain

---

[1] *CR.* 1892—1906; *BCA.* II. sqq.; v. p. 552, bibliography to Ch. XVII.; *KTR.* p. 31, ff. 28, 29.

themselves shew a more elaborate example adapted to accommodate a large number of persons. Owing to the thinness of the soil most of the excavations had to be hewn in the rock, and were often shallow so that they have usually been plundered or at any rate their contents are in poor preservation. Where the bedrock is not reached the cist of the grave is often formed of tiles. At Chersonese cremation is more general than at Olbia although far less frequent than burial, e.g. the passage under the ivth century town-wall contained six urns with ashes and the beautiful jewelry already mentioned (v. pp. 380, 397—399, 402, 410 n. 1, 499 and inset of Plan vii. p. 493). Near by were two columbaria of Roman date with niches for urns. Reference has been made to the practice at Chersonese of laying gold leaves upon the eyes and mouth of the dead (v. p. 507, f. 339): the nearest analogues are in Seleucid graves dug by Loftus at Warka in Mesopotamia and Mycenaean plates from Cyprus: like the funeral masks they seem to have served to make it less painful to look upon the face of the dead at the time of the funeral ceremony, or to prevent the entrance of demons[1].

Bosporus.

It is in the graves about Kerch that most interest may be felt, since these have yielded the most precious spoil. Duhmberg[2] enumerates sundry varieties, simple graves sunk in the earth or hewn out of the rock, covered with boards or tiles or slabs of stone (often enough old gravestones with inscriptions). Sometimes there are cists made of stone slabs. Beside these are the undercut graves and subterranean chambers in which the dead were laid either directly upon the floor as at Olbia or upon a ledge or bench as at Chersonese. Out of 81 graves opened in 1899 only two shewed cremation. Coffins in these lesser graves seem either to have been absent or to have left no traces. These various classes of simple graves are well described in the introduction to *ABC.*[3], and diagrams are added giving the arrangement of the stock sizes of tile to make a cist (Plan B) with plans and sections of stone cists and chambers (Plan C) and accounts of their contents.

The catacombs have been already discussed (v. supra, p. 307), they seem to have exact analogues in other Greek sites. Most characteristic of the environs of Kerch are the more ambitious tombs with barrows. Such occur in other Greek lands and references to their heaping up are common enough in the literature, but I do not know of any Greek site surrounded by the rows and groups of barrows that occur in the neighbourhood of Panticapaeum and Phanagoria (v. p. 435, n. 1). It seems as if native influence had some part in producing this result. It was these conspicuous barrows that first attracted the notice of the various grave robbers of old times and also of the archaeologists of the last century, so that very few are still untouched. Accounts of their contents are to be sought in *ABC.*, and in the older series of the *CR.*,[4]

---

[1] F. H. Marshall, *BM. Jewellery*, III. 196.
[2] *CR.* 1899, p. 27; *BCA.* I. p. 80, see bibliography to Chap. xix. for excavations in Bosporan cemeteries.
[3] Reinach's ed. p. 17 sqq.

[4] e.g. Pavlovskij barrow, *CR.* 1859, Pl. v. pp. 6—15, others on Jüz Oba ridge, ib. pp. ix, x: 1860, pp. iii—vi, Pl. vi.: Vitjazevo near Anapa, 1881, p. iv. 1882—8, Pl. I.—vi. pp. 31—38; Little Bliznitsa, ib. Pl. vii. pp. 76—82.

and a hasty description of many may be found in *KTR*.[1]   Here it will be
sufficient to give some account of the contents of three important tombs;
the Great Bliznitsa and Artjukhov's barrow, both in the Taman peninsula,
and the grave of the Queen in the golden mask at Glinishche north of Kerch.

Great Bliznitsa.

The richest Greek barrow opened near the Bosporus is that called
the Great Bliznitsa or Twin near Vyshe-stebléevka north of Lake Tsukur
upon the Taman Peninsula[2].   Its circumference was about 350 metres and its
height 15.   Operations were begun on the west side and first there was found
an empty masonry chamber with painted architectural adornments (ff. 312, 313).
Near was a plain chamber in which was the tomb of a lady whom Stephani
has called a Priestess of Demeter, as the decorations of her elaborate jewelry

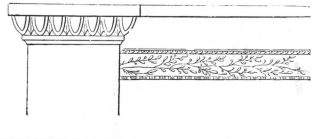

FIGS. 312, 313. *CR.* 1865, p. 14. Great Bliznitsa. Man's Tomb. Painting in Corridor and
Grave-chamber. v. p. 307.

all have reference to the cult of Eleusinian Goddesses.   By this was the place
upon which a second lady had been burnt, and at a lower level a bricked
platform with the traces of the funeral feast.   Here an interesting feature was
a funnel-shaped hole defined by a limestone plate 1·24 m. × ·62 m. in which
was an opening ·27 m. square shut by a stone fitting it exactly.   This

---

[1] pp. 22—69 and 111 sqq.
[2] It is a little difficult to obtain a clear idea of
the disposition of the Great Bliznitsa as its exploration was not conducted continuously but fell
in the years 1864, 1865 and 1868.   Accordingly we
have accounts of the finding of various interments
and objects in them in the formal Report for each

of these years, and in the Supplement to the
Report for the year following each of these we
have Stephani's elaborated account of the objects
themselves. Cf. *CR.* 1864, p. iv sqq., 1865, p. iii
and p. 5, Pl. I.—VI.; 1866, p. 5 sqq., Pl. I.—III.;
1868, p. v; 1869, p. 6, Pl. I.—III.   No plan has
been given.

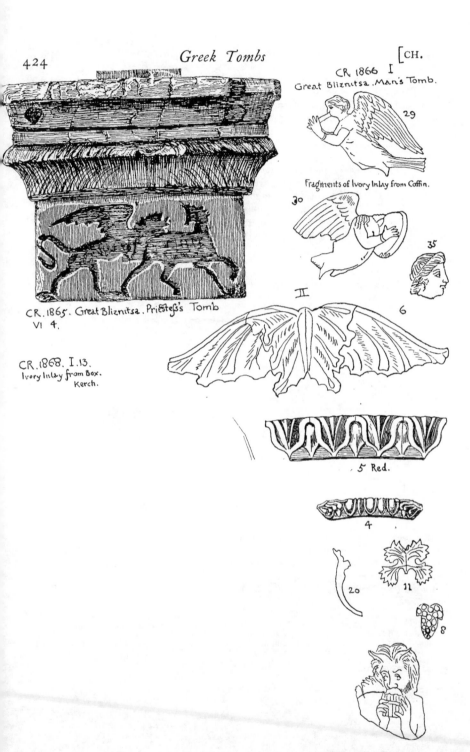

CR. 1866 I
Great Bliznitsa. Man's Tomb.

29

Fragments of Ivory Inlay from Coffin.

30

35

CR. 1865. Great Bliznitsa. Priestess's Tomb
VI 4.

II

6

CR. 1868. I.13.
Ivory Inlay from Box.
Kerch.

5 Red.

4

20

11

8

hole went down into the earth and must have been a βόθρος[1] for offering liquids to the dead. Twenty feet to the s.w. were fragments of a dish.

On the south side of the hill were the traces of another funeral feast, and at a higher level a number of amphorae buried, not far from the empty tomb[2]. In this part also were the traces of a great pyre and another βόθρος. Here belonged a late red-figured vase with Europa[3]. Near by was a stone tomb with a prismatic vault. This had collapsed and crushed the coffin of the man buried beneath it: but precious fragments of its ivory inlay remain (v. f. 314) and some other objects. Finally in 1868 there was discovered the tomb of a third lady yielding only to that of the first lady in richness.

The accounts of the exploration give such uncertain particulars as to the relative positions and levels of these various finds that it is impossible to say exactly in what order the different people were laid to rest in the barrow: but it is clear that they all belonged to one family in spite of the differences of ritual, and they must have lived at about the same time, for gold plates struck from the same dies occur in different tombs, although they are so delicate that they could not have stood much wear. The date is approximately indicated by the stater of Alexander found on the burning place of the second lady, and the style of all the objects confirms this. The most important of the works of art have been discussed under the categories to which they belong, but the inventories of the different tombs have an interest of their own.

FIG. 315. Centre of Gold Calathos from Great Bliznitsa. Priestess's tomb. *CR.* 1865, I. 3. ⅔. v. pp. 56, 391.

The Priestess of Demeter was most completely furnished with all adornments, comprising a best and second-best set. There were in her coffin, itself enriched with inlay[4], a gold calathos for state occasions (f. 315) and a simple

---

[1] Perhaps after all ὀπή would be the right word, cf. Pausanias, x. iv. 10 where we have a very similar case on pure Greek soil (Daulis): v. Frazer, ad loc. for parallels from all parts of the world.

[2] *CR.* 1865, p. iii.
[3] *CR.* 1866, III.
[4] *CR.* 1865, VI. 4, 5 on f. 314.

stlengis, a pair of temple-ornaments (f. 316), and two pairs of earrings, a rich necklace and a simpler one, a pair of gold bracelets (f. 317), four

FIG. 317. Great Bliznitsa. Priestess's Tomb. Gold Bracelet. *KTR.* p. 65, f. 84=*CR.* 1865. II. 6. ¼. v. p. 402.

gold rings[1], twenty-two varieties of gold plates making up 1875 in all[2], gold beads, a pair of boots and a mirror handle. Of other objects found near the most important were the remains of the harness of four horses with bronze bits and highly decorated phalerae[3].

FIG. 316. Great Bliznitsa. Priestess's Tomb. Gold Temple-ornament. *KTR.* p. 59, f. 75=*CR.* 1865, II. 1. ¼. v. p. 394.

The tomb of the third lady, found in 1868, offered remarkable analogies to the Priestess's in the selection of adornments. Again we have a calathos, this time the figures only were of gold not the ground, they comprised a row of Bacchanals going

[1] One with a lion, *CR.* 1865, III. 23 on f. 318.
[2] ib. III. 1, 2—5, 20 on f. 318.

[3] ib. v. VI., cf. supra p. 155 n. 1.

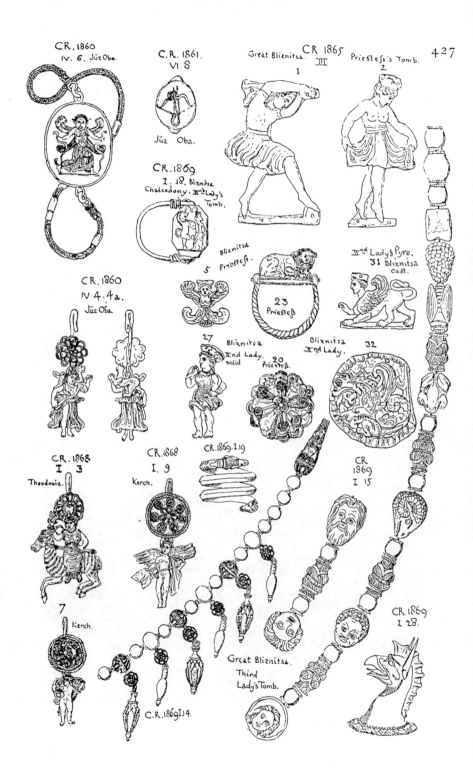

CR. 1860
IV. 6. Jüz Oba.

C.R. 1861.
VI. 8

Jüz Oba.

CR. 1869
I. 18. bliznitsa
Chalcedony. II Lady's
Tomb.

Great Bliznitsa. III
1

CR 1865

Priestess's Tomb.
2

CR. 1860
IV 4. 4a.
Jüz Oba.

5 Bliznitsa
Priestess

23
Priestess

II nd Lady's Pyre.
31 Bliznitsa
cast.

27 Bliznitsa
II nd Lady.
solid

20
Priestess

Bliznitsa
II nd Lady.

32

CR. 1868
I 3

Theodosia.

CR. 1868
I. 9

Kerch.

CR. 1869. I. 19

CR
1869
I 15

7
Kerch.

Great Bliznitsa.
Third
Lady's Tomb.

C.R. 1869.I.14.

CR. 1869
I. 28.

back to the types fixed by Scopas[1], a stlengis (f. 319), earrings, an even fuller
set of necklets—the remarkable collar (f. 320) and two necklaces, bracelets,
rings, one (chalcedony) with an oriental subject, and another in the shape of
a serpent[2], two hundred gold plates in eight varieties some of them identical
with the Priestess's.   So far the correspondence is almost complete ; but the
differences are very curious.   Some may be a matter of date, for of the two
the third lady would appear the later, a glass bottle, an Egyptian Bes and the
Persian stone might point to the orientalizing work whose influence becomes
stronger a very little later.   Original are the golden griffin-heads which
probably adorned the coffin unless they went along the rim of a stephane[3].

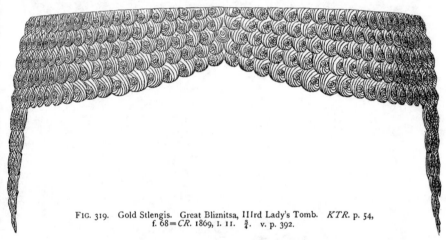

FIG. 319.   Gold Stlengis.   Great Bliznitsa, IIIrd Lady's Tomb.   *KTR.* p. 54,
f. 68 = *CR.* 1869, I. 11.   ¾.   v. p. 392.

   To a kind of childishness we may put down a whole series of miniature
vessels in bronze and clay, a doll and tiny cymbals.   But only a most
perverted taste can have had pleasure in the extraordinary series of terra-cottas[4].
Some are merely Bacchic, some mere genre figures, others caricatures, but
several are most obscene.   They do not stand alone, but in no other Greek
tomb have so many disgusting grotesques been found.   Stephani calls them
ἀποτρόπαια, "lucky," but they go too far in the direction of ἄτοπον καὶ γελοῖον[5].
   The lady (No. II) who was burnt has naturally left us less on the site of her
pyre than her relatives in their graves, still she had her rings and her gold
plates : of these there were 322 in eight varieties, some are interesting as being
identical with those of the Priestess, others for their technique as being cast not
stamped[6], and one for being unique in this whole barrow as shewing traces of
Scythic influence.   It is clearly the barbarous imitation of a Greek group of a
sea-griffin devouring a lioness.   This touch of the native is interesting, as it
strengthens the idea that the great richness of these graves was partly due

---

[1] *KTR.* p. 54, f. 67 = *CR.* 1869, I. 7, 8, 9.
[2] *CR.* 1869, I. 14, 15, 18, 19 on f. 318.
[3] *CR.* 1869, I. 28 on f. 318, v. sup. p. 393, n. 8.
[4] *CR.* 1869, II. III.
[5] Cf. A. J. B. Wace in *BSA.* x. p. 103 sqq. who

asserts the sovran power of grotesques and ob-
scenities against the evil eye and instances these
examples among others, v. supra p. 369, n. 7.
[6] *CR.* 1865, III. 27, 31, 32 on f. 318.

to barbarian views of the next world, although the people's artistic tastes were purely Hellenic.   Finally it is in this tomb that we find the stater of Alexander which fixes the earliest date for the whole barrow.   The βόθρος associated has always claimed the attention of students of funeral beliefs.   It too may be a reflexion of native usage : at any rate the Volga Finns still leave a channel by which nourishment can be poured into the tomb (v. p. 106).

FIG. 320.   Gold Necklet.   Great Bliznitsa.   IIIrd Lady's Tomb.   *KTR.* p. 62, f. 81 = *CR.* 1869, I. 13.
²⁄₃.   v. p. 400.

The decoration of the masonry tomb has been discussed elsewhere. The chamber was quite empty, so on what evidence it is said to have been a man's tomb, is not clear.   The other man's tomb was chiefly interesting for its vault which had fallen in, and for its coffin with ivory inlay (f. 314). Besides there was a most remarkable helmet[1], being a translation into bronze of a soft Phrygian cap, two gold rings, one of which had been long in use, and the usual gold plates, over 60 in five varieties, one like that figured from the Priestess's tomb[2], and others which find their analogues in other Kerch tombs.

The vase with Europa found by the place of the funeral feast belonged to the last red-figured style.

The whole barrow is very remarkable, and it is a pity that a more intelligible account of its contents has never been compiled nor a plan supplied.

[1] *KTR.* p. 48, f. 55 = *CR.* 1866, frontispiece.   [2] *CR.* 1865, III. 5 on f. 318.

Artjukhov's Barrow.

Belonging to the following century, dated by coins of Lysimachus, we have the rich Barrow of Artjukhov whose importance in the history of jewelry has been pointed out above (p. 404). But having regard to this importance it seems worth while to give a more systematic account of its contents[1]. The tumulus was to the north of Sênnája, the ancient Phanagoria on the Taman peninsula, not far from the site assigned to Cepi. It was opened by Tiesenhausen and Lutsenko. In it were three important tombs.

In the east part of the barrow in Tomb I, which was in two compartments, a woman was buried alone; she possessed a gold diadem (f. 322), six necklets[2], four on f. 321, a chain with lion ends and a row of amulets, 3 bracelets, 3 gold earrings; on her left hand she wore a ring with glass mosaic (ib. I. 13), on the right one with garnet and filigree and a plain carnelian : she had also a medallion with a bust of Aphrodite and a gold pin with a tassel (ib. I. 17), also four round gold plaques ; in silver she had by her a cyathus and two other vessels, a spindle and a saucer on a stand, also a bronze mirror. In the outer compartment were a pot, four saucers, three small bottles, two flutes and part of a lock[3].

In Tomb II (plan and section, ff. 323, 324) lay a man and a woman. In the vestibule were little but some vessels whose importance has already been discussed (p. 351).

On the man's body were a golden wreath, a gold ring, a medallion with garnets (II. 3 on f. 321), four silver rings and a gold stater of Paerisades. The woman by him also had a bay wreath, a neckband or frontlet, a neck-ring, a neck-chain ending in oxen's heads, two necklaces, a gold medallion, a gold pin, a pair of gold earrings (f. 322, III. 5), a chalcedony ring (ib. III. 6), and a ring with a shoe-shaped bezel in enamel ; from the inscription on the ring we may call this pair Hestiaeus and Mammia (ib. III. 7, 8), a cameo of Cupid and a butterfly (ib. III. 9), four other rings one with an engraved garnet, three round gold plates, a coin of Lysimachus, eight silver vases including cyathi, a saucer on a stand, a box, a silver spindle, in bronze a mirror-box, a lamp[4] and another box ; also a pelice like the one from Olbia (p. 350, f. 255).

In Tomb III again there lay a man and a woman. The man wore a gold wreath with convolvulus and an iron ring, by him were a stlengis and a few clay pots[5]. The woman also wore a convolvulus wreath, likewise a gold neck-chain, a necklace and bracelet of rock crystal, garnet, chalcedony and smalt, earrings with Erotes, a gold ring with Heracles, an iron finger ring, four gold roundels, and a wrap of felt or fur. By her there were two engraved silver vessels (f. 321, IV., 8, 9), a plain round mirror box, a shell with rouge and white, and several clay vessels.

As has been remarked already, in all there is a love of garnets and stones, of vessels, of reef-knots. Specimens also of certain objects occur in more than

---

[1] For accounts of its excavation v. *CR.* 1879, p. xliv sqq.: for discussion of the contents, *CR.* 1880, p. 6, cf. *KTR.* p. 54 sqq.

[2] *CR.* 1880, I. 2—7.

[3] A good lock with two hasps, von Stern, *Trans. Od. Soc.* XXI. p. 274, Pl. A.

[4] *KTR.* p. 55, f. 69 = *CR.* 1880, p. 19.

[5] For one v. *KTR.* p. 56, f. 70 = *CR.* 1880, p. 21.

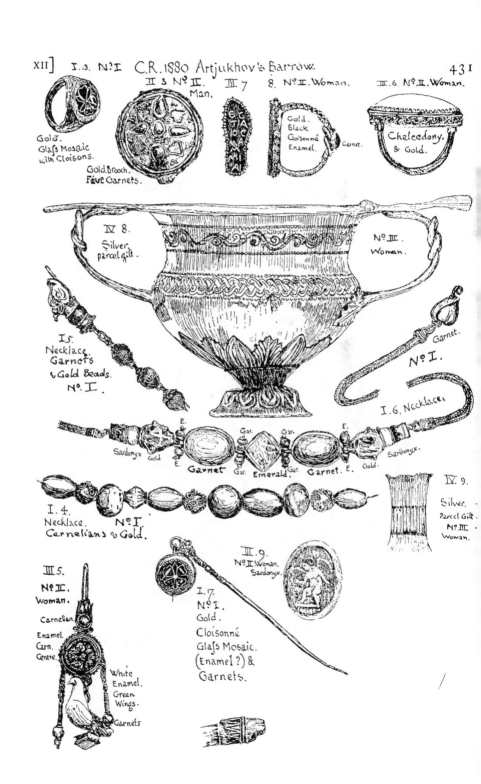

II.3 N.º II.   III.7   8. N.º II. Woman.   III.6. N.º II. Woman.
Man.

Gold.
Glass Mosaic
with Cloisons.

Gold.Brooch.
Five Garnets.

Gold.
Black
Cloisonné
Enamel.   Garnet.

Chalcedony.
& Gold.

IV.8.
Silver,
parcel gilt.

N.º III.
Woman.

I.5.
Necklace.
Garnets
& Gold Beads.
N.º I.

Garnet.

N.º I.

I.6. Necklace.

Sardonyx Gold   E.   Gar.   Gar.   E.   Sardonyx.
          Garnet Gar. Emerald. Gar. Garnet. E. Gold.

I.4.
Necklace.   N.º I.
Carnelians & Gold.

IV.9.
Silver.
Parcel Gilt.
N.º III.
Woman.

III.5.
N.º II.
Woman.

Carnelian.
Enamel.
Carn.
Centre.

White
Enamel.
Green
Wings.
Garnets

III.9.
N.º II. Woman.
Sardonyx.

I.17.
N.º I.
Gold.
Cloisonné
Glass Mosaic.
(Enamel?) &
Garnets.

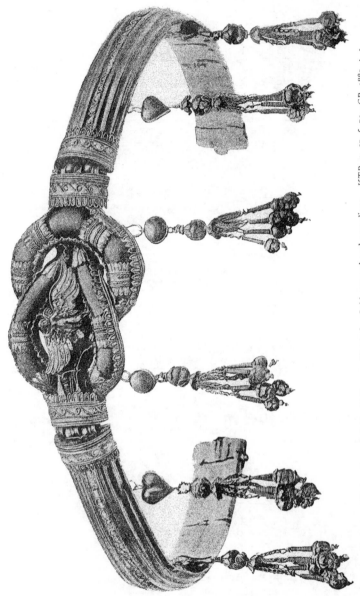

FIG. 322. Diadem from Artjukhov's Barrow, Tomb I. Gold, enamel and carnelians. *KTR.* p. 57, f. 71 = *CR.* 1880, I. I. Slightly reduced. v. pp. 404, 405.

one grave, the gold roundels in I, II and III, the plaques with Aphrodite and Eros (similar to that on p. 407, f. 295 Γ) in I and II, in the same two the silver boxes, spindles, and saucers on stands; plain saucers and two-handled silver vessels in II and III.   The coins of Lysimachus and Pacrisades point to the same time, the end of the iiird century or the beginning of the iind. A tomb opened by Ashik on the way to the old Quarantine in 1839[1] must have been very similar in its contents to any tomb of this barrow.

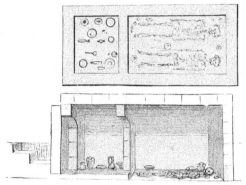

FIGS. 323, 324.   *CR.* 1880, p. 12.   Artjukhov's Barrow.   Tomb II.   Plan and Section.

Glintshche.

As a specimen of a rich tomb of the latest period we may take that opened by Ashik at Glinishche near Kerch in 1837.   It is usually known as the tomb of the Queen with the Gold Mask.   In a barrow he discovered a great marble sarcophagus with a cover ending in pediments.   The skeleton within was that of a woman, wearing the golden mask[2], and wrapped in a woollen robe with a gold pattern sprinkled with gold plates (f. 325).   Her gold wreath was of an ordinary late type with a centre piece of a horseman drinking from a rhyton (ib.)[3].   Her belongings shewed a strange mixture of Greek and barbarian work : the latter would appear to be her own, the other objects heirlooms.   Personal to her must have been her bracelets (f. 327) in gold and garnets, her scent bottle recalling that of Novocherkassk (f. 326, v. p. 409) and the harness adorned with the Bosporan *tamga* ℍ (f. 328).   She wore three rings, one plain, one double and one bearing an Eros rudely engraved upon a garnet (f. 325) : unluckily it does not seem possible to identify a coin[4] found with her; it is in poor preservation.   In strong contrast to this rude contemporary work are the various vessels handed down from Hellenistic times. Chief of these is the great dish in silver and niello which must have been made for one of the Diadochi, an Antigonus or an Antiochus : it can hardly have been less than four hundred years old when it was buried.   On the back is an inscription with the name of King Rhescuporis, and it is usually referred

[1] *ABC.* p. lxiii.   Reinach, p. 20, v. supra p. 351.   [3] *ABC.* iii. 4, 5 = *KTR.* p. 230, f. 204.
[2] ib. 1 = *KTR.* p. 70, f. 94, v. supra p. 390.   [4] *ABC.* LXXXV. 8.

to Rhescuporis II (III) who reigned from 211—228 A.D.[1], but the silver cups, ewers and vase and the bronze basin and jug, also perhaps the sceptre and some of the small things, spoons, rouge pot, bronze pilaster and others must also go back long before the time of the "Gothic" jewels.

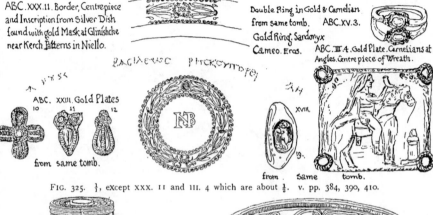

ABC. XXX. 11. Border, Centrepiece and Inscription from Silver Dish found with gold Mask at Glinishche near Kerch. Patterns in Niello.

Double Ring in Gold & Carnelian from same tomb. ABC.XV.3.

Gold Ring, Sardonyx Cameo. Eros. ABC. IV.4. Gold Plate. Carnelians at Angles. Centre piece of Wreath.

ABC. XXIII. Gold Plates 10 11 12 from same tomb.

XVIII. 19. from same tomb.

FIG. 325. ⅓, except XXX. 11 and III. 4 which are about ½. v. pp. 384, 390, 410.

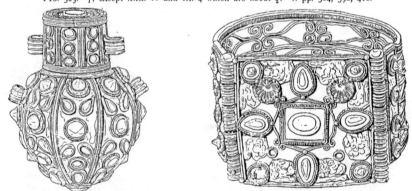

FIGS. 326, 327. Kerch, Glinishche, Tomb of Queen with the Mask. Bottle and Bracelet in Gold and Garnets. *ABC.* XXIV. 25, XIV. 4. ⅓. v. pp. 235, 280, 409.

In finishing this survey of the Greek objects found in South Russia I must ask my readers' indulgence for not being sufficiently acquainted with the finds in pure Greek lands to institute instructive comparisons. I have endeavoured to put within their reach material that is not very accessible to them, and it is for the student of Greece and the Hellenized East to throw light on this material from the observation of other parts of the Hellenic world. Especially I should like to know whether there appears any substantive

---

[1] This because in the tomb at Hadzhi Mushkai, v. *ABC.* Reinach, p. 43, containing almost identical diadems (v. p. 390, n. 7), jewelry (v. p. 408) and harness, *BCA.* XXXVII. p. 33, f. 15, together with old Greek heirlooms, among others apparently a IVth century aryballus, *ABC.* LVIII. 6, 7, were found "indications" of a coin of that king: but the form of the genitive in -ει recalls later coins, v. p. 384.

difference in the ordering of the tombs in South Russia and in Hellas, whether what appears to me quite a singular richness of the former is merely due to the opulence of a commercial community or to the influence of barbarian ideas making people more anxious that the dead should have the richest and fullest provision for the future life : a minor point would be the question whether the

FIG. 328. Harness from Glinishche, Kerch. Leather mounted in Gold set with Carnelians.
KTR. p. 314, f. 279=*ABC.* XXIX. 4. $\frac{2}{3}$. v. p. 318 n. 1.

immense number of barrows about Olbia, Panticapaeum and Phanagoria can be paralleled in Greece or Asia Minor[1], and if not, whether it is merely a question of soil or of influence exercised by the barrow-heaping tribes of the country. It is not for me who have never been in Greece to answer such questions, but I have supplied one term of comparison, may some one who can supply the other bring his knowledge to bear upon the matter.

[1] Mr Wace tells me of such in Thessaly e.g. Larissa, and Pherae, 'Εφ. 'Αρχ. 1909, p. 27 ; Leake, *Northern Greece*, III. p. 367 ; Πρακτικά, 1907, p. 153 sqq.; *JHS.* XX. (1900), p. 20 ; Macedonia, Pydna and Pella, *Annals of Archaeology and Anthropology*, Liverpool, II. (1909), p. 159 ; Pergamum, *Ath. Mitt.* 1907, p. 231 ; 1908, p. 365, and then Sardis which again is not Greek.

CHAPTER XIII.

COLONIZATION AND TRADE.

THE Euxine coast was the first El Dorado, the first mysterious land to draw adventurers across broad seas in search of fame and treasure. Heroes of old had won glory enough by voyages across the Aegean, but they would not have lived upon the lips of men whose wonderland had broadened with their knowledge, had not the poets set their feats ever beyond the bounds of new discoveries. Thus Jason who but crossed from Iolcos to Lemnos[1] must later have sought the golden fleece by sailing εἰς Φᾶσιν ἔνθα ναυσὶν ἔσχατος δρόμος; and Odysseus on his way from Troy to Ithaca must pass through the dangers recounted by sailors returned from the Euxine. Later when the Greeks had dared Italian and Sicilian seas a yet wider scene for adventure was displayed. Even Jason must return by the West, faring up the Ister and down by its other branch into the Adriatic, yet for him the great field of his achievements remained Colchis, the city Cytais—Aea with its king Aeetes and his daughter, Medea the sorceress, skilled in herbs. Now, by the nature of things, Odysseus could not be brought through the Pontus to Ithaca. The winds that blow him into the Western sea have nothing impossible about them. But in the Western sea there was room for all the marvels of the world: if the hero could not sail the Euxine, the wonders of the Euxine could be put in his course through the West. Cities of Italy or Sicily became proud that at their straits, or bays, or headlands, the hero had met adventures which nevertheless still bore every mark of Pontic scene.

A clear case is that of the Cimmerians. Their place was on the Cimmerian Bosporus, a land weird enough with its mud volcanoes and marshes to supply the groundwork for a picture of the Lower World. Yet the perpetual night in which they live, just like the long days of the Laestrygones, points to the far North: and the general build of the poem makes us think of them as far in the West upon Ocean stream. Clearly the poet combines the details of his picture without caring that he takes them from three different quarters of the compass. Poseidonius wished to identify the Cimmerii with the Cimbri of Jutland, so would Professor Ridgeway[2] and Professor Bury[3], but I fear that I cannot do so (v. supra p. 40); for me the Black Sea remains the one historic place for the Cimmerii, and if they appear anywhere else they have come from the Black Sea. Dubois de Montpéreux

[1] Demetrius of Scepsis ap. Strab. I. ii. 38.
[2] *Early Age*, I. p. 390.
[3] *Klio* VI. (1906), p. 79, adducing the splendid story in Procopius *B.G.* IV. 20 (II. p. 567, Bonn)

about the fishermen ferrying souls over to Britain, but the fishermen are not called Cimmerian and I do not see how they come in.

and K. E. von Baer[1] actually make the Black Sea coast the scene of the Odyssey. The latter not only sees the harbour of the Laestrygones in Balaklava Bay, but recognizes in a grove of poplars on the Sea of Azov, near the mouth of the Protoka, the very grove of poplars and willows by which Odysseus lands. But mere descriptions of scenery have no bearing on the question. The Laestrygonian harbour, shut in by overlapping head-lands, is just the port a poet would describe as ideal without any need of Balaklava for a model. It might just as well be Dartmouth or Boscastle which lays claim to a resemblance: such a port is difficult for a sailing ship—we lost a frigate off Balaklava—and its white calm throws into relief the wildness of the inhabitants.

The attempts to set the Nekyia in Campania are very much more forced: there is nothing to play the part of Ocean stream and the etymologies pro-posed do not help at all. Ephorus, to whom they go back, was kind to the patriotism of Circeii and other towns about, and moderns have developed his hypothesis with a perverse ingenuity[2].

Another link with the Pontus is Circe with her island Aeaea, own sister to Aeetes with his city Aea; the account of the island sounds like a stray piece of Colchis, and the lady is skilled in herbs like her niece Medea. Strabo (I. ii. 10) thinks not unreasonably that this is the ground of their relationship.

The view that Odysseus once sailed the Euxine is well stated by von Wilamowitz-Moellendorf, who however puts the Laestrygones on the south coast of Asia Minor, but it is clear that the further north they are the better[3].

When the Odyssey was coming into shape the Asiatic Greeks clearly knew a good deal about the Euxine, and the poet could use that knowledge to provide scenery for his poem. Even in the Iliad (XIII. 5—7) we have the Mare-milkers mentioned, that is he had some idea of the Nomad's life, but their acquaintance was not full and its mysteries were not yet fathomed.

When the mariners of the Aegean first sailed the Euxine and what men they were we cannot say: with our new knowledge of ancient sea powers we must put much further back the time of first exploration. If the pots of the Tripolje culture really point to Aegean influence, this may have been exerted by sea.

Certain spots are said to have once belonged to the Carians: Cios[4], Caria and the Carians' Harbour to the south of Callatis[5], Amastris[6], even the country about the mouth of the Tanais[7], and this may be evidence of ancient settlements of Aegean peoples or may be due to mere coincidence of names. Of the presence of Phoenicians there is no real trace (pace M. Bérard): if they did penetrate into the Euxine they were not the first to sail it. Indeed it is not quite certain that the sailing all came from the south: in the Middle Ages of Greece immigrants from Central Europe may, on striking the Euxine, have

[1] *Ueber die Homerischen Lokalitäten in der Odyssee*, Brunswick, 1878, the final form of an article in *Reden und Aufsätze*, Vol. III.
[2] V. Bérard, *Les Phéniciens et l'Odyssée*, II. p. 311.
[3] *Homerische Untersuchungen*, Berlin, 1884, p. 165; cf. E. H. Berger, *Mythische Cosmographie der Griechen*, Leipzig, 1904, Supplement to Roscher's *Encycl.* pp. 15—31.
[4] *Schol. Ap. Rh.* I. 1177.
[5] Arrian, *Peripl.* 24. 3, also in Mela II. 2 and *Peripl. Anonymi*, 101 (75).
[6] *Schol. Ap. Rh.* II. 943.
[7] Pliny, *NH.* VI. 20 (7). For all these see Neumann, *Hellenen*, p. 340: Bürchner, p. 33.

taken as kindly to sea raiding as did the Goths in the IIIrd century A.D. The old familiarity with the Euxine may have almost faded away when Troy rose to power and could block the way thither, or when new and savage tribes occupied the dangerous coasts on each side of the strait. Certainly the beginning of the last millennium B.C. was a period of groping for more knowledge of the Euxine coast. The Asiatic Greeks knew something of it but not enough to light up every corner, and leave no room for marvels. The hero could always escape into Ocean stream which would bear him to all the wonders of the world.

As we have seen the ordinary man in Greece never advanced much beyond this stage. He always had a vague feeling that the Euxine, even though no longer called Ἄξενος, was dark and strange, he could never disabuse himself of the idea that the Sea of Azov joined the Caspian and the Caspian opened into the outer Ocean.

With the Milesian sailors it was otherwise. Navigation of the Euxine continued to be dangerous, but the dangers were known and the risks reckoned; sudden storms, rocky coasts, hostile tribes and pirates were to be set against the chance of carrying off valuable slaves or making a piratical seizure oneself. With time enterprise became more regular, instead of carrying off slaves men bought them from those who had taken them in war, and peaceful gains became worth winning, the gold of Phasis, the fish of the great northern rivers, in time the hides of the steppes, the corn of the lowlands by the river mouths, the gold of the far interior, Transylvania or perhaps the Altai. But this commerce depended on regular relations being established, such as could only be secured by the founding of factories. Such gradually sprang up round the whole coast wherever it was convenient for Milesian ships to put in for the night, wherever a defensible rock or island commanded a safe cove or a beach upon which the ships could be easily drawn up. Between these settlements a struggle for existence would be inevitable: where suitable topographical conditions occurred in a favourable geographical situation, some spot at which land and sea roads converged, the factory would attract the produce of a wide area and flourish: when communications with the *Hinterland* were difficult the spot remained a mere refuge for the night, and as skill in navigation increased perhaps it faded away. It was by such a process of natural selection that the famous Greek colonies arose at the right points, and have mostly survived to the present day where physical or ethnological conditions have not been utterly changed, whereas when the later Greek statesmen did more than give a town a new name and some splendid buildings, that is when they used their wide knowledge of geography to choose a new site which should enjoy all possible advantages, the cities mostly decayed with the short-lived states of their founders.

We need not then credit the Milesians with a profound knowledge of the *Hinterland* of the Black Sea because the sites they chose have remained the commercial cities of the coast. The permanent settlements if not haphazard were dictated by the comparative success of the factories, and we have clear cases of their missing points of world importance because of local disadvantages. It seems to us a strange oversight that they should have allowed the Megarians to forestall them at Chalcedon and Byzantium, and

no one has refrained from jeering at the blindness of the Chalcedonians themselves: yet the disadvantages of Byzantium on the land side, where until
Roman times its fields were open to Thracian inroads, went far to excuse
those who preferred sites less suitable for the capital of the Eastern Mediterranean, but more favourable for an agricultural colony.   Byzantium, in fact,
had no value until the Milesians had called into existence a great Euxine
trade: their mistake was in not appreciating what they themselves had done[1].

It is hard to know what meaning we can attach to the traditional dates
given by Eusebius and Jerome for the foundation of the Pontic colonies.
The case of Cyzicus which is given three times, B.C. 1267 (Anno Abrahae 747),
B.C. 757 and B.C. 679 is perhaps instructive: the first figure representing the
mythical foundation by the Argonauts, the second the real occupation, the
last some important accession of population or break with the mother city[2];
whereas Sinope is only put down under 631 B.C. although the Armenian
version tells us that Trapezus, its daughter, was settled in 757 B.C.: Chalcedon
685 B.C., Byzantium 653 B.C., Istrus 657 B.C. and Borysthenes 647 B.C. are
quite reasonable.   The movement seems to have gone on about the same
time as that which settled Magna Graecia and Sicily: the early date assigned
to Cumae is due to confusion with Cyme in Aeolis[3].

There is no reason to doubt that during the VIIIth century the north
coast of Asia Minor was studded with Milesian factories, and that during the
VIIth century they were spread more thinly along the Scythian coast.   At the
same time the circumstances of the mother city, want of land, pressure from
Lydia and internal quarrels encouraged citizens to settle permanently in
what had been mere trading stations.   Inasmuch as a considerable number of
citizens was necessary to establish a community that could stand by itself,
the Milesians sometimes allowed men of other states to join in the enterprise.
From the VIth century the finds made upon the coast and in the interior
prove the existence of a great trade between the settlers and the natives, but
when hard times for the Ionians set in, the market which Miletus had made
passed to the Athenians, at any rate as regards pottery (v. supra, p. 339).
On the other hand the Milesians seem to have set the taste of the natives
in gold work so that, their imitations went on recalling rather the Asia Minor
style of the VIth century than the more developed products of later times.

Accounts vary as to the relations between the settlers and the natives.
Ephorus[4] says that until they fell into luxury the Milesians were victorious
over the Scythians and settled the Euxine with famous cities: but it looks
as if he were merely pointing a moral.   On the whole relations after the end
of the piratical stage seem to have been friendly.   The new comers are
generally represented as renting the site of their settlement from the natives.
Of course unfair dealing was always apt to bring armed reprisals and ill-
defended wealth would always be a temptation, but the choice of a site
and speedy fortification made the Greeks fairly safe from mere raids, and both
parties gained by intercourse being on a peaceful footing; the natives valued
the wares brought by the strangers, and the latter recognized that it was not
wise to provoke too far customers who were the masters of the land.

---

[1] v. Polybius, IV. XXXViii. 1—5.
[2] v. Hasluck, *Cyzicus*, pp. 157, 163.
[3] Beloch, *Gr. Gesch.* I. p. 180, n. 1.
[4] ap. Athenaeum, XII. 26.

Trade then was the origin of the Greek settlements on the north coast of the Euxine and each flourished and attracted population according to the commercial advantages of its position. Chersonese is a possible exception but it was trade that kept even Chersonese alive in later times. No doubt some of the colonists carried on agriculture and had their farms near by, but the main part of them exploited commercially the broad lands of which they had seized the gates.

In his accounts of the advantages and drawbacks of the site of Byzantium Polybius (l.c.) gives us a summary of the Euxine trade. The chief exports were cattle and slaves, less important were honey, wax and dried fish, of corn he says that according to the harvests it was imported and exported: to this list we must add hides (δέρματα, v.l. θρέμματα), also salt, timber, some precious stones including amber[1], drugs[2] and perhaps gold.

Of the slaves the greater part came from Asia Minor whose natives were peculiarly fitted for servitude; the Getae also furnished a large supply. Scythian slaves are not specially common; less adaptable than the Asiatics they would be more suitable for outdoor labour than for personal service. The best known instance of their employment is as policemen at Athens.

On the fish trade Koehler has written a whole disquisition called ΤΑΡΙΧΟΣ. He comes to the conclusion that preserved fish of every quality from jars of precious pickle, which corresponded to our caviar or anchovy, to dried lumps answering to our stockfish: sturgeon, bêluga, mackerel, tunny, mullet were all sent to Greece, and later to Rome, from the mouths of the Dnêpr, the straits of Kerch, the fisheries of the Sea of Azov and the mouths of the Don. Of the cattle trade we do not hear so much, but it is not surprising in view of the Nomads living all about. Herodotus (v. 10) tells of the bees beyond the Ister; honey and wax were among the chief products of mediaeval Russia.

The men of Olbia made salt at the mouth of the Dnêpr and the Chersonites later gained it from the same region; near Perekop too were great salterns. This salt was marketable both among barbarians and Greeks. Sadowski has described the old salt-way[3], leading up towards the Amber coast, but as the salt has left no traces the way is purely hypothetical, the coins found at Schubin may just as well have come up from the head of the Adriatic, and Herodotus tells us of no NW. trade route though he describes so fully that leading NE. Constantine Porphyrogenitus[4] and Pope Martin[5] tell of the exchange of salt in Cherson against the corn of Asia[6]. The process of salt-extraction as practised in the XVIIIth century is described by Peyssonel[7]. The Crimean timber was not reckoned as good as that of the opposite coast, and of course in the steppes there was none to spare[8].

These same raw materials meet us in any account of the trade at a Scythian port, e.g. Tanais exports slaves and hides, and nomadic products[9].

As to gold there were many stories to attract enterprise, the gold worn by the Agathyrsi (this seems the most tangible, the Romans dug gold in

[1] Pliny, *NH.* XXXIII. 161 (57), XXXVII. 33, 40 (11), 64 (16), 65 (17), 119 (38).
[2] ib. XXVII. 2 (1), 45 (28), 128 (105); Amm. Marc. XXII. viii. 28.
[3] *Handelstrassen*, p. 88, v. inf. p. 484 n. 6.
[4] *De Adm. Imp.* c. 42 (p. 180, Bonn).
[5] Mansi, *Concil.* XV. pp. 64, 65, Epp. XVI. XVII.
[6] Cf. Shestakov, *Sketches of the History of Cherson*, pp. 68 sqq. (v. inf. 538).
[7] *Comm. de la Mer Noire*, I. p. 169; grain, p. 165.
[8] Theophrastus, *de Plantis*, IV. v. 3.
[9] Strabo, XI. ii. 3 (inf. p. 567).

Transylvania, Constantine, l.c., speaks of a "Gold Coast" between the Dnêstr and Dnêpr), the sacred gold of the Scythians, the gold trappings of the Massagetae and later of the Aorsi, the gold of the griffins and Arimaspi. These added to the rich finds made in tombs—no proof that the gold was abundant, but only that the royal families hoarded it for generations—had made us all believe too easily in a naturally auriferous Scythian area. Now Bertier-de-La-Garde has shewn that there is no real evidence for this, but that gold flowed into Scythia from oversea to pay for exports (v. inf. p. 631).

As to the imports Polybius (l.c.) mentions wine and oil as the chief, but Strabo gives a better account when he says that Tanais received clothing and wine, and everything that belongs to civilized life. That this was just so is shewn abundantly in our earlier chapters.

Products of early Greek industry penetrated the interior (Ionian pots to the Middle Dnêpr, p. 339[1], gold work even to Vettersfelde in Lusatia, p. 236), how far the Greeks themselves voyaged is another matter. I feel less and less inclined to doubt that there was some foundation for the circumstantial story that the Geloni were of Greek blood, and quite believe that Aristeas had wandered up into Asia to the land of the Issedones (v. p. 105 sqq.). He no doubt had heard tell of the gold in the Altai, and they had probably made themselves intermediaries in the fur trade between Permia and Iran, which brought into the far north so many Sassanian dishes. I can find no authority for the use of furs among the Greeks except perhaps those on the coast of the Euxine[2]. Speck (I. p. 117) seems to think that the furs were the object of the NE. caravan route.

We have already seen (supra, p. 359) that the wine trade has left evidence of itself in the amphorae found all along the coast and even in the interior. Beside those of local manufacture we have the stamps of Rhodes and Thasos that occur in large numbers and those of Cnidos and Paros, which are comparatively rare. It is clear that the custom of affixing stamps was not universal, for we know that other wines came into the Pontus. The speech of Demosthenes against Lacritus gives us an idea of the ways of Greek tramps in the second class wine trade, especially as it preserves the agreement made between Artemon of Phaselis, who wished to speculate in the Pontic trade, and Androcles of Athens who advanced him three thousand drachmae for the purpose. Artemon was to sail in the twenty-oared ship commanded by Hyblesius his fellow-citizen, and to take in three thousand jars of Mende wine at Mende or Scione, dispose of it on the Bosporus, or if he liked go on to Borysthenes, take in cargo from the Euxine and bring it all back to Athens on the same ship. Androcles could claim his money twenty days after the return of the ship. He was to have 22·5 per cent interest if the ship left the Pontus by midsummer, 30 if she were later. This high rate gives some idea of the profits Artemon might reasonably make, and incidentally of the risk run. As a matter of fact Artemon did not propose to run any risks. He raised a further loan on the same security, only took in 450 jars of Mende wine, carried it over to Bosporus and there sold it and

---

[1] Cf. *Arch. Anz.* 1911, p. 230, Pasterskoe Gorodishche (Kiev); p. 235, f. 42, Nemirov, Podolia, cf. Spitsyn, "Scythians and Hallstatt," *Bobrinskoj*

Miscellany, St P., 1911, pp. 155—168.
[2] Stele of Greek γουνάριος (furrier), Kerch, VIth cent. A.D., *Trans. Od. Soc.* XXIX. *Minutes*, p. 8.

took on board eighty casks of sour Coan wine, ten or eleven pots of salt fish, a little wool, and two or three bales of goatskins: the wine and fish were for a farmer at Theodosia to give to his labourers.   Lacritus, the defendant, who took the place of Artemon deceased in the meanwhile, represented that this consignment was destined for Athens, but that the ship had been wrecked between Panticapaeum and Theodosia, and all the goods lost.   "As if," said the speaker, "any one ever heard of wine being brought from Pontus to Athens: whereas it is sent there from these parts, from Peparethus and Cos and Thasos and Mende."   As a matter of fact the captain had met a Chian in Pontus, and had borrowed money from him under promise to bring the ship and everything it contained to Chios, strictly against the Athenian Navigation law—it was not even lawful to lend money for a voyage which should not bring corn to Athens.   So now the ship was hidden in a thieves' harbour, waiting to get safely to Chios, and Lacritus was trying to avoid paying his debts because she had been wrecked off Theodosia. Whether this complicated story be true or no it cannot have been contrary to possibility and gives us a vivid idea of what the Pontus trade was like. We have the same tale of rascality in the speech against Phormion, but the documents are not supplied so it is not so instructive.   Here the defendant contends that he paid certain monies to the agent of the prosecutor, but that they were lost in a shipwreck.   An interesting point is that the goods exported from Athens did not always find an instant sale on the Bosporus. It is a pity that we are not told what they were.   The shipwreck was caused by an extra consignment of hides on the deck.

Yet in spite of the high rate of interest charged by the moneylenders we must not imagine that the risk was as great as would appear from these private orations.   Cases naturally arose out of shady transactions or unfortunate ventures and we do not hear of the normal and successful voyages.   In the preliminaries there is no difficulty found in obtaining money for the Pontic trade and nobody thought much of its dangers until something went wrong.

Most interesting was the trade in corn which Polybius says that the Pontus exported or imported according to the yield of each harvest.   Another important factor which varied more gradually was the degree of civilization in which at any given time the coast tribes might happen to be.   When a fresh tribe had lately come to the front with a fresh reinforcement of savagery or when intertribal wars were specially disastrous, the coast strip from which the corn supply was drawn was rendered unavailable, and the limited area of land in the actual possession of the Greek states might be insufficient to supply their needs in a bad year.   For a hundred years before the time of Herodotus the tribes of Scythia seem to have been in fairly stable equilibrium, and the Aroteres to the north of Olbia had, as he says (IV. 17), taken to growing wheat for export, and no doubt the same sort of thing arose in the Eastern Crimea.   So the Euxine for the first time had surplus corn, and the Pisistratids found it worth while to secure this trade by their establishment at Sigeum.   It was this corn which paid for the black-figured vases and archaic gold and bronze work imported into Scythia.   As far as Athens was concerned the Persian wars put a stop to this exchange, but the conditions in Scythia remained the same, and when Athens again obtained access to the

Scythian markets her population was increased and her demand still more[1]. The coming of the Sarmatians seems to have upset the equilibrium. New tribes succeeded to the half-civilized ones, and the state of things shewn by the Protogenes decree (App. 7) would not encourage agriculture in the interior of the country; so too in the Crimea the relations of Greeks and natives were interrupted: even the cornlands of the Bosporan kingdom can hardly have given so full a return as before. Accordingly the time just before Polybius was unfavourable to corn production in Scythia, whereas in other parts of the Greek world it had spread and flourished. Hence the necessity of importing corn into what used to be the granary of Greece. Mithridates again secured peace: his opponents, Scilurus and Palacus, were also almost civilized, and the area under corn in the Crimea no doubt spread. About Olbia the Getae probably prevented much progress unless Scilurus was strong enough to give efficient protection. But Crimean agriculture, although burdened with heavy taxation, could provide in kind 180,000 medimni of corn as tribute and 200 talents in silver, the result of prosperous trading.

The Greek tombs dating from the early centuries of our era shew a fair prosperity all along the Scythian coast; even in a little town like Gorgippia the guild of shipowners could, under royal patronage, set up a temple and statues to Poseidon[2]; but with the approach of fresh tribes things again changed for the worse. We know most of Chersonese, once an agricultural state, self-sufficient but not apparently exporting much; with the loss of territory on the main peninsula and the impoverishment of its own stony soil it became absolutely dependent for all the necessities of life upon supplies drawn from the opposite coast[3]; for these it paid with salt and the products of trade with the interior—a state of things just the reverse of what had been.

Little evidence is left that the Euxine coast traded with the far interior: amber mostly came to the Adriatic; Greek and Roman things may have reached Siberia through Iran; perhaps some of the China trade, interrupted in south-western Asia and travelling by the Oxus from which even if there were no direct water communication it could easily get to the Caspian, debouched at Tanais, though the more usual way was across the Transcaucasian isthmus to Dioscurias or Phasis. This was the trade on which Genoese Caffa and Venetian Tana flourished in the Middle Ages: they relied on very precious goods which could stand the very expensive land transit, not on the bulky raw materials that Bosporus and Olbia had exported: the slave trade was common to both periods; but the Genoese had sometimes to send provisions to Caffa because the Tartars were not yet agricultural, or at any rate were not disposed to sell their corn to strangers with whom they were not on the best of terms. In the xviiith century the Crimea exported some sixty shiploads of barley a year to Constantinople. Though on a smaller scale, the trade described by Peyssonel is essentially similar to that of ancient times. The same would be true of modern times but for the influence of protected

[1] For details of the Bosporan corn trade, v. inf. p. 574. L. Gernet, *Bibliothèque de la Faculté de Lettres de Paris*, xxv. (1909), p. 269, esp. 315—316, "L'Approvisionnement d'Athènes en Blé au Ve et IVe siècles" minimizes the importance of the Pontic corn trade, but Dr Grundy, *Thucydides and the History of his Age*, London, 1911, pp. 74 sqq.,

159 sqq. shews that it was vital not only to Athens but to almost all states of Hellas: Pericles tried to make a corner in it and thereby exercise influence over cities Athens could not reach by arms, this was what they found most intolerable, p. 187.

[2] App. 51 = *BCA*. xxxvii. p. 38, No. 2.

[3] Cf. Pope Martin l.c., Const. Porph. cc. 42, 53.

industries which lessen the import of manufactured articles. Also the export of wheat is drawn from a larger area instead of a narrow fringe along the Dnêpr and Bugh, upon which Olbia had to draw; in 1903 Odessa sent out 2,200,000 tons of grain (in 1908 only 655,000), coming from the governments of Bessarabia, Kherson and Ekaterinoslav, besides what went from Nicolaev and Kherson : the central provinces feed Russia itself, the south-eastern use Taganrog—this had no counterpart in ancient times, as there was no agriculture so far east and Strabo does not give corn as an export of Tanais.

Intercourse with other Mediterranean countries besides Greece and Asia Minor does not seem to have been frequent. In early days we have engraved gems from Western Asia; from the Ist century B.C. we find Italian pots and bronzes with glazed pots, beads and charms from Egypt and Phoenician glass. The epitaphs of foreigners dying in Scythia and the foreign coins which have strayed there all tend to shew that the opposite coast was the land with which the people had most to do : other communications were merely fortuitous. Coins of the Scythian coast hardly occur outside their own region : men of the Euxine, though they did travel for business or pleasure or instruction, and in particular journeyed to Rome on state affairs, have not left many traces of their presence in foreign lands; one or two epitaphs, some dedications made by Bosporan kings and some names in lists of Delphic proxenies, make up the number. The dislocated grammar of the later inscriptions at Olbia and on the Bosporus, the pedantic adherence to Dorism of the Chersonesites, suggest that there was not much going to and fro. It was their place in the scheme of things to stay at home and export corn to feed the great centres of civilization or later to defend them against roving barbarians.

BIBLIOGRAPHY.

Colonization.

Neumann, K. *Die Hellenen im Skythenlande*, p. 335 sqq.

Bürchner, L. *Die Besiedelung der Küsten des Pontos Euxeinos durch die Milesier*, I. Teil. Kempten, 1885. Unluckily the second part which would have dealt with the N. coast has never appeared.

Hertzberg, G. *Kurze Geschichte der Altgriechischen Kolonisation*. Gütersloh. 1892. pp. 24—28.

Trade.

Koehler, H. K. E. ΤΑΡΙΧΟΣ, *Mém. de l'Acad. des Sciences de St P.* Sér. VI., *Sc. Polit. etc.* T. I. (1832), pp. 347—490.

Preller, L. *Ueber die Bedeutung des schwarzen Meeres für den Handel und Verkehr der alten Welt.* Dorpat, 1842.

von Sadowski, J. N. *Die Handelsstrassen der Griechen und Römer an die Gestade des Baltischen Meeres:* deutsch von Albin Kohn. Jena, 1877.

Perrot, G. "Le Commerce des Céréales en Attique." *Revue Historique*, IV. (1877), pp. 1–73.

Mishchenko, Th. G. "Commercial Relations of the Athenian Republic with the Kings of Bosporus." *Kiev University Bulletin*, No. 7 (1878), p. 477.

von Stern, E. R. "The Significance of Ceramic Finds in South Russia for elucidating the Cultural History of the Black Sea Colonies." *Trans. Od. Soc.* XXII. (1900), p. 1.

—— "Die Griechische Kolonisation am Nordgestade des Schwarzen Meeres im Lichte archäologischer Forschung." *Klio*, IX. (1909), p. 139.

Speck, E. *Handelsgeschichte des Altertums.* Vol. I. (1900) *passim* under the heads of various trade articles ; Vol. II. (1901), pp. 445—458.

For mediaeval commerce, Heyd, W. *Histoire du Commerce du Levant au Moyen Âge*, tr. by Furcy Raynaud. Paris and Leipzig, 1886. Vol. II. pp. 156—215, 365—407.

For the XVIIIth century, Peyssonel, *Traité du commerce de la Mer Noire.* Paris, 1787.

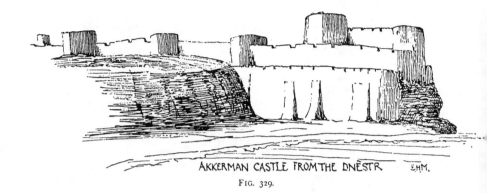

AKKERMAN CASTLE FROM THE DNESTR   EHM.

FIG. 329.

CHAPTER XIV.

TYRAS.

NORTH of the Danube the first Greek colony was Tyras. It has already been shewn (p. 14) that Tyras was at Akkerman, on the right side of the Dnêstr liman, about ten miles from its mouth, and that the statements of Strabo (VII. iii. 16) agree thereto. Ptolemy (III. x. 8) is troubled by conflicting data, the other authorities[1] are perfectly vague. Some confusion was caused by the existence of a second name for the city: Ophiussa. This was probably the real name superseded by that derived from the river and current in the mouths of strangers. Herodotus (IV. 51) mentions the Tyritae, but not the city, yet it was probably founded about the same time as Istrus and Olbia, in the middle of the VIIth century B.C. Its position at the mouth of a great river corresponds to that of the other Milesian colonies. But it never seems to have attained any distinction. It is mentioned rather as a geographical point than as a political entity. It must have had a certain amount of trade; what inscriptions we have deal with trade rather than politics, but that is all. Under certain conditions its position might have strategical importance, but those conditions were not present in ancient or in modern times; formerly it was overshadowed by Olbia, now by Odessa. The Romans may have had some regard for it during the period when it was under their sway, while Olbia still maintained a precarious independence. For that interval it was the last outpost of the power holding the upper Balkan peninsula. This was again its position in its time of greatness in the later Middle Ages, when there

---

[1] Ps.-Scylax, 68; Ps.-Scymnus, l. 803; Steph. Byz. s.v.; Anon. *Peripl.* § 88 (62); Mela II. i. 7; Pliny, *NH.* IV. 82 (26). Amm. Marc. XXII. viii. 41 derives Tyras from Tyros and talks of Phoenicians.

was no Olbia, and it was on the north-eastern frontier of Moldavia, fortified
to resist Russians and nomads alike.　At that time it was the great port
and fortress of the north-western Euxine, and its buildings were worthy of its
greatness.　It is still one of the most complete of mediaeval fortresses with
its keep, inner and outer bailey standing deserted but intact, and now
transferred to the care of the Odessa Archaeological Society. ·It remains
a monument to Genoese, Wallachs and Turks, who strengthened it in turn.
The present name due to the latter means White Fortress, in old Russian
Bêlgorod; the Genoese called it Moncastro.　General Bertier-de-La-Garde
says that it never was Genoese, that the inner and outer baileys were built
by Moldavians under Greek direction, and · the keep constructed by the
Turks when they took the place in 1484[1].

This great fortress has been the destruction of the Greek town, most
of whose site it must cover.　In von Stern's excavations Greek potsherds were
found mixed up with Chinese porcelain and Venetian glass in a way which
shewed that the area had been dug over again and again.　Hence the two
most important Tyras inscriptions were found far from the· town at Korotnoe
and Chobruchi, sixty and seventy miles up the river; and this led to doubt as
to the true site of the city.

The earlier of these[2] is the end of a decree conferring public honours
on one Cocceius, who had approached the Emperor on behalf of the town.
It is "sealed" by the Chief Archon (πρῶτος ἄρχων), four others, the proposer
(εἰσηγητής) and the leading citizens, passed by the Senate and People, executed
and enrolled by the Secretary in the third consulship of Commodus and
that of Antistius Burrus (181 A.D.), year 125 by the Era of Tyras, giving
56 A.D. as the starting-point for the latter.　The later inscription[3] gives a
letter from Ovinius Tertullus, legate of Lower Moesia, covering a letter to
him from the Emperors Severus and Caracalla and another to Heraclitus,
probably the procurator of the province.　The tenor of the correspondence
is that the citizens of Tyras have confirmed to them an immunity· from
customs of which they could not prove the origin, but which was supported
by letters of M. Aurelius and Antonius Hiberus, a predecessor of Tertullus.
But before future citizens whom they may elect can enjoy the privilege their
names must be submitted to the legate; that is a distinct encroachment on the
freedom of the city.　The inscription is dated in the consulship of Mucianus
and Fabianus (A.D. 201), in the 145th year of the Era of Tyras, in the
archonship of P. Aelius Calpurnius.　A very fragmentary inscription[4] mentions
freights, and stamps, and bankers(?), so it also deals with trade.　Fragments
of dedications we have, one in Latin for the preservation of Septimius Severus, Caracalla and Geta (his name erased as usual)[5], and one[6] giving the
name of Priscus the arch]on.　Another, ...ς Κρατίνου Σαράπιδι, Ἴσιδι,/
... θεοῖς συν(ν)άοις χαριστήριον[7], IInd or Ist century B.C., is the only inscription

---

[1] My sketch is very unsatisfactory but it is all
that I had time to make, and I have. never been
able to obtain a photograph of the fortress as seen
from the river.　There are some poor views in
Uvarov, *Recherches*, Pl. XXXII. to XXXV.

[2] App. 3=*IosPE*. I. 2.

[3] App. 4=*IosPE*. I. 3.

[4] *Trans. Od. Soc.* XXIII. p. 3, No. 2=*IosPE*.
IV. 452.

[5] *IosPE*. IV. 2.

[6] *IosPE*. IV. 453=*Trans. Od. Soc.* XXIII. p. 2,
No. 1.

[7] *IosPE*. ·IV. 1; cf. a dedication to Sarapis at
Istrus, Mommsen *R.G.* v. p. 284=*Prov. R.E.* I. p. 310.

that witnesses to the cults of Tyras. If only we had a faithful copy of it, another fragment, ΜΕΣΥΤΗΕΟΣ ΗΙΑΩΗΙΣ[1], might be of interest as it apparently belongs to an early stage in the development of the alphabet almost unrepresented to the north of the Euxine.

Such with the coins is the sum of our materials for the history of Tyras: the lost work of Poseidonius the Olbiopolite (v. p. 465) would have been welcome. Founded presumably in the VIIth century B.C., it was a colony of Miletus, as Scymnus (l. 803) tells us, and the names of the months Artemision and Leneon agree[2]. It has been suggested[3] that Pericles on his expedition to the Pontus in 444 B.C. made Tyras a member of the confederacy of Delos. Some town beginning with T paid a talent after 424 B.C., but there is not evidence enough to justify a restoration (cf. p. 561).

The city probably flourished until the coming of the Sarmatians, when it must have shared the harassments to which Olbia was exposed, falling under the power of native kings (v. p. 119). With Olbia on one side and the towns to the south on the other, it probably submitted to Mithridates (cf. the coin, Pl. I. 6), whose commander Neoptolemus may have founded Turris Neoptolemi at the mouth of the river. Like Olbia, no doubt it suffered from the Getae about 50 B.C., for Dio Chrysostom[4] says they took all the Greek cities on the left of the Pontus as far as Apollonia. During all this period it owed its existence to fishing in the liman, to corn growing on the lowlands by the river and to cattle raising on the steppes; perhaps also to viticulture such as now produces the excellent Bessarabian wine. Accordingly the most common head upon the autonomous coins is that of Demeter (Pl. I. 1—4), crowned with ears of corn, with a bull or a horse on the reverse. Other deities are Apollo (8—10) with a lyre, Athena (11) helmed with the bull, a river god with a fish (13, 14), Dionysus with cornucopia and a bunch of grapes (5—7), Asclepius with the snake upon an altar (12), and Hermes with his petasus and caduceus (Burachkov x. 25).

After the destruction by the Getae we cannot say what came to Tyras. It is tempting to think that it lay waste until 56 A.D., the year of its new era, and that then Ti. Plautius Silvanus, legate of Moesia, who later (about 62) extended his province and made Roman influence reach beyond the Borysthenes, raised the city from its ashes as a frontier defence to Moesia[5].

The retention of its old kalendar argues autonomy. Mommsen quotes many examples of town eras dating back to the year in which a city came definitely under the Roman suzerainty and was at once granted autonomy[6]. But there is a coin ascribed to Augustus (No. 15), and if the ascription be right the town must have been under Roman sway long before. Yet the account of Tomi given by Ovid would make us think that Tyras must have been untenable during the first decades of our era.

In any case we find the town under Roman protection, governed by its

[1] *IosPE*. I. 7; after L. Waxel, *Recueil d'Anti-quités*, No. 6.
[2] Latyshev in *IosPE*. I. 2, 3 and "Kalendars" in Ποντικά, p. 37.
[3] Latyshev, *Olbia*, p. 46 n. citing U. Köhler, "Urkunden u. Untersuch. z. Gesch. d. Delisch-Attischen Bundes," *Abh. d. k. Ak. d. W. zu Berlin*,

1869, pp. 74 and 164 sqq. V. App. 2 = *CIAtt.* I. 37, fr. z''''*7. He has also supplied Νικ[ωνία].
[4] *Or.* XXXVI. p. 49.
[5] App. I = *CIL.* XIV. No. 3608; cf. A. v. Domaszewski, "Die Dislocation des römischen Heeres im J. 66 n. Chr.", *Rhein. Mus.* 1892, p. 207.
[6] *R. Staatsrecht*, III. i. p. 707.

five archons, a senate and a popular assembly. Probably its constitution was much like that of Olbia. From the time of Domitian we have a regular series of Roman coins (Pl. I. 16—27) as far as Alexander Severus (d. 235). It can hardly be a coincidence that in his reign the Goths drew near to the Danube, which they crossed in 238 A.D., and began to cut short the coasts of the Roman Empire. The Tyrani enjoyed the confirmation of their free port not much more than thirty years. Zosimus (I. xlii. 1) expressly names their river as the base of a Gothic raid under Gallienus.

COINS. PLATE I.

Tyras did not begin to coin until the latter part of the ivth century B.C., the earliest coin known seems to be No. 1 (86 grn. = 5·57 grm. Aeginetic drachma *HN.*[2] p. 273), later silver coins are lighter, No. 2 weighs 80·1 grn. = 5·2 grm., and the didrachm, always rudely restruck, 144 grn. = 9·34 grm.

Æ. Head of Demeter r., wheatears in hair. | Horse-protome r. TYPA.

      Giel, *Kl.B.*, No. 3, B. x. 27 ; Orêshnikov, *Cat. Uvarov*, No. 1.

Later it even essayed a gold issue, a stater on the Lysimachean pattern.

N. 129·5 grn. = 8·4 grm. Head of deified Alex- | Pallas Nicephoros throned l. with spear and shield:
  ander, somewhat degraded r. | in exergue trident flanked by dolphins l.; in field
                                      | ΒΑΣΙΛΕΩΣ ΛΥΣΙΜΑΧΟΥ ; under throne TY.

    FIG. 329 *bis.* British Museum, unpublished, cf. *HN.*[2] p. 273. My special thanks are due to Mr G. F. Hill who shewed me the coin, discussed its date and gave me leave to publish it.

The southern neighbours of Tyras did the same and their issues fall into two groups according as the head on the obverse still remains that of Alexander, idealized or degraded, or has been assimilated to the features of Mithridates or Pharnaces[1]: this coin belongs to the ideal group; it may be put down to the late iiird or the iind century B.C.

Most Tyras types are here represented as the series at Odessa is specially rich, but it lacks two coins recalling types of native princes

Æ. Head of Hermes in petasus r. | Caduceus. TYPA.

    B. x. 25, *HN.*[1] p. 234, cf. Pl. III. 23 KAY, 24 Scilurus, Pick XIII. 11 Sarias, and inf. p. 487.

Æ. Head of Demeter under kerchief r. | Fish (?) vertical between two wheatstalks making
                                    | a square with ground line. TYPA.

    Hermitage, B. x. 23 (after von Grimm No. 2); Pick, XII. 16, cf. Pl. III. 20, Canites.

The general question of native kings and their coins touches Olbia more nearly than Tyras (v. p. 487, Pl. III. 20—27). Dionysus and the spread eagle (No. 6) looks Mithridatic (cf. Pl. VI. 8, 9, IX. 16, 17, 23). Of the imperial coppers specimens enough are given to represent each Emperor

---

[1] Pick, op. cit. pp. 64 n. 2, 91, 154, 170, Regling, ib. pp. 591, 606: to the first group belong No. 255, Callatis; Nos. 2471—2473, Pl. v. 6, Tomi: to the latter, Nos. 256—266, Callatis; No. 482, Pl. II. 27, Istrus; Nos. 2474—2486, Pl. XXI. 6, Tomi: cf. Panticapaean staters on this model inf. p. 583, Pl. VI. 19—21. The cities are distinguished by letters under the throne: KAΛ, IΣ, TO.

whose coins are known, the series extending from Domitian to Alexander Severus, and to shew that the types are thoroughly imperial. The coin assigned to Augustus (No. 15) might very well belong to some other town ; Pick does not seem to recognize it. Of the coins put down to Trajan by Jurgiewicz, J. 39 seems to be a poor specimen of No. 17, Hadrian; J. 40 one of the later ones with Heracles reverse.

BIBLIOGRAPHY.

History and Geography.

Becker, P. "Tyras and the Tyritae." *Trans. Od. Soc.* II. p. 416. I have not seen his *Civil Life of the Tyritae.* Odessa, 1849.
Bruun, Ph. "On the Site of Tyras." *Trans. Od. Soc.* III. p. 47 : *Chernomorje*, I. p. 3.
von Stern, E. R. "The Latest Excavations at Akkerman." *Trans. Od. Soc.* XXIII. p. 33.

Inscriptions.

App. 1—4. Becker and Bruun as above.
Jurgiewicz, W. N. "On the Inscription from Chobruchi." *Trans. Od. Soc.* XIII. p. 7.
IosPE. I. 2—7 (with summing up of previous literature), IV. 1—8, 452—455.
von Stern, E. R. "New Epigraphic Material from S. Russia." *Trans. Od. Soc.* XXIII. pp. 1—5, Nos. 1—4.
Latyshev, V. V. "On the Kalendars of Olbia, Tyras and Chersonesus Taurica." *Trans. VIth Russ. Archaeological Congress.* Odessa, 1888, II. p. 56=Ποντικά, p. 37.

Coins.

von Grimm, A. "Die Münzen von Tyras." *Berliner Blätter f. Münz- Siegel- u. Wappenkunde*, VI. (1868), p. 27.
Gardner, P. *British Museum Catalogue of Greek Coins, Thrace, &c.*, p. 13. London, 1877.
Burachkov, P. O. (B.). *General Catalogue of Coins belonging to the Greek Colonies on the N. Coast of the Euxine.* Pl. X.—XII. Odessa, 1884.
Giel, Ch. Ch. (G.). *Kleine Beiträge (Kl. B.) zur Antiken Numismatik Süd-Russlands*, p. 2. Moscow, 1886.
—— "New Additions to my Collection." *TRAS.* V. (1892), Pl. IV. 4, 5.
—— "Coins acquired in 1892, 1893." *TRAS.* VII. (1895), Pl. XVIII. 12—14.
Orêshnikov, A. V. *Catalogue of Antiquities belonging to Ct A. S. Uvarov.* Pt VII. "Coins of Greek Cities N. of the Euxine," pp. 1, 2, Nos. 1—7. Moscow, 1887.
von Sallet, A. *Beschr. d. ant. Münzen d. k. Museen zu Berlin*, I. pp. 31, 32. 1888.
Jurgiewicz, W. (J.). "The Coins of Tyras City." *Trans. Od. Soc.* XV. (1889), pp. 1—12, Pl. I.
Bruun, L. "Ueber die Münzen von T. unter Hadrian." *Zt. f. Numismatik*, XVI. (1888), p. 182.
Pick, B. (P.). *Die Antiken Münzen von Dacien und Moesien* I. Berlin, 1898. Pl. XII. 1—28, XIII. 1—12, p. 919. (Most complete but without the corresponding text.)
Head, B. V. *Historia Numorum (HN.)* [1] p. 234, [2] p. 273. Oxford, 1887, 1911.
Tyras is not included in Koehne's *Description du Musée Kotschoubey (MK).*

Akkerman.

Kochubinskij, A. A. "XV Century Stone Inscriptions from Bêlgorod now Akkerman." *Trans. Od. Soc.* XV. p. 506.
—— "Tura (Tyras)—Bêlgorod-Akkerman and its stone Inscription of 1454." ib. XXIII. p. 79.
—— "On the state of the Fortress of Akkerman." ib. XX. *Minutes*, p. 5.
von Stern, E. R. "An Expedition to Akkerman." ib. XIX. *Minutes*, p. 13.
—— "Latest Excavations at Akkerman," with Plan of Fortress. ib. XXIII. p. 33.
    Also short articles on various details in *Trans. Od. Soc.*
Bertier-de-La-Garde, A. L. "Report on the condition of the Fortress." ib. XXII. *Minutes*, p. 75.

FIG. 330. View of Olbia looking West.

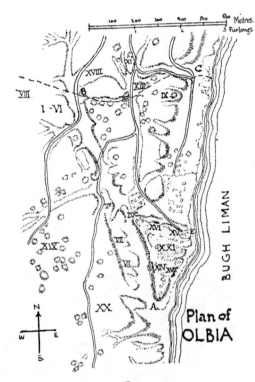

FIG. 331.

AB. Hare's Ravine.
BC, DE. Cross Ravines.
ABC. Extent of earlier town.
ADE. Extent of Acropolis and of Roman town.
VIII, *BC.* Line dividing Ct Musin-Pushkin's land from the common of Parutino.
D. Here six layers of remains going back to VI—VII cent. B.C.
E. Quay, Spring and Prytaneum (?); north of it River-wall and Tower. (*Arch. Anz.* 1910, p. 227; 1911, p. 212.)
I.–VI, VII—VII, XI, XVIII. Hellenistic and Roman Cemeteries.
VIII. Most ancient graves of VII—VI cent. B.C.
IX. Great Barrow with vault (v. p. 420): beneath it (1902–3), Hellenistic House: below all Polygonal wall (*BCA.* XIII.).
X. Corner of Roman City Wall; *CR.* 1902, p. 25.
XI. Barrow of Heuresibius (1900), v. p. 417 sqq., ff. 308, 309.
XII, XIII. Hellenistic Buildings: between them ancient gate and paved way (1907–8); *BCA.* XXXIII. p. 105, f. 2.
XIV. Ancient Town-walls and Roman Tower; *CR.* 1904, Pl. I.
XV, XVI. Town-walls and place of gate; *CR.* 1905, Pl. I.
XVII. Traces of Town-walls; *CR.* 1904, p. 3.
XIX, XX. Graves of vth and ivth cent. B.C. More such north of the boundary.
XXI. Large building on the Acropolis, perhaps a Temple.

CHAPTER XV.

OLBIA.

In the following sketch of Olbia its history and constitution I have been well content to follow Latyshev's "Olbia," of which von Stern says that it is the best of modern books dealing with our region. Therefore I have not given references every time I am indebted to him, but have rather indicated the few cases in which I have presumed to differ. I have accordingly paid less attention to older writers whose views were strangely fanciful, founded upon few inscriptions and very subjective judgements of coins. These vagaries have led our author to undervalue the style of coins as an evidence of date, and in the question of Scythian kings I have preferred to be guided by an experienced numismatist, A. V. Orêshnikov. New inscriptions found since the publication of Latyshev's work have thrown comparatively little fresh light on the history and constitution of Olbia, epigraphic material has been more important on the other sites, but it has added to our knowledge of the cults of Olbia even since the appearance of Miss G. M. Hirst's excellent papers. It is especially upon the purely archaeological side that most progress has been made, and our ideas of the first stages of the city's existence are decidedly more definite.

Olbia[1] is the clearest example of a Milesian colony which seems to have come into being gradually, having developed out of a trading factory.

Berezan.

At least there is a presumption that the early Greek settlement on the island Berezan was the factory surviving on its original site down to the vth century. Not that anything has been found there that can be definitely placed before the earliest finds on the mainland[2], for on both sites Ionian pottery (v. supra, p. 338), archaic terra-cottas and examples of the early Olbian *aes grave* have occurred. Nor indeed are we quite justified in calling Berezan an island, there is every probability that when first settled by the Greeks it was

---

[1] 'Ολβίη or 'Ολβία was the name the inhabitants gave to their city. They called themselves Olbiopolitae (Latyshev, *Olbia*, p. 33). Foreigners spoke of them as Borysthenitae, a name that they themselves kept for the natives dwelling along the river Borysthenes. This river-name was applied to the whole region and by strangers to the city, which is called by Herodotus Βορυσθενειτέων ἐμπόριον or πόλις. They themselves in a decree (App. 5 = *IosPE*. I. 11, early IVth cent. B.C.) apparently erected at the entrance of the Thracian Bosporus and directly concerning strangers and foreign currency in Olbia begin "These are the conditions of free entrance [Εἰς Βο]ρυσσθένη" which Latyshev says must mean the town, but it might well apply to the whole liman—to the port of Borysthenes in the wider sense.

Pliny, *NH*. IV. 82 (26) gives the forms Olbiopolis and Miletopolis which occur nowhere else (for the real Miletopolis near Cyzicus v. Hasluck, *Cyzicus*, p. 74), the former must have existed to account for Olbiopolitae: of the latter we can say nothing. In Anon. *Periplus* (86 (60)) we find 'Ολβία Σαβία, but this is mere dittography, OABIACABIA.

[2] Except perhaps a Geometric pot, *Arch. Anz.* 1910, p. 227, f. 27.

joined to the mainland[1]: geologically it is a piece of the South Russian steppe with cliffs all round and only one or two inconvenient landing places: it is about 1000 yards by 350 (900 × 320 m.), and some mile and a half ($2\frac{1}{2}$ km.) from the land: the sea in between is mostly only three feet deep and nowhere more than six: the island lost 28 yards (25 m.) in breadth in the last century and antiquities have been dredged up from the sea between it and the land, so the question merely seems one of the time when the separation took place. Strabo is the first to mention it as an island but says it had a harbour, which is certainly not the case now: he clearly distinguishes it from Leuce and so does Ptolemy, who calls it Borysthenis though he gives it a wrong position: but later writers hopelessly confuse the two. The suggestion of Papadhimitriu that the settlement upon it was the ἐμπόριον τῶν Βορυσθενεϊτέων of Herodotus (IV. 17), which ought to be right on the coast, would be attractive if it could be reconciled with the archaeological evidence, but von Stern will have it that continuous occupation ceased in the first decades of the vth century B.C. and the natural inference is that shortly before this the site had become detached from the mainland and consequently was no longer a convenient place for trading or living, so that it was finally deserted even by the fishing population:—perhaps the name survived for Herodotus as the traditional centre of the Scythian coast.

The early remains on Berezan fall into two classes, the necropolis and burial pits (v. supra, p. 415) and the houses: in both we can distinguish two periods, the first comprising the end of the VIIth and the first half of the VIth centuries B.C., the second the latter part of the VIth and the first decade or so of the vth. We have many house walls of both periods, the former distinguished by being set upon virgin soil or upon a specially prepared foundation of clay and ashes in layers, such as we also find at Olbia, the latter being built upon made ground, even over older refuse pits, but naturally more perfect; we have for instance the plan of a one-roomed dwelling with a verandah[2], and another with two rooms has walls standing 9 ft. 6 in. high, with door and window complete[3]. The earlier houses are built of larger stones than the later, and in connection with them we have the round foundations or θόλοι(?)[4]. One or two pits von Stern puts at the beginning of the early period as being pit-houses such as the first settlers occupied temporarily, roofing them with sails. In both settlements we find rubbish-pits about 5 ft. deep widening as they go down, store-pits with wider entrances and steps down to them and burial-pits close to or in the houses, as well as in the necropolis, and wells, round in the older, square in the newer

---

[1] Maps. *Trans. VIth Russian Arch. Congress,* Odessa, 1884, I. p. 216, R. A. Prendel, "Archaeological Investigations on the Island Berezan." *CR.* 1907, p. 71, f. 60. History. Bruun, *Chernomorje,* I. p. 14 identified it with the Island of S. Aetherius: this is denied by Latyshev, Ποντικά, p. 285, v. supra, p. 16, n. 3. Ph. Kovalevskij, *Trans. Od. Soc.* XXVI. *Minutes,* No. 361, p. 48 relates its modern military history: S. D. Papadhimitriu, ib. XXIX. p. 97, re-examines the ancient accounts of it. For its connexion with the cult of Achilles Pontarches, v. inf. p. 480. For the pots therefrom bought of Fr. Levitskij and M. Voitinas v. *CR.* 1901, p. 133; 1903, pp. 152, 153, ff. 303, 304; *BCA.* XXXVII. p. 81; for a Naucratis cylix, *BCA.* XL. pp. 142—158; scarabs and beads, ib. pp. 118—120. The first excavations after Prendel's were G. L. Skadovskij's, in 1900 and 1901, to be published with Levitskij's pots in a number of *Mat.* but meanwhile summarized by Pharmacovskij in *Arch. Anz.* 1904, p. 105 and E. von Stern in *Trans. Od. Soc.* XXIII. *Minutes,* p. 88. In these same *Minutes,* XXV. p. 97; XXVII. p. 68; XXVIII. pp. 46, 137; XXIX. pp. 39, 80, von Stern publishes his own excavations from 1902 on; and his reports in good time come out in *CR.* from 1904 on: meanwhile Pharmacovskij summarizes them in *Arch. Anz.* 1905, p. 61; 1906, p. 117; 1907, p. 144; 1908, p. 177; 1909, p. 161; 1910, p. 223; 1911, pp. 228—234, ff. 38—41.

[2] *Trans. Od. Soc.* XXIX. *Minutes,* p. 39.

[3] ib. p. 89, Plan B[8].

[4] *CR.* 1906, p. 51, f. 64.

period.   Further points of distinction are that arrow-heads are mostly flat
(four-sided, v. p. 190, f. 82) in the older, triangular in the newer stratum, and
most important of all the presence of Milesian and other Ionian pottery in the
older layer and of Attic down to the "severe" style in the later (v. p. 338).
These enable the various strata to be dated so confidently.   There is a period
before fish-coins or triangular arrow-heads and with very few black-figured
Attic sherds[1].   The occurrence of the coins when they appear is interesting:
the fish, scattered, in lumps or held in the hand of the dead, among them two of
a new flat-fish type, begin in what is still the first period; the *aes grave*, archaic
Medusa and Pallas, only comes in the later and with it occasionally smaller
pieces of the same type (v. Pl. II.).

From early in the vth century Berezan has ceased to be a place of
permanent habitation.   In spite of considerable excavations hardly anything
of later date has been found upon it, a few amphora necks, a few Roman lamps,
a piece of glass of the IInd century B.C. and several inscriptions to Achilles
Pontarches (e.g. App. 13), but other such were found at Bejkush on the coast
opposite, as well as at Olbia: there can hardly have been three temples to him,
though if there were one on Berezan it would help the confusion with Leuce
in the later authors and might be regarded as the oldest shrine of the community,
unless indeed it was a mere substitute for the temple on Leuce of which the
Olbiopolites may have lost the patronage after the IVth century B.C.   In more
recent times we have to note but a Swedish Runic inscription to the memory
of a Variag[2], a few Cossack pipes, the Turkish fortifications and the monument
to a French lieutenant dating from the Crimean War.

But the island or peninsula is *a priori* the point on which foreign traders
who were not sure of their ground would fix: whereas the inconvenience of the
site once they had established satisfactory relations with the natives would soon
lead them to open an agency on the mainland and this would gradually supersede
the first site, especially if its harbour was spoilt and its communication with the
land cut off.

Olbia.   Site and Excavations.

The site of Olbia itself is perfectly clear.   The city stood on the right bank
of the Bugh liman, there about three miles broad, at a point about a mile south
of the village of Parutino.   About four miles below the city the liman opens
into that of the Dnêpr or rather into a common estuary some nine miles across.
If we follow this common estuary eastwards about nine miles from the mouth of
the Bugh it is narrowed by a sharp promontory Cape Stanislav, and beyond
begins the Dnêpr liman proper.   This Cape Stanislav must be the Cape of
Hippolaus mentioned by Herodotus (IV. 53) and Dio as running out between
the Hypanis and Borysthenes rivers.   From the mouth of the Bugh to the
narrow entrance by Ocháckov is about twenty miles (32 km.), but as was said
before the wide estuaries with shifting channels make it hard to give exact
distances from point to point in any less summary way than measuring them
upon the map (v. supra, p. 15).

Upon the Cape of Hippolaus Herodotus says there was a temple of

---

[1] *Trans. Od. Soc.* XXIX. *Minutes*, p. 88.   [2] *BCA.* XXIII. p. 66.

Demeter (v.l. Μητρός), and Bruun thought that he had found its site a mile to the north of the actual headland[1], but no certain remains have been investigated. At other points in the environs (e.g. Hadzhi Göl, Kisljakovka and Kotseruba and at Bejkush on the Berezan liman) coins and traces of habitation have been reported but no such site has been thoroughly explored; at Nicolaevka a little below Berislav on the Dnêpr was a town of Roman date[2].

The ground covered by the city itself is triangular in shape, the apex pointing to the south. On the west side is a considerable ravine (Hare's Dell, Zájachia Balka, *BDA* on the plan). To the east was the Bugh liman. The northern boundary varied according to the prosperity of the city.

The triangle *ADE* always remained populated. In Greek times it may have formed an acropolis, but only one of its surrounding walls (at xiv on f. 331) can be certainly referred to an early date: in Roman times it contained the whole city and was duly fortified with massive walls (xiv, xv, xvii), in places reaching the enormous thickness of 13 ft. 5 in. (4·70 m.); at xiv they were strengthened by a great tower, 82 × 33 ft. (25 × 10 m.), in the iind or iiird century A.D.; near xvi was a gate of which nothing is left. The work was of three periods; good masonry with a face of massive headers and stretchers having been repaired with poorer work and again patched up very roughly[3].

In Greek times the city stretched as far as the line *BC*. Along the Hare's Dell north of *D* so far no walls have been found, but to the north of *E* are foundations of a piece of river-wall with a tower[4] and along the south side of the ravine *BC* the early settlers seem to have dug a trench which no doubt had a palisade on its inside. Later on a splendid wall was built on the very edge of the ravine north of the trench and the latter was filled up and its site built over. This wall has lost all its facing and almost all its material but has been traced by its foundations 16 ft. (5 m.) thick, built in layers of clay and of charcoal with cinders alternately, a combination which hardens into rock-like consistency. Such foundations were found in the oldest deposits of Berezan and continued in use in Hellenistic Olbia, inasmuch as its natural soil the *loess* is very friable. For this technique Pharmaçovskij quotes the accounts of charcoal under the foundations of the temple at Ephesus[5]. Between xii and xiii were the traces of an early tower and the remains of another with great facing stones: between them was the site of the main gates and a patch of pavement. Cut into the foundations of one tower was a tomb with Attic pots of the ivth century B.C. shewing that the tower must be yet older. In its position the tomb is just comparable to that in the wall at Chersonese (v. inf., p. 499). Another interesting thing about it is that it is covered with a true vault[6]. Here then were the walls and towers that Protogenes repaired (v. inf., p. 461) and of which Dio Chrysostom saw the remains far out in the country. The upper part of the walls was of sun-dried brick and nearly all the solid material went to build the Roman Olbia, and so they lay hid till quite lately.

[1] *Trans. Od. Soc.* v. p. 991.
[2] *BCA.* xxxiv. *Suppl.* p. 140.
[3] *CR.* 1904, pp. 11, 12, ff. 6, 7, 9, Pl. I. (plan of Tower xiv); *Arch. Anz.* 1905, p. 63; 1906, p. 118; 1907, p. 146; *Hermes* (Russian), 1907, p. 19.
[4] *Arch. Anz.* 1911, pp. 211—220 ff. 24, 25.
[5] Diog. Laert. ii. ix. 19; Pliny, *NH.* xxxvi. 95 (21).

[6] Pharmaçovskij has only given a general account of the trench and walls found in 1907 in *Hermes*, 1907, pp. 45–49, 68–70; *CR.* 1907, p. 7 sqq.; *Arch. Anz.* 1908, p. 180; 1909, p. 162; plan, *BCA.* xxxiii. p. 105, f. 2. In the trench was a terra-cotta mould for a woman's face perhaps taken from a work of Calamis, *BCA.* xl. pp. 121—129.

Near *E* is a spring and a considerable space of low ground suitable for beaching ancient ships: under water are the remains of a mole: round about most of the coins are picked up and this was presumably the site of the commercial district.   Here two streets met, one along the back of the river-wall, the other running inland.   Six layers of débris have been distinguished : the sixth or lowest only goes back to the IInd century B.C. and stands in marshy soil.   To the fifth layer belong buildings round a peristyle court (p. 457): on the analogy of the Prytaneum at Priene[1] Pharmacovskij has suggested that they served the same purpose, but he prefers to speak of them as a house: the big supporting wall to the south might be the boundary of the Ecclesiasterium[2].

The city was thickly inhabited right up to the Greek wall.   Excavations on the spots marked IX, XII and XIII shewed foundations of Hellenistic buildings and under those at IX (p. 456) Pharmacovskij unearthed a wall of polygonal masonry that he refers to the archaic period[3].   In Roman times on this very spot was reared a great barrow (v. p. 420), proof positive that by then this area was without the city boundary.   At that time it seems to have been waste land.

Some idea of the changes the city's area underwent may be gleaned from the positions of the burying places of different ages.   It is remarkable that the older the graves the farther they are from the town.   This points to the greatest period of the town having been in the VIIth and VIth centuries B.C. when people went.as far afield as VIII to bury and even across to the next ravine parallel to Hare's Dell.   Less remote are the graves of the Vth and IVth centuries about XIX and XX and to the north on the site of Parutino.   Still closer in were the Hellenistic graves I—VI, VII, and XVIII, whereas Roman interments trespassed on the Hellenistic city.   The time of greatest expansion in Olbia would accordingly coincide with the time of close and often very friendly relations with the Scythic power to which Herodotus and the spoils of Scythic graves with their strong Ionian influence alike bear witness.   This supposes an extremely rapid growth at the very first, which is just what we do see in successful colonies.   Uvarov was not wrong in the main, *BC* really was the line of the old walls although the towers that he found along it have proved to be but barrows IX and XI with retaining walls of masonry.   The many other barrows all about have given the place its name of the Hundred Barrows.

The advantages of the site do not seem very obvious; the chief attraction seems to have been the low-lying space of shore upon which ships could be drawn up, commanded as it was by higher ground itself defended by the ravine on the further side.   Probably too the channel of the Bugh was in ancient times favourable to Olbia: of the alternative sites which suggest themselves, Nicolaev was too far up country, Kherson channel has never been good and there must have been some special reason against Ocháakov, which when in hostile hands was undoubtedly a thorn in the side of Olbia.   Dio Chrysostom[4] says that in his time it belonged to the queen of the Sauromatae.   Be this as it may it was Olbia that the Milesians chose as the point which could control the trade routes of the Hypanis and Borysthenes and become the chief emporium of the North Western Euxine.

---

[1] Wiegand-Schrader, p. 231 sqq.   [3] *CR.* 1903, p. 17, f. 15.
[2] *Arch. Anz.* 1910, pp. 227—234, ff. 28, 29, 32.   [4] *Or.* XXXVI. p. 49.

Until this century the site of Olbia, though ascertained in the time of Pallas, has not been fortunate archaeologically.   The northern necropolis was part of the communal property of the village of Parutino, and was exposed to every kind of predatory digging.   To the south of the line VIII *BC* the main area belongs to Count Musin-Pushkin whose predecessors refused to allow scientific digging while taking insufficient steps to prevent the raids of the Parutino peasants.   Hence the bulk of the inscriptions and objects discovered have lost half their value through their exact place of finding not being known. Even the occasional attempts of archaeologists were unsystematic and ill recorded.   But a new era opened with the advent of Mr Pharmacovskij in 1901 and the conclusion of an agreement between the Archaeological Commission and the owners of the soil.   The opening up of the walls described above gives us the position of the acropolis and the limits of the Roman town.   In the middle of the triangle have been found the remains of a considerable building apparently a temple, and further work may tell us where were the temples of Zeus Olbios and the chapel of Achilles Pontarches. Several inscriptions found to the north of the inner walls indicate the probable position of the temple of Apollo Prostates.

The point whose exploration has been of most interest is that marked IX. This was rendered conspicuous by the great barrow with its chamber and plinth of masonry described above.   Below three layers which had to do with the barrow and so were dated in the IInd century A.D., Pharmacovskij found four others.   The lowest is only represented by a fragment of polygonal masonry referred to the archaic period.   The two layers above this were Hellenistic but the buildings in them were too fragmentary to tell us much except that they were dwelling houses[1].

From the fourth layer, though much disturbed by the heaping up of the barrow, still could be made out the plan of a Hellenistic house.   A comparison of its arrangements with those of other Greek houses shews that it comes between the earlier houses at Priene of the IIIrd century B.C. and that described by Vitruvius which seems to lead on to the Delian type of the Ist century B.C. It is specially close to that called by Vitruvius (VI. 7 (10)) Rhodian.   This as well as the details of style point to the middle of the IInd century B.C.[2]

The house consisted of two systems of chambers each surrounding its court.   Of one not very much is left but of the other a most attractive restoration has been made.   It is just the moment in evolution of the Greek house before the peristyle becomes the same on all four sides.   In our example whereas three sides of the square have each four ordinary Ionic columns, making five spaces, the west has a façade of two stories; the upper is Corinthian having antae with two columns between, while below are two Ionic columns flanked by antae forming what Vitruvius calls the prostas, and again antae at the corners of the court.   The court was paved with cobbles, the centre having a square panel of primitive mosaic made of unshaped pebbles. The design consisted of a circle whose content has perished inscribed in a square, the spandrels being filled with palmettes, the frame outside has a frieze

[1] *BCA*. XIII. Pl. IV. and pp. 98—110.
[2] For a most detailed account of this house, v. *BCA*. XIII. pp. 37—98.   Plans, Pl. VI, VII, X; re-

storations Pl. XI, XII, and *CR*. 1903, pp. 8 sqq. Cf. *Arch. Anz.* 1904, p. 103 with pictures of the mosaic.

of animals arranged in pairs each looking towards a palmette, on each side two winged lions, a lion and a boar and two panthers. The outermost member of the frame is a wave-pattern, broken in the middle of the north and south sides by paths leading out of the centre across the plain pavement to the colonnade. East of the court was a long chamber with a fine view over the Bugh, perhaps a spring and autumn dining room. To the south were large spaces which have not been fully explored owing to the desirability of leaving some part of the barrow untouched. One of them, however, yielded the three precious heads of Asclepius, Hygiea (p. 292, f. 208) and Eros (?). Beyond the north wall of the court was apparently a blank wall.

The entrance was from the NE. An alley ended in a vestibule which led by a narrow passage into the north walk of the peristyle. The narrowing of the passage gave space for a porter's niche between the corner pier and the north anta of the prostas or east face of the house which made the west side of the court. This prostas led into two considerable rooms which with those above them made the chief part of this division of the house. These reception rooms were plastered and painted in the first Pompeian style to imitate marble panelling. To the south were three rooms of one story only ; one of them, which came at the SE. corner of the court, had a great cistern beneath it, fed from the converging roofs of the whole complex of buildings. Further to the west was a store room with seven great pithoi.

The orientation of the house is interesting. In Greece the prostas would have looked south as Vitruvius recommends. But in Olbia that would have made it unbearably hot in summer without there being much gain of warmth in winter. A western aspect is exposed to bad winds off the steppe whereas the breezes from the Bugh are pleasant. Hence the eastern aspect of the prostas. Vitruvius mentions that special arrangements were necessary in the Pontus.* What appliances they had for artificial heat does not appear. The winter snow determined the steep pitch of the roof, about 20°, as we know from a ridge tile[1].

This house was built upon banded foundations of clay and ashes carried right down to virgin earth : hence its erection meant great disturbance of all lower layers. The duration of its existence, about a century, is marked by the lettering of the astynomus stamps on its tiles. It perished by fire towards 50 B.C. ; evidently it succumbed to the Getic storm.

The heaping up of the barrow again disturbed the soil, hence in its mass and in the layers below it are found pottery fragments of all possible periods, beginning with Ionian, through black- and red-figured Attic of various styles to Hellenistic and Roman products, also terra-cottas of corresponding dates. This confusion makes it hard to place particular strata but gives us the right to infer that the site was continuously inhabited from the VIIth century B.C.[2]

The house at *E*, the prytaneum (?), is a little later in date, the peristyle, an irregular oblong with five and four columns a side, being without a prostas; in the middle was an altar once surmounted by a tripod. The entrance was through a vestibule from the street behind the river-wall, and into this the peristyle drained. Between the street and the court was a handsome room

[1] *BCA*. XIII. p. 65, f. 36.   [2] ib. pp. 185—231, v. supra, p. 339.

partly paved with pebble-mosaic like the former in technique, but with simpler patterns—wave, maeander and guilloche : on it was another little altar and terra-cottas of Cybele and a priestess[1]. Destroyed in the Getan sack this house was patched up immediately and again burnt.

History.

The date assigned by Eusebius to the foundation of Olbia (Ol. 33. 2, B.C. 647–6) thus quite agrees with the archaeological evidence[2].   But regard being had to what has been said above about the gradual growth of the factory definite dates are clearly out of place (v. supra, p. 453).

The history of Olbia is divided into two parts at the destruction of the city by the Getae in the middle of the ist century B.C.   During the first part it is that of a typical Greek town, at first prosperous, later on hard pressed by the surrounding tribes, probably more or less tributary to barbarian chieftains, but essentially Greek.   During the later period its population had accepted a strong barbarian element and the town existed at first on sufferance, later by the support of Rome, but there was some connexion with the former inhabitants, it was not an entirely new community upon the old site, for the old personal names lived on though mixed with foreign ones, the Greek language survived in some form, and the institutions (e.g. the names of the months) still shew a resemblance to those of Miletus and her colonies.

During the vith and vth centuries B C. we cannot say that we know any definite events of Olbian history.   Herodotus gives us stories of the relations between the Scythian kings and the Olbiopolites from which we may gather that the princes were attracted by the higher civilization, its conveniences and its pleasures, and established friendly and even intimate relations with the Greeks, whereas the mass of the nation having less chance of enjoying all this was less well-disposed.   But to make the most of every detail of these stories and argue as to the state of architecture in Olbia because the house of Scyles was adorned with sphinxes and griffins, as to its fortifications and sallyports because from a tower a citizen shewed the Scyths their king making one of a Bacchic thiasus, or judge of the size of the town because Scyles could leave his "army" in the προαστεῖον, is to take too literally the stories of Tymnes.   But we can conclude that the Borysthenites had friendly dealings with a fairly powerful nation which proved a very good customer for all their Greek wares.

How the expedition of Darius affected Olbia we do not hear. Presumably it was a source of anxiety and nothing more.   More serious was the expedition of Pericles into the Pontus. Its main effects were probably to strengthen Athenian commerce in this region, from the middle of the vth century the Attic pots come in again (v. p. 339), whether Olbia were enrolled in the Delian confederation we cannot say.   In the new list set out in 424 B.C. there is a town beginning with O (App. 2, cf. pp. 447, 561) but it only paid a talent which is no more than Nymphaeum and perhaps Tyras paid.   From this period we have three epitaphs, the earliest was found beyond the Hares' Dell[3], and also the coins EMINAKO (v. p. 487) who may have been a foreign ruler.

[1] *Arch. Anz.* 1910, pp. 228—234, ff. 28—30; 1911, pp. 207—220, ff..18—23.
[2] Schoene following B gives Ol. 33. 4 but the Oxford MS. seems with A and P to turn the scale against it ; perhaps 33. 3 of F is right: Scaliger gave Ol. 31. 3, B.C. 654 ; cf. Latyshev, *Olbia*, p. 38, n. 2.
[3] App. 4ᵃ=*IosPE.* I. 120 (facs. IV. p. 275 = Roehl, *I. Gr. Antiquissimae*[3], No. 48, perhaps the oldest

From the ivth century a few inscriptions have survived, mostly epitaphs and grants of proxeny[1] to foreigners, Chaerigenes of Mesembria, Hellanicus of Rhodes (?), Nautimus of Callatis and a Dionysius whose city cannot be read. This last stone was found at Chersonese. All this points to lively intercourse with other trading cities.

A decree found at the temple of Zeus Urius at the entrance of the Thracian Bosporus gives regulations for the treatment of foreign money at Olbia[2], directing that all copper and silver and gold other than that of Cyzicus should be exchanged against Olbian currency according to the market and that such transactions should take place "upon the stone in the ecclesiasterium" upon pain of confiscation of the amount in question: but Cyzicene gold (or rather electrum) staters were fixed at 10½ staters (Olbian silver like Pl. iii. 2)[3].

Cyzicene staters have been found in Olbia and in later times their place was taken by those of the Macedonian kings. So far only one autonomous Olbian gold stater (just like Pl. iii. 2) has been discovered[4]. It seems clear that the Olbiopolites mostly used foreign gold such as the Alexanders and Lysimachi, at least a thousand of which were found at Anadol in Bessarabia[5], and that this is meant by the gold pieces mentioned in the decrees thanking Callinicus and later Protogenes (v. inf. pp. 460—462 and 485).

This decree in honour of Callinicus son of Euxenus[6] in the ivth century records the bestowal by the grateful people of praise and a wreath worth a thousand gold pieces to be presented in the theatre at the Dionysia and the setting up of a statue. But what Callinicus had done to deserve this is lost.

The one event in this century for which we have a literary source is a siege of Olbia by Zopyrion recorded by Macrobius[7], for the sake of the extreme measures taken by the citizens to rally to themselves all possible defenders. They set slaves free, gave foreigners the citizenship and cancelled all debts. This means that they must have been reduced to great straits, either that the city was not in a position to resist an attack or that the forces of the invader were overwhelming; in any case the shock to the city's prosperity must have been serious. Almost certainly this Zopyrion was the governor left by Alexander in Thrace after his reduction of that country and his demonstration against the Getae across the Danube. Zopyrion wishing to distinguish himself went farther whether against Getae or Scythians (v. p. 123) and was destroyed with 30,000 men. But what the mutual relations of Olbia, the Scythians, the Getae and Zopyrion may have been we cannot make clear. Also the date of the occurrence is doubtful, Justin says Alexander heard the news just after Arbela, Q. Curtius, when he had returned from India to Persia: and Curtius says that Zopyrion perished in a storm, presumably on shipboard:

N. of the Euxine, cf. pp. 447, 560, 618), *IosPE.* iv. 28 and *Trans. Od. Soc.* xxiv. *Minutes*, p. 39.
[1] *IosPE.* i. 8—10, 14, 15. *BCA.* x. p. i, No. 1.
[2] App. 5=*IosPE.* i. 11.
[3] Latyshev, *Olbia*, p. 48 n. quotes Dittenberger, *Hermes*, xvi. p. 189, cf. *Sylloge*[2], ii. 546. Bertier-de-La-Garde, "Comparative Values," p. 54 sqq. after considering the amount of gold in a Cyzicene and of silver in an Olbian stater declares that this decree put a premium of about 2½ per cent on Cyzicenes

in order to attract gold in its then most general form to the Olbian market.
[4] Burachkov, p. 64, No. 167, Pl. viii. 201, Pick, ix. 1, now at Brussels: a dozen ¼ staters are known, v. p. 485, Pl. iii. 1.
[5] *BCA.* iii. p. 58.   [6] *IosPE.* i. 12.
[7] *Saturnalia*, i. xi. 33. Borysthenitae, obpugnante Zopyrione, servis liberatis dataque civitate peregrinis et factis tabulis novis hostem sustinere potuerunt.

but a governor of Thrace would not want ships to attack the Getae, whereas they would be invaluable against Olbia of which the river side was not fully defended until the time of Protogenes. Bertier-de-La-Garde[1] refuses to believe in the siege of Zopyrion saying that you cannot besiege an unwalled town, but part of the circuit had been completed in stone and the rest was no doubt defended by walls of crude brick or a palisade and ditch for which very likely Protogenes substituted stone. Grote (XII. p. 299) regards Zopyrion as an unknown person and declines to fix any date for his attack upon Olbia.

To the end of the IVth century belongs a tantalizing inscription[2], in praise of a man who appears to have brought the citizens to one mind by arranging an impartial compromise. Presumably there had been a faction fight. Perhaps when the danger from Zopyrion had passed there were difficulties between the old and the newly enfranchised citizens. But this discord may have to do with the subsequent decadence.

Protogenes.

After the attack by Zopyrion, Olbia appears to have begun to decay. Circumstances were no longer favourable. Her customers in European and Asiatic Greece had mostly fallen on evil times, mixed up in the rivalries of various dynasts, or had diverted their attention to the richer regions of Asia laid open to them by the conquests of Alexander. For instance the steady corn production of Egypt must have competed fatally with the fluctuating exports of South Russia. Worse than this, changes in the population of the interior interrupted the trade routes, ruined the Scyth power with which Olbia had established tolerable relations, so that the remnants were driven to encroach upon Olbian territory, and brought new foes from East and West.

This decadence is fully illustrated by the decree in honour of Protogenes to which reference has already been made. It is perhaps the most important epigraphic document from the Scythian region[3].

Its interest may be grouped under two heads, the information it affords as to the tribes surrounding Olbia and her relations with them and the internal economic questions of providing money to buy off these tribes, to fortify the town against them, and to relieve the distress of the citizens due to these exactions and to bad harvests.

The tribes mentioned in the inscription have been already dealt with (p. 118 sqq.[4]). Towards them Olbia stands in no pleasant relation. We hear most of a King Saitapharnes to whom one year the Olbiopolites give four hundred gold pieces (for the question as to what coins are meant, v. p. 459), provided by Protogenes, another year he paid other four hundred pieces to the Saii, perhaps the tribe of which Saitapharnes was king, soon after some part of 1500 gold pieces was spent on "douceurs" ($\epsilon\theta\epsilon\rho\alpha\pi\epsilon\dot{\nu}\theta\eta\sigma\alpha\nu$) to lesser chiefs ($\sigma\kappa\eta\pi\tau o\hat{\nu}\chi o\iota$) and the advantageous preparation of gifts for the king.

---

[1] *Comparative Values*, p. 86, n. 2.

[2] *IosPE.* IV. 456 = *Trans. Od. Soc.* XXIII. p. 9, No. 6.

[3] App. 7. For a full commentary see Boeckh, *CIG.* II. 2058; *IosPE.* I. 16; Schmidt, *Rh. Mus.* IV. (1836), pp. 357 sqq., 571 sqq., and Dittenberger, *Syll.*[2] I. 226.

[4] Braun, *Investigations*, I. pp. 89, 102 sqq., 117, 129, v. supra, pp. 125, 126, puts the inscription in the IInd cent. to suit his theory that the Galatae were the Kelts afterwards known as the Britolagae on the Danube, but originally from further north. Niederle, *Slav. Ant.* I. pp. 303—311, after stating all views comes to no conclusion.

This phrase suggests that the gifts were not merely money (as was said by some in discussing the famous tiara) but money's worth which could be got cheap or dear according to circumstances. Saitapharnes would have been much pleased with Rachumowski's work had it been executed in time. Fitting out an embassy to the king cost 300 gold pieces and could hardly be done for that. Later Protogenes himself went on an embassy to the king and offered him 900 gold pieces—Latyshev suggests that this was two years' tribute with an extra hundred to make up—but he was not satisfied, found fault with the gifts and prepared for war : here the narrative breaks off; but Protogenes had spent 2000 gold pieces on embassies and gifts, besides the 1500 for general purposes most of which went the same way.

On the other side of the stone we find that worse foes have appeared, Galatae and Sciri, and that in fear of them the Thisamatae, Scythae and Saudaratae try to take shelter in the city walls, driving its inhabitants to despair and to the desertion of the city. Also their allies the Mixhellenes to the number of 1500 and all their slaves turn against them. We do not quite see where Saitapharnes and the Saii come in. It is likely that they were on the eastern side of the Hypanis and even of the Borysthenes and so more or less safe. We have no means of saying where Cancytus may have been and τὸ πέραν might conceivably be the Hylaea and the parts beyond, where Herodotus puts the Scythae Nomades, whereas the other tribes were probably to the west and north exposed to the new comers. In any case the danger seems to have passed away after rousing the town to complete its fortifications along the river bank.

The most pressing need was the want of two stretches of wall along the river, that by the harbour and that by the old fish-market. All this Protogenes had to undertake at a cost of 1500 gold pieces; next we are told of five towers restored by him, two by the great gate (v. p. 454), Cathegetor Tower, Waggon-way Tower and Epidaurius Tower, he also built up the three curtain walls (σχοινιαία) between them and he completed another piece of wall from the Tower of Posis to the upper place (this cost a hundred gold pieces), besides building the grain store and the bazaar gateway[1]. All this in the face of difficulties with the contractors so that he had to take the work over himself and repair at a cost of 200 gold pieces the barges kept by the city for the transport of stone. That makes a total of 1800 gold pieces spent upon buildings.

Still larger amounts went to the meeting of other calls on the treasury mostly in times of famine. To begin with Protogenes redeemed for 100 gold pieces the sacred plate of the city which the foreign creditor was just taking to be melted down : next year he paid 300 for a cheap lot of wine bought by the archons under Democon : the following year he sacrificed 200 by selling 2000 medimni of corn at half price. When elected one of the Nine he offered 1500, much of which went in gifts to chiefs. The following harvest was again bad, Protogenes advanced 1000, 300 without interest for a year: he was repaid at the rate of 400 coppers evidently at a loss (v. p. 483). The same year he sold 2500 medimni of corn making an abatement of about

---

[1] See Bertier-de-La-Garde on these walls, *Comparative Values*, p. 86, n. 2.

2270 gold pieces[1]. That amounts to about 4400 making no allowance for loss of interest or on copper repayments. In some of these transactions it is not clear whether the town intended repayment or took as a gift the sum provided. But this does not make much difference as the inscription represents Protogenes as cancelling the debts due to himself from the city by the singular process of crediting it with non-existent surpluses and applying these to the extinction of its debts to himself. All this he did during three years as "financial director of the city's affairs," in the course of which time he used no harsh measures against the tax-farmers, but let them pay at their own convenience, while he submitted to the people at due seasons accounts falsified for the city's benefit. Yet the city proceeds to ask him to sacrifice private debts due to him and to his father amounting to 6000 gold pieces and to remit interest due upon them. In all, then, he spent about 9200 gold pieces on the town of which we seem to hear of 2500 being paid back, though with loss of interest and at a lower rate of exchange: that makes 6700 in public bene-factions and the 6000 of private debts brings the total up to 12,700 gold pieces, a colossal sum. The question that rouses most wonder is how Protogenes and his forbears amassed a fortune from which they could make such sacrifices; whereas no one else in the town is represented as ready or able to help at all[2]. Yet we have another inscription of about the same date, the peculiar lettering is almost identical, saying[3] "Cleombrotus son of Pantacles saw to the building of the Gate and Curtainwall," and the same Cleombrotus[4] dedicates a tower to Heracles with six bombastic elegiac couplets. This man, his converse Pantacles son of Cleombrotus (if this is his father we have the base of his statue dedicated by the people to Heracles, the lettering is a good deal older)[5], Heroson son of Protogenes converse to the hero of the great inscription, two Aristocrates (the name of Protogenes's colleague as envoy to Saitapharnes) and several sons of Aristocrates, several sons of Herodorus, the name of an eponymous priest during his activity, further Heuresibius son of Demetrius, who on *IosPE*. I. 105 made a dedication to Zeus the King, and Agrotas who with his brother Posideus set up a statue to their father Dionysius priest of Apollo Delphinius[6], are all mentioned on a list of citizens[7]. Further Posideus son of Dionysius an Olbiopolite receives proxeny in an inscription at Delos dated about 180 A.D.[8]

This means that unless we have been misled by the customary repetition of ancestral names all these men belong to the first half of the IInd century B.C. Latyshev, who believes that the Galatae mentioned are the forces of the

---

[1] The first dearth runs up the price of corn to ⅔ of a gold piece for a medimnus; P. sells for ₇/₁₀. Next time it goes up to ⅔ and even to 1⅖, P. sells for ₇/₁₆ and ⅓⅔. If we take the gold piece to be an Attic stater of Lysimachus or Alexander, 1⅝ would be about 136 shillings a quarter. Bertier-de-La-Garde (*Comparative Values*, &c. p. 65) says this is an impossible price and supposes the gold pieces to be such as Pl. III. 1 or rather electrum hects of Cyzicus reducing the sums to a fifth of the above, but failure of crops can be absolute in S. Russia and if the exchange of which Polybius speaks (IV. 38, v. p. 440) were prevented siege prices would naturally rule, much higher than anything at Athens, to which all the corn of the Greek world gravitated.

[2] If I were inclined to wild hypotheses I should suggest that Protogenes was really a tyrant who had come into power on the shoulders of the democracy after a rising against an oligarchy devoted to Heracles, dedications to whom by Cleombrotus and Nicodromus, *IosPE*. IV. 459, had been defaced by the people: if not a political tyrant P. must have been a commercial monopolist for he had evidently concentrated into his hands all the money in the town. No doubt he ruled through democratic forms.

[3] *IosPE*. I. 100.   [4] ib. I. 99.
[5] *BCA*. XXXIII. p. 41, No. 1.
[6] *IosPE*. I. 106.
[7] *IosPE*. I. 114, cf. IV. p. 273.
[8] Latyshev in *Journal of Min. Public Instr.* St P. Feb. 1890=Ποντικά, p. 55; also *IosPE*. IV. p. 264 quoting Fougères, *BCH*. XIII. (1889), p. 236.

kingdom of Tyle which fell in 213 B.C., prefers to see grandsons where it is just as possible to see grandfathers. Thereby he puts back Protogenes into the IIIrd century. Protogenes himself is represented in the decree as comparatively young, at least the debts due to his father are remembered apart from those due to him : that is in the list he is maybe a survival from the IIIrd century and Cleombrotus too ; but the lettering of the decree is placed by Mommsen at the end of the IInd century, by Boeckh in the Ist or IInd, by Dittenberger in the IInd century, Latyshev shews that it might be IIIrd, but he is driven thereto by the date of the fall of Tyle. The list of citizens looks if anything later still[1]. Braun's arguments in favour of bringing the Galatae from the Carpathians rather than from Thrace agree with the *prima facie* date of the writing and a fair view of its relation to the document at Delos as dated by Fougères. Altogether I should put the decree in the first half of the IInd century B.C. Some other points in it will be touched on in the review of the institutions of Olbia (p. 474).

A further illustration of financial affairs in the IInd century B.C. is afforded by an inscription[2] giving the fees for sacrificing various beasts. They are fixed by the Seven, apparently the commission that managed the finances of the Gods, twelve hundred coppers, that would be three gold pieces, for a bull, three hundred for a sheep or goat, sixty for some other animal or according to Jernstedt's conjecture for the skin. The fees went to the sacred treasury but that was no doubt used as a reserve for the public needs.

Soon after this we would put the period of vassaldom to Scythian kings (v. p. 119); the danger from that quarter had become more and more threatening and it is conceivable that the suzerainty of a strong ruler like Scilurus was rather a relief, if he protected the city against other barbarians and allowed her merchants to trade in his extensive territories. That this was probably so we judge from the occurrence in his capital Kermenchik (Neapolis?), besides a stone bearing the king's name[3], of three inscriptions recording dedications made by Posideus the son of Posideus to Zeus Atabyrius, Athena Lindia and Achilles, lord of the island (of Leuce)[4], the last in celebration of a victory over the Satarchaei pirates. The same name occurs on a dedication to Aphrodite Euploea found at Olbia[5], and there is good reason to supply it in No. 49, a decree of the men of Cos, and perhaps in No. 48, a decree of the men of Tenedos in honour of an Olbiopolite. There is no call to make Posideus a Rhodian as is usually done because of his dedications to Rhodian deities; he was evidently a seaman by the victory over the pirates, with close connexions with the islands of Asia Minor, and there was special reason for his having to do with Rhodes, just then the chief commercial state of the Aegean and carrying on a great wine trade with Olbia, as we know by the amphora stamps.

Whether the Olbiopolites liked their connexion with Scilurus or not, it came to an end at the defeat of his son Palacus by Diophantus with the forces of Mithridates and Chersonese[6]. That Olbia submitted to Mithridates seems

---

[1] See the forms of Ξ, Π, C, Ꙩ on facsimile *IosPE*. I. 16, Pl. II. (as against Ϲ) and in the list ΛΕΖCⲰ; Ꙩ is placed in the IInd century *IosPE*. IV. 101 at Chersonese. For the dates of lettering in Scythia v. K-W. *Grabreliefs*, p. vii, but Watzinger accepts Latyshev's dating.

[2] App. 8 = *IosPE*. I. 46.
[3] p. 119, n. 5 = *IosPE*. I. 241.
[4] *IosPE*. I. 242—244.
[5] *IosPE*. I. 94.
[6] App. 18 = *IosPE*. I. 185, IV. 67, Strabo, VII. iv. 3, v. inf. p. 520.

implied in the fragmentary decree[1] in honour of...son of Philocrates a master mariner of Amisus thanking him for services in transporting supplies to certain Armenians in Sinope, also in facing a storm to bring home an embassy of the city's and reinforcements granted to it by the king. Rostovtsev[2] refers the former service to a running of the blockade of Sinope in 70 B.C., when Machares had deserted his father; the Armenians being the Cilician troops borrowed from Tigranes, who were holding the city for Mithridates. The second transaction he assigns to the king's last moment of power in 64 B.C. when Olbia wanted support against the threatening Getae and he himself would be glad to secure a *pied-à-terre* with a view to his intended Western campaign. After his death it again became a prey to the indiscriminate attacks of the surrounding tribes. Of this time we have a glimpse in the decree in honour of Niceratus son of Papias[3]. He is praised as a peacemaker among the citizens and a defender of the city against the attacks of outside foes, whose name is not given, but they were probably not the Getae as the scene of his death is laid in the Hylaea. The honours he receives are interesting, a public funeral, on the day of which the workshops were to be closed and the citizens to wear black and attend in order, a gold wreath, an equestrian statue, a yearly rehearsing of his merits at the ecclesia for electing magistrates and at the horse-races in honour of Achilles established by oracle, and the setting forth of the complimentary decree upon a fair white stone to rouse the emulation of others.

Sack by the Getae.

The next event in the history of Olbia is its sack by the Getae. Our authority for it is Dio Chrysostom, who says that the Getae took this and the other Greek cities on the west of the Pontus as far as Apollonia, which happened a hundred and fifty years before. The speech was delivered about 100 A.D.; but we may have to reckon back from the time of Dio's stay at Olbia, which may have been about 83 A.D. So the sack must be put between 67 and 50 B.C. This corresponds exactly with the time when Byrebista had raised the Getae or Daci to greater power (v. p. 123) and no doubt the destruction may be laid at his door. It is borne out by the burnt layer found by Pharmacovskij (v. p. 457), by such expressions as that of the decree in honour of Callisthenes[4] c. 200 A.D. which speaks of his descent from the founders of the city, hardly the first founders of eight hundred years before, and by hints from the other towns affected[5]. Indeed the inscriptions of such towns as Istropolis and Odessus, and the description, maybe exaggerated, of Ovid's life at Tomi present close parallels to the state of things we have found at Olbia.

Dio speaks of this sack as the last and greatest capture, and says that the city had often been taken before: that it had been on the verge we know from several inscriptions, after a capture there would be no decree set up, so we cannot say whether it were actually taken: but there is so far no trace of any such break; when he says "often" Dio is almost certainly exaggerating. Scilurus may well have entered the city and done comparatively little harm.

[1] App. 9=*BCA.* XVIII. p. 97, No. 2.
[2] "Mithridates of Pontus and Olbia," *BCA.* XXIII. p. 21.
[3] *IosPE.* I. 17. Latyshev, *Olbia*, p. 139.
[4] *IosPE.* I. 24.
[5] Latyshev, *Olbia*, p. 147, quotes an article of his own in *Ath. Mitt.* XI. (1886), p. 200, citing inscriptions from Odessus and Istropolis.

Olbian Life.

Reviewing the history of Olbia as far as we have gone we must confess that it is a sufficiently depressing record. The citizens' main occupation was commerce with the natives, a commerce in which the civilized man usually makes unrighteous profits, and one branch of which was no doubt the slave trade ; this was varied by internal disputes of which we have hints from time to time, constant petty wars with ever fresh tribes of barbarians, struggles against bad harvests once exhaustion came to the lands which had at first been so fertile, and ever growing financial difficulties. Yet in spite of these disadvantages, in spite of their severe winter, the Olbiopolites strove to live the life of Hellenes. They must have concentrated into the summer the activities of the whole year, for they endeavoured to keep up the due festivals and games. We read of Dionysia held in the theatre[1] and horseraces in honour of Achilles. Dionysius son of Nicodromus the gymnasiarch seems to have gained some prize abroad perhaps in Athens[2] from which Panathenaic vases were brought back in triumph (supra, p. 347). A special point is the archery contest in which Anaxagoras son of Demagoras made the record shot of 282 fathoms[3], a contest most natural in Scythia. To anticipate, the very archons and strategi in the later period record their victories in running, leaping and throwing the lance and discus (v. p. 473).

Of special interest is an inscription recording a statue by Praxiteles[4], so that the statues of which we hear so often were not all specimens of mere municipal art, and the Hellenistic houses are better than we might expect. Some of the earlier coins also attest a fairly high standard of taste and execution though degeneracy soon sets in.

As regards literature Olbia gave birth to a well-known philosopher Bion[5], but the stories we hear of him suggest not so much a serious thinker as a sophist with keen mother-wit and unstable intellectual interests—he first attended the Academy, then joined the Cynics, passed on to the Cyrenaic school and finally became a pupil of the Peripatetic Theophrastus before setting up for himself at Rhodes. When rivals hinted at his lowly origin, he turned on them and said that his father was a freedman dealing in salt fish and was sold up for cheating the customs, his mother no better than she should be, and he himself, having been the favourite slave of a rhetor who left him all his possessions, began his free life by burning his old master's writings : this was merely inverted boasting, we cannot learn from it anything about life in Olbia: Bion flourished in the iiird century B.C. Sphaerus, his younger contemporary, though called a Borysthenite by Plutarch, is more usually stated to have been a Bosporan[6]. Lastly Suidas[7] speaks of a historian Poseidonius the Olbiopolite who wrote about the phenomena of the ocean and the land of Tyras, also, if it be the same man, Attic and Libyan histories, and a Scholiast on Apollonius Rhodius (ii. 660) says that Dionysius Olbianus (v.l. Ἀλβιανός) ἱστορεῖ τὰς εὐρείας ἠιόνας λέγεσθαι Ἀχιλλέως δρόμον[8].

---

[1] *IosPE.* I. 12.   [2] ib. IV. 459.
[3] p. 66, n. 10 and App. 6=*IosPE.* IV. 460.
[4] v. p. 295, nn. 10, 11.
[5] Cf. Diog. Laert. IV. vii.
[6] Plutarch, *Cleomenes*, II. Diog. Laert. VII. vi.

[7] Lexicon ap. Latyshev, *Olbia*, p. 144. Bekker, p. 877. Müller, *FHG.* III. p. 172.
[8] This is not a confusion with Dionysius Periegetes as he emphasizes the narrowness of the Tendra.

M.

We have one relic of private life at Olbia, an early ivth century letter.

A. Ἀρτικῶν τ[ο]ῖς ἐν οἴκω[ι]
χαίρειν· ἦν ἐγβάλει ἐκ τῆς
οἰκίης ὑμ[ᾶς] Μυλλίων
παρὰ Ἀτάκους, [ἐ]ς τὸ οἴκημα

B. ἦν [π]αρδιδῶι· εἰ δὲ μή,
παρὰ Ἀγάθαρκον εἰς τὰ...
παρὰ Κέρδω[ν]ος ἐρίων
τὸ μέρος κομισάσθω(ι).

So Latyshev reads: Articon to the housefolk greeting; if Myllion from Ataces turn you out of the house (go) into the chamber if he offer it; if not to Agatharcus into the [other?]: let him take the share of the wool from Cerdon[1].

FIG. 332. Letter on lead. Olbia. *BCA.* x. p. 11, No. 7.

V. V. Škorpil[2] has published three more lead tablets from Olbia, two are merely *defixiones*, lists of names of people cursed, one of about the same date as Articon's letter, the other of about the iind century B.C., the date also of the third, apparently an anonymous letter to a judge (?) offering him a bribe (σὲ τειμήσω καί σοι ἄριστον δῶρον παρασκευάσω) if he will deny access to his court to certain dangerous persons enumerated.

Olbia restored.

Poor as was the life of Olbia in the last centuries B.C., it was magnificent compared to that of the resurrected Olbia. Dio tells us about it and his picture is probably true in outline though no doubt the light and shade are exaggerated. We must not forget that we are dealing with a professional rhetorician who wishes to lay stress on the desolation of Olbia, the calamities it had suffered in the past, the hourly dangers from foes outside, the meagreness of the intellectual fare within the citizens' reach, in order to throw up the survival among them of the true Hellenic spirit, of martial courage, proud independence, love of the old national poet and eagerness for any chance of culture.

[1] Cf. G. S[chmidt], *BCA.* xiv. p. 138, Artikon sagt denen im Hause χαίρειν. Wenn euch Mylaion aus der Wohnung hinauswirft, so soll er (der Sklave) zu Atakes' (Sohn) in die Vorratskammern— denn gibt er sie her (gut): wo nicht, soll er zu Agatharkos in die (Kammern) die er von Kerdon hat, die Partie Wolle tragen; Wilhelm, *Jahresh. d. oesterr. Arch. Inst.* xii. p. 118 with a better facsimile thinks nothing lost after τὰ, B. l. 2.

[2] *BCA.* xxvii. p. 68.

His account is that after the capture by the Getae the survivors came together again[1] by the consent of the Scythians themselves, who missed the convenience of Greek trade which had ceased with the disappearance of Greek speakers. It is to this period we would assign the coins of Pharzoeus (one a gold stater Pl. III. 26) and Ininsimeus (Inismeus) which witness to settled relations between Olbia and the natives (v. p. 119). At the time of his visit Dio describes quite another state of things, as one of his main points is the perpetual danger from hostile natives, the greater because the town had not been able to fortify itself properly. He gives a graphic picture of the poor buildings huddled up against a few towers that remained of the old circuit, whereas other towers stood out in the country not looking as if they belonged to the city at all; the sun-baked brick walls had naturally collapsed as soon as they were breached and neglected. He next pourtrays the eighteen year old Callistratus as he rides back from the war girt with a great cavalry sword and dressed after the Scythian fashion in trousers and all, with a little black cloak over his shoulders. The general wearing of black is a curious point as it cannot have been universal in the older Olbia for it is decreed as a sign of mourning (p. 464), Dio derives it from the Melanchlaeni who were never anywhere near Olbia. Yet this barbarous figure (very much like the Bosporans on the walls of catacombs, p. 313 sqq.) is well known for his good looks as well as for his courage, and his features recall the Ionian type, moreover he takes an interest in philosophy and even wishes to follow Dio for the sake of opportunities of study.

Dio then enters into a conversation in which he banters them for their excessive devotion to Homer (even now they only had blind poets to encourage them Tyrtaeus-like) and quotes a couplet of Phocylides :

καὶ τόδε Φωκυλίδου· πόλις ἐν σκοπέλῳ κατὰ κόσμον
οἰκεῦσα σμικρὴ κρέσσων Νίνου ἀφραινούσης

suggesting that there is more sense in it than in the shoutings and leapings of Achilles. For this he is interrupted by a bystander who asks him not to speak against Homer and Achilles, and goes on to explain that the day before the natives had made an attack and killed some sentries and they did not know when they would have peace to listen. And indeed, says Dio, the gates were shut and a flag flying as a signal that hostilities were going on. In spite of this trouble Dio is pleased to find them so anxious to hear and so truly Greek that nearly all had collected round him. So they adjourn to the temple of Zeus where was their place of council and plenty of space and there they range themselves in order about him. Dio is delighted at their old-fashioned look with their long hair and beards. Two citizens had shaved but this was regarded as disgraceful imitation of the Romans. Yet these old-time Greeks could no longer speak Greek clearly (σαφῶς). Dio goes on with his speech about the well-administered city, but is interrupted by one Hieroson (one would like to read Heroson a name so typical of earlier Olbia) and asked to speak in the Platonic style about the government of the universe, inasmuch as Plato is the favourite author next to Homer : and so with great applause he discourses of the government of the universe.

---

[1] The excavations shew a very short interruption, *Arch. Anz.* 1911, p. 217; *BCA.* XXXIII. p. 113.

The whole picture is quite unique, it reminds one of a French *littérateur* giving his experiences of Canadian *habitants*, but actuality underlies its idyllic surface and much is borne out by the inscriptions: Ovid supplies the other side of the picture.

The truth lies among the three.   The stage and main situation are the same in all, but Ovid insists on the barbarism and discomfort, whereas Dio makes us have a kindly feeling for the Borysthenites, he shews them simple, brave, independent yet courteous, keeping in all their barbarism touches of true Hellenism that had died out elsewhere, and feeling in all their ignorance and narrowness aspirations after higher things.   But this is not borne out by the inscriptions, a whole series of which consists of complimentary decrees couched in a turgid style equally full of showy bombast and inextricable anacolutha.   We might yet think that they represented the inarticulate strivings of real gratitude had not chance preserved us one precious document[1], telling us that the Senate and People crown Dadus the son of Tumbagus in recognition of the services he might have rendered had he lived, seeing that he was a well-educated young man of great promise.   That the people should sympathize with a bereaved father is all very well, but such an example shews what a farce the complimentary decrees had become.   It was only necessary to belong to the inner ring of the leading families and you might have any number of lines of ungrammatical rhetoric dedicated to your memory.

From the restored Olbia we have a very considerable number of inscriptions, naturally far more than from the ancient time.   They tell us much of the organization of the city and give us the names of many magistrates and citizens, but very few refer to anything which can be called an event; and very few can be dated.   The chief criterion of date is the assumption of Roman praenomina and nomina in accordance with a fashion which changed with each change of Emperor.

It would seem that for some two hundred and fifty years there was no alteration in the internal economy of Olbia.   All that happened was that the magistrates succeeded each other duly, performed their duties, made some dedication or restoration in their own honour and handed on their offices to other members of the aristocratic families.

Magistrates and citizens alike strove to adorn their city, but rather in a spirit of ostentatious emulation than of civic virtue, and the place must have been full of bad statues and fulsome eulogies.   Dio says the good statues of former times had all been mutilated by the Getae.   Now we read of the building of a gymnasium[2], a portico in the time of Tiberius[3] and another in the time of Severus Alexander[4], a tower[5], an exedra[6] and baths[7] under Septimius Severus, also of restorations, of the theatre[8], a praetorium ($\sigma\tau\rho\alpha\tau\acute{\eta}\gamma\iota\sigma\nu$)[9], the temple of Apollo Prostates[10] and the chapel ($\pi\rho\sigma\sigma\epsilon\upsilon\chi\acute{\eta}$) of Achilles Pontarches[11]; evidently the look of the city was improved during the hundred years following Dio's visit,

---

[1] *IosPE.* I. 26.
[2] App. 10=*IosPE.* I. 22.
[3] *IosPE.* I. 102.
[4] ib. I. add. 97[1].
[5] ib. I. 101.
[6] ib. I. 103.
[7] *IosPE.* I. 97.
[8] ib. I. 104.
[9] ib. IV. 26.
[10] ib. I. 58, 61.
[11] ib. I. 98, at least it was roofed by the archons, who mostly made their offerings to him.

and it is hard to believe that in the preceding century the statues had been left without any attempt to make good the damage[1].

Externally the restored Olbia had dealings with the natives, with the other Pontic cities and with Rome. Refounded by the permission of the Scythians after the Getan power had collapsed, her relations with the natives soon became uncertain. We may believe that Rome helped her to throw off the yoke of Pharzoeus and Inismeus, for in the early years of Tiberius Ababus the son of Callisthenes had already dedicated a portico to Augustus, Tiberius and the People. Such a dedication means gratitude or expectation on the part of Olbia. He is very likely the father of Orontes, son of an Ababus described by the Byzantines as having attained the honour of being presented at the Imperial court[2]. Again in 62 A.D. Ti. Plautius Silvanus[3], legate of Moesia, boasts of having made a Scythian king raise the siege of "Cherronensus which is beyond the Borustenes." To this display of Roman activity is usually ascribed the annexation of Tyras, but this was probably in 56 A.D. However, it must have meant something for Olbia. When Dio says that two citizens were held in contempt for having shaved in imitation of the Romans, we must remember that he had been exiled by the Roman government. The steady attraction of Rome is shewn by the increasing frequency of Roman names, such as Ulpius and Aelius : it must have been much increased by the conquests of Trajan. Antoninus Pius granted help against the Tauroscythae and made them give hostages to the Olbiopolites, so from his time there can have been left but the shadow of independence[4].

However the Olbiopolites themselves did their best in their own way, we hear of generals gaining triumphant victories and making dedications accordingly[5], and of citizens thanked for going out to meet barbarian chiefs, and we may be sure they did not meet them empty handed[6].

Finally the inevitable happened. We find Olbian coins with the image and superscription of Septimius Severus, baths dedicated to Severus and Caracalla while Cosconius Gentianus was legate of Moesia[7], statues of Caracalla and Geta set up by Senate and People and all signs of full Roman sovranty. Possibly the difficulty experienced in the reduction of Byzantium moved Septimius Severus to get all the Pontic towns more in hand. We have coins of Severus, Caracalla and Geta, then an interval and then again those of Severus Alexander.

Meanwhile the Olbiopolites kept up a lively intercourse with other Greek cities, especially those on the Pontus and Propontis. Reference has already been made to a decree of the Byzantines in honour of Orontes son of Ababus[2]. It is written in elaborate Doric and praises Orontes for hospitality to strangers at Olbia and dignity when himself staying at Byzantium.

---

[1] Cf. the decree in honour of Theocles son of Satyrus App. 10, l. 21, ἔργων τε ἐπιμελείαις καὶ κατασκευ(α)ῖς ἐνεκοπίασεν ὡς δι' αὐτὸν περικαλλεστέραν καὶ ἐνδοξοτέραν τὴν πόλιν ἡμῶν γενέσθαι. It seems hard that after this Dio should have spoken of the city as οὐ πρὸς τὴν παλαιὰν δόξαν, and of ἡ φαυλότης τῶν οἰκοδομημάτων.

[2] IosPE. I. 102 (cf. IV. p. 271), Ababus Callisthenis, and IosPE. I. 47, Ὀρόντας...Ἀβάβου...μέχρι τᾶς τῶν Σεβαστῶν γνώσεως προκόψαντος; cf. Deissmann, Licht vom Osten, p. 277, n. 6; so Carzoazus

son of Attalus in the IInd century κινδύνους μέχρι Σεβαστῶν συμμαχίᾳ παραβολευσάμενος whatever that may mean, IosPE. I. 21 : Deissmann, p. 55, n. 7 renders "exposing himself to dangers by the help he gave in the struggle,"—comparing Philippians, ii. 30, παραβολευσάμενος (ℵABD) τῇ ψυχῇ.

[3] App. I = CIL. XIV. 3608.

[4] Julius Capitolinus, Antoninus Pius, c. 9.

[5] IosPE. I. 58.

[6] IosPE. I. 21, 22, 25.

[7] IosPE. I. 97, v. TRAS. VII. p. 74.

More general was the praise offered to Theocles son of Satyrus who died in his year of office as chief archon. Not only did Olbia give him the usual honours decreeing that he should wear a gold wreath at his funeral, his virtues be rehearsed by a herald and a medallion with his bust put upon the gymnasium in whose building he had been concerned, but the foreigners resident in the town had the names of their cities added as joining in the honour paid him[1]. Regular hospitality to foreigners is one of the virtues credited in complimentary decrees. On the other hand one of Dio's hosts draws a most unfavourable picture of the Greeks that came to Olbia, saying that they are mere merchants and bagmen bringing poor rags and bad wine, more barbarous than the Olbiopolites themselves. Let us hope that the architect from Nicomedia and Tomi[2] who built their baths was a little better than this. Further evidence of such intercourse may be seen in the foreign coins that found their way to Olbia, from Amisus, Callatis, Odessus, Tomi, Istrus, Tyras, Cercinitis, Chersonese, Panticapaeum, Phaselis, Thasos, Athens, Locri, Panormus and others, besides the staters of Cyzicus and later of various dynasts, which supplied the lack of local gold, and the Imperial currency. Three gravestones[3] witness to Bosporans living and dying at Olbia and the grave described on p. 420 seems to be that of a woman of Chersonese.

Finally to these citizens of many states was added an entirely fresh element in the Roman soldier and his Thracian auxiliaries[4]. Perhaps from the time of Antoninus Pius there must have been a cohort or ala of such regularly stationed for the defence of Olbia and of Bosporus and Chersonese: from the time of Trajan or Hadrian a detachment was supplied by *Legio XI Claudia*, part of the garrison of Lower Moesia. This continued till at any rate 248 A.D. when two of the soldiers dedicated an altar to Mercury in honour of the consulship of Philip Augustus and Philip the Emperor[5].

Coins give the latest dates, one of Otacilia Philip's wife was found long ago, more recently one of Valerian[6] and even one of Constantius[7]. After this date we can say no more. Only Ammianus Marcellinus (XXII. vii. 40) speaks of Olbia as existing in his time: but that is little to go by. Subsequently someone must have lived on the site, for this very altar was found built into a wall and a few Byzantine coins have been picked up[8]. But of this which may be called the third Olbia we know nothing. Presumably the Goths destroyed the second but it may have been the Carpi or some Sarmatian tribe. The date must have been about the year in which Decius was defeated, rather later than Mommsen puts it[9]. No author found the event worth mentioning, not even Jordanes[10], who knew of the city's existence and even speaks of Borysthenis and Olbia separately; he might well have attributed this exploit to the Goths had they performed it, but they were not very successful against walled cities such as Tomi, Marcianopolis and Cyzicus[11], and the end may not have been an instantaneous catastrophe.

---

[1] For the list see App. 10=*IosPE*. I. 22, cf. a similar list I. 23 with IV. p. 267.
[2] *IosPE*. I. 97, Νεικομ[ηδίως] τοῦ καὶ Τομείτ[ου.
[3] *IosPE*. I. 115—117.
[4] *IosPE*. IV. 32, 34, 35; *BCA*. X. pp. 5, 13, Nos. 4, 8; XXVII. p. 64, No. 4 and Professor Rostovtsev's observations thereon.

[5] App. 14=*BCA*. X. p. 5, No. 4.
[6] *BCA*. XXVII. p. 65; *CR*. 1907, p. 24.
[7] *Arch. Anz.* 1911, p. 221.
[8] ibid.; Uvarov, *Recherches*, I. p. 103, Justin II.
[9] *R.G.* V. pp. 216,285=*Prov.* I. pp. 237,310—312.
[10] *Getica*, V. 32.
[11] Zosimus, I. xlii. xliii. 1.

Institutions.

In the following review of Olbian institutions no attempt is made to trace any development. For the earlier Olbia hints in the Protogenes decree borne out by one or two other inscriptions are all we have to go upon. Probably the forms of the old order survived into the new city though impregnated with an aristocratic spirit. The Nine and Seven do not occur in the later Olbia.

The population of Olbia consisted of citizens, free aliens, and slaves. We hear nothing of metoeci. Only the citizens formed the body politic.

Apparently the constitution was at any rate in theory a pure democracy: we do not know of any class of citizens having any special rights, nor of any division into tribes or φρατίραι. But at any rate in the restored Olbia this democracy had become something very like an oligarchy. For one reason or another the responsible offices of the state are concentrated in the hands of a small number of families and the same names occur again and again[*] shewing that these families held their own for generations. This was in a manner recognized in the formula for complimentary decrees. The rehearsal of a man's merits usually begins by mentioning that his ancestors had benefited the city and held high office[1]. It is interesting that barbarian names are as common as Greek among these Olbian *nobiles*. Olbia never adopted election by lot, the Attic remedy against undue influence, also unlimited reelection was apparently allowed, so the inner ring had the means to maintain its supremacy[2].

The legislative bodies were the Boule and the Ecclesia or Demos. The former seems merely to have had probouleutic functions, propositions being first considered by it and then brought before the ecclesia. The formula for decrees generally mentions both. This formula when fully expressed gives the name of the proposer (ὁ εἰσηγησάμενος) and says that the proposal was stated (εἶπαν) by the archons or in some cases by the archons and the Seven, this was probably because finance, the province of the Seven, was nearly touched by the activity of the citizens honoured[3].

In one complimentary decree the proposal comes from the Synhedri[4], whom Latyshev regards as a permanent committee of the boule like the prytaneis in many cities.

Latyshev analyses the full preambles of the later decrees to extract therefrom some account of the procedure[5]. Apparently the proposer laid his scheme before the boule, and if the boule approved it it was brought before the ecclesia by the archons who probably presided over it. If the proposal is made by several men, e.g. by the synhedri, the statement stands in one name alone unqualified by any magistrate's title. Occasionally instead of the archons we only find the chief or eponymous archon[6].

Quite exceptional is a preamble[7] in which it appears that a resolution

---

[1] *IosPE.* I. 17, 22 (=App. 10), 24, 26.
[2] *IosPE.* I. 16, 22 (=App. 7, 10), 24, 77 (=App. 14).
[3] ib. I. 13, 16 (=App. 7), IV. 456.
[4] *BCA.* XIV. p. 94, No. 1. He proposes to re-store the word in *IosPE.* I. 28 and I. 42, cf. IV. p. 268.
[5] *IosPE.* I. 21, 22 (=App. 10), 24, 27—31, 42.
[6] ib. I. 24.
[7] App. 9=*BCA.* XVIII. p. 96, No. 2.

(γνώμη) voted by the demos on the proposal of the archons was the following year ratified by demos and boule.

The preamble sometimes[1] adds that the ecclesia was crowded or universal (ἐκκλησίας συνηθροισμένης πανδήμου). This gave its decisions no more legal force but added lustre to a complimentary decree.

A decree was then inscribed upon a fair white stone and set up in a conspicuous place. This was probably done under the direction of a secretary, such a γραμματεὺς as is mentioned at Tyras, but there is no direct evidence for this. There was further a town-crier or herald who proclaimed the virtues of deceased benefactors or contracts for which the city asked tenders.

The boule met in Dio's time at the temple of Zeus (Olbios ?), the demos had its ἐκκλησιαστήριον which also served as an exchange[2].

The Ecclesia seems to have had the ultimate decision in all possible matters, foreign affairs, the despatching of envoys and gifts to foreign potentates, war and preparations for it, elections of magistrates (at a special meeting, ἡ ἀρχαιρετικὴ ἐκκλησία), finance including the regulation of the price of corn, of the currency and of customs, the requisition of necessary sums from rich men and the invitation of tenders for various contracts, and finally that which has left most trace to our day the voting of complimentary decrees, privileges and rewards to magistrates, citizens and foreigners. The latter were given citizenship, proxeny, and immunity from import duties. To citizens were given such a title as father of the city[3], wreaths of gold, the setting up of a medallion or a statue, plain or gilded, afoot or equestrian, and lastly the honour of a funeral at the public expense, the shops being closed and the citizens clothed in black.

In case of sudden necessity the archons had the power to summon the ecclesia[4], but in the face of such miscellaneous responsibilities it must have had regular days for meeting, but we know nothing of them.

The dates are sometimes given in the preambles of decrees, but we can deduce nothing from them except that the names of the months, Panaemos, [Metageit]nion, Boedromion, Cyanepsion, [Apa]tureon, Leneon, Anthester[ion], Tha[rgelion], Calamae[on], were such as we meet at Cyzicus and other Milesian colonies[5]. Olbia seems never to have had an era and a simple manner of reckoning dates such as we find in Roman times at Tyras, Chersonese and in the Bosporan kingdom. Years were denoted in earlier times by the name of some priest, probably that of Achilles, in later times by that of the chief archon.

Magistrates.

Executive power in Olbia belonged to colleges of magistrates. The only solitary officials were the king and the director of finances, which office Protogenes, probably appointed for the special need of the time, held for three years:

---

[1] *IosPE.* I. 22 (=App. 10), 24, 27, 28; *BCA.* XIV. p. 94, No. 1.

[2] App. 5=*IosPE.* I. 11.

[3] Maybe not a mere title but the expression of that power concentrated in one magistrate's hands which had become common in the IIIrd century. Rostovtsev, *BCA.* XXIII. p. 18.

[4] App. 7=*IosPE.* I. 16.

[5] Latyshev, "On the Kalendars of Olbia, Tyras, and Chersonesus Taurica" in *Trans. of VIth* (1884) *Russian Arch. Congr.* Odessa, 1888, Vol. II. p. 56 =Ποντικά, p. 25, v. *IosPE.* I. 18, 21, 22, 28, 30, 31, 42 (IV. p. 268); *BCA.* XIV. p. 94, No. 1; XVIII. p. 96, No. 2.

"πάντα διωίκησεν" in an uncontrolled fashion not like a regular magistrate, but he may correspond to the normal Athenian official ὁ ἐπὶ τῇ διοικήσει as Latyshev supposes. There were five archons, six strategi, five agoranomi, a college of Nine and a college of Seven : we do not know the number of the astynomi. Each college had a head as it were eponymous, for in official documents the others are grouped round him as οἱ περὶ τὸν δεῖνα. Each college had its patron deity to which it made a dedication after its year of office—the archons to Achilles Pontarches, the strategi to Apollo Prostates and sometimes to Achilles Pontarches ; the agoranomi to Hermes Agoraeus. The dedication took the form of a Nike, a vase or other ornament, or of an improvement or restoration of a sacred fabric. These dedications are recorded in inscriptions of which many have come down to us especially those of the strategi. The college makes them on behalf of the city, or the prosperity or the full water supply (εὐποσία) of the city, and of the health and in the case of strategi the valour of its members.

As the same man could hold an office more than once we find the same name occurring in different positions in the lists. This was governed either as Latyshev says by seniority or by the number of votes obtained by each in the election which was open by χειροτονία.

Archons and Strategi.

The Archons, a college of five devoted to Achilles Pontarches[1], were the principal magistrates. Their chief, the πρῶτος ἄρχων, in later times gave his name to the year. They seem mostly to have acted as a college and not to have specialized as at Athens. But as a college they seem to have had general supervision over the business of the state. They were the main executants of the will of the ecclesia which they summoned and before which they laid proposals. There is reason to think that they became something in the way of masters of the ecclesia when the government took an aristocratic turn. They certainly had some part in the finances, both as making provision for extraordinary expenditure on presents for Saitaphernes or bargains in wine for the poorer citizens and also as having some responsibility for the coinage. The later coins often bear names and a monogram χ^ρ which probably stands for Ἀρχ(οντος). Latyshev would also explain another monogram common along the whole North Euxine coast $\cancel{\Lambda}$ as Πρῶτος Ἄρχων. In two cases we have names and patronymics on coins which we can match on inscriptions. Compare Α]ΔΟΟΫ ΔΕΛΦΟΥ on Pl. III. 15 with **ΑΔΟΗΣ ΔΕΛΦΟΥ**[2] and ΔΑΔΟC CΑΤ[ΥΡΟΥ] on Pl. III. 16 with ΙΔΑΔΟΝΣΑΤΥ, i.e. οἱ περὶ Δάδον Σατύρου ἄρχοντες or στρατηγοί on a fragment of a stone disk[3], but Niceratus on the coin of Ininsimeus (v. p. 487) is too common a name to identify[4] and the coin ΠΙCΙCΤΡΑΤΟΥ ΔΑΔΑΚΟΥ[5] has so far no corresponding stone.

Mention has been made of archons competing in games and winning prizes, e.g. this Adoes in wrestling and jumping, his (?) son Heuresibius[6]

---

[1] *IosPE.* I. 77 (=App. 13), 78, IV. 17; *BCA.* x. p. 2, No. 2; XVIII. p. 109, No. 14.
[2] Archon, *Trans. Od. Soc.* XXVIII. *Minutes*, p. 32 a, cf. *IosPE.* I. 115, l. 4; *BCA.* XXXVII. p. 78.
[3] *IosPE.* I. 144.
[4] Archons, *IosPE.* I. 78, 81, cf. 21, 101, 122.
[5] Pick, XI. 7; Burachkov, VIII. 173.
[6] App. 13=*IosPE.* I. 77.

M.

in jumping and running, and a colleague in spear and discus throwing; others in other years in running alone. or in throwing the spear and discus[1]. It suggests that their family ties enabled men to attain to be archons comparatively young.   So too the strategi (v. n. 4).

Of the Strategi we can only say that they formed a college of six (in one inscription five are mentioned but that may be an accident) with a ὑπηρέτης whose good service is often recorded[2], were the military leaders for they had victorious triumphs, and made dedications to Apollo Prostates[3], offering Nikai in gold or silver, gold torques, a gold and jewelled belt, silver vases, a tripod, a gold wreath, a statue, a little couch, also χαριστήρια to Achilles Pontarches[4]: they generally set up their inscriptions upon very second-hand stones.   Of the organization of the Olbian forces we know nothing : a signal was run up on the walls in case of attack from the natives.

Finance Magistrates.

The college of Nine had something to do with the finances of Olbia, at least so we gather from a passage in the Protogenes decree : Protogenes on being elected into their body immediately supplies 1500 gold pieces for current expenses, which looks as if his election brought him into direct contact with the financial needs of the state.

We hardly know more of the college of Seven.   They support the archons in speaking for the decrees in honour of Protogenes and of two other bene- factors whose names are imperfect[5], and they are responsible for the tariff of taxes on sacrifices[6].   Probably they administered the sacred treasury and its interests were advanced by Protogenes and the other two men, so the Seven lent their support to their being honoured.   A few coins bear the legend OIEΡTA but we cannot tell why they should have taken part in the issue of this money[7].   Neither the Nine nor the Seven are mentioned in the later Olbia.

Latyshev takes Protogenes to have been occupying a normal post when he was restoring the public finances for three years, and sees in ἐπιμηνιεῦσαι a hint that he was made an ἐπιμήνιος or special monthly magistrate to help the citizens' private money matters and straighten the relations of debtor and creditor chiefly by sacrificing 6000 gold pieces due to himself.   But in such work monthliness does not come in, and ἐπιμήνιος does not seem to be used anywhere in this sense.   It is better to keep to Boeckh's *dilationem per menses dare debitoribus* by in some way pacifying the creditors.

Before we leave the question of finances we may remark that our authorities give us the usual sources for the revenue, duties on imports, direct taxes on places of business[8], fines and confiscations and contributions from rich men, whether forced or voluntary ; the only rather unusual source is

---

[1] *IosPE.* IV. 19, 25 (?).
[2] *IosPE.* I. 53, 57, 68, 69; *BCA.* XXIII. p. 31, No. 6.
[3] *IosPE.* I. 50—74, the last to Phoebus; IV. 15, 16; *BCA.* X. p. 4, No. 3; XVIII. p. 102, Nos. 4, 5 (=App. 11), 6—12; XXIII. p. 30, Nos. 5—7; XXXVII. p. 65, Nos. 1, 2.
[4] *IosPE.* I. 79, 80 (the chief strategus wins the

spear throwing); *BCA.* XXVII. p. 35, No. 32; *Trans. Od. Soc.* XXIX. *Minutes,* p. 61.
[5] οἱ ἄρχοντες καὶ οἱ ἑπτὰ εἶπαν, *IosPE.* I. 13, 16, IV. 456.
[6] App. 8 = *IosPE.* I. 46.
[7] Pl. III. 7; Burachkov, v. 88, 91; Pick, IX. 32 (?), X. 5, 6.
[8] *IosPE.* I. 20 ἐργαστ]ηρίων μίσθω[σις].

the tax on sacrifices, but this did not go strictly speaking to the state[1]. The expenses too were the usual ones, the cost of war, or presents and embassies to stave off war, the keeping up of the fortifications and public buildings and ships, the helping of poor citizens in time of scarcity and the support of dramatic representations, athletic contests and religious ceremony in general. These objects were mostly undertaken by contractors unless, as we have seen, some patriotic citizen came forward; the taxes and even judicial fines were collected by companies of contractors[2].

Minor Magistrates.

The internal order and decency of the town and the conduct of trades and manufactures were the care of a college of five Agoranomi: they suitably made dedications to Hermes Agoraeus[3]: but their choice of a Nike was rather bombastic unless they had very serious disorders to contend with. Their names sometimes occur on amphorae and we have a bronze label off a vessel marked **ΑΓΟΡΑΝΟ|ΜΟΥΝΤΟC | ΑΓΑΘΟ|ΚΛΕΟΥC Β | ΛΕΙΤΡΑ**[4].

The Astynomi cannot be shewn to belong to Olbia but certain amphorae and tiles marked with the name of the maker and of an astynomus designated as such have been generally referred to Olbia (v. supra, p. 360).

Of the Gymnasiarch[5] we know no more than his existence which implies that of Ephebi: it is curious to notice that it was his son that won the race.

The survival of the title King[6], a *rex sacrificulus*, is interesting, but so common in various Greek states that we might expect it. Certain sacrifices could not be offered but by a man clothed in the dignity and name if not the power of the ancient king whose duties as priest were hardly less important to his people than his duties as ruler.

Cults.

The Cults of Olbia have been very fully treated by Miss Hirst and her articles are easily accessible to English readers[7]. There will be therefore no need for me to quote parallels from the other cities of the Euxine coast; perhaps their mutual resemblance has been exaggerated by investigators who have approached them from the standpoint of Greece. I should certainly agree with the conclusion that at Olbia no native deity such as the Tauric Virgin at Chersonese has penetrated into the Greek city.

In making the following summary, though I am much indebted to Miss Hirst by whom the material has been so clearly marshalled, I have been compelled to differ from her conclusions in details. Also I have been enabled to add one or two facts from the latest excavations.

[1] App. 8 = *IosPE*. I. 46.
[2] v. E. Ziebarth, "Das gr. Vereinswesen," XXXIV. *Preisschr. d. Jablonowskischen Gesellschaft*, Leipzig, 1896, p. 23.
[3] *IosPE*. I. 75 (= App. 12), 76.
[4] *Arch. Anz.* 1909, p. 172, f. 35.
[5] *IosPE*. IV. 459; F. Poland, "Gesch. d. gr. Vereinwesens," XXXVIII. *Preisschr. d. Jablon. Ges.*

Leipzig, 1909, p. 538, 92, A*.
[6] *IosPE*. I. 53. Its bearer is one of the strategi, so it can hardly have been a real office.
[7] *JHS.* XXII. (1902), p. 245; XXIII. (1903), p. 24: Russian translation by P. V. Latyshev, brought up to date by V. V. Latyshev in *BCA.* XXVII. (1908), p. 75.

Evidence as to cults of Olbia is derived from the statements of Herodotus and Dio Chrysostom, inscriptions, one or two works of art and coins. These last must be used with caution as often other than religious considerations dictated the choice of types even when these are actually heads or emblems of gods. Achilles Pontarches had perhaps the most interesting and important cult but as in duty bound let us begin with Zeus.

Zeus and Poseidon.

Zeus is mentioned in the inscriptions with various epithets. As Soter he receives the dedication of the decree in honour of Callinicus son of Euxenus[1] and another made by some private citizen on behalf of the peace and safety of the city[2]. With the name Zeus Eleutherius there is a ivth century fragment[3]. In the next century we have Zeus Basileus[4]. As was fitting to Zeus Poliarches was dedicated a tower built by Anaximenes and his brethren, sons of Posideus in the iind century A.D.[5] Most interesting is the title Zeus Olbios. Callisthenes son of Callisthenes is praised for "having been priest of the god who defends our city Zeus Olbios and having [vac.] the god in holy fashion and making petition for good blending of the airs and so obtaining a favourable season[6]."

Evidently Zeus Olbios was the god of Olbia and the giver of Olbos: especially in the form of a good harvest. The two ideas were inextricable. Surely it was in the temple of this Zeus that the council met and before it the open space into which Dio's hearers crowded. A priest of his in Roman times made a dedication to Achilles Pontarches[7]. There is a certain number of coins[8] with a head of Zeus and a sceptre or an eagle on the reverse.

The Rhodian Zeus Atabyrius like Athena Lindia has nothing but the personal reverence of Posideus an Olbiopolite living at Neapolis[9].

Considering that it was an Ionian town depending upon maritime commerce it seems strange that there should be no trace of Poseidon, but his office was taken by Achilles Pontarches and he had no jurisdiction in the Western Euxine. Some writers call the well known head of the River god on the coins (Pl. iii. 4, 5) Poseidon without sufficient reason. The only doubt could be when the head looks right instead of left[10] or the reverse bears a dolphin, but this is a usual type on the smaller coins of Olbia (B. iii. 24) and not a special symbol of the god on the obverse.

Apollo and Helios.

If Zeus appears with most names, by the number of inscriptions Apollo received most honour. As Apollo Prostates[11] the defender he was as we have seen the object of special devotion on the part of the strategi. Their dedications

---

[1] *IosPE.* i. 12.
[2] ib. i. 91, cf. 92.
[3] ib. iv. 458.
[4] ih. i. 105.
[5] ib. i. 101.
[6] ib. i. 24. ἱερεὺς δὲ γενόμενο[ς τοῦ] προ/εστῶτος τῆς πόλεως ἡμῶν θεοῦ Διὸς ᾿Ολβίου [καὶ...] οὐ/σας τὸν θεὸν ἁγνῶς, τῆς τῶν ἀέρων εὐκρα[σίας δεόμενος]/

ἐπέτυχεν εὐετηρίας κ.τ.λ. Could the missing verb be a compound of λούω, a natural rain charm?
[7] *Trans. Od. Soc.* xxvii. *Minutes*, p. 11.
[8] Pl. iii. 12, 13; Burachkov, p. 61, Nos. 147—159, Pl. vi. 105—115.
[9] *IosPE.* i. 242.
[10] B. iii. 23; Pick, ix. 32 inscribed ΟΙ ΕΠΤΑ (?).
[11] Called Phoebus, *IosPE.* i. 58 (in verse), 74.

have been found just to the north of the Roman walls and this probably was the site of the temple[1]. Miss Hirst would see on a coin (Pl. III. 16) a late copy of his cult image apparently wearing a calathos as town deity and thinks that this image, archaic as it is, was preceded by a mere pillar which survives as an accessory on another coin (Pl. III. 17) but was originally the representation of Apollo Hiatros. But for this latter epithet actually at Olbia the only authority is a conjecture[2]. However the epithet occurs at Panticapaeum and Phanagoria and at Apollonia and Istropolis; moreover there is the cylix of the careless red-figured style that Count Bobrinskoj found at Zhurovka near Chigirin, inscribed Δελφινίο(υ) ξυνή(ι) ἰητρô(υ), and this may have come from Olbia[3]. This is rendered probable by the occurrence of the epithet Delphinius which spread from Athens and Miletus[4] to most Ionian cities. In a fuller discussion of the cylix[5] Tolstoi maintains that the Healer and Delphinius are originally independent deities merged in Apollo. Delphinius he derives from δελφύς matrix. Granted that the myth in the Homeric hymn is aetiological should not the explanation be sought in the resemblance of Δελφοί and δελφίς?

Apollo's head occurs on a great number of coins both early and late[6]. The 𝕄 monogram might conceivably stand for Αποллωνος Προcτατογ or perhaps Αχιλλεωc ΠοντΑρχογ just as at Chersonese it is for ΠΑΡΘενογ (v. p. 549).

On the ground of certain coins it has been suggested that Helios was worshipped at Olbia; one might say that it would be the last place in the Greek world where he would be worshipped: a big double countermark with a rayed head on one side and oΛ with two horses' heads on the other stamps them as a temporary issue referred to about the 1st century B.C. The rayed head recalls some Asiatic types, Rhodes, Sinope or Amisus. Pick (p. 150, n. 1) thinks the horses emblems of a wind-god (Pl. III. 11)[7].

Hermes, Dionysus, Ares and Asclepius.

Hermes Agoraeus was patron of the agoranomi[8]. To Hermes too in conjunction with Heracles did Nicodromus the gymnasiarch dedicate a statue of his son Dionysius[9]. To Hermes Ἄρκιος "the reliable" Apaturius[10] inscribed a Panathenaic scyphus, the addition Ἀνθεστήριος suggests the Attic rite

[1] *IosPE.* I. 50—74; IV. 15, 16; *BCA.* x. p. 4, No. 5; XVIII. p. 101, Nos. 4, 5 (=App. 11), 6—12; XXIII. p. 30, Nos. 5—7; XXXVII. p. 65, Nos. 1, 2. See also Ct I. I. Tolstoi, "Cult of Apollo on the Bosporus and at Olbia," *Journ. Min. Pub. Instr.*, St P., 1904, Jan. Farnell, *Cults of the Greek States*, IV. p. 372, quotes Soph. *Trach.* 209 for προστάτης.

[2] *IosPE.* I. 93. ᴋʜ¡ΟΣΟ/ ᵀΙΟ῁ΛΛ῁ΩΝΙΙ Latyshev supplies
...κηίος ὀλ[βιοπολίτης? but one is tempted to suggest Ἀπ]όλλωνι ἰ[ητρῶι? ἱερησάμενον, cf. IV. 27, v. p. 478, n. 12; *BCA.* x. p. 8, Nos. 5, 6, v. p. 479, n. 8.

[3] *Arch. Anz.* 1904, p. 102; *BCA.* xiv. p. 10, v. supra, pp. 176, 361.

[4] Diog. Laert. *Thales*, I. i. 7, so Tolstoi reads; Farnell, *Cults*, IV. p. 147 would bring it from Crete.

[5] *BCA.* XIV. p. 44.

[6] Pl. III. 6, 7, 15—17, cf. B. p. 45, Nos. 39—50, Pl. III. 25—31, p. 70, Nos. 204—228, Pl. VII. 164—VIII. 178; Pick, IX. 30, X. 6, 25—30, XI. 7—20.

[7] Orêshnikov, *Materials touching the ancient Numismatics of the Black Sea coast*, p. 29, Pl. II. 25—27, published a coin of a King Aelis to whom he shews good reason for attributing the suzerainty of Tomi and suggests that he is responsible for the same rayed head on the coins of Olbia, if for a short time he had gained power there, v. Pl. III. 22.

[8] *IosPE.* I. 75 (=App. 12), 76.

[9] *IosPE.* IV. 459.

[10] *Trans. Od. Soc.* XXIII. p. 19: so ib. p. 21 (Berezan), ΙΕΡΗΕΙΜΙΤΟΡΜΕΩ; ib. p. 23 (Olbia), ЄΡΜΗϹ, dotted letters *en barbotine*, Vogell, *Samml.* No. 441, Pl. VII. 8.

χύτροι on the third day of the Anthesteria. To Mercury is inscribed the last epigraphic monument of Olbia, the altar set up by Pyrrus and Bithus for the safety of the Emperor Philip A.D. 248[1]. Hermes also occurs on a few coins[2].

Of Dionysus Herodotus (IV. 78) tells us in the story of Scyles; also there was a theatre and Dionysia[3]. A cylix (p. 351, n. 1) marked ΔΙΟΝΥΣΟΥ hardly counts. Recently a VIth or Vth century graffito from Berezan[4] and part of a stone table with the inscription in IVth century letters Μητ[POBIOΔIONYΣ∧I have given clear material evidence[5] and another fragment of the latter date was set up by his priest Thrasybulus[6].

Ares may have been worshipped at Olbia by the Thracian element perhaps, but there is no evidence. There are coins of Geta (Pl. III. 18) with a standing warrior on the reverse but even if it is Ares it is quite Roman: about as likely to be a real object of a Greek cult as the abstractions on Roman coins.

Asclepius may have had something to do with the tower restored by Protogenes that they called τὸν Ἐπ[ι]δαυρίου. A relief regarded by Uvarov[7] (v. supra, p. 304) as a sacrifice to him seems nothing more than an ordinary funeral feast but these do run into reliefs in honour of Asclepius[8]. There do not seem to be any coins with the head of Asclepius. The marble head found by Pharmacovskij in 1902[9] though undoubtedly Asclepius is no evidence for a real cult of the god.

Dioscuri, Cabiri, Rider God, Good Genius, River God.

The Dioscuri were mentioned in an inscription which has lost their names but the stone shews their caps and stars on a bas-relief above[10]. Also these appear on coins[11] in a way usual throughout the Northern Euxine (e.g. Pl. VI. 1, IX. 28) but differentiated by a dolphin; the other side with a tripod also much resembles Panticapaean coins (Pl. VI. 3, 4). It looks as if the dolphin were the only Olbian element; the issue may be Mithridatic.

For the worship of the Cabiri we have only one piece of evidence: Epicrates son of Niceratus dedicates a statue of his uncle Eubiotus son of Ariston who had served as priest to "the gods in Samothrace[12]".

To Ἀγαθὸς Δαίμων is inscribed a black-glazed cylix of the early IVth century B.C. and what may be a boundary-stone of the IIIrd[13].

Votive reliefs to their own "Rider-god" were set up by Thracian auxiliaries in Roman service[14].

The commonest coins of Olbia, coins which were issued for many generations to judge by the varieties of style, bore on their obverse a horned head with long rough hair and sometimes ox ears (Pl. III. 4, 5). There has been some doubt whom this might represent: the Russian peasants recognise the

[1] App. 14=*BCA*. X. p. 5, No. 4.
[2] Pl. III. 24, 25 : B. VII. 150; VIII. 179; Pick, X. 32, 33.
[3] *IosPE*. I. 12.
[4] *Trans. Od. Soc.* XXVII. *Minutes*, p. 60.
[5] *BCA*. XVIII. p. 109, No. 13.
[6] *BCA*. XXIII. p. 30, No. 4.
[7] *Recherches*, Pl. XIII.
[8] J. E. Harrison, *Prolegomena*, p. 360.
[9] *BCA*. XIII. Pl. III., v. supra p. 297.

[10] *IosPE*. I. 18, description of the stone.
[11] B. VI. 100, 101 ; Pick, X. 31.
[12] *IosPE*. IV. 27 corrected according to *BCA*. X. p. 7, No. 5 in the discussion of the latter, see p. 479, n. 8 : Εὐβίοτος Ἀρίστωνος./Ἐπικράτης Νικηράτου/τὸν θεῖον/θεοῖς τοῖς ἐν Σαμοθράκη[ι]/ἱερησάμενον.
[13] *BCA*. XLII. pp. 134—140, ff. 1—5; *IosPE*. I. 10.
[14] Now in Historical Museum, Moscow, Rostovtsev, *BCA*. XL. Pl. VI. 17—19, 21, 22, *Arch. Anz.* 1911, p. 237, cf. 1904, pp. 11—17, v. inf. p. 546.

Devil and call the place where they are mostly picked up the Devil's Dell; others find him, as they put it, like a Scythian or a Russian peasant; to others he is Poseidon. But no doubt he is really a river god Hypanis or Borysthenes[1]. It is a less crude version of such an idea as the god Gelas on the coins of that city. We can assume some cult of the bountiful river.

Goddesses.

Demeter ranks almost as the city-goddess, wearing as she does on some coins (Pl. III. 3) a mural crown adorned with ears of wheat and on others (Pl. III. 2, 8) wheat-ears alone and so more directly reminding us of the corn trade. Curiously enough her name has not yet appeared upon inscriptions[2], and unluckily an uncertainty of reading in Herodotus (IV. 53, v. p. 454) makes us unable to determine whether she or Cybele had the temple by Cape Hippolaus. It is a question whether she do not appear on the latest *As* from Olbia as Burachkov supposes (v. p. 484).

For Cybele and her cult we have the evidence of an inscription of Roman date recording the erection of a statue to her priestess[3]. Her head appears on a rare coin (Pl. III. 14). Terra-cottas of goddess and priestess were found on the mosaic in the Prytaneum (?).

Aphrodite does not occur on the coins, and the inscription which names her[4] was set up by the Posideus whose taste for exotic deities has been mentioned already (v. p. 463); in any case the epithet Εὔπλοια is interesting: but there is a *graffito* Ἱστιαῖος Ἀφροδίτηι οἶνον[5]. On Berezan G. L. Skadovskij dug up a cylix with the word ΑΠΑΤΟΡΗΣ[6].

Artemis occurs on several coins[7] and on one inscription[8], also round the neck of a vase in the shape of a woman's head stands ΑΡΤΕΜΙΣ ΟΤΙ[9].

There was probably some cult of Hecate at her grove on Kinburn Spit (v. p. 16), though the only inscription from by there is a dedication to Achilles[10].

Thetis is naturally associated with Achilles[11].

A statue of Athena Parthenos was found in 1903[12]. The dedication to Athena Lindia at Neapolis was made by Posideus an Olbiopolite, but that does not prove that this Rhodian cult was established in his own city[13]. It is on the coins that we have most evidence of Athena. Even here it is a question whether Pallas were a native type or had some Athenian connexion. However the *Aes grave* at Olbia seems thoroughly native and some of the earliest examples of it bear Athena helmeted and a fish[14]. Other coppers have a gorgoneion, perhaps still keeping some connexion with Athena, others a beautiful head in which Burachkov may not be wrong in seeing Demeter, though the type also recalls nymphs like Arethusa. Athena may also occur on ordinary coins and is quite common as a countermark (Pl. III. 6, 10)[15].

[1] Two rivers on a late relief, *BCA*. XL. Pl. VI. 19.
[2] Very riskily restored in *BCA*. XIV. p. 98, No. 4.
[3] *IosPE*. I. 107.
[4] *IosPE*. I. 94.
[5] *Trans. Od. Soc.* XXIII. p. 18.
[6] ih. p. 21: *Arch. Anz.* 1904, p. 105.
[7] B. p. 60, Nos. 137—146, Pl. V. 86, VI. 122—128; Pick, X. 14.
[8] *BCA*. X. p. 8, No. 5 *b*. Τιμὼ Ὑψικρέοντος / θυγά- τηρ, / Ἐπικράτου γυνή. / Ἐπικράτης Νικηράτου / Ἀρτέμιδι

ἱερησαμένην, v. p. 482.
[9] *Trans. Od. Soc.* XXIII. p. 19.
[10] *IosPE*. IV. 63, v. p. 481 n. 6.
[11] v. p. 481, *IosPE*. I. 82.
[12] *Arch. Anz.* 1904, p. 106; *BCA*. XIV. p. 69, v. supra, p. 296.
[13] *IosPE*. I. 243.
[14] Pl. II. 2; B. II. 9, 10, 12; *CR*. 1902, p. 24, f. 37.
[15] B. VI. 116—121, 125 is not very clear; Pick X. 15—17, 36, 37, v. inf. pp. 485, 486.

Heracles and Achilles.

Among heroes Heracles who had left a footprint on the Tyras and sons
in the Hylaea[1], undoubtedly received honour at Olbia. A statue of Pantacles
son of Cleombrotus was dedicated to him by the people[2], and his son Cleombrotus,
a contemporary of Protogenes, dedicated to him a tower glorifying himself in
an epigram set out on what seems to have been a ready-shaped Attic grave
stele[3]. He is coupled with Hermes on another inscription also poetical, that
beneath the statue set up by Nicodromus the gymnasiarch after his son's
victory[4].

Latyshev has drawn attention to the curious fact that these last two
inscriptions have been purposely effaced: this may be a coincidence or may
point to a definite destruction of monuments dedicated to Heracles: which
could best be explained by his being regarded as the symbol of some party,
presumably aristocratic, and that party and all its works having been overturned
by opponents. The coins with the head of Heracles are rather rude but are
assigned to the same period, the IInd century B.C. They look however like
poor imitations of Asiatic types rather than the independent expression of
Olbiopolitan worship[5].

The case of Achilles Pontarches allows us to judge for how little in the
matter of worship the coin-types go. Dio says expressly that the Olbiopolites
honour him extraordinarily, and shews them very jealous of his honour when
he ventured to speak lightly of him. Further he says that they had built him
a temple in the city and another in the island called Achilles' Isle. And yet
we cannot point to any coin with his image[6]. On the other hand the inscriptions
bear Dio out fully and are just enough to shew that this was not merely a
matter of the later Olbia.

Mention has already been made of his cult at Leuce and we know that
in the IVth century B.C. Olbiopolites took part in it[7]. But the complimentary
decree[8] expressing thanks for benefits conferred upon citizens visiting the
island suggests that at some time early in the IIIrd century B.C. someone was
living there, presumably a priest, and that he was not under the direct control
of the Olbiopolites: that would not prevent their setting up a decree in honour
of a man who had driven pirates from the island and afterwards came to Olbia
and was useful to the city. That other Greeks made dedications we know
from the graffiti; καὶ τοὶ συνναῦται is surely not Ionic[9]. In later times the
authors all agree that the island was really deserted.

Although Leuce is the most famous Isle of Achilles it is not quite clear
that Dio means it, as in his time the Olbian power could hardly have gone so
far afield. It has therefore been suggested that by this time Berezan had taken
its place, in as much as two dedications[10] have lately been found upon it and

---

[1] Herodotus IV. 82, 8—10.
[2] *BCA.* XXXIII. p. 41, No. 1.
[3] *IosPE.* I. 99, cf. Kieseritzky-Watzinger, 129.
[4] *IosPE.* IV. 459.
[5] Pl. III. 9, 10; B. p. 47, Nos. 51—67, Pl. IV. 32—44; Pick, X. 18—23.
[6] Of those ascribed by Koehne *MK.* I. pp. 84, 85, 88, only the first is possible; and even that dates

from the reign of Caracalla.
[7] *IosPE.* I. 171, 172.
[8] ib. I. 13.
[9] See supra, p. 361 and *Trans. Od. Soc.* XX. p. 169, Pl. I., for that and two other dedications to Achilles.
[10] *BCA.* XVIII. p. 109, No. 14, XXVII. p. 35, No. 32.

two of the first discovered are said to have come thence[1]. But it is clear that these dedications have nothing to do with any temple, for they are scattered along the coast from Koblevka and the Tiligul[2] past Bejkush[3] to Ochakov[4] and again several upon the Tendra or Cursus Achillis[5], one set up by a sailor from Bosporus. Achilles seems even to have invaded the "Grove of Hecate," for an altar to him was dredged up off Kinburn Spit[6]. It is not unlikely that with the changes of these uncertain sandbanks islands may be formed, and afterwards washed away by a new set of the currents or extended to join some existing spit[7]. Such an island in these parts would naturally be sacred to Achilles: but the only permanent ones are Berezan and Leuce, being of such stuff as the mainland is made of.

But though most of the dedications to Achilles are scattered, enough fragments have been found at Olbia to bear out Dio's statement that he had a sanctuary there[8]. We cannot locate the actual site of the temple or as it seems to have been called the chapel ($\pi\rho o\sigma\epsilon\upsilon\chi\dot{\eta}$)[9]: of course it may have been near the shore and handy for people to take the stones away as ballast or building material, but except in the case of a stone found at Odessa[10] this is not a likely explanation of their dispersion in spite of the analogies of the two Tyras inscriptions and the wonderful case at Chersonese[11].

The dedications wherever set up were mostly made by the archons[12], some by the strategi[13], several, as was natural, by priests of Achilles[14], one strangely enough by a priest of Zeus Olbios[15]. It is curious that we do not have Helen, Medea or Iphigenia mentioned though literature always gives Achilles a companion on Leuce[16]. The oldest mention of Achilles[17] except that from Kinburn Spit tells us that there were horse-races in his honour apparently instituted by order of the Pythian prophetess. Achilles is a very common name at Olbia and we also get Brisais[18] from the same associations.

Of the hero Sosias we know but that his place was by the old fish-market[19].

Priests.

Such being the cults of Olbia a word must be said as to the Priests that served them. A priesthood seems to have been an honourable position involving expense and accepted as one of the services to the state expected of an Olbio-polite politician. In the praises of Theocles the son of Satyrus[20] it is mentioned that besides being strategus and archon he had served as priest. So too

[1] *IosPE.* I. 77, 78.
[2] *IosPE.* I. 80, 82, 83.
[3] *IosPE.* IV.17; *Trans. Od. Soc.* XXVII. *Minutes,* pp. 7, cf. 63; 11.
[4] *IosPE.* I. 79. [5] *IosPE.* I. 179—183.
[6] *IosPE.* IV. 63. Ἀχιλλεῖ τὸμ βωμὸν καὶ τὸ κέδρον: this latter perhaps the model of a pine-cone serving as a sea mark; lettering ivth century B.C.
[7] v. p. 16 and Latyshev, "The Island of St Aetherius," *Journ. Min. Pub. Instr.*, St P., May, 1899=Ποντικά, p. 284.
[8] *IosPE.* IV. 18; *BCA.* X. p. 2, No. 2 and some fragments.
[9] *IosPE.* I. 98, v. p. 468, n. 11.
[10] *Trans. Od. Soc.* XXIX. *Minutes,* p. 59.
[11] *IosPE.* IV. 72, v. inf. p. 524, n. 7.

[12] *IosPE.* I. 77 (App. 13), 78, 98 (?); IV. 17, 19(?); *BCA.* X. p. 2, No. 2; XVIII. p. 110, No. 14.
[13] *IosPE.* I. 79, 80; *BCA.* XXVII. p. 35, No. 32; *Trans. Od. Soc.* XXIX. *Minutes,* p. 60.
[14] *IosPE.* I. 81, 82, wherein Thetis is associated with her son, 83; IV. 18, 19(?); *Trans. Od. Soc.* XXIX. *Minutes,* p. 59.
[15] *Trans. Od. Soc.* XXVII. *Minutes,* p. 12.
[16] v. p. 14. Ct I. I. Tolstoi, *Journ. Min. Pub. Instr.* St P., June, 1908, pp. 245—259, "The Myth of the Marriage of Achilles on Leuce," thinks Helen the original mate supplanted by the local heroines.
[17] *IosPE.* I. 17, 1st century B.C.
[18] *BCA.* X. p. 13, No. 8.
[19] App. 7=*IosPE.* I. 16.
[20] App. 10=*IosPE.* I. 22.

Callisthenes son of Callisthenes had been priest of Zeus Olbios[1]. Tryphon son of Tryphon the strategus[2] may not be the same person as the priest of Zeus Olbios[3]. In the time of Protogenes some priest was eponymous but whether that of Apollo Prostates, Achilles Pontarches or possibly Zeus Olbios we cannot say[4].

We have the names of six priests of Achilles Pontarches of whom one served four times and two twice. Hence the office was probably annual. Four of the names are barbarous. This suggests that the priesthood was open to all; not, as might be, closed to the descendants of some priestly house surviving from the old city[5]. Besides these priesthoods of the great patrons of the city we have mention of less important priesthoods probably held for some time. These afford a good excuse for ostentatious folk to set up statues to their relations and glorify themselves. A clear case of this kind of thing is seen in the three statues set up by Epicrates son of Niceratus, one to his uncle Eubiotus son of Ariston priest of the Cabiri[6], one to his wife Timo daughter of Hypsicreon priestess of Artemis and one to his daughter whose name is lost and who does not seem to have held any sacred position[7]. Something the same is the setting up by Agrotas and Posideus of a statue to their father Dionysius priest of Apollo Delphinius[8] and by Socratides son of Philinus to his wife the priestess of Cybele[9].

Of the cult of the Roman Emperors we can only say that it is hard to distinguish evidence for it from the expression of extravagant loyalty. No doubt it existed for the last half century of the city's being[10].

Although religious societies similar to those in the Bosporan kingdom (v. p. 620) existed at Odessus, they have not left any memorials at Olbia.

COINS.   PLATE II.

The most original Olbian pieces are those of cast bronze: Plate II gives nearly all the types and its letterpress the varieties. Coins they were no doubt, at any rate the round ones, but quite unlike any others in the Greek world: the large pieces must have had intrinsic value like the early Italian *aes grave*, taking the place of silver which was probably too scarce for coinage. Coins with intrinsic value ought to shew their mutual relations by their weights, but their extraordinary variability prevents our arriving at an evident conclusion. General Bertier-de-La-Garde (*Comparative Values*, p. 72) gives the weights of 186 specimens and I use his figures founded upon the rejection of pieces in really bad condition. Clearly Nos. 3 and 4, the most modern in style, are on a reduced standard. Taking the Δ which sometimes occurs on No. 4, average weight 112 grm., to mean that it contains 10 units, I have been inclined to take No. 3, average weight 22 grm., to contain 2 units. If we divide the biggest of the old issues into 10, the smaller denominations fall fairly into place.

[1] *IosPE.* I. 24.
[2] ib. I. 57.
[3] *Trans. Od. Soc.* XXVII. *Minutes*, p. 12.
[4] App. 7 = *IosPE.* I. 16.
[5] ib. I. 78, 81, 82; IV. 18, 19; *Trans. Od. Soc.* XXIX. *Minutes*, p. 59; other fragments mentioning priests, *IosPE.* I. 83, 86, 91; IV. 40.

[6] *IosPE.* IV. 27, v. supra, p. 478 n. 12.
[7] *BCA.* x. p. 7, No. 5, v. supra, p. 479 n. 8.
[8] *IosPE.* I. 106.
[9] ib. I. 107.
[10] *IosPE.* I. 97, 97¹, 102, 109; *BCA.* x. p. 6, No. 4 (=App. 14).

	Early Issue.										*Late Issue.*	
Units	1	2	3	(4)	5	(6)	7	(8)	(9)	10	2	10
Types, Nos.	1 h	1 a	2		2 b and 6 a		6			2 a and 1	3	4
Weight {Average	12	28	38		71					117	116	22	112
in grams.}Maximum	16	34	43		76	71		103		127	138	27	120

Bertier-de-La-Garde takes the Δ to be a magistrate's name and thinks that the big coins were bronze obols and the units chalci, eight to the obol Attic fashion in place of Aeginetic twelve. His table would be:

	Early Issue.									*Late Issue.*	
Chalci	1	2	3	(4)	5	(6)	(7)	8		2	8
Types, Nos.	1 b	1 a	2		2 b			2 a and 1		3	4
Average weight (grm.)	12	28	38		71			117	116	22	112

The absence from this of 4 the half-obol is remarkable, though of course it can be made up with two dichalci. He regards the big dolphins as weights not coins, but did not know of No. 6 here published for the first time by the kindness of the British Museum authorities.

Any number of different tables could be drawn up according to different ways of looking at these variable coins but none yet carry conviction. However Bertier-de-La-Garde's further hypotheses deserve stating. He supposes his chalci to have weighed $2\frac{1}{2}$ Aeginetic drachmae of 6·064 grams, and the obol 20 drachmae, so that silver was worth 120 times bronze. Next, just as in the Italian copper we find the *as* reduced to $\frac{1}{3}$ in the IIIrd century B.C., he takes the "Devil" coins (III. 4, 5) to be a token currency of $\frac{1}{3}$ the old weight; transitional is one stamped **APIX** in a wheel like the reverse of No. 1 b[1]. Olbia *asses* circulated in the IIIrd century, for 108 of them were found in piles upon a dish of that date. Copper being then $\frac{1}{120}$ of silver and silver from Alexander's time $\frac{1}{10}$ of gold, gold would be worth 1200 times as much as copper or 400 times as much as the new copper at par. This is just the value at which Protogenes (v. p. 461) accepted the latter, and we can scarcely doubt that it had fallen below par especially if he belonged to the IInd century when the "Devils" are inferior, that is where his service to the city came in, δοὺς χρυσίον πᾶν, χαλκὸν ἐκομίσατο ἐκ τετρακοσίων. It seems however simpler to believe that by his time copper was counted not weighed and that four hundred copper pieces were taken by him for one of gold: this may have been an Attic stater which would be equal to 480 dichalci: the whole drift of the decree is that he was taking less than his due.

The smaller dolphins, mostly so much perished that we cannot establish their true weight, may very likely have been mere tokens: Bertier-de-La-Garde will not see in them coins at all, but from the way that they are held in the hands of the dead on Berezan they seem to correspond to the coins for Charon found elsewhere. On this site two were found shaped like flat-fish instead of dolphins. According to von Sallet[2] the middle sized dolphins with **APIXO** such as Nos. 7 and 8 betokened ἄρριχος a basket of fish, a single fish being reckoned

---

[1] op. c. p. 92 after D. Sestini, *Lett. e Diss. Num.* IV. Florence, 1818, p. 40, No. 4; his Pl. IV. 7 rather recalls my Pl. III. 9.

[2] *Zt. f. Numismatik*, x. p. 144, accepted by Professor Ridgeway, *Origin of Currency*, p. 317.

equal to a smaller dolphin marked ΘΥ[ννός] No. 9.   But against this it must
be urged that the letters ΓΑΥΣ which alternate with ΑΡΙΧ on the coins are
almost certainly short for Pausies or Pausanies[1]; that is that we here have magistrates' names.   Considering the large number of Iranian names beginning with
ΑΡΙ and the known fact that Scyles had a commanding position in the city the
question arises whether even at this early period we have not to do with a
native name.   But this does not explain the : which divides up the word on
No. 8.   With its ΘΥ No. 9 tempts us to see in it a tunny, but why is it in the
shape of a dolphin, which is a natural improvement of a δελφίς ingot, as if one
should put eyes and a snout to a pig of lead ?   Further the fishy wealth of
Olbia was not in tunnies but in sturgeon.   Lastly how should Nos. 1 and 7
bear the same word for a basket ?   Mr J. R. McClean has given ten large
coppers Nos. 1 and 4 and four smaller Nos. 2 and 3 to the Fitzwilliam Museum.
The ΑΡΙΧΟ fish make his reading ΧΑΡΙ[Σ impossible—besides four ounces of
bronze make a weighty symbol for a favour.   So ΑΡΙΧ on the round coins
disposes of Koehler's Τ]ΑΡΙΧ[ΟΣ ; he vainly seeks to distinguish between
tunnies and dolphins, but the back fin of the latter is always characteristic[2].

As to the types, the Pallas is copied from the early coins of Athens.
The Medusa is a current archaic motive, the sea-eagle and dolphin present
the first example of a type which rings the Euxine and is better represented
at Istrus and Sinope[3] than at Olbia.   Nos. 1 and 2 must belong to the
vith century B.C.   The full face Medusa has nothing to do with the fashion
for full faces that prevailed in the ivth century following the wonderful models
from Sicily.   Coins of these types are found not only at Olbia especially on
the edge of the Liman but also on the island Berezan which ceased to be
inhabited soon after the beginning of the vth century, and are associated with
vith century potsherds.   The full face on No. 4 with the more artistic presentment of the eagle and dolphin would appear to belong to the ivth century.
It has a reminiscence of Arethusa, but the way was prepared by the Medusa,
and it has been doubted whether we have not the beautiful Medusa, on the
way to the Rondanini type, others have seen in her a local nymph, but she is
certainly the same head as is seen in profile on the large silver coins Pl. III. 2
and there the evident ears of corn point to Demeter.   No. 3 presents a less
archaic Medusa and the sea-eagle shews that it is not much older than No. 4.

The little coins with ΙΣΤ are a puzzle—the casting technique and place of
finding point to Olbia—v. Sallet (l.c.) thought ΙΣΤ meant ΙΣΤΙΟΝ, Pick (p. 180)
takes it to be ΙΣΤΡΙΗΝΩΝ comparing a coin found by Murzakiewicz on Leuce[4]
bearing a wheel and ΙΣΤΡΙ but struck not cast.   He would refer them to
Istrianorum Portus.   No satisfactory explanation has yet been suggested.
Pharmacovskij[5] puts them down to Istrus itself: Bertier-de-La-Garde (p. 77)
thinks them Olbian small-change tokens[6].

It is hard to distinguish coins of such strange size and shape from the
weights for use in scales.   Bertier-de-La-Garde (p. 78) thinks the large dolphins

---

[1] Cf. Burachkov, Text, p. 37, No. 3, a large
copper, obverse as No. 1; reverse, wheel with
pellets between four spokes, on the rim ΕΠΙΚ.
[2] ΤΑΡΙΧΟΣ, p. 424.
[3] *BMC. Thrace* p. 25; *Pontus*, XXI—XXII.
[4] *Trans. Od. Soc.* III. p. 238, No. 4.

[5] *BCA*. XIII. p. 232, n. 1.
[6] The Schubin coins (Sadowski, op. c., p. 72,
Pl. III. 1, 2, Wheel; 3, Gorgoneion. | Incuse square),
though rather like some of these, are probably not
Olbian, v. supra, p. 440.

like No. 6 and also square blocks with dolphins in relief and magistrates' names (Burachkov III. 16 **KPITOBOY**, VI. 136 **APIΣTOΞ**) all equally weights, deducing therefrom the use at Olbia of a light Phoenician mina of 360 grm. = 5550 grns. divided into 60 Aeginetic drachmae.

PLATE III. 1—19.

As for its *aes grave* so for its silver, but not for gold, Olbia at first used the Aeginetic standard; later on it took to the Attic. Aeginetic are the **EMINAKO** coins (v. p. 487), and the fairly common silver staters, No. 2 weighing about 190 grn. = 12·3 grm. Gold is very rare, the Olbiopolites having evidently used the Cyzicene staters = 10½ local drachmae (v. p. 459); but there are a few small gold pieces, No. 1 weighing 32·8 grn. = 2·13 grm., taken as Attic hemidrachms by G. F. Hill (*Num. Chron.* iv. XII. (1912) Pl. VI. 3) and by Bertier-de-La-Garde who thinks these the gold pieces so freely spoken of in the inscriptions in honour of Callinicus and of Protogenes (v. pp. 459—462), but these are more likely to have been Attic staters, e.g. those of Lysimachus and the unique Olbian gold stater at Brussels (Pick, IX. 1), in type exactly like No. 2; this weighs 132 grn. = 8·51 grm.

The IVth and IIIrd century silver coins mostly bear the head of Demeter, with flowing locks and ears of corn above her forehead; the reverse has on the larger coins the group of the sea-eagle and dolphin, on smaller ones the dolphin with a wheatear or a leaf or alone, like the gold No. 1; these types are not uncommon also upon copper. An interesting type among the earlier coins is No. 3, on which Demeter, still wearing her wheatears, appears in a mural crown as Tyche of the city; the reverse has a magistrate's name and a Scythic archer. On the other coins Demeter is veiled (Pick, x. 9, B. VI. 134).

The commonest type of copper bears a horned river-god with shaggy locks, called by the Russian peasants "Devils"; reverse, a Scythic gorytus and a strange-shaped axe. The series went on for many years: the extremes of style are shewn in Nos. 4 and 5. Each coin bears a monogram or a few letters of a magistrate's name. This series was contemporaneous with the former, as e.g. the ĒK monogram of No. 2 appears on a "Devil" figured by Pick, IX. 27; a specimen countermarked **APIX** has been noted above. The magistrates' names are tabulated in *MK.* I. p. 42, B. p. 45, *Berlin Beschreib.* I. p. 24, *BMC. Thrace*, p. 11. We sometimes find the Demeter head with the bowcase and axe on the reverse; such was No. 11 before being countermarked.

A curious class of coppers is marked by great concavity of the reverse, the edges being bevelled. Hence the small surface of the obverse was more than usually exposed to wear; the head upon it is variously regarded as 'Demeter or Apollo, but No. 9 is very like No. 10, which is certainly Heracles, cf. Pick, x. 19, 20. The reverse has the eagle and dolphin and the letters BΣE. Of similar make are coins with **EIPHBA** (or **BAEIPH**, Pick, x. 26), which look like **ΒΑΣΙΛΕΩΣ ΕΙΡΗΝΑΙΟΥ**, presumably the merely eponymous king. They mostly have Heracles types, and, just as the Heracles inscriptions have been erased (v. supra p. 462), his coins have been stamped with a head of Pallas, cf.

Æ. Head of Pallas helmeted rt. | Owl, ΣBE, oΛBIo.

Pick, X. 15; B. VI. 119.

The only remaining important type is that of Apollo. With the eagle and dolphin reverse he is somewhat uncertain (cf. Pick, IX. 9, but x. 13); on No. 6, the lyre makes him quite clear; two coins with his head are inscribed OIΕΠΤΑ (cf. p. 474, 476), No. 7 with the archer and

Æ. Head of Apollo laur. r.	Bowcase as No. 8 (perhaps the same coin).
	οΛΒΙο, above, οΙΕΠΤΑ below.
Pick, x. 6; B. v. 88.	

Miscellaneous types of interest are,

Æ. 25·8 grn. = 1·67 grm. ⎰Medusa (prob. Demeter	Dolphin, above οΛΒΙο, below ΚΡΙ.
Æ. 94·5 grn. = 6·12 grm. ⎱ as Pl. II. 4) full face.	As No. 2.

The first, Pick, x. 10; B. III. 21; the second, Brit. Mus., *Num. Chron.* 1912, Pl. VI. 4.

Æ. Head of Hermes in petasus r.	Winged caduceus, ΟΛΒΙΟ.
Pick, x. 32; B. VII. 150.	

This is like coins of Tyras (v. p. 448), ΚΑΥ- and Scilurus, Nos. 23, 24; a similar coin (Pick, x. 33) substitutes ΟΛΒΙΟΠΟΛΕΙΤΛΝ as on No. 14 and

Æ. 94·3 grn.=6·11 grm. Head of Pallas in	Spear and shield, ΟΛΒΙΟΠΟΛΕΙΤΩΝ.
helmet r. cf. p. 485.	
Brit. Mus. cf. Æ. Pick, x. 36; B. VI. 116.	

All these coins have the same countermark, a leaf, as on Nos. 13, 14; on No. 12 this has been surcharged with a caduceus suggesting the Hermes coins. Very Mithridatic (cf. Panticapaeum, Pl. VI. 1—4) is

Æ. Winged tripod, above οΛ.	Dolphin, star and caps of Dioscuri.
Pick, x. 31; B. VI. 101.	

The reverse of No. 13 and the eagle of No. 12 recall coins of Mithridates, and may be traces of his power in Olbia. But the reverse of No. 12 is in the BM. specimen practically identical with that of Pharzoeus's gold coin No. 26; on the Odessa specimen the eagle looks the other way.

The various types seem to have succeeded more or less in the order named from the IVth to the Ist century B.C. In the IInd century A.D. we have more coins of Olbia, all of them with the heads or types of Apollo Prostates, to whom so many inscriptions were set up. Probably the ₪ monogram stands here for his name just as at Chersonese it stands for Παρθένος. As Miss Hirst says, No. 16 preserves for us the pose of one cult statue and No. 17 another. But the barbarism of the execution prevents our taking any pleasure in the composition. These coins have the further interest of bearing the names of two archons whom we find mentioned in inscriptions, Adoes Delphi and Dadus Satyri (v. supra p. 473), ✗ clearly = Ἄρχοντος. Pick figures some very rude coins with the name of Olbia and types derived from provincial Roman models, but we will hope that they were the productions of the surrounding savages. One type is interesting, as it shews an ox (Pick, XI. 23), which appears also upon Olbian coins of Severus Alexander. I have reproduced only two in the series of imperial coins of Olbia—they are generally very similar to those of Tyras and other neighbouring cities; they extend from the reign of Septimius Severus to that of Severus Alexander. The coin of Geta, No. 18, has for its reverse a curious representation of Mars, rather a copy of some Roman type than the town statue of Ares; No. 19, Severus Alexander, is presumably the last Olbian coin, though some of later date (v. p. 470), struck elsewhere, have been found on the site.

PLATE III. 20—27.

The historical conclusions that can be drawn from the coins of native kings found about the N.W. Euxine have already been stated (supra p. 119).

In a class by themselves are the silver coins with the name EMINAKo : three finds of them have been made at Olbia, in one case sixteen together in one pot, and they have occurred nowhere else[1].

Æ. 181 grn.=11·73 grm.　Heracles nude but for the lion-scalp, shooting r., within a border of dots.　EMINAKo.	A four-spoked wheel as Pl. II. 2, 5 within an incuse square, dolphins in the spandrels.

The finding place, the reverse and the weight, apparently an Aeginetic stater, suggest Olbia, but the make, with a shallow square, and the obverse (cf. Thasos, Head, *Hist. Num.*², p. 265), recall Thrace : the name looks as likely to be Irano-Scythic as Thracian : the style is late vth century.

Pick divided the later coins, from the IVth century on, according as the rulers whose names they bear may have been lords of Tyras and Olbia respectively. The type, obverse Hermes, reverse caduceus, is common to Odessus (Pick, IV. 19), Tomi (ib. v. 19), which shews other resemblances to native types, Tyras (B. x. 25, cf. *Hist. Num.*¹ p. 234) and Olbia (Pick, x. 32, 33), also to Canites (ib. XIII. 7, perhaps 8), Sarias (ib. XIII. 11), Mostis[2], KAY, No. 23 and Scilurus, No. 24; cf. the caduceus countermark on No. 12: special links are those joining No. 20 to Pick, XII. 16 at Tyras, the monogram which seems to read TOMI on No. 22, whereupon is a head such as appears on the countermark of No. 11, which has the cross-link of Tomitan horse-protomae as though Aelis had spread these over the whole of his dominions. Sarias has divinities on his other coins, Demeter and Apollo, but the head on No. 21 may yet be a portrait; I cannot see the suggested resemblance to No. 5[3]. Tacchella[4] puts down Canites and Sarias as Getan; others of the dynasty would be Adraspus and Acrosandrus (or rather Charaspes and Acrosas)[5]. Two kings named Scostoces would seem to have dwelt in Thrace proper. Besides Nos. 24 and 25 Scilurus has Pick, XII. 5, which I give on p. 50, f. 4, after Koehne's drawing, so as to shew the chariot : on Pick, XII. 4 (reverse like No. 25) he wears a flat headdress, but both that and No. 25 may be portraits[6].

The coin of Pharzoeus shewn, No. 26, is of fair workmanship, but Pick gives two others thoroughly barbarous and of baser gold, which makes Orêshnikov's[7] dating in the 1st century A.D. the more probable. The royal sign on which the eagle stands recurs on the coin of Inismeus, No. 27, and is like the *Tamgi* on Bosporan coins, it just might be conventionalized lightning (supra p. 317 and Pl. VIII. 26). Since my plate was prepared Mr Orêshnikov writes that the Hermitage has acquired a tetradrachm with the magistrate's name Niceratus and the king's spelt Ininsimeus, so it must equal that of the Bosporan Ininthimeus, cf. the two forms Spargapises and Spargapithes in Herodotus : in style the coin is clearly of the 1st century A.D.

[1] *Hist. Num.*² p. 283; *Zt. f. Numismatik*, III. Pl. II. 4; Orêshnikov, *Cat. Moscow University Coins*, p. 15, Pl. I. 9; Bertier-de-La-Garde, op. cit. p. 58, n. 2; *Trans. Od. Soc.* XXV. *Minutes*, p. 54.
[2] G. F. Hill, *Num. Chron.* 1912, Pl. VI. 6.
[3] For both Nos. 21 and 22, cf. W. Wroth, *Num. Chron.* 1899, p. 88: he kindly sent me the casts.

[4] *Rev. Num.* 1900, p. 397, Pl. XII. ; 1903, p. 31, Pl. V.
[5] So Regling in Head's *Corolla Numismatica*, p. 259 ; Pick, p. 520, cf. 601 n. 2; *H.N.*² p. 289.
[6] I cannot agree in assigning to Olbia the coins with KOΣΩN, *HN.*² l.c., cf. *Berlin Beschr.* p. 23.
[7] *TRAS.* IV. p. 14, cf. *Trans. Mosc. Num. Soc.* II. p. 239.

BIBLIOGRAPHY.

Sources.

Nearly all in Latyshev, *Scythica et Caucasica e veteribus Scriptoribus Collecta.* (Supplement to *TRAS.*), St P. 1890–1906. The Indices have not yet appeared.

Herodotus, IV. 17 sqq., 78.

Ps.-Scymnus, ll. 804—812.

Strabo, VII. iii. 17.

Dio Chrysostom, *Or.* XXXVI. (pp. 48—57).

Ps.-Arrian, *Periplus*, 31 (20).

Ptolemy, *Geographia*, III. v. 14; VIII. X. 3.

Stephanus Byz. s.vv. Βορυσθένης and ’Ολβία.

Anon. *Periplus P.E.* 86 (60).

Plutarch, *Vita Cleomenis*, II. Sphaerus Borysthenita.

Diogenes Laertius, IV. vii., *Vita Bionis.*

Eusebius, *Chronici Canones*, ap. Syncellum, p. 402, l. 18: ap. Hieronymum, Ol. 33.

Dexippus, fr. 14: ap. Julium Capitolinum *in Maximo et Balbino*, 16.

Zosimus, I. 42.

Schol. in Apollonium Rhodium, II. l. 660. Dionysius Olbianus.

Pomponius Mela, II. 6.

Pliny, *NH.* IV. 82 (26).

Julius Capitolinus, (*Historia Augusta*), *Vita Antonini Pii*, 9.

Macrobius, *Saturnalia*, I. xi. 33.

Ammianus Marcellinus, XXII. viii. 40.

Jordanes, *Getica*, v. 32.

Inscriptions and History.

Magazine articles whose contents have been summarized in general works are mostly not included. It is impossible fully to separate the historical from the numismatic books.

Blaramberg, J. de, *Choix de Médailles Antiques d'Olbiopolis ou d'Olbia avec une notice sur Olbia.* Paris, 1822. This I do not seem to have seen. As the first attempt at a view of Olbia and its Coinage it has a historical value.

Koehler, H. K. E, "ΤΑΡΙΧΟΣ ou Recherches sur l'histoire et les antiquités des Pêcheries de la Russie Méridionale," *Mém. de l'Acad. Imp. des Sciences de St. Pétersbourg*, VIme Série, T. I., 1832.

Schmidt, W. A. S., "Das olbische Psephisma zu Ehren des Protogenes," *Rhein. Mus.* IV. (1836), pp. 357 sqq., 571 sqq.

Boeckh, A., *CIG.*, Vol. II. Sarmatia. Berlin, 1843.

Uvarov, Ct A. S., *Recherches sur les Antiquités de la Russie Méridionale.* Paris, 1855.

Koehne, B. de, *Description du Musée Kotschoubey (MK)*, I. pp. 1—103, Pl. I. St P. 1857.

Latyshev, V. V., *IosPE.* I. (1885), Nos. 8—172; IV. (1901), 9—63, 456—463, recapitulating Inscrr. published in various periodicals esp. *Trans. Od.· Soc.*; *BCA.* (yearly from 1904), X. p. 1, Nos. 1—12; XIV. p. 94, Nos. 1—7; XVIII. p. 95, Nos. 1—22; XXIII. p. 28, Nos. 1—12; XXVII. p. 35, No. 32; XXXIII. p. 40, Nos. 1, 2; XXXVII. p. 65, Nos. 1—6.

—— *Investigations into the History and Constitution of the City of Olbia.* St P., 1887.

—— Ποντικα, St P. 1909, contains several small articles touching Olbia.

von Stern, E. R., has published in *Trans. Od. Soc.* many Inscrr. some not yet gathered up by Latyshev, e.g. l.c. XXVII. *Minutes*, pp. 7, 12, 64, XXIX. *Minutes*, p. 59.

Hirst, G. M., "The Cults of Olbía," *JHS.* XXII. (1902), p. 245; XXIII. (1903), p. 24. Russian translation with extra notes by Latyshev, *BCA.* XXVII. p. 75.

Rostovtsev, M. I., "Mithridates of Pontus and Olbia," *BCA.* XXIII. p. 21.

—— "Latin Inscription from Olbia," *BCA.* XXVII. p. 64, No. 4.

Škorpil, V. V., "Three Inscribed leaden Tablets from Olbia," *BCA.* XXVII. pp. 68—74.

The regular histories devote few pages to Olbia, e.g. Grote, XII. p. 641 (296—300); Mommsen, *R.G.* v. p. 285=*Provinces* I. pp. 310—312.

Excavations.

Jastrebov, V. N., "Excavations at Olbia," *CR.* 1894, p. 98.

Kulakovskij, J. A., "Excavations at Olbia," *CR.* 1900, p. 3.

Pharmacovskij, B. V., "Excavations on the site of Olbia," *CR.* 1896, p. 200; cf. *JHS.* XVI. (1896), p. 344.

—— "The Vault of Heuresibus and Arete at Olbia," *BCA.* III. p. 1.

—— "Excavations of the Necropolis of Olbia in 1901," ib. VIII.

—— "Excavations at Olbia in 1902-3," ih. XIII.

Accounts of his excavations from 1902—1909 have appeared year by year in *Arch. Anz.* 1904, p. 103; 1905, p. 63; 1906, p. 118; 1907, p. 145; 1908, p. 180; 1909, p. 162; 1910, p. 227; 1911, p. 207 respectively and in *CR.* for the years reported as far as published.

—— Article "Olbia" in Brockhaus-Jefron's *Russian Encyclopaedia*, Suppl. Vol. III.

—— Articles summarizing the work up to 1907 inclusive in *Hermes* (Гермесъ, a New Russian Classical Magazine). St P., 1907.

—— "Olbia 1901—1908, Fouilles et Trouvailles," Communication faite au 2me Congrès International d'Archéologie Classique du Caire, 1909, *BCA.* XXXIII. p. 103.

—— "Olbian Antiquities in the collection of N. Ph. Romanchenko, St P." *BCA.* XLII. pp. 134—143.

Mr Pharmacovskij has very kindly sent me off-prints of most of his articles.

For pots and small antiquities from Olbia see references in Chapter XII. especially to Boehlau, J., *Sammlung A. Vogell*, Cassel, 1908, and to many articles by von Stern and to notices by him in the minutes of nearly every meeting ·in *Trans. Od. Soc.* I have not enumerated the many Olbian articles in its earlier numbers, those dealing with Inscriptions and History are quite superseded by Latyshev; those concerned with the site and excavations unsystematic, the numismatic ones quite fantastic.

Plans of Olbia. Köppen, P. J., *Trans. Od. Soc.* VIII. Pl. IX. made in 1821, reprinted by Blaramberg, op. cit. and by Pharmacovskij, *JHS.* (1896), p. 344 and often in *CR.*

Uvarov, A. S., op. cit., Pl. VIII. A, B, very fanciful.

The Plan, p. 450, f. 331 is that in *JHS.* supplemented by Pharmacovskij in a personal letter for which I am very grateful.

Map of Liman and surrounding country, Ph. Bruun, *Trans. Od. Soc.* v. Pl. 5.

A Bibliography of Berezan has been given on p. 452, n. 1.

Coins.

Besides Blaramberg, Uvarov, Koehne, and casual references in other works enumerated above

BMC. Thrace &c., p. 11. London, 1877.

von Sallet, A., *Zt. für Numismatik*, X. (1883), p. 144.

—— *Beschreibung d. Münzen d. K. Museen zu Berlin* (1888), I. pp. 15—30.

Burachkov, P. O. (B.), *General Catalogue of Coins of Greek Colonies on the N. Coast of the Euxine*, pp. 37—81, Pl. I—IX. Odessa, 1884.

Giel, Ch. (G.), *Kl.B.* p. 1; *TRAS.* v. (1892), p. 344, Pl. IV. 1—4: VII. (1895), p. 217, Pl. XVIII. 1—11.

Head, B. V., *H. Num.*² p. 272.

Oreshnikov, A. V., *Catalogue of Antiquities belonging to Ct A. S. Uvarov*, Pt VII. pp. 3—41. Moscow, 1887.

—— "Coins of Scythian Kings with the name *Olbia*," *TRAS.* IV. (1890) 14—24.

—— *Description of Ancient Greek Coins of Moscow University.* Moscow, 1891.

—— *Materials touching the Ancient Numismatics of the Black Sea Coast*, p. 29. Moscow, 1892.

Antonovich, V. B., *Description of Coins in Kiev University*, pp. 106—112. Kiev, 1896.

Pick, B., *Die antiken Münzen von Dacien und Moesien*, Bd I. Pl. VIII—XII., no text but v. p. 919. Berlin, 1898.

Bertier-de-La-Garde, A. L., *Corrections to Burachkov.* Moscow, 1907.

—— "Comparative values of monetary metals on the Bosporus and Borysthenes, *c.* 350 B.C." Moscow, 1909. (Extract from *Numismatic Miscellany*, Vol. I. Moscow, 1911.)

Pharmacovskij, B. V., "Coins found in 1901," *BCA.* VIII. p. 63, Pl. VI.

—— "Coins found in 1902-3," *BCA.* XIII. p. 233.

Goszkewicz, V. I., *Town Museum, Kherson: Pt I. Coins*, pp. 2—10. Kherson, 1910.

CHAPTER XVI.

CERCINITIS.

Few little towns have had devoted to them so disproportionate an amount of discussion as Cercinitis[1]. Various views about it have been already mentioned as the question had to be taken in connexion with the general topography (p. 17). The evidence for putting it near Eupatoria is the fair agreement with the distance given by the source common to the late Ps.-Arrian and Anon., the fact that this does not contradict the words of the Diophantus inscription, the occurrence of many coins of Cercinitis on this site (they also occur at Chersonese and at other points in the west Crimea) and finally the discovery of remains of a Greek settlement more important than any other in that part of the peninsula.

Between Chersonese and Tarkhankut, the western promontory of the Crimea, the coast forms a kind of quadrant; the only shelter for ships is furnished by a projection southwards breaking the regular curve, and protecting the open roadstead of Eupatoria, so that the modern town faces SE. Two miles to the west is the salt lake of Majnak now, as usual, cut off from the sea. This seems to have been the old harbour, and the old town was on its eastern side. There remain of it a few foundations, among them a grand staircase, some barrows and the site of a cemetery. This last extends as far as the Quarantine on the outskirts of the modern town.

The whole space is defended by a bank across from the lake to the Bay of Eupatoria. The objects yielded by the cemetery date from the vith century B.C. on and include a silver twist (like that figured on p. 208, f. 106, 32), a black-figured lecythus, two red-figured craters, a bronze statuette of Egyptian work and some terra-cottas of all dates, and coins of Cercinitis and Chersonese (of the earlier periods), also of Panticapaeum, Amisus and more rarely Olbia. The middle part of the site has been less dug over. The western part which was the town has the characteristically uneven surface, but the foundations do not present any clear features, though Burachkov claims to have distinguished streets and towers. Lumps of slag, runnings from moulds and imperfect bronze objects make it probable that there was a bronze foundry on

---

[1] The name first occurs in Hecataeus, Fr. 153, ap. Steph. Byz. Καρκινῖτις πόλις Σκυθική. Herodotus IV. 55, 99 mentions a town Καρκινῖτις. On him depends Pomponius Mela II. 4 who mentions the gulf Carcinites and from its name forms that of the town as Carcine; in this he is followed by Pliny, NH. IV. 84, 85 (26), and Ptolemy makes Καρκινίτης a river as well as a gulf and speaks of Κάρκινα πόλις μεσόγειος by misunderstood Herodotean tradition. As his text now stands Strabo (VII. iii. 19; iv. 5) only mentions Καρκινίτης gulf but v. p. 496 infra.

The coins give KAPK and KEPKI. The Inscrr. App. 16, 18 (IosPE. IV. 79; I. 185) have Κερκινῖτις. Ps.-Arrian (30 (19)) and Anon. (83 (57)) in their peripli make Κερκινῖτις 600 stades from Chersonese, Anon. adds the form Κοροvῖτις and speaks of the gulf as Καρκινίτης. There is another Cercina and an island Cercinitis in the lesser Syrtis, cf. כרכה fortress, and some might use this name as an argument for the presence of the Phoenicians in the Euxine. The Italian maps give Crichiniri and such in the W. Crimea (Bruun, Chernomorje, II. p. 8).

the site.   Besides the inscribed stele, others have been found, one with part
of a very rude *Totenmahl*, also a bit of pediment with dentels.   All these are
illustrated in Romanchenko's two papers.   The amphora handles recall those
found at Chersonese.   The barrows occur, some within the defensive bank
(which may be more recent), and some in the open plain.

Mention by Hecataeus proves that the town existed about 500 B.C.
(cf. Jakunchikov's coins).   The one inscription of the ivth century[1] shews
the town to be Dorian, and therefore racially related to Chersonese.   It may
have been an earlier attempt on the part of the founders of the better known
town, more probably it was a sister factory whose development was hindered
by the badness of the Hypacyris route and the indefensibility of its territory.

What degree of autonomy it enjoyed we cannot tell.   Of the three chief
types of coins one would pass as Chersonesan but for the legend; the other
two offer great similarities, but the right of issuing any coins at all argues
formal independence.   Many Chersonesan coins occur on the site, especially
those like Pl. iv. 6, 10.

Probably Cercinitis was at first an independent settlement which was
compelled to lean for help upon Chersonese, whose situation laid it less open
to the attacks of the natives.   On the other hand the open plain about
Cercinitis offered space for a development of agriculture impossible upon
the Lesser Peninsula.   So mutual interest linked the towns very closely
and Chersonese naturally became predominant.   During the ivth and iiird
centuries Chersonese could protect her dependency, but with the organization
of Scythian power under Scilurus, or even before his time, she had to
relinquish it.   By the help of Diophantus it was recovered, but the remains
so far as we know do not shew anything much after the iind century A.D.

COINS.   PLATE IX. 1—3.

Jakunchikov[2] has two coins found on the site but without inscription :

Æ.   17·1 grn. = 1·11 grm.   Horse galloping r. | Rude incuse square.

The later coins are both in make and types very similar to those of Chersonese
(see Pl. iv.).   The head on No. 1 had some resemblance to that on Pl. iv. 17,
especially in the peculiar embattled crown, but it is still more like the Tyche
of Amisus and Heraclea Pontica[3].   This coin also occurs with the magistrate's
name ΠΟΛΥ (Orêshnikov 2).   The axe on No. 2 is rather like that represented on Olbian coins, Pl. iii. 4.   Orêshnikov thinks the head is a dolphin.
This type has several other names ΕΡΜΑ, ΓΕΛΩ, ΙΠΠΟΚΡΑ, ΚΑΛΛΙΑ,
ΚΑΛΛΙΠ (Or. 3—9), ΙΣΤΙ (cf. iv. 14) : the first two of these occur also on
No. 3 (Or. 10, 11), presumably it is of the same date : its types are quite
Chersonesan.   Romanchenko[4] publishes an entirely new type :

Æ.   Head of Heracles r. as at Chersonese, Pl. iv. | Eagle l. upon thunderbolt above H P Ω N, below
9 or 20. | KAPKINI.

[1] *BCA.* X. p. 18, No. 13.   ΑΜΒΑΤΙΑΣΤΑΣ
ΗΡοΔοΤο.
[2] *TRAS. Num. Sect.* I. ii. p. 25, Pl. III. 43, 44.

[3] *BMC. Pontus* II. 10—12 ; XXIX. 19—20.
[4] *BCA.* XXV. p. 187, f. 31.

P. Vacquier (op. cit.) gives several coins of which some are demonstrably strange to Cercinitis, others quite unique, e.g. No. 8:

Æ. Alexander-Heracles r. | Bow and club, between them XEPX above
　　　　　　　　　　　　　| ΒΑΣΙΛΕΟΣ ΣΧΙΛΟΥΡΟΥ

Burachkov (*Trans. Od. Soc.* IX. p. 98) also describes a coin

Æ. Scilurus with sagaris behind him, KEP. | Bow and club, ΒΑΣΙΛΕΟΣ ΣΚΙΛΟΙΡΙΟΥ.

There is nothing improbable in Scilurus having coined at Cercinitis, but no certain examples exist, and it would be a very likely idea for a forger.

Head, *HN.*² p. 279 would distinguish Carcine from Cercinitis following Imhoof-Blumer, "Kleinasiatische Münzen," II. p. 527, Pl. XIX. 25, 26 (*Sonderschr. d. Österr. Arch. Inst.* Wien 1902), who puts down to Tamyrace two coins

Æ. Young Head in helmet l. | Lion not very unlike inf. Pl. v. 10, 11, TAM.

but these have never been found north of the Euxine, and probably belong to some obscure town in Asia Minor.

BIBLIOGRAPHY.

Site and Excavations.

Romanchenko, N. Ph., "Materials for the Archaeology of the District of Eupatoria," *TRAS.* VIII. i—ii. (1895), pp. 219—236.
—— "Excavations in the Environs of Eupatoria," *BCA.* XXV. pp. 172—187, cf. *CR.* 1895, p. 22, 1896, p. 70.
Burachkov, P. O., *Trans. Od. Soc.* XII. (1881), pp. 242—247 and Pl. III. *Trans. Od. Soc.* IX. (1875), pp. 1—133.
Latyshev, V. V., *Mat.* IX. p. 6, treating the Chersonesites' oath.
Bruun, *Chernomorje*, II. p. 6 sqq. and all the literature dealing with the Scythia of Herodotus discuss the question of Cercinitis and the river Hypacyris, v. pp. 17, 33.

Coins.

Friedlaender, G., "Kerkine città del Chersoneso Taurico," *Annali* (*Bulletino*) *dell' Instituto*, XVI. pp. 232-4. Roma, 1844.
Spasskij, G. I. The same article (first in *Trans. Od. Soc.* II. 1848) then "De la situation de l'antique ville de Carcinis et de ses monnaies," *Mém. de la Soc. Imp. d'Arch. de St. P.* IV. (1850), p. 317, and in *Archaeologico-Numismatic Miscellany.* Moscow, 1850.
Koehne, *Musée Kotschoubey*, I. pp. 105—112.
Burachkov as above and in his general Catalogue, p. 95 and Pl. XIII.
Vacquier, P., *Numismatique des Scythes et des Sarmates, Kerkinitis et Tannais*, Paris, 1881; cf. v. Sallet in *Zt. f. Numism.* X. p. 309.
von Sallet, A., *Beschr. der Münzen*, I. p. 1, Pl. I. 1—3. Berlin, 1888.
Orêshnikov, A. V., *Cat. Moscow University Coll.* p. 25. Moscow, 1891.
—— *Materials touching the ancient Numismatics of the Black Sea Coast*, Moscow, 1892, pp. 1—14 and Pl. I.: "Coins of Carcinitis or Cercinitis," reviews all preceding work and gives photographs of Burachkov's coins.
Romanchenko, N. Ph., "On the question of an ancient settlement near Eupatoria," *Archaeological Bulletin* (*Archeologicheskia Izvêstia*), 1894, pp. 9—15, I have not seen but its content is repeated in *BCA.* XXV. p. 187.
Jakunchikov, B. M., "Unpublished and rare Greek Coins," *TRAS. Num. Section*, I. ii. p. 25, Pl. III. 43, 44. St Petersburg, 1909.
Head, B. V., *HN.*² p. 279. Oxford, 1911.
Bertier-de-La-Garde, A. L., "Monetary Novelties," No. 1, *Trans. Od. Soc.* XXX. 1912.

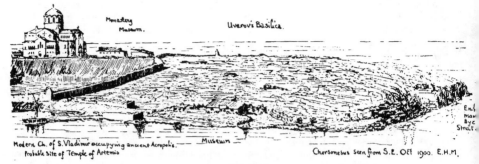

FIG. 333 b.

CHAPTER XVII.

CHERSONESE.

CHERSONESE[1] differs from all the other Greek colonies on the north shore of the Euxine except Cercinitis in being Dorian. It can hardly be a coincidence that like the other Dorian colonies it was founded on a site which however accessible from the sea did not offer special advantages for trade with the interior. Just as Heraclea Pontica, its mother city, had its own territory from which it drew supplies, so for the greater part of its existence Chersonese had mainly to rely on the produce of the Lesser Peninsula which soon became its very own, and in flourishing periods on possessions in the west part of the Crimea. But when the other colonies because of their intimate connexion· with the natives whose hostility might bring ruin fell into decay through the change of population, then rose to importance the

[1] The official title of the city was Χερσόνασος ά ποτὶ τᾷ Ταυρικᾷ (*IosPE.* IV. 71, 72), other Greeks spoke of Χερσοναοΐται οἱ ἐκ τοῦ Πόντου (Ditt. *Syll.*[2] 268, 281, 588); so it was distinguished from Chersonesus in Crete and the various peninsulas Thracian, Cnidian etc. There is always to be feared possible confusion with Chersonesus Taurica, the Crimea (Chersonesus Taurica = the city seems modern Latin), also with the Lesser Peninsula, Strabo's μικρά, which constituted the homeland of the city. The general name was Χερσόνησος or Χερρόνησος, there seems no ancient authority for the fashion of doubling the *n*. Pliny, *NH.* IV. 85 (26), speaks of Heraclea Cherronesus, but that name seems due to his mixing it up with Heraclea Pontica its mother city: many modern writers use it as the full designation. About the IIIrd century A.D. came in the forms Χερσών, Χερσωνίται first found in a frag-

ment of Phlegon of Tralles in the time of Hadrian, but the quotation occurs in late authors who may have substituted the more modern form (e.g. Const. Porph. *de Them.* II. 12, p. 63). Dionysius Exiguus (ap. Mansi, *Concil.* III. p. 366, but cf. p. 383) translates the signature of Bp Aetherius II at the second council of Constantinople A.D. 381 as <T>ersonitanus, whereas his successor at the council of 448 was styled ἐπίσκοπος Χερρόνησου (ib. VIII. p. 239, cf. p. 243): that is the long form did not at once give way to the short. The latter appears in Latin as Chersona in Jordanes (*Get.* V. 32, 37). The Russian chronicle makes it Корсунь, Korsun. The Tartar name was Sary Kermen, the yellow fortress, cf. Selivanov, p. 10, n. 3: Brandes, s.v. Chersonesos (20), *P.-W.* III. p. 2261. I shall call it Chersonese as the anglicized form of the word is familiar though not in its application to this city.

modest commerce of the Chersonesites, safe in their remote corner of a secondary peninsula. So the time when Chersonese was of moment in the world was when it was handing on to the untouched tribes of Russia the religion and culture of Eastern Rome. That is my excuse for continuing my sketch of its history to the time when cut off from the interior by the Mongols it died at the coming of the. Turk.

Since then it has lain desolate. In 1578 Martinus Broniovius de Biezdz-fedea[1], ambassador from Bathóry to the Crim Tartars, visited the site of which he left a high-flown account more indebted to Strabo than to his own eyes. So it remained until the coming of the Russians in 1783, and the speedy foundation of Sevastopol. Chersonese then became accessible to travellers and the first learned folk to see it were Pallas[2], Mrs Guthrie[3], and Dr E. D. Clarke[4]. All these had preconceived ideas of what ought to be found on a classical site, and when nothing of the sort was to be seen, they ascribed the desolation to a Russian passion for destruction. General A. L. Bertier-de-La-Garde[5] has shewn that Pallas and Clarke much exaggerated the damage done. Clarke, more especially after the treatment he had suffered at the hands of the insane Emperor Paul, was no doubt excessively prejudiced against the Russians, and everywhere speaks of the antiquities that he saw as doomed to destruction. As a matter of fact everything he mentions has been preserved unto this day; but the explanation is probably that he visited the country just as real order was being established, and the pioneers of conquest were giving place to a more settled administration which could see to the preservation of antiquities. But during the first twenty years it was small blame to the Russians if they used Chersonese as a quarry for Sevastopol and stripped the town of the ready squared stone that lay on the surface. General Bertier-de-La-Garde argues that during its long decay the city's fine buildings had been dilapidated by its own inhabitants, and that there was nothing but small rough stone left by the time the Russians appeared, but the amount of squared stone walling discovered in recent excavations offers a presumption that much had remained aboveground and was greedily carried off to Sevastopol. It can hardly be held that it was more trouble to cart stone a couple of miles than to quarry it at Inkerman five miles off. Some destruction had already been done by the Turks who are said to have shipped columns across to Constantinople, by the Genoese, and by the Tartars; but at the time of the Russian occupation the remains of the poor Byzantine town stood almost intact surrounded by its walls, and with its gates *in situ*[6]: much in the same way Chufut Kale stands on its hill deserted by all but a Rabbi in charge of the Karaite synagogue, the people having gradually moved to Baghchi Saraj. To charges of reckless destructiveness Russians can reply that the Allies did their share of damage during the siege of Sevastopol.

[1] *Tartariae Descriptio*, Col. Agrip. 1595 reprinted in the Elzevir *Russia seu Muscovia*, Lugd. Bat. 1630, p. 258.
[2] *Tour in Southern Provinces*, Vol. II. p. 55.
[3] *Tour in Taurida made in* 1795, London, 1802, p. 95.

[4] *Travels*, Vol. II. pp. 206, 273, London, 1817, 8vo.
[5] *Mat.* XII. p. 1 sqq.
[6] A view shewing it like this is reproduced in Ainalov, *Monuments of Christian Chersonese*, I. p. 1, f. 2 after Sumarokov, *Leisure of a Crimean Judge*, St Petersburg, 1803, but it is mostly fancy.

The Lesser Peninsula.

The home domain of Chersonese consisted of what Strabo calls the Lesser Peninsula, a triangle of which the base is the line from Inkerman to Balaklava (7½ miles = 12 km.) and the south side the inhospitable coast from the latter to Cape Chersonese about 14 miles (23 km.) following the slight curves. The general line of the north side is fairly straight and extends some 12 miles (20 km.) from the Cape to the head of the North Bay at Inkerman, but the coast is deeply indented and presents a wonderful series of harbours.

This triangle is a plateau which has a general slope towards the north and especially the west (on Map VIII. the heights are marked in feet), from the cliffs at the extreme south, where they reach 1000 feet (304 m.) to the lower cliffs opposite Inkerman, and to the flat Cape Chersonese. The edge of the plateau forms an escarpment overlooking a depression which coincides with the base of the triangle. Further to the east were the mountains of the Tauri, a region that the Chersonesites never seem to have subdued until after the Christian era. This triangle is precisely the limit of the ground occupied by the Allies besieging Sevastopol; they could hold the Sapun and Karagach escarpment against the Russian armies that attempted to relieve the town. It is drained by many ravines which make the inlets of the northern coast. General Bertier-de-La-Garde[1] still further reduces the space owned by the citizens saying that traces of their occupation scarcely extend east of the South Bay of Sevastopol.

This exposed limestone plateau is now mostly barren: it lacks moisture and the soil is very thin: only in the ravines are there attempts at gardening and a few vineyards on the south-eastern slopes above Kadikoj. Yet in ancient times its whole surface was undoubtedly cultivated. Dubois de Montpéreux traced all over it the lines of regular boundary walls and in many places the foundations of the ancient homesteads[2]. Inscriptions give us fragments of a decree concerning the apportionment of land[3] and Agasicles is praised for his services in a redistribution of the vineyards[4]. The produce of the vineyards was exported in amphorae referred to Chersonese on account of Doric names which coincide with those of known Chersonesan magistrates[5]. I have no explanation of the enigma to offer unless it were a great diminution of rainfall; perhaps if sufficient labour and intelligence were applied to the peninsula it could support a considerable population. Nowadays this is not worth while as the valleys along the south coast of the great peninsula are far more attractive; debarred from these by the Tauri the Chersonesites did their best with difficult soil. In later times when decay set in Chersonese had to rely on imported wine and grain paid for with hides and wax from the Pecheneg country[6].

Let us now apply Strabo's description to this country.

---

[1] *BCA.* XXI. p. 192 note.
[2] Dubois de M. I. Pl. XX., XXI. not trustworthy, cf. Pallas, II. p. 66 and Neumann, *Hellenen*, pp. 403 sqq.; Arkas, Pl. IV.; Pechonkin, *BCA.* XLII. pp. 108—126, Pl. III. gives a careful plan of such near C. Chersonese: he figures an ancient stone winevat, p. 111, f. 1.

[3] *IosPE.* IV. 80.
[4] *IosPE.* I. 195 = App. 17. This may refer to land in the west of the Crimea, v. p. 518.
[5] Collected and well annotated by I. I. Makhov, *Bull. Taur. Rec. Comm.* XLVIII. 1912.
[6] Const. Porph. *de Adm. Imp.* c. 53, v. inf. p. 538.

"As you sail out (of the Gulf of Carcinites) you have on your left[1]......a townlet and another harbour of the Chersonesites. For as you continue your sail there stretches out towards the south a great promontory being part of the main Chersonese and upon it is built the city of the Heracleotes, itself called Chersonese. In this is the Sanctuary of the Maiden (a deity after which also is named the cape that runs out in front of the city at a distance of 100 stades and is called Parthenium[2]) with a temple of the deity and an image. But between the city and the cape are three harbours. Then comes Old Chersonese all pulled down and after it a harbour with a narrow mouth, at which point the Tauri did most of their piracies attacking those that took refuge in it: it is called the harbour Symbolôn. And this harbour makes with another called Ctenus an isthmus forty stades broad, this is that which shuts in the lesser Chersonese which we said was a part of the great Chersonese and has in it the town with the same name of Chersonese."

In the next section Strabo remarks that Ctenus is the same distance from the town Chersonese as from the harbour Symbolôn.

Again (l.c. § 7) he speaks of "a place called Eupatorium founded by Diophantus general of Mithridates. It is a cape distant about 15 stades from the wall (τείχους) of the Chersonesites making a fine large bay turned towards the city. Above it is a sea-mere with salt-works. This was where Ctenus was." He next describes how Diophantus fortified the cape and made a mole across to the city (καὶ τὸ στόμα τοῦ κόλπου τὸ μέχρι τῆς πόλεως διέχωσαν, surely this must be a mistake, a bridge or boom would give the easy communication sought) and how when the Scythians tried to pass the ditch across the isthmus towards Ctenus, by filling it up each day with reeds, the king's men burnt them each night and so repelled their attacks (v. p. 519).

With New Chersonese fixed the promontory Parthenium must be that now called Cape Chersonese, the distance of 100 stades agrees fairly well with the actual 85, by land it would agree almost exactly. The three harbours would be Strelets, Reedy and Cossack Bays. The narrow-mouthed harbour Symbolon is clearly Balaklava. Old Chersonese should be somewhere east of Cape Parthenium. Clarke and Pallas say that the isthmus between Cossack Bay and the south-western sea was covered with the remains of a town, and on this the only conceivable site, Kosciuszko-Waluzynicz's excavations exposed two cross-walls with towers and gates, also remains of houses and small antiquities going back to the Greek period of Chersonese. The end of one of

---

[1] VII. iv. 2. The first words Ἐκπλέοντι δ' ἐν ἀριστερᾷ πολίχνη καὶ ἄλλος λιμὴν Χερρονησιτῶν have something wrong with them. Casaubon long ago conjectured Καλὸς λιμήν, C. Müller in a note to Ptol., *Geog.* III. v. 2 (p. 414), suggests καὶ Καλὸς λιμὴν εἶτα δὲ ἄλλος λιμήν, but Latyshev in his comment on the Citizens' oath in *Mat.* IX. p. 8 and in *Journ. Min. Pub. Instr.* St P., 1892, April=Ποντικά, p. 129, thinks that the lacuna was still greater including a description of all the SW. coast of the Crimea. The loss was in any case due to the homoeoteleuta ΚΑΛΟϹΛΙΜΗΝ and ΑΛΛΟϹΛΙΜΗΝ, that is the Fair Haven was mentioned and its name misunderstood. The towns along the west coast of the Crimea would be accounted for and the copyist's mistake easily explained if only we dare put back

the text in some such form as this—

ΕΚΠΛΕΟΝΤΙΔΕΝΑΡΙϹΤΕ
ΡΑΙΕϹΤΙΚΑΛΟϹΛΙΜΗΝ
Κ'ΤΕΙΧΗΧΕΡΡΟΝΗϹΙΤΩ-
ΕΙΤΑΔΕΚΑΡΚΙΝΙΤΙϹ
ΠΟΛΙΧΝΗΚ'ΑΛΛΟϹΛΙΜΗΝ
ΧΕΡΡΟΝΗϹΙΤΩΝ

The lines are hardly shorter than usual, e.g. Kenyon, *Palaeography of Greek Papyri*, pp. 21, 66, Pl. XI. or Schubart, *Pap. Gr. Berol.* 31, Theaetetus.

[2] Latyshev, l.c. first proposed taking this as a parenthesis and so doing away with the idea of two sanctuaries, one in the town, another on the cape. Hence the buildings identified as this temple by Pallas and later travellers are probably but homesteads with well-built refuge towers.

the walls projected into Cossack Bay and formed an island upon which the Byzantines built a monastery answering to the account of the first resting place of S. Clement of Rome. If this fortress was not Old Chersonese it may have been a place of refuge to which cattle might be driven away from inroads of the Tauri, perhaps one of the τείχη referred to in the citizens' oath (v. p. 516)[1].

In 1910 N. M. Pechonkin[2] found pots and other objects beginning like the oldest things from New Chersonese with the end of the ivth century B.C. and going down to the early Roman period, when Strabo speaks of the place as ruined. They do not tell us whether this was the original settlement made in a corner remote from the natives because the Heracleotes were not yet sure of their ground, nor, if so, when the bulk of the population migrated, leaving a mere remnant behind. Pliny (l.c.), who does not seem dependent on Strabo, implies the existence of Old Chersonese by speaking of Cherronesus Nea.

Ctenus is clearly the great bay now called North Bay, the subsidiary Quarantine, Artillery, South, Dock and Careening Bays make it not unlike a comb. Balaklava to Inkerman is nearer sixty than forty stades[3] but this distance just answers to the five miles from Chersonese to Inkerman. Eupatorium fifteen stades from Chersonese must have been a fort made by walling off the end of the North Cape and this is the isthmus towards Ctenus of which Strabo speaks in § 7; not the isthmus Balaklava-Inkerman. Pallas and Clarke misunderstanding this passage saw remains of a wall along the latter line; but General Bertier-de-La-Garde declares that there are no traces of it now and well shews that the population of Chersonese could not have manned so long a wall. No doubt they had observation-posts along the Sapun ridge and relied on the lie of the land for protection. Even so the massive foundations of the scattered homesteads suggest that they were built to offer refuge against sudden raids; there were no open villages.

The value of a *tête-de-pont* like Eupatorium to Diophantus who carried war into the country of the Scyths is evident, saving him from the long march round the North Bay and the dangerous passage of the Chërnaja. The batteries on North Cape remained in Russian possession and the defenders of Sevastopol retired to them by a bridge thrown across from the city and so withdrew.

No attempt has been made to state the many conflicting views as to these various localities, e.g. Burachkov put Eupatorium at Eupatoria regardless of distances. Eupatoria is another instance of singularly unfortunate application of ancient names. Bertier-de-La-Garde[4] denies that Eupatorium was the name of the fortress built by the besieged across the bay; yet this is the natural deduction from Strabo's words; so the Allies had their Fort Victoria. He maintains that the whole story about Scythian siege applies exactly to Cossack Bay and the site of Old Chersonese: the points deciding him are the sea-mere with salterns and the shallowness of the bay which allowed of throwing the mole across it. Von Stern[5] will have none of Old Chersonese but allows the scene of this siege to have been in Cossack Bay, saying that it is a

---

[1] *CR.* 1890, p. 37, and Clarke's plan, II. p. 273.
[2] *Arch. Anz.* 1911, p. 206; *BCA.* XLII. pp. 108—126.
[3] Pallas says that the distance does not look more than 40, op. cit. II. p. 62.

[4] *BCA.* XXI. p. 177 sqq.
[5] *Trans. Od. Soc.* XIX. *Minutes*, p. 99; Hettler's *Zt. f. Alte Gesch.* I. 2, pp. 63—71, and again *Trans. Od. Soc.* XXVIII. *Minutes*, p. 89.

matter of the τείχη or forts of the Chersonesites (v. p. 516) not of the city wall, but this again is straining Strabo's words as he mostly speaks of πόλις. The view in the text has to give up διέχωσαν : 15 stades of mole is too much to ask, however shallow the bay: a bridge is no mean feat. The saltern cannot be reckoned a permanent geographical feature, but there is a lake just inside North Cape[1].

Site and Remains.

The final settlement of the Heracleotes was on a low peninsula between the lesser Round Bay and the Quarantine Bay[2].   Among all the harbours offering this seems to have been chosen because it was well commanded by an easily fortified site yet itself had gently sloping shores suitable for the Greek method of beaching ships.   The western harbours provided no kind of acropolis, the eastern such as South Bay were enclosed by steep cliffs, and North Bay was on too large a scale and too much exposed to enemies.

The space finally enclosed by the walls of New Chersonese is some five eighths of a mile (about 1 km.) long from west to east and 600 yards (550 m.) from north to south occupying the whole of the blunt headland between the two bays.   This gives a circumference of two English miles (3 km.) which can in no way tally with Pliny's five Roman miles[3].   This considerable extent was naturally not built with one effort, but the capricious progress of the work shews less perseverance than might have been expected.   The explanation is

[1] Ptolemy, *Geog.* III. vi. 2, may in the light of this view receive a rather better interpretation than Latyshev's on Map II. (supra, p. 11): long. 60°: lat. 47° 16′ (Symbolon Portus) can be at the head of an inlet running up from the SE. and 61° 15′: 47° 10′ (Ctenus) on a deeper inlet coming from the NW. by "Eupatoria" (60° 45′: 47° 40′). Thus an outline not unlike the actual, though not to be deduced from Ptolemy's data, can be made to fit them. Chersonese so appears between C. Parthenium and Symbolon Portus, i.e. on the site of the old city. Dandace seems to occupy about the place of the new town and perhaps it was the name of one of Strabo's three harbours. Amm. Marc. who mentions it only copies Ptolemy.

[2] The following account of the fortifications of New Chersonese with the deductions which can be drawn from them with regard to the history of that settlement presents, except as regards the open state of the town, the views of General Bertier-de-La-Garde (*BCA.* XXL), who has brought to the solution of the problems a most wonderful combination of qualities, for he is at once a soldier who understands the strategy and tactics of attack and defence, an engineer trained to notice technical points, an archaeologist and so to speak an "oldest inhabitant."   Nothing less than this was required to answer the riddles presented and produce a consistent explanation of all the phenomena. Plan VII may not be quite exact, but Fig. 338 supplements it in the interesting area. The difficulty was that no large-scale plan had been published and the small-scale ones differed surprisingly from each other.   I took as my main basis that given in Brockhaus-Jefron's Russian Encyclopaedia, s.v. *Chersonese,* and on it endeavoured to combine the sectional plans drawn to various scales which have accompanied the yearly reports of the excavations published in *CR.* from 1888—1906 and in *BCA.* (v. Bibliography p. 551). Finally I corrected the fortifications by Bertier-de-La-Garde's Pl. II. &c., and the churches and earlier excavations by Ainalov, *Monuments of Christian Chersonese,* I. "Ruins of Churches,"f. 1, and Mr M. I. Skubetov, draughtsman to the excavations, made some important additions on the rough copy. The death of Mr K. K. Kosciuszko-Walużynicz in December 1907 made it impossible to bring out the full results of his last two years' work.   To him we owe almost all our knowledge of what has been actually found at Chersonese and I am specially indebted to him for his courtesy in giving me information on the spot and in supplying me with the latest results of his researches.   The present Director of the excavations, Dr R. Löper, has continued his predecessor's kindness to me.

A great hindrance to the work is the presence of the monastery, which takes up the best part of the site. Its great church, the chief landmark of Chersonese, is built over the remains of a basilica hastily assumed to be the scene of Vladimir's baptism. Further the operations of military engineers are destructive but unavoidable as the site is of such strategic importance to Sevastopol.

[3] *NH.* IV. 85. This distance must refer to the isthmus of Perekop, cf. Pomp. Mela II. 3, 4, whom Pliny seems to have misunderstood.

that until the 1st century B.C. a wall of crude brick or a palisade was in places defence enough.   During the IVth century when danger was to be feared from the aggressive policy of the Spartocids, Greek poliorcetics were rather elementary, later on it was only a question of barbarian raids almost powerless against any sort of fortification[1].

One exposed point of the position was clearly the lowest part of the site towards its SE. corner (Fig. 338) commanded as it is by a considerable hill to the SW. of it: moreover it was vital to protect the port.   Here accordingly was made the first attempt at fortification, or probably, as von Stern points out[2], the beginning was made here for physical rather than tactical reasons. Between E and B the wall goes down into a deep valley the middle of which about DC is nothing but the old bed of an arm of the harbour.   The foundations actually stand in water and for that reason have not been exposed. In this water crude brick would simply have melted[3]; so from the tower F to the tower C were built the lower courses of a wall, and towers and gates were laid out: the towers had rather shallow projection and the gates were not well commanded by cross fire, but it was early for these improvements.

This whole piece of work is admirable, even extravagant in execution. The stones are large and "rusticated," i.e. carefully smoothed round the edges, the face being left rough; they are laid as headers and stretchers alternately, without mortar but held by swallow-tailed wooden clamps.   The facing is backed with rubble and stones set in clay, total thickness 12 ft. 8 in. (3·85 m.). Upon some stones are masons' marks, notably an N with the archaic slope, later forms point to the IVth century[4].   Deep in the heart of the wall[5] by the gate and dating from its construction is a sepulchral passage, a kind of T-shaped tunnel containing urns within which were ashes and jewelry, the earliest of which is of the IVth century, the latest about a hundred years more recent (v. pp. 380, 397—399, 402, 410 n. 1, 422): members of a distinguished family were successively buried here: having regard to the singular position, may it not be supposed that we have here the family tomb of the builder of the wall?   He may have deserved the honour by his munificent intentions, but he did not execute them.   The curtain walls were nowhere carried up more than nine courses[6]: some of the towers were left even lower (v. elevation on Fig. 338): also the gate E by its position involved a most inconveniently steep approach.   Perhaps because these weak points were observed the work was left incomplete as is shewn by the regularly stepped line of its top courses, quite unlike the look of a wall which has been partly knocked down after having once been finished; further no similar stones have been found used as material in any later building.

A second attempt was made after a short interval which did not give the projecting corners time to weather: the work was more cheaply executed, the stones smaller and far less regular, though still rusticated; there are no masons'

[1] How elementary they were in the Vth century is well shewn by Grundy, *Thucydides and the History of his Age*, Ch. XIII. p. 282 sqq.   Bertier-de-La-Garde thinks that Old Chersonese remained as a refuge until the 1st century A.D. and so the Chersonesites were in no hurry to complete their defence on the new site.

[2] *Trans. Od. Soc.* XXVIII. *Minutes*, p. 113.
[3] Cf. Xenophon, *Hellen.* v. ii. 1—8.
[4] *BCA.* XXI. p. 93, f. 14; similar marks along L-N-O and on the house-walls G-G.
[5] v. inset Plan VII; *BCA.* I. pp. 3—5, ff. 2—4.
[6] Mr Wace suggests a mud brick top to the wall.

marks.   In this style the stepped upper line of the first attempt was brought
to a level, but in other respects the former plans were departed from.   The
unfinished gate E was walled up and the towers were rebuilt with more projection,
thus the depth of this stratum varies from eleven courses at the tower D which
had not been intended by the first building, and seven in the curtain wall by
C to one course on the wall about the gate E (v. elevation on Fig. 338).

FIG. 334.   Gates (E on Plan VII. v. inset) in the Greek Wall of Chersonese.   Eight courses of 1st period, one of 2nd ; above, Roman with
threshold of postern.   The gate was 3·87 m. broad, the passage way
8·39 m. long.   Just within the entrance are portcullis-grooves and
5·33 m. from the face of the wall are projections reducing the opening
to 2·12 m.   To the east of the gate inside was a stair to go up on the
wall.   Three water runnels meeting give the directions of streets, two
"back of the walls," one towards the Acropolis and one towards the
harbour (Fig. 338).   At a lower level than all this was a sepulchral
monument 2·40 m. square as it were a pyramid with three steps (*CR.*
1900, p. 21, f. 43).   The jambs of the gate shewed no signs of any
traffic having passed through it.
From a photograph furnished by Mr Kosciuszko-Walużynicz, who stands
in the gateway.

The plans were changed even during the execution of this small piece of
work.   In the second style the foundations were laid of a wall running east of

tower C to a round tower of the same size (V^1 on Fig. 338)[1]. Then they seem to have decided to include a greater space for the harbour district and the towers A^1 and B were built, but nothing remains to connect B up with a curtain wall. So far they had got by the IIIrd century B.C. Towards the end of the IInd century they began to join up towers C and B by means of a wall jutting out to the west of C and having in it a postern c with a skilfully turned arch : this wall only reached half-way to B^2.

After the middle of the last century B.C., perhaps as a result of experiences in the wars with Scilurus, they tried to make Chersonese more defensible on this side and also more convenient. With the latter intention the existing masonry wall was sacrificed. We have seen that between E and B the wall

FIG. 335. *BCA.* I. p. 29, f. 23. Greek walls at Chersonese looking SE. from near *e* towards *Dd*. Seven courses of first period, four of second with round tower *D*. Upper work and square towers *Dd*, Roman.

descended into a deep valley. The road to the main part of the city followed it down into this marshy depression and then climbed a very steep slope to the gate at about *I*. To remedy this the beginnings of the defensive walls were used as a retaining wall and earth to the depth of about 20 ft. was piled against their outer face to make a causeway.

Another weak point was at the SW. corner L-N, where an enemy might come along a hog's back leading gently down to the town : here again we have IVth century work forming a foundation for the walling of irregularly squared but not rusticated stones characteristic of the Roman period, when the circuit was finally completed in masonry.

[1] *CR.* 1905, Pl. III.
[2] *CR.* 1900, Pl. I. pp. 13, 14, ff. 27—29; *BCA.* XXI. p. 109, f. 16.

From the successive towers A^1, A^2 on the shore of the harbour[1] a wall five times rebuilt runs sw. to B, the most exposed point in the circuit. Hence the original narrow tower of the second Greek period was treated as a mere nucleus thickened at three successive rebuildings. Just by it was a postern b. The piece of wall from B to C rested for its northern half on the Greek wall of the second period, but the latter had been completely earthed over, for there are courses of rough foundation masonry between it and the lowest course of Roman finished walling[2]. A new postern c was built just above the former one. Its object was to allow sallies from b to return to the town without exposing their right flank to an enemy. In the straight piece from C to E (Fig. 335) the three periods of masonry are best seen. At D the second period had designed a weak semicircular tower. The gate at E had long been walled up. It had no proper cross fire to defend it, and was altogether badly placed. The round Greek tower E^1 to the west of it was not a powerful work, in Roman times it was rebuilt in rectangular form[3]. F was a stronger circular tower[4]. No Greek work remains along the slope from F almost to L. At I was the main town gate for traffic approaching from the east and a street led up from it to the Acropolis[5]. J was a tower whose importance came later[6]—between it and the se. corner tower L^7 there were only three ordinary towers as here the ground falls steeply from the foot of the wall. Some way along this space were the main Thermae[8] from which successive lines of water-courses ran between the walls to c, here re-entered the town over the postern and so gained the harbour[9]. The next section L-N ran across a ridge giving easy access to the great gates M, the chief entrance to the town from the plateau, Balaklava and Old Chersonese: the gates were renewed in Byzantine times, and the actual doors stood until the xviiith century. The aqueduct from Jukharin's Ravine entered the town at this point: but the levels were equally favourable for bringing siege engines up to this piece of wall, therefore it was built as early as the ivth century B.C. and in Roman times rebuilt, doubled and strengthened by four towers: in 1894–5 it was mostly cleared away by the War Office[10]. The same applies to the stretch N-O. From O the foundations of the Greek wall go straight on nnw. to P^1, the remains of a round tower; there must have been three towers in between. The Romans turned the wall westwards at a small gate and a tower: their wall makes two more projecting bends with towers, a re-entrant angle by o where a retaining arch carries it over a burial chamber[11], and finally at P^2 reaches the sea at a tower half of which has fallen[12]. This tower commanded the postern p (v. Fig. 336). This western section of the wall is remarkably well designed to secure cross-fire and is further strengthened with an outer wall.

The system of an outer wall was applied also to the other part of the walls resting on Greek foundations. The reports in *BCA.* give it as early Byzantine but one stretch seems according to the graves it disturbs to be rather of the Antonine age[13]. It reaches from the tower J past the gates I to the

[1] *CR.* 1897, pp. 91, 92, ff. 203, 204.
[2] *BCA.* XXI. Pl. VII.
[3] *CR.* 1904, pp. 64—67, ff. 96—102.
[4] *CR.* 1903, Pl. III. i., p. 30, f. 28.
[5] *CR.* 1905, Pl. II.
[6] *BCA.* XVI. Pl. III.
[7] *CR.* 1893, p. 57, f. 35.
[8] Plan *CR.* 1898, p. 113, f. 13.
[9] ib. p. 107, f. 7; 1899, p. 4, Pl. I; 1900, Pl. I.
[10] My plan follows Garaburda as very kindly amended for me by M. I. Skubetov, *Bull. Taur. Rec. Comm.* XLIII. Pl. I., cf. Bertier-de-La-Garde, *BCA.* XXI. Pl. II. pp. 133, 134, ff. 22, 23.
[11] *CR.* 1901, p. 23, f. 46.
[12] *CR.* 1895, p. 102, ff. 253, 254.
[13] *IosPE.* IV. 94, of the time of Commodus.

FIG. 336. *CR.* 1895, p. 103, f. 254. Chersonese. NW. postern *p* with foundation of tower *P²*.

tower *D* which was rebuilt on a square plan without regard to the round foundations of the second period; opposite was built the tower *d* to make the

FIG. 337. Chersonese. View between walls looking NW. On left Roman tower *d*: on right late Greek round tower about which has been built Roman square tower *D*; beyond, Greek wall with two Roman columbaria butting against it: these hide the Gate *E* and the Tower *E¹* is in the bank beyond.

other side of a gateway. The foundations of D rested on an arrangement of beams now rotted away : that is the ground was marshy but not permanently submerged. Attention was next turned to the Southern Extension and this was made into a military quarter by building a tower at V^2 and joining it to A^2 and to C with a small gate c^2 half way. The curtain CB was elaborately strengthened and the tower B once more reinforced. Control of access into the town was secured to the garrison by extending the double wall as far as B where gates h were made just under the great tower ; the wall B—A^2 was also doubled.

As long as the Black Sea was duly policed, there was no great need for sea walls, though some fragments of such are assigned to the Greek period, e.g. A^1-V^1-T^2 (probably Roman) and at "1894" west of R; but after the middle of the IIIrd century pirates' raids had to be taken into account ; hence the coast-line of the city was then guarded with walls, pieces are still found at qq, at H, at $Q\,Q^1$, where we have the inner side of a tower, and near Z. From a point where a line drawn NE. from R cuts the coast, past a square tower and then a convex bend at R, they can be traced fairly continuously round the harbour[2], with big towers at S, T, V^2 and A^2, perhaps another about T^2 between T and V^2. V^3 and the wall running north from it with small towers like v^1 and several little gates $v^2\,v^2$ is of still later date. Nearer to the present water's edge is the line of a quay wall, the flat space between being insufficient for an enemy to form on, and thoroughly well commanded by the defenders.

The parapet and battlements of the walls are nowhere preserved : but a view of a fortified town on the wall of a tomb south of the city shewed battlements, simple on the curtain-walls and overhanging on the towers[3].

The builders of the walls have not left themselves without witnesses. The possible founder has his tomb ; the second attempt agrees in date with Agasicles[4], whose wall building is not put down as his highest achievement. Somewhere in the IInd century A.D. we have the ἐπιμελητής Namuchus[5] directing such work ; of another inscription on some tower but the date 270 = A.D. 245/6 is left[6]. The names of Theodosius and Arcadius may be attached to the building of the military quarter[7], as also that of Domitius Modestus under Valens, Valentinian and Gratian (A.D. 370—375)[8]. Zeno's inscription (A.D. 488) seems to have come from the tower B[9], and to commemorate the last strengthening of it. That of Isaac Comnenus[10] came from near the quay and records the rebuilding of the gates of the Praetorium,

[1] *CR.* 1895, p. 97, f. 244.

[2] *R*, *CR.* 1905, Pl. IV ; 1904, p. 50, f. 92; *S*, 1894, p. 53, f. 71 ; *T*, 1895, p. 87, f. 224; *V*, 1906, p. 62, f. 70, Pl. II.; *A*, 1897, p. 91, f. 203.

[3] *BCA.* XXI. p. 161, f. 29. The writers of the reports in *BCA.* thought that the original area of the city was only half what is contained by the circuit of walls above described : they believed that walls at $G\,G\,G$ were parts of an old Greek circuit connecting F and H, and so all the space west of this line and also that south of E—S would have been additional : in each case they based their conclusions upon burials found within these areas, but the southern extension must have been made in the IVth century B.C. and the Greek walls

L-N-O discovered in 1907—9 shew that the western was quite small only including the space beyond OP^1. As shewn on the plans the walls G, G, and H never seemed suitable for town-walls either in thickness or direction : walls of rusticated ashlar at y are just as solid and certainly belonged to Greek houses, *BCA.* XLII. pp. 102—107, ff. 5—7.

[4] App. 17 = *IosPE.* I. 195.

[5] *IosPE.* I. 202.

[6] ib. I. 211.

[7] App. 22 = *IosPE.* IV. 464.

[8] *BCA.* XXIII. p. 5, No. 2, where Rostovtsev suggests that it was called τὰ Θεωνᾶ, v. inf. p. 531.

[9] App. 23 = *Inscr. Christ.* 7.

[10] A.D. 1059, App. 24 = *Inscr. Christ.* 8.

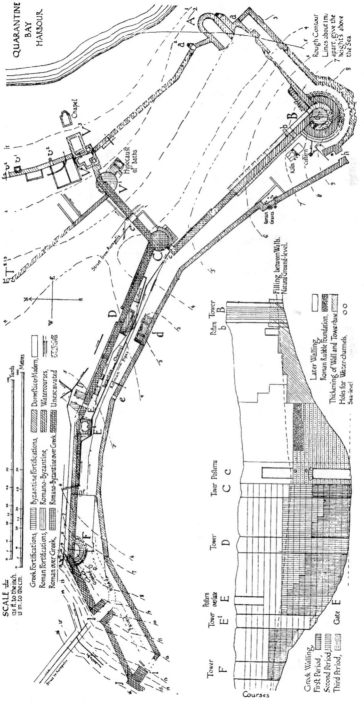

FIG. 338. Supplementary Plan of SE. part of Town-walls (v. explanation to Plan VII.) and Diagrammatic Elevation of Greek Wall from F to B, after Bertier-de-La-Garde, *BCA.* pp. 98, 109, ff. 15, 16.

Mr Skubetov tells me of a Greek Tower (A^1 on Plan VII.) inland of A and a wall joining it to V^1, both discovered in 1907 and not yet published.

perhaps the military quarter. Justinian I also is said by Procopius to have rebuilt the walls of Cherson[1], but the expressions are vague. The greatest recorded trial the wall had to face was the attack ordered by Justinian II (v. inf. p. 532). Bertier-de-La-Garde points out that the topography agrees with the account of the siege given by Theophanes (6203, 581 Bonn), if we take *A* to have been Centenaresius, the tower on the water's edge first taken, *B* Syagrus, and the inner wall which foiled the attack, that from *C* to *V*. The siege which Vladimir laid to the town was not such a test of its fortifications, being ended by treachery. The destruction of the walls was due to the Genoese, especially along the sea-front: all along the land side they could until quite recently be traced, and in some places stood up as much as thirty feet, but of course the ashlar facing of the above-ground walls had gone[2].

Civil Buildings and Necropolis.

Of the buildings of the city there is not much to be said here. From Greek times we have nothing but fragments mostly mutilated by being used in later erections. We can point to worked stones from an Ionic temple about 35 feet high built into Uvárov's basilica (1), but this cannot go back before the IInd or IIIrd century A.D. (v. p. 525): other fragments are still later. Of some interest are the potter's kilns, in one near *Z* were found the clay moulds (v. p. 364), another near *B* seems mainly to have produced amphorae, two are very well preserved west of *R*[3]. From Roman times we have the Thermae (*K*) mentioned above, in connexion with them seems to have been a curious building with elaborate drainage just north of *J*[4], other baths near *V*[1], some ordinary dwelling houses, one *Y* with a hypocaust such as is found so commonly in Britain[5], and a large building *X* in a commanding situation in the western part of the town, possibly the residence of the governors—the palace of which Broniovius speaks[6]—unless the governor lived in the military extension to the SE. Perhaps some interesting building is concealed by the monastery, but it is not very likely. Excavations on this central site might with more probability give us fresh inscriptions. A deep cellar, found in 1904, contained 43 blanks of bronze; it has been supposed that it was the mint[7]. Near by was found a Greek altar with a sculptured snake curled round it, suggesting Asclepius[8]. To the north at *U*, rather towards the sea, there seems in ancient times to have been an open space, later covered with Byzantine houses.

Besides the city of the living the city of the dead yields much to the excavator. At Chersonese it has given up many interesting objects, of which the most important have been noticed in their place in Chapter XI.[9] The

[1] *De Aedificiis* III. 7.
[2] This still has to be guarded against. An attempt was made in 1894 to take away the marble sill of postern *p*. Chersonese stones got as far as Saraj on the Volga, cf. *IosPE.* IV. 72, infra p. 524, n. 7.
[3] *CR.* 1905, pp. 48, 49, Pl. IV.
[4] ib. pp. 40, 41, Pl. II., it was perhaps a fullonica.
[5] *CR.* 1903, p. 28, Pl. III., plan ii.
[6] *CR.* 1903, pp. 26—27, Pl. III., plan i.
[7] *CR.* 1904, pp. 54—57, ff. 76—81.
[8] ib. p. 58, f. 82.
[9] Of the miscellaneous objects on Fig. 339 the stele of Gazurius is interesting for his title (v. inf.

p. 541), for the arms, the looped javelin, the shield (cf. p. 56, f. 10), the typical sword, the mediaeval looking helmet (cf. Boeheim, *Waffenkunde*, p. 39; *Ant. Pergamon*, II. Pl. 45. 2, 47. 2, Text p. 102; Baumeister, p. 2037, f. 2215), the greaves and the gorytus. Kieseritzky-Watzinger (No. 409, Pl. XXVIII.) say there was an upper field with figures of a boy, woman, man and child. For the cups v. p. 361; the earring, p. 409; the leaves for eyes and mouth, p. 422. The fibula indicates connexions with the barbarians and the buckles exemplify just that view of pattern and background on which Riegl laid such stress (v. p. 273).

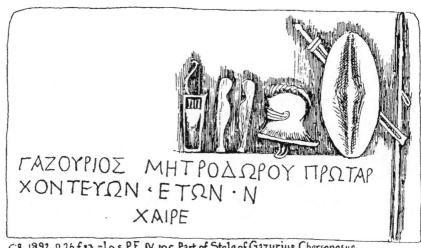

ΓΑΖΟΥΡΙΟΣ ΜΗΤΡΟΔΩΡΟΥ ΠΡΩΤΑΡ
ΧΟΝΤΕΥΩΝ · ΕΤΩΝ · Ν
ΧΑΙΡΕ

CR.1892.p.26.f.13.=I.o.s.P.E.IV.105. Part of Stele of Gazurius. Chersonesus.

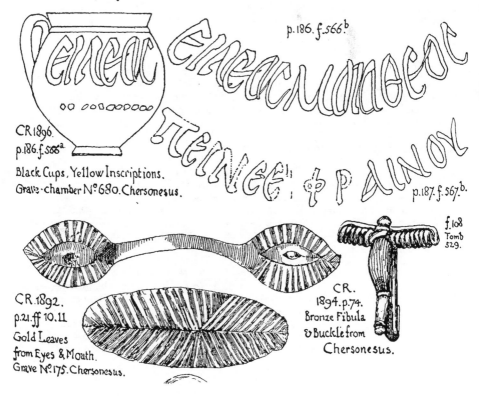

p.186. f.566.[b]

CR.1896.
p.186.f.566.[a]

Black Cups, Yellow Inscriptions.
Grave-chamber N.º 680. Chersonesus.

p.187. f.567.[b]

f.108
Tomb
529.

CR.1892.
p.21.ff.10.11
Gold Leaves
from Eyes & Mouth.
Grave N.º 175. Chersonesus.

CR.
1894.p.74.
Bronze Fibula
& Buckle from
Chersonesus.

different methods of burial have also been discussed in connexion with the usages of the other cities along the same shores (v. p. 421).   But the actual position of the tombs gives us information.   Mention has already been made of the vth century Greek tomb found just inside the Greek gateway *E*.   The idea of the western extension of the city in Roman times, since confirmed by the excavation of the actual town walls, was first arrived at on the discovery of Greek tombs within the present walls.   So too the secondary walls are dated by the fact that they destroy in their course typical tombs of the earlier Roman time.   It is a little hard to make out where each type of tomb prevails, chiefly owing to the somewhat desultory character of the excavations of the necropolis due to the necessity of anticipating the destructive activity of the military engineers.   In general we find, as might be expected, the earlier and richer tombs near the city, the later or poorer ones at some distance, just the opposite to Olbia: the "catacombs[1]" are naturally restricted to places where knolls of rock cropped out.   Most of the necropolis is to the south of the city, for on all other sides it was surrounded by sea.   It extended almost half a mile in this direction well beyond the cross-church.   Whether there were buildings or tombs to the east of the Quarantine Bay is not clear. Clarke on his map and Koehne[2] actually put the city there, but that may be mere carelessness.   In any case Sevastopol has destroyed all traces.

Byzantine Cherson.   Churches.

It is for its Byzantine remains that Chersonese is of interest in the history of Architecture.   These belong to two main periods.   There was an earlier one in which most of the streets follow the old lines, so that the houses are rather irregularly placed, but they are fairly well built, and the churches adorned with marble (mere trade-work from the Proconnesian quarries), some mosaic floors and a little wall-mosaic.   This city seems to have perished by fire and the whole site was laid out afresh.   If there is any truth in the story of the revenge of Justinian II (v. inf. p. 532), his may be the destruction indicated.   The new streets were regular, cutting at right angles the old main street, which went from SW. to NE., but they were narrow and the houses mean and badly built of rough stone with clay for mortar. Byzantine houses are marked *W*.   The churches were in some cases allowed to go to decay, in others restored with the old materials, often on a smaller scale and within the old foundations (Fig. 340, Plans 4, 13).   In everything is seen the increasing poverty of the city.   This rebuilding and the partial reconstructions that preceded it changed the level of the city and caused constant modifications in the various arrangements for water-supply and drainage. Not much is left of the oldest system of which we can only trace the gutters down the middle of each street, in Roman times earthen pipes were more in use, but the late Byzantines reverted to open channels at least for the drains of the Thermae.   Though the aqueduct from Jukharin's ravine was no doubt the chief source of supply, rain-water was collected from roofs, for instance that from tower *B* was stored in a cistern to the west of it[3].   As the surface rose,

---

[1] A large one very well described by Skubetov, *Bull. Taur. Rec. Comm.* XLV.

[2] p. 8; his map, Pl. IX., is correct.

[3] *CR.* 1900, p. 20, f. 40.

the later inhabitants constantly adapted the lower parts of earlier buildings for the storage of food, fish has left most traces, and for middens or cess-pools.

I have been tempted to add a bare enumeration of the chief churches, which, with the subjoined page of ground plans, may be of value to students of Byzantine architecture. The subject was excellently treated by General Bertier-de-La-Garde in 1893[1], but several interesting buildings have been found since he wrote, and perhaps his verdict that Chersonian architecture was extremely poor stands in need of some revision. I received Ainalov's work too late to do more than add references to it. I cannot deal with the innumerable chapels (by 1891 twenty-seven churches and chapels had been found and since then another twenty at least), but will add a list of illustrations shewing the best among the icons and objects of ritual use.

The churches of Cherson were mostly basilicas roofed in wood ; only six have a plan founded upon the Greek cross, and even of these all do not seem to have had domes ; apparently the skill of the local builder was not equal to such difficult construction. All point about NE. towards the summer sunrise.

Of the basilicas the finest, probably the cathedral, was that discovered by Count Uvárov (1, the numbers refer both to Plan VII. and to Fig. 340) in 1853[2]. It measured about 158 ft. long by about 88 broad (48 × 27 m.), including a side chapel. It seems, both on the evidence of coins and of style, to have been built in the VIIth century and restored in the Xth. From the older church survived many remains of pagan buildings : it was paved with excellent mosaic, part of which, much rearranged, is now in the Hermitage. Its walls were also covered with mosaic, at any rate in the apse, for many cubes of coloured glass, especially of the blue ground, have been picked up on the site and on the shore below, as the sea has washed away the NE. corner of the building. Remains of frescoes also occurred, shewing in places three separate layers.

To the south of this is a building in the form of an ace of clubs (2)[3]. A basin in the middle, a system of water-pipes and a big cistern to the SE. shew it to have been a baptistery. The three apses seem to have been vaulted and adorned with mosaic, in which again blue predominated ; even the central space was very likely domed. The lower part of the walls was lined with marble. The walls themselves are carefully constructed of stone, with binding layers of brick so as to sustain a vault. The evidence of coins points to about 600 A.D., which would fit both basilica and baptistery. If Vladimir was christened at Cherson (inf. p. 535) it was most probably in this building. Latyshev, discussing the life of S. Capito (inf. p. 531, n. 4), suggests that this represented the baptistery and church of S. Peter that he built. Almost under the baptistery are the remains of a small apse ; this might go back to S. Capito's time. East of the baptistery was another early church in plan very like No. 10[4]. There were two smaller basilicas[5] SW. of Uvárov's.

[1] *Mat.* XII. p. 21 sqq.; Plans, Pl. III. ff. 14—24.
[2] *Report of Archaeological Explorations made in* 1853, St P. 1855; Tolstoi and Kondakov, *Russian Antiquities*, Pt IV. (St P. 1891), p. 1, f. 1, p. 17, f. 10; *CR.* 1901, p. 33, f. 63: 1904, p. 60, f. 86, is a plan of the whole group shewing an outer narthex and the streets to the west as well; Ainalov, pp. 1—14, ff. 3—16.

[3] First excavated by the Odessa Society in 1876—7, and finished in 1901, v. *BCA.* IV. p. 89, cf. Bertier-de-La-Garde in *BCA.* XXI. p. 70, Pl. I. Ainalov, pp. 15—24, ff. 17a—21.
[4] *CR.* 1904, p. 59, 60, f. 86: not in Ainalov.
[5] Ainalov, pp. 24—29; ff. 22—24.

A building near the sw. gate *M* being a quatrefoil on plan with a central dome and four apses resembles the baptistery but shewed no trace of a basin in its mosaic floor[1]: it may have been secular, but the way it seems to occupy the site of an older kiln recalls the story of S. Capito (p. 531).

Of the same date as Uvárov's basilica and identical with it in plan was one which was found just inside the postern at the NW. corner of the city (3)[2]. It was 122 ft. long and 70 broad (37 × 21 m.): the aisles were paved with mosaic, but the nave with plain marble blocks; the sanctuary also was paved with marble, but in it a darker variety made the pattern of a cross within a circle, the altar being at the centre and below it a cross-shaped excavation for relics. This basilica seems to have been deserted in the xth century and its marbles used up in other buildings[3].

In the western part of the town not far from the monks' garden was discovered in 1889 the best instance of a large church being destroyed and another built on its site, so much smaller that nave and aisles came within the old nave (4)[4]. The older church had marble work identical in style with that of the churches at Ravenna, the presumption being that all was made at Proconnesus. The floor was of rather good mosaic, and the whole has been preserved by the erection of sheds to cover it. The newer church is put together in the rudest way out of fragments of the former, unnecessary columns being built into the walls and the capitals used to pave the sanctuary. There was no pavement in the nave and clay was used for mortar, but the miserable building is interesting as a very late example of an aisled basilica built in the Eastern Church and for its altar being against the wall of the apse instead of on the chord (so too No. 13). It may be assigned to the xiiith century. The very last of these belated Chersonian basilicas was the church of S. George's Monastery, near Cape Fiolente, built after the abandonment of the city about the xvth century[5].

In the centre of the town, about where we should put the Acropolis, stood a considerable group of churches and chapels, including a cross-church (5), a basilica (6) and a church of intermediate type (7). The first (5) being, according to the knowledge of the middle of the last century, the church nearest to the centre of the town was taken as the scene of Vladimir's baptism, and over it has been built the great new church of the Monastery. The remains of the old churches have been quite spoilt[6].

Small-scale plans of eleven churches are given by Bertier-de-La-Garde, but I have mostly used plans on a larger scale than his. Basilicas 10 and 11 are remarkable for their proportionate breadth: 12 is given as an example of the heaping together of sepulchral chapels[7].

---

[1] *BCA.* XLII. pp. 92—102, ff. 1—4.

[2] *CR.* 1901, pp. 25—30, ff. 49—58.

[3] The whole group, Ainalov, pp. 29—43, ff. 25—34, with the cruciform chapel (8) closely recalls that near *Q*, A. 36, ib. pp. 42—46, ff. 35—37, excavated by the Odessa Society in 1877-8.

[4] *CR.* 1889, p. 14. *Mat.* XII. p. 22 and Pl. I., v.—vii; Ainalov, pp. 81—94, ff. 59—68. No. 13 on a hill to the s. outside the town, *CR.* 1902, p. 46, f. 79; Ainalov, pp. 119—121, ff. 84, 85, is another case of one basilica inside another.

[5] Bertier-de-La-Garde, *Trans. Od. Soc.* XXVIII. "On the History of Christianity in the Crimea: a false Millenary" (a history of the Monastery), p. 60, cf. *Museum Worsleyanum*, London, 1794, Pl. CXI., for a view of the church now destroyed.

[6] Tolstoi and Kondakov, op. cit. IV. p. 16, f. 9; *Trans. Od. Soc.* v. Pl. VI.; Ainalov, pp. 46—66, ff. 38—47.

[7] On these Ainalov, pp. 92—98, ff. 69—71, mostly repeats Bertier-de-La-Garde.

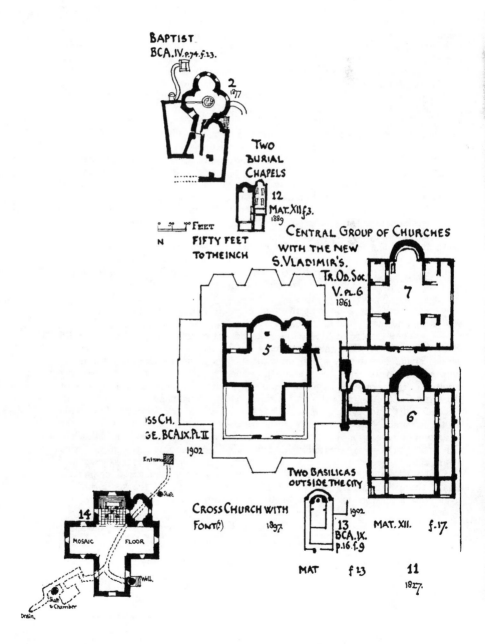

BAPTIST
BCA.IV. p.74.f.23.

2
1877

TWO
BURIAL
CHAPELS

12
MAT. XII.f.3.
1889

0 5   10 FEET
N
FIFTY FEET
TO THE INCH

CENTRAL GROUP OF CHURCHES
WITH THE NEW
S.VLADIMIR'S.
TR. OD. SOC.
V. PL.6
1861

7

5

6

SS CH.
GE. BCA.IX.PL.II
1902

Entrance

Shaft

14

MOSAIC   FLOOR

Shaft
to Chamber

Drain

WELL.

CROSS CHURCH WITH
FONT(?)   1897

TWO BASILICAS
OUTSIDE THE CITY

1902

13
BCA. IX.
p.16.f.9

MAT. XII.   f. 17.

MAT   f 13   11
1827.

Of the cross-churches beside the baptistery (2) and a small one (8) attached to the NW. basilica (3)[1] there may be mentioned one (9) found in 1897, north of the Greek tower *F*; round it ran a complete *peribolos* wall[2]. This church was 24·65 m. (80 ft. 9 in.) long, 19·50 m. (63 ft. 8 in.) broad. Between the arms were various subsidiary chambers, and that to the NE. had a kind of little apse in which was a basin, generally taken to be a font, but it is probably nothing more than a large piscina. In the main apse under the site of the altar was found *in situ* a silver coffer (13·4 × 8·5 × 11·5 cm. = 5¼ × 3¼ × 4½ in.) much the same in form as the two pitched shrines of our mediaeval times[3], adorned with three nimbed heads on each side and one at each end, and crosses on the slopes of the roof. Within was still the relic of an unknown martyr wrapped up in a cloth. Professor Pokrovskij refers the reliquary to the VIth century A.D. In later times the church was divided into separate ossuaries and finally destroyed by fire. The roof was of timber, the walls not being of a character to support vaults.

Remains of a still more remarkable cross-church (14) were explored in 1902[4]. The earlier observers had noticed ruins on a little mound about 450 yards (410 m.) due south of the great south tower *B*. On excavation they proved to consist of a massive wall, including a space 44 × 36 m. (144 × 118 ft.). In the midst was a cruciform church 20 × 21 m. (65 ft. 8 in. × 69 ft.), and to the NE. two chambers filling up the space between it and a hall later turned into a chapel whose apse projected beyond the *peribolos*. Between the east and north arms of the cross was a chamber early pulled down, and corresponding to it on the south another better preserved; this was used as the *diaconicum* and had a basin like that described in the NE. addition of the last church (9) set in similar fashion in a kind of apse, but the eastern arm of the main church is rectangular. At one stage this was lined with seats like a round apse, but originally there was a door at the end of each arm. Finally the whole was walled up and made into an ossuary.

The chief feature of the building besides its remarkable plan is a splendid mosaic floor, better than that removed from Uvárov's basilica. In the square central panel is a high vase flanked by peacocks, and something similar is in the south transept. In the north transept is a design of intersecting squares. The border of the whole is vine-pattern and the greater part of the area is taken up with intertwined straps enclosing medallions with various fruits and vases[5]. The eastern arm had a brick floor. The walls of the church were decorated with frescoes; on them were painted or scratched inscriptions in Greek and Armenian[6]. Only the SE. addition, the *diaconicum*, was vaulted; the rest of the roof was of timber: this arrangement agrees with No. 5. The date seems to be c. 525—550.

The whole building is constructed over six large sepulchral chambers. Below these is a passage hewn out of the rock roughly in the shape of a **y** stretching from the NE. corner of the enclosure, where it is reached by a

---

[1] *CR.* 1901, p. 23, f. 46; cf. p. 510, n. 3.
[2] *CR.* 1897, pp. 97—112, ff. 209, 215—218; 1903, Pl. III. plan i.   Ainalov, pp. 70—80, ff. 54—58.
[3] *CR.* 1897, p. 103, f. 213, 214; cf. Dalton, *Byz. Art*, pp. 563, f. 347, 565, n. 1.

[4] *CR.* 1902, Pl. I. pp. 28—38, ff. 46—57; Bertier-de-La-Garde, *BCA.* XXI. pp. 1—70; Ainalov, pp. 100—118, ff. 75—83a.
[5] *BCA.* IX. Pl. III.
[6] ib. pp. 37—41, ff. 15—19.

square shaft, to the NW., where it ends by a drain-hole through the outer wall, the whole distance being 45·36 m. (148 ft. 6 in.). At two points are dry wells made to help in the excavation or to supply air, and at the end of the short arm just south of the nave of the church is a well with water. This has been regarded as a catacomb in the Roman sense. But Bertier-de-La-Garde shews that it is merely a passage giving protected access to water from a refuge-tower built in the SE. corner of the enclosure, and continued beyond the actual well in hopes of securing a more abundant supply. His other idea that the continuation was the beginning of an underground way to the city cannot vanquish a certain prejudice against admitting the existence of such long secret passages. By an analysis of the coins found in the graves about the church he gives strong reason to suppose that this was never a pagan burying place, but the original Christian cemetery, dating from times before the triumph of the faith, and therefore rich in martyrs' tombs and a suitable place for a fine church though the exposed site needed massive defences.

The church of most complex plan, discovered in 1906 too late for Ainalov or my Fig. 340, stood just to the west of *K*. In essence it was a cross church, but between each of the four arms of the cross was a chapel with an apse, those east of the transepts serving as *prothesis* and *diaconicum*. The end of each transept formed the side of another apsidal chapel, so that the east elevation of the church presented five apses; these apses were covered with half domes and the crossing was domed; the rest of the church was roofed in wood. A square baptistery was added on the north side, and at the west end was an inner and an outer narthex, the latter afterwards turned into chambers: the total length was 25 metres and the breadth 19 (81 × 62 ft.). Most of the coins were of Romanus I, so the church may date from the xth century[1].

One more ecclesiastical antiquity of Cherson the probable site of the tomb of S. Clement of Rome deserves mention because a reasonable hypothesis has endowed it with such an association (v. inf., p. 530). Mention has been made of the islet in Cossack Bay formed about the extreme wall-tower of Old Chersonese[2]. On it we now find the remains of a little monastery. Placed amid the water and connected with the land by a causeway which may have been submerged from time to time it occupies just such a position as might give rise to the tradition of a church built by angels in the sea and approachable but once a year. In fact the earlier legends have nothing miraculous about them, but may be taken to mean that once a year priests and people went by boat six miles (precisely the distance) to celebrate the saint's day. This agrees with the account of how in 862 A.D. Constantine the Philosopher better known as Cyril the apostle of the Slavs found the Saint's relics neglected and carried them off to Rome. He seems to have brought the site into notice again as the buildings, restored shortly after his time, were still seen by Rubruck (c. 1).

---

[1] *CR.* 1906, pp. 66—78, ff. 73—75, Plan IV.

[2] v. Bertier-de-La-Garde *Mat.* XII. Pl. III. fig. 10 and p. 57 sqq.; Ainalov, pp. 137—143, f. 103. Here I should like to give some account of the remarkable Cave-Churches of Inkerman but that would be making too much of a digression, v. *Trans. Od. Soc.* XIV. pp. 166—279, Arkas, Pl. VIII ; D. Strukov, *Ancient Monuments of Christianity in Taurida*, Moscow, 1876; Arsenij I. Markevich,

"Monuments of Christianity near Baghchi Sarai and Karasubazar," *Bulletin of the Tauric Record Comm.* Sympheropol, 1899: there are considerable remains of a basilica, VII—XVI centuries, at Partenit on Aju Dagh, Rêpnikov, *BCA.* XXXII. pp. 91—140, ff. 1—64: and a fairly complete church at Senty, Kuban district, with frescoes, *BCA.* IV. pp. 1—14, ff. 1—9, Pl. 1—9: another on the R. Amhata near by, *BCA.* I. p. 104, and at Demerdzhi near Alushta.

Lesser Byzantine Antiquities.

Students of Byzantine art may be glad to have indicated to them the chief illustrations of smaller objects found at Cherson in that they shew a style as distinct from that of Byzance as that of the architectural monuments[1]. Moreover objects of this style were exported to Russia and served as models at Kiev.

Closely connected in material with the architecture are certain fragments of carved marble used in the adornment of churches[2] referred by Bertier-de-La-Garde to the Proconnesian marble works.

Of painting we cannot judge by the fragments of frescoes and wall-mosaics, but small icons in low relief in various materials shew characteristic Byzantine drawing. Perhaps the earliest is an incised marble plate with the subject of Our Lord and S. Peter walking on the Sea of Galilee[3].

True reliefs in gilt slate are one of SS. George and Demetrius and a fragment with Our Lord in glory[4]. Certain marble reliefs are excessively rude[5], one of a saint inscribed ο]ῦ ὁ Θεὸς τὸ ὄνομ[α οἶδεν][6]. In bone after much the same style we have S. Luke[7]: in cast bronze an Evangelist[8] and an icon of Our Lady Hodegetria[9]. In clay there is a dish with a very archaic presentment of the Saviour (?)[10] and a roundel or pilgrim's badge with S. Phocas who was a great patron of sailors on the Euxine and had a hospital at Cherson[11]. A mould for producing such a roundel with an inscription in honour of S. George was found in 1898[12], also moulds for crosses and other sacred objects[13]. Crosses themselves are common: one[14] has a Slavonic inscription shewing that it was made for the Russian market, and examples of precisely similar style are found at Kiev[15]. An enamel crucifixion of the XIth century is set in the mitre of the Hegumen of the monastery. Interesting for its dumpy archaic style is a bronze censer with several scenes from Gospel history[16].

Of other sacred objects in metal we have many candlesticks both small standing ones[17], and large ones either to hang in church[18] or to stand, such the Russians call *panikadilo*—one of these was made out of a marble club of Heracles set on a base[19], others of old capitals of columns[20]—a bronze discos[21]

[1] Ainalov promises future parts of his *Monuments* dealing with marbles, mosaics and frescoes, with smaller ecclesiastical objects and with the glazed pottery. It is curious how few of the things figured in O. M. Dalton's *Byzantine Art and Archaeology* have analogues at Cherson.

[2] *Mat.* XII. p. 25, Pl. IV. 1: *CR.* 1897, p. 109, ff. 217—219; 1901, p. 32, ff. 60—62; 1904, p. 57, f. 81, p. 61, f. 87.

[3] *Mat.* XXIII. p. 26, f. 40. This and the other objects described by Latyshev in *Mat.* XXIII. are also published by him in the *Byzantine Chronicle* (*Vremennik*), 1899, No. 3; cf. Ποντικά, p. 303, and E. Michon, *Bulletin de la Soc. des Antiquaires de France,* 1900, pp. 332—337.

[4] *CR.* 1894, pp. 55, 56, f. 74; 1893, p. 51, f. 32.

[5] *CR.* 1904, p. 58, f. 83, p. 62, f. 91.

[6] *CR.* 1906, p. 80, f. 79.

[7] *CR.* 1902, p. 40, f. 65.

[8] *BCA.* I. p. 55, f. 51.

[9] *CR.* 1895, p. 94, f. 240; *Mat.* XXIII. 41, f. 44, where the inscription is discussed.

[10] *CR.* 1904, p. 53, f. 74.

[11] *CR.* 1896, p. 166, f. 531. He is fully discussed in *Mat.* XXIII. p. 30, No. 42.

[12] *CR.* 1898, p. 116, f. 16; cf. *Mat.* XXIII. p. 35, No. 43. Another, *CR.* 1905, p. 47, f. 46.

[13] *CR.* 1898, p. 117, f. 17: *Mat.* XXIII. p. 27, No. 41.

[14] *CR.* 1902, p. 40, f. 166.

[15] For a discussion of their peculiarities v. Tolstoi and Kondakov, *Russian Antiquities*, V. p. 32, ff. 21, 22; Kondakov, *Russian Hoards*, I. p. 43—45, ff. 24—27. More specimens are figured in *CR.* 1897, p. 99, f. 210, p. 101, ff. 211, 212; 1899, p. 13, f. 20; 1900, p. 24, f. 58; 1903, p. 25, ff. 18—20; 1905, p. 46, f. 45; *BCA.* XVI. p. 57, f. 14, p. 79, f. 36.

[16] Tolstoi and Kondakov, IV. pp. 34, 35, ff. 27, 28, cf. Dalton, p. 620, f. 393; Kondakov l.c. describes the enamel; better, *Samml. Swenigorodski*, p. 180.

[17] *CR.* 1896, p. 167, f. 535; 1897, p. 111, f. 224; 1900, p. 24, f. 59; 1904, p. 68, f. 103.

[18] *BCA.* XVI. p. 80, f. 37; *Bull. Taur. Rec. C.* XLIV.

[19] *CR.* 1902, p. 34, f. 54.

[20] ib. p. 30, f. 47.　　　[21] *BCA.* I. p. 46, f. 43.

or paten, a hand-censer[1], the end of a crozier[2] and the silver reliquary (p. 512): of secular use were many locks (of a type still made at Tula) and keys[3], weights inlaid with silver[4], a decorated bronze mortar and a cymbal[5].

Rather a different interest attaches to a series of carvings of beasts in bone or ivory (v. p. 335, n. 3). Even better examples of the beast-style, forming a transition between the Oriental and the Mediaeval beast-styles and not without Scythic influence, are to be found in the remains of shallow bowls or dishes of glazed pottery (v. p. 357, n. 5). Very good specimens of the same pottery have occurred at Theodosia. The same kind of monster appears on a gilt bronze buckle from Chersonese[6]. One piece of mediaeval glass is interesting as it bears a shield with a pale and above the date ꟽ°cccxxii[7].

History.

Chersonese was a colony of Heraclea Pontica upon the coast of Bithynia. The mother city was founded by the Megarians (with the help of the men of Tanagra)[8] at the time that Cyrus conquered Media (c. 559 B.C.)[9]. At first a democracy it soon fell under the power of its aristocrats[10].

The foundation of Chersonese itself may possibly have been due to the expelled democrats who here found the freedom they had sought in vain in the former colony. Conceivably, if we do not press the word "soon" too far, the democrats sought refuge in a Heraclean factory already in existence and this accession of strength allowed the transfer of the settlement to a new site[11]. As to the date of the foundation of Chersonese we have no information. Ps.-Scymnus (l. 824) says that in obedience to an oracle the Heracleotes joined with the Delians to colonize a Chersonese. Here Delians is probably a mistake for Delphians and there may well be a confusion with the tradition as to the foundation of Heraclea Pontica recorded by Justin. There is no trace of any Ionic influence in the language or institutions of Chersonese. Pliny[12] says that the towns at this end of the Crimea were called Megarian. No doubt this was in opposition to the Milesian colonies along the rest of the Scythian coast.

Friendly relations between mother and daughter city were always kept up so that even in the time of Hadrian the Heracleotes supported the Chersonesites in their petition for liberty[13]. These relations helped the Chersonesites to remain purely Greek.

Herodotus makes no mention of Chersonese, not much can be deduced from his silence but it was probably later than his time. The first attempt at wall building on the new site belongs to the succeeding century. Bertier-de-La-Garde[14] thinks the most natural point of time for the Heracleotes to found

---

[1] *CR.* 1894, p. 56, f. 75.
[2] *CR.* 1893, p. 74, f. 44.
[3] *BCA.* XVI. pp. 114, 115; XLII. pp. 127—133, Pl. IV—X.
[4] *CR.* 1904, p. 52, ff. 68—71, cf. Dalton, p. 619, f. 392.
[5] *CR.* 1903, p. 36, ff. 49, 50.
[6] *CR.* 1901, p. 31, f. 59.
[7] *CR.* 1895, p. 92, f. 236.
[8] Nymphis, f. 2, *FHG.* III. p. 13, Pausanias, v. xxvi. 6, on the advice of Delphi, Justin, XVI. iii. 4.

[9] Ps.-Scymnus, l. 975.
[10] Aristotle, *Pol.* VIII. (v.) vi. 2.
[11] Ps.-Scylax, § 68, the first author (v. supr. p. 25) to mention Chersonese, calls it ἐμπόριον. But Herodotus applies the same term to Olbia.
[12] *NH.* IV. 85, reading *Megaricae...vocabantur* according to good MSS.; cf. Brandis, s.v. Chersonesus, *P.-W.* III. p. 2265. The ordinary text gives *Megarice...vocabatur.*
[13] App. 20=*IosPE.* IV. 71.
[14] *BCA.* XXI. p. 196, n. I.

a colony in the Crimea would be just after the fall of Theodosia which they had helped against the dynasts of the Bosporus: but von Stern[1] argues that this help was probably rendered because of the Heracleotes already having a colony to protect in the Western Crimea and that the wall is older than the date mentioned. The fact is that we know too little of the history of any of the states concerned. The only hope lies in a complete excavation of the site of Old Chersonese and a determination of the time when it was first inhabited.

Evidence of communication with Athens we have in the vase found in the wall marked as a prize from the Anacia (v. supra, p. 380). Later in the century we have the dedication to Athena Soteira made by a citizen whose name is lost. The statue above was the work of a Polycrates who has been identified with the one mentioned by Pliny[2]. But Chersonese never seems to have been so closely connected with Athens as were the Bosporus and Olbia. Perhaps its Doric sympathies drew it aside and through Heraclea Pontica it had with Asia Minor special ties which strengthened as Athens sank. In the iiird century we have evidence of such ties in a decree granting proxeny to Timagoras of Rhodes[3] and in many coins of states such as Heraclea, Amisus, Sinope, Galatia, Amastris, Magnesia, Teos, and Byzantium and amphorae of Thasos and Rhodes as well as their coins[4].

To the iiird century belongs the well-known citizens' oath[5], certainly one of the three or four most interesting epigraphic finds of South Russia. It is the formula which every Chersonesite had to rehearse before becoming a full citizen and accordingly it enumerates at length the duties of a citizen[6]. But the full detail into which it enters suggests that special dangers had injured or threatened the state and were still to be guarded against. We may compare the party oaths mentioned by Aristotle[7]. The citizen swears by Zeus, the Earth, the Sun, the Maiden, the gods and goddesses of Olympus and the heroes of the land to defend Chersonese, its land, Cercinitis, the Fair Haven and the other Forts (τείχη) against Greek and barbarian alike, to be faithful to the democracy and protect the "saster[8]" and reveal to the damiorgi any plots against it; in case of election to the offices of damiorgus or senator to exercise them faithfully and not to divulge any state secrets; to deal fairly by every other citizen except a renegade: to take no part in any plots[9] internal or external, private or public, but to give information of such, any oaths to the

[1] *Trans. Od. Soc.* XXVIII. *Minutes*, p. 102.
[2] v. p. 295, *IosPE.* IV. 82: *NH.* XXXIV. 91 (19), the Attic form ἐπόησε is some confirmation.
[3] *IosPE.* IV. 64. [4] Bobrinskoj, p. 26.
[5] App. 16, v. p. 645, f. 348 : first published in *Mat.* IX. No. 1 = *IosPE.* IV. 79, cf. *Revue des Études Grecques*, v. p. 403; Ditt. *Syll.*² 461, and Latyshev, Ποντικά, p. 142, for further literature.
[6] For the shorter formula of the Athenian Oath cf. Lycurgus, *in Leocratem* § 77, and Stobaeus, *Florileg.* XLIII. 48. For the Gods invoked and the penalties cf. the treaty between Smyrna and Magnesia ad Sipylum B.C. 244. To this the citizens of each state swore obedience thus "'Ομνύω Δία Γῆν Ἥλιον Ἄρη Ἀθηνᾶν Ἀρείαν καὶ τὴν Ταυροπόλον καὶ τὴμ Μητέρα τὴν Σιπυληνὴν καὶ Ἀπόλλω τὸν ἐμ Πάνδοις (καὶ Ἀφροδίτην τὴν Στρατονικίδα) καὶ τοὺς ἄλλους θεοὺς πάντας καὶ πάσας...εὐορκοῦντι μὲμ μοὶ εὖ εἴη, ἐφιορ-

κοῦντι δὲ ἐξώλεια καὶ αὐτῷ καὶ γένει τῷ ἐξ ἐμοῦ." Ditt. *Inscrr. Or.* 229, cf. *Syll.*² 837 : the oath of Pharnaces I, App. 17ᵃ = *BCA.* XLV. p. 23, No. 1, cf. p. 518 n. 2, is almost identical in its terms.
[7] *Pol.* IX. (V.) 7 (9), 1310 a, and Thuc. VIII. 75.
[8] The word σαστήρ is new. It seems most probably derived from the root of σώζω. Th. Sokolov (*Journ. of Ministry of Pub. Instruction*, St P. Nov. 1902) compares the form ἀρητήρ: and suggests that it means a kind of civil dictator appointed to compose the differences which the document presupposes. He cites Ditt. *Syll.*² 108, a promise of the Athenians to support τὸν ἄρχοντα ὃν εἵλοντο Θετταλοί. Latyshev seems to think it means the established constitution.
[9] E. Ziebarth, *Das gr. Vereinswesen*, p. 94, regards these συνωμοσίαι as more or less permanent political clubs.

contrary notwithstanding, and to give his vote according to justice: finally not to export corn from the plain but to bring it to Chersonese. If he keep the oath may it be well with him and his, if he break it may neither sea nor land bear him fruit nor his women have offspring.

This document shews us the city governed by a democracy with damiorgi and a senate for which every citizen was apparently eligible. The administration of justice was also in the hands of the citizens. The city was predominant ally or mistress of Cercinitis, the Fair Haven and other Forts, and to it belonged a "plain" on which corn was grown. This plain must have been in the western part of the Crimea because legislation was required to ensure that its produce of wheat should be brought to Chersonese. If the plain were merely the plateau of the Lesser Peninsula Chersonese would have been the only conceivable port. This legislation recalls the Athenian regulation of the corn trade.

About the end of the IIIrd century we have several documents that point to the prosperity of the Chersonesites, probably the highest point that the city reached in its earlier history. To it belong the works of Syriscus narrating τὰς ἐπιφανείας τὰς Παρθένου...καὶ τὰ ποτὶ τοὺς Βοσπόρου βασιλεῖς...τὰ θ' ὑπάρ-ξαντα φιλάνθρωπα ποτὶ τὰς πόλεις[1]. In the list of Proxenies conferred by the Delphians we find under the year 195/4 B.C. the name Hymnus, son of Scythas of Chersonese, and under 192/1 those of Phormion son of Pythion and Heraclidas son of Rhisthas, and in another inscription the occasion upon which this privilege was granted to these latter[2]. The Delphians had sent envoys to announce the approaching Pythian games and these envoys reported that the Chersonesites had entertained them sumptuously at the public expense and had passed a decree expressing their general and several regard for the Delphians and sent envoys, Phormion and Heraclidas, to make sacrifices of a hundred beasts to Apollo and twelve to Athena Pronaos (each sacrifice being headed by an ox) and to distribute the meat among the Delphians. Other gifts are recorded as well. Accordingly a decree of thanks was passed in honour of the Chersonesites and they were granted *promantia*, while their envoys were given the proxeny and suitable presents. That they were in a position to make such handsome sacrifices argues a certain prosperity.

This prosperity was probably due to their having gained dominion over the plain and divided it among the citizens. We have a fragmentary list of citizens who bought plots of land and among them the name of Hymnus son of Scythas[3]. The lettering points to a date a few years earlier than the occurrence of his name at Delphi. The same name also occurs upon an amphora, but the lettering seems later[4]. The area of a plot was 100 fathoms square[5], the prices given varied according to the quality or position of the land. The apportionment was carried out by ἐπιμεληταί elected for the purpose. An ἐπιμελητής in such an operation, very likely this one, was Agasicles son of Ctesias[6], who besides holding the regular offices is praised for having made a proposal about a garrison and organized it, set out the boundaries of the vineyards upon the plain, and made walls.

[1] *IosPE.* I. 184, cf. *BCA.* XLV. p. 44, inf. p. 544.
[2] Dittenberger, *Syll.*[2] 268, 281.
[3] *IosPE.* IV. 80, cf. I. 226.
[4] *BCA.* II. p. 23, with C for Σ. A grandson's name perhaps.

[5] 40,000 sq. yds., 8¼ acres, 3·35 hectares: ἑκατώ-ρυγος, sc. κλῆρος, Keil, *Hermes*, 1903, pp. 140-144.
[6] App. 17 = *IosPE.* I. 195: the name also occurs on coins, Giel, *Kl.B.* p. 2: Bertier-de-La-Garde, *Trans. Od. Soc.* XXVI. p. 220, n. 3, pp. 248, 249.

Although we cannot declare that the plateau of the Lesser Peninsula was not called the "Plain," the expression in the oath makes it probable that this word was reserved for the territory in the west part of the Crimea, and this is rendered almost certain by the small area on the plateau suitable for vineyards. It looks then as if the activity of Agasicles was devoted to organizing and defending new possessions on the mainland (he may have built the τείχη so often referred to) and the decree regulated the allotment of them among the citizens. The rectangular division of the plateau probably dates back earlier and formed a model for the allotment of new acquisitions, though the transfer of properties in succeeding ages has introduced certain irregularities now noticeable. Probably most of the wine exported in Chersonesan amphorae was raised on the mainland.

To this prosperous period belong the pieces of frieze from a temple dedicated by Pasiadas son of Artemidorus to Dionysus, to judge by the bucrania and swags of ivy leaves with which they are adorned[1].

The city was of sufficient power to be included in an alliance made in 179 B.C. between the kings Pharnaces I of Pontus, Eumenes II of Pergamum, Prusias of Bithynia, Ariarathes V of Cappadocia, Artaxias of Armenia and Acusilochus, and Gatalus the Sarmatian, and the cities Mesembria, Cyzicus and Heraclea Pontica[2]: but each ally was under express obligations to Rome.

As the second century wore on the position of Chersonese changed for the worse. For one thing Greece was declining, for another she was receiving raw products from Syria and Egypt, now thoroughly opened up; moreover the oath of Pharnaces hints at attempts to destroy the democracy and finally we now hear of Scythians making attacks upon the city or at any rate its possessions: no doubt the coast tribes were being pressed on by Sarmatians behind them. With these Sarmatians accordingly the Chersonesites established friendly relations, so foreshadowing the Byzantine expedient of using distant tribes to make diversions against nearer ones (p. 539); this seems the foundation of the story of Amage queen of the Sarmatians, said with a force of 120 horsemen to have defeated and slain a Scythian king hostile to Chersonese[3].

But this policy was not permanently successful. Our one clear view of Chersonesan history, the story of the campaigns of Diophantus in the last decade of the second century, shews us the Scythians and Tauri united under King Scilurus, and the Rhoxolans, a tribe of Sarmatians, ready to assist them. Scilurus, who has taken the Fair Haven, Cercinitis and the Forts, has built Neapolis, Chabum and Palacium and is at any rate suzerain of Olbia, about this time leaves to his son Palacus a united sovranty and the prospect of adding Chersonese to his dominions[4].

[1] *IosPE.* IV. 87: *Mat.* XII. Pl. IV. v. p. 545, n. 8.
[2] Polybius, XXV. 2 (XXVI. 6). This alliance put an end to a long war in which Pharnaces had seized Sinope and tried to extend his kingdom. It is not clear which side Heraclea took in this, whether she supported Pharnaces against Bithynia that had lately seized most of her territory or joined with her late enemies to resist the encroachments of a new one, whatever her policy she was probably supported by Chersonese; v. Th. Reinach, *Mithridate*, p. 41: Schneiderwirth, *Das Pontische*

Heraklea, II. p. 17. App. 17ª=*BCA.* XLV. p. 23, No. 1 gives the oaths interchanged by Pharnaces and the city: I am specially grateful to Professor Latyshev and Dr Löper for sending me this new find before publication.
[3] Polyaenus, VIII. 56, it seems to fit in here.
[4] See the inscr. of Diophantus, Appendix 18=*IosPE.* I. 185, cf. IV. p. 278, Ditt. *Syll.*² 326, also *IosPE.* IV. 67, further Strabo VII. iii. 17, 18, iv. 3, 7; Justin XXXVII. iii. 1, XXXVIII. vii. 3: the clearest account is in Th. Reinach, *Mithridate*, p. 61 sqq.

The Bosporan kingdom was in equal danger. Help was to be had only from beyond the sea. The Chersonesites called in Mithridates VI, who had lately assumed the government of Northern Cappadocia (Pontus). On their entreaty he sent Diophantus of Sinope the son of Asclepiodorus, giving just the help his ancestor Pharnaces I had promised in his oath. This commander, who seems to have urged the expedition, appears to have spent four years almost continuously in the Crimea, probably from 110 to 106 B.C. We know that the conquest of some Scythians was the first exploit performed by or rather for Mithridates, and Diophantus is understood to have written an account of the country and of his campaigns (Ποντικά) which is quoted in a work on the Red Sea by Agatharchides used by Artemidorus, who wrote in 104 B.C.[1] Now Mithridates only returned from his wild life and succeeded to power in 111 B.C.,[2] so he could scarcely send help before the following year[3].

Diophantus then crossed the Euxine with a fleet in the summer of 110. His first measure was to make a passage with his whole army over to the other side (Inscr. l. 6). This I take to be the making of the mole across the harbour[4]—that is rather a bridge across to the North Cape—and the building of a fort (which he called Eupatorium) to secure the harbour against the pirates of Palacium and to gain free access to the main peninsula so as to turn the enemy's position. When he got into the enemy's country he was attacked by Palacus before he was ready (Inscr. l. 7), but that merely gave him the occasion to set up in honour of Mithridates the first trophy celebrating a victory over the Scythians. This put the neighbouring Tauri into his power and he founded them a city on the spot and settled them together in it. As it was filled with Tauri and naturally in their country, probably it occupied the same site as Palacium on the harbour Symbolon and had nothing to do with Eupatorium: by giving it into the possession of the Chersonesites he could secure to them command of the harbour and people that had so long plagued them, and indeed the Tauri seem to have given them little more trouble, though they were still hostile 150 years later (v. p. 523, n. 2). No accurate writer speaks of Tauri north of the North Bay[5].

Diophantus would naturally leave a garrison in his *tête-du-pont*, and it seems as if it was in his absence that an attack was made on it by the Scythians, who filled the ditch up with reeds which the defenders burnt every night, until they were relieved by the success of the general campaign; the incident may have occurred at any moment in the war[6].

Diophantus, after settling the Tauric question, went off to the Bosporus and reduced it (v. p. 582). Next (probably the following year 109) he returned to Chersonese, took the pick of the citizens and marched into the midst of Scythia (i.e. the Central Crimea) and received the surrender of the royal towns of Chabum and Neapolis and the submission of all the tribes to Mithridates. For this success he received the thanks of the city and afterwards went back to Sinope (Inscr. ll. 9—15).

The pacification, however, was not permanent. The Scythians rebelled

---

[1] Niese, *Rhein. Mus.* XLI. (1887), p. 559.
[2] Th. Reinach, op. cit. p. 55.
[3] Justin puts it well, XXXVII. iii. 1, ad regni deinde administrationem cum accessisset, statim non de regendo, sed de augendo regno cogitavit.
[4] v. supra, pp. 496, 497. Strabo, VII. iv. 7.
[5] This is Selivanov's view, op. cit. p. 22, note 3.
[6] Strabo, l.c., for other views v. supra, p. 497.

and in the latter part of the following year (108) Mithridates sent Diophantus
back to restore his authority.   Diophantus with his own force and the best of
the Chersonesites, undeterred by the approach of winter, set out to recapture
the same royal towns of the Scythians, but the season made the valleys impassable and he turned aside to the plains along the coast of the Western Crimea,
took Cercinitis and the Forts, and laid siege to the Fair Haven.   But Palacus,
believing the season to be in his favour, had collected all his own forces and
further brought up the "Rheuxinali" (Inscr. ll. 15—23).   So Diophantus was
obliged to leave to the citizens of Chersonese the capture of the town commemorated in another inscription[1].   In the battle which followed Strabo (VII.
iii. 17) pits fifty thousand Rhoxolans under their king Tasius against six
thousand hoplites : either Diophantus prevented the junction of the barbarians
or the forces of Palacus were reckoned in with the Rhoxolans.   The event of
the battle had been foreshewn by the Maiden of Chersonese and rendered
certain by the superiority of the Greek arms and tactics.   According to the
accounts none of the barbarian infantry escaped and but few of the cavalry
(Inscr. ll. 23—28).

Diophantus lost no time in following up his victory.   Early in the
following spring (107) he marched to Chabum and Neapolis and compelled
the Scythians to flee or to make terms (Inscr. ll. 28—32).   His next task was
to restore the authority of Mithridates on the Bosporus.   This he seemed at
first to have done without apparently any display of force : but the Scythian
party of Saumacus the foster-son of Paerisades rose in insurrection, slew the
old king and nearly caught Diophantus, who escaped upon a ship sent by
Chersonese.   However Mithridates seems to have sent help to his general,
and Chersonese, exhorted by him, contributed three ships full of chosen
citizens, so that in the early spring (106 ?) he set out thence and captured
Theodosia and Panticapaeum, punished the ringleaders, sent Saumacus off to
Mithridates, and reduced the country to obedience (Inscr. ll. 32—44).

The net result was that Chersonese became tributary to Mithridates in
return for effective protection against the Scythians.   So far as we know the
city was never again in such danger from the surrounding tribes, but its fate
was now intimately linked with that of the Bosporan kingdom.

At first the terms granted it seem to have been easy.   Diophantus is
thanked for supporting the envoys of the city, and it is natural that he should do
all he could for a city which had furnished him with such a valuable *pied-à-terre*
and contributed men to the reduction of the Bosporus.   In return for these
services the senate and people decreed that Diophantus should be crowned
with a gold wreath at the festival of the Maiden, and that the symmnamones
(v. inf. p. 542) should call aloud this honour ; that a bronze statue of him in
full armour should be set up in the Acropolis between the altars of the Maiden
and of Chersonese, and most effectual of all that the decree should be cut upon
the base of the statue.

Still indebted as they might be to Diophantus, the Chersonesites probably
had to contribute their share of the 180,000 medimni of wheat and the 200
talents of silver yearly sent across the Euxine to Mithridates, and according to

---

[1] *IosPE.* IV. 67, very fragmentary, but mentioning the Fair Haven and like the Diophantus
inscription set up in the year when Agelas son of
Lagorinus was king.

Strabo Chersonese remained "from that time until now" under the rulers of the Bosporus.

It was perhaps rather as a subject of Mithridates than as a daughter state and ancient ally that Chersonese sent help to Heraclea Pontica when it was being besieged by Cotta in 72 B.C.[1]: though in the disorganization of the Pontic empire which the wars with Rome had brought about, it would have been possible to escape complying with the commands of the king. What part Chersonese played in the final break up it is impossible to say. The darkness settles down again and all efforts to reconstruct the history of the succeeding period have failed.

It is however difficult to believe that Chersonese had an uneventful history at this time, or that its submission to foreign kings was continuous. We cannot tell exactly what Strabo or his sources meant by "until now," we are certainly not obliged to take it to mean the last year of his life, c. A.D. 19. Pliny (d. 79), whose information as to these parts mostly goes back to the time of Augustus, says of Chersonese *libertate a Romanis donatum* (sc. *oppidum*), but this may refer to Flavian times[2]. That something remarkable happened at Chersonese in 25/24 B.C. we can deduce from the fact that the Era of the city is reckoned from that date. This we may calculate from an inscription relating the restoring of the town walls by the command of the Emperor Zeno. It is dated "in the year 512 in the 11th of the Indiction." Zeno reigned from A.D. 474 to 491, and the only 11th year of an indiction is 488 A.D.[3]

Considering the disturbed state of these regions and the various uprisings and revolutions which even our scanty knowledge of Bosporan history shews (v. inf. p. 589) it is very probable that some fresh start was made by Chersonese in 25 B.C. and even if it were not politically successful, and the Bosporans maintained their hold until after the date of Strabo's death, the new reckoning may have become customary to supplement the clumsy method of eponymous kings or archons[4].

[1] Memnon, c. XLIX. 4. *FHG.* III. p. 551. Bosporus and Theodosia also helped, though Machares afterwards turned against his father.   [2] *NH.* IV. 85.

[3] App. 23: the inscr. has been published about twenty times, v. Bertier-de-La-Garde, *Trans. Od. Soc.* XVI. p. 45; first by Pallas, *Travels in Southern Prov.* Eng. Ed. Vol. II. p. 74, Pl. 5, cf. among others L. de Waxel, *Recueil de quelques antiquités*, Berlin, 1803, No. 5; E. D. Clarke, *Travels*, 8vo, Vol. II. p. 213; Boeckh, *CIG.* 8621; Latyshev, *Inscr. Christ.* No. 7, with photographic reproduction. Two questions have been specially debated; whether the number of the Indiction is 11 or 14, IA or $I\Delta$. The latter would give the date as A.D. 490/1 or 475/6. This last was adopted by Boeckh, who accordingly fixed the era at 36 B.C., and thought that to be the date of the Liberation of Chersonese, mentioned by Pliny. The other question was whether the inscr. belonged to Chersonese at all. One Cousinéry (*Voyage dans la Macédoine*, Paris, 1831, I. pp. 268–269, according to B.-de-La-G.) gives it as from Thessalonica. General Bertier-de-La-Garde (l.c.) discusses the whole subject, shews pretty clearly that the reading is IA and for ever

disposes of Cousinéry by the following arguments. 1. Pallas saw the stone in Hablitz's possession at Sympheropol probably in 1794, and Waxel certainly in 1797, so Cousinéry cannot have seen it at Thessalonica less than forty years before he wrote his book. Hablitz said it came from Chersonese. 2. There is no way by which it could have been brought from Thessalonica to the Crimea. 3. Cousinéry is trying to prove an absurd theory. 4. He says it was kept in Esky Dzhuma in Thessalonica in the cellars: there are no cellars in that mosque and never have been. 5. Cousinéry made corrections of the Byzantine spelling: if allowance be made for these, his errors can be traced to his having used Clarke and Waxel. The evidence of a man of 84 writing about what he could not have seen for 40 years cannot be set against that of intelligent observers like Pallas, Waxel and Clarke.

[4] It is just to this period that Dr Richard Garnett (*Eng. Hist. Rev.* Jan. 1897, *Essays of an Ex-Librarian*, p. 129) would refer the story of Gycia, v. inf. p. 528, assigned by Const. Porph. to the reign of some successor of Constantine I, late in the IVth century A.D.

M.

Roman Period.

At least from the time of their rendering assistance to Heraclea Pontica
the Chersonesites had to reckon seriously with the power of Rome. Their
policy, whenever they were sufficiently free to have a policy, was to use Rome
to free them from Bosporan sovranty or protect them from Bosporan ambition,
but to snatch any opportunity when Rome was occupied to recover independence, sometimes by the risky method of alliance with Bosporus. Even if
we had the history of Chersonese we should scarcely follow all the turns of
such delicate steering, and it is hopeless to reconstruct the course of events
from two or three fragmentary inscriptions and some enigmatic coins. One
stone[1] bears part of the name of King Aspurgus of the Bosporus (8 B.C.—
38 A.D.), but we do not know in what connexion he was mentioned. So
a citizen is praised for having headed a successful embassy to King Polemo,
but whether the first (14 B.C.—) or the second (38—41 A.D.) we cannot tell[2].
Nor can we say what services Cornelius Pudens rendered to the city to earn
him proxeny[3].

Most tantalizing of all is an inscription about a kind of Chersonesan
Protogenes[4]. The hero of it comes back from abroad, encourages the citizens,
drives out a tyrant without loss of life, is elected director of the finances,
restores the fortifications, collects supplies through his own correspondents,
goes on a mission to the Emperor and Senate, and it would seem recovers
the city's hereditary liberty ; finally, on his return wards off an attack
threatened by the tyrant and his picked men, apparently by catching his
children and working on his paternal feelings. His reward is like that of
Diophantus. The lettering shews that the Emperor mentioned is one of the
earliest. It does not seem as if the word tyrant could be applied to one of the
Bosporans, so that quite a new element appears on the scene. It certainly
looks as if the Romans gave help against the tyrant.

Nor do the coins give us enough to construct any definite history,
although a series bearing dates offers more to go upon than usual. Hitherto
the coins had mostly borne the names of magistrates. All the dates have
been collected by Bertier-de-La-Garde[5], the result is they fall into two
divisions, in the former every year from 70 to 78, i.e. A.D. 46 to 54, is represented. Then there is a gap, and the next division has the numbers 103, 104,
109, 111, 120, 131 and 158, so stretching from A.D. 79 to 134. One of the
former division and four of the latter are of gold, including the last (Pl. IV.
25). The coins have most of them a monogram (Παρθένου, v. p. 549), and
further, there occur upon some the legends BACIΛEYOYCAC and EIPHNHC
CEBACTHC[6]. Finally, we have a last series with the word EΛEYΘEPAC,
evidently later than the date-marks.

Bertier-de-La-Garde argues that the first division from A.D. 46 to 54 runs
from the accession of Cotys I to the death of Claudius, and represents a time
during which Chersonese was practically independent. This free position

---

[1] *IosPE.* IV. 147.   [2] *IosPE.* IV. 91.
[3] *IosPE.* IV. 69.   [4] *IosPE.* IV. 68.
[5] *Trans. Od. Soc.* XVI. p. 65.
[6] Βασιλευούσας occurs in Inscriptions, e.g. IV. 70;

and App. 18ª=Ποντικά, p. 314, and agrees with
Παρθένου ; perhaps it is the same on the coins, for
on them the Maiden's figure appears. Orêshnikov,
Num. Misc. II., comes to this view independently.

was probably gained during the struggles of Mithridates VIII and Cotys for the throne of the Bosporus.   It may have been convenient to the Romans to acknowledge it, and if Pliny was up to date this may be the freedom he means[1].   The interruption in the series of dated coins goes from A.D. 54 to 78, beginning with the accession of Nero, whose vigorous foreign policy finally insisted on his head appearing on the coins of Cotys, and ending with Vespasian's reign.   In the early part of this period we know that Rome, through Ti. Plautius Silvanus, helped Chersonese against the Scythians[2].   In 66 A.D. the Jewish King Agrippa speaks of the Crimea as being held by a Roman garrison[3], and Chersonese was no doubt one of its stations: the detachment there being under a centurion according to a tile from Aj Todor[4]. In the latter part of this time the Chersonesites set up a statue to S. Vettulenus Cerialis, legate of Moesia[5].

But we cannot say that Chersonese was quite free of Rome during the second period of dated coins: though some relaxation may tally with the Dacian wars and the preoccupation of the central government therewith during the reigns of Domitian and Trajan, it was still advisable for the city to honour the legate of Moesia with an inscription[6]: also the heads of Apollo on the coins have a curiously imperial look, and the phrase EIPHNHC CEBACTHC (Pl. IV. 23) seems the Roman PAX AVGVSTA: finally, we have the evidence of the coins and bricks found at Aj Todor, the ancient Charax, a station on the south coast of the Crimea west of Jalta[7].

Here everything points to a vexillatio of the Ravenna fleet, some 500 men, as in occupation through the reigns of Vespasian and Domitian, and later the establishment of a vexillatio of the Moesian fleet from Trajan's time to Gordian's.   We may suppose that when the Dacian trouble was over the Romans in due course again turned their attention to Chersonese, just as it·

---

[1] For the significance of a gold coinage cf. Mommsen, *R. Staatsrecht.* III. i. p. 712.

[2] App. I = *CIL.* XIV. 3608 l. 23, Scytharum quoque rege(m) a Cherronensi | quae est ultra Borustenen, opsidione summoto.   This is dated after 62 A.D. when the Vth legion was sent from Moesia to Armenia. Rostovtsev, *BCA.* XXVII. p. 55, No. 1, thinks the physician Vedius Threptus, perhaps the freedman of some distinguished Roman serving in this campaign, was slain by the Tauri at this time; the lettering seems early enough.

[3] Josephus, *B.J.* II. xvi. 4, v. A. von Domaszewski, *Rhein. Mus.* 1892, p. 207, "Die Dislocation des römischen Heeres im Jahre 66 n. Chr."

[4] v. n. 7, Rostovtsev, *Klio,* II. p. 93, *Per L.A.C. centurionem leg. I. Italicae praepositum Vexillationis Moesiae inf.*

[5] *IosPE.* I. 197.

[6] S. Octavius Fronto, c. 92 A.D.   *IosPE.* IV. 93.

[7] M. I. Rostovtsev, *Journ. Min. Publ. Instr.* St P. March, 1900, p. 140, "Roman Garrisons on the Tauric Peninsula" = *Klio,* II. pp. 80—95, gives a particular account of this settlement.   It consisted of a high steep promontory cut off by a brick wall with the outer defence of a ditch some distance beyond, l.c. p. 88; one of the buildings was a hypocaust: to his account R. prefixes a review of the whole history of the Roman occupation and this he has corrected and supplemented in *BCA.* XXIII. p. 1, XXVII. p. 55, XXXIII. p. 20.   I have been content to reproduce his account.   Newer excavations published by him, *BCA.* XL. pp. 1—42, with a good plan have revealed a gate in the outer wall flanked by towers, a cistern or "Nymphaeum" with a mosaic bottom, baths and halls, also outside a temple with votive reliefs to various gods (v. p. 546) and inscriptions set up by *beneficiarii* at their post commanding important cross-roads; cf. *Arch. Anz.* 1911, pp. 234—238; Vinogradov, *Hermes* (Russian), VI. (1910), pp. 248 sqq., 278 sqq.

A find made in 1904 two miles inland of Jalta consisting of many hundred coins and a few other things offered to the goddess·of some barbarous tribe in the hills, shews that a little east of Aj Todor Bosporan influences as measured by the predominance of Bosporan coins over Chersonesan, were in the ascendant, and Bertier-de-La-Garde in treating of it (*Trans. Od. Soc.* XXVII. *Minutes,* pp. 19—27) suggests that Aj Todor, placed at the point where a transverse ridge reached the sea, was a natural Chersonesan frontier post and occupied as such by Roman troops; they would hardly have chosen it of themselves as a post from which to command the sea, since for this it offered no advantages. Rostovtsev thinks it a Tauric oppidum.

was about this time that Arrian was sent on his reconnoitring expedition round the east coast of the Euxine. They were very likely dissatisfied with the use the city had made of its liberty[1]

There probably followed a period of complete subjection, during which the Chersonesites made every effort to obtain a tolerable position, and finally they were given their liberty, that is liberty in the Roman sense, and renewed their issue of coins, this time with the inscription ЄΛЄΥΘЄΡΑC (Pl. IV. 26—29). The late date of these coins is shewn by their style, and this is confirmed by their occurrence at Aj Todor associated with Roman coins of the late IInd and early IIIrd centuries[2].

Nor are we left quite in the dark as to what the Chersonesites may have been doing when the Roman vigilance was relaxed. Whatever their actual freedom they were no doubt allies of Rome, and Rome allowed none of her allies to treat with other states; whereas we have two inscriptions in honour of men who have had to do with the Bosporus: on one the hero besides having held the usual offices is praised for something done, κατὰ Βόσπορον. His last duty seems to have been an embassy to the legate of Moesia[3].

Better preserved and more explicit is an inscription in honour of Ariston, son of Attinas[4]. Besides filling the ordinary offices with singular merit and rendering special services in putting the finances in order, Ariston twice went as ambassador to Rhoemetalces[5] (131—154 A.D.), each time with success, and finally spent six years petitioning the Emperor about the city's freedom. On this service he died apparently without being successful. The petition was afterwards backed up by the mother state, Heraclea Pontica, and Roman resentment was appeased. The Chersonesites duly express their gratitude in more severe Doric than usual[6]. Meanwhile their relations with other towns are shewn by various fragments of proxenies granted among others to Dia... of Heraclea, Pharnaces of Amastris, a ship-master Satyrus probably a Bosporan, and another ship-master, C. Caius Eutychianus of Sinope[7].

---

[1] Phlegon of Tralles, *Olympiades* Lib. XV., fr. 20, as quoted by Const. Porph. *de Them.* II. 12, says that Caesar put Cherson (sic) under his nominee Cotys. As Lib. XV. seems to deal with Hadrian this would be Cotys II (123—131 A.D.) and the experiment would be a possible one on the part of Rome. But we have no reason to reckon Cotys II a special nominee of Hadrian's, whereas Cotys I was put on the throne by Claudius (v. inf. p. 597), and perhaps it refers to his time. Or it may be a case of the old confusion between the Crimea and the town Chersonese, made this time by Constantine who certainly had "Chersonese" before him, "Cherson" was not literary in the IInd century. Rostovtsev in Brockhaus-Jefron thinks that Rome put Chersonese under the Bosporus in order to strengthen the latter for its work of resisting barbarians.

[2] For *ciuitates liberae* see Mommsen, *R. Staatsrecht*, III. i. p. 655 sqq.

[3] *IosPE.* I. 196. Latyshev puts this at 60—70 B.C. and thinks that this man implored the help of Ti. Plautius Silvanus. But for Chersonese Lower Moesia was the only Moesia, so that even after the

division under Domitian, the nearer province would be understood without "Lower," and the inscription can quite well be put later.

[4] App. 19=*IosPE.* I. 199.

[5] The name occurs among the Thracian kings of the time of Augustus. Loewy (*Inschr. Gr. Bildh.* p. 237, No. 337) assigns the inscr. to this date because of the title of Augustus, ποτὶ τὸν θεὸν Σεβαστὸν, but Latyshev (*IosPE.* IV. 280) rightly quotes App. 20=IV. 71, ποτὶ τὸν [θε]ὸν ἁμῶν καὶ δεσπόταν used of Antonine: cf. Deissmann, p. 264, n. 8.

[6] App. 20=*IosPE.* IV. 71. There are mistakes in it and it is obviously a dead dialect, cf. Mommsen, *Provinces*, I. p. 282 note.

[7] App. 18ᵃ=Ποντικά, p. 314; *IosPE.* IV. 70; *BCA.* XIV. p. 104, No. 12; *IosPE.* IV. 72. The fate of this last inscription is a real curiosity of Epigraphy: its right half has been known since 1822; it was found in the ruins of Saraj on the Volga, the capital of the Golden Horde, and copied by the Pastor of the German colony Sarepta. So it found its way into *CIG.* (2134b), and Boeckh thought it might come from Exopolis, a town mentioned by

In the latter half of the second century we have plentiful evidence of the presence of a Roman garrison at Chersonese. Besides the Greek tombstones with Roman names which always mark date we have many epitaphs of Roman soldiers and auxiliaries belonging to regiments known to have been stationed in Moesia during this period[1]. In an African inscription[2] we have the epitaph of a *praepositus vexillationibus Ponticis apud Scythia(m) et Tauricam*, and in one from Vaison[3] perhaps another is mentioned. The head of the detachment at Chersonese appears to have been a centurion (p. 523 n. 4).

Two important documents, both belonging to 185 A.D., throw much light on the Roman forces at Chersonese and their relations with the townsfolk. One is a dedication made in honour of Commodus and of Flavius Sergianus Sosibius *trib. mil. leg. I. Italicae*, no doubt commander of the whole garrison, naval and military, by T. Aur. Secundus Ravenna, trierarch of the Moesian fleet[4]. In the other, the well-known inscription dealing with the τέλος πορνικόν[5], we have mentioned the tribune Atilius Primianus in chief command, a predecessor of his Arrius Alcibiades and a centurion Valerius Maximus, who seems to have exacted the tax and taken too great a proportion of the proceeds for the benefit of the garrison, leaving the town less than the share which had been defined by the Emperors. Hence a correspondence between the central government, the legate of Moesia, the town of Chersonese and the commanders of the Roman soldiers stationed there[6]. Interference with the private concerns of Chersonese could hardly go further.

However, the city must have prospered, as the remains of a fair sized temple, dedicated to Aphrodite and used up in Uvarov's basilica, seem to belong to the beginning of the third century[7], so far as we can judge from the type of name written on the columns. The usual contribution to the cost of a column was five hundred denarii. On the architrave is chronicled a gift of three thousand, the balance left in the hands of [Aur.] Hermocrates after a year of office as agoranomus.

Ptolemy on the Don. The left half was found at Chersonese and published in *Mat.* XVII. No. 2. Latyshev had not recognised its relation to the other fragment, but his restoration has been well borne out upon the whole. On noticing the name in *CIG.* he put the parts together in *Journ. Min. Pub. Instr.* St P. Nov. 1895. The story is of some importance for the causes of the destruction of Chersonese. It is wonderful that a stone should have been carried 800 miles and more.

[1] e.g. *IosPE.* IV. 120, Aur. Victor, *leg. I. Italicae* (in Moesia from 69 A.D., B. Filow, "Die Legionen der Provinz Moesien," *Klio*, Beih. VI. (1906), p. 27, and united with *XI. Claudia* before 211); *IosPE.* I. 222, Aur. Saluianus, *tubicen leg. XI. Claudiae* (v. Filow, p. 66); the names of these legions occur at Aj Todor; we have no clue to the date of Iulius Valens, *IosPE.* IV. 121, as his *leg. V. Macedonica* was in Moesia from 71 to 200 A.D. and again under Aurelian (Filow, p. 64); *IosPE.* IV. 119, Aur. Valens and Ael. Iulius, *coh. I. Cilicum* in Moesia from 134 A.D.; *BCA.* XXVII. p. 58, No. 2, M. Antonius Valens, *coh. II. Lucensium*, in Moesia c. 105 A.D.; ib. XXXIII. p. 20, No. 2, M. Maecilius, *cho. I. Bracaraugustanorum* in Moesia A.D. 99 to 134, both these cohorts were from Spain. Greeks

bearing names such as, *BCA.* X. p. 22, No. 16, Aur. Tyche or *IosPE.* IV. 108, M. Aur. Jason must belong to the same period; Aur. Viator (ib. IV. 122) seems of the IIIrd century.

[2] *CIL.* VIII. 619, cf. *Suppl.* 11780 from Makter quoted by Rostovtsev, *Klio*, II. p. 83.

[3] *CIL.* XII. 1358, Rostovtsev *BCA.* XXXIII. p. 21.

[4] *IosPE.* IV. 94, and ap. Rostovtsev, *Klio*, II. p. 85.

[5] App. 21 = *IosPE.* IV. 81, and Domaszewski, *CIL. III. Suppl.* p. 2243-5, No. 13750 cf. Rostovtsev, l.c. p. 86, and Latyshev, *Mat.* IX. p. 39. For the precise impost see *Journal Asiatique*, VIII. ii. (1883), p. 170, inscr. of the *octroi* exacted at Palmyra A.D. 137, *Hermes* XIX., H. Dessau, "Der Steuertarif von Palmyra," p. 517, Suetonius, *Gaius*, 40. On the collection of this impost by soldiers in Rome v. Rostovtsev, *History of State-contracts in the Roman Empire*, St P. 1899, p. 73; at Palmyra, p. 96; in Egypt, pp. 210, 212 (there is a German Ed.).

[6] Cf. a similar correspondence in the case of Tyras, App. 4 = *IosPE.* I. 3, supra p. 446.

[7] *IosPE.* I. 203—210; Tolstoi and Kondakov, *Russ. Ant.* IV. p. 20, f. 16. *BCA.* III. p. 27, No. 9.

The privileges of the city though boasted upon the series of coins issued at this time did not satisfy the inhabitants and Democrates, the son of Aristogenes, earned praise by paying his own expenses at Rome when going as an envoy for the benefit of the city[1]. At this period the Doric dialect is no longer kept up. Now also comes in the title Protarchonteuon, forming a transition to the πρωτεύων used by Constantine Porphyrogenitus[2]. About the middle of the century Chersonese ceases to coin money[3].

Legendary Wars with Bosporus.

We hear no more of Chersonese, henceforth called Cherson, until the time of Diocletian. In the last chapter (53) of his work on the government of the Empire, Constantine Porphyrogenitus[4] losing sight of any practical purpose goes off into a digression on the history of Cherson[5]. He says that in the time of Diocletian (284 to 303 A.D.) Sauromatus (*sic*) of the Bosporans, son of Crisconorus (Rhescuporis?), marched through Lazice as far as the Halys, where he was met by a force under Constans (this must be for Constantius Chlorus, and gives a date before 292) who being in a weak position urged the Chersonites to make a diversion. Accordingly the President Chrestus, son of Papias, collected a large force of men and artillery in waggons, defeated the Bosporans by a pretended flight, captured their city with their wives and families and compelled the latter to send to Sauromatus to make peace. Sauromatus, who had meanwhile won more advantages over the Romans, was after some negotiations forced to forgo an indemnity, give up his prisoners and retire to Bosporus, whereupon the womenfolk were duly handed back to him unhurt, and the victorious Chersonites returned home. For this the city received true freedom and immunity and rich gifts.

Constantine the Great when troubled by an invasion of the Scythians (Goths) upon the Danube, remembering the help given to his father, called in the Chersonites[6], who under their President Diogenes, son of Diogenes, went with their artillery (χειροβολίστραι) and waggons and defeated the enemy.

---

[1] *IosPE.* I. 200.

[2] *IosPE.* IV. 105, cf. 86, epitaph of Gazurius, v. p. 505, f. 339.

[3] For guesses as to the presence of a Roman garrison at this period v. Rostovtsev in *BCA.* XXIII. p. 1, No. 1, publishing a Latin Inscription of about this date mentioning/ eq(ues) Rom[anus d]ux per qua[driennium leg.] XI. Cl(audiae). In A.D. 245 the Chersonites were restoring their walls, *IosPE.* I. 211: just the time when the barbarians had subdued Olbia and Bosporus. A witness to Roman commerce is a square lead weight inscribed τριούν-κιν Ἰταλικόν, *CR.* 1906, p. 80, f. 80.

[4] For the author v. Krumbacher, *Gesch. d. Byz. Litteratur*², p. 252 sqq.; for the book, J. B. Bury in *Byz. Zt.* XV. pp. 517—577.

[5] ἱστορία περὶ τοῦ κάστρου Χερσῶνος, v. R. Garnett, l.c.; Finlay, *Hist. of Greece*, II. p. 350 sqq.; Gibbon, ed. Bury, II. p. 218. Brandis in *P.-W.* p. 2269 says this is all unhistorical and blames those

who have repeated it, but it is probably drawn from some Chersonian chronicle (each incident is dated by the name of an annual president, e.g. στεφανη-φοροῦντος καὶ πρωτεύοντος Θεμιστοῦ τοῦ Θεμιστοῦ); and represents what the Chersonites believed about their past. Also the story of Gycia is very pleasing, quite worthy of Herodotus. The genesis of the whole is very likely an attempt to explain certain statues existing in Cherson, certain privileges and perhaps the existence of the remains of a great house, ruined and made into a rubbish heap, left in the west part of the town near a postern—this is Mommsen's view, *Provinces*, II. p. 316, note—the whole being combined with traditions of ancient wars against the rulers of the Bosporus and stock stories like David and Goliath and Ali Baba.

[6] Koehne, *Chersonese*, p. 108, puts this at A.D. 318; Stritter, *Mem. Populorum*, IV. p. 537, at 327; Gibbon, l.c. at 332.

Accordingly the Emperor summoned the leaders to Byzance, confirmed the former privileges, and presented them with a golden statue (of himself) in royal crown and robes, a charter of liberties for them and their ships, and a ring with his portrait with which petitions to the Emperor were to be sealed. Also he granted them a yearly allowance of cord, hemp, iron and oil for the artillery and a thousand rations to those who served it, "paid until this day" to their descendants who make up a fixed number in the corps.

Years passed and Sauromatus, grandson of the former Sauromatus son of Crisconorus, sought to avenge his grandfather but was defeated at Capha (Theodosia; this is the first occurrence of the mediaeval name) by the president of Cherson, Byscus[1], son of Supolichus, and the boundary fixed at Capha at the old frontier of the Spartocids (v. inf. p. 557).

After a time another Sauromatus arose and crossed the boundary with a great force collected from the tribes about the Maeotis. The president of Cherson at this time was Pharnacus, son of Pharnacus, who led his army out to meet the enemy and proposed a single combat with the Bosporan king, although he himself was a small man. Sauromatus readily agreed, trusting like Goliath in his height and heavy armour, but Pharnacus had arranged that when he should have manoeuvred his opponent round so that each had his back to his enemy's host, the Chersonites should cry out, "aha." Sauromatus turned his head round at the cry and the scales of his armour opened so that Pharnacus could pierce him with his spear. On seeing their leader slain the host of Sauromatus fled, but the victorious Pharnacus contented himself with drawing the boundary at a line forty miles from Bosporus town, doing no harm to the citizens. In memory of this clemency the Bosporans set up his statue in their city. This was an end to the kingship of the Sauromati in Bosporus.

So far the story is not such as to make it impossible that it should have some foundation. Of course we must make allowance for the patriotism of the Chersonites, who glorify the prowess, cunning and mercy of their leaders, and extend the boundaries of the city's dominion. We can understand too that a confusion should arise between the ethnic name Sauromates and the proper name derived from it[2]. Some of the expressions suggest that the enemy of Cherson was not exactly the rightful ruler of Bosporus, he appears rather as the chief of the barbarians about the Maeotis. The state of things may correspond to a time of confusion in Bosporan affairs, when at once there were two kings, one as it seems the representative of the old reigning house, the other of more recent barbarian origin. At the time indicated for the beginning of these events Thothorses, and after him Rhadampsadius, seem to have been rivals of the last Rhescuporis, and after this we know nothing of the Bosporus. The barbarian element seems to have got out of hand because the Romans were busy with internal affairs and the Danubian difficulties. In earlier times they would not have allowed real wars between their vassals; we may compare the state of things under Pharsanzes, another extra king of Bosporus, who put its fleet at the disposal of the barbarians (v. inf. p. 608).

[1] Cf. Βοΐσκος, *IosPE.* IV. 103; *BCA.* XVIII. p. 118, No. 29.

[2] The forms in -*os* are presumably to be referred to the later date of Constantine or his authority.

Gycia.

Next, Constantine goes on to tell the story of the plot made by a
Bosporan king Asander to avenge his kingdom upon Cherson.   Hearing that
Lamachus the president of Cherson had a fair daughter named Gycia, the
king proposed that his eldest son should marry her and so put an end to
the hostility between the two states.   The Chersonites agreed but only on
condition that the prince should come and live at Cherson and never go back
to see his father at Bosporus, and the condition was accepted.   Now at
Cherson, Lamachus, who was very rich in gold and silver, menservants and
maidservants, flocks and herds and goods, had a house taking up four wards
(*regiones*) of the city in length and breadth : it had its own postern in the
city wall and four towered gates with fair wickets through which each kind of
beast went in and out to its own stable.   Lamachus gave his consent to the
marriage and after a space of two years died, and Gycia was left alone with
Asander's son, for her mother had died long before.   A year after the death
of Lamachus, in the presidency of Zethus son of Zethon[1], Gycia, not desirous
of making a display but wishing to keep bright the memory of her father,
asked grace of the elders of the city that she might yearly all her life long on
the anniversary of his death make a great feast to all the townsmen, their
wives, children and households, so that abstaining from work for that day they
should dance and make merry in public each in his own ward.   In this
proposal she was encouraged by her husband who saw in it an opportunity of
carrying out his treasonable designs against the liberties of Cherson.   After
the feast he sent a trusty slave to Bosporus saying " From time to time upon
the pretext of bringing me presents send me ships and ten or twelve stout
young men over and above the rowers.   Let them wait at Symbolon and
I will send and bring the young men and the presents into the city.   Then
in the daytime in the sight of all I will send away the young men and they
shall hide till dark in the meadow (perhaps the marshes of the Chërnaja
by Inkerman) and then I will bring them by sea round to the harbour Susa
and let them in by my own postern."   So they did and in time there were
assembled in the cellar of the house two hundred Bosporans, only waiting for
the annual feast to burn and slay, the lady knowing nothing of the matter.
Now a slave-girl, trusted by Gycia, had committed some fault and chanced to
have been shut up in a chamber just above the Bosporans; in spinning she
dropped her spindle-whorl and it rolled into a hole in the pavement.   To
reach it she pulled up a brick and through the hole she saw armed men in the
cellar beneath, so she put the brick back carefully and sent for her mistress
and shewed her the sight.   Then Gycia, saying that her offence was fore-
ordained of Heaven (ὁ Θεὸς) that this treachery might be revealed, took her
back into yet closer confidence and commanded her to keep silence : but she
herself opened the matter to two trusty kinsmen and bade them summon
the chiefs of the city in a secret place and let them choose out three men
furnished with ability, able to keep a secret, who should promise under oath
to do what Gycia should ask them, for she must trust them with a matter

[1] Cf. *IosPE.* IV. 86, 96.

most weighty and of great moment to the state.   When the three men came
she made them swear that when she died she should be buried in the midst of
the city.   Then she told them of the two hundred Bosporans hidden in her
house.   Further she said that they were not to forgo the approaching feast
but to celebrate it with moderation.   So she would first seem tired of it and
they likewise would go early as though to bed : but really as soon as the
prince was put off his guard they should all join and pile wood about the
house of Lamachus and prepare covered torches and then stand ready to slay
all that should break out thence ; last of all that she herself should lock the
doors and come out to them, whereupon they should put fire to the whole.
To this they agreed, and on the appointed day the feast was celebrated with
the utmost eagerness, so that they tired early of the dancing and went home.
In her own house Gycia vied with her husband in pressing wine upon all,
only she bade her chambermaids be sober and herself drank watered wine
from a purple goblet but plied her husband withal.   So when the citizens
appeared weary she made her husband go to rest before the former time :
this he did gladly but had not dared say so of himself.   So all the doors were
locked and the keys brought to Gycia who commanded her maids to take her
jewels and any precious things they could hide in the folds of their garments.
Then she stole from her husband as he slept overcome with wine, locked the
bedroom door, went quietly out with her maids from the great gate and gave
the citizens the sign to compass the house with fire.   So it was burnt with all
and everything within it.

When the citizens wished to rebuild it for her, Gycia would not allow
it but bade them rather make a dunghill of the place where such treachery
had been plotted.   And the place is called the look out place of Lamachus
until this day.

When the citizens saw the infinite mercy of heaven towards their city
wrought through Gycia, and that she had spared nothing of her own, in the
street of the city they set up two images of brass pourtraying her in her
youth and beauty as she was at the time when she saved the city : one
shewed her modestly adorned, revealing to the citizens her own husband's
plot ; the other in warlike array attacking the plotters.   Below these the
tale was written and whoever among the citizens wished for the fame of
loving fair things would clean the letters and make clear the writing.

Now when a certain season had passed and Stratophilus son of Philo-
musus was chief ruler of Cherson, Gycia in her great wisdom wished to make
trial of the Chersonites whether they would keep their oath and bury her
in the midst of the city.   So she took counsel with her maids and feigned to
be dead ; and her maids mourned her and gave word to the citizens that
she was dead and asked in what place she should be buried.   Whereupon the
Chersonites took no account of their oath, but carried her without the city to
bury her.   And when the bier was set down at the tomb, Gycia sat up and
looked round on the citizens : " Is this," said she, " your promise under oath ?
Is this how you keep your word ? "   Then the Chersonites, shamed by the
issue of their own ill faith, prayed her to pardon their fault and to cease from
reproaching them.   So they swore a second oath to bury her in the midst
of the city and this indeed they kept ; for during her lifetime they set up her

altar-tomb and raised to her yet another brazen statue and overlaid it with
gold setting it by her tomb for a yet more sure memorial.

This pleasing piece of Chersonian legend does not inspire confidence
in its truth.   Sir Lewis Morris was not violating history when he turned
it into a tragedy and made a few changes to suit his purpose[1]; only he need
not have made the period 970 A.D. after the death of the author who relates it.
As we have seen, Dr Richard Garnett (op. cit.) is dissatisfied with the date to
which Constantine refers it and rightly points out that neither the names nor
the customs still less the general atmosphere suit a presumably Christian town
in the latter part of the IVth century.   But when he comes to putting it
in the 1st century B.C. because at that time there was a real Asander
reigning in Bosporus he is doing more than is possible.   As well fix the date
of Arthur or Vladimir from the contents of the ballads without the help of
external history.   It looks, as I have said, as if the legend had gathered
about some dismantled house (perhaps the Monte Testaccio in the west part
of the city is Λαμάχου σκοπή) and several statues of women, perhaps a
Παρθένος πρόμαχος and a Victory. · As to religion the tone is vaguely
monotheistic unlike the century in which the Maiden gave definite promises
of victory to Diophantus[2].

Christianity.   Byzantine Period.

As to the introduction of Christianity into Chersonese, legend has it that
S. Andrew first preached the gospel here[3].   At the end of the first century we
find it already a place of banishment for Christians, Flavia Domitilla in 92[4],
S. Clement of Rome in 94.   Whatever its foundation, in its final form the story
of S. Clement is full of absurdities, he arrives with many companions and
finds two thousand Christians working in marble quarries and forced to go
45 stades for a drink of water, the Saint at once reveals a clear spring, and
next his preaching daily gains many converts among the townsmen up to
five hundred, and seventy-five churches are built.   This rouses a persecution ;
as nothing touches the Saint he is tied to an iron anchor and thrown into the
sea.   His disciples pray for the sight of his relics and the waters stand up to
leave a path to where the Saint lies in a shrine and the anchor by him within
a church (v. supra, p. 513).   It is revealed to the disciples not to remove the
body, and each year on the day of the martyrdom the miracle is repeated and
this keeps the Chersonites constant in the faith.   But the greatest wonder
is that once the only son of pious parents who had taken him to the shrine
was (for the shewing forth of the Saint's glory) left behind in it, and when the

---

[1] *Gycia: a Tragedy*, London, 1886.
[2] S. P. Shestakov, "Sketches of the History of
Chersonese in the VI—X centuries A.D." ; Pt III. of
Ainalov's *Monuments of Christian Chersonese*,
Moscow, 1908, takes the same view of Gycia as I
do. I find that his very full (140 pp.) treatment of
Chersonian history brings him to much the same
conclusions as I had embodied in my bare outline.
His first chapter, "The Beginnings of Christianity

at Cherson," was contributed to *Serta Borysthenica*
in honour of Professor Kulakovskij, Kiev, 1911.
[3] Ps.-Nestor, p. 7; cf. S. V. Petrovskij, "Apo-
cryphal Tales of Apostolic Teaching on the Black
Sea Shore," *Trans. Od. Soc.* XX. p. 29, XXI. p. 1 ;
Golubinskij, *Hist. Russian Church*[2], I. i. p. 23.
[4] Bruttius, Fr. 3 ap. Hieron. *Chron.* Schoene,
p. 163, says *in insulam Pontianam*; H. Peter,
Hist. Rom. Rell. II. p. 160.

parents returned next year to recover his body they found him alive and leaping, the Saint having fed and guarded him the while[1].

In the time of Diocletian, about 300 A.D., was made a real effort to evangelize Cherson, apparently initiated by Hermon, Bishop of Jerusalem, who is represented as sending out bishops wholesale. It roused violent opposition, the first martyr was S. Basileus and with him his companion S. Ephraim destined for "Turkey," i.e. the steppes. Next suffered SS. Eugene, Agathodorus and Elpidius together. Later Hermon sent S. Aetherius but he was cast ashore off the Dnêpr, on the island Alsos since called by his name (v. pp. 16, 481, n. 7), and died before reaching his see. S. Capito his successor was sent out by Constantine, accompanied by 500 soldiers under the command of Theonas. He passed unscathed through a furnace, which was counted to him for martyrdom, built a church and baptistery and converted the unbelievers. M. I. Rostovtsev suggests[2] that the compiler of the legend brought into connexion the arrival of the bishop, the establishment of the corps of ballistarii which Constantine Porphyrogenitus also assigns to the time of Constantine the Great and the existence of the quarter τὰ Θεωνᾶ, presumably the military quarter, i.e. the south-eastern extension *ABCV*. The Chersonites are represented as obstinate Pagans, but Christianity seems to have prevailed by the middle of the IVth century[3].

Capito, although he does not seem to have attended the Nicene council, marks the regular establishment of the see of Cherson. His successor, Aetherius the Second, signed the minutes of the second council of Constantinople in 381 as "Tersonitanus," and Longinus those of the council of 448 (v. p. 493, n. 1). At Chalcedon in 451 it was finally decided that the Bishop of Cherson was subject to the Patriarch of Constantinople. Franko (loc. cit.) has suggested rather plausibly that the Chersonites affiliated their church to Jerusalem in order to support its claim to autocephaly, as in the time of Hermon, whose date is not far out, the church of Jerusalem was of no great importance. Later on Cherson was advanced to be the seat of an archbishop and finally of a metropolitan.

During the latter part of the IVth century Cherson became a regular place of banishment for persons regarded by the Court with disfavour or suspicion, even pretenders to the throne such as Procopius[4]. This proves that it was not exempt from the observation of the central government. But there is reason to believe that on the whole it was more independent than any other

---

[1] For the history of S. Clement and the miracles at his shrine v. *Menologium Graecum*, Urbino, 1727, Pt I. p. 210; *Trans. Od. Soc.* IX. p. 134; X. p. 139; and P. Lavrov, *Mon. of Chersonèse*, II. Moscow, 1911, "Lives of Chersonian SS. in Graeco-Slavonic Literature," pp. 1—153, 174—180. I have not seen Dr Ivan Franko, "S. Clement at Korsun," *Trans. Shevchenko Soc.* Lemberg, 1902—1906 (Little Russian), cf. his résumé in *Archiv f. Slavische Phil.* XXVIII. (1906), p. 229, "Cyrillo-Methodiana," in which he expresses disbelief in Clement's ever having been at Cherson and ascribes the legends concerning him to Chersonite hagiographers; Gregory of Tours is the first authority for the story, v. Shestakov, op. cit. p. 14

and 54 sqq. Bede knew it in much the same form.
[2] *BCA.* XXIII. p. 5 sqq.
[3] For the seven martyrs of Cherson v. *Acta SS.* (Bollandi) *Martii*, I. p. 639, Mar. 7, and *Menologium Graecum*, Pt III. Mar. 8; also *Trans. Od. Soc.* VII. p. 120. Latyshev gives a full discussion and all texts in *Mém. de l'Acad. des Sciences de St P. Cl. Hist.-Phil.* Sér. VIII. T. VIII. 3 (1906) and a Russian rendering in *BCA.* XXIII. p. 108 sqq., see too Lavrov, op. cit. pp. 154—170, 180—184. The whole question is well dealt with by Shestakov, p. 17 sqq., who is inclined to allow some foundation of truth in the stories: they have a certain interest as being almost certainly the work of Chersonite authors.
[4] Zosimus, IV. 5.

town in the Empire.   For instance it is not included in the Synecdemus of
Hierocles (c. 500).   Not but what in case of need it received help.   Proof
of this is seen in the fact of repairs done to towers and gates by officers of the
Emperor.   Such works were carried out by a Praetorian Prefect Domitius
Modestus under Valens (370—375)[1], a Tribune Fl. Vitus under Theodosius
and Arcadius (383—398)[2], by Count Diogenes under Zeno (488)[3], by
Justinian I[4]; at Bosporus under Maurice in 590 by Eupaterius General
($\sigma\tau\rho\alpha\tau\eta\lambda\acute{\alpha}\tau\eta s$) and Duke of Cherson[5],—a few years previously the Turkish
danger had been serious[6],—and finally by Leo Aliatus Patrician and Praetor
($\sigma\tau\rho\alpha\tau\eta\gamma\acute{o}s$) of Cherson and Sugdaea under Isaac Comnenus in 1059[7]·   In return the city made contributions in kind to the upkeep of the Imperial navy[8].

There was a special coinage for Cherson under Justinian I, under
Maurice and from Michael III and Basil I to Basil II and Constantine IX (XI),
i.e. 866—1025; in all these periods we have other evidence of close dependence, but the types and monetary system are peculiar to Cherson[9].

An interesting exile was Pope Martin (c. 653); he gives a most dismal
account of things, complaining that the town was dependent upon what ships
brought for the very necessaries of life, but there is probably a good deal of
exaggeration in what he says[10].

But much the most important exile was Justinian II, banished in 695,
on whom after his mutilation by the usurper Leontius, as Gibbon puts it,
"the happy flexibility of the Greek language could impose the name
Rhinotmetus."   The story goes that Justinian hearing that some of the
townsmen had hostile designs upon him escaped by the help of others to
the Khan of the Khazars, married his sister and settled at Phanagoria.
However, the Khan was finally bribed by Tiberius III to give him up but
Justinian broke loose and took refuge with the Bulgars and by their help
regained his throne (705).   So he was in a position to avenge upon the
citizens the insults and hostility they had directed against him.   The accounts
of his vengeance are just a string of legends which leave us quite in the dark
as to his real motives.   When he was an exile the governors seem to have
been sent out from Constantinople, but at the time of his vengeance the
Khazars had a representative (*tudun*) in the city and the expeditions seem to
have been as much against the Khazars as against the Chersonites though
the citizens are exterminated once or twice in the course of events.   Finally
it is Bardanes a nominee of Cherson that wins over the soldiers and returns
to Byzance to murder Justinian (711)[11].   The whole story is severely criticized
by Bertier-de-La-Garde[12], he admits however that it agrees remarkably well
with the disposition of the fortifications, and Cherson seems rather more

[1] *BCA.* XXIII. p. 5, No. 2.
[2] App. 22=*IosPE.* IV. 464.
[3] App. 23=*Inscr. Chr.* 7.
[4] Procopius, *de Aedif.* III. 7.
[5] App. 70=*Inscr. Chr.* 99.
[6] A.D. 581, Menander, fr. 64, *FHG.* IV. p. 266.
[7] App. 24=*Inscr. Chr.* 8=*CR.* 1895, p. 88, f. 225.
[8] *Corp. Jur. Civ.* III. Novella 163, c. ii.
[9] Oréshnikov, "Chersono-Byzantine Coins," *Trans. Moscow Numism. Soc.* III. (1905), supple-ments in *Numismatic Miscellany*; Sabatier, *De-*

scription Générale des Monnaies Byzantines, I.
p. 71. Mr Wroth, *Imperial Byz. Coins in the Brit. Mus.* I. p. xviii, hardly seems to recognize the Justinian coinage; no specimens are in the B.M., cf. pp. ciii and 43 n.   He correlates the end of coinage with the capture by Vladimir, p. liii.
[10] Mansi, *Coll. Concil.* XV. pp. 64, 65, Ep. XVI., XVII.   Shestakov, p. 31, takes him literally.
[11] Gibbon, ed. Bury, V. p. 180; Bury, *Later Roman Empire*, II. p. 362.
[12] *Trans. Od. Soc.* XVI. p. 78.

independent than he will allow. Shestakov (pp. 31—35) is less sceptical. The fullest accounts are in Theophanes[1], and Nicephorus Constantinopolitanus (p. 44 sqq.), who used the same source less accurately[2]. The later writers (v. bibliography) merely abbreviate except Constantine Manasses (ll. 3988—4100) whose poetical treatment is quite in place.

During the reigns of the Isaurian dynasty Cherson was a refuge for the Orthodox banished by the Iconoclasts; as such it appears to have made itself more or less independent of the Empire. Several of the letters of Theodore of Studium are addressed to, or speak of, such refugees[3]. At the same time it cultivated friendly relations with the Khazars, perhaps it had only changed a distant overlord for a near one.

Certainly it is represented as a new idea when Petronas Camaterus, a spatharocandidate, who was sent to help the Khan of the Khazars to build himself a capital at Sarkel on the lower Don, and on his way had occasion to call at Cherson, suggests to Theophilus (c. 834) that he should make himself direct master of the city instead of leaving its government to the president (πρωτεύων) with the so-called Fathers of the city. So Theophilus sent this very Petronas as praetor (στρατηγός) and from that day the praetors were sent from Byzance[4]. This is probably the time when Cherson was made a Theme, the xiith[5]. About this time the late life of S. Stephen of Surozh (Sudak) tells of a Russian Bravlin making a successful raid on Cherson: how he got there is a mystery[6], perhaps he is a reflection of Vladimir's attack.

Towards 861 there came to Cherson, Cyril (Constantine) and Methodius, afterwards the apostles of the Slavs, at this time sent by the Patriarch Photius on a mission to the Khazars, or perhaps to the Slavs under the Khazar rule; they also preached to the Goths in the region called Phulla[7]. In Cherson Cyril is said to have learned many languages eastern and northern and some have supposed that it was from their alphabets that he supplied the signs for Slavonic sounds which are wanting in Greek, but Taylor[8] and Jagić[9] have made it probable that these signs are ligatures from the Greek cursive and that their alphabet was already invented[10]. Cyril visited the tomb of Clement and took his relics away to Rome, and "Cersona" appears

---

[1] p. 566 sqq., Bonn=p. 369, de Boor.
[2] v. Krumbacher, *Gesch. d. Byz. Lit.*[2], p. 350.
[3] Shestakov, pp. 38—42; Theodore Stud. *Epp.* I. 31, 48, II. 92.
[4] Const. Porph. *de adm. Imp.* c. 42; v. p. 542, n. 12; cf. Bury, *Hist. E. Roman Empire*, p. 415 sqq.
[5] Id. *de Them.* lib. II. ad fin.
[6] Shestakov, p. 47, cites Vasilievskij, *Russo-Byzantine Investigations*, II. p. 74.
[7] A pun on this word is a clear proof, which has hitherto escaped notice, of a knowledge of Hebrew on the part of Cyril or his biographer; he applies Isaiah LXVI. 19, "I will send...unto the nations, to Tarshish, *Pul* and Lud," where LXX has Φούδ and the Hebrew פול is a mistake for לוד, cf. Gen. x. 6, Vulg. has Africam.
[8] *Alphabet*, II. p. 195.
[9] *Four Palaeographical Articles*, St P. 1884.
[10] This is not the place to go into the complicated questions touching Cyril and Methodius or the vast literature of the subject. The original authorities

which mention the visit to Cherson are "Ein Brief des Anastasius Bibliothecarius an den Bischof Gaudericus" published by J. Friederich in *SB. d. k. Bai. Ak. Phil.-Hist. Cl.* 1892, p. 393; "Translatio S. Clementis," *A A. SS. Mart.* II. p. *19; "Vita Constantini" (O. Slav.), ed. Miklosich and Dümmler, *Denkschr. d. k. Ak. d. W. zu Wien, Phil.-Hist. Cl.* XIX. 1870; the "Vita Methodii" (O. Slav.), *Arch. f. Kunde Oesterr. Geschichtsquellen*, XIII. 1854, passes this episode over; P. Lavrov intends an edition of them all: cf. Hilferding, *Works*, St P. 1868, I. p. 306, "Cyril and Methodius"; L. K. Goetz, *Gesch. der Slavenapostel*, Gotha, 1897, reprinting Latin translations; V. Jagić, "Zur Enstehungsgeschichte d. kirchenslav. Spr." in *Denkschr. d. k. Akad. zu Wien, Phil.-Hist. Cl.* XLVII. (1902) and *Arch. f. Slav. Phil.* XXV. p. 544, XXVIII. pp. 161, 186, 229; "Cyrillo-Methodiana" by V. Lamanskij, A. Brückner, I. Franko; also as touching Cherson, Shestakov, op. cit. p. 48: v. *Encycl. Brit.* [11] s.v. "Slavs"; Bury, op. c. pp. 392—401, 485—488, 500.

in the frescoes of San Clemente[1]. The state of Cherson is described as pitiable, surrounded on all sides by new hordes of barbarians, its immediate environs desert, its own population much mixed and decadent.

In 891, under Leo VI the Chersonites rebelled and killed the governor Symeon, but they do not seem to have established their independence[2]. The importance of Cherson in dealing with the Bulgars and the Khazars and for missionary effort is brought out in this reign by the letters of the Patriarch Nicolaus Mysticus to Symeon of Bulgaria, to an unknown, perhaps Bogas, governor of Cherson, mentioned in them, and to the Archbishop of Cherson[3].

Intercourse with Russians. Vladimir.

In the following century the power of the Khazars had declined through the attacks of the Pechenêgs, and the Eastern Slavs had been united under their Russian (Varangian) leaders, so that they could throw off the Khazar yoke. The Russians descended to the mouth of the Dnêpr in spite of the attacks of the nomads on their flanks and even made expeditions for trade and war across the Euxine. Of all the Greeks the Chersonites came into closest contact with them and their city became a main channel of Greek influence flowing into Russia. Accordingly their interests are carefully guarded in the treaties made by Byzance with Igor (944) and Svjatoslav (972)[4], providing that the Chersonites should be allowed to fish unmolested at the mouth of the Dnêpr (near which they had salt-works), and that their land should be left in peace and even protected from the raids of the Black Bolgars: however the Russians were to support the Emperor in case of Cherson's revolting. It was through the help of Svjatoslav that a Chersonite Calocyrus hoped to become Emperor but failed[5].

The "Notes of the Gothic Toparch" have been fixed astronomically at 961 A.D. in the reign of Svjatoslav by Fr. Westberg who puts the scene of action to the north of the Crimea, but the author's avoidance of all non-classical names makes identification of what he is trying to say hopeless[6].

The conversion of the Russian people to Orthodox Christianity is one of the most important events in European history, and though it was coming about by the direct intercourse of Byzantines and Russians,—Christian tombs dating back a hundred years before Vladimir have been found at Kiev[7],—

---

[1] The relics are usually said to have been long lost and discovered by Cyril, but Franko, l.c., prints a form of the legend which ascribes the discovery to a priest Philip some fifty years before Cyril. Vladimir in 988 also took Clement's relics to Kiev, but then he had force on his side. If we take Brückner's view of Cyril's character, we might think that Photius suggested to Cyril how to make his mission to the West acceptable by using his stay at Cherson to authenticate relics which were sure to be most welcome at Rome.

[2] Theophanes Contin. VI. c. 10, ed. Bekker, p. 360.

[3] Shestakov, pp. 57 sqq.; Migne, *P. G.* CXI. epp. ix, lxviii., cvi.

[4] Ps.-Nestor's chronicle under those years.

Longinov, "Treaties of Peace between Russians and Greeks," *Trans. Od. Soc.* XXV. p. 395.

[5] Stritter, *Mem. Pop.* II. p. 988 from Zonaras XVI. 27, cf. G. Schlumberger, *Un Empereur Byzantin au X⁰ siècle*, p. 560 sqq.

[6] Publ. by Hase, Leo Diaconus, p. 496 sqq.; the whole question is summed up by Westberg, *Mem. de l'Acad. Imp. des Sc. de St P. Cl. Phil.-Hist.* Sér. VIII. T. v. 2 (1901), "Die Fragmente des Toparcha Goticus." I have not seen Kunik, ib. XXIV. (1874), p. 61, Vasilievskij, *Journ. Min. Publ. Instr.* No. 185, who spoke of Moesia, nor P. Miljukov, *Trans. VIII. Russ. Arch. Cong.* (Moscow), 1897, who suggests of Akkerman, Shestakov, op. cit. p. 79.

[7] *BCA.* XXXIV. *Suppl.* p. 169.

Cherson certainly played its part in the process, being generally regarded as
the scene of its most dramatic incident, the baptism of Vladimir, hence the
building of the great church shewn in the view (Fig. 333) and the necessity of
discussing the question[1]. In the Russian *Chronicle* the story goes that in
986 A.D. missionaries from the Muhammadan Bolgars on the Volga, the
Germans, the Jews (Khazars) and the Greeks came to Vladimir one after
another to set forth their faiths, and that next year he in turn sent envoys to
see how the faiths were practised in the various countries[2]. In 988 as though
to take Christianity by force he suddenly descended upon Cherson, encamped
upon the further side of the town in the harbour, and set about starving
it into submission, declaring that he could wait three years : as he did not
succeed he threw up a bank against the wall (to bring his men on a level with
the defenders) but these stole away the earth by a hole in the wall and carried
it into the town. Finally a Chersonite named Anastasius sent Vladimir a
message upon an arrow to say that pipes brought water into the town from
wells to the east of him and bade him cut them off. Vladimir cried out, " If
this prove true, I will be baptized." So the defenders were reduced by thirst.
Then Vladimir sent to the Emperors Basil and Constantine demanding their
sister Anne in marriage and threatening to do the like to Constantinople.
They agreed on condition of his accepting Christianity, and upon this it is
clear that he had already resolved. Thus Anne set out with much weeping
as into slavery, and with her officers and priests, and the Chersonites met her
with reverence. Then Anne's priests baptized Vladimir, naming him Basil in
the church of S. Basil (v.l. Our Lady, in the "Life," S. James), in the midst of
the town where the Chersonites buy and sell ; many of his warriors were also
baptized. So Vladimir took Anne to wife and by the church his palace and
hers are to be seen unto this day. After building a church on the heap of
earth ·stolen from his bank, Vladimir went back to Kiev with his bride,

[1] The principal original authorities for the
baptism of Vladimir and the taking of Cherson are :
Ps.-Nestor, *Russian Chronicle* sub A.M. 6496=
A.D. 988, Laurentian MS. St P. 1897.
This is reprinted by E. Golubinskij, *Hist.
Russian Ch.*², Moscow, 1901, I. i. pp. 225—238, in
columns parallel with a "*Life of Vladimir*" which
agrees with it very closely.
Iacobus Monachus, *Panegyric (Memory and
Praise) of Vladimir*, ib. pp. 238—245.
The "*Special" Life of Vladimir* published by
A. A. Shakhmatov at pp. 1072—1074 in "The
Korsun Legend of Vladimir's Baptism," his contri-
bution to the *Miscellany (Sbornik) of Articles
dedicated by his Admirers to V. I. Lamanskij*, St P.
1908, Vol. II. pp. 1029—1153; besides secondary
Lives of Vladimir discussed by Shakhmatov, pp.
1044—1072.
Leo Diaconus, X. 10 (p. 175).
Anonymus Bandurii, imperfect at the beginning,
reprinted in the Bonn Constant. Porphyrog. III. p.
357, translated with the newly recovered beginning
(after Regel, *Analecta Byzantino-Russica*, St P.
1891) by Golubinskij, op. cit. pp. 248—252.
Cedrenus, II. pp. 443, 444, Bonn.
Zonaras, III. pp. 552, 553, Bonn.
Yahyá of Antioch ap. Baron V. R. Rosen,

" Basil Bolgaroctonus," p. 23, *Miscellany (Sbornik)
of the Imp. Acad. of Sc. St P.* Vol. XLIV. 1883:
The discovery of this last has rendered earlier
treatment of the questions concerned out of date,
cf. Rosen, op. cit. pp. 194, 198, 215; G. Schlumberger, *L'Epopée Byzantine*, Paris, 1896, 1900, Vol. I.
702—end, Vol. II. 1 sqq.; Golubinskij, op. cit.
pp. 105—164; S. Srkulj, "Drei Fragen aus der
Taufe des heiligen Vladimir," in *Arch. f. Slav. Phil.*
XXIX. (1907), pp. 246—281 ; Shakhmatov, op. cit.
and in "Investigations into the most ancient Com-
pilations of the Russian Chronicle," pp. 133—161 ;
*Chronicle of the Progress of the Archaeographic
Commission*, XX. St P. 1908; S. P. Shestakov, op. c.
pp. 82—93, 125—137; A. L. Bertier-de-La-Garde,
"How Vladimir besieged Korsun," *Bulletin
(Izvéstia) of the Imp. Acad. of Sc. St P.*, *Russian
Language Section*, Vol. XIV. 1909. I have not seen
Sobolevskij, *Journ. Min. Pub. Instr.* 1888, June,
"In what year was S. Vladimir Christened?"
[2] Stories of such disputations were in the air,
e.g. the conversion of the Bulgarian Boris in 864,
the preaching of Cyril among the Khazars and the
accounts of how they were Judaized, but the stories
are hard to date, v. J. Marquart, *Ost-Eur. u. Ost.-As.
Streifzüge*, pp. 5—27.

carrying off thither Anastasius and other priests of Cherson, the relics of
S. Clement, holy vessels and icons, also two brazen statues and four brazen
horses afterwards set up in Kiev, but the town he gave back to the Emperors
as a marriage-gift (*vêno*).   The *Chronicle* adds that some said mistakenly that
Vladimir was baptized at Kiev, Vasiliev or elsewhere.

Shakhmatov's "Special" Life agrees with this tale in making the fall of
Cherson due to treachery and in putting Vladimir's baptism there, but in
other respects it differs entirely.   Vladimir sends to demand the daughter
of the prince of Cherson in marriage, on his being refused with scorn he
collects his forces, takes up his position and makes his threat as before ; but
"Vladimir waited six months and the men of Korsun were not starved out :
now in the town was a Variag named Zhĭdĭbern (Norse Sigbjorn) : he shot an
arrow into the company of Variags and said 'take the arrow to Vladimir.'"
He had written on the arrow that he was friendly to Vladimir and that in two
or three years he could not starve Korsun out, "for shipmen come with drink
and food into the town and their road is to the east of thine array."   So
Vladimir cut this road and in three months the men in the town surrendered
through hunger and thirst.   Thereupon Vladimir violates the daughter of the
prince and princess before their very eyes, slays them and gives her in
marriage to Zhĭdĭbern whom he sends to Constantinople to demand for him
the hand of Anne ; and the end is as in the former version.

Bertier-de-La-Garde shews that both these stories are fairly consistent
with the strategical topography of the place, supposing Vladimir had boldly
penetrated to the head of the harbour, and the shipmen landing somewhere
in North Bay brought provisions to the point opposite the town and
across the mouth of the harbour out of sight of Vladimir who could not keep
the sea in winter, the water pipes are of course well known (v. supra, p. 502):
he also shews that both the episodes with arrows are reasonable and supposes
a separate cutting off of the provisions and of the water, as is implied by either
story separately, e.g. shipmen could not bring water for a beleagured town : in
fact that the authors of these two accounts knew a common source in which
appeared all and more than all the incidents that now fill up two stories, the
source being a tale or ballad made up in Vladimir's camp, incorporating
the motive of the vengeance of the rejected suitor.   The Chronicle certainly
implies that the siege took a long time and the "Special" life gives it at not
less than nine months, this would enable us to reconcile the date given by the
Chronicle, 988, which we may take as that of the beginning of the siege with
the date of the capture deducible from Leo Diaconus and defined as between
April and June 989.   A difficulty has arisen because Yahyá of Antioch
confirms the vaguer accounts of Cedrenus and Zonaras telling of a force of
Russians, the origin of the Varangian guard, who were lent to Basil and
Constantine and enabled them to defeat Bardas Phocas at Chrysopolis in the
summer of 988 and at Abydos, April 13, 989.   Yahyá says that (apparently
in 987) the Emperors had to apply for help to an enemy, the prince of the
Russians, and he demanded their sister in marriage, to which they consented
on condition of his being baptized : and afterwards (giving time for the affair
of Cherson), Basil sent bishops who baptized the prince...and they sent him
their sister :...and when the matter of the marriage was decided (not

necessarily after the promised bride had been received), the host of the Russians came and joined the host of the Greeks who were on the side of Basil: the Russians must have arrived between April 4, 988, when Basil published a very despairing preamble to a Novel, and the battle of Chrysopolis in the summer. Bertier-de-La-Garde argues that Vladimir would not have let his men go without getting a hostage for them in the shape of Anne, this being the main object of his marriage, and that Cherson must have been captured before then, in fact the hostilities against Cherson were the hostilities of which Yahyá speaks: besides it would be inconceivable that Vladimir should be besieging the Emperors' town just when he was helping them with picked forces. Srkulj (p. 269) has hit on the explanation without making very much of it, when he suggests that perhaps at the moment the town did not belong to the Emperors. There is no direct evidence for this, but its dependence on Asia Minor is the most constant fact in its history and all Asia was under Bardas Phocas. Hence it appears to me an excellent stroke of policy for Vladimir, when the Emperors delayed his imperial bride, to do them a service, and yet remind them of his power by taking a Greek town belonging to the rebel side: this would palliate the treachery of Anastasius but would not much lessen the disaster in the eyes of Leo Diaconus. The hostility of which Yahyá speaks was the longstanding hostility of the Russians dating from Askold and Dir, now turned to permanent friendship. The Emperors were then constrained by the pressure of the Bulgarian war and the revolt of Bardas Phocas, to promise a Porphyrogenita in marriage to a barbarian, and brought up to execute their promise by the alarming service of the reduction of Cherson[1]. Vladimir had no need of a hostage for his Variags, who as a matter of fact, never came home as a body, but were quite able to take care of themselves, being for the next hundred years the main support of the Empire, always recruited from fresh Norsemen and later on from Englishmen. He was anxious for the matrimonial project because, though he knew the political weakness of the Empire, its prestige attracted him, and he really thought the time had come to adopt the faith and civilization of the Greeks.

    The latest authorities have come to believe that however much truth there may be in the details of the siege the legend of Vladimir's baptism at Cherson was inserted in the chronicle at one of its early remodellings. Shakhmatov supposes that an account of his baptism at Kiev came immediately after the triumph of the Greek missionary which ought to lead up to it (the sending of his own envoys being part of the Cherson story), and it is suggested that the mission was also political to ask for his help against Bardas or the Bulgarians. This would be in 986 and could be brought into agreement with the statement of the Panegyric that he took Korsun in the third year after his baptism; with it independent sources assert that he survived his baptism 28 years in all, and his death in 1015 is well known. It looks therefore as if Vladimir had been baptized at home, at Kiev or Vasiliev in 986, but like Mecztsław of Poland, and Stephen of Hungary[2]

---

[1] For their unwillingness v. *Luitprandi Leg.*   *de adm. Imp.* c. 13, p. 86 sqq.
p. 350 of the Bonn Leo Diac., and Const. Porph.   [2] Golubinskij, I. p. 132 n.

in similar circumstances, he kept it quiet for a while until the taking of Cherson and the marriage with an imperial princess gave him a grand opportunity to make the announcement: foundation for the story that he was christened at Cherson may be sought in the baptism of part of his host or in a misunderstanding of the marriage ceremony: the object of it was a desire to exaggerate the part played by Cherson in the Christianization of Russia. For it was the priests of Cherson that baptized the Russian people in the Dnêpr: Joachim first bishop of Novgorod was from Cherson; the holy and other objects made at Cherson for the Russian market went far and wide, so that many of the oldest pieces are still traditionally called Korsunian, but this attribution does not rest on a very sound basis except as regards crosses of a certain type which do occur at Chersonese, even with Slavonic inscriptions. At Novgorod are two pairs of bronze gates, one pair made at Magdeburg in the xiith century and called Korsunian, the other of Byzantine design said to have been brought from Sigtuna in Sweden. It is possible that the names have been exchanged, but even so we cannot be sure that the Byzantine gates came from Cherson[1]. The Icon called Our Lady of Korsun belongs to a type which derives from Italian painting of the xivth century[2].

Commerce and Diplomacy. Decay.

A certain amount of prosperity seems to have come to the Chersonites from this commerce with the Russians, for whom were destined a hoard of Novgorod *grivnas* (bars of silver) found at Cherson[3], and with the Pechenêgs to whom they exported silk and other stuffs and ribbons dyed to various shades of purple[4]. In return they received hides and wax which they sold at Constantinople. Their ships then went along the coast of Asia Minor and brought cargoes of corn and wine and other such products. Without these the Chersonites could not live. Accordingly if the Chersonites were insubordinate, as perhaps in the reign of Leo, all that need be done was to seize any of their ships and cargoes that might be at Byzance, and shut up the crews and passengers in workhouses, to send and do the same by their ships along the coasts of the themes of the Bucellarii (Bithynia), Paphlagonia and the Armeniac theme (Pontus), meanwhile preventing the native ships from sailing across, and for the praetor to stop the allowance of ten pounds sent to Cherson from the treasury and the other two pounds allowed by treaty and retire to another town. For the Chersonites were equally dependent on selling the produce of the Pechenêgs and buying the provisions of Asia[5].

[1] Tolstoi and Kondakov, *Russian Antiquities*, v., crosses, pp. 32, 33, ff. 21—23, gates, pp. 33—36, ff. 24, 25 ; Kondakov, *Russian Hoards*, I. p. 33 sqq., where a distinction is insisted upon between the elegance of Constantinople work and the heavy oriental style of Cherson. Golubinskij, *Hist. Russ. Ch.* I. ii. p. 48 strongly emphasizes the Korsun influence on Russian architecture, but in plan the early Russian churches are not like the Chersonian.

[2] Kondakov, *Iconography of the B.V.M.: the connexion of Greek and Russian Icon-painting with Italian painting of the early Renaissance*, St P. 1911, pp. 163—165, ff. 112—114.
[3] *CR.* 1889, p. 14.
[4] Const. Porph. *de adm. Imp.* c. 6.
[5] ib. c. 53 fin. ; cf. for earlier times the commerce of the Altziagiri Huns with *Chersona, quo Asiae bona auidus mercator importat,* Jordanes *Get.* v. 37.

Besides the commerce there passed through Cherson most of the diplomatic communications between Byzance and the Pechenêgs[1]: and these latter were most important as by keeping on friendly terms with them the Empire could have the advantage of the Russians, Magyars (Τοῦρκοι) and Khazars, and dearly too did they make the Greeks pay for their services. However the Uzi could be employed against the Pechenêgs and also against the Khazars, and these latter could be kept from interfering with Cherson by the help of the chief of the Alans or the Black Bolgars. So the system of playing off barbarian against barbarian is expounded by Constantine[2].

In 1066 we have a curious story shewing how the barbarians regarded the Greeks. A captain from Cherson made friends with Rostislav Vladimirovich, who was making the Russian principality of Tmutorokan on the east side of the Bosporus too strong, and gave him at a banquet slow poison from under his nail, then he returned and prophesied the prince's death. But the Chersonites stoned him for his pains[3].

With the arrival of fresh hordes of Turkish tribes and the weakening of the Russian power the profitable connexion of the latter with Cherson became difficult and from the time of the Tartar invasion ceased completely. At the same time the declining authority of the Empire (during the Latin usurpation Cherson was Trapezuntine) could no longer afford assistance, indeed, with the growth of Genoese influence in the xivth century, it became hostile to the interests of Cherson. The Italians while feeling their way, dwelt at Cherson and had a consul and even an archbishop there[4], but after establishing themselves firmly at Sudak, Caffa and Cembalo (Balaklava) they boycotted the city and even forbade the Greeks to trade there[5].

It is generally said[6] that the final blow was struck in 1363 by Olgerd the Lithuanian, who having defeated the Tartars and pursued them into their country, took the opportunity of plundering the poorly defended city[7], but I cannot help thinking that the Korsun meant is the Russian town of that name not very far from Kiev, and I find that Bertier-de-La-Garde regards this incursion as mythical. Be that as it may, the inhabitants gradually withdrew to Cembalo and Inkerman, but the episcopal see still bore its old name being even raised to the rank of a metropolis, perhaps to resist the pretensions of the Latin archbishop, and the only events recorded are petty quarrels with other sees as to small border villages: finally it was united with that of Gothia still called after the few Ostrogoths who had remained behind in the Crimea.

Some few people must have remained in 1449 as the Genoese then had a consul at Cherson, but in 1470 there was no one to prevent the Bank of S. George pulling down the walls. We may take 1475 the year of the Turkish conquest to be the end of Cherson as a habitation of men.

---

[1] As of old with the Turks v. Menander, *de Legat.* f. 43, *FHG.* IV. 245.

[2] op. cit. cc. 1—13.

[3] Ps.-Nestor, a. 1066.

[4] In 1303 he was Richard an Englishman, *Trans. Od. Soc.* v. p. 980, Baronii et al. *Ann. Eccl.* Lucca, 1750, XXV. p. 565, A.D. 1333, No. XXXVII. For Italian glass dated 1322, v. p. 515.

[5] A.D. 1350, Niceph. Gregoras XVIII. 2.

[6] Bobrinskoj, p. 162.

[7] Karamzin, *Hist. of the Russian Empire*, Vol. v. c. i., quoting in note 12 Stryjkowski, *Chron. Lith.* XII. ii., but the former dates Olgerd's raid in 1332, and Kojalowicz, *Hist. Lituana*, Danzig, 1650, p. 287, who claims to put Stryjkowski (whom I have not seen) into classical dress, says nothing of Cherson; Solovjëv, *History of Russia*, says nothing either.

Institutions.

The political constitution of Chersonese can only be divined by putting together the scanty hints afforded by the inscriptions and eking them out with analogies drawn from Megara and its other colonies. The authors tell us nothing. Yet even so we can see that the names and duties of the magistrates and most likely the whole spirit of the constitution underwent a complete change in the latter part of the 1st century B.C., perhaps under Roman influence. Hence we must be very chary of applying to one period data derived from another[1].

Chersonese was essentially a democracy, and it preserved the forms and something of the spirit of a democracy to a very late period. Indeed it has been claimed for it that it was the only ancient city state which kept essential autonomy well into the Middle Ages. Yet no doubt it became rather oligarchical after its final submission to Rome under the Antonines.

Sovranty resided in the People (ὁ δᾶμος): but measures brought before it had first been considered by the Senate (ἁ βουλά). Every citizen[2] might aspire to the senate. Proposals might be made either by private individuals[3] or by officials, occasionally νομοφύλακες[4], more often the πρόεδροι[5], who seem to have presided over the senate in Roman times. In earlier times we find the date of the decree in honour of Diophantus[6] expressed by the name of the king, which gave the year, of the προαισυμνῶν and of the γραμματεύς. It would appear that the προαισυμνῶν was the chief of a college of αἰσυμνᾶται corresponding to the prytaneis at Athens with their ἐπιστάτης, and probably holding office for a month. The exact relations of αἰσυμνᾶται and πρόεδροι are not clear. The latter may have taken the place of the former whose name was part of the Megarian heritage: or they may have co-existed, it being mere chance that the words occur in distinct periods: at Athens the πρόεδροι in some degree superseded the prytaneis. Further in connexion with the senate and people there was a Secretary, γραμματεύς[7].

Magistrates.

Until quite a late period the heads of the executive seem to have been the δαμιοργοί. It is to them that the citizens are to reveal all plots against the city. Every citizen was eligible, probably there was some limit of age. How many there may have been we do not know. The chief of them appears to have been said δαμιοργεῖν τὰν [πρώτ]αν ἀρχὰν[8]. The word seems

---

[1] The whole matter was excellently treated by Latyshev in *Journ. of Min. Publ. Instr.* St P. June, 1884, *Classical Sect.* pp. 35—77 : "Epigraphic Data as to the Constitution of Chersonesus Taurica"=*BCH.* IX. (1885), pp. 265—300, 524, 525, and I have followed him closely, but the data supplied by the inscriptions in *IosPE.* IV., especially the Oath, throw considerable fresh light; and also App. 18ª, from *Journ. Min. Publ. Instr.* 1907, March=Ποντικά, pp. 314—331, where Latyshev discusses the recent additions to our knowledge, cf. *BCA.* XXIII. p. 49 sqq.

[2] App. 16=*IosPE.* IV. 79.

[3] *IosPE.* I. 184, cf. *BCA.* XLV. p. 44; IV. 64, 65.

[4] *BCA.* III. p. 21, No. 1; XIV. p. 101, No. 9.

[5] App. 18ª, *IosPE.* I. 188; IV. 71, 72; *BCA.* XIV. p. 103, Nos. (11), 12; also *IosPE.* I. 200.

[6] App. 18=*IosPE.* I. 185, cf. App. 17ª=*BCA.* XLV. p. 23, No. 1.

[7] App. 17ª, 18, 18ª, *IosPE.* I. (190), IV. (97).

[8] *IosPE.* I. 196; the word occurs in another inscription which gives the *cursus honorum, IosPE.* I. 199 (=App. 19); and I have ventured to suggest it for the damaged wreath of App. 17 instead of Latyshev's στραταγήσαντι.

to have gone out about the middle of the IInd century A.D. as it last appears in App. 19 dated by the mention of Rhoemetalces (131—154), whereas in App. 18ᵃ dated A.D. 129—130 we find the first mention of Archons¹ a πρῶτος ἄρχων and four common ones. About this time came the abandonment of the Doric forms in decrees. No doubt they had perished in common speech long before, as even the legal speech was impure. In decrees of the later period, e.g. App. 18ᵃ, the best preserved, we find the chief archon sealing next after the Maiden Queen, the rest of the first two columns (στίχοι) are taken up with thirteen names of prominent citizens, perhaps ex-magistrates, several of them belonging to the same families; in the last column we have four other archons, three nomophylaces, prodicus and secretary. The chief archonship could be held more than once². Gazurius (p. 507, f. 339) is described as πρωταρχοντεύων, and from that, as I have said, it is but a step to the πρωτεύων καὶ στεφανηφορῶν of Constantine Porphyrogenitus.

The Byzantine Governors were called στρατηγοί, Praetors (v. p. 543), and πρωτεύων has the wider meaning of "being a leading citizen³." On a seal (p. 543), it seems a real title. There must have been Strategi in ancient times, but the sixth wreath of Agasicles (App. 17) is doubtful.

The administration of justice was in the hands of the citizens who swore to judge according to the laws. There were magistrates called πρόδικοι who must have had to do with the course of justice, perhaps as at Corcyra they were representatives of the senate in legal affairs⁴.

The νομοφύλακες, five or six in number, were police magistrates⁵. They occasionally proposed measures as a college.

The ἀγορανόμοι looked after the markets. Perhaps it was while he filled this office that Agasicles laid one out. Hermocrates spent the proceeds of his tenure, three thousand pence, on the temple of Aphrodite⁶.

We can deduce the existence of ἀστυνόμοι from the amphora-handles with Doric names found at Chersonese; we find the same names upon coins, their bearers having ascended to be δαμιοργοί⁷ (v. supra, p. 359).

The office of Gymnasiarch, also filled by Agasicles, was rather a liturgy than a magistracy⁸; so too with that of Thiasarch which is coupled with other liturgies, although most probably it was semi-private⁹.

The Priesthood was a post of honour and expense: it was not unusual for statues to be put up to those who had held one, to women as well as men. A priest, no doubt that of the Maiden, is named in dating decrees¹⁰.

There were also ταμίαι τῶν ἱερῶν who were to defray the expenses of erecting a statue to Diophantus and the inscription to Syriscus¹¹.

With the priests are coupled in several inscriptions the Kings whose office was no doubt purely religious¹². That they were eponymous we know

¹ In *IosPE.* IV. 65 the word is only conjectural and not convincing.
² e.g. *IosPE.* I. 196.
³ πρεσβύτερος πόλεως was probably a purely complimentary title, *IosPE.* I. 202.
⁴ App. 18ᵃ, 20, and *IosPE.* I. 196.
⁵ App. 18ᵃ, 19; *BCA.* III. p. 21, No. 1; XIV. p. 101, No. 9; XVIII. p. 114, No. 23.
⁶ *IosPE.* I. 203.
⁷ Makhov, *Bull. Taur. Rec. Com.* XLVIII., sup-

poses that the astynomi were responsible for the coinage as well as the amphorae.
⁸ cf. also Ποντικά, p. 311.
⁹ *IosPE.* I. 200, Democrates, son of Aristogenes; Ziebarth, p. 170, and Poland, p. 28, (v. inf. p. 620, n. 5) think him a public overseer of societies.
¹⁰ App. 18ᵃ, *IosPE.* I. 190, IV. 70; cf. also App. 15, 17, 19, *IosPE.* IV. 86, 87, 92.
¹¹ *IosPE.* I. 184, cf. *BCA.* XLV. p. 44.
¹² App. 15, *IosPE.* IV. 87, 88.

from two inscriptions of the same year[1]. After a reorganization in the last half-century B.C., the fruits of which we can trace in the coinage also, human kings no longer appear and we find the Maiden named as Queen in decrees (e.g. App. 18[a]) and on coins. This change it is hard not to bring into connexion with the establishment of the Chersonesan Era 24 B.C. both on coins and decrees, as the date according to that era is associated with the words βασιλευούσας Παρθένου, or the monogram Ⓡ. As Queen the goddess was the first to seal decrees[2].

The συμμνάμονες only appear as crowning Diophantus and others whom the city honoured, proclaiming their deeds at a festival and writing them in stone. Latyshev takes them to be like ἱερομνάμονες and thinks that they came into the matter because of the religious character of the festival, whereas Th. Reinach calls them *greffiers publics*, which would seem rather to correspond to γραμματεύς, and indeed μνάμων seems to be the old Doric equivalent for γραμματεύς surviving from before the time of writing[3], at least those at Iasus[4], Halicarnassus and Salmacis[5], and Gortyn seem to have been "living archives" especially as regards land: such a function would be closely allied to the proclamation and registering of decrees[6]. We may infer that the college as a whole was called the συμμνάμονες and each individual member a μνάμων[7].

There is no need to do more than mention the ἐπιμεληταί who allotted the fields[8]; or who saw to the building of walls[9]: the same word probably occurs in the tantalizing inscription which also mentions a tyrant, and the citizen who was elected (χειροτονηθείς) to take charge against him[10]. Nor need we make a special office of διοικητής for Ariston (App. 19), who brought the finances into order. Such a reorganizer was necessary from time to time, another of them was Heraclidas, son of Parmenon ἐπὶ τᾶς διοικήσε[ος | ἐ]ὼν[11]. In the same inscription is named a ταμίας, the regular treasurer.

Byzantine Government.

The organization of Cherson under the Byzantines is nowhere clearly described. Until the time of Theophilus it was under its own πρωτεύων καὶ στεφανηφορῶν, assisted by the City Fathers[12]. The στρατηλάτης καὶ δοὺξ Χερσῶνος of Maurice's inscription at Bosporus[13] may be regarded as a military commander sent to help against some special attack of barbarians. The expeditions of Justinian II were probably much like that of Theophilus, reasoned attempts to subject Cherson more directly, and officials were nominated for its government. Its freedom was saved by the ensuing

---

[1] App. 18, *IosPE.* IV. 67; cf. App. 17[a], IV. 77, 80.
[2] Orêshnikov, "Coins of Chersonese &c." *Num. Misc.* II. pp. 13, 14, instances coins of Byzantium whereon goddesses appear holding magistracies, cf. *Zt f. Num.* IX. (1882), p. 147; *Numismatische Zt.* (Wien), XXVII. (1896), p. 27.
[3] *IosPE.* I. 184, 185 (App. 18), IV. 65—67.
[4] *Mithridate*, p. 70, cf. Daremberg-Saglio, s.v. Mnamones.
[5] Ditt. *Syll.*[2] 96, l. 32; 10.
[6] Perhaps at Megara, Ἐφ. Ἀρχ. 1886, pp. 226, 231.

[7] v. Ct I. I. Tolstoi, *Journ. Min. Pub. Instr.* St P. Feb. 1905, *Cl. Sect.* p. 73.
[8] *IosPE.* IV. 80.
[9] *IosPE.* I. 202.   [10] ib. IV. 68.
[11] *BCA.* XVIII. p. 114, No. 23, IIIrd century B.C.
[12] Const. Porph. *de Adm. Imp.* c. 42, οὐκ ἦν στρατηγὸς ἀπὸ τῶν ἐντεῦθεν (Constantinople) ἀποστελλόμενος, ἀλλ' ἦν ὁ τὰ πάντα διοικῶν ὁ λεγόμενος πρωτεύων μετὰ τῶν ἐπονομαζομένων πατέρων τῆς πόλεως.
[13] App. 70 = *Inscr. Christ.* 99.

anarchy. It was under a πρωτοπολίτης and πρωτεύοντες, but the Khazar *tudun* was perhaps the real ruler[1]. The Dux is again mentioned in a fragment which has been referred to the time of Justin II[2]. Theophilus sent Petronas to be the first Praetor raising him two steps from the rank of a σπαθαροκανδιδᾶτος to that of a πρωτοσπαθάριος[3]. This is the regular rank of a praetor of Cherson ; the seals or leaden *bullae* of eight at least have come down to us, all of this highest order save one spatharius, but they ranked last of the στρατηγοί[4] : one is στρατη(γὸς) Χερσόνος καὶ κατὰ Σαρ(μάτας)[5].

We find the names of one or two other magistrates on seals : of Commerciarii or inspectors of customs, five seals have survived, all of spatharocandidati except one spatharius. One man, a spatharius, is described as ἐπὶ τῶν οἰκ(ειακῶν) πρωτεύο(ντι) Χερσόν(ος). The former title designates the manager of the property of the Emperor's privy purse. Whether the office of πρωτεύων continued after the institution of praetors it is hard to say, on this seal it looks like an office, whereas when Calocyrus is described as the son of a πρωτεύων it would seem to mean merely a leading man[6]. Two of Jurgiewicz's seals are not definitely Chersonian, but appear to come from there, upon one of them we have a spatharocandidate ἐπὶ τῶν οἰκειακῶν, on the other a protospatharius as a γενικὸς λογοθέτης or treasurer-general. These seals belong to the x–xiith centuries. The different hierarchical ranks are some measure of the relative importance of the offices.

Cults.

In Chersonese one cult predominated almost to the exclusion of every other—the cult of the Maiden. She was no doubt in the first place a local deity—the same to whom the Tauri offered their human sacrifices[7]. Further she was identified with Artemis, apparently by a series of false etymologies and analogies[8]. The name Taurica suggested ταυροπόλος and ταυρώ : her dwelling in the mountainous belt may have brought to mind, Oriloche[9] : the bloody rites of her sacrifice recalled those of Artemis Orthia at Sparta. Herodotus (iv. 103) identified the Tauric goddess with Iphigenia, who was and was not Artemis Brauronia. Hence a confusion in which mythologists

---

[1] Theophanes, p. 570, Bonn=372 de Boor; Nicephorus C—politanus, p. 46.

[2] *BCA.* XVIII. p. 121, No. 37.

[3] For a table of these orders v. J. B. Bury, "The Imp. Administration System in the IXth Century," p. 22, *Brit. Acad. Suppl. Papers*, I. 1911 ; cf. Hirschfeld, "Die Rangtitel d. röm. Kaiserzeit," *SB. Berlin Akad.* 1901, p. 579 sqq.

[4] Philotheos, Κλητορολόγιον, ap. Bury, op. cit. pp. 137, 138, 147.

[5] Schlumberger, G., *Sigillographie de l'Empire Byzantin*, p. 235 sqq., repeated with additions by Ct I. I. Tolstoi, *TRAS.* St P. II. (1887), p. 28 sqq., Pl. III. : cf. Jurgiewicz, *Trans. Od. Soc.* XIV. p. I, Pl. I. ; XV. p. 41 ; XXI. *Minutes*, p. 39 : Tolstoi and Kondakov, *Russian Antiquities*, IV. pp. 4—7, ff. 4—6 ; K. M. Konstantopoulo, Βυζ. Μολυβδόβουλλα in Svoronos, *Journal International d'Arch. et de Numism.* v. Nos. 120, 121 ; IX. No. 118ª: *BCA.* XX. p. 25.

[6] cf. Const. Porph. op. cit. c. 53, p. 251, Bonn, τοὺς δὲ τούτων πρωτεύοντας.

[7] The native goddess referred to on p. 523, n. 7 was milder, seeming only to have received the jaw-bones of domestic animals as meat-offerings.

[8] For Artemis and the Tauric Maiden v. Roscher, s.v. *Artemis* § 15, I. p. 585, and *Parthenos*, III. p. 1661 ; also Wernicke in *P.-W.* s.v. *Artemis*, Βραυρωνία, Ἰφιγένεια, Ὀρθία, Ὀρσιλόχη, Παρθένος, Ταυροπόλος, pp. 1375—1409 ; Harrison and Verrall, *Myths and Monuments of Ancient Athens*, pp. 394—404 ; Farnell, *Cults*, II. p. 452. Orēshnikov, op. cit., p. 9, vehemently objects to the Maiden being called Artemis ; I should have done better to avoid the name.

[9] v.l. Orsiloche in Amm. Marc. XXII. viii. 34 ; cf. Ant. Lib. 27, citing Nicander, who gives Iphigenia the name Ὀρσιλόχεια.

rejoice. The whole story was brought into artistic shape and popularized by Euripides. But in Chersonese, without troubling about origins, they acquiesced in their Maiden being Artemis: on coins she is the huntress with bow and spear, short chiton and hunting boots. Three attitudes may go back to artistic statues—though the coins are early for such dependence—standing over a deer and driving a spear into its neck from behind (Pl. IV. 16, 27), sitting and looking at the point of an arrow, perhaps with her deer beside her (Pl. IV. 8, 9), and kneeling on one knee with her spear laid down by her and holding a bow in her left hand (Pl. IV. 14); lastly we have what appears to be her cult image, perhaps the ξόανον of which Strabo speaks (VII. iv. 2); she stands as though casting her spear with her right hand, while the left is outstretched with the bow[1]. On her head can be distinguished a mural crown which re-appears on coins bearing her head alone (Pl. IV. 17): that is she also did duty as city-goddess, as Demeter may have done at Olbia[2]: it is in this aspect that she encouraged Diophantus and his army (App. 18, l. 23). Mela (II. i. 3) calls Diana the foundress of the city and the chief festival in the religious year was that of the Παρθένεια. Her altar was on the acropolis and no doubt her temple too with its πρόναον in which decrees of honour could be set up[3]. Near it was an altar τᾶς Χερσονάσου, who must have been rather the local nymph than the Tyche of the city; the gender seems to rule out a Hero Chersonesus whom Orêshnikov[4] sees on certain coins and a bas-relief: perhaps the Nymphs' cave mentioned by Mela (l. c.) belonged to a nymph Chersonesus. A cave called Parthenon is mentioned as the refuge of S. Basileus[5].

On coins besides the heads with mural crowns we have other heads that may be considered to exhibit Artemis (e.g. Pl. IV. 1—5, perhaps 2 and 4 might just conceivably be Apollo). Also the figure of a deer must be referred to her[6]. Lastly the Victory which appears driving a quadriga (Pl. IV. 6) or a biga[7], perhaps even that standing with a wreath[8], must be thought of as an emanation of the Maiden. Even without these nearly two thirds of the coins figured by Burachkov bear the Maiden's image.

A very curious case of the citizens' devotion is furnished by an inscription which thanks Syriscus son of Heraclidas for having laboriously written an account (inter alia) of the manifestations of the Maiden and read it aloud[9]. There can be no doubt that if any priesthood was eponymous it was that of the Maiden. A dedication gives the name of a priest who had also been king[10], and another, probably that of the same Gazurius who was chief archon[11].

Upon the coins Apollo occurs most frequently after the Maiden. Sometimes it is hard to tell which is meant, but in the later series upon

---

[1] Pl. IV. 25, 26, 28, side view: front view Burachkov, XVI. 110. The reliefs from Aj Todor, *BCA.* XL. p. 16, Pl. V. 12—14 only faintly recall these attitudes.
[2] Cf. Ἄρτεμις Τύχη Γεράσων, v. Roscher. I. p. 1628.
[3] *IosPE.* IV. 67.
[4] *Num. Misc.* II. "Coins of Cher." pp. 8, 32.
[5] Cap. 4 of his life, ap. Latyshev, v. p. 531, n. 4.
[6] Pl. IV. 17, 22, the latter looks rather Mithridatic.
[7] Bur. XV. 69.   [8] Pl. IV. 12; B. XVI. 90, 94, 95.
[9] *IosPE.* I. 184 cf. IV. p. 277, giving Wilhelm's

restoration from *Arch. Epigr. Mitth. aus Oesterreich*, XX. p. 87, mostly upheld by new pieces, *BCA.* XLV. p. 44, v. supra p. 517.
[10] App. 15 = *IosPE.* IV. 83, also probably 87, 88.
[11] *IosPE.* IV. 86. Other interesting dedications: ib. IV. 84, IVth cent.; 85, IInd cent., Δῆλιος Ἀπολλᾶ Παρθένωι κατ' ἐνύπνιον, the nomenclature suggests Apollo. Σωτήριχος θεᾶς Παρθένου, *BCA.* XXVII. p. 16, No. 2, may have been a priest or perhaps a ἱερόδουλος.

which his bust appears distinguished by the lyre there can, pace Bertier-
de-La-Garde (v. inf. p. 549), be little doubt[1].   No inscription mentions him.

Athena Sotira receives one dedication, made by a man for his wife (both
names are lost).   The statue above was the work of Polycrates[2].   In date
this was as early as any dedication to the Maiden and in itself one which we
should value specially highly for the name of the artist.   Athena's helmeted head,
in type like that used by Alexander, occurs on a few coins (Pl. IV. 11, 12).

In the Oath of the Citizens the Maiden comes just where the patron of
the city should come (cf. inscription cited on p. 516, n. 6).   Zeus, Earth, and
Sun are invoked without our deducing thence that they had any special cult
at Chersonese, their very natures and offices made them the guardians of all
oaths, still less has the mention of all the gods and goddesses of Olympus any
definite significance, even the heroes of the land need not have had direct
worship paid to them.   The only other inscription mentioning Zeus is a
dedication of a piece of wall to Zeus Soter not earlier than the IInd century A.D.[3]
Zeus is represented on one coin which bears his head on the obverse and
a thunderbolt on the reverse[4].   Coins like Pl. IV. 24 are thought by Koehne
and Burachkov to bear Zeus but the head is more probably that of Asclepius[5].
I(oui) O(ptimo) M(aximo) which instead of D.M. heads the gravestone of M.
Antonius Valens, Rostovtsev explains by a combination of the Roman worship
of Jove and the Spanish habit of dedicating gravestones to upper deities[6].

To Aphrodite was dedicated the temple which dating from the end of
the IInd century A.D. furnished many fragments to Uvarov's basilica[7].   One
coin (Pl. IV. 10) bears a type which resembles rather her head than the
Maiden's, but it does not seem to have been repeated.

In the same basilica that yielded the fragments of Aphrodite's temple
were found pieces of frieze with skulls of oxen and goats (?), and swags of ivy[8],
suggesting that it was to Dionysus that Pasiadas son of Artemi[dorus] king
and priest dedicated it[9].   One type of coin (Pl. IV. 7) with its Janiform head
suggests the Indian Dionysus and Ariadne or some one else of Dionysus' train,
but it is not less like a bearded Hermes.

To Hermes Demoteles son of Theophilus (IInd century A.D.) dedicates as
gymnasiarch epinicia which take the form of five elegiac couplets inscribed
upon a base and containing several new epithets applied to the god, who
is prayed to be gracious to all, ὅσοι κλυτὸν ἄστυ τὸ Δώρου ναίουσιν, an
interesting example of the Chersonesites' long-lived pride in their Doric
descent[10].   He has but few coins which honour his deity: his head appears on
some (Pl. IV. 19, B. XV. 67, 82, 83, 86, XVI. 119) and on others the caduceus,
this is scarcely evidence of an actual cult.

Asclepius with or without Hygiea also appears but rarely upon coins

[1] Pl. IV. 23, 25, 26, 28; B. XV. 43—45, XVI. 99—
101, 106—114.
[2] IosPE. IV. 82, v. supra p. 295, n. 12.
[3] IosPE. I. 202, cf. BCA. XXVII. p. 39.
[4] Giel in TRAS. VII. Pl. XIX. No. 35, a thunderbolt occurs as a countermark on a few other coins,
e.g. Pl. IV. 13.
[5] Of the coin described in BCA. XVI. p. 59, B. β,
I cannot judge; it is said to bear busts of Zeus and
Artemis and EIPHNHC CEBACTHC effaced.

[6] BCA. XXVII. p. 58, No. 2.
[7] IosPE. I. 203, v. supra pp. 295 and 525.
[8] Von Stern, Od. Mus. Guide, p. 79, No. 1;
Mat. XII. Pl. IV. 2, p. 19; IosPE. IV. 87.
[9] Dionys[us restored in BCA. XVIII. p. 114, No.
23, and on an altar (?) at Old Cher., Mat. XII. p. 57,
and Diony]sia, IosPE. I. 184, are very risky:
ΔΙΟΝΥϹΟΥ scratched on a cup, BCA. II. p. 24.
[10] Latyshev, Journ. Min. Publ. Instr. St P.
1907, Class. Section, pp. 261—265 = Ποντικά, p. 311.

M.

(Pl. IV. 29, probably 24; B. XVI. 115—118). According to Latyshev's restoration of one inscription[1], he had a temple in which complimentary decrees were set up perhaps in return for physicians' services. But there is a bare possibility that we have to do with a name like Asclapiodorus.

Many coins exhibit Heracles or his symbols, the lion's head or the club. Inasmuch as the mother city was Heraclea, and Chersonese may itself have been a Heraclea, it is no wonder if there was a cult of Heracles. But his appearance on coins does not go for much. It may have but suggested the name of the city or it may have been mere reproduction of types specially common about the Pontus. The most usual head is Alexandroid[2].

The Dioscuri appear on a bas-relief and on coins[3]. The altar τᾶς Χερσο-νάσου (App. 18, l. 52) and Mela's Nymphs' Cave have already been mentioned.

I cannot admit as evidence of any cult at Chersonese the sherds with two or three letters or a monogram scratched upon them such as HP or HPA, ΔI, ΔAMA, ΔIAI, AΘA, API, APT, for these are the first letters of men's names as well as gods': even CⲰTH begins some human names. It may be no mere chance that ten in von Stern's collection bear HP or HPA but these are common enough initial combinations (v. p. 361).

At Aj Todor (v. p. 523, n. 7) were inscriptions and reliefs dedicated to Jove, the "Thracian Riders," Dionysus, Mithras, Hermes, triple Hecate and (on another site) Artemis, also a cistern inscribed N]ymph[aeum; the temple being outside the wall was accessible to others beside the Roman garrison[4].

Kalendar, Literature and Athletics.

We know four months of the Chersonesan Kalendar, Dionysius, Heracleius, Lyceius and Eu[cleius]. Save for Heracleius, perhaps derived from Heraclea Pontica, they bear out Latyshev's guess that Chersonese used a Kalendar like that of Megara and its colonies, Byzantium and Chalcedon[5].

Of literary activity in Chersonese our only specimens are one or two metrical epitaphs of which perhaps the less said the better[6], and the hymn to Hermes. We do just know the name of one Chersonesite writer Syriscus crowned for celebrating the Maiden's wonders but it seems they had to go to a stranger for any statue which should be an ornament to the city. Still their Doric traditions saved them from falling into the inflated style of the Olbian decrees[7]. The tale of Gycia must reproduce Chersonian tradition, and a good deal of the hagiographical literature to which reference has been made was doubtless written in the city.

As at Olbia, so here we have evidence of the survival of athletic contests[8], in lists of victors in running both long and short distances, throwing the

[1] *IosPE.* I. 189.

[2] Pl. IV. 9, 20; B. XV. 46—53; also a beardless type that may be Heracles, Pl. IV. 18; B. 54—57; lion's head, Pl. IV. 10, 21. The club is very common.

[3] *CR.* 1903, p. 28, f. 25; Orêshnikov, *Num. Misc.* II. "Coins of Chersonese &c." p. 31.

[4] *Arch. Anz.* 1911, pp. 234—238 citing M. I. Rostovtsev *BCA.* XL. p. 1 sqq. Pl. I—v, "The Sanctuary of the Thracian Gods and the Inscriptions of the Beneficiarii at Aj Todor."

[5] App. 18, 17ᵃ and 18ᵃ, *IosPE.* IV. 70, 95 cf. *BCA.* XXIII. p. 61: *Trans. VIth Russ. Arch. Congress,* Odessa, 1886, Vol. II. p. 70=Ποντικά, pp. 40, 319.

[6] *IosPE.* IV. 108, 110, 136, 149; *BCA.* XIV. p. 107, No. 17; p. 111, No. 25; XXXIII. p. 48.

[7] *IosPE.* I. 200 alone approaches them.

[8] *IosPE.* I. 228, better IV. p. 282; *BCA.* X. p. 20, No. 14; *Journ. Min. Publ. Instr.* 1907, *Cl. Sect.* p. 261=Ποντικά, p. 311.

javelin, boxing, wrestling and ἀγκυλομαχία which one would like to translate ju-jitsu. In honour of the victors we have the beginning words of each line of an elegiac epigram which we need not regret. More interesting is a fragment[1] which seems to tell of contests of trumpeters and heralds and of an epigram written by one Marcus. All these inscriptions are shewn by the names and the grammatical forms (ἀκόντιν) to belong to late Roman times, at least the third century. They justify Pliny's praise when he says that in the whole region the Chersonesites kept their Greek civilization specially bright[2].

Coins. Plate IV.

Koehne in his book on Chersonese and later in *MK.* and recently General A. L. Bertier-de-La-Garde have done most to bring the coinage of Chersonese into order. The latter divides its numismatic history into three periods, which he has tabulated as follows[3]:

I. Independence, from middle of IVth century to middle of Ist century B.C. Æ and Æ. Nos. 1—22.	Types: chief, Artemis, Heracles; rarer, Pallas, Hermes, Aphrodite, and Zeus: many secondary, bull, griffin, lion, deer, Nike, etc. XEP; once at beginning XEPΣ; once at end XEPCONHCOY. Names of magistrates except upon the earliest.
II. Autonomy, from middle of Ist century B.C. to latter part of IInd century A.D. Æ and Æ. Nos. 23—25.	Types: Apollo, Artemis; rarer, Zeus, Heracles, Pallas and Nike; secondary, deer, eagle, caduceus. XEP. No magistrates. Dates. 𝕀𝔸ℙ or its varieties.
III. Roman Liberty, to middle of IIIrd century A.D. Æ only. Nos. 26—29.	Artemis (Apollo not allowed by Bertier-de-La-Garde), Asclepius and Hygiea; bull. XEPCONHCOY ΕΛΕΥΘΕΡΑC: no dates, no names, no 𝕀𝔸ℙ.

One or two transitional pieces do not come into this grouping.

The silver coins in the first group are rare. Up to the Mithridatic period Bertier-de-La-Garde[4] makes of them two main divisions according as Heracles appears upon them or not. Upon the greater part the Maiden is unrivalled and these are coined on a standard of about 55 grn. or 3·55 grm. to the drachma, this he identifies with the Phoenician standard. So No. 1 would be half a drachma, No. 3 a lightish drachma, No. 4 a didrachm, No. 5 a tridrachm, No. 13 a tetradrachm: we seem to have the obol of this series in

Æ. 8·5 grn. = ·55 grm. Artemis head l. | Fish over club, below XEP.
Orêshnikov, *Mat.* VII. p. 38, No. 35: weight corrected by B.-de-La-G.

The bull upon club seems to be derived from the coins of Heraclea Pontica[5], but it is such a common type as not to go for much. It is hard to think that it was not regarded as the *armes parlantes* of the Tauric Peninsula.

But No. 9 (141·6 grn. = 9·17 grm.) does not fit in with such a system nor its congeners of half (reverse as Nos. 9 or 8) and quarter (reverse as No. 8) weight. This Heracles class has didrachm, drachma and hemidrachm of the Persian standard, lightened from its 86 grn. drachma, as used in Asia Minor and especially in the mother city Heraclea Pontica with whose types it agrees.

[1] *BCA.* XIV. p. 111, No. 24.
[2] Praecipui nitoris in toto eo tractu custoditis Graecis moribus, *NH.* IV. 85.
[3] "Signification of Monograms 𝕀𝔸ℙ etc.," *TRAS. Num. Sect.* I. (1900), p. 56: Orêshnikov,

op. c., generally agrees but separates a group from c. 110 to 24 B.C. which he calls "Bosporan Influence," and the next he terms "Reign of the Maiden."
[4] *Trans. Od. Soc.* XXVI. pp. 236—248.
[5] cf. *BMC. Pontus*, Pl. XXIX., XXX.

The first attempt to issue coins on this standard approached more nearly to the original weight and the series comes out :—

Didrachm,	164·73　grn. = 10·56 grm.	Heracles as No. 9.	Artemis as No. 9.
Drachma,	80·34　grn. = 5·15 grm.	do.	Artemis slaying deer as No. 16.
Hemidrachma, 39·156 grn. = 2·51 grm.		Peculiar hd of Artemis r.	Bull as No. 8 (B. XIV. 18, 19).

but these are all very rare and of specially good workmanship. Evidently Chersonese struck silver upon one standard, the Persian, for external, on another, the Phoenician, for internal circulation. The two series run parallel as we see both from their style and from the magistrates' names common to both: to make a bridge between the systems was the object of the tridrachm No. 5 equivalent to a Persian didrachm. Orêshnikov[1] does not accept this.

The coins in the top row on the plate belong in style to the second half of the IVth century. The coppers Nos. 6 and 7 are as good in execution. as the silver. The spearman on No. 6 would appear to be a local hero, on the defensive like Chabrias[2]; both the types of No. 7 are interesting, the Janiform head on the obverse is quite unexplained, Orêshnikov supposes it to be the bearded Dionysus and a Maenad ; Head makes the beardless head Dionysus and the other Zeus[3]: the reverse is a favourite motive among the Scythians. The second row represents the following two hundred years: the tetradrachm No. 13 is the largest of a series with a similar head on the obverse, didrachm (B. XIV. 3—5), drachma (B. 1—2) have reverse like No. 16, the half drachma has bow and quiver as on Pl. VI. 5 (B. 22—24). The first trial of Heracles-coin came early in the IIIrd century, the main issue such as No. 9, later, even half-way down the IInd. That coins like Nos. 9 or 13 were circulating at the end of that century is shewn by the countermarks, e.g. the dolphin is Mithridatic, and just traceable on No. 13 under the thunderbolt is 𝔸, the first form of 𝕀𝔸 which marks all the next period at Chersonese.

At the very beginning of the Ist century there was a rough and ready reform of the currency. Under four magistrates, Demetrius, Moeris, Apollonius and Diotimus, any coins of anything like the right weight, e.g. drachmae both of the Artemis and the Heracles series, like Nos. 9 and 13 but smaller, were re-struck to bring them into relation with the tetradrachms of Mithridates and the Roman denarii now the chief currency of the Levant. No. 17 comes from a hoard found in 1853 near Sevastopol and now spread all over Europe, No. 18 (there are coppers very like it, B. XV. 54) is the chief constituent of a hoard found in 1903[4] near Karan, between S. George's Monastery and Balaklava, just north of 979 on Map VIII., apparently in a house or small fort burnt in the Scythian wars. In this hoard were found copper as well as silver coins and not merely new-struck ones as in the former hoard, but coins that had been in circulation previous to the reform, so we may put magistrates' names such as Choreius, Menestratus, Pythion, Promathion, Diagoras, Istron, &c., fairly late. The earliest in style found in the hoard was No. 11, but examples of it occur with Ist century stamps, so its good execution must be due to exact copying of the Alexander type. The head on

[1] *Num. Misc.* II. "Coins of Chersonese &c."
[2] Bertier-de-La-Garde, *Trans. Od. Soc.* XXX. "Monetary Novelties" No. 2: issue numbers A—Σ
occur, also the same magistrates as on No. 7.
[3] *Cat. Uvarov*, p. 42, No. 287 : *HN.*² p. 279.
[4] *Trans. Od. Soc.* XXVI. p. 250.

No. 17 recalls the type of Sinope[1] and the deer is perhaps Mithridatic (cf. Pl. VI. 7). On the smaller denomination, No. 18, the memory of the Heracles series was preserved. No. 19 was found in the Karan hoard and belongs to this date. No. 20 also bears the head of Heracles in a lionskin which has hitherto been restricted to silver but the whole type is very similar to Panticapaean coins (Pl. VI. 12, 14, 16, 24). The 1st century B.C. was the time of chief naval activity on the Euxine, and during it prows commonly occur on coins. This one may have to do with the exploits of Diophantus. The coin has been re-struck, the die seems hardly big enough for the blank, but what it may have been originally cannot be distinguished. Thoroughly Panticapaean is No. 21 with its lion's head (cf. Pl. V. 9) and the star which appears to be Mithridatic (cf. Pl. VI. 3). Certainly the grazing deer on No. 22 is Mithridatic (cf. his later tetradrachms and Pl. VI. 7): so too B. XVI. 97,

| Æ. Artemis like No. 13. | Eagle on thunderbolt (cf. Pl. VI. 11), X E P, countermark 𝔸ℙ. |

It has already been said that great changes took place at Chersonese in the second half of the last century B.C. What they were exactly we cannot tell (v. p. 521), but on monetary affairs we find their influence fundamental. Coins already in circulation were countermarked 𝔸ℙ or later 𝔸ℙ, new ones bear the latter on the die and date-letters appear, the era (v. p. 521) being calculated from 24 B.C. A find in the valley above Jalta, the site of a local sanctuary (v. supra, p. 523, n. 7), has provided a coin of the type common to the second and third period, e.g. No. 26, with an inscription forming a transition between them, obverse XEPCONH EΛEYΘ, reverse ΠΑΡΘΕΝΟC[2]. This confirms the guesses of Becker and other writers that the monograms indicate the Maiden goddess; Bertier-de-La-Garde suggests that the mint came under the direction of the temple authorities instead of the town magistrates, and therefore the goddess's monogram was put on the coins. A difficulty arises as to the interpretation of the obverse type, a bust with a lyre before it (Nos. 23, 25, 26, 28). Bertier-de-La-Garde sees in it Artemis YMNIA and certainly it looks very feminine on e.g. No. 28, and he thinks that the more elaborate monogram 𝔸ℙ[3] stands for ΠΑΡΘένος Ὑμνία: but it might do just as well for ΠΑΡΘένοΥ and on No. 25 the head is certainly masculine, it might be said to be a reminiscence of a Roman Emperor. But after the history of the interpretation of a colossal statue such as "Winckelmann's Muse," certainty in regard to badly executed coins cannot be attained.

In this second period there is a change of metal, no more silver is coined, but we have a small number of gold pieces, corresponding in weight to the Roman or Bosporan aurei (v. p. 632). Their political signification and the dates they bear have been treated in the history of Chersonese[4]. No. 25 with the letters PNH = 158, i.e. 134 A.D., is the last of them.

[1] *BMC. Pontus*, XXII. 11—13.
[2] Bertier-de-La-Garde, *On monograms* 𝔸ℙ *etc.*, p. 60, Pl. VI. 5.
[3] Orêshnikov, *Num. Misc.* II., thinks this not

πapθένos and the bust a personification.
[4] For these see pp. 522, 523, Bertier-de-La-Garde in *Trans. Od. Soc.* XVI. and von Sallet in *Zt f. Num.* and *Berl. Beschr.* I. p. 7.

The third period is marked by the word ΕΛΕΥΘΕΡΑC. Probably in between had been a time of direct subjection to Rome. There is no more question of gold or silver, only of copper. With the archaism of decadence the coins, like No. 27, bear reproductions of types of the first period, Artemis slaying a deer like No. 16 and the bull which appeared already on No. 4, but mostly we have Apollo with the lyre and Artemis standing. It has been suggested that this is a reproduction of a group set up in the city—Artemis in a mural crown, with dart and bow, a stag by her side, not so very unlike Diane de la Biche—but shewing late date by the accumulation of attributes. Asclepius and Hygiea are purely Roman. The tolerable style of Nos. 28 and 29 is due to a raising of craftsmanship accounted for by close communication with more civilized centres. The lettering with clumsy serifs is enough to shew the late date.

BIBLIOGRAPHY.

Sources.

The earlier collected in Latyshev's *Scythica et Caucasica* (*TRAS.* 1890—1906), the Byzantine mostly in Stritter, I. G., *Memoriae Populorum olim ad Danubium, Pontum Euxinum, &c., incolentium.* St P., 1771—1779.

Herodotus, IV. 103.

Ps.-Scylax, 68.

Polybius, XXV. ii. (XXVI. vi.), 12.

Ps.-Scymnus, l. 822 sqq.

Strabo (308), VII. iii. 17, iv. 2—7.

Pomponius Mela, II. i. 3.

Trogus Pompeius ap. Justinum, XXXVII. iii. 1 ; XXXVIII. vii. 3.

Pliny, *NH.*, IV. 85 (26).

Fl. Josephus, *Bell. Jud.* II. xvi. 4.

Phlegon Trallianus, *Olymp.* Lib. XV. fr. 20 (XXII.), *FHG.* III. p. 607.

Memnon, c. XLIX. 4, *FHG.* III. p. 551.

Polyaenus, *Strategemata*, VIII. 56.

Ptolemy, *Geographia*, III. vi. 2.

Ps.-Arrian, *Periplus Ponti Euxini*, 30 (19).

Anonymi *Periplus P.E.* 80 (54).

Ammianus Marcellinus, XXII. viii.

Jordanes, *Getica*, V. 32, 37.

Zosimus, *Historia Nova*, IV. 5.

Procopius, *De Aedificiis*, III. 7.

—— *De Bello Persico*, I. 12.

—— *De Bello Gothico*, IV. 5.

Menander Protector, "Excerpta de Legationibus," c. 43, *FHG.* IV. p. 245.

Theophanes Confessor, Bonn, pp. 173, 510, 537, 566, 570—585, 691=de Boor, 112, 332, 351, 369, 372—380, 451.

Theophanes Continuatus, VI. c. 10, p. 360.

Nicephorus C–politanus, Bonn, pp. 44, 46 sqq.

Constantinus Porphyrogenitus, *De Thematibus*, II. c. 12 (p. 62, Bonn).

—— —— *De Administrando Imperio*, cc. 1—13, 37, 42, 53.

—— —— *De Cerimoniis*, II. c. 54 (p. 794 Bonn).

Leo Diaconus, VI. 9 ; X. 10.

Toparcha Goticus, ad fin. Leonis Diac., Hase, p. 496 sqq., cf. supra, p. 534, n. 6.

Cedrenus, I. pp. 775—784 ; II. pp. 372, 383.

Zonaras, III. pp. 233, 236, 240—242, 513—519.

Anna Comnena, *Alexias*, X. 2.

Constantinus Manasses, ll. 3890, 3988—4100.

Michael Glycas, IV. p. 517 sqq.

Nicephorus Gregoras, XVIII. 2.

Ps.-Nestor, *Chronicle according to the Laurentian Version.* Ed. III. St P., 1897. (The best translation by L. Leger, Paris, 1884.) Introd. p. 7 and under A.D. 944, 945, 971, 988, 989, 1066.

For Hagiographical Literature, most fully collected by P. Lavrov in *Monuments of Christian Chersonese*, II. Moscow, 1911, v. p. 531, nn. 1, 3.

General Histories of Chersonese.

Fuller Bibliographies Al. I. Markevich, "Bibliography of the Crimea," in *Bulletin of the Tauric Record Commission*, Vol. XX. and in Bobrinskoj's *Chersonese*, pp. 188—194. I have not included small articles whose contents have been summarized in general works, especially the first publications of inscriptions, or such as touching on single points are referred to in the footnotes.

Guthrie, Maria, *A Tour performed in the years 1795-6, through the Taurida or Crimea, &c.*, ed. by Matthew Guthrie. London, 1802.

Siestrzencewicz de Bohusz, Mgr S. *Histoire du Royaume* (!) *de la Chersonèse Taurique.* St P., 1824.

Polsberw, L. *De Rebus Chersonesitarum et Callatianorum.* Berlin, 1838.

Koehne, B. de, *Investigations into the History and Antiquities of the city of Chersonesus Taurica.* St P., 1848. This also appeared in the form of "Beiträge zur Geschichte und Archäologie von Cherronesos in Taurien," in *Mém. de la Soc. d'Archéologie et de Numismatique de St P.* (the earlier series of *TRAS.*) Vol. II. pp. 161—241, 301—353 (1848). Pl. X.—XII. XVI.—XX. Vol. III. pp. 1—102. Pl. I. II. (1849). "Herr Stephani und seine Kritik" and "Nachträge." Supplement to Vol. IV. and Pl. I. 3, 4 (1850).

Neumann, K. *Die Hellenen im Skythenlande*, pp. 379—446. Berlin, 1855.

Koehne, B. de, *Description du Musée Kotschoubey (MK.)*, I. pp. 119—267, Pl. II.

Selivanov, S. A. *Chersonesus Taurica.* Odessa, 1898.

Brandis, C. G. in *P.-W. Encycl.* pp. 2261—2269, s.v. Chersonesos (20). Stuttgart, 1899.

Rostovtsev, M. I. in Brockhaus-Jefron *Encycl.* XXXVII. pp. 162—165, s.v. Chersonese. St P., 1904.

Bobrinskoj, Count A. A. *Chersonesus Taurica. An historical Sketch.* St P., 1905.

Kulakovskij, J. A. *The Past of Taurida.* Kiev, 1906.

(Ivanov, Dr E. E. "Chersonesus Taurica, an historico-archaeological Sketch," *Bull. Taur. Record Comm.* XLVI. Sympheropol, 1912.)

Site and Remains.

Martinus Broniovius de Biezdzfedea, *Tartariae Descriptio.* Col. Agrip. 1595. Reprinted in Elzevir *Russia seu Moscouia.* Lugd. Bat. 1630 ; also *Trans. Od. Soc.* Vol. VI. (1867), p. 341.

Pallas, P. S. *Travels through the Southern Provinces of the Russian Empire made in the years 1793— 1794.* Eng. Trans. London, 1802.

Clarke, Dr E. D. *Travels in various Countries.* Pt I. Vol. II. 8vo Ed. London, 1817.

Dubois de Montpéreux, F. *Voyage autour du Caucase*, VI. pp. 130—202, I. Pl. I, 20, 21, II. Pl. 59. Paris-Neuchâtel, 1839-43.

Arkas, Zacharias, *Description of the Heraclean Peninsula and its Antiquities.* (*Trans. Od. Soc.* Vol. II. (1845). Reprinted,) Nicolaev, 1879.

Extracts from the most humble Report of Archaeological Explorations made in 1853. St P., 1855.

(Becker, P. *Die Herakleotische Halbinsel.* Leipzig, 1856.)

Murzakewicz, N. "The Chersonesan Church of S. Vladimir." *Trans. Od. Soc.* V. (1863), p. 996, Pl. VI.

(Mansvetov, D. I. *Historical Description of ancient Chersonese and the Monuments discovered in it.* Moscow, 1872.)

Strukov, D. *Ancient Monuments of Christianity in Taurida.* Moscow, 1876.

CR. 1882-88, p. ccvi., to 1907, contains short Reports of K. K. Kosciuszko-Waluźynicz's excavations, and to these were added from 1890 to 1898, fuller statements in an Appendix; from 1899 these fuller statements were transferred to *BCA.* I. pp. 1—55 ; II. pp. 1—39 ; IV. pp. 51—119 ; IX. pp. 1—62 ; XVI. pp. 37—113 ; XX. pp. 17—100; XXV. pp. 67—171 ; XXXIII. pp. 50—70; XLII. pp. 1—91 (part of the report for 1907 is by M. I. Skubetov, the draughtsman of the excavations), pp. 92—107 by Dr R. Löper (v. supra, p. 498, n. 2).

Arch. Anz. 1900 sqq. contains very short notices of Chersonese.

Tolstoi, Ct I. I. and N. P. Kondakov, *Russian Antiquities in Monuments of Art.* Pts I. pp. 17, 18 (=*KTR.* pp. 18—20), IV. pp. 1—24, V. pp. 27—38. St P., 1889-97.

Bertier-de-La-Garde, General A. L. "Remains of Ancient Constructions in the Neighbourhood of Sevastopol and the Cave-towns of the Crimea." *Trans. Od. Soc.* XIV. (1886), pp. 166—279.
—— "Excavations of Chersonese," *Mat.* XII. St P., 1893.
—— "Chersonese," *BCA.* XXI. St P., 1907.
Malmberg, W. K. "Description of Classical Antiquities found at Chersonese in 1888-9." *Mat.* VII. St P., 1892.
von Stern, E. R. "Report on the position of Old Chersonese." *Trans. Od. Soc.* XIX. (1896), *Minutes*, p. 99.
—— "On the Results of the last excavations at Chersonese." Ib. XXII. (1900), *Minutes*, p. 62.
—— "Bemerkungen zur Topographie und Geschichte des Taurischen Chersonesos" in Hettler's *Zt für Alte Gesch.* I. 2, p. 63—71. Bern, 1900.
—— "On the position of Old Chersonese." *Trans. Od. Soc.* XXVIII. (1907), *Minutes*, pp. 89—131.
Engel, M. *Archaeological Excavations at Chersonese*, 1897—1899. Sevastopol, 1900.
Ainalov, D. V. *Monuments of Christian Chersonese*, I. "Ruins of Churches," Moscow, 1905.
Garaburda, M. I., and M. I. Skubetov, "The defensive Wall of Chersonese," *Bull. Taur. Record Com.* XLIII. Sympheropol, 1909.
Pechonkin, N. M. "Archaeological Excavations on the site of Strabo's Old Chersonese," *BCA.* XLII. pp. 108—126, cf. *Arch. Anz.* 1911, p. 206.
(Vinogradov, Th. A. "Excavations at Aj Todor," *Hermes* (Russian) VI. pp. 248 sqq., 278 sqq., St P. 1910.)

Inscriptions and Historical Details.

Gibbon, E. *Decline and Fall.* Ed. J. B. Bury. London, 1902.
Waxel, L. de, *Recueil de quelques Antiquités trouvées sur les bords de la Mer Noire...en* 1797 *et* 1798. Berlin, 1803.
Karamzin, *History of the Russian State.* Vol. V. c. I.
Boeckh, A. *CIG.* Vol. II. pp. 80—170. Berlin, 1843.
CIL. III. *Suppl.* XIV. p. 392, No. 3608 ; cf. supra p. 525.
Finlay, G. *History of Greece under the Romans.* Ed. H. F. Tozer. Vol. II. p. 350. Oxford, 1877.
Jurgiewicz, W. "Psephisma of Chersonese rewarding Diophantus." *Trans. Od. Soc.* XII. (1881), pp. 1—48.
Burachkov, P. O. "An Attempt to make the Diophantus Inscription agree with the Localities and the Testimonies of Ancient Authors." ib. pp. 222—248.
Schneiderwirth, G. *Das Pontische Heraklea.* Heiligenstadt, 1881-5.
—— (*Zur Geschichte von Cherson in Taurien,* Berlin, 1897.)
Latyshev, V. V. *IosPE.* I. 184—240, IV. 64—190, 464—467. St P., 1885—1901.
—— *Mat.* IX. pp. 1—45 ; XVII. pp. 1—25 ; XXIII. pp. 2—51. St P., 1892-99.
—— *BCA.* I. pp. 56—59 ; II. pp. 61—68, Nos. 1—14 ; III. p. 21, Nos. 1—14 ; X. p. 20, Nos. 14—19, p. 96 ; XIV. p. 100, Nos. 8—37 ; XVIII. p. 114, Nos. 23—39 ; XXIII. p. 35, Nos. 13—21, pp. 49—51, 57—62 ; XXVII. p. 15, Nos. 1—31 ; XXXIII. pp. 43—49, Nos. 3—11.
—— *Inscr. Christianae* (Russian), pp. 7—36, Nos. 7—30.
—— "Epigraphic Data for the Constitution of Chersonesus Taurica." *Journ. Min. Publ. Instr.* St P. 1884, p. 135. Reprinted as "La Constitution de Chersonésos en Tauride d'après des documents Épigraphiques." *BCH.* IX. (1885), pp. 265—300, 524, 525.
—— "On the Kalendar of Ch. Taur." *Trans. VI. Russian Arch. Congr.* II. p. 70. Odessa, 1888. =Ποντικά, p. 40.
—— "Bürgereid der Chersonesiten" (=*Mat.* IX. No. 1). *SB. d. k. pr. Ak. d. W. zu Berlin,* 1892, p. 479. Improved as a separate publication (St P. 1900)=Ποντικά, (St P. 1909) pp. 142—167.
—— "Inschriften aus der Taurischen Chersonesos" (=*Mat.* XVII. 1—17). *SB. Berlin,* 1895, p. 505.
—— "Decree in honour of Dia...the Heracleote." *Journ. Min. Publ. Instr.* St P., 1907, p. 140 sqq. =Ποντικά, p. 314. Ποντικά contains some other minor articles touching Chersonese.
Gilbert, G. *Handbuch der Gr. Staatsalterthümer,* Bd II. p. 188. Leipzig, 1885.
Mommsen, Th. *The Provinces of the Roman Empire* (=*R.G.* V.). London, 1886.
Niese, B. "Straboniana, VI. Die Erwerbung der Küsten des Pontos durch Mithridates VI." *Rheinisches Museum,* XLI. (1887), p. 559.
Bury, J. B. *A History of the Later Roman Empire.* London, 1889.
—— *A History of the Eastern Roman Empire* (A.D. 802—867). London, 1912.
Reinach, Th. *Mithridate Eupator, Roi de Pont.* Paris, 1890.

von Domaszewski, A. "Die Dislocation des römischen Heeres im Jahre 66 n. Chr." *Rhein. Mus.* XLVI. (1892), p. 207.

Bertier-de-La-Garde, A. L. "An Inscription of the Time of the Emperor Zeno in connexion with Fragments from the History of Chersonese." *Trans. Od. Soc.* XVI. (1893), p. 44.

—— "How Vladimir besieged Cherson," *Bulletin (Izvěstia) of the Second Section of the Imp. Acad. of Sciences,* St P. vol. XIV. 1909. (v. under coins.)

von Stern, E. R. "*Graffiti* on ancient Pots from S. Russia." ih. XX. (1897), pp. 163—199.

Rostovtsev, M. I. "Roman Garrisons on the Tauric Peninsula." *Journ. Min. Publ. Instr.* 1900, p. 140. Repeated in *Klio (Beitr. z. Alten Gesch.)* II. (1902), pp. 80—95.

—— "New Latin Inscriptions from Chersonese." *BCA.* XXIII. p. 1, Nos. 1—4; XXVII. p. 55, Nos. 1—3; XXXIII. pp. 20—22.

—— "The Sanctuary of the Thracian Gods and the Beneficiarii of Aj Todor." *BCA.* XL. p. 1, Pl. I—VI.

Garnett, Dr Richard. "The Story of Gycia." *Eng. Hist. Rev.* Jan. 1897 = *Essays of an Ex-Librarian,* p. 129. London, 1901.

Golubinskij, E. E. *History of the Russian Church²,* I. i, ii. Moscow, 1901, 1904.

Keil, B. ΕΚΑΤΩΡΥΓΟΣ. *Hermes,* XXXVIII. pp. 140—144. Berlin, 1903.

Shestakov, S. P. "The Beginning of Christianity in Cherson." *Serta Borysthenica* (in honour of Professor Kulakovskij), p. 183. Kiev, 1906-11.

—— "Sketches of the History of Chersonese in the VI—IXth centuries A.D." In *Monuments of Christian Chersonese,* III. Moscow, 1908.

Makhov, I. I. "Amphora Handles of Ch. T. with names of Astynomi." *Bull. Taur. Rec. Com.* XLVIII. 1912.

—— "Thasian Amphora Handles from Ch. with emblems and names of Astynomi," ib. XLIX. 1912.

Löper, R. "Chersonesan Inscriptions." *BCA.* XLV. pp. 23—70; cf. Latyshev, ib. pp. 132—136.

Coins.

Besides the two works of Koehne whose importance is chiefly numismatic and has made earlier works negligible, and Bertier-de-La-Garde's article on the Zeno Inscription in *Trans. Od. Soc.* XVI.

von Sallet, A. *Zeitschrift für Numismatik,* Berlin.

  I. (1874), pp. 17—31. "Die Münzen von Ch. in der Krim."

  IV. (1877), p. 273—277. "Ein Goldstater der Taurischen Ch. mit dem Beinamen BACIΛΕΥOΥCA und einer Jahreszahl der Chersonesischen Æra."

  X. (1883), p. 143 and XI. (1884), p. 47, Pl. I. 7. "Jahreszahlen auf Münzen der T. Ch."

—— *Beschr. d. Ant. Münzen d. k. Museen zu Berlin,* I. (1888), pp. 2—7.

Gardner, P. *Brit. Mus. Cat. Thrace, Tauric Chersonese, Sarmatia, &c.,* p. 1—3. London, 1877.

Burachkov, P. O. (B.). *General Catalogue of Coins of Greek Colonies on N. Shore of Euxine,* pp. 101—126, Pl. XIV—XVII. Odessa, 1884. (Corrections by Bertier-de-La-Garde. Moscow, 1907.)

Giel, Ch. (G.). *Kl. B.,* p. 2, Pl. I. *TRAS.* v. (1892), p. 346, Pl. IV. 6—12 ; VII. (1895), p. 220, Pl. XVIII. XIX. 15—38.

Orêshnikov, A. V. *Catalogue of the Collection of Antiquities of Ct A. S. Uvarov,* Pt VII. pp. 41—48, Pl. I. Moscow, 1887.

—— *Description of Ancient Greek Coins in Moscow University,* pp. 26—30. Moscow, 1891.

—— *Materials touching the Ancient Numismatics of the Black Sea Coast.* Moscow, 1892, pp. 25—28. "Certain Coins of Ch. T." (i.e. dated coins). Pl. II.

—— *Mat.* VII. p. 33 sqq. "Descr. of Coins found in the Ch. Excavations in 1888-9." St P., 1892.

—— "Chersono-Byzantine Coins." Moscow, 1905, extract from *Trans. Moscow Numismatic Soc.* Vol. III. Supplements in *Numismatic Miscellany,* I. Moscow, 1911.

—— "Coins of Chersonesus Taurica, Kings of the Cimmerian Bosporus and Polemo II of Pontus," extract from *Numismatic Miscellany,* II. Moscow, 1912.

Antonovich, V. B. *Description of Coins in Kiev University.* Pt I. "Ancient Coins," p. 112. Kiev, 1896.

Bertier-de-La-Garde, A. L. "Some new or little-known Coins of Chersonese." *Trans. Od. Soc.* XXVI. (1906), pp. 215—276.

—— "On the meaning of the Monograms ⟨LAP⟩ and ⟨AP⟩ on the Coins of Chersonese." *TRAS. Numismatic Sect.* Vol. I. (1906), pp. 51—79.

—— "A chance find of Antiquities near Jalta." *Trans. Od. Soc.* XXVII. (1907), *Minutes,* pp. 19—27.

—— "Monetary Novelties from the ancient cities of Tauris," ib. XXX. (1912).

—— "Materials for Stathmological Investigations into the Coinages of the ancient Greek cities and kings of Tauris and Sarmatia," pp. 21—25. *Numismatic Miscellany,* II. Moscow, 1912.

Wroth, W. *Imperial Byzantine Coins in the British Museum,* esp. p. ciii. London, 1908.

Head, B. V. *HN.²,* p. 279. Oxford, 1911.

M.

FIG. 341. View of Theodosia c. 1786 looking S.E. *Museum Worsleyanum*, London, 1794, II, Pl. 117.

CHAPTER XVIII.

THEODOSIA AND NYMPHAEUM.

Theodosia.

ALTHOUGH Theodosia and Nymphaeum were soon to become part of the Bosporan kingdom they have not left themselves without witness to their free existence, and the former at any rate always remained a separate title in the rulers' style and a special division of the kingdom. The anonymous *Periplus P. E.* (77 (51)) says that Theudosia, a deserted city with a harbour, lay 280 stades, $37\frac{1}{3}$ miles, from Cazeca, that it was an ancient Greek city, a colony of the Milesians and often mentioned in literature. So far he agrees with Ps.-Arrian (30 (19 H.)), but he adds from some unknown source, "now Theudosia is called in the Alan or Tauric tongue Ἀρδαβδα, = ἑπτάθεος: it is said that exiles from the Bosporus once inhabited it." As an inscription proves it not deserted till after Arrian's time, this is so much against the authenticity of the second half of the Periplus ascribed to him (v. p. 24, n. 3). Ulpian, the scholiast to Demosthenes *in Leptinem*, says that Satyrus died while besieging it and that it had its name from the sister, or according to other authority wife, of Leucon who on capturing the city made it more of a port than before and renamed it[1].

This question of its name is interesting; some authors (v. p. 560) and inscriptions give it as Θευδοσία which in itself is a Doric form[2], others and even inscriptions of the same ruler, Θεοδοσία. On the later coins we have ΘΕΥ (Pl. IX. 7), ΘΕΥΔο[3], on most early ones probably autonomous, ΘΕοΔΕ∩ (Pl. IX. 4 and Jakunchikov's, v. p. 559), ΘΕοΔΕο[4], but ΘΕοΔο (Pl. IX. 6) is almost as early. Koehne[5] has suggested with great probability that these are ἐθνικά from some ungreek name *ΘΕΟΔΕΙΑ and that Leucon made a kind of pun in changing this to the name of his sister which somewhat resembled it and was also a good augury for the newly won city. As to Ardavda Müllenhoff gets the right meaning out of it (v. p. 39) but it has been suggested[6] that this was a mistaken interpretation and that the second half is cognate with *dare* making an equivalent for the Greek name. It is almost certainly Iranian, but we cannot take this as throwing light on the Tauri for it is more probably Alan.

The site has never been systematically excavated, but in the harbour-works carried out in 1894 by that distinguished engineer and archaeologist General Bertier-de-La-Garde there were found inscriptions[7], sculpture

[1] Von Stern, *Theodosia*, p. 12, thinks this a mere scholiast's invention deduced from the text of Demosthenes: a Bosporan Theodosius, v. App. 28.

[2] v. Sandys in Dem. *Lept.* 33. In all but the latest inscriptions both forms end in -ίη.

[3] Bertier-de-La-Garde, "Monetary Novelties," *Trans. Od. Soc.* XXX. No. 10.

[4] Giel, *TRAS.* V. Pl. IV. 14.

[5] *MK.* I. p. 276.

[6] Jurgiewicz, *Trans. Od. Soc.* VIII. p. 9.

[7] *IosPE.* IV. 195, 196 (IVth cent. B.C., cf. v. Stern, *Theodosia*, Pl. X. 2, 1), 197 (IIIrd cent. A.D.), 198.

(v. pp. 296, 298), terra-cottas[1], sherds of pottery[2], some with graffiti, e.g. ΒΟΣΠΟΡΙ+ΟΕΙΜΙΤΟΤΙΜΩΡΙ◊ΣΚVΛΙ⊞ with its early lettering and curious names[3] and the two abecedaria (v. p. 361), also amphora-handles (v. p. 358, n. 8), all proving that the hill whereon stand the remains of the Genoese citadel at the east end of the circuit of mediaeval walls was the site also of the Greek city.   Other excavations made in 1852 by Prince Sibirskij and in 1853 by the great sea-painter Aivazovskij on the initiative of Count Perovskij[4] produced most beautiful gold work which may be referred to the IVth century and terra-cottas decidedly above the average of the Pontic coasts.   But the terra-cottas found in the harbour-works are of quite a distinct class shewing a genuine archaic style of which one or two specimens (v. p. 364) must go back to the VIth century recalling the κόραι of the Athenian Acropolis, and black-figured vases tell of Athenian commerce[5]. That makes the history of Theodosia begin over a century before the first event recorded, the siege laid to it by Satyrus c. 389 B.C. (v. inf. p. 574). We have an incident of this siege preserved by Polyaenus who says that the Heracleotes supported the Theodosians and sent across Tynnichus with the few soldiers they could raise and several buglers to be put into separate boats distant from one another.   So when they sounded the besiegers thought in the darkness that they were so many full complements, and retired before the superior force.   Certain it is that Satyrus died without having taken the city, but Leucon was more successful, although it is probable that he too had to contend with the Heracleotes[6].   It looks as if there was a prolonged struggle on the part of Heraclea Pontica, helped no doubt by her colony Chersonese, to extend her power over Theodosia or at any rate to prevent its falling under that of the Bosporan rulers.   Memnon of Rhodes may have taken the side of Heraclea in this struggle, at least we do not know in what other war he should have opposed Leucon[7]: if so the Heracleotes remained hostile through all Leucon's reign, as Memnon's career only just overlapped his.

However, when at length successful, Leucon took no vengeance on Theodosia but made good use of its natural advantages.   Strabo (VII. iv. 4) says that the harbour was sufficient for as many as a hundred ships, whereas the harbour and docks of Panticapaeum could only accommodate thirty : as a matter of fact the natural harbour has never been very good and the roads though spacious are absolutely open to the SE.; however, that is not a dangerous quarter and the gently shelving beach would allow Greeks to draw their ships ashore.   The piles found in the recent harbour-works may be the remains of a Greek mole or may only go back to Genoese times, they shew that the need of a real harbour had been met before the present final solution of the difficulty.   For Leucon Theodosia had two great advantages over Panticapaeum, it was always free from ice, and it was close to the rich corn-lands instead of being upon the "rugged peninsula."   Accordingly it was here that he made the staple of his corn-trade as we find in the speech of

---

[1] v. p. 363, *Od. Mus. Terra-cottas*, I. p. 21.
[2] Von Stern, *Theodosia*, Pl. II—V.: everything is kept together in the Odessa Mus., v. *Guide*, p. 50 sqq.
[3] *Trans. Od. Soc.* XX. p. 181, Pl. II. No. 49.
[4] *Rep. of Arch. Explor. for* 1853 ; Koehne, *MK.*

[1] p. 274; *ABC.* Pl. XIIa,=supra p. 401, f. 294, Reinach, pp. 52—54; LXXa. 1, 4, 6, 10, p. 117 (Terra-cottas); *KTR.* p. 13 sqq.
[5] Von Stern, *Theodosia*, Pl. II.
[6] Polyaenus, v. xxiii. : VI. ix. 3.
[7] ib. v. xliv. 1, v. inf. pp. 576, 626.

Demosthenes against Leptines, and Strabo speaks of his sending 2,100,000
medimni across to Athens.   Further, its possession made it easy to defend
the whole eastern projection of the Crimea by a ditch running across to the
sea of Azov.

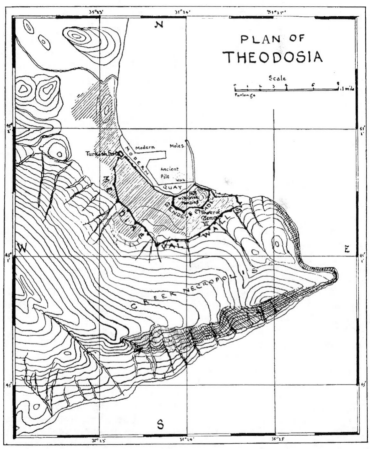

FIG. 342.   After Bertier-de-La-Garde ap. von Stern, *Theodosia*, Pl. 1.   Contours 45 ft apart. $\frac{1}{13400}$.

Leucon and his successors without denying themselves supreme authority
were considerate enough to call themselves archons merely and let the name
of the city be part of their official style (v. p. 576).

It is likely that Theodosia suffered in the wars between Paerisades I and
the Scythians[1], certainly compared with the many ivth century things objects

---

[1] Demosthenes *in Phormionem*, § 8.

of the Hellenistic period are decidedly few : it probably fell into the same straits as Chersonese in the IInd century B.C. It was taken by Diophantus[1] and probably regained some prosperity under Mithridates : yet, perhaps under pressure of his taxation, it was one of the cities which followed the example of Phanagoria and revolted against him[2]. This is the last historical notice of it—the mentions in Mela, Pliny, Ptolemy and later Ammianus are merely geographical—and we might believe the Peripli that it lay desert in Roman times but for pieces of *terra sigillata*[3], the fairly complete series of Bosporan coins found on the site[4], and one or two inscriptions ; the most important, referred by von Stern[5] to the IIIrd century A.D., shewed that there existed at Theodosia just such a religious society as at Tanais and elsewhere in the Bosporan kingdom. A presumption that it continued to have some importance as a frontier port is offered by the existence of a dignitary of the kingdom called the prefect of Theodosia[6].

Von Stern[7] expands two- or three-letter monograms upon sherds into the names of Apollo, Athena, Ares, Hera or Heracles, Artemis, Asclepius and perhaps Demeter : he wishes to regard them as θεοὶ σύνναοι, but men write the name of a god to whom they are making a dedication, even when there is only one in the temple, besides we have no right to make them names of deities at all.

In the very unhistorical wars between Chersonese and Bosporus recounted by Constantine Porphyrogenitus[8], Capha is named as the spot where the Chersonites defeat their enemies and set the frontier against them. That it was inhabited in the succeeding centuries is shewn by Byzantine pottery[9] and by a pillar with epitaphs dated A.M. 6327 = A.D. 819[10].

This name of Caffa is that under which the site of Theodosia became famous. As the chief Genoese mart on the Black Sea it destroyed by its competition the trade of Cherson and ruined its Venetian rival Soldaia (Sudak) which finally came under its authority together with Cembalo (Balaklava). It was far more important than Vospro (Kerch) and even Tana (Azov) in which were quarters for the merchants of each rival city.

The Genoese appear to have established themselves at Caffa shortly after 1266 and the settlement, being the objective of a trade-route reaching to China, flourished exceedingly in spite of the occasional hostility of the Tartar Khans, until the Turks gained control of the Thracian Bosporus. Then the tenure of the Italians became very precarious, it is wonderful that they could hold it at all at such a distance from their base, and the Turks had no difficulty in seizing it in 1475. At that time it seems to have contained a population of about a hundred thousand made up of many creeds and races. When the Genoese were turned out the rest remained and it was quite prosperous under the rule of the Turks who called it Little Stambul. The Sultan kept it directly under himself and did not give it to the Crim Tartars.

[1] App. 18 = *IosPE.* I. 185, l. 41.
[2] v. p. 588, Appian, *Hist. Rom.* XII. (*Mithr.*) 108.
[3] e.g. Von Stern, *Theodosia*, Pl. IX. 100.
[4] Bertier-de-La-Garde ap. Stern, p. 90.
[5] *Trans. Od. Soc.* XXIV. *Minutes*, p. 29 = *IosPE.* IV. 468.
[6] v. p. 612, App. 61, 63 = *IosPE.* II. 29, *BCA.* X.

p. 26, No. 21.
[7] *Trans. Od. Soc.* XX. p. 173, Pl. I. 4—21, cf. supra p. 361.
[8] v. supra p. 526, *de Adm. Imp.* c. 53, pp. 252, 255 Bonn.
[9] Von Stern, *Theodosia*, Pl. VI—VIII.
[10] *CIG.* IV. 9286 ; Latyshev, *Inscr. Christ.* 75.

At the time of the Russian conquest in 1783 it had some 80,000 inhabitants but most of these deserted it, wishing to remain under the Sultan's rule. It was then adorned not only with the churches and walls of the Genoese but with minarets, baths and fountains of Turkish building and surrounded with orchards and gardens. The shortsighted destruction of all these amenities and the wavering commercial policy of its new owners reduced it to a ruin from which it has taken long to recover[1]: but its prosperity is rapidly increasing since Sevastopol has been closed to merchant vessels. Its new harbour is deeper than the roads of Taganrog and Kerch, thus ships which have taken in half their cargo further east here complete their lading[2].

Coins. Plate IX. Nos. 4—7.

The coins go back to the vth century, e.g. No. 4 inscribed ΘΕ οΔ Ελ and

Æ. 3·9 grn. = ·25 grm. Head of Pallas, r. | as No. 4.
B. XVIII. 2 |
Æ. 16·2 grn.= 1·05 grm. Female head in ampyx r. . Ox-head in profile r. (cf. No. 29) ΘΕΟΔΕΟ all as
it seems in incuse square.
Giel, *TRAS.* v. Pl. IV. 14.

Almost as early is a coin in the Jakunchikov collection at St Petersburg[3]:

Æ. Ox-head, three quarters r. | Star, between the six short thick rays ΘΕΟΔΕλ.

The star has been compared to that on coins of Chersonese (Pl. IV. 21) and Panticapaeum (Pl. VI. 3) and the general similarity of design regarded as evidence for a monetary league, but the Theodosian coin seems very much earlier than the other two. Found at Theodosia all these coins no doubt belong there in spite of the unexpected form of the inscriptions. The charging ox upon the reverse of Nos. 5 and 6 appears on coins of Heraclea Pontica and Chersonese (Pl. IV. 4, 5, 8, 16) and would seem to point to an alliance. The largest silver coin, recently acquired by Bertier-de-La-Garde[4],

Æ. 72·8 grn. = 4·72 grm. Head of Heracles | Club, beneath ΘΕΥΔΟ
bearded r. |

also recalls Heraclea, but almost certainly belongs to a time when autonomy had been lost, as does No. 7 with a similar inscription, though the resemblance between the latter and the commonplace types of Leucon II (Pl. VI. 16, 17) does not amount to very much, and cannot be adduced as proof that it belongs to a time of subjection. Burachkov's XVIII. 4—7 belong to other cities. The standard seems to be Aeginetic as the coins fit into the Panticapaean series[5].

---

[1] For the present state of the walls, v. *BCA.* XXVIII. pp. 45, 91.

[2] For a convenient account of Caffa in Genoese times, fuller than von Stern, *Theodosia*, pp. 25—31, v. W. Heyd, *Histoire du Commerce du Levant au Moyen Âge*, Paris and Leipzig, 1886, II. pp. 156—215, 365—407, cf. G. L. Oderico, *Lettere Ligustiche*, Bassano, 1792; M. G. Canale, *Nuova Istoria della Repubblica di Genova*, Florence, 1858–60, II. pp. 399–457, III. pp. 234–241. Many documents and inscriptions are in various numbers of *Trans. Od. Soc.* (v. von Stern, op. c. p. 25, n. 1) and *Atti della Società Ligure di Storia Patria*, VI—VII. 2, 1867–79, P. A. Vigna, "Codice Diplomatico delle Colonie Tauro-Liguri, A.D. 1453-75." Peyssonel, *Commerce,*

witnesses to its prosperity under Turkish rule and E. D. Clarke, *Travels*, II. p. 144 sqq. and Pallas, *Travels*, II. p. 265, to its subsequent ruin. Vinogradov, Lagorio and K. Neumann criticize the methods of the government.

[3] *TRAS. Num. Sect.* I. iii. (1909), p. 171: I am very grateful to the owner for sending me a cast.

[4] "Monetary novelties," Pl. I. 10, *Trans. Od. Soc.* XXX.

[5] v. p. 631 : B. XVIII. 2 would be ¼ obol, Terlecki's coin just similar but ·5 grm. ½ obol, Giel's, 1⅓, IX. 4, three and Bertier-de-La-Garde's, 5 or 6 obols, see his "Materials for Stathmological Investigations," *Num. Misc.* II. p. 26, Nos. 49—53.

Sources and Inscriptions mentioning Theodosia.

Θεοδοσία(η), App. 18, 26, 27, 42, 61, 63 (=*IosPE*.
I. 185, II. 343, 6, 36, 29; *BCA*. X. p. 26,
No. 21) and *IosPE*. II. 345.
Strabo, VII. iv. 4, 6.
Mela, II. I. 3.
Pliny, *NH*. IV. 86 (26).
Ptolemy, *Geogr*. III. vi. 2; VIII. X. 4.
Ammianus Marcellinus, XXII. viii. 36.

Θευδοσία(η), App. 29, 29³, 30, 35 (= *IosPE*.
II. 344, 11, 346, 15) and *IosPE*. II. 10, 347,
IV. 400 (Θευδοσιεύς), 418, 419.
Demosthenes *in Lacritum* 31—34 (MSS. with o):
—— *in Leptinem*, 33, Schol.
Ps.-Scylax, 68.
Ps.-Arrian, 30 (19 H.).
Appian, *Hist. Rom*. XII. 108.
Polyaenus, V. xxiii.
Stephanus Byz. s. v.; ἐθνικά, Θευδοσιανός καὶ
Θευδοσιεύς (some MSS. with o, also s. v. Νύμφαιον).
Harpocration, s. v.
Anonymi *Periplus P. E.*, 77 (51), 78 (52).

Ancient History and Antiquities.

Inscriptions found there, *IosPE*. IV. 195—198, 468 = *Trans. Od. Soc.* XXIV. *Minutes*, p. 29.
Neumann, K., *Hellenen*, pp. 464—469.
Koehne, B. de, *Musée Kotschoubey*, I. p. 271—320.
Vinogradov, V. K., *Theodosia*. Theodosia, 1884.
Lagorio, F., "Four Periods in the Life of Theodosia," *Trans. Od. Soc.* XV. (1887), p. 404.
Kulakovskij, J. A., *The Past of Tauris*, Kiev, 1906.
von Stern, E. R., "Theodosia und seine Keramik" (Russian and German), Pt III. of *Das Museum
d. kais. Odessaer Gesellschaft für Geschichte und Altertumskunde*, Odessa, 1906.
    This last sums up all there is to be known of Theodosia; unfortunately I had not received it
when I compiled the above outline: however I found that on the whole the author confirmed my
conclusions and I had very little to add, and I have been allowed to take from it the plan: details
of the latter and of his discoveries while carrying out the harbour works are added by Bertier-de-
La-Garde, p. 85 sqq.

Nymphaeum.

At Nymphaeum[1] (Eltegen, v. p. 20) we can clearly trace the old harbour
(cf. Strabo, l. c. πόλις εὐλίμενος), an acropolis, φρούριον (Appian l. c.), set upon
the cliffs and defended by a bank, a lower town and a necropolis. The
excavations carried out by Kondakov (who found the interesting tombs with
things in the Scythic style and an early coffin, v. pp. 208, f. 106, 210, 214,
f. 115 and 329) and Verebrjusov[2] and of late years by Mr Novikov its owner,
whose collection has been acquired by the Hermitage, have mainly yielded
minor antiquities including a fine Panathenaic vase, but there is a fair number
of inscriptions, mostly epitaphs[3]. Most interesting of these is the first, Πύρρος
Εὀρυνόμο Ἡρακλεώτας with its suitable mixture of dialects[4]. We gain more
from the dedication $\frac{Δ/\sim/}{ΑPM[o}$, Ἀρμοδίῳ[5], with its early vth century writing and
Attic associations, from the agonistic(?) list of citizens published by Škorpil
l. c.[6], which shews that early in the IIIrd century B.C. there was an Ionic
population with many Attic names and a small barbarous element, and from
the inscription on Glycaria's fountain (see below).

[1] Νυμφαῖον, usual form, Aeschines *in Ctesiphontem*, 171; Strabo VII. iv. 4; Appian, *Mithridates*, 108: Ptolemy, III. vi. 2; Steph. Byz. s. v.
who prefers the ἐθνικὸν Νυμφαιεύς to Νυμφαίτης
which seems supported by the ΝΥΜΦΑΤΟΣ of the
ill-recorded *IosPE*. II. 201 taken by V. V. Škorpil,
BCA. XLV. p. 14 as a genitive; Anon. *Peripl. P. E.*
76 (50); Harpocration s. v.: Ps.-Scylax 68 has
Νυμφάια, its coins ΝΥΝ and ΝΥΜ; Pliny, *NH*.
IV. 86, Nymphaeum. Škorpil gives an exhaustive

account, *Trans. Od. Soc.* XX. p. 16, cf. also Brandis,
s. v. Bosporos (2) in *P.-W.* III. p. 769.
[2] *CR*. 1876, pp. x--xxv; 1878, p. xxxvii; 1879,
pp. lxii—lxvii; 1880, pp. xiv—xvi.
[3] *IosPE*. II. 288, IV. 287, 325, 361, *BCA*. III.
p. 44, No. 10 of the IVth cent. B.C., *IosPE*. IV.
274 of the IIIrd, II. 102, 204, IV. 226, 276, 375,
BCA. XIV. p. 121, No. 43 of Roman date.
[4] Collitz-Bechtel, III. i. 3083.
[5] *BCA*. X. p. 25, No. 20.
[6] *IosPE*. IV. 205, cf. ib. 432.

We cannot tell whether Nymphaeum was originally founded by the Athenians in order to secure a share of the Bosporan corn-trade or acquired by them subsequently. It is generally thought to have been one of the gains of the Euxine expedition which Pericles made in 444 B.C. shortly before the Spartocids seized the power at Panticapaeum which was probably not strong enough at the moment to raise any objection. The archaic writing of the dedication to Harmodius suggests that the Athenians were honouring their hero at an earlier date than this. We know from Craterus (ap. Harpocrat.) that Nymphaeum was a member of the Delian league and paid a talent, hence Köhler has been able to restore its name from ΝΥ. He has also restored ΚΙΜ to Κιμμερικόν, Opuk, and ΠΑΤ to Πατραεύς the village near the monument of Satyrus (v. pp. 20, 23, 573) but this is all very doubtful[1]. If right it tends to shew that Athens made a serious attempt to establish herself on the Bosporus.

In any case these possessions became untenable when she lost command of the sea after Aegospotami B.C. 405. The Athenian commander Gylon handed the place over to Satyrus and received Cepi in exchange. No doubt he was fined for this by the Athenians and Aeschines calls it treachery, some have thought that the fine was merely the formal disapproval of an act which must not be allowed to set a precedent. Aeschines discredits his statement by calling the Bosporan rulers enemies whereas we know that very shortly after they were on excellent terms with Athens. Probably Gylon was in a difficult position and contrived to extract from an inevitable loss to his country a personal advantage to himself.

Škorpil[2] has published an inscription found in the sea off Eltegen: in it the praise of As]ander's wife Glycaria is put into the mouth of a wayfarer who has drunk his wine with water from a fountain by her tomb: the stone is in shape suitable for the keystone of a rustic arch and has a hole for a water pipe. There is quite a good case for the restoration of the husband's name and for identifying him with King Asander who married his known wife Dynamis rather late in life: the lettering is very like their inscriptions (v. pp. 591, 592 n. 7, 593 nn. 4–6). Škorpil goes on to suggest that Nymphaeum was Asander's home or appanage and would thereby explain the next fact about it recorded in history, its rebellion against Mithridates (Appian, l.c., v. p. 588).

Pliny speaks of the town as a thing of the past (l.c. fuere oppida... Nymphaeum Dia); it may have suffered in the troublous times about the beginning of our era, but there are three or four gravestones of Roman date and the name survives in *Periplus* Anonymi and the Peutinger Tables. However, the harbour probably began to silt up in the early centuries of our era and there seems no evidence of the town's existence in Christian times.

The coins of Nymphaeum (Pl. IX. 8, 9 Aeginetic ½, 2 and 5 obols[3]) are of silver and go back to the vth century: all bear on one side the head of a Nymph, on the other ΝΥΜ, ΝΥΝ or ΝΥ, a vine-leaf and grape-cluster.

---

[1] App. 2=*IG.* (*CIAtt.*) I. 37; "Urkunden z. Gesch. d. Attischen-Delischen Bundes," *Abh. d. k. Akad. d. W. zu Berlin*, 1869, Nos. 24, 25, pp. 74, 75, 165, 167, cf. supra pp. 447, 458.

[2] *BCA.* XXXVII. pp. 14—22, with Rostovtsev, who disclaims responsibility for any theorizing:

['Ασ]άνδρου Γλυκάρεια δάμα[ρ], | παρὰ πυραμίδος σευ
ἀγχίκρηνον ὕδωρ | εἵλκυσα σὺν Βρομίωι·
δίψος δ' ἀμπαύσας | τοῦτ' ἔφρασα· καὶ ζώ[ουσα] |
καὶ φθιμένη σώζ[εις] | τοὺς ἐπιδευ[ομένους].

[3] Bertier-de-La-Garde, "Mat. for Stathmological Investigations," p. 45, No. 159, 76 grm. = 4·93 grm.

Juz Oba.

View from Kerch Roads

FIG. 343 a.

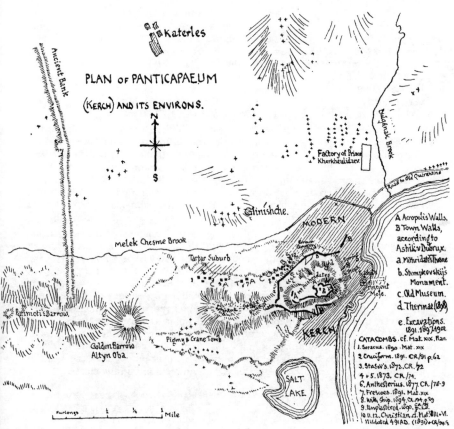

Katerles

PLAN OF PANTICAPAEUM

(KERCH) AND ITS ENVIRONS.

N
S

Ancient Bank

Factory of Prince
Kherkheulidzev.

Dulqnak Brook

Road to Old Quirantine

Glinishche.

MODERN

Melek Chesme Brook

Tartar Suburb

KERCH

Patinioti's Barrow.

Golden Barrow
Altyn Oba.

Pigmy & Crane Tomb

SALT
LAKE

Furlongs   ¼   ½   1 Mile

A Acropolis Walls,
B Town Walls,
according to
Ashik v Dubrux.
a. Mithridates Throne
b. Stempkovskij's
Monument.
c. Old Museum.
d. Thermae (1898)
e. Excavations.
1891. 1897.1902

CATACOMBS. cf. Mat.xix. Plan.
1. Soracus. 1890 . Mat. xix
2 Cruciform. 1891. CR/91 p.62
3. Stasov's. 1872. CR. /72
4 + 5. 1873. CR. /74.
6. Anthesterius. 1877. CR. /78-9
7. Frescoes. 1891. Mat. xix
8. With ship. 1894. CR.94 p.99
9. Unplastered. Woo. p.29.
10.11.12. Christian d. Mat.VIII+VI.
1 undated 491AD. (1890)+CR/94.9

FIG. 344.

Golden Barrow Long Rock Sugarloaf Mount Mithridates Kerch Bulganak Royal Barrow

looking N.W. Oct 1900. E.H.M.

FIG. 343 b.

CHAPTER XIX.

BOSPORUS.

THE Bosporan kingdom was the agelong rival of Chersonese and in every way opposed to it. As the latter was the last Greek city to remain an autonomous democracy, so the Bosporus offers the first example of the type of state in which a monarch made a Greek city his capital and from it ruled a barbarous population. So the rule of the earlier Spartocids fore-shadowed the Hellenistic states that arose after Alexander's death, because on the Bosporus Hellenistic conditions appeared independently. As else-where, the rulers treated the Hellenic cities with great favour and spared their susceptibilities, but they could not allow them real autonomy. The commercial Ionians of Panticapaeum were probably very well suited with their rulers, who on the whole allowed their trade to prosper, defending them against the natives of the interior and the pirates of the coast with more consistent success than democracy could have secured. We only hear of revolts when the dynasty had become effete or a foreign conqueror had imposed intolerable burdens to provide material for his ambitious schemes. Full light upon the actual development of this original form of state would be very welcome, but save for an inaccurate list of rulers in Diodorus, very scanty references in other authors and a few fragmentary inscriptions, we are left in the dark. We have a little more information about the last century B.C. when the Bosporus was brought into close connexion with the kingdom of Pontus and the general course of history. Again the darkness closes down and of the Bosporan kingdom for three hundred and fifty years after Christ we know but the names and dates of its kings and their faithful defence of an outpost of civilization against a weight of barbarism to which at last they had to give way.

Site of Panticapaeum.

The position of the various towns that made up the kingdom of Bosporus has been already discussed in the general survey of the coast (pp. 20—23 and Map III.). The actual site of Panticapaeum should present a certain amount of interest: but there is nothing above ground to attract the archaeologist.

71—2

The mighty masonry of some of the tombs has been described (pp. 194, 294). Upon the sketch plan prefixed to this chapter have been marked the lines of the walls surrounding the acropolis (Mount Mithridates) and the lower city as seen by Dubrux and Ashik in the early part of last century. They differ much from those shewn by Dubois de Montpéreux and may be almost as fanciful. But the general lie of the land necessitates something similar well agreeing with Strabo's description (VII. iv. 4): "Panticapaeum is a hill encircled all about by dwellings in a circuit of 20 stades. To the east is a harbour and docks for about 30 ships: it has also an acropolis." The latter is evidently Mount Mithridates surmounted by a chapel to the memory of Stempkovskij the archaeologist, mayor of Kerch during the twenties, and by the curiously cut mass of rocks called the throne of Mithridates. This must have formed the basement of a considerable building.

Half way down the hill there runs round it a kind of terrace approached by a fine flight of steps. On its widest part stands the old Museum, built on the model of the "Theseum" at Athens; it was destroyed during the war by the carelessness of the allies, who let the Turks amuse themselves by smashing all its contents, and since then it has been left as a memorial of Western civilization[1]. Happily the practice of forwarding the more valuable finds to the Hermitage was already long established and Lutsenko the director had sent away everything of great importance. The present Museum is in the town. To the east of Mount Mithridates are traces of the ancient mole jutting out from the oldest part of the modern town—the site of the former Turkish fortress and the ixth century church of S. John[2].

The modern town is mostly on the north of the hill on very low ground which was probably harbour in ancient days. The present bay is silting up with the accumulations of the brooks Melek-Chesme and Bulganak and the deposit left by the strait current. The houses only climb up the lower slopes of the hill. All the sides of the latter are of made earth full of débris of antiquity, but it has been turned over and over by all kinds of excavators, so that finds made there are not very instructive. In general about the Bosporus the excavations have yielded many beautiful objects, but very little information as to the history and topography of the various sites[3]. Diggings to the NW. of Mount Mithridates (Fig. 344, *e*) shew that spot to have been inhabited in the vth century B.C. but to have been the extreme limit of the town in that direction, as a little further on were found tombs of that date and a kind[4] of Monte Testaccio. Further to the east about (*d*) discoveries were rather more interesting. Here Duhmberg found the cellars of considerable houses[5] with fragments of painted wall plaster, flooring and pillars. Near here have also occurred a few pieces of mediocre sculpture. This district must have been covered with fairly rich houses in the 1st century B.C. The only public building yet explored is the Bath-establishment of the same date uncovered in 1898 (see plan and explanation p. 565, f. 345). This part of the town perished by fire and sword; skeletons were found head downwards in a well.

---

[1] W. H. Russell ap. McPherson, p. 41.

[2] *BCA.* XXXII. pp. 69—74, ff. 39—44.

[3] Older things seem now appearing (as against p. 338), Ionian pots and archaic jewelry, *Arch. Anz.* 1911, p. 205, ff. 14, 15; 1912, pp. 333—337, ff. 16—18,

20, 21, p. 346, ff. 31, 32; cf. *BCA.* XLV. pp. 92—110, Pl. VII—XIII.

[4] *CR.* 1891, p. 25, 1899, p. 17, f. 26. For the types of tombs about Kerch, v. p. 422.

[5] *CR.* 1899, p. 19, f. 28.

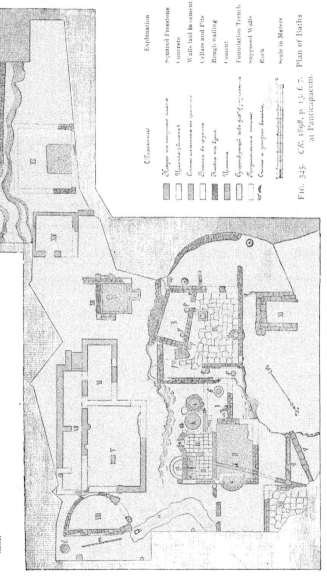

I. Furnace-room; *a*, stove; *b*, ash-pit. II. Caldarium with concrete floor; *c*, niche; *d*, drain. III. Tepidarium; *e*, raised stone stage; upon it traces of semicircular basin *f*, united to outer basin *g*. IV. Frigidarium; next it round bath *h*, and waste-pit *i*; *k*, over-flow pipe. V. Ambulatio surrounded by columns, into it opened VI. Exedra adorned in incrustation-style like the earlier Pompeian houses. VII. Passage. VIII. Semicircular basin of later date; *l*, well still holding water; *m*, earthen supply-pipe; *n*, leaden pipe taking surplus water to the town. IX. Open paved court with another well *o*. X. Store-room with grain pits *pppp*. XI. Kiln with half-baked tiles and net-weights. XII. (with drain *qq*), XIII., XIV., XV. Private houses. XVI. Narrow paved lane.

Explanation

Squared Freestone
Concrete
Walls laid in cement
Cellars and Pits
Rough walling
Cement
Foundation Trench
Supposed Walls
Rock

Scale in Meters

Fıɢ. 345. *CR.* 1898, p. 13, f. 7. Plan of Baths at Panticapaeum.

Although the baths were supplied by a well, and there was a fountain at the foot of Mount Mithridates near the sea, water was probably a difficulty with the men of Panticapaeum : hence the numerous large cisterns that have been found on the slopes of the hill. At this day there is no water in Kerch fit to make tea with, except what is fetched from Taman on the other side of the strait.

Phanagoria and Gorgippia.

Phanagoria was certainly near Sênnája, but the topography of the town has never been explored. It seems to have covered a considerable area, but the sea has encroached upon the northern part of it. The actual site of the town was what is now a more or less level space about three quarters of a mile long and half a mile broad between the farms of Borovik and Semenjaka. From the middle of the sea-board a mole ran out about 350 yards (320 metres). The town-site is surrounded by mounds of rubbish containing tombs ; and barrows line for a mile and a half in every direction the roads leading to the other towns of the Taman peninsula. To the south ran the old branch of the Kuban now filled up.

No Greek buildings have been excavated but architectural fragments, bases of statues and inscriptions have been found built into the ruins of Byzantine date. The site of the acropolis cannot be pointed out[1]. Dubois de Montpéreux as usual saw walls and gates and streets, but the oldest inhabitant knew nothing of them. The ruins seen by De La Motraye[2] were probably mediaeval. In Tartar times the peninsula of Taman was more thickly inhabited than now[3].

Inscriptions mention several buildings which are likely to have had some architectural importance, a gymnasium[4], a Caesareum[5], colonnades round the temple of Aphrodite Apaturias[6] and outside the town the temple of Artemis Agrotera[7].

At Gorgippia (Anápa) nothing seems visible, but inscriptions are continually being discovered; these mention temples of Aphrodite Nauarchis[8] and of Poseidon[9], a $πρό[ναον]$[10], a $τέμενος τοῦ μεγάλου θεοῦ$ and an $ἐργαστήριον$[11].

Tanais.

It is generally thought that there were two settlements called Tanais, a later, of which we have the remains at Nedvigovka, and an earlier, which is that mentioned by the ancient authors[12]. It is curious that it is not noticed by

[1] Appian, XII. 108.
[2] *Travels*, II. p. 48.
[3] K. K. Görtz, *Archaeological Topography of the Taman Peninsula*, pp. 87—126, Plan 3, and *Historical Review of Archaeological Investigations and Discoveries on the Taman Peninsula from the end of the XVIIIth Century to* 1859, pp. 7—10, 71, 105 and Plan. It is well to renew the caution against confusing Suvorov's Fort Phanagoria just E. of Taman, with the ancient city : e.g. Clarke's marbles "from the ruins of Phanagoria" came from Taman, *Travels*, II. p. 82. The old name of Taman is unknown, in Const. Porph. it is Ταμάταρχα and in old Russian Tmutarokan.

[4] *IosPE*. II. 360, cf. *BCA*. III. p. 50, No. 17.
[5] App. 68 = *IosPE*. II. 362.
[6] στοαὶ περινάοι *IosPE*. II. 352.
[7] App. 29 = *IosPE*. II. 344.
[8] App. 47 = *BCA*. XXIII. p. 46, No. 32.
[9] App. 51 = *BCA*. XXXVII. p. 38, No. 2.
[10] *IosPE*. IV. 430.
[11] *BCA*. XXXVII. pp. 61, 63, Nos. 43, 46.
[12] Strabo, XI. ii. 3; Alexander Polyhistor ap. St. Byz. s. v. calls it Ἐμπόριον a term used of it by Strabo and occurring in inscriptions on the new site; Eustath. in Dion. Per. l. 663; Ptolemy, III. v. 12, perhaps means the new town : see also Pliny, *NH*. VI. 20 (7).

Ps.-Scymnus who speaks at length of the river and mentions the small settlements on the Taman peninsula.   Pliny says that this region was held first by Carians, then by Clazomenians and Maeonians, lastly by men of Panticapaeum, while Strabo directly states that it was a colony of Bosporans: it seems to have enjoyed a certain amount of independence as he speaks of some Maeotae obeying the Bosporan rulers and some the holders of the trading station on the Tanais.   Polemo I found this freedom not to his liking and utterly destroyed the settlement (c. 15—7 B.C.).   It had a great trade with both European and Asiatic nomads taking their slaves and hides and other nomadic products and giving in exchange clothing and wine and articles of civilized life.   In front of it at a distance of a hundred stades lay the island of Alopecia with a mixed population.

Leontiev, who has done more than anyone else for Tanais[1], was inclined to seek the older Tanais at Elisavetovskaja in the delta: P. Butkov[2] wished to put it, as well as the mediaeval Venetian colony Tana, at Azov, explaining the lack of remains by the wholesale blowing up of the Turkish fortress after the Treaty of Belgrade in 1739.   Mr A. A. Miller's excavations at Elisavetovskaja, 1908—1910, have not been sufficient to settle the question[3]. He shews by a map of the mouths of the Don (l.c. p. 86) that the upper section of the delta (v. Map IX.) was once divided by a considerable channel into two halves, to the north a marsh, to the south a long stretch of sandy ground even now mostly raised above the spring floods: this stretch is covered with barrows for four miles, and half way along the old channel which bounded it to the north, is the site of a town with an outer bank, an inner enclosure and a "hard" or jetty (Plan l.c. p. 120).   The barrows are Scythic in type save for an absence of horse-gear, but are full of Greek amphorae and other pots: the town-site yields similar ware giving the date as the IIIrd century B.C., but some things from the barrows are much older, the sheath (p. 270, f. 186) came from here and another almost as early[3].   But so far there are no inscriptions or other evidences of a real Greek settlement[4] and I am much more inclined to think that we have here Alopecia and the κατοικία μιγάδων ἀνθρώπων.   It happens that coming up the east coast, along which the traffic went, you would get to it just a hundred stades before reaching the spot where the town seems to have started anew about 100 A.D.

That this place has a right to the name Tanais the inscriptions prove; but as nothing on the site goes back B.C. the presumption is that the old town was elsewhere.   Probably some change in the river channels made it advisable to re-establish the settlement between the villages of Nedvigovka and Sinjavka upon the north side of the northernmost arm of the Don now called the Dead Donets.   Above a high cliff sloping steeply down to the river, a space about 700 feet square was surrounded by a bank; outside this was a ditch omitted on the side next the river.   To the east and west were ravines which helped to isolate the site.   At the corners of the square and in

[1] *Propylaea* (Russian), IV. p. 387: *Extract from Rep. of Arch. Explor. in* 1853 (St. P. 1855) pp. 65 —121, cited in Latyshev, *IosPE.* II. pp. 225, 226.

[2] *Drevnosti,* i.e. *Trans. Mosc. Archaeol. Soc.* III. (1873) pp. 155—168. Epitaph of a Consul at Tana, A.D. 1362, *CR.* 1890, p. 41, f. 20.

[3] *BCA.* XXXV. pp. 86.—130, Pl. v. ff. 23, 24 late Sc. sheath and rhyton = *Arch. Anz.* 1910, pp. 202— 206, ff. 5,6; also ib. 1911, p. 197, f. 5, VIth cent. sheath.

[4] A Panathenaic Amphora, *Arch. Anz.* 1912, p. 374, ff. 66, 67, late Vth cent. B.C. looks more like it, cf. *BCA.* XLV. p. 83, Pl. VI.

the middle of the north and west sides were towers. There was a gate at the
NE. angle and another in the middle of the south side from which a way led
down to the river. By the sw. angle below the cliff was a Monte Testaccio.
The barrows of the necropolis had mostly been rifled in ancient times but
Professor Veselovskij had some success in 1908[1], finding evidence of both

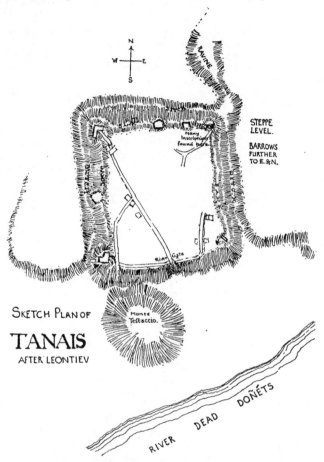

FIG. 346. Nedvigovka. Scale about $\frac{1}{5400}$ or 150 yards to the inch.

interment and cremation with interesting cinerary urns of slip ware and
IInd century jewelry of some pretensions, especially an earring with a large
Nike pendant[2]. In the middle of the town was the market-place as shewn

[1] *Hermes* (Russian), 1909, p. 246 sqq.; *Arch.*   [2] l.c. p. 150, f. 10.
Anz. 1909, pp. 140—145, ff. 1—6.

by remains of its paving; there were also two wells. All the masonry was exceedingly poor except one wall which may have belonged to a temple. The town was destroyed suddenly so that stores of wheat in the cellars were not removed: in cellars, too, were found candelabra and a lamp of bronze, the most elegant bronzes found in South Russia (v. p. 381, n. 13). The earliest inscriptions belong to the time of Sauromates I about the beginning of the IInd century A.D.,[1] the latest to that of Ininthimeus in A.D. 237[2]. Beside those set up by the religious societies and one or two private dedications, one of which seems to mention the docks (v. p. 619), no doubt to be placed on the sandy belt of beach where coins are still found, we have a whole series commemorating the erection of various buildings: walls[3], towers[4], gates[5], a market-place[6] and a spring beautified so as to be a tower[7]. Soon after the date of the last the town must have been destroyed probably by the Goths and Borani who were threatening the Bosporus about that time. Barbarous wallings and coins which go down to Rhescuporis the Last A.D. 338 and Valens shew that it was not entirely deserted. The cause of its brief prosperity is referred by Leontiev to the disturbance of the trade routes in Western Asia due to the decay of the Parthian power and its wars with Rome. So Tana which later flourished in the same neighbourhood was indebted to the decay of the Caliphate and to the Crusades. Tanais had no coins of its own. Those referred to it by Burachkov (XXIII. 1 *a*) and P. Vacquier[8] do not belong to it.

History.

We have no data telling us just when Panticapaeum[9] was founded by the Milesians[10]. Eusebius puts the foundation of Trapezus, a colony of Sinope, at 756 B.C., but the Greeks do not seem originally to have approached the Cimmerian Bosporus from that side, the Caucasus coast discouraged them. On the left side of the Euxine Istrus and Olbia are given as founded in the middle of the VIIth century and Panticapaeum was probably rather later. It was reckoned the mother of the cities on the Bosporus and was most likely the first of them[11].

[1] *IosPE.* IV. 446, 449, A.D. 123.
[2] App. 59=*IosPE.* II. 434.
[3] *IosPE.* IV. 447, A.D. 163; II. 431, [431 *bis*], c. A.D. 220.
[4] *IosPE.* II. 427, A.D. 188; 428, A.D. 192.
[5] *IosPE.* II. 432, c. A.D. 230, 435.
[6] App. 55=*IosPE.* II. 430, A.D. 220.
[7] App. 59=*IosPE.* II. 434, A.D. 236.
[8] *Numismatique des Scythes etc.* Tannais (sic), p. 103, Pl. I. 9.
[9] The true name of the European capital was Panticapaeum (Ptolemy, Παντικαπαία, Eustochius ap. St. Byz. s. v., Παντικάπη), but Greeks living at a distance sometimes said Bosporus without precising further that they meant the town Panticapaeum. To the people of the country Bosporus meant the land on each side of the strait with all the Greek cities except Theodosia which lay rather apart. The name Bosporus for the city prevailed in Byzantine times, e.g. Procopius *de Aedif.* III. 7,

and Vospro as a synonym for Kerch survived into the middle ages. Bosphorus is the usual Latin and English form but Pliny and Tacitus use the more correct Bosporus—in inscriptions, e.g. *IosPE.* II. 36 (=App. 42), 42, 355, 358 (v. inf. p. 598, n. 7, p. 613, n. 12), we have Βούσπορος by mistaken pedantry. The word is probably not Greek but Thracian. (Brandis, *P.-W.* p. 741.)
[10] No importance need be attached to Steph. Byz. s. v. ᾠκίσθη δὲ παρὰ Αἰήτου παιδός, λαβόντος τὸν τόπον παρὰ 'Αγαήτου τοῦ Σκυθῶν βασιλέως καὶ καλέσαντος τὴν πόλιν ἀπὸ τοῦ παραρρέοντος ποταμοῦ Παντικάπου. At the traditional period of Aeetes there were yet no Scythians in the country. The name is not Greek and may have something in common with that of the river Panticapes. The coins with ΑΠΟΛ may point to a Greek name Apollonia, v. p. 628.
[11] Ammianus Marcell. XXII. viii. 26.

72

Phanagoria[1], the capital of the Asiatic shore, was the only town not Milesian. Arrian (ap. Eustath. l.c.) names as its founder Pha(e)nagoras of Teos fleeing from the violence of the Persians. It always seems to have kept a character of its own perhaps due to this different origin.

Hermonassa is said by Eustathius (l.c.) to have been Ionian and founded by one Hermon, but he quotes Arrian as saying that it was an Aeolian colony named after Hermonassa, wife of Semandrus of Mytilene. Κλαζομενίων σκοπαί[2], on the coast of the Maeotis between Tyrambe and Cimmerice, kept alive the name of non-Milesian adventurers.

Cimmeris is definitely called a foundation of the Bosporan tyrants[3]. So by its name was Gorgippia, and perhaps Stratoclia[4]; Portus Sindicus was also a secondary foundation. To judge by the agonistic catalogue[5], Gorgippia contained a considerable Dorian element. Eumelus brought Dorians over from Callatis[6]. Cepi we know to have been Ionian[7].

Whenever Panticapaeum and the Greek towns about it may have been founded, we get no ray of light upon their history until the vth century. Then Diodorus Siculus gives us what purports to be a list of Bosporan rulers for two centuries. Unfortunately his information is not even consistent with itself and one of the two dated inscriptions shews that his chronology is purely artificial—that he has fitted the regnal years of Bosporan kings to the list of Athenian archons by a secondary calculation, not by using direct evidence that they answered each to each. Further his text is in a bad state, the numbers being as usual specially liable to error; but when his light fails we realize how hard it is to supply any sort of continuous list.

The first entry in the history of the Bosporan kingdom runs[8]: "In the archonship of Theodore at Athens (438/7 B.C.)...those who had held the kingship of the Cimmerian Bosporus, they bore the name of Archaeanactids, had ruled forty-two years. And Spartacus took over the rule and ruled seven years."

Who were the Archaeanactids[9] we do not know and it does not seem much use bringing them into connexion with Archaenax of Mytilene. Their name would seem to point to their being a privileged family from whom magistrates were chosen, such as were the Codridae at Athens. Their ancestor had a very suitable name for the founder of such a house, so suitable as to make one doubt his existence. Diodorus uses the title king very vaguely, probably they were not really kings, if only their rule had gone back to time immemorial we might have thought of the title as surviving from primitive usage; but if we are to believe Diodorus—and he is our only informant—their rule came into being but forty-two years

[1] Φαναγορία, passim; Φαναγόρεια, Ps.-Scymn. l. 886; Φαναγόρειον, Strabo, XI. ii. 10; Φαναγόρη, Dion. Per. l. 549, Φαιναγόρα, Eustath. in eundem; Φαναγόρου πόλις Ps.-Scylax, 72, Anon. 73 (46); Phanagorea, Pomp. Mela, I. 112. It took the name of Agrippias Caesarea in honour of Agrippa's settlement of Bosporan affairs under Augustus Caesar: v. Latyshev, *IosPE.* II. Introd. p. xxxviii.
[2] Strabo, XI. ii. 4, cf. Pliny, *NH.* VI. 20 (7). "Clazomenian" pots from Taman are probably only late Milesian, Pharmacovskij, *Arch.Anz.* 1912, p. 337.
[3] Ps.-Scymn. l. 898.
[4] Pliny, *NH.* VI. 18 (6): Stratocles in App. 27 =

IosPE. II. 6 was probably a Spartocid.
[5] *IosPE.* IV. 432, cf. *Mat.* XXIII. p. 64.
[6] Diod. Sic. XX. xxv.
[7] Κῆπός τ' ἀποικισθεῖσα διὰ Μιλησίων, Ps.-Scymn. l. 899; Κῆποι, Aeschines *in Ctes.* 171; Strabo, XI. ii. 10; Cepoe, Mela, I. 112; Pliny, *NH.* VI. 18 (6). The inhabitants used the ἐθνικόν Κηπίτης, *BCA.* XXIII. p. 42, No. 26, IVth cent. inscr. at Panticapaeum.
[8] Diod. Sic. XII. xxxi. 1.
[9] v. S. A. Zhebelëv, "The Bosporan Archaeanactids," *Journal Min. Pub. Instr.* St P. 1902, March, p. 130.

before in 480 B.C. If they were a clan with a hereditary claim to government they must have gone much further back ; Zhebelëv remarks that Diodorus does not generally go back before that date, so his first year for their power seems quite meaningless. If they had held power only for forty years they must have been parvenu tyrants.

How Spartacus or rather Spartocus (so his descendants always wrote the name on their inscriptions) took over the power we know not: the usual idea that he was a Thracian mercenary leader who made a *coup d'état* has everything in its favour[1]. Spartocus reigned for seven years. So Diodorus says in two places (XII. xxxi. 1 and XII. xxxvi. 1), but he is made to die in B.C. 433/2, which gives him only five years of reign. In the latter passage his successor is called Seleucus and reigns forty years (so the best MS. P[atmius], vulg. four). In the next passage touching Bosporus (XIV. xciii. 1) we hear nothing of Seleucus, but are told that in B.C. 393/2 died Satyrus son of Spartocus king of Bosporus having ruled forty-four years (so P., vulg. δεκατέσσαρα, edd. τετταράκοντα to make it agree with the archon-date and XII. xxxvi. 1). Before P. was discovered it was usually assumed that between Seleucus with his four years and Satyrus with his fourteen a *Spartocus II had dropped out. Now it is generally thought that Latyshev[2] is right in supposing that Seleucus—a name neither Greek nor Thracian and never heard of before the time of Seleucus Nicator though so familiar after-wards—is a mistake for Satyrus whose single reign took up the time formerly assigned to Seleucus, *Spartocus II and Satyrus. Diodorus goes on to say that Satyrus dying in 393/2 B.C. was succeeded by Leucon his son who reigned for forty years and in the next passage (XVI. xxxi. 6) that Leucon having ruled forty years died in 354/3 B.C., and was succeeded by his son "Spartacus"(II), who reigned five years till his death in 349/8 when "Parysades" his brother began his reign of thirty-eight years (XVI. lii. 10), and after his death a civil war followed in 310/9 B.C.[3] There was no reason to doubt this series until an inscription found in the Piraeus in 1877 shewed that in 347/6 B.C.[4] the Athenians had received from the joint rulers of the Bosporus, Spartocus and Paerisades (so always in inscriptions) envoys to announce the death of their father Leucon and were setting up a decree complimentary to them and their brother Apollonius who remained in a private station. This means that Leucon did not die till about the preceding year or perhaps the one before that[5], just the date given by Diodorus for the death of Spartocus II himself. Schaefer's explanation is no doubt right that Diodorus, calculating back from 310/9 when he had definite information about the Bosporus, knew that Paerisades had reigned thirty-eight years but did not know that five of

---

[1] On the Thracian names of Spartocus, Paerisades = (Πατροκλέης) and Camasarye, v. W. Tomaschek "Die Alten Thraker," III. in *Sitzber. d. kk. Akad. zu Wien.* CXXXI. pp. 44, 18, and 49.

[2] *Journ. Min. Pub. Instr.* St P., June, 1894, "On the History of the Bosporan Kingdom," I. = Ποντικά, p. 174.

[3] XX. xxii., being the beginning of an extract which goes into details of Bosporan history and augurs a firstrate source.

[4] App. 28 = Kumanudis, Ἀθήναιον, VI. p. 152 sqq.; A. Schaefer, *Rhein. Mus.* XXXIII. p. 418 sqq., cf. XXXVIII. p. 310; *CIAtt.* IV. ii. 109 b ; Ditt.[2] I. 129; *BCH.* v. pl. 5 ; Hicks[2] Hill, 140.

[5] In App. 34 = *CIAtt.* II. i. 311 ; Ditt.[2] I. 194, a year and a half had passed after the liberation of Athens from Demetrius Poliorcetes before the Athenians had sent corn and congratulations upon that event, v. infra p. 580.

these ran concurrently with the reign of Spartocus II whom he regards as reigning before Paerisades from 354/3 to 349/8.

Hence, instead of letting Leucon's forty years begin in 388/7, Diodorus had to push back his accession to 393/2. But I believe that he left the discrepant forty-four years to Satyrus and that the readings of the MSS. in both places where the latter was mentioned (XII. xxxvi. I (MSS. Σέλευκος), P. τεσσαράκοντα vulg. τέσσαρα and XIV. xciii. I, P. τετταράκοντα τέτταρα vulg. δεκατέσσαρα) go back to this number. Diodorus is almost as much out about Spartocus I to whom he gives seven years although the dates are but five years apart. The whole confusion shews that Diodorus took some fixed date and calculated back from it adjusting the result to the tables of Athenian archonships.

Paerisades was succeeded in 310/9 by Satyrus II who only reigned nine months being slain in battle with a younger brother Eumelus who also slew another brother Prytanis[1]. Eumelus reigned five years and five months (B.C. 309—304/3) and was killed in a carriage accident leaving the throne to his son Spartocus who reigned for twenty years (303—283 B.C.)[2]. So far, thanks to Diodorus, we can establish the chronology more or less (see table inf. p. 583) and it remains to fill in this outline by the testimony of other authors and of inscriptions.

Of Spartocus I we know nothing more. His short reign must have been fully taken up with establishing the authority of the new dynasty. How far that authority stretched we cannot tell.

Satyrus I devoted himself to rounding off the kingdom. We find him holding Cepi before the collapse of the Athenian sea power (405 B.C.) when Gylon the Athenian governor handed him over Nymphaeum and received Cepi in exchange (v. supra p. 561). This acquisition of Nymphaeum was the first enlargement of the kingdom of which we hear. Henceforward there was no more need for the dyke just to the west of Kerch on the boundary of strictly Panticapaean territory. It was probably Satyrus that secured the whole eastern end of the "rugged" peninsula by the dyke which runs across from Opuk-Cimmericum to the Maeotis. Nymphaeum gave Satyrus a harbour less liable to be ice-bound than Panticapaeum, but in pursuance of the same policy he set before himself the task of adding the port of Theodosia to his dominions. The harbouring of Bosporan exiles[3] was probably a mere pretext. In this he was not successful but he left things so far advanced that his son Leucon could fulfil his desires. It is extremely improbable that a ruler who held Cepi and went as far afield as Theodosia should have allowed Phanagoria to continue perfectly free; we may assume that if he did not receive it from Spartocus, it was his first objective[4].

That Satyrus had yet extended his power over barbarians to the east and like his successors called himself king of certain native tribes is unlikely, but we cannot be sure, inasmuch as from his time we have no inscriptions,

---

[1] Diod. Sic. xx. xxii.—xxvi.
[2] Diod. Sic. xx. c. 7.
[3] Anon. *Peripl.* 77 (51).
[4] Brandis *P.-W.* III. p. 767, holds that Phanagoria was independent until the time of Mithridates.

It is hard to reconcile this with the inscriptions either from its immediate neighbourhood (*IosPE.* II. 343 Leucon) or its actual site (*IosPE.* IV. 418 Paerisades) and the general situation required its early annexation.

but he is mentioned by Lysias and by Isocrates[1], who represents him as well disposed to Athens and allowing Athenian grain vessels special facilities for which he received the thanks of the city.   On the other hand he seems liable to suspicion and capriciously condemns to confiscation and death the speaker and his father Sopaeus or Sinopeus one of his chief ministers, though afterwards repenting and marrying his son to the speaker's sister.   We hear of exiles and plots, so all Bosporans were not satisfied with his rule.   Strabo (XI. ii. 7) mentions on the Asiatic shore near Patraeus[2], a tumulus raised to the memory of King Satyrus.   It is likely to have been the first of the name who best deserved such a monument after his long reign and great services.

The tale of Tirgatao[3] does not fit any known Satyrus, but Latyshev is inclined to refer it to Satyrus I.   The story goes that Hecataeus king of the Sindi, having been driven from his kingdom, was reinstated by Satyrus who gave him his daughter in marriage and bade him slay his former wife Tirgatao, a Maeotian princess of the tribe of the Ixomatae; Hecataeus out of love to her spared her life, but put her in prison.   She, however, escaped to her own people, married her father's successor, roused her tribe against the Sindi, overran the kingdom of Hecataeus and did harm to that of Satyrus.   The two kings sued for peace and handed over Metrodorus son of Satyrus as a hostage: but meanwhile tried to get Tirgatao assassinated.   She foiled the plot, slew the hostage and renewed the war with such success that Satyrus died of chagrin and his son and successor Gorgippus had to buy peace with rich gifts.

The main reason for supposing that the story applies to Satyrus I, is that all the rulers of Bosporus subsequent to his time claimed to be kings of the Sindi: a good reason against is that Satyrus died at the siege of Theodosia and was succeeded by Leucon: also that we do not hear again of the Ixomatae until much later and that Metrodorus is a late type of name[4]. However, in the same generation as Leucon I there was a Gorgippus, the father of Comosarye wife of Paerisades I[5], and Latyshev suggests that he at first divided the kingdom with Leucon ruling the Asiatic side and founding Gorgippia.   The inscription[6] on which Leucon is called Archon of Bosporus and Theodosia does not help to prove that his authority was limited to the part west of the strait inasmuch as it was found near Lake Tsukur.   But that sometime in the IVth century a Gorgippus had quasi-sovran rights in Gorgippia we know from tile-stamps with ΓΟΡ|ΓΙΠ|ΓΟ|Υ[7]. But these would suit another Gorgippus mentioned with another Satyrus by Dinarchus[8] about fifty years later, and the repetition of the same names in the family makes identification impossible.   It is quite likely that in the

---

[1] *Pro Mantitheo*, § 4, 393 B.C. speaking of 405 B.C.   *Trapeziticus*, 3–5, 11, 20, 35, 51, 52, 57, B.C. 394; the speaker is a young Bosporan, name unknown.

[2] This may or may not be the Πατρασύς (MSS. Πάτρασις) of Hecataeus ap. St. Byz. s.v.

[3] Polyaenus, VIII. lv.   For the name v. supra, p. 39.

[4] It seems to occur upon tiles as ΜΗΤΡΟC where the C does not =Σ but is a sign of abbreviation by suspension, cf. ΣΑΤΥC for Σατύρου, ΑΠΟC

for Ἀπολλωνίου, ΚΡΑΤΙΓC, ΤΙΜΟC, &c.: v. *CR.* 1861, p. 176; Giel, *Kl. B.*, p. 41; *BCA.* XI. p. 155; III. p. 162; Škorpil in *Bobrinskoj Miscellany*, p. 33, nn. 4, 8, 9.

[5] App. 30 = *IosPE.* II. 346.

[6] App. 26 = *IosPE.* II. 343.

[7] *Mat.* XVII. p. 71, No. 7; Škorpil l.c. n. 5; cf. ih. n. 11 and *ABC.* Reinach, p. 135, No. LXVIII. a gold cylinder inscribed Ὀρχάμο τοῦ Γοργίππο.

[8] *In Demosthenem*, 43.

unknown times after B.C. 250 the decadent Bosporan kingdom may have acquiesced in the independence of the Sindi and been incapable of resisting the spirited Tirgatao. That Strabo (XI. ii. 10) seems to call Gorgippia βασίλειον τῶν Σινδῶν points to their somewhat recent independence.

Satyrus died while besieging Theodosia¹. His operations had been rendered null by the aid of the Heracleotes who sent across the ingenious Tynnichus². Leucon I, his son, is always regarded as one of the most enlightened of Greek rulers. He was successful in reducing Theodosia and made it the great port for the shipment of corn. He is said to have named the town anew after his sister or wife—what may have been its precise state previously we do not know. Master of Theodosia he developed the agriculture of the flat district between that town and the Bosporus. The open country had been subject to the steppe Scyths who even pushed their raids across the strait on the ice to the country of the Sindi³. No doubt fear of such inroads led the minor cities more readily to acquiesce in the spread of a strong central power. The agricultural inhabitants of the plain were reduced to serfdom and the Bosporan kingdom was ready to become the granary of Greece.

Naturally the closest ties sprang up between such a country and the chief commercial and manufacturing state of Hellas, Athens, and it is in this connexion that we hear most of Leucon and his successors. In this, too, he completed the policy of Satyrus⁴.

Of these friendly relations we hear in Demosthenes. In order to equalize the burdens of the Social War, B.C. 356, Leptines proposed that all immunities decreed to individual citizens, except descendants of Harmodius and Aristogeiton, should be revoked. This was bad policy in the case of foreigners who had merely complimentary citizenship and Demosthenes opposed it; the case of Leucon and his sons was a very good one for his purpose. Moreover Demosthenes had family relations with the Bosporan rulers, for Gylon his maternal uncle had been under their protection since he had handed Nymphaeum over to them, and either now or subsequently the orator received from them a yearly allowance of a thousand medimni of corn⁵.

So Demosthenes sets forth at length the advantages reaped by Athens from the good will of Leucon⁶. In a normal year Athens imported 800,000 medimni of corn of which half came from Bosporus. On these 400,000 medimni Leucon remitted the export duty of 3⅓ per cent amounting to 13,000 medimni and further, both at Panticapaeum and at his new staple of Theodosia, gave the ships bound for Athens facilities to load first. Moreover, three years before, in time of famine, he sent enough corn (presumably

---

¹ Harpocration, s. v., cf. supra p. 556.
² Polyaenus, V. xxiii. For Heraclea's policy in this matter see supra, p. 516, but Chersonese had long been existing, witness Ionian pots found there, v. Add. We cannot say to what date should be referred the war between Heraclea and Bosporus mentioned by Aristotle, *Oeconomica*, II. ii. 8.
³ Herodotus, IV. 28.
⁴ For variations in Athenian commerce as measured by the ceramic finds v. supra pp. 338 n. 1, 339, 442: for the Pontic corn-trade besides Gernet and Grundy whose opinions are noticed on

p. 443 n. 1, see G. Perrot, "Le Commerce des Céréales en Attique au IVe Siècle avant notre Ère." *Revue Historique*, IV. (1877), pp. 1—73; Th. G. Mishchenko "Commercial Relations of the Athenian Republic with the Kings of Bosporus," *Kiev University Bulletin*, No. 7 (1878), p. 477: H. Francotte, "Le pain à bon marché et le pain gratuit dans les cités grecques," *Mélanges Nicole*, p. 135; A. E. Zimmern, *The Greek Commonwealth*, Oxford, 1911, p. 356.
⁵ Dinarchus *in Dem.* § 43.
⁶ Dem. *in Lept.* 29—40.

at the normal rate) to let the Athenians make fifteen talents profit on the surplus. Strabo (VII. iv. 6) may mean this same consignment when he speaks of 2,100,000 medimni sent by Leucon from Theodosia. Such an amount would about represent the Attic wheat deficit in a thoroughly bad year: or it may be the total of several consignments. There is no reason to suppose that there was any question of a gift in either case. The 15,000[1] medimni sent by Spartocus III (v. infra) is quite a different thing if only for the small amount of corn involved.

The ordinary price for corn was 5 drachmae a medimnus. No doubt the Bosporan rulers were themselves large sellers: no doubt, too, they did a profitable business with other states and the fisheries provided another source of revenue. No wonder that Bosporus could afford the wine and oil, the pottery and manufactures of Greece, even if money had to be spent on tribute to threatening Scythian tribes, on the support of Greek, Thracian and native mercenaries and on a fleet to keep down the neighbouring pirates. Perhaps it was for this purpose that later Spartocus II and Paerisades wanted the crews granted them in the inscription[2] set up to them in the Piraeus.

But from Athens the Spartocids received also less material recognition. From the same inscription we know that Satyrus had been honoured in some way, from Demosthenes and the same source we know that Leucon was publicly praised by the Athenian state, granted the citizenship and immunity from civil burdens and crowned at the Panathanaea with a golden wreath worth 1000 drachmae: which wreath according to custom was duly inscribed and dedicated to Athena Polias: further that the decree conferring these honours was set up, as Demosthenes tells us, in triplicate, in the Piraeus, at Bosporus and in the temple of Zeus Urius at the entrance of the Euxine. The decree of immunity was necessary because there was always money belonging to the Spartocids lying at Athens and some ingenious citizen might have proposed an antidosis. That is why the proposal of Leptines had a material importance. But it was the insult of withdrawing a privilege granted as a courtesy which would have done the harm. No doubt the Spartocids' vanity was flattered by these compliments. As Perrot remarks they never seem to have sought the glory of success at the great Hellenic games, at which Sicilian princes loved to display their magnificence. Probably the descendants of a Thracian condottiere could not gain admittance. But it was some consolation that the "eye of Hellas" enrolled them among her citizens and allowed the distant Bosporans to enter for the Panathenaic games and bring home prize amphorae (v. pp. 347, 626).

In later times the compliments paid went even farther. Dinarchus (l.c.) accuses Demosthenes of corrupt motives in proposing that Birisades [*sic*] and Satyrus and Gorgippus should have bronze statues in the Agora. The inscription from the Acropolis in honour of Spartocus III (B.C. 287/6)[3], speaks of such statues set up to his ancestors in the Agora and in the Emporium and of an offensive and defensive alliance concluded with them, and proposes to

---

[1] So Perrot p. 64. Edd. restore πεντακοσίους.　　[3] App. 34 = Ditt.[2] I. 194.
[2] App. 28 = Ditt.[2] I. 129.

set up to him two statues, one in the Agora by his ancestors and one upon the Acropolis, as well as the usual inscriptions and wreaths.

Leucon had to do not merely with Athens. We have the first few words of a decree in his honour passed by the common assembly of the Arcadians soon after 369 B.C.[1] Perhaps he employed Arcadian mercenaries or granted them such a favour as the Mytilenians a few years later. These he let off with 1⅓ per cent export duty on 100,000 medimni of corn a year: above that figure they had to pay the usual 1⅔ per cent[2].

He left behind him as good a reputation as was possible for a man who was regarded as a τύραννος[3]. To have looked after his soldiers' morals by stopping their pay when they got into debt through vice or gambling[4], is counted to him for righteousness by Latyshev, who reckons among *minus laudabilia* his saying that a tyranny has need of bad men[5] and the devices for foiling conspiracies of which Polyaenus (VI. ix. 2, 3) tells us, though one of these, enlisting the support of the trading class by borrowing its money, is not indefensible and the other not more treacherous than necessary: both shew that the Bosporan Greeks had the spirit not to submit quite tamely: the financial operation (ibid. § 1) of calling in all the coinage and reissuing it at double its face value seems to have been regarded as doing no harm to anyone: it may have begun a practice which disfigured Bosporan coin with countermarks but the style of extant coins subjected to the process points to a later ruler of the name. Polyaenus (V. xliv. 1, see inf. p. 626) also relates the trick played upon Leucon towards the end of his life by Memnon of Rhodes who was in the employ of the Heracleotes, the consistent foes of the Bosporan kings.

Besides the decree of the Arcadians three other inscriptions on the Bosporus record his name. In one from the Taman peninsula[6] he is only styled archon of Bosporus and Theodosia. In another from Kerch he bears the titles of archon of Bosporus and Theodosia and king of the Sindi, Toretae, Dandarii and Psessi[7]. The natural inference is that the former inscription belongs to a time when he had not yet conquered the native peoples. Latyshev argues from this and from the story of Tirgatao (v. supra p. 573) that at first he was not ruler of the Asiatic side of the strait, but the stone comes from there and the document would not have been dated in his archonship had he not at the time borne rule in that district. Hence we may infer that Satyrus set the reduction of the neighbouring Greek communities as the limit of his policy and that Leucon raised the dynasty from being archons of a few coast towns to being also kings of wide stretches of country and populous if barbarian tribes in the interior—and he it was who left the greatest name to posterity. Towards the end of his reign he seems to have admitted his sons to power, as they are thanked with him by the Mytilenians.

[1] *IosPE*. II. 4, Kerch.
Ἔδοξεν τοῖς Ἀρκάσιν ·Λεύκωνα
[τὸν Σατύ]ρο(υ) Παντικαπαῖταν....
[2] Ditt.[2] 914=*IG.* XII. (*IGins*) ii. p. 2 No. 3: already in 428 B.C. the Mytilenians had been getting corn from the Pontus, Thuc. III. ii. 2.
[3] Cf. Chrysippus ap. Plut. *de Stoicorum Repugn.* 20; Strabo, VII. iv. 4; Dio Chrys. *de*

Regia Pot. II. 77.
[4] Aeneas, *Com. Poliorc.* V. 2.
[5] Athenaeus, VI. 71 (p. 257 e).
[6] App. 26=*IosPE*. II. 343.
[7] App. 27=*IosPE*. II. 6; in App. 29=*IosPE*. II. 344 he only appears as the father of Paerisades. For the tribes see supra pp. 24, 127, 128.

From the joint reign of Spartocus II and Paerisades I (349/8—344/3) the only monument is the Piraeus inscription from which we learn the true chronology of these rulers, the precise honours paid them by Athens and the existence of a third brother Apollonius, who though a private person received compliments by way of afterthought[1]. The inscription is headed with a bas-relief shewing three figures, but unfortunately the heads have been mutilated so we cannot judge whether any barbarous traces were left in the family type[2].

Paerisades when reigning alone (344/3—310/9) continued the policy of Leucon[3] and is classed with him as a mild and capable ruler. He may even claim to surpass him; Strabo (VII. iv. 4) says he was reckoned a god, whether before or after death we cannot tell: here again we find the Bosporus anticipating Hellenistic custom. However, he had his difficulties as about 330 B.C. commerce in Bosporus was utterly disorganized by a war with the Scythian king[4]. Probably the nomads had made a raid into the country about Theodosia, but war with the eastern tribes may be referred to. In this direction Paerisades enlarged his authority or at any rate his pretensions. It is hard to believe that we can trace the fluctuations of his power in the changes of his title; kings do not give up titles when they no longer represent facts, George III called himself king of France: the leaving out of tribes may be due to mere questions of space[5], but the addition of new tribes no doubt indicated fresh conquests.

Paerisades at first adopted Leucon's style as in App. 29 which is just like App. 27 except that there was no room for Psessi or their name has perished[6]. Next instead of enumerating the last tribes separately, he summed them up as Μαϊτῶν πάντων[7], further he added Θατέων[8] and dropped the πάντων[9], and made the final addition of Δόσχων[10]. No doubt these last two tribes stood apart from the Maeotae. The Sindi also are counted separately being the first Maeotian tribe to form part of the Bosporan state and being apparently less barbarous than the others.

One inscription[9] is abnormal in that Bosporus is left out, also its whole form is unusual: still it falls into place as coming before Paerisades conquered the eastern tribes, a more satisfactory criterion than the absence of Bosporus, which must surely be a slip. Schaefer[11] has based upon this the view that it belongs to a time when Spartocus ruled Bosporus and Paerisades Theodosia and the Maeotian tribes—a most unnatural combination. The stone was found at Kerch so in such a case it must have been dated by Spartocus.

The whole dominion of Paerisades is well summed up in the epigram:

Εἰκόνα Φοίβωι στῆσε, Ἀντίσστασι, Φανόμαχός σο[υ],
ἀθάνατον θνητῶι πατρὶ γέρας τελέσας,
Παιρισάδεος ἄρχοντος ὅσην χθόνα τέρμονες ἄκρ[οι]
Ταύρων Καυκάσιός τε ἐντὸς ἔχουσιν ὅροι[12].

---

[1] His name occurs on tiles Giel, *Kl. B.* p. 41; *BCA.* III. p. 162.
[2] App. 28 = Ditt.[2] 129: *BCH.* V. pl. 5.
[3] cf. Dem. *in Phorm.* § 36.   [4] ibid. § 8.
[5] e.g. App. 29 = *IosPE.* II. 344.
[6] In *IosPE.* IV. 419 we seem to have fragments of the same formula.
[7] *IosPE.* II. 10, 11 (= App. 29³), 345, IV. 418.

[8] App. 30 = *IosPE.* II. 346.
[9] App. 31 = *IosPE.* II. 8.
[10] *IosPE.* II. 347, v. p. 128, n. 8.
[11] op. c. also Latyshev *IosPE.* II. p. xxiii.
[12] *IosPE.* II. 9: the genitive in -εος is most used by Paerisades I, *IosPE.* II. 9, 10, 345, 347, IV. 418: -ους comes in II. 11, 344, 346 = App. 29³, 29, 30. Later kings of the name use -ου.

M.

These were the natural boundaries which could only be easily passed towards the NE. where the frontier was no doubt very variable.   Polyaenus (VII. xxxvii.) has his anecdote about a Paerisades, probably the first of the name, how that he had one change of raiment for setting the battle in array, another for the fighting and a third for purposes of flight.   The device seems to have stood him in better stead than it did Ahab.

Paerisades married Comosarye daughter of Gorgippus[1].   This Gorgippus may have been Leucon's brother if the story of Tirgatao applies to Satyrus I: in any case he was probably a member of the ruling family as his daughter's name is, like Spartocus and Paerisades, Thracian, and his own name recurs in the history and geography of Bosporus.

Paerisades had three sons at least, Satyrus II, who succeeded him, Eumelus and Prytanis[2].   Most probably he had another, Gorgippus, and towards the latter part of his reign had associated Satyrus and Gorgippus with him in the power.   That would account for Demosthenes having carried the proposal to set up the statues of all three Pontic tyrants as Dinarchus (l.c.) puts it, and would agree with the phrasing of inscriptions[3] which begin Παιρισάδης καὶ παῖδες give proxeny to so and so.   These inscriptions testify that they treated not merely Athenians but also Piraeans (i.e. Athenian colonists at Amisus) and Chalcedonians well.

Probably the reign of Paerisades represents the highest prosperity of the Bosporus kingdom under its own ruling house.   The native tribes were weak or well kept in check by its. vigorous ruler.   As the granary of Greece it was sure of a constant income flowing in from a certain market.   Athens its best customer was indeed declining but was not yet utterly fallen.   But with the opening up of Asia to Greek enterprise new corn supplies were made accessible and new competitors appeared in markets whose purchasing power was lessened owing to the draining of Greece by wars and emigration.

The country was made the less ready to bear this adverse change by the exhaustion produced by a year's civil war, 309/8 B.C.   When Paerisades died Satyrus his eldest son was his natural successor.   We hear nothing of Gorgippus.   However, Eumelus a younger son disputed his claim and Diodorus (xx. xxii.—xxvi.) gives us a detailed account of the struggle.

Eumelus allied himself with Aripharnes king of the Thateis who lived beyond a river Thates.   Satyrus invaded their country with two thousand Greek and two thousand Thracian mercenaries and Scythian allies numbering twenty thousand and more foot and ten thousand horse.   He made a laager with his provision waggons and joined battle against the enemy who had twenty thousand horse and twenty-two thousand foot.   Neither side seems to have used any Bosporan Greeks.   After a doubtful struggle Satyrus was victorious and Eumelus and Aripharnes retired to the latter's royal fastness, obscurely described as a, kind of pile village surrounded by the river and rendered unapproachable by great cliffs and a thick forest.   Two ways only led to it, one well guarded by the high towers of the royal castle, the other leading through marshes and only secured by wooden fortifications. Satyrus, after preliminary plundering of the open country, made his

---

[1] App. 30=*IosPE.* II. 346.
[2] Acis, v. p. 585, n. 4, was, to judge by the   lettering, his daughter.
[3] *IosPE.* II. 1 (=App. 32) and 2.

approaches in form, took the wooden fortifications and began to cut a way through the forest, though his men were much harassed by the enemy's sharpshooters. Ultimately when by the fourth day the attack was approaching the castle, Meniscus the captain of the mercenaries had to give way to the defenders and Satyrus coming to his support was wounded and died that same evening.   Meniscus raised the siege retiring to Gargaza and brought the king's body back across the strait (τοῦ ποταμοῦ regarded as mouth of the Tanais) to Prytanis at Panticapaeum.

Prytanis laid Satyrus in the royal tomb and hasted to Gargaza where he assumed the power.   Eumelus proposed a partition, but Prytanis refused it and hurried back to Panticapaeum to establish his authority. Thereupon Eumelus and his barbarian allies advanced and took Gargaza and other places, forced Prytanis to a combat, defeated him and shut him in a headland by the Maeotis : Prytanis capitulated and promised to leave the country, but when he came to the capital Panticapaeum, made a last attempt to seize the power, failed, fled to Cepi and there was slain.   This last attempt seems to have exasperated Eumelus who proceeded to exterminate the house of Spartocus and the adherents of Satyrus, and only Paerisades the young son of Satyrus escaped. He took refuge with Agarus king of the Scythians.

These massacres roused the indignation of the citizens : but Eumelus called a mass-meeting, defended his actions, restored the ancestral government (τὴν πάτριον πολιτείαν ἀποκατέστησε), conceded again the immunity which the dwellers in Panticapaeum had enjoyed in the time of their forbears and promised to exempt everyone from the direct taxation, doing all this to gain the affection of the masses.   So he ruled his subjects according to law and aroused much admiration by his merits : moreover he was a benefactor to the other Greeks about the Pontus, to the men of Byzantium and Sinope and especially to the citizens of Callatis.   For when Lysimachus besieged them and there was lack of corn in the city, he received a thousand of them and granted them lands upon the Psoas.   Further, he earned universal praise by restraining the piracies of the Heniochi, Tauri and Achaei and conquered for his kingdom much land of barbarous tribes.   Indeed he formed the project of uniting all the tribes about the Pontus and might have succeeded but for `his strange death.   Jumping from a runaway waggon (it had four horses, four wheels and a tilt (v. p. 51, f. 6)) he got his sword caught in a wheel and was whirled round and round and killed after a reign of five years and five months (309/8—304/3).

I have given rather a full summary of the story of Eumelus found in Diodorus because it seems evidently to go back to an extract from some history of, or panegyric written for Bosporus. It gives us an insight into the relations between the Bosporan state and the surrounding tribes indicating what a part they played in its internal affairs.   The river Thates with the fastness of Aripharnes and the town of Gargaza are quite unknown[1], but everything points to the country between the lower Kuban and the

---

[1] Unless Thates (v.l. Θάψιν) and Gargaza be Ptolemy's Ψάθις and Gerusa as Wesseling and Ortelius suggest. Ψόας too is unknown and not unlike Ψάθις, but Latyshev, *Journ. Min. Pub. Instr.*   St P. Apr. 1894 = Ποντικά, p. 171, conj. Θιαννῖτιν χώραν for Ψόαν καὶ τὴν χ., comparing ἐν Θιαννέοις in App. 49 = *IosPE*. II. 353.

outliers of the Caucasus.   What may have been the rights and immunities
restored by Eumelus to the citizens of Panticapaeum we cannot tell.   They
were probably rather shadowy.   At least the citizens take singularly little
part in their rulers' struggle.   Eumelus may represent a reaction of the
barbarian element against the Hellenic.   In other things besides his scheme
of general conquest he appears as a forerunner of Mithridates the Great.

There are no lapidary inscriptions in honour of Satyrus II, Prytanis or
Eumelus, but the names occur upon tiles[1].

Spartocus III, son of Eumelus, reigned from 304/3 to 284/3 B.C.   He is
the last king of whom Diodorus (xx. c. 7) speaks.   As we have seen the
Athenian inscription[2] tells us that in 287/6 B.C., a year and a half after
expelling the garrison of Demetrius Poliorcetes, in return for a present of
15,000 medimni of wheat Athens decreed Spartocus the usual honours : she
could offer no other reward.

In his own country several inscriptions date from his reign, but do not
tell us much about him[3]: the first calls him archon alone, the next (and II. 35)
king alone, the last two give him both titles (e.g. 348 ἄρχοντος καὶ βασιλεύοντος).

His son Paerisades II reigned from 284/3 till after 252 B.C., for in the
latter year he presented a vase to Apollo at Delphi[4].

In one inscription he is spoken of as archon of Bosporus and Theodosia
and king of the Sindi, Maeotae and Thateis[5].   In the others he is only king[6].

The tiles[7] with the names Spartocus and Paerisades seem to belong to
these kings to judge by the lettering (Π, Ο, Σ) and grammatical forms
(genitive Παιρισάδου) but there is very little to go upon as also in the question
of the coins (v. inf. p. 584 sqq.).

As Boeckh and after him Latyshev have well explained, the Spartocids
at any rate from the time of Leucon when they had extended their power
over neighbouring barbarian tribes, had borne a double title.   In the Greek
cities of the Bosporus and in Theodosia they professed to fill the more or
less constitutional office of Archon, though their authority was such that
other Greeks thought of them as τύραννοι and called them as much when they
did not wish to be polite[8].   Otherwise they spoke of them as δυνάσται or
ἡγεμόνες.   Demosthenes speaks of Leucon as archon, the official decrees of
the Athenian people give no title at all : no one could tell but that Paerisades
and Spartocus II and Spartocus III were private individuals.   So thanks
are given for acts which were obviously political without any mention of the
state which performed them.   That the Spartocids were really the whole
state we see from decrees of proxeny being made out in their name[9].

Naturally there was no need of such careful regard for the feelings of
barbarous tribes and the Spartocids could proclaim their power for what it

[1] *CR.* 1861, p. 176; Giel, *Kl. B.* p. 41; *BCA.*
III. p. 162; XI. p. 156. Škorpil, *Bobrinskoj Mis-*
cellany, p. 33, nn. 9—11.
   [2] App. 34=*CIAtt.* II. 311, Ditt.[2] I. 194.
   [3] *IosPE.* II. 13 (=App. 33), 14, 348, 349: cf. 35.
   [4] Latyshev, *Journ. Min. Publ. Instr.* St P.
1899, Nov. p. 55 (=Ποντικά, p. 301) n. 3 quoting
Homolle *BCH.* VI. p. 164, n. 4.
   [5] App. 35=*IosPE.* II. 15.

   [6] *IosPE.* II. 16, 17 (=App. 36), 35, [350].
   [7] *CR.* 1861, p. 176; Giel, *Kl. B.* p. 41; *BCA.*
III. p. 162 (ΠΑΙΡΙΣΑ
              ΠΡΥΤΑΝΗ, ih. p. 163, cannot be
fitted in); XI. p. 156; Škorpil, *Bobrinskoj Misc.*,
p. 33, nn. 6, 7.
   [8] e.g. Dinarchus *in Dem.* 43.
   [9] *IosPE.* II. 1 (=App. 32), 2.

was and call themselves kings. Whatever may have been the concessions
made by Eumelus to gain the acquiescence of the mob they probably did
not amount to much more than words. The constitution of their fathers and
their forbears' immunity were sounding phrases, and if the ruler could remit
the taxes paid by the citizens of the chief town it shews that he was entirely
independent of them. So his successor Spartocus becomes rather careless
of a distinction which was becoming an anachronism in the world of the
Diadochi—and Paerisades II after the last regular appearance of the ancient
formula called himself simply king. Later historians not unnaturally tended
to call all members of the house kings in whatever connexion they may have
been mentioning them.

We have an inscription[1] which mentions a king Spartocus (IV), son
of Paerisades. The lettering suggests the middle of the IIIrd century.
Latyshev makes him son to Paerisades II. Another son of his was Leucon[2]
who during his father's lifetime made a dedication to Apollo Hietros. The
combination of names recalls to Latyshev the story referred to by Ovid in
the *Ibis* (l. 309):

Aut pia te caeso dicatur adultera, sicut
    Qua cecidit Leucon vindice dicta pias[3].

Neither king would seem to have reigned long: hence we have but one
coin and one inscription from the time of Spartocus and only coins from that
of Leucon II, if indeed all the coins are not still later. The tile with the
name of Leucon is still unpublished. Škorpil seems to refer it to Leucon I[4].

Then follows a break of about seventy years into the earlier part of which
there probably come the King Aces and the Archon Hygiaenon, but as we
know their names from tiles and coins only, they are better discussed in
connexion with the coins of the Spartocids (p. 583). The friendly relations
with Chersonese chronicled by Syriscus (p. 517) came just at this time.

We next have a glimpse of the Bosporan kings in the middle of the
IInd century in an inscription honouring as King and Archon Paerisades
Philometor, son of King Paerisades and of Queen Camasarye Philotecnos,
daughter of Spartocus, and now married to Argotes son of I...thus[5].
Latyshev[6] has identified these persons with pious donors recorded in inscriptions in the temples of Branchidae and Delphi. At the former place
under the year 156/5 we have the name of Queen Camasarye[7] and under
the following year Haussoullier restores that of Paeris]ades[8].

Further Homolle[9] has published a decree of the Delphians in honour of

---

[1] App. 37 = *IosPE*. II. 18.
[2] App. 35 = *IosPE*. II. 15.
[3] Cf. Schol. Ask. ap. R. Ellis; Latyshev, *Sc. et
Cauc.* II. p. 106: Leucon unus ex Ponticis regibus
Spartacon fratrem suum interfecit qui cum
uxore sua solebat adulterari. Postea idem Leucon
interfectus est ab uxore sua: unde Arion:
"Leucon occidit fratrem pro coniuge eumque
    Coniux et causa mortis utrique fuit."
C. von Mure, ibid., preserves the name Alcathoe
but makes her wife to Spartacus.

[4] *Bobrinskoj Misc.* p. 33.
[5] App. 38 = *IosPE*. II. 19. Tomaschek, "Alten
Thraker," p. 49 suggests Ἰ[σάν]θου, cf. ih. p. 9.
[6] *Journ. Min. Pub. Instr.* Nov. 1899, p. 52 =
Ποντικά, p. 298.
[7] *CIG.* 2855.
[8] *Revue de Philologie*, n. s. XXII. (1898) p. 113—
131 quoted by Latyshev, op. c. p. 53, n. 3. Ditt.[2]
133 still follows Boeckh in making C. wife to
Prusias II.
[9] *BCH.* XXIII. (1899), I—VI. p. 96.

βασι/[λεὺς Παιρι]σάδ[ας] καὶ βασίλι/[σσα Καμασαρ]ύα βασιλέως Σπα/[ρτόκου.
It seems rather earlier in date than the Branchidae entries. We learn from it
that Camasarye's father, who cannot be the Spartocus IV of whom we have
already treated, bore the title of king. As Latyshev says, both Paerisades
and Camasarye belonged to the royal house and were probably cousins, or
uncle and niece: perhaps Paerisades was the son of Prytanis (v. p. 580, n. 7);
he certainly seems not to have been in as direct succession as his wife and to
have ranked rather as king-consort. She survived him and from the form
of the Bosporan inscription was regent in the time of her son Paerisades
Philometor, even associating in her power her second husband Argotes. In
view of this we cannot be sure that the Paerisades mentioned at Branchidae
was her husband rather than her son and accordingly lose the *terminus post
quem* for the accession of Philometor that Latyshev wishes to fix. Still
considering the natural longevity of the Spartocids it is possible that
Philometor whose reign began with a minority may be the Paerisades whom
we find reigning in the last decade of the century, we can at least be sure
that he too belonged to the royal house.

Paerisades the Last ruled a kingdom no longer strong enough to make
head against the barbarians, who increased their demands for tribute, and
who seem to have had the sympathy of a large party of the population.
Accordingly Paerisades put himself under the protection of Mithridates VI
Eupator king of Pontus, and thereby brought his kingdom into the main
stream of history.

Mithridates employed as his agent in the Crimea Diophantus, whose
exploits are related in the great Chersonesan inscription[1]. After defeating
Palacus, Diophantus went to the Bosporus and there was most successful
(presumably in the winter of B.C. 110, inscr. l. 10), apparently relieving
Paerisades from his enemies, but leaving him the semblance of authority. So
things remained for about three years, during which Diophantus was breaking
the power of the western Scythians. However, in the autumn of 107, when
Diophantus was actually at Bosporus seeing after the interests of Mithridates,
the Scythians under Saumacus[2], who had been brought up by Paerisades,
rose and killed the old king and nearly caught Diophantus, who escaped on a
ship sent by Chersonese. Diophantus raised a force among the men of that
city, received support from Mithridates, and in the following spring crushed
the revolt and took Saumacus prisoner. It is quite possible that Saumacus
was the legitimate representative of the Spartocids naturally opposed to the
intervention of Mithridates and like Eumelus relying on native support, but
after his failure Diophantus could establish his master's unlimited authority
over the kingdom.

Neither among the Spartocids nor still less among the later kings can
we find a place for Leucanor and Eubiotus of whom Lucian[3] speaks, though
the older investigators even assigned coins to the latter.

---

[1] App. 18=*IosPE*. I. 185: for the question of the dates and general account of Diophantus, v. p. 519.
[2] Besides Pl. VI. 22, he coined silver, v. R. Keil, "König Saumakos," *Zt. f. Numismatik*, VIII. p. 329 B. XXV. 37, 17·75 grn.=1·15 grm. Rayed hd r. | ox-hd r. ΒΑΣ ΣΑΥΜ.
[3] *Toxaris*, §§ 44 and 54.

TABLE OF THE SPARTOCIDS.

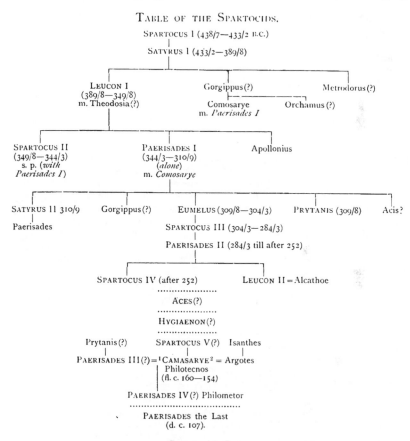

SPARTOCUS 1 (438/7—433/2 B.C.)

SATYRUS 1 (433/2—389/8)

LEUCON I (389/8—349/8) m. Theodosia(?)   Gorgippus(?)   Metrodorus(?)

Comosarye m. *Paerisades I*   Orchamus(?)

SPARTOCUS II (349/8—344/3) s. p. (*with Paerisades I*)   PAERISADES I (344/3—310/9) (*alone*) m. *Comosarye*   Apollonius

SATYRUS II 310/9   Gorgippus(?)   EUMELUS (309/8—304/3)   PRYTANIS (309/8)   Acis?

Paerisades   SPARTOCUS III (304/3—284/3)

PAERISADES II (284/3 till after 252)

SPARTOCUS IV (after 252)   LEUCON II = Alcathoe

....
ACES(?)
....
HYGIAENON(?)
....

Prytanis(?)   SPARTOCUS V(?)   Isanthes

PAERISADES III(?) = [1]CAMASARYE[2] = Argotes
Philotecnos
(fl. c. 160—154)

PAERISADES IV(?) Philometor

....
PAERISADES the Last
(d. c. 107).

Spartocid Coins.

Numismatists[1] have made so much history out of the Bosporan coins that it is impossible to treat the coins and the history apart, but as regards the Spartocid period they have thrown on it very little real light. Even did we know the names and dates of all the kings we could scarcely assign them their coins, for in dealing with remote cities, using imitative types, style becomes a most untrustworthy criterion, we cannot even be sure that there was steady decadence, at any time a good engraver might come across from Asia and raise the level.

[1] Since Koehne's day attention to publishing Spartocid coins has been given by Prince Sibirskij (quite fantastic), Chabouillet, von Sallet, Orêshnikov (*Zur Münzkunde d. Cim. Bosp.*, the most valuable), Burachkov, Podshivalov (*Trans. Od. Soc.* XV. p. 13, the best photographs), Imhoof-Blumer (who puts them all into the IInd century B.C.), Latyshev (from the historical side, *IosPE*. II. p. xxix.), Giel, Škorpil (Hygiaenon) and Bertier-de-La-Garde, *Num. Misc.* II. "Mat. for Stathmological Investigations," p. 58, who alone gives all the weights, see Bibliography.

Coins bear three names known in Bosporan history, Spartocus, Leucon and Paerisades, and one, Hygiaenon, that occurs on Bosporan tiles with the title of Archon; a fifth name, Aces, otherwise unknown but not without analogues, appears on a coin assigned to the Bosporus on the ground of its close resemblance to the staters of Paerisades and Hygiaenon.

One thing is clear, that we have no coins of the older Spartocids who refrained from the title of king except in connexion with the barbarous tribes. There is no coin older than Spartocus IV, or at most Paerisades II. Coinage was the only sovran act that we can attribute to the cities of Panticapaeum and Phanagoria.

Spartocus only coined silver, Leucon only copper, and Aces only gold; Hygiaenon certainly coined gold and silver, perhaps copper as well. Electrum and gold staters and a silver tetradrachm bear the name Paerisades. The gold coins go together being all modelled on the staters of Lysimachus and shewing on the reverse his Pallas Nicephoros (cf. p. 448, f. 329 *bis*).

The eleven surviving staters with the name Paerisades all come under the description applied to Pl. VI. 20, 21, but they seem to fall into four groups as they differ among themselves in execution and the cast of features upon the obverse and also in the monograms upon the reverse and in weight. These particulars, the history and the chief publications of each coin, may be tabulated as follows:

I. EL. 130·7 grn. = 8·47 grm.   EP in field; nothing under seat. Once Pr. Sibirskij's, now Giel Coll.
    MK. II. p. 33, No. 2; Chabouillet, I. 5; Orêshnikov, Title-page; Burachkov, XXIV. 6;
    Podshivalov, I. 3; Giel, *TRAS.* v. 52.

II. N·. 130·3 grn. = 8·44 grm.   ⩕ in field; ⩖ under seat. Artjukhov's Barrow, Grave II: Hermitage.
     CR. 1880, II. 4, 5; Or. I. 1; B. p. 215; Pod. I. 1.

     N·. 130·9 grn. = 8·48 grm.   ⩕ in field and ⩑ : nothing under seat. Acad. Sciences, St P.
     CR. 1880, II. 6, 7; Or. I. 2; B. p. 216; Pod. I. 2.

III. N·. 130·9 grn. = 8·48 grm.   ⩖ under seat.   Paris.
     MK. II. p. 33, No. 1; Chab. I. 3; Or. I. 3; Pod. p. 21.

     N·. 130·3 grn. = 8·44 grm.   ⩖ under seat.   Glasgow, Hunter Coll.
     Pl. VI. 20: Chab. I. 4; Pod. p. 21; Macdonald, II. p. 229, XLV. 5.

     N·. 130·1 grn. = 8·43 grm.   ⩖ under seat.   St Florian, Austria.

     N·. 130 grn. = 8·42 grm.   ⩖ under seat.   Giel Coll.
     Giel, *TRAS.* v. 53.

     N·. 127·6 grn. = 8·27 grm.   No monograms.   Kerch: ⎫ Terlecki Coll. now
     N·. 129·3 grn. = 8·38 grm.   ΔІ in field; ⩕ (?) under seat.   Temrjuk: ⎬ Prowe.
     Both in letters from V. V. Škorpil and I. Terlecki: Orêshnikov, *Num. Misc.* II. (1912).
     "Coins of Chersonese &c." p. 37, Pl. I. Nos. 2, 3, puts the first in Group II, the second in a
     group by itself, but to my eye the Hunter specimen links them together.

IV. N·. 125·8 grn. = 8·15 grm. ⎫ K in field; ⩕ under seat. Siverskaja: Hist. Mus. Moscow.
     N·. 127·3 grn. = 8·25 grm. ⎭
     Pl. VI. 21.   Or. I. 4, 5; Pod. II. 14, 15.

Burachkov's XXIV. 5 is a forgery; Mr Alexêev's reputed specimen no one seems to have seen.

With the staters goes the tetradrachm lately acquired by H.I.H. Alexêj Michailovich:

Æ. 217·6 grn. = 14·1 grm. Hd of Paerisades r., │ Pallas Nicephoros as before; Φ in field; nothing
    bearded and filleted.   │   under seat.
Photograph and letter from Orêshnikov: v. *Num. Misc.* II. p. 39, f. 13; Bertier-de-La-Garde, l.c.

I cannot feel that there is much essential difference between the first three groups. The head in all is decidedly idealized though the Ammon horn of the Alexander model is not reproduced, it is a kind of compromise; the work on Sibirskij's example is finer than on the others, and the hair is rather stiff in group III, none come near a good Lysimachus; so too the average weight is decidedly inferior to the general run of the Lysimachi in the Anadol hoard buried somewhere circa B.C. 270[1]. The time of Paerisades II is possible, and the style of the things in Artjukhov's barrow (v. p. 430) agrees, unless our judgment of it is founded on this very coin, but if we knew of a Paerisades about 200 B.C.—perhaps the father of Philometor might do—he would suit the coins better. The head on the tetradrachm is certainly a portrait, for it has a slight beard not unlike those worn by Prusias I and II (B.C. 220—149)[2], and this makes for about the same date; the features to my eye resemble those on Sibirskij's stater. Group IV shews the light weight and rude workmanship of the Pseudo-Lysimachian staters issued in the western Euxine towards the end of the IInd century B.C. and first half of the Ist: on such appear the features of Mithridates and Pharnaces, and no doubt we have here those of Paerisades, probably Philometor or a later king if such there were: they shew a decided resemblance to Spartocus. The monogram under the seat is no doubt ΠΑ for Panticapaeum, cf. the BY of Byzantium and the TY of Tyras (v. supra p. 448). The trident and dolphins in the exergue also appear in the western Euxine.

There is therefore no proof that the unique stater at Paris inscribed ΒΑΣΙΛΕΛΣ ΑΚΟΥ (131·17 grn. = 8·5 grm.; the head has the horn of Ammon, and so is not a portrait[3]) belongs to a king of Bosporus; accordingly Chabouillet (p. 3) assigns it to a Thracian or Scythian dynast: Imhoof-Blumer (op. c. p. 35) was first to prefer Bosporus on account of the general likeness: judging by weight and style it ought to come rather earlier than the better Paerisades coins though the A (also found on the tetradrachm) and the absence of Athena's spear suggest lateness; the name would be the masculine counterpart of Ἀκίς which has occurred in the Spartocid house[4].

As to Hygiaenon the tiles with ΑΡΧοΝΤοΣ / ΥΓΙΑΙΝοΝΤοΣ[5] settle the matter, and so Aces is probably Bosporan also: Hygiaenon's silver coin[6]

Æ. 55·6 grn. = 3·6 grm. Head of Archon r. much as on Pl. VI. 19.	Horseman charging r. with raised spear, chlamys flying behind. In front, Ⱨ; below, ⳰⳰⳰; between, ΑΡΧοΝΤοΣ / ΥΓΙΑΙΝοΝΤοΣ.

was first found and next the gold stater (Pl. VI. 19)[7], lastly Škorpil has announced a copper (l.c. Pl. I. 3),

Æ. Head r. with long back hair.	Starry caps of Dioscuri, between them cornucopiae, below ΥΓΙΑ.

but he tells me that Bertier-de-La-Garde doubts its belonging to Hygiaenon.

[1] *BCA.* III. p. 58.
[2] Imhoof-Blumer, *Porträtk.* p. 33, IV. 17, 18.
[3] *Pace* Orêshnikov, *Num. Misc.* II. p. 41, f. 14.
[4] Ἀκὶς Παιρι[σάδεος ἀνέθηκεν
   Ἀ]φρο[δίτηι...*BCA.* XVIII. p. 125, No. 40.
[5] First published by McPherson, *Kertch*, p. 72; cf. *CR.* 1861, p. 176; another stamp with A, 1868,

p. 125: full list Škorpil, "The date of the Archon Hygiaenon's rule," *Bobrinskoj Misc.* pp. 34, 35, ff. 1, 2.
[6] E. Muret, *BCH.* VI. p. 211; Škorpil, l.c. p. 37, Pl. I. 2, figures a better specimen.
[7] Orêshnikov, *Trans. Moscow Num. Soc.* II. 1899; *Num. Misc.* II. Pl. I. 1; Škorpil, l.c. Pl. I. 1.

The silver coin looks of the IInd century, the lettering of the tiles IIIrd, the stater in weight 129·32 grn. comes between the better and the worse Paerisades, but the style is better than any, the hair rather recalls the Panticapaean "macaroni" (v. inf. p. 628). The head is certainly a portrait though slightly idealized, it is without the divine horn or the regal diadem. The sum of all this points to Aces in the latter part of the IIIrd century followed by Hygiaenon and a Paerisades early in the IInd[1].

Leucon's coins, being copper, are naturally much the commonest. They are rough in style and rather worn. The lettering on all three varieties (Pl. VI. 16, 17, 18) is very similar, and there is no reason to give them to more than one king. The heads of Heracles (Pl. VI. 16, occasionally the reverse has the bow the other way up and above the club[2]) and of Athena are derived from types of Alexander, but that is the only guide to the date. Against putting them down to Leucon II, of whom Ovid speaks, is the presumption that he had a short reign, but we are hardly justified in inventing for them a Leucon III in the IInd century B.C.

Spartocus has only left one single coin (Pl. VI. 15, in the Rumjantsev Museum at Moscow) in poor preservation; von Sallet thought the E was Є, and put it accordingly into the IInd century, assigning it to Spartocus, the father of Camasarye. On the whole the general style points that way rather than to the IIIrd, and further the head bears a distinct resemblance to the Paerisades on the worst variety (Pl. VI. 21), i.e. probably to his grandson Philometor.

Mithridates and Pharnaces.

Mithridates, by defending Chersonese and driving the Scythians out of the Bosporus, gained throughout the Greek world the reputation of a champion of Hellenism. Also he added to his ancestral dominions a district from which in the future he could draw men, money and supplies. The Crimea and Sindica paid him a tribute of 180,000 medimni of wheat and 200 talents of silver[3], and we find troops from these parts enumerated among his forces[4]. Not less valuable was the access he thereby gained to recruiting grounds which supplied levies more martial if not more trustworthy than the commercial Greeks. It was because he had profited by continuous relations with the barbarians of the interior and had long been used to enrol under his banners Scythians, Tauri and Sarmatae, as well as Bastarnae, Thracians and Kelts further west, that he formed his great scheme of marching on Italy from the north and rolling up all these nations to overwhelm it[5]. It is probably at this time that Mithridates received the allegiance of Olbia formerly subject to Scilurus (v. p. 463). Neoptolemus was his most likely agent, as we find his name attached to a tower at the mouth of the Tyras, and probably Tyras town also joined him.

---

[1] Th. Reinach, *Mithridate*, p. 190, n. 4, p. 301, makes Hygiaenon rebel against Mithridates in 86 B.C.; but he did not know the stater and cannot have paid enough attention to the lettering of the tiles.

[2] Burachkov, XXIV. 1.
[3] Strabo, VII. iv. 6.
[4] Appian, XII. 15, 41; Bosporans even captured Roman standards, Orosius, VI. xxi. 28.
[5] Appian, XII. 15, 41, 57, 69, 109.

At first Mithridates seems to have ruled by deputy the provinces that his deputy had won for him[1]. The first war with Rome forced him to subject them to a heavy tribute and probably interfered with their trade, also the Scythian danger may have appeared less serious now that it had been diverted; similar causes acted in Colchis and both dependencies revolted[2]. Colchis was quickly reduced and Mithridates put in as viceroy his son of the same name.

Against Bosporus a large expedition was being prepared when Murena, wishing for a cheap triumph, alleged that the Roman power was the real objective of so powerful a force and claimed to be merely anticipating Mithridates in declaring war. So for two years the attention of the king was occupied by the "second" war with Rome. After the defeat of Murena and the conclusion of peace (81 B.C.) Mithridates was free to deal with Bosporus, which he speedily reconquered. About this period come the exploits of Neoptolemus, who defeated the natives both on the ice and on the water of the Bosporus[3], but an expedition against the wild tribes of the Caucasus coast was destroyed. Meanwhile Machares was installed as viceroy of Bosporus (B.C. 79)[4]. What his title may have been we do not know, as no coins bearing his name have come down to us. At first during the course of the ensuing war with Rome he continued faithful and forwarded to his father reinforcements and provisions, so that he was allowed to add to his dominions the satrapy of Colchis[5]. Accordingly he refused supplies to Cotta during the siege of Heraclea (72 B.C.)[6]. But when Fortune had definitely declared herself upon the side of Rome and Mithridates in great straits after the disastrous retreat from Cyzicus sent across for help, Diocles, his envoy to the Scythians, deserted to Lucullus, taking with him the money entrusted to him, and Machares withheld his support. During the flight of Mithridates into Armenia, Machares was practically independent, still he had the grace to send grain to besieged Sinope. Finally he gave in to Lucullus and made a treaty with him, offering him a gold wreath and supplying with corn the besiegers of Sinope instead of the beleaguered city[7]. At this juncture Olbia appears to have sent help to the besieged[8].

After his final defeat in 67 B.C. and the desertion of Tigranes, when the West, the South and the East were closed to him, Mithridates put his hopes in the North. Colchis had not followed its ruler Machares in his desertion, but seems to have reverted to a kind of neutral independence. He found there no opposition to his flight, and wintered in Dioscurias (66/5 B.C.)[9]. From here he stirred up the Iberians and Albanians and gave Pompey some trouble in his pursuit. When the latter arrived in the basin of the Phasis Mithridates had fled; his last hope was to win back the kingdom of Machares. He could not go by sea, for a Roman squadron was watching the coast. He had to make his way along the steep southern slope of the Caucasus, through

---

[1] So he did in Colchis, Strabo XI. ii. 18, ἐπέμπετο δ᾽ ἀεί τις τῶν φίλων ὕπαρχος καὶ διοικητὴς τῆς χώρας.
[2] B.C. 83, Appian, XII. 64 : Reinach, *Mithridate*, p. 301.
[3] Strabo, VII. iii. 18.
[4] Appian, XII. 67.
[5] Memnon, f. 53.
[6] Memnon, f. 49.
[7] B.C. 70, Appian, XII. 83 ; Memnon, f. 54.
[8] *BCA.* XXIII. p. 21 sqq., v. supra, p. 464.
[9] Appian, XII. 101 sqq.

tribes whose reputation for savagery was unsurpassed in the ancient world. The Heniochi were friendly, but the Zygi were so hostile that he had to take to boats and so get round to the Achaei, who were also well disposed[1].

When Machares learned that his father had come through this unexampled journey he did not dare to measure his strength against even such a small force as he had brought, but sent envoys to try and turn away his wrath, and knowing him too well to have faith in their efficacy, burned all the ships he could and put the strait between his father and himself. When other ships were found and sent after him, he slew himself after having been ruler of Bosporus fourteen years and almost independent for the last seven (71—65 B.C.)[2].

Although the last acts of Mithridates and his death are the most dramatic events in the history of Bosporus (well is the hill of Kerch called Mount Mithridates), they are too familiar to make it necessary that I should describe them in detail[3]. Filled with his great scheme of invading Italy from the north, Mithridates relaxed no efforts to collect and equip an army ; for this he disdained neither bond nor free, spared no wood, not even the oxen for the plough, laid the heaviest taxes upon even the smallest property and allowed his agents to make these exactions insolently, being unable to look after them himself because of some disfiguring disease which kept him in his castle. Further, the Roman fleet was blockading the whole peninsula[4] and an earthquake (64 B.C.) added to the economic ruin[5]. Moreover, in spite of his energy and the fact that the aged king had created a new army and a new fleet, all felt that the star of Rome was in the ascendant and had lost their former confidence and loyalty. Finally the Roman deserters who formed a corps whose very position made them trustworthy, were disturbed at the prospect of attacking their motherland of Italy.

The spark to make the explosion came from Phanagoria. Castor the governor, illtreated by one of the king's eunuchs, slew him and roused the people. The acropolis held out. In it were five children of Mithridates, who gave themselves up. One, Cleopatra, would not yield and was rescued by her father. Following Phanagoria's example, Chersonese, Theodosia, Nymphaeum, and the other places of which Mithridates had lately got possession, revolted. Then he began to have doubts of his own troops. In a last hope of strengthening himself he sent two of his daughters as brides to Scythian kings asking for speedy help ; but their military escort slew the eunuchs in charge and handed the girls over to Pompey. Yet even so Mithridates did not despair of his Italian campaign. Then his favourite son Pharnaces, whom he had designated as his heir, fearing that on the failure of this great emprise the forces of the kingdom would be utterly exhausted and the Romans embittered beyond hope of appeasement, determined to seize the kingdom while there was yet a kingdom to seize. His plot was discovered and his confederates tortured, but he was spared. The very next night he went and tampered with the Roman deserters and easily won them over and

[1] Strabo, XI. ii. 13; Appian, XII. 102, says the Achaei were put to flight. The tribes do not seem to have been as hostile as they might have been. Perhaps Machares, to ensure his convoys on their way across to Sinope, had been putting down their piracies.

[2] Appian, XII. 102 ; Dio Cassius, XXXVI. l. 2, says he was slain by his own friends.
[3] Reinach, pp. 402 sqq. ; cf. Appian, XII. 107 ; Dio Cassius, XXXVII. X. 4 sqq. ; Orosius, VI. iv., v.
[4] Plutarch, *Pompey*, XXXIX.
[5] Dio Cassius, XXXVII. Xi. 4 ; Orosius, VI. v. 1.

the fleet too.   In the confusion many corps came over because they thought
the matter already decided.

Mithridates went out to speak to the rebels, but it was too late, he barely
escaped from them alive.   Returning to the castle he watched from the
terrace while Pharnaces was crowned king with a strip of papyrus from a
temple near.   When there came again none of his messengers whom he sent
asking to be allowed to depart safely, he thanked his faithful friends and
guards and sent them over to the new king.

So he prepared to die.   The poison which he carried with him failed to
act, though it sufficed for his two daughters Mithridatis and Nyssa.   Too
weak to slay himself, he had to ask this last service of Bituitus, a Gaulish
chieftain who had long followed him faithfully[1].   So he died at the age of
sixty-nine, having been overlord of the Bosporus for more than forty years.
Pharnaces sent the body over to Sinope, where it was buried by Pompey in
the royal tomb.

Pharnaces asked either for all his ancestral dominions, or at least for the
Bosporus as ruled over by Machares.   Pompey, while admitting him as a
friend and ally of the Roman People in return for the service he had done
in ridding it of its great enemy, granted him the Bosporus only, and exempted
from his rule the city of Phanagoria, because it gave the signal for revolt[2].

With this arrangement Pharnaces had to be content, and he occupied
himself in extending his power over the tribes to the east of the Maeotis, so
that his frontiers reached to the Tanais.   One of these tribes, the Dandarii,
he conquered by flooding their country from an arm of the Hypanis, so they
must have dwelt in its northern delta[3].   About 48 B.C. he thought that the
Romans being preoccupied with the civil war, he had an opportunity of
regaining his father's kingdom.   First he seems to have retaken Phanagoria
(if indeed he could keep his hands off it so long), but treated it with
clemency[4].   Next he overran Colchis and the former kingdom of Pontus,
defeating Cn. Domitius Calvinus and fancying himself as great as his father.
However, he received the news that Asander, whom he had left as governor
of Bosporus, had revolted, so he turned back and on his way encountered
Caesar at Zela, to be utterly defeated (B.C. 47)[5].

He made his peace with Rome as best he could, and fled back to
Bosporus, for he did not despair of regaining his authority there.   So he
raised a force of natives and recovered Theodosia and Panticapaeum, but was
hemmed in and slain by Asander.

Now Asander had risen in the hope that the Romans would be favourable
and give him the dominion of the country : but Caesar, disgusted by his
treachery, named as king one Mithridates, said to be son of the great
Mithridates by a Gaulish mistress, Adobogionis, wife of Menodotus of
Pergamum.   However, this Mithridates of Pergamum was defeated and slain
by the native claimant, and for the next few years the Romans were much too
taken up with their own affairs to disturb Asander[6].

---

[1] B.C. 63, Dio Cassius, XXXVII. x. 4.
[2] Appian, XII. 113.
[3] Strabo, XI. ii. 11.
[4] Appian, XII. 120 ; cf. Dio Cassius, XLII.

ix. 2.
[5] Dio Cassius, XLII. xlv.—xlvii.
[6] Strabo, XIII. iv. 3 ; Dio Cassius, XLII. xlviii.
3, 4 ; A. Hirtius, *Bel. Alex.* 78.

Little light is thrown by coins upon the history of Bosporus under Mithridates or Pharnaces. The former struck his large silver in Asia Minor and left the cities their small change : certain copper coins with the monogram ₧ have been referred to him coining for some reason under the name of Eupator, but their style seems later (v. p. 603). Pharnaces issued gold staters as Great King of Kings from A.B. (see below) 243 to 247 = B.C. 55 to 51, when, as far as we know, his rule was confined to Bosporus (Pl. VI. 23).

GENEALOGY OF KINGS OF PONTUS AND BOSPORUS : B.C. 100 TO A.D. 100.

Rulers claiming Bosporus in capitals. Pretenders' names in brackets.

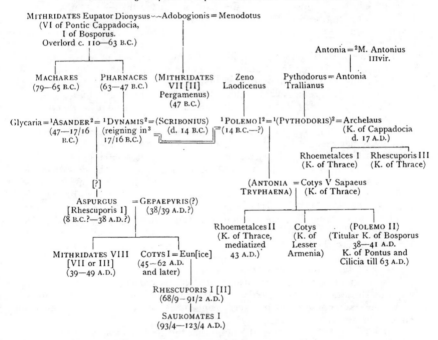

Mithridates Eupator, besides being the most picturesque figure in Bosporan history, did it a very definite service, being held responsible for the introduction into it of the era by which subsequent kings dated their coins and inscriptions[1]. This Bosporan era, as we shall call it, inasmuch as it was used on the Bosporus much longer than anywhere else, originated in Bithynia,

[1] Pharnaces I in App. 17ᵃ = *BCA*. XLV. p. 23, n. 1 (v. p. 518), seems to make B.C. 179 the 157th year of an era otherwise unknown, perhaps reckoned from B.C. 336, the accession of Mithridates, son of Ariobarzanes, whom Löper calls Ctistes, giving as his successors Mithr. II, Ariobarzanes, Mithr. III, Pharnaces I, Mithr. IV Philopator Philadelphus, Mithr. V Euergetes and Mithr. Eupator, to whom as against E. Meyer and Reinach he restores the traditional VI.

where it probably commemorated the year in which Zipoetes raised that principality to the rank of a kingdom. The point from which it is reckoned is the autumnal equinox of B.C. 297 = A.U.C. 457[1]. The months are those of the Macedonian Kalendar; we have no names of Bosporan months before its introduction, probably they were after the Milesian pattern as at Olbia and Tyras (p. 472). The era first appears upon the coins of Nicomedes II in B.C. 148/7 and continues till the death of Nicomedes III in B.C. 74/3. Mithridates, during a close political and commercial alliance with Bithynia, issued his famous tetradrachms bearing date A.B. (Anno Bithyniae seu Bospori) 202 = B.C. 96/5 and subsequent years, and staters from A.B. 205 = B.C. 93/2. They probably circulated in Bosporus, and were in themselves sufficient to familiarize his subjects with the era. Pharnaces II also put these dates on his coins, which were no doubt issued in Bosporus. The first coin distinctively Bosporan on which the era is used bears date A.B. 281 = B.C. 17/6 (Fig. 347) and belongs to Dynamis, wife of Asander, ruling alone after her husband's death. The first dated inscription bears the name of Aspurgus and the year ‾ ▩T usually read ΓΙ T, but quite possibly ЄκT, giving the dates A.B. 313 or 325 = A.D. 17 or 29[2]; the last date known is A.B. 794 = A.D. 497/8[3].

Asander and Dynamis.

The first mention of Asander seems to be in the Nymphaean inscription quoted on p. 561, according to which he had a first wife Glycaria. It would also be a witness to his importance at Nymphaeum, and this may have been the reason why that city revolted before any other. The literary references do not tell us who he was, but speak of his personal antagonism to Pharnaces: this makes it hard to understand why the latter, during his time of power, did not make away with him and how his daughter Dynamis came to be Asander's wife. The most natural explanation is that he had his own following in the country, due, it is suggested, to his representing the Spartocid tradition, and was too strong to be attacked; so Pharnaces early in his reign, when Asander would be about fifty, thought that he would attach him to himself by giving him his daughter to wife, and afterwards trusted him to the extent of leaving him in charge of the kingdom during his expedition to Asia. The common idea that Asander at the age of 63 married Dynamis just after he had killed her father is almost too much even for the 1st century B.C.[4]; it is founded on the gratuitous assumption that Pharnaces only had one daughter, the one whom he offered in marriage to Caesar before Zela[5]. The account of Asander in Dio Cassius (LIV. xxiv.) is that he married Dynamis, daughter to Pharnaces

---

[1] Cary, *Histoire des Rois de Thrace et de ceux du Bosphore Cimmérien éclaircie par les médailles*, Paris, 1752, and Froelich, *Regum Veterum numismata anecdota aut perrara notis illustrata*, Vienna, 1752, as summarized by Eckhel, *D.N.V.* Pars I. vol. II. p. 381, ap. Latyshev, *IosPE.* II. Introd. p. xxxiii, fixed the first year of the era at 297 B.C. All have agreed, and Th. Reinach, *Trois Royaumes*, p. 130, has traced it to its Bithynian source. Löper (loc. cit. and *Bull. Russ. Arch. Inst. at Constantinople*, VIII. p. 160) thinks an inscription of Mithridates Euergetes at Ineboli is dated by A.B., cf. *Num. Chron.* Ser. IV. Vol. V. (1905), p. 113.

[3] *BCA.* X. p. 90, No. 107.   [2] *IosPE.* II. 364.

[4] Škorpil, *BCA.* XXXVII. p. 21; Prince Sibirskij, *Trans. Od. Soc.* X. p. 56; Bertier-de-La-Garde, ih. XXIX. (1911), "Coins of Rulers of the Cimmerian Bosporus determined by Monograms," p. 181. To this last article, though I have not been able to accept all its positions, I have been most indebted throughout the next fifteen pages.

[5] Appian, XIII. 91.

and so granddaughter to Mithridates[1], and that by 14 B.C. he was dead and his wife, after taking over the power, had married first an adventurer Scribonius and afterwards the Roman nominee Polemo. Lucian[2] says that Asander was raised by Augustus from ἐθνάρχης to king, was a first-rate soldier at the age of ninety and starved himself to death at the age of ninety-three when he saw his men deserting to Scribonius[3]. This would place his birth about 108 B.C. Strabo adds (VII. iv. 6) that he defended the isthmus across to the Maeotis with a wall 360 stades long with ten towers to the stade, trusting thereby to keep off the Scythians without paying them tribute[4].

On the east side of the Maeotis he established his rule as far as the Tanais[5], and probably repressed the pirates unlike the Bosporan rulers who gave them a refuge and market for their spoils[6]: sea-power is suggested by his coins and his admiral's dedication[7]. This inscription proves that his royalty was recognized by Rome (in it first occurs the epithet φιλορώμαιος) and mentions his wife Dynamis. The evidence of coins bears out the other information, but just fails to tell us anything fresh. We have his gold coins for 29 years. For the first ten or so they weigh the same as those of Pharnaces, 125·6 grn. = 8·14 grm., afterwards coming down to the weight of a Roman aureus, 123·9 grn. = 8·03 grm.[8] For the first three years he bore the title of archon and put on his coins the heads of Octavian (1 and 2) and Antonius (3[9]). In the fourth he also figures as king and lets his own head appear, and so henceforth, e.g. Pl. VI. 26 with date KH = 28: unluckily he did not use the Bosporan era, and we do not know from what date to reckon.

His wife Dynamis represented the Mithridatic tradition and put the date A.B. 281 (= B.C. 17/16, A.U.C. 737/8) on her solitary stater, which shews us that in that year she was reigning alone as queen and had not yet married Scribonius. Reckoning back 28 complete years we have B.C. 44 = A.U.C. 709/10 as the latest date when Asander can have begun to coin as archon. That would just allow us to suppose that as long as Caesar, the friend of Mithridates Pergamenus, was alive he kept quiet, but on the news of his death took the title of archon, received the acquiescence of Octavian, then fully occupied in avenging his uncle's murder, and put his effigy upon his coins. For this he substituted that of Antony upon the latter's coming

FIG. 347.
Gold Stater of Dynamis,
123·9 grn. = 8·03 grm.
ΑΠΣ = A.B. 281 = A.D. 17/16.
Orêshnikov, *Cat. Uvarov Coll.*
Pl. II. 471.

east in A.U.C. 712' and next year was allowed by the concurrence of Octavian

[1] Cf. App. 41 = *IosPE.* II. 356.

[2] If *Macrobii* be Lucian's, c. 17.

[3] Dio Cassius, LIV. xxiv. 4, implies some interval between the death of Asander and the appearance of Scribonius.

[4] Because of the length mentioned this wall is generally supposed to be across the isthmus of Theodosia, and the remains of a bank there still exist: but even this has only half the breadth required, and at this time the kings of Bosporus ruled as far as Chersonese and did not want protection on this line. Strabo (VII. iv. 1), speaking of the isthmus of Perekop, says that it is forty stades broad, but that other authors give it as 360. This 360 may be due to his authority reckoning

right across from the bay of Carcinites to the open Maeotis at Genichesk, then it is not far out. A wall 360 stades long, with ten towers to the stade, would take up a most enormous force to defend it; one of 40 stades would naturally be very closely fortified. The mention of the number of the towers suggests that Strabo meant the isthmus of Perekop and merely adopted the wrong reckoning of the distance across, v. supra, p. 16, n. 6.

[5] Strabo, XI. ii. 11. [6] ib. XI. ii. 12.

[7] App. 39 = *IosPE.* II. 25.

[8] Bertier-de-La-Garde, *Trans. Od. Soc.* XXIX. p. 207. *BMC. Pontus etc.* Pl. X. 10 shews ΘK = 29.

[9] (1) Giel, *Kl. B.* Pl. II. 22; (2) B. XXV. 41 after Sibirskij; (3) Orêshnikov, *Cat. Uvarov,* p. 62.

and Antony to assume the style of king, a licence attributed by Lucian to
Augustus. This is essentially Orêshnikov's explanation and does account for
the facts—only it requires us to assume that Asander died early in his year 29
and that Dynamis issued her coin very soon after. As archon, Asander
hastily coined a great deal of bronze bearing a ship's prow all restruck on
already existing coins either of Panticapaeum and Phanagoria or of Sinope
and Amisus (v. inf. p. 630 and Pl. vi, 24, 25), but as king he seems to have
confined himself to gold. Perhaps he had supplied the demand by his hasty
reminting. Apparently he feared that to assume the title of archon, strike
coins and reckon his rule from the date of his rebellion against Pharnaces, a
rebellion so definitely disapproved by Caesar, would have been to flout the
suzerain claims of the Romans and might lead to their sending fresh nominees
like Mithridates of Pergamum, or at any rate make them unready to allow
him the full title of king, the unauthorized assumption of which they could not
have overlooked. In any case we may reckon the extreme years of his rule
B.C. 47/46 = A.U.C 707/8 = A.B. 251 and B.C. 17/16, A.U.C. 737/8 = A.B. 281[1].

Dynamis then was queen in this latter year, but on the appearance of an
adventurer Scribonius[2], who claimed to be a grandson of Mithridates named
by Augustus to succeed upon Asander's death, she took him for her husband.
Upon this Agrippa, who was at Sinope settling the affairs of Asia, sent across
Polemo, king of Asiatic Pontus, to slay Scribonius and take possession of the
kingdom. He found that the Bosporans had already unmasked and slain the
impostor, but were by no means ready to accept as king the member of an
upstart dynasty, and they did not yield to Agrippa's decision until he came
himself to support it. This is all put down to the year A.U.C. 740 = B.C. 14 =
A.B. 283[3].

Dynamis professed special gratitude to Augustus. Accordingly she set up
statues to him at Panticapaeum[4] and Phanagoria[5]. At the latter town she also
set up one to Livia[6]. In these, no more than upon her stater or the complimentary inscription of the Agrippeans[7], is there any mention of her husband.
It has been supposed that they were the expression of her gratitude for the
alliance with Polemo, but rather she was still hoping for the favour of being
left alone as queen-regent to bring up her son, or more probably grandson,

---

[1] For Asander, v. p. 591 n. 4 and the following:
von Sallet, whose Doctor's dissertation was *De
Asandro et Polemone...quaestiones chronologicae et
numismaticae*, Berlin, 1865, amplified into *Beitr. z.
Gesch. u. Num. d. Kön. d. Cim. Bosp. u. d. Pontus*,
ib. 1866, thinks Julius Caesar recognized A. so
that his coins begin in A.U.C. 708/9 = B.C. 46/5 :
Waddington, *Rev. Num.* n.s. XI. (1866) p. 417,
dates his archonship from the death of Pharnaces,
B.C. 47 : Burachkov, *General Catalogue*, pp. 190,
230, Pl. XXV. 41—50, begins with 45 B.C., and Giel,
Kl. B. pp. 10—12, Pl. II. 22, agrees with von
Sallet : these are all well summarized by Latyshev,
IosPE. II. pp. xxxv—xxxvii, but he comes to no
conclusion. Giel, *TRAS.* VII. p. 225, Pl. XIX. 60
goes over to Orêshnikov's view as put forth in
Catal. of Ct Uvarov's Coins, Pt VII. pp. 62—68,
v. esp. No. 471, the stater of Dynamis, supra
Fig. 347. Brandis, s.v. Bosporus, *P.-W.* III.
pp. 777—779, makes Asander date from his first

rising against Pharnaces in 48/7, and so gives
Dynamis some years of solitary reign. But he
sees the head of Asander on all his coins alike,
which is absurd : Asander certainly did not put
his own head upon the coins of years 1 and 2,
though Wroth, *BMC. Pontus*, p. xxxi, and Regling
with Hennig (*Berliner Münzblätter*, XXIX. 1908,
p. 86) think that he did in year 3. These latter
take the head on years 1 and 2 to be Antony ; I am
very much inclined to find Antony on all three
years. I regret not having seen V. Voigtius, *De
Asandro Bospori Rege*, Kiev, 1894.

[2] Dio Cassius, LIV. xxiv. 4—6.

[3] Eutropius, VII. 9, (Augustus) omnes Ponti
maritimas ciuitates R. adjecit imperio ; Dio
Cassius, l.c. ; Eusebius, Ol. 191. 3.

[4] App. 40 = *IosPE.* IV. 201.

[5] ib. II. 354.

[6] ib. IV. 420.

[7] App. 41 = *IosPE.* II. 356.

Aspurgus. But the success of Scribonius shewed that this could not be allowed by Rome, though it was probably for this that the Bosporans fought against Polemo. Dynamis, as a daughter of Pharnaces, must have been an elderly bride and probably did not long trouble Polemo, as within a few years we find him married to Pythodoris[1].

Polemo I and Pythodoris.

Polemo had no possible right to the Bosporus. The princes, vassals of the Empire, formed at this time a special class whose members from Mauretania to Bosporus and from Judaea to Thrace intermarried and were regarded as interchangeable[2]. Polemo was raised into this class by Antony. His father Zeno, a rhetor of Laodicea, had bravely defended his native city against the Parthians, the son was made king, first of Lycaonia, next of Pontus and finally of Little Armenia. Although he supported Antony at Actium he did not lose the favour of Augustus, and Agrippa thought him a suitable instrument for securing the obedience of the Bosporus[3].

His second wife Pythodoris belonged to a similar family. Her father Pythodorus was a great man at Tralles, as rich as a king and a close friend of Pompey's. This brought upon him confiscations, but his wealth carried him through[4]. He married Antonia, eldest daughter of the triumvir by his second wife Antonia[5].

So Polemo and his wife belonged to the Antonians, but this did not prevent their being highly favoured by Augustus. Towards the end of his life he reigned over most of the countries that formed the kingdom of Mithridates. He subdued Colchis[6], continued the conquest of the eastern coast of the Maeotis, and on a lack of obedience on the part of the colony of Tanais utterly ravaged it[7].

Polemo met his death while making a treacherous attack upon the Aspurgians, whom Strabo (XI. ii. 11; XII. iii. 29) regards as a tribe of barbarians living in a space of five hundred stades between Phanagoria and Gorgippia. This is the first we hear of the Aspurgians, and it can hardly be a coincidence that Aspurgus is the name of the next king of whom we know, the rightful heir of Asander. It would. be natural to suppose them to be a political party of his adherents having its chief strength in that part of the country but that the name occurs in inscriptions[8], ὁ ἐπὶ τῶν Ἀσπουργιανῶν being one of the officers of the Bosporan monarchy in the latter part of the IIIrd century A.D.: Rostovtsev[9] suggests that Aspurgus founded a military

---

[1] I cannot but think that she was only divorced and regained power, so that the ⋈ coins (Pl. VII. 1) were struck by her from A.B. 289=B.C. 9/8 to A.B. 304=A.D. 7/8 perhaps as regent for Aspurgus.

[2] P. C. Sands, *The Client Princes of the Roman Empire under the Republic*, just stops short of this period.

[3] Strabo, XII. iii. 29; viii. 16.

[4] Strabo, XIV. i. 42.

[5] Mommsen, *Eph. Epigr.* I. p. 272.

[6] Strabo, XI. ii. 18.

[7] Strabo (XI. ii. 3) speaks of this having taken place νεωστί: and from this it has been argued that Polemo lived to within a few years of 19 A.D., when Strabo was still writing: but as we do not know his method of composition or to how much revision he subjected his notes, this is no criterion. The sack of Tanais may have happened thirty years before.

[8] *IosPE.* II. 29 (=App. 61), 431, 431 *bis*.

[9] *BCA.* X. p. 15.

settlement, perhaps made up of mercenaries whom he had used against Polemo and established on the land side of the Taman Peninsula. This region would, as Brandis (p. 780) says, be called τὰ Ἀσπουργιανά and count as a local division of the kingdom beside ἡ νῆσος and the others (v. p. 613). That Strabo was so little clear about them would argue that Polemo's death was not very fresh in his mind, but we have no information as to when it happened. It seems likely that the Bosporan coins, which begin in A.B. 289 = B.C. 9/8, imply that he was no longer king; in any case Pythodoris married Archelaus, king of Cappadocia, about 8 A.D. Polemo struck a few pieces, but they are not connected with Bosporus (Pl. vi. 27): as he did not represent the Mithridatic tradition he did not use the Bosporan era.

Pythodoris succeeded to Polemo's kingdom, but we do not know whether Bosporus was included: Strabo (xii. iii. 29) says nothing of it in his account of her dominions, but that may refer to after 17 A.D., when she had been left a widow by Archelaus. She seems to have retained her rule in Asia Minor until succeeded by her grandson Polemo II, and also directed affairs in Thrace, where her eldest daughter Antonia Tryphaena was married to King Cotys V Sapaeus. She has left coins with the dates 60 and 63 of the Actian era, both with heads of Augustus and one dated 60 with that of Tiberius. The reverse types, Capricorn (Pl. vi. 28) and Scales, refer to the horoscope of Augustus, his conception and birth[1].

Aspurgus to Rhescuporis I.

The assertion of Roman power by the forced marriage of Dynamis to Polemo, almost coinciding with the assumption by Augustus of the sole right to coin gold and the limitation of all other coining rights, is the starting point of a period in Bosporan history beset with curious difficulty due to the jealousy with which the Romans controlled the issues of the Bosporan mint. For the first few years it was absolutely closed: then in A.B. 289 = B.C. 9/8 there begins the series of dated aurei which continues almost uninterrupted until the ivth century A.D.; this would furnish a satisfactory chronological framework but for the fact that non until A.B. 377 = A.D. 80/1, save for two significant exceptions, do we find a full name and a king's portrait upon a gold coin[2]. Instead we have but monograms: ⚹ (Pl. vii. 1), A.B. 289—304 = B.C. 9/8 to A.D. 7/8; ⚹ (ib. 2), A.B. 305, 306 = A.D. 8/9, 9/10; ⚹ and the like (ib. 3), A.B. 307—310 = A.D. 10/11—13/14; ⚹ and the like (ib. 4), A.B. 311—334 = A.D. 14/15—37/8; ⚹ (ib. 6), A.B. 334, 335 = A.D. 37/8—38/9; then two aurei with the name Mithridates, A.B. 336 (ib. 10), 338 = A.D. 39/40, 41/2; afterwards ⚹ (cf. ib. 19), A.B. 342—357 = A.D. 45/6—60/1; ⚹ (ib. 22), A.B. 359 =

---

[1] Orêshnikov, ap. Giel, *Kl. B.* p. 12, and *Bulletin of the Tauric Record Commission*, xxxiv. Sym;pheropol, 1902, "Pythodoris and her house in the Pontic Kingdom"; he is largely indebted to Mommsen, *Ephem. Epigr.* I. p. 270, II. p. 250. W. v. Voigt, *Philologus*, lviii. (1899) p. 175 does not agree, and refers the scales to Tiberius, cf. Manilius, I. 507, iv. 548, and Housman ad loc.

[2] The table on p. 611 gives every year of the Bosporan era that appears on a coin during this period.

A.D. 62/3 and ⟨monogram⟩ (Pl. VII. 23), A.B. 365—374 = A.D. 68/9—77/8; the heads too rarely present recognizable features, though after Bertier-de-La-Garde's exposition (v. inf. p. 601) we may take it that they all represent Romans and not Bosporan rulers. ⟨monogram⟩ and ⟨monogram⟩ are certainly for Cotys and Rhescuporis, as dated inscriptions attest, unfortunately they do not exactly determine the accession of either, but when ⟨monogram⟩ was appearing upon coins an inscription mentions Aspurgus and uncertainties rise. The coppers have not even dates, those with ⟨monogram⟩ and ⟨monogram⟩ are quite puzzling, they do not bear portraits either : those with ⟨monogram⟩ and ⟨monogram⟩ are not all certainly contemporaneous with the gold that bears those marks. Mithridates and Gepaepyris appear in full upon coppers, but they are certainly as exceptional as that king's gold: Cotys and Rhescuporis use names as well as monograms, one gets round the law by an artifice, the other at last attains freedom to put his image and superscription on both gold and copper. The heads on the coppers with monograms are some help in checking the dates on the gold, being mostly inscribed Roman portraits. In one case (ib. 21) Nero allows not even a Bosporan monogram, just as he has his own on gold in A.B. 359 (ib. 22): occasionally we have heads of Bosporan rulers apparently defined by the monograms ⟨monogram⟩, ⟨monogram⟩, ⟨monogram⟩ and ⟨monogram⟩. This is all that the coins yield readily and certainly.

Before embarking upon conjectures it seems best to see what is definitely known from authors and from inscriptions, both sources of knowledge being very scanty just when the monograms are most enigmatic. The first name we meet is that of Aspurgus mentioned in no author; but a *servi manumissio* from Phanagoria tells us that he was reigning in A.B. 313 = A.D. 17, or else perhaps A.B. 325[1]. We have no certain knowledge of the limits of his reign, though the coins allow us to make a guess at any rate at the closing date.

On the base of his statue[2] were set out his titles, from which we know that he ruled over the whole Bosporan kingdom and right up to Tanais ; but Chersonese is not mentioned, for it had now regained its freedom, though somehow his name occurs in an inscription there[3]. We learn also that he was acknowledged by Rome (φιλόκαισαρ as well as φιλορώμαιος) and was called the son of Asander ('Ασανδρ(όχ)ου). Coins (e.g. Pl. VII. 20) and inscriptions[4] shew that he was father to Cotys; Tacitus and Petrus Patricius call Cotys brother to Mithridates VIII (III), so we have the names of two sons. It is at least possible that Gepaepyris was his wife (v. p. 601).

Dio Cassius (LIX. xii. 2) says that in 39 A.D. Gaius granted to Polemo the son (or rather grandson) of Polemo all his father's dominions. Later on (LX. viii. 2) he says that in 41 A.D. Claudius granted Bosporus to Mithridates, a descendant of the great Mithridates, and ceded to Polemo part of Cilicia in exchange. But we have the aureus (Pl. VII. 10) with an Emperor's head on one side and on the other Nike, the name of Mithridates in full and the date A.B. 336 = A.D. 39/40, and another with the date A.B. 338 = A.D. 41/2

---

[1] *IosPE*. II. 364, v. supra p. 591.
[2] App. 42 = *IosPE*. II. 36.
[3] *IosPE*. IV. 147.
[4] App. 44, 45 = *IosPE*. II. 32, 37.

to shew that he was exercising sovran rights long before the grant to Polemo was revoked[1]. We do not know the reasons for the Roman policy: perhaps Gaius, who had his intuitions, distrusted Mithridates, and the highly connected Zenonids took the opportunity of a change at Bosporus to urge a claim, which, though Polemo II does not seem to have gone to the country, brought him compensation nearer home. The coins of Polemo and his mother Antonia Tryphaena have nothing to do with Bosporus (Pl. vii. 8, 9)[2].

Besides the gold coins Mithridates issued coppers with his own head and name, and the club, lion-skin and quiver of Heracles and the trident of Poseidon on the reverse (Pl. vii. 11). Others have the head and the name of Queen Gepaepyris[3], which also appear on the obverse of coins like Pl. vii. 7 with a goddess in a calathos and veil on the other side.

These were numismatic audacities, no one else dared to put his full name directly on to a coin until leave was given forty years later, and they symbolized a revolt on the part of Mithridates against his position as a vassal of Rome, a position he felt unworthy of his great ancestry. The emblems of Heracles and Poseidon refer to a descent from them to which the later Bosporan kings laid claim[4], we do not know how it was traced. But it was of Mithridates the Great that his namesake was most proud and this pride became the inspiration of his life. If, as Latyshev supposes, what Petrus Patricius[5] says of Mithridates Iberus really applies to Bosporanus, and in giving him a brother and successor Cotys he seems to shew his own mistake, Mithridates disregarding his mother's advice really made preparations for war against the Romans and when their suspicions were aroused sent his brother Cotys to Rome to allay them. He however revealed the whole scheme and received the kingdom for himself, being conducted back by a force under Didius Gallus. Tacitus gave an account of all this in a lost book of the Annals; the end of the story which is preserved[6] recalls that of Satyrus and Eumelus.

Didius Gallus withdrew with the main part of his army and left Cotys, quite a young man, under the protection of Julius Aquila and a few cohorts. Mithridates was regarded as crushed, but he began to win over deserters and rouse the native tribes till he had sufficient force to drive the king of the Dandaridae (or Dandarii) out of his kingdom, also he made Zorsines, king of the Siraci, resume hostilities. So Cotys and Aquila made friends with Eunones, king of the Aorsi, who supplied them with cavalry. Aquila and his allies routed their enemy who could not make a stand at Soza in the country of the Dandaridae, because that tribe was not well disposed, but Zorsines attempted to defend Uspe in the country of the Siraci, a place set in a strong position beyond the river Panda and defended by wooden walls and earthworks. This was stormed and quarter was refused. The fate of Uspe struck terror into the Siraci and Zorsines made his peace with Rome, prostrating

---

[1] Giel, *TRAS.* vii. p. 225, Pl. vii. 62; v. p. 354, Pl. vi. 67; Bertier-de-La-Garde, *Trans. Od. Soc.* xxix. p. 177, Nos. 70, 71.

[2] In App. 43=*IosPE.* ii. 400, from Anapa, dated A.B. 338, the king's name has been erased. On the whole the scratches are more like Mithridates than Polemo, and so Stephani restored it. The erasure may have been due to the hatred of Cotys: Latyshev restores Polemo's name and

suggests on the strength of it that Polemo ruled on the Asiatic side and Mithridates on the European, but there is no real evidence for this; however the epithet φιλογερμάνικος would suit Polemo better.

[3] Burachkov, xxvi. 93.

[4] App. 54=*IosPE.* ii. 41.

[5] *FHG.* iv. p. 184, fr. 3.

[6] *Ann.* xii. 15—21.

himself to the Emperor's statue.   So the Roman force returned after coming within three days' journey of the Tanais.   On its way back some of the troops were wrecked on the Tauric coast and slain by the natives.

Mithridates could not trust Cotys (proditor olim, delnde hostis, cf. Pet. Patricius), and did not regard the guarantee of Aquila as sufficient.   He dressed the part of the suppliant king, prepared a suitable speech[1] and threw himself at the feet of Eunones.   Eunones raised the suppliant and sent envoys to Rome asking that Mithridates be spared the indignity of a triumph and the punishment of death.   Claudius having decided that the trouble and risk of so distant an expedition were too great[2], said that he was quite prepared to exact the due penalty of Mithridates, but. that he preferred to spare the conquered.   So Mithridates was brought to Rome where he was thought to have borne himself too insolently for his position, crying aloud so as to be heard by all, "I was not brought back to you, but came back : if you do not believe me, let me go and then see if you can. bring me back."   He lived at Rome until the time of Galba who had him executed for taking part in the conspiracy of Nymphidius[3].   All this is related by Tacitus under the year 49 A.D., no doubt the year that Mithridates appeared in Rome after his long struggle.   Cotys had been on the throne for more than four years, as we have a coin of his (with the monogram 𝕭𝕬𝕶) dated A.B. 342 = A.D. 45.

Ancient authors tell us no more about Cotys, but we have several inscriptions with his name.   Two are *servorum missiones* (cf. App. 43) and merely give us the dates 57 and 59 A.D. and tell us that like all his successors he bore the names Tiberius Julius[4].   On the base of a statue of his preserver Nero he is the first Bosporan king to proclaim himself "pious and high priest of the Augusti[5]," while an inscription on a fountain[6] claims that he has raised again the glory of his land and house, and holds all the sceptres of the Inachii (=Achaei).   In two mutilated inscriptions of Rhescuporis I (II), Latyshev has been able to restore the name of Cotys (which alone can fit) with all but absolute certainty, so shewing that his wife's name was Eun[ice] and that Rhescuporis was his son[7].

We do not know in what year Rhescuporis came to the throne and no author mentions him.   All we hear of the Bosporus at this time is that in A.D. 66 Herod Agrippa says that the Heniochi, Colchi, Tauri, Bosporans and peoples round the Maeotis are now kept in order by 3000 hoplites and forty

---

[1] *Ann.* XII. 18 : Mithridates terra marique Romanis per tot annos quaesitus sponte adsum : utere, ut voles, prole magni Achaemenis, quod mihi solum hostes non abstulerunt.

[2] c. 20 : sed disserebatur contra suscipi bellum avio itinere, inportuoso mari : ad hoc reges feroces, vagos populos, solum frugum egenum, taedium ex mora, pericula ex properantia, modicam victoribus laudem ac multum infamiae si pellerentur. A good summary of the disadvantage of punitive expeditions.

[3] Plutarch, *Galba*, 13, 15.

[4] *IosPE.* IV. 204, Kerch : *BCA.* XXVII. p. 38, No. 34 from Duzu Kale near Novo-Mikhailovka on the coast E. of Anapa, from which the stone was probably brought. It contains the first mention

of Jews in these parts, no doubt from the διασπορά in Asia Minor bearing out Kulakovskij in his review of *IosPE.* II. in *Journ. Min. Publ. Instr.* St P., May, 1891, p. 180 n. ; v. inf. p. 622, n. 1.

[5] App. 44 = *IosPE.* II. 32.

[6] App. 45 = *IosPE.* II. 37.

[7] *IosPE.* II. 355, Phanagoria, dated A.D. 71, on the base of a statue of Vespasian, κ[ύριω]ν τοῦ σύμπαντος Βοσσπόρου; *BCA.* XXXVII. p. 70, No. 7 :
[τὸ]ν ἐκ προγόνων βα[σιλέων βασιλέα μέγαν]
Τιβέριον Ἰούλιον Ῥησ[κούποριν, βασιλέως Κότυ-]
ος καὶ βασιλίσσης Εὐν[είκης (?) υίόν, φιλοκαίσα-]
ρα καὶ φιλορώμαιον, ε[ὐσεβῆ, ἀρχιερέα τῶν Σε-]
βαστῶν διὰ βίου καὶ ε[ὐεργέτην τῆς πατρίδος]
ὁ δῆμος Γοργιππέω[ν..................]
ρον τὸν ἴδιον εὐεργέ[την].

warships (cf. p. 523)[1], but these two inscriptions and two manumissions, one dated A.D. 79, the other, A.D. 81[2], belong to his time ; several more mention him as the father of Sauromates his successor[3].

In A.B. 377 = A.D. 80/1 the Bosporan rulers in the person of Rhescuporis obtained what they had been striving after for three generations, the right to put their names and portraits upon their coins. But we cannot exactly fix the year of his death, for A.B. 388 = A.D. 91/2 is the last year in which he coined, whereas we have no aureus of his successor Sauromates until A.B. 390 = A.D. 93/4.

Coins with monograms.

If we now turn back to correlate these few facts just outlined with the contemporary coins it appears that for the last half of the period we are not entirely at a loss and it is best to see what we can make of it before attempting the first half. The coinage with the name of Mithridates is the definite expression of his bid for more freedom if not for independence, of his pride in his divine ancestors and his regard for Gepaepyris, of whom more later : the dates shew that he exercised sovran rights during some three years A.D. 39/40 to 41/2 before his first defeat, but as no coin of ☒ (obviously Cotys) bears date before 45/6 it looks as if it took four years before Cotys was well on his throne: the next bears 48/9, leaving an interval which it is tempting to connect with the second resistance of Mithridates ending in A.D. 49.

Cotys, as might be expected, shewed great subservience to Rome. On coppers with his monogram we have mostly Roman portraits, Claudius and Agrippina (Pl. VII. 19), Britannicus, Nero and Poppaea[4], the latter with the epithet Σεβαστή granted in A.D. 62 and so the latest coin of Cotys, as no aureus is known after 60/1[5]. Still Bosporan likenesses do occur, his own, one marked with ☒ and one, a woman's, with ☒ apparently a posthumous honour paid to those rulers[6]. Also he found an excuse to put his whole name and his father's on to a coin by displaying his pride in the honours accorded him by the Romans, on the obverse the sella curulis, wreath and sceptre[7] labelled TEIMAI ΒΑCΙΛΕWC ΚΟΤΥΟC and on the reverse various arms and ΤΟΥ ΑCΠΟΥΡΓΟΥ (Pl. VII. 20). But Nero put an end to this and we have a solitary aureus with his monogram ☒ dated A.D. 62/3 (Pl. VII. 22) and answering to it a copper with nothing Bosporan at all (ib. 21) : this we can correlate with the presence of the Roman troops of which Herod Agrippa spoke. Buffer states were out of fashion: Claudius had annexed Thrace, in the following year (63) Nero annexed Pontus, reducing Polemo II to a small part of Cilicia: so he seems to have mediatized Cotys.

We cannot be sure that all this does not belong to the next reign which

---

[1] Josephus, *Bell. Jud.* II. xvi. 4 ; A. von Domaszewski, *Rh. Mus.* XLVII. (1892), p. 207.

[2] *BCA.* XLV. p. 10, No. 2; App. 46 = *IosPE.* II. 52.

[3] *IosPE.* II. 38, 39, 358 ; IV. 446.

[4] Burachkov, XXVII. 105, 111 : *BMC. Pontus*, XI. 14 ; 9, 13 ; 10—12 ; XII. 1.

[5] Koehne, *MK.* II. p. 226, claims one for A.B. 362

= A.D. 65/6, but Bertier-de-La-Garde, *Trans. Od. Soc.* XXIX. p. 163, rejects it.

[6] l.c. p. 162, Pl. II. 34, 30, 31 ; Bur. XXVII. 105 (= *BMC. Pontus*, XI. 13), 113, 106.

[7] Cf. coins of Juba II and Ptolemy of Mauretania, L. Müller, *Num. de l'anc. Afrique*, III. pp. 106, 129.

may have begun any time between A.D. 62 and 68/9. Rhescuporis seems to have decided at once for Vespasian, an aureus of the latter year with ⟨monogram⟩ bears that emperor's portrait and to him he probably owed his recognition as king, hence the laudatory inscription cited above (p. 598 n. 7) : we have three more aurei with the monogram of Rhescuporis dated A.B. 369, 370, 374 = A.D. 72/4, 77/8, but none from the time of Titus. Domitian must have regarded Rhescuporis with special favour, as instantly upon his accession his head appears on the reverse of an aureus and on the obverse he allowed the king to put his own bust and the inscription BACIΛEWC PHCKOVΠOPIΔOC. As the year A.B. 377 expired a fortnight after Domitian's accession (Sep. 13 A.D. 81), this is a remarkable example of the swiftness of the Roman posts, and the quickness with which coin-dies were sunk[1]. In A.B. 383 and 384 (Pl. VII. 24) appears the full name Tiberius Julius Rhescuporis but he soon reverted to the shorter style in which he was followed by his successors.

In copper he at first continued the types of Cotys with the arms and the TEIMAI (cf. Pl. VII. 20) and Nero's reverse (cf. ib. 21) : later he launched out into portraits, his own bust flanked by the club and trident on one side of a coin and his queen's on the other or both facing each other on the obverse, or else a full length shewing him seated on the curule chair and holding his sceptre (ib. 25) a new version of the TEIMAI, putting his foot on the neck of one of two crouching captives or again riding swiftly with uplifted spear (cf. Pl. VIII. 4) : further we have a view of a town gate with an equestrian statue over the arch (cf. ib. 2), and a reverse with Nike. All these point to successful wars with barbarians[2]. Two more of his coppers are used by Bertier-de-La-Garde[3], to support his view that this Rhescuporis was the son of Aspurgus and that the latter also bore the name Rhescuporis as well : on the obverse of each is the head of a long-haired king and BACIΛEWC PHCKOVΠOPIΔOC, on the reverse ⟨monogram⟩ and a female head wearing in one case a calathos (as inf. Pl. VII. 7) in the other a stlengis[4]; either of them would be a goddess or a Roman lady, perhaps Livia, in a goddess's attributes. He regards it as a coin rendering posthumous honour to the king's father, like those of Cotys mentioned above, arguing that you would not have a king's monogram on the same coin on which he had been allowed to display his full name and that we know from e.g. Pl. VII. 20 that a king could put his father's name in full : but there is nothing surprising in the use of an old die for the reverse after the whole name had been allowed[5] and we have good reason for thinking that Cotys not Aspurgus was father to this Rhescuporis[6], finally we have no real evidence that Aspurgus was called Rhescuporis at all.

This idea had originally been suggested by Burachkov to account for the monogram ⟨monogram⟩ known to belong to the time of Aspurgus : but if we are to guess at monograms I am inclined to see in ⟨monogram⟩ the same name as in

---

[1] General Bertier-de-La-Garde tells me Turkish ships cross from Constantinople in three days.
[2] Burachkov, XXVII. 121—131 ; *BMC. Pontus*, XII. 5—11.
[3] *Trans. Od. Soc.* XXIX. p. 164, Pl. II. 32, 33.
[4] *BMC. Pontus*, XII. 4.

[5] A stranger thing is a coin with BÃE on the reverse and the same monogram countermarked on the obverse. Giel, *TRAS.* v. Pl. VI. 60.
[6] This disposes of an interpretation of the monogram on Pl. VII. 25 as τοῦ 'Ασπούργου: it might be the date ΑΟΤ=A.B. 371=A.D. 74/5.

⚏ with the insertion of B for βασιλεύς: and it can hardly be chance that in ⚏ we can see ΑΠΡ three important letters of Ἀσπούργος: the addition of the Σ would introduce too great complications. So too it can hardly be a coincidence that the B comes just when there was a new emperor whose names Tiberius Julius were borne by all the successors of Aspurgus and most likely were adopted by him in connexion with the conferment upon him of the kingly title[1]. On the reverse of coppers, except on Pl. VII. 5, ⚏ accompanies a portrait which is probably Aspurgus: on the obverse appear first Tiberius and then Gaius with their superscriptions[2].

Again it can hardly be chance that in ⚏, a woman's monogram as we know from coins struck in her honour by Cotys (v. p. 599), we can see the characteristic letters of ΒασίλισσΑ ΓΗΠαίπυΡις[3], a name that we read upon the coins of Mithridates VIII, and only their mother could appear upon the coins of both brothers—the φιλορώμαιος mother of whom Petrus Patricius speaks. It looks therefore as if Aspurgus began by putting his simple monogram ⚏ on his coins in A.B. 307 and 310 = A.D. 10/11, 13/14, received the title of king from Tiberius in A.B. 311 = A.D. 14/15 and died in A.B. 334 = A.D. 37/8 leaving his wife Gepaepyris as regent until Mithridates came of age in A.B. 336 = A.D. 39/40. This minority raised the hopes of the Zenonids and led to Polemo II's empty claim. The monograms ⚏ and ⚏ kept the Λ as part of ΒΑσιλεύς, perhaps the top line is a survival from the Π in ⚏ .

I have hazarded the suggestion that Dynamis lurks in ⚏ indicating that she was the head of the Anti-Polemonian or Aspurgian party though she must have been very aged: but her rival Pythodoris also ruled at the age of sixty. Of ⚏ I have no interpretation: perhaps it belonged to an elder brother of Aspurgus; there may be a T in it accounting for the top line.

As to the portraits on these gold coins from A.B. 289 to 374 there can be scarcely any doubt but that they are meant to represent Romans and that very little attempt was made to secure a resemblance, though fathers and sons or very near relations are made somewhat alike: Roman officials would have demanded closer portraiture[4]. Until A.B. 310 = A.D. 13/14 we have the same face on the obverse: its disappearance after that year points to Augustus. Its companion on the reverse goes on one more year and has been called Agrippa. The next face on the obverse as it takes the place of Augustus is clearly Tiberius and persists not merely to A.B. 333 = A.D. 36/7, as we might expect, but to 335. The reason suggested is that on the reverse they took to putting the next heir to the Empire, first perhaps the younger Drusus, then from A.B. 321 = A.D. 24/5 a son of Germanicus, finally to be defined as Gaius. When the latter came to the throne, there being no obvious heir, they left the two heads as before, a precedent for the Emperor's predecessor or parent taking the obverse and himself the reverse. The two staters of Mithridates VIII

---

[1] So *IosPE.* IV. 203 mentioning Cotys, son of Ti. Julius, may as well be Cotys I as II or III: but it does not tell us anything. The style Ti. Julius is established for all kings except those known only by coins or imperfect inscriptions.

[2] B. XXVI. 84—88; *BMC. Pontus*, XI. 5, 6.
[3] Bertier-de-La-Garde, op. cit. p. 159, reads HP... or HPA....
[4] There are numberless views: I give Bertier-de-La-Garde's, op. cit. pp. 166—179.

have not been explained as on the first Gaius ought to appear, but both have the same head and it persists as that of Claudius on the regular obverses until A.B. 359 = A.D. 62/3, except that Agrippina appears for the one year A.B. 352, the first of Nero's reign. On the reverses we have Britannicus till 346 and then Nero. The ⵗ coins all have Vespasian on the obverse and on the reverse a purely conventional Titus, but Domitian appears on the first gold coin with a king's name, A.B. 377; from that year the Bosporan king occupies the obverse and the Emperor the reverse.

If we are at a loss with regard to the gold coins which do bear dates, even worse is the case of the coppers with the monograms ⵗ, ⵗ :
ⵗ occurs on not less than twenty varieties: the monogram (as almost always on Bosporan coins) is on the reverse and so in many cases is a numeral letter. The same applies to coins with ⵗ, save that there are only three varieties and all have numerals[1]: one has Δ, another, Pl. VII. 13, like the identical ⵗ coin (ib. 5), ⵏ, the third, Pl. VII. 12, unlike ⵗ's similar coin (ib. 18), I. Roughly speaking the size of the coin increases with the numeral it bears, so the numbers do not give dates but values presumably in chalci or lepta. Bertier-de-Là-Garde's inference is that ⵗ came first, produced several issues and then introduced the novelty of value-marks kept up by his successor ⵗ and by ⵗ under whom the reckoning by chalci soon gave way to that by *asses* practised in later times (v. p. 633). According to this ⵗ and ⵗ must have been contemporaneous with ⵗ, ⵗ and ⵗ and consequently, as two kings cannot fill the same state at the same time, these latter monograms must be those of officials regulating the coinage, and having in view the close relations between Bosporan and Roman gold we must pronounce these officials to have been Roman: but it is not clear that once value-marks were introduced they were never dropped, but were used

---

[1] Cf. Pl. VII. 12—18, *BMC. Pontus*, pp. 44, 45; Podshivalov, *Trans. Od. Soc.* XV. pp. 28—36; Burachkov (B.) XXIV. 11—26 and p. 226, No. 32; Giel (G.), *Kl. B.* II. 20; *TRAS.* V. vi. 59; Orêshnikov (Or.) *Mat. for Num. Bl. Sea Coast*, pp. 15—20; Bertier-de-La-Garde (BG.) *Trans. Od. Soc.* XXIX.

Publ.	Obv.	Rev.	Diam. in mm.
Coins with ⵗ:			
B. 11.	Sarapis.	Cornucopia, A.	14
B. 18.	Athena.	Dog.	15
B. 25.	Dionysus.	Cista mystica, B.	17
B. 22.	Ammon.	Uraeus.	18
B. 20.	Dolphin.	Monogram only.	19
Pl. VII. 14.	Athena.	Horse-head.	20
B. 13.	Lion, star.	Wreath, palm, Γ.	20
B. 14.	„	Monogram only.	20
G. *Kl. B.*	Perseus.	„	20
G. *TRAS.*	Youth's hd.	„	20
Pl. VII. 15.	Apollo.	Tripod, myrtle, Δ.	21
B. 16.	Demeter.	Ox-head.	21
Pl. VII. 16.	Poseidon.	Dolphin, E.	25
B. 21.	Zeus.	Eagle, ⵏ.	28
Pl. VII. 17.	Perseus.	Herm, palm, Z.	21

Publ.	Obv.	Rev.	Diam.
B. 24.	Hermes.	Caduceus, Z.	21
B. p, 226.	Athena.	Twined snakes.	25
B. 26.	Hermes.	Caduceus, Z.	27
Pl. VII. 18.	Helios.	Crescent, star.	30
Or.	Heracles.	Lionskin, club, bow-case, I, in myrtle-wreath, cf. Pl. VII. 11.	32
BG. I. 12.	„	„ without I.	32

Coins similar in style, no monogram; cf. B. 11, 24:

	Obv.	Rev.	
BG. II. 20.	Sarapis.	Cornucopia, A.	14
BG. II. 22.	Hermes.	Caduceus, B.	15
BG. II. 21.	„	„ Z.	20

Coins with ⵗ:

	Obv.	Rev.	
BG. I. 18;	Heracles.	Snake, apple-tree of Hesperides, Δ.	20
Or. *Cat.*			
Uvarov, p. 76.			
Pl. VII. 13.	Ares.	Trophy, ⵏ.	20
Pl. VII. 12.	Helios.	Crescent, star, I.	24

For "indications" of Pl. VII. 17 worn on crowns v. pp. 388, f. 285, 390.

continuously, and on this depends the comparative chronology suggested : also the monograms ⚉, 𝕂𝕅𝔼, 𝔸ℙ are similar to 𝔹𝔸ℙ, 𝔹𝔸𝕂, 𝔹𝔸𝔹 in application and execution, nor is there any change in the coinage as though with the appearance of the latter group a new authority had assumed control, so that it is unlikely that the persons represented by the former group stood in an entirely different relation to the coinage from that in which the kings 𝔹𝔸ℙ etc. stood.

The extraordinary variety of types on the coins of 𝔹𝔸𝔹 makes it hard to say that they point in any particular direction unless perhaps to Asia Minor, but we cannot see in this the influence of Pythodoris under whose tutelage Bertier-de-La-Garde would put both these mysterious kings. It appears to me that in these miscellaneous types a king who was limited in real authority even as regards the coinage of gold, tried to symbolize his pretensions and ancestry : Bertier-de-La-Garde[1] cites a parallel in Juba II of Mauretania, husband of Cleopatra Selene, whose position was very like that of a Bosporan king. He seems to have taken a pleasure in varying his coins, some with Latin, some with Greek, some with Punic inscriptions, and types recalling different divinities and the glories and cults of Africa and Egypt[2]. So 𝔹𝔸𝔹 hints at a descent from Poseidon (Pl. vii. 16) and Heracles (the coin with a reverse like Pl. vii. 11), ancestors of the later Bosporan kings, and also at a connexion with Mithridates VI, by putting Helios = Mithras with a Mithridatic profile and the star and crescent, the old badge of his house (Pl. vii. 18), Perseus, the eponymous ancestor of the Persians (Pl. vii. 17), Sarapis, the god of Sinope, Dionysus, whose name was adopted by Mithridates, though he has not dared repeat the most characteristic types used by the great king.

These Mithridatic reminiscences made Orêshnikov (l.c.) read 𝔹𝔸𝔹 as Βασιλέως Εὐπάτορος and assign the coins to Mithridates the Great[3] ; while those with 𝔹𝔸𝕄 he put down to Mithridates VIII imitating his great ancestor, pointing out that numbers 4 and 6 taken as regnal years would suit the part of his reign before he was dethroned and 10 his last bid for royalty[4]. The attribution to Mithridates VI is impossible on the ground of style (e.g. Pl. vii. 16 is nearer akin to vii. 11 than to the splendid issues of the great king) and the numerals 1—7, 10 on 𝔹𝔸𝔹 coins led me to attribute both series to Mithridates VIII, hence the position in which they appear on Pl. vii. This ground fails me, and though I do not consider it inconceivable that a *poseur* like Mithridates VIII may have used two monograms besides his whole name, adopting the surname Eupator but just lacking courage to put it at full length because that would be open defiance to Rome before he was ready, and may have chosen the many types setting forth the ancestry of which we know that he was proud, I fear that until inscriptions are discovered throwing light on the period between B.C. 16 and A.D. 14 we must give up hope of reading the riddle of these monograms.

---

[1] *Trans. Od. Soc.* XXIX. p. 150.
[2] L. Müller, *Numismatique de l'Afrique Ancienne*, III. p. 103 sqq.
[3] Imhoof-Blumer, *Porträtk.* p. 36 and Wroth, *BMC. Pontus etc.*, p. xxx. n. 1 agree.

[4] He cites from Chaudoir, *Corrections...à Sestini*, p. 70 a lost coin like vii. 12 but with ΚΛΑΥΔΙΟΥ round the head which would settle the matter: Bertier-de-La-Garde explains the inscription as a fake.

During this dark period some close connexion was formed between the Bosporan house and the royal house of Thrace. The Thracian names of Spartocus and Paerisades indicate too remote a link to account for the appearance on the Bosporus of the names Cotys, Rhescuporis and a century later Rhoemetalces[1], which go back generations in the Thracian dynasty. We do know of a link in that Pythodoris, second wife of Polemo I, married her daughter Antonia Tryphaena to Cotys V Sapaeus of Thrace and became regent of the country, but the Zenonids were only interlopers on the Bosporus and Antonia's son, Polemo II, never established his claim to it, so it would scarcely be through them that the Bosporan dynasty (*pace* Bertier-de-La-Garde l.c.) adopted Thracian names. If Gepaepyris was Thracian[2] she would be a more likely person. The descent claimed from Eumolpus (App. 54) shews pride in the Thracian connexion. I have referred to the probability that Aspurgus took the names Tiberius Julius on being granted the kingly title at the accession of the Emperor Tiberius.

Sauromates I and Cotys II.

Ti. Julius Sauromates I, son of Rhescuporis, reigned according to his coins (Pl. VIII. 1) from A.B. 390 to 420 = A.D. 93/4 to 123/4. His coppers are similar to his father's (v. p. 600 and Pl. VII. 19, 20, 25) only that upon some appears the head of the Emperor[3] or that of an Empress or goddess (cf. VII. 7 reverse). The superscriptions are sometimes extraordinarily ill written testifying to Bosporan ignorance of Greek[4]. A new variety of the gateway coin shews two towers, a kneeling captive and a tree or flames behind the arch (Pl. VIII. 2). The portraits of the king upon his large bronzes are very characteristic with his mild expression, long hair and prominent nose[5]. His inscriptions[6] give us his full title—he revives the style βασιλεὺς βασιλέων used by Pharnaces and perhaps by Asander—tell us of buildings undertaken for or by him, and shew that in his time Tanais was already re-established, but on the new site. The Latin inscription is a compliment from the colony of Sinope. He is the first to express upon inscriptions the claims to descent from Poseidon and Heracles that his father indicated upon his coins and Rhescuporis II[7] stated most elaborately. To this king's reign we must refer a revolt quelled by Trajan of which Jordanes speaks[8], if we are to believe in it at all. Pliny the Younger[9] tells us of envoys sent by Sauromates to Trajan.

Ti. Julius Cotys II, son of Sauromates, reigned from A.B. 420 to 429 = A.D. 123/4 to 132/3. In his first year his admiral defeated the Scythians[10].

[1] Bertier-de-La-Garde, op. cit. p. 186–8, well explains him as the representative of a younger branch whose founder received this name before the Thracians were mediatized in 43 A.D.

[2] So Tomaschek, *Die alten Thraker*, p. 51.

[3] Burachkov, XXVIII. 151–4.

[4] Orêshnikov, *Mat. for Num.* p. 21.

[5] Sauromates, son of Rhescuporis, must be the original of Sauromatus, son of Crisconorus, the enemy of Cherson in Const. Porph. *de Adm. Imp.* c. 53: the legend has no value as Bosporan history though some as Chersonian literature, v. p. 526.

[6] *IosPE.* II. [26, 38], 39, 40 (Latin), 352, 358, 401, IV. 202 (?), 446, *BCA.* XXIII. p. 46, No. 32 (=App. 47), XXVII. p. 37, No. 33 (?) from Partenit, probably brought there as building material.

[7] *IosPE.* II. 41(=App. 54) and 358.

[8] *Romana*, 267, Traianus...Bosforanos Colchos edomuit postquam ad feritatem prorupissent; perhaps a mere exaggeration of Eutropius VIII. 3, regem...Bosporanorum...in fidem accepit.

[9] *Epp.* LXIII, LXIV, LXVII.

[10] *IosPE.* II. 27, his only other inscription is IV. 421 = App. 48.

Phlegon of Tralles says that the Emperor gave him the crown and put Cherson under him[1]. Arrian in his *Periplus* (26 (17 H.)) is made to tell the Emperor that he extended his information to include the north coast of the Euxine in case he should wish to interfere in Bosporan affairs on the occasion of the death of Cotys which had recently occurred. Brandis[2] has suggested that the forger who added the second half of the Periplus introduced this local name in order to make a transition to his own work. But there is nothing unlikely in disturbances on the Bosporus at the time of Cotys's death as Rhoemetalces his successor does not seem to have been his son, but the representative of a younger branch, yet the dated aurei overlap by a full year[3].

The bronze coins of Cotys are much like his father's : new types present the temple of Jupiter Capitolinus with KA ΠE and the king's monogram 𝕭𝕬𝕶 within a wreath (Pl. VIII. 5). His gold coins and those of Rhoemetalces and Eupator are a good deal alloyed and the British Museum Catalogue even reckons them electrum.

Rhoemetalces and Eupator.

Ti. Julius Rhoemetalces, as his coins shew, reigned from A.B. 428 to 450 = A.D. 131/2 to 153/4 ; they are fairly continuous, but there is a curious gap between A.B. 434 and 439 (Pl. VIII. 6). In his second year he set up an inscription to Hadrian as τὸν ἴδιον κτίστην[4]. Later on he may have had some idea of making himself more independent, for twice the Chersonesans sent Ariston to him to discuss an alliance[5] and some cause of trouble arose between him and the Roman provincial authorities. However the Emperor Antoninus Pius sent him back to his kingdom[6]. His coppers present much the same types as those of his predecessors, without the new ones added by Cotys II[7]. O. Rossbach[8] supposes that a bust in the National Museum at Athens is a portrait of Rhoemetalces, but there are other possibilities.

The name of Ti. Julius Eupator shews that in spite of their Thracian names the Bosporan kings had not forgotten the Mithridatic tradition. His coins extend from A.B. 451 to 467 = A.D. 154/5 to 170/1 (cf. Pl. VIII. 7). Then follow three years without any issue ; these may be assigned either to Eupator or to his successor Sauromates or to an interregnum or struggle. Lucian makes one of his characters in "Alexander or the False Prophet" meet at Aegiali the envoys of Eupator journeying into Bithynia to fetch the yearly subsidy[9] and fare in their ship to Amastris. His inscriptions are all from Tanais[10] where there was much building activity in his time.

---

[1] καθυπέταξεν, ap. Const. Porph. *de Them.* II. 12; Steph. Byz. s.v. Βόσπορος ; v. sup. p. 524 n. 1.

[2] *P.-W.* III. p. 783, more at length, *Rh. Mus.* LI. p. 1. C. Patsch defends its genuineness in *Klio*, IV. pp. 68—75 : v. supra p. 24.

[3] *BMC. Pontus*, p. 61, Cotys, ΘKY = 429 A.B.

[4] *IosPE.* II. 33, other inscriptions II. 353 (=App. 49), 437. *BCA.* XLV. p. 9, No. 1 is a private dedication to Hadrian (?).

[5] App. 19=*IosPE.* II. 199, v. sup. p. 524.

[6] Iulius Capitolinus in *Script. Hist. Aug.* "Vita Antonini," c. 9, Rhoemetalcen in regnum Bosporanum audito inter ipsum et curatorem negotio

remisit. Brandis, *P.-W.* III. p. 784, translates *curator* by *Vormund* suggesting that Rhoemetalces was a minor under a guardian.

[7] B. XXIX. 179—190.

[8] Svoronos, *Journal Internat. d'Archéologie Numismatique*, IV. (1901), pp. 77—82, Pl. IV.

[9] c. 57, ἀπιόντας ἐπὶ κομιδῇ τῆς ἐπετείου συντάξεως, so Brandis translates, *P.-W.* III. p. 787, not paying tribute as P. C. Sands, op. cit. p. 135, says. Cf. infr. p. 608 n. 2.

[10] *IosPE.* II. 422 (=App. 50), 438, 439 ; IV. 447; the latter has a fine example of the Bosporan state mark, v. p. 317, f. 227, p. 318, n. 1.

The coins of Eupator are very uneven in workmanship, so much so that some rude specimens have been assigned to an unnecessary *Eupator II[1]. Eupator uses the coin types brought in by Cotys II (substituting his own monogram ⟨monogram⟩) as well as the ordinary ones[2].

Whether this points to his being more directly linked to him or no we cannot say: the mutual relations of Cotys II, Rhoemetalces and Eupator are unknown[3]. The next king Ti. Julius Sauromates II was son of Rhoemetalces.

Sauromates II, Rhescuporis II, Cotys III, Sauromates III.

After the three years' gap mentioned above the coins of Sauromates II run without any decided break from A.B. 471 to 507 = A.D. 174/5 to 210/11 (cf. Pl. VIII. 9). He is not mentioned by any author but appears in a good many inscriptions[4]. In the first he thanks Caracalla as a benefactor of himself and his kingdom: another (App. 52) speaks of him as having gained victories over Scythians and Siraci, received the submission of the Tauric land and made the sea safe for ships to go to Bithynia. Indeed the reign of Sauromates marks the end of a peaceful stretch in Bosporan history and the beginning of long wars with the natives; to this corresponds the way the quiet scenes depicted in the earlier catacombs (e.g. p. 313, f. 223) give place to combats in the later (pp. 314—319, ff. 224—230[5]). His coinage is interesting: besides continuing the types of Rhoemetalces[6] he issued a series of large coppers[7] of unusually good workmanship with the labours of his ancestor Heracles (e.g. Pl. VIII. 11). Other new types are those of the captive and trophy[8], the eagle displayed holding a wreath[9] and a figure of a goddess (Aphrodite Urania?) sitting on a throne crowned with a mural crown, holding the apple in one hand and a long sceptre in the other (Pl. VIII. 12, 14). Before her sometimes stands Eros[10]. This type survived in utter degradation upon the coins of later kings. A more important innovation was the substitution in some of his staters of very decided electrum for gold, an important step in a degradation which ended in the miserable coins of the later kings[11].

Ti. Julius Rhescuporis II son of Sauromates, king from A.B. 507 to 525 = A.D. 210/1 to 228/9, is usually considered to be the husband of the queen with the gold mask (v. p. 433). From his time we have many inscriptions mostly

---

[1] Koehne, *MK.* II. p. 313, cf. v. Sallet, *Zt. f. Num.*, IV. p. 309.

[2] Pl. VIII. 8; B. XXIX. 191—202.

[3] *BCA.* X. p. 29, No. 22 mentions a son of Rhoemetalces, Tib. Julius...Eupator or Sauromates we cannot say.

[4] *IosPE.* II. 34, 57, 357, 427, 428, 445 (=App. 53), *BCA.* XXXVII. p. 38, No. 2 (=App. 51), on the analogy of the last his name is probably to be supplied in *IosPE.* II. 402 (=App. 69) and certainly in II. 423 (=App. 52): II. 47 is doubtful, much more so *BCA.* X. p. 29, No. 22. In *IosPE.* II. 41, 43, 430—431 *bis*, IV. 194 he appears only as father to Rhescuporis II. His *tamga* (cf. p. 318, n. 1) adorns App. 52 and *BCA.* XL. p. 113, No. 112, v. p. 614, n. 2. *BCA.* XLV. p. 51, No. 5 at Chersonese seems to mention this king's warlike operations.

[5] Rostovtsev, *Bobrinskoj Miscellany* "Painting of the 1891 Catacomb," p. 127, n. 2.

[6] B. XXX. 218—227, XXXI. 250, 251.

[7] B. XXX. 230—238, marking a real reform of the copper currency, v. p. 633.

[8] B. XXXI. 252—254.

[9] Pl. VIII. 13: B. XXXI. 246—249.

[10] Rostovtsev, op. c. p. 150, n. 1, arguing that the figures, formerly described as Sarapis and Isis (v. supra p. 310), are really chthonian deities into whom the deceased is to be merged, suggests that on these coins we have the queen merged in a similar goddess and on those (B. XXX. 228, 229) which shew Heracles with club and trident crowned by Nike, the king merged in his divine ancestors: he compares the stele described on p. 304, n. 4.

[11] Taraktash hoard, A. Ch. Steven, *Bulletin of Tauric Record Comm.* XLIII. 1909, p. 99, as quoted by Latyshev, Ποντικά, p. 123, n. 1.

from Tanais where much was doing in his reign[1]. Two stones[2] witness to the gratitude of the citizens of Prusias ad Hypium : another[3] set up by the city of Amastris calls the king Philhellene, proof positive that he was a barbarian. His "aurei" are some of gold and some of electrum (Pl. VIII. 15, 16) ; the coppers mostly shew the king on horseback with a spear (type of Pl. VIII. 10) and the seated Aphrodite : a new and elaborate type[4] shews a trophy with supporters and a crouching captive below. The abundant coinage of Rhescuporis gives place in A.B. 524 to an issue of his son Ti. Julius Cotys III : in 525 both coined aurei reduced by 5 grn. probably thus raising funds for a civil war[5]. Cotys III's coins go on till A.B. 530 = A.D. 233/4 (e.g. Pl. VIII. 17).

After his father's death Cotys did not reign alone for we have coins (e.g. Pl. VIII. 18) bearing the name Sauromates (III) and dates from A.B. 526 to 529 = A.D. 229/30 to 232/3. Their names appeared together in an inscription of a society at Gorgippia[6], so presumably their relations were friendly. To Sauromates III is referred a hopelessly corrupt manumission[7], otherwise he is unknown ; Cotys is mentioned in several inscriptions from Tanais[8]. The degradation of the coinage now proceeded rapidly. Cotys III has "aurei" of gold, electrum and silver, Sauromates III of electrum and silver and perhaps even potin. Their coppers shew few types and poor design.

Later Kings.

However, worse was speedily to come. The coinage shews that the kingdom was fast declining and that divided rule produced its natural effect. Whether the division was effected peacefully we cannot tell ; but it is probable that, as in the Empire itself, mutually hostile claimants to the crown held different parts and tried to dethrone each other. Further the execution of the portraits is so poor that it is impossible to be sure to how many persons belong the various heads marked Rhescuporis. The regnal years are as follows. Coins with the name Rhescuporis appeared during the year A.B. 530 = A.D. 233/4 (Pl. VIII. 19), the last year of Cotys, and A.B. 531 = A.D. 234/5 the first of Ininthimeus whose coins (Pl. VIII. 20) go on till A.B. 536 = A.D. 239/40[9]. Then begin other coins marked Rhescuporis which go on without any considerable break until A.B. 572 = A.D. 275/6. There is a good deal of variety among the portraits on these coins but different writers put the change at different times : Mionnet and Sabatier take A.B. 550 = A.D. 253/4, for which year there seem no Rhescuporis coins, and just at that moment Pharsanzes strikes coins with the dates A.B. 550 (Pl. VIII. 21), 551 = A.D. 253/4, 254/5[10] : Orêshnikov[11] finds at A.B. 560 = A.D. 263/4 a new head and a better style (v. Pl. VIII. 22 and 23), leading off with a real gold aureus : whereas Koehne (l.c.) refuses to make any

---

[1] *IosPE.* II. 41 (=App. 54), 42, 43, 48, 429, 430 (=App. 55), 431, 431 *bis*, 446—451, IV. 194, *BCA.* XXXVII. p. 1, No. 1 : not all of them, e.g. II. 447 (=App. 56), mention him, the year number being sufficient dating : in II. 432, 453, IV. 433 he is given as the father of Cotys.

[2] *IosPE.* II. 43 and IV. 194 (from Esky-Krym, a new place for Bosporan inscriptions).

[3] ib. II. 42.

[4] B. XXXII. 284.

[5] Bertier-de-La-Garde, "Materials for...Stathmological Investigations," p. 87, n. 46.

[6] App. 57 = *IosPE.* IV. 433.

[7] *IosPE.* II. 54.

[8] *IosPE.* II. 432, 452 (=App. 58), 453, [455].

[9] B. XXXII. 316; Giel, *TRAS.* V. p. 360, says 535.

[10] Koehne, *MK.* II. p. 332.

[11] *Cat. Uvarov,* p. 113.

distinction; certainly the variation in style of Eupator or Sauromates II is just as great. This evidence may be interpreted according to taste. One and the same king may have been enthroned in A.B. 233, deposed the following year in favour of Ininthimeus, restored in 239, again driven out by Pharsanzes during the year 254, and re-established under more favourable conditions so that in a few years he could make improvements in the coinage and rule undisturbed till his death in A.B. 572 = A.D. 275/6[1], or again there may have been a whole series of shortlived princes bearing or adopting the same royal name and struggling with various rivals or rebellious subjects. This is what we usually find towards the end of an oriental dynasty. Certainly the appearance of Pharsanzes, as has been already remarked, coincides with the time when on the extinction (or rather effacement) of the old loyal dynasty, the Borani and Goths were allowed by upstart kings to use against Roman Asia the harbour and ships of Bosporus[2]. It is clearly useless to number these later Rhescuporids.

Ininthimeus (A.D. 234—239) apparently belonged to the old house, at least he used the names Tiberius Julius, but a different *tamga* ⇄ (v. p. 318, n. 1), on inscriptions at Tanais[3], the latest found on the site. Shortly after the town must have succumbed probably to the very movement of the barbarians that brought the Borani to the Bosporus. A Ti. Julius Rhescuporis has left us inscriptions from Panticapaeum itself[4], dated A.B. 546, 547 = A.D. 249, 250, and these tell us that he claimed the kingdom by hereditary right.

Evidently A.B. 572 = A.D. 275/6 must have been a critical year on the Bosporus. The date is borne by the last coin of the Rhescuporis series, by the whole issue of Sauromates IV (Pl. VIII. 24) of whom we know no more, and by the first coin struck by Tiberius Julius Teiranes whose series (Pl. VIII. 25) breaks off at A.B. 576 = A.D. 279/80, the latest from Taraktash (v. p. 606, n. 11). In his honour and that of his queen Aelia all the great men of the kingdom from Theodosia to τὰ Ἀσπουργιανά joined to set up a dedication to Zeus and Hera the Saviours[5], so he must have ruled on both sides of the strait.

Thothorses succeeded to Teiranes and we find his coins for most years from A.B. 575 to 605 = A.D. 278/9 to 308/9 (e.g. Pl. VIII. 26)[6]. In time he corresponds to the legendary Sauromatus son of Crisconorus in Constantine Porphyrogenitus. No inscription names Thothorses, but one dated A.B. 603 = A.D. 306 throws an interesting light on the career of a Bosporan in his reign[7]. One Sogùs son of Olympus after spending sixteen years in Roman territory where he bore the name of Aurelius Valerius Olympianus and rose to be

---

[1] Orêshnikov, p. 116.

[2] Zosimus, I. 31: Βορανοὶ δὲ καὶ τῆς εἰς τὴν Ἀσίαν διαβάσεως ἐπειρῶντο, καὶ ῥᾷόν γε κατεπράξαντο ταύτην διὰ τῶν οἰκούντων τὸν Βόσπορον, δέει μᾶλλον ἢ γνώμῃ πλοῖά τε δεδωκότων καὶ ἡγησαμένων τῆς διαβάσεως. ἕως μὲν γὰρ βασιλεῖς αὐτοῖς ἦσαν παῖς παρὰ πατρὸς ἐκδεχόμενοι τὴν ἀρχήν, διά τε τὴν πρὸς Ῥωμαίους φιλίαν καὶ τὸ τῶν ἐμπορίων εὐσύμβολον καὶ τὰ παρὰ τῶν βασιλέων αὐτοῖς ἔτους ἑκάστου πεμπόμενα δῶρα, διετέλουν εἴργοντες ἐπὶ τὴν Ἀσίαν διαβῆναι βουλομένους τοὺς Σκύθας, ἐπεὶ δὲ τοῦ βασιλείου γένους διαφθαρέντος ἀνάξιοί τινες καὶ ἀπερριμμένοι τῆς ἡγεμονίας κατέστησαν κύριοι, δεδιότες ἐφ᾽ ἑαυτοῖς τὴν διὰ τοῦ Βοσπόρου τοῖς Σκύθαις ἐπὶ τὴν Ἀσίαν· δεδώκασι

πάροδον, πλοίοις αὐτοὺς οἰκείοις διαβιβάσαντες, ἃ πάλιν ἀναλαβόντες ἀνεχώρησαν ἐπ᾽ οἴκου.

[3] *IosPE*. II. 433, 434 (= App. 59), [435].

[4] *IosPE*. II. 44, 45, 46 (= App. 60).

[5] App. 61 = *IosPE*. II. 29, v. p. 612: App. 62 = *IosPE*. IV. 211 probably belongs to this reign.

[6] Giel, *TRAS*. V. p. 360, makes him begin at A.B. 583 = A.D. 286/7 but there seems no reason to doubt the earlier years quoted by Koehne *MK*. II. p. 357: Orêshnikov, *Cat. Uvarov*, p. 118 raises no objection: Giel is sole authority for the year 605. Note the special *tamga* on his coin.

[7] App. 63 = *BCA*. X. p. 26, No. 21: cf. the σεβαστόγνωστος Roman knight in App. 60.

personally honoured by Diocletian and Maximian, and after passing through much tribulation returns to be governor of Theodosia and builds a προσευχή in fulfilment of a vow.

Rhadamsadius (Rhadamsades, Rhadampsadius) coined from A.B. 605 to 619 = A.D. 308/9 to 322/3 (e.g. Pl. VIII. 27)[1] thus overlapping with Rhescuporis the Last. Rhadamsadius is mentioned in two inscriptions[2], but both are imperfect beyond satisfactory restoration. One mentions Rhescuporis as well and Latyshev restores it as if it belonged to the time when the two kings reigned together, but the stone is lost and the reading unintelligible. Koehne gives coins of Rhescuporis the Last for most years between A.B. 608 = A.D. 311/2 and A.B. 631 = A.D. 334/5: Podshivalov[3] instances some with the date A.B. 600 = A.D. 303/4 at the beginning and A.B. 638 = A.D. 341/2 at the end and Imhoof-Blumer follows him in this[4], but the coins (e.g. Pl. VIII. 28) are so miserably executed that Orêshnikov[5] is quite right in doubting these figures. Giel (l.c.) after a new examination declares that his earliest coin is A.B. 615 = A.D. 318/9. The name is written in either nominative or genitive in endless ways; Giel[6] gives thirteen varieties. One of these misunderstood gave birth to a mythical king CVΓΓHC who has been finally disposed of by Giel[7].

Koehne has been followed by many other investigators in his endeavour to make out two dynasties during the latter part of the Bosporan kingdom. He makes Rhescuporis, Sauromates IV and Rhescuporis the Last the representatives of the old line and Pharsanzes, Teiranes, Thothorses and Rhadamsadius members of a foreign dynasty. But we cannot establish two lines of kings; each set is fairly complementary to the other and the overlappings, about A.D. 253/4, 272 and 318—321, are quite intelligible without such a supposition : the words of Zosimus do not necessarily imply it.

The series of coins which gives us each king's name and date fails us in 342 A.D. and the general idea used to be that the Bosporan kingdom soon came to an end and Panticapaeum was destroyed by the Huns[8].

In A.D. 362 envoys from the Bosporans approached Julian asking leave to pay tribute (annua complentes sollemnia) and live peaceably in their own territories[9]. Perhaps what they really wanted was help against the barbarians. Certain it is that there were movements of Goths and Huns passing from the Crimea to the Caucasian mainland in close neighbourhood to the Greek cities, but what destruction they wreaked was not fatal, for it is certain that the old population went on digging catacombs and using the Bosporan era and bearing Iranian names until the end of the vth century (v. p. 320), and probable that kings bearing the names of Tiberius Julius and more or less representative of the ancient line may have survived in the town until the centralizing policy of Justinian undertook their duties of government and defence.

---

[1] As to the first date Giel, *TRAS.* v. p. 359, says that what Koehne read as ЄX should be Ŀ X making 606. As to the later limit there exist several pieces with ΘIX but on one of them Giel has seen clear traces of an attempt to alter the die to BIX and so thinks the Θ in all cases a mistake, but Koehne, *MK.* II. p. 365, quotes at any rate 616 and 617.

[2] App. 64, 65 = *IosPE.* II. 49, 312[1] (p. 309).

[3] *Beschr.* p. 24, Nos. 75, 79.

[4] *Porträtköpfe*, Pl. v. 16 and p. 38.

[5] *Cat. Uvarov*, p. 119, but in "Coins of Cher. T., Kings of Bosp. Cimm. &c.," *Num. Misc.* II. Pl. I. 13, p. 47, he publishes with reservations one dated ΘAX = A.D. 342/3.

[6] *TRAS.* VII. p. 228.

[7] *TRAS.* v. p. 359.

[8] Mommsen, *Provinces*, I. p. 315.

[9] Amm. Marc. XXII. vii. 10.

M.

The main evidence for this is the inscription of Ti. Julius Doeptunes[1] in which the old Bosporan formulae are preserved untouched, except that the old invocation Ἀγαθῇ Τυχῇ is flanked with a cross, the epithet εὐσεβής comes before the rest, and the titles ἔπαρχος and κόμης applied to two officials concerned shew the influence of Christian Constantinople. Of the date only the unit Θ remains, but the ten looks like Ο and as in its general disposition the inscription is so like those of the earlier kings that in a time of change it cannot be separated from them by a very great interval, I should be inclined to supply Χ for the hundred and make the whole ΘΟΧ, A.B. 679 = A.D. 383.

The earliest dated Christian inscription has the year A.B. 601 = A.D. 304/5[2]. In 325 Cadmus Bishop of Bosporus signed the decisions of the council of Nicaea; later in the century no doubt Christianity became dominant. We have a cross[3] set up to a Deacon in the year A.B. 733 = A.D. 436/7 and there is the whole catacomb with its walls covered with psalms, prayers and responses dated A.B. 788 = A.D. 491 and others similar but undated[4]. Christian burials are concentrated in two regions, one spot in the Glinishche and one on the north slope of Mount Mithridates near the catacombs.

At the same time we must admit the presence of Goths even in the towns; for as Škorpil points out[5], we find them buried with their characteristic jewelry in these same Christian cemeteries and in catacombs hard by[6].

In the time of Justin (A.D. 518—527) says Procopius[7] the Bosporites who had been independent found it necessary to add themselves to the Empire. The Huns had lately utterly destroyed Cepi and Phanagoria[8] and they feared the same fate for Bosporus. Justinian tried to assure the peace of the Bosporus by supporting Grod or Gordas, a converted Hun, as prince of the neighbouring barbarians, but he infuriated his compatriots by melting down their idols and selling the metal in the city. Under his brother Mugel or Moagerius they rose up against him, slew him and attacked Bosporus where they slew the imperial officers. So Justinian had to send considerable forces and re-establish the imperial authority[9]. Presumably it was at this time that he rebuilt the fortifications that had fallen into decay[10]. From henceforward Bosporus has no independent existence. Sometimes it is subject to the Empire, sometimes to the Huns, later to the Khazars, but it does not keep the same individuality that Chersonese kept and there is not the same temptation to follow its history through the dark ages[11].

[1] App. 66 = *IosPE.* II. 49¹, p. 292.
[2] *Trans. Od. Soc.* XXII., *Minutes*, p. 59: +ἐνθάδε κατάκι/τε Εὐτρόπις χα ꝝ.
[3] Latyshev, *Inscr. Christ.* 86.
[4] Kulakovskij in *Mat.* VI.; *Röm. Quartalschrift*, VIII. pp. 49—87, 309—327, Pl. II, III; cf. supra, p. 320.
[5] *BCA.* XXIII: p. 31.
[6] e.g. MacPherson, Pl. V : von Stern *Trans. Od. Soc.* XX. p. 1; Pharmacovskij *Arch. Anz.* 1905, p. 60 = *CR.* 1904, pp. 71, 78, v. supra p. 385, where dishes with figures of Constantius afford some idea of the date.
[7] *de Bello Persico*, I. 12.
[8] Procopius, *de B. Goth.* IV. 5 : yet we find Phanagoria mentioned in the time of Justinian II; Theophanes (de Boor), p. 373; Niceph. C-politanus (Bonn), p. 46.
[9] Malalas (Bonn), p. 431 : Theophanes (de Boor), p. 175, v. supra, p. 532.

[10] Procopius *de Aedif.* III. 7, cf. Latyshev, *Inscr. Christ.* No. 98. This obligation fell on later emperors, e.g. Maurice App. 70 = *Inscr. Christ.* No. 99, and was carried out through imperial officials—no doubt the Bosporan dynasty was extinct.
[11] The history of Bosporus between the last Rhescuporis and Justinian is gradually brought out by a controversy between Latyshev and Kulakovskij: cf. Latyshev, *IosPE.* II. 49¹, p. 292; *CR.* 1882–8, p. 22; Kulakovskij, "Review of *IosPE.* II.," *Journ. Min. Pub. Instr.* May 1891, p. 181; *Mat.* VI. p. 24: *Röm. Quartalschrift*, VIII. pp. 49, 309 sqq. Latyshev, *TRAS.* V. p. 373; *Mat.* XVII. p. 59; *Inscr. Christ.* No. 98; Kulakovskij, *Vizantijskij Vremennik*, II. (1895), p. 198, III. (1896) p. 1 ; *The Past of Taurida* (Kiev, 1906), p. 55 sqq. See also Bertier-de-La-Garde, *Trans. Od. Soc.* XVI. p. 82. Brandis, *P.-W.* II. p. 786.

LATER KINGS OF BOSPORUS AND THEIR DATED COINS.

		A.D.	B.C.
Mithridates VI (I of Bosporus) Eupator Dionysus, coined BΣ—AΛΣ, A.B. 202–231, B.C. 96—67. (Machares)			110?–63
			79—65
Pharnaces, coined ΓΜΣ—ΖΜΣ, A.B. 243—7, B.C. 55—51.	A.U.C.		63—47
Asander, unrecognised. (Mithridates VII Pergamenus)	707/8—709/10		47—44
Archon, years of rule, 1—4	709/10—712/3		44—41
King, years of rule, 4, 6—10, 12, 14, 16—18, 20—25, 27—29	712/3—737/8		41—17/16
Dynamis (alone)	737/8 AΠΣ 281		17/16
(Scribonius)			15 (?)
Polemo I	740—		14—9/8 (?)

			A.D.	B.C.
Dynamis or Aspurgus (?)	Coins with 𝔐 ΘΠΣ-AYΣ, ΓYZ, ΔYΣ, ᏰYΣ, ΘYΣ, T, BT, ΔT		289—304	B.C. 9/8—A.D. 7/8
Aspurgus (?)	„ „ ᴋᴺᴱ	ET, ᏰT	305, 306	8/9—9/10
Aspurgus	„ „ ᴬᴾ and the like,	ZT, IT	307, 310	10/11—13/14
Aspurgus	„ „ ᴷᴬᴾ AIT, ΓIT, EIT—HIT, KT, AKT, ΓKT—ΔΛT		311—334	14/15—37/8
Gepaepyris (?)	„ „ ᶠᴬ	ΔΛT, EΛT	334, 335	37/8—38/9
(Polemo II)				(38—41)
Mithridates VIII.	Full Name	ᏰΛT, HΛT	336, 338	39/40—41/2
?	Coins with ᴮᴬᴱ ⎫			39 (?)—49 (?)
?	„ „ BΛ𝐌 ⎭			
Cotys I	„ „ ᴮᴬᴷ BΜT, EΜT, ᏰΜT, ΘΜT, NT, BNT—ZNT		342—357	45/6— ⎧Copper⎫ 60/1 ⎩till 62⎭
(Nero)	„ „ ᴺᴷ	ΘNT	359	62/3
Rhescuporis I	„ „ ᴷᴬᴴ	EΞT, ΘΞT, OT, ΔOT	365—374	68/9—77/8
„	Full Name	ZOT, ΘOT—ΔΠT, ᏰΠT, HΠT	377—388	80/1—91/2 (93)
Sauromates I		9T (?), Γ9T—H9T, Y—HT, IY—KY	390—420	93/4—123/4
Cotys II		KY—ΓKY, EKY—ΘKY	420—429	123/4—132/3
Rhoemetalces		HKY—ΔΛY, ΘΛY—BΜY, ΔΜY—NY	428—450	131/2—153/4
Eupator		ANY—ΔΞY, ᏰΞY, ZΞY	451—467	154/5—170/1 (173)
Sauromates II	AOY—HOY, ΠY, AΠY, ΓΠY—H9Y, Φ—ΓΦ, EΦ—ZΦ		471—507	174/5—210/1
Rhescuporis II		ZΦ—ΓKΦ, EKΦ	507—525	210/1—228/9
Cotys III		ΔKΦ—ΛΦ	524—530	227/8—233/4
Sauromates III		ᏰKΦ—ΘKΦ	526—529	229/30—232/3
Rhescuporis III		ΛΦ, AΛΦ	530, 531	233/4, 234/5
Ininthimeus		AΛΦ, BΛΦ, ΔΛΦ—ᏰΛΦ	531—536	234/5—239/40
Rhescuporis		ᏰΛΦ, HΛΦ—ΘΜΦ	536—549	239/40—252/3
Pharsanzes		NΦ, ANΦ	550, 551	253/4, 254/5
Rhescuporis	ANΦ—BNΦ, ZNΦ—ΔΞΦ, BOΦ		551, 552, 557—564, 572	254/5—267/8, 275/6
Sauromates IV		BOΦ	572	275/6
Teiranes		BOΦ—ᏰOΦ	572—576	275/6—279/80
Thuthorses		EOΦ, ᏰOΦ, HOΦ, AΠΦ—X, ΔX, EX	575—605	278/9—308/9
Rhadamsadius		EX—ZIX, ΘIX (?)	605—619 (?)	308/9—322/3
Rhescuporis		HX—ΘKX, ΛΛX, HΛX, ΘΛX (?)	608—639 (?)	311/2—342/3

Every known gold or silver coin of these Bosporan rulers from Pharnaces to Ininthimeus is noted with its weight in Bertier-de-La-Garde's "Materials for Stathmological Investigations," *Num. Misc.* II., and this table is in close agreement with his: he adds one to the numbers of the Rhescuporids (v. p. 600).

Officials of the Bosporan Kingdom.

We have already seen how the Spartocids at first ruled as archons in the Greek cities, then assumed the title of kings over various barbarian tribes and finally imitated the other rulers of their time and called themselves, at any rate in ordinary usage, kings of the whole Bosporus.   Considering their preponderance as evidenced by the absence of all mention of senate or people they can hardly be said to have had a constitutional position.   Mithridates introduced the purest orientalism and this probably characterized all his successors.

The growth of the king's title has been followed as it developed into the sonorous formula used by Rhescuporis II[1].   Even this did not express enough for subjects who address Sauromates II as ὁ ἴδιος [θεὸς] καὶ δεσπότης or σωτήρ[2], and Teiranes and his queen as οἱ ἴδιοι θεοὶ καὶ εὐεργέται[3].

The king was surrounded by his court and some of the administrators of the government bore titles derived from his household, having as usual developed out of his personal attendants.   After the time of Mithridates VIII the Bosporans seem to have dropped out of the social class of client kings, we hear no more of the ruling queens who are characteristic of the period of transition and probably a harem system was established[4].   Others of the official hierarchy bore territorial titles.   Latyshev[5] has given the general outlines of this organization pieced together from indications centuries apart in date.   But there is every reason to believe that the Bosporan kingdom was thoroughly conservative and the picture is probably right, it remains but to fill in the details which have come to light since Latyshev wrote.   The chief interest in the matter is that the Bosporan kingdom as a survival of Hellenistic states throws light on the manner in which such personal officers of the ruler, always the main officials of an Eastern state, passed into the organization of the later Roman Empire.

We have a list of the chief grandees in an inscription at Panticapaeum set up by them in honour of Teiranes and his queen Aelia[3].   They call themselves ἀριστοπυλεῖται "officers of the Sublime Porte", and include Menestratus prefect of the Kingdom (ὁ ἐπὶ τῆς βασιλείας)[6] and of Theodosia[7], Phannes commander of the Thousand[8] and prefect of the Aspurgiana[9], Phanes the chief secretary of state (ἀρχιγραμματεύς), Chariton the captain (λοχαγός)[10], Phidanûs formerly governor of the city (πρὶν πολειτάρχης), Leimanus actual governor of the city, Èuius and Eros former finance ministers (ἐπὶ τῶν λόγων), Psycharion actual finance minister, Alexander formerly private secretary (ἐπὶ τῆς πινακίδος), Menestratus under secretary of state (γραμματεύς), and perhaps Bardanes ἐπὶ τ(ῶν?) Παιρισάδου[11].   These state officials[12] with many private persons seem

---

[1] App. 54 = *IosPE*. II. 41.
[2] *IosPE*. II. 357, 358.
[3] App. 61 = *IosPE*. II. 29.
[4] A eunuch is commemorated in *IosPE*. II. 121.
[5] *IosPE*. II. Introd. p. liv.
[6] Cf. *IosPE*. II. 46 (= App. 60), 187, 363, 423 (= App. 52, 193 A.D.), 433, and *BCA*. XXXVII. p. 38, No. 2 (= App. 51), πρῶτος ἐπὶ τῆς β.
[7] Cf. App. 63 = *BCA*. X. p. 26, No. 21.
[8] χειλιάρχης, cf. *IosPE*. II. 41 (A.D. 193), 46

(= App. 54, 60), 357.
[9] Cf. *IosPE*. II. 431 (c. A.D. 220), 431 *bis*.
[10] Cf. at Phanagoria, *IosPE*. II. 363 and at Gorgippia, 402 (= App. 69), IV. 436 a, *BCA*. XXXVII. p. 44, No. 3.
[11] Reading l. 35, Ἰώδας [β'] · Βαρδάν(ης) Οὐ- ...π...ὁ ἐπὶ τ(ῶ)ν Παιρισάδου· Σ[τ]οσ- ά(ρ)[ακος] κ.τ.λ.: for Latyshev's text, v. p. 657.
[12] The ἐπιμηνίσαντες may have served as officers of the society, so too the γραμματεύς.

to have formed a religious society with Julius Chopharnes as priest. Other inscriptions mention ὁ ἐπὶ τῆς νήσου[1], ὁ ἐπὶ τῆς Ὀργιππίας[2], ὁ ἐπὶ τῶν ἱερῶν[3].

Clearly the country was divided into districts and their rulers were apparently little satraps. The west side of the strait was called the kingdom *par excellence*, the peninsula of Taman or perhaps its northern part about Fontan formed the island[4], the country between Phanagoria and Gorgippia was called τὰ Ἀσπουργιανά, perhaps ὁ ἐπὶ τῶν Ἀ. was a later name for ὁ ἐπὶ τῆς νήσου. Gorgippia as a frontier port at one extremity and Theodosia in a similar position at the other each had its own governor. Pluralism was allowed, for instance Menestratus has two adjoining prefectures. The officials went into retirement after holding office, none of them were appointed for life. Prominent families might have more than their share of office, e.g. Ulpius Parthenocles and Ulpius Antimachus were prefects of the kingdom and the island and very likely brothers[5]. As to the time when these offices came into being, ὁ ἐπὶ τῆς νήσου is mentioned in the time of Aspurgus and the others probably go back to the same period.

The court officers (οἱ βασιλικοί?)[6] were as follows : ὁ ἐπὶ τῆς αὐλῆς[7], the ἀρχικοιτωνείτης[8], the κραβάτριος[9], maybe the same or his underling, ὁ ἐπὶ τῆς πινακίδος[10] apparently the king's private secretary, and ὁ περὶ αὐλὴν γα[ζοφύλαξ], if rightly restored, the court treasurer[11].

The πολείταρχαι of Panticapaeum were presumably presidents of the municipality nominated by the crown like the *gradonachalnik* of certain Russian towns. Phanagoria or rather Agrippias Caesarea may have preserved special privileges even after its reduction by Pharnaces, it seems to have treated directly with Rome in a surprising manner[12]. Its magistrates are called Archons in 307 A.D.[13] : its Demos is mentioned in the time of Dynamis[14] and in the IInd century A.D. a Demos and perhaps a Boule too[15] : we also meet with the titles of λοχαγός[16] and ὁ ἐπὶ τῶν ἱερῶν[3].

So too we learn that the Demos survived at Gorgippia in the time of Cotys I[17] ; here besides the governor, who was no doubt nominated by the king, were ἐνκυκλίων οἰκονόμοι and ἱερῶν οἰκονόμοι[18]. The ὀρφανοφύλαξ[19] was also probably in the service of the state rather than an officer in a society (v. pp. 624, 625) and the same applies to the Gymnasiarch[20], who may have been fulfilling a liturgy rather than practising a profession.

However ὁ ἐπὶ τοῦ παιδαγωγίου at Panticapaeum was surely head of a state school[21]. Minor officials were Soracus who collected fines (δικῶν πράκτωρ)[22],

[1] *IosPE*. II. 36 (=App. 42), 254 (130 A.D.), 359.
[2] *IosPE*. IV. 434 ; *BCA*. XXIII. p. 46, No. 32 ; XXXVII. p. 38, No. 2 (=App. 47, 51).
[3] At Phanagoria, *IosPE*. II. 352, 353 (=App. 49), A.D. 151 : at Gorgippia, IV. 434.
[4] Cf. Ps.-Scymnus, l. 891. Denys Perieg. l. 549.
[5] v. p. 318, *IosPE*. II. 26.   [6] *IosPE*. IV. 359.
[7] v. p. 302, f. 215 ; *IosPE*. II. 48, 65, 342 ; *BCA*. X. p. 32, No. 24, A.D. 214.
[8] *IosPE*. II. 428, A.D. 192.
[9] *IosPE*. II. 297, κραβατάριος, *BCA*. X. p. 65, No. 68, 140 A.D.
[10] *IosPE*. II. 29, 49[1] (=App. 61, 66), 131.
[11] *IosPE*. IV. 202, c. 100 A.D. As uncertain is β]ασιλικὸν ταμ[ίαν at Taman, *Trans. Od. Soc*,

XXVIII. *Minutes*, p. 24.
[12] *CIL*. VI. 5207 found at Rome : Ἥδυκος Εὐόδου/ πρεσβευτὴς Φανα/γορειτῶν τῶν κα/τὰ Βόσπορον.
    Ἀσποῦργος Βιομ/άσου υἱὸς ἑρμηνε/ὺς Σαρματῶν Βω/σπορανός.
[13] *IosPE*. II. 363.
[14] App. 41=*IosPE*. II. 356.
[15] *IosPE*. II. 359, 360.   [16] *IosPE*. II. 363.
[17] *BCA*. XXXVII. p. 70, No. 7 ; v. p. 598, n. 7.
[18] Both in App. 51=*BCA*. XXXVII. p. 38, No. 2 ; cf. *IosPE*. IV. 434, for the latter and ὁ ἐπὶ τῶν ἱ.
[19] *IosPE*. IV. 434 ; cf. *BCA*. XXXVII. p. 46, No. 7.
[20] *IosPE*. II. 403.
[21] *BCA*. XIV. p. 117, No. 39.
[22] v. p. 319 ; *IosPE*. IV. 342.

and the interpreters ἑρμηνεῖς[1] under a chief mentioned on a building at Taman[2]. The ἐπιμεληταί[3] often mentioned as carrying out particular tasks were chosen *ad hoc* and were not as such regular magistrates: ἔπαρχος and κόμης (App. 66) were probably Roman titles not Bosporan offices.

Army and Fleet.

The military forces of the kingdom had always to be kept efficient. Many are the epitaphs of Bosporans who fell in the continuous struggle against the surrounding tribes. Their ordinary equipment is shewn on frescoes and grave reliefs (v. pp. 301—304, 313—319, ff. 214—216, 218, 223—225, 227, 230) but there was a body of Bosporans armed in Roman fashion[4]. We cannot discern their organization: there were chiliarchs[5], λοχαγοί[6], occurring in all three towns, they may be commanders of local forces. At Gorgippia there was also a ταγμα]τάρχης, if that is right[7], and στρατηγοί[8]. At Panticapaeum a special part of the cemetery was set apart and marked στρατηγῶν[9], and near by was buried a στρατηγὸς Τυκανδειτῶν[10]. The native arm was stiffened with Roman troops at any rate during the IInd century A.D.[11] Apparently they consisted not of legionaries but of auxiliaries. We have the gravestones of privates in the Cyprian cohort[12] and the princeps and centurion of the Thracian cohort[13]. There was also a σπείρη Βοσποριανὴ πρώτη[14].

The fleet was almost as important as the army. We hear of Spartocus II and Paerisades asking for Athenian crews (supra, p. 575), the services rendered by Eumelus in putting down piracy have been duly chronicled and the later kings boast of similar exploits. The northern dominion of Mithridates was founded on sea-power and his admiral Neoptolemus won a battle in the strait itself. Asander's success would seem to have been due to a naval victory, at least a ship's prow occurs on all his coins (Pl. VI. 24—26), and we find his ναύαρχος setting up a monument to Poseidon Sosineos and Aphrodite Nauarchis, deities singularly nautical[15]. So in the time of Cotys II the admiral Tryphon celebrates a victory over the Scythians[16].

Magistrates of Tanais.

We do not know what may have been the exact relations between Tanais and the Bosporan kingdom or its internal constitution before its destruction by

[1] *IosPE.* II. 86², p. 296; Aspurgus in *CIL.* VI. 5207, v. p. 613, n. 12, was probably in Roman service.
[2] *BCA.* XL. p. 112, No. 28, *Tamga* of Sauromates II (v. p. 655), Δι' ἐπιμελείας Ἡρα/κᾶ Ποντικοῦ ἀρχερ/μηνέως Ἀλανῶν/έ[ν τῷ] εφ' (=A.D. 208).
[3] *IosPE.* II. [33], 48, 49, 49¹ (=App. 65, 66), 50, 312, 353 (=App. 49), cf. n. 2.
[4] Tacitus, *Ann.* XII. 16, cf. Arrian, Ἔκταξις κατ' Ἀλανῶν, 3 where they come after the Italians and Cyrenaeans. Gattion σπειραρχής; *IosPE.* IV. 293, was probably officer in such a corps not as Poland, *Gesch. d. gr. Vereinswesen* (v. p. 620, n. 5), pp. 153, 359 says, the head of a band of mystics: so too the men with native names and the title *princeps*, *IosPE.* II. 28, 278, 182², p. 303.
[5] *IosPE.* II. 29, 41, 46 (=App. 61, 54, 60), Phanagoria, 357.

[6] Panticapaeum, *IosPE.* II. 29, Phanagoria, 363; Gorgippia, II. 402 (=App. 69), IV. 436 a; *BCA.* XXXVII. p. 44, No. 3.
[7] *IosPE.* IV. 431, perhaps πολει]τάρχης.
[8] *IosPE.* II. 404; *BCA.* XXXVII. p. 38, No. 2= App. 51.
[9] *BCA.* III. p. 33, No. 1. [10] *IosPE.* IV. 297.
[11] v. Rostovtsev, *Journ. Min. Pub. Instr.,* St. P., March, 1900, p. 144; cf. *BCA.* x. p. 14.
[12] *IosPE.* II. 293; *BCA.* III. p. 39, No. 5; cf. Cichorius in *P.-W.* IV. s.v. *cohors,* p. 277.
[13] *IosPE.* II. 290; cf. Cichorius, l.c. p. 341.
[14] Ditt. *Inscr. Orientis,* 489; *Olympia,* v. p. 538 No. 447; cf. Cichorius, l.c. p. 255. A second cohort is mentioned *CIL.* X. 270* but seems doubtful.
[15] *IosPE.* II. 25 (=App. 39).
[16] *IosPE.* II. 27.

Polemo[1], but the town was rising again under Sauromates[2], and from the time of Eupator and his successors we have several inscriptions recording how various officials made restorations of towers, walls, a gate, a fountain and an agora. The settlement consisted of two communities distinguished as Ἕλληνες καὶ Ταναεῖται[3], each with its head, the Hellenarch[4] and the Archon of Tanais (App. 52) or Ταναειτῶν[5]. This last office appears in commission in App. 55 which mentions four or five men. This double character is also indicated by the custom of speaking of benefits conferred τῇ πόλει καὶ τοῖς ἐμπόροις (e.g. App. 55), but it is not clear which corresponds to which, nor whether as places ἡ πόλις and τὸ ἐμπόριον were distinct or no.

Supreme over both communities and their magistrates was the royal Legate[6]: he was often one of the great officers of the kingdom, the grand chamberlain (App. 52), the prefect of the Aspurgiana[7], the prefect of the kingdom[8], but sometimes he was chosen from the Tanaites, e.g. Chophrasmus son of Phorgabacus, Legate in A.D. 236 (App. 59), appears in several lists of private citizens.

In App. 52 we have apparently four στρατηγοὶ τῶν πολειτῶν as well as the archon of Tanais and the Hellenarch. Minor officers were the διάδοχος (App. 59) and the revenue officer, but he may have been employed in the kingdom rather than in the town as he is called Hellenarch late revenue officer[9].

The architects and ἐπιμεληταί[10] hardly count as public officials. They were probably chosen for each separate job, though the architect Aurelius Antoninus[11] evidently got most of the town's work.

Cults.

The religious history of the Bosporan kingdom is especially interesting in its later stages. A Graeco-Iranian population in the presence of a Jewish ferment developed a syncretistic popular religion organized in private societies which seem more completely than in the Empire to have superseded the hierarchies of the old Hellenic gods. The names of these survive in official documents of the latest period but their personalities seem faded and the combinations of deities which occur and the epithets applied to them shew a pantheistic tendency. Somehow it seems quite natural that the Hellenic religion should not have flourished in a country in which the bay and myrtle, so interwoven with their cult, could not be made to grow in spite of efforts made by Mithridates and others definitely for the sake of ritual needs[12].

Of the old Hellenic gods Zeus did not apparently attract the worship of the Bosporans. There is a dedication to Zeus γενάρχης made by one of the

---

[1] v. p. 594; Strabo, XI. ii. 3, 11.
[2] *IosPE.* IV. 446.
[3] *IosPE.* II. 428.
[4] *IosPE.* II. 423 (=App. 52), 427, 428, 430 (=App. 55)—432, 434 (=App. 59).
[5] *IosPE.* II. 427.
[6] ὁ πρεσβευτής, *IosPE.* II. 422, 430 (=App. 55), 431, 431 *bis*, 433, 434 (=App. 59), 435, IV. 447, called ὁ πρεσβεύσας II. 428 and ὁ ἐκπεμφθεὶς ὑπὸ τοῦ

βασιλέως εἰς τὸ ἐμπόριον, App. 52.
[7] *IosPE.* H. 431, 431 *bis*.
[8] *IosPE.* II. 433.
[9] *IosPE.* II. 432 πρὶν προσοδικός.
[10] *IosPE.* II. 427, 428, 430 (=App. 55), 431, 431 *bis*, 434 (=App. 59).
[11] *IosPE.* II. 429, 430, 433, 434.
[12] Theophrastus, *de Plantis*, IV. v. 3; Pliny, *NH.* XVI. 137 (59).

kings about the Christian era[1] and a few coins bear his head[2]. The great inscription in honour of Teiranes[3] is addressed by a religious society under a priest to Zeus Σωτήρ[4] and Hera Σώτειρα but this is hardly the personal Zeus. In this rather general sense he is joined with Aphrodite and Ares at Tanais[5], and in the pagan formula for the manumission of slaves[6] he is called as a witness together with Ge and Helios. The head of this latter appears on a coin of Gorgippia (Pl. IX. 22) and on two of 𝔅𝔄𝔈 and ᗷᗩᐱ (Pl. VII. 12, 18): this seems merely personal to these rulers.

Poseidon was the patron of the gild of shipowners at Gorgippia where he had a temple[7], otherwise he was regarded less as a god than as an ancestor of the royal house: as such his name appears in the genealogical boasts of the later kings[8], and Sauromates II put on his coins a figure combining his attributes with those of Heracles[9]. As Σωσίνεος he obtains with Aphrodite Nauarchis a dedication from Asander's admiral[10], and appears on coins which may be referred to that king (Pl. V. 28, VI. 12, 13; also VII. 16).

The chief deity of ancient Panticapaeum was Apollo especially with the epithet Hietros[11], his priest is the only one regularly mentioned in inscriptions. The supposition has already been mentioned that the Greek name of Panticapaeum was Apollonia because of the coins marked ΑΠΟΛ (v. p. 628, and Pl. IX. 10): these early coins also sometimes bear the head of Apollo[12]. He was also called Phoebus[13]. Apollo was worshipped at Phanagoria where he may have been patron of the games, at least Mestor makes his dedication to him[14] ἀγωνοθετήσας. Here too he bears the epithet Hiatros[15]. In later times there was an Apollo ἀτελής, the infinite, at Dioclea perhaps a suburb of Phanagoria[16], and at Tanais Apollo received a dedication[17]. His head is common upon coins of the 1st century B.C. Apparently he and his tripod were Mithridatic types[18].

Hermes is not directly mentioned in inscriptions but the great games at Gorgippia were Hermaea[19]. His head only occurs on 𝔅𝔄𝔈 coins[20]: his figure is common on the walls of "catacombs" in company with Calypso (v. pp. 309—311, 319—321).

Dionysus has one dedication made to him simply[21], and another[22] under the

[1] *IosPE.* IV. 200.
[2] Burachkov, XXII. 161—167; XXIV. 21, 22 B̊ÆE.
[3] App. 61 = *IosPE.* II. 29.
[4] There are a few *graffiti*: ἄμ]φωτις Διὸς Σωτήρ[ος from Kerch, *Arch. Anz.* 1910, p. 209; ἱερ]ὸς Διὸς Φιλίου, ib. 1908, p. 171, and Τίβης Διὶ Πατρῴῳ καὶ Ἴτης, ib. 1907, p. 139.
[5] App. 52 = *IosPE.* II. 423.
[6] *IosPE.* II. 54, 400 = App. 43.
[7] App. 51 = *BCA.* XXXVII. p. 38, No. 2; perhaps App. 69 = *IosPE.* II. 402.
[8] *IosPE.* II. 41 (= App. 54), 358, 361.
[9] B. XXX. 228, 229, v. p. 606: his trident appears on many royal coins, e.g. Pl. VII. 11, VIII. 6.
[10] App. 39 = *IosPE.* II. 25; the combination of god and goddess finds a close parallel at Mylasa, Π. Ἀσφάλειος and Ἀ. Εὔπλοια, *P.-W.* s.v. Aphrodite, I. p. 2755.
[11] *IosPE.* II. 6 (= App. 27), 10, 15 (= App. 35),

supra, p. 477 and p. 581; Ct I. I. Tolstoi, *Journ. Min. Publ. Instr.* St P., Jan. 1904, Class: Sect. pp. 1—15, "The Cult of Apollo on the Bosporus and at Olbia"; Roscher, I. p. 433; Farnell, *Cults*, IV. pp. 233, 409.
[12] B. XIX. 25 and 48.
[13] In verse, v. supra, p. 577; Ἀπόλλων Κυλιάνιος, *IosPE.* IV. 407, is probably a man's name and patronymic, so Škorpil, *BCA.* XL. p. 115 quoting an amphora-stamp with the same genitive.
[14] *IosPE.* II. 345.   [15] *IosPE.* II. 348.
[16] *IosPE.* II. 351.
[17] App. 50 = *IosPE.* II. 422.
[18] Panticapaeum, Pl. V. 24—27, VI. 2—6, 9, 11; B. XX. 98—100, XXI. 101—143, XXII. 144—151; Phanagoria, Pl. IX. 16—18; B. XXIII. 12—18 b; Gorgippia, Pl. IX. 23, 24; B. XXIII. 5 c: B̊ÆE, Pl. VII. 15.
[19] *IosPE.* IV. 432.
[20] B. XXIV. 23, 24, 26.
[21] App. 37 = *IosPE.* II. 18.
[22] *IosPE.* IV. 199, IV C. B.C.

strange epithet ἀρείῳ; no doubt he was honoured in the theatre mentioned by Polyaenus (v. xliv. 1). Mithridates called himself Dionysus, so no wonder the god's head appears on many coins which may be referred to his time[1].

Ares had a temple and statue at Panticapaeum restored by a Sauromates[2], he is also mentioned in a Tanais inscription[3]. He occurs upon coins of ΚΑΡ and ΒΑΜ (Pl. vii. 5, 13).

Asclepius appears upon one inscription[4]. It was in his temple at Panticapaeum that his priest Stratius dedicated the bronze vessel that had been burst by the frost to the standing wonder of the Greeks[5]; he figures on no coin[6].

Heracles received a dedication on each side of the strait[7]. His head appears on coins of Leucon after an Alexander model (Pl. vi. 16) and in another type on later coins of Panticapaeum[8]: his club and lion-skin adorn those of ΒΑΕ and Mithridates VIII and his club alone issues of many subsequent kings (v. p. 633 and Pl. vii. 11, viii. 7). He is claimed as an ancestor by Sauromates I[9] and Rhescuporis II[10]. Sauromates II put all his labours on his coins[11].

Quite unexplained so far are the deities to whom Comosarye makes her dedication[12] ἰσχύρωι θειωῖ Σανέργει καὶ Ἀστάραι. Mr S. A. Cook, late Fellow of Gonville and Caius College[13], to whom I applied for help under the impression that at any rate Ἀστάρα was clearly Semitic and a form of 'Ishtar, Astarte, would not allow even so much; the Phoenician form always has the second *t*, the Aramaic changes away the *s*, e.g. Atargatis, and there is no possibility of the Ethiopic form which would agree occurring here: but he hardly allows enough for the Greek distortion of loan-words[14], and I still dare suppose Astara a form of Astarte: so she becomes almost indistinguishable from Aphrodite Apature herself; and if we remember that in Strabo's story[15] Heracles had his part in the deceit which she used towards the giants, we might see in the strong god Sanerges such a deity as the East loved to join with Astarte and the West usually identified with Heracles. In Sanerges may lurk the names of the Babylonian deities San or Nergal or even both combined[16].

From Asia Minor came Mên[17] who appears in the ist century B.C. upon coins of Panticapaeum, Phanagoria and Gorgippia. Probably[18] his presence here is in connexion with the star and crescent badge of Mithridates. Reinach

---

[1] Panticapaeum, Pl. vi. 8 and a full length figure with lioness and thyrsus on the large Mên coins vi. 10: Phanagoria, B. xxiii. 24 *b* and the uncertain coins, Pl. ix. 21, cf. Giel, *Kl. B.* Pl. iv.
[2] *IosPE.* ii. 47.
[3] App. 52 = *IosPE.* ii. 423.
[4] *IosPE.* ii. 30, dedicating a table.
[5] Strabo, ii. i. 16.
[6] B. xxiv. 22 is Ammon, *BMC. Pontus*, p. 44.
[7] *IosPE.* ii. 24, 350.
[8] B. xxii. 181, 182; also Theodosia, v. p. 559.
[9] *IosPE.* ii. 358.
[10] App. 54 = *IosPE.* ii. 41.
[11] e.g. Pl. viii. 11; B. xxx. 230 sqq.; Giel, *TRAS.* v. Pl. vii. 74—77.
[12] App. 30 = *IosPE.* ii. 346.
[13] I offer him my best thanks.
[14] The loss of the *t* in Greek may be paralleled by its loss in Hamilcar, cf. מלקרת: and there does

occur a later Babylonian form אסתרא Eṣtrā with an Aramaic termination, as used by Syrians and Mandaites, Nöldeke, *Encycl. Bibl.* ii. p. 1404 s.v. Esther.
[15] Strabo, xi. ii. 10: Ἐτυμολογοῦσι δὲ τὸ ἐπίθετον τῆς θεοῦ μῦθόν τινα προστησάμενοι, ὡς, ἐπιθεμένων ἐνταῦθα τῇ θεῷ τῶν Γιγάντων, ἐπικαλεσαμένη τὸν Ἡρακλέα κρύψειεν ἐν κευθμῶνί τινι, εἶτα τῶν Γιγάντων ἕκαστον δεχομένη καθ᾽ ἕνα τῷ Ἡρακλεῖ παραδιδοίη δολοφονεῖν ἐξ ἀπάτης.
[16] The combination of the two names Sanerges and Astara is curiously like the names of two otherwise unknown deities שנגלא ואשירא in an Aramaic inscription at Teima in N. Arabia, *C. I. Semit.*, Pt. ii. Tom. i. No. 113, l. 16 kindly pointed out to me by Professor Bevan. We have learnt nothing certain since Koehler published his *Dissertation* in 1805.
[17] *HN.*² p. 281 he is called Mithras.
[18] Pl. vi. 10, B. xxii. 179, Giel, *Kl. B.* Pl. iv. 6, B. xxiii. 6 *c.*

M.

calls by his name the dancing terra-cotta figures in Phrygian costume (v. pp. 346, 368).

Another Asiatic deity who occurs in terra-cottas is Mithras (ib.). Mithridates does not seem to have sought to spread his ancestral cult outside Cappadocia. We cannot put a name to the "Great God" at Gorgippia (v. p. 566).

As to other gods who only occur on coins there is no reason to take this as evidence of special cult. Pan whose head appears on most of the autonomous coins of Panticapaeum (and through imitation on some of Phanagoria, Pl. IX. 15) does not seem to have been held in any particular honour there, he served but as the *armes parlantes* of the city[1]. The caps of the Dioscuri are similarly represented on the coins of the Euxine cities either as patrons of sailors or because of some monetary agreement, but they were not worshipped specially so far as we can tell (Pl. VI. 1, IX. 22, 28). Sarapis comes on the coins of ℞𝔼 among many exotic types (p. 602, n. 1), figures with Isis and Harpocrates upon a ring[2] which argues at any rate private devotion and with Hermes on a stele[3]; allied divinities occur in burial vaults (v. pp. 310 and 606, n. 10): ℞𝔼 also put the head of his ancestor Perseus with his harpé upon a coin (Pl. VII. 16).

The chief deity of the whole kingdom was no doubt Aphrodite Urania[4]: the centre of her worship was on the east side of the strait where she had a temple in Phanagoria and one called τὸ Ἀπάτουρον on the south side of Lake Corocondamitis[5]: after this sanctuary she is described in inscriptions as Ἀπατουρίας[6] or more often Ἀπατούρου μεδέουσα[7]. Strabo (l.c.) calls the goddess ἡ Ἀπάτουρος but the Berezan graffito (p. 479) Ἀπατόρης does not support this form, nor does the inscription found by De La Motraye[8] on an unidentified site near the Upper Kuban ⊗Ε.. ΑΓΑΤΟΡΟΙΙΙ.ΜΑ+ΙΙΙΑΡℳΙΙ>ΙΙ, as it is to be restored θε[ᾶι] Ἀπατόρο μ[εδεούσηι ὁ δεῖνα] with Ct I. I. Tolstoi[9] rather than θε[ῶι] Ἀπατόρω[ι κ.τ.λ. with Boeckh and Latyshev[10].

The word Apaturos must be an importation of the Teians. It is connected with the Apaturia the celebration of which Herodotus (I. 147) regards as the true mark of the Ionians: this was a festival of the clan[11]. The aetiological myth repeated by Strabo about Aphrodite deceiving the giants and handing them over to Heracles, like other myths explaining the name from ἀπάτη, are founded on a false etymology[12].

Without any epithet we find Aphrodite even at Phanagoria where she

---

[1] In *HN.*[2] p. 281 it is called a bearded Satyr.

[2] *ABC.* XVIII. 7.

[3] *Arch. Anz.* 1912, p. 347: for Sarapis and Isis at Olbia, v. ib. p. 366 and supra Addenda to p. 478.

[4] *IosPE.* II. 347.

[5] Strabo, XI. ii. 10; Pliny, *NH.* VI. 18 (6): oppidum paene desertum Apaturos: Hecataeus ap. Steph. Byz. s.v. seems to call the lake Ἀπάτουρος.

[6] *IosPE.* II. 352.

[7] *IosPE.* II. 343 (=App. 26), IV. 418 Phanagoria: II. 19 (=App. 38), 28 Kerch. This last (243 A.D.) has Ἀφρ. Οὐρανίᾳ Ἀπατούρῃ μεδεούσῃ, probably a mistake for Ἀπατούρου or perhaps Ἀπατούρης, cf. Apatura, the late form of the placename, Menander Prot. *FHG.* IV. p. 245, fr. 43; *Geog. Rav.* II. 12; cf. Jessen in *P.-W.* I. p. 2671, s.v. Apature; Tomaschek, ib. p. 2681, s.v. Apaturos.

[8] *Travels*, London, 1723, II. pp. 48—51, XXVII.

[9] *Journ. Min. Publ. Instr.* St P., May 1909, pp. 216—221.

[10] *IosPE.* II. 469: the spacing cannot be relied on and though the alphabet must go back to the VIth or early Vth century it cannot be before the differentiation of Ω; the bas-relief figured above it shewing Poseidon, Aphrodite, Eros, Ares and Hephaestus can hardly belong: an archaic original could not possibly have assumed such a form even under the hand of an XVIIIth century engraver.

[11] ἀπατόρια: ὁμοπάτρια *Schol. in Ar. Acharn.* l. 146.

[12] p. 617, n. 15, cf. Toepffer, *P.-W.* I. p. 2679, s.v. Apaturia, and Farnell, *Cults*, II. p. 657.

must be Apature[1] and at Panticapaeum[2] where she is also called Nauarchis[3] and at Tanais[4]. As Nauarchis she had a temple built to her at Gorgippia A.B. 407 = A.D. 110[5]. Aphrodite does not occur on the coins of the cities upon the Bosporus. It is only from the days of Sauromates II[6] that she suddenly becomes the most important type. She is seated on a throne with a staff in one hand and an apple or patera in the other[7], wearing a high headdress, and before her stands Eros. This aspect is clearly far removed from the ordinary Aphrodite such as we see in many terra-cottas (v. p. 367, nn. 1, 2) which have no cult significance, whereas this throned type probably represents the cult image. As such she has affinity with chthonian goddesses, as Rostovtsev suggests (v. supra, p. 606, n. 10) or with the Asiatic goddesses whose names are so variously represented by the Greeks; he sees her head upon such coins as Pl. VII. 7 or IX. 19. Astara[8] is probably another name for her.

Other nature goddesses appear on the Bosporus. We have dedications to the Mother[9], the Phrygian Mother[10] from her priestess, and even to the mysterious Ἀγγιστις[11]. To this Mother may be referred many terra-cottas (v. supr. p. 368). Here seems to belong a late *graffito* θεᾶς μεγά[λης][12].

Artemis of Ephesus[13] was the same kind of deity. More Hellenic was the hunting goddess Artemis Agrotera[14], whose temple on the Taman peninsula has all vanished, perhaps owing to the same volcanic agency that threw up the inscription which records its existence[15]. Artemis seems to have protected the docks at Tanais[16]. A few coins bear her head (Pl. IX. 13), but the browsing deer that mostly goes with it is a Mithridatic emblem (Pl. VI. 7, IX. 18).

A dedication to Demeter dating from Leucon I[17], another set up by a priestess of the goddess[18], yet another with the epithet Thesmophoros[19] and the tomb called the Great Bliznitsa wherein was buried a family specially devoted to Demeter (v. supr. p. 423), all point to her worship having flourished in the IVth and IIIrd centuries B.C., while a fragmentary inscription with ritual directions as to certain mysteries which may be those of Eleusis[20] marks a revival in Roman times[21]. The rape of Core or her head alone often adorns the walls of catacombs.

Quite isolated is a little altar inscribed Βάθυλλος Δέρκιος | Ἑκά[τη]ι Σπάρτης μεδεούσ[ηι][22]. Since Hecate does not seem to have had any special connexion with Sparta, perhaps Bathyllus came from there.

[1] IosPE. II. 349.
[2] IosPE. II. 21, 22; BCA. XVIII. p. 125, No. 40, v. supra, p. 585, n. 4.
[3] App. 39=IosPE. II. 25; cf. Εὔπλοια at Olbia, IosPE. I. 94 and supra p. 479.
[4] App. 52=IosPE. II. 423.
[5] App. 47=BCA. XXIII. p. 46, No. 32.
[6] B. XXXI. 239 sqq. inf. Pl. VIII. 12, 14.
[7] For a similar composition in terra-cotta v. ABC. LXIX. 9, cf. supra, p. 368.
[8] App. 30=IosPE. II. 346.
[9] IosPE. II. 16.
[10] App. 36=IosPE. II. 17.
[11] IosPE. II. 31, cf. Roscher s.v. Agdistis in his Mythol. Encycl. I. p. 100.
[12] BCA. III. p. 163.
[13] IosPE. II. 11 (=App. 29[a]), Kerch. BCA. XXXVII. p. 37, No. 1, Gorgippia.

[14] App. 29=IosPE. II. 344, cf. Roscher, I. p. 581; P.-W. II. p. 1378; Farnell, II. pp. 450, 562.
[15] In ancient times there were earthquakes on the Bosporus, and one split a hill and revealed gigantic bones. Theopompus Sinop. ap. Phleg. Trall. de Mirab. XIX. (48).
[16] IosPE. II. 421, Θεᾷ Ἀρτέμ[ι|δι μ]εδεού|[ση]ι ΝΕΩΟΥΩΙ | κ.τ.λ. wherein ΝΕΩΡΙΩΝ or ΝΕΩΡΙΟΥ seems to lurk.
[17] IosPE. II. 7.
[18] IosPE. II. 20.
[19] App. 33=IosPE. II. 13.
[20] IosPE. II. 342, Taman: L. Ziehen, Leges Gr. sacr. e tit. coll. p. 250, No. 86, thinks it dealt with mysteries of Isis or Bendis.
[21] Rostovtsev, Bobrinskoj Misc. p. 121.
[22] IosPE. II. 23, IVth or IIIrd cent. B.C.

It is rather surprising that we have no documentary evidence of any cult of Athena upon the Bosporus. Her head occurs on a few coins (Panticapaeum, Pl. VI. 14 ; Leucon, VI. 17 ; ᚹᚩ, VII. 14), but these are merely reproductions of Alexander's types.

Phanagoras appears upon the coins of the city that he founded (Pl. IX. 12), and he was no doubt the object of a heroic cult[1].

Finally there was the cult of the Augusti[2] of whom the kings proclaimed themselves perpetual high priests. In accordance with this the ladies of the imperial house appear on coins with the attributes of goddesses (Agrippias Caesarea, Pl. IX. 19, 20; Gepaepyris, VII. 7). In spite of their addressing their kings as gods (v. p. 612)[3], it is not likely that the Bosporans actually worshipped them as such.

A document which illustrates religious beliefs at Panticapaeum, but can scarcely be regarded as evidence for a definite cult, is a *defixio*, as usual a tablet of lead rolled up and pierced with two nails[4]; it bears two curses, in one Hermas, Hecata, Pluto, Leucothea and Phersephona, each and all called Chthonian, Artemis Strophaea and Demeter Chthonia and the Chthonian heroes are invoked; in the other the Chthonian Hermas, Hermas (l. Hecata), Plutodotas, Praxidica, Phersephona, the heroes and Demeter. The chthonian side of gods appears in the catacombs but again this does not imply that the living paid it so much regard as Rostovtsev (l. cit.) argues.

Religious Societies.

More interesting than the official religion in the Bosporan kingdom were the semi-private societies[5] (θίασοι, σύνοδοι)[6]. These seem to have had three distinguishable objects, the worship of certain deities, the due burial of the members, and the education of the young; this last would appear to have been a subsequent development, but we cannot say whether the other two were original or whether one grew out of the other.

The societies, introduced from Asia Minor[7], spread equally in all the cities of the Bosporan kingdom, but it is only lately that we have ascertained that everywhere existed certain features which the inscriptions of Tanais (Nedvigovka), preserved by the conditions of the site, have made most intelligible to us. It is only at Tanais that we have complete catalogues[8] of

[1] In *HN.*[2] p. 494, he is called a Cabiros.

[2] From the time of Dynamis, *IosPE.* IV. 201 (=App. 40); then II. 32 (=App. 44), 39, 41 (=App. 54), 352, 355, 360; *BCA.* XXXVII. p. 70, No. 7, v. p. 598, n. 7.

[3] App. 61 = *IosPE.* II. 29.

[4] *Arch. Anz.* 1907, p. 127: another, *CR.* 1868, p. 122, v. E. M. Pridik, *Journ. Min. Publ. Instr.* St P. Dec. 1899, Cl. Sect. pp. 115—124.

[5] Treated in the accounts of Tanais given by Stempkovskij its discoverer, Leontiev its first excavator, *Propylaea* (Russian), IV. p. 387 sqq. and *Extract from the Report of Arch. Explor. for* 1853, pp. 65—121, in the remarks of Stephani on publishing newly discovered inscriptions, *CR.* 1869, p. xxii ; 1870/71, p. xxiii, p. 228 sqq., more broadly by Pomjalovskij, *Trans. VIth Russ. Arch. Congress* (Odessa), II. (1888) pp. 24—28, and by Latyshev,

IosPE. II. p. 246; their organization has been well studied by E. Ziebarth, "Das griechische Vereinswesen," esp. pp. 58—60, 207—211, No. XXXIV of *Preisschriften der Jablonowski'schen Gesellschaft*, Leipzig, 1896, and again by F. Poland, "Gesch. des gr. Vereinswesens," No. XXXVIII. ib. 1909, and the character of their religion by E. Schürer, *Sitzber. d. k. Pr. Akad. d. Wiss. zu Berlin*, 1897, I—XXXII. pp. 200—225, "Die Juden im bosporanischen Reiche und die Genossenschaften der σεβόμενοι θεὸν ὕψιστον ebendaselbst," cf. his *Gesch. d. jüdischen Volkes im Zeitalter Jesu Christi*[3], III. pp. 53—63 (references are to his article in *SB.*), but some important material has appeared since they wrote.

[6] For the words v. Poland, pp. 16 sqq., 158 sqq.

[7] Poland, p. 23.

[8] App. 53, 56, 58 ; *IosPE.* II. 437—467, IV. 449; Ziebarth, p. 59, Poland, p. 284.

societies with their officers and members; from Gorgippia come many
fragments of such documents, enough to shew a general correspondence
together with considerable divergence in detail and names of officers unknown
elsewhere[1]; from Theodosia we have a list of names of members, but the
heading and the titles of the officers are lost[2]; still smaller are fragments
from Zjuk (Heracleum or Zenonis Chersonesus)[3] and Opuk (Cimmericum)[4].

At Panticapaeum have been found no fragments that can be held exactly
to correspond to the general catalogues, but we have many gravestones erected
to the memory of one or more officers or members of a society and bearing
the list of officers whereby we see that the terminology was practically the
same as at Tanais, and so presumably the objects of the societies[5]. The two
or three inscriptions from near Phanagoria shew rather a different terminology
and offer one more indication that Phanagoria was not quite as the other towns[6].

The earliest of the θίασοι in the Bosporan kingdom is that which in the
middle of the IInd century B.C. set up a stele to Aphrodite Urania, Lady of
Apaturon, on behalf of Paerisades Philometor, Camasarye and Argotes[7].
The head was called a συναγωγός, the members θιασῖται, and their names are
appended. This organization seems to have been devoted to one deity in the
ancient Pantheon—it was not in any sense monotheistic. Another catalogue
from Panticapaeum, of which we have part of the heading, seems to have been
dedicated θεᾷ σ[ωτείρᾳ][8], in which the personality of the goddess may or may
not be fading, as we should expect at so late a date. The courtiers of Teiranes
(App. 61) appear to have formed a society with a priest, a γραμματεύς(?) and
νεώτεροι under a novice-master Coties.

The catalogues from Tanais are headed by a dedication θεῷ ὑψίστῳ[9], or
have the phrase εἰσποιητοὶ ἀδελφοὶ σεβόμενοι θεὸν ὑψιστον[10]. At Gorgippia
we have θεῷ δικαίῳ as well as θεῷ ὑψίστῳ[11]. Τὸ ὑψίστῳ was often added the
further epithet ἐπηκόῳ[12] at Tanais[13], and at Panticapaeum[14]. We have also
manumissions of slaves made θεῷ ὑψίστῳ παντοκράτορι εὐλογητῷ[15]. The whole
form of these documents and the epithets of the deity are clearly due to
Jewish influence, although they end with the pagan formula ὑπὸ Δία, Γῆν,
Ἥλιον[16]. The purely Jewish manumission also occurs[17], so we are justified in
supposing that it was in the presence of Jews that the pagan gave place to

[1] *IosPE.* II. 402 (=App. 69)—418, IV. 433
(=App. 57)—443; *BCA.* III. p. 52, XXXVII. p. 38,
No. 2 (fairly complete=App. 51)—p. 60, No. 41.
[2] *Trans. Od. Soc.* XXIV. *Minutes*, p. 29, E. von
Stern=*IosPE.* IV. 468.
[3] *IosPE.* IV. 206.
[4] *BCA.* XL. p. 92, No. 1.
[5] *IosPE.* II. 19 (=App. 38), 57—65 (cf. supra
pp. 301, 302, ff. 214, 215), IV. 207—211 (=App. 62),
212, 469; *BCA.* X. p. 31, Nos. 23—27; XXVII. p. 42,
No. 1; XXXIII. p. 22, No. 1; XXXVII. p. 1, Nos. 1, 2;
XL. p. 104, No. 18; *Trans. Od. Soc.* XXVI. *Minutes,*
p. 61; XXVII. *Minutes*, p. 18. *BCA.* XL. No. 18,
and *IosPE.* IV. 207, belong to the same society.
App. 62, *BCA.* X. Nos. 23—25 and XXXVII. No. 1
are painted, not incised.
[6] *IosPE.* II. 365 (four members together), IV.
421 (=App. 48); *BCA.* XIV. p. 116, No. 38.
[7] App. 38=*IosPE.* II. 19.
[8] *IosPE.* II. 57 (late IInd century A.D.): Latyshev

supplies θεασ[εῖται] (IV. p. 286), but the analogies
he quotes, IV. 433 (=App. 57), 434, are not exact.
[9] *IosPE.* II. 437, 439, 445 (=App. 53), cf. 451.
[10] *IosPE.* II. 449, 450, 452 (=App. 58), 456.
[11] *IosPE.* IV. 430; 436b, ὑψίστῳ.
[12] θεοὶ ἐπήκοοι, v. O. Weinreich, *Ath. Mitt.* 1912,
pp. 1—68: at Olbia, v. Add. to p. 468.
[13] *IosPE.* II. 438, 446, 447 (=App. 56), 448, 454,
455, 457, and probably *BCA.* XIV. p. 134, No. 55,
a private dedication found at Rostóv.
[14] App. 63=*BCA.* X. p. 26, No. 21.
[15] *IosPE.* II. 400 (=App. 43), 401; 54, made θεῷ
ΤΗϹΜΑϹ καὶ Παρθέ[νου, is hopelessly corrupt: and
BCA. XLV. p. 10, No. 2, Phanagoria, imperfect.
[16] Cf. the oaths, App. 16, 17³.
[17] *IosPE.* II. 52 (=App. 46), 53, Kerch; 364,
Phanagoria; *BCA.* XXVII. p. 38, No. 34, Duzu
Kale near Novo-Mikhailovka, probably brought
from Bosporus: perhaps *BCA.* XXXVII. p. 74, No. 8,
Gorgippia; *IosPE.* IV. 204, Kerch.

monotheistic societies whose cult was, as it were, unsectarian, as Schürer says, neither Judaism, nor Paganism, but a *Neutralisirung* of both[1].

All these epithets are practically confined to Greek as spoken by Jews and have their equivalents in Hebrew or Aramaic, as pointed out by Schürer. In the manumission θεῷ ὑψίστῳ παντοκράτορι εὐλογητῷ recalls LXX. κύριος ὁ θεὸς ὁ παντοκράτωρ = יְהֹוָה אֱלֹהֵי־צְבָאוֹת, e.g. Amos iii. 13, and εὐλογητός = בָּרוּךְ. Ζεὺς ὕψιστος is fairly common in Roman times, but points to similar eastern influences. Deissmann (op. cit.) is inclined to minimize these, but the Jewish element cannot be ignored. In Palmyra we get several examples of Διΐ ὑψίστῳ ἐπηκόῳ, once translated [מנא]ורח טבא וֻגֻעֻמא שמה בריך, "He whose name be ever blessed, the good, the merciful," where ὕψιστος seems to equal εὐλογητός.

Θεὸς ὕψιστος, though occurring in heathen inscriptions, is comparatively rare, whereas it is a common combination in Jewish Greek[2], LXX., and Apocrypha, answering to the Hebrew אֵל עֶלְיוֹן, Gen. xiv. 18, etc.

The word σεβόμενοι had the technical sense of Gentiles who had adopted some of the Jewish faith without submitting to all the requirements of the Mosaic law, e.g. often in the Acts, as of Lydia σεβομένη τὸν θεὸν (xvi. 14)[3]. It is true that this phrase only comes in a small class of the Tanais inscriptions: but we cannot thence argue that this worship was confined to that class. Among the semi-pagan sects of the IVth and Vth centuries was that of the ὑψιστάριοι to which once belonged the father of Gregory Nazianzen[4]. That the god of the Tanaites was originally Zeus is rendered probable by the frequent survival of an eagle upon the pediments above the inscriptions, though it is reduced to a mere decoration and as such is even doubled. Until Schürer had shewn the true connexions of this ὕψιστος θεὸς analogies pointed in the direction of Sabazius, as a close parallel had been found at Pirot (Serdica)[5] in

---

[1] The Jews in the Bosporan kingdom are fully discussed by Schürer, op. cit. who shews that they had suffered Gentile influence, as is proved by App. 46 = *IosPE.* II. 52, which is modelled on a legal form of manumission by which a slave was fictively sold to a heathen deity without becoming a temple-slave or owing any other duty to the god than reverence. (See also Deissmann, *Licht vom Osten*, p. 233.) This in the Jewish form is expanded to "worship and regular attendance at the synagogue," whose members took the responsibility of the transaction. The slave seems to have been a Gentile; in all cases he bears a name unknown among any Jews. For προσκαρτέρησις cf. the use of προσκαρτερεῖν in the Acts i. 14, ii. 42, vi. 4, and especially ii. 46 and elsewhere in the New Testament (Deissmann, op. cit. p. 66). In later times we have many Jewish epitaphs often adorned with the seven-branched candlestick, Levites' trumpet, Aaron's rod, etc.: *IosPE.* II. 304—306, IV. 404, 405, 426, cf. E. Lutsenko, "Ancient Jewish Funeral Monuments discovered in the mounds of Phanagoria," *Travaux de la IIIᵉ Session du Congrès Internat. des Orientalistes*, St P. 1876, Vol. I. pp. 575—580, Pl. I—VIII. In the Byzantine period we know of the presence of Jews at Phanagoria from Theophanes (p. 357 de Boor), v. Kulakovskij's review of Schürer, *Journ. Min.*

Pub. Instr. St P. 1898, April. No doubt these Crimean Jews converted the Khazars. For the whole question of the Jews in the Crimea and the Karaim besides the authorities referred to by Schürer, v. "Alt-Jüdische Denkmäler aus der Krim mitgetheilt von Abr. Firkowitsch, geprüft von A. Harkavy," *Mém. de l'Acad. Imp. des Sc. de St P.*, VIIᵉ série, T. XXIV. No. 1, 1876.

[2] e.g. inscription from Athribis *BCH.* XIII. (1889) p. 178.

[3] So Josephus *Antt. Jud.* xx. viii. 11 calls Poppaea θεοσεβής.

[4] *Orat.* XVIII. 5: Migne *P.G.* XXXV. p. 989 sqq. Ἐκεῖνος τοίνυν...ῥίζης ἐγένετο βλάστημα οὐκ ἐπαινετῆς ...ἐκ δυοῖν τοῖν ἐναντιωτάτοιν συγκεκραμένης, Ἑλλη-νικῆς τε πλάνης καὶ νομικῆς τερατείας· ὧν ἀμφοτέρων τὰ μέρη φυγὼν ἐκ μερῶν συνετέθη. Τῆς μὲν τὰ εἴδωλα καὶ τὰς θυσίας ἀποπεμπόμενοι τιμῶσι τὸ πῦρ καὶ τὰ λύχνα· τῆς δὲ τὸ σάββατον, αἰδούμενοι καὶ τὴν περὶ τὰ βρώματα ἔστιν ἃ μικρολογίαν τὴν περιτομὴν ἀτιμάζουσιν. Ὑψιστάριοι τοῖς ταπεινοῖς ὄνομα καὶ ὁ Παντοκράτωρ δὴ μόνος αὐτοῖς σεβάσμιος.

[5] Latyshev, *IosPE.* II. p. 246, quoting Domaszewski, *Arch.-epigr. Mitth. aus Oest.* X. (1886) p. 238, No. 2, also Ziebarth, p. 57; Schürer, p. 212; von Stern, *Trans. Od. Soc.* XXIV. *Minutes*, p. 35; Poland, p. 216.

Serbia, a dedication made θεῷ ἐπηκόῳ ὑψίστῳ by a θία[σος] Σεβαζιανός. Perhaps the personality of Sabazius, in whose honour the thiasus had been named, had faded with time. Certainly there is no reason to call the Bosporan deity Sabazius, though they both had come to be much the same kind of divinity.

The lists of θιασεῖται or συνοδεῖται at Tanais are arranged according to three formulae. The most usual[1] after the invocations to the deity and to good luck and after naming the reigning king begins ἡ σύνοδος ἡ περὶ ἱερέα τὸν δεῖνα and gives the list of officers and then that of the members. The next[2] begins the enumeration thus ἡ σύνοδος περὶ θεὸν ὕψιστον καὶ ἱερέα κ.τ.λ. Finally we have lists which appear to contain names of new members or mere associates; they run εἰσποιητοὶ ἀδελφοὶ σεβόμενοι θεὸν ὕψιστον ἐγγράψαντες ἑαυτῶν τὰ ὀνόματα περὶ πρεσβύτερον τὸν δεῖνα[3].

In the second variety the deity is reckoned as if he were the chief officer of the society; in the development of mystic doctrine either the deity has descended among his worshippers or they have raised themselves almost to his level. This then would seem an innovation appearing in A.D. 220—228, but two inscriptions which do not shew it are assigned to the reign of Cotys A.D. 227—233[4], so perhaps not all societies adopted it. The examples of affiliated associations seem to belong to the same decade.

As to numbers, Poland (pp. 284, 285) remarks that societies in the earlier days were rather small, ranging from some 15 to 30; inscriptions of the second variety, with which II. 445 and 454 must be included, shew 40 as the norm plus additions which can be seen to be such; the affiliated associations are naturally quite small, about 20, II. 452 enumerates only eleven members.

The officers of a society at Tanais usually appear more or less in this order (ἱερεύς), (πατὴρ συνόδου), συναγωγός, φιλάγαθος, παραφιλάγαθος, γυμνασιάρχης, νεανισκάρχης, and (γραμματεύς): I have bracketed those which are not always present. The presence of a ἱερεύς[5] argues that there was a sacrificial ritual, the πατὴρ συνόδου seems rather to have held the position of a patron or an honorary senior than a real office[6], while the συναγωγὸς was the working president[7]; the γυμνασιάρχης and νεανισκάρχης shew that the society concerned itself with the education of the young; perhaps if we had complete lists we should find that the πρεσβύτερος of an affiliated association was the νεανισκάρχης of the parent society. The γραμματεύς only appears in one or two of the earlier societies. What were the duties of the φιλάγαθος and παραφιλάγαθος we cannot divine[8]. Ziebarth (p. 146) is inclined to believe in a kind of *cursus honorum*, a regular promotion from office to office, but Poland (p. 338) does not concur. The heading of the Theodosian list has unfortunately perished. At Gorgippia we learn most from the inscription set up to Poseidon[9] by the

---

IosPE. II. 437—445 (=App. 53), 454: 453 and 455 cannot be restored to fit into any regular formula: 453 seems to call full members ἀδελφοί.

[2] *IosPE.* II. 446, 447 (=App. 56), 448, 451; the first two name the same priest and are taken to belong to the same society, although there is but five years between them, and yet only two names are common to the two lists.

[3] *IosPE.* II. 449, 450, 452 (=App. 58), 456, [459].

[4] *IosPE.* II. 454, 455.

[5] Poland, p. 339.

[6] So Poland, p. 371, against Ziebarth, p. 154.

[7] Ziebarth, p. 149.

[8] In Chalcedon societies the φ. had ritual functions, Ziebarth, p. 155; in Egypt the word seems a mere honorific title, Poland, p. 413.

[9] App. 51=*BCA.* XXXVII. p. 38, No. 2: App. 69 (=*IosPE.* II. 402) had, I think, the same dedication.

gild of ship-owners (Merchant Venturers) in the time of Sauromates II.   It
looks as if the gild was open to others besides ship-owners, seeing that all the
chief men of the state were members (v. p. 625), even the king, who had paid
an entrance-fee towards restoring the temple[1].   Probably too the deity had,
like his worshippers, lost touch with the sea and become very like the θεὸς
ὕψιστος.   The gild is called a θέασος, feminine on the analogy of σύνοδος used
in *IosPE*. IV. 434.   The officers besides the usual Priest[2] and συναγωγὸς[3]
included φροντισταί[4], elsewhere unknown, but the ἱερῶν οἰκονόμος, like the
obviously secular officials and probably even the γυμνασίαρχος[5] and ὀρφανοφύλαξ[6] of other inscriptions (to judge by their places in the list), were not, as
such, officers of the society (v. p. 613).   The number of members at Gorgippia
was particularly large : one list[7] has not less than 150 names.

At Panticapaeum there is direct evidence mostly of the burial-club side of
the societies ; we have no lists of members but epitaphs beginning ἡ σύνοδος
ἡ περὶ ἱερέα or συναγωγόν (the absence of the priest may indicate a society of
less distinctively religious character), followed by the names of the officers
given more or less fully and that of the dead man.   We have two inscriptions
of one society with the same officers[8]; in one the members call the dead man
τὸν ἴδιον ἀδελφόν, an expression Poland (p. 54) had sought in vain to
exemplify.   Unusual is the case in which a society honours its παραφιλάγαθον
διὰ βίου with an engraved gold wreath-strip[9].   Failing full lists an epitaph[10]
giving all the identical officers that we had at Tanais proves the existence of a
precisely similar organization with the same purposes including the care of the
young.   Only the γραμματεὺς is absent, and he occurs in some cases[11], and in
others we find a πραγματᾶς occupying the same place[12].   In view of this
terminological identity and of the fact that the θεὸς ὕψιστος ἐπήκοος was
worshipped at Panticapaeum we may take it that the burial societies at the
latter place worshipped him, and that had we yet any gravestones from Tanais
we should find that the religious societies there were also burial-clubs.

It may be by chance that the two or three inscriptions from Phanagoria
bear a character of their own, but it might be urged that though the Jews were
in special force there, still paganism made of the great shrine a stronghold.
There is a hieratic stamp about the σύνοδος whose officers are a νακόρος, a
ἱερεὺς and a ἱερομάστωρ as well as the γραμματεὺς and φιλάγαθος[13]; the
ἱερομάστωρ comes again in an inscription from Akhtanizovka[14].   He seems to
correspond to the ἱεροποιός[15], an assistant to the priest in other societies.   No
doubt the spirit of their worship changed, but it looks as if the Phanagorites
remained in a sense faithful to Aphrodite Apature[16].   A very late list from Taman[17]

---

[1] Latyshev quotes this meaning of εἰσαγώγιον
from Ditt.[2] 734, l. 52, but prefers "remission of
customs duty."

[2] Cf. *BCA*. XXXVII. p. 44, No. 3, v. inf. p. 625,
n. 15.

[3] Cf. *IosPE*. IV. 434; *BCA*. III. p. 52; XXXVII.
pp. 45, 46, Nos. 5, 6.

[4] *IosPE*. IV. 434; *BCA*. XXXVII. pp. 44, 46,
Nos. 3, 6.

[5] *IosPE*. II. 403.

[6] *IosPE*. IV. 434.

[7] App. 69=*IosPE*. II. 402.

[8] *IosPE*. IV. 207; *BCA*. XL. p. 104, No. 18.

[9] *IosPE*. IV. p. 125, n. 2; *BCA*. XXVII. p. 43.

[10] App. 62=*IosPE*. IV. 211, cf. ib. 209, 210,
212.

[11] *IosPE*. IV. 209, 212 ; perhaps App. 61=II. 29.

[12] *IosPE*. II. 61, 62 (v. supra p. 301, f. 214), 63;
Poland, p. 378, thinks him a finance officer.

[13] App. 48=*IosPE*. IV. 421.

[14] *BCA*. XIV. p. 116, No. 38.

[15] Ziebarth, p. 151 ; Poland, p. 390.

[16] Poland, p. 191, remarks that the worship of
A. Urania flourished just in the same regions as
that of θεὸς ὕψιστος.

[17] *IosPE*. II. 389.

has only the words συνθειασεῖται and τῶν ἀγίων, both peculiar, distinguishable among the names.

Besides their direct religious and educational objects the societies had much social importance. Evidently they included among their members the most distinguished citizens. At Tanais, for instance, Chophrasmus, son of Phorgabacus, appears as priest of a society[1] in the years 220 and 225 A.D., and in the former year he was apparently Hellenarch[2]; in 236 A.D. he becomes legate[3]. So Ζηνῶν Φάννεως, who comes first among the private members of his society[4], is prefect of the Aspurgiana and legate. The names of various ἐπιμεληταί who carried out public works for the town, sometimes at their own expense, reappear among the θιασῖται and so too those of the architects[5].

At Bosporus the Teiranes stele seems to shew all the court enrolled in a society; no wonder Julius Sambion was πατὴρ συνόδου when ὁ ἐπὶ τῆς αὐλῆς[6], Daphnus who held the same post was a συνοδίτης (v. p. 302, f. 215), and Sogus, whose distinctions are set forth in App. 63[7], probably set up the προσευχὴ for the benefit of a σύνοδος. At Gorgippia we have as members of the θέασος ναυκλήρων[8], apparently the king himself[9], the πρῶτος ἐπὶ τῆς βασιλείας, ὁ ἐπὶ τῆς Γοργιππίας[10], a ἱερῶν οἰκονόμος, who is probably the same as ὁ ἐπὶ τῶν ἱερῶν[11], several ἐνκυκλίων οἰκονόμοι and στρατηγοί[12], and other lists shew λοχαγοί[13]. The ὀρφανοφύλαξ[14] was also a state-official, and ἱερεῖς when they stand low on the list are probably not the society's priests[15]. Membership was confined to men and apparently to soldiers, at least at Panticapaeum, where the reliefs set up by the σύνοδοι always represent the deceased as such: either he is leaning on a pillar with his bow-case hung up behind him (p. 301, f. 214) or he is riding out in full equipment with or without an attendant (p. 302, f. 215). I cannot agree with Poland (p. 72) that they were no true societies but rather lists of the chance participants in an annual celebration, who had their names cut on a stone just as nowadays they might be photographed in a group.

It is quite possible that this organization may have helped the Greeks in their resistance to barbarization, though the names in the lists shew that by the IIIrd century A.D. the members were mostly of native blood, and the grammar makes one feel that Greek was hardly a living tongue, or rather was not being treated with due respect as a dead language. The use of the cases and the construction of the sentences are so bad that it is sometimes hard to establish the exact sense[16], while other mistakes seem due to phonetic decay[17].

In any case the religious societies in the Bosporan kingdom offer an interesting example of that trend towards monotheism which prepared the triumph of Christianity.

[1] *IosPE.* II. 446, 447 (=App. 56).
[2] *IosPE.* II. 430 (=App. 55), 431, 431 *bis.*
[3] App. 59=*IosPE.* II. 434.
[4] *IosPE.* II. 446.
[5] v. p. 615, nn. 10, 11 : Ziebarth, p. 209.
[6] *BCA.* x. p. 32, No. 24.
[7] *BCA.* x. p. 26, No. 21.
[8] App. 51=*BCA.* XXXVII. p. 38, No. 2.
[9] Cf. App. 57=*IosPE.* IV. 433.
[10] Cf. *IosPE.* IV. 434.
[11] ibid., Poland, p. 391, takes him to be an assistant to the society's priest.

[12] Cf. *IosPE.* II. 404; in 402 (=App. 69) l. 32 I cannot allow myself to see the word.
[13] App. 69, *IosPE.* IV. 436a; *BCA.* XXXVII. p. 44, No. 3.
[14] ih. p. 46, No. 7 (?); *IosPE.* IV. 434; Poland, p. 405.
[15] *IosPE.* II. 402 (=App. 69), 404, 410; Poland, p. 340.
[16] e.g. in App. 58=*IosPE.* II. 452, the doubt whether there were one πρεσβύτερος or four, and the confusion of cases in App. 51.
[17] e.g. ω for ου, App. 52, l. 17, cf. App. 47, l. 11.

The Bosporans kept up the gymnastic exercises of Hellas, but we have not so much evidence of it as in Chersonese and Olbia.   Only at Gorgippia have we a considerable inscription[1], which tells us that early in the IIIrd century B.C. that city held a festival of the Hermaea at which was a long race (δόλιχος). There was also a kind of all-round contest in ε[ὐε]ξία, into which, strength, beauty, agility and skill in arms all probably entered.   Other early lists of citizens from Panticapaeum[2] and Nymphaeum[3] were also probably agonistic. Phanagoria can shew its Agonothetes in the time of Paerisades I[4].   The Panathenaic vases which I have mentioned several times (p. 347) are also a proof that the Bosporans were not unsuccessful in their cultivation of athletics, though we do not know of their having distinguished themselves in the great games of the mother country.   The occurrence of the title gymnasiarch among the officers of religious societies proves that to the end bodily exercises were practised.   Professors of gymnastics were imported from Sinope[5].

The Bosporans' taste and practice in art has been sufficiently treated (p. 294). Memnon made use of their taste in music by sending with his envoy to Leucon the famous citharoedus Aristonicus of Olynthus.   The latter was instructed to begin his performance as he approached the shore, so that to hear him the whole population should assemble in the theatre, and accordingly its full numbers might be ascertained[6].   We have the stele of an αὐλητρὶς from Myrmecium[7].   A VIth century "Pseudo-Panathenaic" vase from Kerch with a contest of flute players matched by a genuine inscribed one of the VIth century from Elizavetovskaja (Tanais, v. p. 567) with lyrists argues some success in music[8].

In literature they have nothing to boast of.   Sphaerus, a rather obscure philosopher, a pupil of Zeno and Cleanthes, lived at the court of Ptolemy Philopator[9].   He also helped Cleomenes. in his schemes for regenerating Sparta.   Yet the Bosporan kings tried to patronize letters.   One of them who had received a full Greek education came to Smyrna while seeing the sights of Ionia.   Polemo of Smyrna, the chief sophist of the town, so far from politely waiting upon him, would not even go to see him when invited, and made the king come to him with a present of ten talents[10].   The king must have been Sauromates I, Cotys II or Rhoemetalces, during whose reigns Polemo flourished.   The long extract in Diodorus (v. p. 578) presumably comes from the works of some native author: but the historians of Mithridates and his deeds seem to have been from Asia Minor.

We can only judge of Bosporan literature by one or two metrical inscriptions[11] and epitaphs, of which there are about thirty.   The earliest of these, one of the very earliest inscriptions from the north of the Euxine, being written boustrophedon, is a failure[12].

[1] *IosPE.* IV. 432 = *Mat.* XXIII. p. 64.
[2] *IosPE.* II. 55, 56.   [3] *IosPE.* IV. 205.
[4] *IosPE.* II. 345.
[5] *IosPE.* II. 299.
[6] Polyaenus v. xliv. I.
[7] *BCA.* XXIII. p. 44, No. 29.
[8] *Arch. Anz.* 1912, pp. 339, 374, ff. 23, 24, 66, 67 : Radlov in *BCA.* XLV. pp. 76—91, Pl. V, VI.
[9] *FHG.* III. p. 20 ; Diog. Laert. VII. vi. 177, 178 enumerates his very miscellaneous works : but Plutarch, *Cleomenes* II., calls him a Borysthenite.

[10] Philostrat., *Vitae Sophistarum,* I. iv. 25, p. 229.
[11] *IosPE.* II. 9, v. p. 577, and 37 = App. 45.
[12] App. 25 (S. slope of Mt Mithridates) = *BCA.* X. p. 63, No. 66, cf. XXIII. p. 63 ; *Mélanges Nicole,* p. 301, No. 1 ; Crönert, *Wochenschr. f. Kl. Phil.* Oct. 24, 1906 ; A. Τύχ|ων|ος.   B. Σήμα|τι τῶιδ' | ὑπόκει|ται ἀνὴρ | [π]ολλο[ῖ]σι ποθει|νός.   C. Ταύροις εἰνί (?) Τύχων |||| τῶνο[μ]|α δ' ἐστὶ Τύχ[ω]ν εοι.   In C are evidently attempts at a pentameter. Crönert's τῶνομα δ' ἐστὶ Τύχων καὶ πατρὸς δ' ἐστὶ Τύχωνος makes too free with the lettering.

Other early verses are better[1], and the epitaphs of Lysimachus[2] and Glycaria (v. p. 561) are still simple. Those of Roman date are either monotonous[3] or artificial, full of phrases which recur in the Anthology[4] or Kaibel's collection. This is particularly true of a series from a spot in the Glinishche, which must have been an aristocratic cemetery[5].

A very literary composition is the epitaph of Sabbion, whose special delight was in the Muses[6]. By the irony of fate Vergilius Aephnidius has the worst of probably unintentional hexameters[7], but some Bosporan knew enough Homer to scratch half a line on a stone and make but two mistakes[8]. An epitaph in verse was often earned by death in battle with the natives.

Ordinary gravestones tell us of strangers sojourning in Bosporus, besides Romans and Jews (v. pp. 614, 622, n. 1). We have near neighbours whose ἐθνικὰ point to city patriotism within the kingdom, men of Nymphaeum, Theodosia, Hermonassa and Cepi[9], and several Chersonesites[10] and an Odessite[11], but no Olbians. Most foreigners came from the opposite coast Amastris and Amisus[12], Heraclea Pontica[13], and especially Sinope[14], also Tium and Paphlagonia[15]. Of more distant cities that sent men to die in Bosporus may be mentioned Mantinea, Mytilene, Chios, Colophon, and even far off Cyprus and Syracuse[16]. The foreign coins found come from the same Asiatic cities (among them in the early period from Cyzicus[17]), and offer further evidence of the close communication between the opposite coasts of the Euxine, which found its full expression in the Empire of Mithridates.

BOSPORUS COINAGE, CITY ISSUES. PLATES V, VI. 1—14, IX. 10—29.

To the exceptional constitution of the Bosporan kingdom correspond its monetary issues, so much can be discerned, but the want of data forbids us from tracing this correspondence into any great detail. just as the rulers of the country long refrained from assuming any higher title than king with respect to the cities, so they refrained from the royal prerogative of coining. It is clear that they kept to this rule until the latter half of the IIIrd century at least, and the comparative rarity of Spartocid coins in the precious metals as compared with the abundant city issues argues that their interference in the matter was exceptional. The common coins with Leucon's name may have been called out by some emergency and do not represent a great addition to

---

[1] Hedeie, *IosPE*. II. 370 cf. *BCA*. XXIII. p. 56; Hecataeus a foreigner, *BCA*. III. p. 36, No. 3; Sanon, XIV. p. 123, No. 46.

[2] *IosPE*. II. 171.

[3] e.g. Chreste, p. 301, f. 213, Timotheus, App. 67 = *IosPE*. II. 383.

[4] *IosPE*. IV. 221, cf. *Anth. Pal.* VII. 516.

[5] Cf. *Mélanges Nicole*, l.c.; *IosPE*. II. 86, in which the youth is called λόγων φίλος; IV. 256, 317, set up by a thiasus; *BCA*. X. p. 71, No. 77; XIV. p. 120, No. 42: others of the group, *IosPE*. IV. 218, *BCA*. X. p. 49, No. 46, p. 66, No. 69, and part of XIV. p. 124, No. 47, the most elaborate of all, are in Iambics: this and two similar ones, *IosPE*. II. 298, 299 commemorate people of Sinope, as 286 a woman of Amisus.

[6] *IosPE*. II. 197.

[7] *IosPE*. IV. 330. Not so bad as Zeilas of Tarsus, *BCA*. XLV. p. 16, No. 7, set up in his life-time to his wife "one of the Pierian Muses": above is a funeral feast.

[8] *IosPE*. IV. 409 = *Il.* X. 242.

[9] *IosPE*. II. 201, cf. supra p. 560, n. 1; IV. 400, 334; *BCA*. XXIII. p. 43, No. 26.

[10] *IosPE*. II. 302, 302¹, 303, IV. 402.

[11] *IosPE*. II. 295.

[12] *IosPE*. II. 285, 286, 286¹, 287.

[13] *IosPE*. II. 289, cf. supra p. 560.

[14] v. n. 5 and *BCA*. X. p. 67, No. 71; XVIII. p. 132, No. 49; XXVII. p. 50, No. 8.

[15] *IosPE*. II. 301, 296.

[16] *BCA*. III. p. 51, No. 17; *IosPE*. II. 294, II. 468 and IV. 403, 401, II. 292, 300.

[17] e.g. *ABC*. Reinach, p. 130.

the currency. There are points of resemblance between certain royal coins and others issued by the cities, but in the uncertainty of historical and stylistic criteria we do not gain from these much help in dating either.

With the entrance of Mithridates the coinage becomes quite different and types which ultimately go back to his inspiration become dominant : but he did not deprive the cities of the right of coining, not even of the right of coining silver. He allowed them to issue the small silver change and copper required to supplement the splendid tetradrachms which he made the chief currency of his dominions. To his time belong Dionysiac types. During the unsettled half-century that succeeded, naval power was all-important on the Euxine, and naval types are very general upon the coins, especially during the time of Asander. From this time the mints become royal mints, only, as it seems, Phanagoria, which had been granted exceptional privileges and had taken the name of Agrippias Caesarea, continued to issue copper after the other cities had given up coining. The coinages of Nymphaeum and Theodosia, even the latter's last (IX. 7) so-called Leuconian type, have no affinity but their Aeginetic weight with that of the Bosporan towns and have been treated separately.

The first group of coins is common to Panticapaeum, Apollonia and Phanagoria. The metal is silver and the reverse has almost always an incuse square. The type is a lion-scalp (v. 3—6. IX. 10, 11) treated in some cases in quite an archaic manner. The smaller coins of the class are very small indeed, some of these have an ant instead (v. 1, 2). The incuse square is sometimes plain, quadripartite or with pellets, sometimes of the swastika or mill-sail pattern : a few members of the group have a ram's head with a fish below it ; it is remarkable that an example at Berlin[1] has this more developed type overstruck with a quadripartite square inscribed ΓΑΝΤ. The legends are ΑΠ or ΠΑ (reading either way), ΑΠοΛ, ΠΑΝΤ, ΠΑΝΤΙ and ΦΑ. The ant has been supposed to refer to Myrmecium, the little town to the NE. of Kerch: and Apollonia has been thought to be the true Greek name of Panticapaeum. These coins have been referred to Apollonia in Thrace[2], but they are found on the Bosporus. Their issue must have continued for most of the vth century[3].

This name of Apollonia may account for a severe head of Apollo on the obverse of a late coin of this early series[4] and upon the reverse of one[5] of the next group, which belongs to the time of greatest prosperity under the established Spartocids. This group is marked at Panticapaeum by heads of Pan, whose presence merely expresses the first three letters of the city's name. His head appears in wonderful variety, bearded and beardless, at first with straight fine hair (v. 7, 9—13), then it becomes more bold and curly (v. 8, 15), and finally is conventionalized in a way which recalls Mucha's posters of fifteen years ago with their decorative "macaroni" (v. 16—23). The later straight and rough treatments which shade into one another correspond to the time when full, or nearly full faces were in vogue on coins; the last style returns to profile. In this style the use of the drill has been allowed to produce round blobs (there is no other word) in the features and a monotonous quality of

[1] *Beschr.* I. p. 9, Pl. II. 13.
[2] *BMC. Thrace,* &c. p. 87.
[3] Giel, *Kl. B.* Pl. III., shews 43 of them.
[4] Burachkov, XIX. 25, reverse, ram's head and ΠΑΝΤΙ in square, 15·7 grn. = 1·02 grm., 1½ obols(?).
[5] B. XIX. 48=*MK.* I. p. 345 ; obverse, Pan bearded l., 195·4 grn. = 12·66 grm., stater.

treatment (see the folds in the neck of the ox on v. 17). Often the presence of the ivy wreath goes with the later style. This Pan class of coin seems to have gone right through the ivth century and survived into the iiird. In the iind and perhaps even in the 1st it appears to have been occasionally revived in inferior specimens (vi. 1, ix. 15).

The finest examples are furnished by the magnificent gold staters which are the glory of the Panticapaean mint ; these are in three varieties, according as the head of Pan, or, as some call him, a bearded Satyr, is in full face (v. 8), or turned to the left (v. 7) or in profile, but wreathed with ivy (v. 16). The reverse always bears a horned griffin. The types of the silver are more varied. Mostly we find lions (e.g. v. 11—13, the latter has been taken to be a complete allegory of Bosporus conquering Chersonese !), demi-lions (v. 10) or lion-faces (v. 9, 14); further, we have ox-heads (v. 15, 17), supposed by Orêshnikov to be in allusion to Bosporus. On copper the types of this period include demi-griffins (v. 18), lion-heads (v. 20), each with the sturgeon below, ox-heads similar to v. 15, and, most important of all, the bow and arrow (v. 19, ix. 15) which connects on with Leucon's reverse (vi. 16). To the ivth century belong some good coins of Phanagoria with quite distinctive types, Phanagoras, ox or demi-ox and wheatear (ix. 12 and B. xxiii. 2, 4 *b*).

The issues of the late iiird and iind centuries are marked by a predominance of Apolline types. The earliest of these (v. 25) still has macaroni treatment of the hair. The change seems to be about the time of Spartocus, on whose coin we have the bow in case, which we also find on some of the later Pan coins (v. 23), on a great countermark over a Pan coin (v. 21) and on the Theodosian coins which recall those of Leucon by their obverse (ix. 7 ; cf. vi. 17). But one copper issue (v. 24) almost exactly reproduces the coin of Spartocus (vi. 15) and the monogram might read ΣΠ. Similar coins occur in silver (B. xxi. 107, 112), and v. 26 is a degenerate variety. With Apollo go such types as the dolphin (vi. 2), the eagle (B. xxi. 102), and the horse (v. 25, 27), also Poseidon (v. 28). We now find fuller legends such as ΠΑΝΤΙ and ΠΑΝΤΙΚΑΠΑΙΤΩΝ. It is hard to know whether degraded Pans such as vi. 1 or ix. 15 should be classed with these or referred to a later assertion of coining rights ; vi..1 has Mithridatic affinities. To the iind century would seem to belong the first issue of Gorgippia, which may be even earlier to judge by the lettering (ix. 22).

During the Mithridatic period Dionysus (who was incarnate in the great king) appears on most of the coins, the three cities of Panticapaeum, Phanagoria and Gorgippia striking identical types[1] on blanks of a new fabric. To shew their identity in type and monogram I have given vi. 9, ix. 17 and ix. 24, so vi. 8, 10 recur at the other two towns, and ix. 16, 18, 23 have analogues at Panticapaeum. The balaustion is peculiar to Phanagoria, but the head of Artemis on ix. 13 is like that on vi. 7, which is clearly shewn to be Mithridatic by the characteristic pasturing deer, the mark of Mithridates' later tetradrachms (cf. Pl. iv. 22 at Chersonese)[2], and the star and crescent of ix. 14 is the well-known sign of the Achaemenid house. The last coin has no legend; ix. 21 is also distinguished by no legend to shew its minting place, but its

---

[1] Giel, *Kl. B.* Pl. iv., shews them well.   [2] Rather than the goddess's attribute.

monogram is Mithridatic, and it is commonly found on the Bosporus and undoubtedly belongs there[1].

No one has unravelled the confusion of issues which reigned on the Bosporus in the time following Mithridates.   There was such a restriking and countermarking of coins as has hardly ever been known.   The various short-lived governments seem to have wished to make political capital by making their emblems appear on the coinage as soon as possible; but to determine the order of these restrikings is difficult.

Such a coining contest seems to have gone on between Asander and his opponents.   The copper coins that are certainly his are marked by prows, emblems apparently of a naval victory, and we have an inscription dedicated by his admiral to naval deities[2].   On the other side we have the Mithridatic tradition of which Pharnaces was the embodiment.   To this belong the deer, eagle, tripod, stars, cornucopia and pilei, Apolline and Dionysiac emblems[3]; this side, too, made a bid for naval victory with a prow.   Further, there is an occasional reversion to autonomous types, such as we see in the Pan of VI. 1, the griffin wing of VI. 4 or the balaustion of IX. 14[4].   A very clear case of the Mithridatic tradition is seen in VI. 5 and 6, where Apollo's head recalls the king's features, and the types on the other side come from him, and yet VI. 6 is struck upon a coin of Asander as archon.   So VI. 11, a city coin, is struck over the unassigned coin IX. 21.   The eagle does not seem to be the Roman type, as it occurs on Mithridatic coins, e.g. of Sinope[5], and Asander has struck VI. 25 on VI. 11, itself already restruck.   All Asander's large bronzes are struck upon coins of Panticapaeum or Phanagoria.   The smaller ones, as Pl. VI. 24, are struck upon those of Amisus and Sinope[6].

So the big countermark put upon the Poseidon-prow coins (VI. 12) as on VI. 13 is exceedingly like the Pallas on VI. 14, which has a prow on its reverse.   To which side these stamps belonged we cannot distinguish.   With this interchange of monetary courtesies the city issues of the Bosporus come to an end.   Save only Phanagoria, granted an exceptional position by Agrippa and accordingly renamed Agrippias Caesarea, issued IX. 19 and 20 ; the head on the obverse seems decidedly like that of Livia, whether she were represented as a mortal or a goddess.   A similar head appears on coins of Gepaepyris (VII. 7), Cotys I, Rhescuporis I and Sauromates I, but local coining can hardly have survived into these latter reigns; the reverse types are quite common-place.

As to the standards upon which the minting of the precious metals in Panticapaeum and Phanagoria proceeded, it is, as usual, an article of Bertier-de-La-Garde's which gives most help[7].   With the archaic vth century silver coins he does not deal directly, but though remarking on their likeness to the Samian[8], many specimens of which have been found on the Bosporus, thinks

---

[1] For the coins with BÃE, VII. 14—18, B. XXIV. 11—26, v. p. 602.

[2] App. 39=*IosPE*. II. 25.

[3] *BMC. Pontus*, Introduction, p. xv sq.

[4] For this coin v. *Zt. f. Numismatik*, XX. p. 254, Pl. IX. 1, 2, where Imhoof-Blumer assigns this and a similar coin bearing a leather helmet on the obverse to Phanagoria.   Sinope had a very similar issue, cf. also *Kl. B.* Pl. V. 1, 2.

[5] *BMC. Pontus*, Introduction, p. xv, No. 1, Pl. XXIII. 2; Orêshnikov, *Cat. Uvarov*, p. 62.

[6] Asander's VI. 24 and *BMC. Pontus*, X. 8 on ib. III. 6 (Amisus) and XXIII. 2 (Sinope).

[7] *Numismatic Miscellany*, I. Moscow, 1909, "The Comparative Value of Monetary Metals on the Bosporus and Borysthenes in the middle of the IVth century B.C."

[8] *BMC. Ionia*, p. 350, Pl. XXXIV. 4—7.

that the Aeginetic system suits them best[1]. .Head[2] refers them to the Phoenician or Asiatic.   No electrum was coined at Panticapaeum at any time.

In the ivth century Panticapaeum coined in gold and copper, but no doubt the silver, still Aeginetic, was the real basis[3]. We have the stater (v. 17), the tetrobol (v. 15), the triobol (v. 9, 11, 12, 13, 14, and other varieties with Pan and lion), the diobol with a ram on the reverse, perhaps to be referred to the older series[4], the obol (v. 10, other varieties with young Pan and demi-lion or griffin)[5], similar types served for the half- and quarter-obol[6]. Stirred by the success of Philip's gold staters Panticapaeum attempted its issue of gold; of the two earlier varieties (v. 7, 8) 14 and 16 specimens are known, all extremely close to 140·4 grn. = 9·1 grm., and 46 of the later rather broader sort (v. 16) are nearly as exact. This unique weight has been generally supposed to be an Attic stater raised because gold was cheap at Panticapaeum owing to the produce of the Ural or Altai mines. But Bertier-de-La-Garde shews that this abundance of gold was mythical (v. supra p. 441), and that electrum was there a little dearer than elsewhere, 7·41 times silver, citing Demosthenes[7], who says that there a Cyzicene = 28 Attic drachmae. Assuming therefore that the unusual weight is due to a desire to make the gold coin commensurate in value with the silver unit he finds that to take the gold coin as equal to nine silver staters (v. 17) brings out the monetary ratio of gold to silver as 11·6 : 1, and the commercial as 12 : 1, again a little more than in Greece, but much the same as he had reached at Olbia, allowance being made for more alloy in the Olbian silver, and he thinks that we have in the gold piece, which weighs exactly an Egyptian *Kat*, 1½ drachmae or 9 obols Aeginetic, the very rare hects[8] (young Pan : demi-griffin l., 22·8 grn. = 1·5 grm.) being half-drachmae : so a silver stater would be exactly worth a gold obol. Unfortunately for Panticapaeum this ingenious adjustment was spoilt by the drop in gold down to ten times silver after Philip's coining and Alexander's conquests: also the 6°/₀ extra was just enough to make its gold sought after but not enough to give it an independent position in the market, and it suffered the fate of good coin, going straight out of the country, to the great loss of the town which had bought its gold rather dear. This last consideration brought ill success to a final attempt to coin gold, this time Attic staters; five are known just like v. 16 but, though perfectly preserved, weighing only 132 grn. = 8·55 grm. (one is 8·34), and a solitary half-stater, 66·4 grn. = 4·3 grm.[9]   The

---

[1] His last article, kindly sent to me in slip-proof, "Materials for Stathmological Investigation into the coinages...of Tauris and Sarmatia," *Num. Misc.* II. 1912, gives (pp. 26—36) weights of 585 coins of this early silver, dividing them into seven groups (one transitional) and sixty sorts denominated according to the average of each sort: sometimes two sorts make a continuous series and any division between them must be arbitrary (e.g. coins like v. 2 range from ·07 to ·25 grm., is ·14 grm. to be denominated an ⅓ or a ¼ obol?); I give his denominations for those I figure and for one or two larger ones, but these again are too rare for us to be sure of their proper weight: v. 1 is ⅓ obol; v. 2, IX. 11, ¼ obols; v. 4, 5, 6, IX. 10, diobols; v. 3, triobol; IX. 12 (cf. Panticapaeum, *Cat. Uvarov*, 366, 67·2 grn. = 4·35 grm.), pentobol; Giel, *Kl.B.* III. 18 (91 grn.

= 5·89 grm.), a drachma; Brussels (131·8 grn. = 8·54 grm.), 9 obols. I had put down v. 5, 6 as obols but they are clearly very light terms of series averaging 1·39 and 1·44 grm. He allows several issues of ½ obols (e.g. B. XIX. 9, like my v. 5, 4·6 grn. = ·3 grm.) and more doubtfully of 1, 1½ and 4 obols.

[2] *HN.*[2] p. 280; cf. *BMC. Thrace*, p. 87.

[3] Bertier-de-La-Garde, op. cit. pp. 36—40, enumerates 24 sorts and 213 coins, cf. *Comp. Values*, p. 34, n. 2.

[4] B. XIX. 26 (27 grn. = 1·74 grm.).

[5] B. XX. 65, 66, 87.

[6] Giel, *TRAS.* v. Pl. v. 29 (5·55 grn. = ·36 grm.), 30 (3·24 grn. = ·21 grm.).

[7] *In Phormionem*, § 23.

[8] B. XX. 61, *BMC. Thrace*, p. 4. No. 4.

[9] Bertier-de-La-Garde, *Comp. Values*, p. 51.

example of Philip and Alexander had been irresistible, but subservience to it was also useless and the city issued no more gold : for the IIIrd century Panticapaeum, like most cities, left coining to foreign kings. A fresh start with silver was made early in the IInd century by Panticapaeum, Phanagoria, and now also Gorgippia : it was on the reduced Attic standard, not the cistophoric[1]. There is nothing to guide us in classifying the denominations of the copper token currency.

The coinage of the Sindi belongs to the vth century before they came under the power of the Spartocids. Hecataeus, the name of their king at this period, if genuine, shews that the Greeks had already established a footing among them, and the coins are quite Greek imitated from familiar types: IX. 25 points to Heraclea Pontica, 26 to Teos, from which Phanagoria was colonized, and the owl suggests Athens or Sinope; the standard is Aeginetic[2].

The one coin of Dioscurias (IX. 28) appears to be Mithridatic. The Colchian coins (IX. 29)[3] are quite archaic, but no definite meaning can be attached to their types, which rather recall Samos.

One thing is clear throughout the Bosporus, that the coin types had not the slightest religious significance. The types of the main series were either canting heraldry or commercial, the imported types were purely political.

BOSPORUS ROYAL ISSUES. PLATES VI. 15—28, VII, VIII.

The royal issues have been discussed in the course of the history so far as they bore upon it, and the chief types of each king have been passed in review. As to their weights and denominations, the solitary silver coin of Spartocus appears to be a didrachm, that of Hygiaenon a drachma, and that of Paerisades a tetradrachm, all of the lightish Attic standard current in their day, and the gold staters correspond (v. p. 584). Later on those of Mithridates weigh about 128·86 grn. (= 8·35 grm.), those of Pharnaces and of Asander down to about B.C. 33, 125·6 grn. (= 8·14 grm.), the later issues of Asander and Dynamis (v. p. 592, f. 347), 123·9 grn. (= 8·03 grm.), just a trifle more than the Roman aureus with which they competed. The earlier gold coins with monograms average 122 grn. (= 7·91 grm.); Mithridates VIII 121·1 grn. (= 7·85 grm.), Cotys I and Rhescuporis 121·6 grn. (= 7·88 grm.), thus declining much less quickly than the Roman gold. When Rhescuporis was allowed to put his full name on coins he came down to 120·8 grn. (= 7·83 grm.), Sauromates I to 120·2 grn. (= 7·79 grm.) and Cotys II to 119·75 grn. (= 7·76 grm.)[4]. At this weight the coins remained fairly constant, but under this king the gold begins to be much alloyed, so that it passes into electrum, which is almost white under Sauromates II, after whose time the weight also becomes very uncertain. Under Cotys III the electrum was debased to mere silver, Sauromates III was satisfied with potin ; Ininthimeus returned to electrum, but the following Rhescuporis and Pharsanzes mostly

[1] v. 25 is a tetradrachm ; VI. 8, a didrachm, cf. VI. 15 ; v. 26, VI. 7, IX. 16, 22, 23, drachmae ; v. 27, IX. 13, tetrobols and v. 28 a diobol, or perhaps all three half-drachmae.

[2] IX. 25, 26, 27, all diobols. The other coins, B. XXIII. 1*d*—7, fit into the series, p. 631, n. 1, as

3, ½ and ¼ obols.

[3] P. A. Pakhomov, "Coins of Georgia," Pt I. *TRAS. Num. Sect.* I. iv. (1909), p. 6.

[4] Bertier-de-La-Garde, *Trans. Od. Soc.* XXIX. pp. 207—213, cf. *BMC. Pontus*, p. XXXiii.

coined potin, though there is a momentary reversion to gold of light weight 39·4 grn. (= 2·55 grm.)[1]. Soon after this the series passes into bronze with no definite weight and hardly any shape, but the king's name and the date distinguish the degenerate aureus.

The subsidiary signs of these royal coins have been specially studied by Bertier-de-La-Garde[2]. The coins of the gold series in certain years between A.B. 299 and 359 bear unexplained dots (VII. 4). Then between A.B. 418 and the time of utter degradation we have various marks, some, e.g. the club (VIII. 7, 20, 27) and the trident (VIII. 6), doubtless refer to the king's ancestry ; others, the star (VIII. 9)—which is a star and not a ✳ = sesterce[3]—crescent, bird, wreath, rosette (VIII. 15), dots (VIII. 17, 18, 21), and letters (VIII. 23), seem to mark the different issues in any given year when more than one issue was called for ; they are commonest under Eupator and Sauromates II.

The numbers upon the coins of B̂AE, BΛΛ and B̂AP (VII. 15—18, 12, 13, 5) have already been shewn to be marks of value, the unit perhaps being some fraction of the chalcus, but they are rather surprising, as 1—7, 10 do not fit into any familiar system; probably because they did not go with the Roman coinage to which the Bosporan was subordinated they gave way to a new series of numbers; B̂AP's ordinary coins have 6 and 12, Mithridates VIII's 12, Cotys I's 4, 6, 8, 12, 24, those of later kings till Sauromates II some 24 and all 48. At its heaviest the 48 weighs about the same as a Roman dupondius and the smaller denominations correspond roughly to Roman coins on the assumption that the unit is the half-ounce: probably this was an adaptation of the old local fraction of the chalcus to the Roman system.

By the earlier part of the reign of Sauromates II the copper coinage was a good deal debased and a new issue restoring the size of the principal coppers was made, perhaps at the command of Septimius Severus, whose head appears as a subsidiary mark (VIII. 14) or countermark upon the new coins. To prevent confusion with the former reduced copper there was introduced the new set of types mentioned above (p. 606) and new marks of value indicating at first a very small unit—Bertier-de-La-Garde suggests a scruple—as the smaller coins bear such large numbers as 96 and 144 (VIII. 13) ; but the main bulk have either a star (VIII. 12) or a star and B (VIII. 10, 11, 14) as being more convenient than the larger numbers, and indicating one and two *asses* respectively. But the reform was short-lived, and soon after Rhescuporis II the coppers lose all regularity of weight and become debased even before the gold, which had kept a good standard for nearly two centuries, followed its example.

---

[1] *MK.* II. p. 332.
[2] Bertier-de-La-Garde, "*Différents* on Bosporan Coins," *Numism. Misc.* I, Moscow, 1911, cf. *BMC.*

Pontus, p. xxxiv.
[3] *pace* Mommsen-Blacas, *Hist. de la Mon. Rom.*, III. pp. 19, n. 3, 294.

BIBLIOGRAPHY.

Sources.

All but the latest collected in Latyshev's *Scythica et Caucasica* (*TRAS.* 1890—1906).
Hecataeus, fr. 161, 164, 165, 198 : ap. Steph. Byz. s.vv. Δανδάριοι, Φαναγόρεια, 'Απάτουρον, Πάτρασις.
Herodotus, IV. 12, 28.
Lysias, *pro Mantitheo*, § 4.
Isocrates, *Trapeziticus*, §§ 3—5, 11, 20, 35, 51, 52, 57, 58.
Aeneas Poliorceticus, v. 2.
Demosthenes, *in Leptinem*, §§ 29—40, et Schol.
        in Phormionem, §§ 8, 23, 36.
        in Lacritum, §§ 31, 32, 34, 35.
        Vita Demosthenis Zosimi.
Aeschines, *in Ctesiphontem*, § 171.
Dinarchus, *in Demosthenem*, § 43.
Ps.-Scylax, 68, 72.
Aristotle, *Oeconomica*, II. ii. 8 (1347 *b*).
Theophrastus, *de Plantis*, IV. v. 3 ; xiv. 13.
Polybius, IV. xxxviii. 4.
Ps.-Scymnus, ll. 835–7, 886—899.
Diodorus Siculus, XII. xxxi. 1 ; xxxvi. 1 ; XIV. xciii. 1 ; XVI. xxxi. 6 ; lii. 10 ; xx. xxii—xxvi ; c. 7.
Strabo, II. i. 16 ; VII. iii. 8 ; 17 ; 18 ; iv. 3—7 ; XI. ii. 3—19 ; XII. iii. 29 ; XIII. iv. 3 ; XIV. i. 42.
Fl. Josephus, *de Bell. Jud.* II. xvi. 4.
Plutarch, *Vita Periclis*, XX.
      Vita Luculli, XXIV.
      Vita Pompeii, XXXII, XXXV, XXXVIII—XLII.
      περὶ τῶν Στωικῶν ἐναντιωμάτων, 20.
Dio Chrysostom, *de Regno*, §§ 75—77.
Memnon, c. XLIX. 4, LIII, LIV : *FHG.* III. pp. 551, 555.
Phlegon Trallianus, *Olymp.* Lib. XV. fr. 20 (XXII), *FHG.* III. p. 607.
        de Mirabilibus, XIX. (48).
Dionysius Periegetes, ll. 548—553, cf. Eustathium ad loc.
Arrian, ῎Εκταξις κατ᾽ 'Αλανῶν, §§ 3' 18.
Ps.-Arrian, *Periplus*, 26 (17), 29, 30 (19).
Ptolemy, *Geographia*, III. vi. 2—4 ; v. viii. 5—8 ; VIII. x. 4 ; xviii. 3.
Appian, *Hist. Rom.* Lib. XII. (*Mithridatica*), 15, 41, 64, 67, 69, 78, 83, 91, 101—121.
Lucian, *Alexander vel Pseudopropheta*, 57.
      Macrobii, 17.
      Toxaris, passim.
Polyaenus, *Strategemata*, V. xxiii ; xliv. 1 ; VI. ix. 1—4 ; VII. xxxvii ; VIII. lv.
Harpocration, s.vv. Θευδοσία, Νύμφαιον.
Dio Cassius, XXXVI. l. 2 ; XXXVII. x. 4—xiv. 3 ; XLII. ix. 2 ; xlv—xlviii ; LIV. xxiv. 4—6 ; LIX. xii. 2 ;
    LX. viii. 2.
Athenaeus, VI. 71 ; VII. 21 ; XII. 26.
Diogenes Laertius, VII. 6.
Philostrati, *Vitae Sophistarum*, I. iv. 25, p. 229.
Steph. Byz. s.vv. Βόσπορος, 'Ερμώνασσα, Κοροκονδάμη, Μαιῶται, Μυρμήκιον, Παντικάπαιον, Τάναις, Ταυρική,
    Ψησσοί.
Eusebius, *Chronici Canones*, Ol. 191. 3 (Sync. 594, 4), 220. 2 (ap. Hieron.).
Zosimus, *Historia Nova*, I. xxxi—xxxii.
Procopius, *de Bello Persico*, I. 12.
      de Bello Gothico, IV. 5.
      de Aedificiis, III. 7.

Anonymi *Periplus P.E.* 62 (21)—77 (51).
Petrus Patricius, fr. 3, *FHG.* IV. p. 184.
Theophanes Confessor, p. 175, de Boor.
Constantinus Porphyrogenitus, *de Them.* II. 12.
         de Adm. Imp. 37, 42, 53.
Johannes Malalas, p. 431, Bonn.

Cicero, *de Imperio Cn. Pompei,* IV. 9; IX. 22.
  pro Murena, XV—XVI (32—34).
A. Hirtius, *de Bello Alexandrino,* c. 78.
Livy, *Epitome,* LXXXXVIII, CI, CII, CXIII.
Justini *Epitome,* XXXVII. iii. 1, XXXVIII. vii. 3—10.
Ovid, *Ibis,* l. 310, et Scholia ad loc.
Pomponius Mela, I. 109—115; II. 2, 3.
Pliny, *NH.* IV. 86, 87 (26); VI. 17—20 (5—7); VII. 88 (24); XVI. 137 (59); XXV. 6 (3).
Tacitus, *Annals,* XII. 15—21.
Pliny the younger, *Epist.* LXIII, LXIV, LXVII.
Julius Capitolinus (*Hist. Aug.*), *Vita Antonini Pii,* 9.
Eutropius, VII. 9; VIII. 3.
Ammianus Marcellinus, XXII. vii. 10; viii. 26, 30.
Orosius, VI. iv, v. 1—7; xxi. 28.
Jordanes, *Romana,* 267.

General Histories.

For works before the time of Boeckh see Latyshev, *IosPE.* II. p. xvi n. 1.

Boeckh, *CIG.* II. pp. 90—107.
Ashik, Anton, *Bosporan Kingdom,* with many plans and drawings mostly superseded by *ABC.,* but not all. III Parts, Odessa, 1848-9.
Spasskij, Greg., *The Cimmerian Bosporus with its Antiquities and Notabilities.* Moscow, 1846.
—— *Archaeologico-Numismatic Miscellany* (a reprint of older treatises). Moscow, 1850.
Sabatier, P., *Souvenirs de Kertsch et Chronologie du Royaume de Bosphore.* St P. 1849.
Grigoriev, V. V., "The Kings of the Cimmerian Bosporus," *Journal of the Ministry of the Interior.* St P. 1851 = *Russia and Asia* (collected papers). St P. 1876, pp. 322—417.
Antiquités du Bosphore Cimmérien (ABC.). St P. 1854 (Reinach's Reprint, Paris, 1892).
Neumann, K., *Die Hellenen im Skythenlande,* pp. 469—570. Berlin, 1855.
Koehne, B. de, *Musée Kotschoubey (MK.),* Vol. I. p. 268 sqq. and all Vol. II. St P. 1857.
MacPherson, D., *Antiquities of Kertch.* London, 1857.
Sibirskij, Prince A., "A glance at the Autonomy and History of Panticapaeum," *Trans. Od. Soc.* VI. pp. 119—174.
Latyshev, V. V., Introduction to *IosPE.* II. pp. ix—lvi. St P. 1890.
—— Russian translation with some additions to the notes, Ποντικά, pp. 60—128. St P. 1909.
Brandis, C. G., *P.-W. Encycl.* s.v. Bosporos (2 and 3), II. pp. 757—788. Stuttgart, 1899.
Kulakovskij, J. A., *The Past of Taurida.* Kiev, 1906.
von Stern, E. R., *Theodosia,* gives a résumé of Bosporan History, pp. 6—22. Odessa, 1906.

Sites and Remains.

Motraye, A. De La, *Travels.* English Ed. London, 1723.
Guthrie, M., *Tour through Taurida.* London, 1802.
Pallas, P. S., *Travels in the Southern Provinces of the Russian Empire,* II. pp. 264—341. English Ed. London, 1802.
Clarke, E. D., *Travels in Various Countries,* II. pp. 64—152. 8vo. Ed. London, 1817.
Dubois de Montpéreux, F., *Voyage autour du Caucase,* Vol. v. Atlas, I. Pl. 2, 9—12, II. Pl. 42, 43, IV. Pl. 3—30. Paris and Neuchâtel, 1838—1843.

The older excavations are mostly summarized in Ashik, op. cit., *ABC.* and the course of research by P. M. Leontiev, *Propylaea* (Russian), I. ii. pp. 67—101. Moscow, 1856. Discoveries made in 1853 are given in the special report for that year (St P. 1855); later results appear year by year in *CR.* from 1859, and from 1899 in greater detail in *BCA.* I. pp. 80—93; II. pp. 40—60; IX. pp. 73—177; XVII. pp. 1—76; XXV. pp. 1—66; XXX. pp. 1—98; XXXV. pp. 12—47; XL. pp. 62—91, in the form of reports from the Directors of the Kerch Museum, Kareisha, Lutsenko, Verebrjusov, Gross, Duhmberg and Škorpil. There are summaries in *Arch. Anz.* by Kieseritzky, 1903, p. 83, and Pharmacovskij, 1904, p. 106; 1905, p. 60; 1906, pp. 110—113; 1907, pp. 126—140; 1908, pp. 164—174; 1909, pp. 149—156; 1910, pp. 207—216; 1911, pp. 198—205; 1912, pp. 338—348.

(Stempkovskij, I. A., *Investigations as to the position of ancient settlements on the shores of the Euxine.* St P. 1826.)

Dubrux, P., "Description of Ruins and traces of ancient Towns and Fortifications along the European shore of the Cimmerian Bosporus" (written in 1828—1833), *Trans. Od. Soc.* IV. (1858) pp. 3—84, plans i—iii; cf. also Latyshev's "Correspondence of Olenin and MS. of Dubrux," *Trans. Od. Soc.* XV. (1889), pp. 61—149.

(Blaramberg, J. de, "Observations on some points touching the ancient Geography of Taurida," *Trans. Od. Soc.* II.): review by Koehler and Graefe, ib. v. (1863), pp. 957—963.

(Ashik, A., *Hours of Leisure and Letters on the Antiquities of Kerch.* Odessa, 1851.)

Becker, P., "Kerch and Taman," *Propylaea,* III. pp. 349—382. Moscow, 1857.

Thompson, R. and J. Hogg, "Sketches of Kertch, its larger tumuli and some other remains," *Trans. Roy. Soc. of Literature,* Ser. II. Vol. VI. pp. 100—129. London, 1859.

Goertz, K., *Archaeological Topography of Taman Peninsula.* Moscow, 1870; reprinted St P. 1898.

—— *Historical View of Archaeological Investigations and Discoveries in the Taman Peninsula from 1800 to 1859.* Moscow, 1872; reprinted St P. 1898.

Bruun, Ph., "Various names of Kerch and its Environs in Ancient and Mediaeval Times," *Chernomorje,* II. p. 299. Odessa, 1880.

Kondakov, Tolstoi and Reinach, *Antiquités de la Russie Méridionale.* Paris, 1891.

See also the bibliographical notes to each section of Chapter XI.

For Tanais v. pp. 567, 620.

Plans. Panticapaeum: Blaramberg, op. cit. Pl. 1; Dubrux, op. cit. Pl. II; Ashik, *Bosp. Kingdom,* I. Pl. IV; *ABC.* Map I; Dubois de Montpéreux, op. cit. I. Pl. 2 inset; Thompson and Hogg, op. cit. p. 100, Pl. 1; *Mat.* XIX. Pl. I; *CR.* 1889, p. 17, f. 26.

Phanagoria: Goertz, *Arch. Top.* Pl. 3; *Hist. View,* Pl. I.

Tanais and Mouths of the Don: Report for 1853; *Propylaea,* IV. p. 387; *BCA.* XXXV. p. 86, f. 1.

Inscriptions and Historical Details.

Boeckh, A., *CIG.* II. pp. 90—170.

Latyshev, V. V., *IosPE.* II. St P. 1890; IV. 199—451, 468—478, St P. 1901; *Mat.* IX. pp. 46—64; XVII. pp. 26—71; XXIII. pp. 52—75; since 1900 *BCA.* II. pp. 69—72, Nos. 1—4; III. pp. 33—52, Nos. 1—17; X. pp. 25—97, Nos. 20—109; XIV. pp. 116—137, Nos. 38—55; XVIII. pp. 125—133, Nos. 40—50; XXIII. pp. 39—65, Nos. 22—34; XXVII. pp. 37—39, Nos. 33, 34; XXXVII. pp. 36—64, Nos. 1—46, pp. 71—77.

—— *Collection of Greek Inscriptions of Christian Times,* 77—107. St P. 1896.

—— *Mélanges Nicole,* p. 301 sqq. Geneva, 1905.

Trans. Od. Soc. XXIV. *Minutes,* p. 29; XXVI. *Minutes,* pp. 59—62; XXVII. *Minutes,* pp. 17, 18, 61, 62 XXVIII. *Minutes,* pp. 23—31, 133, 134; XXIX. *Minutes,* pp. 11—15, 63—65; XXX. *Minutes,* pp. 4—11.

Kulakovskij, J. A., Review of *IosPE.* II. *Journ. Min. Public Instr.* St P. May, 1891, p. 171.

Škorpil, V. V., *BCA.* III. pp. 122—165; XI. pp. 19—166; XXVII. pp. 42—54, Nos. 1—13; XXXIII. pp. 22—32, Nos. 1—14; XXXVII. pp. 1—10, Nos. 1—11; pp. 14—35; XL. pp. 92—117, Nos. 1—28; XLV. pp. 9—22, Nos. 1—14.

Latyshev's publications supersede all former ones such as appeared in *Trans. Od. Soc., CR.* and separate brochures.

For Inscriptions found outside S. Russia and bearing on Bosporan history v. App. 2, 28, 34, and supra pp. 576, 581 sqq., 613, n. 12.

Koehler, H. K. E., *Dissertation sur le Monument de Comosarye.* St P. 1805.

Mommsen, Th., "De Titulo Reginae Pythodoridis," *Ephem. Epigraphica,* I. pp. 270—276. Rome, 1872.

—— "Reges Thraciae inde a Caesare Dictatore," *Ephem. Epigraphica,* II. pp. 250—263. Rome, 1873.

—— *The Provinces of the Roman Empire* (=R.G. v.), I. 312—319. London, 1886.

Schaefer, A., "Athenischer Volksbeschluss vom J. 346," *Rheinisches Museum,* XXXIII. p. 418. Bonn, 1878.

Schaefer, A., "Die Regierungszeit des Königs Paerisades von Bosporus," *Rhein. Mus.* XXXVIII. Bonn, 1883.

Perrot, G., " Le Commerce des Céréales en Attique au IVᵉ Siècle avant notre ère," *Revue Historique*, IV. pp. 1—73. Paris, 1877.

Mishchenko, Th. G., "Trade Relations of the Athenian Republic with the Bosporan Kingdom," *Bulletin of the University of Kiev*, VII. (1878) p. 477.

Francotte, H., "Le pain à bon marché et le pain gratuit dans les cités grecques," *Mélanges Nicole*, p. 135. Geneva, 1905.

Gernet, L., "L'Approvisionnement d'Athènes en Blé au Vᵉ et IVᵉ siècles," *Bibl. de la Fac. de Lettres de Paris*, XXV. (1909) p. 269.

Grundy, G. B., *Thucydides and the History of his Age*, pp. 74 sqq., 159 sqq. London, 1911.

Gilbert, G., *Handbuch der griechischen Staatsalterthümer*, II. p. 188. Leipzig, 1885.

Reinach, Th., *Trois Royaumes d'Asie Mineure*, p. 201. Paris, 1888.

—— *Mithridate Eupator*. Paris, 1890.

von Domaszewski, A., "Die Dislocation d. röm. Heeres im Jahre 66 n. Chr.," *Rhein. Mus.* XLVII. p. 207. Bonn, 1892.

(Voigtius, W., *Symbolae ad Regum Sociorum P.R. Condicionem Cognoscendam*, Fasc. I. " De Asandro Bospori Rege." Kiev, 1894.)

—— "Quo Anno Agrippa Expeditionem Ponticam fecerit," *Griechische Studien für H. Lipsius*, pp. 127 —134. Leipzig, 1894.

(Ortmann, K., *De Regno Bosporano Spartocidarum*. Diss. Halensis Sax. 1894.)

(Melnikov-Razvedenko, S., " The Cimmerian Bosporus in the Spartocid Epoch," *Collection of Materials for a description of the Caucasus*. Tiflis, 1896.)

Latyshev, V. V., "On the History of the Bosporan Kingdom, I." (MS. P of Diodorus), *Journ. Min. Publ. Instr.* St P. June, 1894.

—— "On the History of the Bosporan Kingdom, II." (Camasarye), *Journ. Min. Publ. Instr.* St P. Nov. 1899.

—— "The Inscription of Eupaterius," *Vizantijskij Vremennik*, I. (1894) pp. 662—672. St P. and *Trans. Od. Soc.* XXI. pp. 245—250. Odessa, 1898.

—— "Agonistic Catalogue from Gorgippia" (*IosPE*. IV. 432), *Journ. Min. Publ. Instr.* St P. March, 1896.

—— "Site of Gorgippia," *Jour. Min. Publ. Instr.* St P. Nov. 1898.

All with some reviews reprinted in Ποντικά. St P. 1909.

Bonnell, E., *Beiträge zur Alterthumskunde Russlands*, II. pp. 619—785. St P. 1897.

Rostovtsev, M. I., "Roman Garrisons on the Tauric Peninsula," *Journ. Min. Publ. Instr.* St P. March, 1900 = *Klio*, II. pp. 80—95. Leipzig, 1902.

—— "Inscription from Eltegen" (with V. V. Škorpil): *BCA.* XXXVII. pp. 14—22. St P. 1910.

—— "Wall Paintings of the grave chamber opened at Kerch in 1891," *Bobrinskoj Miscellany*, pp. 118—154. St P. 1911.

Zhebelëv, S. A., "The Bosporan Archaeanactids," *Journ. Min. Publ. Instr.* St P. March, 1902.

Tolstoi, Ct I. I., "The Cult of Apollo on the Bosporus and at Olbia," *Journ. Min. Publ. Instr.* St P. Jan. 1904.

—— "ΑΠΑΤΟΡΟ on the Monument found by De La Motraye," *Journ. Min. Publ. Instr.* St P. May, 1909.

For the Religious Societies v. p. 620, n. 5.

Coins.

Besides the works of Koehne, Spasskij, Sabatier, Grigoriev, etc., given above.

Chabouillet, A., " Dissertation sur un Statère d'or du roi inconnu Acès ou Acas," *Mém. de la Soc. des Antiquaires de France*, XXIX. 3ᵉ Sér. 9, pp. 1—63. Paris, 1866.

Sallet, A. von (*Beiträge zur Geschichte und Numismatik des Cimmerischen Bosporus und des Pontus*. Berlin, 1866).

—— "Zur Numismatik der Könige von Pontus und Bosporus, I." *Zt. f. Numismatik*, IV. p. 229 ; do. II. ib. p. 304. Berlin, 1877.

—— *Beschr. d. Ant. Münzen d. k. Museen zu Berlin*, I. (1888) pp. 8—15.

Froehner, W., *Catalogue de Médailles du Bosphore Cimmérien formant la Collection de Mr Lemmé à Odessa*. Paris, 1872.

Gardner, P., *British Museum Catalogue (BMC.), Thrace, &c.*, pp. 4—10, 87. London, 1877.

Wroth, W., *BMC. Pontus, &c., and the Kingdom of Bosporus*, pp. xxviii—xxxviii, 1—5, 42—82. London, 1889.

Sibirskij, Prince A., "Silver and Copper Coins of Pharnaces," *Trans. Od. Soc.* x. (1877) p. 26.

—— "Hypothesis of the Ancestry of Asander," *Trans. Od. Soc.* x. (1877) p. 56.

    (Fragments of his *Catalogue des Médailles du Bosphore Cimmérien* (?), of which only three copies exist. Its only importance is for its illustrations.)

Keil, R., " König Saumakos," *Zt. f. Numismatik*, VIII. p. 329. Berlin, 1881.

Burachkov, P. O. (B.), *General Catalogue of Coins belonging to the Greek Colonies on the N. Coast of the Euxine*, pp. 129—289, Pl. XVIII—XXXII. (with corrections by Bertier-de-La-Garde, Moscow, 1907). Odessa, 1884.

Podshivalov, A. M., *Beschr. d. unedirten…Münzen von Sarm. Eur., Chers. Taur. und Bosp. Cim. aus d. Samml. A. M. P.* (also in Russian). Moscow, 1882.

—— (*Moscow Publ. and Rumjantsev Museums, Num. Cabinet*, Pt I. Moscow, 1884.)

—— *Monnaies des rois du Bosph. Cim., Dynasties des Spartocides et des Achéménides (Eupator I*). (I have used the Russian Version in *Trans. Od. Soc.* XV. (1889) pp. 14—40.) Moscow, 1887.

—— "Certain data for historical investigation into the rulers of the Cim. Bosp. according to epigraphic and numismatic monuments," *Trans. VIth Russian Arch. Congress*, II. p. 72. Odessa, 1888.

Imhoof-Blumer, F., *Porträtköpfe auf antiken Münzen Hellenischer und Hellenisirter Völker*, p. 34 sqq. Pl. IV, V. Leipzig, 1885.

Giel, Chr. (G.), *Kleine Beiträge zur antiken Numismatik Südrusslands (Kl. B.*), pp. 3—43. Moscow, 1886.

—— "On Bosporan coins with the monograms ℞, etc." *Trans. VIth Russian Arch. Congr.* Vol. II. p. 104. Odessa, 1888.

—— "New Acquisitions of my Collection." *TRAS.* V. p. 347 sqq., Pl. IV. 13—VII. 84. St P. 1892.

—— "Description of Coins added to my Collection in 1892 and 1893." *TRAS.* VII. p. 222 sqq., Pl. XIX. 29—XX. 23. St P. 1895.

Orêshnikov, A. V., *Zur Münzkunde des Cimmerischen Bosporus*. Moscow, 1883.

—— " The Cimmerian Bosporus in the Epoch of the Spartocids according to Inscriptions and Royal Coins." *Trans. VIth Russian Arch. Congress*, II. pp. 80—103. Odessa, 1888.

—— *Catalogue of the Collection of Antiquities of Ct A. S. Uvarov*, Pt VII. pp. 48—123, Pl. II—IV. Moscow, 1887.

—— " Nouvel Essai de chronologie des monnaies d'Asandre," *Annuaire de la Soc. française de Num.* 1888, pp. 5—9.

—— *Description of Ancient Greek Coins in Moscow University*, pp. 31—50. Moscow, 1891.

—— *Materials touching the Ancient Numismatics of the Black Sea Coast*. Moscow, 1892.

    p. 15. Coins with monograms ℞ and ℞. (Cf. *Annuaire de la Soc. française de Num.* 1889, pp. 56 sqq.)

    p. 21. Coins of the Bosporan King Sauromates I with barbarous inscriptions.

    p. 24. Coins of Eupator II.

—— "A gold stater of the Archon Hygiaenon," *Trans. Moscow Numismatical Society*, Vol. II. 1899.

—— "Pythodoris and her family in the Pontic Kingdom," *Bulletin of the Tauric Record Commission*, No. 34. Sympheropol, 1902.

—— "Cilician Coins of King M. Antonius Polemo," *Trans. Mosc. Num. Soc.* II. 1899.

—— "Coins of Chersonesus Taurica, Kings of the Cimmerian Bosporus and Polemo II of Pontus," *Numismatic Miscellany*, Vol. II. Moscow, 1912.

Antonovich, V. B., *Description of Coins in Kiev University*, Pt I. pp. 113—133. Kiev, 1896.

Hennig, R., "Die Regierungszeit des Asander," *Berliner Münzblätter*, n.f. XXIX. p. 85. 1908.

Bertier-de-La-Garde, A. L., "Comparative Values of monetary metals on the Bosporus and Borysthenes, c. 350 B.C." *Num. Misc.* Vol. I. Moscow, 1909.

—— " *Différents* (symbols) on Royal Bosporan coins of the Roman Period." ib. Moscow, 1911.

—— "Coins of rulers of the Cimmerian Bosporus determined by Monograms," *Trans. Od. Soc.* XXIX. (1911) pp. 117—232.

—— "Materials for Stathmological Investigations into the coinages of the ancient Greek cities and kings of Tauris and Sarmatia," *Numismatic Miscellany*, II. Moscow, 1912.

Škorpil, V. V., "The question when the Archon Hygiaenon ruled," *Miscellany of Archaeological Articles presented to Ct A. A. Bobrinskoi on the XXVth anniversary of his Presidency of the Archaeological Commission*, pp. 31—44. St P. 1911.

Head, B. V., *HN.*[2] pp. 280, 281, 494, 495, 499—505. Oxford, 1911.

APPENDIX

I have followed Latyshev (or in the case of Nos. 1, 2, 17[a], 28, 34 other editors) in his supplements, punctuation, accentuation, etc., except where I have noted divergent readings and in some inscriptions of which I have kept the precise spelling. I have not given more than one or two references to the literature of each inscription, the rest can be found under these or in the notes on the pages cited. Conventions as in *JHS*. except that { } enclose letters omitted by the engraver's carelessness. I have not always expanded obvious abbreviations. Names and facts occurring in these Inscriptions but not mentioned in the Text have not been indexed.

1. *CIL.* XIV. 3608. Near Tibur, cf. pp. 447, 469, 523.

TI. PLAUTIO M.F. (ANI)
SILVANÓ AELIAN(O)
PONTIF. SODALI AUG.
III vir. A.A.A.F.F., Q(uaestori) Ti. Caesaris
5 Legat. leg. V. in Germaniá
Pr. Vrb., Legat. et ComitI Claud.
Caesaris in Brittannia, ConsuIf,
Procos. Asiae, Legat. pro praet. Moesiae
In qua plura quam centum mill.
10 ex numero Transdanuvianor.
ad praestanda tributa cum coniugib.
ac lIberIs et principibus aut régibus suIs
tránsdúxit. Motum orientem Sarmatar.
compressit quamuIs parte{m} magná{m} exercitús
15 ad expedItionem in Armeniam mIsissct.
Ignotos ante aut infensos P.R. réges signa
Rómána adórátúros in rIpam quam tuebatur
perduxit. Régibus Bastarnárum et
Rhoxolánorum fIlios, Dácorum fratr(u)m
20 captos aut hostibus éreptos remIsit ; ab
aliquIs eórum opsides accépit ; per quem pácem
próvinciae et confirmauit et protulit,
Scythárum quoqué rége(m) a Cherróne(n)si,
quae est ultrá Borustenen, opsidióne summóto.
25 Primus ex ea próvincia magnó trItici modo
annónam P.R. adlevavit. Hunc légátum in
(in) Hispániam ad praefectur. Vrbis remissum
Senatus in praéfectura triumphalibus
ornamentIs honoravit, auctóre Imp.
30 Caesare Augusto Vespasiáno verbis ex
órátióne eius q(uae) i(nfra) s(cripta) s(unt) :
Moésiae ita praéfuit ut non debuerit in
me differri honor triumphálium eius
ornámentórum ; nisi quod látior eI
35 contigit mora titulus Praéfecto Vrbis.
Hunc in eadem praeféctúra Vrbis Imp. Caesar
Aug. Vespásianus iterum cos. fécit.

2. *IG. (CIAtt.)* I. 37 (after G. F. Hill, *Sources for Greek History*, p. 156, No. 308). Athens (424 B.C.), cf. pp. 447, 458, 561.

fr. z''''*2 : T T Νύ[μφαιον?]
              T T '[Ἐράκλεια?]
fr. z''''*7 : T 'O[λβία]
               T T T[ύρας]
               T · Τα[μυράκε]
              .X X Κα[ρκίνε]
              .X X Κιμ[μερ...]
              .X X Νικ[ονία]
              .. X Πατ[ρασύς]
              — — Κερ[ασός]
              — — Δα[νδάκε]

3. *IosPE.* I. 2. Tyras, Chobruchi. 181 A.D. cf. pp. 446, 541.

5 θειότ[ατος — — — — — 'Ρωμαίων αὐτοκράτω]-
ρ ηὔξησ[ε τὴν πόλιν ἡμῶν? — — —   ]
10 παρὰ τοὺς ἡγο[υμένους? — — —τῶν τῷ δήμῳ]
συμφερόντω[ν — — — — ὠφελίμου ἀν]-
δρὸς γεγονότ[ος..................... δε]-
δόχθαι τῇ βουλῇ καὶ τῷ δήμῳ Κο[κκήιον — — — —]·
νον τετειμῆσθαι χρυσῷ στεφάνῳ κ[αὶ τύπ]ῳ ἐπι[χρύσῳ?],
15 τό τε ψήφισμα τελειωθὲν ὑπὸ τοῦ γραμμ[ατέως]
τῆς πόλεως Οὐαλερίου 'Ρούφου δοθῆναι τῷ π[ατρὶ]
αὐτοῦ Κοκκηίῳ Οὐάλεντι καὶ τὸ ἀντίγραφον ἀ[ποτε]-
θῆναι εἰς τὰ δημόσια.—Ἐγένετο ἐν Τύρᾳ πρὸ ε' καλ. Μα-
ίων αὐτοκράτορι Κομόδῳ τὸ γ' καὶ 'Αντιστίῳ Βούρ-
20 ρῳ ὑπάτοις, ὡς δὲ Τυρανοὶ ἄγουσιν, ἔτους εκρ', ἀρχόντων δὲ τῶν περὶ Θεόδωρον Βοήθου, μηνὸς 'Αρτεμεισι-
ῶνος λ'. Ἐσφραγίσαντο· Θεόδωρος Βοήθου πρῶτος ἄρχων· Κ[α]ῖσαρ Ζούρη ἄρχων· Λαισθένης Μοκκα
ἄρχων· Αἴλιος Λούκιος ἄρχων· Οὐαλεριανὸς Που-
25 τικοῦ εἰσηγητής· Τι.β. Κλαύδιος 'Αντ[ισθένη]ς· Σεπτού-
μιος 'Ιεροσῶντος· Πίδανος Πιτφαρ[νάκ]ο[υ· Οὐα]λ[έρ]ιος
Βασσιανοῦ· 'Ιερώνυμος 'Αρτεμιδώρο[υ]· Θεοδ[ᾶς 'Αρτε]μι-
δώρου· Χρύσιππος Χρυσίππου· Νίγερ 'Αρτεμιδώρου· Μακάριος 'Αρτεμιδώρου· Διονυσόδωρος 'Αχιλλαίου·
30 Λούκιος Σατορνείλου· Φιλόκαλος Φιλοκάλου· Διονύσιος Πίσκα. 'Ηρακλέων Σωμᾶ· Δελφὸς Δελφοῦ.
Οὐαλέριος 'Ρούφος γραμματεὺς ἐτελείωσα τὸ
ψήφισμα.

4. *IosPE.* i. 3, Pl. i. Tyras, Korotnoe, A.D.
201, cf. pp. 446, 525.

[EXemplum epistulae ad Tertullum].
[Misimus tibi epistulam ad Heraclitum, unde]
[intelleges, quid statuerimus de immunitate],
[quam Tyrani sibi concessam esse contendunt].
[Quam licet admittere non soleamus nisi pri]-
1 [vile]gii auct[oritate perpensa et origine immu]-
nitatis inspecta, quod us[urpatum esse diu qua]-
qua ratione videbatur, cum iusta [moderati]-
one servavimus, ut neque ipsi cons[uetudi]-
5 ne diuturna pellerentur et in poste[rum]
decreta civium adsumendorum consi[liis]
praesidis provinciae c(larissimi) v(iri) perpenderentu[r].

EXemplum epistulae ad Heraclitum.
Quamquam Tyranorum civitas or(i)ginem
10 dati beneficii non ostendat nec facile, quae
per errorem aut licentiam usurpata sunt, prae-
scriptione temporis confirmentur, tamen,
quoniam divi Antonini parentis nostri litte-
ras, sed et fratrum imperatorum cogitamus, item
15 Antonii Hiberi gravissimi praesidis, quod attinet
ad ipsos Tyranos quique ab iis secundum leges
eorum in numerum civium adsumpti sunt, ex pristino more nihil mutari volumus. Retinere
igitur quaqua ratione quaesitam sive possessam
20 privilegii causam in promercalibus quoque rebus, quas tamen pristino more professionibus
ad discernenda munifica mercimoniorum eden-
das esse meminerint. Sed cum Illyrici fructum
per ambitionem deminui non oporteat, sciant
25 eos, qui posthac fuerint adsumpti, fructum
immunitatis ita demum habituros, si eos legatus
et amicus noster v. c. iure civitatis dignos esse de-
creto pronuntiaverit. Quos credimus satis a-
bundequ(a)e sibi consultum, si grati fuerint, exi-
30 stimaturos, quod origine beneficii non quaesita
dignos honore cives fieri praeceperimus.

Ὀουίνιος Τέρτυλλος ἄρχουσι, βουλῇ, δήμῳ Τυρανῶν χαίρειν.
Ἀντίγραφον τῶν θείων γραμμάτων, πεμ-
35 φθέντων μοι ὑπὸ τῶν κυρίων ἡμῶν ἀνει-
κήτων καὶ εὐτυχεστάτων Αὐτοκρατόρων,
τούτοις μου τοῖς γράμμασιν προέταξα, ὅ-
πως γνόντες τὴν θείαν εἰς ὑμᾶς μεγαλο-
δωρίαν τῇ μεγάλῃ αὐτῶν τύχῃ εὐχαριστή-
40 σητε. Ἐρρῶσθαι ὑμᾶς καὶ εὐτυχεῖν πολ-
λοῖς ἔτεσιν εὔχομαι. Ἀπεδόθη πρὸ
ιγ΄ καλανδῶν Μαρτίων, Ληναιῶνος η΄.
Ἀνεστάθη ἐπὶ Μουκιανοῦ καὶ Φαβιανοῦ
ὑπάτων, ἐν τῷ εμρ΄ ἔτει,
45 ἀρχῆς Π(οπλίου) Αἰλίου Καλπουρνίου.

4ᵃ. *IosPE.* i. 120 (iv. p. 275). Olbia, cf. p. 458,
n. 3.

+ Α Ρ Μ [ι ⊙ Σ Τ
⊙ Δ Ι Φ [Ι Λ ⊙
Ε Ι Μ Ι Μ
Ν Η Μ Α

5. *IosPE.* i. 11. Anadolu Kavak (Temple of
Zeus Urius), cf. pp. 459, 472, 485.

1 [Εἰς Βο]ρυσσθένη εἰσπλεῖν τὸν βου-
[λόμε]νον κατὰ τάδε· ἔδοξε βουλῆι
[καὶ δή]μωι, Κάνωβος Θρασυδάμαντο[ς
εἶπε·] εἶναι παντὸς χρυσίου ἐπισήμο(υ)
5 [κα]ὶ ἀργυρίο(υ) ἐπισήμου εἰσσαγωγὴ[ν
κ]αὶ ἐξαγωγήν· ὁ δὲ θέλων πωλεῖν [ἢ
ὠν]εῖσθαι χρυσίον ἐπίσημον ἢ ἀργύ-
[ριο]ν ἐπίσημον πωλείτω καὶ ὠνείσθ[ω
ἐπὶ] τοῦ λίθου τοῦ ἐν τῶι ἐκκλησιασ[τη-
10 ρίωι·] ὃ[ς] δ᾽ ἂν ἄλλοθι ἀποδῶται ἢ πρίη-
[ται, στε]ρησεῖται ὁ μὲν ἀποδόμενος το[ῦ
πωλουμέν]ου ἀργυρίου, ὁ δὲ πριάμενος τῆ[ς
τιμῆ]ς, ὅσου ἐπρίατο· πωλεῖν δὲ καὶ ὠν[ε-
ῖσθαι] πάντα πρὸς τὸ νόμισμα τὸ τῆς
15 [πόλε]ως, πρὸς τὸν χαλκὸν καὶ τὸ ἀργύριο[ν
τὸ] Ὀλβιοπολιτικόν· ὃς δ᾽ ἂν πρὸς ἄλλο [τι
ἀποδ]ῶται ἢ πρίηται, στερήσεται ὁ μὲν· [ἀ-
ποδ]όμενος ο(ὗ) ἂν ἀποδῶται, ὁ δὲ πριάμ[ε-
ν]ος ὅσου ἂν πρίηται· πράξονται δὲ πα[(ὁ)ς
20 πα]ρὰ τὸ ψήφισμα τι παρανομο(ῦ)ντας
οἳ ἂν τὴν ὠνὴν πρίωνται τῶν παρανο-
μησάντων δίκηι καταλαβόντε[ς·]
τὸ δὲ χρυσίον πωλεῖν καὶ ὠνεῖσθ[αι τὸ]-
ν μὲν στατῆρα τὸν Κυζικηνὸν ἐ[νδεκά]-
25 το(υ) ἡμιστατήρο(υ) καὶ μήτε ἀξιώτερο[ν μή]-
τε τιμιώτερον, τὸ δ᾽ ἄλλο χρυσίον τὸ [ἐ-
πίση]μον ἅπαν καὶ ἀργύριον τὸ ἐπίση[μον
π]ωλεῖν καὶ ὠνε(ῖ)σθαι ὡς ἂν ἀλλ[ήλους]
πείθωσι· τέλος δὲ μηδὲν [πράττειν μήτε
30 χρ]υσίου ἐπισήμου μήτ᾽ ἀργυ[ρίου ἐπιση-
μ]ου μήτε πωλο(ῦ)ντα μήτ᾽ [ὠνούμενον. .

6. *IosPE.* iv. 460. Olbia, cf. pp. 67, 465.

Φημὶ διακοσίας τε
καὶ ὀγδοήκοντα ὀργυιὰς
καὶ δύο τοξεῦσαι
κλεινὸν Ἀναξαγόραν
υἱὸν Δημαγόρεω,
Φίλτεω δὲ πα...

A (contd).

7. *IosPE.* i. 16, Pl. ii. Olbia, cf. pp. 104, 118,
125–6, 259, 388, 443, 459–463, 471–
474, 481–485, 488.

A.

Ἔδοξε βουλῆι καὶ δήμ[ωι] εἰκάδι, οἱ ἄρχο[ν-
τ]ες καὶ οἱ ἑπτὰ εἶπαν· Ἐπειδὴ Ἡροσῶν τε ὁ Πρ[ω].
τογένους πατὴρ πολλὰς καὶ μεγάλας
χρείας παρείσχηται τῆι πόλει καὶ εἰς χρη-
5 μάτων καὶ εἰς πραγμάτων λόγον, Πρωτογένης τε διαδεξάμενος τὴμ παρὰ τοῦ πατρὸς εὔνοιαν πρὸς τὸν δῆμον διὰ βίου δια-
τετέλεκεν λέγων καὶ πράττων τὰ βέλ-
τιστα· καὶ πρῶτομ μὲν παραγενομέ-
10 νου Σαϊταφάρνου τοῦ βασιλέως εἰς Κάγκυ-
τον καὶ ἀπαιτοῦντος τὰ δῶρα τῆς παρόδου,
τῶν δὲ κοινῶν ἐξηπορημένων, ἐπικληθεὶς
ὑπὸ τοῦ δήμου ἔδωκε χρυσοῦς τετρακοσίου[s]·
τῶν τε ἀρχόντων θέντων τὰ ἱερὰ ποτήρι-
15 α εἰς τὴν τῆς πόλεως χρείαν πρὸς Πολύχα[ρ]-
μον πρὸς χρυσοῦς ἑκατὸν καὶ οὐκ ἐχόντων
λύσασθαι, τοῦ δὲ ξένου φέροντος ἐπὶ τὸν
χαρακτῆρα, αὐτὸς ὑπεραποδοὺς τοὺς ἑκατὸν χρυσοῦς ἐλύσατο· τῶν τε περὶ Δημοκῶν-
20 τα ἀρχόντων ἀγορασάντων λυσιτελῶς οἶνον
χρυσῶν τριακοσίων, οὐκ ἐχόντων δὲ τὴν τιμὴν
διαλῦσαι, ἐπικληθεὶς ὑπὸ τοῦ δήμου ἔδωκε τοὺς
τριακοσίους χρυσοῦς· ἐπί τε Ἡροδώρου ἱέρεω σιτοδείας οὔσης καὶ πωλουμένου τοῦ σίτου εἰς πέν-
25 τε, καὶ διὰ τὸν κίνδυνον τὸν ἐπιφερόμενον οἰομένου δεῖν τοῦ δήμου παραθέσθαι σῖτον ἱκα-
νὸν καὶ εἰς ταῦτα παρακαλοῦντος τοὺς
ἔχοντας, πρῶτος παρελθὼν ἐπηγγείλατο μεδίμνους δισχιλίους εἰς δέκα, καὶ
30 τῶν λοιπῶν παραχρῆμα κομισαμένων τὴν τιμήν, αὐτὸς ἐνιαυτὸν συμπ[ε]-
ριενεγχθεὶς τόκον οὐδένα ἐπράξατο· ἐ-
πί τε τοῦ αὐτοῦ ἱέρεω ἀθρόων παραγενο-
μένων Σαΐων ἐπὶ τὴν τῶν δώρων κομι-
35 δήν, οὐ δυναμένου δὲ τοῦ δήμου δοῦναι αὐτοῖς, ἀξιώσαντος δὲ Πρωτογένην
βοηθῆσαι τοῖς καιροῖς, παρελθὼν ἐπηγγε[ί]-
λατο χρυσοῦς τετρακοσίους· αἱρεθεὶς τε
τῆς τῶν ἐννέα ἀρχῆς οὐκ ἐλαττόνωμ
40 μὲν ἢ χιλίων καὶ πεντακοσίων χρυσῶν
πρόδεσιν ἐποιήσατο ἐπὶ ταῖς μελούσαις
προσόδοις, ἐξ ὧμ πολλοὶ μὲν σκηπτοῦχοι
ἐθεραπεύθησαν εὐκαίρως, οὐκ ὀλίγα δὲ
δῶρα παρεσκευάσθη τῶι βασιλεῖ λυσιτελῶ[s]·
45 πραθέντος τε τοῦ στόλου εἰς βασίλεια
κατὰ τὸ ψήφισμα, ἐν ὧι ἔδει τοὺς ἀγορά-

σαντας λαβεῖν παρὰ τῆς πόλεως χρυσο[ῦς]
τριακοσίους, καὶ ἀγοράσαντος Κόνωνος, δι-
ὰ τὸ δὲ τὰ χρήματα μὴ δύνασθαι
50 δοῦναι τοὺς ἄρχοντας, ἀλλ᾽ εἶναι παρὰ τοῖς τελώναις, δια[λ]υσαμένων τὴν ὠ.
νὴν πρὸς τὴμ πόλιν, καὶ διὰ ταῦτα τρί[s]
ἀναπραθείσης τῆς ὠνῆς καὶ τὸ τρίτον
ἀγοράσαντος Φορμίωνος, σινιδὼν
55 Πρωτογένης διότι μεγάλοις διαπτώ-
μασι περιπεσεῖται ἡ πόλις, αὐτὸς παρελθὼν εἰς τὴν ἐκλησίαν ἔδωκε τοὺς τριακοσίους χρυσοῦς· πάλιν τ᾽ ἐπὶ Πλειστάρχο(υ)
ἱέρεω σιτοδείας γενομένης ἰσχυρᾶς καὶ πω-
60 λουμένου τοῦ σίτου εἰς μέδιμνον καὶ δύο τρι-
τεῖς, προδήλου δὲ ὄντος ἔσεσθαι τιμουστέ-
ρου, ὥσπερ δὲ καὶ ἐγένετο παραυτίκα ὁ μέδι-
μνος χρυσοῦ καὶ δύο τριτῶν, καὶ διὰ ταῦτα
διαγωνιάσαντος τοῦ δήμου καὶ οἰομένου
65 δεῖν σιτωνῆσαι, εἰς δὲ ταῦτα χρείας παρα-
σχέσθαι τοὺς εὐπορουμένους, πρῶτος συν-
ελθούσης ἐκλησίας ἐπηγγείλατο εἰς τὴν
σιτωνίαν χρυσοῦς χιλίους, οὓς παραυτίκα ἐ-
νέγκας ἔδωκε, ὧν τοὺς τριακοσίους ἀτόκους
70 εἰς ἐνιαυτόν, καὶ δοὺς χρυσίον πᾶν χαλκὸν
ἐκομίσατο ἐκ τετρακοσίων· πρῶτος δ᾽ ἐπηγγείλατο πυρῶν μεδίμνους δισχιλίους πεντακοσίους, ὧν τοὺς πεντακοσίους μὲν ἔδωκεν
εἰς τέτταρας καὶ ἑκτέα, τοὺς δὲ δισχιλίους εἰ[s]
75 δύο καὶ ἑπτὰ χαλκοὺς ἡμιέκτεα, καὶ τῶν λοιπῶν τῶν
ἐν τούτωι τῶι καιρῶι ἐπαγγειλαμένων παραχρῆμα τὰς τιμὰς κομισαμένων ἀπὸ τῶν
πορισθέντων χρημάτων, αὐτὸς συμπεριε-
νεγχθεὶς ἐνιαυτὸν τὴν τιμὴν ἐκομίσατο τό-
80 κον οὐδένα πραξάμενος, καὶ διὰ τὴμ Πρωτο-
γένους προθυμίαν πολλὰ μὲγ χρήματα, οὐ-
κ ὀλίγος δὲ σῖτος ἐπορίσθη τῶι δήμωι· τοῦ τε
βασιλέως Σαϊταφάρνου παραγενομέ-(νομε)
νου εἰς τὸ πέραν ἐπὶ θεραπείαν, τῶν δὲ ἀρχόν-
85 των συναγόντων ἐκλησίαν καὶ τήν τε πα-
ρουσίαν δηλωσάντων τοῦ βασιλέως καὶ ὅ-
τι ἐν ταῖς προσόδοις ἐστὶν οὐδέν, παρελθὼν
Πρωτογένης ἔδωκε χρυσοῦς ἐνακοσίους· τῶ[ν]
δὲ πρεσβευτῶν λαβόντων τὰ χρήματα καὶ ἀ-
90 [Α]ριστοκράτους, τοῦ δὲ βασιλέως τὰ μὲν δῶρ[α
μεμψ]αμένου, εἰς ὀργὴν δὲ καταστάντος κα[ὶ
τὴν] ἀνάζευξιν ποιησαμέν[ου, μετα.ρ........
...] καὶ τοῖς προστάταις.ανα[ξίως, ὧν ἕνεκεν (?)
95 συν]ελθὼν ὁ δῆμος περίφ[οβος ἐγένετο καὶ
πρεσ]βευτὰς ἐπὶ τ — — — —
— — σω — —

1. 58 perhaps Πλειστάρχο[υ].

B (contd).

7. *IosPE*. I. 16 (contd).

B.

ἔτι δὲ τοῦ πλείστου μέρους τοῦ πρὸς τὸμ ποτ[α]-
μὸν τῆς πόλεως ἀτειχίστου ὄντος, τοῦ τε κα[τὰ]
τὸν λιμένα παντὸς καὶ τοῦ κατὰ τὸ πρότερ[ον]
ὑπάρχον ἰχθυοπώλιον, ἕως οὗ ὁ ἥρως ὁ Σωσίας,
5 τῶν δὲ αὐτομόλων ἐπαγγελλόντων Γαλά-
τας καὶ Σκίρους πεποιῆσθαι συμμαχίαν καὶ δύναμιν συνῆχθαι μεγάλην καὶ ταύτην τοῦ χει-
μῶνος ἥξειν ἐπαγγελλόντων, πρὸς δὲ τούτοις Θισαμάτας καὶ Σκύθας καὶ Σαυδαράτας ἐπι-
10 θυμεῖν τοῦ ὀχυρώματος, δεδιότας ὡσαύτως καὶ
αὐτοὺς τὴν τῶν Γαλατῶν ὠμότητα, καὶ διὰ
ταῦτα πολλῶν ἐχόντων ἀθύμως καὶ παρεσκε-
ασμένων ἐγλείπειν τὴμ πόλιν, ἅμα δὲ τῶι και·
ἄλλα γεγενῆσθαι ἐλαττώματα πολλὰ
15 κατὰ τὴγ χώραν, ἐφθάρθαι μὲν τὴν οἰκετεί-
αν ἅπασαν καὶ τοὺς τὴμ παρώρειαν οἰ-
κοῦντας Μιξέλληνας οὐκ ἐλάττους ὄν-
τας τὸν ἀριθμὸν χιλίων καὶ πεντακοσίων,
τοὺς ἐν τῶι προτέρωι πολέμωι συμμαχήσαντας
20 ἐν τῆι πόλει, ἐγλελοιπέναι δὲ πολλοὺς μὲν
τῶγ ξένων, οὐκ ὀλίγους δὲ τῶμ πολιτῶν, ὧν ἕ-
νεκεν συνελθὼν ὁ δῆμος διηγωνιακὼς καὶ τὸγ
κίνδυνον τὸμ μέλλοντα καὶ τὰ δεινὰ πρὸ ὀ-
φθαλμῶν ποιούμενος παρεκάλει πάντας
25 τοὺς ἰσχύοντας βοηθῆσαι καὶ μὴ περιιδεῖν τὴν ἐκ
πολλῶν ἐτῶν τετηρημένημ πατρίδα ὑποχείριον γενομένην τοῖς πολεμίοις, οὐδενὸς δ᾽ ἐπιδι-
δόντος ἑαυτὸν οὔτ᾽ εἰς ἅπαντα οὔτ᾽ εἰς μέρη ὧν
ἠξίου ὁ δῆμος, ἐπηγγείλατο αὐτὸς κατασκευᾶν
30 ἀμφότερα τὰ τείχη καὶ προθήσειμ πᾶσαν τὴν
εἰς αὐτὰ δαπάνην, καίπερ αὐτῶι προκειμένων
οὐκ ἐλασσόνωγ χρυσῶν ἢ χιλίων καὶ πεντακοσίων, καὶ εὐθὺς ἐνέγκας εἰς τὴν ἐκλησίαν χρυσοὺς
πεντακοσίους εἰς τοὺς ἀρραβῶνας ἀπέδοτο πάν-
35 τα τὰ ἔργα ὑπὸ κήρυκα, καὶ παρὰ τὸ τὴν ἀρίθμη-
σιν ποιήσασθαι ἐξ ἑτοίμου τοὺς ἐργώνας οὐκ ὀλίγα χρήματα περιεποίησε τῆι πόλει· ἔτι δὲ πολλῶν ἐργωνῶν ἐγκαταλιπόντων τὰ ἔργα Πρωτογένης τῆι πόλει τὰ μὲν ἔργα αὐτὸς συνετελέ-
40 σατο, διάπτωμα δὲ τῶι δήμωι οὐδὲν ἀνή-
νεγκεν, ἀναλώσας τε εἰς ἀμφότερα τὰ τείχη
χρυσοὺς χιλίους πεντακοσίους καὶ τὸ πλεῖστον
διαλύσας χρυσίον ἐκομίσατο χαλκὸν ἐκ τετρα-
κοσίων· κατεσκεύασε δὲ καὶ τοὺς πύργους κακῶς δι-

45 ακειμένους, τοὺς πρὸς ταῖς μεγάλαις πύλαις ἀμ-
φοτέρους καὶ τὸγ Καθηγήτορος καὶ τὸγ κατὰ τὴν
ἁμαξιτὸγ καὶ τὸν Ἐπ[ι]δαυρίου· ἐπεσκεύασε δὲ
καὶ τὸ σιτόβολον· κατεσκεύασε δὲ καὶ τὸμ πυλῶ-
να τὸν ἐπὶ τοῦ δείγματος· ἔτι δὲ τῆς πόλεως
50 ναῦλον τελούσης τοῖς ἄγουσι τοὺς λίθους ἰδιώ-
ταις διὰ τὸ τὰ πλοῖα τὰ δημόσια κακῶς διακεῖσ-
θαι καὶ μηθὲν ἔχειν τῶν ἁρμένων, ἐπηγγείλατο
καὶ ταῦτα κατασκευᾶν, ἀναλώσας τ᾽ εἰς ταῦτα
πάντα χρυσοὺς διακοσίους λόγον ἤνεγκε παρα-
55 χρῆμα, ὧν ἕνεκεν ὁ δῆμος πολλάκις αὐτὸγ καὶ
πρότερον ἐστεφανωκὼς καὶ τότ᾽ ἐστεφάνωσεν
ἐπὶ τῆι τοῦ λόγου ἀποδείξει· ἔτι δὲ λοιπῆς οὔσης
ἀσυντελέστου τῆς κατὰ τὸμ Πόσιος πύργον σχοι-
νιαίας εἰς τὸν ἐπάνω τόπον, ἐπικαλεσάμενος ὁ
60 δῆμος ἠξίωσε καὶ ταύτην συντελέσασθαι τε-
τάρτην οὖσαν σχοινιαίαν, Πρωτογένης δὲ οὐ-
δὲμ βουλόμενος ἀχαριστεῖν ὑπέμεινε καὶ ταύτην τὴν τειχοδομίαν, εἰς ἣμ προέθηκε χρυσοὺς ἑ-
κατόν· ἐπὶ δὲ τῆς κοινῆς οἰκονομίας καὶ ταμιεί-
65 ας γενόμενος καὶ χειρίσας τὰς μεγίστα(ς) τῆς πόλ[ε]-
ως προσόδους οὐδένα μὲν τῶν τελωνῶν ἐκ τῶν
ὑπαρχόντων ἐξέβαλε, οὐδενὸς δ᾽ ἀπηλλοτρί-
ωσε οὐδὲν τῶν ὑπαρχόντων, συμπεριενεχθεὶς
δὲ τοῖς καιροῖς αὐτῶν πᾶσι, τοῖς μὲν ἀφέσεις ἐ-
70 ποιήσατο τῶγ χρημάτων, τοῖς δὲ συμπεριενεγ-
χθεὶς χρόνον ὅσον ἠβούλοντο τόκον οὐδένα ἐ-
πράξατο· πλεῖστα δὲ χειρίσας τῶγ κοινῶν, τρία δὲ
ἔτη συνεχῶς πάντα διώκησεν ὀρθῶς καὶ δικαίως, τοὺς μὲν λόγους ἐν τοῖς ὡρισμένοις χρόνοις ἀ-
75 ποφέρων, τὰ δ᾽ ἀπὸ τῶμ προσόδωμ πίπτοντα
ἐν τοῖς τῆς πολιτείας χρόνοις παραδεξάμενος
εἰς κομιδὴν τε τῆς γεγενημένου τούτου ἐπ᾽ ἀ-
ληθείας, ἐξ ὧν ἀπέλυσε μὲν τὴμ πόλιν ὀφειλη-
μάτων, παρέλυσε δὲ τόκων· τῶν δ᾽ ἐν τῆι πόλει
80 κακῶς διακειμένων πάντων διά τε τοὺς πολέ-
[μ]ους καὶ τὰς ἀφορίας, καὶ τῶν ὑπαρχόντων εἰς τὸ
[μη]θὲν ἡκόντων, ζητήσαντος ὑπὲρ τούτων τοῦ
[δή]μου ἐπιμηνιεῦσαι καὶ προνοῆσαι χρησίμως
[τοῖ]ς τε δανεισταῖς καὶ τοῖς χρήσταις, ὀφειλομένων
85 [α]ὐτῶι καὶ πατρὶ χρυσῶν ἑξακισχιλίων πρῶτος
[ἐ]πέτρεψε τῶι δήμωι ὃν ἂμ βούληται τρόπον χρή-
[σασθαι] αὐτῶι, ἀξιώσαντος δὲ ἄφεσιν ποιήσασ-
[θαι] τοῖς χρήσταις ἀφῆκε πᾶσι καὶ οὐδὲν ἄ-
[λλο ποθεινό]τερον αὑτῶι νομίσας εἶναι
90 [τοῦ παρὰ τοῦ δήμου αὑτῶι] ὑπάρχειν εὔνοιαν τοῦ ἰδ-
[ίου ———————————— τ]εθραυσμένος τοῖς ὑπα-
[η ————————————— χρυσ]οῦς οὓς ἅπασι τοῖς
[————————————— πρὸς οὐ]θένα ἐ-
95 [————————————————] τειχ

8. *IosPE.* ι. 46. Olbia, cf. pp. 463, 474.

  Έπταδεύσαντες
  έπεμελήθησαν τοῦ
    θησαυροῦ·
  Ήρόδοτος Παντακλέους,
5 Έπιχάρης Διονυσοφάνους,
  Ποσειδώνιος Εύκράτους,
  Άδείμαντος Άπα[τ]ουρίου,
  Ίστικ[ῶ]ν Μητροδώρου,
  Λεοντομ[έ]νης Ήροσῶντος,
10 Ήρακλείδης Εύβίου.
  Τούς θύοντας άπάρχεσθαι
  [ε]ίς τὸν θησαυρόν·
  βοὸς μὲν χιλίους διακοσίους,
  ίερείου δὲ κ[α]ὶ αἰγὸς τριακοσίους,
15 [τ]έ[ρφ]ους δὲ ἐξήκοντα.

9. *BCA.* XVIII. p. 96, No. 2. Olbia, cf.
      pp. 463, 472.

 1 ['Επὶ ἄρχοντος......]ς τοῦ μετὰ Ποσίδεον Ἀναξα-
  [γόρου, μηνὸς Μεταγειτ]νιῶντος ϛκ΄, ἥν ὁ δῆμος ἐψη-
  [φίσατο γνώμην κυρῶσα]ι ἔδοξε βουλῇ καὶ τῷ δήμῳ. "Αρ-
  [χοντες οἱ περὶ Ποσίδεο]ν 'Αναξαγόρου εἶπαν· ἐπειδὴ
5 [.........ὁ δεῖνα] Φιλοκράτο[υ] 'Αμισηνὸς κυβερ-
  [νήτης ὢν πρότερόν τε χο]ρήγια [β]ασι[λικὰ?] τοῖς μεθηδρασ-
  [μένοις ὑπὸ τοῦ βασιλέως Μ]ιθραδάτου Εύπάτορος Άρμε-
  [νίοις κομίσαι πλέων? κ]ατὰ Σινώπης ἐφιλοτειμήθη
  [καὶ νῦν τούς τε ἡμετέρους πρεσ]βευτὰς καὶ [τ]ὴν ὑπὸ τοῦ βασι-
10 [λέως πεμπομένην βοήθειαν?] τῷ δήμω[ι] ἀναλαβεῖν ἄπα-
  [σαν ὑποσχόμενος? χρήσιμ]ον ἑαυτὸν παρέσχετο τοῖς
  [πολίταις προθυμίας οὐδε]μᾶς λιπόμενος, καὶ ἀνα-
  [χθεὶς εἰς θάλασσαν παντοδ]απῶν πνευμάτων καὶ ἐναν-
  [τίον πνεόντων ἐφιλοτειμήθ]η ἐνπελαγίξων κρατήσαι
15 [καὶ ἔσωσε τούς πλέοντας εὐνο]υς ὑπάρχων, τῶν δὲ πρότε-
  [ρον...................]ων τοῖς ἡμετέροις τόποις
  ....μεθεδραξομένους
  .... τοῦδε το[ῦ
  .... τού]τωι

l. 8. πλέων Rostovtsev for Latyshev πλέουσι?

10. *IosPE.* I. 22, see next page.

11. *BCA.* XVIII. p. 104, No. 5.
   Olbia, cf. pp. 37, 474, 477.

 1 Ἀγαθῆι τύχηι.
  Ἀπόλλωνι Προστάτηι
  οἱ περὶ Ἀρχίδημον Δα-
  δάκου στρατηγοί· Ἀχίλ-
5 λητος Νεικηράτου, Ἀσπούργος Παρσπανάκου, Ζου-
  ρόξις Γετομούσου, Διονύσιος Ἑρμογένους, Βάξα-
  γος Ἀμωρομάρου παῖδα
10 κατέατησαν δῶρον ὑπέρ
  τῆς πόλεος καὶ τῆς ἑαυ-
  τῶν ὑγείας.

12. *IosPE.* I. 75. Olbia, cf. pp. 37,
      475, 477.

 1 Ἀγαθῆ τύχη.
  Ἐπὶ ἀρχόντων
  τῶν περὶ Ποντικὸν
  Νεικίου οἱ περὶ Διογέ-
5 νης Μακεδόνος ἀγορα-
  νόμοι· Κιλίκας Μυρότου,
  Σόσσιος Κάρπου,
  Σώμαχος Σαμάγου,
  Ἱλίτας Ἡλίου Ἐ{ρ}μ{η}ι Ἀγοραίωι
10 ἀνέθ{η}καν Νείκην ἀργυρέαν
  ὑπέρ τῆς πόλεως εὐσσταθί-
  ας καὶ τῆς ἑαυτῶν ὑγείας.

13. *IosPE.* I. 77. Probably Berezan,
   cf. pp. 37, 453, 473, 481.

 1 ['Αγ]αθῆι τύχ[ηι.
  Ἀχιλλέϊ Ποντ[άρχηι
  οἱ] περὶ Ἀναξι[μέ-
  ν]ην Σωκράτ[ους]
5 τὸ δ' ἄρχον[τες·]
  Πουρθαῖος [Πουρ]-
  θαίου, Δημήτρ[ιος]
  Ἀχιλλέος, Εὐρ[ησί-
  β]ιος Ἀδόου, Ἀ[μω-
10 ρ]όμαρος Εὐρησ[ιβί]-
  ου ὑπὲ[ρ] εἰρήνης κ[αὶ]
  πολυκαρπ[ία]ς κα[ὶ ἀν]-
  δραγαθίας τῆς π[όλε]-
  ως καὶ τῆς ἑαυτ[ῶν ὑγεί]-
15 ας.
   Πουρθ[αῖ]ος Πο[υρθαί]-
  ου ἀρχοντ[ε]ύων ἐν[είκα
  λ]όγχαι, δίσκ[ωι. Ε]ὐρησ[ίβιος
  Ἀ]δόου ἀρχον[τ]εύων ἐ[νείκα
20 δρόμ[ωι], π[α]ιδόμ[ατι].

81—2

10.　*IosPE.* I. 22.　Olbia, cf. pp. 388, 468–470, 472, 481.

1　Ὅσαι πόλεις ἐστεφάν[ω]σαν [Θ]εοκλέα Σατύρου ἥρωα χρυσέοις στεφάνοις·

Ὀλβιοπολεῖται,	Ἡρακλεῶται,	Τιανοί,	Τομεῖται,	Μείλητος,	Χερσόνησσος,
Νεικο[μ]ηδεῖς,	Βυζάντιοι,	Προυσεῖς,	Ἰστριανοί,	Κύζικος,	Βόσπορος,
Νεικαιεῖς,	Ἀμαστ[ρ]ιανοί,	Ὀδησσεῖται,	Καλλατιανοί,	Ἀπάμεια,	Τύρα, Σινώπη.

5　Ἐπὶ ἀρχόντων τῶν περὶ Θεοκλέα Σατύρου τὸ δ´,
μηνὸς Βοηδρομιῶνος ει´, ἐκκλησίας γενομένης
πανδήμου, εἰσηγησαμένου Ἀντι[φ]ῶντος Ἀναξιμέ-
νους, οἱ ἄρχοντες εἶπαν· Ἐπ{ε}ὶ Θεοκλῆς Σατύρου, ἀ-
νὴρ γενόμενος ἐκ προγόνων λαμπρῶν κ(α)ὶ πολλὰ
10　τῇ πατρίδι ἡμῶν καταννσαμένων ἔν τε πρεσβείαις καὶ (ἀ)ρ-
χαῖς πάσαις καὶ εὐεργεσίαις τῶν καθ´ ἕνα πολειτῶν τε
καὶ τῶν ἐπιδημούντων παρ´ ἡμᾶς ξένων, κατηκολούθησεν
ὁ ἀνὴρ τῷ τῶν προγόνων ἀξιώματι καὶ τὸ λαμπρὸν καὶ εὔ-
νουν πρὸς τὴν πατρίδα διε[δ]είξατο, ὡς καὶ οἱ πρόγονοι αὐτοῦ,
15　ἔν τε ἤθει χρηστῷ καὶ τρόπῳ ἀγαθῷ καὶ εὐνοίᾳ τῇ κοινῇ περὶ πάντα πᾶσιν διαφερούσῃ, ὡς διὰ τὸ μέτριον αὐτοῦ καὶ περὶ τὴν πατρίδα φιλόστοργον καὶ περὶ τοὺς Ἕλληνας φιλόξενον νεικῆ-
[σα]ι μὲν τοὺς προγόνους τοὺς ἑαυτοῦ, ἰσόρ{ρ}οπον δὲ καταστῆ-
ναι τοῖς τὰ μεγάλα τὴν πατρίδα ἡμῶν εὐεργετηκόσιν, εἴς τε πρεσ-
20　βείας αὐτὸς ἑαυτὸν ἑκοντὴν παρέχων ἄοκνον, ἔργων τε ἐπιμελείαις καὶ κατασκευ(α)ῖς ἐνεκοπίασεν ὡς δι´ αὐτὸν περικαλλεστέραν καὶ ἐνδοξοτέραν τὴν πόλιν ἡμῶν γενέσθαι, ἀρχαῖς τε
αἷς ἦρξεν καὶ ἱερατείᾳ καὶ στρατηγί(α)ις καὶ λειτουργίαις ἁπάσαις ἑαυτὸ[ν]
ἀφελῶς τῇ πατρίδι εἰς ἅπαντα ἐπεδίδου, ἥρεμόν τε ἑαυτὸν παρέχων
25　καὶ ἴσον πᾶσιν, καθαρῶς ἅπαντα καὶ δικαίως διοικῶν· ἄρχων
τε τὴν μεγίστην ἀρχὴν τὸ τετράκις—καθότι τοιούτων
ἀνδρῶν χρεία ἦν ἄρχειν καὶ πλειστάκις—, πᾶσαν ὁμόνοιαν
πολειτευόμενος, τοῖς μὲν ἡλικιώταις προσφερό-
μενος ὡς ἀδελφοῖς, τοῖς δὲ πρεσβυτέροις ὡς υἱός,
30　τοῖς δὲ παισὶν ὡς πατήρ, πάσῃ ἀρετῇ κεκοσμημένος,
ὑπὸ τοῦ βασκάνου δαίμονος ἀφῃρέθη μὴ διατελέσας
τὴν ἀρχήν, ὥστε ἐπὶ τούτοις τοὺς πολείτας καὶ τοὺς ξένους
διὰ τὸ ἀφῃρῆσθαι τοῦ προεστῶτος τῆς πόλεως καὶ τὰς πόλεις, ὧν
35　ἐπεδήμουν οἱ (ξ)ένοι, στεφανωθῆναι τὸν Θεοκλέα χρυσῷ στεφάνῳ καὶ ἀναγορευθῆναι ὑπὸ τοῦ κήρυκος, ὅτι ἡ βουλὴ καὶ ὁ δῆμος
καὶ αἱ πόλεις τῶν παρεπιδημούντων ξένων στεφανοῦσιν Θεοκλέα Σατύρου νεικητὴν γενόμενον τῶν ἀπ´ αἰῶνος περὶ τῶν κοινῇ
πᾶσιν διαφερόντων καὶ τῶν τῇ πόλῃ συμφερόντων, καὶ ἀνατεθῆναι αὐ-
40　τοῦ εἰκόνα ἔνοπλον δημοσίᾳ ἐν τῷ γυμνασίῳ, οὗ τῆς κατασκευ-
ῆς τὴν ἐπιμέλειαν αὐτὸς πεποίητο· τὸ δὲ ψήφισμα τοῦτο ἀναγραφῆ-
ναι εἰς στήλην λευκόλιθον καὶ ἀνατεθῆναι ἐν τῷ ἐπισημοτάτῳ τῆ[ς]
πόλεως τόπῳ εἰς τὸ μαθεῖν πάντας τὸν ἄνδρα πρὸς ἀνδρε(ία)ν μὲν
εὐτολμον καὶ πρὸς ἀρετὴν δὲ ἄοκνον καὶ πρὸ(ς) πολείτας σωτή-
45　ριον καὶ πρὸς ξένους φιλάνθρωπον, ᾗ ἱς προτροπὴν τῶν τὴν πόλιν φιλεῖν καὶ εὐεργετεῖν δυναμένων.

11.　*BCA.* xviii. p. 104, No. 5 ;
12.　*IosPE.* I. 75 ;
13.　*IosPE.* I. 77 ;
　　　see p. 643.

14.　*BCA.* x. p. 6, No. 4.　Olbia,
A.D. 248, cf. pp. 470, 478,
482.

Pro salutem
Imp. D. NN.
Philippo Aug.
III et Philip-
5 po Imp. II Coss.
ara Merc-
urio posu[e(runt)]
Py(y)rrus Bi-
thus Mil(ites).

So Latyshev, but he admits
the possibility of
l. 7 posuị.
ţ Py(y)rus Bi-
thus Mil(es).

15. *IosPE.* iv. 83. Chersonese, cf. pp. 541,
544·

Βίων Σιμία.
'Αντιβίων Βίωνος τοῦ Σιμία βασιλεύσας
ὑπὲρ τοῦ πατρὸς Παρθένωι ἱερεὺς ἐών.

16. *IosPE.* iv. 79. Chersonese, v. Fig. 348,
cf. pp. 490, 516, 517, 540, 621.

1 'Ομνύω Δία, Γᾶν, "Αλιον, Παρθένον,
[θ]εοὺς 'Ολυμπίους καὶ 'Ολυμπίας
[κ]αὶ ἥρωας ὅσοι πόλιν καὶ χώραν
καὶ τείχη ἔχοντι τὰ Χερσονασι-
5 τᾶν· ὁμονοησῶ ὑπὲρ σωτηρίας
καὶ ἐλευθερίας πόλεος καὶ πολιτᾶν καὶ οὐ προδωσῶ Χερσόνασον
οὐδὲ Κερκινῖτιν οὐδὲ Καλὸν λιμένα οὐδὲ τἄλλα τείχη οἰδὲ τᾶς ἄλ-
10 λας χώρας ἂν Χερσονασῖται νέμον-
ται ἢ ἐνέμοντο οὐθενὶ οὐθὲν οὔτε "Ελ-
λανι οὔτε βαρβάρωι, ἀλλὰ διαφυλαξῶ τῶι δάμωι τῶι Χερσονασιτᾶν, οὐδὲ καταλυσῶ τὰν δαμοκρατίαν οὐ-
15 δὲ τῶι προδιδόντι καὶ καταλύοντι ἐ-
πιτρεψῶ οὐδὲ σιγκρυψῶ, ἀλλὰ ἐ-
ξαγγελῶ τοῖς δαμιοργοῖς τοῖς κατὰ πόλιν· καὶ πολέμιος ἐσσοῦμαι τῶ[ι]
ἐπιβουλεύοντι καὶ προδιδόντι ἢ ἀφι-
20 στάντι Χερσόνασον ἢ Κερκινῖτιν ἢ
Καλὸν λιμένα ἢ τὰ τείχη καὶ χώραν
τὰν Χερσονασιτᾶν· καὶ δαμιοργησῶ
καὶ βουλευσῶ τὰ ἄριστα καὶ δικαιότα-
τα πόλει καὶ πολίταις καὶ τὸν ΣΑΣΤΗ-
25 ΡΑ τῶι δάμωι διαφυλαξῶ καὶ οὐκ ἐ-
χφερομυθησῶ τῶν ἀπορρήτων οὐθὲν οὔτε ποτὶ "Ελλανα οὔτε ποτὶ βά[ρ]-
βαρον, ὃ μέλλει τὰμ πόλιν βλάπτειν·
οὐδὲ δωρεὰν δωσῶ οὐδὲ δεξοῦμα[ι]
30 ἐπὶ βλάβαι πόλεος καὶ πολιτᾶν· οὐδὲ
ἐπιβουλευσῶ ἄδικον πρᾶγμα οὐδενὶ οὐθὲν τῶμ πολιτᾶν τῶμ μὴ ἀφε-
στακότων, οὐδὲ τῶι ἐπιβουλεύο[ντι
[ἐπιτρεψῶ οὐδὲ συγκρυψῶ οὐθὲν οὐθε]-
35 νί, ἀλλ' ἐξαγγελ[ῶ] καὶ κρινῶ ψά[φωι]
κατὰ τοὺς νόμους· οὐδὲ συνωμο[σί]-
αν συνομοῦμαι οὔτε κατὰ τοῦ κοιν[οῦ]
τοῦ Χερσονασιτᾶν οὔτε κατὰ τῶμ [πο]-
λιτᾶν οὐδενὸς, ὃς μὴ ἀποδέδεικτ[αι
40 π]ολέμιος τῶι δάμωι· εἰ δέ τινι συν[ώ-
μο]σα καὶ εἴ τινι καταλέλαμμαι ὅρ[κωι
ε]π' εὐχαῖ, δι[α]λυ[σ]αμένωι μὲν ἄμειν-
νόν εἴη καὶ ἐμοὶ καὶ τοῖς ἐμοῖς, ἐμμ[έ-
ν]οντι δὲ τὰ ἐναντία· καὶ εἴ τινά κ[α
45 σ]υνωμοσίαν αἰσ[θ]ωμαι ἐοῦσαν [ἢ γιγ]-
νομέναν, ἐξ[ε]ξαγγελῶ τοῖς δαμ[ιορ-
γ]οῖς· οὐδὲ σῖτον ἀπὸ τοῦ πεδίου ἀ[πα-
γ]ώγιμον ἀποδωσοῦμαι οὐδὲ ἐξ[α]-
ξῶ ἄλλαι ἀπὸ τοῦ πεδίου, ἀλλ' [ἢ εἰς
50 Χ]ερσόνασον. Ζεῦ καὶ Γᾶ καὶ "Αλιε [καὶ]
Παρθένε καὶ θεοὶ 'Ολύμπιοι, ἐμμένο[ν]-
τι μέμ μοι εὖ εἴη ἐν τούτοις καὶ αὐ[τῶι]
καὶ γένει καὶ τοῖς ἐμοῖς, μὴ ἐμμέν[ον]-
`τι δὲ κακῶς καὶ αὐτῶι καὶ γένει καὶ [τοῖς]
55 ἐμοῖς, καὶ μήτε γᾶ μοι μήτε θάλασ]-
σα καρπὸν φέροι μήτε γυν[αῖκες εὐτε-
κ]νοῖεν μήτε........ θανα...

FIG. 348. The Chersonesan Oath.

17. *IosPE.* I. 195.   Chersonese, cf. pp. 388, 495, 517, 540, 541.   1—8 are in wreaths.

A.   *B.*

ὁ δᾶμος 'Αγασικλῆ Κτη[σία].

1	2	3	4	5	6	7	8
εἰσαγησα-	ὁ{ο}ρ[[ξ]αντι	τειχοπο-	[ποήσαντι(?)]	[δαμιοργ]ή-	[ἱερατ]εύ-	γυμνασι-	ἀγορανο-
μένωι τὰν	τὰν ἐπὶ τοῦ	ήσαντι.	· τὰν ἀγορ-	[σ]αντι.	[σ]αντι.	αρχήσαντι	μῆ[σα]ντι
φρου[ρὰ]ν	πεδίου		[άν]				
καὶ κατασκευ-	ἀμπελείαν.			No. 5. Latyshev supplies [στραταγ]ή[σ]αντι.			
άξαντι.							

17ᵃ. *BCA.* xlv. p. 23, No. 1.   Chersonese, cf.
pp. 516, 518, 540, 590.   Ed. R. Löper.

[............. ἀλλὰ]
1 [συνδιαφυλαξοῦμεν τὰν αὐτοῦ βασ]ιλεί[αν]
    [κατὰ τὸ δυνατόν, ἐμμένοντ]ος ἐν ταῖ ποθ' ἁ[μὲ]-
    [s φιλίαι τήν τε ποτὶ 'Ρωμ]αίους φιλίαν διαφυλάσ-
    [σοντος καὶ μηδὲ]ν ἐναντίον αὐτοῖς πράσ-
5 [σοντος· εὐ]ορκοῦσι μὲν ἀμῖν εὖ εἴη, ἐπιορκοῦ-
    [σι δὲ τὰ ἐ]ναντία. ὁ δὲ ὅρκος οὗτος συνετε-
    [λέ]σθη μηνὸς 'Ηρακλείου πεντεκαιδεκάτα[ι],
    βασιλεύοντος 'Απολλοδώρου τοῦ 'Ηρογεί-
    του, γραμματεύοντος 'Ηροδότου τοῦ 'Ηρο-
10 δότου.—"Ορκος, ὃν ὤμοσε βασιλεὺς Φαρνάκης
    πρεσβευσάντων παρ' αὐτὸν Μάτριος καὶ 'Ηρακλε[ί]-
    ου· 'Ομνύω Δία, Γῆν, "Ηλιον, θεοὺς 'Ολυμπίους πάντας
    καὶ πάσας· φίλος ἔσομαι Χερσονησίταις διὰ παν-
    τός, καὶ ἂν οἱ παρακείμενοι βάρβαροι στρατεύωσιν
15 ἐπὶ Χερσόνησον ἢ τὴν κρατουμένην ὑπὸ Χερσο-
    νησιτῶν χώραν ἢ ἀδικῶσιν Χερσονησίτας, καὶ ἐπι-
    καλῶνταί με, βοηθήσω αὐτοῖς, καθὼς ἂν ᾖ μοι και-
    ρός, καὶ οὐκ ἐπιβουλεύσω Χερσονησίταις κατ' οὐδένα
    τρόπιν, οὐδὲ στρατεύσω ἐπὶ Χερσόνησον, οὐδὲ
20 ὅπλα ἐναντία θήσομαι Χερσονησίταις, οὐδὲ πράξω
    κατὰ Χερσονησιτῶν ὃ μέλλει βλάπτειν
    τὸν δῆμον τὸν Χερσονησιτῶν, ἀλλὰ συν-
    διαφυλάξω τὴν δημοκρατίαν κατὰ τὸ
    δυνατόν, ἐμμενόντων ἐν τῆι πρὸς ἐ-
25 μὲ φιλίαι καὶ τὸν αὐτὸν ὅρκον ὁμοσάντων,
    τήν τε πρὸς 'Ρωμαίους φιλίαν διαφυλασσόν-
    των καὶ μηδὲν ἀντίον αὐτοῖς πρασσόν-
    των. εὐορκοῦντι μὲν εὖ εἴη, ἐπιορκοῦντι δὲ τά-
    ναντία. 'Ο δὲ ὅρκος οὗτος συνετελέσθη ἐν
30 τῶι ἑβδόμωι καὶ πεντηκοστῶι καὶ ἑκατοστῶι
    ἔτει, μηνὸς Δαισίου, καθὼς βασιλεὺς Φαρνάκ[ης]
    ἄγει.

18. *IosPE.* I. 185, see next page.

18ᵃ. *Journ. Min. Publ. Instr.* Mar. 1907, p. 140
        = Ποντικά, p. 314.   Chersonese, Anno
        154 = A.D. 179, cf. pp. 522, 540—542, 546.
1 ['Αγαθᾶι τύχαι].
    [Πρόεδροι Χερσονασιτᾶ]ν τᾶ(ν) ποτὶ τᾶι Ταυρικᾶ[ι
    εἶπαν· 'Επειδὴ Δια .... Δ]ημητρίου 'Αρακλεώτας
    [πρότερόν τε........ σεμνῶι κεχ]ραμένος ἄθει τὰν καλο-
5 [κἀγαθίαν ....]ας εὐχραστον πέφανε[ν
    καὶ νῦν ποτὶ πάντας τοὺς πολείτ]ας ἀγάπα[ν] γνασίαν
                                                ἐνδείκν[υ-
    ται .... φιλ]ικᾶι καὶ ἰσαδέλφωι εὐνοίαι τα[..
    .... γ]εγεννάμέν[ο]s πολείτας ἄριστα σε-
    [.:...... πράσσων τὰ συμφ]έροντα ἀμεῖν διατελεῖ. Δι' ὃ
                                                δεδό-
10 [χθαι τᾶ βουλᾶ καὶ τ]ῷ δάμῳ ἐπαινέσαι μὲν ἐπὶ τούτοις
                                                Δια-
    [........ Δημη]τρίου 'Αρακλεώταν, δόμεν δὲ αὐτῷ προξε-
    [νίαν, πολειτείαν], ἔσπλουν τε καὶ ἔκπλουν ἐν εἰράναι
                                        καὶ πολέ-
    [μωι ἀσυλεὶ ἀσ]πονδεὶ αὐτῷ τε καὶ ἐκγόνοις αὐτοῦ καὶ
                                        χράμα-
    [σι, μετοχ]άν τε πάντων τῶν ἐν τᾶ πόλει, ὧν καὶ τοῖς
                                        ἐνφύλτ-
15 οις τ]ῶν ἀστῶ[ν] μέτεστιν. Τὸ δὲ ψάφισμα τοῦτο ἀναγρα-
    [φᾶ]μεν λευκολίθου στάλαι καὶ θέμεν ἐν τῷ ἐπισαμοτάτῳ
    [τ]ᾶς ἀκροπόλιος τόπῳ. Ταῦτ' ἔδοξε βουλᾶι, δάμῳ
                                        βασιλευ-
    ούσας Παρθένου, ἔτεος ρνδ', ἱερέος δὲ Χρηστίωνος τοῦ Βο-
    ίσκου, μανὸς 'Αρακλείου η', γραμματεύοντος 'Αρίστωνο[s]
20 'Αττίνου. 'Εσφραγίσαντο α' στίχωι· θεὰ βασίλισσα
    Παρθένος, Τ. Φλάουιος 'Αρίστων υἱὸς Φλαουίου 'Αρίσ-
    τωνος τοῦ 'Αγεπόλεως πρῶτος ἄρχων, Ζῆθος
    'Αρίστωνος, Τ. Φλάουιος Πυθόδοτος υἱὸς Φλαουί-
    ου 'Αγεπόλεως, Εὐρύδαμος Διοσκουρίδου, Τ. Φλάουιο[s]
25 'Αγέπολις υἱὸς Φλαουίου 'Αρίστωνος, Τ. Φλάουιος Παρθε-
    νοκλῆς υἱὸς Φλαουίου [Π]α[ρθε]νο[κλέου]s· β' στίχωι· 'Α-
    θήναιος Διογένους, 'Ερμοκλῆς 'Απολλωνίου, Φιλόμου-
    σος 'Απολλωνίδου, Δημοκράτης Βοΐσκου, 'Ηρόξενος
    Βοΐσκου, 'Αρίστων 'Αντιλόχου, Ποντικὸς 'Ι[λ]άρου, Ζῆθος
30 Πυθοδότου· γ' στίχωι· Θεαγένης Διογένους ἄρχων, 'Αρίσ-
    των 'Απολλωνίου ἄρχων, "Ηραιος Χηματίνου ἄρχων, Πα-
    τέ[ρ]ων 'Ασκληπιάδου ἄρχων, Ζῆθ(υ)ος 'Απολλωνίου νό-
    μων φύλαξ, Πυθόδ(ω)ρος Χρηστίωνος νόμων φύλαξ, Δα-
    μοκλῆς Λαγορείνου νόμων φύλαξ, Μητρόδωρος Διοσκου-
35 ρίδου πρόδικος καὶ ὁ γραμματεὺς τῆς βουλ[ῆς] 'Αρίστων 'Ατ-
    τίνου.
    l. 16. Latyshev στάλα[s] but cf. *BCA.* xlv. p. 52, No. 6.

18. *IosPE.* I. 185. Chersonese, cf. pp. 119, 121, 388, 463, 490, 491, 496—498, 518—520, 540—542, 546, 582.

I . . . . σω . . . .
ὁ δεῖνα . . . .]ιθο[υ ε]ἶπαν· Ἐπ[ειδὴ Διόφαντος Ἀσκλαπι]οδώρου Σινωπεὺς φίλος [μὲν καὶ
εὐεργέτας ἀμῶν ἐ]ών, πιστε[υ]όμενος δὲ [καὶ τιμώμενος οὐ]θενὸς ἦσσον ὑπὸ βασιλέος Μιθραδά[τα] Εὐπά-
[τορος, δι]ὰ παντὸς ἀγαθοῦ παραίτιος γίνεται [ἑκάστωι ἀ]μῶν, ἐπ[ὶ τ]ὰ κάλλιστα καὶ ἐνδοξότατα.τὸν
5 [βασ]ιλέα προτρεπόμενος· παρακληθεὶς δ᾽ὑπ᾽αὐτο[ῦ καὶ τ]ὸν ποτὶ Σ[κ]ύθας πολεμον ἀναδεξάμενος
[καὶ π]αραγενόμενος εἰς τὰν πόλιν ἀμῶν, ἐπάνδρως παντὶ τῶι στρατοπέδῳ τὰν εἰς τὸ πέραν διάβα-
[σι]ν ἐποήσατο· Παλάκου δὲ τοῦ Σκυθᾶν βασιλεῖος αἰφνιδίως ἐπιβαλόντος μετὰ ὄχλου πολλοῦ, παρα-
[τα]ξάμενος ἐν χρ[ε]ίαι, τοὺς ἀνυποστάτους δοκοῦντας εἶμεν Σκύθας τρεψάμενος πρῶτον ἀπ᾽αὐ-
[τῶ]ν ἐπόησε βασιλέα Μιθραδάταν Εὐπάτορα τρόπαιον ἀναστᾶσαι· τοὺς δὲ παροικοῦντας Ταύρους ὑ-
10 [φ᾽ἑ]αυτὸν ποησάμενος καὶ πόλιν ἐπὶ τοῦ τόπου σινοικίξας, εἰς τοὺς κατὰ Βόσπορον τόπους ἐχω[ρ]ί-
[σθη] καὶ πολλὰς καὶ μεγάλας ἐν ὀλίωι χρόνωι πράξεις ἐπιτελέσας πάλιν εἰς τοὺς καθ᾽ἀμὲ τόπους [ἐ]πέ-
[στ]ρεψε καὶ παραλαβὼν τοὺς ἐν ἀκμᾶι τῶν πολιτᾶν εἰς μέσαν τὰν Σκυθίαν προῆλθε· παραδόντων δὲ
[αὐτ]ῶι Σκυθᾶν τὰ βασίλεια Χαβαίους καὶ Νέαν πόλιν, σχεδὸν πάντας ὑπακόους συνέβα γεν[έ]σθαι
[βασ]ιλεῖ Μιθραδάται Εὐπάτορι· ἐφ᾽οἷς ὁ δᾶμος εὐχαριστῶν ἐτίμασε ταῖς καθηκούσαις αὐτὸν τιμαῖς,
15 [ὡς] ἀπολελυμένος ἤδη τᾶς τῶν βαρβάρων ἐπικρατείας. Τῶν δὲ Σκυθᾶν τὰν ἔμφυτον
[αὐ]τοῖς ἀθεσίαν ἐκφανῆ καταστασάντων καὶ τοῦ μὲν βασιλέϊος ἀποστάντων, τὰ δὲ πρά-
[γμ]ατα εἰς μεταβολὰν ἀγαγόντων, δι᾽ἃς αἰτίας βασιλέϊος Μιθραδάτα Εὐπάτορος Διόφαντον
[πά]λιν ἐκπέ[μ]ψαντος μετὰ στρατοπέδου, καίπερ τοῦ καιροῦ συγκλείοντος εἰς χειμῶνα, Διό-
[φα]ντος ἀναλαβὼν τοὺς ἰδίους καὶ τῶν πολιτᾶν τοὺς δυνατωτάτους ὥρμασε μὲν ἐπ᾽αὐτὰ
20 [τὰ β]ασίλεια τῶν Σκυθᾶν, κωλυθεὶς δὲ διὰ χειμῶνας, ἐπιστρέψας ἐπὶ τὰ παραθαλάσσια Κερκινῖτιν
[μὲν] ἐλάβετο καὶ τὰ Τείχη, τοὺς δὲ τὸν Καλὸν λιμένα κατοικοῦντας πολιορκεῖν ἐπεβάλετο· Παλά-
[κου] δὲ συν[ε]ργεῖν τὸν καιρὸν ἑαυτῶι νομίζοντος καὶ συναγαγόντος τοὺς ἰδίους πάντας, ἔτι δὲ
[καὶ τ]ὸ τῶν Ῥευξιναλῶν ἔθνος συνεπισπασαμένου, ἃ διὰ παντὸς Χερσονασιτᾶν προστατοῦσα
[Παρ]θένος καὶ τότε συμπαροῦσα Διοφάντωι, προεσάμανε μὲν τὰν μέλλουσαν γίνεσθαι πρᾶξιν .
25 [διὰ τ]ῶν ἐν τῶι ἱερῶι γενομένων σαμείων, θάρσος δὲ καὶ τόλμαν ἐνεποίησε παντὶ τῶι στ[ρα]τοπέ-
[δωι· Δ]ιοφάντου δὲ διαταξαμένου σωφρόνως, συνέβα τὸ νίκαμα γενέσθαι βασιλεῖ Μιθ[ρ]αδά-
[ται Εὐπ]άτορι καλὸν καὶ μνάμας ἄξιον εἰς πάντα τὸν χρόνον· τῶν μὲγ γὰρ πεζῶν ἤτοι τις [ἢ] οὐ-
[δεὶς ἐσώθ]η, τῶν δὲ ἱππέων οὐ πολλοὶ διέφυγον· οὐδένα δὲ χρόνον ἀργὸν παρείς, παραλαβὼν
[τὸ στρατόπεδον, ἄκ]ρου τοῦ ἔαρος ἐπὶ Χαβαίους κ[α]λὶ Νέ[αν π]όλιν ἐλθὼν παντὶ [τῶι βα]ρ[εῖ

II.

30 . . . . . .]σ . ω . .[. . . . . ὥστε τοὺς μὲν . . . .
. . . . .]φθγεῖν, [τ]οὺς δὲ λοιποὺς Σκύθας περὶ τῶν καθ᾽ ἑαυτο . . . .
τωι βουλεύσασθαι. Εἴς τε τοὺς κατὰ Βόσπορον τόπους χωρισ[θεὶ]ς καὶ [καταστα]-
σάμενος καὶ τὰ ἔν[θ]ινα καλῶς καὶ συμφερόντως βασιλεῖ Μιθραδάται Εὐπ[άτορι],
τῶν περὶ Σαύμακον Σκυθᾶν νεωτεριξάντων καὶ τὸν μὲν ἐκθρέψαντα αὐτὸν [βα]-
35 σιλέα Βοσπόρου Παιρισάδαν ἀνελόντων, αὐτῶι δ᾽ ἐπιβουλευσάντων, διαφ[υγὼν τὸν]
κίνδυνον ἐπέβα μὲν ἐπὶ τὸ ἀποσταλὲν ἐπ᾽ αὐτὸν ὑπὸ τῶν πολιτᾶν πλοῖον, παρα[γενό]-
μενος [δὲ] καὶ παρακαλέσας τοὺς πολίτας, συνεργὸν πρόθυμον ἔχων τὸν ἐξ[απο]-
στέλλοντα [β]ασιλέα Μ[ι]θραδάταν Εὐπάτορα, παρῆν ἔχων ἄκρου τοῦ ἔαρος [στρα]-
τόπεδον πε[ζ]ι[κό]ν τε καὶ ναυτικόν, παραλαβὼν δὲ καὶ τῶν πολιτᾶν ἐπιλέ-
40 κτους ἐμ πληρώμασι τρισί, ὁρμαθεὶς ἐκ τᾶς πόλεος ἀμῶν παρέλαβ[ε]

18.   *IosPE*. i. 185 (contd).

μὲν Θεοδοσίαν καὶ Παντικάπαιον, τοὺς δὲ αἰτίους τᾶς ἐπαναστάσεο[ς]
τιμωρησάμενος καὶ Σαύμακον τὸν αὐτόχειρα γεγονότα βασιλέος Παιρι-
σάδα λαβὼν ὑποχείριον εἰς τὰν βασιλείαν ἐξαπέστειλε, τὰ δὲ πράγματα [ἀ]-
νεκτ[ά]σατο βασιλεῖ Μιθραδάται Εὐπάτορι. Ταῖς τε πρεσβείαις ταῖς ἀποστελ-
45 λομέναις ὑπὸ τοῦ δάμου συνεργῶν εἰς πᾶν τὸ συμφέ[ρ]ον Χερσονασίταις εὔ-
νουν ἑαυτὸν καὶ φιλότιμον παρέχεται. Ὅπως οὖν καὶ ὁ δᾶμος τοῖς εὐεργέταις
ἑαυτοῦ τ[ὰς] καθηκούσας φαίνηται χάριτας ἀποδιδούς, δεδόχθαι τᾶι βου-
λᾶι καὶ τῶι δάμωι στεφανῶσαι Διόφαντον Ἀσκλαπιοδώρου χρυσέωι στεφάνωι Παρθενείοις ἐν τᾶι πομπᾶι, τὸ ἀνάγγελμα ποιουμένων τῶν συμμναμόνων·
50 "Ὁ δᾶμος στεφανοῖ Διόφαντον Ἀσκλαπιοδώρου Σινωπέα ἀρετᾶς ἕνεκα καὶ εὐνο[ί]-
ας τᾶ[ς] εἰς αὑτόν"· σταθῆμεν δὲ αὐτοῦ καὶ εἰκόνα χαλκέαν ἔνοπλον ἐν τᾶι ἀκροπό-
λε[ι] παρὰ τὸν τᾶς Παρθένου βωμὸν καὶ τὸν τᾶς Χερσονάσου, περὶ δὲ τούτων ἐπιμε-
λ[ὲς] γενέσθαι τοῖς ἐπιγεγραμμένοις ἄρχουσι, ὅπως ὅτι τάχιστα καὶ κάλλιστα
γ[έ]νηται· ἀναγράψαι δὲ καὶ τὸ ψάφισμα εἰς τὰν βάσιν τοῦ ἀνδριάντος, τὸ δὲ εἰς
55 ταῦτα γενόμενον ἀνάλωμα δόμεν τοὺς ταμίας τῶν ἱερῶν. Ταῦτ' ἔδοξε βουλ[ᾶι]
καὶ [δ]άμωι μηνὸς Διονυσίου ἐννεακαιδεκάται, βασιλεύοντος Ἀγέλα τοῦ Λ[α]-
γορίνου, προαισυμνῶντος Μήνιος τοῦ Ἡρακλείου, γραμματεύοντος Δα[μασι-
κλ]εῖος τοῦ Ἀθαναίου.

18ᵃ.   Ποντικά, p. 314, see p. 646.

19.   *IosPE*. i. 199.   Chersonese, cf. pp. 295, 524, 540—542, 605.

Ἀρίστωνα Ἀττινᾶ τὸν φιλόπατριν.

1	2	3	4	5
πρεσ-βεύοντα ὑπὲρ τᾶς ἐ-λευθερίας πο-τὶ τὸν θεὸν Σε-βαστὸν ἐξα-ετίαν καὶ ἀ-ποκαμόν-τα.	προδική-σαντα.	νομοφυ-λακήσαν-τα.	δαμιορ-γήσαντα καλῶς.	πρεσ-βεύσαντα ποτὶ βασι-λέα Ῥοιμητά[λ]-καν περὶ συμ-μαχίας κα[ὶ] ἐπιτετευ-χότα

6	7	8	9	10
ἱερα-τεύσαν-τα καλῶς καὶ ἰκόνι χαλκέα ι.	διοικήσαν-τα καὶ φωτί-σαντα χρή-ματα τᾶι πόλει.	πρεσ-βεύσαντα ποτὶ βασιλέ-α Ῥοιμητάλ-καν τὸ δεύτε-ρον καὶ ἐπι-τετευχό-τα. Κηφισόδοτος [ἐ]πόησε.	δαμιορ-γήσαντα καὶ εἰκόνι τελέ[αι].	πολειτευ-ό]μενον κα-λῶς.

1—10 are in wreaths.

20.   *IosPE*. iv. 71, see p. 650.

21. *IosPE.* IV. 81. Chersonese (cf. *Mat.* IX. p. 39). 185 A.D., cf. p. 525

I.

```
. . . ουλ . .
. . . οις ευδ . . .
. . [rasura] Εὐτυχ . . . .
. . . σωφρο?]σύνης καὶ κοσ[μιότητος? . . . .
. . . . Ἀτειλ[ί]ῳ Πρειμιανῷ χειλιάρχῃ κ[αὶ Οὐαλερίῳ Μαξίμῳ ͱ . . . . . . . . . . .
. . . . . . . . . . . . . . . . . . ὅπως μὴ προφάσει τούτων ει . . . . . . . . . . . . . . .
. . . . . . . . . . . . . τῆς αὐ]τοκρατορικῆς ἀντιγραφῆς καὶ·τῆς τῶ[ν . . . . . . . . . . . . . .
. . . . . . . . . . . . . προτεθῆναι δημοσίᾳ, ὅπως πᾶσιν φανεραὶ εἴ[εν . . . . . . . . . . . . . .
. . . . . . . . . . . . γρα]μμάτων καὶ ἐκ τούτων ἴστε ὅτι οὐδὲν νεωτερισθήσε[ται . . . . . . . .
```

II.

```
10 . . . . . . . . . . . . . . . . . ψ]ήφισμα πρὸς μὲ ἀπεστείλατε, οὗ τὸ ἀντίγραφον ὑποταγῆναι ἐκ[ί.
λευσα . . . . . . . . . . . . . . . Ἀτ]ειλίῳ Πρειμιανῷ χειλιάρχῃ καὶ Οὐαλερίῳ Μαξίμῳ ͱ· καὶ νῦν δὲ
[ . . . . . . . . . . . . ταῦτα τ]ὰ γράμματα ὁμοίως προτεθῆναι φροντίσατε. Ἐρρῶσθαι ὑμᾶς εὔχομαι.
```

III.

—CC

```
. . . . . . . . . . . . . . . γράμμασι βασιλικ]οῖς καὶ ὑπομνήμασιν πιστεύοντες ὑπατικῶν καὶ ἀποφάσεσιν χει-
[λιαρχῶν . . . . . . . . . . . . . . ]ν τοῦ τέλους τοῦ πορνικοῦ πολλὴν ἀμεριμνίαν ἐθαρροῦμεν ἔχειν
15 . . . . . . . . . . τῆς πο]λειτικῆς ἐπιτειμίας ἐχομένων καὶ ἡ τῶν βασιλευόντων ἐκύρωσεν
. . . . . . . . . . . . . καὶ ἡ τῶν ἀποφηναμένων ἠσφαλίσατο γνώμη μετὰ τοῦ μηδὲν ἐπικοι-
[νοῦσθαι? . . . . . . . . . . ]ι τὰ ἡμέτερα δίκαια· ἐπεὶ δὲ παρακεινεῖν τὰ οὕτως ἀσφαλῶς ὁρισθέντα οἱ νῦν
. . . . . . . . . . . . . ἐφ᾽ οἷς κωλύονται ἀδίκως καὶ βιαίως τινὰ πράττοντες, ἀλλὰ καὶ δι᾽ ἐν.
. . . . . . . . . . . . . τὴ]ν ἀξίωσιν φανερὰν σοι ποιῆσαι ἐπὶ σὲ πεποιήμεθα τὸν εὐεργέτην
20 . . . . . . . . . . . . ἡμεῖν τὴν ἀσφάλειαν τὴν τῶν δεδωρημένων καὶ τῶν κεκριμένων
. . . . . . . . . . . . . . α[ς]· ὑπέρθεσιν δὲ τῆς μηνύσεως τῶν βιαζομένων ἡμᾶς οὐδεμί.
[αν . . . . . . . . . . . . ]εσθαι κατ᾽ἀρχὰς ὑπὸ τῆς σῆς φιλανθρωπίας τοὺς ἐπὶ τοῖς καιροῖς
. . . . . . . . . . . . . . π]ερὶ τοῦ πράγματος τούτου ἀρχῆθεν ἐπιζήτη(σ)ις γενομένη καὶ θε.
. . . . . . . . . . . . . . τὴν πρ]ὸς τοὺς βασιλέας ἡμῶν δέησιν φανεράν σοι πεποιήκαμεν καὶ τὴν
25 . . . . . . . . . . . . . τῶν συμφ]ερόντων ἡμεῖν γραμμάτων προετάξαμεν καὶ τὰ ὑπομνήματα τὰ
[τῶν ὑπατικῶν καὶ τὴν ἀπόφασι]ν τὴν τοῦ χειλιάρχου, ἐπειδὴ καὶ τάξιν ταύτην ἔλαβεν ἀπὸ τῶν δωρησα.
[μένων . . . . . . . . . . . γνώμη]ν περὶ τούτου ἀποφήνασθαι κελευσθέντα χειλίαρχον περιορισθεν-
[τ . . . . . . . . . . ] κηδεμόνα σε γενόμενον φυλάξειν μὲν τὰ μετὰ τοσαύτης καὶ σκέψεως
[καὶ . . . . . . . . . . . ]αι ἐπὶ τόποις τοῖς εἰς τοῦτο τὸ τέλος ἀνήκουσι, εὐλογίστως δὲ προσήσεσθαι
30 . . . . . . . . . . . . δέησιν, ἧς οὐδὲν ἀναγκαιότερον ἀνθρώποις καὶ βίου σώφρονος γνωρίζουσι
[τὸ χρήσιμον καὶ ἠθῶν] εὐχομένοις φυλάσσεσθαι σεμνότητα. CC
```

IV.

```
                                                        Τίνα ἐπέστειλα Ἀτειλίῳ Πρειμι-
[ανῷ καὶ ἄλλοις περὶ τοῦ πορνικοῦ τέλ]ους ὑποταγῆναι ἐκέλευσα προνοῶν μήτε ὑμᾶς παρὰ τὰ δεδογμένα ἐνοχλεῖ-
[ς]εσθαι μήτε τοὺς ἡμεῖν ὑπηρ]ετοῦντας ὑπερβαίνειν τὸν περιγεγραμμένον ὅρον. CC
```

V.

```
[Ut scias quae sint officia militum a]gentium in vexillatione Chersonessitana d(e)capitulo lenocini quod su[b-
35 . . . . . . . . . . . misi tibi exem]plum sententiae Arri Alcibiadis tunc trib(uni) praepositi eiusdem vexill[a-
tionis . . . . . . . . . . . . . . ]us tam intentionem eius quam manifeste determinatam partem ad ius p[er
tinentem . . . . . . . . . . ] et quoniam idem Alcibiades videri non (po)potest su(b) te npus v(e)ntu[rum ?
. . . . . . . . . . . . . recupe]randae vectigalis quantitatis sponte suscepisse, cum sententiam su[b] iu[di-
cii forma . . . . . . . . . . ]pridem et dixerit et proposuerit et omnibus annis fisco pariaverit, dubium n[on
40 est, . . . . . . . . eandem? vectigalis] quan(tita)tem et circa disciplina(e) ratione(n) et observare et obtin[ere
. . . . . . . . . . . . eius sententiae ?] exemplum parate nanu scriptum unde de plano recte legi possit iuxta
. . . . . . . . . . . . pro]positum esse cura.
```

VI.

```
                         E(xemplum) e(pistulae). Quid scripserim Atilio Primiano tr[ib.
. . . . . . . . . . . ]rio comilitonum, quod ad ne (e)idem tribunus propter capitulum le[no-
cini . . . . . . . . . . s]ecundum forna n sententiae Arri Alcibiadis tunc trib(uni) dictae om . . .
45 . . . . . . . . . . us disciplinain vel cum iniuria aut contumelia paganorum comuit . . .
```

VII.

```
                         E(xemplum) e(pistulae). Qvid ad decretum Chersonessitanorum rescripserim c[o-
gnoscetis ex iis quae . . . . . . . . . ]es svbici praecepi et rursum admoneo caveatis, ne sub obtentu h[uius
modi inquisitionis milites ordinata]m iam pridem placitam ac cust(o)ditam cum dispendio vestrae exsist[ima-
tionis . . . . . . . . . . . . . . ]nquietent vel innovare quid temptent.
```

```
50 [προετέθη siue ἀνεστάθη ?] ἐπὶ ἀρχόντων τῶν περὶ Μ(άρκον) Αὐρ(ήλιον) Βασιλειδιανὸν Ἀλέξανδρον.
[Ἐπρέσβευον ? . . . . . . . Τ.] Φλ(άουιος) Ἀρίστων καὶ Οὐαλέριος Γερμανός.
```

M.   82

19. *IosPE.* 199, see p. 648.

20. *IosPE.* iv. 71. Chersonese, cf. pp. 524, 541. Fragment *b*, *BCA.* xxiii. p. 57.

a.

1   Ἀγαθᾶι τύχαι.
Π[ρό]εδροι Χερσονασειτᾶν τᾶν ποτὶ τᾷ Ταυ-
ρικᾶι εἶπαν· Ἐπειδὴ τοὶ εὐσεβέστατοι πα-
τέρες Ἡρακλεῶται οἰκείωι πάθει τὰν ὑπὲρ
5 τᾶς ἁμετέρας σωτηρίας ἐποάσαντο φρον-
τίδα πάσαι σπουδᾶι καὶ πάσᾳ φιλοστοργίᾳ
κεχραμένοι γνασίωι πρεσβείαν τε ποτὶ τὸν·[θε]-
ὸν ἁμῶν καὶ δεσπόταν Αὐτοκράτορα Τῖτον Αἴλι[ον]
Ἀδριανὸν Ἀντωνεῖνον ἰκετεύσουσαν ἐξέ-
10 πενψαν ὑπὲρ ἀμὲς ἐν οὐδενὶ ὀλιγωρή-
σαντες, τάς τε θείας ἀποκρίσεις καὶ τὰς
εὐμεναθείσας εὐεργεσίας ἠξίωσαν
δι᾽ ἀνδρῶν ἐπισαμοτάτων Ἡρακλείδου
Μενεσθέος καὶ Πρόκλου Μέμνονος διαπε[ν]-
15 ψάμενοι δά(λ)λους ποάσασθαι εἰς τὸ φανε-
ρὰν αὐτῶν τὰν καλοκἀγαθίαν γενέσθαι, ἀμὲ[ς]
πασσυδὶ ταῖς πρεπούσαις ἀμοιβαῖς ἀμείψα-
σθαι καθᾶκον ἐψαφισάμεθα· δι᾽ ἃ δεδόχθαι τᾷ
[βουλᾷ κ]αὶ τῶι δάμωι ἐπαινέσαι μὲν ἐπὶ τούτοι[ς
20 τὰν πρό]γονον ἀ[μῶν . . . πό]λιν καὶ πράτ[αν
ἐν τῷ Πόντῳ? . . .

b.

1 [.............T. Φλάουιος.........υἱὸς Φλ]αουίου Εὐρυδά-
[μου............................᾽Α]πολλώνιος Ζήθου·
[.......................ὁ δεῖνα Χ]ρηστίωνος Τ. Φλά-
[ουιος.................υἱὸς Φλαουίου]Ἀπολλωνίου·Διοσκου-
5 [ρίδας.....................Ἀπολλ]ώνιος Ἀρίστωνος᾽Ἀττίνας
[᾽Αρίστωνος?.....................Τ.] Φλάουιος Παρθενοκλῆς
[υἱὸς Φλαουίου Παρθενοκλέους? στίχο]ς γ´· Γάιος Ἰούλιος
Αἰμι(λ)ιανὸς
[.....................ὁ δεῖνα]᾽Ιουλίου ἄρχων· Μάρκος Οὔλπιος
[.....................᾽Ηρακ]λείδης Θεαγενίωνος ἄρχων· Βοϊο-
10 [κος.....................]· Νάνων Καλλιστράτου·᾽Ροῦφος Ν
[.....................ὁ δεῖνα]᾽Αππα·᾽Ιουλιανὸς Ἀκύλαν ἄρχων·
Φιλ[ο
............καὶ ὁ γραμμ]ατεὺς τῆς βουλῆς Τ. Φλ. Ἀγε-
πολ[ις].

21. *IosPE.* iv. 81, see p. 649.

22. *IosPE.* iv. 464. Chersonese, cf. pp. 504, 532.

1 [Ἐ]πεὶ¹ τῶν Δεσποτῶν ἡμῶν, τῶν ἐωνν.²
Α{ὑ}γού{σ}τον τῶν ἀνεική
των κὲ φφιλλ³ Θεοδ[ο]
ίσου κὲ Ἀρκαδίου καὶ ἐ
5 πεὶ τῆς πράξεως τοῦ πωλὰ
καμόντος Φλ. Βίτου τριβού(νου) καὶ
τῶν μηχανι(κῶν) οἰκ[ο]δομήθη τὸ τῖχ(ος) [τῆς]⁴
Χ[ερ]σῶνο[ς⁵ δι᾽] Εὐθηρί..ου τοῦ [μ]εγαλο-
[πρεπεστάτου κόμητος⁶?]

So Shestakov, op. c. p. 7, n. 3.
¹ Lat. ὑπὲρ.   ² αἰωνίων.   ³ Φλαβίων.
⁴ om. Lat.   ⁵ Lat....εον[τος.   ⁶ om. Lat.

23. *Inscr. Christ.* 7.   Chersonese, A.D. 487–8, cf. pp. 504, 521, 532.

1 ✝Αὐτοκράτωρ Κέσαρ Ζήνων εὐσε[β]ὴς νικ[ητὴς]✝
τροπεοῦχος μέγιστος ἀεισέβαστος·
φιλοτιμησάμεην ἡ αὐτῶν εὐσέβια, ὡς ἐ[ν]
πάσαις ταῖς πόλεσιν, καὶ ἐν ταύτη τῇ αὐτοῦ
5 πόλι, ἐδωρήσατο χρημάτων δόσιν, τὰ συνα-
γόμενα ἐκ τοῦ πρακτίου φημὶ τοῦ ἐνταῦθα
βικαράτου τῶν καθοσιωμένων βαλλισ-
τραρίων· δι᾽ ὧν ἀνανεοῦντε[ς] τὰ τίχη πρὸς
σωτηρίαν τῆς αὐτῆς πόλεως καὶ εὐχαρισ-
10 τοῦντες ἀνεθήκαμεν τόδε τὸ τίτλον
εἰς μνημόσυνον ἀείδιον τῆς αὐτῶν
✝βασιλίας✝
✝Ἀνενεώθη δὲ ὁ πύργος οὗτος πρά-
ττοντος· τοῦ μεγαλοπρ(επεστάτου) κόμ(ητος)
15 ✝Διογένου ː ἔτους: φιβ´ ː ἐν ἰνδ(ικτιῶνι) ια´✝

24. *Inscr. Christ.* 8.   Chersonese, A.D. 1059 cf. pp. 504, 532.

1 ✝Ἐγένωντο αι πορται του πραιτοριου
σιδηραι, ἐνεκενήσθησαν καὶ
αἱ λοιπαὶ τῆ κάστρη ἐπὶ Ἰσακίου
μεγάλου βασιλέ(ως) καὶ αὐτωκράτωρο(ς) Ρωμέ(ων)
5 τῆ Κομνηνῇ ϟ Αἰκατερίνης τῆς εὐσεβεστάτης
Αὐγούστης διὰ Λέοντ(ος) π(ατ)ρικίου ϟ ϛρατηγοῦ Χερ-
σωνο(ς) ϟ Σουγδ(αιας) τῇ Ἀλιάτ(ου), μη(νὸς) Ἀπρι[λλίου]
Ἰνδ(ικτιωνος) ιβ´, ἔτ(ους) ͵ϛφξϛ✝

I have only put the accents that are present on the stone.

25. *BCA.* x. p. 63, No. 66. Kerch, cf. p. 626.

A front of slab.   B back.

               ΣΗΜΑ

TYX   TITꓕ⅄Δ

               VΓOKEI

ꝀⅤ   TΑIΑⅬΗΡ

—— Break.   -O-Λ-Λ-O-

OΣ   ΣIΓOOII

               ⅬΟΣ

C round edge.

TΑVI OIΣ EIITVXⰆN TⰆΝO

    IoƎⱢ--ꓕⱯ⅃I⅃ƷƎΔΑ

26. *IosPE.* II. 343. Taman Peninsula near L. Tsukur. Leucon I, cf. pp. 573, 576, 618.

1 Δήμαρχος Σκύθεω
  ἀνέθηκεν Ἀφροδίτ[ηι]
  Οὐρανίηι Ἀπατούρο(υ)
  μεδεούσηι,
5 ἄρχοντος
  Λεύκωνος Βοσπόρ[ο](υ)
  καὶ Θεοδοσίης.

27. *IosPE.* II. 6. Bosporus. Leucon I, cf. pp. 128, 570 n. 4, 576, 577, 616.

1 Στρατοκλῆς ὑπὲρ πατρὸς τοῦ ἑαυτοῦ
  Δεινοστράτο(υ) ἱερησαμένου Ἀπόλλωνι Ἰητρῶι
  ἀνέθηκεν Λεύκωνος ἄρχοντος Βοσπόρο(υ)
  καὶ Θεοδοσίης καὶ βασιλεύοντος Σινδῶν,
5 Τορετέων, Δανδαρίων, Ψησσῶν.

28. *IG.* II. (*CIAtt.* IV. ii.) 109 *b*; Ditt. *Syll.*[2] I. 129. Piraeus. Ol. 108. 2 = B.C. 347/6, cf. pp. 571, 575, 577.

Σπαρτόκωι, Παιρισάδηι,
Ἀπολλωνίωι, Λεύκωνος παισί.

  Ἐπὶ Θεμιστοκλέους ἄρ[χ]οντο[s]
  ἐπὶ τῆς Αἰγηῖδος ὀγδό[η]s πρι[τ-
5 a]νείας, ἧι Λυσίμα[χ]ος Σωσιδή[μ-
  ου Ἀχα]ρ[ν]εὺς ἐγραμμάτευε Θε[ό]-
  φιλος [Ἀλι]μούσιος ἐπεστάτε[ι],
  Ἀνδροτίων Ἄνδρωνος Γαργήτ[τι]ος [ε]ἶπ[ε]ν· π[ε]-
  ρὶ ὧν ἐπέστειλε Σπάρτοκος κ[αὶ] Παιρ[ισάδη]-
10 s καὶ οἱ πρέσβεις οἱ ἥκοντ[ε]s π[α]ρ' αὐτῶν ἀπ[α]-
  γγέλλουσιν, ἀποκρί[ν]ασθαι αὐ[τ]οῖ[s], ὅτι ὁ [δῆ]-

28 (contd).

μος ὁ Ἀθηναίων ἐπαινεῖ Σπάρτ[ο]κον καὶ Παιρισάδην ὅτι εἰσὶν ἄνδρες [ἀ]γα[θ]οὶ καὶ ἐπ[αγ]-
γέλλονται τῶι δήμωι [τ]ῶι Ἀθηναίων ἐπιμ[ελ]-
15 ήσεσθαι τῆς ἐκ[π]ομπῆς τοῦ [σ]ί[τ]ου, καθάπερ ὁ
πατὴρ αὐτῶν ἐπεμελεῖ[τ]ο [κα]ὶ ὑ[π]ηρετήσειν π-
ροθύμως ὅτου ἂν ὁ δῆμ[ος] δ[έη]τα[ι], καὶ ἀπαγγ[έ]-
λλειν αὐτο[ῖ]s το[ὺ]s π[ρέσβ]εις, ὅτι ταῦτα ποι-
οῦντες οὐδενὸ[s] ἀτυχήσο[υ]σιν τοῦ δήμου το-
20 ῦ Ἀθηναίων· [ἐπ]ε[ι]δὴ δὲ [τὰ]s δω[ρειὰ]s δίδοασι-
ν Ἀθηναίοι[s ἅσ]περ Σ[άτ]υ[ρ]ος καὶ Λεύκων ἔδοσαν, εἶναι [Σπ]α[ρτ]ό[κ]ωι [κ]αὶ Παιρισάδει τὰς δ-
ωρειὰς ἃs [ὁ δῆμ]ος ἔδωκε Σατύρωι καὶ Λεύκωνι καὶ στεφ[ανοῦν] χρυσῶι στεφάνωι Παναθη-
25 ναίοις το[ῖς μεγ]άλοις ἀπὸ χιλίων δραχμῶν
ἑκάτερ[ο]ν· [ποιε]ῖσθαι δὲ τοὺς στεφάνους τοὺς ἀθλοθέ[τας] τῶι προτέρωι ἔτει Παναθηνα-
ίων τῶν μεγ[άλ]ων κατὰ τὸ ψήφισμα τοῦ δήμου
τὸ πρότερον ἐψηφισμένον Λεύκωνι καὶ ἀνα-
30 γορεύειν, ὅτι στεφανοῖ ὁ δῆμος ὁ Ἀθηναίων
Σπάρτοκον καὶ Παιρισάδην τοὺς Λεύκωνος
παῖδας ἀρετῆς καὶ εὐνοίας ἕνεκα τῆς εἰς τ-
ὸν δῆμον τὸν Ἀθηναίων· ἐπειδὴ δὲ τοὺς στεφάνους ἀνατιθέασι τῆι Ἀθηνᾶι τῆι Πολιάδι,
35 τοὺς ἀθλοθέτας εἰς τὸν νεὼ ἀνατιθέναι τοὺς στεφάνους, ἐπιγράψαντας· "Σπάρτοκος
καὶ Παιρισάδης Λεύκωνος παῖδες ἀνέθεσα-
ν τῆι Ἀθηναίαι, στεφανωθέντες ὑπὸ τοῦ δήμου τοῦ Ἀθηνα[ί]ων·" τὸ δὲ ἀργύριον διδόναι το-
40 ῖς ἀθλοθέταις εἰς τοὺς στεφάνους τὸν τοῦ
δήμου ταμίαν ἐκ τῶν εἰς τὰ κατὰ ψηφίσματα
τῶι δήμωι με[ρι]ζ]ομένων· τὸ δὲ νῦ[ν] εἶναι παρ-
αδοῦναι τοὺς ἀποδέκτας τὸ εἰς [τ]οὺς στεφ[ά]-
νους ἐκ τῶν στ[ρ]ατιωτικῶν χρ[η]μάτων· ἀναγ[ρ]-
45 άψαι δὲ τὸ ψήφισμα τόδε τὸγ γραμματέα τῆς
βουλῆς ἐν στήληι λιθίνηι καὶ στῆσαι πλη[σ]-
ίον τῆς Σατύρου καὶ Λεύκωνος, εἰς δὲ τὴν ἀν[α]-
γραφὴν δοῦναι τὸν ταμίαν τοῦ δήμου τριά[κ]-
οντα δραχμάς· ἐπαινέσαι δὲ τοὺς πρέσβει[s]
50 Σῶσιν καὶ Θεοδόσιον, ὅτι ἐπιμελοῦνται [τῶ]-
ν ἀφικν[ν]ουμένων Ἀθήνηθεν εἰς Βόσπορον [κα]-
ὶ καλέσαι αὐτοὺς ἐπὶ ξένια εἰς τὸ πρυτα[νε]-
ῖον εἰς αὔριον· περὶ δὲ τῶν χρημάτων τῶν [ὀφ-
ει]λ[ο]μένων τοῖς παισὶ τοῖς Λεύκωνος ὅπως
55 ἀν ἀπολάβωσιν, χρηματίσαι τοὺς προέδ[ρους
οἳ] ἂν λάχωσι προεδρεύειν ἐν τῶι δήμωι [τῆι
ὀγ]δόηι ἐπὶ δέκα πρῶτον μετὰ τὰ ἱερά, ὅ[πως ἀ-
ν] ἀπολα[β]όντες τὰ χρήματα μὴ ἐγκαλῶσ[ι τῶι]
δήμωι τῶι Ἀθηναίων· δοῦναι δ[ὲ τὰ]s στρ[ατεγ-
60 α]s ἃs αἰτοῦσι Σπάρτοκος καὶ Παιρισ[άδης, τ-
οὺ]s δὲ πρ[έ]σβεις ἀπογράψαι τὰ ὀνόμα[τα τῶν
ὑπ]ηρε[σι]ῶν ὧν ἂν λάβωσιν τῶι γραμμα[τεῖ τῆ]-
s βουλῆς· οὓς δ' ἂν ἀπογράψωσιν, εἶνα[ι ἐν τῶι]
τ[ετ]αγμένωι ποιοῦντας ἀγαθὸν ὅ τι [ἂν δύνω]-
65 νται τοὺς παῖδας τοὺς Λεύκωνος. Π[ολύευκτ-
ο]s Τιμοκράτου Κριωεὺς εἶπε· τὰ [μὲν ἄλλα κα-
α]θάπερ Ἀνδροτίων, στεφανῶσα[ι δὲ καὶ Ἀπολ]-
λώνιον τὸν Λεύκωνος υἱὸν ἐκ τῶ[ν αὐτῶν].

29. *IosPE.* II. 344. Akhtanizovka. Paerisades I,
cf. pp. 22, 128, 295, 566, 576, 577, 619.

1 Ξενοκλείδης Πόσιος ἀνέθηκε
τὸν ναὸν Ἀρτέμιδι Ἀγροτέραι
ἄρχοντος Παιρισάδους τοῦ
Λεύκωνος Βοσπόρου καὶ Θευδο-
5 σίης καὶ βασιλεύων Σινδῶν
καὶ Τορετῶν καὶ Δανδαρίων.

29ª. *IosPE.* II. 11. Kerch.   Paerisades I,
cf. pp. 128, 577, 619.

1 [Ὁ sive ἡ δεῖνα] Κοιρ[άν]ου ἀνέθηκεν
[ὑπὲρ τ]ῆ[s θυ]γατρὸς Ἰτίης Ἀρτέμιδ[ι]
Ἐφεσείηι ἀρ[χοντο]s Παιρισάδους Βοσπόρου
καὶ Θευδ[οσίης] καὶ βασιλεύοντος
5 Σινδ[ῶν καὶ Μαϊτ]ῶν πάντων.

30. *IosPE.* II. 346. Taman Peninsula. Paerisades I, cf. pp. 22, 128, 296, 573, 577,
578, 617, 619.

Κομοσαρύη Γοργίππου θυγάτηρ, Παιρισάδους [γυ]ή,
εὐξαμένη
ἀνέθηκε ἰσχυρῶι θεῶι Σανέργει καὶ Ἀστάραι, ἄρχοντος
Παιρισάδους
Βοσπόρου κα{ὶ} Θευδοσίης καὶ βασιλεύοντος Σ[ινδ]ῶν
καὶ Μαϊτῶν πά[ντων]
καὶ Θατέων.

31. *IosPE.* II. 8. Kerch. Paerisades I, cf.
pp. 128, 577.

1 Φαινίππου ἀ[νάθημα ὑπὲρ τοῦ]
ἀδελφοῦ Ἀρτε[μιδώρου? τοῦ . . . . . .]-
. .]ο(ν), ἄρχοντος Παιρ[ι]σάδ[εος Θεοδο]-
σίης καὶ βασιλεύοντος Σινδ[ῶν
5 καὶ Μαϊτῶ?]ν καὶ Θατέων.

32. *IosPE.* II. 1. Kerch. Paerisades I, cf.
pp. 578, 580.

1 [. . . . . ω]ι Διον[υσίου] Πειρα[εῖ προξενία].
Παιρισάδης καὶ παῖδε[s . . . . ωι]
Διονυσίου Πειραεῖ καὶ [ἐκγόνοις],
ἔδοσαν προξενίαν κ[αὶ ἀτέλει]-
5 αν πάντων χρημάτω[ν ἐν παν]-
τὶ Βοσπόρωι, αὐτοῖς κα[ὶ θεράπου-
σι]ν τοῖς τούτων, καὶ ε[ἴσπλουν
καὶ ἔ]κπλουν καὶ πολέ[μου καὶ εἰ-
ρήνης] ἀσυλεὶ κα[ὶ ἀσπονδεί].

l. 6 Ditt. (*Syll.*² 134) σύμπα[σι]ν·

33. *IosPE.* II. 13. .Kerch.   Spartocus III,
cf. pp. 580, 619.

[Ἡ δεῖνα . . . .]σθένους γυνὴ
[ἀνέθηκε Δή]μητρι Θεσμοφόρωι
ἄρχοντος Σπαρτόκου
τοῦ Εὐμήλου.

34. *IG.* II. (*CIAtt.* II. i.) 311; Ditt. *Syll.*² 194.
Athens. Ol. 123. 3 = B.C. 286/5, cf. pp.
571, 575, 580.

1 [Ἐπὶ Δ]ιοτίμου ἄρχοντος ἐπὶ τῆς Ἀντι[γονίδος (?) ἐ-
βδό]μης πρυτανείας, ἧι Λυσίστρατ[ος Ἀριστομά-
χου] Παιανιεὺς ἐγραμμάτευεν · Γα[μηλιῶνος ἔνηι
καὶ] νέαι, ἐνάτηι καὶ εἰ[κοσ]τῆι τῆ[s πρυτανείας·
5 ἐκκ]λησία· τῶν προέδρ[ων ἐπε]ψ[ή]φιζε . . . .
. . .]οσθένου Ξυπετ[αιὼν καὶ συμπρόεδροι· ἔδο-
ξε]ν τῶι δήμωι· Ἀγύρ[ριος Καλλιμέδοντος Κολλυ]-
τεὺς εἶπεν· ἐπειδὴ [πρότερόν τε οἱ πρόγονοι οἱ]
Σπαρτόκου χρείας [παρέσχηνται τῶι δήμωι καὶ]
10 νῦν Σπάρτοκος πα[ραλαβὼν τὴν εἰς τὸν δῆμον οἰ]-
κειότητα κοινῆι [τε τῶι δήμωι χρείας παρέχε]-
ται καὶ ἰδίαι Ἀθη[ναίων τοῖς ἀφικνουμένοις]
πρὸς αὐτόν· ἀνθ᾽ [ὧν καὶ ὁ δῆμος ὁ Ἀθηναίων αὐτοὺς]
πολίτας ἐποιή[σατο καὶ ἐτίμησ]εν [εἰκόσιν χαλ]-
15 καῖς ἔν τε τῆι [ἀγορᾶι καὶ] ἐν τῶι ἐμπορίωι [καὶ]
ἄλλαις δωρεα[ῖς, αἷς προσήκει τιμᾶσθαι τοὺ[s]
ἀγαθοὺς ἄνδ[ρας, καὶ διέθε]το ἐάν τις βαδίζε[ι]
ἐπὶ τὴν ἀρχὴν τ[ὴν τῶν προγόνω]ν αὐτοῦ ἢ τὴν Σπα[ρ]-
τόκου βοηθε[ῖν παντὶ σθένε]ι κ[α]ὶ κατὰ γῆν καὶ
20 κατὰ θάλατ[ταν· ἔτι δὲ Σπάρτ]οκος ἀφι(κ)ομένης
πρεσβείας [παρ᾽ Ἀθηναίων ἀκ]ούσας ὅτι ὁ δῆμος
κεκόμιστ[αι τὸ ἄστυ συνή]ᾳθη τοῖς εὐτυχήμασ[ι]
τοῦ δή[μου καὶ δέδωκεν σῖτ]ου δωρεὰν μυρίου[s]
καὶ πε[ντακισχιλίους με]δίμνους, ἐπαγγέλλε[τ-
25 αι δὲ καὶ ἐς τὸ λοιπὸν χρ]είαν παρέξεσθαι τῶι
[δήμωι καὶ βοηθήσ]ειν καθό]τι ἄν δύνηται καὶ ταῦ-
[τα πράττει προαιρούμε]ος διαφυλάττειν τὴν [ε-
ὔνοιαν τὴν εἰς τὸν δῆμ]ον τὴν παραδεδομένην
[αὐτῶι παρὰ τῶν προγόνω]ν· ὅπως ἄν οὖν φαίνηται
30 [ὁ δῆμος χάριτος μεμνη]μένος (?) πρὸς τοὺς εὐνους
[διὰ τοῦ ἔμπροσθεν χρ]όνου διαμ(ε)μενηκότας αὐ-
[τῶι, τύχηι ἀγαθῆι δε]δόχθαι τῶι δήμωι ἐπ[αινέ-
σαι μὲν τὸν βασιλέ]α Σπάρτοκον Εὐμήλου [Βοσ-
πόρου καὶ στεφανῶ]σαι χρυσῶι στεφάνωι [ἀπὸ - - -
35 δραχμῶν ἀρετῆς] ἕνεκα καὶ εὐνοίας ἥν ἔχω[ν δι-
ατελεῖ πρὸς τὸν] δῆμον καὶ ἀνειπεῖν τὸν στέ[φα-
νον Διονυσίων] τῶν μεγάλων τραγωιδοῖς ἐν τῶι
[ἀγῶνι, τῆς δὲ π]οιήσεως τοῦ στεφάνου καὶ τῆς ἀ-
[ναγορεύσεως] ἐπιμεληθῆναι τοὺς ἐπὶ τῆι διο[ι-
40 κήσει· στῆσαι] δ᾽ αὐτοῦ καὶ εἰκόνα χαλκῆ(ν) ἐν τῆι
[ἀγορᾶι παρὰ] τοὺς προγόνους καὶ ἐάν περ ἐ[ν ἀκρο-
πόλει· ὅπω]ς ἂν δὲ καὶ εἰδῆι ὁ βασιλεὺς Σπάρτ[ο-
κος τὰ ἐψηφ]ισμένα τῶι δήμωι, χειροτονῆσαι πρέ-
[σβεις τρε]ῖς ἄνδρας ἐξ Ἀθηναίων ἁπάντων, οἵτι[ν-

34. *IG*. II. 311 (contd).

45 ἐs αἱρεθέ]ντεs ἀπαροῦσιν καὶ τό τε ψήφισμα ἀ[π-
οδώσου]σιν καὶ ἀπαγγελοῦσι τὴν εὔνοιαν ἥν
[ἔχει πρὸ]s αὐτὸν ὁ δῆμος καὶ παρακαλοῦσιν αὐ[τ-
ὸν βοηθ]εῖν τῶι δήμωι καθότι ἂν δύνηται, δοῦ[ν-
αι δὲ ἐφό]δια τῶν πρέσβεων ἑκάστωι τὸ τετα[γ-
50 μένον]· ὅπως ἂν δὲ καὶ ὑπόμνημα ἦι τῆς οἰκειό-
[τητος κ]αὶ τῶν δωρειῶν τῶν προστιθεμένων αὐτῶι πρ]ὸς ταῖς ὑπαρχούσαις, τὸν γραμματέα τὸν
[κατὰ π]ρυτανείαν ἀναγράψαι τόδε τὸ ψήφισμα
ἐν στ]ήληι λιθίνηι καὶ στῆσαι ἐν ἀκροπόλει, τὸ
55 [δὲ ἀν]άλωμα τὸ γενόμενον μερίσαι τοὺς ἐπὶ τῆι
[διο]ικήσει.

Ὁ δῆμος.

l. 24, Ditt. πε[ντακοσίους.
l. 26 supplevi βοιηθεῖν, cf. Ditt. ad l. 48.

35. *IosPE*. II. 15. Kerch. Paerisades II,
cf. pp. 128, 580, 581, 616.

Λεύκων Παιρισάδου ἀνέθηκε τὸν ἀνδριάντα Ἀπόλλωνι
['Ι]ητρῶ[ι ἰ]ερησάμενος, ἄρχοντος Παιρισάδου τοῦ Σπαρ-
τόκου Βοσπόρου καὶ Θευδοσίης καὶ βασιλεύοντος
Σινδῶν καὶ Μαϊτῶν πάντων   καὶ Θατέων.

36. *IosPE*. II. 17. Kerch. Paerisades II,
cf. pp. 580, 619.

Βασιλεύοντος Παιρισάδου τοῦ Σπαρτόκου Ἐστιαία
Μηνοδώρου θυγάτηρ ἱερωμένη ἀνέθηκεν Μητρὶ Φρυγίαι.

37. *IosPE*. II. 18. Kerch.
Spartocus IV, cf. pp.
581, 616.

[Βασιλ]ε(ύ)οντος Σπαρτόκου
τοῦ Παιρισάδου ['Α]γλα[ὸ]s
Ἡρακλείδου Διονύσωι.

38. *IosPE*. II. 19, cf. *CR*. 1877, p. 246=*KTR*.
p. 29, f. 26. Kerch. Paerisades IV (?),
cf. pp. 581, 618, 621.

1 Παιρισάδου. Καμασαρύης. Ἀργότου.
Ὑπὲρ [ἄ]ρχοντος καὶ βασιλέως
Παιρ[ισ]άδου τοῦ βασιλέως Παιρισάδου φιλο[μ]ήτορος καὶ βασι-
5 λίσσης Καμασαρύης τῆς Σπαρτ[ό-
κ]ου θυγατρὸς φιλ[ο]τέκνο[υ καὶ]
Ἀργότου τοῦ Ι . . . θου βασ[ιλίσ]-
σης Καμασαρ[ύη]ς ἀνδρὸς [ὁ συνα]-
γωγὸς Θεόκρι[το]s Δημη[τρίου καὶ]
10 οἱ θιασῖτα[ι] ἀνέθηκ[αν τὴν στή]-
λη[ν] 'Αφροδ[ε]ίτῃ Οὐ[ρανίᾳ, Ἀπατού-
ρ]ου μεδεούσῃ . . . .
Θεόκριτος Δημ[ητρίου], κ.τ.λ.

39. *IosPE*. II. 25. Kerch. Asander and
Dynamis, cf. pp. 561, 592, 614, 616,
619, 630.

1 Βα[σιλεύοντος βασιλέως βασιλέων]
μεγάλου Ἀσάνδρου [φιλ]ορωμαίου σωτῆ-
ρος καὶ βασιλίσσης Δυνάμεως Παν-
ταλ[έω]ν ναύαρχος Ποσιδῶνι Σωσινέ-
5 [ω]ι καὶ Ἀφροδίτηι Ναυαρχίδι.

40. *IosPE*. IV. 201. Kerch. Dynamis, cf.
pp. 561, 593, 620.

[Α]ὐτοκράτορα Καίσαρα θεὸν
[θ]εοῦ υἱὸν Σεβαστὸν τὸν ἑαυτῆς
[σ]ωτῆρα καὶ εὐεργέτην
[β]ασίλισσα Δ[ύνα]μις φιλορώμαιο[s].

41. *IosPE*. II. 356. Phanagoria, Semenjaka's
Farm. Dynamis, cf. pp. 592, 593, 613.

1 [Β]ασίλισσαν Δύναμιν φιλορώμ[αιον,
τὴ]ν ἐκ βασιλέω[s μεγάλου Φα[ρνάκου
το]ῦ ἐκ βασιλέως βασιλέων Μιθ[ραδά-
το]υ Εὐπάτορος [Διο]νύσ[ο]υ,
5 [τὴ]ν ἑαυτῶν σ[ώτειραν κ]αὶ εὐε[ργέ-
τι]ν [ὁ δ]ῆμ[ος ὁ Ἀγριπ]πέω[ν].

42. *IosPE*. II. 36. Kerch. Aspurgus, cf. pp. 128, 569, 596,
613.

1 Βασιλέα μέγαν Ἀσποῦργον φιλορώμαιον, τὸν ἐκ βασιλέως Ἀσανδρόχου,
φιλοκαίσαρα καὶ φιλορώμαιον, βασιλεύοντα παντὸς Βοσσπόρου, Θεοδοσίης
καὶ Σινδῶν καὶ Μαιτῶν καὶ Ταρπείτων καὶ Τορετῶν, Ψησῶν τε καὶ Τανα[ε]ιτῶν,
ὑποτάξαντα Σκύθας καὶ Ταύρους, Μενέστρατος β΄ ὁ ἐπὶ τῆς νήσου τὸν ἑαυτοῦ σω-
5 τῆρα καὶ εὐεργέτην.

43. *IosPE*. II. 400. Anapa, A.B. 338 = A.D. 41.
[Mithridates VIII ?], cf. pp. 597, 616, 621.

1 Θεῶι ὑψίστωι παντο-
κράτορι εὐλογητῷ, βα-
σιλεύοντος βασιλέ-
ως [. . . . .] φιλο-
5 γερμα[νί]κου καὶ φιλοπάτ-
ριδος, ἔτους ηλτ΄, μη-
νὸς Δείου, Πόθος Στ-
[ρά]τωνος ἀνέθηκεν
τ[ῆ]ι [προσ]ευχῆι κατ' εὐχ[ὴ]-
10 ν θ[ρ]επτὴν ἑαυτοῦ, ἧ ὄνομα Χ[ρ]ύσα, ἐφ' ᾧ ᾖ ἀνέπα-
φος καὶ ἀνεπηρέαστο[s]
ἀπὸ παντὸς κληρον[όμ]-
ου ὑπὸ Δία, Γῆν, Ἥλιο[ν].

l. 4, Lat. suppl.
[Πολέμωνος]
Stephani
[Μιθρα]δα[το]ν,
which seems to
suit the traces
on the stone
better.

44. *IosPE.* II. 32. Kerch. Cotys I,
cf. pp. 596, 598, 620.

1 [Αὐτοκράτορα Νέρωνα Κλαυδίου] υἱὸν Κ[α]ίσ[αρα
Σεβαστόν, ὕπατον τὸ τρίτ]ον, δημαρχικῆς ἐξου[σίας
τὸ πέμπτον, πατέρα πα]τρίδος, τὸν ἑ[α]υτοῦ σωτ[ῆρα
καὶ εὐεργέτην, Κότυς] ὁ Ἀσπούρ[γ]ου [β]α[σ]ι[λεὺς φι-
5 λόκαισαρ καὶ φιλορώ]μαιος, εὐσεβής, ἀρχιε[ρεὺς τῶν
Σεβαστῶν διὰ βίου καθ]ιέρωσεν.

45. *IosPE.* II. 37. Hadzhi Mushkaj. Cotys I,
cf. pp. 596, 598, 626.

Τήνδ' ἀρετὴ κρήνης πολλὴν | λιβάδ' ἐξανέδειξεν
υἱός | Ἀσπούργου, εὐσεβέος | Κότυος,
γαίης καὶ προγόνων | πατρώïον ἀραμένοιο
κῦδος | κεἰναχίων σκῆπτρ' ἐπέχοντος ὅλα.

46. *IosPE.* II. 52. Kerch. A.B. 377 = A.D. 81.
Rhescuporis I, cf. pp. 599, 621, 622.

1 Βασιλεύοντος βασιλέως Τιβερίου Ἰουλίου Ῥησκουπόριδος φιλοκαίσαρος καὶ φιλορωμαίου, εὐσεβοῦς, ἔτους ζοτ' μηνὸς Περει[τί]-
5 ου ιβ', Χρήστη γυνὴ πρότερον Δρούσου ἀφείημι ἐπὶ τῆς [προ]-
σευχῆς θρεπτόν μου Ἡρακλᾶν
ἐλεύθερον καθάπαξ κατὰ εὐχή[ν]
μου ἀνεπίληπτον καὶ ἀπα[ρ]ενό-
10 χλητον ἀπὸ παντὸς κληρονόμ[ου·
τ]ρέπεσ(θ)αι αὐτὸν ὅπου ἂν βού-
λ[ητ]αι ἀνεπικωλύτως καθὼς ε[ὐ]-
ξάμην, χωρὶς ἰς τ[ὴ]ν προ[σ]ευ-
χὴν θωπείας τε καὶ προσκα[ρτε-
15 ρ]ήσεω[ς], συνεπινευσάντων δὲ
καὶ τῶν κληρο(ο)νόμων μου Ἡρα-
κλεί[δο]υ καὶ Ἑλικωνιάδος,
συνε[πιτ]ροπεουσης δὲ καὶ τῆ[ς]
συναγωγῆ[ς] τῶν Ἰουδαίων.

47. *BCA.* XXIII. p. 47, No. 32. Anapa. A.B.
407 = A.D. 111. Sauromates I, cf. pp.
566, 604, 613, 619, 625.

1 Βασιλεύοντος βασιλέως
Τιβερίου Ἰουλίου Σαυρομά-
του φιλοκαίσαρος καὶ φιλορωμαίου εὐσεβοῦς
5 θεᾷ Ἀφροδείτῃ Ναυαρχίδι
εὐξάμενος τὸν ναὸν ἀ-
νήγειρεν Φαρνακίων Πό-
θου ὁ ἐπὶ Γοργιππείας ἐκ
τῶν ἰδίων ἀναλωμάτων
10 ἐν τῷ ξυ' ἔτει
καὶ μηνὶ Δαεισίου.

48. *IosPE.* IV. 421. Taman. Cotys II,
cf. pp. 604, 621, 624.

. . . .
[Βασιλεύοντος βασι]-
1 λέως [Τιβερίου Ἰουλίου]
Κότυος, υἱ[οῦ βασιλέως]
Σαυρομάτου, [φιλοκαίσα]-
ρος καὶ φιλορωμαίου,
5 εὐσεβοῦς, ἡ σύνο-
δος, ἡ περὶ νακόρον
Βάγην Σωσιπάτρου.
καὶ Ἱ[ρ]έα Στράτωνα
Ὀν.. . . .ρου καὶ ἱερομά-
10 στορα Ἀπολλώνιον Χρυ-
σαλίσκου καὶ γραμμα-
τέα Ἀγαθοῦν Πολεμοκρά-
του καὶ φιλάγαθον Μυρεῖ-
νον θ' καὶ οἱ λοιποὶ θιασεῖται
15 Καλοῦς Μυρείνου
Μέγης Μηνᾶ
Δημοκράτης Δάδα
Ἀρισταγόρας Ἀγαθοῦ
Δάδας Ἀπολλωνί[ου]
20 . . . . . . Ἡλίττα
. . . .

49. *IosPE.* II. 353. Phanagoria.
A.B. 448 = A.D. 151. Rhoemetalces,
cf. pp. 579, 605, 613.

1 Τιβέριος Ἰούλιος βασιλεὺς
Ῥοιμητάλκης, φιλόκαισαρ καὶ φι-
λορωμαιος, εὐσεβής, τὰς ὑπὸ
Λη+ οδώρου ἀνατεθείσας γέας
5 ἐν Θιαννέοις καὶ τοὺς πελάτας
κατὰ τὸν παρακείμενον τελαμῶνα χρόνωι μειωθέντα συναθρόι-
σας ἅπαντα καὶ πλεονάσας ἀπε-
κατέστησε τῆι θ[ε]ῶι σῶα, δι' ἐπι-
10 μελεί[α]ς Ἀ[λ]εξάνδρου Μυρείνου
τοῦ ἐπὶ τῶν ἱερῶν. ημν', μηνὶ
Ἀπελλαίωι κ'.

50. *IosPE.* II. 422. Tanais. Eupator,
cf. pp. 605, 616.

1 Ἀ[γ]αθῇ τύχῃ.
Βασιλεύοντος βα-
σιλέως Τιβερίου
Ἰουλίου Εὐπάτο-
5 ρος φιλοκαίσαρος
καὶ φιλορω[μ]αίου
εὐσεβοῦς θεῷ Ἀπόλ-
λωνι εὐ[ξ]άμενος Ἀν-
τίμαχος Χαριτω- . . .
10 [νος πρεσβε]υτ[ή]ς . . . .

51. *BCA.* xxxvii. p. 38, No. 2, Pl. ii. Anapa.
Sauromates II, cf. pp. 566, 606, 612–616,
621, 623, 625.

1 ['Αγαθῇ τύχῃ].
Βασιλεύοντος βασιλέως Τιβερίου Ἰουλ]ίου Σαυρομάτου φιλοκαίσαρος καὶ φιλορωμαίου,] εὐσεβοῦς τοῦ ... ἔτους .. μην]ὸς Δαισίου. Θεῷ Ὑπο-
5 σριδῶρος [ἐπὶ] βασιλέως Σαυρομάτου, υἱοῦ μεγάλου βασιλέως Ῥοιμητάλκου, θέασος ναυκλήρων,
οἱ καὶ ποιήσαντες· τὰ ἀγάλματα καὶ τὸν ναὸν ἐκ
θεμελίων ἀναστήσαντες, εἰς ἃ καὶ [ἐ]τείμησεν ὁ βασιλεὺς τὸν θεὸν καὶ τὴν θέασον [εἰ]σαγώγιον ἀρτα-
10 βῶν χειλίων. Θεασεῖται περὶ ἱερέ[α]ν Ἀθηνόδωρον
Σελεύκου πρῶτον ἐπὶ τῆς βα[σι]λείας καὶ συναγωγὸν Μοιρόδωρον Νεοκλέους ὁ ἐπὶ τῆς Γοργιτείας
καὶ φροντιστὰς Κοσσοῦν Ἄττα Κοσσοῦ καὶ Φαρνάκην Νού-
μηνίου ἱερῶν οἰκονόμος. Θε[α]σεῖται Πανταλέων
15 Φαρνάκου στρατηγόν, Μοιρόδω[ρος Ἀταμ]άξου στρατ-
[ηγός]
Χρηστίων Πάπα, Μακάριος Ἀθη[νοδώρου ....]
ἐνκυκλίων οἰκο[νόμ]ος, Γάγανο[ς .... ἐν]-
κυκλίων οἰκο[νόμο]ς, Ἀσπούρ[γος .... ἐνκυκλίων]
οἰκονόμο[ς .... κ.τ.λ.

At least 16 lines of names similar to those in No. 69.

53. *IosPE.* ii. 445. Tanais. Sauromates II,
cf. pp. 606, 620, 621, 623.

1 Θεῷ ὑψ[ί]στῳ. Τινο Eagles. Ἀγαθῆι τύχηι.
Βασιλεύον[τος β]ασι[λέω]ς Τιβ(ερίου) Ἰουλ(ίου) Σαυρομάτου
φιλοκαίσαρ[ος κα]ὶ φιλο[ρ]ωμαίου εὐσεβοῦς, ἡ σύνοδος
ἡ περὶ ἱ[ερέα Ἰού?]λιον Σα . χάδου καὶ πατέρα σ[υ]νόδου
5 Χορούα[θον ....] καὶ συναγωγὸν Ἀρδα[ρίσκ]ον
[Σ]υνεγδή[μου καὶ φιλάγαθ]ον Διαγ[όραν?..]βλωνά-
κ[ον] καὶ
[π]αραφιλάγαθ[ον Χόφρασμ?]ον Ψοργαβά[κου] καὶ
[νεαν]ισ-
[κ]άρχην Δημή[τριον Ἀπολ]λωνίου καὶ γυμ[να]σιά[ρχην]
Βα-
[σι]λείδην Θεον[είκ]ο[υ καὶ Ἀτ]ή[α]ν Ἡρακλείδου
[γρ]α[μμα]τ[εὺ]ς
10 [συν]όδου· οἱ λ[οιποὶ θια]ο[ῖτ]αι· Ἀρδαρ[ίσκ]ος Ζ[η-
νοδότ]ον, Δη[μήτ]ριος .... ου, Λείμανος Φί[δα],
[Μί]δαχ[ος Στυρ?]άνο[υ, Ἀσκ]ληπιάδης Οὐαλ[ερ]ίου,
κ.τ.λ.

20 more lines of names and a mutilated date.

52. *IosPE.* ii. 423. Tanais.
A.B. 490 = A.D. 194.
Sauromates II, cf. pp.
120, 318, 606, 612,
615—617, 619.

....
1 χειλίους, πολ[ε]μήσας
δὲ καὶ Σιραχοὺς καὶ Σκύ-
θας καὶ τὴν Ταυρικὴν ὑ-
πόσπονδον λα[β]ὼν, (ἐ)λεύ-
5 θερ]ον ἀπέδει[ξ]ε [ἐν] Πόν-
τ[ῳ], Βειθυνίᾳ τοῖς [π]λέου-
σι τὸ πέλαγος ἐ[πὶ σ]τρα-
τηγῷ πολειτῷ[ν .... Ζή]-
νωνος [Δ]άδα Ε[ὐ]ί[ο]υ, καὶ
10 Ἰουλ(ίου) Δ .. ονου κα(ὶ) Ἰουλίου
Ῥ]όδω[νο]ς τῶν πρὶν ἐπὶ [τῆ]ς
βασιλε[ία]ς, Ζήνων β´ τοῦ [Δ]ά-
δ[α] ἐκπ[εμφ]θεὶς ὑπὸ τοῦ
βασιλέ[ως] εἰς τὸ ἐμπόριον
15 καθιέρω[σ]α Διί, Ἄρη καὶ
Ἀφροδίτη ἐπὶ Βορά-
σπω [Β]άβου ἄρχοντ(ος) Τα-
νάεως καὶ Ἑλ]ληνάρχ(ου)
Ῥόδωνος Χαρίτ[ω]νος
20 ἐν τῷ ϙυ´, Δύ[σ]τρου α´.

Tamga
of Sauro-
mates II.

54. *IosPE.* ii. 41. Kerch.
A.B. 512 = A.D. 216.
Rhescuporis II, cf. pp.
597, 604, 607, 612, 614,
616, 617, 620.

1 ['Αγαθῇ τύχῃ].
Τὸν] ἀφ' Ἡρακλέους καὶ Εὐμόλ-
πο]υ τοῦ Ποσειδῶνος καὶ ἀπὸ
προγόνων βασιλέων βασιλέ-
5 α Τιβέριον Ἰούλ[ι]ον Ῥησκούπο-
ριν, υἱὸν μεγάλου βασιλέως
Σαυρομάτου, φ[ι]λοκαίσαρα
καὶ φιλορώμα[ι]ον, εὐσεβῆ, ἀρχιερέα τῶν Σεβαστῶν διὰ
10 βίου, Οὔλπιος Ἀντισθένης
Ἀντιμάχου χειλιάρχης
τὸν ἑαυτοῦ σωτῆρα καὶ
δεσπότην τειμῆς χάριν
ἐν τῶι βίῳ ἔτει
15 καὶ μηνὶ Λώωι κ´.

55. *IosPE.* ii. 430. Tanais.
A.B. 517 = A.D. 220. Rhescuporis II, cf. pp. 569,
607, 615, 625.

1 Ἀγαθῆι τύχηι.
Ἐπὶ βασιλεῖ Ῥησκουπόριδι, υἱῷ .
μεγάλου βασιλέως Σαυρομάτου, κα[ὶ]
Ζήνων Φάννεως πρεσβευτῇ βα-
5 σιλέως Ῥησκουπόριδος, καὶ Χο-
φάρνου Σανδαρζίου, Βάβος Βαιο-
ράσπου, Νιβλόβωρος Δοσυμοξάρ-
θου, Χοράσβος Σανδαρζίου στρατεύον-
τες Ταναειτῶν, Χόφραρμος Φοργα-
10 βάκου, Βασιλείδης Θεονείκου Ἑλ-
ληνάρχης ἐξαρτίσας τὴν ἀγορὰν
ἐκ τῶν ἰδίων ἀναλωμάτων ἀπεκα-
τέστησα τῇ πόλει καὶ τοῖς ἐμπόροις διὰ ἐπιμελητῶν Ζήνωνα Φάι-ν-
15 ν]εως, Φαρνόξαρθον Ταυρέου,
Φαλδάρανος Ἀπολλωνίου καὶ
[ἀρ]χιτέκτονων Διοφάντου Νε-
οπόλιον κα[ὶ] Αὐρηλίου Ἀντωνείνου, Ναύακος Μευάκου.
20 Ἐν τῷ ϛιζ´.

56. *IosPE.* II. 447. Tanais. A.B. 522 = A.D. 225. Rhescuporis II, cf. pp. 37, 607, 620, 621, 623, 625.

1   Ἀγαθῇ τύχῃ.
Θεῷ ὑψίστῳ ἐπηκόωι ἡ σύνοδος περὶ θεὸν ὕψιστον καὶ ἱερέα Χόφρασμον
Φοργαβάκου καὶ συναγωγὸν Εὐπρέπην
5 Συμφόρου καὶ φιλάγαθον Ἀντίμαχον Πα-
σίωνος καὶ παραφιλάγαθον Σύμφορον Δημητρίου καὶ γυμνασιάρχην Β[αλ]ῶδιν Δημητρίου
καὶ νιανισκάρχην Σαυάνων Χοφράσμου καὶ οἱ
λοιποὶ θιασῶται· Μηνόφιλος Μόσχα, Ἀβρόξεος
10 Ἀρίστωνος, Σωτηρικὸς Ποπλίου, Φα[ῦ]χος Ποπλίου,
Μια ... ηδος Ἀντιμάχου, Ῥαχοίσακος Εὐνοίκου, Λοι-
άγας Βαλωδίου, Μέγις β′, Εὐτύχης Ἀντιμάχου, Δυνά-
των Δημητρίου, Ἰραύαδις Δημητρίου, Σύμφορος Καλ-
λισθένου, Ἀσπάνδανος Λειμάνου, Ἀρδάγδακος Πο-
15 πλίου, Μάδωϊς Σαμβατίωνος, Νάβαξος Κίμβρου, Μίδα-
χος Ἀρδάρου, Φορίανος Ἀντισθένου, Ῥαχοίσ[ακος]
Ῥασσ[ό]-
γου, . ανάθακος Ζευάκου, Ἡρακλείδης Μαρκεανοῦ,
...κος Σιανάκου, Ὀχωδίακος Δούλα, Γάος, Πάναυχος Ἀρ-
[δάρ]ου, Ὀσμάρακος Ἀμαιάκου, Ψυχαρίων Τρύφω[ν(ος),
Ἀρ]ίστων
20 [Μενεσ]τράτου, Ὀδίαρδος [Δ]ημητρίου, Σύμφορος Χο-
..... κ]αὶ εἰσβε .... α Ὀκξύμακο[ς ...
.......]οθαι[..... Δ]ιοφάντου, Εὐτ[ύχης ..
........], Ἀμαρδίακος Μεν[ε]στρ[ά]του, [....
... Ἀλ]εξάνδρου, Γώσακος Ἀσπά[κ]ου, Ἀραούη[β]ος
25 . δύλλο(υ), Δαλόσακος Συμφόρο[υ, Ἀ]ρδόναστος
Σώφρ(ο)νος, Βάγδοχος Συμφόρου, Σα ... σ[κ]ος Ἀμ-
αειάκου, Γωδίγασος Συμφόρου, Χ . κιος Ἀ[θην]οδώ-
ρου, Ξιαμφώκανος Ἀντιμάχου, Αὐβα-
δαγ ...... ναείστου.

30 Ἐν τῷ βκφ′ ἔτει κ(α)ὶ μηνὶ [Περ]ειτίου κ′.

57. *IosPE.* IV. 433. Anapa (?). Cotys III and Sauromates III, cf. pp. 607, 621, 625.

1   ... Ἀλέ]ξανδρος Νουμηνίου, Σ[τ]α ...

['Αγαθ]ῆ τύχηι.
[Βασιλεύοντος βασιλέ]ως Τιβερίου Ἰουλίου [Κότυος]
[υἱοῦ μεγάλου βασι]λέως Ῥησκουπόρι[δος, φιλο-]
5 [καίσαρος καὶ φιλορω]μαίου εὐσεβοῦς, ἔ[τους? ...
.... μηνὸς Πανή]μου ζ′. Θεασεῖται ο[ἱ .....
.... βασιλέως] Σαυρομάτου κ[........
...............] βασιλέως Κό[τυος ....
.... Νουμ]ήνιον Ἄττα, Σ[.....
... Νεοκλ[έους ...
... π]ολειτῶ[ν ...
.. Μυρ]είνο[υ? ...

58. *IosPE.* II. 452. Tanais. A.B. 525 = A.D. 229. Cotys III, cf. pp. 607, 620, 621, 623, 625.

[Ἀγαθῆ]ι τύχῃ.
Θε[ῷ ὑ]ψίστῳ ε[ὐχή].
Βα[σ]ιλεύοντ[ος] βασιλέ[ως Τιβερίου
Ἰ]ουλίου [Κό]τυος φιλοκα[ίσαρος] καὶ φι-
5 [λορωμαίο]υ εὐσεβοῦς, εἰσποιητοὶ
ἀδ[ελφοὶ σ]εβόμενοι θεὸν ὕψιστον,
ἐνγρ[άψαντ]ες ἑαυτῶν [τ]ὰ ὀνόματα
[π]ερὶ πρεσ[β]ύτερον Μ ...... ρκανιοσα Ἡ-
ρακ[λείδ]ου καὶ Ἀρίστωνα [Μ]ενεστράτου καὶ Καλλι-
10 γ[ένη]ν Μύ[ρω]νος, Ἀλεξίωνα Πατρόκλου, Εὐτυχιανὸς
Μ[... ου, Εὐτ]ύχης Θεαγένου, Σωζομενὸς Στυράνου,
Μάης Σαλᾶ, [Φα]δίο[υς Φιλ]ήμονος, [Δ]ιονύσιος Σόγου,
Εὐ-
τυχιανὸς Γοργίου, Δαλόσακος Συ[μ]φόρου, Καρδ[ίο?]υς
Δά-
δα, Φόσακος β′, [Δι]όφαντο[ς] Διο[ν]υσίου, Εὐτύχης
15 Ἀντιμάχου, Αάδας Χοδιακ[ο]υ, Σαμβίων Ἑλπιδίωνος, Μυρεῖνο[ς] Μασπ[ο]ῦ, Ἀσκλᾶς Ἡρακλεί-
[δ]ου. Τὸν δὲ τελαμῶ[ν]α ἐδωρήσατο τοῖς ἀδελ-
[φ]οῖς Σαμ[βίω]ν Ἑλπιδίωνος. Φούρτας Ἀγαθοῦ, Ἀγαθή-
μερος Ποπλίου.
20 Ἐν τῷ εκφ′ ἔτει, Γορπιαίου α′.

l. 8, Μαρκεανόν (?), cf. *IosPE.* II. 447, l. 17.

The names of the last two members have been subsequently added in small letters.

59. *IosPE.* II. 434. Tanais. A.B. 533 = A.D. 237. Ininthimeus, cf. pp. 318, 569, 608, 615, 625.

1   Ἀγαθῇ   τύχῃ.
Βασιλεύοντος   βασιλέως Τιβερίου Ἰουλίου   Ἰνινθιμαίου φιλοκαίσαρος καὶ   φιλορωμαίου, εὐ-
5 σεβοῦς,   χρόνῳ ἤμε-
ληθεῖσαν   τὴν κρή-
νην (ἀ)νοικοδόμηθη ἐκ θεμελίων καὶ γέγονε πύργος ἐπὶ π[ρ]ε[σ]-
βευτῇ Χόφρασμον Φοργα[β]βάκου
10 κ(α)ὶ Ἑλληνάρχη Ψυχαρίωνα Φιδάνοι
καὶ διαδόχῳ Ἡρακλείδην Ἄττα καὶ δι-
ὰ ἐπιμελητῶν [Π]άπα Χρήστου καὶ Ἀντίμαχον Κίμβρου καὶ Ἔρωτος Μαστοῖ, Σαμ-
βατίωνα Σι[ρ]άνου, Μενέστρατον Φαδινά-
15 μου, Φιδάνους Κίμβρου, Ὀφθαίμακος
Ἀψάχου, Κοσσοῦς Ἡρακλείδου, Μύριππος
Ἡδύκωνος, διὰ ἀρχιτέκτονος Αὐρηλίου Ἀντωνείνου. Ἐν τῷ γλφ′, Γορπιαίῳ
λ′.

60. *IosPE.* II. 46. Kerch. A.B.
546 = A.D. 250. Rhescu-
poris III, cf. pp. 608, 612,
614.

1 Ἀγαθῆι τύχηι.
Βασιλεύοντος βασιλέως
Τιβερίου Ἰουλίου Ῥησκουπόριδος
φιλοκαίσαρος καὶ φιλορωμαίου,
5 εὐσεβοῦς, τὸν σεβαστόγνωστον
Αὐρήλιον Ῥόδωνα Λολλαίου, τὸν
ἐπὶ τῆς βασιλείας καὶ χειλίαρχον
καὶ ἱππέα Ῥωμαίων, Αὐρ. Κέλσος β'
νεώτερος Ἡρακλεώτης τὸν
10 εὐεργέτην ἐν τῷ ϛμφ' ἔτε[ι]
καὶ μηνὶ Γορπιαίῳ ζ'.

61. *IosPE.* II. 29. Kerch. Teiranes, cf. pp. 558, 594, 608,
612—616, 620, 621, 625.

On *A*, the face of the pedestal.

1 Ἀγαθῆι   Two   Τύχηι.
Βασιλεύ-   Busts   Βασιλέω[ς]
οντος   Τιβερίου
Ἰουλίου Τειράνου φιλοκαίσαρος καὶ φι[λο]-
5 ρωμαίου εὐσεβοῦς, θεοῖς ἐπουραν[ί]-
οις Διὶ Σωτῆρι καὶ Ἥρᾳ Σωτείρᾳ ὑπὲρ
βασιλέως Τειράνου νείκης καὶ αἰωνί[ου]
διαμονῆς καὶ Αἰλίας βασιλίσσης
ἀνέστησαν τὸν τελαμῶνα [οἱ ἀρι]-
10 στοπυλεῖται τοῖς ἰδίοις θεοῖς καὶ εὐεργέταις, ἱερατεύοντος Ἰουλ(ίου) Χοφά[ρ]-
νου Ἀφροδεισίου πρὶν λοχα[γο]ῦ,
καὶ οἱ λοιποὶ ἀριστοπυλεῖται·
Μενέστρατος Γ[ο]σ[ε]μφλί[ου]? ἐπὶ τῆς
15 βασιλείας καὶ ἐπὶ τῆς Θεοδ[οσίας],
Φάννης Σακλέως χειλιάρχης καὶ ἐπ[ὶ]
τῶν Ἀσπουργιανῶν, Φάνης Ἀγαθοῦ
ἀρχιγραμματεύς, Χαρίτων Νείκη-
φόρου λοχαγός, Φιδάνους Θεαγ[γέ]-
20 λου πρὶν πολειτάρχης, Λείμαχ[ος]
Φίδα πολειτάρχης, [Ε]ὔιος Μενεσ-
τράτου, Ἔρως Ῥαδαμάσεως πρὶν ἐ-
πὶ τῶν λόγων,

On sides *B* and *C* are 50 ll. of names
including

24 Ψυχαρίων Σόγου ἐπὶ τῶν λόγων,
28 Ἀλέξανδρος β' πρὶν ἐπ[ὶ]
τῆς πινακ(ίδος?),
34   Μενέστρατος [β']
γραμματεύς· Ἰώδας Βαρδάνου
... π .. ὁ ἐπὶ τ(..) Παιρισάδους · · οσ-
42   καὶ οἱ ἐπιμη-
[ν]ίσαντες· Μαρκιαν[ὸς] Πατερ[ίου],κ.τ.λ.
76 Βίων β'.   Νεώτεροι οἱ [περὶ τοῦ]
Κοτίους .. λειο[υ], Διονύσιος ...

M.

62. *IosPE.* IV. 211. Bosporus. (Teiranes?),
cf. pp. 608, 621, 624.

1 Ἡ σύνοδος ἡ περὶ ἱ[ε]-
ρέα Πάππον [Ἀρ]θαράκο[υ]
καὶ πατέρα Ψίδαν καὶ συ-
ναγωγὸν Ἑκατᾶ[ν] καὶ φιλά[γα]-
5 θον Δάδαν [καὶ] παραφιλάγαθον Φιλώταν, γυμνασιάρ-
χην Δάδαν Ἀν[τ]ι[μ]άχου
[κα]ὶ νεανισκάρχην Γ'... ον
καὶ [οἱ λοι]π[οὶ] συνοδεῖτα[ι]
10 ἀνέστησα[α]ν Ἡ ...... ην
Εὐαρέστου σ[υνοδείτην? μνή]-
μης χάριν ἐν [τῶι ... ἔτει],
μηνὸς Περ[ειτίου ..].

Painted not incised.

63. *BCA.* x. p. 26, No. 21.
Kerch. A.B. 603 = A.D. 306.
(Thothorses), cf. pp. 558,
608, 612, 621.

1 Οἱῷ ὑψίστῳ
ἐπηκόῳ εὐ-
χήν. Αὐρ(ήλιος) Οὐαλέ-
ριος Σόγους Ὀ-
5 λύμπου, ὁ ἐπὶ
τῆς Θεοδοσίας,
σεβαστόγνω-
στο(ς), τειμηθεὶς ὑ-
πὸ Διοκλητια-
10 νοῦ καὶ Μαξιμιανοῦ,
ὁ καὶ Ὀλυμπιανὸς
κληθεὶς ἐν τῷ ἐ-
παρχείῳ, ὁ πολλὰ
ἀποδημήσας καὶ
15 ἀποστρατήσας ἔτη
δέκα ἓξ καὶ ἐν πολ-
λοῖς θλίψεις (sic) γενό-
μενος, εὐξάμενος
ἐκ θεμελίου οἰκο-
20 δομήσας τὴν προσ-
ευχὴν ἐν τῷ γχ'.

64. *IosPE.* II. 49. Kerch.
Rhadamsadius,
cf. p. 609.

[Ἀγαθῇ] τύχῃ.
[Τὸ ....]ον Ῥαδαμσαδίου το[ῦ]
[βασιλέως κατεσκ]ευάσθη δι' ἐπιμελίας
.· .... ς καὶ Θεοδο[σίο]υ Πατ[ρ]έ[ως].

65. *IosPE.* II. 312¹ (p. 309). Kerch. Rhadamsadius and Rhescuporis, cf. p. 609.

1 ΑΓΑΘΗ   [τύχῃ]
ΑΠΟΛΓΕΠΙ   [βασιλέων?]
ΡΑΔΑ⊔Ψ   [αδίου καὶ Ῥη]-
CΚΟΥΠΟΡ   [ίδος, ἀνεσ]-
5 ΤΑΘΟΗ   [ύργος? ἐπιμελ]-
ΕΙΛΘ

The stone is lost and all the readings doubtful.

66. *IosPE.* II. 49¹ (p. 292). Kerch. A.B. 679
= A.D. 383 (?). Doiptunes, cf. pp. 320,
610, 613, 614.

1 † Ἀγ[αθῇ τύχ]η.
✠Ἐπὶ Τιβερίου Ἰουλίου Δοιπτούνο[υ]?
βασιλ(έως) εὐσεβο[ῦ]ς φιλοκέσαρος καὶ
[φ]ιλορωμέου [ἀν]έστη ὁ πύργος οὗ-
5 [τος] καὶ ἐπὶ ἐπάρχο[υ] Εἰσγουδίου
[καὶ ἐ]πὶ τοῦ κόμ(ητος) Ὀπαδίνου τοῦ [ἐ]-
πὶ τῆς πιζνα[κ]ίδος καὶ ἐπὶ τοῦ πρω-
[τεύοντος? ...]τα Σαναγου καὶ ἐπὶ τοῦ
[ἐπιμελητο]ῦ? τοῦ ἐπὶ τοῦ ἔργου
10 [. .... μηνὸς Γ]ο]ρπιαίου κο ..
.... ἔτ(ους) θο[χ'?].

83

67. *IosPE.* II. 383, Fig. 349 }
68. *IosPE.* II. 362, Fig. 350 } , see p. 660.

69. *IosPE.* II. 402. Anapa. Fitzwilliam Museum. E. D. Clarke's copy made when the stone was less broken and corrected in Porson's hand is in the University Library, Cambridge. Sauromates II (?). The first three lines restored by comparing the stone and No. 51, and various corrections introduced in the names, cf. Fig. 351 and pp. 37, 606, 612, 614, 616, 621, 623—625.

1 Βασιλεύοντος βασιλέως Τιβερ[ίου Ἰουλίου Σαυρομάτου φιλο]-
καίσαρος καὶ φιλορωμαίου εὐσε[βοῦς · τοῦ ... ἔτους .. μηνὸς Ἀρτε]-
μισίου. Θεῷ Π{ο}σιδῶνος ἐξ[...........................
     Then only stray names : l. 4, Πόθου; l. 9, Πόθου Χρηστίωνος; l. 10, Νουμίνιος;
     l. 11, Γοργ]όσα Ζαξζοῦς; l. 12, ... κράτους; l. 16, Ἀλέξανδρος; l. 17, .. ου Κοσσο[ῦς
     l. 18, . ου Κοσσοῦ[ς; l. 19, Ἀλεξάνδρου
20 Μυρίσκου · Νεοκλῆς Θ — — — —
     ων β΄ Φαρνάκου · Τειμό[θεος — — —
     Γλύκων Σωσία · Γοργία[ς — — —
     . άάτας Ἱππαρείνου · — — —
     ... Φαρνάκου λοχ[αγὸς — —
25 Φα[ρ]ναξ[ίων Ἰα — — — — — — — — — — — — — Μοι]-
     ροδώρου Λεφαοσα · Ἀρίστων Π[— — — —
     ωνο[ς] Ζαβαγίου · Ἀθηνόδωρος Πόθου — — — —
     της Πάπα Χώλου · Χρηστοῦς Μυρίσκου Μυρείρου
     [Κ]όνου · Νεοκλῆς Φαρνακίωνος Χάρδει · Σ(?)έρεις Φανδαράξου ἱ[ε-
30 ρ]εύς · Πάππος Φαρνακίωνος · Γάστεις Ἀγαθοῦ Κέφθου · Ἀθηνόδ[ω]-
     ρος Φαρνακίωνος Ἀτία · Νεοκλῆς Πόθου Θεοτείμου · Πόθος Μαρίου
     ν(?)ηγος · Τειμόθεος Ψινίθα · Πάπας Χρηστίωνος · Ἑρμῆς καὶ Ἀγαθοῦς [υἱ-
     οὶ] Χρηστίωνος Ἑρμοῦ · Λυσίμαχος β΄ · Παπίας Χρηστοῦ · Ἄγρων Γάσ[τ]ε[ι
     Μ]ακάριος Φαρνακίωνος · Ἀρίστων Βαγίου · Σαφάσας Χρηστίωνος ·
35 [Φα]ρνάκης β΄ Ἔρωτος · Φιλοδέσποτος Φαρνάκου Ἔρωτος · Πόθος
     [β΄] Χρυσοχόου · Πόθος Πάπα · Ἔρως Φαρνακίωνος Ἔρωτος · Πραξ[ί]-
     ας Χρυσώτου · Ποθείνος Τεργονίου · Ἀθηνόδωρος Μυρίσκου · Ἀ[ρ]-
     ςτων Χρηστίωνος · Ζαξζοῦς Τειμοθέου · Ἀθηνόδωρος Νεοκλ[έ-
     ου]ς Ἡγουμενοῦ · Πάπας Μυφαγόρα Κοσσοῦ · Ἀτταμάζα[ς Πάπου(?) ·
40 Κο]σσοῦς καὶ Ἀθηνόδωρος υἱοὶ Βάγητος · Δ[αμόσ]τρα[τος] Ἁγίου · Μηνό-
     [δωρ]ος Βωράκου · Φαρνακίων Ἑρμαδίωνος · Ατακούας Πάππου Κόνου ·
     Κοσσοῦς Ἀγαθοῦ Γοργίου · Πάβας Φαρνάκου Τράγου · Φαρνακίων Ἀγα-
     [θοῦ Ρο]ργίου · Ποθεῖνος β΄ Γναφίσκου · Αταμάζας Κάρσα · Προσδοκίων
     ...... α · Πόθος Πάππου · Νουμήνιος Ποθείνου · Χάχας Γοργόσα
45 Π ... ο .... παπ ..... Κυράθωνος · Χρηστίων Θέκα · Δημήτρι-
     [ο]ς Ἑρμ[οῦ] Φ .... Πάννυχος Φαρνακίωνος · Ἡγουν-
     [μ]ενὸς .... κ]αὶ Νουμήνιος υἱ-
     οὶ Νουμηνίου] .... Νε]οκλῆς Ἀγαθοῦ
     . αγυ ... Πο .... [Ἀτακ]ούας Ἀγαθοῦ Φαρ-
50 [ν]ακίω[νος ....] Πυθώρου · Ρόδων
     .... Φαρνα[κίω]νο[ς] ... μη .. [Κοσσοῦ Ν]ουμήνιος Ἔρωτος ·
     [Χρ]ηστίων Πανταλέοντος .... ος Φαρνακίωνος · Ἱππαρείνος Χάρδει ·
     — — — — — — Χρηστὸς Χρηστοῦ · Πάππος Θέκα · Κατόκας Δάδου
     — — — — — π ... Πάππος Ἑρμῆ · Γλύκων Ἀγαθοῦ · Χρηστοῦς Πάπ-
55 [που — — — — Μ]ο{ι}ρόδωρος Λιμνάκου · Μαστοῦς Κοθίνα · Πόθος Ατ-
     [ία?] — — ο — ος Ἀγαθοῦ · Πάπας Ἀξία · Σιαγοῦς Χρηστίωνος Φαρ-
     [να] — ... κ .... φο .. ς [Κ]ρησία · Πάππος Γοξίνου · Νυμφαγόρας Σαμβίω-
     [νο]ς .... Ἑρ .... Φα[ρ]νάκης Φαρνακίωνος Ἡγουμενοῦ · Ἡρακλ[έ-
     ω]ν Νεοκλέ[ου]ς · Χρ[η]σ[τί]ων Ἑρμοῦ · Κόθις Ἀρίστωνος · Ποθίσκος Ἀγαθ[οῦ] ·
60 Ἀ[ξί]ας Ἀλφ[οκ]ράτου Σεγυοῦς Σαρμάτα · Ἑρμαδίων Νουμηνίου Χρηστοῦ.

FIG. 351. *BCA*. x. Pl. 1.

67. *IosPE.* II. 383.
Taman.   Fitzwilliam
Museum, Cambridge.
Cf. p. 627.

Fig. 349. *BCA.* x. p. 95.

1   Τειμόθεος Δάσειος χαῖρε.
Τειμόθεος ὁ πάτρας ὅσιος φώς· παῖς δὲ Δάσειος,
τρὶς δεκά(δ)ας ἐτέων τερματίσας ἔθανες.
Α τάλαν, οἰκτείρω σε πολυκλαύστωι ἐπὶ τύμβωι·
5   νῦν δὲ σὺν ἡρώων χῶρον ἔχοις φθίμενος.

68. *IosPE.* II. 362. Taman. Fitzwilliam Museum, Cambridge. Cf. p. 566.

Fig. 350. *BCA.* x. p. 93.

δι]-

1 ἀ τὰς ἀπὸ αὐτῶν εἰς α[ὐ]τὸν γενομένας τειμὰ[ς . . . .
αις τε καὶ ἀνεισφορίαις ἀπάσαις ταῖς κατὰ τὴν βֿασιλείαν · · · ἱερέα ἀπο]-
δειχθέντα τοῦ Καισαρείου διὰ βίου εἰς·γένος . . . .
τας ἀνέστησεν τειμῆς χάριν σὺν τῷ καὶ ἐπι[. . . . . . τὴν ἠ]-
5 μέραν αὐτῶν ὑπό τε ἐμοῦ καὶ τῶν ἐκγόνω[ν μου . . . .

69. *IosPE.* II. 402, Fig. 351, see pp. 658, 659.

70. *Inscr. Christ.* 99, p. 105, Pl. XI.
Taman.   A.D. 590.   Maurice, cf. pp.
318, 532, 542, 610. On each side of
the text stands a Nike with a wreath
and below it two *Tamgi*, ⲧⲧ and ꙁ,
v. p. 318, n. 1.

I   + Πρὸς τοῖς λοιποῖς
μεγάλοις ϗ θαυμαστοῖς
κατορθόμασι ϗ τόδε τὸ(δ)
λαμπρὸν ἐν Βοοσπόρω
5   κεσάριον ἀνενέωσεν
Μ[αυρ]ίκις ὁ εὐ[σ]εβ(έστατος) ϗ θεοφύλακ(ι)τ(ος) ἡμῶ⳿
δεσπότης διὰ τοῦ γνησίου αὐτοῦ
δούλΗ ΕὐπατερίΗ, τΗ ἐνδοξοτάτου
9   στρατηλάτ(υ)ου καὶ δουκὸς Χερσῶνος. Ἰνδ(ικτιῶνος) η΄.

COIN PLATES

The following Persons and Institutions possess important collections of Greek coins from South Russia and to most of them as indicated below I am indebted for casts:

H.I.H. the Grand Duke Alexander Michailovich; his is perhaps the richest of all. It includes the coins collected by A. M. Podshivalov and by Chr. Giel (**G.**) and described in their writings (v. supra pp. xxx, xxxii, 638).

The Hermitage (**H.**); no Catalogue published, but Koehne in *MK.* (v. p. xxx) often indicates what coins were there even in his time: it receives the results of excavations.

The Historical Museum at Moscow contains Burachkov's coins (**B.** p. xxix) and others (Mosc.).

The Rumjantsev Museum at Moscow, Catalogue by Podshivalov (p. xxxii).

The University of Moscow, Catalogue by Orêshnikov (p. xxxii).

The University of S. Vladimir, Kiev, Catalogue by Antonovich (p. xxix).

The Museum of the Odessa Historical and Archaeological Society (**O.**), specially rich in Olbia and Tyras.

The University of New Russia, Odessa, also has some coins.

The Museums at Kherson (Catalogue by Goszkewicz, p. xxviii), Chersonese, Theodosia and Kerch.

Mr B. M. Jakunchikov at St Petersburg collects Greek coins in general (v. *TRAS. Num. Sect.* 1. ii. pp. 7—59).

Mr Th. I. Prowe at Moscow.

The Countess Uvarov at Porêchje (**U.**), Catalogue by Orêshnikov (p. xxxii).

Mrs L. I. Kuris and Mr P. A. Mavrogordato at Odessa: the latter has recently sold in western Europe many coins which were not required for the Odessa Society's Museum.

General A. L. Bertier-de-La-Garde at Jalta, especially rich in Chersonese (**BG.**). This collection is destined to join that at Odessa.

Dr I. A. Terlecki at Kerch (to whom my best thanks are due for making me practically acquainted with Bosporan coins and letting me have a selection (**M.**) which has conveniently filled up certain gaps): some of his best coins have passed to Mr Prowe.

The K. Münzkabinet, Berlin, Catalogue by von Sallet (v. p. 489).

The Cabinet des Médailles, Paris.

The British Museum (**BM.**), which has much increased its series especially from Mr Mavrogordato since the publication of its Catalogues (**BMC.**) *Thrace, Tauric Chersonese and Sarmatia*, by P. Gardner, 1877; *Pontus and Bosporus*, by W. Wroth, 1889.

The Imperial Cabinet at Vienna, the Royal Cabinets at Brussels and Copenhagen, the Hunterian Museum at Glasgow, the St Florian Collection at Enns, have important pieces. The Fitzwilliam Museum (**FW.**) at Cambridge possesses a fine series of Olbian *Asses* and about a hundred ordinary coins.

A Corpus of these coins has been undertaken by the Grand Duke in conjunction with the staff of the Hermitage, but meanwhile the numismatic literature of our region (v. the various Bibliographies) is unsatisfactory. Koehne's *Musée Kotschoubey* (**MK.**), the first real attempt to deal with it as a whole, quite superseded all that went before but is now out of date and withal very rare. Burachkov's *General Catalogue* (**B.**) is also a rare book and both text and plates are very untrustworthy, but Bertier-de-La-Garde's *Corrections* have to a great extent made up for this and since, as figuring over a thousand coins, it is still the means by which specimens are identified, I have given many references to it.

Pick's plates (**P.**) of Olbian and Tyran coins are just what was wanted, but there is no text, only a note on p. 918 to state in what collections the specimens he figures are preserved : the materials for his text have been handed over by the Berlin Academy to the Russian compilers of the Corpus. Articles by Jurgiewicz (**J.**) (on Tyras), by Podshivalov (on the Bosporus), and by Giel in his *Kleine Beiträge* (**Kl. B.**) and "Accessions to his Collection" (**TRAS.** v and vii), have been of real value, and more recently Orêshnikov's (**Or.**) and Bertier-de-La-Garde's (**BG.**) work. How much I am indebted to these my text has shewn : copies of several of these more recent articles I have furnished with a running analysis in English and placed in the Medal Room of the British Museum where they are generally accessible.

These plates have been something of an afterthought, and I have been able neither to choose the very best specimens nor to reproduce the coins quite as I should wish, but pending tthe publication of the Corpus it seemed necessary to bring the more important coins before my readers : these nine plates, though they fall short of the spacious collotypes now customary, offer a fairly representative selection giving a sufficient idea of the city issues and an example of very nearly every ruler ; the descriptions make up for some deficiencies with data from better specimens : that is enough to render intelligible the short account of the coinage in connexion with history and religion appended to the chapter devoted to each state. I have mostly chosen the commoner $_c$o$_i$n$_s$ just because they are common and therefore truly typical. These I found ready to hand in the Odessa collection to which half the coins belong ; it was put at my entire disposal by the Director, Professor E. R. von Stern, to whom my best thanks are due. But a desire to add rarer specimens because they illustrated some particular point has involved my giving much trouble to those who have the keeping of the originals. Most of all are my thanks due to Mr A. V. Orêshnikov, keeper of the Historical Museum at Moscow : to him I sent an unconscionable list of desiderata from among Burachkov's coins. The courtesy of Mr O. F. Retovski of the Hermitage was the more to be appreciated in that it was as a complete stranger that I applied to him for casts from that collection and the Grand Duke's, including Giel's. General Bertier-de-La-Garde kindly sent me most delicate impressions from certain of his important coins of Chersonese. Nearer home I am glad to acknowledge the help given me in the B. M. by the late Mr Warwick Wroth, Mr G. F. Hill and Mr H. Mattingly. The Hunterian Paerisades was cast for me by the late Professor J. Young of Glasgow. Recognition is also due to the technical skill of Mr Ready at the B. M. and of the late Mr H. A. Chapman at the Fitzwilliam. The latter made the casts from my sealing-wax impressions and took the photographs from which the blocks were prepared as well as many other photographs needed for this book.

With regard to the weights given for the gold and silver coins I must explain that I had not the time to weigh those from which I took impressions in the Odessa Museum : but the weights of nearly all these specimens have been published by Bertier-de-La-Garde in his *Materials for Stathmological Investigation*, and so I have been able to supply them : but in some few cases, which did not come within his purview, the weight is given in brackets and is that of the specimen of the same coin given in the publication cited in the last column of the description.

PLATE I. TYRAS

PLATE I.

TYRAS.

Metal	Wt. grn. grm.	Obverse	Reverse	Coll.	Publication
Æ.	{ 86 { 5·57	Demeter three-quarters l., ears of corn on forehead.	Bull butting l.: above, TYPANΩN; in field, A.	BM.	P. XII. 10.
Æ.	{ 80·2 { 5·2	Demeter facing, ears of corn on forehead.	Bull butting l.: above, T]YPAN.	O.	{ B. X. 1, 2. { J. 1.
Æ.		Demeter front, ears of corn on forehead.	Cista Mystica: TYPA; monogram ПΨ.	O.	{ B. 18. { P. XII. 15. { J. 2.
Æ.		Demeter r., under kerchief.	TYPA in wreath.	O.	J. 9.
Æ.		Dionysus (?) r., laur.	Cornucopia: TYPA.	O.	{ B. 16. { P. XII. 21. { J. 12.
Æ.		Dionysus r., laur.	Eagle standing on thunderbolt: below, TYPAN.	O.	{ B. 19. { J. 13.
Æ.		Dionysus (?) r., laur.	Bunch of grapes: TYPA.	O.	{ B. 28. { J. 14.
Æ.		Apollo l., laur.	Horse's head and neck r.: TYPA.	B.	{ B. 6. { P. XII. 11.
Æ.		Apollo l., laur.	Similar.	O.	{ B. 11. { P. XII. 12.
Æ.		Apollo l., laur.	Lyre: TYPA.	O.	{ B. 22. { P. XII. 17.
Æ.		Athena r., helmed.	Bull butting l.: above, TYPA.	O.	B. 26.
Æ.		Asclepius r.	Altar with snake: TYPA.	O.	{ B. 24. { P. XII. 19.
Æ.		Rivergod r.	Fish l.: TYPA.	O.	{ B. 13. { P. XII. 22.
Æ.		Rivergod (?) l.	Fish: TYPANΩN.	O.	J. 6.
Æ.		Augustus (?) l.: KAI[CAP] CEBACTO[C.	Spread eagle r.: TYPA]NωN (?).	O.	J. 110.
Æ.		Domitian r., laur.: ΔO]METIANOC [KAICAP.	Tyche (?) in calathos, seated l., on throne, holding out patera: TYPA in exergue.	O.	{ B. XI. 31. { P. XII. 23 { J. 32.
Æ.		Hadrian r., laur.: AΔPIANOC KAI AY.	Club of Heracles vertical: TYPA.	O.	J. 41.
Æ.		Antoninus Pius r., laur., dot-border: AY]TANTΩNEINONCEB.	Heracles standing with lion-skin and club, hd to r.; dot-border: TYPA[N]ΩN.	O.	{ B. 35. { P. XII. 25. { J. 49.
Æ.		M. Aurelius r., laur.: BHP]ICCIMOC KAICAP.	Pallas standing with spear, shield and helmet, hd to l.: TYPA NΩN.	O.	{ B. 36. { P. XII. 26. { J. 59.
Æ.		Commodus, bust r., laur.: AYK AI KOMOΔOC.	Eagle standing l. looking r., with wreath in beak: TYPANΩN; B.	O.	{ B. 49. { J. 74 (76)
Æ.		[Sep. Severus r., cf. 22.]	Winged Victory r., with palm and wreath: TY PANΩN; Δ.	O.	B. 57.
Æ.		Sep. Severus, bust r., laur: AYTKAICEΠCEBHPOC ΠEP.	Heracles with club, lion-skin and apples, hd to r.: TYPA NΩN; Δ.	BM.	{ B. 55. { Cf. P. XIII. { J. 79.
Æ.		Julia Domna, bust r.: IOYΛΔO MNACE.	Tyche (as 16): TYPANΩN; Δ.	O.	{ B. 59. { J. 81.
Æ.		Caracalla, bust r., laur.: AYTKMAYPCEY HPOC ANTΩNI	As 22.	O.	{ B. XII. 66. { J. 94.
Æ.		Geta, bust r.: ACEΠΓET KAICAP.	[As 20.]	O.	J. 104.
Æ.		Al. Severus, bust r.: AYTKM]AYP CEB [AΛEΞANΔ.	Winged Victory l., with palm and wreath: TYPA]NΩN, crescent in field.	O.	{ B. 74. { J. 108.
Æ.		J. Mammaea, bust r.: IOYΛIA MAMMAIA CEB.	River-god seated r. by urn from which stream flows: TYPANΩN, Δ and crescent.	O.	J. 109.

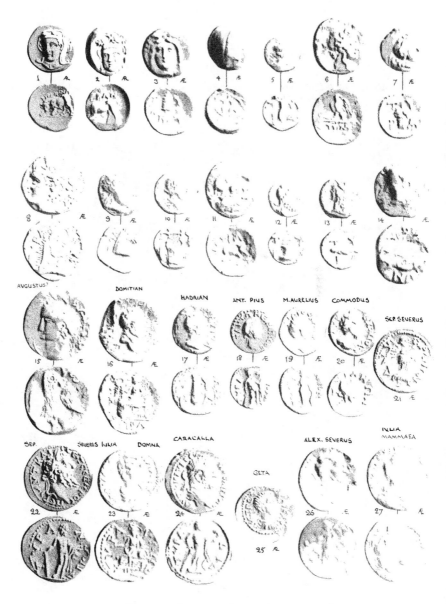

CITY AND IMPERIAL ISSUES (PP. 447—449)

PLATE II, OLBIA

M.

84

PLATE 11.   OLBIA.   AES GRAVE AND CAST PIECES, ALL B

No.	Weight grn. grm. High. Low. Aver.			Obverse	Reverse
1.	2130 138	1605 104	1790 116	Archaic Medusa facing, tongue hanging out.	Sea-eagle, wings extended, upon dolphin: APIX.
[1 a.	525 34	324 21	431 28	Same smaller.	Four-spoked wheel: APIX.
[1 b.	247 16	154 10	185 12	Same smaller.	Same smaller.
[2 a.	1960 127	1574 102	1806 117	Pallas helmed l., before her dolphin.	Four-spoked wheel: ΓΑΥΣ.
[2 b.	1173 76	1033 67	1096 71	Same smaller.	Same smaller: pellets in quarters.
2.	663 43	509 33	586 38	Same smaller.	Same smaller: ΓΑΥΣ.
3.	417 27	278 18	340 22	Medusa facing.	Eagle upon dolphin: ΟΛΒΙΗ.
4.	1852 120	1605 104	1728 112	Demeter (?) facing: necklace, ears of corn in hair.	Eagle upon dolphin: ΟΛΒΙΗ, beneath sometimes Δ.
[5 a.			41·8 2·7	ΙΣΤ.	Four-spoked wheel.
[5 b.			20·8 1·35	ΙΣΤ.	Same smaller.
			12·6 ·82	ΙΣΤ.	Same smaller.
6.			1592 103	Dolphin.	(Flat.)
[6 a.			1111 72	Dolphin.	(Flat.)
				[Dolphin.]	APIXO.
8.				[Dolphin.]	APIX:O.
9.				Smaller dolphin.	ΘΥ.
[10.				Flat fish.	

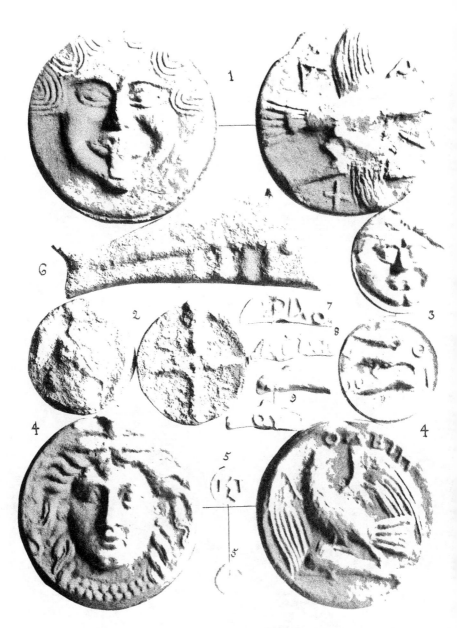

AES GRAVE (pp. 482—485)

PLATE III. OLBIA. NATIVE KINGS

ng	Me-tal	Wt. grn. grm.	Obverse	Reverse	Coll.	Publication
	_N._	32·8 2·13	Head of Demeter l.	Dolphin l.: below, ΟΛ.	O.	B. IV. 45. P. IX. 18.
	_R._	189 12·25	Demeter l., crowned with corn.	Sea-eagle upon dolphin; in field, trident: ΟΛΒΙΟ: above, monogram.	O.	B. VI. 135. P. IX. 2.
	Æ.		Demeter l., mural crown adorned with ears of corn.	Kneeling shooting l. a Scythic archer with bow-case: above, ΣΩΣΤΡΑ;in exergue,[ΟΛΒΙΟ].	O.	B. VII. 152. P. X. 1.
	Æ.		Horned river-god l.	Bow-case and quiver, axe: below, ΟΛΒΙΟ; above, ΙΦ.	O.	Cf. B. IX. 214.
	Æ.		Same, later style.	Same: other letters above.	O.	Cf. P. IX. 27.
	_R._	52 3·37	Apollo r., laur.: countermark, helmeted Pallas.	Three-stringed lyre: above, ΟΛΒΙΟ; on each side, monogram.	O.	B. V. 83. P. X. 25.
	Æ.		Apollo (?) r., laur.	Archer as 3: ΟΙ ΕΠΤΑ.	B.	B. 91. P. X. 5.
	Æ.		Demeter r.	Bow-case: below, ΟΛΒΙΟ.	O.	B. 87. P. X. 6.
	Æ.		Heracles in lion-scalp r. (perhaps Apollo or Demeter).	Eagle upon dolphin: above, ΟΛΒΙΟ; below, ΒΣΕ.	O.	B. IV. 64.
	Æ.		Heracles in lion-scalp r.: countermark, Pallas.	Club horizontal: above, ΟΛΒΙΟ; below, ΕΙΡΗΒΑ.	B.	B. 42. P. X. 20.
	Æ.		Same or Demeter l.: large countermark, Helios rayed, cf. 22.	Like 5: large countermark, two demi-horses springing apart: ΟΛ.	B.	B. VI. 102. P. IX. 31.
	Æ.		Zeus r.: countermark, caduceus.	Eagle standing l.: ΟΛΒΙΟ Π]ΟΛΙΤΕ[ΩΝ; ⋈.	O.	B. 111. P. XI. 4.
	Æ.		Zeus r.: countermark, myrtle-branch.	Sceptre vertical: ΟΛΒΙΟΠΟ ΛΙΤΕΩ[Ν.	O.	B. 105. P. XI. 3.
	Æ.:		Cybele in calathos and veil: countermark, myrtle-branch.	Tympanum: ΟΛΒΙ; monogram. ΟΠΟΛΙΤ[ΕΩΝ	B.	B. VIII. 151. P. X. 35.
	Æ.		Apollo bust r., before him bow-case: [ΟΛΒΙΟΠΟΛΕΙΤωΝ]; ⤬.	Eagle l. looking back with wreath: ΑΔΟΟ[Υ ΔΕΛ]ΦΟΥ.	O.	B. 170. Cf. P. XI. 9.
	Æ.		Apollo r.: ΟΛΒΙΟΠΟ.	Apollo standing with bow and patera (?): ΔΑΔΟΟCCΑΤΥ[ΡΟΥ].	H.	B. VIII. 178. P. XI. 19.
	Æ.		Apollo leaning on a pillar: ΟΛΒ[ΙΟΠΟΛΕΙΤω]Ν.	Lyre: Δ]ΑΔ[ΟCC]ΑΤΥ[ΡΟΥ (?).	H.	B. 180. P. XI. 20.
	Æ.		Bust of Geta r.: ΚΑCΕΠΤΙΓΕΤΑ.	Mars in full armour standing r.: ΟΛΒΙΟΠΟ ΛΕΙΤΩΝ Α.	H.	B. 190. P. XII. 1.
	Æ.		Bust of A. Severus r., laur.: ΑΥΤΚΜΑΥΡCΕΥΑΛΕΞΑΝΔΡΟC.	Spread-eagle with wreath: ΟΛΒΙΟ ΠΟΛΙΤΩΝ.	O.	B. 193.

NATIVE KINGS.

ng	Me-tal	Wt. grn. grm.	Obverse	Reverse	Coll.	Publication
ITES	Æ.		Two heads r. (Demeter and Cora?) nearer wearing kerchief.	Two stalks of wheat: ΒΑΣΙΛΕΩΣ ΚΑΝΙΤΟΥ; in exergue, ΒΑΚ.	H.	P. XIII. 6. MK. I. p. 24.
IAS	Æ.		Bearded head r., wreathed (?).	Bow in case: ΒΑΣΙ ΣΑΡΙ.	BM.	P. XIII. 10. Num. Chron. n.s. XIX. p. 88.
LIS	Æ.		Rayed head facing.	Two B]ΑΣΙ[ΛΕΩΣ; monogram stars: ΑΙΛΙΟΣ ΤΟΜΙ (?).	BM.	Ib. p. 89.
AV-	Æ.		Hermes r., in petasus.	Winged caduceus: ΒΑΣΙ ΚΑΥ.	G.	TRAS. v. 4.
URUS	Æ.		Similar.	Caduceus: ΒΑ]ΣΙΛ[ΕΩΣ ΣΚΙΛΟΥΡΟ[Υ.	O.	B. IX. 203.
	Æ.		Bearded head in pointed cap r.: countermark, saltire.	Bow-case between ear of corn and club: B]ΑΣΙΛΕΩ[Σ ΣΚ]ΙΛΟΥ[ΡΟΥ; to l. vertically ΟΛΒΙο.	B.	B. 207.
ZOEUS	_N._	130·8 8·48	Hd of Pharzoeus r., filleted.	Eagle r., standing on royal sign: ΒΑΣΙΛΕΩΣ ΦΑΡΖΟΙΟΥ; ΟΛ; ⋈.	G.	TRAS. v. 3. P. XII. 6.
MEUS	_R._	60·2 3·9	Hd of Ininsimeus r.; royal sign: ΒΑCΙΛΕΩC ΙΝΙCΜΕΩC.	Tyche in mural crown r.: ΟΛΒΙΟΠΟΛΕΙΤΕΩΝ: monograms ⤬; CAT.	O.	B. 212. P. XII. 9.

ORDINARY COINS (pp. 459, 473 sqq., 485, 486): NATIVE KINGS (pp. 119, 121, 487)

PLATE IV. CHERSONESE

PLATE IV.

CHERSONESE.

No.	Me-tal	Wt. grn. grm.	Obverse	Reverse	Coll.
1.	Æ.	27·47 1·78	Artemis l. in coif.	Fish and club : XEP.	O.
2.	Æ.		Artemis (?) r. laur.	Club and XEP in wreath.	O.
3.	Æ.	53 3·43	Artemis almost full face, filleted.	Half bull butting l., bow : XEP.	BG.
4.	Æ.	98 6·35	Same.	Bull butting l.: below, club and fish : XEP.	BG.
5.	Æ.	151·7 9·83	Artemis l. filleted.	Bull butting r., club : XEP, K.	H.
6.	Æ.		Artemis as Nike with torch driving quadriga, r.	Naked spearman in pileus with shield kneeling l.: I, XEP below.	O.
7.	Æ.		Janiform head : Artemis l., bearded Dionysus (?) r.: above, HP.	Lion attacking deer r.: XEP.	B.
8.	Æ.		Artemis seated r. looking at arrow-point : by her deer.	Bull butting l. over club : XEP.	B.
9.	Æ.	141·6 9·18	Heracles r. in lion-scalp.	Artemis seated l. looking at arrow point : AΠOΛΛΩNIOY, XEP.	BM.
10.	Æ.		Artemis (Aphrodite ?) r. in coif.	Lion's face full and club : XEP.	O.
11.	Æ.		Athena r. helmed.	Griffin r.: above, XEP : below, HPAKΛEIOY.	BG.
12.	Æ.		Athena as above.	Nike moving l. with wreath : in front XEP, behind wing AΓOΛΛ.	G.
13.	Æ.	212·3 13·76	Artemis r., quiver behind : three countermarks : 1, [monogram] in a circle of dots ; 2, dolphin ; 3, thunderbolt.	Bull butting l.: above, club and XEP ; below, IΣTPΩNOΣ (?).	B.
14.	Æ.		Artemis kneeling r. on r. knee, holding bow in r. hand and picking up arrow in l.	Griffin l.: above IΣTIEIO ; below, XEP.	O.
15.	Æ.		Artemis r. laur.	Deer kneeling l.: XEP above, below ΞENOKΛE.	O.
16.	Æ.		Artemis l. slaying deer with spear in r. hand : she wears short chiton and endromides, has a quiver on her shoulder and strung bow in l. hand. XEP.	Bull butting l. over club : below, quiver ; between, ΔIAΓOPA.	O.
17.	Æ.	57·9 3·75	Artemis r. in earrings and mural crown as Tyche ; behind, quiver.	Deer standing r.: below, MOIPIOΣ ; on r. side XEP : restruck.	O.
18.	Æ.	28·2 1·83	Young Heracles, fillet, r.	Club between XEP and ΔIOTIMOY.	BG.
19.	Æ.		Hermes in petasus r., caduceus behind ; dot-border.	Cornucopia between XEP and ΠYΘIΩNO[Σ.	BG.
20.	Æ.		Heracles r. in lion-scalp.	Prow l.: above, XEP ; below, ΣIΛANOY : countermark, [monogram].	BG.
21.	Æ.		Lion's head r.	Six-rayed star, between rays XEP and three pellets.	O.
22.	Æ.		Artemis r.; behind, quiver.	Deer grazing r.: below, XЄP : between its feet [monogram] reversed.	G.
23.	Æ.		Apollo r. hair done effeminately : before him lyre ; behind, branch : EIPHNHΣ ΣEBAΣTHΣ : dot-border.	Artemis r. in mural crown holding out bow in l. hand, poising dart in r.: ETOYΣ PK ; [monogram] : cf. 25 : counter-mark, erect Artemis.	O.
24.	Æ.		Zeus (Asclepius?) r. filleted : XEP.	[As 25, no date.]	O.
25.	N.	107·4 6·96	Apollo l. laur.: before him snake : XEP : dot-border.	Artemis as on 23 : PNH in field and [monogram] : dot-border.	O.
26.	Æ.		Apollo filleted r.: before him lyre : XEP : dot-border.	Artemis as on 23 but by her r. side stag : EΛEYΘEPAΣ : dot-border.	O.
27.	Æ.		Artemis as on 16 : below, XEPΣ : dot-border.	Bull butting l.: below EΛEYΘEPAΣ : dot-border.	O.
28.	Æ.		Apollo r. very effeminate, lyre : EΛEY-ΘEPAΣ : dot-border.	Artemis r. with stag as 26, side view : XEPCONHCOY : dot-border.	O.
29.	Æ.		Asclepius as on Roman coins : EΛEY-ΘEPAΣ : dot-border.	Hygieia : XEPCONHCOY : dot-border.	O.

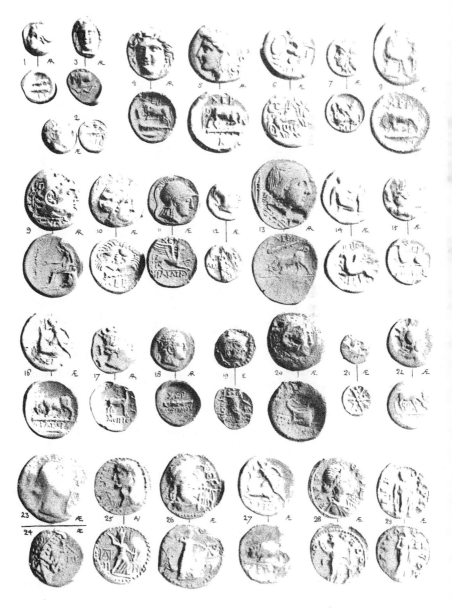

ANCIENT COINS (pp. 522, 523, 540—550)

PLATE V. PANTICAPAEUM

PLATE V.   PANT

No.	Me-tal	Wt. grn. grm.	Obverse
1.	Æ.	1·54 / ·1	Ant.
2.	Æ.	2 / ·13	Ant.
3.	Æ.	42·3 / 2·74	Lion-scalp facing.
4.	Æ.	25·6 / 1·66	Same.
5.	Æ.	16·4 / 1·06	Same, less rude.
6.	Æ.	16·08 / 1·04	Same.
7.	N.	140·1 / 9·08	Pan l., straight hair and beard, poin ears.
8.	N.	140·43 / 9·1	Pan ¾ l., curly hair and beard.
9.	Æ.	23·15 / 1·5	Pan r., straight hair and beard.
10.	Æ.	10·6 / ·69	Pan l., straight hair and beard.
11.	Æ.	33·64 / 2·18	Pan ¾ r., straight hair and beard.
12.	Æ.	40·1 / 2·6	Pan ¾ l., beardless, straight hair.
13.	Æ.	40·1 / 2·6	Pan l. almost facing, bearded, crowned.
14.	Æ.	37·6 / 2·44	Pan ¾ l., beardless, ivy-crowned.
15.	Æ.	44·8 / 2·9	Pan as 8.
16.	N.	140·5 / 9·1	Pan l., ivy-crowned, macaroni and beard.
17.	Æ.	182·3 / 11·81	Pan l., ivy-crowned, beardless, m roni hair.
18.	Æ.		Pan r., macaroni hair and beard.
19.	Æ.		Pan l., as 16.
20.	Æ.		Pan l., as 17.
21.	Æ.		Same with countermark of star.
22.	Æ.		Pan r., beardless, macaroni hair.
23.	Æ.		Similar.
24.	Æ.		Male head r., beardless.
25.	Æ.	245·8 / 15·93	Apollo (?) l., laur.
26.	Æ.	54·3 / 3·52	Apollo r., laur.
27.	Æ.	33·7 / 2·18	Apollo r., laur.
28.	Æ.	20·2 / 1·31	Poseidon r., filleted.

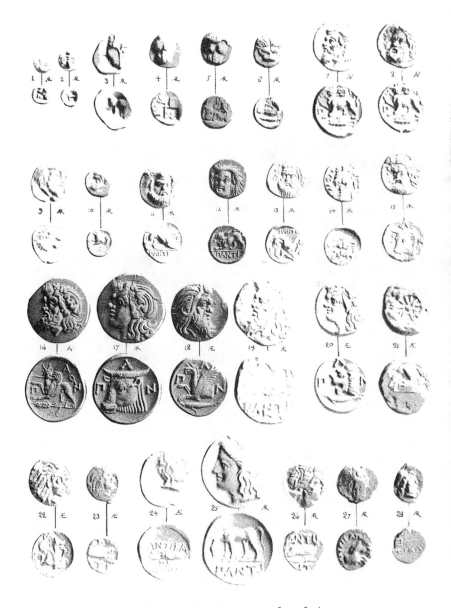

EARLIER CITY ISSUES (pp. 627—631)

PLATE VI. PANTICAPAEUM. BOSPORUS KINGS B.C.

PLATE VI. PANTICAPAEUM (CONTD). BOSPORUS. KINGS B.C.

King	Metal	Wt. grn. grm.	Obverse	Reverse	Coll.
	Æ.		Pan l., ivy-crowned, bearded.	Cornucopia between two starred pilei: ΠΑΝΤΙ.	O.
	Æ.		Apollo r., laur.	Dolphin l.: ΠΑΝ.	BM.
	Æ.		Eight-rayed star: ΠΑΝΤΙΚΑΠ.	Tripod-lebes.	M.
	Æ.		Griffin's wing.	Tripod-lebes: ΠΑΝ.	M.
	Æ.		Young head r., (Apollo) wearing wreath with pendent tie.	Quiver with strap and bow. ΠΑΝΤΙΚΑ ΠΑΙΤΩΝ	M.
	Æ.		Same, struck on coin of Asander, cf. 24.	Pegasus pasturing l. do.	B.
	R.	55 3·56	Bust of Artemis r., bow and quiver.	Deer pasturing r. 𝕂 do.	G.
	R.	104·9 6·8	Dionysus r., wreathed.	Ivy-wreath encircling 𝕂 above. ΠΑΝΤΙ ΚΑΠΑΙ ΤΩΝ	B.
	Æ.		Same head.	Thyrsus leaning against tripod-lebes. ΝΕ 𝕂 ΠΑΝΤΙΚΑ ΠΑΙΤΩΝ	O.
	Æ.		Bust of Men or Mithras r., in laur. Phrygian cap with crescent and star on forehead.	Dionysus standing l., do. in l. hand thyrsus, in r. grape-cluster, at his feet panther l. 𝕂	O.
	Æ.		Apollo r., laur.: struck upon B. XXIII. 25, cf. inf. IX. 21.	Eagle displayed upon ΠΑΝΤ thunderbolt. Monogram.	B.
	Æ.		Poseidon filleted r.	Prow l.: ΠΑΝΤ.	BM.
	Æ.		Same.	Same: countermark, Pallas helmed r.	B.
	Æ.		Pallas helmed r., as countermark of 13.	Prow r., ΠΑΝ.	BM.

BOSPORUS. KINGS.

King	Metal	Wt. grn. grm.	Obverse	Reverse	Coll.
Spartocus	R.	119·9 7·77	Filleted hd of Spartocus r.	Bowcase: ΒΑΣΙΛΕΩΣ [ΣΠΑΡ]ΤΟΚΟΥ: 𝕂	Rumjan-tsev.
Leucon	Æ.		Alexandroid Heracles in lion-skin r.	Club and bow: ΒΑΣΙΛΕΩΣ ΛΕΥΚΩΝΟΣ.	B.
,,	Æ.		Pallas helmed r.	Thunderbolt: do.	O.
,,	Æ.		Oval shield, spear behind diagonally.	Dagger(?) quiver(?): do.	H.
Hygiaenon	N.	129·3 8·38	Hd of Hygiaenon (?) r., no fillet.	Athena seated l., Nike on r. hand, spear against r. shoulder, l. arm on shield with gorgoneion: in exergue trident l., flanked by dolphins. ΑΡΧΟΝΤΟΣ ΥΓΙΑΙΝΟΝΤΟΣ. Under Nike 𝕂, under seat ╬	Prowe.
Paerisades	N.	130·3 8·44	Head r., filleted.	Same, worse style. ΒΑΣΙΛΕΩΣ ΠΑΙΡΙΣΑΔ[ΟΥ. Under Nike (?), under seat ╬	Hunter.
,,	N.	125·8 8·15	Head r., filleted.	Same, worse, under Nike K, under seat 𝕂	Moscow
Saumacus	Æ.		Rayed head facing.	Thunderbolt. ΒΑΣΙ[ΛΕΩΣ ΣΑΥ[ΜΑΚΟΥ]	BM.
Pharnaces	N.	126·4 8·19	Filleted head of Pharnaces r.	Throned Apollo l., ΒΑΣΙΛΕΩΣ r. hand holds ΒΑΣΙΛΕΩΝ bay-wreath out ΜΕΓΑΛΟΥ towards lebes- ΦΑΡΝΑΚΟΥ tripod, left arm rests on lyre: in field l. ivy-leaf(?): to r. ΖΜΣ =247, B.C. 51.	G.
Asander Archon	Æ.		Beardless hd r., Asander (?): re-struck on coin of Amisus. BMC. Pontus III. 6.	Prow, l. ΑΡΧΟΝΤΟΣ ΑΣΑΝΔΡΟΥ.	O.
,,	Æ.		Same hd but wreathed r.: re-struck on VI. 11, itself on IX. 21.	Similar.	O.
King	N.	124 8·03	Asander filleted r.	Nike l. with wreath ΒΑΣΙΛΕΩΣ and palm. HK=28. ΑΣΑΝΔΡΟΥ	BM.
Polemo I.	R.	[54·15 3·51]	Bust of Polemo r., filleted.	Eight-pointed star. ΒΑΣΙΛΕΩΣ ΠΟΛΕΜΩΝΟΣ ΕΥΣΕΒΟΥΣ	O.
Pythodoris	R.	53·9 3·35	Hd of Augustus r., filleted.	Capricorn r. ΒΑΣΙΛΙΣΣΑ ΠΥΘΟΔΩΡΙΣ ΕΤΟΥΣ Ξ	BM.

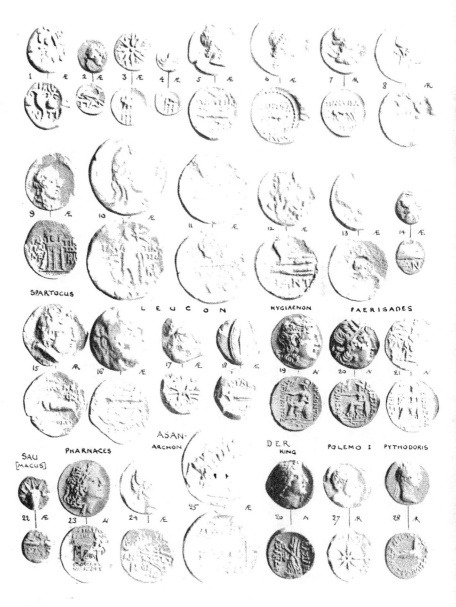

LATER CITY ISSUES (pp. 628—632). KINGS B.C. (pp. 582—586, 590—595, 611)

PLATE VII. BOSPORUS KINGS 1st CENTURY A.D.

PLATE VII. BOSPORUS. KINGS, 1st CENTURY A.D.

No.	King	Me-tal	Wt. grm.	Obverse	Reverse
1.	(monogram)	N.	121·9 / 7·9	Hd of Augustus l., bare; circle.	Beardless male head (Agrippa?), bare, r.; circle. (monogram)
2.	(monogram)	N.	121·75 / 7·89	As above.	Same head. (monogram)
3.	(monogram)	N.	120·3 / 7·83	As above.	Same head. (monogram)
4.	(monogram)	N.	122·8 / 7·96	Hd of Tiberius, r., bare; circle.	Beardless male head (Drusus?) r.; circle. (monogram)
5.	,,	Æ.		Bearded hd. r., helmed (Ares?) .·.	Trophy; dot-border. ,,
6.	(monogram)	N.	116·7 / 7·56	Head of Tiberius, r., new type; circle.	Gaius (?) r.; circle. (monogram)
7.	GEPAEPYRIS	Æ.		Bust of G. draped and diademed r.: [BACIΛICCHC ΓHΠAIΠYPEΩC].	Female bust draped, in calathos and veil r. (Livia as Aphrodite?). IB.
8.	POLEMO II	R.	[50·6 / 3·28]	Hd of P. r., diademed; dot-border: BAΣIΛEΩΣ ΠOΛEMΩNOΣ.	Nero r., laur.; dot-border: ETOYΣ IH.
9.	POLEMO AND TRYPHAENA	R.	51·7 / 3·35	Similar.	BAΣI ΛIΣΣHΣ ΤΡΥΦΑΙ encircled by diadema. NHΣ
10.	MITHRIDATES VIII [III]	N.	121·1 / 7·85	Head of Gaius (?) r., laur.; dot-border.	Nike l., with wreath and palm: BAΣIΛEΩΣ MIΘΡIΔATOY.
11.	,,	Æ.		Hd of M. r., diadem: dot-border: BACIΛEΩC MIΘPAΔATOY.	Bow-in-case, lion-skin on club, trident; dot-border: IB.
12.	BAM (monogram)	Æ.		Beardless male bust r., wearing rayed crown; dot-border.	Star and crescent; dot-border: BAM; I.
13.	,,	Æ.		Bearded hd r., helmed (cf. 5): ·. BA M.	Trophy, helmet below; dot-border. (symbol)
14.	(monogram)	Æ.		Similar head.	Hd and neck of horse r. (monogram)
15.	,,	Æ.		Hd of Apollo r., laur. within bay-wreath; dot-border.	Tripod with cover to r., bay-branch; dot-border: to l. (monogram) to r. Δ.
16.	,,	Æ.		Hd r., long hair, beard, diadem, trident: king as Poseidon (?): dot-border.	Dolphin r.; dot-border.: below, E, above, (monogram)
17.	·,,	Æ.		Hd of Perseus l., winged, in front harpe, dot-border.	Bearded Herm looking r., at base palm-branch (monogram), I. and wreath:
18.	,,	Æ.		Male head rayed r.	Star and crescent, dot-border. (monogram)
19.	COTYS I	Æ.		Head of Claudius r., laur.: TI KΛAYΔIOV ΣEBAΣTOV KAIΣAPOΣ.	Head of Agrippina Junior l.: IOVΛIAN AΓPIΠ-ΠINAN ΣEBAΣTHN. (monogram)
20.	,,	Æ.		Curule chair, on it crown, on r. sceptre surmounted by human hd l.: TEIMAI BAΣIΛEΩΣ KOTVOΣ.	Round shield, behind it spear, above to l. horse-hd l., to r. rayed hd l.; below to l., helmet r., to r., sheathed sword: TOY AΣΠOYPΓOV. KΔ.
21.	NERO	Æ.		Hd of Nero r., laur.: NEPΩNOΣ KΛAVΔIOV KAIΣAPOΣ ΣEBAΣTOV.	MH in wreath.
22.	,,	N.	122·8 / 7·96	Hd of Claudius r., laur.: circle.	Hd of Nero r., laur.: circle. (monogram)
23.	RHESCUPORIS	N.	122·2 / 7·92	Hd of Vespasian r., laur.: circle.	Hd of Titus r., bare: circle. (monogram)
24.	,,	N.	121 / 7·84	Bust of Rhescuporis r., draped and diademed; dot-border: TIBEPIOΣ IOVΛIOΣ BAΣIΛEVΣ PHΣKOVΠOPIΣ.	Hd of Domitian r., laur.: dot-border.
25.	,,	Æ.		R. seated r. on curule chair holds man-headed sceptre: TIBEPIOΣ IOVΛIOΣ BAΣIΛEVΣ PHΣKOVΠOPIΣ. (symbol)	Round shield, behind it spear, above, to l. horse-hd, to r. plumed helmet; below axe l., sheathed sword r.: TEIMAI BAΣIΛEΩΣ PHΣKOVΠOPIΔOΣ. MH.

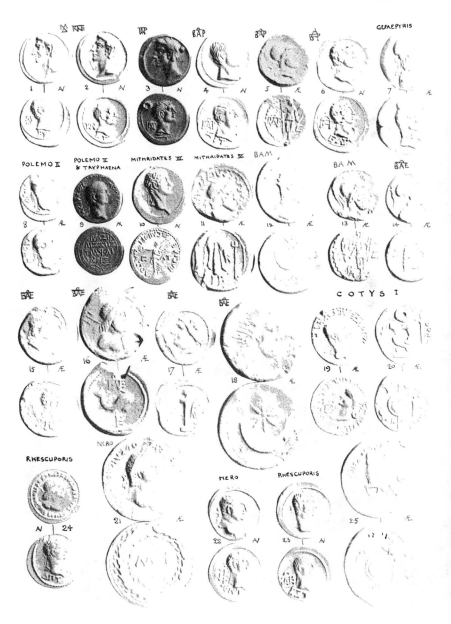

KINGS IST CENTURY A.D. (pp. 595—604, 611, 632, 633)

PLATE VIII. BOSPORUS, LATER KINGS

PLATE VIII. BOSPORUS. LATER KINGS.

No.	King	Metal	Wt. grn. grm.	Obverse	Reverse
1.	SAUROMATES I	N.	119·75 / 7·76	Bust of S. r., diademed and draped; dots: BACIΛEWC CAYPOMATOY.	Head of Trajan r., laur.; dot-border.
2.	„	Æ.		Bust of S. l., diademed and draped: TI.] IOYΛIOY BACIΛEWC C]AYPOMATOY.	City-gate, tree behind on r., captive crouching r.; MH.
3.	„	Æ.		Bust of S. r., facing queen (?) l.; below MH.	King as on VII. 25. TIBEPIOC IOYΛIOC BACIΛEYC CAYPOM[ATHC.
4.	COTYS II	Æ.		Bust of C. r., diademed and draped: BACIΛEWC KOTYOC.	Horseman (king?), wearing cuirass, chlamys and bow-case, galloping r. and hurling spear: below MH..
5.	„	Æ.		Temple of Capitoline Jove: KA ΠE.	Wreath surrounding BAK and KΔ.
6.	RHOEMETALCES	N.	119·6 / 7·75	Bust of R. r: BACIΛEWC POIMHTAΛKOY.	Antoninus Pius r.
7.	EUPATOR	N.	119·4 / 7·74	Bust of E. r., club: BACIΛEWC EYΠATOPOC.	M. Aurelius r., facing L. Verus l.
8.	„	Æ.		As 5.	Wreath surrounding BAEY and KΔ.
9.	SAUROMATES II	EL.	120·1 / 7·78	Bust of S. r: BACIΛEWC CAVPOMATOV.	Sep. Severus r., star.
10.	„	Æ.		As above.	King wearing cuirass and cloak on horse r., r. hand raised, l. holds spear: in field star and B.
11.	„	Æ.		[As above.]	Heracles r., shooting Stymphalian birds: star and B.
12.	„	Æ.		[As above.]	Aphrodite (?) in calathos, chiton and peplos sits l. on ornamented throne: in outstretched r. hand patera (?), in l. long sceptre: star and B.
13.	„	Æ.		[As above.]	Eagle l., wings open, beak turned back, holds wreath: PMΔ.
14.	„	Æ.		[As above.]	As 12, degraded: in field bust of Sep. Severus, star and B.
15.	RHESCUPORIS	N.	118·5 / 7·68	Bust of R. BACIΛEWC PHCKOVΠOPIΔOC.	Head of Caracalla: star.
16.	RHESCUPORIS	EL.	117·7 / 7·63	Bust of R. BACIΛEWC PHCKOVΠ[OPIΔOC].	Bust of Emperor r.
17.	COTYS III	R.	118·36 / 7·67	Bust of C. BACIΛEWC KOTVOC.	Bust of Emperor.
18.	SAUROMATES III	R.	114·9 / 7·45	Bust of S. BACIΛEWC CAVPOMATOV.	Bust of Emperor. ·.·
19.	RHESCUPORIS	R.	123·5 / 8	Bust of R. BACIΛEWC PHCKOVΠOPIΔO.	Bust of Emperor.
20.	ININTHIMEUS	R.	103·6 / 6·71	Bust of I. BACIΛEWC ININΘIME[OV].	Bust of Emperor: club.
21.	PHARSANZES	POT.	[115·7 / 7·5]	Bust of Ph. BACIΛEWC ΦAPCANZOV.	Bust of Emperor: two dots.
22.	RHESCUPORIS	POT.	[110·3 / 7·15]	Bust of R. BACIΛEWC PHCKOVΠOPIΔOC.	Valerian and Gallienus facing.
23.	RHESCUPORIS	POT.	[113 / 7·32]	Bust of R. BACIΛEWC PHCKOVΠOPIΔOC.	Bust of Emperor r.: K.
24.	SAUROMATES IV	POT.	113·4 / 7·35	Bust of S. BACIΛEWC CAVPOMATOV.	Bust of Emperor.
25.	TEIRANES	Æ.		Bust of T. BACIΛEWC TEIPANOV.	Bust of Emperor.
26.	THOTHORSES	Æ.		Bust of Th. BACIΛEWC ΘOΘWPCOY.	Bust of Emperor.
27.	RHADAMSADIUS	Æ.		Bust of R. BACIΛEWC PAΔAM[CAΔIOV?].	Bust of Emperor: club.
28.	RHESCUPORIS	Æ.		Bust of R. BAC]IΛEWC PICKOVΠO[PIΔOC].	Bust of Emperor.

LATER KINGS (pp. 604—611, 632, 633)

PLATE IX. SMALLER STATES

PLATE IX.

SMALLER STATES.

CERCINITIS.

No.	Metal	Wt. grn./grm.	Obverse	Reverse	Coll.	Publication
1.	Æ.		Hd of Tyche (Artemis?) l., wearing mural crown bearing ☉ between two palmettes: dot-border.	Horseman galloping r., with spear and bowcase: below, KAPKI; above horse's croup HPAK sideways.	B.	B. XIII. 1. / Or. *Mat for Num.* I. 1.
2.	Æ.		Bearded figure l., seated on rock, holding axe (?): to left sideways, KEPKI.	Horse walking l., off fore-leg raised: below, KAΛΛIA.	O.	B. 2. / Or. 7.
3.	Æ.		Artemis l., in earrings and necklace: above KEP.	Deer in same pose: above, ΓE.	BM.	B. 10. / Or. 10.

THEODOSIA.

No.	Metal	Wt. grn./grm.	Obverse	Reverse	Coll.	Publication
4.	R.	40·4 / 2·62	Hd of Pallas r., helmed.	Bucranium with hanging garland. ΘE-OΔ-EΩ.	B.	B. XVIII. 1. / *TRAS.* V. 13.
5.	Æ.		Beardless head l.	Bull butting r.: above, ΘE.	G.	B. 3.
6.	Æ.		Similar.	Similar: ΘEOΔO[Σ].	G.	*TRAS.* v. 15.
7.	Æ.		Pallas helmed r.	Bow-case and club: below, ΘEY.	B.	B. 8.

NYMPHAEUM.

No.	Metal	Wt. grn./grm.	Obverse	Reverse	Coll.	Publication
8.	R.	5·39 / ·35	Hd of Nymph l., in ampyx.	Vine-spray and bunch of grapes: above, NY.	BM.	B. 11.
9.	R.	25·9 / 1·68	Similar.	Similar: NYN in incuse square.	B.	B. 10.

APOLLONIA.

No.	Metal	Wt. grn./grm.	Obverse	Reverse	Coll.	Publication
0.	R.	22·4 / 1·45	Lion-scalp.	Incuse square in four compartments: AΠOΛ.	FW.	*Kl.B.* III. 15.

PHANAGORIA.

No.	Metal	Wt. grn./grm.	Obverse	Reverse	Coll.	Publication
1.	R.	2·78 / ·18	Similar.	Incuse square: in compartments ΦA and pellets.	M.	Cf. B. XIX. 4.
2.	R.	68·7 / 4·35	Hd of Phanagoras l., in pileus.	Bull butting r.: above, ΦANA: in exergue grain of corn.	BM.	B. XXIII. 5 b.
3.	R.	24·5 / 1·58	Hd of Artemis r., quiver behind.	Rose: ΦANAΓO-PITΩN.	BM.	B. 6 b.
4.	Æ.		Rose.	Star with small crescent.	BM.	*Zt. f. Num.* XX. ix. 2.
5.	Æ.		Pan bearded r., restruck on coin of Panticapaeum, countermark star (?).	Bow and arrow: ΦA.	O.	B. 10 b.
6.	R.	56 / 3·63	Dionysus r., laur.	Filleted thyrsus: ΦANAΓO PITΩN.	O.	B. 1 b.
7.	Æ.		Dionysus r., laur.	Tripod, thyrsus ΦANAΓOP against it: ITΩN tol. [symbol], tor. [symbol].	O.	B. 12 b.
8.	Æ.		Artemis r., quiver behind.	Kneeling deer ΦANAΓO l., below, PITΩN.	O.	B. 21 b.

AGRIPPIAS CAESAREA.

No.	Metal	Wt. grn./grm.	Obverse	Reverse	Coll.	Publication
9.	Æ.		Female bust r., in veil and calathos: Livia as Aphrodite(?): dot-border.	Sceptre: KAI-ΣA; below, H; PE-ΩN dot-border.	O.	B. 1 e.
0.	Æ.		Bust of Livia veiled, stephane.	Prow l., AΓPIΠ·ΠEΩN, H; dots.	O.	B. 1 f.

UNKNOWN. PHANAGORIA (?).

No.	Metal	Wt. grn./grm.	Obverse	Reverse	Coll.	Publication
1.	Æ.		Dionysus r., in ivy-wreath.	Bow-case and quiver. [symbol].	O.	B. 25–30 b.

GORGIPPIA.

No.	Metal	Wt. grn./grm.	Obverse	Reverse	Coll.	Publication
2.	R.	56 / 3·63	Helios r., in rayed crown.	Cornucopia betw. two stars: ΓOPΓIΠ.	G.	*TRAS.* V. 5
3.	R.	61·7 / 4	As 16.	Stag running r.; behind, a filleted thyrsus: ΓOPΓIΠ-ΠEΩN.	BM.	B. 2 c.
4.	Æ.		As 17.	As 17 but ΓOP-ΓIΠ-ΠE-ΩN.	O.	B. 5 c.

SINDI.

No.	Metal	Wt. grn./grm.	Obverse	Reverse	Coll.	Publication
5.	R.	20·4 / 1·32	Heracles hd r., in lion-skin.	Horse-head in incuse square: above, ΣINΔΩN.	O.	B. 7 d.
6.	R.	14·2 / ·92	Griffin seated r., before him ear of corn.	As 25.	B.	B. 1 d.
7.	R.	19·14 / 1·24	Heracles kneeling r. stringing bow (?).	Owl displayed in incuse square: above, ΣINΔΩN.	B.	B. 5 d.

DIOSCURIAS.

No.	Metal	Wt. grn./grm.	Obverse	Reverse	Coll.	Publication
8.	Æ.		Two star-crowned caps of Dioscuri.	Thyrsus vertical: ΔI-OΣ-KOY-PIA-Δ-OΣ.	O.	*BMC.* p. 5. / Pl. I. 11.

COLCHI.

No.	Metal	Wt. grn./grm.	Obverse	Reverse	Coll.	Publication
9.	R.	[34·2]	Male head r.; dotted border.	Bull's head r.; line-border.	O.	*BMC.* p. 4. / Pl. I. 9.

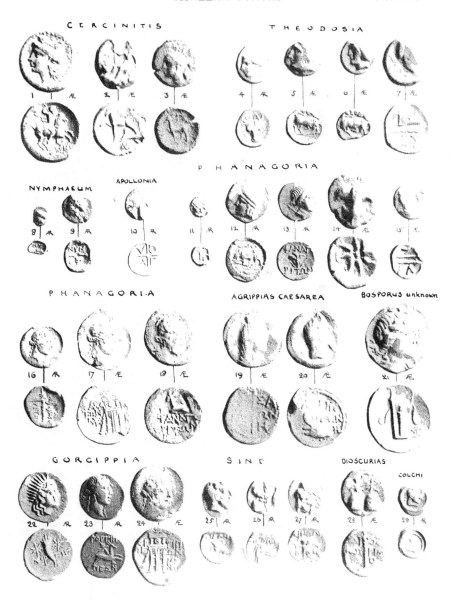

CERCINITIS (pp. 491, 492), THEODOSIA (pp. 555, 559), NYMPHAEUM (p. 561).
APOLLONIA (pp. 20, 569, 628), PHANAGORIA, ETC. (pp. 628—632)

INDEX

Arabic and Small Roman Numbers refer to the pages. Italics distinguish those upon which a subject is mainly treated from the many casual mentions of it.

A Large Roman Number following a geographical name indicates the Map upon which it may most conveniently be found. If this indication is absent, it means that I have not succeeded in exactly locating the place, but its Government and District will be found in the Text.

Greek words are inserted where they would come if transliterated into Latin, save that αι, οι appear as if αι, οι, κ as if k. Greek words next each other are put in the right Greek order.

Inscriptions in the Appendix are not directly indexed, as references to them are given for names and facts of importance where these occur in the Text.

The Coin-plates are also not indexed as direct inspection of them is quicker than the use of an index.

Add. = Addenda (v. p. xxxvi): e.g. "287 Add." means that a subject not mentioned on p. 287 appears in the Addenda thereto; "516 and Add.", that something is mentioned both on p. 516 and in the Addenda thereto.

Modern Names are furnished with accents when I know the pronunciation, but this is very difficult to arrive at, geographical names being mostly non-Russian and surnames very irregular.

Ababus Callisthenis, 469
Abakán Steppe, I. 241
Abasgi, I. 24, 129
Abazá, Mme J. Th., 177
ABC. xxx
Abercromby, J. on Finns, 105 n. 3, 106 n. 1, 257 n. 5
Abicht, K. 33
Abii, 114 n. 3
Abkházes, 24, ·129
Aborace, 23
Abu Sir (Egypt), coffins from, 322 n. 1, 323 n. 1
Abydos (Hellespont), 536
Academy of Sciences of St P., Publications of, xxv
Acanthus, 287 Add., 289, 299, 300 f. 212, 324—326 ff. 234—236, 328, 353—355 ff. 259—261, 384, 390, 391 f. 287
Accipenser stellatus, Huso, Sturio, 6
Aces, 581, 583—586
Achaei (Caucasian tribe), IX. 24, 128, 579, 588, 598
Achasa regio, VI. 114 n. 3
Achilles, cult and legend of at Leuce, 14 n. 2, 361, 463: at Olbia, 467; horse-races, 464; Pontarches, 452 n. 1, 453, 456, 468, 473, 474, 476—482, priest of, 472, 482
   arms of, v. Nereids; sarcophagus, 298; at Scyros, 285 —287 Add.
Achillis Cursus (Tendra), 4, 14—16, 465, 481
Achillis Vicus, III. 21; columns at, 23
Achúev, IX.; fishing, 6
Acinaces, 71, 86
Acis Paerisadis, 578 n. 2, 583, 585 n. 4
Acorn, 388, 400
Acra (Acrae), III. 20, 22, 23
Acropolis, Athens, 350; Chersonese, 500, 502, 510, 520; Nymphaeum, 560; Olbia, 454, 456; Panticapaeum, 564; Phanagoria, 566, 588
Acrosandrus (Acrosas), 123, 487
Acroterium, painted, 300, 331; plaster, 373 f. 277; terra-cotta, 364; wooden, 323, 324 f. 234
Actors, 358, 367, 369
Adagúm, R., IX. 216
Addenda, xxxvi—xl
Adders, 6
ἀδελφὸς εἰσποιητός, 621, 623; ἴδιος, 624
Admiral, 586, 587, 592, 604, 614, 616

M.

Adobogionis, 589, 590
Adoes Delphi, 473, 486
Adraspus (Charaspes), coins of, 123, 487
Aea, 436, 437
Acaea, 437
Acetes, 436, 437, 569 n. 10
Aegean, 436, 437; coasts harried by Goths, 126 culture, its analogies with Tripolje, 134, 135, 141, 142
Aeginetic standard, 448, 483—487, 559, 561, 630—632
Aelia, Queen, 608
Aelis, coins of, 119, 477 n. 7, 487
Aelius Iulius, 525 n. 1
Aeolians, 570
Aepolium, 13
Aes grave, v. *Asses*
Aeschines, 561
Aeschylus on Scyths, 50
Aesculapius, v. Asclepius
Aetherius I, Bp of Chersonese, 531; his island, 16 n. 3, 531
Aetherius II, Bp of Chersonese, 493 n. 1, 531
Africa, officer from, 525
Agaetes, 569 n. 10
Agarus, 579
Agasicles Ctesiae, (App. 17), 360, 495, 504, 517, 518, 540 n. 8, 541; crowned, 388
Agate, bottle, 235; engraved, 411—413 ff. 298, 300; lion, 405
Agathocles Agathoclis, 475
Agathodorus, S., 531
Agathon, on Scythic bow, 66
Ἀγαθὸς Δαίμων, 478
Agathyrsi, I. 27, 28, 36, 43, *102,* 440; vase, 54 f. 8, 55
Agathyrsus, eponymous hero, 43
Agelas Lagorini, 520 n. 1
Aggistis, 619
Agonistic lists, 626
Agonothetes, 616, 626
Agoranomus, 473, 475, 477, 525, 541; on amphorae, 359
Agri, 128
Agriculture, Siberian, 246
Agricultural Scythians, 27—31, 175; opposed to Nomads, 36 sqq.; legends apply to, 44
Agrigentum, coin-type of, 263

86

87

M.

M·

M.

Index